International Directory of

COMPANY
HISTORIES

International Directory of

COMPANY

HISTORIES

VOLUME 77

Editor

Jay P. Pederson

ST. JAMES PRESS

An imprint of Thomson Gale, a part of The Thomson Corporation

Detroit • New York • San Francisco • San Diego • New Haven, Conn. • Waterville, Maine • London • Munich

International Directory of Company Histories, Volume 77

Jay P. Pederson

Project Editor
Miranda H. Ferrara

Editorial
Virgil Burton, Donna Craft, Louise Gagné, Peggy Geeseman, Julie Gough, Linda Hall, Sonya Hill, Keith Jones, Lynn Pearce, Holly Selden, Justine Ventimiglia

Editorial Systems Implementation Specialist
Mike Weaver

Imaging and Multimedia
Leslie Light, Michael Logusz

Composition and Electronic Prepress
Gary Leach, Evi Seoud

Manufacturing
Rhonda Dover

Product Manager
Gerald L. Sawchuk

LIBRARY OF CONGRESS CATALOG NUMBER 89-190943

ISBN 1-55862-581-X

This title is also available as an e-book
ISBN 1-55862-625-5

BRITISH LIBRARY CATALOGUING IN PUBLICATION DATA

International directory of company histories, Vol. 77
I. Jay P. Pederson
33.87409

Printed in the United States of America
10 9 8 7 6 5 4 3 2 1

Contents

Preface

The St. James Press series *The International Directory of Company Histories* (*IDCH*) is intended for reference use by students, business people, librarians, historians, economists, investors, job candidates, and others who seek to learn more about the historical development of the world's most important companies. To date, *IDCH* has covered over 7,750 companies in 77 volumes.

INCLUSION CRITERIA

Most companies chosen for inclusion in *IDCH* have achieved a minimum of US$25 million in annual sales and are leading influences in their industries or geographical locations. Companies may be publicly held, private, or nonprofit. State-owned companies that are important in their industries and that may operate much like public or private companies also are included. Wholly owned subsidiaries and divisions are profiled if they meet the requirements for inclusion. Entries on companies that have had major changes since they were last profiled may be selected for updating.

The *IDCH* series highlights 10% private and nonprofit companies, and features updated entries on approximately 50 companies per volume.

ENTRY FORMAT

Each entry begins with the company's legal name; the address of its headquarters; its telephone, toll-free, and fax numbers; and its web site. A statement of public, private, state, or parent ownership follows. A company with a legal name in both English and the language of its headquarters country is listed by the English name, with the native-language name in parentheses.

The company's founding or earliest incorporation date, the number of employees, and the most recent available sales figures follow. Sales figures are given in local currencies with equivalents in U.S. dollars. For some private companies, sales figures are estimates and indicated by the abbreviation *est*. The entry lists the exchanges on which the company's stock is traded and its ticker symbol, as well as the company's NAIC codes.

Entries generally contain a *Company Perspectives* box which provides a short summary of the company's mission, goals, and ideals; a *Key Dates* box highlighting milestones in the company's history; lists of *Principal Subsidiaries*, *Principal Divisions*, *Principal Operating Units*, *Principal Competitors*; and articles for *Further Reading*.

American spelling is used throughout *IDCH*, and the word "billion" is used in its U.S. sense of one thousand million.

Users of the *IDCH* series will notice some changes to the look of the series starting with Volume 77. The pages have been redesigned for better clarity and ease of use; the standards for entry content, however, have not changed.

SOURCES

Entries have been compiled from publicly accessible sources both in print and on the Internet such as general and academic periodicals, books, and annual reports, as well as material supplied by the companies themselves.

CUMULATIVE INDEXES

IDCH contains three indexes: the **Index to Companies**, which provides an alphabetical index to companies discussed in the text as well as to companies profiled, the **Index to Industries**, which allows researchers to locate companies by their principal industry, and the **Geographic Index**, which lists companies alphabetically by the country of their headquarters. The indexes are cumulative and specific instructions for using them are found immediately preceding each index.

SUGGESTIONS WELCOME

Comments and suggestions from users of *IDCH* on any aspect of the product as well as suggestions for companies to be included or updated are cordially invited. Please write:

The Editor
International Directory of Company Histories
St. James Press
27500 Drake Rd.
Farmington Hills, Michigan 48331-3535

St. James Press does not endorse any of the companies or products mentioned in this series. Companies appearing in the *International Directory of Company Histories* were selected without reference to their wishes and have in no way endorsed their entries.

Notes on Contributors

M. L. Cohen
Novelist and researcher living in Paris.

Jeffrey L. Covell
Seattle-based writer.

Susan B. Culligan
Minnesota-based writer.

Ed Dinger
Writer and editor based in Bronx, New York.

Robert Halasz
Former editor in chief of *World Progress* and *Funk & Wagnalls New Encyclopedia Yearbook*; author, *The U.S. Marines* (Millbrook Press, 1993).

Frederick C. Ingram
Utah-based business writer who has contributed to *GSA Business*, *Appalachian Trailway News*, the *Encyclopedia of Business*, the *Encyclopedia of Global Industries*, the *Encyclopedia of Consumer Brands*, and other regional and trade publications.

Kathleen Peippo
Minneapolis-based writer.

Sara Poginy
Ohio-based writer.

Nelson Rhodes
Editor, writer, and consultant in the Chicago area.

Carrie Rothburd
Writer and editor specializing in corporate profiles, academic texts, and academic journal articles.

David E. Salamie
Part-owner of InfoWorks Development Group, a reference publication development and editorial services company.

Frank Uhle
Ann Arbor-based writer; movie projectionist, disc jockey, and staff member of *Psychotronic Video* magazine.

A. Woodward
Wisconsin-based writer.

List of Abbreviations

¥ Japanese yen
£ United Kingdom pound
$ United States dollar
A.E. Anonimos Eteria (Greece)
A.O. Anonim Ortaklari/Ortakligi (Turkey)
A.S. Anonim Sirketi (Turkey)
A/S Aksjeselskap (Norway)
A/S Aktieselskab (Denmark, Sweden)
AB Aktiebolag (Finland, Sweden)
AB Oy Aktiebolag Osakeyhtiot (Finland)
AED Emirati dirham
AG Aktiengesellschaft (Austria, Germany, Switzerland, Liechtenstein)
ARS Argentine peso
ATS Austrian shilling
AUD Australian dollar
ApS Amparteselskab (Denmark)
Ay Avoinyhtio (Finland)
B.A. Buttengewone Aansprakeiijkheid (The Netherlands)
B.V. Besloten Vennootschap (Belgium, The Netherlands)
BEF Belgian franc
BHD Bahraini dinar
BRL Brazilian real
Bhd. Berhad (Malaysia, Brunei)
C. de R.L. Compania de Responsabilidad Limitada (Spain)
C.A. Compania Anonima (Ecuador, Venezuela)
C.V. Commanditaire Vennootschap (The Netherlands, Belgium)
CAD Canadian dollar
CEO Chief Executive Officer
CFO Chief Financial Officer
CHF Swiss franc
CIO Chief Information Officer
CLP Chilean peso
CNY Chinese yuan
COO Chief Operating Officer
COP Colombian peso
CRL Companhia a Responsabilidao Limitida (Portugal, Spain)
CZK Czech koruna
Co. Company
Corp. Corporation
D&B Dunn & Bradstreet
DEM German deutsche mark
DKK Danish krone
DZD Algerian dinar
EEK Estonian Kroon
EGP Egyptian pound
ESOP Employee Stock Options and Ownership
ESP Spanish peseta
EUR euro
FIM Finnish markka
FRF French franc
G.I.E. Groupement d'Interet Economique (France)
GRD Greek drachma
GmbH Gesellschaft mit beschraenkter Haftung (Austria, Germany, Switzerland)
HKD Hong Kong dollar
HUF Hungarian forint
I/S Interesentselskap (Norway)
I/S Interessentselskab (Denmark)
IDR Indonesian rupiah
IEP Irish pound
ILS new Israeli shekel
INR Indian rupee
IPO Initial Public Offering
ISK Icelandic krona
ITL Italian lira
Inc. Incorporated (United States, Canada)
JMD Jamaican dollar
K/S Kommanditselskab (Denmark)
K/S Kommandittselskap (Norway)
KG Kommanditgesellschaft (Austria, Germany, Switzerland)
KGaA Kommanditgesellschaft auf Aktien (Austria, Germany, Switzerland)
KK Kabushiki Kaisha (Japan)
KPW North Korean won
KRW South Korean won
KWD Kuwaiti dinar
LBO Leveraged Buyout
Lda. Limitada (Spain)
L.L.C. Limited Liability Company (United States)
Ltd. Limited (Various)
Ltda. Limitada (Brazil, Portugal)

Ltee. Limitee (Canada, France)

LUF Luxembourg franc

mbH mit beschraenkter Haftung (Austria, Germany)

MUR Mauritian rupee

MXN Mexican peso

MYR Malaysian ringgit

N.V. Naamloze Vennootschap (Belgium, The Netherlands)

NGN Nigerian naira

NLG Netherlands guilder

NOK Norwegian krone

NZD New Zealand dollar

OAO Otkrytoe Aktsionernoe Obshchestve (Russia)

OMR Omani rial

OOO Obschestvo s Ogranichennoi Otvetstvennostiu (Russia)

Oy Osakeyhtiö (Finland)

PHP Philippine peso

PKR Pakistani rupee

PLC Public Limited Co. (United Kingdom, Ireland)

PLN Polish zloty

PTE Portuguese escudo

Pty. Proprietary (Australia, South Africa, United Kingdom)

REIT Real Estate Investment Trust

RMB Chinese renminbi

RUB Russian ruble

S.A. Société Anonyme (Belgium, France, Greece, Luxembourg, Switzerland, Arab speaking countries)

S.A. Sociedad Anónima (Latin America, Spain, Mexico)

S.A. Sociedades Anônimas (Brazil, Portugal)

S.A.R.L. Sociedade Anonima de Responsabilidade Limitada (Brazil, Portugal)

S.A.R.L. Société à Responsabilité Limitée (France, Belgium, Luxembourg)

S.A.S. Societá in Accomandita Semplice (Italy)

S.A.S. Societe Anonyme Syrienne (Arab speaking countries)

S.R.L. Sociedad de Responsabilidad Limitada (Spain, Mexico, Latin America)

S.R.L. Società a Responsabilitá Limitata (Italy)

S.R.O. Spolecnost s Rucenim Omezenym (Czechoslovakia

S.p.A. Società per Azioni (Italy)

SAA Societe Anonyme Arabienne

SAR Saudi riyal

SEK Swedish krona

SGD Singapore dollar

Sdn. Bhd. Sendirian Berhad (Malaysia)

Sp. z.o.o. Spólka z ograniczona odpowiedzialnoscia (Poland)

Ste. Societe (France, Belgium, Luxembourg, Switzerland)

THB Thai baht

TND Tunisian dinar

TRL Turkish lira

TWD new Taiwan dollar

VAG Verein der Arbeitgeber (Austria, Germany)

VEB Venezuelan bolivar

VND Vietnamese dong

YK Yugen Kaisha (Japan)

ZAO Zakrytoe Aktsionernoe Obshchestve (Russia)

ZAR South African rand

ZMK Zambian kwacha

Acosta Sales and Marketing Company, Inc.

6600 Corporate Center Parkway
Jacksonville, Florida 32216
U.S.A.
Telephone: (904) 281-9800
Fax: (904) 281-9966
Web site: http://www.acosta.com

Private Company
Founded: 1927
Employees: 11,000
NAIC: 424410 General Line Grocery Merchant Whole-
  salers; 424420 Packaged Frozen Food Merchant
  Wholesalers

■ ■ ■

Privately owned Jacksonville, Florida-based Acosta Sales
and Marketing Company, Inc. is one of North America's
largest sales and marketing agencies serving the foodservice and grocery industries. The company's primary
service is headquarters selling, acting as a marketing and
sales agent for about 1,300 consumer products manufacturers, helping them to gain placement on the shelves
of top supermarkets and other retail outlets, such as
convenience stores, drugstores, and mass merchandisers.
Another Acosta service available to clients is retail
fieldwork. Acosta sales representatives visit stores to
ensure that client products are properly displayed, are
not out of stock or beyond their expiration date, are accurately priced, and are presented to consumers in the
best way possible. Acosta also offers space technology
services that help clients through the use of sophisticated

software to determine the ideal location on the shelves
of local retailers. Finally, Acosta is involved in category
management, offering clients a wide range of advanced
management tools to help in decision making, including
consumer insights, syndicated data analysis, pricing and
ad tracking, customer reviews, client scorecarding, and
the use of Acosta's web-based communication tool,
TeamNET.

COMPANY ROOTS DATING TO THE 1920S

The man behind the Acosta name was Louis T. (Lou)
Acosta, who in 1927 opened a small food product sales
and marketing agency that took the name L.T. Acosta
Company, Inc., servicing the Jacksonville area. In 1956,
Lou Acosta persuaded Robert H. (Hy) Albritton, owner,
president, and CEO of Common & Co. Food Brokers,
to merge his company into L.T. Acosta Co. and become
Acosta's executive vice-president. With Lou's retirement
in 1959, Hy Albritton became president of L.T. Acosta
Co. By the end of 1974, Acosta had grown from 11
employees to 27. It remained a small, single-market sales
agency, employing a little more than a dozen people
generating annual sales of $500,000, when Delmer (Del)
Dallas took over as president in 1974. He would be the
man most responsible for transforming Acosta into a
regional powerhouse. Dallas grew up on a Mississippi
farm, and then worked his way through Mississippi State
University, where he received a marketing degree in
1953. He went to work for Procter & Gamble in sales
and sales management, a job that took him throughout
the southeastern United States. He then took a management position at a P&G subsidiary, the Clorox

---

COMPANY PERSPECTIVES

Founded in 1927, Acosta is a professional services company dedicated to delivering results and currently represents more #1 and #2 brands than any other sales agency in North America. That's why companies choose Acosta to help them chart a course aimed toward success.

Company, before moving to Jacksonville in 1966 to become a partner at Acosta.

After becoming Acosta's president, Dallas began an expansion program. The first step was to break out of the Jacksonville market by opening a Tampa, Florida office. At the time, it was something of a bold step, because food sales and marketing agencies generally limited themselves to a single market. Acosta was one of the first to represent manufacturers in more than one market. In 1977, Acosta opened an office in Birmingham, Alabama, and in 1981, opened an office in Miami, Florida, allowing the agency to offer service throughout the entire state of Florida.

In 1983 Dallas began to expand the business beyond Florida through the acquisition of Raley Brothers in the state of Georgia to become a regional player. By the end of the decade Acosta entered the Carolinas, but the 1990s would see a host of changes in the food business that forced regional agents such as Acosta to grow ever larger in order to compete.

INDUSTRY CHANGES IN THE 1990S

At the start of the 1990s, the supermarket industry was composed of a lot of small local and regional chains. In 1992 the top five chains accounted for less than 20 percent of all grocery sales, but as mass retailers including Wal-Mart began to sell groceries the dynamics in the industry changed. Groceries were already a low-margin business, and in order to compete with Wal-Mart, which could use its size to drive hard bargains with suppliers and offer low prices to consumers, supermarket chains had to become larger as well. Because of low financing costs, chains found it easier to buy stores than to build them, leading to a wave of major mergers. By the end of the 1990s the top five grocery chains controlled 40 percent of all sales, and the consolidation trend continued. Faced with only a handful of powerful supermarket chains to sell to, manufacturers began to

consolidate in order to maintain their own competitive edge. As a result, ever larger manufacturers were selling to nationwide chains, and both wanted to deal with national sales and marketing agents rather than contend with scores of regional sales agents. Hence, the sales and marketing agents themselves were forced to consolidate, as the weaker players were swallowed by the stronger until only a few survivors were left. Acosta was one of those survivors.

As Dallas was growing Acosta, he also was grooming his successor, Gary Chartrand. A New Hampshire native, Chartrand was a veteran of The Carnation Company when Dallas recruited him for Acosta in 1983. Chartrand became president in 1993, was named chief executive officer in 1996 (the same year Dallas retired at the age of 65), and was elected chairman of the board in 1998.

It was not until 1998 that Acosta began its transformation from a regional company to a national concern wielding tremendous power. Chartrand explained to *Jacksonville Business Journal* in a 2001 profile, "The best way to protect our company was to be coast to coast." The plan was to buy the best in class in each market. The first in a series of steps to Acosta's becoming a national player was the merger in July 1998 with PMI-Eisenhart, serving the Midwest. The pace picked up considerably in 1999. First, in June 1999, Acosta acquired Kelley-Clarke, a leading agency in the West, then two months later northeast agency MAI was added, and finally in August 2000 Acosta reached an operating agreement with Luke Soules, which did business in Texas and New Mexico. (Acosta would acquire Luke Soules outright in 2003.) "In about 15 months," Chartrand told *Jacksonville Business Journal,* "we took the company from [doing business] in about 25 percent of the country to 100 percent." The first contract for national representation, courtesy of Minute Maid, was soon forthcoming in September 1999.

Chartrand, unlike some of his chief rivals, did not take on significant institutional debt to achieve the company's growth. Instead, according to the *Florida Times Union,* "Acosta negotiated deals where, not only were the sellers paid over a period of years, but the majority of the sellers were retained to work in the business, giving them a powerful incentive to both make the deals work and to grow the business in markets they already know well. 'The way he put it together, frankly, is brilliant,' said Tony Marinatos, managing director of Chartwell Capital Management a private Jacksonville investment firm."

One of Acosta's three chief national rivals, Dallas-based Marketing Specialists Corp., incorporated in 1998 and borrowed money to finance a series of acquisitions.

KEY DATES

1927: L.T. Acosta opens L.T. Acosta Company, Inc., a family-run, single-market food broker, servicing the Jacksonville, Florida, area.

1956: Louis Acosta persuades Robert H. (Hy) Albritton, president and owner of Common & Co. Food Brokers, to merge with L.T. Acosta Co.

1959: L.T. Acosta retires and Hy Albritton becomes president and CEO of L.T. Acosta Co.

1974: Hy Albritton retires and Del Dallas becomes president of the company; an expansion plan is initiated, and Acosta becomes one of the first companies to offer manufacturer representation in more than one geographic area.

1977: Acosta opens an office in Birmingham, Alabama.

1981: Acosta opens its Miami, Florida office, offering Florida statewide service.

1983: Acosta acquires Raley Brothers, located in the state of Georgia, its first acquisition outside Florida.

1989: Acosta enters the Carolinas market.

1993: Gary Chartrand becomes president of Acosta.

1996: Chartrand is named Acosta's CEO.

1998: Acosta merges with PMI-Eisenhart, a leading agency in the Midwest.

2002: Acquisitions of top agencies in Canada make Acosta the leading foodservice sales agency in North America.

2003: Acosta acquires Luke Soules.

The new business failed to perform as hoped, and the company filed for Chapter 11 bankruptcy protection in May 2001. After they filed for bankruptcy, Acosta reached a transition agreement with Marketing Specialists to assist the estate in the collection of its receivables and to hire some of its employees. All told, Acosta hired more than 1,700 of Marketing Specialists' 5,700 employees. Some, but not all, of Marketing Specialists' clients transitioned their business to Acosta and its competitors.

Even as Acosta was becoming a national force, it was taking steps to become involved in international markets. Knowing full well that retailers would go global, the company formed a consortium of leading consumer products distributors around the world. For the most part, Acosta helped manufacturers interested in global expansion make connections with these distributors. It was then paid finders' fees by the distributors.

INTERNATIONAL ACQUISITIONS IN THE EARLY 2000S

Acosta completed its first international acquisitions in 2002, in one stroke picking up four regional sales and marketing companies in Canada: Ontario-based Thomas, Large & Singer; Quebec-based Belgo International; Western Canada's Tees & Persse Brokerage; and Trebley Atlantic, based in the Maritimes. The resulting Acosta Canada would have 300 employees working out of 13 offices spread from coast to coast. The deals also made Acosta the largest sales and marketing firm in North America. To serve its clients wherever they did business, Acosta forged alliances with local brokers that allowed it to spread its influence globally.

Acosta expanded on other fronts in the early 2000s. It created a subsidiary, MatchPoint Marketing, to handle a full range of promotional, advertising, and other related projects for clients. It also created another subsidiary, Natural/Specialty Sales Inc., a national sales and marketing solution designed exclusively to serve manufacturers of natural, organic, gourmet, and ethnic foods.

While Acosta and the other large sales and marketing companies that survived the consolidation of the 1990s had no choice but to grow ever larger or perish, both manufacturers and grocers were not necessarily pleased with the reduction of local and regional sales and marketing agents. According to a 2001 *New York Times* article, "With so few brokers to choose from, a manufacturer is left in a bind, because it is hard to find an agent who does not already represent a competing brand." With only three national sales and marketing agencies (after the demise of Marketing Specialists), the fourth largest brand and smaller in a particular category was essentially out of luck. "The consolidation also ties the hands of manufacturers of the three top-selling brands in any category because they have nowhere else to go. 'It's not like you can drop your broker if you don't like the service,' said a manufacturer of a top-selling snack food … . 'The other two are working for your competitor.'" The alternative was for manufacturers to create their own direct sales forces, but that could cost as much as 6 percent of the product's wholesale price, at least twice as much as what a broker charged. On the other hand, grocers had their own complaints that the shelves were not as well maintained as before, and that the introduction of new products and changes in prices were often delayed. "Now, there may be only one broker working an entire aisle, so there's no fight there, no competition," Richard T. Frede, vice-president of Schnuck Markets, a Midwest supermarket chain, told the *Times*. "It makes them real lethargic resetting the shelves."

Acosta continued to expand its domestic business, and was especially interested in building Acosta's presence in so-called perimeter areas of the supermarket, such as fresh foods, which not only accounted for a third of all supermarket sales but was also the fastest growing area of the store. To this end, in July 2003 Acosta acquired The Vaughn Group, a fresh foods sales and marketing agency serving the Texas market. Later in 2003, Acosta strengthened its fresh foods business in the Mid-Atlantic region by acquiring Priority Foods Brokers, which served the Baltimore, Maryland, and Washington, D.C. markets. In June 2004, Acosta looked to the West Coast, acquiring Infinity Food Marketing and Carman & Associates, two major meat and seafood sales and marketing agencies serving northern California. The addition of Cincinnati-based Reliance Foods Brokerage L.L.C. in October 2004 bolstered Acosta's fresh food business in the Midwest. Then, in November 2004, Acosta acquired Premier Food Marketing, Inc., a sales and marketing agency specializing in bakery products in New England, the Eastern Great Lakes area, the New York Metropolitan area, and the Mid-Atlantic states. Also during this period, Acosta acquired Specialty Partners, Inc., a specialty and natural foods sales and marketing company, a move that strengthened Acosta's position in natural foods and specialty products in the Northeast, Midwest, and Southeast.

In 2005 Chartrand told *Supermarket News* that the emphasis on fresh foods was "paying huge dividends. In the meat and deli area, for instance, we now have new national clients in ConAgra, Sara Lee and Hormel."

Chartrand also told the trade publication that Acosta planned to make further acquisitions in "adjacencies," such as consumer marketing and research. To help in providing direction, Chartrand hired a chief strategy officer to build research and advanced-analytics to plot the company's future course, as well as a chief information officer to make sure that the company's information technology capabilities kept pace with its ambitions.

Ed Dinger

PRINCIPAL SUBSIDIARIES

MatchPoint Marketing; Natural/Specialty Sales Inc.

PRINCIPAL COMPETITORS

Advantage Sales and Marketing, L.L.C.; CROSSMARK.

FURTHER READING

Barker-Benfield, Simon, "Jacksonville, Fla.-Based Marketing Firm Absorbs Competitor's Business," *Florida Times-Union*, June 1, 2001.

———, "Super Marketers: Locally Based Acosta Puts Products on Stores' Shelves, and It Is the Biggest Company of Its Kind in the Nation," *Florida Times-Union*, June 25, 2001, p. FB-10.

Longo, Don, "Middle Management," *Progressive Grocer*, November 15, 2005, p. 98.

Merrefield, David, "Acosta Does Battle Against Downtime," *Supermarket News*, August 23, 2004, p. 20.

———, "Gary Chartrand; Chairman and CEO, Acosta Sales and Marketing Co.," *Supermarket News*, July 25, 2005, p. 106.

Murphy, Kate, "Food Brokers Are Bigger, So Shelves Look Smaller," *New York Times*, September 2, 2001, p. BU4.

Skidmore, Sarah, "Jacksonville, Fla., Businessman Dies of Cancer," *Florida Times-Union*, June 15, 2004.

Stuart, Devan, "Giant Food Marketer Goes International," *Jacksonville Business Journal*, May 4, 2001.

AGORA SA

Agora S.A. Group

—■—

Czerska 8/10 00-732
Warsaw,
Poland
Telephone: +48022055504002
Fax: +48-22-555-4850
Web site: http://www.agora.pl

Public Company
Incorporated: 1989
Employees: 3,586
Sales: £11.5 million (2004)
Stock Exchanges: Warsaw London
Ticker Symbol: AGO
NAIC: 511110 Newspaper Publishers; 511120 Periodical Publishers; 513110 Radio Broadcasting

■ ■ ■

Polish media company Agora S.A. Group is one of the true economic success stories to emerge from Eastern Europe since the demise of Communism in the late 1980s. The flagship of the Warsaw-based company is daily newspaper *Gazeta Wyborcza* (Election Gazette), boasting the highest circulation in Poland. A major part of *Gazeta's* success has been its use of 20 local editions that combine national news and advertising with local content and ads. Another element of the *Gazeta* formula is regular daily national supplements dedicated to subjects such as real estate, travel, and automobiles. A weekend women's magazine also is included. In addition, Agora publishes *Nowy Dzien* (New Day), a national daily in the mold of *USA Today,* a free national news-

paper called *Metro,* and 14 mass circulation magazines. The Collections division publishes collections of literature and has expanded to include music CDs. The company also has been involved in radio since the mid-1990s and owns about 30 stations, including one super-regional news radio station. Agora also runs one of Poland's largest outdoor advertising companies and one of the country's top Internet portals. Agora is eager to add television stations to its portfolio as well. It is a public company, listed on both the Warsaw and London Stock Exchanges.

ORIGINS DATING TO 1980S "SOLIDARITY" MOVEMENT

A Communist country since the end of World War II, Poland began the process of casting off its form of government in 1980 with the launch of a trade union federation at the Gdansk Shipyards called *Solidarnosc,* or Solidarity. Led by Lech Walesa, Solidarity became the center of a broad anticommunist movement that included diverse elements such as members of the Catholic Church and the radical left. Although driven underground by the government, Solidarity remained a vital force, preventing the government from launching its own tepid reform program in the late 1980s. Nationwide strikes in 1988 forced open talks with Solidarity, which was legalized in April 1989 and permitted to participate in the upcoming elections it had forced upon the government. As part of the agreement, Solidarity would be permitted to publish its own newspaper for the election campaign. Walesa offered the editorship of the newspaper to Adam Michnik, a philosopher, historian, writer, and longtime leading dis-

COMPANY PERSPECTIVES

We endeavor to live by the values which guided us when we founded the company and which continue to be our key tenets—truth, tolerance, respect for human rights and solidarity with the less fortunate. We promote these principles in our media—the newspaper, radio stations and on-line—and we strive to act on them as a company.

sident who was imprisoned for six of the previous 25 years for his activities. To organize and run the newspaper, Michnik turned to Helena Luczywo, editor of one of Poland's most important underground newspapers.

Luczywo's parents, both Jews, fled Poland to the Soviet Union during World War II, avoiding the fate of some three million Polish Jews killed during the Holocaust. Her family returned to Warsaw after the war and was essentially apolitical until 1968 when the Polish government turned anti-Semitic and her parents were fired from their jobs. Luczywo was far from a radical at this point, choosing to get married and have a child. She found work as an English interpreter and translator, and then in 1976 she was hired by a Swedish TV crew interviewing workers persecuted by the Polish government. It was an eye-opening experience for Luczywo, who decided to get involved in the opposition movement. She joined some friends and began publishing the underground newspaper *Robotnik* (The Worker), which in its very first issue advocated Polish independence. After the government crackdown on Solidarity in 1981 and the beginning of mass arrests she sent her daughter to live with her parents and spent a year leading a furtive life relying on fake identification papers. Luczywo now began publishing a new underground paper, *Tygodnik Mazowsze* (Mazovia Weekly). In 1986 she was able to secure an exit visa and spent several months in the United States as a fellow at Radcliffe's Bunting Institute. Able to devour the wealth of newspapers and magazines available at the Harvard University library, she became familiar with contemporary Western media. She returned to Poland and edited *Tygodnik Mazowsze* until Michnik approached her in 1989 about editing the first legally independent newspaper in all of the Soviet bloc of Eastern European countries.

Luczywo brought with her the staff from *Tygodnik Mazowsze* and established *Gazeta Wyborcza*, named the Election Gazette because its immediate function was to promote the slate of Solidarity candidates in the upcoming election. Michnik, Luczywo, and her staff set up shop in an empty nursery school, where Michnik used a bathroom as his office and the reporters worked at tables and sat on chairs intended for small children. They even held staff meetings outside in the sandbox. The first issue, which displayed the Solidarity logo, was just eight pages in length and was essentially devoted to profiles promoting the eight Solidarity candidates for office. All 150,000 copies were sold.

Even before the first issue was printed, Michnik and Luczywo knew they wanted to publish a truly independent newspaper. They formed a parent company for the paper called Agora, which in Polish meant a place to exchange views freely. Walesa, on the other hand, believed that *Gazeta* should be owned by Solidarity. This disagreement escalated further when *Gazeta* backed Walesa's opponent in the 1990 presidential election. Infuriated, Walesa wanted the Solidarity logo removed from the paper and Michnik fired. In September 1990 Solidarity's National Committee denied *Gazeta* the right to use its logo and slogan, although Michnik stayed on. He had tendered his resignation but Luczywo and other members of the paper persuaded him to remain.

FINDING A PLACE IN THE NEWS ECONOMY: 1990S

With the demise of Communism, *Gazeta*, like all of Poland, struggled to find its way in a new and unfamiliar capitalist system. Newspapers had functioned traditionally as political platforms, but now had to find a way to serve readers in a different manner, and make money. New to the mass market, Agora turned to advice from abroad. At a media conference held in Prague in 1990, *New York Times* publisher Arthur Sulzberger, Jr., spoke and impressed Luczywo with the concept of a newspaper trying to meet the needs of as many readers as possible. In response to this advice, she pushed *Gazeta* to print regional editions and she supported the idea of supplements. While Luczywo was proving herself to be a quick learner editorially, she realized she was out of her element when it came to the business side. Fortunately, she had a childhood friend who had become a Citibank executive to turn to: Wanda Rapazcynski.

Like Luczywo's parents, Rapazcynski's parents (the father Jewish, the mother Catholic) fled to the Soviet Union where they became friends. Their daughters became friends as well in postwar Warsaw, but unlike Luczywo, Rapazcynski immigrated to the United States in response to the government's anti-Semitic campaign in 1968, giving up her studies in psychology at the

KEY DATES

1989: Agora and Gazeta Wyborcza is founded.
1993: Cox Enterprises acquires an interest in the company.
1995: The company moves into radio.
1999: An initial public offering of stock is made.
2002: Prnszyński i S-ka Czasopisma is acquired, adding several magazine titles.
2004: Agora becomes involved in book publishing.

University of Warsaw. She married her Polish émigré boyfriend and had a child while earning a doctorate in psychology at the City University of New York. By 1982 she grew disenchanted with her field and elected to earn an M.B.A. from Yale University. Two years later she went to work at Citibank, ultimately becoming a vice-president and the head of product development. In January 1990 Rapazcynski's work brought her to Poland in search of business opportunities for Citibank. She looked up Luczywo, whom she had only seen twice in the previous 22 years. Within a matter of minutes she volunteered to help with *Gazeta.* "I felt that I owed a debt," she told *Fast Company* in a 2000 profile. "These people were here during martial law and communist rule. I wasn't."

For the next two years, Rapazcynski continued to hold down her Citibank job in New York, offering business advice for Agora and *Gazeta* over the phone, and spending her vacations working in Poland. The strain became too much and in 1992, when her daughter was beginning boarding school, she decided to quit her well-paying job at Citibank and move back to Warsaw for a less than certain career with Agora.

Rapazcynski played a key role in changing the culture at *Gazeta,* where people were lackadaisical, an attitude bred by decades of Communist rule during which there was no reward for doing good work. But perhaps of even more importance was her job of attracting investors in *Gazeta.* The owners of the *New York Review of Books* lent the paper $300,000 for printing supplies in 1990, but finding someone to make a more significant investment in Agora proved difficult. Rapazcynski's daughter wrote 400 letters to U.S. foundations, but no one was willing to take a chance on a country whose future was so uncertain. Some foreign media companies were willing to acquire control of *Gazeta,* but the paper did not want to give up its hard-earned independence. Finally, Rapazcynski was able in 1993 to convince Cox Enterprises Inc., the Atlanta-based media company, to acquire a 12.5 percent stake in Agora without exercising any editorial influence. The money was used to computerize the newspaper and build a new $21 million printing plant.

The relationship with Cox was beneficial in a number of other ways. Given that Poland's democracy was still in a fragile state, Rapazcynski told the *Financial Times,* "It was a very comforting thought that if someone tried to arrest us, there would be someone in Washington to scream loudly." The Cox connection also helped Agora to receive $8 million in debt financing from the European Bank for Reconstruction and Development. Moreover, Cox was generous in providing advice. In 1995, having already established *Gazeta* as the top newspaper in Poland, Agora was ready to diversify and become involved in radio. Cox, owner of a number of U.S. radio stations, helped Agora draw up a business plan and dispatched some radio consultants to Poland. At the time, Polish radio stations were national and offered a mix of music and news. Cox advised Agora to invest in local radio and create focused formats. What Agora learned through market research was that an oldies format would prove popular with Polish listeners between the ages of 25 and 45, the most coveted advertising demographic. The concept proved to be a winning one, and Agora was able to diversify beyond *Gazeta.* In 1997 Agora bought a 12 percent interest in a pay television station run by Canal Plus of France, but it was sold in 2001 because it was too small a stake to have commercial impact.

GOING PUBLIC IN 1999

Agora hired Credit Suisse First Boston to help with an initial public offering (IPO) of stock to fuel further growth. At the bank's behest Rapazcynski was named Agora's president to provide reassurance to investors, and then the company was prepared for the IPO. Shares were first sold to 1,600 employees for just 24 cents each based on years of service. Given that the general offer price would be 100 times that amount, a large number of employees became instantly wealthy. In addition, Agora set up a charitable trust, which would receive 7.5 percent of the issued shares, to be distributed to Polish charities and benefit the entire country. The 1999 IPO proved highly successful, raising $93 million for Agora, which allowed it to build a new office complex and printing facilities. By the end of the year, *Gazeta* boasted an average daily circulation of 560,000 and ad sales of $123 million. In addition, its five-year-old radio division, with 13 local stations and one national station, was growing quickly. Ad revenues grew from $2.7 million in 1998 to $7 million in 1999.

Agora looked to develop into a true media empire with the start of the new century. On the print side, *Metro,* a *Gazeta* insert first published in 1998, became a separate free newspaper published twice a week in Warsaw in 2001. Two years later it began to be published Monday through Friday, and then in November 2004 it expanded beyond Warsaw and the concept was introduced in nine other cities. In April 2005 another nine cities were added. In 2005 Agora filled out its slate of newspapers with the launch of a national daily called *Nowy Dzien* (New Day). Agora also moved beyond *Gazeta*'s magazine inserts to establish a full-fledged magazine operation, jumpstarted by the 2002 acquisition of the titles published by Poland's Prnszyñski i S-ka Czasopisma, including *Good Housekeeping, Hearth & Home, House Beautiful, Flower and Garden, Bouquets, Beautiful Gardens, Cuisine, Fine Cooking, My Child—The Monthly for Caring Parents, Automotive Magazine, Poster Automotive Magazine, Science,* and *Life.* Later in 2002 Agora acquired several titles from the Motor Media Project, including category leader *Motorcycle World* as well as yearly *Motorcycles of the World* and quarterlies *Motorcycle World Library* and *Moped World.* Most of the acquired periodicals would be given significant facelifts, and Agora also would launch original titles, such as *Avanti,* a new women's shopping magazine introduced in 2004, and *Logo,* a men's quarterly offering advice and shopping tips, which premiered in 2005. Agora also entered the book publishing field in June 2004 with the publication of a 40-volume collection of 20th-century literature, the success of which led to the publication of a 20-volume encyclopedia, travel books, collections of fairy tales, and a collection of classical music CDs.

In other media ventures, Agora launched an Internet portal in 2000, and became involved in outdoor media with the acquisition of AMS, Poland's largest billboard advertising firm. A gaping hole in Agora's holdings remained television, however. The country had only two commercial stations, and it was uncertain when more licenses would be issued. There was a good chance, however, that Agora eventually would add television to its growing list of media assets.

Ed Dinger

PRINCIPAL OPERATING UNITS

Gazeta Wyborcza; Nowy Dzien; Metro; Collections; Magazines; Outdoor; Radio; Internet.

PRINCIPAL COMPETITORS

Axel Springer AG; 4Media S.A.; ZPR Group.

FURTHER READING

Bobinski, Christopher, "Growing Voice of Dissent," *Financial Times,* March 25, 1998, p. 7.

Eade, Philip, "Wanda Rapaczynski," *Euromoney,* December 2000, p. 29.

Green, Peter S., "Daily Thrives on Its Values," *International Herald Tribune,* March 31, 1999, p. 11.

Harding, James, "News Moguls Retain Their Common Touch," *Financial Times,* May 5, 2000, p. 18.

Kruger, Pamela, "'The Best Way to Keep the Devil at the Doors Is to Be Rich,'" *Fast Company,* November 2000, p. 152.

Michaels, Daniel, "Polish Journey: Newspaper That Once Battled Communists Courts IPO Buyers," *Wall Street Journal,* March 3, 1999, p. 1.

Perlez, Jane, "Warsaw Journal: Paper's Fare Adds the Spice of Life to Politics and the Poles Devour It," *New York Times,* June 5, 1993.

Simpson, Peggy, "In Poland, Women Run the Largest News Organization," *Nieman Reports,* Winter 2001, p. 80.

Williamson, Elizabeth, "For Polish Radicals, Stock Bounty Puts Fat on Lean Years," *Wall Street Journal,* July 13, 2000, p. A1.

Albany Molecular
Research, Inc.

—————■—————

21 Corporate Circle
Albany, New York 12212
U.S.A.
Telephone: (518) 464-0279
Fax: (518) 464-0289
Web site: http://www.albmolecular.com

Public Company
Incorporated: 1991
Employees: 805
Sales: $169.5 million (2004)
Stock Exchanges: NASDAQ
Ticker Symbol: AMRI
NAIC: 541710 Research and Development in the Physical Sciences and Engineering Sciences

■ ■ ■

Albany Molecular Research, Inc. is a chemistry-based drug discovery, development, and manufacturing company. The company performs research and development work for major pharmaceutical and biotechnology companies, identifying and developing compounds for applications in the drug market. Albany Molecular offers services that encompass the entire development cycle of a drug, from lead discovery through lead optimization, preclinical testing, clinical trials, and commercial manufacturing. The company operates overseas through subsidiaries in Singapore and India.

ORIGINS

Founders Chester Opalka and Thomas D'Ambra helped legitimize a new way of doing business in the pharmaceutical industry, forsaking stable employment and draining personal bank accounts to carve a new niche in the industry. Opalka and D'Ambra first met while working for a pharmaceutical company named Sterling Winthrop, Inc. Opalka joined the company in 1970 after he earned an undergraduate degree in chemistry from Niagara University. Opalka served in various capacities during his 20-year tenure at Sterling Winthrop, linking up with D'Ambra midway through his stay at the company.

D'Ambra joined Sterling Winthrop in 1982, bringing with him an undergraduate degree in chemistry from the College of Holy Cross and a doctorate degree from the Massachusetts Institute of Technology, which he earned the year he joined the medicinal chemistry department at Sterling Winthrop. During his seven-year stay at Sterling Winthrop, D'Ambra participated in drug research programs in the endocrine, cardiovascular, and analgesic therapeutic areas, work that provided the inspiration for Albany Molecular. He was impressed not by the work that was being done, but by the work that was not being done, watching as numerous projects with potential were abandoned because of a shortage of chemists. "We saw an opportunity to build a company to provide high-value research and development," D'Ambra said in a May 29, 2000 interview with *Business Week*, explaining the premise behind Albany Molecular.

D'Ambra left Sterling Winthrop in 1989, giving up his post as senior research chemist to begin an entrepreneurial career. Albany Molecular was not his first attempt at launching a start-up venture; he cofounded Coromed, Inc. in 1989, hiring Opalka in early 1991 as a senior research chemist. The pair left Coromed in 1991 to start Albany Molecular, an effort that would require each partner to forego any form of salary for an undetermined length of time. Opalka refinanced his house, while D'Ambra's wife worked in a tollbooth to help pay the couple's bills.

The venture was a gamble of sorts because in 1991 major pharmaceutical companies, often collectively referred to as "Big Pharma," rarely looked for outside help in their drug development efforts. It was up to Opalka and D'Ambra to convince Big Pharma to outsource the methodical chemical research required to turn a compound into a marketable pharmaceutical.

Initially, the scope of Albany Molecular's business was limited. Major pharmaceutical companies were willing only to outsource custom synthesis and process research to such third-party outfits as Albany Molecular. D'Ambra, who took charge of leading the company while Opalka took the title of vice-president, made the best of the situation, however, achieving what would be his company's landmark success during its formative years.

Not long after starting out, the company was hired to purify a substance from a mixture of compounds, an effort that failed with its original intent but eclipsed all hopes in every other respect. D'Ambra and the rest of the nascent company's scientific team were unable to meet the objectives of the original assignment, but the effort resulted in discovering a new way to synthesize fexofenadine. D'Ambra patented the process, licensing it to Aventis S.A. in 1995. The technology enabled the production of the active ingredient of Allegra, which received Food and Drug Administration approval in 1996, quickly becoming the second-leading allergy

medication. Allegra was a so-called "blockbuster" drug, akin to drilling and striking oil, generating revenues that enriched Aventis and provided the major source of income, through royalty payments, for Albany Molecular for the next decade.

The licensing agreement with Aventis enabled Albany Molecular to post its first profit in 1995, marking the beginning of a string of profitable years that would extend into the 21st century. The process developed by D'Ambra became the financial lifeblood of the company, both in terms of the revenue collected directly from the licensing agreement and from the new business opportunities created by the company's success in drug discovery chemistry. In an April 4, 2005 interview with *Chemical Market Reporter*, the company's senior vice-president, Michael Trova, marked the ten-year anniversary of the seminal achievement by noting, "1995 was in fact the first example, that we're aware of, of a medicinal chemistry-related project being outsourced." Albany Molecular's pioneering work convinced Big Pharma that outsourcing drug discovery chemistry worked, leading drug companies to assign far greater responsibilities to companies of Albany Molecular's ilk.

With a steady stream of cash coming in (the company collected more than $20 million a year from the Aventis deal during the latter half of the 1990s), D'Ambra and Opalka presided over an enviable operation. Start-up ventures in the pharmaceutical industry generally took years before becoming profitable, but Albany Molecular was not only profitable, it was recording substantial profits in relation to its revenue volume. In 1998, for example, the company recorded $33.9 million in revenue, from which it posted $10.4 million in net income.

While it was demonstrating such financial vitality, D'Ambra and Opalka decided to sell the company on Wall Street, completing an initial public offering of stock in early 1999. With the proceeds from the public offering, the founders pressed ahead with increasing capacity, broadening their service offerings, and increasing the size of their customer base. They began making a series of investments and acquisitions, building the company along two lines, its chemistry services contract business with other pharmaceutical companies and its drug discovery platform that called for collaborations with pharmaceutical and biotechnology firms.

INVESTMENTS AND ACQUISITIONS AT THE START OF THE 21ST CENTURY

Albany Molecular's business model, a chemistry services platform on one side and a drug discovery platform on

KEY DATES

1991: Albany Molecular is founded.
1995: The company formulates the active ingredient in Allegra.
1999: The company completes its initial public offering of stock.
2003: The acquisition of Organichem Corp. is completed.
2005: Laboratory facilities are established in Singapore and India.

the other, offered the company the best of both worlds in the pharmaceutical industry. Its contract business offered potentially steady, short-term growth opportunities, while its drug discovery business offered potentially big rewards in the long term. With its footing firmly established by the dawn of the 21st century (the company placed fourth on *Business Week*'s list of the 100 fastest-growing companies in 2000), Albany Molecular began to bolster its size and capabilities, becoming a more comprehensive player in the industry niche it had helped to create.

Perhaps the most important development was the company's acquisition of a minority interest in Organichem Corp., which was created after a management-led buyout of Nycomed-Amersham's pharmaceutical plant in December 1999. The plant, located in Rensselaer, New York, was situated on a 25-acre site that included a pilot plant, 170,000 liters of reactor capacity, and the capability of large-scale manufacturing, having been engaged in producing drugs for more than a century. Albany Molecular acquired its stake, a 37.5 percent interest, before the end of 1999, intending to exercise its options to acquire full control over the company by the end of 2002.

Albany Molecular's financial success continued as the company entered the 21st century. Revenues swelled to $69 million in 2000 and net income increased to $23.5 million, enabling the company to raise $119.5 million in a secondary stock offering during the year.

Opalka retired in 2000, leaving D'Ambra to superintend the fortunes of the pair's entrepreneurial creation. D'Ambra's biggest complaint was voiced in an October 23, 2000 interview with *Investor's Business Daily*: "We can't grow fast enough to keep up with demand for the potential contracts that are out there."

His most pressing problem was finding enough chemists to perform the work the company was obtain-

ing. D'Ambra spent $1 million on recruiting chemists in 1999, adding 45 chemists during the year. In 2000, he added another 45 chemists, as he struggled to find the personnel to keep pace with Albany Molecular's bounding growth.

His efforts at expanding the company's business offered no respite in recruiting qualified personnel. In February 2000, he completed the $2.3 million acquisition of American Advanced Organics, a Syracuse, New York-based developmental-scale contract manufacturer that was renamed the Syracuse Research Center. D'Ambra set his acquisitive sights to the west at the end of the year, spending $22.4 million for a drug discovery company based outside of Seattle, Washington, named New Chemical Entities Inc. New Chemical Entities, which was renamed AMRI Bothell Research Center, possessed a library of more than 100,000 natural compounds that D'Ambra could use to discover and to create new drugs.

Against the backdrop of recessive economic conditions during the first years of the decade, Albany Molecular recorded impressive growth. Between 2001 and 2003, revenues nearly doubled to $196.3 million, propelled by the growth of the company's contract business. After acquiring laboratory facilities outside of Chicago in late 2001 and announcing a $30 million expansion plan the following year, the company completed its acquisition of Organichem in 2003, purchasing the 62.5 percent it did not already own.

After years of uninterrupted financial progress, Albany Molecular hit a bump in the road during its 13th year in business. The company cited increasing competition from Asia, the closure of its laboratory operations in Chicago, and decreased royalties from Allegra as causes for an $11.6 million loss in 2004. Revenues suffered as well, dropping from $196.3 million to $169.5 million. D'Ambra responded to the difficult year by initiating significant changes in 2005 that promised to mark the beginning of a new era of existence for Albany Molecular.

EXPANSION OVERSEAS IN 2005

D'Ambra sought to improve the company's financial performance by expanding overseas, taking his first steps in a globalization plan in early 2005. In February, the company was preparing to begin production at its new research center in Singapore, where it could benefit from reduced operating costs and access to a relatively inexpensive pool of chemists.

"Our customers are under a lot of pressure and looking for cost savings," D'Ambra explained in a February 7, 2005 interview with *Chemical Market*

Reporter. "So we believe this step is important to maintaining our leadership position, particularly in the early stages of chemistry outsourcing."

By the time the Singapore facility had gained its first customer in mid-2005, Albany Molecular was establishing another overseas research center in Hyderabad, India, aping the trend established by its customers, drug companies, of reducing research and manufacturing costs by moving operations overseas. Further, chemists, increasingly in short supply in the United States, were relatively abundant in India, where they typically earned $1,000 per year, helping to lower Albany Molecular's operating costs by approximately 75 percent.

As Albany Molecular concluded its first 15 years in business, further international expansion was expected. Company officials were scouting locations in Eastern Europe, South America, and China, hoping to increase Albany Molecular's exposure to worldwide markets and to insure a steady supply of qualified scientists. The company had achieved much during its first decade and a half in business, but in one sense its enviable success posed an important question about its future. Allegra royalty payments, which had proved instrumental to the company's rise, were beginning to decline, with patents scheduled to expire in 2013.

One of D'Ambra's most daunting challenges was weaning Albany Molecular off its dependence on Allegra-related income, an objective that seemed to be within his grasp considering the company's pioneering record of accomplishments in providing chemistry services to pharmaceutical companies. D'Ambra's chances of future success also were improved by the comprehensive capabilities the company was able to acquire from the riches of its Allegra work. In the years ahead, Albany Molecular, supported by its contract business for steady financial gains and its drug discovery platform for large financial rewards, promised to play a prominent role in the industry niche it had helped to create.

Jeffrey L. Covell

PRINCIPAL SUBSIDIARIES

AMR Technology Inc.; AMRI Bothell Research Center Inc.; Albany Molecular Research Export Corporation; Organichem Corporation; Albany Molecular Research Singapore Research Centre, Pte. Ltd.; Albany Molecular Research Hyderabad Research Centre, Pte. Ltd. (India).

PRINCIPAL COMPETITORS

ArQule, Inc.; Array BioPharma Inc.; Discovery Partners International, Inc.

FURTHER READING

Aaron, Kenneth, "New York's Albany Molecular Buys Seattle-Area Drug-Discovery Company," *Times Union,* December 21, 2000.

"Albany Molecular Purchases Chicago Research Facility for $10 Million," *Chemical Market Reporter,* October 1, 2001, p. 16.

"Albany Molecular Research: All R&D, All the Time," *Business Week,* May 29, 2000, p. 192.

Alva, Marilyn, "Albany Molecular Research Inc.," *Investor's Business Daily,* October 23, 2000, p. A12.

Boswell, Clay, "Albany Molecular Plans to Go Global with New Singapore Research Centre," *Chemical Market Reporter,* February 7, 2005, p. 8.

DerGurahian, Jean, "Albany, N.Y., Biotech Firm Reports Doubled Revenue in 2000," *Times Union,* March 11, 2001.

"Discovering Outsourcing Increases," *Chemical Market Reporter,* April 4, 2005, p. 14.

"For Albany Molecular, Proprietary Technologies Are Key to Success," *Chemical Market Reporter,* November 20, 2000, p. 29.

Furfaro, Danille T., "Albany, N.Y., Molecular Research Inc. Details $30 Million Expansion Plan," *Times Union,* May 30, 2002.

Moorse, Alan, "Albany Molecular Co-Founder Opalka Retiring But Keeping Hand in Business," *Capital District Business Review,* August 28, 2000, p. 5.

Schmitt, Bill, "Albany Buys Drug Services Firm," *Chemical Week,* January 3, 2001, p. 13.

Scott, Alex, "Albany Molecular Acquires Majority Stake in Organichem," *Chemical Week,* January 15, 2003, p. 22.

Wechsler, Alan, "Albany Molecular Makes Gains," *Times Union,* May 11, 2005.

———, "Albany, N.Y., Drug Research Firm Weighs Overseas Manufacturing," *Times Union,* May 20, 2004.

———, "Sales Rise, But Profits Drop for Albany Molecular Research Inc.," *Times Union,* November 5, 2003.

Alimentation Couche-Tard
Inc.

———■———

1600 Saint-Martin Boulevard East
Tower B, Suite 200
Laval, Quebec H7G 4S7
Canada
Telephone: (450) 662-3272
Fax: (450) 662-6648
Web site: http://www.couche-tard.qc.ca

Public Company
Incorporated: 1985
Employees: 34,000
Sales: CAD 10.21 billion (2005)
Stock Exchanges: Toronto
Ticker Symbol: ATD
NAIC: 445110 Supermarkets and Other Grocery (Except
   Convenience) Stores

■ ■ ■

Alimentation Couche-Tard Inc. operates nearly 5,000 stores in Canada and the United States, ranking as Canada's largest retailer and the third largest convenience store chain in North America. The company's stores, more than 3,000 of which sell motor fuel, range in size from small, 400-square-foot units to 10,000-square-foot units, each designed to give customers a local, neighborhood feel. Alimentation Couche-Tard's stores operate under the names Couche-Tard, Mac's, and Circle K.

ORIGINS

Alain Brouchard orchestrated the phenomenal rise of Alimentation Couche-Tard ("food for those who go to bed late") in the retail industry, creating one of the titans of the convenience store sector. A native of Chicoutimi, Quebec, he fulfilled, and most likely greatly exceeded, a goal to build his own retail business, completing a mission conceived during his childhood. "I come from a very entrepreneurial family and I'd always been in the store business," he explained in an October 2002 interview with *Report on Business Magazine.*

"Even as a teenager, I worked in a store, stocking the shelves. I saw firsthand the opportunity to build my own company."

Although Brouchard technically did not build his own company from the ground up, his achievements on the expansion front thoroughly obliterated any sense of an Alimentation Couche-Tard existing before his arrival. Brouchard, via acquisition, started with 12 stores; 20 years later, after a spate of acquisitions and a relentless march across North America, he was preparing to open his 5,000th store.

After working in Chicoutimi stores, Brouchard moved south as a young adult. During the late 1970s, he managed two convenience stores in suburban Montreal. The experience confirmed his affinity for the convenience store format, spurring him to make his first entrepreneurial move when he was in his mid-30s. In 1985, he spent CAD 170,000 to purchase a dozen stores operating under the name Couche-Tard. The small chain, which began as a single store at the beginning of the decade, became Brouchard's vehicle for expansion, a modestly sized business that he used to create a retail behemoth. Brouchard first launched his attack in Quebec before expanding throughout eastern Canada, westward

COMPANY PERSPECTIVES

Couche-Tard's unique operational approach combines the strengths of a large organization and the advantages of benchmarking with the benefits of local management and entrepreneurship in each store. So Couche-Tard is a family of autonomous business units that prosper by showcasing their brands while leveraging the critical mass of the parent company. With such a structure, we can compete with the smallest chains through a personalized approach to better seize local opportunities and minimize costs. Similarly, we outperform other chains by developing operational systems that maximize efficiency, by investing in new marketing concepts that improve profit margins, and by benefiting from supply synergies to lower product costs.

across all Canadian provinces, and down into the United States. By the time he celebrated the 20th anniversary of acquiring Alimentation Couche-Tard, Brouchard had cleared the way for expansion into Mexico.

Brouchard was at his most aggressive in terms of expansion at the dawn of the 21st century, leading the company forward at such a blistering pace that progress during his first 15 years in charge could be dismissed as insignificant. The period was important, however, because it confirmed Brouchard's talents as a retail executive, established the foundation for Alimentation Couche-Tard's transcontinental expansion at the start of the 21st century, and included impressive growth, which only paled in significance when compared with the company's assault on North American rivals in the new millennium. Brouchard bolted out of the blocks, increasing the size of the chain from 12 stores to 116 stores by the end of 1986. Over the course of the ensuing decade, Alimentation Couche-Tard's store count nearly tripled, reaching 310 units by the end of 1996, when sales totaled CAD 259 million. Up to that point, Brouchard had confined his efforts to his home province, creating the leading convenience store chain in Quebec. In 1997, the essence of his acquisition campaign changed character, marking a turning point in Alimentation Couche-Tard's history and signaling the beginning of Brouchard's bold bid to become the largest convenience store operator in North America.

Once Brouchard began expanding geographically, Alimentation Couche-Tard entered a new phase of development, taking the first evolutionary step toward assuming a transcontinental profile. The process happened quickly and it was propelled in large part through acquisitions. The start of the new era began with Brouchard's acquisition of C Corp. Inc. in 1997. A subsidiary of Provigo Inc., C Corp. operated 245 convenience stores in Quebec under the Provi-Soir banner and 50 other stores in Ontario and Alberta under the names Winks and Red Rooster. It was a landmark acquisition, one that Brouchard had been pursuing for five years. "This acquisition is the most important in our history and the most important in the Quebec convenience store industry," he said in an announcement quoted in the April 14, 1997 issue of *Business Wire.*

His next statement indicated the significance of the deal, explaining that the addition of the 50 stores in Ontario and Alberta "would allow us to expand our horizons and will provide an important stepping stone for our national expansion."

With the acquisition of C. Corp., Alimentation Couche-Tard swelled to a 630-unit chain in 1998, nearly doubling in size, with CAD 509 million in sales. Within a few short years, it would take less than a month for the company to match the revenue volume recorded in 1998.

NATIONAL DOMINANCE IN 1999

Brouchard's next move on the acquisition front established Alimentation Couche-Tard as a retailer with a formidable presence. In 1999, he completed another deal that had been five years in the making, purchasing Silcorp Ltd., a Scarborough, Ontario-based chain with 813 stores throughout Canada. The acquisition, which saw Alimentation Couche-Tard purchase a retailer larger than itself, created the first national convenience store chain in Canada, completing Brouchard's ascension to the top of the country's retail ranks. Under Alimentation Couche-Tard's ownership, the stores acquired from Silcorp formed a second brand that operated under the name Mac's, giving Brouchard control over more than 1,600 stores, including more than 200 units in the western provinces. The company's sales, not surprisingly, increased exponentially, reaching CAD 1.6 billion in 2000, three times the total registered two years earlier.

In the wake of the acquisition of Silcorp's stores, Alimentation Couche-Tard pressed ahead cultivating its business in central and western Canada with its Mac's brand and in eastern Canada with its Couche-Tard brand. Brouchard, while discussing the merits of the Silcorp purchase, revealed his intentions to expand to the south. But before he made the international leap, he and his executives developed what they called the company's

```
┌─────────────────────────────────────────────┐
│                                               │
│              KEY DATES                        │
│                    ■                          │
│                                               │
│  1985:  Alain Brouchard buys 12 stores for CAD│
│         170,000.                              │
│  1997:  The acquisition of C Corp. expands    │
│         Alimentation Couche-Tard beyond       │
│         Quebec's borders for the first time.  │
│  1999:  Alimentation Couche-Tard becomes the  │
│         first national convenience store      │
│         chain in Canada after acquiring       │
│         Silcorp Ltd.                          │
│  2001:  Alimentation Couche-Tard enters the   │
│         U.S. market with the purchase of      │
│         Johnson Oil Co.                        │
│  2003:  The purchase of 1,663 Circle K stores │
│         makes Alimentation Couche-Tard the    │
│         fourth largest convenience store      │
│         chain in North America.               │
│  2005:  Revenues surpass CAD 10 billion as the│
│         company becomes the third largest     │
│         convenience store operator in North   │
│         America.                              │
│                                               │
└─────────────────────────────────────────────┘
```

"Strategy 2000/Store 2000" plan. An important part of the strategy called for decentralized management and creating an eclectic array of stores in terms of size, design, and merchandise mix, ultimately aiming at a chain in which each store reflected its neighborhood. Brouchard, as the century began, made it clear that his objective was to usurp the position held by 7-Eleven, Inc., the largest convenience store chain in North America, but unlike 7-Eleven, which presented customers with identical images of itself at each of its locations, Brouchard wanted individual stores tailored to their communities. As he pressed ahead with expansion, his differentiation strategy spawned stores ranging in size from 400-square-foot, shopping mall-based stores to 10,000-square-foot locations frequented by truckers. A motley collection of stores appeared, including one located in a basement with no windows, which was designed with a submarine theme. Executives at 7-Eleven likely were not beguiled by Alimentation Couche-Tard's many guises, but if they were, the arrival of Brouchard on their home soil in 2001 left no doubt about the intentions of Canada's king of retailing.

When Brouchard first discussed expanding into the United States with the press, he thought his foray would start in the Pacific Northwest. Instead, he made his first move in the Midwest, acquiring Johnson Oil Co. in June 2001. Johnson, which operated its stores under the Bigfoot banner, owned 225 stores in Illinois, Indiana, and Kentucky, a network that Brouchard planned to expand to more than 600 stores. Next, after completing several smaller acquisitions, Brouchard strengthened his position in the Midwest by purchasing another larger convenience store chain. In August 2002, he spent CAD 120 million to acquire 285 stores from bankrupt Daisy Mart Convenience Stores Inc., a company founded in 1939 that, after rapid expansion left it awash in debt, filed for Chapter 11 in 2001. The addition of the stores, which were located in Ohio, Kentucky, Pennsylvania, Michigan, and Indiana, made Alimentation Couche-Tard the eighth largest convenience store chain in North America. Brouchard, who presided over a chain of 2,400 outlets after the Daisy Mart purchase, did not intend to ease back on his expansion efforts. "The first goal is 6,000 stores," he declared in an October 2002 interview with *Report on Business Magazine.* "It will take a few years to get there, but it will happen," he vowed.

ACQUISITION OF CIRCLE K IN 2003

Following the Daisy Mart acquisition, Alimentation Couche-Tard maintained a presence in six states, far from the geographic footprint Brouchard envisioned for his company. He wanted to do in the United States what he had done in Canada: create a nationwide chain of convenience stores. An enormous opportunity to take a major step toward achieving his goal was presented in 2002, when ConocoPhillips Co., the largest petroleum refiner in the United States, announced plans to divest the majority of its vast retail marketing network because management believed there were better business opportunities in the wholesale market than in the retail market. Brouchard saw his chance to leap past his closest rivals and he took it, reaching an agreement with ConocoPhillips in October 2003 to acquire the refiner's chain of Circle K stores. In December 2003, the CAD 1.1 billion deal was concluded, giving Brouchard 1,663 stores in 16 states and franchise relationships with more than 350 franchised and licensed stores. The acquisition, which included roughly 700 stores in California and Arizona, had a tremendous effect on Alimentation Couche-Tard's stature, enabling the company to leapfrog from the number seven position in North America's convenience store market to the number four position. Alimentation Couche-Tard entered 2004 trailing only 7-Eleven, Royal Dutch/Shell Group of Companies, and BP PLC.

In the wake of the Circle K acquisition, considerable effort was directed at integrating the chain into Alimentation Couche-Tard's operations. Previously, the stores acquired by Alimentation Couche-Tard had been rebranded as either Mac's or Couche-Tard units, but the

Circle K stores retained their name, giving Brouchard a three-pronged approach to expansion. He resumed his acquisition campaign roughly a year after inking the Circle K deal, completing transactions that chipped away at 7-Eleven's lead. In November 2004, Brouchard acquired 21 stores in Arizona from Shell, and announced plans to acquire several more regional chains in 2005.

As Brouchard celebrated his 20th year of ownership in 2005, Alimentation Couche-Tard stood as a towering force with a network of nearly 5,000 stores. After purchasing 19 stores in the Augusta, Georgia, area in February and another nine stores in Illinois in April, the chain consisted of 4,853 stores. Sales totaled CAD 10.2 billion by the end of the company's fiscal year in 2005 and net income reached CAD 199.5 million. Brouchard revealed during the year that within two years he would complete another major acquisition, one that was expected to add hundreds of stores to the company's portfolio of properties. As he plotted his company's continued growth and pursued his goal of reaching 6,000 stores, few industry observers doubted the capabilities of someone who had parlayed a CAD 170,000 investment into a CAD 10 billion retail empire.

Jeffrey L. Covell

PRINCIPAL SUBSIDIARIES

Mac's Convenience Stores L.L.C.; Magasins Couche-Tard Inc.; Magasins Couche-Tard Inc.; 2966565 Canada Inc.; Actigaz Inc.; 9006-7141 Québec Inc.; C Corp. Inc.; The Circle K Corporation.

PRINCIPAL COMPETITORS

7-Eleven, Inc.; Exxon Mobil Corporation; Royal Dutch/Shell Group of Companies.

FURTHER READING

"Canadian Chain Makes First Foray into U.S., Snaps up MW Marketer for $65.8 MM," *Oil Express,* May 21, 2001, p. 3.

"Canadian C-Store Chain Plays in Peoria," *Oil Express,* November 24, 2003, p. 4.

"ConocoPhillips Sells Circle K for $830 Million," *Oil Daily,* October 7, 2003.

"Couche-Tard Acquires R-Con Centres Inc. Holder of Mac's Master Franchise in Manitoba," *Canadian Corporate News,* August 22, 2001.

"Couche-Tard Buys R-Con Centres, Eyes U.S. Expansion," *NPN International,* November-December 2001, p. 7.

"Couche-Tard's Takeover of Circle K Stores Coincides with Sunbelt Squeeze," *Oil Express,* December 15, 2003, p. 3.

Frayer, Janis Mackey, "How Convenient," *Report on Business Magazine,* October 2002, p. 35.

King, Laura, "ConocoPhillips Offloads Circle K," *Daily Deal,* October 7, 2003.

Mackinnon, Jim, "Dairy Mart to Live on As Brand Only Under New Ownership," *Akron Beacon Journal,* August 22, 2002.

McCarthy, Erin, "More Than Gasoline, Lotto Tickets and Cigarettes," *Display & Design Ideas,* October 2003, p. 22.

Schnitzler, Peter, "Bigfoot Parent Enjoys Convenient Gains," *Indianapolis Business Journal,* May 28, 2001, p. 29B.

Squier, Suzy, "Couche-Tard Leads the Way in Canada's Convenience Market," *DSN Retailing Today,* September 6, 2004, p. 8.

Allergan, Inc.

———————•———————

2525 Dupont Drive
Irvine, California 92612-1531
U.S.A.
Telephone: (714) 246-4500
Fax: (714) 246-4971
Web site: http://www.allergan.com

Public Company
Incorporated: 1948 as Child Institute, Inc.
Employees: 5,030
Sales: $2.05 billion (2004)
Stock Exchanges: New York
Ticker Symbol: AGN
NAIC: 325411 Medicinal and Botanical Manufacturing;
    325412 Pharmaceutical Preparation Manufacturing

■ ■ ■

Allergan, Inc. is a global provider of specialty pharmaceutical products in three main areas: eye care, neuromodulators, and skin care. Allergan (pronounced AL-ergan) is one of the world leaders in ophthalmic pharmaceuticals, developing, manufacturing, and marketing products used in the treatment of glaucoma, cataracts, dry eye, eye infections, and conjunctivitis. The firm's largest single product, however, is the neuromodulator Botox, which is responsible for about one-third of overall revenues. Botox is used both therapeutically to treat various neuromuscular disorders, such as crossed eyes, uncontrolled blinking, and sustained muscle spasms, and cosmetically to erase facial wrinkles. Allergan's skin care line focuses on treatments for psoriasis and acne.

Allergan markets its products in more than 100 countries around the world, with international sales accounting for about 30 percent of the total. The firm maintains three research and development facilities located in Irvine, California; High Wycombe, England; and Dublin, Ireland, and manufactures most of its products at its own plants situated in Waco, Texas; Westport, Ireland; and São Paulo, Brazil.

OPHTHALMIC BEGINNINGS

In 1948 Gavin S. Herbert, Sr., started a small business in a laboratory above one of his Los Angeles drugstores. Incorporated as Child Institute, Inc. because the original intention was to market a product to stop thumb sucking, an idea quickly abandoned, the company turned its attention to ophthalmic products. Stanley Bly, who had only a bachelor's degree in chemistry, created the business's first product, an antihistamine eye drop named Allergan. The name was derived from a combination of the words *allergy* and *neoantergan,* a main ingredient. Under the new company name Allergan Pharmaceuticals, Inc., adopted in 1950, Bly developed additional products, including a cortisone eye drop, Cortefrin. The small business was assisted by the salesmanship of Herbert's son, Gavin Herbert, Jr., a 19-year-old student at the University of Southern California.

In 1953 Bly's sudden death almost caused the company to close. Sales at that time were approximately $25,000, and many of Bly's product formulas were undocumented. A young associate professor at the University of Southern California's School of Pharmacy, John Biles, reformulated Allergan's products and saved

COMPANY PERSPECTIVES

Our Vision/Our Mission: To continue as an innovative, technology driven, global health care company focused on pharmaceuticals in specialty markets that deliver value to customers, satisfy unmet medical needs and improve patients' lives.

To become the partner of choice for ever better health care through the value of our tech-nological in-novation, industry leadership, partnering skills and relationships, worldwide infra-structure, research and manufacturing capabilities. To develop a level of understanding of our customers in order to implement operational strategies that provide the greatest value for our customers and stockholders.

the company from failure. The next year, Allergan continued to struggle when Gavin Herbert, Jr., was drafted into the navy during the Korean War and Herbert, Sr., was involved in an automobile accident and was hospitalized for several months. Herbert, Jr., kept the company alive by commuting from his station in San Diego to Los Angeles on weekends. In 1957 Gavin Herbert, Jr., was discharged from the navy and Allergan sales had reached $100,000.

In the late 1950s Allergan moved out of the upstairs laboratory into a 6,000-square-foot space in a converted Los Angeles theater. With the assistance of Jack Browning, an ad agency executive and former employee of SmithKline & French, Allergan also launched its first marketing plan. A key element of that plan was the advent of Allergan's first national product, Prednefrin, a corticosteroid launched in 1958. By 1962 Allergan was a million-dollar company and the company moved its operations to a 30,000-square-foot plant in Santa Ana, California.

Allergan continued to grow in the 1960s, with an increased focus on in-licensing products such as Herplex. Herplex, introduced by Allergan in 1965, was the first antiviral approved by the Food and Drug Administration (FDA) for use in the United States and the second drug of any type to be approved after the emergence of new FDA rules requiring that manufacturers prove the efficacy of all new drugs. The new FDA rules provided Allergan with a competitive advantage over larger companies, who were less adaptable. Dean McCann, who later became the company's senior vice-president of

legal affairs, began advising Allergan in compliance with the FDA rules as early as 1957.

CONTACT LENS CARE MARKET BEGINNING IN 1960

In 1960 hard contact lenses first became available. Allergan demonstrated its propensity to take advantage of new technology when it entered the contact lens market that year. Liquifilm, a wetting solution for hard contact lenses, became an important vehicle for Allergan's ophthalmic products.

Allergan began to develop a global outlook in 1964, when it created its first foreign distributorships in Puerto Rico and Iraq. That same year, Allergan established its first foreign subsidiary in Canada. The company's only competition abroad was Alcon, and Allergan's growth in the international market and the success of its hard contact lens care products combined to bring sales growth of 20 to 25 percent during the 1960s.

Allergan achieved $10 million in sales by 1970, and in October of that year the company went public through an initial public offering that issued 280,000 shares at $15 a share. In advance of taking the company public, a long-term plan for managing growth had been developed. Toward the realization of that plan, Allergan purchased 24 acres from the Irvine Ranch Company and, in 1968, built its Von Karman production facility on that site. In 1971 Allergan erected its first office building in Irvine, California, where it remained headquartered in the early 21st century.

By the mid-1970s, the company had become a major ophthalmic producer, meeting a growing demand for soft contact lens products. Soft contact lenses had become available in 1970, and Allergan became a contractual supplier of soft contact lens solutions to industry giant Bausch & Lomb. Allergan's two lens products were HydroCare, introduced in 1974, and the Soflens enzymatic cleaner, which debuted in 1975, went on to become the company's first $100 million product, and was credited by some with saving the soft lens market. The company's international business flourished because of the success of Allergan's soft contact lens cleaner, which had become the focus of Allergan's European sales because it required no regulatory approval. Allergan established its first manufacturing sites outside the United States in the 1970s, in Puerto Rico and Ireland. The company's operations realized growth of 30 percent in net profits between 1970 and 1975, with total sales reaching $33 million in the latter year.

This period of growth was bolstered by a thriving U.S. ophthalmic market, estimated at a value of $90

KEY DATES

1948: Gavin S. Herbert, Sr., incorporates Child Institute, Inc.

1950: Under the new name Allergan Pharmaceuticals, Inc., the firm introduces its first product, an antihistamine eye drop named Allergan.

1958: Company launches its first national product, Prednefrin, a corticosteroid.

1960: Allergan enters the contact lens care market with launch of Liquifilm wetting solution.

1964: First foreign subsidiary is established in Canada.

1970: Company goes public.

1971: Allergan moves into new headquarters in Irvine, California.

1975: Soflens enzymatic lens cleaner becomes Allergan's first $100 million product.

1980: SmithKline Corporation acquires Allergan.

1986: Company acquires American Medical Optics and changes its name to Allergan, Inc.

1989: SmithKline merges with Beecham Corporation, spinning off Allergan as a newly independent, public company.

1991: Allergan acquires Oculinum, Inc., maker of Type A botulinum toxin soon marketed as Botox.

1995: Sales surpass the $1 billion mark.

1996: Company introduces Alphagan, a treatment for glaucoma.

1998: New CEO David Pyott launches a major restructuring.

2002: Company gains FDA approval for the cosmetic use of Botox; Allergan's ophthalmic surgical and contact lens care unit is spun off to shareholders.

2005: Allergan reaches an agreement to acquire Inamed Corporation for $3.2 billion.

million at the manufacturer's level in 1975. Business that year rose by 18 percent (an average increase would be 10 to 12 percent), because of price increases and an exacerbated allergy season. In 1975 Allergan held approximately 30 percent of the hard contact lens market and increased its considerable share of prescription ophthalmics by 27 percent.

In 1977 Allergan was reincorporated in Delaware. In 1978 Gavin Herbert, Sr., Allergan's cofounder and

chairman, died. Gavin Herbert, Jr., succeeded his father, adding chairman to his titles of president and chief executive officer. Growth continued in the latter half of the 1970s, with revenue rising from $46.4 million in 1978 to $62.6 million in 1979.

SMITHKLINE ERA: 1980-89

SmithKline Corporation (soon renamed SmithKline Beckman Corporation) purchased Allergan for $260 million, and Allergan became a wholly owned subsidiary in 1980. That year, Allergan approached $100 million in sales, a 20 percent increase for the decade. For Allergan, the association with a larger pharmaceutical company was a way to combat its dependence on in-licensing and development. As a subsidiary of Smith-Kline, Allergan was able to create new products through its first research program. For SmithKline, the purchase of Allergan was the first step in its implementation of a new strategy. In 1970, large profits generated by Thorazine had become a double-edged sword when the patent expired, due to SmithKline's shortsighted lack of investment in research and its failure to develop new ventures. Ten years later, SmithKline President and CEO Henry Wendt recognized that the company was again becoming dependent on a single product, the anti-ulcer drug Tagamet, with a patent that would expire in 1993.

The purchase of Allergan was Wendt's first step forward in a new strategy to link diagnostic and therapeutic products. In addition, the purchase was to be a catalyst for new partnerships resulting in lucrative research and innovation. Accordingly, SmithKline put Allergan scientists to work, seeking applications of the research knowledge that produced Tagamet to cures for eye or skin diseases.

During its period as a SmithKline subsidiary, Allergan completed several important acquisitions. In 1984 the company purchased Laboratories Dulcis du Dr. Ferry, S.A., a French firm specializing in ophthalmic prescription drugs. The deal helped Allergan gain entrance into several major European markets. Two years later Allergan acquired American Medical Optics (AMO) from American Hospital Supply Corporation for $165 million. AMO produced intraocular lenses implanted by ophthalmic surgeons to replace a person's natural lenses clouded by cataracts. This venture outside the pharmaceutical market prompted the firm in 1986 to shorten its name to simply Allergan, Inc.

A third major mid-1980s acquisition moved Allergan into the market for contact lenses themselves. At the time, the potential market for soft contact lenses was enormous. In 1984, according to *Industry Week*, 120 million Americans suffered from a vision problem, but only 12 percent wore soft contact lenses. Two additional factors made soft contacts a lucrative product: a shorter lifespan (soft lens wearers replaced lenses every 15 months or so), and the advent of tinted lenses, used by more than 20 percent of wearers who had no vision problems. Finally, the availability and increased affordability of soft contact lenses for astigmatic wearers caused the traditional 10 percent increase in new wearers to jump to 20 percent between 1982 and 1984, according to *Industry Week.*

In 1984 SmithKline strengthened its investment in Allergan, which then held 20 percent of the contact lens solutions market, when it acquired, for $155 million, International Hydron, the number two maker of soft contact lenses (behind the industry giant Bausch & Lomb, which held 40 percent of the lens and solutions business). International Hydron became part of Allergan in 1987. At the time of SmithKline's purchase, the contact lens market was reshuffling; some 20 companies had folded in the 1970s, but the remaining 30 businesses were struggling to maintain their positions behind Bausch & Lomb and to take advantage of the unprecedented market potential of soft contacts. Billion-dollar companies such as Nestlé and Johnson & Johnson began eyeing the market as its potential became apparent.

By 1987, the $500 million contact lens care market was growing at about 20 to 25 percent annually, and Allergan and its competitors were locked in fierce competition. Allergan stepped forward with an innovative new product, Ultrazyme Enzymatic Cleaner, the first weekly enzymatic cleaner that could be used during disinfection. This product was responsive to an increased focus on better lens care, as studies began to demonstrate that unsanitary lenses led to eye problems. Between 1980 and 1989, Allergan's sales increased from $100 million to $800 million.

Allergan employed two strategies to manage this rapid growth: updating its information systems and restructuring its human relations departments. Michael Garrison, who sold computers for General Electric Company prior to becoming Allergan's director of information management, developed innovative information strategies for Allergan in the late 1980s. These computer-based systems included an in-house voicemail system that linked ophthalmologists directly to Allergan; a million-dollar campaign to provide laptop computers for all 300 U.S. sales representatives to increase territory management; and the donation of computers and communication software to doctors' offices, which made briefs written to support products being considered for FDA approval instantly available for downloading by Allergan researchers.

William C. Shepherd, who would become president of Allergan's U.S. operations and, later, CEO, envisioned a strengthened human resources structure that would enable the company to manage and increase its sales and promote itself as the world's leading eye care company. Supporting 20 percent annual growth and rapid expansion, Allergan restructured its human resources department, utilizing both centralized and decentralized models. Shepherd hired Rick Hilles, who later became Allergan's senior vice-president of human resources, to create and implement this new structure. Hilles divided the company into six strategic operating areas (SOAs) and separated the responsibilities of the human resources department into two separate areas. A decentralized area focused on specific market segments and goals, while a centralized structure provided technological benefits, information flow, research and development, marketing, manufacturing, and overall management. The restructuring was publicly lauded when Allergan received the 1991 Optimas Award.

INDEPENDENT AND PUBLIC AGAIN: 1989

Allergan again became a public company in 1989, when SmithKline merged with Beecham Corporation (to form SmithKline Beecham plc), spinning off Allergan as a distribution to shareholders. The transition period posed problems for Allergan, which had high costs, inefficient manufacturing systems, gaps in new product development, and large debt. The eye-care market was no longer growing at the dramatic pace of the 1980s. Sales had moved away from traditional contact lenses, as disposable lenses and fashion glasses, neither of which were sold by Allergan, took the industry lead. With ophthalmologists spending less, Allergan's diagnostic equipment business also was experiencing little profit.

Allergan's business strategy had become unmanageable because it forced the company to compete over too broad a range of business sectors: from pharmaceuticals to consumer products to diagnostic eye care instruments. In 1990 Allergan was close to a billion-dollar company, but its stock had fallen from $25 (at the time of its spinoff) to $15 a share. Investment analysts began to advise investors that Allergan was prime for a takeover, pointing to Nestlé's Alcon Laboratories as a potential purchaser.

Allergan changed its business strategy to reflect market needs in the early 1990s. Under the leadership of President and CEO William Shepherd, Allergan reshaped its operations with a three-pronged strategy: making more money available for research and development, containing costs, and implementing quality.

Between 1989 and 1991, Allergan reduced employment by 10 percent, consolidated some manufacturing operations, reduced its debt, and improved its cash flow, resulting in the elevation of its price on the stock market. In addition, in 1991 the company's board of directors approved a plan to realign Allergan into market-focus business groups with a regional structure giving the company a global focus on the Americas, Europe, Pan-Asia, and Japan.

With a new focus on specialty pharmaceuticals, Allergan began to emerge as a developer of therapeutic products. In 1991 Allergan acquired Oculinum, Inc. and gained an advantage as the only firm marketing Type A botulinum toxin, a product of the bacterium that causes botulism that had been shown to be safe and effective in treating neuromuscular disorders. Botox, the market name for the substance manufactured by Oculinum, Inc., generated $5 million in sales during its first year. Also in 1991, Allergan researcher David Woodward patented a composition that could be used in treating glaucoma. At that time, most glaucoma treatments inhibited the formation of fluids. The new Allergan composition, a derivative of protoglandin (a fat molecule produced in the eye), helped the eye drain, relieving fluid pressure.

A product generating less excitement was Allergan's first one-bottle contact lens disinfecting solution, Ultra-Care Disinfectant/Neutralizer. Allergan was late to enter the one-step market, and its solution was considered inferior to its competitors by analysts, according to the *New York Times*. In 1992 Allergan sold its North and South American contact lens business, and in 1993 the company sold its remaining contact lens business. The company retained its lens care operations, which received a boost with the 1994 introduction of Complete, a new one-bottle solution.

In 1993 Allergan became involved in a proxy battle, as a result of new rules adopted that year by the Securities and Exchange Commission. The State of Wisconsin Investment Board in Madison rallied support from other institutions to put Allergan's "poison pill" shareholders' rights plan to a vote by the holders. Allergan's management position was that shareholder control of the plan would render the board impotent in case of a sudden takeover. Allergan's shareholders, however, passed what became one of the first successful shareholder solicitations by a slight majority (52 percent) at the April 1993 annual meeting.

The early 1990s restructuring improved Allergan's growth, with sales increasing from $762 million in 1991 to $858 million in 1993. Acquisitions marked the years 1994 and 1995. In 1994 Allergan acquired the Ioptex Research global intraocular lens product line. Among the 1995 acquisitions were Optical Micro Systems, Inc., a maker of cataract surgery equipment; Laboratorios Frumtost, S.A., a Brazilian manufacturer of ophthalmic and other pharmaceutical products; and the worldwide contact lens care product operations of Pilkington Barnes Hind. The last of these included the Consept F cleaning and disinfecting system and significantly increased the company's contact lens care product operations in Japan. In late 1995 Allergan launched Azelex cream for the topical treatment of mild to moderate acne of the skin; the product was well received by the market.

LATE 1990S: NEAR MERGER WITH PHARMACIA & UPJOHN, NEW LEADERSHIP, RESTRUCTURING

Increasing competition and acquisition-related costs led to sagging profits for Allergan in the mid-1990s. In early 1996 Allergan entered advanced merger discussions with Pharmacia & Upjohn Inc., but the merger was blocked by AB Volvo, which held a minority stake in Pharmacia & Upjohn. Soon thereafter, Allergan announced a restructuring that included the elimination of about 450 jobs and 1996 pretax charges of about $75 million. The company enhanced its research and development efforts through collaborative agreements in 1996 with SUGEN, Inc., for research into treatments for ophthalmic diseases, such as age-related macular degeneration and diabetic retinopathy, and with Cambridge NeuroScience, Inc., for research into new treatments for glaucoma and other serious ophthalmic diseases. Also in 1996 Allergan received FDA approval for the Alphagan ophthalmic solution for the treatment of open-angle glaucoma and ocular hypertension. By the late 1990s Alphagan was the company's largest selling eye care pharmaceutical product.

In 1997 Allergan expanded its burgeoning skin care line through the FDA approval of Tazorac for the treatment of plaque psoriasis and acne. Also receiving FDA approval in 1997 was Array, a multifocal intraocular lens used to help cataract patients see well over a range of distances, a global market leader since its debut. Although overall sales had surpassed the $1 billion mark in 1995, growth stalled in 1997, with net sales falling slightly, from $1.15 billion in 1996 to $1.14 billion in 1997. With the company's financial performance and stock price continuing to disappoint a number of institutional investors, Shepherd retired at the end of 1997 after 31 years with Allergan. Taking over as president and CEO at the beginning of 1998 was David Pyott, who had been head of Novartis AG's nutrition division, which included the Gerber Products Company baby food unit. Taking over as chairman was Herbert W. Boyer, a biochemist, member of the Allergan board since 1994, and a founder of Genentech Inc.

Under the new leadership, Allergan began a three-year restructuring effort in 1998 whereby five of its ten plants would be closed and its workforce reduced by 550 people, or 9 percent. Allergan subsequently posted a net loss of $90.2 million for the year, due to a restructuring charge of $74.8 million and asset write-offs of $58.5 million. The company in 1998 also contributed $200 million to a new subsidiary, Allergan Specialty Therapeutics, Inc. (ASTI), which was then spun off to shareholders as a dividend. ASTI was charged with conducting research into new pharmaceutical products in the area of retinoids, which held promise for treating such diseases as diabetes and cancer. Allergan retained first crack at any products developed by the quasi-independent ASTI; it had the option to buy the spinoff back, and was likely to do so. Offloading some of its R&D enabled Allergan to increase R&D expenditures without having its earnings-per-share dragged down. Meanwhile, in 1998 the company also entered into a multiyear alliance with the Parke-Davis Pharmaceutical Research Division of Warner-Lambert Company to investigate retinoids for the treatment of metabolic diseases. Among other late 1990s R&D efforts were the attempt to expand the approved uses of Botox to include treatment of migraine headaches, chronic tension headaches, lower back pain, cerebral palsy, and such cosmetic uses as brow furrows; the development of Restasis, a drug for the treatment of moderate to severe dry eye; and the development of Abrevia, a treatment for allergic conjunctivitis.

In April 1999 a seemingly revitalized Allergan announced a $70 million expansion of its R&D campus at the Irvine headquarters and the addition of 300 new research scientists and other professionals. The expansion was slated for completion in 2004. Although the company had been hurt by stagnating sales of its contact lens care lines, which accounted for about 28 percent of overall sales in 1998, large increases in the sales of Botox and of eye care pharmaceuticals, most notably Alphagan, led to an 11 percent increase in overall sales in 1998.

EARLY 2000S: RIDING BOTOX AND EYE CARE PHARMACEUTICALS TO NEW HEIGHTS

Revenues expanded smartly in the early 2000s, fueled not only by skyrocketing sales of Botox but also by steadily increasing sales of ophthalmic pharmaceuticals. By 2003 Botox was generating $564 million in revenues,

representing one-third of the company total, with sales increasing more than 25 percent each year. One factor driving these figures was the securing in 2002 of FDA approval for cosmetic use of Botox, specifically to temporarily relieve brow furrows. Botox had been used for years for "off-label" antiaging purposes, but the approval meant that Allergan could begin advertising cosmetic use of Botox directly to consumers. Nevertheless, the company was quick to point out that 60 percent of its Botox revenues in 2003 was derived from therapeutic uses and that the drug had been approved for as many as 20 different applications by regulatory agencies in 73 countries. In 2004, when the FDA approved the use of Botox to treat hyperhidrosis (excessive underarm sweating), sales of the drug reached $705 million, or 34 percent of overall sales.

Sales of ophthalmic pharmaceuticals, meanwhile, were expanding at a rate of more than 10 percent per year. The glaucoma treatment Alphagan still led the way through 2004, but its sales had peaked the previous year when the first generic form of the drug was approved by the FDA. By this time, however, Allergan had already introduced a new glaucoma drug, Lumigan, which was approved by the FDA in 2001. By 2004 sales of Lumigan had reached approximately $225 million, not far behind the $266 million generated by Alphagan that year. Allergan's eye care pharmaceutical line was further bolstered with several more FDA approvals: Restasis, for treatment of chronic dry eye, December 2002; Zymar, for bacterial conjunctivitis, March 2003; and Elestat, for relief of itching associated with allergic conjunctivitis, December 2003.

In 2001, as expected, Allergan bought back ASTI for $71 million. A much more significant deal occurred in June 2002 when the company spun off its ophthalmic surgical and contact lens care unit to shareholders, creating a newly independent, public company called Advanced Medical Optics, Inc. Although the divested operations accounted for one-third of sales, their sales were increasing only 2 percent a year. Gavin Herbert, Jr., still on the company board, expressed his displeasure at this move, telling *Business Week,* "it felt as if he [Pyott] was chopping off our right arm." Pyott, however, had concluded that the surgical devices and lens care unit was a drag on the much faster growing, more promising pharmaceutical operations. Following the divestment, Allergan was solely focused on pharmaceuticals for three main markets: ophthalmic, neurological, and dermatological.

As part of its drive to build up its drug pipeline, Allergan acquired Oculex Pharmaceuticals, Inc. for $223.8 million in November 2003. Oculex, of Sunnyvale, California, was developing a drug for the treatment of major sight-threatening diseases of the eye, including macular edema and age-related macular degeneration and had developed a proprietary, biodegradable applicator to deliver the drug to the back of the eye. Also in the pipeline were proposed new uses of Botox, including the treatment of spasticity, migraines, and urologic conditions such as overactive bladder. Allergan was moving aggressively to expand its Botox franchise as other drug makers were beginning to inch closer to bringing direct competition to market. The most immediate threat appeared to be Reloxin, a drug under development by Ipsen Ltd. based on the same ingredient as Botox. Any launch of Reloxin, however, was not expected until 2008 at the earliest. Allergan, meanwhile, suffered a setback in September 2004 when the FDA rejected its application for oral tazarotene for the treatment of psoriasis, requesting additional study. The company was already marketing a gel form of tazarotene under the brand Tazorac.

Allergan enjoyed its best year yet in 2004 as sales surpassed the $2 billion mark, and profits were a record $377.1 million. Late the following year, Allergan made a bold move to significantly enhance its position in the cosmetic medicine sector when it reached a definitive pact to acquire Inamed Corporation for $3.2 billion. Allergan's offer thwarted a bid by one of its rivals, Medicis Pharmaceutical Corporation, to acquire Inamed. Based in Santa Barbara, California, Inamed had developed a product line, highly complementary to that of Allergan, that included dermal fillers used to smooth out lines and folds around the mouth and chin, silicone-gel breast implants (which the FDA had preliminarily reapproved for sale earlier in 2005), and the Lap-Band, a device used in stomach reduction surgery. Inamed also held the U.S. rights to Ipsen's Reloxin, but Allergan planned to divest those rights in order to gain U.S. regulatory approval of the takeover.

Heidi Feldman
Updated, David E. Salamie

PRINCIPAL SUBSIDIARIES

Allergan Optical Irvine, Inc.; Allergan Sales Puerto Rico, Inc.; Herbert Laboratories; Oculex Pharmaceuticals, Inc.; Allergan America, LLC; Allergan Holdings, Inc.; Allergan Puerto Rico Holdings, Inc.; Allergan Sales, LLC; Allergan Specialty Therapeutics, Inc.; Pacific Pharma, Inc.; Allergan Productos Farmaceuticos S.A. (Argentina); Allergan Australia Pty Limited; Allergan N.V. (Belgium); Allergan Produtos Farmacêuticos Ltda. (Brazil); Allergan Inc. (Canada); CrownPharma Canada Inc.; Allergan Laboratorios Limitada (Chile); Allergan de Colombia S.A.; Allergan A/S (Denmark); Allergan France

S.A.S.; Pharm-Allergan GmbH (Germany); Allergan Asia Limited (Hong Kong); Allergan India Private Limited (51%); Allergan Botox Limited (Ireland); Allergan Sales, Limited (Ireland); Allergan Services International, Limited (Ireland); CrownPharma Limited (Ireland); Allergan Pharmaceuticals Holdings (Ireland) Limited; Allergan S.p.A. (Italy); Allergan K.K. (Japan); Allergan NK (Japan); Japan International YK; Allergan Korea Ltd.; Allergan, S.A. de C.V. (Mexico); Allergan Servicios Profesionales, S. de R.L. de C.V. (Mexico); Pharmac, S.A.M. (Monaco); Allergan B.V. (Netherlands); Allergan Scrvices BV (Netherlands); Allergan Holdings BV (Netherlands Antilles); Allergan New Zealand Limited; Allergan AS (Norway); Allergan Singapore Pte. Ltd.; Allergan Pharmaceuticals (Pty.) Ltd. (South Africa); Allergan, S.A. (Spain); Allergan Norden AB (Sweden); Allergan AG (Switzerland); Allergan Optik Mamulleri Sanayi Ve Ticaret Limited (Turkey); Allergan Holdings Limited (U.K.); Allergan Limited (U.K.); Allergan de Venezuela, S.A.

PRINCIPAL COMPETITORS

Alcon Laboratories, Inc.; Bausch & Lomb Inc.; Pfizer Inc.; Novartis AG; Merck & Co., Inc.; Dermik Laboratories, Inc.; Galderma Laboratories, L.P.; Medicis Pharmaceutical Corporation; Bristol-Myers Squibb Company; Schering-Plough Corporation; Johnson & Johnson; Solstice Neurosciences Inc.; Ipsen Ltd.; Inamed Corporation; Mentor Corporation; Merz GmbH & Co. KGaA.

FURTHER READING

"Allergan Inc.," *Wall Street Journal,* December 7, 1993, p. B4.

"Allergan Pharmaceuticals," *Wall Street Transcript,* March 22, 1976, p. 1.

"Allergan Shareholders Pass Proposal Forcing Vote on Poison Pill," *Wall Street Journal,* April 28, 1993, p. A6.

Altman, Lawrence K., "Botulinum Toxin's Promise As Drug May Rival Its Potential As Weapon," *New York Times,* March 10, 1998, p. F7.

Baiocchi, Chris, "'New Allergan': Less Fat, More Brains," *Orange County (Calif.) Business Journal,* May 17, 1999, pp. 3, 19.

Barron, Kelly, "Making Eyewash Sexy," *Forbes,* March 6, 2000, p. 72.

Berman, Dennis K., and Rhonda L. Rundle, "Allergan Offers to Purchase Inamed," *Wall Street Journal,* November 15, 2005, p. A3.

Chen, Ingfei, "Toxin to the Rescue," *Science News,* January 19, 1991, pp. 42-43.

Chernoff, Joel, and Patricia Limbacher, "3 Companies in Proxy Battles," *Pensions and Investments,* April 19, 1993, pp. 1, 34.

"Companies Seek to Test Cancer Drug on People," *Journal of Commerce,* December 1, 1993, p. 5A.

"Composition May Help in Treating Glaucoma," *New York Times,* May 11, 1991.

Crabtree, Penni, "Irvine, Calif.-Based Eye Care Firm Awaits Results of Restructuring," *Orange County (Calif.) Register,* November 15, 1998.

"Drugs and Biotech: New Hope for the Dead?," *Fortune,* November 29, 1993, p. 32.

Filipowski, Diane, "Allergan's Structuring for Success," *Personnel Journal,* March 1991, pp. 56-57.

Frank, Robert, "Allergan Inc. Plans to Spin Off Optical-Device Unit to Holders," *Wall Street Journal,* January 22, 2002, p. A4.

Greene, Jay, "Allergan's Botox, Made from Toxin, Used to Fight Wrinkles," *Orange County (Calif.) Register,* February 16, 1998.

Kelleher, James B., "Allergan Spinning Off Its Eye-Care Unit," *Orange County (Calif.) Register,* January 23, 2002.

Knap, Chris, "Irvine, Calif.-Based Allergan May Have New Migraine Remedy," *Orange County (Calif.) Register,* April 21, 1999.

Lev, Michael, "Allergan Gains from a Reduction," *New York Times,* December 5, 1991, p. C8.

Lipin, Steven, and Stephen D. Moore, "Pharmacia & Upjohn's Plan to Acquire Allergan Inc. Is Blocked by AB Volvo," *Wall Street Journal,* May 14, 1996, p. A3.

Marcial, Gene G., "Allergan: Seeing Past the Myopia," *Business Week,* February 5, 1990, p. 78.

McCusker, Tom, "Using Technology to Listen Better," *Datamation,* January 15, 1988, pp. 38-42.

McMenamin, Brigid, "Blurred Vision," *Forbes,* March 23, 1998, p. 142.

"1991 Optimas Awards," *Personnel Journal,* January 1991, p. 53.

O'Reilly, Brian, "Facelift in a Bottle: Allergan, the Drug Company That Makes Botox, Has a Fresh Glow," *Fortune,* June 24, 2002, pp. 101-02, 104.

Perkes, Courtney, "Allergan to Buy Inamed," *Orange County (Calif.) Register,* December 22, 2005.

Reed, Vita, "Allergan Broadens Eye Offerings with Oculex Acquisition," *Orange County (Calif.) Business Journal,* October 27, 2003, pp. 1, 19.

——, "Allergan Touts Drug Pipeline As Fuel for Growth," *Orange County (Calif.) Business Journal,* June 25, 2001, pp. 1, 81.

——, "Beyond Botox: Allergan Working Pipeline," *Orange County (Calif.) Business Journal,* October 10, 2005, pp. 3, 13.

Rundle, Rhonda L., "Allergan CEO Shepherd Set to Retire, with Pyott from Novartis As Successor," *Wall Street Journal,* October 6, 1997, p. B7A.

——, "Allergan Opens Eyes with Cataract Ads," *Wall Street Journal,* March 8, 1999, p. B6.

——, "Allergan Plans Job Cuts, Charge of $103 Million," *Wall Street Journal,* September 16, 1998, p. B6.

——, "Allergan Signs Definitive Pact to Buy Inamed for $3.2 Billion," *Wall Street Journal,* December 21, 2005, p. C3.

——, "Allergan's Inamed Bid Reflects Boom in Cosmetic Treatments," *Wall Street Journal,* November 16, 2005, p. B3.

Rundle, Rhonda L., and Sarah Lueck, "FDA Clears Botox for Cosmetic Use," *Wall Street Journal,* April 16, 2002, p. D6.

Schack, Justin, "David Pyott of Allergan: Eyes on the Prize," *Institutional Investor,* September 2000, pp. 30, 32.

"SmithKline Beckman Unit to Acquire French Company," *Wall Street Journal,* February 2, 1984, p. 11E.

"SmithKline Plans to Buy Allergan for $259 Million," *Wall Street Journal,* December 7, 1979, p. 14.

"SmithKline: Reducing Its Dependence on Drugs," *Business Week,* November 14, 1983, pp. 211-12.

Stephens, Harrison, *Allergan's First Fifty Years,* Lyme, Conn.: Greenwich Publishing Group, 2000, 112 p.

"Takeover Defenses, One Step Backward in the Proxy Arena," *Mergers & Acquisitions,* September/October 1993, pp. 11-12.

"Tale of a Topnotch Team," *Insight Magazine,* Irvine, Calif.: Allergan, Inc., March 1994.

Verespej, Michael, "Eye-to-Eye Combat," *Industry Week,* October 15, 1984, pp. 30-32.

——, "Nowhere to No. 2," *Industry Week,* October 1, 1984, pp. 87-88.

Weintraub, Arlene, "He Bet on Botox—and Won," *Business Week,* October 13, 2003, pp. 126, 128.

Winters, Patricia, "Lens-Care Battle in Sight," *Advertising Age,* October 19, 1987, p. 12.

Wolfson, Bernard J., "Allergan's Answer," *Orange County (Calif.) Register,* October 15, 2002.

——, "To Analysts, Allergan a Vision of Success," *Orange County (Calif.) Register,* April 22, 2001.

Alliant Techsystems Inc.

5050 Lincoln Drive
Edina, Minnesota 55436
U.S.A.
Telephone: (952) 351-3000
Fax: (952) 351-3009
Web site: http://www.atk.com

Public Company
Incorporated: 1990
Employees: 14,000
Sales: $2.8 billion (2005)
Stock Exchanges: New York
Ticker Symbol: ATK
NAIC: 332993 Ammunition (Except Small Arms) Manufacturing; 332995 Other Ordnance and Accessories Manufacturing

■ ■ ■

In 1990 Honeywell Inc. spun off its defense-related business to form a new company, Alliant Techsystems Inc. Alliant quickly became a leading producer of conventional munitions. The company grew an aerospace business with the acquisition of Hercules Aerospace Company in 1995 and Thiokol Propulsion in 2001. A series of subsequent acquisitions has positioned Alliant as a producer of precision weapon systems.

HONEYWELL'S INVOLVEMENT IN THE DEFENSE INDUSTRY: 1941-89

Honeywell's entrance into the defense industry came in 1941, when the war in Europe and Japan's occupation of China led the administration of Franklin D. Roosevelt to begin preparations for the possibility that the United States might be involved in the conflicts. At the time the company, then called Minneapolis-Honeywell, was one of the few U.S. manufacturers with the workforce, facilities, tooling, and expertise to produce precision instruments and controls for the military.

Minneapolis-Honeywell's first military contracts were for an automatic system for releasing payloads at high altitudes for precision bombing. The company's chairman, Harold Sweatt, assigned the company's heating regulator division to develop the system. The company's volume of military business expanded rapidly after the Japanese attack on Pearl Harbor and the U.S. entry into World War II. During the course of the war, the firm turned out turbo engine regulators and complex automatic ammunition firing control devices, among other items, and served as the only U.S. manufacturer of tank periscopes.

At the end of the war Sweatt was determined to keep Minneapolis-Honeywell in the electronic controls business. The most lucrative customer at the time was the Pentagon, which was gearing up for cold war hostilities with the Soviet Union. These circumstances drew Minneapolis-Honeywell even deeper into the stable and lucrative government contracting business. In addition, research dollars provided for Pentagon projects were almost always applicable to commercial projects. The formula worked in reverse as well. Minneapolis-Honeywell purchased the Micro Switch division of First Industrial in 1950. The company's switches were used to operate relays in vending machines and other manually operated devices, but they soon found military ap-

COMPANY PERSPECTIVES

Our ability to successfully compete against larger, more established companies in our industry is due in large measure to our size and speed. Unlike our competition, we are not dependent upon large platforms or programs of record that often constrain the ability to think out of the box. As a result, we are able to bring to the market non-traditional approaches to the way business has always been done in our industry—and we do so with speed and innovation.

plications in battle tanks, artillery, and guided missile systems.

Minneapolis-Honeywell's brief association with the radar powerhouse Raytheon, coupled with their subsequent computer venture, Datamatic, firmly established the company's reputation as a high-technology electronics manufacturer. It led to increased activity in aviation control systems and the company's eventual participation in the manned space program.

In 1964, after shortening its name to Honeywell, the company opted out of the competition for major defense and space projects. Honeywell simply was not in a position to compete economically with such industry giants as Boeing, General Electric, or General Dynamics. Instead, Honeywell concentrated on working as a subcontractor within a narrow range of electronics systems. The company's profitable defense systems businesses, however, created public relations difficulties. Headquartered in the politically liberal state of Minnesota, Honeywell endured a series of protests launched by groups opposed to American involvement in the Vietnam War.

As the war effort in Vietnam wound down during the administrations of Richard Nixon and Gerald Ford, defense budgets were scaled back. This produced less work for Honeywell's defense businesses and later caused the company to reduce its operations. In 1982 Chairman James Renier carried out a corporate downsizing that claimed 3,500 jobs. With this restructuring Honeywell abandoned its adversarial position in the marketplace in relation to IBM and later sold off much of its computer manufacturing assets.

In 1986 and 1988 Honeywell's defense businesses recorded tremendous losses, stemming from huge cost overruns. Unable to collect for the losses and penalized for the late delivery of products under contract, Renier decided to immediately reduce Honeywell's exposure to Pentagon projects. He initially attempted to reposition much of the government defense business toward commercial aviation and flight control markets. In the short run the strategy appeared effective. At this time the company's defense and aerospace operations comprised nearly half of Honeywell's total income and a significant portion of its total profits.

Renier, however, was determined to refocus Honeywell on its core commercial operations. While they made money, its defense businesses, specifically the Defense & Marine Systems division, were not as profitable or promising as other groups in the company. Thus it was felt that defense operations were diluting the company's profitability. In addition, the lessening in tensions between the United States and the Soviet Union raised increasing questions about the long-term viability of involvement in the defense market.

FORMATION OF ALLIANT TECH-SYSTEMS IN 1990

Renier decided to organize the Defense & Marine Systems and Test Instruments divisions along with the Signal Analysis Center into a separate corporate entity. The new entity would operate as an independent subsidiary until it could be sold, preferably to another defense contractor. After several months, however, no company stepped forward with an acceptable bid. Eager to dispense with the low-margin division and to get on with the business of running Honeywell, Renier decided to distribute shares in the new entity to Honeywell shareholders. To do this, the subsidiary would have to be prepared for life as an independent corporation.

Renier offered the chairmanship of the new company to Toby G. Warson, a former naval commander and CEO of Honeywell's subsidiary in the United Kingdom. Completing the management team were Kenneth Jenson, a former executive in the division, and Dean Fjestul, the head of finance for Honeywell Europe. With his management team in place, it came time to choose a new name. (Renier asked that the new company not use the venerable Honeywell name.) The management eventually settled on the name Alliant Techsystems. This name was based on the word alliance, which they believed accurately described the relationship the new company hoped to maintain with the U.S. Department of Defense.

After a distribution of one Alliant share for every four Honeywell shares, Alliant began business as an independent company in October 1990. It entered the market with a 50-year history, 8,300 employees, and a position as the Pentagon's 17th largest contractor. Its operations were divided into four main units: precision armament, ordnance, marine systems, and information storage systems. At the time of the company's creation, Alliant consisted of two groups, six divisions, and two operations, representing tremendous bureaucracy and redundancy. One of Warson's first actions as chairman was to consolidate the work functions among the company's various fiefdoms and, in the process, to eliminate 800 administrative jobs.

Within months the operation had been streamlined into a manufacturing and materials arm and an engineering and technology center. Sales were handled by four market groups that were organized in the same fashion as the Department of Defense. In another important move, Warson used the company's entire first quarter operating income to pay for Alliant's restructuring costs and to partially pay down debt. Still, Alliant was saddled with a $14 million charge for legal and administrative costs, $30 million in severance payments, a $165 million loan from Honeywell, and a $60 million dividend payment to Honeywell. This brought the new company's debt-to-equity ratio to a precarious 1.4 to one.

EFFECT OF THE PERSIAN GULF WAR ON SALES

With 1989 earnings of $53.8 million on sales of $1.14 billion, it seemed that Alliant was off to a difficult start. But the company gained its independence only three months after the Iraqi invasion of Kuwait. Suddenly, the

dynamics of Pentagon work changed drastically. The invasion, coupled with the evaporation of the Soviet military threat because of the collapse of communism, forced U.S. military strategists to focus their combat planning on a new type of enemy, the well-armed third world dictator. Battling this type of opponent did not require nuclear weapons or new weapons platforms.

With the demise of the Soviet military machine, the administration of George H.W. Bush increasingly turned to lower-cost improvements in existing weapons systems, those necessary to battle armies such as Iraq's. Alliant was perfectly suited for this approach to modernization. In 1990 Warson told *Industry Week,* "If you look at the U.S. defense budget, it's clear that the major new weapons systems—for instance the B-2 bomber, the advanced tactical fighters, new tanks and submarines—are in trouble. The Pentagon is looking for ways to enhance existing systems and to improve the performance of the individual soldier. And that's the market we're in."

Warson noted that budget constraints were likely to preclude the Army from replacing its aging Abrams tanks. Instead, he suggested that the Pentagon would opt to upgrade the weapons by equipping them with the new 120mm ammunition that Alliant made. By and large, the company's products were cheap and effective, and because ammunition, a large part of Alliant's production, had to be continually replaced, the company was assured of a more stable market than airplane, rocket, and submarine builders could enjoy.

As the confrontation in Kuwait became a shooting war and Operation Desert Shield was transformed into Desert Storm, more than 1,300 Alliant workers represented by the Teamsters went out on strike in a dispute over wages, benefits, and the terms of another contract. These workers, who manufactured 25mm shells for the Bradley Fighting Vehicle, were quickly replaced by managers struggling to keep production running.

The strike, a notably unpopular one because of the timing, was short-lived, however, as both sides managed to resolve the dispute. Alliant served the war effort well, turning out 120mm uranium-tipped antitank shells, 30mm bullets for the A-10 Warthog and Apache helicopter, and a variety of other ordnance. In addition, Alliant was the sole manufacturer of MK 46 and MK 50 antisubmarine torpedoes, although none were employed during the war.

Alliant continued to gain momentum after the Gulf War was over. Warson carried out a successive wave of consolidations, mostly within the management ranks, dropping a further 800 employees by October 1991. In addition, the number of layers of management was cut from 14 to seven. This enabled the company to compete more efficiently for the dwindling number of Pentagon contracts for new weapons systems.

The one weak spot in Alliant's organization was the company's Metrum Information Storage division. Metrum, Alliant's only nonmunitions unit, manufactured data recording and storage devices. While half of Metrum's sales were to commercial customers, the unit suffered from numerous production setbacks that forced the company to write off millions of dollars. The Metrum division was eventually sold. Still, by 1992 Warson had made tremendous progress in clearing up Alliant's balance sheet. With a manageable debt of $148 million and interest payments under control, it was expected that Alliant would work its debt off the books by 1994.

With a strong financial position, Warson hoped to broaden Alliant's markets by acquiring another company or establishing a joint venture. His first effort in this direction met a swift rebuke. Warson proposed merging the ordnance division of Stamford, Connecticut-based Olin Corporation into those of Alliant, and he had even sealed the $68 million agreement when the U.S. Federal Trade Commission became involved, opposing the sale on the basis that the combination would leave the Pentagon with only one supplier of specialized munitions.

Warson and his colleagues at Olin argued that the market could support only one manufacturer. Far from conspiring to gouge the Pentagon with monopoly pricing, Warson argued that, by preventing the two companies from realizing economies of scale under reduced orders, the Pentagon would in fact be shelling out more for its ammunition. Despite gaining the support of the army for its case, Alliant called off the proposed merger in December 1992.

A NEW BUSINESS PLAN FOR THE 1990S

Because the company's business was heavily dependent on military contracts, the continuing decrease in the size of the U.S. defense budget posed a threat to Alliant's profitability. Between 1985 and 1993 the U.S. weapons-procurement budget plummeted by more than half, and further cuts loomed in the future. "It's important that we manage our business to the realities of the marketplace during this period of rapid change in the defense industry," Warson told the *Wall Street Journal* on January 28, 1993. To reduce costs, Alliant shed another 1,700 employees in 1993, dropping the company's total below 4,000. Alliant also scaled back production of its Adam land mine, disposable AT-4 infantry weapon, and MK 46 torpedo. With the savings from these curtailed

operations, Alliant hoped to raise profit margins to offset the impact of declining sales, which dropped from $1.1 billion in 1992 to $800 million in 1993.

Alliant ultimately recognized that its continued survival would require strategic shifts as well as organizational restructuring. As the July 13, 1994, *Wall Street Journal* explained, Alliant strove to gain "entry into new markets" instead of relying for business predominantly on waning government procurement contracts. In 1993, for instance, Alliant formed a joint venture with the Ukrainian government to dismantle stockpiles of munitions left over from the Soviet Union. In this way the company sought to apply its substantial expertise in munitions handling to an arena that was not dependent on the Pentagon's budget.

As a further effort to widen the scope of its business, Alliant acquired the aerospace division of Hercules Inc. in 1995. The aerospace operations of Delaware-based Hercules produced rocket motors for space launch and strategic nuclear missiles. This market segment was a new realm for Alliant, but it provided the company with an array of opportunities since the demand for communications satellites was growing rapidly. Such satellites provided mobile telephone services, direct-to-home television feeds, and paging and messaging services. According to the November 10, 1995, *Wall Street Journal,* analysts speculated that more than 350 satellites would be sent into space between 1995 and 2000. Armed with the capacity to manufacture the rocket motors used to launch these satellites, which it had gained by purchasing Hercules, Alliant was ideally situated to capitalize on the boom. Nevertheless, to ensure continued profitability, the company cut its workforce by an additional 20 percent (about 700 jobs) in 1995.

Alliant also began to eliminate units that did not conform to its new strategy. In December 1996 the company sold its Marine Systems Groups, which produced torpedoes, mine-detection equipment, and other naval weaponry, to General Motors' Hughes Electronics. The move enabled Alliant to reduce its debt by an additional $89 million and to concentrate more fully on its profitable rocket technology.

Alliant instituted other changes as well. Instead of continuing to compete head-on with defense industry giants such as Boeing and Raytheon, Alliant began to forge partnerships with them. In June 1995, for example, Alliant was awarded a multimillion-dollar contract from the McDonnell Douglas Corporation to produce solid rocket propulsion systems for the Delta III space launch vehicle. In addition to its 1997 contract with the Lockheed Martin Corp. to manufacture a component of the F-22 Raptor fighter jet, Alliant received a long-term contract from the Boeing Co. in June 1998, worth $750 million, to manufacture solid rocket boosters for Boeing's Delta space launch vehicles.

Of course, Alliant did not abandon its lucrative position in the munitions industry. While the end of the cold war had changed the needs of the U.S. military, the outbreak of bloody regional conflicts in the former Yugoslavia and in various parts of Africa underscored the importance of basic munitions. With the U.S. Congress reluctant to devote vast sums to develop entirely new weapons platforms, the Department of Defense focused heavily on upgrading the capabilities of existing ammunition and electronic warfare and surveillance systems. Alliant strove to meet these needs. The company's low-cost mortar and artillery fuses led the field, and Alliant was also the sole provider of VOLCANO and Shielder antitank systems.

Alliant's strategy of creating new markets while simultaneously bolstering its existing sectors proved to be successful. After a dismal year in 1995, in which Alliant's net income dropped as a result of restructuring charges, the company's sales and profits rose in 1996 and 1997. In 1998 Alliant's net income rose, and the ratio of its total debt to capitalization declined. Sales in 1999 grew 1.4 percent to reach $1.09 billion. Even more telling was the tectonic shift in Alliant's commercial-to-military sales ratio. In 1995, 3 percent of Alliant's sales were to commercial clients, with the remaining 97 percent going to the military. Fueled by its burgeoning aerospace sector, 16 percent of Alliant's sales were to commercial clients by 1999, with 84 percent to the military.

With a new chairman and CEO in place by January 1999, Alliant's future looked hopeful. Paul David Miller had served 30 years with the U.S. Navy, retiring as an Admiral in 1994. He had also headed up Litton Industries, Inc.'s Litton Marine Systems before signing with Alliant. The company's chief assured stockholders that Alliant's defense business would remain stable and that its role in solid propulsion would continue to expand.

HOMELAND DEFENSE TAKING ON NEW MEANING: 2000–05

The outgoing Clinton administration increased the defense budget, driving up stock of weapons builders to record levels, according to a November 2000 *Los Angeles Times* article. The upward trend for the industry continued, when the defense-minded George W. Bush administration came on board. As 2001 began, Minnesota had a senator, Mark Dayton, on the Armed Services Committee improving the prospects for companies in that state with regard to defense contracts.

According to Alliant President Scott Meyers, the company was ready. Weapons in the pipeline were in sync with the U.S. military's move toward high-tech warfare, including the two-barreled, computerized Objective Individual Combat Weapon, in development, which offered bursting ammunition and long-range precision. "As the military downsizes and the likelihood of fighting in urban areas increases, the military wants a greater ability to wage war from afar," Meyers told the *Star Tribune* in March 2001.

Attacks on American soil a few months later and subsequent talk of American military action abroad further drove up Alliant's prospects. The company had taken over the production of the government's only small-caliber ammunition manufacturing facility in 2000. But Miller had additional plans for Alliant.

"In the Navy in the early 1990s, Admiral Miller championed the shift to 'adaptive joint forces'—military jargon for increased cooperation among the Navy, Army and Air Force. And he foresaw the move to the lighter, more precise weapons that has been behind his push to transform Alliant," Amy Cortese reported for the *New York Times*.

Miller had asked Daniel J. Murphy, another ex-admiral, to make a recommendation regarding the company's proposed entry into the precision guided missile business. The consultant role led to a job with Alliant beginning in 2001; he turned down one with Lockheed Martin.

Early in 2002, Alliant announced the addition of a third business, Precision Systems Group, joining Alliant's other two businesses, defense and aerospace, and charged to develop precision guided weapon systems. The company also announced a management change: head of the Utah-based aerospace group, Paul Ross, would succeed Meyers as president. Nick Vlahakis, head of the defense group, was named senior vice-president and COO.

Alliant was at the same time on an acquisitions spree. In rapid succession it acquired and assimilated Alcoa's solid rocket booster maker Thiokol Propulsion, in 2001; missile-guidance electronics company Science and Applied Technologies, Inc. and a high-tech gun operation of Boeing's, in 2002; and composite space structure business Composite Optics, Inc. and two Allied Aerospace's units, in 2003.

Murphy, who directed the Precision Systems Group as it gathered the pieces of an entire weapons system, succeeded Miller as CEO in October 2003. Miller continued on as chairman of the board.

Meanwhile, the ammunition business grew. Late in 2001, the company had acquired Blount International's commercial ammunition businesses, becoming the nation's largest manufacturer of ammunition. For the war in Iraq, Alliant supplied all of the Army's small-arms ammunition for rifles and machine guns, about half of the medium-caliber rounds coming from armored vehicles and tanks, as well as parts for more sophisticated weaponry, according to the *New York Times*. Munitions sales climbed during the end of 2002 due to military sales and the Blount acquisition.

With nearly half of Alliant's aerospace revenue derived from NASA, the Columbia explosion in February 2003 also rocked Alliant's price per share. The company under Miller had been outperforming heavy hitters in the industry and the Standard and Poor's 500.

Twelfth among American defense companies in terms of revenue, Alliant needed to continue to pick its battlefield carefully: "We are very selective in the pursuits that would have us go head to head with the giants in our industry," Murphy told the *Twin Cities Business Monthly* in 2004. "We enter a competition with a very large defense contractor only after careful analysis of our likelihood of a win."

Precision-guided weaponry, a niche expected to grow rapidly in support of the 'war on terror,' spelled opportunity for Alliant. The company bested Lockheed for a laser guided mortar shell contract in December 2003. The U.S. Army contract, an estimated $500 million, ran through 2008.

During its first full year of operation, fiscal 2003, Precision Systems produced $649 million in sales. Murphy expected double digit growth during the decade, according to *Twin Cities Business Monthly*. Ammunition and aerospace sales helped finance the growth of the smaller operation.

Alliant's stock, which had begun underperforming after the loss of the Space Shuttle Columbia, continued to lag behind others in the defense industry and the S&P 500. Thiokol Propulsion had been making shuttle rocket boosters for 21 years; the company took much of the blame for the 1986 Challenger disaster. Additionally, investors had yet to fully come on board with the Alliant of the future.

During the first half of 2004, the company purchased Mission Research Corp., bringing in more technology expertise. Miller stepped down as chairman at the end of fiscal 2005, succeeded by Murphy. Under his leadership, Alliant had grown from $1.1 billion in revenue to $2.8 billion.

With critical high-tech expertise in place, Murphy turned his attention to organic growth. He also had his eyes toward the sky as the Space Shuttle Discovery prepared for takeoff. On the ground back in Minnesota outside Alliant's headquarters, antiwar protesters held vigil, hearkening back to the company's Honeywell days.

John Simley
Updated, Rebecca Stanfel; Kathleen Peippo

PRINCIPAL DIVISIONS

Precision Systems; ATK Thiokol; Ammunition; Advanced Propulsion & Space Systems; ATK Mission Research.

PRINCIPAL COMPETITORS

Aerojet-General Corp.; General Dynamics Corporation; Raytheon Company.

FURTHER READING

"Alliant to Cut 30% of Work Force; Posts Loss of $90 Million," *Wall Street Journal*, January 28, 1993, p. B4.

"At Military Contractor, Strikers Face Winter's Chill and Neighbors' Wrath," *New York Times*, February 16, 1991, p. 10.

Cole, Jeff, "Re-Entry Mission: U.S. Rocket Makers Rely on Foreign Rivals for New Shot at Space," *Wall Street Journal*, November 10, 1995.

Cortese, Amy, "Quiet, but Central, Role for Ammunition Maker," *New York Times*, March 23, 2003, p. 4.

Crock, Stan, "The Little Contractor That Could," *Business Week*, July 4, 2005, p. 78.

Cruz, Sherri, "Technology to the Defense," *Star Tribune*, March 18, 2001, p. 1D.

Davies, Phil, "With a Bullet," *Twin Cities Business Monthly*," pp. 46-49.

DePass, Dee, "Alliant Launches Ad Campaign," *Star Tribune*, March 29, 2005, p. 2D.

———, "Nine Years on the Protest Line," *Star Tribune*, November 4, 2005, p. 1D.

———, "Rocket Man," *Star Tribune*, July 10, 2005, p. 1D.

Flanigan, James, "New Growth, Role for Defense in a Changing World," *Los Angeles Times*, November 19, 2000, p. C1.

"FTC Seeks to Block Merger of Defense Firms," *Washington Post*, November 7, 1992, p. C1.

Hinds, Gary, "Minneapolis-Based Aerospace Company Promotes Utah Executive," *Knight Ridder/Tribune Business News*, February 27, 2002.

"Honeywell Board OKs Spin-Off of Defense Units," *Electronic News*, October 1, 1990, p. 6.

"Honeywell Defense Business Can't Find Buyer; Spin-off Set," *Electronic News*, July 30, 1990, p. 27.

"Linkage Plan of Olin, Alliant Is Called Off," *Wall Street Journal*, December 9, 1992, p. A4. Miller, James, "Alliant

Techsystems to Pay $465 Million for Hercules Inc.'s Aerospace Business," *Wall Street Journal,* July 13, 1994.

"Precision Pick on Target," *Barron's,* June 17, 1991, pp. 44-45.

Price, Dave, "Who Will Become Next CEO, President of Alliant Techsystems?" *Finance and Commerce Daily Newspaper,* January 25, 2003.

"Sink or Swim," *Forbes,* October 14, 1991, pp. 66-71.

"Toby Warson Dives for Profits," *Industry Week,* December 3, 1990, pp. 35-38.

Wall, Robert, and Barry Rosenberg, "Company Makeover," *Aviation Week & Space Technology,*" June 14, 2004, pp. 53-53.

alpha airports group plc

Alpha Airports Group
PLC

———— ■ ————

Europa House
804 Bath Road
Cranford, Middlesex TW5 9US
United Kingdom
Telephone: +44 (0) 20 8580 3200
Fax: +44 (0) 20 8580 3201
Web site: http://www.alpha-group.com

Public Company
Incorporated: 1994
Employees: 5,431
Sales: £487.8 million (2005)
Stock Exchanges: London
Ticker Symbol: AAP
NAIC: 445292 Confectionery and Nut Stores; 445310
    Beer, Wine, and Liquor Stores; 446120 Cosmetics,
    Beauty Supplies, and Perfume Stores; 448310
    Jewelry Stores; 451211 Book Stores; 453220 Gift,
    Novelty, and Souvenir Stores; 453991 Tobacco
    Stores; 488119 Other Airport Operations; 722310
    Food Service Contractors; 722320 Caterers

■ ■ ■

Alpha Airports Group PLC is an England-based supplier of support services for airlines and airports. The Flight Services division prepares in-flight meals, offers security and other services such as equipment management, and handles in-flight retail. The Retail side operates airport concessions such as restaurants, newsstands, and duty-free stores. Alpha Flight Services, which accounted for more than half of turnover and two-thirds of employees, operates at more than 60 airports in Europe, the Middle East, Australia, and the United States; Alpha Retail is active in about two dozen airports.

FLOATED IN 1994

The Forte Group's airport services division was spun off as Alpha Airports Group PLC in a successful February 1994 initial public offering (IPO). Shares began trading at 140p. Alpha's market capitalization was £211 million and its annual revenues were about £423 million, split evenly between flight catering and the less lucrative airport retail operations.

Forte had originally launched its airport services unit in 1955. In 1970 it merged with another large hotels group, Trust Houses Ltd., which had begun to provide its own catering service at airports; a majority owned joint venture, John Gardner (London) Limited, owned Gardner Merchant Caterers Limited, one of Europe's leading contract caterers.

Alpha's predecessors began serving European airports, as well as institutions, in the 1970s and 1980s. An operation was set up at Paris's Orly Airport in 1971, followed the next year by another at Schiphol in Amsterdam. A base at New York's JFK International was acquired in 1985.

By the mid-1990s, it accounted for nearly half the meals served on planes departing British airports. It also had operations at four sites in Continental Europe and in New York City. Altogether, Forte Airport Services was making 45 million meals a year. An equally large business was the network of duty-free stores. Overall, Forte Airport Services had 6,000 employees.

COMPANY PERSPECTIVES

Alpha's appreciation of the needs of international business comes not simply through talking to our partners, but also through our own global network. Our people are as talented at making travel special around the world as they are in the U.K.

Alpha's success extends much further than our core business in the U.K. With Duty Free stores as far afield as Florida and the Maldives, a network of flight kitchens in four continents, a strategic partner in Singapore, a distributor in Nepal, and retail bar and restaurant outlets in Stockholm and Jersey, we're as international as our many global partners.

With such a variety of audiences and cultures to serve, Alpha's inherent flexibility is a critical strength of the brand. Every inflight menu or airport retail concept is carefully tailored to its particular market, making the very most of local opportunities to maximise profit for our airport and airline partners.

Wherever your business is focused, Alpha's international expertise can make a difference to your business.

Forte had amassed a £1 billion debt along with its diversified holdings. A plan to sell Airport Services and contract caterer Gardner Merchant to the Compass Group in 1992 was called off as Forte Chairman Rocco Forte thought the offer of £530 million for the pair was too low. Three-quarters of Gardner Merchant was sold instead to management for £400 million, and Alpha was spun off.

The newly independent Alpha was quick to invest in far-flung flight catering operations in a bid to obtain global reach. It soon acquired a 49 percent holding in Australia's leading independent flight caterer, Connat Flight Services Pty. Ltd., for AUD 7.5 million (£3.6 million) in June 1994; this was raised to an 85 percent holding within a couple of years. It also bought a pair of small Florida flight kitchens owned by Jerry's, and set up the Allied Caterers joint venture in Trinidad. Alpha divested its flight caterer in Portugal, acquired several years earlier, after that country's national airline formed its own catering unit.

Reston, Virginia-based ground handler DynAir Services was acquired from defense services specialist DynCorp for $122 million (£79 million) in September 1995. DynAir operated at 52 locations in the United

States, and was beginning to operate as far abroad as Russia. It had sales of $131 million a year. According to *The Times,* Alpha had been courting DynAir for three years.

Forte had retained a 25 percent stake in Alpha after the IPO. It was later acquired by the Granada group, and in November 1996 Harrods owner Mohamed Al Fayed bought the holding in Alpha from Granada for £52 million. Fayed also owned a chain of ten airport stores called Signature.

Alpha's loss-making U.S. catering operations were sold off in 1996 for £6.8 million. Alpha acquired a 60 percent holding in Sri Lanka's Orient Lanka duty-free store for $18 million.

RECONFIGURING IN THE LATE 1990S

Alpha had about 12,000 employees in the late 1990s. One new hire was Kevin Abbott, a former board director at Rexham, who took over from the original chief executive, Paul Harrison, in October 1997 after Harrison left to join the Standard Chartered bank.

Sales for fiscal 1998 were £702 million. Its retail division had more than 100 outlets, most of them in the United Kingdom, operating under names including The Beauty Centre, Glorious Britain, and A Taste of Ulster. It suffered a loss of business, however, after the British Airport Authority established its own World Duty Free chain.

The company, with a £73 million debt, lacked the capital to develop its three divisions: retail, flight services, and ground handling. Expecting to raise £70 million, Alpha did put its duty-free stores on the block in February 1998, but canceled the sale several months later after failing to find a suitable buyer in the midst of the Asian financial crisis. It was able to finance growth, however, through a new £100 million credit line.

In June 1999, Alpha bought the Gatwick flight kitchen of British Airways for £14 million. At the same time, it obtained a ten-year contract to supply British Airways with in-flight meals at Gatwick and eight regional British airports. Alpha Catering Services was then supplying more than 12 million meals a year to British Airways via 95,000 flights a day.

Alpha's U.S. ground handling business, Dynair, was sold to SAirGroup's Swissport International for $155 million (£100 million) in August 1999. By this time, Dynair was active at 57 airports in the United States, Italy, and Russia. The fragmented ground handling busi-

KEY DATES

1955: Forte Group launches an airport services business.
1970: Forte merges with Trust Houses Ltd.
1971: The first Continental airline catering unit is set up at Paris-Orly.
1994: Forte Airport Services is spun off as Alpha Airports Group PLC.
1995: Alpha acquires U.S. ground handler DynAir Services.
1996: The U.S. flight catering operations are divested.
1999: DynAir is sold to SAirGroup's Swissport International; the European Union eliminates duty-free sales.
2001: Alpha buys a majority holding in the Royal Jordanian catering operation.
2004: The "Blue Sky" concept promises to revolutionize in-flight meal service.

ness was beginning to consolidate as local monopolies in Europe were opened to competition.

Revenues fell about 20 percent to £515 million in 1999-2000, in large part due to the elimination of duty-free sales within the European Union. Nevertheless, pretax profits rose £3.6 million to £19.3 million. Alpha was countering the loss of duty-free business by developing branded retail outlets. During the fiscal year, Harrods sold its 27 percent interest to Servair, Air France's catering unit.

NEW HORIZONS AFTER 2000

While no frills budget airlines such as easyJet grew in popularity, Alpha developed café-style offerings to feed their passengers. In 2000 the company was working to provide passengers the opportunity to order meals online at the same time they bought their tickets. Alpha also teamed with Virgin Express Tax Free Shop in the spring of 2001 to improve the food and retail offered onboard the Virgin Express airline.

Alpha acquired a 51 percent holding in Royal Jordanian's catering unit for £8.8 million ($12.6 million) in the summer of 2001. This was an important strategic move into a fast-growing aviation market. "We will make Alpha Jordan a showcase for our international customers and thus aim to become the undisputed flight caterer of choice in future privatizations in this develop-

ing Middle East region," said Alpha CEO Kevin Abbot.

The company's flight catering business fell off temporarily in the industrywide aviation slowdown following the September 11, 2001 terrorist attacks on the United States, resulting in layoffs of more than 900 workers. In-flight and duty-free sales, however, were rising.

Alpha was expanding in Continental Europe and niche international markets in Australia, the Middle East, and India. It sold off a stake in Inflight Sales Group in 2002, relinquishing the North American in-flight catering business.

Alpha doubled the capacity of its flight kitchen in Cardiff to 10,000 meals a day. Alpha also had been updating its airport retail concept, and was benefiting from increasing traffic at Britain's regional airports. The logistics and IT infrastructure also was being upgraded.

In 2004 Alpha benefited from a pick-up in long haul air travel following the end of the Iraq war, particularly at its Jordan base. Alpha acquired a 60 percent holding in Istanbul Duty Free in November 2004. Turkey's tourism traffic was booming. Alpha was also boosting its stake in its Italian affiliate, Servair AirChef S.R.L.

Turnover for the fiscal year ended January 2005 (not including joint ventures) was £487.8 million, up 11 percent from the previous year. Pretax profit was down a third to £11.7 million; the deadly South Asia tsunami of December 2004 had some impact on the company's duty-free trade. Alpha then had about 5,500 employees.

The company was expanding into Eastern Europe via the spring 2005 acquisition of a majority stake in Romania's Abela Rocas S.A. for £3.4 million (EUR 5 million). Abela Rocas had been founded in 1993 by the Albert Abela group and had annual revenues of 281 billion. It catered up to 5,000 airline passengers a day and had operated airport foodservice.

While it was expanding its geographic horizons, Alpha also was venturing into new concepts in airline food. Its "Blue Sky" meals promised to streamline the aerial dining experience by offering meals on disposable mats rather than the traditional tray. This simplified cleanup for the flight attendants and allowed passengers to leave their seats without having to wait for their trays to be collected.

In October 2005, longtime client Thomsonfly replaced Alpha with rival LSG Sky Chefs. Alpha had been supplying meals to Thomsonfly, formerly Britannia Airways, for three decades.

Frederick C. Ingram

PRINCIPAL SUBSIDIARIES

Abela Rocas S.A. (Romania; 64.1%); Alpha Airport Holdings B.V. (Netherlands); Alpha Airport Holdings (UK) Limited; Alpha Airport Services Inc. (U.S.A.); Alpha Airports Group (Jersey) Limited; Alpha Airport Catering (Ireland) Limited; Alpha Catering Services Limited; Alpha Flight Services B.V. (Netherlands); Alpha Flight Services Ireland Limited; Alpha Flight Services Overseas Limited (Jersey; 80.4%); Alpha Flight Services Pty. Limited (Australia); Alpha Keys Orlando Retail Associates LLP (U.S.A.; 85%); Alpha MVKB Maldives Pvt Limited (60%); Alpha Overseas Holdings Limited; Alpha Retail Catering Sweden AB; Istanbul Duty Free Ic ve Dis Ticaret A.S. (Turkey; 60%); Jordan Flight Catering Company Limited (Jordan; 41%); Orient Lanka Limited (Sri Lanka).

PRINCIPAL DIVISIONS

Flight Services; Retail.

PRINCIPAL COMPETITORS

Compass Group; DFS Group; Gate Gourmet; LSG Sky Chefs; Sodexho Ltd.

FURTHER READING

"Airline Firm Alpha Hires City Agency," *PR Week,* March 10, 1994.

"Alpha Airports' Blue Sky Sounds Death Knell for In-Flight Trays," *AFX UK Focus,* March 31, 2005.

"Alpha Airports in Talks to Acquire DynAir Services Group," *World Airport Week,* August 22, 1995.

"Alpha Airports to Sell Retail Operation," *Scotsman,* April 24, 1998, p. 27.

"Alpha Halts Duty-Free Stores Sale," *Scotsman,* August 11, 1998, p. 22.

Barrow, Martin, "Alpha Chief to Quit As Profits Edge Up to £22m," *Times,* April 26, 1997, p. 28.

Bennett, Neil, "Alpha Airports—Tempus," *Times,* February 4, 1995.

Blackwell, David, "Alpha Airports Valued at £211M in Flotation," *Financial Times,* January 26, 1994, p. 24.

———, "Alpha Depressed by BA Loss," *Financial Times,* September 23, 1995, p. 10.

———, "Finance and the Family—Forte Spreads Wings," *Financial Times,* January 29, 1994, p. 4.

Boschat, Nathalie, "Alpha Airports to Launch Online Catering Service," *Dow Jones International News,* March 30, 2000.

"Britain's Alpha Buys Majority Stake in Jordan Unit," *Reuters News,* August 2, 2001.

"British Airports Group Acquires Additional Stake in Australian Caterer," *Asian Aviation News,* April 21, 1995.

"British Alpha Airports Group Takes Over Abela Rocas Romania," *Rompres,* April 13, 2005.

"CEO Interview: Kevin Abbott, ALPHA Airports Group PLC," *Wall Street Transcript Europe,* February 8, 1999.

Cunliffe, Peter, "Alpha Cuts Back Workforce," *Express,* February 1, 2002.

Curphey, Marianne, "Alpha Wins DynAir After 3-Year Pursuit," *Times,* August 9, 1995.

Daeschner, Jeff, "Alpha Airports Sees Benefit from US Disposal," *Reuters News,* October 11, 1996.

Davitt, Dermot, "Alpha Stokes the Fires of Ambition," *Duty-Free News International,* October 15, 2002, pp. 104+.

Dyer, Jeff, "Alpha Airports to Pay $122M for DynAir," *Financial Times,* August 9, 1995, p. 17.

Feltsted, Andrea, "New Appetite for In-Flight Meals Lifts Alpha Shares," *Financial Times* (London), September 27, 2002, p. 26.

"Forte Emerges from His Father's Shadow," *Independent* (London), November 23, 1993, p. 26.

Gilchrist, Susan, "Alpha Buys 49% Stake in Connat," *Times,* June 2, 1994.

"Independents' Day: DynAir Gains Synergy with Alpha," *Airports International,* July 1, 1996, p. S27.

Mahlich, Greg, "Forte's ALPHA Airports Sees Debt Falling," *Reuters News,* January 25, 1994.

Milton, Tina, and Dermot Davitt, "Alpha Acquisition to Drive International Expansion at Istanbul," *Duty-Free News International,* November 15, 2004, p. 1.

Pauling, Tim, "Alpha Looks to Future Growth," *Aberdeen Press & Journal,* March 31, 2000.

Rimmer, John, "Ambitious Alpha Plots Global Retail Expansion Programme," *Duty-Free News International,* October 1, 2004, p. 1.

Rowe, Richard, "Three's a Crowd," *Airports International,* July 1, 1998.

Tate, Michael, "Alpha's Air Fare on Menu at £230M," *Observer,* January 23, 1994, p. 2.

———, "Alpha Wants to Feed Aussies Pie in Sky," *Observer,* September 15, 1994, p. 2.

———, "Forte Eyes £70M Alpha Sell-Off," *Observer,* January 1, 1995, p. 1.

"UK Alpha Airports Steps Up Retail," *Reuters News,* July 13, 1999.

Waller, Martin, "Listing for Air Offshoot Will Shrink Forte Debt," *Times,* October 14, 1993.

Walsh, Dominic, "Alpha Suffers 'Shock' Contract Loss to German-Owned Rival," *Times* (London), October 26, 2005, p. 63.

Weir, Keith, "Forte Says More Disposals to Come," *Reuters News,* December 4, 1995.

White, Sally, and John Carrington, "Trust Houses and Forte in Surprise Merger," *Times,* May 4, 1970, p. 17.

Willcock, John, "Alpha Moves Towards an International Image," *Independent* (London), August 13, 1997, p. 18.

Young, Andrew, "Alpha Aims to Jettison Retail Arm," *Reuters News,* February 17, 1998.

American Ecology Corporation

——— ■ ———

300 E. Mallard Drive, Suite 300
Boise, Idaho 83706
U.S.A.
Telephone: (208) 331-8400
Toll Free: (800) 590-5220
Fax: (208) 331-7900
Web site: http://www.americanecology.com

Public Company
Incorporated: 1984
Employees: 178
Sales: $54.2 million (2004)
Stock Exchanges: NASDAQ
Ticker Symbol: ECOL
NAIC: 562211 Hazardous Waste Treatment and Disposal; 562112 Hazardous Waste Collection

■ ■ ■

American Ecology Corporation delivers waste treatment and disposal services to producers and handlers of hazardous, toxic, and low-level radioactive wastes (LLRW). Its subsidiary, US Ecology, provides nuclear waste services and hazardous waste services to industrial, medical, academic, and government customers across the nation. The U.S. Army Corps accounts for about 30 percent of the company's sales; other customers include nuclear plants, steel mills, petrochemical facilities, and academic and medical institutions. The company handles non-hazardous, hazardous, and radioactive waste at facilities in Idaho, Nevada, Texas, and Washington state.

1984-2000: A KEY PLAYER IN THE LOW-LEVEL RADIOACTIVE WASTE MARKET

In 1984, Teledyne Inc. spun off two of its subsidiaries, US Ecology Inc. and Teledyne National Corp., both of which were engaged in the disposal of waste materials. W. E. Prachar became president and chief executive of the newly created American Ecology Corp., which, by 1985, consisted of three subsidiaries: US Ecology, the nation's oldest commercial low-level radioactive waste disposal company, providing site clean-up and transportation and packaging services for low-level radioactive and hazardous waste, and seminars in waste management nationwide; National Ecology, a resource recovery firm operating a refuse-derived fuel plant for the county of Baltimore, and offering design and engineering services in the resource recovery area to industry and municipalities; and Detox Inc., specializing in the treatment of contaminated groundwater.

The following year, California's Department of Health Services accepted US Ecology's bid to design, build, and operate the state's first site for the disposal of low-level radioactive waste from Arizona, California, and the Dakotas. Five years earlier, in 1980, the federal government had passed the Low-Level Radioactive Waste Policy Act, which required that each state in the nation develop a facility to handle its LLRW waste before 1993. This waste typically consisted of contaminated clothing, laboratory waste, filter materials, equipment, and plumbing and cleaning material from power plants, hospitals, research institutions, and industries that used radioisotopes. California was one of the nation's largest generators of low-level radioactive waste, and the

COMPANY PERSPECTIVES

∎

Our growth is straightforward. We aggressively price commodity services while seeking to expand higher value niche services and increase waste volume throughout. We also strive to deliver customer service second to none. This strategy, which takes advantage of the largely fixed cost nature of the disposal business while responding to customer needs, has been a proven recipe for success.

California site was the first of its kind to be built in the United States in fulfillment of both federal and state requirements.

In fact, US Ecology's history stretched further back than its history with Teledyne. It began providing nuclear waste services since 1953 and hazardous waste services in 1968. From 1963 to 1978, when the company was still Nuclear Engineering Co. Inc., it operated Maxey Flats dump site in Fleming County, Kentucky, for the Commonwealth of Kentucky. In the mid-1980s, an EPA investigation found reason to believe that these facilities were threatening to cause or were causing the discharge of contaminants into the environment, resulting in groundwater pollution, and the EPA informed American Ecology in 1986 that US Ecology was potentially responsible for investigative and remedial actions involving the dump site. American Ecology, in turn, sued its insurers when it learned that Superfund cleanup costs did not fall within the insurance policy's definition of property damage. Later, in 1988, it filed suit for the Eastern District of Kentucky against the Commonwealth of Kentucky, seeking recovery for costs incurred and to be incurred by US Ecology in connection with remedial action at Maxey Flats.

Despite the bad press and costs associated with Maxey Flats, American Ecology continued to grow; by 1987, it was well established in its market. The company operated two of three existing LLRW treatment and disposal sites in the United States, in Nevada and Washington, for treatment and disposal of low-level radioactive waste and two hazardous waste disposal facilities in Nevada and Texas. Its application for a license to operate a low-level radioactive waste site in California was pending. The Central States Low-Level Radioactive Waste Compact, one of several regional companies, or compacts, established as a result of the Federal Low-level Radioactive Waste Policy Act of 1980, selected US Ecology to develop and operate a regional low-level radioac-

tive waste disposal facility to serve Arkansas, Kansas, Louisiana, Nebraska, and Oklahoma. The company began working closely with state officials and eventually selected a site in Nebraska to begin operating in 1993.

However, American Ecology suffered uneven cash flow, and, as a result, the company made several internal changes. In 1989, it sold National Ecology to a subsidiary of Babcock and Wilcox. Two years later, it moved its corporate headquarters from Louisville, Kentucky, to Houston, Texas, and Harry Phillips, Jr., owner of Phillips Investments Inc. and former director of Browning-Ferris Industries Inc., one of the nation's largest waste collection and disposal companies, replaced Prachar as chief executive after Philips increased his ownership to approximately 36 percent of the company's stock. The company also moved US Ecology's headquarters to Sacramento, California, to facilitate construction and operation of California's planned Ward Valley waste disposal facility in the Mojave Desert.

1990S: ACQUISITIONS AND ONGOING DIFFICULTIES

The early 1990s were good years at American Ecology. Under Phillips leadership, the company's sales rose from $56 million in 1991 to $72 million in 1994. The company's income increased 70 percent in 1992, with revenues up by 27 percent from 1991's $71 million total. In 1993, American Ecology embarked on a strategy of enhanced service capabilities and expansion throughout the United States and Mexico through acquisition. Its first purchase was Waste Processor Inc., a publicly held, Texas-based environmental services company that provided hazardous and industrial waste transportation and onsite remediation. Waste Processor's assets included transportation terminals in Texas, a fleet of trucks, and a hazardous waste transport permit from the Texas Railroad Commission. Also in 1993, US Ecology's disposal facility in Washington became slated to operate as a regional disposal facility.

Acquisitions continued throughout 1994 when American Ecology acquired Gibralter Chemical Resources, Inc., a hazardous waste disposal, fuels blending, solvent recycling, and transportation company located in Winona, Texas. It also purchased Quadrex Recycle Center, a radioactive waste processing facility in Oak Ridge, Texas.

A year later, American Ecology reorganized itself into two operating units. It consolidated its nuclear waste business under US Ecology, headquartered in Oak Ridge, Tennessee, and its chemically related business under American Ecology Chemical Services, headquartered in Houston. Corporate headquarters for the

KEY DATES

1984: Teledyne spins off two subsidiaries, US Ecology Inc. and Teledyne National Corp., which become American Ecology Corporation.

1985: US Ecology contracts to develop and operate California's first disposal site for low-level radioactive wastes.

1987: Central States Low-Level Waste Treatment Contract selects US Ecology to develop its low-level radioactive waste facility.

1989: The company sells its subsidiary, National Ecology Inc.

1991: Harry Phillips, Jr., replaces W. E. Prachar as chief executive; American Ecology moves to Louisville, Kentucky; US Ecology moves to Sacramento, California.

1993: American Ecology purchases Waste Processor, Inc.

1994: American Ecology purchases Gibraltar Chemical Resources, Inc. and Quadrex Recycling Center.

1995: The company reorganizes into two operating units: US Ecology and American Ecology Chemical Services; Jack Lemley becomes chief executive officer.

1999: American Ecology sues the states of Nebraska and California.

2002: Steve Romano becomes the chief executive officer and moves the corporate headquarters to Boise, Idaho.

2004: American Ecology sells its Oak Ridge facility.

entire company moved to Boise, Idaho. Also in 1995, Jack Lemley succeeded Phillips as chief executive officer and president. Lemley had been a director of American Ecology since 1992, having served before that as chief executive of Transmarche-Link JV, which designed and built the Channel Tunnel providing train service between England and France.

However, problems also began to mount in the early 1990s. Neither development of the Ward Valley site or the site in Nebraska proceeded smoothly. Five years after the state of California contracted with US Ecology to develop its LLRW site, Interior Secretary Babbitt finally approved the transfer of federal lands for the site in Ward Valley. In 1998, a year after negotiations began for the Central Interstate Low-Level Radioactive Waste

facility in Nebraska, that state denied American Ecology the license to construct the five-state waste facility. Lemley, then the company's chief executive, testified before the Senate Armed Services Strategic Forces Subcommittee in 1998 that the 1980 Low-level Radioactive Waste Act was a "political failure." In 1999, American Ecology sued the state of Nebraska for rejecting its license application and sought reimbursement for the $94 million it paid out in development costs for the proposed multistate dump site. It also sued the state of California for the $80 million it spent on development costs on the Ward Valley dump after the federal government denied the state's request to buy land for the proposed facility at the end of the decade.

The company experienced losses of $49.8 million on revenues of $67.9 million in 1995, the same year that U.S. Geological Survey data showed radioactive waste had long been leaking from its site in Beatty, Nevada. The company insisted that the leakage occurred when workers whom it later dismissed improperly dumped liquid wastes in the facility, but "American Ecology's record is horrible," was the opinion of Senator Barbara Boxer in *Business Week* in 1996, referring to Maxey Flats' place on the Superfund list in 1986 and the 1978 lawsuit by the state of Illinois seeking $97 million in damages after radioactivity polluted a lake near the Sheffield dump. In 1992, US Ecology began to implement the EPA-approved plan of constructing a clay cap on the 20-acre Sheffield landfill and cleaning up contaminated groundwater.

Critics, including environmentalists as well as Native Americans, who considered the land at Ward Valley sacred, pointed to the company's finances and to American Ecology's history of problems at its sites. They worried that plans to dig unlined trenches at Ward Valley could result in contamination of the Colorado River. After Deputy Interior Secretary Garamendi accused the company of using 1950s technology for a facility that would operate well into the 21st century in a 1996 *Business Week* article, American Ecology insisted its operations would be safe because the waste would be placed in sealed containers before burial. Others thought the company's financial woes too great for it to survive.

It was not until 1998, American Ecology's first profitable year since 1994, that the company began to experience a turnaround. In 1996, the company had losses of $11.9 million; the following year, it earned $1.43 million on revenues of $41.5 million. In 1998, with revenues of $39 million, American Ecology turned over its former low-level waste site at Beatty, Nevada, to the State of Nevada Health Division for permanent custody. This marked the first time a commercial low-level waste disposal company had closed such a facility and returned it to the state's nuclear licensing agency for long-term care and control. The company also took on a contract with Virginia Electric Power Company to decontaminate, refurbish, rewind, and upgrade seven large electrical motors used to circulate cooling water inside nuclear power reactors.

Having made the decision to focus on its core business of low-level radioactive waste services and disposal facilities, in 1999 American Ecology sold all the assets of its two waste transportation related businesses: American Ecology Transportation, a hazardous and non-hazardous waste transportation service provider, and Surecycle, a business division that operated a scheduled, containerized hazardous waste collection service in the Gulf Coast market. In 2000, it sold its Nuclear Equipment Service Center in Oak Ridge, Tennessee, to Alaron.

In an effort to recoup costs for the development of potential sites in California and Nebraska, in 2000 American Ecology became embroiled in a legal fight over whether Nebraska was justified in rejecting its license application, seeking reimbursement for some $94 million in development costs. It also sued the state of California for the $80 million it spent on development costs on the Ward Valley dump after the federal government denied the state's request to buy land for the proposed facility. The case against California was remanded for trial in 2001, while the court ruled in favor of the company and against Nebraska in 2002.

More acquisitions and sales following during the next five years. In 2000, American Ecology opened the El Centro landfill municipal solid waste recycling and disposal facility outside Corpus Christi, Texas. In 2001, it acquired Envirosafe Services of Idaho, Inc., which it renamed US Ecology of Idaho and whose principal operation was hazardous waste treatment and disposal. Also in 2001, the Illinois Department of Nuclear Safety accepted permanent custody of the low-level environmental waste disposal site that US Ecology had operated from 1968 to 1978.

Steve Romano became chief executive of American Ecology, replacing Jack Lemley, who retired in 2002. Romano had 22 years of experience in waste management, including positions with the U.S. Nuclear Regulatory Commission, the Idaho National Environmental and Engineering Laboratory, and the Wisconsin Department of Natural Resources. During Romano's first year, the company moved its headquarters to Boise and added to its 18-person staff. It also sold subsidiary American Ecology Recycle Center, which provided low-level radioactive waste processing and environmental remediation services.

Also in 2002, American Ecology closed its Oak Ridge, Tennessee plant, purchased in 1994, which had since lost more than $45 million, laying off about 20 percent of its workforce. It sold the plant in 2004, marking its exit from all non-core businesses in order to concentrate on the treatment and disposal of hazardous waste at its Nevada, Idaho, and Texas sites and low-level radioactive waste at its Washington, Idaho, and Texas sites. The company was again ready for new beginnings in 2005 when it received a contract from Honeywell International to treat contaminated groundwater. Also in 2005, the company resumed full treatment services in a new hazardous waste treatment building at its Texas facilities.

Carrie Rothburd

PRINCIPAL SUBSIDIARIES

US Ecology of Idaho Inc.

PRINCIPAL COMPETITORS

Clean Harbors; Envirocare; Waste Management.

FURTHER READING

Antosh, Nelson, "American Ecology Clears Hurdle for Waste Dump," *Houston Chronicle*, May 13, 1995, p. 2.

Bowles, Jennifer, "California Examines Ways to Store Nuclear Waste," *Press-Enterprise*, November 5, 1999.

Harrison, Tom, "American Ecology Says Signs Point to Resolution of Financial Woes," *Nucleonics Week*, December 5, 1996, p. 5.

Hord, Bill, "American Ecology Stock Sinks on Woes," *Omaha World Herald*, October 21, 1999, p. 20.

Schine, Eric, "Nuclear Waste with Nowhere to Go," *Business Week*, June 10, 1996, p. 44.

Wald, Matthew L., "Marketplace: Some Say 'Not in My Backyard' While Others See Opportunity," *New York Times*, February 2, 1993, p. D8.

Zuercher, Richard R., "Ward Valley Compromise May Put LLW Project Back on Track," *Nucleonics Week*, March 31, 1994, p. 4.

Apple Computer, Inc.

1 Infinite Loop
Cupertino, California 95014
U.S.A.
Telephone: (408) 996-1010
Fax: (408) 974-2113
Web site: http://www.apple.com

Public Company
Incorporated: 1977
Employees: 13,426
Sales: $13.93 billion (2005)
Stock Exchanges: NASDAQ
Ticker Symbol: AAPL
NAIC: 334111 Electronic Computer Manufacturing;
334119 Other Computer Peripheral Equipment
Manufacturing; 511210 Software Publishers

∎ ∎ ∎

Apple Computer, Inc. designs, manufactures, and markets personal computers, software, networking solutions, and peripherals, including a line of portable digital music players. Apple's product family includes the Macintosh line of desktop and notebook computers, the iPod digital music player, the Mac OS X operating system, the iTunes Music Store, the Xserve G5 server, and Xserve RAID storage products. The company's products are sold online, through third-party wholesalers, and through its own chain of stores. Apple owns approximately 125 retail stores in the United States, as well as stores in Canada, Japan, and the United Kingdom.

ORIGINS

Apple was founded in April 1976 by Steve Wozniak, then 26 years old, and Steve Jobs, 21, both college dropouts. Their partnership began several years earlier when Wozniak, a talented, self-taught electronics engineer, began building boxes that allowed him to make long-distance phone calls for free. The pair sold several hundred such boxes.

In 1976 Wozniak was working on another box, the Apple I computer, without keyboard or power supply, for a computer hobbyist club. Jobs and Wozniak sold their most valuable possessions, a van and two calculators, raising $1,300 with which to start a company. A local retailer ordered 50 of the computers, which were built in Jobs's garage. They eventually sold 200 to computer hobbyists in the San Francisco Bay area for $666 each. Later that summer, Wozniak began work on the Apple II, designed to appeal to a greater market than computer hobbyists. Jobs hired local computer enthusiasts, many of them still in high school, to assemble circuit boards and design software. Early microcomputers had usually been housed in metal boxes. With the general consumer in mind, Jobs planned to house the Apple II in a more attractive modular beige plastic container.

Jobs wanted to create a large company and consulted with Mike Markkula, a retired electronics engineer who had managed marketing for Intel Corporation and Fairchild Semiconductor. Chairman Markkula bought one-third of the company for $250,000, helped Jobs with the business plan, and in 1977 hired Mike Scott as president. Wozniak worked for Apple full time in his engineering capacity.

COMPANY PERSPECTIVES

The company is committed to bringing the best personal computing and music experience to students, educators, creative professionals, businesses, government agencies, and consumers through its innovative hardware, software, peripherals, services, and Internet offerings. The company's business strategy leverages its unique ability, through the design and development of its own operating system, hardware, and many software applications and technologies, to bring to its customers new products and solutions with superior ease-of-use, seamless integration, and innovative industrial design.

Jobs recruited Regis McKenna, owner of one of the most successful advertising and public relations firms in Silicon Valley, to devise an advertising strategy for the company. McKenna designed the Apple logo and began advertising personal computers in consumer magazines. Apple's professional marketing team placed the Apple II in retail stores, and by June 1977, annual sales reached $1 million. It was the first microcomputer to use color graphics, with a television set as the screen. In addition, the Apple II expansion slot made it more versatile than competing computers.

The earliest Apple IIs read and stored information on cassette tapes, which were unreliable and slow. By 1978 Wozniak had invented the Apple Disk II, at the time the fastest and cheapest disk drive offered by any computer manufacturer. The Disk II made possible the development of software for the Apple II. The introduction of Apple II, with a user manual, at a consumer electronics show signaled that Apple was expanding beyond the hobbyist market to make its computers consumer items. By the end of 1978, Apple was one of the fastest-growing companies in the United States, with its products carried by over 100 dealers.

In 1979 Apple introduced the Apple II+ with far more memory than the Apple II and an easier startup system, and the Silentype, the company's first printer. VisiCalc, the first spreadsheet for microcomputers, was also released that year. Its popularity helped to sell many Apple IIs. By the end of the year sales were up 400 percent from 1978, at over 35,000 computers. Apple Fortran, introduced in March 1980, led to the further development of software, particularly technical and educational applications.

In December 1980, Apple went public. Its offering of 4.6 million shares at $22 each sold out within minutes. A second offering of 2.6 million shares quickly sold out in May 1981.

Meanwhile Apple was working on the Apple II's successor, which was intended to feature expanded memory and graphics capabilities and run the software already designed for the Apple II. The company, fearful that the Apple II would soon be outdated, put time pressures on the designers of the Apple III, despite the fact that sales of the Apple II more than doubled to 78,000 in 1980. The Apple III was well received when it was released in September 1980 at $3,495, and many predicted it would achieve its goal of breaking into the office market dominated by IBM. However, the Apple III was released without adequate testing, and many units proved to be defective. Production was halted and the problems were fixed, but the Apple III never sold as well as the Apple II. It was discontinued in April 1984.

The problems with the Apple III prompted Mike Scott to lay off employees in February 1981, a move with which Jobs disagreed. As a result, Mike Markkula became president and Jobs chairman. Scott was named vice-chairman shortly before leaving the firm.

Despite the problems with Apple III, the company forged ahead, tripling its 1981 research and development budget to $21 million, releasing 40 new software programs, opening European offices, and putting out its first hard disk. By January 1982, 650,000 Apple computers had been sold worldwide. In December 1982, Apple became the first personal computer company to reach $1 billion in annual sales.

The next year, Apple lost its position as chief supplier of personal computers in Europe to IBM, and tried to challenge IBM in the business market with the Lisa computer. Lisa introduced the mouse, a hand-controlled pointer, and displayed pictures on the computer screen that substituted for keyboard commands. These innovations came out of Jobs's determination to design an unintimidating computer that anyone could use.

Unfortunately, the Lisa did not sell as well as Apple had hoped. Apple was having difficulty designing the elaborate software to link together a number of Lisas and was finding it hard to break IBM's hold on the business market. Apple's earnings went down and its stock plummeted to $35, half of its sale price in 1982. Mike Markkula had viewed his presidency as a temporary position, and in April 1983, Jobs brought in John Sculley, formerly president of Pepsi-Cola, as the new president of Apple. Jobs felt the company needed Sculley's marketing expertise.

KEY DATES

1976: With $1,300, Steve Jobs and Steve Wozniak found Apple Computer, Inc.

1980: Apple converts to public ownership.

1982: Apple becomes the first personal computer company to reach $1 billion in annual sales.

1985: John Sculley assumes the helm after a management shakeup that causes the departure of Jobs and several other Apple executives.

1991: PowerBook line of notebook computers is released.

1994: Power Macintosh line is released.

1996: Acquisition of NeXT brings Steve Jobs back to Apple as a special advisor.

1997: Steve Jobs is named interim chief executive officer.

1998: The all-in-one iMac is released.

2000: Jobs, firmly in command as CEO, oversees a leaner, more tightly focused Apple.

2001: The iPod is released; Apple opens its first retail store in Virginia.

2003: Apple opens its first store in Japan.

2005: The release of a video iPod, the fifth generation of the device, pushes total iPod unit sales to 30 million.

1984 DEBUT OF THE MACINTOSH

The production division for Lisa had been vying with Jobs's Macintosh division. The Macintosh personal computer offered Lisa's innovations at a fraction of the price. Jobs saw the Macintosh as the "people's computer," designed for people with little technical knowledge. With the failure of the Lisa, the Macintosh was seen as the future of the company. Launched with a television commercial in January 1984, the Macintosh was unveiled soon after, with a price tag of $2,495 and a new 3-inch disk drive that was faster than the 5 1/4-inch drives used in other machines, including the Apple II.

Apple sold 70,000 Macintosh computers in the first 100 days. In September 1984 a new Macintosh was released with more memory and two disk drives. Jobs was convinced that anyone who tried the Macintosh would buy it. A national advertisement offered people the chance to take a Macintosh home for 24 hours, and over 200,000 people did so. At the same time, Apple sold its two millionth Apple II. Over the next six months Apple released numerous products for the Macintosh, including a laser printer and a hard drive.

Despite these successes, Macintosh sales temporarily fell off after a promising start, and the company was troubled by internal problems. Infighting between divisions continued, and poor inventory tracking led to overproduction. Although originally a strong supporter of Sculley, Jobs eventually decided to oust the executive; Jobs, however, lost the ensuing showdown. Sculley reorganized Apple in June 1985 to end the infighting caused by the product-line divisions, and Jobs, along with several other Apple executives, left the company in September. They founded a new computer company, NeXT Incorporated, which would later emerge as a rival to Apple in the business computer market.

The Macintosh personal computer finally moved Apple into the business office market. Corporations saw its ease of use as a distinct advantage. It was far cheaper than the Lisa and had the necessary software to link office computers. In 1986 and 1987 Apple produced three new Macintosh personal computers with improved memory and power. By 1988, over one million Macintosh computers had been sold, with 70 percent of sales to corporations. Software was created that allowed the Macintosh to be connected to IBM-based systems. Apple grew rapidly; income for 1988 topped $400 million on sales of $4.07 billion, up from income of $217 million on sales of $1.9 billion in 1986. Apple had 5,500 employees in 1986 and over 14,600 by the early 1990s.

In 1988, Apple management had expected a worldwide shortage of memory chips to worsen. They bought millions when prices were high, only to have the shortage end and prices fall soon after. Apple ordered sharp price increases for the Macintosh line just before the Christmas buying season, and consumers bought the less expensive Apple line or other brands. In early 1989, Apple released significantly enhanced versions of the two upper-end Macintosh computers, the SE and the Macintosh II, primarily to compete for the office market. At the same time IBM marketed a new operating system that mimicked the Macintosh's ease of use. In May 1989 Apple announced plans for its new operating system, System 7, which would be available to users the next year and allow Macintoshes to run tasks on more than one program simultaneously.

Apple was reorganized in August 1988 into four operating divisions: Apple USA, Apple Europe, Apple Pacific, and Apple Products. Dissatisfied with the changes, many longtime Apple executives left. In July 1990, Robert Puette, former head of Hewlett-Packard's personal computer business, became head of the Apple USA division. Sculley saw the reorganization as an attempt to create fewer layers of management within Apple, thus encouraging innovation among staff. Analysts credit Sculley with expanding Apple from a consumer and education computer company to a business computer company, one of the biggest and fastest-growing corporations in the United States.

Competition in the industry of information technology involved Apple in a number of lawsuits. In December 1989 for instance, the Xerox Corporation, in a $150 million lawsuit, charged Apple with unlawfully using Xerox technology for the Macintosh software. Apple did not deny borrowing from Xerox technology but explained that the company had spent millions to refine that technology and had used other sources as well. In 1990 the court found in favor of Apple in the Xerox case. Earlier, in March 1988, Apple had brought suits against Microsoft and Hewlett-Packard, charging copyright infringement. Four years later, in the spring of 1992, Apple's case was dealt a severe blow in a surprise ruling: copyright protection cannot be based on "look and feel" (appearance) alone; rather, "specific" features of an original program must be detailed by developers for protection.

MISMANAGEMENT, CRIPPLING AN INDUSTRY GIANT: 1990S

Apple entered the 1990s well aware that the conditions that made the company an industry giant in the previous decade had changed dramatically. Management recognized that for Apple to succeed in the future, corporate strategies would have to be reexamined. Apple had soared through the 1980s on the backs of its large, expensive computers, which earned the company a committed, yet relatively small following. Sculley and his team saw that competitors were relying increasingly on the user-friendly graphics that had become the Macintosh signature and recognized that Apple needed to introduce smaller, cheaper models, such as the Classic and LC, which were instant hits. At a time when the industry was seeing slow unit sales, the numbers at Apple were skyrocketing. In 1990, desktop Macs accounted for 11 percent of the PCs sold through U.S. computer dealers. In mid-1992, the figure was 19 percent.

But these modestly priced models had a considerably smaller profit margin than their larger cousins. So even if sales took off, as they did, profits were threatened. In a severe austerity move, Apple laid off nearly 10 percent of its workforce, consolidated facilities, moved production plants to areas where it was cheaper to operate, and drastically altered its corporate organizational chart. The bill for such forward-looking surgery was great, however, and in 1991 profits were off 35 percent. But analysts said that such pitfalls were expected, indeed

necessary, if the company intended to position itself as a leaner, better-conditioned fighter in the years ahead.

Looking ahead is what analysts say saved Apple from foundering. In 1992, after the core of the suit that Apple had brought against Microsoft and Hewlett-Packard was dismissed, industry observers pointed out that although the loss was a disappointment for Apple, the company wisely had not banked on a victory. They credited Apple's ambitious plans for the future with quickly turning the lawsuit into yesterday's news.

In addition to remaining faithful to its central business of computer making (the notebook PowerBook series, released in 1991, garnered a 21 percent market share in less than six months), Apple intended to ride a digital wave into the next century. The company geared itself to participate in a revolution in the consumer electronics industry, in which products that were limited by a slow, restrictive analog system would be replaced by faster, digital gadgets on the cutting edge of telecommunications technology. Apple also experimented with the interweaving of sound and visuals in the operations of its computers.

For Apple, the most pressing issue of the 1990s was not related to technology, but concerned capable and consistent management. The company endured tortuous failures throughout much of the decade, as one chief executive officer after another faltered miserably. Scully was forced out of his leadership position by Apple's board of directors in 1993. His replacement, Michael Spindler, broke tradition by licensing Apple technology to outside firms, paving the way for ill-fated Apple clones that ultimately eroded Apple's profits. Spindler also oversaw the introduction of the Power Macintosh line in 1994, an episode in Apple's history that typified the perception that the company had the right products but not the right people to deliver the products to the market. Power Macintosh computers were highly sought after, but after overestimating demand for the earlier release of its PowerBook laptops, the company grossly underestimated demand for the Power Macintosh line. By 1995, Apple had $1 billion worth of unfilled orders, and investors took note of the embarrassing miscue. In a two-day period, Apple's stock value plunged 15 percent.

After Spindler's much publicized mistake of 1995, Apple's directors were ready to hand the leadership reins to someone new. Gil Amelio, credited with spearheading the recovery of National Semiconductor, was named chief executive officer in February 1996, beginning another notorious era of leadership for the beleaguered Cupertino company. Amelio cut Apple's payroll by a third and slashed operating costs, but drew a hail of criticism for his compensation package and his inability to relate to Apple's unique corporate culture. Apple's financial losses, meanwhile, mounted, reaching $816 million in 1996 and a staggering $1 billion in 1997. The company's stock, which had traded at more than $70 per share in 1991, fell to $14 per share. Its market share, 16 percent in the late 1980s, stood at less than 4 percent. *Fortune* magazine offered its analysis, referring to Apple in its March 3, 1997 issue as "Silicon Valley's paragon of dysfunctional management."

Amelio was ousted from the company in July 1997, but before his departure a significant deal was concluded that brought Apple's savior to Cupertino. In December 1996, Apple paid $377 million for NeXT, a small, $50-million-in-sales company founded and led by Steve Jobs. Concurrent with the acquisition, Amelio hired Jobs as his special advisor, marking the return of Apple's visionary 12 years after he had left. In September 1997, two months after Amelio's exit, Apple's board of directors named Jobs interim chief executive officer. Apple's recovery occurred during the ensuing months.

Jobs assumed his responsibilities with the same passion and understanding that had made Apple one of the greatest success stories in business history. He immediately discontinued the licensing agreement that spawned Apple clones. He eliminated 15 of the company's 19 products, withdrawing Apple's involvement in making printers, scanners, portable digital assistants, and other peripherals. From 1997 forward, Apple would focus exclusively on desktop and portable Macintoshes for professional and consumer customers. Jobs closed plants, laid off thousands of workers, and sold stock to rival Microsoft Corporation, receiving a cash infusion of $150 million in exchange. Apple's organizational hierarchy underwent sweeping reorganization as well, but the most visible indication of Jobs's return was unveiled in August 1998. Distressed by his company's lack of popular computers that retailed for less than $2,000, Jobs tapped Apple's resources and, ten months after the project began, unveiled the massively successful iMAC, a sleek and colorful computer that embodied Apple's skill in design and functionality.

Because of Jobs's restorative efforts, Apple exited the 1990s as a pared-down version of its former self, but, importantly, a profitable company once again. Annual sales, which totaled $11.5 billion in 1995, stood at $5.9 billion in 1998, from which the company recorded a profit of $309 million. In 1999, sales grew a modest 3.2 percent, but the newfound health of the company was evident in a 94 percent gain in net income, as Apple's profits swelled to $601 million. Further, Apple's stock mustered a remarkable rebound, climbing 140 percent to $99 per share in 1999. By the decade's end,

"interim" was dropped from Jobs's corporate title, signaling Jobs's return on a permanent basis and fueling optimism that Apple could look forward to a decade of vibrant and consistent growth.

2001: IPOD, CATALYST TO GROWTH

Apple's turnaround was confirmed in the first years of the 21st century, as the company strode toward its 30th anniversary exuding an unprecedented degree of strength. At the heart of the company's surging growth was a digital music player branded as iPod. Introduced in late 2001, the device featured five gigabytes (GB) of storage, enabling the user to store approximately 1,000 songs on a player that was smaller than a deck of playing cards. Retailing for $399, the iPod represented another example of Apple's skill in designing an elegant and functional product, a product that became one of the most sought after consumer electronics items during the first half of the decade. Succeeding generations of iPods hit the market and scored resounding success, driving the company's financial growth. A 10 GB model was introduced in mid-2002, followed by the iPod Mini, iPod Shuffle, and iPod Nano, together representing a massive new source of revenue for the company. The fifth generation of the iPod debuted in 2005, a device available in a 30 GB or 60 GB model that was capable of storing and playing video files. By the time the video iPod arrived in stores, Apple derived roughly 35 percent of its revenue from iPods. Between 2001 and 2005, thanks primarily to the popularity of iPods, the company's sales nearly tripled, increasing from $5.3 billion to $13.9 billion. Apple controlled more than 75 percent of the $2.5 billion digital audio player market in the United States.

As the company enjoyed escalating sales midway through the decade, it also celebrated the success of a new dimension to its business. In 2001, the company opened its first retail outlet, a 6,000-square-foot store located in Tysons Corner, Virginia, that became the first unit of a chain of Apple-owned stores. By 2005, the company operated nearly 125 stores in the United States and a handful of stores in Canada, Japan, and the United Kingdom. With an expanding retail arm devoted to highlighting an impressively popular selection of products, Apple approached its 30th anniversary in a stronger position than ever before in its history. In the years ahead, the company's well-established ability to develop singular products for the digital marketplace promised to deliver impressive growth and excite the interests of consumers worldwide.

Scott Lewis
Updated, Jeffrey L. Covell

PRINCIPAL SUBSIDIARIES

Apple Computer, Inc. Limited (Ireland); Apple Computer Limited (Ireland); Apple Computer International (Ireland).

PRINCIPAL COMPETITORS

Compaq Computer Corporation; Dell Computer Corporation; International Business Machines Corporation; Microsoft Corporation; Hewlett-Packard Company.

FURTHER READING

Ahrens, Frank, "Apple Set to Open in Japan First Retail Store Outside United States," *America's Intelligence Wire,* November 27, 2003.

"Apple Crumble," *Economist (US),* July 12, 1997, p. 54.

Bartholomew, Doug, "What's Really Driving Apple's Recovery," *Industry Week,* March 15, 1999, p. 34.

Breen, Christopher, "Video iPod Arrives," *Macworld,* December 2005, p. 18.

Burrows, Peter, "Apple May Be Holding Back the Music Biz," *Business Week,* December 19, 2005, p. 40.

"Dell CEO Says iPod Helped Turn Around Apple," *PC Magazine Online,* November 15, 2005.

"An Even Better iPod," *PC Magazine Online,* May 17, 2002.

"Everybody Wants a Piece of the iPod," *America's Intelligence Wire,* October 27, 2003.

Fawcett, Neil, "Can Microsoft Put Apple Together Again?," *Computer Weekly,* August 14, 1997, p. 17.

Frieberger, Paul, and Michael Swaine, *Fire in the Valley: The Making of the Personal Computer,* Berkeley, Calif.: Osborne-McGraw-Hill, 1984.

Hogan, Thom, "Apple: The First Ten Years," *A+: The #1 Apple II Magazine,* September 1987.

Kirkpatrick, David, "The Second Coming of Apple," *Fortune,* November 9, 1998, p. 86.

Kupfer, Andrew, "Apple's Plan to Survive and Grow," *Fortune,* May 4, 1992.

Merrion, Paul, "Inventor of Music Player Takes a Bite Out of Apple," *Crain's Chicago Business,* November 28, 2005, p. 2.

Pollack, Andrew, "Apple Shows Products for Its Macintosh Line," *Time,* March 4, 1992.

Quittner, Joshua, "Apple Turnover?," *Time,* October 2, 1995, p. 56.

Rebello, Kathy, "Apple's Daring Leap into the All-Digital Future," *Business Week,* May 25, 1992.

Rebello, Kathy, Michele Galen, and Evan I. Schwartz, "It Looks and Feels As If Apple Lost," *Business Week,* April 27, 1992.

Rose, Frank, *West of Eden,* New York: Penguin Books, 1989.

Schlender, Brent, "Something's Rotten in Cupertino," *Fortune,* March 3, 1997, p. 100.

Seitz, Patrick, "Apple Sees Healthy "iPod Economy,'" *Investor's Business Daily,* December 5, 2005, p. A5.

"Will Apple Push 'Intel Inside'?," *Business Week Online,* December 16, 2005.

Wong, May, "Apple Sets Pace in Consumer Electronics," *America's Intelligence Wire,* December 15, 2005.

Zachary, G. Pascal, and Stephen Kreider Yoder, "Apple Moves Its Microsoft Battle to the Marketplace," *Wall Street Journal,* April 16, 1992.

Azerbaijan Airlines

—■—

May 28 str., 66/68
Baku, AZ-1010
Azerbaijan
Telephone: (994-12) 493 40 04
Fax: (994-12) 497 28 04
Web site: http://www.nac-azal.com

State-Owned Company
Incorporated: 1992
Employees: 6,000
NAIC: 481111 Scheduled Passenger Air Transportation;
481112 Scheduled Freight Air Transportation;
481212 Nonscheduled Chartered Freight Air Transportation

■ ■ ■

Azerbaijan Airlines (AZAL) is the national airline of Azerbaijan, an oil-rich former Soviet republic. It operates a network of scheduled routes throughout the former Soviet republic and its neighbors, the Middle East, Europe, and Asia. More than one million people fly the airline each year.

AZAL has a very diverse fleet for its size, consisting of aircraft made in Russia, the Ukraine, the United States, and Europe. The fleet even includes helicopters, of both European and Soviet origin. The company that runs the airline is also in charge of Azerbaijan's civil aviation authority and airports.

ORIGINS

Azerbaijan has had scheduled air service since 1923, when German-made Junkers aircraft of the day plied a route between the republic's capital of Baku (a port on the Caspian Sea) and Tbilisi in Georgia. In 1990, Azerbaijan announced that it was setting up its own airline independent of Aeroflot, the behemoth that had previously handled air services for the Soviet republics. Azerbaijan Airlines (AZAL) was officially established on August 17, 1992, according to *Airline Business*. Its first president was Vagif Sadykhly. According to *Flight International*, it was one of nearly 70 airline companies being set up across the Commonwealth of Independent States (CIS).

Formed from the regional branch of Aeroflot, Azerbaijan Airlines, also known as Azerbaijan Hava Yollari, soon spread its wings into the world outside the Soviet Union that had been Aeroflot's exclusive domain. A scheduled Baku-Istanbul route was launched in January 1991 in partnership with the Turkish state airline, and the cargo enterprise Aviasharg was created with the United Arab Emirates.

State Concern of Civil Aviation included Azerbaijan Airlines as well as the country's civil aviation authority and air traffic control. It employed about 6,000 people and, according to the *European,* was reaping profits of more than $25 million a year.

AZAL inherited a huge fleet from Aeroflot, including more than 20 Soviet-made Tupolev airliners, some regional airliners and freighters, 90 light aircraft, and 50 helicopters. It was quick to lease a pair of Boeing 727s, however, that once belonged to Pan Am (and were built in 1968). AZAL had an extensive involvement with ALG, the U.S.-based lessor of these Boeing 727s. It had a transatlantic charter cargo joint venture with ALG's Buffalo Airways, which was also training AZAL aircrews to Western standards in Dallas, Texas.

Azerbaijan worked out a deal to acquire Boeing airliners (of the 737, 757, 767, and 777 models) in the mid-1990s in exchange for the amount of fuel the more efficient planes were expected to save compared with the old Tupolevs, reported the Interfax news agency. AZAL also was operating ten smaller Yakovlev Yak-40 tri-jets, a massive Ilyushin Il-76 freighter, and several Antonov turboprops.

A new rival, Imair, emerged in 1994. The growth of tiny Azerbaijan's aviation industry was disproportionate to its population of just seven million, as foreign investment poured in, looking to exploit the country's enormous oil reserves. Whereas these brought business and cargo traffic from abroad, Azerbaijan Airlines also was charged with maintaining air links to the country's isolated communities.

NEW LEADERSHIP, NEW ROUTES IN THE MID-1990S

In November 1994 AZAL began a route to Dubai, which, along with Istanbul, was a key source of Western goods. It was soon also flying to Tehran, Tel Aviv, Moscow, Saint Petersburg, London, and China. Service to several regional destinations was suspended in mid-1998 due to low margins and the need to repair three Yak-40 aircraft.

With the exception of a few major cities, service to neighboring CIS countries was suspended as well in January 1999. These routes were generally unprofitable as well and were facing new competition from trains. The main reason for the suspension was that it owed money to its neighbors. According to the Trend news agency, domestic flights accounted for only about 16 percent of AZAL's traffic in 1998.

According to *Flight International,* the airline's fortunes took a leap forward in May 1996 when Djanguir Askerov became AZAL's director-general. A pilot himself, Askerov reorganized AZAL into five units: the airline, airports, air traffic control, in-flight catering (a joint venture with Abela of Dubai), and cargo.

The country invested in a new air traffic infrastructure, including a new airport terminal and new air traffic control facilities (air traffic control had to deal not only with arrivals and departures, but with more than 1,600 overflights a month, noted *Flight International.*) The national airline was running out of aircraft, however, due to a lack of spare parts, an official told *AssA-Irada.* In 1999, AZAL was down to seven Tupolevs and two Boeing 727s.

In spite of the new infrastructure, leading foreign airlines (British Airways, Lufthansa, KLM) were shutting down their operations in the country due to high fees, poor service, and the widespread practice of bribery, reported Russia's ITAR/TASS News Agency. Azerbaijan President Geidar Aliyev promised a crackdown on corruption.

NEW WESTERN PLANES IN 2000

Azerbaijan's border dispute with Armenia had delayed financing for two new Boeing 757s from the U.S. Eximbank. The $66 million loan guarantee was the Eximbank's first transaction for Azerbaijan, according to *Air Transport Intelligence.* The financing also was guaranteed by the Azerbaijan government and the International Bank of Azerbaijan. The United Kingdom's Export Credit Guarantee Department guaranteed financing for the aircrafts' Rolls-Royce engines.

The first of these Boeing 757s was delivered in the fall of 2000. The planes offered the carrier unprecedented range, comfort, and efficiency on long-haul international routes. They also helped project a modern image to the world. Interestingly, the second Boeing 757 to be delivered arrived in December laden with medical supplies due to a recent earthquake in Azerbaijan. In January 2001, AZAL used one of the planes to begin operating a Paris-Baku route in collaboration with Air France.

Azerbaijan, a predominantly Muslim country, experienced a reduction in air traffic following the September 11, 2001 terrorist attacks on the United States. AZAL was able to remain profitable through 2001, however, and even make progress toward paying off its debt. The airline was soon shopping for more new aircraft as it retired its aging Soviet models. AZAL ordered its first Western-made helicopters in October 2002, purchasing six for EUR 52 million from Eurocopter. AZAL used helicopters to ferry personnel and equipment oil rigs in the Caspian Sea.

In July 2004, two of AZAL's airliners were impounded by Turkey over a 12-year-old debt owed by Azerbaijan's Agriculture Ministry to a Turkish company. In the same month, AZAL ordered new Ukrainian-made, 52-passenger An-140 turboprops to replenish its regional fleet, paying about $36 million for four planes.

```
┌─────────────────────────────────────────┐
│                                           │
│            KEY DATES                      │
│            ───────■───────                │
│                                           │
│   1923:  Azerbaijan gets its first        │
│          scheduled air service,           │
│          from Baku to Tbilisi.            │
│   1992:  Azerbaijan sets up its own       │
│          airline independent              │
│          of the Soviet Union's Aeroflot.  │
│   2000:  AZAL acquires two new long-range │
│          Boeing 757 airliners.            │
│   2002:  The first Western-made           │
│          helicopters are acquired.        │
│   2005:  Routes are added to the Indian   │
│          subcontinent.                    │
│                                           │
└─────────────────────────────────────────┘
```

The company also was ordering four aircraft from Airbus, three A319 mid-size airliners and one Airbus Corporate Jetliner (ACJ), for use as an official state aircraft. These were all powered by CFM International engines. AZAL had a large number of aircraft types for such a small company, from manufacturers in Russia, Ukraine, Europe, and the United States.

In 2005 AZAL began serving the Indian subcontinent with flights to Delhi and Karachi. Azerbaijan and Pakistan were working to build trade between the two predominantly Muslim countries. AZAL's code-share partners included Pakistan International Airlines, Emirates Airlines, Air France, and Austrian Airlines.

Azerbaijan Airlines continued to buy aircraft from the former Soviet states. In August 2005 it ordered three Ilyushin Il-76 freighters to be built in nearby Uzbekistan (it had lost one of its Il-76s in a China crash the previous year). AZAL ended 2005 with bad news; one of its brand new An-140 airliners crashed into the Caspian Sea, killing all 23 aboard. The company attributed the accident to instrument failure.

Frederick C. Ingram

PRINCIPAL COMPETITORS

Aeroflot Russian Airlines JSC; El Al Israel Airlines Ltd.; Imair; IranAir; Turkish Airlines Inc.

FURTHER READING

"AZAL Buys 3 Modern Il-76 Airplanes," *Asia Africa Intelligence Wire/AssA-Irada,* August 19, 2005.

"AZAL Files Lawsuit Against Turkish Company," *AssA-Irada,* July 27, 2004.

"AZAL Launches Regular Baku-Paris-Baku Flights," *AssA-Irada,* February 22, 2001.

"AZAL Paying Off Loans," *AssA-Irada,* November 14, 2001.

"AZAL Running Out of Planes," *AssA-Irada,* May 29, 1999.

"AZAL Signs Deal for An-140s," *Flight International,* July 6, 2004, p. 10.

"Azerbaijan Airlines Starts Delhi-Baku Flights—Indian Agency," *BBC Monitoring International Reports,* July 18, 2005.

"Azerbaijan Resumes Cargo Plane Flights to China," *Business Daily Update,* November 15, 2004.

"Azerbaijan to Get 12 Boeing Liners in Exchange for Fuel," *RusData DiaLine—BizEkon News/Interfax,* August 13, 1993.

"Azerbaijani Plane Crashes Off UAE," *Gulf News,* July 14, 1998.

"Azerbaijan's Aliyev Set to Get Tough on Corruption," *ITAR/TASS News Agency,* April 14, 2000.

"Azeri Airline Suspends Flights to Most CIS Destinations," *BBC Monitoring Former Soviet Union—Economic/Trend,* January 2, 1999.

"Azeri National Airline Resumes Some Regional Flights," *BBC Monitoring Former Soviet Union—Economic/Trend,* December 22, 1998.

Blacklock, Mark, "Regional Rivalries," *Airline Business,* November 1993, p. 41.

Chuter, Andy, "Azerbaijani Airlines Look West to Help Expansion," *Flight International,* September 3, 1997, p. 14.

——, "Bridge Building in Baku," *Flight International,* November 26, 1997.

"CIS Authorizes New Operator Licences," *Flight International,* March 11, 1992.

Dunn, Graham, "Azerbaijan Airlines Orders Three A319s, One ACJ," *Air Transport Intelligence,* August 25, 2004.

"Eurocopter Sells Six Helicopters to Azerbaijan," *Agence France Presse—English,* October 2, 2002.

"Ex-Soviet Republic Takes Ex-Pan Am 727," *Flight International,* January 13, 1993.

Kjelgaard, Chris, "Eximbank, ECGD Guarantee Azerbaijan 757 Financings," *Air Transport Intelligence,* April 28, 2000.

Morrow, David, "Azerbaijan Airlines Gears Up for 757 Operations," *Air Transport Intelligence,* October 10, 2000.

"Security Beefed Up at Baku Airport, Official Says," *BBC Monitoring International Reports/Turan,* April 6, 2004.

Shulman, Viktor, "Azerbaijan Opens Its Own Airlines," *TASS,* December 11, 1990.

Sultanova, Aida, "Azerbaijani Plane Crash That Killed 23 Caused by Instrument Failure, Panel Says," *America's Intelligence Wire/AP Worldstream,* December 29, 2005.

"Three CIS States Operate Boeings," *Flight International,* November 25, 1992.

"Turkey Impounds Another Azeri Passenger Aircraft, Ship Over Debts," *BBC Monitoring International Reports/Azad Azarbaycan TV,* July 21, 2004.

"2001 Proves Profitable for AZAL," *AssA-Irada,* February 4, 2002.

Verchere, Ian, "Azeri Ambition Shines Through Peeling Paint," *European,* November 9, 1995, p. 32.

Wastnage, Justin, "Azerbaijan Goes on Upgrade Trail; Airbus and Boeing Asked to Provide Proposals for Four Narrowbodies, While Flag Carrier Also Seeks Turboprops," *Flight International,* September 10, 2002, p. 16.

Zaitsev, Tom, "Azerbaijan Airlines Stakes Claim on Baku-Moscow Route," *Air Transport Intelligence,* October 10, 2003.

BB Holdings Limited

60 Market Square
PO Box 1764
Belize City, 2272660
Belize
Telephone: (501) 227-2660
Fax: (501) 227-5474
Web site: http://www.bbholdingslimited.com

Public Company
Incorporated: 1984 as Belize Holdings Limited
Employees: 30,700
Sales: $1.38 billion (2005)
Stock Exchanges: London NASDAQ
Ticker Symbol: BBHL
NAIC: 561720 Janitorial Services; 551112 Offices of Other Holding Companies; 522110 Commercial Banking

■ ■ ■

BB Holdings Limited is a Belize-based holding company with two primary assets: OneSource Inc., one of the world's leading outsourced facility services companies; and Belize Bank Ltd., the leading financial institution in Belize. OneSource, which was formed from the U.S. branch of Denmark's ISS, operates primarily in the United States, and is one of that market's leading outsourced services providers. The company employs some 31,000 people and operates in nearly 200 major metropolitan areas in 45 states, as well as in Puerto Rico. OneSource's operations include janitorial and maintenance services, contract cleaning, landscape

services, and related facility support services. Belize Bank is the largest full-service bank in Belize, claiming a 50 percent market share in that country. Belize Bank operates 12 branches throughout Belize, with headquarters in Belize City. Listed on the London Stock Exchange and the NASDAQ, BB Holdings is controlled by the highly controversial Michael Ashcroft, who holds dual citizenship in Belize and the United Kingdom, acts as Belize's ambassador to the United Nations, serves as treasurer, and major financial backer, to England's Conservative Party, and is one of the United Kingdom's 15 richest people. In 2005, BB Holdings restructured, demerging its interests in England and Ireland into a separate, publicly listed company, Carlisle Group Limited. BB Holdings reported revenues of nearly $1.4 billion in 2005.

FIRST FORTUNES IN THE 1970S

BB Holdings stemmed from the financial wheelings and dealings of Michael Ashcroft, son of a British civil servant who parlayed a £15,000 loan into a financial empire worth billions of dollars. Ashcroft's father had been stationed in Belize city, then the capital of the British Honduras. Ashcroft, although born in England in 1946, spent a great deal of his youth in the former British colony. Returning to England during the 1960s, Ashcroft spent some time hitchhiking around Europe, before briefly acting as a manager of a rock and roll band. In mid-decade, however, Ashcroft had gone to work for British tobacco giant Rothmans, where he received his first management experience. By the end of the decade, Ashcroft had moved on to the Pritchard Services Group, a provider of janitorial and security services. The ambi-

COMPANY PERSPECTIVES

BB Holdings Limited is a leader in the outsourced facilities services market in the United States serving a broad range of commercial, industrial and municipal clients. The Company also has a financial services business based in Belize which is the largest full service, commercial and retail banking operation in the country. Our success is based on partnership: we not only seek customer feedback, we rely on it to deliver the superior services our customers need to maximize efficiency and maintain a competitive edge.

tious Ashcroft quickly rose in ranks, becoming a member of Pritchard's international acquisitions team. Pritchard later grew into a major internationally operating services group, and by the 1980s, more than half of its revenues came from the United States.

By the early 1970s, however, Ashcroft became determined to strike out on his own. In 1973, Ashcroft borrowed £15,000 in order to buy up his own janitorial services company. Throughout his career, in fact, Ashcroft often returned to the services industries, as he multiplied his fortunes. By 1977, Ashcroft had successfully expanded his janitorial services company, which he sold that year for £1.3 million. With the proceeds from that sale, Ashcroft bought out another company, Hawley, a manufacturer of tents and other outdoor equipment that was then close to bankruptcy.

Hawley became Ashcroft's vehicle to his first real fortune. Into the 1980s, Ashcroft used Hawley to make a dazzling series of acquisitions, transforming Hawley into a business services group, ranging from janitorial services for hospitals and offices, to automobile auction services, and later with a focus on the security services industry. By 1981, Hawley had made its first acquisitions in the United States, and its total revenues had grown to nearly $27 million. In 1986, Hawley bought out Ashcroft's former employer, Pritchard Services, leaping to the second place in the U.S. services industry. The following year, Hawley boosted its security services operations as well, acquiring Crime Control Inc., based in Indianapolis, for $50 million. That purchase gave the company the fourth place spot in the U.S. security market. Through the acquisition of dozens of companies, Hawley had built itself into an international empire with revenues of more than $1.3 billion.

By the end of 1987, however, Hawley had transformed itself again. In that year, the company acquired U.S. security services leader ADT. Founded in 1874 as American District Telegraph, ADT originally served as a provider of telegraph delivery services. In the 1880s, ADT introduced call boxes to allow customers to communicate with its offices; this activity led the group to begin offering security services in the 1890s. By the dawn of the 20th century, ADT's messengers also began doubling as night watchmen. Acquired by Western Union, which was then acquired by AT&T, ADT became that group's specialist security services business, growing into a U.S. market leader.

The addition of ADT transformed Hawley into the leading security services business in the United States, and also refocused the majority of its revenues on the U.S. market. As a result of the acquisition, Hawley changed its name to ADT Inc. and decided to refocus its business around security services. In 1987, therefore, the company sold its U.S.-based facility services business to Denmark's ISS, which by then had developed into one of the world's largest outsourced services providers.

BUILDING A BELIZE BASE IN THE 1980S

In the meantime, Ashcroft had returned to Belize, which had gained its independence from England in 1981. Ashcroft recognized an opportunity to build a new financial empire, as well as a means of gaining political influence. Ashcroft became a major contributor to the country's People's United Party, which later became Belize's ruling party. Ashcroft himself was named Belize's ambassador to the United Nations.

In 1984, Ashcroft set up a new holding company, Belize Holdings (BHI), which became the vehicle for a parallel acquisition spree made by Ashcroft during the 1980s, which fell beyond the scope of his Hawley business. By the late 1980s, BHI had become one of the largest holding companies in Belize, with interests ranging from telecommunications (Ashcroft's holdings later included control of the country's telephone monopoly) to property, shipping, and citrus fruits. In 1987, BHI led the formation of Belize Bank, which took control of the leading Belize bank, originally founded as the Bank of British Honduras in 1902 and taken over by the Royal Bank of Canada in 1912. Belize Bank became the country's largest financial institution, controlling some 50 percent of the market.

BHI represented just one part of Ashcroft's sprawling (and, as some claimed, willfully complex) business interests. Another of Ashcroft's holdings was Aaxis Limited, registered in Bermuda and publicly traded in Canada. Indeed, by the early 2000s, Ashcroft was said

KEY DATES

1973: Michael Ashcroft, formerly employed by Pritchard Services, borrows £15,000 in order to acquire a cleaning services company in England.

1977: Ashcroft sells the cleaning company for £1.3 million, and then acquires Hawley, a manufacturer of tents and outdoor equipment then close to bankruptcy.

1981: Hawley makes its first U.S. purchase.

1984: After launching Hawley on a massive acquisition drive, Ashcroft creates Belize Holdings Limited (BHI) as a vehicle for a number of personal investments.

1986: Hawley acquires Pritchard Services.

1987: Hawley acquires security services company ADT and then sells its facility services operations to ISS International, which renames its U.S. operations as ISS Inc.; BHI forms Belize Bank and acquires the Belize operations of Royal Bank of Canada.

1997: Ashcroft sells ADT to Tyco International for $4 billion, becoming Tyco's largest shareholder; Ashcroft acquires ISS Inc. through another holding company, Aaxis Limited, for $1.

1998: BHI acquires Aaxis for $88 million; Ashcroft acquires Carlisle Holdings, listed on the London Stock Exchange.

1999: BHI acquires Carlisle, and then changes its name to Carlisle Holdings Limited.

2001: Carlisle acquires control of Belize Telecommunications Ltd., the monopoly telephone business in Belize; Centre Point Ltd., a London-based staffing services specialist, is acquired.

2005: Company is renamed as BB Holdings, spinning off its U.K. and Ireland businesses as Carlisle Group Limited.

to have been involved in "thousands" of companies over his 30-year career.

Ashcroft himself took up residence in the United States, where he remained through much of the 1990s. Into the late 1990s, however, Ashcroft moved back to England, where he acquired another publicly listed holding company, Carlisle Holdings. Ashcroft also became a major contributor to the suffering Conservative Party. Ashcroft, whose contributions grew to as much as £3 million per year, was later made the party's secretary. Ashcroft also began lobbying for a nomination into the House of Lords. This effort, coupled with his often highly intricate business dealings, led him into direct confrontation with the country's elitist establishment. In the end, however, Ashcroft won the day, receiving his peerage and becoming "Lord" Ashcroft.

REDEVELOPED FOR THE 2000S

By then, Ashcroft had become one of England's 15 wealthiest people. A major milestone for Ashcroft came with his agreement to sell ADT to Tyco International in a deal worth some £4 billion. As a result of that deal, Ashcroft became Tyco's largest shareholder, and received a seat on its board of directors.

Ashcroft was far from retirement, however, and had already begun to build a new business empire. Into the mid-1990s, ISS Inc., the renamed U.S. arm of ISS International, had slipped into losses. By 1996, ISS Inc.'s losses neared $250 million. Worse, the company was discovered to have falsified its accounts for years. The resulting scandal sent ISS International's stock price plummeting.

The difficulties at ISS Inc. came to the attention of Ashcroft, who recognized a new business opportunity. In January 1997, ISS International agreed to sell ISS Inc. to Ashcroft's Aaxis Limited for the symbolic price of just one U.S. dollar. Once again, Ashcroft had returned to the services sector.

Ashcroft promptly replaced management at ISS Inc. and sold off its underperforming operations. Ashcroft now began shuffling his other holdings in order to create a new, more focused vehicle for the services business. As part of this process, Ashcroft transferred some of BHI's holdings to Carlisle Holdings, while selling off others, including his controversial shipping business (suspected by some of providing a "flag of convenience" for drug runners). In November 1997, Aaxis agreed to be acquired by BHI for $88 million. The company then renamed its services business as OneSource.

In 1999, Ashcroft merged London-based Carlisle into Belize-based BHI, then renamed the enlarged holding company as Carlisle Holdings Limited. The "new" Carlisle now was domiciled in Belize. Carlisle grew into the 2000s, acquiring other parts of Ashcroft's investment empire, such as his personal stake in Belize Telecommunications Ltd. (BTL), the country's telephone monopoly. That deal gave Carlisle direct control of 51 percent of BTL. It also gave Ashcroft the opportunity to reshuffle other pieces of his holdings, transferring a number of Carlisle assets to Ashcroft's personal accounts. Carlisle also continued building up its assets, buying up Centre Point Group, a leading London-based staffing services specialist in 2001. This acquisition boosted the U.K. wing of Carlisle's services operations, known as Carlisle Facilities Services.

In 2005, Ashcroft decided to refocus his services businesses along geographic lines. In August of that year, Carlisle announced that it was changing its name, to BB Holdings. Following that change, the company announced that it was spinning off its U.K. and Ireland-based operation into a new holding company, Carlisle Group Limited, which was also incorporated in Belize. In this way, BB Holdings was refocused around a dual core of Belize Bank and the U.S.-oriented OneSource. Ashcroft, already one of the United Kingdom's wealthiest people, hoped to unlock more shareholder value from his network of holdings and investments.

M. L. Cohen

PRINCIPAL SUBSIDIARIES

OneSource Inc. (U.S.A.); Belize Bank Ltd.

PRINCIPAL COMPETITORS

Service Management International Ltd.; Franz Haniel and Cie GmbH; Al Hamed Enterprises (Group of Cos.); Initial Contract Services USA; Grupo Ferrovial S.A.; Somers Building Maintenance Inc.; Rentokil Initial PLC; Sacyr Vallehermoso S.A.; Care Services Ltd.; Service-Master Co.

FURTHER READING

Atkinson, Dan, and David Teather, "A Round Peg in the Square Mile," *Guardian,* July 17, 1999.

Durman, Paul, "How Tories' Ashcroft Turned $1 into $88m," *The Times,* July 10, 1999, p. 1.

Fisher, Daniel, "Do As I Say," *Forbes,* January 8, 2001, p. 62.

Lappen, Alyssa A., "Cleaning Up," *Forbes,* June 15, 1987, p. 118.

Scott, David Clark, "Solid Growth in Belize Belies Crisis in Mexico," *Christian Science Monitor,* February 13, 1995, p. 8.

Birse Group PLC

Humber Road
Barton-on-Humber,
North Lincolnshire DN18 5BW
United Kingdom
Telephone: +44 01652 63322244 0161 486 9191
Fax: +44 01652 633360
Web site: http://www.birse.co.uk

Public Company
Incorporated: 1970
Employees: 1,227
Sales: £332.87 million ($631.80 million) (2005)
Stock Exchanges: London
Ticker Symbol: BIE
NAIC: 237990 Other Heavy and Civil Engineering
Construction; 236115 New Single-Family Housing
Construction (Except Operative Builders); 237110
Water and Sewer Line and Related Structures
Construction; 237310 Highway, Street, and Bridge
Construction; 531190 Lessors of Other Real Estate
Property; 531210 Offices of Real Estate Agents and
Brokers; 532412 Construction, Mining and Forestry
Machinery and Equipment Rental and Leasing;
551112 Offices of Other Holding Companies

■ ■ ■

Birse Group PLC is a major U.K. construction company
operating primarily in the civil engineering and public
works sectors and focused especially on the northern
England region. The company acts as a holding company
for a number of more or less autonomous subsidiaries
operating in specific construction sectors. Civil

Engineering remains the group's dominant activity, accounting for nearly 70 percent of total revenues, which
were £332.87 million ($630 million) in the company's
2005 fiscal year. The company's civil engineering activities are guided by Birse Civils Limited (Birse CL), which
operates on a national basis and represents one of the
oldest parts of the company's activities. Other components of the group's civil engineering division include
Birse Metro, which is an important contractor for the
London Underground, as well as other public transport
infrastructure projects, and Birse Rail, which acts as a
contractor for U.K. railroad projects. Into the mid-
2000s, Birse has been restructuring its building and
construction division, exiting a number of underperforming sectors, such as home building, where the
company did not have the scale to compete on a national
level. Birse's Building division contributed 18 percent to
group turnover in 2005. The company's third major
division is its Process Engineering, operating in the water
systems and water and waste treatment sectors, and adding 12 percent to the group's turnover. Other Birse
operations include plant and equipment hire. Birse
Group is listed on the London Stock Exchange, and is
led by Chairman Peter G. Watson.

FOUNDING A CIVIL ENGINEER-ING GROUP IN THE 1970S

Peter Birse founded the construction company bearing
his name in 1970 in Barton-on-Humber. Civil engineering played a major role in the group's growth from the
start. Through the 1970s, the company focused especially
on public works projects for local and regional
authorities. By the beginning of the 1980s, Birse had

COMPANY PERSPECTIVES

Birse Group plc is the ultimate parent company of a group of companies whose principle activities comprise construction, plant hire and related services. Its strategy is: "to leverage a group of construction related autonomous businesses each focused on the customer and its core competencies, operating safely and self funded, run by directors who think and behave like owners."

built the company into a major player in the northern region's construction market. Birse launched the company on a national expansion in the 1980s, in part by forming partnerships with other construction groups. An example of this was a joint venture project formed with the Farr Group in the early 1980s to build a section of the London M25 motorway, which opened in 1985. Nonetheless, the company remained primarily a regionally focused group: the company's well-developed knowledge of its local markets was considered a strength.

During the 1980s, Birse also extended its operations to include water and waste treatment systems, and similar process engineering projects. The company again sought out partnerships for these operations, notably through a joint venture formed with fellow contractor ACER. Birse also developed its own plant and equipment hire wing, BPH. By the end of the 1980s, Birse had become an important "junior league" building contractor. The company's annual revenues also grew strongly, multiplying by more than three times from the early 1980s to nearly £200 million by 1989. The company's profits grew strongly during this time as well, multiplying by some 500 percent. As a smaller player, Birse's primary focus remained on contracts ranging up to a maximum of £50 million.

Birse went public in 1989, listing its shares on the London Stock Exchange in September of that year. The public offering brought in a major shareholder and partner, Bilfinger & Berger, based in Germany. The partnership with the larger construction group enabled Birse to begin competing for larger contracts of more than £50 million for the first time. The company also began an aggressive push to triple its revenues into the early 1990s, including a major expansion of its road-building operations in the United Kingdom.

Yet the collapse of the British construction sector in the late 1980s, and the long economic slump that followed, soon brought Birse into difficulties. The company

faced trouble on various fronts. On one hand, the drop in new construction meant fewer contracts for Birse. On the other hand, many of its clients were struggling; in 1991, for example, the company was forced to write off more than £500,000 in bad debts from two private property developers. The following year, Birse lost one of its largest contracts at the time, when the development consortium behind it was forced into bankruptcy. By 1992, Birse itself had slipped into losses.

A NICER APPROACH IN THE 1990S

Birse managed to return to profitability in 1995. Yet the recession era had marked the company in more ways than one. Already considered a tough contractor in the 1980s, the company developed a reputation as one of the industry's most aggressive by the mid-1990s, not only toward its subcontractors, but also toward its clients in an effort to meet ambitious expansion targets. Yet the commitment to that expansion during the difficult economic period brought about a shift in the group's management culture. As one company executive told *The Times*: "We expanded at a bad time. This wasn't a fun industry to be in at that time. The business had evolved into something we didn't want it to be. What I think brought the problem to Peter Birse's attention was when we started to lose customers who had been with us for many years, and people started leaving the company after just a few months."

Birse added: "Slowly, imperceptibly (the business) was starting to operate in an aggressive and confrontational way. There was fear in the workforce as the new style began to bite." By the mid-1990s, Birse recognized that he needed to take action to revitalize the company he founded. Birse hired a team of industrial psychologists, or "performance coaches," to intervene, bringing a series of training sessions in an effort to reinvent the company's culture. Birse himself made headlines by offering a public apology to the company's clients and subcontractors, as well as to its employees.

Although greeted with some skepticism, Birse's cultural turnaround appeared to be working into the second half of the 1990s. The change in culture enabled the company to focus its efforts on developing more open and efficient partnerships, slashing costs by some 20 percent or more. The company also instituted a shift in its operations, de-emphasizing its road-building work in order to boost the share of building construction in its turnover to some 70 percent before the end of the decade. As part of that effort, the company sold off its small, money-losing housing division in 1995.

This effort paid off, for example, with the winning of a contract to build an extension for a hospital in

KEY DATES

1970: Peter Birse founds Birse Group, with a focus on the civil engineering sector.

1989: Birse goes public with a listing on the London Stock Exchange.

1995: After several years of losses, Birse becomes profitable.

1997: Peter Birse apologizes for the company's aggressiveness and institutes a companywide corporate culture change.

2001: Peter Birse retires.

2002: The company restructures, creating three primary subsidiaries, Birse CL, Birse Build, and Birse Process.

2005: The company focuses on civil engineering, selling off parts of Birse Build, which is also refocused on the northern England region.

Anlaby. Yet the company's primary growth remained in the civil engineering sector. In 1999, for example, the company won a bid to build Wessex Water's new sewage treatment plant in Bridport. The company also won a contract to build a materials recovery and energy center at the Port Talbot waste treatment plant in 2001.

CIVIL ENGINEERING FOCUS IN THE 2000S

Peter Birse's retirement in 2001 brought a new management team into place, led by Chairman Peter G. Watson. The company now redeveloped its strategy for the 2000s, focusing its operations more tightly on its strong civil engineering component. In 2002, the company underwent a corporate restructuring, creating three primary divisions: Civil Engineering, Process Engineering (including water and wastewater treatment), and Construction. As part of that restructuring the company created three new autonomously operating subsidiaries, Birse Build, Birse CL, and Birse Process. These were further broken down into subsidiaries targeting dedicated markets, such as Birse Metro and Birse Rail, operating in the subway and railroad markets, respectively, under Birse CL.

By the mid-2000s, the company's civil engineering operations had clearly taken the lead in the group's continued growth. The company decided to refocus itself around a civil engineering core, selling off part of its troubled, money-losing Birse Build subsidiary. As

part of that effort, the company also reduced Birse Build's geographic focus, eliminating its southern England and Midlands region operations to concentrate on its northern England home base. Birse also sold off some of its other noncore operations, such as The Cabin Company, a leading provider of onsite cabins and accommodations.

Birse's civil engineering business in the meantime continued to enjoy growth. In December 2005, for example, the company won its bid for a £3.4 million road improvement contract for the M20 highway. After more than 25 years, Birse remained a prominent name in the British construction sector.

M. L. Cohen

PRINCIPAL SUBSIDIARIES

Birse Civils Ltd.; Birse Construction Limited; Birse Water Limited; Birse Rail Limited; Birse Metro Limited; Birse Process Engineering Limited; Birse Build Limited; Birse Stadia Limited; Birse Properties Limited; BPH Limited; Birse Group Services Limited; IT Incorporated Limited; Minerva Creative Solutions Limited; New Start Ventures Limited.

PRINCIPAL COMPETITORS

AMEC PLC; Balfour Beatty PLC; Taylor Woodrow PLC; George Wimpey PLC; Mowlem PLC; Laing O'Rourke PLC; Foster Wheeler Ltd.; Tarmac Ltd.; Interserve PLC; Morgan Sindall PLC; Skanska Construction Group Ltd.; Alfred McAlpine PLC.

FURTHER READING

"Birse Civils Awarded £3.4m Motorway Contract," *Contract Journal,* December 1, 2005.

"Birse Gets Nose in Front to Take Sewage Odour-Reduction Work," *Contract Journal,* November 9, 2005, p. 8.

"Civil Engineering Saves Birse's Bacon," *Contract Journal,* July 9, 2003, p. 7.

Cowing, Emma, "Birse Shares Rocket As Founder Bows Out," *Scotsman,* August 17, 2001, p. 2.

Dearlove, Des, "When the Snarling Had to Stop," *The Times,* June 18, 1998, p. 6.

Goddard, Andrea, "Birse Shares Climb As Litigation Ends," *Financial Times,* February 26, 2004, p. 28.

Leitch, John, "Birse Moves into the Black," *Contract Journal,* July 10, 2002, p. 9.

———, "Birse on Defensive Over Cash Shortage Rumours," *Contract Journal,* November 28, 2001, p. 3.

McCormick, Helen, "On Track for Growth," *Contract Journal,* September 1, 2005, p. 28.

O'Brien, James, "Birse Can Build on a Strong First Half," *Birmingham Post,* December 12, 2003, p. 21.

Tyler, Richard, "Birse Sees Records Fall—Good and Bad," *Birmingham Post,* July 4, 2003, p. 21.

White, Dominic, "Bugs Bunny, Mr. Blobby and the Caring Side of Builders," *Daily Telegraph,* August 17, 2001.

Boston Scientific Corporation

———■———

1 Boston Scientific Place
Natick, Massachusetts 01760-1537
U.S.A.
Telephone: (508) 650-8000
Fax: (508) 647-2393
Web site: http://www.bostonscientific.com

Public Company
Incorporated: 1979
Employees: 17,500
Sales: $5.62 billion (2004)
Stock Exchanges: New York
Ticker Symbol: BSX
NAIC: 339112 Surgical and Medical Instrument Manufacturing

■ ■ ■

Boston Scientific Corporation is a pioneer in providing medical devices for less invasive surgical procedures, ranking as a leader in the market for coronary stents. The company's medical devices are used in a variety of interventional medical specialties, including interventional cardiology, peripheral interventions, vascular surgery, electrophysiology, neurovascular intervention, oncology, endoscopy, urology, gynecology, and neuromodulation. Boston Scientific operates on a global basis, maintaining overseas manufacturing operations in Ireland and Costa Rica.

EARLY HISTORY: 1969-79

Boston Scientific Corporation was founded in 1979 by John Abele and Peter Nicholas, who met while watching their children play soccer. Nicholas, a Wharton M.B.A., had worked for pharmaceutical company Ely Lilly & Co. since 1968. Nicholas was mainly interested in management; Abele was more technically oriented. He had majored in philosophy and physics at Amherst and had been employed selling medical devices for Advanced Instruments, Inc. In 1968 Abele met Itzak Bentov, inventor of a steerable catheter that was used in less invasive surgical procedures. With financial backing from Cooper Laboratories, Abele began marketing the device through Medi-Tech, Inc., a company in which Abele had acquired an equity interest. In 1969 Medi-Tech introduced its first products, a family of steerable catheters that were used in some of the first less invasive procedures.

By the time Abele and Nicholas met, Cooper Laboratories wanted to sell the medical device company. Abele and Nicholas founded Boston Scientific Corporation for the purpose of acquiring Medi-Tech, Inc. The two men received $500,000 in bank financing and raised another $300,000.

In its first year Boston Scientific reported revenues of about $2 million. Its first products included catheters for gall bladder surgery. The early 1980s marked a period of active marketing, new product development, and organizational growth. The company focused on catheters and other products that could be used as alternatives to traditional surgery. As medical imaging techniques improved, less invasive procedures became more feasible. The catheters allowed doctors to perform surgical procedures through little incisions. Such procedures were also much less expensive. The company soon expanded its line of catheter-based devices to include heart, vascular, respiratory, gastrointestinal, and urological applications.

CAPITAL NEEDS AFFECTING GROWTH: 1980S

By 1983 sales were $16 million. To meet the company's voracious working capital needs, Abele and Nicholas sold a 20 percent interest in Boston Scientific to Abbott Laboratories in return for $21 million, which Abbott would pay over the next four years. The company needed large amounts of working capital, because of the long lead-time between product development and product marketing. In addition, the medical devices that Boston Scientific made required approval by the U.S. Food and Drug Administration (FDA), a process that typically took several years. As a result, the company lost $900,000 in 1988 on sales of nearly $100 million. After learning how to shorten the approval time from the FDA, Boston Scientific again became profitable. By 1991 sales had reached $230 million, with earnings of $42 million.

GOING PUBLIC AND ACQUISI-TIONS: 1992-2000

Boston Scientific went public in May 1992 with an initial public offering (IPO) of 23.5 million shares priced at $17 a share that raised $400 million in capital. Following the IPO, cofounders Nicholas and Abele and their families owned two-thirds of the firm's stock. Nicholas was in charge of the firm's management; Abele had removed himself from day-to-day operations around 1990. Abbott Laboratories sold its shares back to Boston Scientific at the time of the IPO.

The company had four operating divisions: Medi-Tech, which specialized in radiology; Mansfield, for

cardiology; Microvasive Endoscopy for gastroenterology; and Microvasive Urology. Boston Scientific would typically introduce a device for use in less critical places, such as the urinary tract, then apply it to higher-risk situations, such as those in cardiology. This helped speed up development of new products. The company posted 40 percent revenue growth for the first half of 1992, while earnings for the same period grew by 28 percent compared to the same period in 1991. For the year, Boston Scientific had revenue of $315 million.

In 1993 sales reached $380 million, while net income rose to nearly $70 million. Between 1994 and 1995 sales rose from $449 million to $1.2 billion, as the company began an aggressive four-year program of strategic acquisitions. International sales accounted for about one-third of the firm's 1995 revenue.

Beginning in the fall of 1994, Boston Scientific acquired nine companies over a 16-month period, spending about $2.5 billion. During this period it acquired several companies that made niche products that could be marketed worldwide. It paid $400 million for Meadox Medicals Inc., an Oakland, New Jersey-based producer of blood vessel replacement devices. Heart Technology Inc. of Redmond, Washington, was acquired for $450 million; it made surgical tools to unclog arteries. By acquiring Meadox, Boston Scientific gained graft technology that would have taken five years to develop. Heart Technology's single product, Rotablator, was a catheter with a spinning diamond bit that cleaned out clogged arteries. Rotablator's sales had skyrocketed from zero in 1993 to $80 million in 1995.

At the end of 1995 Boston Scientific's market capitalization had grown to $8.5 billion, compared to $1.5 billion at the end of 1994. Its workforce had grown from 2,000 to 8,000 employees. Its product line increased from 3,000 to 8,000 items. With the help of Andersen Consulting, the company was developing a global systems project that would standardize business practices for the firm and its new acquisitions.

In the latter half of the 1990s, trends supporting demand for medical devices included political pressures to develop new cost-effective technology; demand for fast, effective, and safe procedures; and a broad international market. The FDA responded to pressure to reduce its review time for certain types of new devices to 90 to 120 days instead of 18 months or more. Boston Scientific's main business, products for interventional cardiology, served a $3 billion global market that was expected to grow at least 15 percent annually. Its other markets, neurointerventional medicine and endoscopy, were each growing at 15 to 20 percent annually. At the end of 1996 the company had a direct sales force in 17

KEY DATES

1969: Medi-Tech Inc., partially owned by John Abele, introduces its first products, a family of steerable catheters.

1979: Boston Scientific is founded by John Abele and Peter Nicholas for the purpose of acquiring Medi-Tech, Inc.

1992: Boston Scientific makes first public stock offering.

1994: Boston Scientific begins a string of acquisitions that will raise revenue to $2.84 billion in 1999.

2001: Medinol files a lawsuit against Boston Scientific, accusing the company of stealing its stent-manufacturing technology; Boston Scientific settles the lawsuit in 2005, paying Medinol $750 million.

2004: Boston Scientific introduces TAXUS Express, a drug-coated stent that quickly becomes the company's main source of revenue.

countries and distributors in 85 additional countries. Its strategy was to acquire or develop niche products and market them worldwide. Foreign sales accounted for 38 percent of Boston Scientific's revenue in 1996 and were expected to reach 50 percent in the next several years.

Reviewing Boston Scientific's performance in its January 13, 1997 issue, *Medical Economics* asked the then rhetorical question, "What could go wrong with such a success story?" Unfortunately for Boston Scientific and its investors, the correct answer was, "Plenty."

GROWTH AND SETBACKS: 1997-2000

Boston Scientific continued to grow through acquisitions in 1997. Target Therapeutics, Inc. made products used to treat patients with strokes, including microcatheters and microcoil products for access to the small blood vessels of the brain, heart, and extremities. A new coil that Target developed received FDA approval in 1995; it offered a relatively safe and cost-effective treatment for patients with brain aneurysms. Boston Scientific acquired Target Therapeutics for about $1.1 billion in stock in 1997. The acquisition gave Boston Scientific immediate leadership in neurosurgical products and a line or products to treat aneurysms, and expanded its overseas sales.

By mid-1997 Boston Scientific's rapid growth rate was expected to level off at about 25 percent annually. The company announced it would spend $300 million to upgrade five manufacturing facilities. In addition, it was incurring significant costs in integrating more than a dozen acquisitions made since late 1994. According to *Forbes,* Boston Scientific's main product line—balloons for angioplasty—were becoming a commodity. Surgeons were showing a preference for balloons with stents attached to keep arteries open. While Boston Scientific marketed such devices in Europe, it did not sell them in the United States. The U.S. market leader in this area was Johnson & Johnson, and Medtronic, another competitor, received approval for its stent-balloon-combination in June 1997.

Boston Scientific's stock took two significant tumbles during 1997. One occurred when its first-quarter profits failed to meet Wall Street's expectations; stock fell 33 percent. The second occurred after the company warned that its third-quarter earnings would also fall short. In September 1997 profits plummeted 17 percent, from $76 a share to around $63. For 1997, Boston Scientific had revenue of $1.87 billion and earnings of $139.3 million.

In mid-1998 Boston Scientific announced it would spend $2.1 billion to acquire Schneider Worldwide, the vascular devices unit of Pfizer, Inc. Schneider sold surgical stents and artery-clearing devices used in balloon angioplasty. The acquisition was Boston Scientific's largest to date and gave the company a major position in the growing cardiovascular stent market. For 1997, Schneider had worldwide sales of $330 million. It was headquartered near Zurich, Switzerland, and had 2,200 employees worldwide, about 1,200 of whom were in the United States.

In October 1998 Boston Scientific announced a recall of its coronary stent delivery system called "NIR on Ranger with Sox." The company had received more than 100 reports of balloon leakage in the system. The product began shipping in August 1998 to 200 hospitals and medical centers in the United States. By the time of the recall, about 36,000 systems had been shipped and an estimated 25,000 were in use. The recall raised regulatory concerns at the FDA, which had not been notified of manufacturing changes in the stent system. The system had been developed with business partner Medinol Ltd., based in Tel Aviv, Israel.

In November 1998 the company announced it had found about $45 million of "questionable sales" at its Japanese subsidiary for the current year, and an additional $40 million of "improper sales" in previous years. The announcement, coupled with the firm's product recall, pushed Boston Scientific's stock down 11 percent to around $46. The stock had reached a high of $81 in August prior to the recall. For 1998 Boston Scientific reported revenue of $2.23 billion and a net loss of $264 million.

In February 1999 Boston Scientific announced it would cut about 2,000 jobs in 1999 as part of its restructuring following its recent string of acquisitions. About 1,500 of the eliminated positions would affect Schneider employees. The company also expected to spend about $62 million on severance costs.

At the end of 1998 rumors surfaced that James R. Tobin would succeed Peter Nicholas as Boston Scientific's CEO. Tobin resigned in December 1998 as CEO of Biogen Inc., a biotechnology company. Tobin was named CEO of Boston Scientific in March 1999 and assumed the position in June, replacing Peter Nicholas, who remained as chairman. Tobin's assignment essentially was to turn the company around. Over the next 14 months he would eliminate 1,900 jobs and close manufacturing operations in three states. During this period Boston Scientific's stock would lose about two-thirds of its value, fallout from the product recalls and Japanese scandal. To help finance its acquisition of Schneider Worldwide, Boston Scientific raised $500 million through a secondary stock offering in mid-1999.

Following its five-year string of acquisitions, Boston Scientific was organized into six divisions. EP Technologies specialized in cardiac electrophysiology. Medi-Tech was a leading developer and supplier of minimally invasive and surgical devices for peripheral vascular disease management, including balloon catheters and metallic stents. Microvasive Urology manufactured diagnostic and therapeutic products for stone management, incontinence, and prostate disease. Microvasive Endoscopy focused on providing devices and services for gastrointestinal endoscopic procedures. Boston Scientific Scimed Inc. was the company's primary cardiology unit. Target Therapeutics was a leader in neuroendovascular intervention, manufacturing medical devices to treat the brain and other hard-to-reach parts of the body in a minimally invasive manner.

In June 1999 the company received a new patent covering a process for injecting genes into the heart that would allow it to enter the gene therapy field. The process could stimulate the formation of blood vessels and would be used to treat patients with serious heart problems. The patent originated in gene research conducted by CardioGene Therapeutics Inc., which Boston Scientific acquired in July 1998.

In August 1999 Boston Scientific recalled two of its medical laser systems used in treating heart disease, the Rotablator RotaLink Advancer and RotaLink Plus systems. The systems employed a high-speed drill that used a blade to clear plaque from a clogged artery. After the company received complaints that the systems' brake failed to stop the drill from moving through the artery after it had already cleared the blockage, it issued a voluntary recall. The company had sold about $60 million worth of the Rotablator systems in the first half of 1999 and expected no further sales for the rest of the year.

For 1999 the company reported revenue of $2.84 billion and net income of $371 million. Revenues for the first half of 2000 were expected to suffer from a lack of new products. In the latter half of 2000 the company was planning to introduce a gold plated stent. Analysts noted that Boston Scientific was lagging behind its two major competitors, Guidant Corporation and Medtronic Inc., in introducing new stents, which typically had one-year life cycles.

Between July 1999 and February 2000 the company's stock price fell by 57 percent, from around $46 to $19 a share. In 2000, Tobin created a new business unit focused solely on heart stents and stent-delivery systems. These had been manufactured by the company's Minneapolis-based Scimed division, which would continue to provide cardiologists with products such as balloon catheters, guide wires, and guide catheters. In addition, Tobin announced he would be naming a chief technology officer to the newly created position.

In March 2000 Boston Scientific received FDA approval to resume marketing its NIR on Ranger with Sox coronary stents, after solving the leakage problems.

In July 2000 Boston Scientific continued its reorganization, cutting 1,000 positions in Minnesota, Washington, and Massachusetts, while adding 100 employees to its Miami operation and 800 jobs to company plants in Ireland. In Miami, some 300 jobs involving the production of biopsy forceps would be transferred to a lower-cost foreign contract manufacturer, while 400 positions for workers making guidewires were added. About 850 workers were dismissed from the company's Watertown, Massachusetts, plant. Facilities in Plymouth, Minnesota, which employed about 750 workers, and Redmond, Washington, with about 350 employees, were to be closed. One of the Watertown sites became the headquarters to the company's Medi-Tech division, which developed vascular surgery and radiology products. The reorganization was expected to save about $70 million in 2001 and $145 million in 2002.

Difficulties between Boston Scientific and Medinol Ltd., its key supplier of coronary stents, led to delayed product launches, according to some analysts. As a result, the company's stock plunged more than $7 in one day in July 2000 to close at $18.56. Also affecting the stock price were the company's lower than expected second-quarter sales and a poor outlook for the rest of 2000. Boston Scientific subsequently entered negotiations to acquire Medinol Ltd., of which it already owned part, as a means of becoming more competitive with rival companies that already made their own stents.

Meanwhile, the episode of fraudulent sales reports for the period from January 1997 through June 1998 from Boston Scientific Japan was resolved with the Securities and Exchange Commission, whose report chastised the company for lacking effective controls at the time.

Legal difficulties pocked Boston Scientific's progress during the first years of the new century, marring what otherwise would have been a period of remarkable achievement. The company's problems with Medinol flared during the first half of the decade, ignited by the U.S. Justice Department's discovery in 2000 of a secret factory operated by Boston Scientific. Medinol accused Boston Scientific of using the factory, dubbed "Project Independence," to copy its technology. Medinol filed a lawsuit against Boston Scientific in 2001, and Boston Scientific quickly countersued, claiming that Medinol's owners were "abusive and obstructionist," according to the September 22, 2005 edition of the *Boston Globe*. The court battle raged for years, ending in September 2005 when Boston Scientific agreed to pay $750 million to settle claims that it broke its contract and stole technology. The settlement ended the relationship between the two companies, including Boston Scientific's 20 percent ownership share in Medinol.

DRUG-COATED STENTS FUELING GROWTH IN THE EARLY 21ST CENTURY

Boston Scientific executives preferred to remember the period for the stunning success it achieved with a new type of stent. The introduction of drug-coated stents during the first half of the decade represented the most important event in the medical device industry, touching off a race for market share between Boston Scientific and Johnson & Johnson. Drug-coated stents hindered the re-clogging of blood vessels, called restonosis, caused by the formation of scar tissue, thereby increasing the effectiveness of angioplasty, one of the most common medical procedures performed. Johnson & Johnson beat Boston Scientific to market, introducing its Cypher medicated stent in 2003, but Boston Scientific more than compensated for the delay, emerging as the leader in the two-company race. Results of a clinical trial in late 2003 demonstrated that Boston Scientific's medicated stent, named TAXUS Express, worked better than expected, proving to be more flexible and easier to

install than Johnson & Johnson's Cypher. "Most analysts and physicians expected that Boston Scientific's drug-coated stent would be inferior to Johnson & Johnson's, but would be close enough," an analyst explained in a September 16, 2003 interview with the *Saint Paul Pioneer Press*. "There weren't many who thought it would be better."

Boston Scientific began selling TAXUS stents in March 2004 and 70 days later the company controlled 70 percent of the drug-coated stent market. The financial rewards were enormous, providing Boston Scientific with roughly 40 percent of the $5.6 billion it collected in sales in 2004.

Boston Scientific's success with Taxus was even more remarkable considering the problems the company experienced during its first year in the drug-coated stent market. The company recalled the product three times in 2004 after receiving complaints in June about the delivery systems doctors used to implant the stents in blood vessels. Occasionally, the balloon used to expand the stent in the blood vessel failed to deflate properly, a problem Boston Scientific eventually fixed by making changes at its manufacturing plants in Minnesota and Ireland. Despite recalling approximately 100,000 stents, the company maintained its large lead in the market.

As Boston Scientific prepared for the future, its overwhelming lead in the drug-coated stent market sparked hoped for financial success in the years ahead, but the company's stalwart market position was vulnerable on two fronts. Rivals Medtronic Inc. and Guidant Corporation were preparing to introduce their own medicated stents, perhaps as early as 2006, which promised to intensify the race for market share and lower the price of drug-coated stents. Further, in mid-2005 a U.S. District Court jury found that Boston Scientific infringed on two stent patents held by Johnson & Johnson, a ruling that could force Boston Scientific to pay more than $1 billion in damages.

David P. Bianco
Updated, Jeffrey L. Covell

PRINCIPAL SUBSIDIARIES

Advanced Bionics Corporation; BSC Finance Corp.; BSC International Corporation; BSC International Holding Limited (Ireland); Cardiac Pathways Corporation; Catheter Innovations, Inc.; Corvita Corporation; Enteric Medical Technologies, Inc.; EP Technologies, Inc.; Boston Scientific Technologie Zentrum AG; Boston Scientific Foundation, Inc.

PRINCIPAL COMPETITORS

Cook, Inc.; Johnson & Johnson (Cordis Unit); Endo-Sonics; Medtronic Inc.; Guidant Corporation; Conor Medsystems Inc.

FURTHER READING

Ante, Spencer E., "Crashing the Stent Party," *Business Week,* October 31, 2005, p. 82.

Barrett, Amy, "The Wrong Way to Run a Recall," *Business Week,* August 30, 2004, p. 52.

"Boston Scientific Corp.," *Insiders' Chronicle,* November 2, 1992, p. 3.

"Boston Scientific Corp. Closing 350-Employee Redmond Location," *Puget Sound Business Journal,* July 14, 2000, p. 15.

Bray, Hiawatha, "Acquisitive Boston Scientific Corp. to Purchase Target Therapeutics, Inc.," *Knight-Ridder/Tribune Business News,* January 21, 1997.

Heuser, Stephen, "Boston Scientific Reaches $750M Settlement with Medinol," *Boston Globe,* September 22, 2005.

———, "Boston Scientific Warns on Revenue," *Boston Globe,* September 8, 2005.

Jordon, Steve, "Boston Scientific, Guidant Settle Patent Litigation," *America's Intelligence Wire,* February 20, 2004.

Kerber, Ross, "Boston Scientific Acquired California Medical Device Maker for $740 Million," *Boston Globe,* June 2, 2004.

———, "Boston Scientific Dealt Stent Setback," *Boston Globe,* June 22, 2005.

———, "Natick, Mass.-Based Medical Device Maker to Cut 2,000 Jobs Worldwide," *Knight-Ridder/Tribune Business News,* February 11, 1999.

Koenig, Bill, "Bloomington, Ind., Medical Device Maker Files Patent-Infringement Suits," *Knight-Ridder/Tribune Business News,* March 22, 1999.

Lutton, Christine, "Growth Spurt," *Forbes,* July 1, 1996, p. 16.

Maiello, Michael, "Revisionist History," *Forbes,* February 28, 2005, p. 42.

Mangan, Doreen, "Why Medical-Device Stocks Belong in Your Portfolio," *Medical Economics,* January 13, 1997, p. 55.

Marcial, Gene G., "Boston Scientific: Anemic—for Now," *Business Week,* December 6, 2004, p. 158.

McCartney, Jim, "Boston Scientific's Drug-Coated Stent Performs Better Than Expected in Trial," *Saint Paul Pioneer Press,* September 12, 2003.

McDonald, Duff J., "Cashing in on the Best New Multinationals," *Money,* May 1996, p. 136.

McLaughlin, Tim, "SEC Order Raps Boston Scientific for False Sales," *Reuters,* August 21, 2000.

McMenamin, Brigid, "An Odd Couple," *Forbes,* October 17, 1994, p. 58.

Mullich, Joe, "Online Recruiting Gets Scientific," *InternetWeek,* July 10, 2000, p. 46.

Padley, Karen, "Plymouth, Minn., Medical Device Firm's Workers Staying Put So Far," *Knight-Ridder/Tribune Business News,* October 20, 1998.

Pascavis, Travis, "Boston Scientific's Stock Is Cheap for a Reason," *Morningstar.com,* July 18, 2000.

Peltz, Michael, et al., "Buttressing Balance Sheets," *Institutional Investor,* January 1993, p. 55.

"Pffft," *Forbes,* July 28, 1997, p. 248.

Simons, John, "Not for the Faint of Heart," *Fortune,* August 9, 2004, p. 164.

Sohmer, Slade, "Emerging As a Global Sales Success," *Sales & Marketing Management,* May 2000, p. 124.

Solo, Sally, "Boston Scientific," *Fortune,* April 5, 1993, p. 97.

Stevens, Tim, "Multiplication by Addition," *Industry Week,* July 1, 1996, p. 20.

"Why Boston Scientific Is Pumping Again," *Business Week Online,* September 2, 2004.

Woods, Jenny, "Week in Review," *Minneapolis-St. Paul City Business,* July 21, 2000, p. 39.

Brammer PLC

—■—

Claverton Court, Claverton Road
Wythenshawe, Manchester M23 9NE
United Kingdom
Telephone: +44 0161 928 3363
Fax: +44 0161 941 5742
Web site: http://www.brammer.plc.uk

Public Company
Incorporated: 1920 as H. Brammer and Company
Limited
Employees: 2,782
Sales: £290 million ($538.2 million) (2004)
Stock Exchanges: London
Ticker Symbol: BRAM
NAIC: 423840 Industrial Supplies Merchant Wholesalers; 332991 Ball and Roller Bearing Manufacturing; 333612 Speed Changer, Industrial High-Speed Drive, and Gear Manufacturing; 333613 Mechanical Power Transmission Equipment Manufacturing; 333911 Pump and Pumping Equipment Manufacturing; 333912 Air and Gas Compressor Manufacturing; 333999 All Other General Purpose Machinery Manufacturing; 334511 Search, Detection, Navigation, Guidance, Aeronautical, and Nautical System and Instrument Manufacturing; 334513 Instruments and Related Product Manufacturing for Measuring, Displaying, and Controlling Industrial Process Variables; 532310 General Rental Centers; 532420 Office Machinery and Equipment Rental and Leasing

■ ■ ■

Brammer PLC is Europe's leading distributor of replacement industrial components, focusing on Bearings, Power Transmission belts and other components, and Fluid Power components. Twice the size of its largest competitors, Dexis in France and Eriks in The Netherlands, Brammer nonetheless controls just 3 percent of the heavily fragmented European replacement components market. Into the mid-2000s, Brammer has been capitalizing on this situation, initiating a drive to deepen its European penetration. As part of that effort, the company launched a rebranding exercise in 2004, designed to regroup all of its subsidiaries under the single Brammer name upon completion. Brammer continues to generate much of its revenues from the United Kingdom, where it operates from 136 locations. France is the group's next largest market, with 41 locations, followed by Spain, Germany, and the Benelux markets, as well as Austria, the Czech Republic, and Hungary. Altogether, Brammer operates from 253 locations. A growing part of this comes as part of Brammer's Insites service, which places Brammer employees inside client corporations, taking over their inventory and purchasing needs. As of 2005, the company operated nearly 50 Insites locations, primarily in the United Kingdom and in France. Brammer was originally founded by Harry Brammer, inventor of the V-link transmission belt system, among other inventions. The company went public in 1954 on the London Stock Exchange. David Dunn is current company CEO and chairman.

INVENTIVE ORIGINS IN THE 1920S

Harry Brammer was a noted Yorkshire area inventor in the post-World War I era, when he founded his own company in order to exploit one of his inventions, the V-Link transmission belt system. Brammer was credited with a number of other inventions, including the first bicycle toe-clip system. With £3,000 in start-up capital, Brammer launched H. Brammer and Company Limited in 1920, opening a factory in Leeds. The V-link belt became an important component of the growing automotive industry, and later also became known as the Brammer belt.

Brammer went public in 1954, listing on the London Stock Exchange, and remained a small company focused on its core of transmission belt manufacturing into the 1960s. In 1967, Brammer nearly was acquired by friendly rival Croft Engineering (that company's founder had held a seat on Brammer's board of directors), which was then threatened by a hostile takeover bid. Part of Croft's defense involved a takeover of Brammer, for some £2.5 million. Although Brammer's board, which held some 27 percent of the company's stock, agreed to the deal, the acquisition by Croft ultimately failed.

With its independence upheld, Brammer decided to launch its own expansion drive at the end of the 1960s. Rather than increase its industrial belt business, however, Brammer sought new, complementary areas of operations. The company made its first acquisition in early 1968, acquiring Ixion Drives. The following year, the company made a new acquisition, paying £675,000 to acquire Bearing Services, based in Manchester. Bearing Services supplied replacement industrial bearings to the local market, and formed the basis of what was to develop into Brammer's single largest division.

Both acquisitions helped Brammer grow strongly into the early 1970s, driving its profits to more than £1 million for the first time in 1971; by the end of 1974, the company's profits had topped £2 million. By then, Brammer also had launched its first efforts to enter the continental European market. In 1973, the company bought a major share in France's Transmondiale, a subsidiary of Renault, which operated in the industrial bearing replacement and distribution market. The shareholding gave Brammer a foothold in the French market, which remained the group's second largest market after the United Kingdom into the next century.

Brammer next eyed entry into the German market, and in 1973 the company bought two companies located in Bielefeld. The first, Asemissen, specialized in the distribution and wholesaling of automotive components, and the second, Annex, specialized in the distribution and wholesaling of automotive accessories. These acquisitions became part of Brammer's intention to establish itself in the automotive components market in the United Kingdom as well. The company achieved this in 1973 through the acquisition of ES Heap & Co., a well-known supplier of automotive components, based in Yorkshire, with four branches, as well as a business supplying the supermarket channel. On the industrial side, Brammer made a tentative effort to move overseas, buying up Florida Bearings and Antilles Bearings, related companies operating in Miami and Puerto Rico, respectively.

SHIFTING FOCUS IN THE 1980S

The difficult years following the Arab Oil Embargo in the early 1970s cut short Brammer's automotive components ambitions. By 1976, the company was forced to sell off its ES Heap subsidiary, as well as another business, Replacement Services. The company ultimately withdrew entirely from the automotive components market in 1977. By then, however, the company had put into place a new strategy focused on boosting its industrial services offerings, in a move meant to provide the company with greater stability and resistance against the cyclical automotive market. The company also had some success on the automotive front as well, developing its own synthetic belt in 1976.

Brammer returned to the United States, this time acquiring two businesses, Master Pumps and Pope Machinery, including six distribution centers. These additions, the new synthetic belts, and the tighter focus on the industrial market helped Brammer exhibit strong growth through the end of the 1970s, boosting its turnover from £21 million at mid-decade to more than £39 million at decade's end.

By the early 1980s, Bearing Services had grown into Brammer's most important source of revenues; by 1982, that division accounted for some three-quarters of the company's total sales. Bearing Services also had captured the lead in the British bearing market. Brammer launched a new bid to diversify beyond its core industrial components products, in order to reduce its reliance on that single division. In 1983, therefore, the company

KEY DATES

1920: Inventor Harry Brammer establishes H. Brammer and Company Limited in Leeds, England.

1954: Brammer goes public on the London Stock Exchange.

1968: The company diversifies by acquiring Ixion Drives.

1969: Brammer acquires Bearing Services, which becomes a major part of company operations.

1983: United Electronic Holdings is acquired.

1985: Brammer acquires ESE in order to block a hostile takeover attempt.

1992: Brammer acquires Roulement Service, in France, as part of a strategy to become a pan-European supplier.

1999: The company adopts a new strategy to become a one-stop supplier for the European market.

2000: Brammer acquires Carim B.V. (Netherlands), 51 percent of THF (Germany), Grupo Rabinad (Spain), Carl Fischer (Germany), and Anderlecht Bearing Service (Belgium).

2003: Brammer acquires full control of THF.

2004: The company sells the Livingstone Hire electronic rentals division; all international subsidiaries are rebranded under the single Brammer name.

2005: The company acquires 51 percent of MHBH in the Czech Republic as part of an expansion into Central Europe.

paid £5 million to take over United Electronic Holdings, a company that operated a chain of stores selling accessories for the hi-fi and video equipment markets.

Brammer's growth attracted the interests of a number of competitors during the 1980s, a period marked by a frenzy of hostile takeovers and the rise of a new breed of corporate raiders. Among those interested in Brammer's collection of companies, including its dominant status in the British replacement bearings market, was Bunzl. That company began buying up shares in Brammer, before launching a takeover bid worth £117 million. Brammer, perhaps remembering the Croft defense in the 1960s, fought back, turning around to launch a friendly acquisition offer for Energy Services and Electronics (ESE). Although Brammer faced competition for that company from a Dutch-owned rival, the company held firm and raised its offer, in part because Bunzl had made its own takeover conditional on Brammer dropping the ESE bid. In the end, Brammer won the day, acquiring ESE for £44 million in 1985. Bunzl dropped its takeover bid soon after.

The ESE purchase proved a transforming one for Brammer, adding a new electronics rentals division, grouped around Livingston Hire, to the company's operation, while boosting its electronics offering. As a result, Brammer restructured, selling off a number of businesses, such as subsidiaries Brammer Transmission and Russells Rubber. The company, now regrouped around a dual core of Bearing Services and Rentals, had significantly reduced the former's share of its operations, down to just 35 percent. In the meantime, the ESE purchase helped raise the group's electronics operations to 35 percent of its revenues.

PAN-EUROPEAN LEADER IN THE NEW CENTURY

Brammer continued to display its flexibility in adapting its business structure to changing market conditions. In the early 1990s, with the creation of a single European market, the company adopted a new strategy of developing itself into a pan-European market leader. The group's Bearing Services division provided the spearhead for this effort, and in 1992, the company expanded its French position, through the acquisition of Roulement Service. That company, founded in Alsace in 1974, had developed a similar profile to Brammer's, with a 10 percent share of the French replacement bearings market, and a 3 percent share of the power transmission sector. The company also grew in Spain, buying up Rodamientos, the largest industrial components replacement provider in the country. By the mid-1990s, Brammer's European expansion had taken it to The Netherlands and Germany, as well. The company's electronic rental division played a strong part in the group's growth into the mid-1990s, becoming the European leader in the sector.

Toward the end of the decade, Brammer's domestic growth had slowed due to a softening market. Instead, the company stepped up its effort to build its European presence. Into the early 2000s, the company launched a series of acquisitions, including the 2000 purchase of the French distribution operations of Germany's Freudenberg & Co. That purchase boosted Brammer's power transmission distribution business. The company returned to France that year, buying up Somelec S.A., a company that calibrated and maintained electronic testing equipment, and two other businesses, Climats and Sapratin, specialized in the sale and maintenance of climatic systems used during the testing of electronic components.

The company's acquisitions continued, with the 2000 acquisition of The Netherlands' Carim B.V., a distributor of bearings and power transmission products, and 51 percent of THF, based in Germany. In 2001 the company bought up Grupo Rabinad in Spain and German bearings and power transmissions specialist Carl Fischer. The company also added Belgium's Anderlecht Bearing Service that year.

The slump in the electronics and telecommunications sectors brought the company's electronic rentals division into difficulty, with main subsidiary Livingstone Hire slipping into the red by 2003. Brammer announced its intention to exit the market, and in 2004 completed the sale of Livingstone Hire in a management buyout. Instead, Brammer now announced that it intended to set itself up as a one-stop supplier for Europe's increasingly international manufacturing market. As part of that effort, the company launched a two-step rebranding exercise, designed to bring all of its subsidiaries under the single Brammer name.

Brammer moved to consolidate its holdings into the mid-2000s. The company took full control of THF in 2003, then bought up full control of KNS Aandrijftechniek in The Netherlands the following year. By 2005, the company had begun to look toward Central Europe as well. After moving into Hungary, in September 2005, the company announced an agreement to acquire 51 percent of MHBH, a specialist industrial services company, in the Czech Republic. As part of that agreement, Brammer gained the option of taking full control of MHBH by 2009. As the leader in the highly fragmented European market, Brammer looked forward to strong growth in the years to come.

M. L. Cohen

PRINCIPAL SUBSIDIARIES

AKN GmbH (Austria); Britannia Wälzlager & Industrietechnik GmbH (Austria); Brammer Belgium N.V.; AWEXIM Brammer S.R.O. (Czech Republic); Roulement Service S.A.S. (France); THF Brammer GmbH & Co. KG (Germany); AKN Carim (Holland); KNS Aandrijftechniek BV (Holland); Brammer Magyarorszag Kereskedelmi es Szolgaltato Kft (Hungary); USA Brammer, S.A. (Spain); BSL Brammer Limited.

PRINCIPAL COMPETITORS

Dexis S.A.; Eriks N.V.; Deetwyler AG; Wyko PLC; Orefi S.A.; Econosto N.V.; Gruppo Minetti S.p.A.; Biachi S.p.A.

FURTHER READING

"Brammer (BRAM)," *Investors Chronicle,* September 16, 2005.

"Brammer Goes Continental," *Engineer,* October 12, 2001, p. 11.

"Brammer in Talks As It Bids to Seal Deals," *Birmingham Post,* September 2, 2004, p. 25.

"Brammer Receives Bid for Livingston Rental Business," *Electronics Weekly,* January 21, 2004, p. 1.

"Brammer Sales Slump," *Birmingham Post,* November 19, 1998, p. 22.

"Brammer Takes a Look on the Bright Side," *Birmingham Post,* March 17, 1999, p. 19.

Locke, Malcolm, "Brammer Aims for One-Stop Status," *Birmingham Post,* April 8, 2004, p. 19.

Tomlinson, Michael, *Yorkshire Inventor: Tales of Harry Brammer, Inventor Extraordinaire,* London: William Session Limited, 1999.

Brunswick Corporation

1 North Field Court
Lake Forest, Illinois 60045-4811
U.S.A.
Telephone: (847) 735-4700
Fax: (847) 735-4765
Web site: http://www.brunswick.com

Public Company
Incorporated: 1907 as Brunswick-Balke-Collender Company
Employees: 25,600
Sales: $5.92 billion (2005)
Stock Exchanges: New York Chicago Pacific London
Ticker Symbol: BC
NAIC: 333618 Other Engine Equipment Manufacturing; 336612 Boat Building; 339920 Sporting and Athletic Goods Manufacturing; 713950 Bowling Centers

■ ■ ■

Brunswick Corporation, the oldest and largest manufacturer of recreation and leisure-time products in the United States, has used its commercial successes in billiard and bowling products to become the world's leading manufacturer of marine engines and pleasure boats. Brunswick began as a family firm, merged to become the Brunswick-Balke-Collender Company in 1884, and was renamed the Brunswick Corporation in 1960. During the 1980s the company, which once described itself as the "General Motors of Sports," moved to dominate the marine and powerboat industry, while in the 1990s

Brunswick expanded its recreational offerings to include bicycles, wagons, sleds, camping equipment, ice chests, and exercise equipment. In the early 2000s, however, the company divested most of its nonmarine recreational operations, and completed a string of boating-related acquisitions, to fulfill then CEO George W. Buckley's vision of making Brunswick the "Toyota of Boating"; by 2005 nearly 83 percent of revenues was generated by the firm's marine engine and boating businesses, while fitness equipment contributed about 9 percent and bowling and billiards just 8 percent. Its stable of industry leading brands includes Mercury and Mariner engines; Sea Ray, Sea Pro, Sea Boss, Bayliner, Boston Whaler, Crestliner, and Hatteras boats; Life Fitness, Hammer Strength, and ParaBody fitness equipment; Brunswick bowling and billiards equipment; and Valley-Dynamo pool, air hockey, and foosball tables. The company also operates around 130 Brunswick bowling centers in the United States, Canada, Europe, and Japan. About 32 percent of company revenues are derived outside the United States.

EARLY HISTORY

John Moses Brunswick was born in 1819 in Bremgarten, Switzerland. At 14, Brunswick immigrated to the United States. He landed in New York City and worked briefly as an errand boy for a German butcher but soon relocated to Philadelphia, Pennsylvania, where he served a four-year apprenticeship in a carriage shop. In 1839 he moved to Harrisburg, Pennsylvania, where he worked as a journeyman carriage maker, and married Louisa Greiner. The Brunswicks moved to Cincinnati in 1840.

At Brunswick, we believe our strengths are many, and we intend to vigorously use them. The continuing challenge is to uncompromisingly execute that strategy and build upon the six competitive operating platforms that have served us so well in both solid or uncertain economic times. These platforms are to: Steadily and relentlessly reduce costs, the ultimate competitive weapon, to improve our operations and performance; Identify and deploy leading-edge technologies to distinguish our products from those of our competition and to increase our operating efficiencies; Market and build our brands with care and thoughtfulness, nurturing and bolstering our already strong positions in the marketplace; Improve every aspect of our distribution channels to better develop mutually beneficial partnerships with our dealers and distributors to enrich the entire consumer experience; Enhance our customer responsiveness by listening to the voice of the customer and touching that customer, before, during and after the sale; Develop and stretch our people so that they can fully contribute their talents and creativity to strengthen our organization. Most any company can invest in machinery, marketing and technical tools. We believe our advantage is in the people we hire and how we lead, inspire, develop and motivate them.

Brunswick found work as a carriage maker for several local firms until 1841, when a major economic downturn severely depressed the market for carriages. During the depression he worked as a steward on an Ohio River steamboat, then as a commercial trader. Though he prospered financially he became ill, and after spending several months in bed Brunswick used his accumulated commercial profits to open his own carriage shop in 1845.

Brunswick's Cincinnati, Ohio, woodworking shop began by making functional, high-quality carriages. Brunswick was willing to expand his product line and the shop soon began to produce cabinetwork, tables, and chairs. Brunswick boasted that "if it is wood, we can make it, and we can make it better than anyone else."

Brunswick's willingness to diversify was more than a manifestation of the pride that he took in his work; it

was also an early attempt to broaden his product line to counteract fluctuations in the business cycle. For many years Brunswick's growth was internal, but in later years the firm acquired outside businesses to expand its product line.

BEGAN MANUFACTURING BILLIARD TABLES IN THE 1840S

By the mid-1840s the economy had begun to recover and with it came increased manufacturing activity. In this environment Brunswick began to prosper, and he became active in local political, religious, and social circles. Legend has it that in 1845, at a lavish dinner party, John Brunswick was led into another room where his host proudly displayed a fancy billiard table, which had been imported from England. Brunswick saw the opportunity to expand his woodworking business. Thus began Brunswick's long association and ultimate domination of the sporting goods market.

Billiards long had suffered from a poor reputation. Indeed, sports in general had very limited mass appeal in the United States prior to the 1850s. Sporting equipment was ornate and was designed for sale to men of wealth. Brunswick's first tables were elaborate luxury items, and as such found a limited market.

In 1848 Brunswick expanded his market by sending his half-brothers, David and Emanuel Brunswick, to Chicago to establish a sales office and factory. Other sales offices were opened in New Orleans, Louisiana, and St. Louis, Missouri, while half-brothers Joseph and Hyman Brunswick worked in the firm's Cincinnati offices. In 1858 the business was reorganized as J. M. Brunswick & Brother. In 1866 the company was renamed J. M. Brunswick & Brothers when Emanuel Brunswick joined Joseph and John Brunswick as a principal in the firm.

CREATION OF BRUNSWICK-BALKE-COLLENDER COMPANY IN 1884

By the late 1860s the U.S. billiards market was dominated by three firms: Brunswick, Julius Balke's Cincinnati-based Great Western Billiard Manufactory, and a New York-based company named Phelan & Collender, run by Michael Phelan and his son-in-law, H. M. Collender. In 1873 Brunswick merged with Balke to form the J. M. Brunswick & Balke Company. In 1884, following the death of his father-in-law in 1879, Collender merged with Brunswick & Balke, to form the Brunswick-Balke-Collender Company, the largest billiards equipment maker in the world.

During the 1870s Brunswick's half-brothers left the firm to start rival firms and billiard parlors in Chicago

KEY DATES

1845: John Moses Brunswick opens a carriage shop in Cincinnati, soon expanding into the production of billiards tables.

1873: J. M. Brunswick & Brothers merges with Julius Balke's Great Western Billiard Manufactory to form J. M. Brunswick & Balke Company.

1884: Company merges with H. M. Collender's company to form Brunswick-Balke-Collender Company, the world's largest maker of billiards equipment.

1907: Brunswick-Balke-Collender is incorporated.

1924: Company goes public.

1956: Brunswick begins production of automatic pin-setters for bowling alleys.

1960: Company enters the boating market and changes its name to Brunswick Corporation.

1961: Brunswick acquires Kiekhaefer Corporation, maker of Mercury outboard motors.

1965: In the wake of a crash of the bowling industry, Brunswick begins acquiring bowling centers.

1982: After fending off a hostile takeover bid by the Whittaker Corporation, Brunswick divests its medical-supply business.

1986: Company acquires the pleasure-boat manufacturers Bayliner Marine Corp. and Ray Industries, maker of Sea Ray boats.

1997: Exercise equipment maker Life Fitness is acquired.

2000: Company launches program to divest its outdoor brands and narrow focus to marine engines, pleasure boats, and bowling, billiards, and fitness equipment.

2001: Hatteras Yachts, Inc. is acquired.

2002: Company expands into marine electronics by acquiring Northstar Technologies, Inc.

2004: Brunswick acquires the Crestliner, Lowe, and Lund aluminum-boat brands; the Verado engine is introduced.

and San Francisco. It is not entirely clear under what circumstances each of them left, but by 1872 Brunswick's son-in-law, Moses Bensinger, and two longtime employees were vice-presidents at Brunswick.

During this period of rapid growth John Brunswick remained in Cincinnati while Bensinger, who increasingly directed the company's day-to-day operations, greatly expanded the company's Chicago facilities. In July 1886 John Brunswick died. He was succeeded by H. M. Collender, who served as president until his own

death in 1890. Julius Balke, too ill and old to take over as president, stepped aside, and, after buying out another vice-president, Bensinger was named president of Brunswick-Balke-Collender.

Bensinger aggressively expanded the firm's product line. Since many billiard tables were being sold to taverns, he expanded the company's line of carved wooden back bars. Back bars covered the wall behind a bar and served a functional and decorative purpose. They were intricate and elaborate status symbols and also greatly enhanced Brunswick's reputation for fine craftsmanship. Initially the bars were custom built, but their popularity soon had the company's Dubuque, Iowa, factory operating at full capacity. Before long Brunswick bars were installed across the United States and Canada.

ADDITION OF BOWLING PINS AND BALLS: 1880S

In the 1880s Bensinger added another product line, bowling pins and bowling balls. Taverns had begun installing lanes, interest seemed to be growing, and Bensinger was determined to be ready for this new market. He actively promoted bowling as a participatory sport and helped to standardize the game. Bensinger also was instrumental in organizing the American Bowling Congress in 1895. Although the company continued to expand its markets and product lines, bowling was to become the financial backbone of the firm.

Throughout this growth and expansion, Brunswick remained a family firm. John Brunswick's surviving son, Benedict Brunswick, and Julius Balke, Jr., were Brunswick executives, and Bensinger's son, Benjamin Bensinger, worked first as a clerk, then as a salesman, and was rapidly moving his way up in the company. In 1904, upon the death of his father, Benjamin Bensinger became the president of Brunswick-Balke-Collender, at age 36. The firm had several sales offices, and manufacturing plants in Chicago, Cincinnati, Dubuque, and New York, and in 1906 Bensinger opened a large manufacturing plant in Muskegon, Michigan. The Muskegon plant, which grew to over one million square feet in the 1940s, became the cornerstone of the firm's manufacturing, producing such products as mineralite (hard rubber) bowling balls. In the meantime, Brunswick-Balke-Collender was incorporated in 1907.

DIVERSIFICATION DURING PROHIBITION ERA: 1920-33

In the 1910s the temperance movement threatened not only the fixtures and bar business but also billiards and bowling. In 1912, in anticipation of Prohibition, which started in 1920, Brunswick suspended its bar-fixtures operations, which accounted for one-fourth of annual sales, and sought to replace it with automobile tires and the world's first hard-rubber toilet seats. Rubber products best utilized the firm's existing facilities. By 1921 the Muskegon plant was producing 2,000 tires a day. When the price of rubber tripled in 1922, Brunswick sold its tire line to B.F. Goodrich, who began to manufacture tires under the Brunswick name as the Brunswick Tire Company.

Brunswick also began to manufacture wood piano cases and phonograph cabinets. Edison Phonograph was the principal buyer of Brunswick's cabinets. The demand for phonographs was so strong that Bensinger decided that Brunswick should manufacture its own line of phonographs. By 1916 the Muskegon plant was producing Brunswick phonographs and putting them on the market for $150, 40 percent less than comparable models. In 1922 it also began producing records under its own label. Jazz greats such as Duke Ellington, Cab Calloway, and Benny Goodman and classical artists such as Irene Pavlovska and Leopold Godowsky all recorded on the Brunswick label. In 1925 Brunswick teamed up with General Electric Company to manufacture an all-electric phonograph called the Panatrope, which came equipped with or without a radio. In 1930 Brunswick sold the Brunswick Panatrope & Radio Corporation to Warner Brothers for $10 million.

The company had gone public in 1924, and in 1930 Benjamin Bensinger was named chairman of the board and his oldest son, Bob Bensinger, became president. Bob Bensinger had worked for the firm since 1919 and with his brother, Ted, guided Brunswick through the Great Depression. Even with the repeal of Prohibition in 1933 and the popularity of pool halls, the Great Depression was hard on Brunswick. The company marketed a line of tabletop refrigerators called the Blue Flash and a successful line of soda fountains to replace its once-thriving bar and fixture business.

During World War II Brunswick found new markets and new products and once again prospered. United Service Organizations (USO) centers and military bases eagerly purchased billiard and bowling equipment. Brunswick also made wartime products, including mortar shells, flares, assault boats, fuel cells, floating mines, aircraft instrument panels, and aluminum litters.

POSTWAR ERA: PINSETTERS AND OUTBOARD MOTORS

At the end of the war Brunswick became involved in a high-stakes battle with the American Machine and Foundry Company (AMF) over the automatic pinsetter for bowling alleys. AMF produced pinsetters in the late

1940s but these proved unreliable. In 1952 AMF installed an improved version of its machine and called it a pinspotter. Brunswick, which had toyed with the idea of an automatic pinsetter as early as 1911, had to develop a working pinsetter quickly or risk losing its domination of the bowling market. Telling customers that it would be "worth waiting for," Brunswick scrambled to develop its own machine. In 1954 Brunswick formed the Pinsetter Corporation with Murray Corporation of America. By the time the pinsetters were in production in 1956, Brunswick had bought out Murray, and Brunswick aggressively sold its machine to a rapidly expanding market.

Brunswick's policy of selling pinsetters on credit, suburban expansion, and an aggressive advertising campaign all combined to make bowling centers enormously popular in the late 1950s. After the introduction of the pinsetter the company prospered as never before. Sales, which had been $33 million in 1954, jumped to $422 million in 1961. Although Brunswick's earnings did not leap correspondingly—sales were up almost 13-fold, but earnings increased just less than six times—Ted Bensinger, named CEO in 1954, received most of the credit for Brunswick's gains. Brunswick acquired 18 new firms to further diversify its markets. Such companies as MacGregor Sports Products, Union Hardware, Zebco, Owens Yacht Company, and Larson Boats made Brunswick a major force in equipment for golf, roller skating, fishing, and boating (the move into boating began in 1960 with the purchases of Owens and Larson). Brunswick's most important purchase proved to be the 1961 acquisition of the Kiekhaefer Corporation, which built Mercury outboard motors.

Brunswick also sought firms outside recreational sports, and in 1959 it purchased A.S. Aloe and entered the medical-supply business. To complement the Aloe purchase Brunswick also acquired Sheridan Catheter & Instrument Corporation in 1960, Roehr Products Company in 1961, and Biological Research in 1961. Brunswick's medical-supply business became known as the Sherwood Medical Group. Brunswick also developed a popular line of school furniture in the 1950s and kept active in its defense-products division. The company, meanwhile, changed its name to Brunswick Corporation in 1960.

FURTHER DIVERSIFICATION MOVES IN THE 1960S AND 1970S

An unexpected decline in the bowling industry, which represented 60 percent of sales, in the early 1960s presented Brunswick with serious financial problems. Jack Hanigan was brought in as president in November 1963 to handle Brunswick's financial problems. Ted

Bensinger became chairman and he and his brother both remained on the board of directors into the 1970s. Hanigan aggressively sought to reorganize Brunswick and to position the firm for future expansion. In 1965 he formed a technical and new-business division which developed, among other things, Brunsmet, a metal-fiber product. In 1967 Hanigan merged this division and the defense division into the technical-products division. Hanigan also created a bowling center operations division, which began acquiring some of the nation's troubled bowling centers; the company thus began operating bowling centers in 1965 as part of an effort to recoup losses it was incurring when bowling center owners were unable to pay for Brunswick pinsetters bought on credit. The new divisions, along with further expansion of the company's medical lines, growth of the Kiekhaefer-Mercury products, and the recovery of bowling in the late 1960s, all helped Brunswick to reach record sales of $450 million in 1969.

The 1973-74 oil embargo caused problems at Brunswick, particularly in its profitable marine-engine division, but the company was able to further diversify its products and remained strong. The technical-products division continued to grow, producing, among other things, radomes and metal-fiber camouflage. Hanigan retired as chairman and CEO in 1976 and was replaced by K. Brooks Abernathy.

To promote stability Brunswick had been organized into four business groups: marine, medical, recreational, and technical. Jack Reichert, president of the Marine group, became president of Brunswick in 1977 as sales topped $1 billion for the first time. Not content, Brunswick moved into energy and transportation control systems by acquiring Vapor Corporation for $92 million in 1978, as well as actively expanding its international markets.

FOCUSING ON MARINE AND RECREATION PRODUCTS IN THE 1980S AND 1990S

Brunswick successfully fought a hostile takeover bid by the Whittaker Corporation in 1982. Whittaker wanted Brunswick's Sherwood Medical Group medical-supply business. Whittaker was forced to withdraw its offer when American Home Products Corporation stepped in as a white knight, and Sherwood was sold to American Home Products in March 1982 for $425 million in Brunswick stock. In April 1982 Reichert took over as CEO of Brunswick. Reichert sought to decentralize Brunswick to improve efficiency and stress quality output. The firm's 11 sectors were reduced to eight, corporate staff was cut, and executive perquisites were trimmed, reducing bureaucratic costs. Reichert trans-

ferred division staff to production sites in an attempt to enhance product quality. He also moved to include hourly employees as shareholders and increased pension payments to former employees.

During the latter half of the 1980s, Brunswick made a series of significant moves aimed at not only reasserting itself in the field of recreation but also making recreation the company's main focus. In 1986 Brunswick acquired two pleasure-boat manufacturers, Bayliner Marine Corporation and Ray Industries (maker of Sea Ray boats), for $773 million. These purchases, along with the acquisitions of MonArk Boat Company, Marine Group, Inc., Fisher Marine, and Starcraft Power Boats in 1988, made Brunswick the world's largest manufacturer of pleasure boats and marine engines. These companies also made Brunswick vulnerable to fluctuations in marine sales.

Brunswick had enjoyed six consecutive years of record earnings from 1982 through 1988. That string of record years ended in 1989, when restructuring charges arising from a downturn in the marine market resulted in a net loss. In 1989 and 1990 Brunswick disposed of the business units that had theretofore comprised its technical and industrial products divisions, leaving it with only its marine and recreation groups and a much smaller technical group of businesses.

Although the company returned to profitability in 1990, the economic downturn of the early 1990s severely depressed sales of pleasure boats and outboard motors, leading to net losses in 1991 and 1992 and net earnings of only $23.1 million in 1993. While weathering these rough seas, Brunswick put major acquisitions on hold and determined to concentrate solely on its marine and recreation segments. In February 1993 the company announced that it would divest its technical group. The sale to the newly formed Technical Products Group, Inc. was not culminated until April 1995, having been delayed by U.S. government investigations of its defense businesses. Also divested in 1995 was the company's Circus World Pizza operation, while 1996 saw the closure of a noncompetitive golf shaft business. Meanwhile, in April 1993 Brunswick moved into its new world headquarters building in Lake Forest, Illinois.

With Reichert planning to retire in 1995, Brunswick brought in John P. Reilly, formerly with Tenneco Inc., as president and heir apparent in the fall of 1994. He was forced out after only nine months, however, following reported conflicts among top executives. Subsequently, Reichert was succeeded in mid-1995 by Peter N. Larson, a former Johnson & Johnson executive.

In order to guard against future economic downturns, downturns that always hit the pleasure boat market particularly hard, Brunswick in the mid-1990s concentrated on expanding its recreational offerings to a wider variety of consumable goods, which tend to counterbalance such durable goods as boats. In anticipation of this expansion, Brunswick in the fall of 1995 created an Indoor Recreation Group to encompass the bowling and billiards operations, while an Outdoor Recreation Group featured the Zebco fishing equipment business. In early 1996 the company acquired Nelson/Weather-Rite, a unit of Roadmaster Industries Inc. that made camping equipment, for $120 million. Brunswick renamed this unit American Camper; it held the number two position in the U.S. market and offered sleeping bags, tents, backpacks, and other products under the American Camper, Remington, and Weather-Rite brand names. American Camper became part of the Outdoor Recreation Group, as did Igloo Holdings Inc. after it was acquired in January 1997 for about $154 million in cash; Igloo was a market leader in ice chests, beverage coolers, and thermoelectric cooler/warmer products. Two months later, the Hoppe's line of hunting accessories was purchased from Penguin Industries, Inc.; Hoppe's, also added to Outdoor Recreation, was number one in gun cleaning and shooting accessories.

Brunswick next aimed to become a leader in the bicycle market. After spending $190 million in January 1997 to buy Roadmaster's bicycle division, which included the Flexible Flyer line of sleds and wagons, and the Roadmaster brand name, Brunswick in the spring of 1997 acquired Bell Sports Corp.'s Mongoose, a San Jose, California-based maker of higher-end mountain and BMX bikes, for $22 million. That same summer the company formed a Brunswick Bicycles division within the Outdoor Recreation Group to oversee the Roadmaster and Mongoose operations, and to launch a new brand that fall called Ride Hard aimed at the middle-tier of the market between the lower-end Roadmaster and higher-end Mongoose. The acquisition spree continued in July 1997 as Brunswick paid Mancuso & Co. $310 million for Life Fitness, maker of stationary bicycles, treadmills, stairclimbers, rowers, cross trainers, and strength training equipment for fitness centers worldwide. Two other fitness equipment makers were added later in 1997 and in 1998: Hammer Strength and ParaBody. After sales of $3.16 billion in 1996, Brunswick's sales for 1997 jumped 16 percent. Net earnings were down in 1997, however, but only because of a $98.5 million strategic charge for streamlining and consolidating various operations and for exiting from the manufacture of personal watercraft.

After various Asian markets were weakened by the economic crisis that hit the region starting in 1997, Brunswick launched a cost-cutting program in October 1998 involving the elimination of 750 jobs, or 3 percent of the workforce, and the divestment or closure of a plant in China making pinsetting equipment and 15 bowling centers in Asia, Brazil, and Europe. An additional 280 jobs were cut when an Illinois bicycle plant was closed and some of the operations shifted to Mexico; this move was prompted by an influx of less expensive bicycles from Asia. Around this same time, about two dozen boat builders won a $133 million antitrust verdict against Brunswick in a lawsuit that accused the company of engaging in various illegal practices in the sale of stern-drive and inboard engines. Brunswick appealed this verdict, but in the meantime additional lawsuits were soon filed against the company, which quickly faced potential damages approaching $1 billion. Eventually the company began settling the claims out of court, and in 1999 Brunswick recorded a charge of $116 million to cover the costs of the settlements. As a result, profits that year totaled just $37.9 million on revenues of $4.28 billion.

EARLY 2000S: NARROWING FOCUS TO MARINE, BOWLING, BILLIARDS, AND FITNESS

Early in 2000 Brunswick announced a restructuring of its troubled bicycle division, which continued to be buffeted by competition from lower-cost producers in China and Taiwan. The company elected to close its three bicycle manufacturing plants in Mexico and Illinois and begin buying bikes from sources in Asia. But this move was soon deemed a half-measure by the company board, which ousted Larson from the CEO slot in June 2000 to pave the way for a more fundamental overhaul. Named to succeed Larson was George W. Buckley, previously head of the Mercury Marine division. Buckley was charged with divesting the firm's entire portfolio of outdoor brands, including fishing, camping, bicycle, cooler, marine accessories, and hunting sports accessories. The aim was to narrow Brunswick's focus to marine engines and pleasure boats, and bowling, billiards, and fitness equipment. A pretax loss of nearly $410 million recorded in connection with these discontinued operations led to a net loss of $95.8 million for 2000.

The divestment program proceeded apace. In 2000 Brunswick's camping business was sold off, followed by the 2001 sales of the bicycle business to Pacific Cycle, Igloo to Westar Capital L.L.C., Zebco's North American unit to W.C. Bradley Company, and Hoppe's to Michaels of Oregon. This process was completed in early 2002 when Zebco's European business was sold to the operation's management. In the meantime, while contending with another cyclical downturn in the boating business, Buckley launched an acquisition spree aimed at filling in gaps in its lineup of boats and making an aggressive push into boat parts and accessories.

During 2001 Brunswick acquired Princecraft Boats Inc., maker of fishing, deck, and pontoon boats and Canada's leading boatbuilder; Sealine International, a British producer of luxury sport cruisers and motor yachts; and Hatteras Yachts, Inc., a leading manufacturer of luxury sportfishing convertibles and motor yachts. In 2002 Brunswick expanded into marine electronics by acquiring Northstar Technologies, Inc., a world leader in premium marine navigation electronics, including global positioning systems (GPS); Northstar was the basis for the newly formed Brunswick New Technologies division. This deal was followed up by the 2003 purchase of a 70 percent stake in Navman NV Limited, a maker of marine navigation and GPS-based products headquartered in New Zealand. Brunswick purchased the remaining shares in Navman in 2004. Also in 2003, the company began building a significant business in boat parts and accessories by purchasing Land 'N' Sea Corporation and Attwood Corporation. In the meantime, Brunswick in 2002 successfully launched the Bayliner 175, which at a package price under $10,000 was the least expensive Bayliner offered in several years.

Building on its longstanding expertise in billiards, Brunswick in 2003 also acquired Valley-Dynamo, LP, a maker of not only pool tables but also air hockey and foosball tables. Brunswick, already the leader in the commercial and home billiards market, now added the leader in coin-operated tables. As the boating market began to recover in 2003, Brunswick enjoyed its best year since 1998, posting profits of $135.2 million on sales of $4.13 billion. In April 2004 the company filled in another gap in its boating line by acquiring three aluminum-boat businesses from Genmar Holdings, Inc. for $191 million. The three brands—Crestliner, Lowe, and Lund—produced fishing, pontoon, deck, and utility boats ranging from 10 feet to 25 feet. They generated combined sales of $311 million for the year ending in June 2003. Then in December 2004 Brunswick edged into the saltwater fishing boat sector by spending $50.1 million for Sea Pro Boats, Inc. and Sea Boss Boats, LLC, makers of the Sea Pro, Palmetto, and Sea Boss brands. By plugging the various holes in his marine portfolio, Buckley was seeking to bolster the position of his company's dealers, who could offer their customers an increasingly wide-ranging selection of boats and engines. Among numerous new products launched in 2004, the most significant was the Verado engine, a four-stroke model, and the first turbocharged outboard, and one that was quieter than the competition, more fuel efficient, and less polluting. Critically acclaimed (*Boating Life* magazine called it the biggest advance in outboard motors in 30 years) the Verado generated high, sustained demand in the months after its introduction. Brunswick's engine division's sales jumped from $1.91 billion in 2003 to $2.64 billion in 2005. Brunswick also sought to bolster its international sales in 2004 by forming an umbrella organization, Brunswick European Group, for its marine operations in Europe, Africa, and the Middle East.

The acquisitions spree continued in 2005. In March the firm acquired Albemarle Boats, a maker of offshore sportfishing boats of 24 to 41 feet in length based in Edenton, North Carolina. Albemarle fit in well alongside Hatteras, which produced boats 50 feet and longer in length. In May 2005 Brunswick purchased Triton Boat Company, L.P., a leading maker of fiberglass bass and saltwater and aluminum fishing boats based in Ashland City, Tennessee. Kellogg Marine, a leading distributor of marine parts and accessories in the Northeast, was acquired in July.

By this time Brunswick was the clear world leader in pleasure boats, had built the nation's largest boating parts-distribution network, and had become the dominant player in marine electronics through Brunswick New Technologies. The latter was the company's fastest-growing business; its 2005 revenues of $356 million represented a 76 percent jump over the previous year. Overall revenues for 2005 reached a record $5.92 billion, a 13 percent increase over 2004, while profits surged 43 percent, to a record $385.4 million. Buckley's vision of turning Brunswick into the "Toyota of Boating," giving its dealers the opportunity to sell fully equipped, reliable boats and to offer a full range of Brunswick craft, seemed close to being realized. The company was increasingly shipping boats to its dealers with Brunswick-built instruments and gauges already installed, and it was encouraging the dealers to equip the boats with Mercury motors rather than those of its competitors, an endeavor made easier by the hot-selling Verado engine line. Given his success at so boldly turning the company's fortunes around, it was no surprise that Buckley would become a candidate to run an even larger enterprise, and in December 2005 he left the firm to become chairman, CEO, and president of 3M Company. Dustan E. McCoy was immediately selected to succeed Buckley as chairman and CEO, having served as president of the Brunswick Boat Group since its founding in 2000. McCoy planned to lead Brunswick in the same direction, improving the company's product reliability and distribution network and continuing to seek acquisitions to fill in gaps in the product portfolio. Going forward, the 160-year-old company ironically now seemed even more vulnerable to a downturn in the boating industry as its boating operations generated close to 83 percent of overall revenues.

Timothy E. Sullivan
Updated, David E. Salamie

PRINCIPAL SUBSIDIARIES

Brunswick International Limited; Sea Ray Boats, Inc.

PRINCIPAL COMPETITORS

Genmar Holdings, Inc.; Ferretti Group; Bombardier Recreational Products Inc.; Marine Products Corporation; Yamaha Motor Co., Ltd.; AMF Bowling Worldwide, Inc.

FURTHER READING

Arndorfer, James B., "Betting Big on Boats: Brunswick Depends on Pleasure Craft, but Market Is in the Tank," *Crain's Chicago Business,* November 12, 2001, p. 4.

———, "Brunswick's Ambitious Diversification Push Sails Away," *Crain's Chicago Business,* May 1, 2000, p. 3.

Baldo, Anthony, "Brunswick: Not Just a Takeover Play," *Financial World,* May 17, 1988, p. 11.

Bettner, Jill, "Bowling for Dollars," *Forbes,* September 12, 1983, p. 138.

Borden, Jeff, "Bowl Them Overseas: Brunswick Rolls in Asia, S. America," *Crain's Chicago Business,* October 16, 1995, pp. 17, 20-21.

"Brunswick Corp. Opts to Pay $65 Million in Rift over Pricing," *Wall Street Journal,* December 23, 1999, p. C14.

"Brunswick's Dramatic Turnaround: An Interview with CEO Jack F. Reichert," *Journal of Business Strategy,* January/February 1988, p. 4.

"Brunswick to Sell Some Outdoor Lines to K2," *Wall Street Journal,* October 16, 2000, p. B33.

Burton, Jonathan, "Up Periscope," *Chief Executive,* December 1998, pp. 22-23.

Byrne, Harlan S., "Riding High Again," *Barron's,* May 23, 1994, p. 26.

Carrel, Elisabeth, "Brunswick to Buy Yacht Maker," *Chicago Daily Herald,* October 25, 2001, p. 3.

David, Gregory E., "Sea Horses: Brunswick Powers Ahead of Outboard Marine in the Rebounding Boating Business," *Financial World,* November 8, 1994, pp. 34, 36.

Dubashi, Jagannath, "Bumbling Brunswick," *Financial World,* May 30, 1989, p. 30.

Flight, Georgia, "Powerboating's New Powerhouse: With a Shrewd Marketing Strategy and Lots of Advanced Technology, CEO George Buckley Turned 160-Year-Old Brunswick into the Biggest Player in the Pleasure Craft Business," *Business 2.0,* November 2005, pp. 62+.

Fritz, Michael, "Brunswick Seeks Kingpin," *Crain's Chicago Business,* August 1, 1994, p. 1.

Gallagher, Leigh, "Brunswick Keeps Rolling with Newly-Formed Bike Division," *Sporting Goods Business,* July 21, 1997, p. 13.

Gibson, Richard, "Brunswick Faces Fewer Motor Orders," *Wall Street Journal,* May 22, 2001, p. B11A.

———, "Brunswick Must Pay $133 Million in Engine Case," *Wall Street Journal,* June 22, 1998, p. A6.

———, "Personality Rift, Reported U.S. Inquiries Dog Brunswick," *Wall Street Journal,* August 12, 1994, p. B4.

Heist, Lauren, "Brunswick Lands Another Marine Company," *Chicago Daily Herald,* July 12, 2005, p. 3.

Kelly, Kevin, and Richard A. Melcher, "Men Overboard in Boatland," *Business Week,* August 22, 1994, pp. 30-31.

Kogan, Rick, *Brunswick: The Story of an American Company: The First 150 Years,* Lake Forest, Ill.: Brunswick Corporation, 1995, 153 p.

Melcher, Richard A., "Brunswick Wades into New Waters," *Business Week,* June 2, 1997, pp. 67, 70.

Miller, James P., "Brunswick Corp. to Reduce Staff by About 3%," *Wall Street Journal,* October 2, 1998.

Murphy, H. Lee, "Amid Downturn at Brunswick, Its Billiard Unit on the Rebound," *Crain's Chicago Business,* August 27, 1990, p. 6.

———, " Brunswick Broadens Line by Heading Out to Sea," *Crain's Chicago Business,* January 17, 2005, p. 12.

Oneal, Michael, "Can Brunswick Weather Rougher Seas?," *Business Week,* September 5, 1988, p. 66.

Palmer, Jay, "Rough Seas: But Recovery Looms for Brunswick," *Barron's,* October 14, 1991, pp. 16-17.

"Revving Up Brunswick," *Financial World,* October 15, 1981, p. 31.

Rodengen, Jeffrey L., "A Great American Empire," *Boating,* September 1987, p. 71.

———, *Iron Fist: The Lives of Carl Kiekhaefer,* Fort Lauderdale, Fla.: Write Stuff Syndicate, 1991, 640 p.

———, *The Legend of Mercury,* Fort Lauderdale, Fla.: Write Stuff Enterprises, 1998, 207 p.

Rudnitsky, Howard, "Any Offers?," *Forbes,* October 15, 1990, p. 48.

Siler, Julia Flynn, "Has Brunswick Gone Overboard in Powerboats?," *Business Week,* August 7, 1989, p. 27.

Silvestri, Scott, "End of Road for Bikes: Brunswick to Close Cycle-Making Operations," *Chicago Daily Herald,* January 14, 2000.

Slutsker, Gary, "Toes in the Water," *Forbes,* March 15, 1993, pp. 70, 72.

Tatge, Mark, "Brunswick Says It Will Take Charge of $185 Million," *Wall Street Journal,* January 14, 2000, p. B10.

Tita, Bob, "Aiming to Be 'Toyota of Boating,'" *Crain's Chicago Business,* May 16, 2005, p. 16.

Walzer, Emily, "Brunswick to Divest Outdoor Brands," *Sporting Goods Business,* August 4, 2000, p. 20.

Weinschenk, Carl, "Brunswick Changes the Landscape," *Boating Industry,* January 1987, p. 13.

BANKERS SINCE 1672

C. Hoare & Co.

37 Fleet Street
London, EC4P 4DQ
United Kingdom
Telephone: +44-20-7353-4522
Fax: +44-20-7353-4521
Web site: http://www.hoaresbank.co.uk

Private Company
Incorporated: 1672
Employees: 220Total Assets: £1 billion ($1.8 billion)
  (2004 est.)
NAIC: 522110 Commercial Banking; 522120 Savings
  Institutions; 522210 Credit Card Issuing; 523110
  Investment Banking and Securities Dealing; 523930
  Investment Advice; 523991 Trust, Fiduciary, and
  Custody Activities

■ ■ ■

C. Hoare & Co. is one of England's oldest banks, and
also claims to be the country's last independently
operating, privately owned deposit-taking bank. Founded
in 1672, C. Hoare & Co. remains a Hoare family business; all of the company's shareholder-partners are
members of the family. While small by modern banking
standards, with just £1 billion ($1.8 billion) in total as-
sets and only 220 employees, Hoare's strength lies in its
commitment to its niche market: catering to the banking needs of the wealthy and very wealthy. With only
10,000 customers, the company is able to offer highly
personalized services unavailable at larger banks. Many
of the bank's customers and their families have been

clients for generations, and the bank, which has never
advertised, accepts new clients only on the basis of
recommendations from existing clients. Even so,
prospective clients must still qualify before being taken
on by the bank. C. Hoare offers a full range of banking
services, including interest bearing accounts; deposit accounts; loans, mortgages and overdrafts; credit cards;
electronic payments; and foreign exchanges services. The
company's investment operations also include retirement
and pension products. C. Hoare also operates a trust
corporation, Messrs. Hoare Trustees, which offers trustee,
executor, and custodial services, as well as tax completion and planning services. Alexander S. Hoare, the
11th generation at the head of the bank, serves as its
CEO.

DEPOSIT TAKING IN THE 17TH CENTURY

C. Hoare & Co. stemmed from the very beginnings of
the British banking industry. Anti-usury laws had
prevented the development of modern banking into the
17th century. Yet the development of a monetary system
based on gold and silver brought a need for a place to
deposit these metals by traders and others. As goldsmiths
already had vaults to safeguard their goods, they began
accepting deposits of coins and other valuables in
exchange for a fee. Depositors were then issued a receipt.
At first, these receipts were simply used by the depositor
seeking to reclaim his goods from the goldsmith. Before
long, however, depositors began using the receipts, or
notes, as means of making partial payments. Often
enough, the gold transferred between the depositor and

COMPANY PERSPECTIVES

A bank dedicated to high quality personal service is a rarity today. At C. Hoare & Co., we combine an intelligent, professional approach to banking and investment management with care and courtesy. Our exclusive service is delivered by experienced managers who know and understand their customers.

Founded over 300 years ago, we are still owned and managed by the Hoare family. Our strengths lie in our continued independent ownership, our long banking history and our commitment to providing services of the highest standard.

the recipient remained in the goldsmith's vault, and the only item changing hands was the goldsmith's receipt.

By 1633, the goldsmith notes had become accepted proof of a person's ability to pay for a transaction. More and more goldsmiths began accepting deposits, becoming known as "keepers of running cashes." By 1660, the goldsmith's notes had themselves become an early form of banknote, and were accepted as a form of money. Commonly issued as £1 and £5 notes, the goldsmith receipts gave rise to the expression "good as gold." This early banking system encouraged more goldsmiths to take deposits, and by the mid-1670s the city of London featured more than 40 goldsmith-bankers.

Because the goldsmith's notes had become an acceptable form of money, depositors rarely withdrew the actual gold backing their receipts. An important step forward toward the modern banking industry came when goldsmiths began issuing loans based on a percentage of the gold in their vaults, giving rise to the fractional reserve banking system on which the modern banking industry was founded.

The Hoare family's involvement in the London banking industry began in the 1670s, when Richard Hoare, son of a successful horse trader, completed an apprenticeship as a goldsmith. Hoare opened his own business, in Cheapside, London, under the sign of the Golden Bottle. While practicing his trade as a goldsmith, Hoare also began taking deposits and issuing notes, before developing lending and other banking services. By 1690, the banking side of Hoare's business was becoming dominant, as evidenced by his decision to move his shop to Fleet Street, already becoming an important financial and legal center in London.

Hoare quickly became a prominent banker and attracted a number of noteworthy customers, among them John Dryden, Samuel Pepys, and Catherine of Braganza, the wife of King Charles II. Hoare was later knighted by Queen Anne, and also, in 1712, became the mayor of London. Hoare's sons took over the business after his death, and continued to focus on the company's banking business. Although still trading under the "Gilded Bottle" sign, the Hoares reduced their goldsmithing activities and instead began developing their banking features. The company also used its depositor's gold for investment purposes. In the first decades of the 18th century, for example, the Hoares became prominent investors in the South Sea Company, buying its stock at a low price, and then selling its shares as that company's stock soared into the early 1720s.

The arrival of Hoare's grandson, Henry Hoare, marked the family's emergence as a dedicated bank. The third generation of Hoares guided the bank for more than 60 years, overseeing the development of new products and banking services, such as printed checks and passbooks. The Hoare family's bank became one of the city's most prominent, attracting notable customers such as the painter Thomas Gainsborough, furniture makers Thomas Chippendale & Son (who also built the furniture for the bank), and later, Jane Austen and Byron, as well as a number of prime ministers and other noted politicians and aristocrats of the day. In keeping with the bank's standing, and the standing of its customers, the Hoare family rebuilt the Fleet Street location in 1829.

With the creation of the Bank of England, banking emerged as a business in its own right, no longer directly associated with the goldsmith trade. Growing numbers of private deposit-taking banks appeared throughout the country, and by the mid-19th century the country numbered some 4,000 banks. Problems of insolvency, however, brought pressure from the British government to reduce the number of banks while increasing their scale, creating a more stable banking system.

C. Hoare & Co., as the bank came to be known, had survived its own difficult periods. The bank's commitment to family ownership became a source of difficulties in itself. In the mid-19th century, the bank's operations came under control of Peter and Henry Hoare. Yet the two came into conflict over their differing but deeply held religious beliefs, and as a result, the operation of the bank was split between the two, with each leading the bank for six-month shifts. This difficult management structure was compounded by a string of unwise investments, leading the bank into financial problems. The arrival of the next generation of Hoares did little to help the company, in part because the sons of Peter and Henry Hoare, rebelling against their own religious education, proved to be poor managers.

THE LAST INDEPENDENT IN THE 21ST CENTURY

Faced with insolvency, C. Hoare & Co. nonetheless clung to its commitment to remain a private, independent, and Hoare family-controlled bank. Nonetheless, the bank developed a more careful system of choosing its managers, insisting the family members seeking to enter the business first develop professional experience outside of the company.

C. Hoare & Co. weathered its crisis and successfully rebuilt its business into the early years of the 20th century. The British banking sector underwent a new upheaval in the years following World War I. During this period, many of the country's smaller, private deposit-taking banks were bought up by or merged into a smaller number of larger, often nationally operating banks. C. Hoare & Co. became one of the few to remain committed to its independent, private ownership. Nonetheless, the bank underwent a restructuring at the end of the 1920s, transforming itself from a partnership to an unlimited liability company in 1929. A new seven-member shareholder structure was established; each of the bank's seven partners were drawn, however, from the pool of Hoare family members. At the time, the bank had just 20 employees.

As one of the last remaining private banks, Hoare successfully exploited its niche of catering to England's wealthy. Whereas the company counted a number of celebrities among its client base, it particularly attracted customers from the large and nearby legal industry; a number of firms became bank customers. The bank's small size, and restrained client base, allowed it to develop highly personalized services for its wealthy customers, who were often underserved at larger banks. Into the next century, C. Hoare & Co. grew steadily, building up a total assets base of more than £1 billion ($1.8 billion), administered by some 220 employees.

By the dawn of the 21st century, C. Hoare had been turned over to the 11th generation of the Hoare family, including CEO Alexander Hoare and his cousin Venetia Hoare, who became the bank's first-ever female partner. The new generation helped modernize the bank, introducing computer technology and enabling a limited level of online access for its customers. Nonetheless, the bank emphasized its personal services. As Alexander Hoare told the *Financial Times*: "Self-service banking is a solution to a problem we don't have—which is useless service. The customers like speaking to a human who recognizes their voice and who understands their needs."

Remaining committed to its independence, C. Hoare & Co. also resisted the temptation to expand beyond banking and offer diversified products, such as insurance. Nonetheless, in the mid-2000s the company prepared a new investment management product, a multi-manager investment fund led by Northern Trust and combining the products of two other specialist providers. As such, C. Hoare & Co. presented itself as a "manager of multi-managers." With 333 years of history behind it, C. Hoare & Co. had established itself as a modern niche player in the British banking industry.

M. L. Cohen

PRINCIPAL SUBSIDIARIES

Messrs. Hoare Trustees.

PRINCIPAL COMPETITORS

Coutts & Co.; Drummonds; Childs & Co.; Cazenove & Co.; Lazard LLC.

FURTHER READING

Brown, Mark, "Hoare Enters the Modern Age," *Euromoney,* January 2004, p. 6.

Cope, Nigel, "Hoare Welcomes Competitors for the Posh Pound," *Independent,* May 29, 2001, p. 15.

Gimbel, Florian, "A History That's Still in the Making," *Financial Times,* November 10,. 2003, p. 4.

———, "C. Hoare to Become a 'Manager of Multi-Managers' After 300 Years," *Financial Times,* October 20, 2003, p. 2.

Harris, Clay, "Good Luck Rubs Off on C. Hoare & Co.," *Financial Times,* May 26, 2005, p. 24.

Harris, Derek, "Cashing in on Tradition," *The Times,* October 6, 1993, p. 33.

Merrell, Caroline, "Billionaires Join Queue to Sign Up for Bank That Likes to Say: 'Maybe,'" *The Times,* October 22, 2005, p. 67.

Morais, Richard C., "Service Is Never Out of Fashion," *Forbes,* November 28, 2005.

Reece, Damian, "Hoare & Co. Suffers Profits Downturn," *Independent,* August 31, 2005, p. 57.

Camden Property Trust

3 Greenway Plaza, Suite 1300
Houston, Texas 77046
U.S.A.
Telephone: (713) 354-2500
Toll Free: (800) 922-6336
Fax: (713) 354-2700
Web site: http://www.camdenliving.com

Public Company
Incorporated: 1993
Employees: 1,640
Sales: $433.1 million (2004)
Stock Exchanges: New York
Ticker Symbol: SPT
NAIC: 525930 Real Estate Investment Trusts

■ ■ ■

Camden Property Trust is a Houston, Texas-based real estate investment trust (REIT) that specializes in the development, acquisition, and management of luxury and middle-market apartment complexes. All told, the company is involved in about 200 urban and suburban communities, containing more than 65,000 units, making it the fifth largest, publicly traded, multifamily property firm in the United States. About one-quarter of the apartments are located in Texas, with the rest spread across a dozen other states, including Arizona, California, Colorado, Florida, Georgia, Kentucky, Missouri, Nevada, North Carolina, Pennsylvania, Virginia, and Washington, D.C. Camden is listed on the New York Stock Exchange.

ROOTS DATING TO CENTURY DEVELOPMENT AND THE EARLY 1980S

Camden started out in 1982 as the residential arm of Century DevelopmentCentury Development, the Houston company owned by Houston real estate developer Kenneth Schnitzer, known as an aggressive and hard-nosed negotiator. Born in Houston in 1929, Schnitzer began his career, after dropping out of both the universities of Texas and Houston, working in his family's paper distribution business, Magnolia Paper Company. He also married into money, the Weingarten family of Houston supermarket fame, the first of four times he was wed. In 1952, while still working as an executive at Magnolia, Schnitzer completed his first real estate deal, constructing a three-story office building on credit near Rice University. His appetite whetted, Schnitzer became involved in the development of ever larger office buildings in Houston. He truly made his mark in Houston real estate, however, in the 1970s with the development of Greenway Plaza, a project that required the buying of 350 homes to secure enough land. He succeeded and eventually built ten office towers, a 400-room hotel, and the Houston Summit Arena, which became the home to the Houston Rockets professional basketball team and the Houston Aeros of the now defunct World Hockey League of the 1970s. Schnitzer was owner of the Aeros and co-owner of the Rockets.

In the early 1980s Schnitzer's Century Development began building high-rise condominiums in Houston and Austin, Texas. According to *Forbes* in a 1987 article, "There weren't a lot of takers, especially after oil prices and the Mexican Peso started crashing in 1982. So the developers started renting the units. That didn't go over too well, either. Then, in late 1983, someone decided he could unload the condos through syndicated partnerships." Century was the most aggressive of the syndicates, pitching the idea that investors could enjoy federal tax breaks in the near term, then receive a big payoff when the Houston economy rebounded. Heading up Century's effort was Richard J. Campo, who was just in his late 20s. A graduate of Oregon State University, he came to work for Schnitzer in 1976, and then in 1982 cofounded the syndication unit.

The syndication plan did not pan out for investors as advertised, however. Congress passed the Tax Reform Act of 1986 that gutted the tax breaks on which the plan hinged. Campo seized on what he called "desyndication" as a way to salvage as much from the situation as possible. "What he did," wrote *Forbes,* "was unwind the deal, make some money in the process but keep the investors content enough with their own losses so that he could do business with them again." In short, the condos went back to the developers and the investors avoided any liability for the mortgages. Although investors lost money, they knew that if it had not been for Campo, they would have lost even more, and many of them were willing to trust him on future projects.

Along with partner D. Keith Oden, Campo broke away from Schnitzer by engineering a leveraged buyout of Century's syndication division in 1986, renaming it Centeq Companies. Schnitzer would become caught up in the savings and loan scandal of the 1980s, be convicted on federal fraud charges, and then be acquitted on appeal before dying of lung cancer in 1999 at the age of 70. Campo and Oden, in the meantime, began assembling a portfolio of Texas apartments that by 1990 numbered 2,500.

Not until the Tax Reform Act of 1986 eliminated tax shelters did it change the nature of the real estate

industry by making REITs a truly viable investment vehicle. REITs had been created by Congress in 1960 as a way for small investors to become involved in real estate in much the same way as mutual funds. REITs could be taken public and their shares bought and sold like stock. Like stock companies, REITs were subject to regulation by the Securities and Exchange Commission. Unlike stock companies, however, REITs were required by law to pay out at least 95 percent of their taxable income to shareholders each year. This stipulation severely limited the ability of REITs to retain internally generated funds, and so during the first 25 years of existence, REITs were only allowed to own real estate, a situation that hindered their growth because third parties had to be contracted to manage the properties. The 1986 act finally permitted REITs to provide customary services for property, in effect allowing the trusts to operate and manage the properties they owned. Despite these major changes in law, however, REITs were still not embraced by investors. In the latter half of the 1980s, banks, insurance companies, pension funds, and foreign investors provided the bulk of real estate investment funds. But a glutted marketplace resulted, leading to a shakeout. It was only when real estate became available at distressed prices in the early 1990s that REITs finally became an attractive mainstream investment option and many real estate firms used their holdings as a foundation on which to form a REIT and take it public, starting in 1993. Many of these new REITS carved out niches, such as office buildings, shopping malls, or apartments, and then used their newly minted shares as a way to acquire more property.

FORMING AS A REIT IN 1993

Campo and Oden incorporated Camden Property Trust in May 1993, with their niche the upper end of the apartment market. An initial public offering of shares was completed in August of that year, raising $218 million. The new REIT then bought 20 Texas apartment complexes, 17 of which were owned or controlled by Centeq. Altogether, Camden started out with about 7,000 apartments.

In the mid-1990s REITs in the different real estate sectors began to consolidate as it became apparent that they needed a sizable market capitalization if they wanted to attract institutional investors and capital for continued growth; any REIT that did not continue to grow knew it was destined to be left by the roadside. Determined to be one of the chosen, Camden had grown aggressively since going public, so that by the end of 1996 it owned more than 19,000 apartments in Texas and Arizona, although most of its properties were still located in Houston. The REIT completed its first major acquisi-

KEY DATES

1982: Houston-based Century Development forms a syndication unit.

1986: Richard Camp and Keith Oden acquire the syndication unit, renamed Centeq Companies.

1993: Centeq forms the basis of a new real estate investment trust: Camden Property Trust.

1997: Paragon Group, Inc. is acquired.

1998: Oasis Residential, Inc. is acquired.

2005: Summit Properties Inc. is acquired.

tion in April 1997, a deal agreed upon in late 1996. At a cost of $328 million in stock and the assumption of $288 million in debt, Camden picked up Dallas-based Paragon Group Inc., which owned interests in nearly 17,000 apartments in Texas, Florida, Missouri, and North Carolina. Unlike Camden, Paragon had not been aggressive on the acquisition front, and as a result saw its stock slip to $15 a share, compared with the $21.25 per share price when the REIT went public in 1994. The addition of Paragon was important for Camden in a number of ways. It gave the company assets worth more than $1 billion, a cutoff point for many institutional investors, who refused to buy stock in REITs with less than that amount. The deal also bolstered Camden's position in the Dallas market and gave it a beachhead in several desirable markets, including St. Louis; Charlotte, North Carolina; Kansas City, Missouri; Louisville, Kentucky; Tampa-St. Petersburg, Florida; and Orlando, Florida. As a result, Camden gained flexibility, able to shift construction and acquisition resources to markets enjoying growth and pulling back in cities not faring as well.

In addition to integrating the Paragon assets over the course of 1997, Camden completed three smaller acquisitions, costing $46 million, while spending another $192 million in new development. The REIT ended the year with ownership interests in nearly 35,000 apartments, generating income just shy of $200 million, a significant increase over 1996's $111.6 million. It also closed 1997 by reaching agreement on another major acquisition, paying $53 million in stock and assuming $451 million in debt to add Las Vegas-based Oasis Residential Inc. When the deal closed in April 1998, Camden added another 15,000 apartments, giving the REIT more than 51,000 units and a significant presence in Nevada, Colorado, and California markets. Camden

also began a program in 1997 to balance out its geographic mix, leading to a three-year effort to sell off nonstrategic assets, which between 1997 and 2001 would total more than $600 million.

In addition to being a successful consolidator and turning itself into a super-regional REIT, Camden proved to be a savvy developer as well in 1998 when it bought the 700 acres of a private airport located close to Houston's upscale Westchase District for $53 million. It then sold off 500 of the acres for $35 million to the Sunrise Colony Co., which planned to develop a private country club community that would include a world-class golf course and 1,200 homes. Camden sold off another 100 acres to recoup the rest of the $53 million it laid out, and was left with 100 acres for development that was essentially cost-free. The REIT planned to build some 2,000 apartments on the site in the years to come, with Campo telling the *Houston Chronicle,* "It will allow us to control multifamily development in that area for a long time." Because the land was essentially free, Camden would also be put in a favorable competitive position in terms of rental rates.

With the addition of Oasis, Camden enjoyed another jump in revenues, from $200 million to $324 million in 1998. Because of market conditions it was difficult to raise capital to complete large acquisitions, but Camden's development pipeline permitted it to continue its growth pattern. Six communities composed of 2,500 apartment units were completed in 1999 at a total investment of $185 million. The REIT also took steps to provide for further development opportunities. It bought a 38-acre parcel in Dallas's Central Business District, earmarked for a luxury 1,200-unit apartment community, as well as a ten-acre development site located in downtown Long Beach, California, close to the convention center, where it planned to build 240 high-rise condominiums, a 550-apartment complex, as well as a 500-room hotel. Revenues continued to rise steadily, topping $371 million in 1999, a 14.7 percent improvement over 1998.

LAUNCH OF BRANDING STRATEGY IN 2000

Again Camden did not grow externally in 2000, but it still added apartments through development, completing the construction of four new communities and gaining nearly 1,500 apartments. It also broke ground on an apartment community on its Long Beach property in 2000. More so, the REIT launched a branding strategy in 2000, pursuing the theme of "Living Excellence," an effort to build value in the Camden name, not only with investors but the real estate industry, and ultimately with customers.

A combination of low mortgage rates that made house buying attractive and an oversupply of apartments created more challenges for everyone in the apartment field. Camden was especially affected by the terrorist attacks of September 11, 2001, because it owned properties located close to Dallas's airport and the American Airlines headquarters. Camden saw overall occupancy rates decline somewhat, but only allowed price reductions as a last resort. Instead, the company preferred to offer such incentives as repainting apartments or installing ceiling fans, steps that pleased tenants but also enhanced the value of the real estate. Camden also took a hit on its balance sheet because of the meltdown in the Internet sector, writing off several million dollars in investments in Internet companies serving the apartment market. Revenues reached $411 million in 2002 and grew only slightly in 2003 to $416.5 million. New developments were a key element in maintaining a modicum of momentum for Camden.

In 2003 the REIT unveiled several new communities: Camden Ybor City in Tampa, Florida's historic district; Camden Vineyards in California's fast-growing Inland Empire; Camden Tuscany in San Diego's Little Italy District; Camden Sierra at Otay Ranch in Chula Vista, California; and Camden Oak Crest in Houston.

Although difficult conditions continued in some markets in 2004, Camden, because of its diversified approach, continued to prosper. For the year it recorded $433.1 million in revenues and realized a net profit of $41.4 million. In the final months of the year it also agreed to the first major acquisition in six years: the $1.9 billion purchase, including the assumption of debt, of Charlotte, North Carolina-based Summit Properties Inc. It was an important move for Camden, allowing it to keep pace with rivals in a real estate sector that remained fragmented but was beginning to see consolidation heat up. With the addition of Summit, Camden became the fifth largest public owner of multi-family real estate properties. Summit was especially strong in two of the nation's strongest apartment markets: Washington, D.C., and southeast Florida. It also gave Camden a beachhead on which to grow along the East Coast.

All told, Camden was well positioned for ongoing growth: It enjoyed a geographically balanced portfolio of properties, was present in 16 of the top-20 job growth markets in the country, and boasted a development pipeline of $1.1 billion worth of construction projects.

Ed Dinger

PRINCIPAL SUBSIDIARIES

Camden Operating, L.P.; Camden Development, Inc.; Camden Realty, Inc.; Camden Builders, Inc.

PRINCIPAL COMPETITORS

Apartment Investment and Management Company; Archstone-Smith Trust; Equity Residential.

FURTHER READING

Allen, Kathy, "Return of the REITS: Camden Creates Trust to Buy Apartments," *Houston Business Journal,* August 16, 1993, p. 4.

Barrett, William P., "Six Bites from One Apple," *Forbes,* September 7, 1987, p. 88.

Bivins, Ralph, "Building Greater Trust," *Houston Chronicle,* August 9, 1997, p. 1.

———, "How Camden Got 100 West Side Acres for Almost Nothing," *Houston Chronicle,* May 30, 1999, p. 8.

———, "Schnitzer Has Left Large Mark on Houston," *Houston Chronicle,* July 19, 1996, p. 1.

Burke, Erica, "Strength in Numbers," *Construction Today,* May 2005, p. 93.

Pacelle, Mitchell, "Camden Property to Buy Paragon in REIT Merger," *Wall Street Journal,* December 17, 1996, p. C.

Smith, Ray A., "Camden Property Agrees to Acquire Summit Properties," *Wall Street Journal,* October 5, 2004, p. A8.

Cameco Corporation

2121 11th Street West
Saskatoon, Saskatchewan S7M 1J3
Canada
Telephone: (306) 956-6200
Fax: (306) 956-6201
Web site: http://www.cameco.com

Public Company
Incorporated: 1987
Employees: 1,538
Sales: CAD 1.04 billion (2004)
Stock Exchanges: Toronto Montreal New York
Ticker Symbol: CCO; CCJ
NAIC: 212291 Uranium-Radium-Vanadium Ore
  Mining

■ ■ ■

Cameco Corporation is the largest uranium producer in the world, accounting for one-fifth of the world's production. Cameco and two other uranium producers, the French-owned AREVA Group and the Australian-owned Rio Tinto Group, control 60 percent of the world's uranium supply. Cameco is a vertically integrated uranium company, involved in mining the metal ore, processing it, making fuel rods, and, through a 31.6 percent stake in Bruce Power Partnership, operating four Canadian nuclear reactors. The company also is involved in gold production, holding a 52.7 percent interest in Centerra Gold Inc., the largest, Western-based gold producer in central Asia and the former Soviet Union. Cameco's mining operations are conducted in Saskatch-

ewan, where the largest known deposit of high-grade uranium is located, and in Wyoming and Nebraska. The company's uranium refining and conversion facilities are located in Ontario, where the reactor plants it manages are also located. Uranium is used to generate 16 percent of the world's electricity.

ORIGINS

There was a time when the business of mining for uranium appeared destined for exponential growth. During the 1970s, soaring oil prices helped promote nuclear power as an alternative energy source, and uranium, the radioactive metal used to fuel reactors, stood to gain considerably in value. More common than tin and 500 times more common than gold, uranium possessed unique properties: Its atomic structure could be changed in a process that released energy in the form of heat, which, inside a nuclear reactor, could be harnessed to generate electricity, producing one of the cleanest sources of energy available. Concern about a reactor meltdown and the creation of radioactive waste historically had held the growth of the nuclear power industry in check, but by the late 1970s, the attitude toward nuclear-generated electricity was changing. By the end of the decade, there were plans to build 50 new nuclear plants in the United States alone. The price of concentrated uranium ore, known as "yellowcake," shot upward because of the anticipated demand, surpassing $40 per pound. A new era of power generation appeared to be imminent, but on March 28, 1979, the hopes of the nuclear industry and the prospects of uranium miners were crushed shortly after 4 a.m.

When the Three Mile Island nuclear facility near Middletown, Pennsylvania, recorded the most serious accident in the history of the U.S. commercial nuclear power industry, an industry on the verge of major expansion was forced to retreat. The accident, deemed a partial meltdown (roughly half of the core melted during the early stages of the incident), caused no deaths or injuries to plant workers or residents of the nearby community, but it raised the specter of worst-case consequences and stripped the nuclear power-generation movement of its momentum. In the wake of the accident, efforts to build the previously planned 50 new nuclear plants were abandoned, causing the price of concentrated uranium ore to fall substantially. From a business standpoint, the Three Mile Island accident was a public relations disaster for proponents of nuclear-generated power and the commercial interests supporting the nuclear industry, a disaster that was greatly exceeded when the worst-case scenario played itself out seven years later. In April 1986, an explosion at the nuclear facility in Chernobyl destroyed the core of reactor number four, triggering a second explosion and a fireball two minutes later that blew off the reactor's steel and concrete lid. At least 5 percent of the radioactive reactor core was released into the atmosphere and downwind, eventually causing 56 fatalities, either from the explosions, or from radiation, thermal burns, or thyroid cancer.

Cameco was formed in the wake of the Chernobyl disaster, unfurling its corporate banner for the first time as faith in nuclear-generated power reached an all-time low and uranium prices continued to plummet. The company was a newcomer to uranium mining in name only, however. Cameco was created through the merger of two companies, the Saskatchewan Mining Develop-

ment Corporation and Eldorado Nuclear Limited, each a holder of substantial uranium assets. Eldorado was established in 1926, a founding date that would make it the oldest company in the uranium business in North America. Eldorado, which became a Canadian Crown corporation during World War II, also developed into one of the largest companies in the uranium business in North America, accumulating substantial uranium mining interests in Saskatchewan and uranium processing facilities in Ontario, the only such facilities in Canada. The Canadian government first began exploring the possibility of privatizing the company in 1984, discussions that led to its merger with Saskatchewan Mining Development Corp. Saskatchewan Mining, a provincially owned Crown corporation, had established itself as the lowest-cost producer of uranium in Canada by the time of the merger, using its uranium mining operations and reserves in Saskatchewan to distinguish itself. The merger in 1988 created one of the largest integrated uranium mining and processing companies in the world, boasting $1.6 billion in assets under the Cameco name.

Cameco, impressive in size and scope, began operating under less than favorable conditions considering the damage caused by the accidents at Three Mile Island and Chernobyl. By the late 1980s, the price of uranium had fallen to $10 per pound, down substantially from prices that eclipsed $40 per pound a decade earlier. For Cameco and the rest of the uranium industry, the prevailing attitude toward nuclear-generated power provided little encouragement that the 1990s would bring growth. The decade, in fact, brought even bleaker conditions to the uranium industry, as the fall of the Soviet Union delivered a third, decisive blow to the industry. The end of the Cold War brought the end of the nuclear arms race and created another problem for uranium producers. The radioactive material in many nuclear warheads was converted to commercial use (during the early 21st century, reactor fuel made from scrapped Soviet nuclear weapons powered one out of every ten homes in the United States), glutting the uranium market. With the construction of new nuclear plants on hold indefinitely and the existing reactors feeding off stockpiles of uranium, the market for the ore dwindled. Mines were sold or closed down, as depressed prices and excess inventories encouraged or forced many of the smaller operators to exit the business. One of the exceptions to the trend was Cameco.

EXPANSION IN THE 1990S

While other uranium concerns made a retreat, Cameco pressed ahead, increasing its already stalwart position in the uranium market. The company aggressively pursued new prospecting grounds, using the anemic conditions

KEY DATES

1988: Cameco, incorporated the previous year, begins operating following the merger of the Saskatchewan Mining Development Corporation and Eldorado Nuclear Limited.

1991: Cameco completes its initial public offering of stock.

1996: Cameco acquires Power Resources, Inc., the largest uranium producer in the United States.

1998: The acquisition of Uranerz Exploration and Mining Limited gives Cameco access to uranium deposits at Rabbit Lake and McArthur River, two of the largest deposits in the world.

2001: Cameco takes a 15 percent interest in Bruce Power Partnership, giving it control over four nuclear reactors in Ontario.

2003: Russia announces it will limit exports of uranium, causing prices to rise.

2004: Cameco's revenues eclipse CAD 1 billion.

hobbling its industry to its advantage by acquiring terrain that likely contained high-yield, low-risk deposits. In 1991, as it prepared to embark on its expansion plan, the company completed its initial public offering (IPO) of stock, selling 10.4 million shares at CAD 12.50 per share in its debut on the Toronto and Montreal Stock Exchanges in July. At the time of the IPO, which netted the company CAD 130 million in proceeds, Cameco accounted for 10 percent of the world's electrical utility fuel requirements and 20 percent of its uranium conversion services. The company began trading on the New York Stock Exchange in 1996, the year it entered the gold production business through an investment in a gold mine in Kyrgyzstan. The year also marked the acquisition of Power Resources, Inc., a U.S.-based uranium mining company, and Central Electricity Generating Board Exploration (Canada) Ltd., a company involved in Canadian uranium exploration. Cameco paid $105 million for the two companies, gaining the greatest boost to its stature from the addition of Power Resources, which ranked as the largest uranium producer in the United States. The acquisition increased Cameco's reserves and resources by 10 percent.

Cameco's most aggressive moves occurred at the end of the 1990s, when the uranium industry was in its

deepest doldrums. In 1998, the company paid CAD 489 million for Uranerz Exploration and Mining Limited and Uranerz U.S.A., Inc. Uranerz Exploration, based near Cameco in Saskatoon, held a 33.33 percent interest in the Key Lake and Rabbit Lake uranium mines and a 27.92 percent interest in the McArthur River uranium project, all of which were located in northern Saskatchewan. The acquisition added greatly to Cameco's holdings, particularly the McArthur River property, then under development, which ranked as the world's largest known high-grade uranium deposit. Cameco's chief executive officer at the time, Bernard Michel, noted the significance of the purchase in a company press release issued on August 11, 1998. "This acquisition," he said, "increased Cameco's uranium reserves and resources and uranium production levels by about 30 percent, solidifying Cameco's already strong position in the global uranium industry." Cameco began mining at McArthur River in 1999 and achieved commercial production in late 2000.

As Cameco entered the 21st century, the uranium industry continued to limp along, its customers still feeding off excess inventories. Cameco, as it had been doing since its inception, responded to the dour state of its industry by broadening its interests. In 2000, the company expanded its capabilities beyond mining and refining uranium and entered the generation business, signing a memorandum of understanding with British Energy PLC to acquire a 15 percent interest in Bruce Power Partnership. The deal, concluded in April 2001, put Cameco in charge of four nuclear reactors in Ontario, an arrangement that made Cameco the exclusive supplier of fuel to the reactors. In 2003, the company increased its stake in Bruce Power, paying CAD 209 million to gain a 31.6 percent interest in the partnership. Gerald W. Grandey, Cameco's chief executive officer, commented on the move in a February 16, 2003 interview with *Canadian Corporate News,* one month after being promoted to the chief executive office. "The increased ownership," he said, "is consistent with our objective to leverage our unparalleled uranium assets into a greater role in the nuclear industry."

2020 BECKONS

Grandey's commitment, and the commitment demonstrated by his predecessors, to increase Cameco's exposure in the nuclear industry began to look astute not long after the Bruce Power deal. There were a number of factors at work, including the pressing energy needs of a host of nations and the fact that uranium stockpiles were not inexhaustible, but once Russia, the world's second largest exporter of uranium, announced in October 2003 that it would limit exports to conserve fuel for the reactor plants it planned to build, the price of uranium began to rise energetically. After decades of either declining or stagnating in price, the value of uranium began to appreciate, and the one company more than any other that stood to gain was the world's largest uranium producer, Cameco, the "Saudi Arabia of uranium," as the head of an investment firm referred to the company in the November 28, 2005 issue of *Forbes Global*.

After 25 years of being relegated to the backwaters of the energy field, nuclear-generated power had become popular again. Between 1985 and 2003, half of the commercial stockpile of enriched uranium was exhausted, but Cameco's hopes for a lucrative future were based on more than just the gradual depletion of excess inventories. Between the beginning of 2004 and October 2005, the price of uranium nearly tripled, rising to $33 per pound. Analysts expected the price to reach $45 per pound by 2007. The reason for Cameco's optimism and the optimism underpinning pundits' prognostications was the enormous number of nuclear energy projects being announced midway through the decade. In January 2005, China was preparing to award an $8 billion contract to build four reactors, the largest nuclear power construction project in the world. By 2020, China planned to build 27 reactor plants to meet its target of increasing its nuclear energy output fivefold. India, desperate to meet the energy needs of its population, planned to increase its nuclear power capacity by a factor of eight by 2020, an objective it intended to meet by building 31 reactors. Russia, aiming for the same target year, planned to build 25 new reactors. Cameco, as it listened to the ambitious construction plans being announced, holding in its hands one-fifth of the world's supply of uranium, looked toward the future with a degree of confidence unprecedented in its history. The company, able to survive in the worst of times, seemed guaranteed to thrive in the best of times.

Jeffrey L. Covell

PRINCIPAL SUBSIDIARIES

Cameco Bruce Holdings Inc.; Cameco Bruce Holdings II Inc.; Centerra Gold Inc. (52.7%); UEM Inc. (50%); Bruce Power Limited Partnership, I.P (31.6%).

PRINCIPAL COMPETITORS

Rio Tinto Group; AREVA Group; WMC Resources Ltd.; Uranium Resources, Inc.

FURTHER READING

"Cameco Announces Close of Bruce Power Deal," *Canadian Corporate News*, February 16, 2003.

"Cameco to Acquire Canadian Nuclear Fuel Fabricator," *Canadian Corporate News*, December 2, 2005.

Hoover, Ken, "Cameco's Persistence Led to Glowing Gains," *Investor's Business Daily*, December 5, 2005, p. B22.

Serafin, Tatiana, "Going Nuclear," *Forbes Global*, November 28, 2005, p. 52.

"Uranium Company Jumps into Canadian Nuclear Venture," *Energy Daily*, October 16, 2000, p. 3.

"Uranium Demand Rises As Interest in Nuclear Rekindles," *America's Intelligence Wire*, October 14, 2005.

"Uranium Prospects Are Glowing: Asian Projects, Dwindling Stockpiles Lifting Uranium Prices," *America's Intelligence Wire*, January 5, 2005.

"Where Mining Gold Is the Easy Part," *Business Week*, October 29, 2001, p. 4.

Carhartt, Inc.

———— ■ ————

5750 Mercury Drive
Dearborn, Michigan 48126
U.S.A.
Telephone: (313) 271-8460
Toll Free: (800) 833-3118
Fax: (313) 271-3455
Web site: http://www.carhartt.com

Private Company
Incorporated: 1884 as Hamilton Carhartt & Co.
Employees: 4,000
Sales: $324 million (2004 est.)
NAIC: 315225 Men's and Boys' Cut and Sew Work
   Clothing Manufacturing; 315228 Men's and Boys'
   Cut and Sew Other Outerwear Manufacturing

■ ■ ■

Carhartt, Inc. is a leading U.S. producer of workwear, including overalls, jeans, coveralls, jackets, and other items favored by those in the construction and farming industries. The company's garments are sold primarily at smaller retail outlets catering to blue-collar customers. Carhartt's products, which include flame resistant clothing, thermal underwear, footwear, and a full range of outerwear, are renowned for their durability. The company maintains 13 manufacturing facilities in the United States, as well as production plants in Mexico and Europe. Carhartt sells its merchandise in the United States, Europe, and Japan.

EARLY HISTORY

The company's founder, Hamilton Carhartt, was born in Macedon Locks, New York, in 1855 and was raised in Michigan and Wisconsin, where his father, Dr. George Carhartt, was a physician and surgeon. Although his family distinguished itself mainly in the learned professions, Hamilton Carhartt had an interest in commercial pursuits. He left school in 1882 to enter the furniture business, first in Grand Rapids, Michigan, and then, in 1884, in Detroit.

There Carhartt established a wholesale furniture business under the name Hamilton Carhartt & Co. In 1889, he converted the business from home furnishings into one devoted exclusively to manufacturing apparel for working men. His first products were overalls made of duck (a tightly woven cotton fabric) and denim fabrics for railroad workers.

In 1905 the business was incorporated as Hamilton Carhartt Manufacturer, Inc.; it was reincorporated as Hamilton Carhartt Cotton Mills in 1910. By this time Carhartt had grown to include two mills in South Carolina and Georgia, as well as plants in Atlanta; Detroit; Dallas; San Francisco; Walkerville, Ontario; Vancouver, British Columbia; and Liverpool, England. The Walkerville plant was devoted to the manufacture of gloves.

By 1925 Carhartt had established a new plant in Paris and had an office and warehouse in New York City. A third mill was operating in Alabama. Hamilton Carhartt Junior—Manufacturer, a subsidiary specializing in young men's working apparel, had operations in Los Angeles and Philadelphia. The company was producing work clothing, overalls, shirts, hunting wear, pants, and shoes.

1920S-30S: ECONOMIC DOWNTURNS

The Cotton Depression of the 1920s and the Great Depression of the 1930s resulted in Carhartt losing all of its locations except its plants in Atlanta, Detroit, and Dallas. Moreover, the firm sold its rights to market in Texas, most of the southern states, and in southern California, Europe, and Canada. Carhartt unsuccessfully attempted to launch a sportswear line during this time.

With the assistance of the people of Irvine, Kentucky, a new plant was completed at the beginning of 1932 for just over $35,000. The new facility employed 20 people when it opened. In 1937 Hamilton Carhartt, age 82, was killed in an automobile accident; his son Wylie Carhartt assumed control of the corporation.

Despite economic challenges, the Carhartt firm had a solid reputation for quality clothing. It had built this reputation for durable work and outdoor clothing by using heavyweight 100 percent cotton duck for most of its products. The tightly woven material provided strength and durability as well as wind and snag resistance. All Carhartt duck products also had triple chain stitching over felled main seams. This method locked the seams in place, giving them great strength and making it very difficult to pull them apart. The strength of the fabric was also increased by using double fill yarn, where two yarns were twisted together and used as one.

KEEPING IT IN THE FAMILY: 1950S-60S

Wylie Carhartt was succeeded in 1959 as head of the company by his son-in-law, Robert C. Valade, who had begun his career at Carhartt in 1949. During the 1960s

Carhartt began to enjoy larger revenues from chain store sales. This enabled the company to repurchase selling rights in territories it had been forced to sell back in the 1930s. Under Valade's leadership Carhartt would grow from sales of $2 million in 1960 to more than $300 million in the mid-1990s.

In 1960 the firm made two significant acquisitions: Crown Headlight of Cincinnati, Ohio, and W.M. Finck & Co. of Detroit, an overalls manufacturer. Following the acquisitions the firm began selling garments under the label of Carhartt Headlight & Finck. Carhartt also acquired E.F. Partridge in Georgia, which effectively gave the company the right to sell garments in the South again. In 1965 Carhartt, Inc., a Michigan corporation, was formed from the merger of Hamilton Carhartt Overall Co., Inc., a Georgia corporation, and W.M. Finck & Co., a Michigan corporation.

ACQUISITIONS AND EXPANSIONS: 1970S-80S

In 1971 Carhartt established its first contemporary subsidiary, Carhartt South, Inc., to produce jeans, after acquiring a plant in Drew, Mississippi. In 1976 Carhartt formed another subsidiary, Carhartt Midwest, Inc., after purchasing the assets of Shane Manufacturing Co., Inc. The new subsidiary had plants in Evansville, Indiana, and Sebree, Kentucky. In 1978 the acquisition of Gross Galesburg Co. in Galesburg, Illinois, resulted in the formation of a third subsidiary of the same name.

In 1980 Carhartt Midwest expanded into a plant and warehouse in Madisonville, Kentucky. The next year it purchased another plant in Providence, Kentucky, and subsequently closed its Evansville, Indiana, plant. In 1982 Carhartt launched its first national marketing program with national advertising. During the latter half of the decade Carhartt streamlined its organizational structure by merging its subsidiaries with the parent company to form divisions. In 1989 the company built a new distribution center and a new sewing plant on its property in Madisonville, Kentucky. Cutting operations from all plants except Galesburg were then centralized in the former sewing plant at Madisonville. An additional plant was acquired in Edmonton, Kentucky.

EXPANDING CAPACITY: 1990S

Carhartt's sales reached a record $92 million in 1990. The firm expanded its capacity in 1992 by purchasing a 64,000-square-foot sewing plant in Glasgow, Kentucky. That year the company's Gross Galesburg division was renamed Muleskins Division and began concentrating its production on sweatshirts. The Muleskins Division was discontinued shortly thereafter.

KEY DATES

1884: Hamilton Carhartt & Co. is founded as a furniture business.
1889: Business converts to apparel manufacturing.
1925: The company establishes a plant in France.
1960: Sales reach $2 million.
1965: After several name changes, Carhartt, Inc. becomes the company's official corporate title.
1982: Carhartt launches its first national advertising program.
1991: Carhartt apparel appears in New York City fashion shows for the first time.
1997: Carhartt unveils its first line of apparel designed for women.
2004: Through a partnership with Red Wing Shoe Co., Carhartt begins selling a line of footwear.

Work wear was showing signs of becoming a fashion trend in the late 1980s and early 1990s, so Carhartt displayed its outdoor working man's collection for the first time at fashion shows in New York in 1991. The company had been selling its clothes in Japan strictly as fashion items since 1987.

Revenues in 1992 reached an estimated $102 million. Expansion continued in 1993 with the completion of a new 100,000-square-foot distribution center in Glasgow, Kentucky. The firm also purchased an 80,000-square-foot sewing plant in Camden, Tennessee, that began production in mid-July.

Workwear as a fashion trend became very popular in 1993, helping Carhartt toward its 1993 sales goal of $120 million. Top rap and hip-hop groups were wearing Carhartt work clothing on televised videos as well as on CD covers and in performances onstage. Carhartt clothes were even featured in the pages of *Vogue* and *Harper's Bazaar.*

The company was challenged to keep up with demand as trendy urbanites snapped up the firm's limited supply, making it difficult to service the traditional Carhartt market. Mark Valade, Robert Valade's son and vice-president of marketing at the time, told *Sales and Marketing Management,* "We're really having a problem balancing the traditional retailer and the new retailer." All of the firm's manufacturing plants were operating at capacity, and a second distribution center was opened. Still, the company did not have

enough product to supply everyone in 1993, and was forced to turn down accounts from department and specialty store chains because it did not have the production capacity to meet demand.

Carhartt's facility in Irvine, Kentucky, which was originally constructed in 1932, was converted to administrative offices and warehousing as the firm embarked on construction of a new 70,000-square-foot sewing plant there.

Further expansion took place in 1994, as Carhartt broke ground on a new central Kentucky cutting center in Glasgow, Kentucky. The company also purchased a 120,000-square-foot sewing plant in McKenzie, Tennessee, from competitor OshKosh B'Gosh, Inc. In 1995 the firm bought a 90,000-square-foot sewing plant in Dover, Tennessee, and a 26,882-square-foot sewing plant in Marrowbone, Kentucky, in 1996. The McKenzie plant was subsequently closed in 1999.

Internationally, London-based Work in Progress owner Ben Joseph, Carhartt's designated licensee and distributor in the United Kingdom, began promoting Carhartt clothing in England and Ireland in 1995. By 1998 he was also distributing for Carhartt in Europe, with combined revenues reported to be $8 million.

In the fall of 1997 Carhartt introduced a women's line and an Extremes line. Carhartt Extremes was a line of outdoor clothing designed to withstand the harshest weather conditions in wet and cold environments. After testing the women's line the previous fall, the company rolled out its new line of work wear for women at more than 100 stores. It was the first line of Carhartt garments designed specifically for women. Orders met and then exceeded expectations.

THE LATE 1990S AND BEYOND

In 1998 Carhartt began construction of the new 350,000-square-foot Robert C. Valade distribution center in Hanson, Kentucky. It opened in May 1999. When Carhartt awarded a contract for the distribution center to a nonunion design-and-build contractor, the company became involved in a dispute with the local building and construction trades council and the AFL-CIO, which threatened to boycott Carhartt products. Although there was never an official boycott, many union members were awaiting the outcome of the dispute before purchasing Carhartt apparel. The dispute was settled in November 1998 when Carhartt agreed to work with appropriate union building and construction trades councils in the construction of future projects, but planned to complete the Hanson facility with the existing contractor and subcontractors. Carhartt had traditionally been a unionized manufacturer, and union workers were a major customer segment. Carhartt had won the AFL-CIO labor management award in 1992.

Carhartt also expanded its marketing efforts in 1997 and 1998 through national sponsorships. It began supporting Professional Bull Riders events in November 1997, and in January 1998 began sponsoring one of the riders, Troy Dunn, who went on to win the title of World Champion in both 1997 and 1998. In the spring of 1997 Carhartt began its role as official national sponsor of Stihl Timbersports. Soon thereafter, Carhartt became a national sponsor of the Future Farmers of America (FFA) as well as the official sponsor of the FFA Home and Community Development Proficiency Award. As a national sponsor of the National High School Rodeo Association, Carhartt supported events all over the country.

Revenues for 1998 reached an estimated $307 million, triple the figure reported in 1992. Wholesale revenues in the United States were about $255 million, while $50 million was credited to Europe and the United Kingdom and $2 million to Japan. However, sales were flat from 1997 to 1998, a fact the company attributed to an unusually warm winter, given a common perception that Carhartt was a seasonal clothing company for fall and winter.

In 1998 Mark Valade became president of Carhartt following the death of his father, Robert Valade. His mother, Gretchen Carhartt Valade, became board chairperson. For the 1998-99 selling season Carhartt introduced a new merchandising concept for stores carrying its products, employing three unique fixtures: a workhorse fixture that expanded from one to two levels of hanging garments, a wall unit, and an accessory fixture. The module was designed to leverage Carhartt's brand power by organizing its full range of apparel and accessories in one easy-to-shop location. New signage was provided to identify the brand and call attention to the company's newer lines. The fixtures were interchangeable regardless of store format, an important consideration since Carhartt apparel was sold in a variety of retail outlets including discount and department stores, farm stores, and uniform outlets. Following a successful test run, the new shop initiative was rolled out to about 100 stores nationwide in 1998, with an additional 90 stores set to come on board in 1999.

In late 1998 the company began focusing on "first layer" clothing, such as T-shirts and jeans, for workers to wear in warmer weather. Even though work clothes had become a popular form of casual wear, all of the company's clothes continued to be designed for workers, especially construction workers. The company's marketing manager visited construction sites throughout the country to find out what workers wanted. Interestingly,

he found that workers would often purchase Carhartt clothing for casual dress; then, as the clothes faded or lost their new look, the consumer would then wear the clothes for work.

With the construction of a 200,000-square-foot factory in Penjemo, Mexico, in September 1998, that would employ 500 union workers, Carhartt began making new products outside the United States. However, the company planned to continue making its core products at its existing U.S. facilities.

CARHARTT ENTERING ITS THIRD CENTURY OF BUSINESS

As Carhartt entered the 21st century, the company focused on increasing its manufacturing output to meet escalating demand and ensuring that it did not stray from its core customer base. The growing popularity of the Carhartt brand outside its niche, an occurrence that would be applauded by most companies, was a concern for the company as it entered its third century of business. "They know who their loyal audience is—workers, not the fashionistas who are going to be on to something else in three months," an advertising executive remarked in a July 15, 2002 interview with *ADWEEK Midwest Edition.*

Carhartt did not mind the business coming from outside its mainstay market, but it was not going to tailor its products or its marketing to attract fashion-conscious customers and risk losing its identity. "We don't want to lose our roots as basic work wear," a Carhartt distributor said in a May 3, 1999 interview with *Crain's Detroit Business.*

Aside from staying true to its core demographic, Carhartt's progress during the first half of the decade was marked by two notable events. In early 2004, the company signed a partnership with Minnesota-based Red Wing Shoe Co., a manufacturer of shoes and rugged work boots. Under the terms of the deal, Red Wing agreed to provide Carhartt with a line of professional-grade footwear to be sold under the Carhartt brand. The new line of footwear encompassed 22 models by late 2005, giving the company access to a market in which 40 million pair of work boots were sold annually in the United States. The other significant event during the first half of the decade was reported in mid-2005, when Carhartt, which had obtained textiles from the United States and Europe throughout its history, announced it was exploring sourcing opportunities in Asia. The company was considering acquiring $40 million worth of fabric and garments from manufacturers in India, interested principally in purchasing denim and knitted items. Company officials also were exploring business opportunities in China and Taiwan.

David P. Bianco
Updated, Jeffrey L. Covell

PRINCIPAL SUBSIDIARIES

Carhartt Workwear (Netherlands).

PRINCIPAL DIVISIONS

Carhartt North America; Carhartt Europe.

PRINCIPAL COMPETITORS

Levi Strauss & Co.; OshKosh B'Gosh, Inc.; Williamson-Dickie Manufacturing Company.

FURTHER READING

"Branding News: Carhartt Repositions As Workwear Brand," *Marketing,* December 1, 2004, p. 9.

"Carhartt (Finally!) Works Its Way into the Promotional Industry," *Wearables Business,* February 2001, p. 8.

"Carhartt, A Brief History," Dearborn, Mich.: Carhartt, Inc., 1998.

"Carhartt of US May Buy US$40 Mln Worth of Textiles from India," *Asia Africa Intelligence Wire,* May 17, 2005.

Hogue, Leslie Green, "Carhartt Heir's New Business Can Be Beat," *Crain's Detroit Business,* August 2, 1999, p. E9.

———, "Work-Wear Fad Builds Carhartt Clothing Brand," *Crain's Detroit Business,* May 3, 1999, p. 17.

Irwin, Tanya, "Carhartt Puts Perich to Work," *ADWEEK Midwest Edition,* July 15, 2002, p. 5.

"Michigan-Based Outfitter Plans Footwear with Minnesota's Red Wing Shoe Co.," *Saint Paul Pioneer Press,* February 21, 2004.

"Oshkosh Negotiating to Sell Its Jeans Plant to Carhartt," *Daily News Record,* January 27, 1994, p. 10.

Parola, Robert, "Rugged Carhartt Gets Down to Fashion," *Daily News Record,* April 10, 1991, p. 5.

———, "Workwear Grows New Fashion Muscle," *Daily News Record,* May 19, 1993, p. 4.

"Retail Choice: Carhartt," *Marketing,* April 20, 2005, p. 14.

Regenstein, Elliot, "Profile in Marketing: Mark Valade," *Sales and Marketing Management,* September 1993, p. 12.

"Shelf Containment," *Chain Store Age Executive with Shopping Center Age,* February 1999, p. 78.

Smith, Jennette, "Going Mobile," *Crain's Detroit Business,* March 15, 2004, p. 3.

Spevack, Rachel, "Workwear Jumps from Hip-Hop to Mainstream," *Daily News Record,* November 15, 1994, p. 6.

"Work Clothes Maker Reaches Accord with Owensboro, Ky., Trades Council," *Knight-Ridder/Tribune Business News,* November 25, 1998.

Cepheid

———— ∎ ————

904 Caribbean Drive
Sunnyvale, California 94089
U.S.A.
Telephone: (408) 541-4191
Fax: (408) 541-4192
Web site: http://www.cepheid.com

Public Company
Incorporated: 1996
Employees: 212
Sales: $52.9 million (2004)
Stock Exchanges: NASDAQ
Ticker Symbol: CPHD
NAIC: 334516 Analytical Laboratory Instrument
   Manufacturing

∎ ∎ ∎

Cepheid makes equipment capable of performing genetic analysis for medical, life sciences, and biothreat markets. The company's two major products are the SmartCycler and the GeneXpert, which enable rapid genetic testing of organism- and genetic-based diseases by automating complex laboratory procedures. The SmartCycler system integrates DNA amplification and detection, two of the three major processing steps involved in nucleic acid testing. Customers for the company's SmartCycler include the Centers for Disease Control and Prevention, the U.S. Food and Drug Administration, the National Institutes of Health, and the U.S. Army Medical Research Institute for Infectious Diseases. Cepheid's GeneXpert system adds the third primary processing

step, sample preparation, to the capabilities of the SmartCycler. The GeneXpert system is sold in the biothreat market and the clinical genetic assessment market. Through a partnership with Northrop-Grumman Corp., Cepheid developed the Biohazard Detection System for the U.S. Postal Service, which is capable of detecting anthrax and other deadly pathogens. The U.S. Postal Service intends to have Biohazard Detection System units installed at 283 mail-processing centers throughout the country.

ORIGINS

Cepheid was founded by three partners, Thomas L. Gutshall, Kurt Petersen, and M. Allen Northrup. Of the three, Petersen was the visionary, the innovative scientist who, with a passion for the potential of micro-electromechanical systems (MEMS), embodied the essence of Cepheid. "Kurt was the true pioneer of this industry," a MEMS industry analyst said in an April 2, 2001 interview with *Forbes*. "Many of the current MEMS applications are a direct result of Kurt's work."

A graduate of the University of California at Berkeley who earned his doctorate degree from the Massachusetts Institute of Technology, Petersen contributed significantly to the advancement of micromachining technology and its commercialization. A paper he wrote nearly 20 years before cofounding Cepheid was a seminal piece entitled "Silicon as a Mechanical Material," lending legitimacy to Petersen's entrepreneurial career. In 1982, he helped start his first company, cofounding Transensory Devices, a company that operated essentially as a research and development laboratory drawing on his

COMPANY PERSPECTIVES

Genetic testing involves a number of complicated steps, including sample preparation, amplification and detection. Based on state-of-the-art microfluidic and microelectronic technologies, our easy-to-use systems integrate these steps and analyze complex biological samples in our proprietary test cartridges. We are focusing our efforts on those applications where rapid genetic testing is particularly important, such as the infectious disease, cancer and biothreat testing markets.

expertise from his position as vice-president of technology. A short time later, Petersen launched another venture, starting a company named NovaSensor that represented one of the first successful MEMS companies. Petersen left NovaSensor in 1995 before the company was involved in several acquisitions and mergers that subsumed his creation. One year after he left NovaSensor, he collaborated with Gutshall and Northrup to form Cepheid in August 1996, a company that operated in virtual anonymity for the first five years of its existence.

Cepheid, as a corporate title, was chosen to convey the expectations of its principal founders. The term Cepheid referred to a class of stars with exceptionally regular periods of light pulsation that scientists used as reference standards for distance in the universe. With his company, Peterson intended to make MEMS-based instruments capable of analyzing deoxyribonucleic acid (DNA) quickly, instruments that could be used for a variety of purposes, such as distinguishing different types of cancer, detecting dangerous bacteria in meat and shellfish, and diagnosing sexually transmitted disease in urine samples, among a litany of other uses. "Cepheid is going to be a reference standard for DNA analysis," Peterson explained in an October 13, 2001 interview with the *San Jose Mercury News*.

As Cepheid set out to become the archetype of its nascent industry, Petersen took the titles of president and chief operating officer. Gutshall took the helm, assuming the posts of chairman and chief executive officer. Northrup did not take an active role in running the company until a year after its formation, when he accepted the positions of vice-president of research and chief technology officer, but his contribution to Cepheid's founding were instrumental, nevertheless. Northrup, between 1991 and 1997, served as the principal engineer at the Microtechnology Center of Lawrence Livermore National Laboratory, where the three partners

licensed a technology that served as Cepheid's foundation at its birth. Starting out, Petersen, Gutshall, and Northrup focused their efforts on the detection and analysis of nucleic acid, particularly DNA, a process that involved three primary steps: sample preparation, the isolation of target cells and the separation and purification of their nucleic acids; amplification, a chemical process that creates large quantities of DNA; and detection, the method of determining the presence or absence of the target DNA generally through the use of fluorescent dyes. From Livermore, the three partners licensed technology that enabled them to integrate amplification and detection, which became the central element of the instruments developed under the Cepheid banner during the company's first decade of existence. With the technology licensed from Livermore, Cepheid's small staff of scientists began work on developing a commercially viable product, focusing its efforts on creating a device capable of quickly analyzing DNA. The process was slow and costly.

Without a marketable product, Cepheid languished in obscurity, racking up debt throughout the late 1990s. Living largely off funding from government agencies, the company labored to bring its first product to market, a device dubbed the SmartCycler that debuted in May 2000, four years after the company was incorporated. In the years leading up to the release of the SmartCycler, a device possessing unique improvements on Livermore's fast-cycling technique for preparing DNA samples, Cepheid's financial record was bleak. In 1998, revenue totaled $3.5 million, a volume matched the following year, but losses during the two years eclipsed $11 million. To help pay down some of the company's debt, Gutshall led the company toward its initial public offering (IPO) of stock in June 2000, one month after the release of the SmartCycler. The proceeds from the IPO provided some relief, but 2000 ended with another financially woeful result. Cepheid generated $7 million in revenue during the first year of the SmartCycler's presence on the market, but it lost nearly $15 million during the year.

CEPHEID THRUST INTO THE LIMELIGHT: 2001

Cepheid's fortunes did not improve until disaster struck. The SmartCycler, geared for genomics research and medical applications such as diagnosing diseased tissue, failed to elevate the company's stature in the months after its IPO. The company continued to operate as a little-known biotechnology concern involved in life sciences research, struggling to make its mark and forced to contend with problems associated with operating in the public sector. As Cepheid reached its fifth

KEY DATES

1996: Cepheid is founded.
2000: The company first product, the SmartCycler, is released.
2002: Cepheid, as part of partnership led by Northrop-Grumman Corp., is awarded a pre-production contract with the U.S. Postal Service to install biodetection units at 14 mail-sorting facilities.
2004: GeneXpert, the company's second-generation analyzer, is released.

anniversary, its efforts to compete against a larger and more established competitor, Salt Lake City, Utah-based Idaho Technology Inc., caused the company to fall short of its quarterly revenue projection, evoking the displeasure of Wall Street. Worse still, Cepheid's relationship with its most important distributor, Fisher Scientific Co., soured. Fisher filed a lawsuit against Cepheid, delivering another blow to the company's esteem among analysts. Cepheid's stock, which debuted at $6 per share, plummeted to a near record low of $1.53 per share when trading closed on September 10, 2001. The following morning, disaster struck. When terrorists attacked the World Trade Center Towers in New York City and The Pentagon in Washington, D.C., the specter of bioterrorism ratcheted up within the space of hours. Fear spread throughout the nation, as pundits traded theories about the possibilities of other types of attacks against the country, including the release of deadly pathogens on the public. Cepheid, as one of the few companies capable of producing rapid and accurate biodetection units, quickly drew national interest. When trading on Wall Street resumed on September 17, 2001, Cepheid's stock nearly doubled in value. When anthrax spores sent through the U.S. mail killed five people, the threat of bioterrorism became a reality, further increasing the value of Cepheid's work. Petersen and Gutshall, who had labored in Sunnyvale largely without notice, became sought after experts in the field of biodetection, making television appearances on *Good Morning America* and CNN.

The attacks of September 11 brought widespread attention to Cepheid's expertise. Federal agencies used the company's technology to detect anthrax and identify its possible sources. The U.S. Army asked the company to develop a way to test for plague and botulism germs. Most important, the fear created from the anthrax at-

tacks that ensued in the months following the attacks on the World Trade Center Towers and The Pentagon led to a partnership with Northrop-Grumman Corp., a massive defense contractor. In May 2002, Cepheid announced it was part of a consortium led by Northrop-Grumman that the U.S. Postal Service (USPS) had selected for a pilot program to install germ detectors at post office sites nationwide. In December 2002, the USPS awarded the consortium a pre-production contract for biothreat detection systems to be installed and tested at 14 mail-sorting facilities, the first step toward the potential installation of biodetectors at USPS sites throughout the country.

Although the threat of bioterrorism raised Cepheid's profile, it did not cure its financial problems. The company consistently lost money during the first years of the decade, racking up nearly $70 million in losses between 2000 and 2003. Revenues more than doubled during the period, but the $18.5 million registered in 2003 hardly represented a towering volume of business. Cepheid's leadership changed during this period, as Gutshall passed the reins of command in 2002 to John L. Bishop, who had spent the previous decade serving as president of Vysis, a genomic disease management company. When Bishop joined the company, the hopes for future profitability were pinned on the success of the company's next-generation device dubbed GeneXpert, a test version of which was delivered to the U.S. Army Medical Research Institute of Infectious Diseases in early 2002. Unlike SmartCycler, GeneXpert handled all three stages of processing nucleic acid. Processing with SmartCycler required sample preparations to be performed separately, but GeneXpert simplified DNA identification by performing all three steps in one machine.

FUTURE HOPES RESTING ON GENEXPERT

As Cepheid prepared for its 10th anniversary, the tone of the occasion was expected to be influenced by the success of the company's GeneXpert system and its ability to increase its presence in a variety of markets. In 2004, there were developments that boded well for a celebratory party in 2006. Early in the year, the USPS approved the contract bid of the Northrop-Grumman-led consortium. According to the terms of the contract, Cepheid was slated to install 1,784 systems to detect anthrax at 283 mail-sorting facilities, which was expected to be completed during Cepheid's 10th anniversary. At the heart of the company's biodetection units was the company's GeneXpert technology, a comprehensive DNA analysis system that made its commercial debut in the company's third fiscal quarter of 2004. Initially GeneXpert was launched in the biothreat market, a release that was expected to be followed by its debut in the clinical market in 2005 once approval from the U.S. Food and Drug Administration was received. Financially, 2004 ended with one extremely encouraging result that was tempered by the blemish of another annual loss. Revenues for the year leaped to $52.9 million, markedly higher than the $18.5 million generated in 2003. The year ended with a $13.8 million loss, however. As Cepheid's executive staff looked ahead, the likelihood of a financially successful second decade of business rested on the embrace of GeneXpert and succeeding technologies not only in the biothreat market, but also in clinical and industrial markets.

Jeffrey L. Covell

PRINCIPAL SUBSIDIARIES

Cepheid SA (France).

PRINCIPAL COMPETITORS

Applied Biosystems Group; QIAGEN N.V.; Bio-Rad Laboratories, Inc.

FURTHER READING

"Cepheid Delivers GeneXpert to U.S. Army," *Medical Letter on the CDC & FDA,* January 27, 2002, p. 12.

Emert, Carol, "Detecting Disease," *San Francisco Chronicle,* October 21, 2001, p. E1.

Jacobs, Paul, "Sunnyvale, Calif., Maker of Disease Detector Is Suddenly a Hot Commodity," *San Jose Mercury News,* October 13, 2001.

Marcial, Gene G., "Sniffing for Anthrax," *Business Week,* January 19, 2004, p. 92.

Rafkin, Louise, "The Visionary," *Forbes,* April 2, 2001.

Tansey, Bernadette, "Biotech Firms Turn to Antiterrorism Efforts," *San Francisco Chronicle,* March 9, 2003, p. I1.

Cisco Systems, Inc.

170 West Tasman Drive
San Jose, California 95134-1706
U.S.A.
Telephone: (408) 526-4000
Toll Free: (800) 553-6387
Fax: (408) 526-4100
Web site: http://www.cisco.com

Public Company
Incorporated: 1984
Employees: 34,000
Sales: $24.8 billion (2005)
Stock Exchanges: NASDAQ
Ticker Symbol: CSCO
NAIC: 334210 Telephone Apparatus Manufacturing;
    334418 Printed Circuit Assembly (Electronic As-
    sembly) Manufacturing; 334419 Other Electronic
    Component Manufacturing; 511210 Software
    Publishers; 541512 Computer Systems Design
    Services

■■■

Cisco Systems, Inc. is a leading supplier of communications and computer networking products, systems, and
services. The company's product line includes routers,
switches, remote access devices, protocol translators, Internet services devices, and networking and network
management software, all of which link together
geographically dispersed local area networks (LANs),
wide area networks (WANs), and the Internet itself.
Cisco serves three main market segments: large organizations, including corporations, government entities, utilities, and educational institutions; service providers,
including Internet service providers, telephone and cable
companies, and providers of wireless communications;
and small and medium-sized businesses whose needs
include operating networks, connecting to the Internet,
and connecting with business partners. Increasingly,
Cisco's products are appearing in the consumer
marketplace. Cisco operates globally, deriving roughly
44 percent of its sales from overseas business.

BEGINNINGS IN MULTIPROTO-COL ROUTERS

Cisco Systems was founded in December 1984 in Menlo
Park, California, by a husband and wife team from
Stanford University, Leonard Bosack and Sandra Lerner.
Bosack was the manager of the computer science
department's laboratory, and Lerner oversaw the
computers at the graduate school of business. At Stanford, Bosack devised a way to connect the two local area
networks in the respective departments where he and his
wife worked, 500 yards across campus.

Lerner and Bosack initially tried to sell the internetworking technology that Bosack had developed to existing computer companies, but none were interested. They
then decided to start their own business, Cisco Systems,
based on this technology (they came up with the name,
a shortened form of San Francisco, while driving across
the Golden Gate Bridge). Bosack and Lerner were joined
by colleagues Greg Setz, Bill Westfield, and Kirk
Lougheed, as cofounders. Stanford University later tried
to obtain $11 million in licensing fees from the new

COMPANY PERSPECTIVES

A new way to connect. To interact, open a dialogue, spark an idea, or nurture a society. The power of individual imaginations coming together in the network. At the point where technology and people touch, Cisco invents new ways to multiply and enhance the power of the network. Information and creative energy. Converged systems and personal services. Universal links and close relationships. Communication and community. The network powered by Cisco is changing the way we work, live, play, and learn. Everywhere you look.

company, because Bosack had developed the technology while an employee at the university, but eventually the university settled for $150,000 and free routers and support services.

The company was established on a very tight budget. In fact, Bosack and Lerner had to mortgage their house, run up credit card debts, and defer salaries to their friends who worked for them in order to get the venture off the ground, and, even after two years of business, Lerner maintained an outside salaried job to supplement the couple's income.

Cisco's primary product from the beginning was the internetworking router, a hardware device incorporating software that automatically selects the most effective route for data to flow between networks. Cisco's routers pioneered support for multiple protocols or data transmission standards, and could therefore link together different kinds of networks, those having different architectures and those built on different hardware, such as IBM-compatible personal computers, Apple Macintosh computers, UNIX workstations, and IBM mainframes. Cisco thus became the first company to provide a commercial multi-protocol router when it shipped its first product in 1986, a router for the TCP/IP (Transmission Control Protocol/Internet Protocol) protocol suite. A year later, Cisco was selling $250,000 worth of routers per month. Sales for the fiscal year ending July 1987 were $1.5 million, and the company had only eight employees at the time.

Cisco initially marketed its routers to universities, research centers, the aerospace industry, and government facilities by contacting computer scientists and engineers via ARPANET, the precursor to what would become the Internet. These customers tended to use the TCP/IP

protocols and UNIX-based computers. In 1988, the company began to target its internetworking routers at mainstream corporations with geographically dispersed branches that used different networks. To that end, Cisco developed routers serving an even greater array of communications protocols and subsequently distinguished its routers by enabling them to support more protocols than those of any other router manufacturer. By the late 1980s, when the commercial market for internetworking began to develop, Cisco's reasonably priced, high-performance routers gave it a head start over the emerging competition.

Although Cisco had a high rate of sales growth, the young company was still short of cash; in 1988 Bosack and Lerner were forced to turn to a venture capitalist, Donald T. Valentine of Sequoia Capital, for support. Valentine, however, required that the owners surrender to him a controlling stake in the company. Valentine thus became chairperson and then hired an outsider, John Morgridge, as the company's new president and chief executive officer. Morgridge, who had an M.B.A. from Stanford University, was chief operating officer at laptop computer manufacturer GRiD Systems Corp. and prior to that had spent six years as vice-president of sales and marketing at Stratus Computer. Morgridge replaced several Cisco managers, who were friends of Bosack and Lerner, with more qualified and experienced executives. In February 1990, Cisco went public, after which Bosack and Lerner began selling their shares. Sales for the fiscal year ending July 1990 were $69.8 million, net income was $13.9 million, and the company had 254 employees.

Under Morgridge, Bosack had been given the title of chief scientist and Lerner was made head of customer service. However, Lerner reportedly did not get along well with Morgridge and, in August 1990, she was fired, whereupon Bosack also quit. When they left the company, Bosack and Lerner sold the remainder of their stock for $100 million, for a total divestiture of about $200 million. The couple subsequently gave away the majority of their profits to their favorite charities.

EARLY 1990S: RAPID GROWTH AS NETWORKS PROLIFERATE

Meanwhile, Morgridge built up a direct sales force to market the products to corporate clients. At first, Cisco's corporate clients were the scientific departments of companies which already maintained large internal networks. Later, Cisco was able to market its products to all kinds of major corporations to help them link the computer systems of their headquarters, regional, and branch offices. As Cisco's client base grew, the company's greatest challenge became meeting customer support

KEY DATES

1984: Cisco Systems, Inc. is founded by Leonard Bosack and Sandra Lerner.

1986: Company ships its first product, a router for the TCP/IP protocol suite.

1988: Donald T. Valentine, a venture capitalist, gains control of the company; John Morgridge is named president and CEO.

1990: Company goes public; Lerner is fired and Bosack quits.

1993: Cisco completes its first acquisition, that of Crescendo Communications.

1994: Revenues exceed $1 billion for the first time.

1995: John T. Chambers is named CEO.

1996: Company acquires StrataCom, Inc., maker of switching equipment, for $4.67 billion.

1998: Cisco's market capitalization passes the $100 billion mark.

1999: Company acquires 17 businesses, including Cerent Corporation, maker of fiber-optic networking equipment, for $7.2 billion.

2000: Company's market capitalization reaches $450 billion.

2003: Cisco acquires Linksys Group, beginning a push into the consumer marketplace.

2005: The $6.9 billion acquisition of Scientific-Atlanta, Inc. is announced.

service needs. The large size of the network systems for which Cisco supplied products made the user support task especially complex.

The company grew at a tremendous rate as its market rapidly expanded. In the early 1990s, companies of all sizes were installing local area networks (LANs) of personal computers. As such, the potential market for linking these networks, either with each other or with existing minicomputers and mainframe computers, also grew. Cisco's sales jumped from $183.2 million in 1991 to $339.6 million in 1992, and net income grew from $43.2 million to $84.4 million during the same period. In 1992, *Fortune* magazine rated Cisco as the second fastest growing company in the United States. In its role as the leading internetworking router provider, Cisco could redefine and expand the market as it grew.

While new communications technologies became widespread, Cisco adapted and added the capabilities of handling new protocols to its products. In the fall of 1992, Cisco introduced Fiber Distributed Data Interface (FDDI) and Token-Ring enhancements to its high-end router. Around the same time, the company also introduced the first Integrated Services Digital Network (ISDN) router for the Japanese market.

Until 1992, Cisco's products had not addressed IBM's System Network Architecture (SNA), a proprietary network structure used by IBM computers. In September 1992, however, after IBM announced plans to license its Advanced Peer-to-Peer Networking (APPN) protocol used for SNA, Cisco responded by announcing plans for a rival Advanced Peer-to-Peer Internetworking (APPI) protocol for supporting SNA. By August 1993, Cisco had decided not to develop a rival protocol, because IBM made it clear that APPN would be a more open, multivendor protocol than originally intended. Cisco then proceeded to work with IBM on further defining the APPN standard and bought a license to use APPN technology.

The emergence of asynchronous transfer mode (ATM) technology as a new standard method for multiprotocol data communications posed a challenge to Cisco and the router industry. ATM is a cell-switching technique that can provide high-speed communications of data, voice, video, and images without the use of routers. In early 1993, Cisco entered into a joint development project with AT&T and StrataCom to develop standards that would ensure that ATM operated within existing Frame Relay networks. Cisco also became one of the four founding members of the ATM Forum to help define the emerging standard. In February 1993, Cisco announced a strategy to include ATM among the protocols supported by its products. In 1994, Cisco introduced its first ATM switch.

In January 1993, Cisco introduced a new flagship product, the Cisco 7000 router, which featured a 50 percent improvement in performance over the AGS+, Cisco's existing high-end router. In June of that year, Cisco introduced a new low-end, lower-priced product line, the Cisco 2000 router family. The Cisco 2000 was aimed at companies desiring to link their smaller, remote branches or even remote individual employees, but unwilling to pay a premium price. Also during this time, the first network with over 1,000 Cisco routers was created.

International sales became an important part of Cisco's business. Subsidiaries were established in Japan and Australia, and a European Technical Assistance Center was established in Brussels, Belgium. In March 1993, Cisco Systems (HK) Ltd. became a new subsidiary in Hong Kong. International sales steadily increased, accounting for 35.6 percent of sales in 1991, 36 percent in 1992, 39 percent in 1993, and 41.9 percent in 1994.

Most of Cisco's international sales were through distributors, whereas in the United States the majority of sales (65 percent in early 1994) were made directly to the end users.

Cisco also began to market its technology, especially its software, more aggressively to long-distance telephone companies, as the deregulation of U.S. telephone carriers enabled these companies to provide more kinds of data communications products and services. For example, Cisco entered into a joint marketing agreement with MCI International to integrate Cisco's routers into end-to-end data networks over telephone lines. In 1992, Cisco entered new distribution agreements with Bell Atlantic Corp. and U.S. West Information Systems Inc. Cisco also signed marketing agreements in 1993 with Pacific Bell, whereby Cisco became a preferred router supplier for the company's network systems.

Cisco similarly began contracting with major European telecommunications companies at about the same time. British Telecom became an original equipment manufacturer (OEM) client of all of Cisco's products. Other European telecommunications compa-nies that entered into OEM relationships with Cisco included Alcatel of France and Siemens A.G. of Germany. Olivetti of Italy agreed to market Cisco's products under a value-added reseller agreement late in 1992.

Cisco made other strategic alliances to position itself better in the maturing internetworking market. To reach out to less technical clients, Cisco entered into joint agreements with Microsoft Corporation to market Cisco's first PC-based router card with Microsoft's Windows NT Advanced Server networking software through Microsoft's marketing channels. Similarly, Cisco established a partnership with Novell to integrate Cisco's routers with Novell's Netware network software so as to provide links between Netware and UNIX-based networks. Additionally, Cisco began working with Lan-Optics Ltd. to develop remote-access products.

1993-94: FIRST WAVE OF ACQUISITIONS

In September 1993, Cisco made its first acquisition. For $95 million, it acquired Crescendo Communications, which had pioneered products for a new technology called Copper Distributed Data Interface (CDDI). Crescendo's development of ATM technology was also a leading reason for the acquisition. Crescendo Communications was renamed the Workgroup Business Unit, and its switching technologies under development were later incorporated into Cisco's routers. Cisco made its second acquisition, that of Newport Systems Solutions for $93 million in stock, in August 1994. Newport

Solutions sold the LAN2LAN product line, software used in linking local area networks.

Early in 1994, Cisco announced a new networking architecture, CiscoFusion, to provide clients with a gradual transition from routers to the new switched networking technologies of ATM and LAN switching. CiscoFusion allowed users to take advantage of both routing and switching techniques. As part of this architecture, several new switching products were introduced in March 1994, including the ATM Interface Processor and the Catalyst FDDI-to-Ethernet LAN switch. The latter was the first new product of the Workgroup Businesses Unit since the acquisition of Crescendo.

During this time, Cisco moved its headquarters from one end of Silicon Valley to the other, from Menlo Park to a newly constructed office building complex in San Jose, California. The growing size of the company had necessitated larger office space. The company's workforce had grown from 1,451 in July 1993 to 2,262 in July 1994, as Cisco hired talent from smaller, struggling networking companies which were laying off personnel. In 1994, Cisco topped $1 billion in sales, ending the year on July 31, 1994, with $1.24 billion in net sales, a 92 percent increase over the previous year, and $314.9 million in net income, 83 percent more than in 1993. Later in 1994, in October, Cisco completed two more acquisitions of firms involved in the switching sector. It spent $240 million for Kalpana, Inc., a maker of Ethernet switching products; and $120 million for LightStream Corp., which was involved in ATM switching and Ethernet switching and routing.

ASTOUNDING GROWTH UNDER JOHN CHAMBERS STARTING IN 1995

In January 1995 John T. Chambers was named CEO of Cisco, with Morgridge becoming chairman and Valentine vice-chairman. Chambers, who had previous stints at IBM and Wang Laboratories before joining Cisco in 1991, stepped up the company's acquisition pace to keep ahead of its rivals and to fill in gaps in its product line, aiming to provide one-stop networking shopping to its customers. The company completed 11 acquisitions in 1995 and 1996, including Grand Junction, Inc., maker of Fast Ethernet and Ethernet switching products, purchased for $400 million in September 1995; and Granite Systems Inc., a maker of high-speed Gigabit Ethernet switches, bought for $220 million in September 1996.

The largest deal during this period, however, was that of StrataCom, Inc., a $4.67 billion acquisition completed in April 1996. StrataCom was a leading supplier of ATM and Frame Relay WAN switching equipment capable of handling voice, data, and video. The addition of Frame Relay switching products to the Cisco portfolio was particularly important as that technology was being rapidly adopted by telecommunications companies needing to increase the capacity of their networks. The deal was also a key step in Cisco's attempt to move beyond its core customer area of "enterprise" customers (large corporations, government agencies, utilities, and educational institutions) into the area of telecommunications access providers, an area in which it faced entrenched and formidable competition in the form of such giants as Alcatel, Lucent Technologies Inc., and Nortel Networks Corporation.

Cisco continued its blistering acquisitions pace in 1997 and 1998, completing 15 more deals. The largest of these was the April 1998 purchase of NetSpeed, Inc., a specialist in digital subscriber line (DSL) equipment, an emerging technology providing homes and small offices with high-speed access to the Internet via existing telephone lines. Another emerging networking technology was that of voice-over-IP (Internet Protocol), which essentially enables the routing of telephone calls over the Internet. The acquisitions of LightSpeed International, Inc. in April 1998 and Selsius Systems, Inc. in November 1998 helped Cisco gain a significant presence in the Internet telephony sector. The areas of DSL and voice-over-IP provided additional examples of Cisco's strategy of acquiring its way into emerging networking sectors.

By the late 1990s Cisco Systems was the undisputed king of the networking world. In July 1998 the company's market capitalization surpassed the $100 billion mark, just 12 years after its initial public offering, a time frame believed to be a record for achieving that level. Revenues reached $12.15 billion by 1999, a more than sixfold increase over the 1995 result of $1.98 billion. During 1999 Cisco became even more acquisitive, snatching up an additional 17 companies, in the process gaining presences in two more emerging areas: fiber-optic networking and wireless networking. Several fiber-optic companies were acquired, including start-up Cerent Corporation, which was purchased for about $7.2 billion in the company's largest acquisition yet. Fiber-optic networks were particularly being built by telecommunications firms aiming to take advantage of their capacity for handling massive quantities of voice, video, and data, making Cisco's entry into this segment of vital importance.

In late 1999 Cisco announced that it would acquire the fiber-optic telecommunications equipment business of Italy's Pirelli S.p.A. for about $2.2 billion, gaining Pirelli gear that takes a beam of light and breaks it into as many as 128 "colors," each of which can carry a separate stream of voice, data, or video. Cisco's key wireless acquisition also came in late 1999 with the announcement of the $800 million purchase of Aironet Wireless Communications, Inc., maker of equipment that creates LANs without wires in small and medium-sized businesses. The technology was also expected to be transferred to the home environment, where Cisco aimed to capture what was predicted to be an area of rapid early 21st century growth: the networked home.

During 1999 Cisco also acquired GeoTel Communications Corp., a maker of software for routing telephone calls, for about $1.9 billion.

By early 2000, following 1999's frenzied bull market in high-tech stocks, Cisco's market value surpassed $450 billion, making it the third most valuable company in the world, behind Microsoft and General Electric Company (for a brief period in late March, Cisco actually ranked as the most valuable company in the world, with a total market capitalization of $555 billion). Revenues were soaring, as were earnings, which reached $906 million for the second quarter of the 2000 fiscal year alone. Rather than slowing it down, Chambers planned to increase the company's acquisition pace, with the addition of as many as 25 companies during 2000. Through acquisitions and strategic alliances with such industry giants as Microsoft, Hewlett-Packard Company, and Intel Corporation, Chambers aimed to increase Cisco Systems' revenues to $50 billion by 2005.

TRANSFORMATION IN EARLY 2000S

Chambers only made it halfway toward his financial goal by 2005, but the fact that Cisco doubled its revenue volume during the first part of the decade represented a remarkable achievement considering the prevailing conditions in the technology sector. Chambers, described as irrepressibly optimistic and relentlessly upbeat by industry observers, was slow to react to what became the most severe downturn in the history of the industry. Rivals Lucent Technologies and Gateway, Inc., among others, slashed overhead and trimmed their operations as market conditions soured, but Chambers remained sanguine until he was forced to recognize the severity of the situation. During a two-week trip abroad in March 2001, he met with numerous customers, hearing from each that spending was to be drastically reduced in the coming months. Chambers returned home and began what he referred to as "the most challenging time in my business career," in a November 24, 2003 interview with *Business Week*. He laid off 8,500 workers, nearly one-fifth of Cisco's payroll, and implemented sweeping changes throughout the company, reigning in the freewheeling attitude toward expansion that had led to the acquisition of 73 companies between 1993 and 2000 and replacing it with discipline, order, and restraint. "Process was a dirty word at Cisco, including for the CEO," Chambers conceded in his interview with *Business Week*.

Although Chambers admitted he was late in recognizing the seriousness of the situation, his actions ensured that further layoffs were not needed. The company, adhering to a more austere, focused strategy, made great gains as conditions in the technology sector began to improve. Between 2001 and 2003, Cisco's share of the $92 billion communications-equipment market increased from 10 percent to 16 percent, the biggest increase in the company's history. Significantly, the return of favorable economic conditions did not signal the end of wholesale changes at Cisco. Chambers began steering Cisco in a new direction following the downturn in the technology sector, opening a new avenue of growth for the company to exploit in the years ahead.

Throughout its development, Cisco had shied from entering the consumer market, preferring the stability and relatively higher profit margins enjoyed by selling networking equipment to corporations and communications providers. In 2003, Chambers began to change tack, beginning with the purchase of Linksys Group, a manufacturer of wireless routers for consumers. The foray proved successful, encouraging Chambers, who was back to his ebullient self, to delve deeper into the consumer market. In July 2005, he purchased a manufacturer of networked DVD players named KISS Technology, a small acquisition that served as a stepping stone for a massive acquisition announced later in the year. In November 2005, Cisco announced it was acquiring Scientific-Atlanta, Inc., a Lawrenceville, Georgia, manufacturer of cable television set-top boxes. Cisco agreed to pay $6.9 billion for Scientific-Atlanta, which generated $1.9 billion in revenue in 2005, using the purchase to complete what industry insiders referred to as the "quadruple play" package. Cable and telephone companies were interested in providing a bundle of services to their customers, a package of converged networks that included broadband Internet access, Internet-based telephone service, wireless calling, and video services such as video-on-demand. Cisco was well equipped to provide the first three types of services, but it lacked the ability to provide anything substantial in the video realm. The purchase of Scientific-Atlanta gave Chambers quadruple play capabilities, opening a new, vast market for the company. "Once you add video," Chambers explained in a November 21, 2005 interview with *Business Week Online*, "not just in products, but in being able to integrate them all together, that gives us leadership that is very, very unique."

As Cisco prepared to enter what was being billed as the "bundle wars," the company stood poised to reap the benefits of Chambers bold move.

Heather Behn Hedden
Updated, David E. Salamie; Jeffrey L. Covell

PRINCIPAL SUBSIDIARIES

Cisco Systems Canada Limited; Cisco Systems Europe, S.A.R.L. (France); Cisco Systems Import/Export Corporation (U.S. Virgin Islands); Cisco Systems Belgium, S.A.; Cisco Systems Limited (U.K.); Cisco Systems Australia PTY. Limited; Nihon Cisco Systems, K.K. (Japan); Cisco Systems de Mexico, S.A. de C.V.; Cisco Systems New Zealand Limited; Cisco Systems (HK) Limited (Hong Kong); Cisco Systems GmbH (Germany); Cisco Systems (Italy) Srl; Cisco Systems GmbH (Austria); Cisco do Brasil Ltda. (Brazil); Cisco Systems (Korea) Ltd.; VZ, Cisco Systems, C.A. (Venezuela); Cisco Systems South Africa (Pty) Ltd.; Cisco Systems Sweden Aktiebolag; Cisco Systems (Switzerland) AG; Cisco Systems Capital, B.V.; Cisco Systems International Netherlands, B.V.; Cisco Systems Czech Republic, s.r.o.; Cisco Systems Spain, S.L.; Cisco Systems Argentina S.A.; Cisco Systems Chile, S.A.; Cisco Sistemas de Redes S.A. (Costa Rica); Cisco Systems Malaysia, Sdn. Bhd.; Cisco Systems (USA) Pte. Ltd., Singapore; Cisco Systems Thailand, Ltd.; Cisco Systems Peru, S.A.; Cisco Systems Greece, S.A.; Cisco Systems Poland, Sp. zo.o; Cisco Systems Israel, Ltd.; Cisco Systems Internetworking Iletsim Hizmetlieri Ltd. Sirketi (Turkey); Cisco Systems (India), Ltd.; Cisco Systems Capital Corp.; Cisco Systems (Taiwan), Ltd.; Cisco Systems (Colombia), Ltda.; Cisco Technology, Inc.; Cisco Systems Sales & Service, Inc.; Cisco Systems Co. (Canada); Telebit Corporation; Cisco Systems Danmark AS (Denmark); Cisco Systems Norway AS; Cisco Systems Hungary, Ltd.; Cisco Systems Management B.V.; Cisco Systems (Puerto Rico) Corp.; Cisco Systems Finland Oy; Cisco Systems (China) Networking Technologies Ltd.; Cisco Systems Romania SRL; Cisco Systems Croatia Ltd. for Trade; Cisco Systems Slovakia, spol. sr.o; Latitude Communications Pte. Ltd. (Singapore); Protego Networks LLC; Radiata, Inc.; Telebit Corporation; Topspin Communications LLC.

PRINCIPAL COMPETITORS

ADC Telecommunications, Inc.; Alcatel; Cabletron Systems, Inc.; Compaq Computer Corporation; D-Link Corporation; ECI Telecom Ltd.; Fujitsu Limited; Hewlett-Packard Company; Intel Corporation; International Business Machines Corporation; Juniper

Networks, Inc.; Kingston Technology Company; Lucent Technologies Inc.; Madge Networks N.V.; Microsoft Corporation; Motorola, Inc.; MRV Communications, Inc.; NEC Corporation; Network Associates, Inc.; Newbridge Networks Corporation; Nokia Corporation; Nortel Networks Corporation; Novell, Inc.; Sterling Software, Inc.; Telefonaktiebolaget LM Ericsson; 3Com Corporation.

FURTHER READING

Baker, Stephen, "Cisco's Telecom Two-Step in Europe," *Business Week* (international edition), October 11, 1999.

Baum, Geoff, "John Chambers," *Forbes* ASAP, February 23, 1998, pp. 52-53+.

Burrows, Peter, "Cisco's Comeback, " *Business Week,* November 24, 2003, p. 116.

Byrne, John A., "The Corporation of the Future," *Business Week,* August 31, 1998, pp. 102+.

Carlsen, Clifford, "Rolling on the Info Superhighway," *San Francisco Business Times,* August 20, 1993, p. 6A.

Carroll, Paul B., "Cisco Systems Will Acquire StrataCom, Computer Switch Maker, for $4 Billion," *Wall Street Journal,* April 23, 1996, p. A3.

"Cisco's Bold New TV Bet," *Business Week Online,* November 21, 2005.

Clark, Don, "Cisco Is Buying GeoTel for $1.92 Billion in Stock," *Wall Street Journal,* April 14, 1999, p. A3.

Daly, James, "John Chambers: The Art of the Deal," *Business 2.0,* October 1999.

Deagon, Brian, "High-Tech Industry Returns to Mergers As Growth Strategy," *Investor's Business Daily,* November 30, 2005, p. A4.

Donnelly, George, "Acquiring Minds: Cisco and Lucent Buy into the Telecom Revolution with Strategies That Clash and Converge," *CFO Magazine,* September 1999.

Emigh, Jacqueline, "Cisco Unveils ATM Interfacing Router," *Telephony,* February 1, 1993, pp. 24+.

Goldblatt, Henry, "Cisco's Secrets," *Fortune,* November 8, 1999, pp. 177-78+.

Gomes, Lee, "Cisco Tops $100 Billion in Market Capital," *Wall Street Journal,* July 20, 1998, p. B5.

Hutheesing, Nikhil, and Jeffrey Young, "Curse of the Market Leader," *Forbes,* July 29, 1996, pp. 78+.

Ingram, Matthew, "Cisco's Purchase of TV Box Maker Either Bold or Desperate," *New Zealand Herald,* December 6, 2005.

Kupfer, Andrew, "The Real King of the Internet," *Fortune,* September 7, 1998, pp. 84-86+.

Mardesich, Jodi, "Cisco's Plan to Pop Up in Your Home," *Fortune,* February 1, 1999, pp. 119-20.

Maurer, Harry, "Cisco Dials Scientific-Atlanta," *Business Week,* December 5, 2005, p. 32.

Mullaney, Timothy J., "Cisco: Paging Dr. Info Tech," *Business Week,* July 11, 2005, p. 78.

Musich, Paula, "Cisco Chief Plots Router Course: Outlines Plans for ATM Technology," *PC Week,* September 13, 1993, pp. 49+.

———, "Cisco Revamps Router Strategy: Shifts Product, Distribution Tactics for Maturing Market," *PC Week,* November 22, 1993, p. 123.

———, "Cisco, Wellfleet Ride Router Market to Success," *PC Week,* December 14, 1992, pp. 163+.

Osterland, Andrew, "No Kidding. Cisco Isn't Done Yet," *Financial World,* January 21, 1997, pp. 62-64, 66.

Pitta, Julie, "Long Distance Relationship," *Forbes,* March 16, 1992, pp. 136+.

Poe, Robert, "Cisco Strikes the Mother Lode with New Router," *America's Network,* June 15, 2004, p. 8.

Reinhardt, Andy, "Meet Mr. Internet," *Business Week,* September 13, 1999, pp. 128-31+.

Reinhardt, Andy, Peter Burrows, and Amy Barrett, "Cisco Crunch Time for a High-Tech Wiz," *Business Week,* April 28, 1997, pp. 80+.

Schlender, Brent, "Computing's Next Superpower," *Fortune,* May 12, 1997, pp. 88-90+.

Schonfeld, Erick, "Cisco and the Kids: Are They As Scary As They Look?," *Fortune,* April 14, 1997, pp. 200-02.

Thurm, Scott, "Cisco to Acquire Networking Firm Cerent," *Wall Street Journal,* August 26, 1999, p. A3.

———, "For Cisco, Focus on Small Companies Pays Off," *Wall Street Journal,* May 27, 1999, p. B8.

———, "Joining the Fold: Under Cisco's System, Mergers Usually Work; That Defies the Odds," *Wall Street Journal,* March 1, 2000, pp. A1, A12.

Thurm, Scott, and Deborah Ball, "Cisco to Buy a Pirelli Unit for $2 Billion," *Wall Street Journal,* December 20, 1999, p. A3.

Tully, Shawn, "How Cisco Mastered the Net," *Fortune,* August 17, 1998, pp. 207-08, 210.

Coachmen Industries, Inc.

—■—

2831 Dexter Drive
Elkhart, Indiana 46514
U.S.A.
Telephone: (574) 262-0123
Fax: (574) 262-8823
Web site: http://www.coachmen.com

Public Company
Incorporated: 1964
Employees: 4,416
Sales: $865.1 million (2004)
Stock Exchanges: New York
Ticker Symbol: COA
NAIC: 336213 Motor Home Manufacturing

■ ■ ■

Coachmen Industries, Inc., based in Elkhart, Indiana, is one of the nation's leading recreational vehicles (RVs) manufacturers, and is also involved in the modular housing industry. The public company, listed on the New York Stock Exchange, is composed of seven main subsidiaries. The cornerstone is Coachmen Recreational Vehicle Company, which has been manufacturing motorhomes and travel trailers since the early 1960s. Georgie Boy Manufacturing, L.L.C. concentrates on Class A motorhomes, and Viking Recreational Vehicles, L.L.C. offers lightweight, folding camping trailers. An offshoot of Viking, Prodesign Products, L.L.C., produces a wide variety of fiberglass and thermoformed plastic items used in the RV as well as automotive, marine, heavy truck, and medical industries, including raised roofs, shower pans, storage boxes, and medical trays. Coachmen's modular home business is conducted through three subsidiaries. All American Homes, L.L.C. produces homes in its Kansas and Colorado plants that range from 900-square-foot ranch homes to 3,000-square-foot two-story colonial models. Mod-U-Kraf Homes, L.L.C. is a Virginia company that makes ranch, Cape Cod, and two-story homes 1,200 to more than 4,000 square feet in size. Miller Building Systems, Inc. focuses on pre-engineered metal buildings for telecommunications and other commercial uses.

ORIGINS DATING TO THE EARLY 1960S

Coachmen's home of Elkhart, Indiana long ago claimed the title of RV capital of the United States and became the rightful location for the RV Museum and Hall of Fame. In the early 1930s Wilbur Schult, a native of Elkhart, attended the World's Fair, where he saw a homemade trailer and was inspired to build his own and in the process launched the town's RV industry. Coachmen was begun in 1964 by three tight-knit brothers from the Elkhart area: Claude, Thomas, and Keith Corson. Claude, re-garded as the idea man between the three, was credited with the thought of putting a 5,000-square-foot building they owned in Middlebury, Indiana, to use by going into the travel trailer business. Keith was put in charge of production, and Tom, who quit his job at an Indiana investment firm to join his brothers, became the man responsible for finance and marketing.

In the first year of operation, Coachmen produced a dozen travel trailers as well as 80 truck caps and a single truck camper. It was a modest beginning, but a beginning nonetheless, and the company moved beyond camping trailers to include motorhomes.

Coachmen not only survived the 1960s, it found a way to set itself apart from the competition by introducing what it called the "buck stops here" warranty. At the time, RV manufacturers offered a warranty only on what they actually constructed. As a result, if customers had a problem with a component, such as a refrigerator or stove, they had to deal directly with the individual supplier, with whom they carried little weight. Coachmen removed the inconvenience by taking responsibility for everything included in their products. The company became the one who dealt with the component supplier, and because of the amount of business they offered, they were better able to gain satisfaction. It was an idea that proved popular with customers and was eventually adopted industrywide.

Coachmen began to grow steadily. In 1968 it acquired Viking Boat Company, which produced boats, but in the early 1970s would begin to manufacture fold-down camping trailers as well. Trailer production was moved to Michigan and in 1976 the Viking Recreation Vehicle division was formed. Coachmen continued to run the Viking Boat Company as a separate unit until it was sold in 1982 to Murray Chris-Craft. Also during its first 20 years of existence, Coachmen attempted to diversify into aircraft parts and made an early stab at manufactured housing. Both failed, and in 1978 Coachmen closed its only manufactured housing plant after a decade of trying because Tom Corson believed that the operation was too small to compete effectively. He would not stay out of the business for long, however.

GOING PUBLIC IN THE LATE 1960S

In 1969 Coachmen went public to fuel further growth. In July 1969 it completed a pair of acquisitions: Space Age Camper and Enterprises Inc. One of the Corson brothers, Claude, soon left. Forever restless, he quit in 1970 to pursue other business ideas. Keith at the age of 46 would leave for similar reasons a dozen years later, telling the *New York Times* in 1982, "I've been pretty much in the same job for 18 years and decided it was time to take a look at things." He would eventually return and serve as Coachmen's president until his retirement in 2000.

Coachmen enjoyed strong growth through much of the 1970s. It gained a listing on the American Stock Exchange in 1972, and used its increased leverage to complete several acquisitions. In 1974 Coachmen added Flannigan Industries, Inc. and Elkhart-based Lux Co., Inc. Fan Coaches Co. Inc. of La Grange, Indiana was bought in 1978 to fill in the low end of Coachmen's RV lines, followed later in the year by the acquisition of Sportscoach Corp. of America, operating out of California, a major market for RV sales but one in which Coachmen had always been weak. It was also in 1978 that Coachmen moved from the American Stock Exchange to the New York Stock Exchange.

Coachmen's momentum was blunted by poor economic conditions in 1979, when fuel shortages led to high gasoline prices, making such heavy gas users as RVs less attractive to the buying public. Moreover, high interest rates further dampened consumer interest. As a result, by 1982 about half of RV manufacturers were put out of business. To hang on until a recovery mounted, Coachmen was forced to shutter five plants. It lost money in both 1979 and 1980 before returning to the black in 1981 when it recorded a net profit of $2.9 million.

MEMBERSHIP IN *FORTUNE* 500 IN THE 1980S

With business back on track in the early 1980s, Tom Corson looked to grow again. Viking added a new line of truck campers in 1981, and Coachmen opened a new plant in Angel, Oregon. Corson also resumed his diversification efforts. In November 1980 Coachmen acquired C/P Products Corp. to build a major RV parts-and-accessories business, including thousands of items, such as sun roofs and tire carriers. It also provided a hedge against a poor economy, when RV owners might be reluctant to buy a new vehicle but were increasingly interested in fixing up what they already owned. Corson also reentered the modular home business, acquiring

KEY DATES

1964:	The company is founded by three Corson brothers.
1969:	Coachmen is taken public.
1978:	Stock is listed on the New York Stock Exchange.
1984:	Coachmen is listed among the Fortune 500.
1997:	Cofounder Tom Corson is succeeded as chairman and CEO by daughter Claire Skinner.
2000:	Mod-U-Kraf Homes and Miller Building Systems are acquired.

Marlette Homes, Inc. and All American Homes, Inc. in 1982, which would become a key element in Coachmen's portfolio of subsidiaries. At this stage, however, the modular home business was barely profitable. Overall, Coachmen's sales reached $263 million in 1982 and soared to $450 million in 1983, placing the company among the prestigious *Fortune* 500.

The good times never proved long-lasting for Coachmen, as it suffered yet another reversal of fortune in the mid-1980s. The company decided to centralize its manufacturing and engineering operations to cut production costs, then reversed field and decided to disperse its plants in order to be closer to its markets, as well as to overcome a problem of all its products starting to look alike. The change in course took about three years longer than anticipated, and as a result engineering costs created a bloated research and development expense. Coachmen also lost money in Texas, where the economy was devastated by a downturn in the oil and gas industry. It finally closed its Texas plant in 1987. Also during this rough patch, Coachmen sold off its parts and accessories businesses:

United Sales of Texas and CoachLite Supply Co. in 1984, and C/P Products in 1985. Business bottomed out by the end of 1987 and Coachmen appeared to be rebounding in 1988 when difficult economic conditions once again took their toll and the company closed the decade with two more losing years, including a net loss of nearly $11.5 million in 1989.

During the first half of the 1990s, Coachmen divested itself of noncore businesses it had ventured into in the 1980s, such as ambulances through the 1986 acquisition of Southern Ambulance Builders, Inc., and tried to narrow its focus to RVs and modular homes. Viking also sold off its truck camper division in the early 1990s. One of the keepers, however, was the $12.8

million 1995 acquisition of Georgie Boy Manufacturing, Inc.

As the economy picked up in the 1990s, modular home sales took on increasing importance for Coachmen. In 1996 All American contributed $98.7 million in sales, or 16 percent of the company's $606.4 million total revenues, and a sizable portion of Coachmen's more than $29.6 million in net income.

In 1997 Corson began thinking about turning over the reins of the business and settled on his daughter, Claire C. Skinner, as his successor. Skinner had first gone to work for her father at the Elkhart plant at the age of nine gathering screws from the floor for reuse at nine cents an hour. By the time she was ready for college, Skinner had no intention of working in the RV field. She attended Southern Methodist University in Dallas, earning a degree in journalism and marketing, but she found she missed the family business and entered into a management training program at Coachmen's Grapevine, Texas office, and soon became familiar with all aspects of the RV industry. Again, she grew disenchanted with the business, and this time left for law school at Notre Dame, followed by two years in Chicago working as an attorney. Her love for the family business was rekindled once more and finally in 1983 she returned and stayed. Three years later she was named president of the company's largest subsidiary, the flagship Coachmen RV unit. By the time her father was ready to step away from the chairmanship and CEO position, Skinner was well seasoned and the perfect choice to succeed her father. Her uncle, Keith Corson, remained on the management team as president and chief operating officer until he retired in 2000.

Coachmen enjoyed a strong 1998, when revenues increased to $756 million, a 14 percent increase over 1997's $661.6 million. Net income showed even greater improvement, from $24.8 million in 1997 to more than $33 million in 1998, a 34 percent increase. The company's prospects also appeared bright. In the short run, the company benefited from a robust economy that spurred sales of both RVs and modular homes, but a longer-term trend was also hopeful: the baby boom generation was beginning to enter into its 50s, the prime demographic for buyers of RVs. As a result, Coachmen and other RV manufacturers expected to enjoy a 20- to 25-year period of high demand.

Coachmen experienced another record-setting year to close out the 1990s, building sales to $847 million, although net income slipped to $29.5 million due to investment in new technology, start-up costs for new production capacity, and some accounting changes. Nevertheless, Coachmen entered the new century on a high note. In 2000 it was once again aggressive on the acquisition front. It used $10 million in stock to acquire Mod-U-Kraf Homes, Inc. in June 2000. Based in Rocky Mount, Virginia, Mod-U-Kraf had been in the modular home business since 1971. Later in 2000 Coachmen paid $27.3 million in cash and the assumption of $16.6 million in liabilities to acquire Miller Building Systems. Also based in Elkhart, the company was founded by Otto Miller, who in 1967 had cofounded Cliff Industries, which grew into one of the country's largest modular home manufacturers. Miller's latest venture now joined forces with Coachmen's All American Homes division, which had become the largest U.S. builder of modular homes. The year 2000 also was marked by an attempted hostile takeover of the company. Thor Industries Inc. of Jackson Center, Ohio, made a nearly $290 million offer for Coachmen in April 2000. The board of directors quickly rejected the bid, calling it inadequate. Thor, which owned 3 percent of Coachmen stock, urged stockholders to withhold votes for the company's board at the annual shareholders' meeting the following month, but the board remained intact and the Thor threat dissipated.

RV sales had generally proven to provide an early warning sign of economic downturns. The recession of the early 2000s was no exception, as Coachmen experienced a significant drop in revenues to $710 million, especially in the fourth quarter when sales fell off 30 percent from 1999, from $206.7 million to $144.1 million. As a result, net income for the year plummeted to just $2.2 million. To weather these difficult times, Coachmen was quick to take steps to minimize the damage, lessons learned from previous down cycles. Primarily, payroll was cut and production facilities were consolidated. In addition, Coachmen eliminated the few sidelines in which it participated other than RV manufacturing and modular homes. It exited the van conversion business by selling Coachmen Automotive, the furniture industry with the sale of the Lux Company, and RV retailing by shutting down four RV dealerships, although two locations were retained for support purposes and research and development efforts.

With the full force of the recession now being felt, Coachmen could not avoid losing money in 2001, but the company was able to return to profitability in 2002,

netting $9.9 million on sales of $665.2 million. Coachmen had not turned the corner completely, however. In 2003 it experienced an up-and-down year. In the end, sales increased to $711.1 million but net income slipped to $7.4 million. Business was much better in 2004, when the company posted record sales of more than $865.1 million, to go with net income of $15.3 million, the company's best year since 1999. With the demographics still favoring it, Coachmen appeared well positioned now to enjoy a long stretch of success.

Ed Dinger

PRINCIPAL SUBSIDIARIES

Coachmen Recreational Vehicle Company, L.L.C.; Georgie Boy Manufacturing, L.L.C.; Viking Recreational Vehicles, L.L.C.; Prodesign Products, L.L.C.; All American Homes, L.L.C.; Miller Building Systems; Mod-U-Kraf Homes, L.L.C.

PRINCIPAL COMPETITORS

Fleetwood Enterprises Inc.; Thor Industries, Inc.; Winnebago Industries, Inc.

FURTHER READING

"Coachmen: Riding High in a Roaring RV Market," *Business Week,* January 16, 1984, p. 108.

Cuff, Daniel F., "One of the Founders Resigns at Coachmen," *New York Times,* May 19, 1982.

Heikens, Norm, "Elkhart, Ind., Modular Building Manufacturers to Unite," *Indianapolis Star,* August 25, 2000.

Hornaday, Bill W., "CEO of Indiana-Based Coachmen Industries Stays Level-Headed About Compensation," *Indianapolis Star,* May 24, 2004.

Magary, Don, "Coachmen's Tom Corson," *RV News,* June 1996.

Martin, Jennifer, "Elkhart, Ind.-Based RV Maker's Shareholders Vote to Keep Board of Directors," *Indianapolis Star,* May 5, 2000.

Taub, Stephen, "Coachmen Makes a U-Turn," *Financial World,* July 12, 1988, p. 11.

Cochlear Ltd.

14 Mars Road
Lane Cove, New South Wales 2066
Australia
Telephone: (+61) 2 9428 6555
Toll Free: (800) 620 929
Fax: (+61) 2 9428 6353
Web site: http://www.cochlear.com.au

Public Company
Incorporated: 1982
Employees: 700
Sales: AUD 344.9 million (2004)
Stock Exchanges: Australian
Ticker Symbol: COH
NAIC: 339113 Surgical Appliance and Supplies
Manufacturing

■ ■ ■

Cochlear Ltd. develops implantable hearing devices that help the hearing impaired hear. The devices use a combination receiver and stimulator implanted in the ear that works in concert with a microphone and a speech processor to give deaf patients the ability to perceive most environmental sounds and speech. Cochlear Ltd. dominates the market for implantable hearing devices, controlling an estimated 70 percent of the global market. More than 60,000 patients have had the implant surgery successfully performed. The company's implants, which are branded under the "Nucleus" name, are sold throughout the world through a network of Cochlear Ltd. subsidiaries and offices. Cochlear Ltd. also

develops implants for individuals who are deaf in one ear, marketing the implants, which are anchored to the patient's bone, under the "Baha" name.

ORIGINS

Graeme Clark devoted his life's work to discovering a way to help the profoundly deaf hear, a mission that owed its inspiration to his deaf father. Clark, born and raised in Australia, witnessed firsthand the difficulties endured by those who lived in silence, an empathy that drove him to pursue an academic career aimed at finding a solution to the affliction. In 1967, while working as a research professor at the University of Melbourne, Clark came across a scientific paper detailing the use of electrical stimulation to help a deaf person receive hearing sensations. The idea was purely theoretical, one that drew its fair share of critics who believed the concept was too dangerous or too complicated, or both. Undaunted by consensus, Clark, who would become regarded as the father of the "Bionic Ear," pressed ahead with his research, devoting years to exploring the practicality of an implantable hearing aid.

Clark's research centered on the cochlea, the spiral-shaped cavity of the inner ear that resembled a snail shell. The cochlea, or inner ear, contained tens of thousands of fragile hair cells essential for hearing, nerve endings that Clark hoped to stimulate electronically with an implantable device. Although his belief in developing a cochlear implant put him on the fringe of the scientific and medical community, Clark was nonetheless highly regarded, winning an appointment to chair the Department of Otolaryngology at the

University of Melbourne in 1970. (Otolaryngology is the branch of medicine that deals with the diagnosis and treatment of diseases of the ear, nose, and throat.)

Funding for his research work on cochlear implants was hard to come by, however. He and his staff were forced to seek donations from the public and solicit financial help from organizations such as the Lions Club and Rotary Club. He labored for a decade with meager resources, at last receiving a research grant in 1977 for "The Development of a Hearing Prosthesis."

With the money from the grant, Clark neared completion of his scientific work, determined to find a way to place an electrode securely within the inner ear. A trip to Minnamurra Beach in New South Wales provided the inspiration for solving the difficult problem. Clark found a small Turban-shell on the beach and began experimenting with a blade of grass. The following year, Clark was ready to unveil his creation, a debut that made medical history.

In 1978, the first prototype prosthesis was implanted by Clark and colleagues at The Royal Victorian Eye and Ear Hospital. Rod Saunders, a 71-year-old who had lost his hearing at age 46, was the first recipient of the multi-channel cochlear implant, the first medical device to restore brain function prosthetically. Several weeks after the procedure, the implant was successfully "switched on," when all ten electrodes began working. Saunders recognized the tune "Waltzing Matilda," and when Australia's national anthem was played at the demonstration, he delighted the crowd by standing at attention. During a May 27, 2004 interview aired on the Australian Broadcasting Corporation, Clark recalled his reaction to Saunders regaining his hearing. "When he heard speech, I knew that all our hard work had been successful," Clark recounted. "It was one of the most wonderful experiences of my life. I was so overcome, I went into the next-door laboratory and did what's not very Australian—I burst into tears of joy."

Clark's hard work represented one of the most significant medical breakthroughs of the century. His system consisted of three principal parts: a receiver/stimulator, a microphone, and a speech processor. The microphone picked up speech and other sounds, which the speech processor coded into electrical signals. Unlike a conventional hearing aid, which just made sounds louder, Clark's speech processor selected certain important information in the speech signal and produced a pattern of electrical pulses that were sent to the receiver/stimulator implanted in the cochlea. The receiver/stimulator contained tiny electrodes—a pair of electrodes represented a "channel"—that conveyed the information to the brain via auditory nerves in the inner ear, enabling the recipient to perceive most environmental sounds and speech.

The ten-channel implant that allowed Rod Saunders to hear silenced Clark's skeptics and opened the doors to funding that supported further development of the cochlear implant. In 1979, a group of medical equipment manufacturers operating under the name Nucleus expressed its interest in commercially developing Clark's inner ear implant, interest that was also expressed by the Australian government, which awarded a public interest grant to fund the commercial development of Clark's Bionic Ear. Once criticized to the point of ridicule for his belief that a cochlear implant was possible, Clark no longer had to rely on donations from outside the medical community, as the remarkable success of his work attracted the attention and the support of those willing to invest in making the cochlear implant available worldwide. Cochlear Ltd., formed in 1982, became the corporate entity through which the collaborative effort of Clark, Nucleus, and the Australian government sought to bring the cochlear implant to market.

EXPANSION IN THE 1980S

Cochlear Ltd. led a high-profile existence during its first decade in business, as word of the company's namesake product spread beyond Australia's borders and captured the attention of the worldwide medical community. After George Watson became the second recipient of Clark's implant in 1980, the work of turning the prototype into a commercially available device began in earnest. In 1982, the year Cochlear Ltd. was formed, the first device for clinical trial worldwide was implanted at the Royal Victorian Eye and Ear Hospital, the Nucleus CI22, a 22-channel implant. The international trial proved to be successful, completing an important step before approval from the U.S. Food and Drug Administration (FDA) was obtained. In preparation for the implant's approval by the U.S. regulatory body, Cochlear Ltd. established a physical presence in the United

States. In 1984, a small team of Cochlear Ltd. officials opened a subsidiary named Cochlear Corp. in Englewood, Colorado, just outside of Denver. The year also marked the first time the cochlear implant surgery was performed in Europe.

Nearly 20 years after Clark's research began, a major milestone was reached. In 1985, the FDA approved the Nucleus multi-channel cochlear implant for profoundly hearing impaired adults. (Profoundly hearing impaired, or PHI, was classified as hearing loss of more than 90 decibels, which meant a PHI classified individual had no useful hearing. Severely hearing impaired, SHI, reflected a hearing loss of between 70 decibels and 90 decibels, leaving the individual with some residual hearing.)

Obtaining FDA clearance, the first of its kind, represented a major step toward Clark's goal of distributing his implants worldwide, essentially assuring that regulatory bodies in other countries also would approve the use of the implants. Officials at Cochlear Ltd. did not celebrate the occasion for long, however. The year also included the first use of the implants on

children. At the Royal Victorian Eye and Ear Hospital, the proving ground for Clark's work, the first two research pediatric cochlear implant procedures took place, setting in motion clinical trials for children in the United States by the following year.

Acceptance of Clark's work was broadening with each passing month during the 1980s, and Cochlear Ltd. fleshed out its physical presence to keep pace with the growing demand for the revolutionary device. In 1987, the year the Australian Postal Service issued a "Bionic Ear Stamp," the company established its European headquarters in Basel, Switzerland, giving it offices to serve what would be one of its most important financial markets. In 1989, an Asian headquarters was established in Tokyo, four years after the first Nucleus cochlear implant surgery was performed in Japan.

Cochlear Ltd. began the 1990s with another achievement to celebrate, an event that confirmed the company as the preeminent concern serving the deaf worldwide. In 1990, the FDA approved the Nucleus Cochlear Implant System for children aged two to 17 years, the first cochlear implant to be approved for pediatric use by any regulatory body. Clearance by the FDA, as it had five years earlier, conferred market supremacy to Cochlear Ltd., giving the company an enormously significant stamp of approval that helped it maintain its lead over rival companies who had developed their own versions of Clark's cochlear implant. As the regulatory bodies in other countries gave their nod to Cochlear Ltd.'s implants, the number of recipients mushroomed, increasing at a fantastic rate. By 1992, the 5,000th Nucleus implant surgery had been performed. In 1994, the number of Nucleus recipients reached 10,000. The following year, after more than demonstrating itself to be a commercially viable company, Cochlear Ltd. completed its initial public offering of stock, debuting on the Australian Stock Exchange.

Cochlear Ltd.'s activities, from the moment of its creation, were directed toward building a worldwide infrastructure and making improvements in the design of the company's implant system. The exponential increase in the number of Nucleus recipients testified to the company's worldwide reach, while progress on the engineering front occurred on a consistent basis, yielding smaller, more effective implant systems. One improvement of note was achieved in 1998, a year in which the 20,000th person received a Nucleus cochlear implant. Cochlear Ltd. unveiled the ESPrit in 1998, the first multi-channel speech processor worn entirely behind the ear, an innovation that eliminated the long cables required by previous speech processors that were attached to the recipient's belt. Other advances in design and technology followed, but the company's most significant progress at the dawn of the 21st century was achieved in bringing different types of implants to market. The diversification strengthened Cochlear Ltd.'s already stalwart market position, making for a successful completion to the company's pioneering first 25 years in business.

ACQUISITIONS IN THE 21ST CENTURY

The new century began with a nod of approval from the FDA, giving Cochlear Ltd. a new type of implant to offer to the hearing impaired. In 2000, the Nucleus 24 Multichannel Auditory Brainstem Implant (ABI) was approved for use in teenagers and adults with neurofibromatosis Type II, a neurological disease that causes tumor growth along nerves in the spine and neck. The removal of the tumors often required part of the auditory nerve to be removed as well, causing total loss of hearing. Cochlear Ltd.'s ABI restored some of the hearing lost by placing a receiver deep in the brain. The company's efforts to develop devices complementary to its cochlear implant also led to a partnership with Switzerland-based Phonak Group, a leading maker of hearing devices, to create an implantable hearing aid for those with less severe hearing loss, but Cochlear Ltd.'s greatest achievement in this direction occurred via an acquisition in early 2005. In March, the company acquired Sweden-based Entific Medical Systems for AUD 195 million. Entific developed a bone-anchored hearing implant system for individuals with malformed ear canals who were deaf in one ear. The company's implant system, marketed under the name "Baha," offered a hearing solution to an estimated 250,000 people worldwide.

As Cochlear Ltd. looked to the future, the company maintained a formidable lead over competitors. The company controlled an estimated 70 percent of the worldwide market for hearing device implants, holding sway over rivals Advanced Bionics Corp., based in California, and Austria-based Med-El Corp. In the years ahead, the company was expecting to achieve earnings growth of more than 20 percent annually, as it applied its technological expertise to next-generation implants and pursued Clark's mission of enabling the deaf to hear.

Jeffrey L. Covell

PRINCIPAL SUBSIDIARIES

Cochlear Corporation; Cochlear AG (Switzerland); Cochlear Europe Limited (U.K.); Cochlear GmbH (Germany); Cochlear France S.A.S.; Cochlear Benelux N.V. (Belgium); Cochlear Italia S.R.L. (Italy); Cochlear Sweden Holdings; Nihon Cochlear Co. Limited (Japan); Cochlear (HK) Limited (Hong Kong); Cochlear (HK) Limited (China).

PRINCIPAL COMPETITORS

Advanced Bionics Corporation; MED-EL Corporation; Medtronic, Inc.

FURTHER READING

Austin, Marsha, "FDA Approves Englewood, Colo.-Based Firm's Hearing Device for the Deaf," *Denver Post,* October 24, 2000.

Eakin, Jan, "Rival's Pain Assures Cochlear a Better Hearing," *Australasian Business Intelligence,* October 23, 2002.

Einhorn, Bruce, "Listen: The Sound of Hope," *Business Week,* November 14, 2005, p. 68.

"Electronic Brain Implant Helps Patients Regain Hearing After Cranial Nerve Surgery," *FDA Consumer,* January 2001, p. 7.

"FDA Approves Marketing of Cochlear Implant for Children," *FDA Consumer,* October 1990, p. 2.

Foley, Brett, "Cochlear Must Hatch Turnaround Strategy," *Australasian Business Intelligence,* April 29, 2004.

Greenblat, Eli, "Cochlear Expands Reach with Entific Buy," *Australasian Business Intelligence,* March 6, 2005.

Matterson, Helen, "Cochlear Hears Rumblings in US," *Australasian Business Intelligence,* September 22, 2004.

CommScope, Inc.

1100 CommScope Place SE
Hickory, North Carolina 28603
U.S.A.
Telephone: (828) 324-2200
Toll Free: (800) 982-1708
Fax: (828) 328-3400
Web site: http://www.commscope.com

Public Company
Incorporated: 1997
Employees: 4,300
Sales: $1.15 billion (2004)
Stock Exchanges: New York
Ticker Symbol: CTV
NAIC: 334220 Radio and Television Broadcasting and Wireless Communications Equipment Manufacturing

■ ■ ■

CommScope, Inc. is a Hickory, North Carolina-based company that designs and manufactures coaxial and fiber optic cable and related products used by cable and satellite television providers and other applications, including data networking, Internet access, wireless communications, and telephony. The company also specializes in making products that bridge the gap between older analog cabling that still dominates the world's communications infrastructure with newer digital networks, thus becoming a specialist in what is called the "last mile," the direct link to the customer, who gains a powerful digital connection to a predominantly analog world. CommScope products are covered by more than 1,100 global patents and patent applications. The company maintains a dozen manufacturing facilities around the world, including four plants in North Carolina as well as domestic plants in Alabama, Nebraska, and Nevada. International production facilities are located in Belgium, Ireland, Brazil, Australia, and the People's Republic of China. CommScope is a public company listed on the New York Stock Exchange.

BEGINNINGS DATING TO THE 1950S

The origins of CommScope date to 1953 and the start of Superior Cable Corporation in Hickory, North Carolina. The man behind the founding of Superior was Harry G. Burd, who had spent his career in the wire and cable business. After he retired as the vice-president of sales for Anaconda Wire and Cable in the early 1950s, he served as a consultant for Ansonia Electrical Company, a leader in the development of plastic-covered telephone wire, which was on the cutting edge of technology compared with the lead-sheathed, paper-insulated cable that was in use. Burd conducted a market study to determine the demand for plastic-covered telephone cable, but Ansonia ignored his advice to build a cable plant in the Southeast, at a time when the southernmost cable plant was located in Trenton, New Jersey.

Burd decided to build a southern cable plant himself and took on a partner and chief engineer named Jim Robb, whom he met when Robb worked for the Rural Electrification Administration, the federal program to

COMPANY PERSPECTIVES

CommScope combines technical expertise and proprietary technology with global manufacturing capability to provide customers with high-performance wired or wireless cabling solutions.

wire rural America. Because they did not want to be too far removed from the major markets of Pennsylvania, Ohio, and New York, they agreed on a general location of a cable plant in Virginia or the Carolinas. Because textile work was similar in nature to cable making, involving winding and unwinding processes and an emphasis on tension, they began looking to North Carolina. After considering several towns in the state, they settled on Hickory, primarily because the town was eager to attract new industry and offered financial assistance in buying the land and building the plant. Thus Superior Cable Corporation was incorporated in 1953 and in July 1954 it began producing the new plastic-covered telephone wire.

Very soon after its launch, Superior began its own research and development efforts. By mid-1955 it was producing Super Splice sleeves, developed by Robb, that facilitated the joining of plastic-sheathed wires. The product was quickly accepted by the industry and opened the door for Superior to sell its wire to companies such as Southern Bell Company in Atlanta. Superior also found an innovative way to help in determining the length of buried telephone cable, critical because the cable had to be connected to devices called loading coils at precise intervals in order to improve transmission. Superior marked the footage on the outside of its cable, starting at zero. A simple calculation was now all that was required to determine cabling distances and marked cable quickly became a standard. Superior was overwhelmed with orders.

It was also in the 1950s that Superior began to produce Community Antenna Television (CATV) coaxial cable that would find an increasing market as the cable television industry began to take shape. In 1961 Superior created a separate division called Communications Systems Construction Planning Engineering, which it wanted to market as Comm/Tech, but a Chicago company had already trademarked the name. Taking the suggestion of Superior's advertising manager, the unit took the name of Comm/Scope. It developed complete CATV systems and in 1964 the CommScope name was applied to Superior's new coaxial cable.

CHANGES IN OWNERSHIP: 1960S-90S

In the mid-1960s Superior caught the attention of Continental Telephone Company, a rising force in telecommunications that had started out by combining a number of small independent midwestern telephone companies. After acquiring a large California company, Continental contacted Robb, who by this time was serving as Superior's president, and proposed that Continental, which was by far Superior's largest customer, should acquire Superior, making it the core of its manufacturing operation. It was an arrangement that served the interest of both parties, and so in March 1967 Continental acquired Superior, and CommScope became a Continental division.

CommScope remained part of Continental for nearly a decade, and then in 1975 Continental put Superior on the block. It was sold piecemeal, with Alcatel and Corning ultimately ending up with two of the pieces. A management team led by Frank Drendel acquired CommScope. Drendel grew up in the Midwest where he became familiar with coaxial cable by installing television cable for a Continental cable subsidiary, DeKalb-Ogle, while attending Northern Illinois University. His education was interrupted by a stint in the Army during the Vietnam War, and after finishing his degree in 1970 he went to work for Continental's cable subsidiary, Continental Transmission, one of the top cable TV operators in the country. He quickly made chief executive officer but the Federal Communications Commission soon required telephone companies to divest their co-located cable properties and Time Warner bought the property. Drendel went to work as a vice-president of operations for another cable operator, Cypress Communications, only to have Time Warner buy that business as well. He next took an assignment with Continental and moved to Hickory to lead Superior's Comm/Scope unit. When Superior began selling off units shortly after he arrived, he decided to buy the CommScope product line, engineering the first leveraged buyout in the cable business.

Under Continental, CommScope had lost its edge competing in a crowded field of suppliers, doing just $10 million in annual sales. Moreover, cable system construction had fallen off dramatically. Drendel told *CED* in a 2002 profile, "There were 15 companies in our business and we were ranked 15th, but I was young, and I was sure you couldn't keep cable down." He explained there was an additional factor: "I needed a damn job!" Drendel and Jerald Leonhardt, who became CommScope's chief financial officer, along with a group of Hickory-area investors, acquired CommScope in 1976. Four years later Drendel hired another key

KEY DATES

1953: Superior Cable Corporation is founded in Hickory, North Carolina.

1964: Superior begins marketing coaxial cable under the CommScope name.

1967: Continental Telephone acquires Superior and CommScope becomes a division.

1976: CommScope is bought by a management-led investor group.

1977: CommScope is merged with Valtec.

1980: Valtec is acquired by M/A-COM.

1986: CommScope is sold to General Instrument Corporation.

1988: CommScope is taken private.

1990: General Instrument again acquires the company.

1997: General Instrument spins off CommScope as an independent, public company.

2004: Connectivity Solutions is acquired.

member of his management team: Brian Garrett, CommScope's president and chief operating officer.

As Drendel had foreseen, the cable industry could not be kept down, and he and his team began to build CommScope into a major cable suppler. Drendel also anticipated the future importance of fiber optics to the cable industry, and in 1977 merged CommScope with Valtec, Inc., a leader in fiber optic technology. Drendel's foresight would also be evident in the role he played in the creation of C-SPAN, the cable channel devoted to televising Congress, as well as the later movement to make television a digital medium.

In 1980 Valtec sold out to M/A-Com Inc. in order to strengthen both of its units, and CommScope now became part of M/A-Com's Cable Home Group and Drendel became a vice-chairman of the parent company while continuing to head CommScope. In 1983 CommScope established its Network Cable division to become involved in making cable for computer networks and other specialized wire markets. CommScope swapped corporate parents in 1986 when the Cable Home Group was sold to General Instrument Corporation. Now a General Instrument division, CommScope continued to be led by Drendel, who became chairman and CEO of the subsidiary. Two years later, in 1988, Drendel bought back a significant interest in CommScope once again, leading another group of investors, but its independence would last just two years. In 1990, General Instrument,

which itself was being bought by New York's Forstmann, Little & Co., reacquired CommScope.

1997 SPINOFF AND POSITIONING FOR A NEW CENTURY

In the mid-1990s CommScope enjoyed a major growth spurt, gaining a global market share for coaxial cable of more than 50 percent, and building annual sales to $572.2 million in 1996. To meet rising demand it acquired plants in Elm City, North Carolina, and Scottsboro, Alabama. Fortunately, CommScope was not wholly dependent on the cable television industry, which was struggling in the mid-1990s. In 1997 General Instrument decided to split into three separate, publicly traded companies, a move intended, according to the *New York Times,* "to distance itself from the stumbling cable industry." The largest of the three companies, accounting for two-thirds of General Instrument's revenues, would be NextLevel Systems, supplier of set-top boxes, cable modems, and other products for voice, data, and video networks. Its creation was intended to sever General Instrument's association with the cable industry, which had proven to be a damper on growth. The second spinoff was General Semiconductor, maker of electronic components, and the third was CommScope, which would once again attempt to fly solo.

The CommScope spinoff was completed in July 1997. Its shares were distributed to General Instrument shareholders and then listed on the New York Stock Exchange. The company got off to a modest start. Sales improved to $599 million in 1997 but tailed off to $572 million in 1998 due to a drop in international sales caused by an economic crisis in Asia. Nevertheless, CommScope expanded its operations in 1998 by acquiring a coaxial cable manufacturing plant in Seneffe, Belgium. Then, in 1999, the company launched a five-year, $135 million expansion in the Hickory area to beef up its fiber optic and wireless manufacturing and research and development capabilities. The first step was the $7 million purchase of a former printing plant in Newton, North Carolina. Business also improved dramatically in 1999. Sales surged to $749 million, and operating income increased from $72.8 million in 1998 to $117.5 million, as gains were made by all three of CommScope's principal product categories: CATV/Video, wireless and other telecom, and local area networks (LANs).

CommScope appeared well positioned for the new century, but it would have to contend with a severe downturn in the telecommunications industry and a recession. The year 2000 started out well and resulted in CommScope realizing record results by year's end. Sales increased 27 percent to $950 million and earnings improved by 22 percent. The company also bought a coaxial cable plant in Brazil, which would allow it to begin supplying the South American market in 2001. It expanded its business in the western portion of the United States by opening a manufacturing and distribution facility in Nevada, as well as beginning construction on a new corporate headquarters in Hickory. But amid these positive developments uncertainty was brewing in the telecommunications industry, which would suffer through a very difficult 2001. CommScope experienced a 22 percent drop in sales and earnings were cut by more than two-thirds, but it still fared better than most companies in the industry and took advantage of the situation to buy Lucent Technologies' fiber optic cable unit in a joint venture with Japan's Furukawa Electric Co.

CommScope hoped to be ready to benefit from an expected rebound in telecommunications, but conditions only grew worse with the meltdown of the dotcom sector, and this time even CommScope was not left unscathed. Sales fell below $600 million and the company lost $67.2 million, its first losing year; the price of its stock plummeted as well. In order to cut costs, CommScope was forced to slash its workforce at the end of the year. Tough times persisted in 2003, as sales slipped further, totaling $573 million for the year, and the company lost another $71 million.

CommScope had always taken a long-term approach and just as Drendel had believed cable TV could not be kept down in the 1970s, the company was now confident that the widespread demand for broadband communications would bode well for its strategy of producing the products to achieve the "last mile" connections to customers. That belief would begin to be borne out in 2004 when CommScope rebounded with a record year. A major factor was the acquisition of Connectivity Solutions from Avaya, Inc. for $250 million in cash plus stock and the assumption of liabilities. Connectivity Solutions was a major brand in structured cabling for LAN solutions and greatly enhanced CommScope's global position in the enterprise LAN business. CommScope finished 2004 with sales of $1.15 billion and net income of nearly $75.8 million. The company had to contend with rising costs of materials and continued to maintain a short leash on costs, but enjoyed another strong year in 2005. The company also opened its first broadband cable manufacturing facility, located in the People's Republic of China, the first step in a new global manufacturing initiative that would cut costs and solidify CommScope's position in the world market.

Ed Dinger

PRINCIPAL SUBSIDIARIES

CommScope, Inc. of North Carolina; CommScope Nevada, L.L.C.; CommScope Optical Technologies, Inc.; CommScope International Holdings, L.L.C.

PRINCIPAL COMPETITORS

Amphenol Corporation; Corning Incorporated; General Cable Corporation.

FURTHER READING

Beck, Kirsten, and Will Workman, "Man in the Middle: Frank Drendel Supplies the Cable in Cable Television and the Cement in the Information Highway," *CED,* November 2002.

Boraks, David, "AT&T Deal Could Boost Hickory, N.C., Cable Maker's Sales," *Charlotte Observer,* January 19, 1999.

Dickson, Glen, "GI Goes Under the Knife," *Broadcasting & Cable,* January 13, 1997, p. 132.

Landler, Mark, "General Instrument to Split into 4 Public Companies," *New York Times,* January 8, 1997, p. D7.

Martin, Edward, "The Cable Guy," *Business North Carolina,* December 2000, p. 22.

Shain, Andrew, "Firm with Half the World Market in Coaxial Cable to Go It Alone," *Charlotte Observer,* January 8, 1997.

Companhia de Tecidos Norte de Minas - Coteminas

Av. Magalhães Pinto 4000
Montes Claros, Minas Gerais 39404-166
Brazil
Telephone: (55) (38) 3215-7777
Fax: (55) (38) 3217-1633
Web site: http://www.coteminas.com.br

Public Company
Founded: 1969
Employees: 12,576
Sales: BRL 1.42 billion ($485.32 million) (2004)
Stock Exchanges: São Paulo OTC
Ticker Symbol: CTNM3, CTNM4; CDDMY; CTMD Y
NAIC: 313111 Yarn Spinning Mills; 313113 Thread Mills; 313210 Broadwoven Fabric Mills; 313311 Broadwoven Fabric Finishing Mills; 313312 Textile and Fabric Finishing (Except Broadwoven Fabric) Mills; 314129 Other Household Textile Product Mills; 315119 Other Hosiery and Sock Mills; 315221 Men's and Boys' Cut and Sew Underwear and Nightwear Manufacturing; 315223 Men's and Boys' Cut and Sew Shirt (Except Workshirt) Manufacturing; 315231 Women's and Girls' Cut and Sew Lingerie, Loungewear and Nightwear Manufacturing; 315232 Women's and Girls' Cut and Sew Blouse and Shirt Manufacturing

∎ ∎ ∎

Companhia de Tecidos Norte de Minas - Coteminas is the parent company of a group that collectively forms Brazil's second largest manufacturer of textiles and ready-to-wear clothing. The company's 11 factories turn out such textile products as polyester threads and cotton-made fabrics, yarn, and knitwear, home products including towels and bed linens, and clothing including T-shirts, underwear, and bathrobes. Coteminas has merged with Springs Industries Inc. of Fort Mill, South Carolina, to form Springs Global S.A., a Brazil-based company, but both companies retain some independent operations.

JOSÉ ALENCAR'S BOOTSTRAP CAPITALISM: 1945-92

Coteminas was founded by José Alencar Gomes da Silva, one of 15 children of a man who owned a small store. He went to work at the age of 14 as a clerk in a fabric shop. With his earnings he bought a food wagon that he operated in a hotel in Muriaé, the nearest city to his birthplace in the state of Minas Gerais, sleeping on a cot at the end of a corridor to save money. In 1949, at the age of 18, he borrowed money from his older brother Geraldo to open A Queimadeira, a fabric shop in Caratinga, Minas Gerais. Next, he manufactured and sold cheap cloths. After Geraldo died, he assumed control of A União dos Cometas, a textile wholesaler that Geraldo had founded with three friends. Gomes da Silva bought out these partners and, in 1965, founded Wembley S.A. (originally Wembley Roupas S.A.), a clothing firm that was to become the holding company for Coteminas (and that owned 24 percent of Coteminas's stock in 2005).

Gomes da Silva founded Coteminas in Montes Claros, Minas Gerais, in 1969, in partnership with Luiz de Paula Ferreira. The company's first mill, opened in 1976, was financed with funds from the state government. The same agency also financed the birth of other textile producers that would later become part of the Coteminas group, such as Coteminas do Nordeste S.A. (Cotene); Cotenor S.A. Indústria Têxtil; and Companhia Central Brasileira de Acabamentos Têxteis (Cebractex). Coteminas first made yarn and gray (unfinished) fabric. Although, in 1990, the Brazilian government liberalized its trade policies, allowing the entrance of cheap clothing and textiles from Far East firms, Coteminas remained competitive by modernizing its spinning, weaving, preparation, dyeing, and finishing operations, which enabled it to turn out consumer goods as well as yarn and gray fabric.

ADDING CLOTHING TO TEXTILES: 1992-97

Between 1985 and 1994, the net worth of Coteminas increased from $40 million to $492 million. The enterprise became a publicly owned company in 1992, when it collected $14 million for shares sold. Two years later, the company collected another $53 million from the sale of shares. In that year, 1994, Coteminas earned $46.6 million on sales of $164 million, and by mid-1995 the company's shares of stock had increased sevenfold in value since it first went public three years earlier. Coteminas also established a new woven-textile operation named Embratex from its own resources, building a plant in Campina Grande in the state of Paraíba.

Another new enterprise founded by Gomes da Silva in 1994 was Wentex Têxtil S.A., whose role was to manufacture T-shirts and sell them for as little as 75 cents each, cheaper even than the Chinese were charging on average. He took in $35 million from the sale of Wentex shares but kept total control of the voting capital. By this time, however, Gomes da Silva, usually referred to simply as José Alencar, was devoting himself chiefly to politics, having run unsuccessfully the previous year for governor of Minas Gerais. His 30-year-old son, Josué Christiano, was put in charge of Wentex, which, like Coteminas, was based in Montes Claros. Trained in Brazil as a civil engineer, Josué Christiano had next been an honor student at Vanderbilt University's graduate school of business.

Wentex had one advantage over the Chinese competition: the cost of energy in Brazil was less than half of that in China. Josué Christiano also kept costs down by purchasing the raw material, cotton, directly, without dealing through middlemen. Manufacturing expenses were reduced by totally mechanizing nine of the 14 steps to completion. Soon Wentex was turning out 62 million T-shirts a year, two a minute, or four times quicker than the national average. The cost of production to make this cotton-and-polyester-blend shirt was 11 cents cheaper than the average Chinese price.

Before the end of 1995 Josué Christiano obtained BRL 60 million (about $62 million) from investors for a new Wentex factory to be built in Campina Grande to produce more than 82 million T-shirts and 24,000 metric tons of knitwear per year. By late 1997 Josué Christiano was Brazil's leading T-shirt manufacturer, producing not only for Coteminas under the brand name Jamm but also for rival Companhia Hering under the latter's own brand name. During the year Cotene, Cotenor, Cebractex, Wentex, and Empresa Brasileira de Fiação e Tecidos S.A. (Embratex) were merged into Coteminas. Also that year, Coteminas acquired a number of brands, including Artex, Santista, Calfet, and Garcia, and formed a joint venture with Artex, principally to produce and distribute bed linen and terrycloth towels.

Up to this time Coteminas had been mainly producing private-label goods for big chains such as the Brazilian subsidiaries of Carrefour S.A. and Wal-Mart Stores Inc., but now it was beginning to market its own brands of socks, towels, handkerchiefs, and bed linens. Coteminas capped off an extremely busy 1997 by selling shares, both in Brazil and abroad. When the offering closed on December 3, the company had raised $96.6 million, of which some 35 percent came from international investors, including the pension funds of California teachers and General Motors Corp. workers.

To this point Coteminas's advantages were clear and well understood. All its factories and mills were located in regions that received government development aid. The factories in Paraíba benefited from the poverty of Brazil's northeast that permitted the enterprise to pay wages far below the average in the more prosperous south of the country. The cost of electricity in the northeast was also lower. Moreover, in partnership with other enterprises, Coteminas was constructing a thermoelectric power plant in Natal, Rio Grande do Norte, and a hydroelectric dam in Minas Gerais, to lower its costs even more. But the company's direction toward consumer products required a number of changes in its marketing and administration.

THE SPRINGS CONNECTION: 2001-05

The devaluation of Brazil's unit of currency, the real, in early 1999 made Coteminas's products cheaper abroad and gave impetus to an effort to grow by exporting, although initially exports formed only a small part of its revenues. In 2001 Coteminas signed an agreement with Springs Industries Inc. of Fort Mill, South Carolina, to manufacture bedding and bath products for Springs. These products were to be marketed under the Springs name or as part of its private-label programs. Coteminas now had 11 plants in four states, including what it claimed to be the world's largest open-end yarn factory. The company was producing 88,000 metric tons of material a year, compared to only 8,000 in 1991. By taking Coteminas public instead of borrowing funds for expansion at high interest rates, the Gomes da Silva family had reduced its stake in the company to less than 50 percent, but it retained 70 percent ownership in terms of voting rights. Its debt-to-equity ratio was an enviably low 14 percent, with most of the debt linked to a long-term loan from the International Finance Corporation.

Now recognized throughout Brazil as a self-made rags-to-riches tycoon, José Alencar was elected vice-president of the nation in 2002, as the running mate of the new president, Luiz Inácio Lula da Silva. This had drawbacks as well as advantages. From Rio de Janeiro, Larry Rohter of the *New York Times* reported, "Mr. da Silva's running mate, Vice President-elect José Alencar,

has acknowledged that his textile company, the country's second largest, is being investigated on charges of fraud in connection with cotton acquisitions at government-sponsored auctions. Mr. Alencar's son, who runs the company, has admitted manipulating cotton prices to qualify for government subsidies but denies that the action was illegal."

Coteminas bought out its partner, Artex, in the Toalia joint venture in 2001 and merged Toalia S.A. Indústria Têxtil into its own operations. In 2003 Coteminas's factories accounted for one-eighth of Brazil's consumption of natural fibers. The United States was its chief export market. Coteminas's bath-ensemble and bedsheet exports to the United States were being provided to Springs exclusively, but it was selling beach towels and bathrobes there directly. Its 2004 net sales of BRL 1.42 billion ($485.32 million, at the average currency rate for the year) was second to that of Vicunha Têxtil S.A. among Brazilian manufacturers of clothing and textiles, but Coteminas had the highest net profit, and the value of its real estate was also higher than its competitors. Of its output of 121,313 metric tons of material, threads, yarn, and woven fabric accounted for 53 percent; home products for 45 percent; and clothing (T-shirts, underwear, and socks) for the remaining 2 percent. Also in 2004, Coteminas acquired majority control of Companhia Tecidos Santanense, a textile company with $110 million in annual revenue, and opened a towel factory in La Banda, Santiago del Estero, Argentina.

Four of Coteminas's 11 factories were in Montes Claros. Two were in Natal and Campina Grande. The other three were in Macaba, Rio Grande do Norte; João Pessoa, Paraíba; and Blumenau, Santa Catarina. These plants were accounting for one-eighth of Brazil's consumption of cotton. Under the Artex brand, Coteminas was turning out bathrobes, bath towels, and bedspreads, both all-cotton and blends, bearing the Disney label and Disney figures. It was also producing cotton and cotton-polyester bedsheets and pillowcases and cotton tablecloths. Santista-brand goods were cotton and cotton-polyester bath towels, cotton and cotton-polyester sheets, pillowcases, and bedspreads, and cotton-polyester tablecloths. Cotton bath towels, cotton-polyester bedsheets and bedspreads, and cotton-polyester throw pillows were being produced and marketed under the Garcia label. Cotton bath towels and cotton-polyester bedsheets and pillowcases also bore the Calfat label.

Coteminas signed, in October 2005, a merger pact with Springs Industries to create what the two companies said would be the world's largest home-textiles producer. The new entity, Springs Global S.A., was to be based in Brazil, with Josué Christiano and his Springs counterpart serving as co-chief executive officers. Coteminas would receive a 50 percent stake in Springs Global, either directly or through a holding company of which it would be a wholly owned subsidiary. A portion of the business of both companies would remain outside the new entity, however, including Coteminas's denim- and twill-fabrics businesses. Coteminas would choose four of the eight members of the Springs Global board. Although Springs Industries had more than twice the number of plants as Coteminas, a wider range of products, and nearly four times the annual revenue, it was suffering from problems of productivity and was seeking to reduce its U.S. operations. Springs Industries had already moved most of its towel and bedding production to Coteminas.

Robert Halasz

PRINCIPAL SUBSIDIARIES

Companhia de Tecidos Norte de Minas - Coteminas (Argentina); Coteminas International Ltd.; Fiação Canada S.A.; Wentex International Ltd.

PRINCIPAL COMPETITORS

Grendene S.A.; Companhia Hering; São Paulo Alpargatas S.A.; Vicunha Têxtil S.A.

FURTHER READING

Bueno, Denise, "Este tigre cresceu no nordeste," *Exame,* March 12, 1997, pp. 40-41.

"Coteminas Kicks Off Foreign Campaign," *Corporate Finance,* February 1998, p. 12.

"Coteminas: The Big Boy," *Home Textiles Today,* Brazil supplement, September 8, 2003, p. 4.

Furtado, José Maria, "Mas como é mesmo o nome dela?" *Exame,* June 21, 1995, pp. 57-58.

Galuppo, Ricaro, "Quem faz o pano faz a roupa," *Exame,* January 14, 1998, pp. 35-39.

Hogsett, Don, "Springs Global to Be Public," *Home Textiles Today,* November 7, 2005, pp. 1, 23.

"International Spin," *Business Latin America,* July 1, 2002, p. 6.

Lazaro, Marvin, "Springs Extends Reach with Brazilian Deal," *Home Textiles Today,* August 20, 2001, pp. 1, 23.

Onaga, Marcelo, "A vez da Coteminas," *Exame,* October 26, 2005, p. 115.

Rohter, Larry, "Brazil's New Cabinet Offers Surprises, and Draws Criticism," *New York Times,* December 22, 2002, p. 12.

"Small Is Difficult," *Economist,* December 6, 1997, Latin America supplement, p. 19.

Smith, Geri, et al., "The New Latin Corporation," *Business Week,* October 27, 1997, p. 82.

"Springs Will Not Abandon U.S.," *Home Textiles Today,* October 31, 2005, pp. 1, 23.

CoolSavings, Inc.

—————■—————

360 N. Michigan Ave., Ste. 1900
Chicago, Illinois 60601
U.S.A.
Telephone: (312) 224-5000
Fax: (312) 224-5001
Web site: http://www.coolsavings.com

Public Company
Incorporated: 1997
Employees: 133
Sales: $38.3 million (2004)
Stock Exchanges: OTC
Ticker Symbol: CSAV
NAIC: 454110 Electronic Shopping and Mail-Order
Houses; 541613 Marketing Consulting Services

■ ■ ■

CoolSavings, Inc. offers interactive marketing services to publishers and advertisers. The company matches marketers with their target consumers using a unique process of collecting detailed, permission-based information, including demographics and personal interests. CoolSavings' broad distribution network includes four "marketing channels," CoolSavings.com, an Internet coupon site; CoolSavings Marketing Network, an Internet-based promotions distribution network; Technology Licensing; and Direct Mail.

CoolSavings also provides "lead generation, e-mail, coupon and loyalty programs across its extensive network of company-owned Branded Web Properties and top partner sites."

In the fall of 2005 the company announced plans to become a private subsidiary under parent Landmark Communications, Inc.

SEARCHING FOR WAYS TO SAVE; EVOLVING TECHNOLOGY: 1894-1997

Since early days, people have used coupons. In 1894, Asa Candler, the druggist who purchased the Coca-Cola recipe for $2,300, issued the first recorded American coupon, a hand-written piece of paper that offered customers a free glass of the fountain drink. In 1895, C. W. Post introduced the first grocery coupon. The coupon offered a discount of one cent towards the new cereal Grape Nuts. The Great Depression made coupons even more popular throughout the 1930s as people searched for new ways to save money. In 1957, the Nielsen Coupon Clearing House was opened, becoming the first clearinghouse devoted to coupon redemption and creating a new industry. By 1965, about one half of Americans used coupons and ten years later, over 60 percent clipped them. But with the birth of the Internet and new technology, coupon clipping would take on a whole new shape.

In 1995, a new company, CoolSavings, Inc., was born with the hopes of rising to the needs of consumers and retailers alike. The mission was simple: provide consumers with a convenient way to find a deal, and match those consumers with retailers who would offer what they wanted. But in the world of business, most things are not simple and the question would prove to be age-old: how would people handle change?

In just three short years, the mission seemed as though it was coming to fruition when the company was able to report having more than 900,000 consumers in its database. The problem, however, was that retailers were nervous. The Internet was still relatively new and there were no real projections for the success of Internet promotions. Although CoolSavings was offering a unique marketing strategy, some retailers decided to try their hands at launching their own web sites.

Consumers were slow to sign up. The company offered the convenience of online, printable coupons, but it also required people to download specific software in order to use the site. In addition, in order to download a coupon, it was mandatory to enter specific demographics, including name, age, and occupation. To many, this felt like an invasion of privacy.

A NEW PATENT AND A NEW SPOKESPERSON: 1998-99

CoolSavings' answer to the issue of privacy was a patent. In 1998, the company received a patent for its revolutionary tool that would calm consumers and thrill retailers.

CoolSavings announced that it had received a U.S. patent for compiling demographics and providing information to retailers, yet retaining the privacy of consumers. "The patented CoolSavings program acts as a target marketing tool for advertisers and a privacy advocate for consumers," said Steven M. Golden, the company's then-chairman and CEO. In addition to being a unique direct marketing tool, the patent also acted as a significant roadblock to any future competition for CoolSavings. To protect its patent and to block future competitors from opening their doors, the company began filing patent-infringement lawsuits against nine of its rivals.

Though the company had built a database of over four million shoppers by 1999, it felt the need to move to a new level in brand-building. In October, it announced the launch of a $15 million offline advertising campaign, featuring its piggy bank logo in the role of CEO of the company. "Today, we are launching the next phase in our brand-building efforts with an aggressive advertising campaign designed to distinguish us as one of the leading destinations for consumer savings offering a strong value proposition and a unique brand icon," said Steven M. Golden. By using the pink piggy bank in a talking, moving role, CoolSavings became one of the first Internet companies to use a talking icon to identify its brand to consumers.

A QUICKLY PROGRESSING COMPANY: 2000

In 2000, American shoppers celebrated the Third National Coupon Month and CoolSavings celebrated having built a database of over eight million permission-based members. Parents took part in Coupon Month by teaching their children how to save money with coupons. Meanwhile, CoolSavings steadily moved its way up the industry ladder by announcing an initial public offering. Some 3.3 million shares of common stock were offered. According to the *IPO Reporter*, CoolSavings' net proceeds would be about $45.8 million and would be used for general corporate purposes.

Indeed, as the year progressed, 2000 proved to be a successful one for CoolSavings. In July, the company was ranked the Internet's number one coupon site, nearly doubling its nearest competitor, according to a new reporting system created by Media Metrix, an Internet and digital media measurement company. Based on the same company's findings, CoolSavings was also rated as one of the 50 most visited sites on the Internet.

Along with these successes, the company was able to settle "seven of the nine suits it filed, with most of the defendants agreeing to pay royalty fees to use the patent," according to *Crain's Chicago Business*. The company said the deals were based on putting aside ongoing legal battles and focusing on just competing in the business world. Though the more than two years of bickering were over between CoolSavings and the majority of its competitors, the defendants in two other suits were filing countersuits foreshadowing possible challenges for the company.

Also in 2000, CoolSavings managed to report record financial results for the second quarter. Net revenue increased 324 percent to $8.9 million from $2.1 million. Steven Golden commented, "We have successfully developed a complete infrastructure of e-marketing solutions to help advertisers incentivize customers from acquisition to loyalty, while reducing costs along the way."

KEY DATES

1995: CoolSavings, Inc. is launched.
1998: The company is granted a patent for unique privacy-retaining tool.
2000: CoolSavings is rated the number one source for Internet coupons.
2001: The company is delisted from the NASDAQ.
2002: CoolSavings sees record number of new member registrations.
2004: CoolSavings acquires Planet U.
2005: The company launches new FreeStyle Rewards program; announces plans to be taken private.

A ROLLER COASTER YEAR: 2001

The year 2001, however, brought financial woes for CoolSavings as it faced many of the same challenges that other dotcoms were facing. One of these challenges was lack of investor appetite for such companies. The company also began to face mounting losses, declining cash, and a stock price that had not topped $1 since the beginning of the year, threatening possible delisting by the NASDAQ. Adding to CoolSavings' problems, the company's revenue-generating patent came under scrutiny by the U.S. Patent and Trademark Office, a direct result of challenges from two defendants of patent-infringement suits filed by CoolSavings. The two companies, Catalina Marketing Corp. and BrightStreet, Inc., "brought countersuits against the company and petitioned the Patent Office, claiming that CoolSavings' patent is not valid," according to *Crain's Chicago Business*. If CoolSavings lost the patent, it would no longer be able to receive royalties and could face patent-infringement litigation itself, possibly not allowing the company to continue to do business in the same way.

The year did bring several new endeavors. In March, CoolSavings announced a new service for shoppers called CoolShopper. "CoolShopper, [is] a powerful comparison shopping search engine that enables members to identify a comprehensive list of products, brands and merchants," said the company in a news release. The product was fashioned following CoolSavings' continuous goals of providing services to consumers while delivering targeted advertising and incentives for retailers. It was another tool to help consumers make informed shopping decisions, while also giving them more control over their shopping experience. According to Steven M. Golden, "at the same time, CoolShopper will contribute sig-nificant value for our wide range of advertisers by delivering interested, qualified shoppers to their store or site."

Another new endeavor was a joint venture with Time, Inc. called CoolParenting. The venture would allow advertisers to target the specific needs of new parents and children by offering product discounts, samples, and content particularly for them.

In July 2001, Matthew Moog advanced to the role of president and CEO of CoolSavings from his previous posts as president and COO. He had been working in various roles at the company since 1998, including serving as executive vice-president of sales and marketing.

Bad news came for CoolSavings in the fall of 2001 when it received word from the NASDAQ Listing Qualification Panel that it had been delisted from the market. The company had failed to maintain a market valuation of at least $5 million and a bid price of at least $1 per common share for 30 consecutive trading days. The NASDAQ also raised concerns that the company might have violated NASDAQ's voting rights rule.

Though experiencing several challenges, the company continued to look ahead, as Internet coupons grew in popularity with American consumers. According to *Information Week*, online shoppers were attracted to such coupons more than others: "they redeem Web vouchers either online or in stores three times as often as those they receive in the mail or newspapers."

In November 2001, CoolSavings launched new software that would allow advertisers to generate coupons and email them to their customers or place them on their web sites. The new hosting software, called "Coupon Technology Solution," was made available to retailers who wished to broaden their distribution of coupons while keeping closer track of their consumers. This was a huge step for companies who wished to "use online campaigns as testing grounds to target a particular demographic, then hone their direct-mail and other initiatives," said Matthew Moog. Previously the software was only used by CoolSavings' database of households who had to register at the site and download the software in order to get coupons.

NEW TOOLS AND NEW VENTURES: 2002-04

According to *CNN.com*, in 2000 and 2001, "63% of people in the United States used the Internet at least once and many are 'extremely enthusiastic' about it as a tool."

Clearly the popularity of the Internet was constantly increasing, but with the fall of many other dotcom businesses, CoolSavings faced several challenges. But in the spring of 2002, CoolSavings appeared to persist despite tough economic times and the decline of others in its sector. In May, the company announced having over 20 million members in its database of consumers.

Also, Media Metrix reported the company as the 32nd most visited web property on the Internet.

Putting a spin on the "old" way of reaching people, CoolSavings debuted a new Co-Op direct mail marketing program in July. The mailer featured the pink piggy bank icon and was targeted toward registered CoolSavings members who were active shoppers and who had given permission to receive special offers from advertisers. The mailer was preceded by an email that alerted consumers to look for the mailer in their mailbox. Additionally, it was followed by an email that reminded shoppers of the offers they had received.

CoolSavings also declared that it had officially launched the CoolSavings Marketing Network, an Internet distribution network for coupons and samples. The CoolSavings Marketing Network combined the Company's Coupon Technology and its partnerships with top web properties in order to offer consumers even more promotional offers. The company stated that the CoolSavings Marketing Network was the largest distributor of online print-at-home grocery coupons, offering a variety of offers from advertisers such as General Mills, 3M, and Dannon.

In 2003, CoolSavings was able to announce a first in its company history: net income profitability. At the end of the second quarter, the company's financials were looking up, with a net increase in cash for the third consecutive quarter and a 69 percent growth in revenue for the quarter as compared to the same quarter the year before. Again, CoolSavings boasted a membership base that continued to grow, registering nearly two million shoppers in the quarter and recording over 18.5 million member visits.

Though the future was looking brighter, some retailers were expressing mixed thoughts about Internet coupons. In light of some incidents that occurred with shoppers using fraudulent Internet coupons, some supermarkets banned the coupons. CoolSavings urged supermarkets to continue to accept legitimate coupons and reject only coupons for free products, which the company did not support.

In early 2004, as CoolSavings moved out of debt and "into the black," it announced the acquisition of Planet U, a company it had previously sued for patent-infringement. "Planet U's vision was to work with the grocery stores to mine their frequent shopper card databases to deliver personalized rewards based on shop-

pers' past purchases," said research analyst Jim Nail. "Planet U was just too early."

CoolSavings did not disclose the terms of the deal, but did mention that it hoped the acquisition would help evolve the company into more of a loyalty marketing company.

In an era of tired consumers, bombarded with spam and unsolicited calls, and with the increasing popularity of the Do-Not-Call list, it became necessary for advertisers to find new ways to reach shoppers. CoolSavings continued to follow the trends of the times with the announcement of its new Lead Generation Network Services in the fall of 2004. Through these services, advertisers were able to target specific consumers and deliver a variety of offers, such as samples, coupons, travel brochures, and free newsletters. The consumers, with their permission, received information, tailored to their personal needs.

For the quarter ending December 31, 2004, CoolSavings reported record fourth quarter revenues. The company stated that it ended the year strongly due to investments and acquisitions made, as well as new product development. Though the acquisitions made did require a monetary investment, the company noted that those investments helped build a strong foundation for CoolSavings, and would help provide increased revenues and operating margin improvements.

BUILDING ON A STRONG FOUNDATION: 2005

CoolSavings started 2005 with the launch of a new consumer rewards program called FreeStyle Rewards. FreeStyle Rewards was a loyalty program that awarded points to consumers based on dollars spent. In fact, it rewarded one of the highest average points-to-dollar ratios in the industry. The program also answered the demands of consumers for cash rewards, granting them with a Debit MasterCard instead of a Gift Card. CoolSavings cited the program as being an opportunity to provide services to an ever growing group of retailers and consumers.

In the fall of 2005, CoolSavings announced that it would be going private. Its main investor, Landmark Communications, Inc., a private media company, bought out the shares of two other investors, gaining control of 91.7 percent of CoolSavings' stock. Executives at CoolSavings seemed positive about the change, noting that Landmark "does not expect to make any significant changes in CoolSavings management or immediate business strategy."

Going private would save the company about $1 million per year in legal, audit and insurance fees, and would allow the company to focus on building the business as opposed to "public filings and investor calls."

One could not argue with the fact that times had drastically changed since Asa Candler hand-wrote the first coupon. Technology had improved and the birth of the Internet had changed many things, including the way consumers shopped. According to data released by the U.S. Census Bureau, as of 2003, 127 million Americans were using the Internet. At least 54 percent were using the Internet for the purchase of products or services. Naturally, Internet shoppers were always looking for a deal. As a marketing services company, CoolSavings hoped to build on what it had already constructed. Thus far, CoolSavings had proven its ability to be flexible, to bend and evolve with the times. As the company prepared to go private, it could still be expected to serve the ever changing needs of consumers.

Sara Poginy

PRINCIPAL COMPETITORS

Catalina Marketing Corporation; E-centives, Inc.; Life-Minders, Inc.; Mypoints.com, Inc.; Netcentives, Inc.; Yesmail, Inc.

FURTHER READING

Abrams, Rhonda, "A Presence on the Net Is Essential, *AZCentral.com*, November 7, 2005.

Baeb, Eddie, "Internet Coupon Firm's Technology Gets Clipped; Patent Problems Add to CoolSavings' Woes," *Crain's Chicago Business*, March 19, 2001, p. 4.

Beardi, Cara, "CoolSavings Promotes Pink Piggy to 'CEO' Slot: $15 Mil Effort Hits Network TV As Web Site Touts Its Shopping," *Advertising Age*, October 18, 1999, p. 8.

"CoolSavings.com," *Target Marketing*, May 2001, p. 96.

"CoolSavings Granted Patent," *Promo*, August 1998.

"CoolSavings Launches New Lead Generation Network Services," *Business Wire*, August 2, 2004.

Garry, Michael, "Practices Mixed on Internet Coupons," *Supermarket News*, September 15, 2003, p. 47.

Heun, Christopher, "Clipping Coupons Online Just Got Easier—Software Gives Companies More Freedom to Generate Coupons and E-Mail Them to Customers," *Information Week*, November 26, 2001, p. 32.

Rewick, C. J., "Cyber-Coupon Web Site Lets Shoppers Surf for Savings," *Crain's Chicago Business*, June 15, 1998, pp. 3+.

Rose, Barbara, "Chicago-Based Online Marketer CoolSavings Buys Firm It Once Sued," *Chicago Tribune*, February 10, 2004.

Saunders, Christopher, "E-centives, CoolSavings End Patent Battle," *ClickZ Internet Advertising News*, September 29, 2000.

Singh, Shruti Date, "Going Private Saves Firm a Cool $1 Million; CoolSavings Merging with Its Biggest Investor," *Crain's Chicago Business*, September 19, 2005, p. 4.

Stenger, Richard, "Who Should Oversee the Internet? How About Oprah?," *CNN.com*, July 10, 2001.

Wolverton, Troy, "CoolSavings Settles E-Coupon Patent Dispute," *CNET News.com*, July 10, 2000.

Wolverton, Troy, "CoolSavings Settles Patent Suit," *CNET News.com*, December 13, 2000.

Cymer, Inc.

———————■———————

17075 Thornmint Court
San Diego, California 92127
U.S.A.
Telephone: (858) 385-7300
Toll Free: (888) 692-9637
Fax: (858) 385-7100
Web site: http://www.cymer.com

Public Company
Incorporated: 1986 as Cymer Laser Technologies, Inc.
Employees: 770
Sales: $418.0 million (2004)
Stock Exchanges: NASDAQ
Ticker Symbol: CYMI
NAIC: 333298 All Other Industrial Machinery Manufacturing

■ ■ ■

Cymer, Inc. is the leading supplier of excimer lasers, which are used in the manufacture of semiconductors. Excimer lasers deliver deep ultraviolet photolithography light sources in highly narrow bandwidth, enabling complex circuit designs that deliver high processing speeds. Cymer controls more than 90 percent of the worldwide market for excimer lasers, conducting its assembly, integration, and testing activities at a 265,000-square-foot facility in San Diego, California. The company also maintains a refurbishing facility in Korea. Cymer's customers include all three manufacturers of deep ultraviolet photolithography systems, ASML Holding N.V., Canon Inc., Nikon Corp., and numerous semi-

conductor manufacturers, including Advanced Micro Devices, Inc., Intel Corp., Toshiba Corp., and Texas Instruments Inc.

ORIGINS

At one point, when Robert P. Akins and Richard L. Sandstrom reached a crossroads in their careers, they thought about running a hamburger outlet together. It would have been an odd choice for two physicists with Ph.D.s who had just abandoned work on the Strategic Defense Initiative, but for a brief period, while mulling their future over beers at a beach bar named Belly Up, the pair thought about buying a hamburger franchise instead of continuing their development of excimer lasers. Had their discussion reached a different conclusion, Cymer would not have been formed, advances in computer processing power likely would have been stunted, and the Wendy's restaurant chain, having just opened its 3,000th unit, would have gained one more outlet.

Akins and Sandstrom met at the University of California's San Diego campus (UCSD). Akins arrived in 1969 and spent the next five years pursuing studies in two different directions, earning a bachelor's degree in physics and a bachelor's degree in literature. He chose to continue his education in physics, thinking his career opportunities would be greater in the sciences, and, as a graduate student at UCSD, he met Sandstrom, who had earned a bachelor's degree in physics. Akins earned his doctorate degree in optical information processing, a form of computing in which light replaces electricity. Sandstrom concentrated his work on the behavior of laser light as it traveled through the atmosphere.

COMPANY PERSPECTIVES

Virtually every late generation consumer electronic device—whether a PC or laptop, cellular phone, pager, PDA, internet server, modem, appliance or automobile—contains a semiconductor manufactured using a Cymer light source. Today's advanced devices require smaller, faster chips with increased power and functionality, and the chipmakers turn to Cymer to provide the light source critical to producing these chips.

After earning their degrees (Sandstrom, according to Akins, was the more talented scientist of the two), the pair joined a defense contractor based in San Diego named HLX Inc. They spent six years working together at HLX, lending their talents to projects related to laser-induced nuclear fusion, a satellite-to-submarine laser communications link, and the Strategic Defense Initiative. It was heady work, leaving each a bit disillusioned and restless after a half-dozen years. "When the technology starts to get overwhelming," Sandstrom said in a February 24, 1997 interview with *Forbes*, "you want to be a farmer." Akins echoed the sentiment, telling *Forbes*, "We wanted to spend the productive years of our lives doing something more aligned with the real world."

They left HLX and spent several weeks playing frisbee on a beach near Del Mar, California, plotting their next move at the Belly-Up. "It was 1985," Akins noted in his *Forbes* interview, and "fast-food franchises were hot."

Once Akins and Sandstrom shelved plans to buy a Wendy's restaurant, they turned their attention to the high-technology world they left behind, their spirits evidently refreshed. At HLX, they were working with excimer lasers, a type of laser developed by IBM that used a mixture of reactive and inert gases to produce deep ultraviolet light (DUV). Akins and Sandstrom realized that excimer laser technology was not suitable in orbit during the course of their research at HLX, but they believed that there were other applications that might work, a belief that was held by Akins in particular. Sandstrom was recognized as the superior scientist, while Akins was hailed as the visionary, perceiving potential in technology that others did not see. Supported by Akins's vision and Sandstrom's scientific acumen, and little else, Cymer Laser Technologies, Inc. (the name was shortened later) was formed in 1986 to explore the potential of excimer laser technology in commercial applications.

Akins and Sandstrom briefly tried to apply excimer laser technology to the medical device industry before Akins guided the company in the proper direction. The semiconductor industry became the focus of the company's efforts, but it would be years before the two would meet in the marketplace. Cymer was just beginning the long research and development phase of its existence; the semiconductor industry did not yet require the advanced capabilities of excimer laser technology. The demands of semiconductor manufacturing needed to catch up to Akins's vision, and Akins needed to make his vision a reality. "For a long time," Akins said in a December 2, 2002 interview with the *San Diego Business Journal*, Cymer's excimer laser technology "was a solution looking for a problem."

The gap separating the two, a gap that represented the time it would take for Cymer to become a financially healthy enterprise, narrowed as research and development work progressed under Sandstrom's guidance and as Moore's Law proved itself to be an accurate and predictable phenomenon in the semiconductor industry.

In 1965, Gordon Moore, a cofounder of Intel Corporation, was writing an article, titled "Cramming More Components onto Integrated Circuits," when he made the observation that each new generation of memory chips contained roughly twice as much capacity as their predecessors, with 18 to 24 months separating each generation. The observation formed the basis of what became known more than a decade later as Moore's Law, that the number of components on chips roughly doubled at a regular, exponential rate. As Akins and Sandstrom worked on making the performance and stability of their technology suitable for its commercial debut, the concept of exponential increases on the other side of the technological gap worked in their favor. Originally, semiconductor manufacturers used visible light in a manufacturing process called photolithography, the imaging of complex circuit patterns onto chips through camera-like imaging tools known as steppers and scanners. Once a wafer of crystalline silicon was coated with light-sensitive chemicals and put into a stepper, the stepper sent pulses of light through a stencil dictating the circuit pattern. Moore's Law postulated that the complexity of the circuit pattern would increase exponentially over a relatively short, predictable period of time, but the complexity of the pattern depended on the thinness of the circuit lines, which, according to the laws of optics, could be only as thin as the wavelength of light shining through the stencil. Consequently, as engineers tried to squeeze more electronics onto a wafer, increasingly narrower wavelengths were needed. Eventually, Akins realized, semiconductor manufacturers would need the precision of excimer lasers, but as Cymer was

KEY DATES

1986: Cymer is founded.
1988: The company receives $3.2 million in venture capital.
1995: Excimer lasers become the tools of choice in the semiconductor industry.
1996: Cymer completes its initial public offering of stock.
1999: The company controls more than 90 percent of the worldwide market for excimer lasers.
2003: A downturn in the semiconductor industry leads to a $15.4 million loss for the year.
2004: As market conditions improve, financial vitality returns to Cymer; sales eclipse $400 million for the first time in the company's history.

starting out, no one needed light sources as precise as the company's prototype laser.

By the time Cymer was founded, semiconductor manufacturers had stopped using visible light and relied on the shorter wavelengths of invisible ultraviolet light. Cymer's hopes of entering the market rested on the development of its technology and weaning chipmakers off of ultraviolet light emitted by hot mercury gas, the prevailing type of light source used during the late 1980s. The development of its technology, an effort spearheaded by Sandstrom, was forced to subsist on meager financial resources, relying initially on the help of the machine shop at UCSD. The company lacked the capital to have the components of its laser manufactured by others, so Sandstrom and Akins made the components themselves with the lathes and milling machines at their alma mater. "We'd go in on a Saturday morning at 9 a.m. and come out at 7 or 8 p.m. with one set of electrodes," Akins recalled in his February 24, 1997 interview with *Forbes*.

"When it came time to pay for the equipment and materials, the guy who ran the shop told us, 'I'll just keep this thing [the invoice] in the bottom drawer until you guys get the money to pay for it.'"

By the end of 1986, the invoice at the machine shop totaled $250,000, a bill the company was unable to pay until it received its first infusion of capital from outside investors in 1988. The money, $3.2 million invested by a venture capitalist, provided some relief, but additional rounds of financing were sporadic. The company eked by on funds obtained from government grants, investments by foreign companies, and by selling a few lasers for use on pilot projects. Both Akins and Sandstrom took out second mortgages on their homes to keep the company financially alive.

A TURNING POINT IN 1995

The lean times continued into the 1990s, testing the resolve of Akins and Sandstrom. In 1990, the capability of mercury ultraviolet light, with a wavelength of 0.48 micron, looked to be headed toward obsolescence as engineers began designing chips with circuit lines thinner than 0.5 micron, but scientists were able to circumvent the laws of optics, further delaying the need for Cymer's excimer laser technology. By coating wafers with new high-resolution photoreactive chemicals, semiconductor manufacturers were able to etch lines thinner than mercury ultraviolet light's wavelength, pushing the limits of the light down to 0.35 micron, the specification required for advanced chips that would be in use until the late 1990s. Fortunately for Cymer, the company did not have to wait until the 21st century for the market to demand a product on which it had been working since 1986. By 1995, chipmakers realized they soon would need the capabilities of Cymer's technology. Orders for the company's laser, which used a mixture of krypton and fluoride to deliver a 0.25 micron beam, began coming in, pushing revenues for 1995 up to $18 million. Cymer's business began to grow vigorously the following year, when it completed its initial public offering of stock in September. By the end of 1996, after orders increased 350 percent, revenues hit $65 million.

Once the semiconductor industry turned to excimer lasers, Cymer grew at a blistering pace. Equipment suppliers to semiconductor companies such as Intel, NEC, and Motorola desperately needed ultraviolet lasers, and Cymer, one of only three companies in the world capable of making an excimer laser, quickly dominated the market it had helped to create. By the end of the 1990s, the company had installed its 200th DUV excimer laser in Japan, which gave it control of more than 80 percent of the market there. Worldwide, the company maintained an installed base of more than 800 lasers by the end of the decade, a total that amounted to more than a 90 percent share of the total excimer laser market. Cymer's dominance translated into rapid financial growth, lifting sales to $366 million in 2000, more than five times the total collected four years earlier.

INDUSTRYWIDE DOWNTURN AT THE START OF THE 21ST CENTURY

As Cymer entered the 21st century, it maintained its overwhelming control over the global market for excimer lasers, but the early years of the decade brought the company's incredible pace of growth to a halt. The semiconductor industry, a notoriously volatile market, experienced what arguably was the greatest downturn in its history. Companies worldwide felt the pinch of a slumping market, and Cymer was no exception. Between 2000 and 2002, revenues slipped from $366 million to $288 million. Net income during the period plunged from $63 million to $13 million. In 2003, the pattern continued, but with far greater severity. The company lost $15.4 million during the year on sales of $265 million.

As Cymer prepared for its 20th anniversary and the years beyond, the company occupied enviable ground. Its dominant market position began to deliver better financial results once conditions in the semiconductor market improved. In 2004, when refurbishing activities were included for the first time on the company's balance sheet, Cymer generated $418 million in revenue and posted $43 million in net income. The company, in a development agreement with Intel, was busy working on a production-worthy extreme ultraviolet (EUV) source, which was expected to be completed by the end of the decade. In the interim, the company's domination of the market for DUV lasers promised to deliver continued financial growth. The announcement in late 2004 that Coherent, Inc.'s subsidiary, Lambda-Physik, was exiting the excimer laser business in the semiconductor industry made Cymer's already stalwart market position even more formidable. After a decade of development followed by a decade of market supremacy, the Akins-led company promised to play a prominent role in the advances in semiconductor technology for years to come.

Jeffrey L. Covell

PRINCIPAL SUBSIDIARIES

Cymer B.V. (Netherlands); Cymer Japan, Inc.; Cymer Korea, Inc.; Cymer Singapore Pte. Ltd.; Cymer Southeast Asia, Ltd. (Singapore); Cymer Semiconductor Equipment (Shanghai) Co. Ltd. (China).

PRINCIPAL COMPETITORS

Jenoptick Aktiengesellschaft; Gigaphoton, Inc.; Komatsu Ltd.

FURTHER READING

Bengston, Stacey, "Cymer, Inc. Has Announced Appointment of Edward Brown Jr. As Its New President and Chief Operating Officer," *San Diego Business Journal,* September 12, 2005, p. 35.

"Cymer of U.S. Installs 200th DUV Laser in Japan," *AsiaPulse News,* November 23, 1999.

"Cymer Receives First Order from Korean Chip Manufacturer," *AsiaPulse News,* April 24, 2001, p. 648.

Freeman, Mike, "San Diego-Based Laser Maker Due $20 Million in Funding from Intel," *San Diego Union-Tribune,* January 27, 2004.

Gaut, Stephen, "Rancho Bernardo, Calif., Laser Tech Products Firm to Buy Massachusetts Firm," *North County Times,* November 21, 2000.

———, "San Diego-Based Laser Tech Group Plans Office in South Korea," *North County Times,* November 8, 2000.

Graves, Brad, "Laser-Like Vision," *San Diego Business Journal,* December 2, 2002, p. 44.

McHugh, Josh, "Laser Dudes," *Forbes,* February 24, 1997, p. 154.

Phelps, Christi, "Cymer Laser Technologies Closes Deal for $3.2 Million," *San Diego Business Journal,* July 4, 1988, p. 2.

Slavin, Terrence, "Illuminating the Semiconductor Industry," *San Diego Business Journal,* March 27, 2000, p. B4.

Danaher Corporation

2099 Pennsylvania Ave. N.W., 12th Floor
Washington, D.C. 20006-1813
U.S.A.
Telephone: (202) 828-0850
Fax: (202) 828-0860
Web site: http://www.danaher.com

Public Company
Incorporated: 1969 as DMG, Inc.
Employees: 37,000
Sales: $6.89 billion (2004)
Stock Exchanges: New York Pacific
Ticker Symbol: DHR
NAIC: 336399 All Other Motor Vehicle Parts Manufacturing; 326211 Tire Manufacturing (Except Retreading); 334514 Totalizing Fluid Meter and Counting Device Manufacturing

■ ■ ■

Danaher Corporation owns a number of industrial and consumer product manufacturers. Originally a real estate investment trust (REIT), it became an aggressive consolidator in the 1980s under the direction of the Rales brothers. Three main qualities they sought in acquisition targets were strong brands, market leadership, and proprietary technology.

The company achieved the status of a *Fortune* 500 company barely two years after the Rales brothers took over in 1984. Revenues climbed from $300 million to $1 billion within a decade, and by 2004 the company was approaching $7 billion while averaging dozens of

acquisitions a year. Of three business reporting segments, Professional Instrumentation and Industrial Technologies account for about 40 percent of sales each; Tools & Components provides the remainder.

ORIGINS

Danaher had its origins in 1969 when its predecessor, DMG, Inc., was organized as a Massachusetts real estate investment trust (REIT). DMG restructured in 1978, becoming a Florida corporation under the name of Diversified Mortgage Investors, Inc. (DMI). In 1980 a new holding company was formed under the name DMG, Inc., of which DMI became a subsidiary.

Until 1984 all operations of DMG had been in real estate, but that year the holding company underwent a major transformation when it acquired two new subsidiaries. Continuing its real estate operations in the DMI subsidiary, DMG entered the business of tire manufacturing with its acquisition of Mohawk Rubber Company and entered into the manufacture and distribution of vinyl building products with its purchase of Master Shield Inc. In 1984 Steven and Mitchell Rales, the majority stockholders of DMG, Inc., named the reorganized holding company Danaher Corporation, after a favorite mountain stream in western Montana. Steven M. Rales, 33 years old at the time, became the chief executive officer and chair of the board of the new company. Danaher was reorganized as a Delaware corporation in 1986.

Danaher's founders developed a carefully considered strategy of acquisition that was centered around the purchase of companies that had "high performance potential" but were not, for a variety of reasons, performing their best at the time of purchase. They also sought to acquire companies with well-known trademarked brands, high market shares, a reputation for innovative technology, and extensive distribution channels on which to build. Once acquired, Danaher's subsidiaries were grouped according to product lines and potential markets. If a company did not perform well after acquisition, Danaher's directors divested it and used the resulting capital to invest in new technologies or industries.

IN THE *FORTUNE* 500 BY 1986

Utilizing this strategy, Danaher acquired another 12 companies within two years of its founding. By then, Danaher was listed as a *Fortune* 500 company, and revenues had climbed from $300 million in 1984 to $456 million by 1986. The 14 subsidiaries were grouped into four business units: automotive/transportation, instrumentation, precision components, and extruded products. At least 12 of Danaher's products were market leaders.

The automotive/transportation unit produced and marketed tools for the professional auto mechanic as well as transportation parts. This unit consisted of well-known companies and leading market brands including Coats, a highly regarded trademark of wheel service products (such as tire changers and wheel balancers), Matco Tools, Jacobs Engine Brake, and Fayette Tubular Products, which was a leader in car air-conditioning parts.

The instrumentation unit of Danaher manufactured counting and sensing instruments, including devices that kept track of motion (magnetic encoders, electronic counters, and electronic voting machines), and instruments measuring and recording temperature. This unit boasted such prestigious companies as Veeder-Root, which supplied instruments for four out of five gas pumps worldwide, Dynapar, Partlow, and QualiTROL.

The precision components unit manufactured such diverse products as Swiss screw machine parts, the famous Allen wrench, and drill chucks. Finally, the extruded products unit, manufacturing vinyl siding and plastics, included Mohawk Rubber, Master Shield, and

A. L. Hyde Company, a leading American plastics manufacturer. Most of these would be sold off in a few years. Among Danaher's biggest customers were petroleum, aerospace, telecommunications, electronics, and automotive firms, including Toyota and Honda.

Chairman and CEO Steven Rales and Executive Committee Chairman Mitchell Rales maintained that they were seeking the best, not just good, but superior products and service; not just to be a leading company, but a world leader. According to analysts, they had become skilled in aggressive competition, divestment of unprofitable businesses, consolidation of facilities, and debt and cost reduction. Each year the company grew by more than 8 percent and boasted record sales. In 1987 net sales increased 141 percent over 1986.

RESTRUCTURED FOR THE 1990S

During 1989 Danaher reassessed and restructured. George M. Sherman, an executive officer from Black & Decker, became president and chief executive officer, bringing to Danaher his own corporate vision, which included increasing the company's hitherto negligible international sales. Danaher's 14 subsidiaries were reduced to 12 (and shortly thereafter grew to 13), while its four business segments were reduced from four to three: tools, process/environmental controls, and transportation.

The tool unit was greatly expanded by Danaher's 1989 merger with Easco Hand Tools, Inc., and by 1991 tools made up 49 percent of Danaher's sales.

The entirely new process/environment unit reflected a new emphasis on environmental instruments and machines, which included Veeder-Root's underground fuel storage sensors, Dynapar's motion control devices, and QualiTROL's instruments for measuring pressure and temperature, used widely by the electrical transformer industry. The A.L. Hyde Company belonged to the "process/environment" category by virtue of its extruded plastics production. This business segment was by far Danaher's fastest growing.

Transportation, accounting for 29 percent of Danaher's sales in 1991, included such leading brand names as Hennessy/Ammco (producing wheel balancers, tire changers, brake repair lathes), Jacobs Braker (producing engine retarders for heavy diesel trucks), and Fayette Tubular Products for car air-conditioning components.

Danaher's reorganization and streamlining contributed to its continued record sales, growth, and development of new products. In 1991 Sears, Roebuck & Co. selected Danaher as its only source for the manufacture of the Craftsman brand of mechanic's hand

KEY DATES

1969: DMG, Inc. REIT is established.
1978: DMG becomes Diversified Mortgage Investors, Inc. (DMI).
1980: New holding company is formed under DMG name.
1984: DMG acquires Mohawk Rubber Company and Master Shield Inc.; holding company is renamed Danaher Corporation.
1986: After two-year acquisition spree, 14 subsidiaries are regrouped into four business units.
1989: Four business units are cut to three; Easco Hand Tools is acquired.
1995: Total revenues exceed $1 billion.
1998: Fluke Corp. is acquired for $625 million.
2001: A $5.5 billion takeover attempt of Cooper Industries is unsuccessful.
2003: Revenues exceed $5 billion.
2004: The $750 million acquisition of Denmark's Radiometer A/S is Danaher's most expensive to date.

tools. Danaher was already marketing the Jacob Engine Brake diesel engine retarders in Japan, and, in 1991, Danaher acquired Normond/CMS, the leading manufacturer and marketer in Great Britain of environmental products. Danaher was already the leading supplier of hand tools to the National Automotive Parts Association.

The recession of the late 1980s and early 1990s affected Danaher, though not severely. Facilities were consolidated and some restructuring occurred (the firms Dynapar and Veeder-Root were combined into Danaher Controls, for instance, to eliminate duplicate services), but net sales of $832 million in 1991 were only 1 percent below the previous year, and in 1992, sales increased significantly to $897 million, the best year in the company's history for per share earnings. CEO George Sherman attributed the relatively mild effects of the recession to the company's investment in capital spending and in research and development at a time when most other firms practiced a timid "wait and see" policy.

With the worst of the recession over by 1993, Danaher's fortunes seemed secure. In part this was because of increasingly stringent environmental regulations and the growing demand for such environmental products as underground storage tank monitoring devices and fuel pump computers. This was already Danaher's

fastest growing segment of business. Medical technology was another increasingly important area. International markets also continued to grow in importance. Under the presidency of George Sherman, Danaher's international sales were rising significantly, to just over 10 percent of total sales, and market analysts predicted that the percentage would double by the year 2000.

A BILLION-DOLLAR COMPANY IN 1995

The acquisitions continued in the mid-1990s. German industrial timer manufacturer Hengstler GmbH was one of a half-dozen controls businesses acquired in 1994. The next year, Danaher divested its Fayette auto parts business for $155 million, but bought two more tool companies, Delta Consolidated Industries Inc. and Armstrong Brothers Tool Co. By 1995, Danaher had total sales of about $1.3 billion and 10,000 employees. Joslyn Corporation, a venerable Chicago maker of switches and controls, was acquired in 1995 for roughly $250 million. Acme-Cleveland Corp., a manufacturer of industrial controls and test equipment such as used in the telecommunications industry, was acquired for $200 million in 1996.

A number of motion control brands were added in the late 1990s. Danaher bought Pacific Scientific for $460 million in 1998, beating out a hostile bid by Kollmorgen Corp., which was itself acquired by Danaher two years later for $240 million. An even larger purchase in 1998 was that of Fluke Corp., which produced electronic test tools. The $625 million Danaher paid for the acquisition was a company record. Anther motion control company was acquired in 2000: American Precision Industries Inc., for $185 million.

STILL GROWING BY ACQUISITION AFTER 2000

Revenues were $3.8 billion in 2000, with net earnings of $324 million. While Danaher continued its acquisition strategy, it made headlines for one enormous deal that got away. Hand tools manufacturer Cooper Industries rejected a massive $5.5 billion takeover bid in August 2001.

COO Lawrence Culp was promoted to president and CEO in 2001. The company cut 1,100 jobs in 2002 as it restructured in a slow economy.

From 2002 through 2004, Danaher made several major acquisitions and picked up dozens of smaller companies. It also sold off some assets.

Two businesses were acquired from Marconi plc in February 2002. Marconi Commerce Systems, formerly

Gilbarco, was picked up for $309 million. It was a leading global provider of retail gasoline dispensers, automation equipment, and environmental products and services. Danaher paid $400 million for Marconi Data Systems, formerly Videojet Technologies. The company made two other deals that month. It bought the Pennon Group plc's Viridor Instrumentation Limited for $137 million. Viridor made instruments for analyzing water and other fluids and materials. Danaher also completed the sale of its API Heat Transfer, Inc. unit to Madison Capital Partners for $63 million. In October 2002, Thomson Industries Inc., a leading U.S. manufacturer of linear motion control products, was obtained for $147 million.

Danaher spent $312 million in 2003 to acquire a dozen smaller businesses. A similar amount was spent on ten smaller companies and product lines in 2004. All of these were incorporated into Danaher's Professional Instrumentation and Industrial Technologies units.

There were three major acquisitions in 2004. Denmark's Radiometer A/S, bought in January for $750 million, including assumed debt, produced blood gas diagnostic instruments for use in hospitals. Kaltenbach & Voigt GmbH (KaVo) was purchased in May 2004 for about EUR 350 million ($412 million). KaVo was a leading dental equipment manufacturer. Trojan Technologies, Inc., based in Canada, made ultraviolet water disinfection equipment. It was obtained in the fourth quarter for $185 million.

The company had 35,000 employees; about 17,000 were located in the United States. International sales accounted for more than a third of the company's 2004 revenues of $6.9 billion. Most of this was from acquisitions, noted *Forbes;* since 2001, Danaher had acquired a total of 47 companies for $3.4 billion. The company's net earnings were up to $746 million.

The acquisition of Linx Printing Technologies plc, a publicly traded U.K. specialist in product identification, was completed in January 2005. Linx had sales of about $93 million a year. The buy cost Danaher about $171 million. In the middle of the year, Danaher paid $85 million to buy Pelton & Crane, a maker of equipment for dentists' offices.

Leica Microsystems, a German producer of surgical microscopes and other professional instruments, was acquired in the summer of 2005. The cost was about $550 million. Leica Microsystems also made equipment for the semiconductor industry, but antitrust regulators compelled Danaher to divest this. Danaher made a $1 billion bid to buy another spinoff of the famous Leica optics firm called Leica Geosystems, but lost out to Hexagon AB of Sweden.

The company remained an enthusiastic practitioner of the lean manufacturing practices it had been using since the 1980s. Implementing such systems at newly acquired companies was one way it made them more efficient.

Sina Dubovoj
Updated, Frederick C. Ingram

PRINCIPAL SUBSIDIARIES

Acme-Cleveland Corp.; American Precision Industries Inc.; Armstrong Tools Inc.; Danaher Tool Group LP; Fluke Corp.; Delta Consolidated Industries Inc.; Easco Hand Tools Inc.; Gems Sensors Inc.; Gilbarco SpA (Italy); Hengstler GmbH (Germany); Hennessy Industries, Inc.; Holo-Krome Company; Jacobs Vehicle Systems Inc.; Kaltenbach & Voigt GmbH (Germany); Kollmorgen Corporation; Leica Microsystems (Germany); Linx Printing Technologies plc (UK); Matco Tools Corporation; OECO LLC; Pacific Scientific Company; Qualitrol Corporation; Radiometer S/A (Denmark); Thomson Industries Inc.; Trojan Technologies, Inc. (Canada); Veeder-Root Company; Videojet Technologies; Warner Electric Gmbh (Germany).

PRINCIPAL DIVISIONS

Professional Instrumentation (Environmental, Medical Technology, Electronic Test), Industrial Technologies (Motion, Product ID); Tools & Components (Mechanic's Hand Tools).

PRINCIPAL COMPETITORS

3M Precision Optics, Inc.; Cooper Industries Inc.; Johnson Controls, Inc.; The Stanley Works.

FURTHER READING

Berselli, Beth, "Danaher Acquiring Tool Firm; Deal Valued at $625 Million," *Washington Post,* April 28, 1998, p. C1.

———, "Danaher to Buy Pacific Scientific; D.C. Conglomerate's Offer Tops Kollmorgen's Hostile Bid," *Washington Post,* February 3, 1998, p. D3.

Brown, Warren, "Danaher Makes Power Play for Chicago Manufacturer," *Washington Post,* August 28, 1995, p. F11.

"Danaher Corp.," *Washington Post,* October 22, 1992, p. D13.

"Danaher Corp.: Leaner Machine," *Baseline,* June 10, 2005.

"Danaher Forms Industrial Groups," *Industrial Distribution,* August 1991, pp. 11-12.

"Danaher: Riding the Rales; The Rales Brothers Build Their Dream Conglomerate," *Financial World,* September 18, 1990.

"Danaher Takeover of Easco Likely: Shareholders to Vote Today on Proposal," *Washington Post,* June 7, 1990, p. E1.

Gubernick, Lisa, "Raiders in Short Pants," *Forbes,* November 18, 1985.

Ichniowski, Tom, "A Portrait of the Takeover Artist As a Young Man," *Business Week,* August 22, 1988.

MacDonald, Elizabeth, and Michael K. Ozanian, "Bending Metal, Bending Rules," *Forbes,* February 28, 2005, p. 106.

Madigan, Sean, "Cooper Rejects Danaher's $5.5B Bid," *Washington Business Journal,* August 10, 2001, p. 61.

Morrison, Mitch, "Danaher Pumped Over Marconi Deal: Dispenser-Equipment Business Down to Three Companies," *Convenience Store News,* February 11, 2002, p. 16.

Potts, Mark, "Danaher Corp.," *New York Times,* September 20, 1990, pp. C4, D4.

Saunders, Laura, "How to Fight the IRS," *Forbes,* January 22, 1996, p. 64.

"The Washington Area's Largest Companies," *Washington Post,* April 8, 1991, p. WB11.

Woo, Junda, "Shareholder Can Bring Derivative Suit After Merger," *Wall Street Journal,* August 7, 1992, p. B2.

Jet2.com
The low cost airline

Dart Group PLC

Building 470
Bournemouth International Airport
Christchurch, BH23 6SE
United Kingdom
Telephone: 44 (0) 1202 597676
Fax: 44 (0) 1202 593480
Web site: http://www.dartgroup.co.uk

Public Company
Incorporated: 1983 as Channel Express Group Limited
Employees: 1,700
Sales: £268.0 million (EUR 389 million) (2005)
Stock Exchanges: AIM
Ticker Symbol: DTG.L
NAIC: 484110 General Freight Trucking, Local; 481111
Scheduled Passenger Air Transportation; 481112
Scheduled Freight Air Transportation; 481211
Nonscheduled Chartered Passenger Air Transportation; 492110 Couriers; 551112 Offices of Other
Holding Companies

■ ■ ■

Dart Group PLC is the holding company for several
subsidiaries providing temperature-controlled distribution and aviation services in the United Kingdom and
Europe. The distribution side has been delivering fresh
flowers and grocers to U.K. wholesalers since its Channel Island beginnings in the early 1970s. By 1978, the
company was operating its own planes and in 2001
began flying passenger flights. In 2003 Dart launched a
low cost passenger airline known as Jet2.com.

More than one million passengers a year fly Jet2.
com, which has bases in Leeds, Manchester, Belfast, and
other cities and flies as far as Hungary and Spain. Dart
owns about two dozen jets and also has an aviation parts
trading business. The fleet of subsidiary Fowler Welch-
Coolchain has about 750 refrigerated trailers, covering a
network from the Netherlands to northern England.

ORIGINS

Dart Group PLC traces its origins to two businesses
formed in 1971 by Art Carpenter. Carpenter's Air
Services contracted space on cargo airlines to ship fresh
flowers from the Channel Island of Guernsey, while
Carpenter's Transport arranged for their wholesale
delivery.

Another produce, flower, and freight shipping business, Express Air Freight (CI), was set up in 1975 with
Art Carpenter as director. Express Air Freight began using its own aircraft, a Handley Page Dart Herald, in
1978. The next year, another company, Express Air
Services, was formed to take over the aviation operation.
In 1980 Express Air Services won its first mail contract,
flying between Bournemouth, Bristol, and Liverpool.

In 1983 three new companies with the Channel
Express name were formed to take over the Express
Air activities. They were taken over by Channel Express
Group Ltd., led by Phillip Meeson, a pilot himself and
five-time British Aerobatic champion who had previously been successful in automobile retailing and
distribution. In the same year, the company was organized into two divisions, Aviation Services and

Distribution. Under Meeson, Channel Express invested heavily in new equipment and vehicles.

GOING PUBLIC IN 1988

By 1985, the company had three Dart Heralds in its fleet. Aviation services was growing, with new contracts to deliver parcels and newspapers, while the distribution business was also seeing more volume. The company had 200 employees by 1988, as well as 31 trucks, 46 trailers, and seven Dart Herald planes. The company added a new aircraft type, the Lockheed Electra, in 1989. Three more were added within five years and Dart also worked out a deal with Zantop Airlines of the United States to lease additional Electras as needed.

In 1988, Channel Express Group PLC had an initial public offering on the U.K. Unlisted Securities Market. Shares began trading on the London Stock Exchange in 1991, when the company was renamed Dart Group PLC, after the Rolls Royce-manufactured powerplants in its Dart Heralds. Three years later, these planes began to be replaced by Fokker F27s, which were also powered by Dart engines.

Benair Freight Ltd., a freight forwarding company with offices in the United Kingdom and Far East, was acquired in 1990. It was renamed Benair Freight International Ltd. four years later. Benair developed a specialty in shipping tropical fish and other time-sensitive cargo.

Dart also owned Deltec Aviation Services Ltd., an avionics repair company. It acquired Bourne Aviation Supply Limited, an aircraft parts distributor, in 1992 for about £1 million.

Dart Group had annual revenues of more than £30 million by the early 1990s. The company struggled to maintain its margins in a global economy troubled by military conflict in the Persian Gulf. The Channel Express unit, long identified with the island of Guernsey, was developing into a regional European cargo carrier. It was handling shipments for the likes of UPS and British Airways World Cargo.

Another temperature-controlled distributor, Fowler Welch Ltd., was acquired in 1994. Fowler Welch was based in Spalding, Lincolnshire, and handled horticultural products as well as the region's produce. The existing Channel Express distribution business was merged with Fowler Welch in 1996. Dart was investing millions in capital upgrades at its Fowler Welch facilities, expanding its 90,000-square-foot temperature controlled warehouse in Spalding to 150,000 square feet. By this time, Fowler Welch had about 200 trucks and 300 trailers. It was delivering for several major U.K. super-markets as well as about 40 wholesale markets.

JETS ACQUIRED 1996

In 1996, the Channel Express Air Services unit began acquiring Airbus A300 airliners for conversion into freighters by BAE Systems Aviation Services, a process which took about four months. The first aircraft was dubbed the "Eurofreighter." By 1998, the company had three of these jets in the fleet.

In 1999 the temperature-controlled distribution business continued to grow with the £14.2 million purchase of the Coolchain Group. Coolchain was based in Teynham, Kent, a fruit-growing area, and had annual revenues approaching £20 million. The Coolchain buy was augmented the next year by the acquisition of A Wood & Son. Fowler Welch and Coolchain were merged into Fowler-Welch Coolchain Ltd. in 2003.

In 1999, a Netherlands subsidiary called Fowler Welch BA was set up to handle international trade, while the Aviation Services division set up a Parts Trading unit. The company also opened a 40,000-square-foot, state-of-the-art distribution center in Portsmouth.

Dart Group had almost 1,500 employees in 2000. Revenues were about £131.5 million and rose dramatically in 2001 to £190.9 million, when pretax profits were about £9 million.

The fleet continued to expand. A Boeing 737 airliner was added, while the F27 fleet was upgraded. The company began to fly people via summertime charter routes. The last of the Lockheed Electras was retired in 2003.

JET2.COM LAUNCHED 2003

The new passenger charter operation thrived even in the post-9/11 environment. In February 2003, the company's Channel Express (Air Services) subsidiary launched a scheduled passenger airline, dubbed Jet2.com, out of Leeds Bradford Airport. It aimed to serve both business and leisure travelers, offering connections to European capitals and sun and ski destinations. By the end of the year, Jet2.com was operating scheduled routes to Alicante, Amsterdam, Barcelona, Belfast, Faro, Geneva, Malaga, Nice, Palma, and Prague. The company

KEY DATES

1971: Carpenter's Air Services and Carpenter's Transport are formed to ship and distribute fresh flowers from Guernsey.
1975: Express Air Freight (CI) is formed.
1978: Express Air begins operating its own airplane.
1983: Channel Express companies take over Express Air activities; Aviation Services and Distribution divisions are formed.
1988: Channel Express Group Ltd. goes public on the U.K. Unlisted Securities Market.
1990: Freight forwarder Benair Freight Ltd. is acquired.
1991: Shares migrate to the London Stock Exchange; company is renamed Dart Group PLC.
1994: Super Dart Heralds begin to be phased out in favor of Fokker F27 aircraft; Fowler Welch is acquired.
1996: Airbus A300 jets are acquired for conversion into freighters.
1999: Coolchain Group is acquired; new distribution center opens in Portsmouth.
2001: Passenger charter flights begin.
2003: Jet2.com low cost airline is launched in Leeds; Fowler Welch and Coolchain merge.
2004: Jet2.com opens base in Manchester.
2005: Benair subsidiary and F27 aircraft are sold off; shares migrate to AIM exchange.

had a fleet of a half dozen Boeing 737s, all owned rather than leased (a couple of its A300 "Eurofreighters" were leased). Some were the QC, or Quick Change model, which could be converted between passenger and cargo configurations in 30 minutes. Another eight Boeing 737s were ordered during 2003.

Dart Group continued to fly high in 2004. Its Channel Express (Air Services) subsidiary was designated the Royal Mail's leading aircraft provider, calling for seven Boeing 737s to be dedicated to the account. The passenger airline, Jet2.com, continued adding routes (Belfast-Prague). It opened a second hub in Manchester International Airport, the largest in the North, with the first flight going to Budapest. In September, Jet2.com counted its millionth passenger. In spite of cheap fares, from about £15 to £32, the new airline was beating others in customer satisfaction and on-time performance.

Turnover reached £268 million in the fiscal year ended March 2005. Pretax profit was £13.5 million, 50 percent higher than in the previous few years. The company had 1,700 employees, about 500 of them at Jet2.com, which had flown 1.3 million passengers during the year. In the summer, Dart Group's shares migrated from the London Stock Market to its affiliated AIM exchange, which had less cumbersome regulatory requirements.

ALL-JET FLEET IN 2005

In January 2005, the company sold off its last Fokker F27 turboprop. Dart Group announced the purchase of its largest aircraft yet in July 2005, two Boeing 757s which had a capacity of 235 passengers each (100 more than Jet2.com's Boeing 737s). This was added to an existing fleet of 20 Boeing 737s. The temperature-controlled fleet of subsidiary Fowler Welch-Coolchain had 660 vehicles, covering a network ranging across Maasland in the Netherlands, Portsmouth, Teynham in Kent, Spalding in Lincolnshire, and Gateshead in Tyne & Wear.

In August 2005, the company sold Benair Freight International Limited and Benair Freight Pte to the global logistics and marine services giant Gulf Agency Company for £5.1 million ($9 million). Benair then had five offices in the United Kingdom and one in Singapore. The divestiture allowed Dart to focus on its two main businesses, temperature-controlled distribution and aviation services.

By this time, Jet2.com had added new bases in cities including Blackpool and Edinburgh. It was adding new destinations and stepping up frequencies on existing routes to at least daily flights in most instances. Fowler-Welch Coolchain was also advancing, spending £880,000 ($1.5 million) to have GPS provider Thales UK outfit its 750 refrigerated trailers with a satellite tracking and temperature monitoring system.

Frederick C. Ingram

PRINCIPAL SUBSIDIARIES

Channel Express (CI) Limited (Guernsey); Channel Express (Air Services) Limited; Fowler Welch-Coolchain BV (Netherlands); Fowler Welch-Coolchain Limited.

PRINCIPAL DIVISIONS

Distribution; Aviation.

PRINCIPAL COMPETITORS

Air Partner PLC; British Midland Airways Ltd.; Christian Salvesen PLC; easyJet plc; Exel plc.

FURTHER READING

"Channel Express Buys 2 F27 Freighters from Aramco," *Reuters News,* September 12, 1995.

"Channel Express Clinches Lease Deal with Zantop," *Reuters News,* April 18, 1994.

"Company Results: DART—Food Distribution and Aviation Svcs—Good Value," *Investors Chronicle,* November 24, 2000, p. 83.

———, *Report and Accounts 2005,* Christchurch, England: Dart Group PLC, 2005.

"Fowler Welch—Distributor with Fresh Ideas," *Commerce New Media,* September 9, 1998.

"French Thales Tracking Technology to Secure UK Fowler Welch Coolchain Fleet of Trailers," *French News Digest,* December 5, 2005.

"GAC Acquires Benair Freight International," *Middle East Company News,* September 3, 2005.

Murphy, Bob, "Channel Express Says Airbus Freighter Gets U.S. OK," *Reuters News,* May 14, 1997.

———, "Dart UK Buys 2nd Airbus for Channel Express," *Reuters News,* June 18, 1997.

"Special Services for Perishables: A Profile of Benair Special Services—Provider of Proactive, Round-the-Clock, International Delivery Service for Perishable Products," *Frozen and Chilled Foods,* March 1, 2002, p. 27.

SERVICES YOU COUNT ON

The Empire District
Electric Company

602 Joplin Street
Joplin, Missouri 64801
U.S.A.
Telephone: (417) 625-5100
Toll Free: (800) 206-2800
Fax: (417) 625-5146
Web site: http://www.empiredistrict.com

Public Company
Incorporated: 1909
Employees: 855
Sales: $325.5 million (2004)
Stock Exchanges: New York
Ticker Symbol: EDE
NAIC: 221121 Electric Bulk Power Transmission and
    Control

■ ■ ■

The Empire District Electric Company is a small Joplin, Missouri-based utility company that supplies electricity to more than 155,000 customers located in a 10,000-square-mile territory that includes southwestern Missouri and neighboring parts of northeast Arkansas, southeast Kansas, and northeast Oklahoma. It also provides water service to three Missouri communities. In addition, Empire invests in nonregulated businesses through subsidiary EDE Holdings, Inc., including fiber optic and Internet services, customer information software services, and close-tolerance custom manufacturing. Empire is a public company and has been listed on the New York Stock Exchange since 1946.

COMPANY HERITAGE DATING TO THE 1800S

The demand for electricity in the area served by Empire grew out of the zinc and lead mines that operated in the tri-state area of Missouri, Kansas, and Oklahoma. In 1870 "black jack" (sphalerite, the chief ore of zinc) was discovered in Galena, Kansas, which set off a flurry of mining activity and the birth of what became known as the "Empire District" or "Little Empire," a name applied by investors alluding to New York's nickname as the Empire State. The Empire name stuck and would be forever linked to the region, even after mining activity eventually petered out in 1970.

Around 1890 electric power was introduced to the larger mining operations, which until then had been mostly small affairs that relied on the brute force of men and mules. With the dawn of the 20th century it became increasingly apparent that the generation and distribution of electricity to the mines had to be better organized and that there needed to be a combination among smaller power companies to create a larger, more cohesive unit. Papers were filed in Topeka, Kansas, in 1909 and The Empire District Electric Company was born. The utilities brought together under the Empire rubric were Consolidated Light, Power and Ice Company (which had previously acquired Missouri Ice & Cold Storage Company and Southwest Missouri Light Company); the Spring River Power Company; The Galena Light, Heat and Power Company; and the Joplin Light, Power, and Water Company. All told, the combination owned 109 miles of transmission line and was able to produce eight megawatts of power, a far cry from the company's 1,100 megawatts of capacity a century later, serving 2,400

COMPANY PERSPECTIVES

From the early mining camps to the diverse array of industry found across the four-state region today, the "Empire District" is alive and thriving, in no small part, due to the leadership, courage, and spirit of The Empire District Electric Company.

customers. Much of the power was provided by two facilities: the Lowell Dam, built at the junction where Shoal Creek flows into Spring River near Baxter Springs, Kansas; and a 5,000-horsepower, Westinghouse steam generator called "Old Kate," which Spring River had acquired in 1906. "Old Kate" had gained fame by supplying the power needs of the 1904 St. Louis World's Fair.

In 1910 Empire became part of the Cities Service Company, now known as CITGO Petroleum Corporation. It was established by Henry Latham Doherty, whose life was a typically 19th-century rags-to-riches tale. Despite growing up poor and going to work as an office boy at the age of 12, he taught himself engineering science and by the age of 20 had become the chief engineer of Columbus Gas Company in Ohio. In 1905 he launched his own company, Henry L. Doherty & Son, offering technical and financial advice to utilities, and also serving as an investment vehicle. He quickly amassed a fortune, but was far from satisfied. Doherty envisioned a huge company that could provide utility services to the fast-growing cities of the western portion of the United States. In 1910 he formed Cities Service, a holding company composed of three main subsidiaries: Denver Gas and Electric, Spokane Gas and Fuel, and Empire District Electric. It later changed its name to Cities Service Power & Light Co.

Far more generating capacity would be needed to meet the demand of the Empire District mines, and so even as Empire was being organized in the summer of 1909 work was begun on the Riverton Generating Station, which became operational in July 1910. In addition to "Old Kate," it included two 7,500-kilowatt Westinghouse turbines and 16 boilers. It was likely that the two units were rebladed several years later, increasing their capacity to 10,000 kilowatts. In 1913 "Old Kate" was supplemented by a 2,000-kilowatt low-pressure turbine that used the steam exhaust of the larger unit, creating one of the first combination engine turbo installations in the United States. Also in 1913, work was completed on the Ozark Beach Dam. The additional

capacity gained through these installations was not great enough, however, to meet the demand for electricity created by the nation's entry into World War I in 1917, when the company began constructing a 10,000-kilowatt turbine generator and soon added another 12,500-kilowatt unit, supplied with steam from 16 boilers. Neither worked particularly well, so that after the war the smaller unit was replaced by another 10,000-kilowatt unit and the larger was returned to the factory and rebuilt.

During this period, Empire District added capacity through the acquisition of small utilities. Columbus Electric Company was added in 1910, followed a year later by Empire Electric Power & Supply Company. The company also acquired Neosho Electric Light Company in 1916 and Baxter Springs Electric Company in 1919. Empire continued to act as a consolidator in the region in the 1920s and 1930s. In 1922, an Oklahoma cousin that took the Empire District Electric Company was brought into the fold. Ozark Power & Water Company was added in 1927, as was Taney Light & Water Company, Electric Utilities Company, and Joplin Municipal System in 1929. Then, in 1936, Empire acquired Mid-West Development Company.

During the 1920s mining production soared in the area, and Empire extended its service to many new communities and added a 25,000-kilowatt turbine generator in 1925, and because there was an increasing demand for the more efficient 60-cycle current, three years later a 25,000-kilowatt frequency changer was installed, allowing the company to provide either 25- or 60-cycle current. A year later, in 1929, the need for extra capacity would wane, as the stock market crashed and the United States was cast into the Great Depression of the 1930s. Only with the United States' entry into World War II in December 1941 did the country's industry begin to truly rebound. Most of the readily accessible deposits of lead and zinc in the Empire District had long since been extracted, leaving only low-grade ore, which was only profitable if the prices were high enough. During World War II and for two years afterward, the U.S. government subsidized the production of lead and zinc, greatly needed in the war effort. As a result of price supports, mining activities picked up during this period and Empire benefited.

GAINING INDEPENDENCE IN THE 1940S

In 1935 the United States enacted the Public Utility Act, part of which allowed holding companies like Cities Service to own only one of the public utilities: electric light, power, or gas. By this time, Cities Service had become heavily involved in gas and oil exploration and

---

KEY DATES

1909: The Empire District Electric Company is formed.
1910: Empire becomes part of Cities Service Company.
1944: Cities Service spins off Empire.
1946: Empire gains a listing on the New York Stock Exchange.
1970: Asbury Generating Station becomes operational.
1995: State Line Power Plant opens.
2001: EDE Holdings, Inc. is formed for nonregulated businesses.

---

production, and elected to remain involved in this business and divest its other utility assets, including Empire. Although holding companies were given until 1940 to complete the disposition, Cities Service did not spin off Empire as an independent public company until 1944. As part of the plan, Cities Service added other subsidiaries it owned: Ozark Utilities Company; Lawrence County Water, Light & Cold Storage Company; and Benton County Utilities Corporation. Two years later, in 1946, Empire received a listing on the New York Stock Exchange.

After the government removed price supports for lead and zinc production, mining activity fell off somewhat in the Empire District but picked up again in 1950 when lead and zinc increased in price on their own and production was spurred without the need of a subsidy. Although Empire welcomed the extra business from mines and lead smelting and processing, since the end of the war it had pursued a diversification effort, placing more emphasis on residential customers and farmers. By the early 1950s, Empire served about 124 communities in its four-state territory with a combined population of 300,000. The primary communities served included Joplin and Webb City, Missouri; Galena, Kansas; and Picher, Oklahoma. The company served 8,000 farms directly as well as the area's REA (Rural Electrification Act of 1936) cooperatives. As dairy and poultry farming played a more prominent role in the area's economy, these rural customers became an increasingly important part of Empire's customer base.

In addition, after the war Empire launched a campaign to attract other industries to the area as a way to bring stability to its business, which had long been subject to the cyclical nature of the mining industry. By

1950 the effort succeeded in bringing nearly 100 new manufacturing plants, employing 2,400 people, to the Empire District. Moreover, a pair of Shell Pipe Line pumping stations were constructed in the area and a U.S. Army camp reopened.

With the expansion of its customer base came the need for further generating capacity. In 1950 a new 30,000-kilowatt turbo-generator went on line at the Riverton facility. A year later construction began on a 40,000-kilowatt steam turbine, which went into service in 1954. The cooling system of the generator was later improved, boosting its output to 54,000 kilowatts. From 1959 to 1966 Empire pursued another period of significant expansion because of increased demand for electricity, due in part to promotional programs touting electric space heat and electrical appliances, spending about $25 million during this period on new transmission and distribution facilities. One of the generators was reengineered to add 7,000 kilowatts and a new 12,000-kilowatt combined-cycle gas turbine generator was put in operation in 1964. In addition, Empire built new substations and high-voltage transmission lines, which not only strengthened the system internally but allowed Empire to link up with the greater electrical grid of the Midwest. Also in 1964, Empire opened a state-of-the-industry operations and communications center in Joplin.

Even these additions failed to keep pace with demand for electricity in the area, prompting yet another capital project, the $26 million, coal-fired, 200-megawatt Asbury Generating Station, which was begun near Asbury, Missouri, in 1967 and went on line in June 1970. It was a "mine-mouth" plant, which burned coal from the nearby Empire Mine. The new capacity also helped to replace the loss of the Lowell Dam, which went out of service in 1969. Then, in 1975, the twin 10,000-kilowatt Westinghouse turbines that entered service in 1910 were retired. To make up for some of this loss in capacity, Empire added a 90-megawatt combustion turbine peaking unit near LaRussell, Missouri, in 1978. A second unit of the same size was put on hold when the company was able to procure 80 megawatts of power from a 650-megawatt Kansas City-area plant, but was eventually added in 1981. Both generators relied on oil but were converted to natural gas in 1994.

Further changes in the 1980s included the addition of a second generator at Asbury, a 20-megawatt unit that drew on the excess boiler capacity of the original unit. The "mine-mouth" facility would switch to a cleaner-burning blend of low-sulfur Wyoming coal and native coal in 1990 in order to meet more stringent air quality control regulations. Furthermore, in the 1980s, Empire installed a pair of refurbished 16,000-kilowatt

Westinghouse generators capable of using either natural gas or diesel fuel. They were put in operation at the close of 1988.

The need for more capacity continued in the 1990s and into the new century. The State Line Power Plant with a 98-megawatt combustion turbine was opened west of Joplin in 1995, and two years later the facility added a 150-megawatt combustion turbine. In 1998 work began on a project to add another 350 megawatts of power: a second 150-megawatt combustion turbine was added to State Line, and the waste heat produced by the two units was used to generate another 200 megawatts of steam-powered combined-cycle energy. The work was completed in 2001 and the electricity entered the Empire system.

DEREGULATION LOOMING IN THE 1990S

The 1990s also brought the possibility of deregulation, as was occurring throughout the country, especially in California. A number of states held off on deregulation, waiting to see what transpired with the "California experiment." Empire, straddling four states, began to prepare for the effects of deregulation in all four states, and participated in the shaping of legislation and regulations that would replace the current system. While deregulation lingered, Empire took steps to diversify and become involved in nonregulated businesses, positioning the company as a regional supplier of choice for energy and energy-related products, including monitored security systems, electrical system surge protection, fiber optic cable leasing, and the sale of natural gas to industrial customers. As part of this effort, Empire launched a branding effort, introducing a new logo and a marketing slogan, "Services You Count On," in 1997.

Empire closed the century by agreeing to merge with Kansas City-based UtiliCorp United, Inc., a deal that would leave UtiliCorp the surviving entity. But in early 2001, at the 11th hour, UtiliCorp pulled out of the deal, which it was allowed to do without penalty, according to the merger agreement, if regulatory approvals were not received by the end of 2000. Although Missouri and Oklahoma had approved the combination, Arkansas rejected it and Kansas had yet to issue a ruling. Hence Empire remained an independent utility, but because a number of people left the company, uncertain of what would happen following the merger, Empire had to fill the gaps that had been created in the work-force by the proposed merger.

By this time, the California experiment had turned into the California disaster and later played a major role in the Enron scandal, making the four states Empire served reluctant to enact deregulation legislation. Empire continued to pursue nonregulated businesses, and in 2001 created EDE Holdings, Inc. to house those assets. The subsidiary made some minor acquisitions in 2002 and 2003, but set an ambitious goal of EDE contributing as much as 10 percent of Empire's earnings within five years. Nevertheless, the delivery of electricity remained the core of the company. To ready itself for the district's future power needs, Empire began work in 2005 on a new 155-kilowatt combustion turbine addition at Riverton, scheduled to become operational in the spring of 2007.

Ed Dinger

PRINCIPAL SUBSIDIARIES

EDE Holdings, Inc.; Empire District Industries, Inc.; Fast Freedom, Inc.; Conversant, Inc.; Mid-America Precision Products, L.L.C.; Utility Intelligence, Inc.; EDE Property Transfer Corporation.

PRINCIPAL COMPETITORS

Ameren Corporation; Aquila, Inc.; Great Plains Energy Incorporated.

FURTHER READING

"Empire District Electric's Business More Diversified," *Barron's National Business and Financial Weekly,* November 14, 1955, p. 35.

"More Diversified Market Area Favoring Empire District Electric," *Barron's National Business and Financial Weekly,* April 5, 1954, p. 29.

"New Industrial Customers Aid Midwestern Utility," *Barron's National Business and Financial Weekly,* November 14, 1955, p. 35.

Owens, Ross, "Empire Strikes Back: Empire District Electric," *InfoWorld,* October 5, 1998, p. 91.

"Sidewalks Carry More Than Pedestrians," *Transmission & Distribution World,* June 2000.

Wicker, Ken, "Asbury Power Plant, Asbury, Missouri," *Power,* August 1, 2005, p. 34.

(D

THE F. DOHMEN CO.

The F. Dohmen Co.

W194 N11381 McCormick Drive
Germantown, Wisconsin 53022
U.S.A.
Telephone: (262) 255-0022
Toll Free: (800) 444-4496
Fax: (262) 255-0041
Web site: http://www.dohmen.com

Private Company
Incorporated: 1858
Employees: 950
Sales: $2.14 billion (2004)
NAIC: 422210 Drug and Druggists' Sundries Whole-
saling

■ ■ ■

The F. Dohmen Co. is a private, family-owned pharmaceutical wholesaler, one of the top ten in its industry in
the United States. The company distributes generic and
brand-name drugs, medical products, surgical supplies,
and other related products. Its subsidiary DDN/Obergfel
is a leading specialist in pharmaceutical logistics. Its
services include specialized transportation and warehousing of pharmaceuticals, technical services such as data
management, planning, and design of reports and forms,
and financial services such as invoicing and debit and
credit issuance. Another F. Dohmen subsidiary, RE-
STAT, is the fourth largest prescription benefit manager
in the United States. RESTAT serves large employers
such as government agencies and schools as well as
unions, insurance companies, and other employers, in

providing prescription drug discounts and other services
that hold down prescription drug costs. Dohmen also
participates in two distribution networks. Dohmen
Distribution Partners Southeast is a regional drug
wholesaler with headquarters in Birmingham, Alabama.

Dohmen Distribution Partners L.L.C. is a regional
cooperative of independent pharmacy owners in the
Midwest. F. Dohmen's JASCORP division is a maker of
pharmacy-related software products. F. Dohmen operates warehousing and distribution facilities in Wisconsin,
Minnesota, and Kentucky. The company headquarters
were originally in Milwaukee and are now in Germantown, Wisconsin. Its subsidiaries and divisions operate
out of Germantown, Kenosha, and West Bend, Wisconsin. F. Dohmen Co. was founded in 1858, and
remains in the hands of the Dohmen family.

19TH-CENTURY ROOTS

The founder of F. Dohmen, Frederick Dohmen, trained
in pharmacy in his native Germany, and then immigrated
to the United States as a young man. He arrived in New
York in 1855, visited Chicago and St. Paul, and settled
in Milwaukee by 1856. Milwaukee at that time was a
midsized town with a total population of roughly 35,000
and a substantial number of German immigrants.
Dohmen worked at two drugstores owned by fellow
Germans, and then around 1858 he opened his first
store. This was a retail drugstore, which probably also
sold groceries, hardware, paint, and other things.

By around 1862, Dohmen had apparently tired of
the retail end of the business and moved into wholesale

The F. Dohmen Co. has been serving the pharmacy industry for over 140 years and is among the longest, continuously operating wholesale distributors of pharmaceutical and related products in North America. Utilizing a strategy of innovation and diligent market analysis, the F. Dohmen Co. has developed a wide variety of programs and services to assist the independent pharmacist with their day-to-day business needs. The F. Dohmen Co. takes pride in being an industry leader always with the focus of delivering outstanding value to their customers. Because of the innovative programs and services we offer, the F. Dohmen Co. has continued to grow.

pharmaceutical distribution. Around that year, he established a partnership with two others, forming Dohmen, Schmitt & Schulder. This company imported, and then distributed around the Midwest, patent medicines, chemicals, plant extracts and other botanicals, oils, dyes, adhesives, and other goods including snuff and stove polish. This business had its ups and downs, suffering through the so-called Panic of 1873 and ensuing bad years, and later rising to prominence as a founder of a statewide pharmaceutical association. By 1882, Dohmen's partners had left the business, so in 1883 the company reformed under the name F. Dohmen Co. Ltd.

By the early 1890s, F. Dohmen had become a large enterprise, occupying three addresses on Milwaukee's East Water Street. Dohmen's two sons entered the business, and were secretary and treasurer by 1892. That year, a huge fire swept through East Water Street and the surrounding Third Ward district. The heat was so fierce that it exploded trains loaded with oil in the nearby train yard, and by the time the fire had burned out, it had destroyed some 15 city blocks. Dohmen's employees had had some time to move things out of the building before the fire struck, and this later caused a contentious argument with the company's insurer. A private detective claiming to represent several insurance companies demanded that F. Dohmen Co. settle its claims for fire damage at a discount, or else he would reveal evidence that the company committed fraud. The detective said he had proof that goods said to have been destroyed in the fire had actually been safely retrieved. Frederick Dohmen refuted the detective's allegations, and this led to lawsuits and appeals that dragged on for years. The

company was finally vindicated in 1898, but the bad publicity and uncertainty had taken a toll on Frederick Dohmen's health. Only two months after the last court case was decided, Dohmen died suddenly while bowling. His wife died two days later. The presidency of the company passed to Dohmen's son William, and other top posts were taken by Dohmen's other son and his nephew.

LASTING THROUGH THE GREAT DEPRESSION

F. Dohmen Co. seemed to hold steady over the early years of the 20th century, operating in much the same manner as it always had. Meanwhile, the drug industry was changing as pharmaceutical production incorporated modern industrial methods. The number of products Dohmen and its competitors sold increased greatly. Brand-name drugs were hugely in demand in the 1910s and 1920s, and such companies as Dohmen had to risk buying popular remedies that might soon go out of fashion. Modern manufacturing methods also allowed suppliers to cut prices, so that the wholesale drug market became much more volatile.

Glenn Sonnedecker's history of the early years of the F. Dohmen Co., *Supply Line to Health,* characterizes the years between 1900 and the Depression as a period of "consolidation rather than innovation" (p. 35). Company literature exclaimed that F. Dohmen was enlarging its facilities and putting out untold new and better products from its laboratories. Yet the physical plant remained much the same through this period, and the laboratory was principally used for making simple herbal preparations such as essence of peppermint. Other laboratory work involved packing bulk ingredients into smaller packages and bottles, labeling products, and preparing orders for shipping.

Two grandsons of the founder entered the business in 1911 and 1912. In 1916, the company increased the number of members of its board of directors, and the name changed from F. Dohmen Co. Ltd. to The F. Dohmen Co. The company remained profitable through the 1920s, which was a period of general prosperity in the United States. The company got through the Depression of the 1930s by relying on surpluses built up in the good years. The company's president, William Dohmen, died in 1938.

ESSENTIAL RENOVATION IN THE 1950S

After William's death, leadership of the firm passed to the brothers Fred W. and Erwin J. Dohmen. The company made few changes, and in fact operated in

KEY DATES

1858: Frederick Dohmen opens his first pharmacy.

1883: F. Dohmen Co. Ltd. is founded in Milwaukee.

1892: A huge fire wipes out much of the company's neighborhood.

1916: The company name is changed to The F. Dohmen Co.

1954: The company moves to a new plant in Milwaukee.

1980: F. Dohmen leaves Milwaukee for new quarters in Germantown, Wisconsin.

1988: Robert Wendland becomes the first non-Dohmen to run the company.

1992: F. Dohmen buys Northwestern Drug Co., doubling its size.

1995: John Dohmen, fifth generation of the founder's family, becomes CEO.

1999: The company opens a new distribution center in Anoka, Minnesota.

2004: Revenue surpasses $2 billion.

what seemed a pointedly antiquated manner. Erwin Dohmen wrote the company's advertising copy, which was interspersed with folksy wisdom and politically conservative points of view. Fred W. Dohmen died in 1947, and Erwin died in 1952. That year, Fred W.'s son Fred H. Dohmen became president of the company. Fred H. had studied business and marketing at the University of Wisconsin, and he was adamant that the company make major changes to adapt to postwar conditions. Although sales increased in the booming years after World War II, Dohmen saw its profits fall. Its staff worked overtime, but its outdated facilities could not keep up with demand.

The company had long harbored a plan to use some land owned by the Dohmen family for a new plant. But this plot turned out to be insufficient for the facility Fred Dohmen wanted to build. The company finally settled on land on Milwaukee's South Side, and an entirely new plant opened in 1954. At the same time, the company revamped its financial structure, revised its articles of incorporation, and began to make its order-processing more efficient. The first years of Fred H.'s presidency, the company lost money. But after the new building was finished and employees had adjusted to new ways of doing business, F. Dohmen Co. became profitable again. By 1957, revenue had increased 50

percent compared with before the move. The company became fully computerized in the 1960s, moving with the times now rather than lagging behind.

CHANGES IN THE 1980S AND 1990S

The next big change came in 1980, when F. Dohmen moved again, to even bigger and more technologically advanced quarters in Germantown, Wisconsin. The new facilities were cutting edge, described in a profile of the company in the *Business Journal-Milwaukee* (May 29, 1993) as "a technological Disney World." The move came at a time when the healthcare industry was encountering new conditions that led to rapid growth at F. Dohmen. During the 1980s, the federal government changed the way it reimbursed hospitals for Medicaid and Medicare, the two big government-funded health programs. As a result, some third-party players in the healthcare market, including wholesale drug companies, were able to offer new services. F. Dohmen began taking over drug inventories for hospitals, and the company's business grew at what was evidently an extraordinary rate. As a private company, F. Dohmen did not release sales figures, but in the aforementioned profile, a company spokesperson claimed that the company had grown "by leaps and bounds," and that revenue at the end of the 1980s stood at $115 million. At that time, F. Dohmen continued to serve a mostly regional market of the Upper Midwest.

The company acquired some new divisions and subsidiaries over the late 1970s and 1980s. Its Aim-Rite division developed software for pharmacies and serviced and maintained computer software and hardware used by pharmacies. F. Dohmen also formed a division called RxESTAT in the mid-1980s. This was a prescription drug benefit management business, later renamed RESTAT. As F. Dohmen grew, it made organizational changes as well. The company developed an employee stock ownership plan in the mid-1980s, allowing its workers to buy into the private company. Then in 1988, the company appointed a new president, the first in its history without the surname Dohmen. This was Robert Wendland.

Wendland oversaw a merger that doubled the size of the company in 1992. Competition had drastically thinned the field of wholesale pharmaceutical companies. Whereas there were more than 150 wholesalers in 1980, by 1992 there were only about 75. Minneapolis-based Northwestern Drug Co. was nearly identical in size to F. Dohmen, and its president was interested in combining the two firms. After several years of talks, F. Dohmen acquired Northwest Drug, taking over its name and management. The new company was now the 12th largest in the wholesale pharmaceutical industry. Even without taking on Northwest, F. Dohmen's revenues were growing at close to 10 percent annually. Within a few years, revenue was close to $500 million, and the company predicted that it would pass $1 billion by 2000.

CONTINUED GROWTH IN THE LATE 1990S AND 2000S

In September 1995, Robert Wendland stepped down from the presidency and John Dohmen became the fifth generation of Dohmens to lead the company. F. Dohmen was still expanding, with its new divisions now reaching millions of individual customers and serving hundreds of pharmacies. The company's warehouse, storage, and order fulfillment facilities were state-of-the-art, operating with a completely paperless computerized system for maximum efficiency. Although the company had been in the hands of the same family for more than 130 years by the mid-1990s, F. Dohmen was at this point completely geared toward the future, investing in new technology and finding new service niches to fill. It combined a longstanding Dohmen logistical division called DDN with a California company called Obergfel Brothers to create a new subsidiary, DDN/Obergfel, with expertise in distribution and logistics for the pharmaceutical and biotech industries. As pharmacy and biotech continued to grow in the 1990s, outsourcing logistics, including storage, warehousing, shipping, and regulatory compliance, became an attractive option, creating a ready market for DDN/Obergfel. RESTAT, the drug benefit plan management subsidiary, housed only 70 employees in a made-over Indiana schoolhouse in the mid-1990s. A decade later, it had grown to be the fourth largest such firm in the nation.

F. Dohmen moved up the ranks into the top ten firms in the wholesale pharmaceutical industry in the late 1990s. The company continued to form innovative new businesses, responding to needs it discovered through its long and thorough acquaintance with the pharmacy market. It opened a new distribution center in Anoka, Minnesota, in 1999, and formed a new division serving the specific medical-surgical market, called Dohmen Medical L.L.C. F. Dohmen expanded into southeastern markets in 2002, forming Dohmen Distribution Partners Southeast, based in Birmingham, Alabama. The company also increased its market penetration into Michigan with another distribution network of independent pharmacies, Dohmen Distribution Partners. F. Dohmen passed its revenue goals, hitting the $2 billion mark by 2004. The company had been tradition-bound and backward looking early in the 20th century, when it was already a venerable firm. Changes since World War II had kept the company up-to-date, growing and changing with a rapidly evolving industry. From a small regional player, F. Dohmen in the mid-2000s had become one of the largest companies in a consolidating marketplace.

A. Woodward

PRINCIPAL SUBSIDIARIES

DDN/Obergfel; RESTAT.

PRINCIPAL DIVISIONS

JASCORP; Dohmen Distribution Partners L.L.C.; Dohmen Distribution Partners Southeast L.L.C.

PRINCIPAL COMPETITORS

McKesson Corporation; Amerisource Bergen Corporation; Cardinal Health, Inc.

FURTHER READING

Dohmen, Fred H., *Policies and Operations of the F. Dohmen Company, Wholesale Druggists,* Milwaukee, Wis.: F. Dohmen Co., 1939.

Dries, Michael, "Dohmen Fills Growth Prescription with Acquisition, Technology," *Business Journal-Milwaukee,* May 29, 1993, p. 30B.

———, "Where Innovation, Pharmaceuticals Flow," *Business Journal-Milwaukee,* February 11, 1995, p. 1A.

Harris, Fleming, Jr., "Dohmen Sports New Warehouse, New Approach," *Drug Topics,* August 2, 1999, p. 65.

Kueny, Barbara, "Dohmen Foresees Growth in Claims Processing Unit," *Business Journal-Milwaukee,* May 28, 1990, p. X29.

Sauer, Mike, "Innovations and Reinventions," *Corporate Report Wisconsin,* December 1, 1996, pp. 29-31.

Sonnedecker, Glenn, *A Supply Line to Health,* Germantown, Wis.: F. Dohmen Co., 1993.

Flowserve Corporation

5215 N. O'Connor Boulevard Suite 2300
Irving, Texas 75039
U.S.A.
Telephone: (972) 443-6500
Fax: (972) 443-6800
Web site: http://www.flowserve.com

Public Company
Incorporated: 1912
Employees: 13,000
Sales: $2.4 billion (2003)
Stock Exchanges: New York
Ticker Symbol: FLS
NAIC: 333911 Pump and Pumping Equipment Manufacturing

■ ■ ■

Flowserve Corporation is a global leader in the design, manufacture, marketing, and maintenance of fluid-handling equipment. It is the world's second largest producer of industrial pumps as well as valves. Formed in 1997 through the merger of Durco International and BW/IP, Inc., Flowserve operates in 56 countries. Flowserve sells its flow management equipment—which includes engineered pumps, precision mechanical seals, valves, and a range of services—primarily to the petroleum, chemical, and power industries. The company's growth strategy focuses mainly on acquisitions and alliances, although it faces formidable competitors as the industrial flow management industry undergoes a wave of consolidation. Flowserve's many brands include Durco (pumps), Valtek (valves), and GASPAC (seals).

DURCO: 1912–97

Flowserve was created in the July 1997 merger of Durco International and BW/IP, Inc. At the time it joined forces with BW/IP, Ohio-based Durco International, which was known as the Duriron Company until shortly before the merger, had enjoyed ten years of record growth. Launched in 1912 as a foundry, Duriron had been producing chemical fluid handling equipment for more than 80 years. By the 1980s, the company had built a solid reputation for making the specialized equipment needed to move fluids in the chemical process market. BWI/IP was even older, dating back to the 1872 founding of Byron Jackson.

In the 1990s, Duriron embarked on a massive reorganizing effort. With more than 85 percent of its sales derived from the chemical industry, the company was buffeted by the "peaks and valleys" of that cyclical business, according to the *Plain Dealer*. Seeking to enter new segments of the fluid management industry, Duriron began to forge alliances and acquire companies that operated outside its chemical niche. This strategy proved successful, and by 1995, the chemical industry provided only about half of Duriron's business.

Equally important to Duriron's agenda in the 1990s was its expansion into international markets. Since most American industries were well established, few major chemical, petroleum, or other processors needed to invest significantly in costly new pumps and valves. But in less developed countries (and especially in the Middle East,

Latin America, and Asia), the demand for flow management equipment was huge, as entire process industries were being created virtually from scratch. Recognizing that its future hinged on these new markets, Duriron embarked on another spate of acquisitions to gain entry. Duriron's strategy was successful. Between 1985 and 1995, international sales as a portion of the company's total revenue rose from 15 percent to about 33 percent.

Although Duriron's 1996 sales reached $605.5 million (a gain of nearly 13.7 percent from 1995), the company was falling behind in the rapidly consolidating flow management industry, as its competitors grew dramatically larger through mergers and takeovers. Duriron's ability to expand through further acquisitions of its own was particularly limited by its comparative lack of operating capital. To remain a major force in the industry, Durco (as Duriron had rechristened itself in 1997) would need to find new ways to grow.

BW/IP'S GROWTH AND DEVELOPMENT IN THE 1980S AND 1990S

Like Durco, BW/IP was a leader in the manufacture of industrial pumps, although its strength was in the production of specialized pumps for the petroleum and power industries. But the petroleum industry, like the chemical process industry Durco served, was cyclical. In addition, because petroleum industry revenues had flattened in the late 1980s and early 1990s, BW/IP's growth had slowed as well. To protect itself from the vagaries of the petroleum industry, therefore, BW/IP sought to enter new markets.

Like Durco, BW/IP sought to use targeted acquisitions to achieve its goals. In 1996, for example, BW/IP acquired the Anchor/Darling Valve Company, which was an American manufacturer of high-specification, custom-engineered valves for the power and marine industries. A few months later, BW/IP purchased Stork

Popmen B.V. This Dutch company manufactured pumps for the petroleum industry and offered BW/IP access to lucrative European markets. As a result of these efforts, BW/IP's sales rose 9 percent in 1996, to $492 million. Nevertheless, again paralleling Durco, BW/IP was hindered by its lack of capital. Many of its key customers in the petroleum industry were true global companies, who required products and services across the world, a reach that BW/IP simply did not have.

Durco, too, was limited in its efforts to achieve a global presence. As Bernard Rethore, BW/IP's president, chairman, and chief executive officer (CEO), would later explain to the *Wall Street Transcript*, both companies "recognized that to serve our customers in the chemical, petroleum, and power markets on a world basis we needed to have a larger footprint, a greater scope as a company. As BW/IP and Durco, we couldn't do that because each company was too small." In late 1996, executives from the two companies began informal discussion about the potential for joining forces. The advantages of a merger became more apparent after ITT Industries Inc. paid $815 million to acquire Goulds Pumps Inc. in April 1997, thereby becoming the world's largest pump manufacturer. The industry "was consolidating and turning cutthroat," an executive at another industrial pump company told *Business Week*. Faced with the prospect of being left hopelessly behind, BW/IP and Durco pledged to merge.

FLOWSERVE BORN IN 1997

The union of the two companies was a merger of equals, effectuated by a stock-for-stock exchange in July 1997. BW/IP's Rethore was selected as the new company's chairman and chief executive, and William Jordan (the president, chairman, and CEO of Durco) served as the president and chief operating officer (COO) of the new corporate entity. To reflect that the merger had created a new company with a broader range of products and services, BW/IP and Durco elected to take a new name. They settled on Flowserve because it "symbolizes the fact that ... we will adopt an expanded vision of serving all the flow control needs of our customers in the 21st century," Rethore proclaimed in a press release. After closing BW/IP's headquarters in Long Beach, California, and Durco's in Cleveland, Ohio, Flowserve opened global corporate headquarters in Irving, Texas.

Almost immediately after the merger, Flowserve launched a $92 million integration program that consisted of 45 distinct projects. Although BW/IP and Durco each had carved out areas of focus in the wider flow management industry, there was a considerable degree of overlap. To eliminate these redundancies, Flowserve merged the two companies' pump, valve, and

KEY DATES

1997: Durco acquires BWIP, becomes Flowserve Corporation.

1998: Flowserve acquires Lokeren NV, ZAR Beheer, BTR Engineering Limited, and Valtek Engineering; company acquires remaining share of ownership of Durametallic Asia.

1999: Flowserve acquires Innovative Valve Technologies Inc.; company announces significant layoffs as part of restructuring program.

2000: Flowserve announces acquisition of the Ingersoll Pump Unit of Ingersoll-Dressler; company receives contract to provide pumps to the Athabasca Oil Sands Project.

2002: The United Kingdom's Invensys Flow control is acquired.

2004: Remainder of Australia's Thompsons Kelly & Lewis (TKL) is acquired.

2005: Interseal is acquired.

seal businesses into three streamlined divisions: Rotating Equipment, Flow Control, and Fluid Sealing.

The new company also decided to focus on certain core areas, which necessitated shedding extraneous operations. To this end, Flowserve sold its Metal Fab Machine Corp. to Senior Engineering Group PLC for $19 million in November 1997. Moreover, as part of a cost-cutting program, Flowserve shuttered its high-cost pump manufacturing plant in Charleroi, Belgium, and transferred production to two factories in The Netherlands. It also opened a valve production factory in 1997 in Bangalore, India, so that it could reduce labor and materials costs.

In addition to honing its existing operations, Flowserve also sought to enter a different, and lucrative, sector of the flow management industry: service and repair. Whereas the pump and valve business was subject to the cyclical downturns of the petroleum and chemical markets, the service and repair of existing equipment was not. In 1997, Flowserve formed the ServiceRepair Division, which focused on tending to the flow management equipment it had already installed. Flowserve would "go beyond just manufacturing," Rethore told the *Wall Street Transcript* and would provide "cradle-to-grave" service on its equipment.

By the close of 1997, the merger looked to be an unequivocal success. Sales for the year surpassed $1.15

billion, with nearly half of the total generated by operations outside the United States. With 44 manufacturing facilities and 88 service and quick response centers, the company was better positioned to provide a broader array of goods and services to a wide range of customers. Flowserve's net profit for 1997 was $51.6 million.

Investors and industry analysts had high expectations for Flowserve in 1998. The company's sales were balanced, with about one-third of total sales derived from the petroleum industry, one-third from the chemical sector, and one-third from power and other industries. As these markets tended to follow different cycles, Flowserve appeared to be less vulnerable to downturns than BW/IP and Durco had been on their own.

TROUBLES IN 1998

In early 1998, however, both the petroleum and chemical markets softened simultaneously, as the Asian economic crisis of 1997 spread around the globe. By the end of 1998, oil prices (when adjusted for inflation) were at their lowest level in the United States since the Great Depression of the 1930s. The chemical market was plagued by overcapacity, and prices there also dropped, reaching global all-time lows. As a result, the industries involved in these sectors postponed orders for new equipment.

Despite this untimely confluence of events, the company continued to integrate its operations. In 1998, Flowserve inaugurated its Flowserver initiative, a multi-year program intended to coordinate the myriad businesses within the company. Flowserver was predicted to have a $120 million price tag, with an expected completion date of 2001. The centerpiece of Flowserver was the establishment of an integrated information technology system that would consolidate computing and coordinate planning.

Flowserve also increased its efforts to enter new markets. The company made five important acquisitions in 1998, all of which expanded its global reach. In May, Flowserve purchased the Valtek Engineering Division of Rolls-Royce plc. With annual sales of about $20 million, this unit was the British licensee for a number of Valtek control valve products. The acquisition strengthened Flowserve's position in Europe, the Middle East, and Africa. In October, Flowserve bought the remaining 49 percent ownership interest in Durametallic Asia, a fluid sealing manufacturer, from its joint venture partner, the Sanmar Group. In December, Flowserve purchased a mechanical seal business that operated in Australia and New Zealand from an Australian licensee and distributor, BTR Engineering Limited. During the year,

Flowserve also acquired ARS Lokeren NV of Belgium and ZAR Beheer BV of The Netherlands. These European valve repair companies bolstered Flowserve's position in the profitable market for repairing flow management equipment.

Flowserve pursued the service end of the market in other ways in 1998 as well. Early in the year, the company consolidated its two most service-oriented divisions, ServiceRepair and Fluid Sealing, into a new division called Flow Solutions. This new unit was to be the centerpiece of Flowserve's drive to capture a greater share of the service market. As the company announced in a press release, "service and repair [will] be a fundamental part of Flowserve's growth strategy." To improve on its network of service centers, the company built new facilities in locations such as Antwerp, Belgium, and Wilmington, North Carolina. By the end of 1998, Flowserve presided over 85 service centers in 23 countries.

Despite its many activities during 1998, however, Flowserve's sales and profits dropped as a result of the economic conditions afflicting its primary customers. Annual sales fell to $1.08 billion, while net earnings slid to $48.9 million. The company attributed the 6 percent drop in profits primarily to fallout from Asia's recession. Nevertheless, Rethore emphasized to the *Dayton Daily News* that the company had "dealt effectively with the negative impacts on [its] business of global economic turmoil, dramatically lower oil prices, and weakened chemical markets."

RETRENCHMENT AND GROWTH TO CLOSE OUT THE CENTURY

In 1999 and 2000, Flowserve continued its two-pronged strategy of integrating the sprawling businesses of BW/IP and Durco into a cohesive framework on the one hand and gaining a larger presence in international markets on the other. Flowserve had new leadership to aid it in its mission. President and COO Jordan had left the company in October 1998 and was replaced by C. Scott Greer in July of the following year. Rethore remained chairman and CEO, although he planned to relinquish his duties as chief executive after Greer became more familiar with Flowserve's operations.

In November 1999, Flowserve made an important acquisition when it purchased Houston, Texas-based Innovative Valve Technologies Inc. for $15.7 million and the assumption of $84 million in debt. With 63 operating locations and annual revenues of more than $154 million, Innovative was a leader in maintenance, repair, and replacement services for valves, piping, and other flow management systems. "Through this acquisition,

we will significantly expand our technical service and repair capabilities," Greer explained to *Petroleum Finance Week*. In addition to strengthening Flowserve's place in the service sector, the acquisition also positioned the company more strongly in critical emerging markets in the Middle East.

Flowserve also won two major contracts in 1999: one to provide flow management equipment to Suncor Energy's Millennium Project and one for AEC Pipelines' oil sands pipeline expansion. Although the petroleum industry had curtailed a number of projects, oil sands exploration (the extraction of oil from tar sands) continued because of the comparatively low costs involved and the high quality of the crude oil produced. The contracts were worth a total of $10 million.

Despite these considerable advances, Flowserve's 1999 sales were hindered by the continued overall weakness of the petroleum and chemical markets. Sales dropped 2 percent to $1.06 billion, and profits fell to $12.2 million. Faced with these difficulties, as well as with the continued need to eliminate certain redundancies that had persisted since the merger, Flowserve announced early in 2000 that it would close ten facilities and lay off 9 percent of its workforce (about 600 people).

Nevertheless, Flowserve continued to view expansion as the key to its future success. With the stated goal of becoming a $2.5 billion company by 2004, Flowserve made the largest acquisition in its history to that point, when it agreed to buy the Ingersoll-Dressler pump unit of the Ingersoll-Rand Co. in February 2000. The $775 million purchase resulted in the second largest pump company in the world. "This type of acquisition has such a high level of hard synergies that we'll be able to take out excess capacity in the industry," Greer told the *Dow Jones News Service*. Also in February 2000, Flowserve announced that it had won a contract to provide $20 million worth of pumps for the Athabasca Oil Sands Project. One of its largest pump contracts ever, the deal held great promise for the company.

In light of developments such as these, Rethore was optimistic about Flowserve's future prospects. "As our markets recover, and they will, as we acquire successfully and well, and we will, and as we build further the internal operational excellence of this company, as we will, I believe our increasing success will be rewarded," he told the *Wall Street Transcript*.

MORE DEALMAKING AFTER 2000

Flowserve completed its acquisition of Ingersoll-Dresser in September 2001; it was required by antitrust regulators to sell off its Tulsa plant. Flowserve was cutting 1,100 jobs in all to save $75 million a year. It was also updating its newly acquired plants with state-of-the-art, computerized tooling. Flowserve posted a loss of $1.5 million in 2001 though sales rose to $1.9 billion.

Flowserve continued in its role as industry consolidator after 2000, buying companies and trimming their workforces. The company made another large buy in 2002, outbidding Tyco to acquire the Flow Control Division of the United Kingdom's Invensys plc for $535 million. The business had sales of more than $500 million a year; the buy made Flowserve number two in the world market for valves as well as pumps, with more than 14,000 employees overall. Flowserve said it was expecting to gain up to $15 million a year in synergies. Following a familiar pattern, the company shuttered a half-dozen North American plants and cut about 450 jobs following the acquisition.

Rising energy costs had oil producers buying more new equipment from Flowserve. Revenues for 2003 were reported at $2.4 billion, though the company would end up restating figures from 2000 to the first quarter of 2004. In the midst of internal audits and SEC inquiries, the company's top finance jobs became something of a revolving door.

A North American pump service alliance was formed with John Wood Group PLC in mid-2004. "This ... is in direct response to our customers' increasing demand for life cycle cost management service from a single-source supplier," said the head of Flowserve's Pump Division.

The company made a couple of big deals Down Under. In 2004, Flowserve bought out its local partner in Australia's Thompsons, Kelly, & Lewis (TKL) for $11 million. TKL had previously been majority owned by Invensys subsidiary BTR Engineering (Australia). The company produced centrifugal pumps, railroad components, and other steel products. The TKL buy was followed up the next year by the purchase of Ludowici Ltd.'s Interseal mechanical seal business, based in Perth.

The company continued to shed non-core assets. The divestment of Flowserve's Government Marine Business Unit (GMBU) was announced in late 2004. Curtis-Wright Corp. bought it for $28 million. The GMBU specialized in supplying pump technology for naval vessels and had sales of about $26 million a year.

Flowserve was paying off its debt which stood at about $650 million at the beginning of 2005. Its General Services division, whose 600 employees maintained non-Flowserve brands, was up for sale. The company also divested its French distributor Flowserve France, which was acquired by FCX.

Flowserve Corporation and its chairman and CEO C. Scott Greer paid fines to settle an SEC case involving Regulation FD, or fair disclosure. Neither admitted or denied guilt. The charges involved a private meeting with analysts in which company officials allegedly reaffirmed a previously issued forecast.

Greer left the company when his contract expired in mid-2005. He was succeeded as president and CEO by former COO Lewis M. Kling. Towards the end of the year, the company was completing a much delayed Form 10-K for 2004 while it continued to review reports for previous years.

PRINCIPAL SUBSIDIARIES

Flowserve Argentina S.A.; Flowserve Australia Pty. Ltd.; Flowserve (Austria) GmbH; Flowserve FSD N.V. (Belgium); Flowserve Belgium N.V.; Flowserve do Brasil Ltda.; Flowserve Ltda. (Brazil); Valtek Registros, Ltda. (Brazil); Flowserve Canada Corp.; Flowserve Canada Holding Corp.; Flowserve Canada Limited Partnership; Flowserve Nova Scotia Holding Corp. (Canada); Flowserve Chile S.A.; Flowserve Shanghai Limited (China); Flowserve Colombia, Ltda.; Flowserve Europe Holding ApS (Denmark); Flowserve Finance ApS (Denmark); Naval OY (Finland); Flowserve Flow Control S.A.S. (France); Flowserve Pleuger S.A.S. (France); Flowserve Polyvalves S.A.S. (France); Flowserve Pompes S.A.S. (France); Flowserve Sales International S.A.S. (France); Flowserve S.A.S. (France); Argus GmbH & Co. K.G. (Germany); Deutsche Ingersoll-Dresser Pumpen GmbH (Germany); Flowserve Ahaus GmbH (Germany); Flowserve Essen GmbH (Germany); Flowserve Dortmund Verwaltungs GmbH (Germany); Flowserve Dortmund GmbH & Co. KG (Germany); Flowserve Flow Control GmbH (Germany); Gestra GmbH & Co. KG (Germany); IDP Pumpen GmbH (Germany); Ingersoll-Dresser Pumpen GmbH (Germany); IPSCO GmbH (Germany); Pleuger Worthington GmbH (Germany); Audco India Ltd. (50%); Flowserve Microfinish Pumps Pvt. Ltd. (India; 76%); Flowserve India Controls Pvt. Ltd.; Flowserve Microfinish Valves Pvt. Ltd. (India; 76%); Flowserve Sanmar Limited India (40%); Limitorque India Limited (24%); PT Flowserve (Indonesia; 75%); Flowserve Spa (Italy); Ingersoll-Dresser Pumps S.p.A. (Italy); Worthington S.p.A. (Italy); Flowserve Japan K.K.; Niigata Equipment Maintenance Co., Ltd. (Japan; 50%); Niigata Worthington Company Ltd. (Japan; 50%); Flowserve SAAG Sdn Bhd (Malaysia; 70%); Flowserve (Mauritius) Corporation; Flowserve S.A. de C.V. (Mexico); Fabromatic BV (Netherlands); Flowserve B.V. (Netherlands); Flowserve Global Lending BV (Netherlands); Flowserve International B.V. (Netherlands); Flowserve Repair & Services BV (Netherlands); Flowserve Finance B.V. (Netherlands); Flowserve Flow Control Benelux BV

(Netherlands); Flowserve New Zealand Limited; Gestra Polonia SP. z.o.o. (Poland); Flowserve Portuguesa Mecanismos de Controlo de Fluxos, Lda (Portugal); Arabian Seals Company, Ltd. (Saudi Arabia; 40%); Flowserve Abahsain Co. Ltd. (Saudi Arabia; 60%); Flowserve Flow Control Pte Ltd (Singapore); Flowserve Pte. Ltd. (Singapore); Limitorque Asia Pte Ltd (Singapore; 60%); Flowserve South Africa (Proprietary) Limited; Flowserve S.A. (Spain); Flowserve Spain S.A.; Gestra Espanola, S.A. (Spain); Flowserve Sweden AB; NAF AB (Sweden); Palmstierna International AB (Sweden); Flowserve International S.A. (Switzerland); Flowserve S.A. (Switzerland); Ingersoll-Dresser Pump Services Sarl (Switzerland); Flowserve (Thailand) Limited; Audco Limited (UK); Flowserve Flow Control (U.K.) Ltd.; Flowserve Flow Control Limited (UK); Flowserve International Limited (UK); Flowserve Limited (UK); Flowserve Pumps Limited (UK); Flowserve UK Finance Limited; Ingersoll-Dresser Pumps Newark Ltd. (UK); IPSCO (UK) Limited; PMV Controls Limited (UK); BW/IP New Mexico, Inc.; Flowcom Insurance Company, Inc.; Flowserve Holdings, Inc.; Flowserve International, Inc.; Flowserve Management Company (Business Trust); Flowserve U.S. Inc.; PMV Inc; Flowserve de Venezuela S.A.; Hot Tapping & Plugging C.A. (Venezuela).

Rebecca Stanfel
Updated, Frederick C. Ingram

PRINCIPAL DIVISIONS

Flow Control Products; Pumping Systems; Sealing Solutions; Services.

PRINCIPAL COMPETITORS

IDEX Corporation; Roper Industries, Inc.

FURTHER READING

Bohman, Jim, "Dallas-Based Pump and Valve Maker to Eliminate 600 Jobs," *Dayton Daily News,* December 28, 1999.

———, "Flowserve Reports 2001 Losses," *Dayton Daily News,* February 6, 2002, p. 2E.

———, "1998 Earnings; Flowserve Pins Drop on Industry," *Dayton Daily News,* February 10, 1999.

Cecil, Mark, "Flowserve Feels It's Necessary to Divest," *Mergers & Acquisitions Report,* February 14, 2005.

"CEO/Company Interview: C. Scott Greer, Flowserve Corporation," *Wall Street Transcript,* November 2000.

"CEO Interview: Bernard G. Rethore, Flowserve Corp.," *Wall Street Transcript,* May 3, 1999.

"Companies Continue to Feel Wrath of Reg FD," *Financial Analysis, Planning & Reporting,* May 1, 2005.

Fletcher, Sam, "Flowserve to Take $27 Million Charge As Part of Restructuring Plan," *Oil Daily,* January 5, 2000.

"Flowserve and Wood Group Form North American Service Alliance," *Market News Publishing,* July 26, 2004.

"Flowserve to Close Six Facilities, Cut 450 Workers," *Associated Press Newswires,* June 5, 2002.

"Flowserve to Restate Financial Results," *Associated Press Newswires,* February 7, 2005.

"Flowserve Will Acquire Innovative Valve Technologies," *Petroleum Finance Week,* November 29, 1999.

Freestone, Ann, "Renee Hornbaker Integrating Companies for Success," *Strategic Finance,* October 2000, p. 43.

Hay, Andrew, and Dan Lalor, "Flowserve Buys Invensys Unit for $535M," *Reuters News,* March 22, 2002.

Jordan, John M., and Shauna R. Steigerwald, "At-the-Machine Programming Helps Company Keep Grip on Pump Factory Overhaul," *Modern Machine Shop,* January 1, 2003, p. 120.

Montgomery, Christopher, "Flowserve Restates Results for 45 Months," *Dayton Daily News,* February 4, 2004, p. D3.

"More Mergers in Valve Industry," *Water Technology,* June 1, 1997.

Murray, Matt, "Durco and BW/IP to Merge in Deal of $435.6 Million," *Wall Street Journal,* May 5, 1997.

"Plumbing Company to Cut 1,100 Jobs As Part of Acquisition," *Associated Press Newswires,* August 16, 2000.

"SEC Files Settled Regulation FD Charges Against Flowserve Corporation, Its CEO, and Director of Investor Relations," *SEC News Digest,* March 24, 2005.

Solomon, Deborah, "Moving the Market: SEC Case Takes Fair Disclosure to a New Level," *Wall Street Journal,* March 25, 2005, p. C3.

Solov, Diane, "Duriron Co. Making the Most of Strong Markets," *Plain Dealer,* June 26, 1996.

Tate, Pamela, "Flowserve Financial Chief Resigns," *Dow Jones News Service,* June 15, 2004.

Willetts, Susan, "Flowserve Corp. in Pact to Buy Ivensys Bus for $535M," *Dow Jones International News,* March 22, 2002.

Williams, Christopher, "Flowserve Backs 2001 EPS View 'In Neighborhood of $2,'" *Dow Jones News Service,* February 10, 2000.

FOOD FOR THE POOR, INC.

Food For The Poor, Inc.

550 SW 12th Avenue, Building 4
Deerfield Beach, Florida 33442
U.S.A.
Telephone: (954) 427-2222
Toll Free: (800) 427-9104
Fax: (954) 570-7654
Web site: http://www.foodforthepoor.com

Nonprofit Company
Incorporated: 1982
Employees: 232
Operating Revenues: $643.5 million (2004)
NAIC: 624110 Child and Youth Services; 624120 Services for the Elderly and Persons with Disabilities; 624190 Other Individual and Family Services; 524210 Community Food Services; 62422 Community Housing Services; 624230 Emergency and Other Relief Services; 813110 Religious Organizations; 813212 Voluntary Health Organizations

■ ■ ■

Food For The Poor, Inc. is a Christian charity that provides food, health, social, economic, and emergency relief services in 16 countries in Latin America and the Caribbean. The nonprofit organization helps those most in need through feeding, housing, medical assistance, education, water projects, micro-enterprise programs, and emergency relief operations.

The group, which uses 96 percent of its funds on programs, partners with Caritas in the Dominican Republic and Guatemala; The Order of Malta in

Honduras and Guatemala; the Episcopal Diocese of Honduras; Roman Catholic dioceses in Belize, Grenada, Haiti, Jamaica, and El Salvador; Operation Compassion; thousands of churches of all denominations; missionaries; and nongovernmental organizations (NGOs) throughout the Caribbean and Central America.

1982 TO THE MID-1990S: PROVIDING FOOD, HEALTHCARE, SOCIAL, AND ECONOMIC RELIEF

Ferdinand Mahfood cofounded Food For The Poor, Inc. (FFP) with his brother, Robin Mahfood, in 1982. Two of four brothers of Lebanese extraction involved in the import-export business between Jamaica and the United States, Ferdinand had undergone a religious conversion in 1980 during which he determined to help the destitute of Jamaica. With the support of his two other brothers, Joseph and Samuel, he established his nonprofit organization and began to collect funds from North American and European benefactors.

Throughout the 1980s, FFP expanded its scope and streamlined its distribution system. In addition to food, it began to ship medical supplies and equipment and educational materials. To ensure that its aid was meaningful in every case, FFP would send a project specialist to the area in need to assess the situation and to help develop a long-term recovery plan. The agency then shopped on the world market for specific items and shipped them duty-free to local allied Third World churches, missionary programs, and charity organizations. FFP's allied programs arranged for the direct distribution of the items. In this way, FFP eliminated

COMPANY PERSPECTIVES

■

As good stewards of your donated dollars, we take our responsibility as a Christian charity very seriously and we are always working hard to find the most efficient and cost-effective means of securing goods and shipping them. For 23 years, we have worked hard to keep our operating costs as low as possible to keep your donation hard at work serving the poor.

many of the overhead costs that other international relief efforts incurred, while making certain that the items it purchased reached their intended audience. FFP also ensured a low administrative cost for the agency.

FFP expanded into other areas of assistance in the 1980s, including microenterprise programs. Mahfood's goal for those his organization served was that they break free from the cycle of poverty. He believed that education and self-help must fortify charity work to make a true difference. To this end, FFP began to support programs that taught recipients how to raise livestock and develop small businesses; it also provided agricultural assistance to independent farmers throughout the 1980s. In addition, FFP began to build small houses for poor families in 1982, first in Jamaica, a nation whose economy had begun to decline in 1974 as a result of rising fuel costs and recession, and then in Haiti in 1989.

By 1995, FFP was supplying more than $37 million in program services to the destitute poor. Haiti was a primary target for the agency that year as it endeavored to meet requests that had gone unfulfilled during the United Nations' three-year embargo on the country. In all, FFP provided more than $9.4 million in aid to Haiti in 1995, through goods as well as financial support to a variety of relief programs that included hospitals, orphanages, schools, a home for people with physical handicaps, and a village for the elderly. FFP also ran a full service hospital and outpatient clinics in Haiti, as well as providing assistance in the form of food, medicine, and medical equipment to all of the hospitals in Haiti.

1995-99: AN EMPHASIS ON DISASTER RELIEF AND HOMES FOR THE POOR

Also established in the mid-1990s was the organization's Caribbean Hurricane Relief Program, which provided

emergency assistance to Caribbean countries affected by storms during the 1996 hurricane season. These countries included Antigua, Dominica, St. Lucia, St. Vincent, Trinidad, and Granada, nations that did not otherwise receive aid from the United States or other industrialized nations. The goal of this program, according to Ferdinand Mahfood in a 1996 press release, was "to be prepared before the [hurricane] season starts with supplies and funds. It is difficult for the poor residents of these countries to provide for themselves under good conditions. Even a minor storm can have devastating effects for families for many years—and some may never recover from the financial setback."

FFP continued building houses for poor families in Jamaica and Haiti in the late 1990s. In Jamaica, FFP built 2,000 homes after the government agreed to donate approximately 200 acres of land and the necessary infrastructure to support the new community roads, sewer connections, and electricity. Restrooms and shower facilities for the community as a whole were communal. According to Mahfood in a press release, "No one should have to bathe or do other private things in public. Building community showers and restroom facilities is a step in the right direction." In 1998, the agency expanded its building program to El Salvador, and in 1999, it partnered with the American-Nicaraguan Foundation (ANF) to begin construction on Villa Nueva, 263 new homes on close to 90 acres of land in northwestern Nicaragua.

Villa Nueva's occupants came from a community that had been flooded out by Hurricane Mitch. Each family involved was required to send two workers to the construction teams that built the homes, which when finished, were handed over to the female heads of family. Assigning home ownership to women went against the established norms of the region; however, FFP opted to do so, as it explained in a 1999 press release, because of the high rate at which husbands abandoned their families in northwestern Nicaragua and women were "left to fend for themselves and their children with no property and little or no income." By giving women legal ownership of the new homes, "[w]e're trying to make the rebuilding efforts an opportunity for the women of the region to improve their position in society. By placing the homes we build under the names of the women, we give them a power in the family they usually don't have," explained Ferdinand Mahfood.

Also in 1999, FFP began a several-year partnership with the U.S. Department of Agriculture (USDA) and shipped 13 million pounds of food on Christmas Day to Central America. Part of the U.S. government's Presidential Initiative 416B, a program that ships surplus agricultural commodities to developing countries to al-

KEY DATES

1982: Ferdinand Mahfood and Robin Mahfood found Food For The Poor (FFP); the agency starts its home building program in Jamaica.

1996: The agency starts its Caribbean Hurricane Relief Program.

1998: The agency expands its building program to El Salvador.

1999: FFP partners with the American-Nicaraguan Foundation (ANF) to begin construction on Villa Nueva; the agency begins its partnership with the U.S. Department of Agriculture.

2000: Robin Mahfood becomes president of the organization.

2003: FFP initiates its Prison Ministry Department.

2005: The agency is ranked as the 13th largest international charity and the third largest international charity in the United States by the Chronicle of Philanthropy and the 22nd largest by the Non-Profit Times.

leviate hunger, FFP's effort targeted children, the elderly, and community aid families. Children were weighed and examined before and after the distribution of commodities, and parents were taught proper nutrition and feeding habits for their families.

2000-05: UNPRECEDENTED AND ONGOING GROWTH

Ferdinand Mahfood retired in 2000 and Robin Mahfood took over as head of FFP. In 2001, the USDA awarded FFP about $25 million in commodities for distribution in Jamaica, El Salvador, Guatemala, Nicaragua, and Guyana. In December 2002, Food For The Poor received a three-year award of 53 million pounds a year of nonfat dry milk from the USDA, for distribution in 14 countries. This assistance, which also targeted children, the elderly, infirm, and homeless persons, reached more than four million people.

During the 2002 hurricane season, FFP relied upon its warehouse in Spanish Town, Jamaica, to supply other relief agencies, including the U.N. World Food Program, the International Red Cross, the Salvation Army, and CARE, with food, water, and relief supplies. In direct response to hurricane Ivan, FFP increased production from 250 homes per month to 500 homes and began to distribute dry food throughout Jamaica. With funds

from Alcoa Foundation, it began to teach fishermen in two Jamaican communities a more sustainable and environmentally friendly technique of fishing. It purchased boats and fishing and cooling equipment so the fisherman could fish further out in the water away from endangered reefs. Elsewhere in the Caribbean, in the Bahamas, Granada, and Haiti, FFP met the devastating results of the hurricane season with $35 million in relief assistance.

In 2003, FFP, by then the largest relief organization operating in the Caribbean and the third largest charity in the United States, experienced unprecedented growth. Total support received during 2003 was $465 million, up from $351 million the year before. According to President Robin Mahfood in a press release, the agency had "continued to streamline all of [its] operations," and this, combined with its increased scale of operations, had reduced its operating expense ratio to 4.7 percent in 2003, a drop of slightly more than 4 percent since 1999.

The agency distributed more than 3,000 containers of aid to 16 countries in 2003, an increase of close to 2,500 containers from 2002. It built 2,391 homes for families (although slightly more than 100 of these could not be occupied because of inadequate sewage and other concerns). In another new initiative, The Prison Ministry Department of FFP paid out $2,000 in 2003 to buy the freedom of 15 prisoners in Jamaica who had been incarcerated for nonviolent crimes, such as theft of food or traffic violation, and were being held only because they lacked the funds to pay their fines.

Based on its belief that poverty consisted not just of low income but included the undermining of the means of achieving physical and social access to healthcare, in 2004, FFP embarked on a joint project with St. Joseph's Hospital in St. Andrew, Jamaica, to open Our Lady of the Poor free clinic. The hospital donated six rooms, which FFP paid $1 million to refurbish. The clinic, which aimed to provide proper healthcare to improve the standard of life for the poor, could accommodate 100 clients a day.

That same year, FFP partnered with the Salvation Army to provide accommodations for the homeless in Kingston, Jamaica. After ascertaining that many of those using the facilities lacked the means of supporting themselves, FFP arranged to include programs that would boost their income-earning skills, teaching them methods of chicken rearing and how to operate a sewing machine. It also began building 500 units in the Ellerslie Penn community of Spanish Town, Jamaica, where to date it had built more than 300 houses.

The agency's outstanding growth continued through 2004. FFP distributed a record 5,852 trailers of food and other assistance that year, drawing on total support received of $643 million. Again in 2004, the USDA donated 9,000 metric tons of commodities to FFP under the McGovern-Dole International Food for Education and Child Nutrition Program. In conjunction with Caritas Arquidiocesana, FFP established a direct feeding program in Guatemala that served 118,000 children, mothers, teachers, caregivers, and volunteers. FFP also built about 4,300 basic homes for families in 2004. Its prison release program, which had expanded to include Guatemala, Honduras, and Guyana, operated twice yearly, at Christmas and Easter.

During 2005, FFP distributed more than 34,000 trailers of assistance valued at more than $3 billion and completed 7,002 houses. It had built more than 33,000 housing units in the Caribbean and Central America since 1982. The agency was ranked as the 13th largest international charity and the third largest international charity in the United States by the *Chronicle of Philanthropy* and the 22nd largest by the *Non-Profit Times.* Its overhead ratio dropped to below 4 percent.

Carrie Rothburd

FURTHER READING

FitzRoy, Maggie, "Barbara 'Speechless' at Village Site: Beaches Waitress Raises Funds for Jamaica's Poor," *Florida Times-Union,* November 2, 2005, p. L1.

"Food for the Poor Receives Milk Shipment," *Gleaner,* August 26, 2003.

Freeze.com LLC

868 3rd Street South Suite 102
Waite Park, Minnesota 56387
U.S.A.
Telephone: (320) 203-7157
Fax: (320) 253-2225
Web site: http://www.freeze.com

Private Company
Founded: 2000
Employees: 40
Sales: $18 million (2004 est.)
NAIC: 454111 Electronic Shopping; 541613 Marketing
   Consulting Services

■ ■ ■

Freeze.com LLC is a private company that produces and provides free screensavers and graphics for personal computers. The company operates several web sites, including freeze.com, screensaver.com, my.freeze.com, ringtone.com, and wallpapers.com. Freeze also offers e-mail services. Founders Rob and Ryan Weber began the St. Cloud, Minnesota company while college students and have received growing recognition since then. Freeze.com earns its revenue by providing personal demographic information to direct marketers by way of site registrations.

1990S-2001: RISING ENTREPRENEURIAL STARS

In the 1990s twins Rob and Ryan Weber were eager to buy their first home computer. The two found jobs at a local McDonald's and worked their way well beyond their minimum wage beginnings. Rob and Ryan Weber bought a computer and soon found their passion for the Internet and its ability to generate business.

The Webers began a sports card trading site on the Internet when they were only 16. The site attracted visitors through "fan pages" dedicated to information and statistics on famous athletes. The two also created page space for rent on their site that served as a want-ad page for other people selling sports cards and merchandise. It seemed as though the teens had a knack for marketing. The venture brought in roughly $500 a month, and taught the brothers a lesson in just what the Internet could do if one was enterprising and inventive.

Over the next few years the Webers attended St. Cloud State University and continued their Internet business. Rob and Ryan became computer consultants while in college but were disappointed when their consulting fees earned them less than $10,000 a year. The brothers decided to dive into an Internet business when one of their clients sold the web site they had helped him create for a million dollars.

They had been providing consultation that had helped their clients get rich and decided then that they could develop their own business and reap the benefits directly.

The Weber brothers spent time researching what people were interested in on the Internet and discovered that many searches sought free items. They developed an Internet site that directed people to other sites offering giveaway promotions. The "free stuff" site became one of the top Internet sites, with over 23,000 visitors a day.

The Webers further developed their site by adding newsletters to draw in visitors looking for web sites featuring their specific interests. According to a *Star Tribune* interview, the Weber twins were making "between $50,000 and $90,000 a month." Most of the revenue came from advertising space the brothers sold to direct marketing companies whose sales were largely based on volume distribution of their ads. The young entrepreneurs knew they had found a business worth pursuing.

By 2000, Rob and Ryan Weber had been honored as Minnesota's Collegiate Entrepreneurs of the Year and had been chosen as the runners-up for North American Collegiate Entrepreneurs of the Year. Many young college students had always worked their way through school but few brought in figures rivaling those of the Webers.

A key break for the fledgling business came when San Jose business and tech guru Young K. Sohn met the twins. Sohn was president of Agilent Technologies' Semiconductor Products Group and helped attract needed capital investment to Freeze. Sohn served as a director for the company board, adding experience and know-how to the Internet start-up. Sohn noted in a *St. Cloud State Alumni* magazine interview that although he had contributed to the success of the company, he recognized the Webers' talent early on. "It was clear to me they were a lot smarter than me in web-based marketing ...; they have the agility, drive and maturity it takes." Sohn brought in $300,000 of key investment money in 2000.

In the beginning success came fairly easily to the new company. The Webers decided to debut the company under the name Freeze.com but in 2000 the company found out that it had never owned the rights to the domain name. An unscrupulous person had elicited $2,600 from Freeze and had pretended to sell rights that were not actually owned. When the Webers later learned they had been conned the site was established enough that the company thought it wise to buy the name Freeze.com from the rightful owner, a lesson that cost the company $37,000.

During the height of the dotcom crash the company, like many Internet start-ups, took a hit.

Sales revenue dropped significantly and Freeze.com did what it could to survive. The Webers and nine newly hired employees earned money doing online advertising for many direct marketing companies. Freeze.com created banner ads that appeared on search engine web sites and kept a modest amount of revenue coming in to keep the company afloat.

The move to work with direct marketers came out of survival mode and the dotcom uncertainty, but it influenced the direction of the company over the next few years. In 2001 Freeze.com changed its focus to attracting Internet users through free offers, mainly screensavers, ring tones, and wallpapers for computer and cell phone users and tying the free deals to site registration. The company then sold the information to direct marketers. The information had value because it included a lot of demographics that the marketers could use to direct their sales to target specific consumers. The more hits for screensavers at Freeze.com, the wider the audience for product pitches by such advertisers as Sears, eBay, Discover Card, and T-Mobile USA.

Since 2000 the employees at Freeze had been designing some of its own screensavers, although the company still had licensing agreements with other computer graphic artists as well. The screensavers included images that were wholesome in character. Scenes ranged from underwater aquariums with exotic fish, to fireplaces with roaring fires and winter village scenes reminiscent of a Thomas Kincaid painting. Wallpapers.com featured celebrity pictures as well as typical calendaresque renderings of puppies and kittens. The sites linked to one another, which allowed for increased traffic flow.

Shortly after the business began to take off, older brother Aaron joined the company. It had become a true family affair. The Webers' mother, Deb Childers, became Freeze.com's marketing director and their father provided some of the photographic artwork that was available on company sites. The company bought its own 7,500-square-foot headquarters in Waite Park, a neighboring city to larger St. Cloud, after outgrowing its previous location.

2003 AND BEYOND: EXPANSION AND INVESTMENT

By 2003 the company saw sales around the $12 million mark. The redirection paid off with increased revenue for the company. The Webers claimed to have as many as 85 million users registered by 2004. Rob Weber had goals he shared in a 2004 interview with

```
┌─────────────────────────────────────────────────┐
│                                                 │
│              KEY DATES                          │
│              ───────■───────                    │
│                                                 │
│  1998:  Twins Rob and Ryan Weber develop online │
│         director of free products.              │
│  2000:  Webers found Freeze.com LLC.            │
│  2003:  Freeze buys ScreenSaver.com.            │
│  2004:  Freeze is ranked the 31st fastest grow- │
│         ing new business in the United States.  │
│  2005:  Webers are named Young Entrepreneurs of │
│         the Year by the Small Business          │
│         Administration.                         │
│                                                 │
└─────────────────────────────────────────────────┘
```

Dick Youngblood of the *Star Tribune*. Weber stated that he would like Freeze.com to be at $100 million in revenue in the next five years.

According to a Nielsen Net Ratings publication, Freeze.com was ranked ninth among the top advertisers by company. The poll, released in June 2004, linked Freeze among web giants Net Flix, Dell Computer, and SBC Communications.

A series of acquisitions later that year helped the Webers begin to set a pace for their $100 million goal. The company bought out competitor ScreenSaver.com in August 2004. After finding success with its purchase of ScreenSaver, Freeze turned its attention to Rhode Island based Mediawave. In a deal that was touted as being a win-win for both companies, Mediawave sold its consumer software division to Freeze in December 2004.

The division, Rhode Island Soft Systems, was another screensaver and software company started by Eric Robichaud, a fellow teenage Internet developer who was 19 when he launched the company. Rhode Island Soft Systems had previously been a supplier of screensavers to Freeze.com. The Internet graphics community was a close-knit bunch. Ironically, it was Robichaud who helped develop Freeze's earlier acquisition ScreenSaver.com. The deal with Mediawave was reported to be between $750,000 and $1 million cash.

A controversy was brewing in February 2005, when the director Kyle Ohme of IT services at Freeze commented to reporters about vulnerabilities in Microsoft software. In a statement responding to the article in *InformationWeek,* Scott Larson from Aurora, Colorado, took aim at Ohme saying, "He was eager to slam Microsoft's vulnerabilities, while quoting an individual whose site provides a haven of downloadable adware programs. Mr. Ohme's site is responsible for hundreds of hours of spyware and antivirus cleanup at our organization. We now block access to his site and his products."

Despite the controversy Freeze.com stated on its web site that it complied with the Can-Spam Act of 2003. The company-issued privacy policy available on its web site stated, "Freeze is dedicated to following only responsible and ethical e-mail practices. Freeze takes a stance against unsolicited commercial e-mail and is continually updating its policies and procedures with the Can-Spam Act of 2003."

In March 2005, the company's founders were honored by the U.S. Small Business Administration as Young Entrepreneurs of the Year. The following June *Entrepreneur Magazine* ranked Freeze.com the 31st fastest growing new business in the United States.

Freeze initiated an affiliate program called Freeze Cold Cash which paid out one dollar for every U.S. install of its screensavers and $.10 for every international install. The referral system brought many new registrants to its directory worldwide.

In November 2005, Freeze.com chose BlueArc Corporation and its Titan core storage system for its server network. Kyle Ohme explained the choice in a *Market Wire* article: "As our business is growing quickly and stakes are higher than ever, we require a scalable, and robust platform that we can rely on day in and day out. Storage is not just about retaining assets, it's about performance, and better performance offers a better user experience. Millions of people a day will indirectly use this storage—to choose any other NAS platform to power our network is not a risk I was willing to take."

The company was rewarded for its commitment to technological improvement when *Network World Magazine* named Freeze.com an "Enterprise All-Star."

Freeze was lauded for its ability to streamline data center operations and scale IT operations during its period of rapid growth. Ardence, Inc. was credited with supplying Freeze with its award-winning software by creating on-demand streaming capabilities. *Network World* praised Freeze.com for its "exceptional use of network technology to further business objectives. In particular, we like the company's new-style approach to server management, and the big performance and productivity gains it has reaped as a result. Freeze.com exemplifies the All-Star concept."

In December 2005 Freeze.com broke ground on a new building site for its world headquarters. The new facility was needed to allow for the predicted growth of the company. In October 2005 Alta Communications, a

Boston-based investment equity firm provided the financial backing to Freeze.com needed for its future development.

In January 2006 company President Robert Weber was listed in *Twin Cities Business Monthly* as a Minnesota Top 20 Emerging Leader. At that point, the company appeared well on its way to exponential growth over the next decade. The continued influx of investment from savvy tech millionaires and the growing Internet left Freeze.com in a particularly solid place among the very best of online marketers. Nonetheless, the public was tiring of online solicitation and it remained to be seen if more aggressive regulation and monitoring would affect the industry. Company disclaimers aside, sites such as Freeze.com met with more resistance from governmental and non-governmental sources who attempted to reign in spyware and adware that generated millions of complaints in the Internet community.

Susan B. Culligan

PRINCIPAL SUBSIDIARIES

Freeze Media LLC.

FURTHER READING

Foley, John, "You Call This Trustworthy Computing?" *InformationWeek,* February 14, 2005, p. 20.

Larsen, Scott, "Less Than Trustworthy?" *InformationWeek,* February 28, 2005, p. 10.

"New, Moving and Expanding, Freeze Acquires Rhode Island Soft System," *St. Cloud Times,* January 31, 2005.

Peterson, Erin, "College Students/CEO," *Twin Cities Business Monthly,* June 2005.

Stape, Andrea, "Mediawave Sells Its Consumer Software Division," *Providence Journal,* December 3, 2004, p. E1.

"What's Sneaking into Your Computer," *Wall Street Journal,* April 26, 2004.

Youngblood, Dick, "Youthful Entrepreneurs Navigated a Tangled Web," *Star Tribune,* September 22, 2004, p. 1D.

FTI Consulting, Inc.

900 Bestgate Road, Suite 100
Annapolis, Maryland 21401
U.S.A.
Telephone: (410) 224-8770
Toll Free: (800) 334-5701
Fax: (410) 224-8378
Web site: http://www.fticonsulting.com

Public Company
Incorporated: 1982 as Forensic Technologies International
  Corporation
Employees: 1,035
Sales: $427.0 million (2004)
Stock Exchanges: New York
Ticker Symbol: FCN
NAIC: 541611 Administrative Management and General
  Management Consulting Services; 541990 All Other
  Professional, Scientific and Technical Services

■ ■ ■

FTI Consulting, Inc., established as an expert witness service provider, has gained national recognition by helping troubled companies with forensic accounting and litigation support services. When the stormy seas of corporate scandal began to subside so did FTI's main source of income. In response the firm has begun to broaden its consulting services and enter international markets.

CONSULTANTS CREATING OPPORTUNITY: 1982-97

Daniel W. Luczak and Joseph R. Reynolds, Jr., both engineers, founded Forensic Technologies International Corporation in 1982, making the transition from consultants to a full-time business operation. Initially, the pair assisted lawyers with expert witnesses, paper management, and jury psychology, according to the *Washington Post.*

In 1986, the firm established a West Coast office. Its focus was the development of computer-generated animations for courtroom use. The firm would pay nearly $600,000 for computers to start the endeavor and then needed to sell lawyers on the concept. Meanwhile, on the other side of the country, the Annapolis office geared up its visual communications capability. The dual endeavors were the genesis of the company's litigation communications services business.

Forensic Technologies was hired in 1988 by the State of Illinois to determine the cause and origin of a central telephone office fire and make recommendations geared to prevent future disasters. The firm earned its first multimillion-dollar fee for a single matter event. The next year, a product defect case in the construction industry with an exposure in excess of $1 billion elevated Forensic Technologies' reputation as provider of complex technical investigations and litigation services.

Original outside investors stepped aside with the completion of a senior management buyout in 1992. Jack Dunn, formerly a managing director with an investment, came aboard to direct an acquisition and expansion drive. Also during the year, a Chicago office opened, bringing litigation, communications, jury consulting, and engineering services to the Midwest.

In May 1996, Forensic Technologies completed an initial public offering to fund the purchase of complementary companies. The firm raised $11.1 million on the NASDAQ, becoming one of the first public litigation-support services companies, according to the *Washington Post*.

A 1997 acquisition of an insurance claims management firm brought the company into a new line of business. A trial reach and consulting firm also was acquired that year. The addition of the new businesses plus internal growth boosted total revenue to $44.2 million, $13.6 million more than generated in 1996. A total of 46 percent of the company's 1997 revenue came from the company's visual communication services, such as computer animations and graphic illustrations.

NEW NAME REFLECTING NEW LINES OF BUSINESS: 1997-2001

In light of ever expanding offerings, the firm changed its name to FTI Consulting, Inc. during 1998. FTI entered the world of financial consulting that year with the purchase of Virginia-based Klick, Kent and Allen Inc. and New York City-based Kahn Consulting Inc. The Applied Sciences division's investigation and analysis capability grew with the addition of Ohio-based S.E.A., Inc. *Business Week* named FTI one of its small "Hot Growth Companies."

In 1999, FTI stock began trading on the American Stock Exchange.

In February 2000, FTI acquired a company with a specialty in airline bankruptcies, New Jersey-based Policano & Manzo. The $50 million stock and cash deal propelled it into the ranks of U.S. financial restructuring leaders. Robert Manzo and Michael Policano gained 5.1 percent of FTI stock each and the distinction as the company's largest individual stockholders. FTI's Financial Consulting division opened offices in four major U.S. cities and began a healthcare consulting and healthcare fraud investigation practice out of its ex-

panded New York office. The Litigation Consulting division also expanded into New York City.

When FTI shifted its emphasis to financially troubled companies in 1998, the company grew and drew the interest of Wall Street. Inclusion in the Russell 2000 index, beginning in 2000, increased its visibility among institutional investors. FTI Consulting Inc.'s fortunes rose as others' declined.

"It helped analyze evidence for O.J. Simpson's defense. One of its experts was central to the defense of Shane S. DeLeon, who was convicted last year in the hit-and-run death of American University student Matthew Odell. FTI's software for courtroom evidence display was used by lawyers for George W. Bush in a Tallahassee trial that was key to the outcome of the presidential election," Terrence O'Hara wrote in the *Washington Post* in August 2001.

Financial accounting now brought in about 50 percent of FTI's revenues and more than three-quarters of the company's core earnings. FTI was up against workout specialists, such as Los Angeles-based Houlihan Lokey Howard & Zukin, as well as giant accounting firms including Ernst & Young, for business. Its ability to compete was dependent on retaining the myriad of lawyers, accountants, and scientists brought into its ranks by way of acquisitions.

The restructuring segment of the business helped 2001 results beat those of 2000. Earnings climbed from $2.6 million to $16.5 million on revenue of $135 million and $166.4 million, respectively.

A CHANGE IN COURSE: 2002-05

FTI moved to buy PricewaterhouseCoopers' bankruptcy, turnaround, and business restructuring services division in 2002. The U.S. Business Recovery Services operation, a leading bankruptcy, turnaround, and business restructuring service provider with more than 350 employees, practiced across the country, including in New York, Dallas, Los Angeles, Chicago, and Atlanta. FTI planned to sell its low-performing Applied Sciences division, which investigated accidents for corporate clients, to avoid conflict of interest with the clients gained in the PricewaterhouseCoopers purchase and reduce the incurred debt. FTI completed the acquisition in September 2002 for $145 million in cash and three million company shares.

The purchase helped boost 2002 profits to $34.9 million from $12.9 million in 2001. The scrutiny of accounting firms by the Securities and Exchange Commission (SEC) had served to aid FTI's growth spurt. Conflict of interest issues had the industry splitting off

KEY DATES

1982: Forensic Technologies International Corporation is founded.

1986: The firm enters the litigation communications services business.

1988: The firm earns its first multimillion-dollar single matter fee.

1989: A case with exposure in excess of a billion dollars elevates the firm's reputation.

1992: Management buyout of the original investors is completed.

1996: The firm's initial public offering funds expansion.

1998: The name is changed to FTI Consulting, Inc.

1999: Trading begins on the American Stock Exchange.

2000: Policano & Manzo is acquired.

2002: PricewaterhouseCoopers' Business Recovery Services division is acquired.

2003: The firm opens a London office.

their recovery practices. During 2002 FTI benefited from record bankruptcy levels, increasing 6 percent to 1.58 million with 38,540 from businesses.

But as the economy improved, FTI's stock price began to slide. Investors were concerned with the firm's dependency on the bankruptcy services side of its business for revenue and earnings, with about 70 percent of its business tied to restructuring. After its Applied Sciences division was divested, FTI's remaining businesses included bankruptcy services, forensic accounting, and litigation services.

In 2003, FTI bought an SEC investigation specialist, a dispute advisory operation, and competing economic consulting business. In October a London office opened. The European practice opened the door to a less crowded market. Fewer U.S. technology and telecom businesses were in need of restructuring while more competitors had entered the industry during the onslaught of business failures. Moreover, the U.S. economy was on the road to recovery. But changing conditions in Europe led restructuring businesses to look across the pond and in Asia for troubled companies, according to *Investment Dealers' Digest*.

News of the resignation of 13 managing directors resulted in a significant downturn in FTI's stock price in January 2004. The directors, all from Policano & Manzo,

had accounted for as much as 21 percent of FTI's cash flow. Wall Street was concerned with the company's ability to retain other key people.

By mid-year 2004, net income as well as stock price was on the slide as corporate America reined in accounting or governance failings—FTI had done work for WorldCom, Adelphia, and Enron. In response FTI had set its sights on building its economic consulting business and conventional corporate restructuring.

In the spring of 2005, FTI bought Cambio Health Solutions, adding hospital restructuring to its list of services. A combination of problems, such as high capital costs and reduced Medicaid reimbursements, was sending single nonprofit hospitals into restructuring or seeking a buyer and FTI was positioning itself to help out, according to a May 2005 *Corporate Financing Week* article. FTI was expected to expand its consulting business to more industries.

In July, FTI said it planned to make its first foray into the public debt market. Lizzie Newland reported for the *Knight-Ridder Tribune Business News* on July 20, 2005, "Besides providing fuel for acquisitions, the $300 million from the debt offering would allow FTI to be much more aggressive in its stock repurchase program, which is set to end in October."

In September, FTI revealed plans to relocate headquarters from Annapolis to Baltimore. Driven by growth, the move was planned for mid-December. In November, FTI announced an agreement to purchase economics consulting firm Competition Policy Associates, Inc. The acquisition, valued at approximately $70 million, added "depth and breadth in the anti-trust, merger/acquisition, regulatory, healthcare and financial arenas" and opened the way for new opportunities internationally, top executives explained in a *PR Newswire* article. The deal was expected to be completed in early 2006.

Kathleen Peippo

PRINCIPAL COMPETITORS

CRA International, Inc.; LECG Corporation; Navigant Consulting, Inc.

FURTHER READING

"The BBJ Index," *Baltimore Business Journal*, March 30, 2001, p. 26.

Berselli, Beth, "A Case for Courtroom Presentations," *Washington Post*, June 8, 1998, p. F5.

Dang, Dan Thanh, "FTI Bolsters Bankruptcy Services Unit," *Sun* (Baltimore), July 25, 2002, p. 1C.

Duhigg, Charles, "FTI Digs Out the Numbers That Tell the Troubled Tale," *Washington Post,* July 28, 2003, p. E10.

Glator, Jonathan D., "New Venture Hopes to Offer Some Peace of Mind to CEOs," *New York Times,* November 4, 2002, p. C9.

Higgins, Marguerite, "FTI Consulting Sees Growth in Bad Times," *Washington Times,* February 18, 2003, p. C9.

Lemke, Tim, "Managerial Drain Jolts FTI Outlook," *Washington Times,* February 10, 2004, p. C9.

"Moving the Market—Tracking the Numbers," *Wall Street Journal,* June 16, 2004, p. C3.

Newland, Lizzie, "FTI Consulting Inc. to Sell $300 Million in Notes," *Knight-Ridder Tribune Business News,* July 20, 2005.

"Non-Profit Hospitals Surface As Targets," *Corporate Financing Week,* May 30, 2005, p. 5.

O'Hara, Terrence, "It's a Grand Time to Be a Workout Artist," *Washington Post,* August 13, 2001, p. E1.

Patalon, William III, "Amid 3 Takeover Deals, FTI's Earnings Disappoint," *Sun* (Baltimore), July 8, 1998, p. 1C.

———, "Surprise Goodbyes Fuel FTI Stock Dive," *Sun* (Baltimore), January 29, 2004, p. 1D.

"PWC Plans to Revisit Restructuring Practice," *Mergers & Acquisitions Report,* June 20, 2005.

"Restructuring Pros Look Overseas: More Rivals, Fewer Opportunities Stateside Lead U.S. Firms to European Shores," *Investment Dealers' Digest,* October 13, 2003.

"Results Improved at FTI Consulting," *Washington Post,* February 13, 2002, p. E9.

Sentementes, Gus G., "FTI Delays Equity Offering Until Early Next Year," *Sun* (Baltimore), November 27, 2002, p. 1C.

Wadhams, Nick, "FTI Consulting to Relocate to Baltimore," *America's Intelligence Wire,* September 28, 2005.

genzyme

Genzyme Corporation

—————— ■ ——————

500 Kendall Street
Cambridge, Massachusetts 02142
U.S.A.
Telephone: (617) 252-7500
Toll Free: (800) 436-1443
Fax: (617) 252-7600
Web site: http://www.genzyme.com

Public Company
Incorporated: 1981
Employees: 7,100
Sales: $2.2 billion (2004)
Stock Exchanges: NASDAQ
Ticker Symbol: GENZ
NAIC: 325412 Pharmaceutical Preparation Manufacturing; 325414 Biological Product (Except Diagnostic) Manufacturing; 339112 Surgical and Medical Instrument Manufacturing; 621511 Medical Laboratories

■ ■ ■

Genzyme Corporation is a leading biotechnology company that focuses on five business areas: therapeutics, renal, transplant, biosurgery, and diagnostics/genetics. Genzyme's specialty is developing treatments for rare diseases, particularly those related to genetic disorders and organ transplants. The company's most important product is Cerezyme, which is a treatment for Gaucher's disease, an enzyme-deficiency condition. Through Genzyme Molecular Oncology and Genzyme Biosurgery, the company develops gene-based cancer treatment products

and manufactures orthopedic medical and surgical products, respectively.

ENZYME TECHNOLOGY IN THE EARLY 1980S

In 1981, Henry Blair founded Genzyme to produce products based on enzyme technologies. With the help of venture capital funding, Blair acquired Whatman Biochemicals Ltd., which became Genzyme Biochemicals. In 1982, Blair acquired a British catalog business, Koch-Light Laboratories, a supplier of chemicals to the pharmaceutical industry. The pharmaceutical manufacturing arm of Koch Laboratories in 1986 became Genzyme Pharmaceutical and Fine Chemicals based in Haverill, England.

Despite these developments, Genzyme struggled until 1983, when Dutch-born Henri Termeer left Baxter Travenol (now Baxter International) to become company chairman at Genzyme. Termeer studied economics at the University of Rotterdam and earned an M.B.A. at the University of Virginia before joining Baxter in 1973. After undergoing two years of training in Chicago, Baxter assigned him to run its largest overseas sales organization in Germany. The position gave him valuable experience in managing a major business operation. By the time he joined Genzyme, Termeer was one of Baxter's executive vice-presidents. He was recruited to Genzyme by the venture capital firm Oak Investment Partners, which had substantial investments in the start-up company.

Termeer took a personal risk in moving to Genzyme, sacrificing half his salary and a comfortable lif-

estyle in southern California for forbidding office space
in Boston's notorious "Combat Zone," the city's red
light district. The company employed only 11 people.

On assuming the chairmanship, Termeer immediately began a search for investment capital. He
formed an advisory board, consisting of a group of
eminent MIT scientists to identify promising new areas
for product development. While many biotechnology
companies worked to develop huge blockbuster drugs,
Genzyme crafted a niche strategy focusing on less
glamorous products that could be sold readily. This
strategy proved to position the company well, even as it
developed longer-term products.

Genzyme aggressively pursued its strategy first
through developing expertise in engineering and
modifying enzymes and carbohydrates. Enzymes are
proteins that essentially act as catalysts for many cellular
processes, whereas carbohydrates often coat proteins and
govern their interactions with other substances or
chemicals. The company's expertise in these areas yielded
readily marketable products. Genzyme developed and
marketed a product called cholesterol oxidase, including
an enzyme that worked as the active agent in cholesterol
tests.

In 1983, Termeer became president of Genzyme
and in 1985 he was named chief executive officer. In
1986, Genzyme became a public company with an initial
public offering that raised $28.2 million. In the same
year, the company opened a Japanese subsidiary financed
by Japanese sales and built a manufacturing facility in
Cambridge, Massachusetts, for the production of medical grade hyaluronic acid. Genzyme also raised $10 mil-
lion to finance the development of Ceredase through a

research and development limited partnership. Genzyme
divested Koch-Light Laboratories in 1987.

In 1988, the company, with partial funding from
the Department of Trade & Industry, opened a
pharmaceutical chemical plant in Haverville, United
Kingdom, doubling Genzyme's manufacturing capacity.
In addition, the company received U.S. Food and Drug
Administration approval to market the antibiotic clinda-
mycin phosphate for the treatment of serious hospital
infections.

In 1989, Termeer acquired Integrated Genetics (IG)
of Framingham, Massachusetts, a move that industry
observers termed a masterstroke. Termeer's successful
negotiations for the company stemmed from a
coincidental meeting with IG Chairman Robert
Carpenter. Both attended a reunion of Baxter alumni in
Chicago, and the two alums accompanied one another
on the return flight to Boston. Although mired in
financial difficulty, IG possessed superior technology. In
1988, Termeer unsuccessfully bid for IG when its stock
hovered at $5 per share. But Carpenter was willing to
deal in 1989 after trying to sell out to a large
pharmaceutical company. Several weeks after the airplane
flight, Carpenter accepted Genzyme's offer for less than
$3 a share in Genzyme stock, amounting to $31.5
million. The acquisition considerably strengthened Genzyme's expertise in molecular biology, protein chemistry,
carbohydrate engineering, nucleic acid chemistry, and
enzymology.

In the same year, Genzyme raised $39.1 million in
a public stock offering and another $36.8 million
through a research and development limited partnership
to develop four hyaluronic acid (HA) based drugs to
reduce the formation of postoperative adhesions. The
company also formed its Genzyme Diagnostics Division.
By the end of 1989, Genzyme reported revenues of $34.1
million.

THE EARLY 1990S: PRODUCT
BREAKTHROUGHS, CORPORATE
STRATEGIES

By far Genzyme's most lucrative, if not controversial,
product was the drug Ceredase, approved by the U.S.
Food and Drug Administration in 1991. The drug was
the first effective treatment for Gaucher's disease, a rare
but previously untreatable and potentially fatal genetic
disorder. The illness, which afflicted about 20,000 people
worldwide in the early 1990s, most commonly strikes
Jews of East European descent. The victims of the disease
lack a natural enzyme that metabolizes fats, causing lip-
ids, or fatty substances, to mass in the liver, spleen, and
bone marrow, resulting in a variety of crippling condi-

KEY DATES

1981: Henry Blair founds Genzyme.
1983: Henri Termeer becomes Genzyme chairman.
1988: Genzyme opens pharmaceutical chemical facility in the United Kingdom.
1991: Ceredase gains FDA approval.
1994: Genzyme receives FDA approval to market Cerezyme; Genzyme Tissue Repair Division is formed.
1997: Genzyme acquires PharmaGenics, Inc. to create Genzyme Molecular Oncology.
1999: Genzyme Surgical Products is formed.
2004: Genzyme acquires Ilex Oncology Inc.
2005: Genzyme acquires Bone Care International Inc.

tions and years of painful physical deterioration. Genzyme's scientists successfully produced the missing enzyme, which could be infused intravenously and consequently reverse the lipid buildup, allowing patients to live normal and active lives with few side effects.

Although Ceredase won praise as a life-saving treatment, it also drew criticism for being the most expensive drug ever sold, running on average $150,000 per patient a year. As a result, the drug became a vehicle for criticism of high drug prices. In 1992, the Office of Technology Assessment, a nonpartisan Congressional research agency, issued a report accusing Genzyme of pricing the drug so high that patients would have to exhaust their lifetime insurance to buy Ceredase for two or three years. The report noted that the real costs and risks of developing the drug were low because most of the work was done by government researchers. The federal agency stated that the pricing also raised serious questions concerning whether the government should participate in developing drugs with little or no control over their final pricing. Company Chairman and President Henri Termeer said the agency's report was flawed and that the high cost stemmed from the enormous expense of producing the product. To assuage criticism, Genzyme agreed to give Ceredase to patients whose insurance benefits ran out. Nevertheless, others also voiced complaints. Speaking on behalf of the National Organization for Rare Disorders, Abbey S. Meyers, the organization's president, stated in the *Wall Street Journal* on May 20, 1994 that "we were appalled" at Genzyme's pricing of Ceredase. This criticism was the latest in complaints about the exorbitant cost of biotech-

nology drugs. In Congressional hearings, patients had complained about the cost of the anemia drug erythropoietin, or EPO, from Amgen Inc., which cost between $4,000 and $6,000 a year, and Genentech Inc.'s human growth hormone at $12,000 to $18,000 a year. But Ceredase's price far surpassed either of these two drugs and quickly drove the issue onto the legislative agenda.

Ceredase was in fact enormously expensive to make, relying on enzyme extraction from placentas from hospitals around the world. The harvesting of the material was done by a unit of the Institut Merieux of Paris. The production of a year's supply for the average patient required approximately 20,000 placentas equaling about 27 tons of material. In 1994, Genzyme supplied Ceredase to 1,100 patients. The drug's high price stemmed also from its applicability to only a small number of patients, placing the primary burden for paying the research costs and a return to investors on those being treated. Genzyme argued, moreover, that Ceredase differed from other drugs in a critical respect that influenced its price. Typically, drug prices were set to be competitive with existing treatments, including surgery and hospitalization, in spite of production costs. But since Ceredase was the only existing treatment for Gaucher's disease, the price reflected the drug's full production and marketing costs.

Genzyme's monopoly on Ceredase was protected under the Orphan Drug Act, passed in 1983 to give seven-year exclusive rights to drug companies that produce drugs for rare diseases (those afflicting less than 200,000 people). According to Termeer, the Act attracted the capital investment needed to research and develop the drug. In 1994, Genzyme received FDA approval to market Cerezyme, a genetically engineered replacement for Ceredase. The company also hoped to benefit from Orphan Act designation for various projects concerning cystic fibrosis, Fabry's disease, and severe burns.

By 1991, Genzyme raised nearly $100 million for research and development while retaining control over its equity and production rights, a stark contrast to many young biotechnology firms that had to sacrifice these assets to finance themselves. Nearly half the funds, $47.3 million, came from a public offering of Neozyme I Corp., formed by Genzyme in 1990 to research and develop six healthcare products. In 1992, the company formed Neozyme II to fund other Genzyme projects. The companies operated primarily as paper businesses to finance research and development projects and retain rights to the products. If the projects proved successful, Genzyme could buy back the rights.

In 1991, Genzyme also took IG laboratories (the genetic testing services business) public, raising another $14.1 million. Genzyme reported revenues of $121.7

million, more than double 1990 revenues of $54.8 million. In addition, Genzyme announced that it would build new corporate headquarters and manufacturing facilities in Boston on a 51-acre site along the Charles River. The company looked at sites in more than a dozen states, narrowing its choice to two in Massachusetts, Boston and Cambridge, both with international scientific reputations. These sites were close to Genzyme's current headquarters in Cambridge and close to large clusters of biotechnology companies. Boston's offer of a sizable state-owned parcel that could be quickly developed, plus many inducements, including breaks on city and state taxes and government assistance with site planning, road construction, utility rates, and others, clinched the deal. Regional economists hoped that Genzyme's $110 million facility would be one anchor of a thriving regional biotechnology industry, bringing thousands of new research and manufacturing jobs to raise the city and Massachusetts out of recession. Genzyme also ran a pilot production facility in Framingham, Massachusetts, and operations in The Netherlands, Japan, and England.

CONTINUING DIVERSIFICATION AND GROWTH INTO THE MID-1990S

Genzyme's other corporate moves in 1991 included the selling of its interest in GENE-TRAK systems for $10 million and the acquisition of Genecore International's diagnostic enzyme business. The acquisition gave Genzyme worldwide diagnostic sales, production capacity, and inventory, as well as related patent and distribution rights. The company also established Genzyme, B.V., a European subsidiary in Naardan, The Netherlands, to manage the development and regulatory approval of Genzyme's biotherapeutic products.

Genzyme's research achievements for 1991 included beginning clinical development of Thyrogen, a thyroid stimulating human hormone for use in the diagnosis and treatment of thyroid cancer. Genzyme also initiated clinical development of HAL-S synovial fluid replacement, a treatment for tissue damage resulting from arthroscopic surgery. In addition, Genzyme and Tufts University scientists jointly performed breakthrough analysis concerning the role of a key protein responsible for cystic fibrosis, a lung disease. In 1992, the researchers innovated a method to mass-produce this protein for the treatment of the disease by genetically altering mice with a human gene governing production of the protein and then harvesting it from fat globules in the mouse's milk. The discovery marked the first time that animal milk was used to produce proteins of this type.

In 1992, Genzyme developed technology to make purer and stronger pharmaceuticals and to simplify the pharmaceutical preparation process. Genzyme won FDA orphan drug designation for several treatments, covering Cystic Fibrosis Transmembrane Conductance Regulation (r-CFTR), Cystic Fibrosis Gene Therapy (CFGT), Thyrogen Cancer Agent, and Vianain Enzymatic Debridement Agent for treating severe burn patients. In 1994, the company received FDA approval to sell Cerezyme, the genetically engineered replacement for Ceredase.

By the early 1990s, Genzyme had become a large and thriving diversified company, in contrast to many biotechnology firms plagued by clinical failures, cuts in research, layoffs, and funding troubles. In 1994, Repligen Inc. of Cambridge, Massachusetts, announced layoffs of one-third of its staff after failing to find financial backing. Synergen Inc.'s stock plunged on news that its leading drug failed in clinical trials, compelling the Boulder, Colorado firm to cut more than half of its payroll. Glycomed Inc. of Alameda, California, eliminated 30 percent of its workforce to conserve cash. Cambridge Biotech Corp. of Worcester, Massachusetts, a once-leading biotech firm, filed for Chapter 11 protection. Signaling the industry's poor health, Oppenheimer Global Bio-Tech Fund, a specialty mutual fund for stock investors, announced that it was shifting investment strategy to focus on "emerging growth" stocks. With these reversals, investor confidence plummeted, causing financing to dry up and research projects to be dropped, and leaving many smaller firms vulnerable if their flagship drugs failed to pay off. To raise cash, several companies licensed their main products at minimal sale prices. Other companies canceled plans to add manufacturing capacity and sold facilities and leased them back. The main culprit for the industry's woes was a string of clinical failures, as some biotech firms prematurely initiated clinical studies to gain the broadest possible market exposure for their products. Still, in 1994 more than 100 biotechnology products were either in final Phase III clinical tests or awaiting FDA marketing approval.

Genzyme and other large biotechnology companies capitalized on the industry fallout by buying financially troubled firms and products at low prices. Genzyme aggressively began acquiring companies in the late 1980s as part of a broad strategy to minimize risk. Aside from the acquisitions of Integrated Genetics and Gencore International in 1992, Genzyme acquired Medix Biotech, Inc., a producer and supplier of monoclonal and polyclonal antibodies, immunoassay components, and immunodiagnostic services. In the same year, the company's U.K. subsidiary, Genzyme Limited, bought Enzymatix Limited of Cambridge, United Kingdom, which was integrated into Genzyme's Pharmaceutical and Fine Chemicals division. Genzyme also acquired Vivigen, a genetics testing laboratory in Santa Fe, New Mexico.

In 1993, Genzyme acquired both Virotech of Russelsheim, Germany, a producer and distributor of in-vitro diagnostic kits, and Omni Res srl of Milan, Italy, a producer and seller of immunobiological products. Acquisitions in 1994 included a Swiss pharmaceutical concern, Sygena Ltd.; BioSurface Technology Inc., a developer of wound healing products; and TSI Inc., a former high-flying drug testing company that expanded too rapidly and posted major financial losses. The TSI acquisition was made by Genzyme Transgenics Corp., created by Genzyme in 1993 to promote and develop technology combining recombinant microbiology and experimental embryology to produce specialized proteins from animal milk. The TSI purchase made Genzyme Transgenics (73 percent owned by Genzyme) the largest player in the emerging biotechnology market called "pharming," where genetically altered farm animals were used to produce pharmaceuticals.

Genzyme's diversification moves generally received praise, but they also raised speculation that the company would face difficulty integrating the various operations. Moreover, despite the company's numerous acquisitions, its major revenue producer was still just one product, Ceredase/Cerezyme. Beyond this product, Genzyme's line of future drugs contained no blockbuster moneymakers, a strategy originally crafted by Termeer to minimize risk. Unlike many of its competitors, Genzyme had yet to experience any major disappointments in clinical trials on near-term drug development projects.

In 1995, Genzyme's next project, a range of hyaluronic acid (HA) products, also looked promising. Hyaluronic acid contains a polysaccharide found in a variety of human tissues that can be used to prevent postoperative adhesions following abdominal, gynecological, cardiac, and orthopedic surgery. Noting that hyaluronic acid could be used by virtually all surgeons, Genzyme predicted that the market for the drug would be about $1.3 billion, four times that for Ceredase. Unlike the Ceredase market, however, Genzyme faced several competitors for hyaluronic acid, including major pharmaceutical companies. Other products also were being developed to serve the same purpose. In addition, concerns arose that the product was unlikely to be universally effective in preventing postoperative adhesions, and thus the marketing of the drug would be split with competing products. Nevertheless, Termeer expressed confidence in the drug and said that Genzyme would beat competitors to the market by at least five years.

Genzyme's diversification also included a move into gene therapy. Although its leading product, Ceredase, and its genetically engineered successor, Cerezyme, proved highly effective, the company began working with scientists at the University of Pittsburgh and at IntroGene B.V., a biotech firm in Rijswijk, The Netherlands, to develop a gene therapeutic treatment to replace the drugs. The new therapy, if successful, would correct the enduring genetic defects responsible for Gaucher's disease. In addition, in 1995 Genzyme planned to spend $400 million to research and develop gene therapy to treat cystic fibrosis, the most common fatal hereditary disease in the United States. These moves stemmed in part from attempts to avoid obsolescence as the revolutionary developments in gene therapy, still mostly in the exploratory stage, threatened to bypass biotechnology developments.

By the mid-1990s, Genzyme continued to be well positioned to capitalize on emerging technologies and to minimize risk if several of its products failed. The company arose in 1981 to become one of the top five biotechnology companies in terms of sales. Nevertheless, the biotechnology field remained highly competitive, with numerous rivals in the United States and elsewhere, many of which had greater resources than Genzyme. With large pharmaceutical and biotechnology companies as competitors, the prospect loomed that these companies would develop more effective products and marketing strategies. Indeed, Genzyme's competitive pressures were most acute in the therapeutics field. Although no alternatives existed for Ceredase and Cerezyme, another company was attempting to make an alternative product using an enzyme in insect cells. Genzyme's hyaluronic acid products for postoperative adhesions faced competition from both HA-based and non-HA-based products. The company anticipated that the chief competitive factor would be the measure of acceptance by surgeons depending on product performance and price. Several academic and commercial enterprises were engaged in developing therapies to treat either the symptoms or the cause of cystic fibrosis. A number of groups were developing gene therapy approaches to the disease and received government approval to conduct limited human trials. Other organizations were investigating pharmacological and biological agents that would alleviate the symptoms of the disease. A leading biotech firm, Genentech Inc., had already received FDA marketing approval for its product, Pulmozyme. With these competitive elements, any one of these groups could develop gene therapy products or drug therapies before Genzyme, or obtain patent protection that would effectively bar the company from commercializing its technology.

Nevertheless, Genzyme's aggressive strategy had paid off in the past and appeared to position the company well for future developments.

RESURGENCE OF THE BIOTECH-NOLOGY INDUSTRY IN THE LATE 1990S

In the second half of the decade Genzyme devoted increased attention to developing gene therapy programs for a wider range of diseases. In addition to continuing its search for better cystic fibrosis treatments, pledging an additional $400 million to its cystic fibrosis research programs in 1995, the company began exploring alternative genetic treatments for lysosomal storage disorders, notably Gaucher disease and Fabry disease. These alternative treatments were aimed at creating genetic material that would enable patients suffering from these disorders to generate deficient enzymes naturally. During this period the company also developed new therapies for Pompe disease (another lysosomal storage disorder), renal disease, and hypothyroidism in recovering cancer patients. Renagel, a kidney therapy designed to control blood phosphate levels in hemodialysis patients, was launched in 1999, and within one year was being used by more than 30,000 patients.

In the mid-1990s the company also deepened its involvement in cancer research. In 1995 Genzyme Transgenics was the first company to develop a monoclonal antibody in the milk of a transgenic goat. Through this process, which spliced human genetic material into the DNA of milk-producing mammals, researchers were able to produce recombinant human proteins for use in a range of disease therapies. Genzyme took further steps toward expanding its cancer research capabilities in 1996, when it reached an agreement with Imperial Cancer Research Technology Ltd. in the United Kingdom to establish a joint venture dedicated to researching cancer gene therapies. In 1997, the company created a new division devoted to studying cancer vaccines on the molecular level.

In the mid-1990s Genzyme undertook a radical corporate restructuring. The plan called for the eventual partitioning of the company's diverse interests into separate divisions, each of which would have its own "tracking stock." The move effectively established separate companies within the corporation. The realignment began in 1994 with the purchase of BioSurface Technology Inc., which Genzyme converted into a new division, Genzyme Tissue Repair. This new division brought together Genzyme's four existing tissue repair research projects and was launched with eight products in various stages of development and an initial investment of $26 million. At the same time, Genzyme's other research programs were brought together within a larger division, called Genzyme General.

The strategy behind Genzyme Tissue Repair involved the integration of three of Genzyme's specialties—enzymes and recombinant proteins, biomaterials, and cell culture techniques—to develop new approaches to skin grafts and cartilage restoration. Proceeding from advances made in Sweden over the previous seven years, Genzyme Tissue Repair began research on a new method of growing cartilage cells in 1995, and by 1997 its Carticel therapy was demonstrating success with patients suffering from damaged knees. At the same time the division also developed a skin graft product, Epicel, for use with burn victims.

In the wake of the successful integration of Genzyme Tissue Repair into the Genzyme Corporation, the company created a third division, Genzyme Molecular Oncology, in 1997, to study the potential uses of microbiological solutions in the development of a cancer vaccine. The Genzyme Surgical Products Division followed in 1999, with a mission to develop medical instruments and biomaterials for cardiovascular therapies and general surgical uses. In 2000 the company announced its plan to acquire Biomatrix, Inc., which eventually would become its fifth division, Genzyme Biosurgery. This diversification resulted in steady growth, culminating in record net earnings of more than $142 million for 1999.

DIVERSIFICATION IN THE 21ST CENTURY

Genzyme's progress during the first years of the 21st century was highlighted by its diversification away from orphan drug development. The concentration on rare diseases, Termeer's strategic focus during his first 20 years at the helm, proved to be worthwhile, enabling Genzyme to establish monopolies in small, underserved markets, but new avenues of growth were needed. To meet the company's financial targets and to please analysts, Termeer began developing a broader portfolio of products, assuming a more diversified stance largely through acquisition. In August 2003, he acquired Fremont, California-based SangStat Medical Corp., a developer of drugs designed to treat the immune system. The $600 million acquisition, which gave Genzyme, among other products, an anti-organ rejection drug named Thymoglobulin, was followed several months later by a $1 billion acquisition. In February 2004, Genzyme agreed to acquire San Antonio, Texas-based Ilex Oncology Inc., a purchase that underscored Termeer's commitment to diversifying beyond orphan drug development. The most significant gain in the acquisition was Ilex's Campath, a cancer drug approved for the treatment of certain types of leukemia, but the purchased also added other promising treatments in the oncology field, such as clofarabine, a drug designed to combat certain cancers and tumors. "Our objective here is to build a sustainable and competitive commercial oncology business," a Genzyme senior executive explained in a February 27, 2004 interview with the *Boston Globe*. "We've been active in the development stage, but we feel it's important to acquire some revenue and a commercial presence in the space."

New markets and new assets provided substantial financial growth to Genzyme, fulfilling the objective of Termeer's diversification program. Between 2000 and 2004, the company's revenue volume nearly tripled, jumping from $752 million to $2.2 billion. Operating profit increased robustly as well, swelling from $143 million to $252 million. Looking ahead, Termeer planned to continue expanding Genzyme's product portfolio through acquisitions, building the company's core competency in orphan-drug development by adding capabilities in more mainstream treatments. In mid-2005, Termeer took another step in this direction, acquiring Bone Care International Inc. for approximately $600 million. The addition of Bone Care, which possessed a treatment called Hectorol for the treatment of chronic kidney disease, diversified Genzyme's renal care business, accelerating its commercial entry into earlier stages of chronic kidney disease. As Termeer pressed forward with his diversification and expansion program, further additions to the company's operations were anticipated.

Bruce P. Montgomery
Updated, Stephen Meyer; Jeffrey L. Covell

PRINCIPAL SUBSIDIARIES

Genzyme Transgenics Corporation; IG Laboratories, Inc. (69%).

PRINCIPAL DIVISIONS

Genzyme Biosurgery; Genzyme General; Genzyme Molecular Oncology.

PRINCIPAL COMPETITORS

Abbott Laboratories; Chiron Corporation; Genentech, Inc.; Johnson & Johnson.

FURTHER READING

Abate, Tom, "Biotech Firms Transforming Animals into Drug-Producing Machines; Transgenic Creatures Carry Human DNA That Produce Proteins," *San Francisco Chronicle*, January 17, 2000.

Alster, Norm, "Henri Termeer's Orphan Drug Strategy," *Forbes*, May 27, 1991, pp. 202-05.

Convey, Eric, "Genzyme Makes Move in New Direction," *Boston Herald*, January 23, 1996.

Diesenhouse, Susan, "Boston Over Cambridge in a Biotechnology Race," *New York Times*, December 25, 1991.

Fitzgerald, Dennis, "Genzyme Buys Ilex," *Daily Deal*, December 22, 2004.

"Genzyme, Bone Care International Announce Shareholder Approval of Merger," *Asia Africa Intelligence Wire*, June 30, 2005.

"Genzyme Buys PharmaGenics to Create Cancer Focus," *Pharmaceutical Business News*, February 7, 1997.

"Genzyme Celebrates Four Major Openings in Europe," *Manufacturing Chemist*, October 2005, p. 5.

Heuser, Stephen, "Genzyme Halts Drug Test After Death," *Boston Globe*, September 17, 2005.

Hilts, Philip J., "U.S. Agency Criticizes High Price of Drug," *New York Times*, October 6, 1992.

Krasner, Jeffrey, "Genzyme Battles an Old Adversary," *The Boston Globe*, January 25, 2005.

———, "Genzyme in $1 Billion Deal for San Antonio Cancer Drug Firm," *Boston Globe*, February 27, 2004.

Marcial, Gene G., "What Other Biotechs See in Bioenvision," *Business Week*, May 2, 2005, p. 100.

Morse, Andrew, "Genzyme Aims for Pharma Status," *Daily Deal*, March 1, 2004.

Newman, Anne, "Biotech Bonanza," *Business Week*, October 31, 2005, p. 42.

Rosenberg, Ronald, "Genzyme's Plan to Beat Obsolescence," *Boston Globe*, January 8, 1995.

———, "New Competitor Looms for Cambridge Drug Maker," *Boston Globe*, April 29, 2000.

Schwartz, John, and Carolyn Friday, "Beating the Odds in Biotech," *Newsweek*, October 12, 1992, p. 63.

Shaw, Craig, "Genzyme Builds Base, Awaits Upside Volume," *Investor's Business Daily*, August 27, 2004, p. B8.

Stecklow, Steve, "Genzyme Receives FDA Approval to Sell Cerezyme," *Wall Street Journal*, May 25, 1994.

Stipp, David, "Biotechnology Firms Find Themselves in Cash Crunch," *Wall Street Journal*, July 26, 1994, p. B10.

———, "Genzyme to Buy BioSurface, Merge It into a New Unit with Separate Stock," *Wall Street Journal*, July 26, 1994, p. B4.

———, "Stock Swap for TSI Set by Genzyme Transgenics Corp.," *Wall Street Journal*, June 16, 1994, p. B7.

Tanouye, Elyse, "What's Fair?: Critics Say Many New Drugs Are Priced Far Too High," *Wall Street Journal*, May 20, 1994, p. R11.

Tsao, Amy, "Genzyme: Beyond 'Orphan' Diseases," *Business Week Online*, January 12, 2004.

Zitner, Aaron, "Change in Drug Rules Expected; Senate Committee Said to Favor 'Fast Track' Approval Process," *Boston Globe*, June 12, 1997.

Guardsmark, L.L.C.

—————■—————

10 Rockefeller Plaza
New York, New York 10020-1903
U.S.A.
Telephone: (212) 765-8226
Toll Free: (800) 238-5878
Fax: (212) 603-3854
Web site: http://www.guardsmark.com

Private Company
Incorporated: 1963
Employees: 18,500
Sales: $509 million (2005 est.)
NAIC: 541380 Testing Laboratories; 561611 Investigation Services; 561612 Security Guards and Patrol Services

■ ■ ■

Guardsmark, L.L.C. is a leading security company. Related services include drug testing, investigation and background checks, and consulting. The company is active in 400 North American cities. According to the company, Guardsmark hires only one in every 50 applicants. A lengthy written application, background check, and drug test await job seekers.

ORIGINS

Guardsmark, L.L.C. was founded in Memphis, Tennessee, in July 1963 by Ira A. Lipman. Lipman was just 22 years old when he started the company but had years of experience helping at his father's detective agency, including traveling cross country to drum up sales. He told *Business Week* that he started Guardsmark with a $1,000 loan from his father, who was not interested in providing guard services himself. A full-page ad in a regional edition of *Fortune* was an early, low-budget marketing coup for the company, Lipman added.

Guardsmark expanded in its first dozen years through internal growth and a couple of acquisitions. The center of its business was guarding factories, but it also worked in other settings, including screening for weapons at airports. After attracting some venture capital, branch offices were added in Boston, Atlanta, and San Francisco. Fifteen percent of company stock was floated publicly in 1970, raising $2 million, as Guardsmark acquired Lipman's father's detective agency. It was taken private again by Lipman in 1979, however.

By 1974, the company had 32 offices coast to coast and annual revenues of $20 million, about one-tenth those of industry leader Pinkerton's Inc. Guardsman was the seventh largest security firm in the United States, according to *Business Week,* and the only major nonunion player. The market remained highly fragmented, with at least 3,000 smaller firms competing. Lipman made a brash prediction to *Business Week*: "During my lifetime, Guardsmark will ... be bigger than Brink's and Pinkerton's."

A BOOMING INDUSTRY IN THE 1980S

The industry was growing quickly from a shift to outsourcing of security by corporations. Guardsmark attained revenues of $56 million in 1983. Four years later, when sales were about $100 million a year, Lipman told

Forbes that the typical company could save 30 percent by outsourcing its security.

Part of Guardsmark's pitch was the selectivity of its hiring. The company was then hiring about one in two dozen applicants. In 1976, after a shooting incident in Arkansas involving one of its employees, the company became the first security firm to license the Minnesota Multiphasic Personality Inventory (MMPI) from the University of Minnesota. Guardsmark developed a comprehensive drug testing program in the 1980s. A bachelor's degree became a prerequisite for managerial positions in 1981. The company eventually hired a psychologist to direct its human resources.

Although Guardsmark charged more than twice the average for its guards, according to *Time,* the extensive screening helped keep unfortunate incidents, and insurance rates, down. In addition, fewer than 1 percent of Guardsmark's guards carried firearms, noted *Forbes,* offering more savings on liability insurance. Overall the industry average was around 10 percent, reported *Time* in 1992.

RAISING STANDARDS IN THE 1990S

By 1990, Guardsmark had almost 8,000 employees. It was active in more than 400 cities and had more than 80 branches. According to *Crain's New York Business,* the Persian Gulf War in the early 1990s prompted new interest in security among U.S. companies concerned with the possibility of retaliation by terrorists. The total number of security firms in the United States was estimated at 13,000.

Increased crime during slow economies made the security business resistant to recessions. In the downsizing of the early 1990s, many companies were concerned about potential threats from angry former employees.

More were requiring photo ID badges and other measures recommended by Guardsmark to control building access.

A wave of stories relating to public shootings gripped the American media. Some of these involved security guards gone bad, reported *Time* magazine in its scathing March 1992 exposé of the $15 billion private security industry, which employed about one million people, nearly twice as many as were in public law enforcement. *Time* described the industry as "a virtual dumping ground for the unstable, the dishonest and the violent," but praised Guardsmark for going against the grain through its rigorous selection process. For his part, Ira Lipman was publishing ads and articles calling for higher standards for the industry.

Guardsmark had 9,400 employees in 1995, when revenues were $175 million. A notable new hire was Weldon L. Kennedy, formerly deputy director of the FBI, who became Guardsmark's vice-chairman in April 1995.

By the end of the decade, Guardsmark was celebrating annual sales of more than $300 million. After growing at a double-digit rate for more than 20 years, it was the country's fifth largest security firm. It boasted a greater than 90 percent customer retention rate. The company had about 115 branch offices in the United States and Canada and employed around 14,000 employees. Further, the company was held up as an example of excellence by *Time* magazine as well as business guru Tom Peters.

RECORD REVENUES IN 2000 AND BEYOND

Revenues reached a new record, $342 million, in 2000, when the company employed 15,500 people. In September of that year, it announced that it had attained no-cost health insurance for all of its employees, a first among national security firms. Guardsmark said its employee turnover was a fraction of the industry average. By taking better care of its people than its rivals, it was able to attract better and more loyal staff. The company had become, according to Lipman, the largest private employer of former FBI personnel. Associates told the *Memphis Business Journal* that the firm's growth was due in large part to the dedication and focus of founder Ira Lipman. By this time, three of his sons had been brought into the business.

Guardsmark kept its offices open 24 hours a day in the immediate aftermath of the September 11, 2001 terrorist attacks on the United States. The company's thorough background checking of employees played in

KEY DATES

1963: Guardsmark is founded by Ira Lipman.
1970: Guardsmark goes public.
1974: Revenues reach $20 million.
1979: Guardsmark is taken private again.
1995: Guardsmark has 9,400 employees and revenues of $175 million.
1999: Revenues exceed $300 million.
2005: Revenues exceed $500 million.

its favor in the anxious corporate environment that followed. Reflecting the need for security in an uncertain world, the company began using the slogan, "The time for urgency is now." Officials told the journal *T&D* that Guardsmark was constantly updating its training to meet new threats. Employment and revenues reached record heights in 2002 as the company opened 17 new offices.

The atmosphere of heightened security helped Guardsmark get legislation passed to allow private security companies better access to government records for background screening of prospective employees. Guardsmark had been lobbying for the changes since the 1980s. It later emerged in the *New York Post* and other papers that 30 senior officials at the company had paid $200,000 to five senators sponsoring the legislation, which was not technically illegal but did raise eyebrows among public watchdogs.

A new limited liability company, Guardsmark, L.L.C., was formed in 2003. However it was structured, the company was continuing to grow. Revenues exceeded $500 million by 2005. Guardsmark then had about 18,500 employees. It was a big corporate family, but not an overly friendly one; workers were ordered not to "fraternize on or off duty." The controversial policy was upheld by the National Labor Relations Board in June 2005. "A security officer who is overly familiar with a fellow security officer or a client's employee may overlook signals that, if detected, could be instrumental in preventing workplace violence," explained the company.

Frederick C. Ingram

PRINCIPAL COMPETITORS

Borg-Warner Security Corporation; Kroll Inc.; Securitas Security Services USA, Inc.; Wackenhut Corporation.

FURTHER READING

Behar, Richard, "Thugs in Uniform: Underscreened, Underpaid and Undertrained, Private Security Guards Are Too Often Victimizing Those They Are Hired to Protect," *Time,* March 9, 1992.

Brosnan, James W., "Lipman Gives, Gets in D.C.—Security Measure 'A Good Bill,' Says Sponsor Alexander," *Commercial Appeal,* April 25, 2003, p. C1.

"Companies Increase Security with Employee ID Badges," *Charlotte Observer,* August 12, 1999.

Crabtree, Penni, "Private Investigators Now Use High-Tech Tools to Handle White-Collar Crime Wave," *Memphis Business Journal,* February 12, 1990, pp. 1+.

Flack, Stewart, "Making Crime Pay," *Forbes,* May 18, 1987, p. 238.

Franklin, Deborah, "What This CEO Didn't Know About His Cholesterol Almost Killed Him," *Fortune,* March 19, 2001, pp. 154+.

Gault, Ylonda, "Security: No Longer Sleeping Watchman," *Crain's New York Business,* March 18, 1991, p. 5.

"Guard Services Not Created Equal on Drug Testing; Guardsmark Tests Everyone; Competitors Let Client Decide," *Corporate Security,* February 28, 2002, p. 11.

"Guardsmark Chairman Donates Rare Wiesenthal Drawings," *Memphis Business Journal,* March 16, 1999.

Haffenreffer, David, and Weldon Kennedy, "The Cost of Security," *Money & Markets,* CNNfn, March 21, 2003.

"How Guardsmark's Lipman Sells Security; Determined to Be a Leader in His Field, He Abandons the Industry's Stodgy Ways," *Business Week,* March 24, 1975, p. 114Q.

Joyce, Amy, "Undercover Friends; Firms That Discourage Mixing Have It Wrong," *Washington Post,* August 21, 2005, p. F4.

Lipman, Ira A., *How to Protect Yourself from Crime,* 4th ed., Pleasantville, N.Y.: Readers Digest, 1997.

"A Man the Guard Firms Love to Hate," *Time,* March 9, 1992.

McKenzie, Kevin, "Guardsmark Wins Case on No-Compete Policy," *Commercial Appeal,* December 4, 1996, p. B4.

———, "Veteran FBI Agent Finds Security at Guardsmark," *Commercial Appeal,* March 16, 1997, p. A1.

Morris, Vincent, "Schumer Shocker As Bill Boosts Donor," *New York Post,* April 24, 2003, p. 2.

———, "Workers Pre$$ed to Hop on Chuck Wagon," *New York Post,* April 25, 2003, p. 2.

Peters, Tom, *Liberation Management: Necessary Disorganization for the Nanosecond Nineties,* London: Macmillan, 1992.

"Private Security, Public Responsibility: Why Guardsmark Is 100 Percent Drug Free," *Security Management,* February 2003, p. 31.

Romans, Christine, and Pat Kiernan, "How Businesses Can Do the Right Thing," *Money Gang,* CNNfn, September 23, 2002.

Sewell, Tim, "Guardsmark Expanding into International Markets," *Memphis Business Journal,* June 19, 1995, pp. 1+.

Taylor, Chris, "Survivors: Training to the Rescue," *T&D,* October 2003, pp. 29+.

"There Are 13,000 Private Security Firms, But There's Only One Guardsmark," *Security Management,* October 2003, pp. 44+.

Thornburg, Linda, and Susanne Taylor, "The Changing of the Guards," *HRMagazine,* July 1992, pp. 50+.

Guardsmark, L.L.C.

Timson, Judith, "The Power of Friends at Work," *Globe and Mail* (Canada), October 19, 2005, p. C2.

Wellborn, Bill, "'Engine' of Guardsmark, Inc., Driving Firm Toward $1 Billion," *Memphis Business Journal*, June 9, 2000.

Hampton Affiliates, Inc.

9600 SW Barnes Road, #200
Portland, Oregon 97225
U.S.A.
Telephone: (503) 297-7691
Toll Free: (888) 310-1464
Fax: (503) 203-6607
Web site: http://www.hamptonaffiliates.com

Private Company
Incorporated: 1942 as Willamina Lumber Co.
Employees: 1,500
Sales: $1 billion (2004 est.)
NAIC: 113110 Timber Tract Operations; 113310 Logging; 321113 Sawmills; 321212 Softwood Veneer and Plywood Manufacturing; 321911 Wood Window and Door Manufacturing; 321912 Cut Stock, Resawing Lumber, and Planing; 423310 Lumber, Plywood, Millwork, and Wood Panel Merchant Wholesalers

■ ■ ■

Hampton Affiliates, Inc. is a vertically integrated lumber company and one of Oregon's top timber firms. It owns more than 155,000 acres of timberland, produces about 1.4 billion board feet of lumber annually, and has tree farms and mills in Oregon and Washington. Through its Hampton Distribution Companies division, Hampton distributes doors and windows. Hampton supplies homebuilding centers through its stud lumber and distribution operations.

1942-79: A LOCAL LUMBERYARD DIVERSIFYING AND EXPANDING

In 1935, L. M. "Bud" Hampton began operating a lumberyard in Tacoma, Washington. After World War II created a tight lumber market and made raw materials hard to find, he purchased a sawmill and 11,000 acres of timberland near Willamina, Oregon. The Willamina Lumber Co., founded in 1942, assured a supply of product for Hampton's retail yard.

Hampton "had an innate intelligence" for business, according to his son, John, in a 2005 *Oregon Business* article, but his early missteps almost cost him his initial investment. "He was learning as he went. He had no experience with planning. [The company has] been close to broke three times and it was always because my father had some kind of expansion plan."

However, Willamina Lumber recovered from Bud Hampton's mistakes and grew, and in 1950, with lumber prices rising, Bud encouraged John to form a sales company, Hampton Lumber Sales, to buy and sell lumber from outside mills. John Hampton had joined the family company, doing night shift at the mill, after completing a degree in economics at the University of Washington and serving briefly in the U.S. Navy. In 1955, Bud's other son, Charles, took charge of the company's newly founded Canadian subsidiary, Hampton Lumber Mills, Ltd. in Boston Barr, British Columbia.

John Hampton assumed responsibility for plant development and timber acquisition at Willamina Lumber in 1960. That same year, Willamina Lumber sold its modern plywood mill, completed in 1959, in

Redcrest, California, to Pacific Lumber Co. as part of a move to get out of the plywood business and focus on lumber mill operations. The proceeds from the sale went toward improving the company's two, 100,000-feet per eight-hour shift, mills. Between 1960 and 1966, the company progressed from a simple green dimension mill with annual shipments of 18 million feet to a versatile plant with dry kilns, high speed planing mill, automated packaging and wrapping station, and byproduct program. The company sold its waste wood as pulp chips and shavings, and marketed its sawdust. In 1966, John Hampton became president of Willamina Lumber, while brother Charles became vice-president of the company.

In 1970, under the direction of CEO John Hampton, Willamina Lumber diversified further with the formation of Hampton Tree Farms in western Oregon. The company also began a program of intensive forest management. After a fire burned Hampton Lumber Mills, Ltd.'s processing plant early in the year, Willamina began construction of a high-recovery sawmill to process 50 million board feet per year.

By the end of the 1970s, the company started to use an assumed business name as an umbrella for all its ventures. The newly formed Hampton Affiliates had five subsidiaries: Hampton Lumber Sales, Hampton Industrial Forest Products, Hampton Hardwoods, Inc., Hampton Power Products, and All-Coast Forest Products. In 1979, the company built a new facility, a $9 million wood products expansion at Willamina, which employed 145 workers. The expansion housed a new small log mill, a veneer mill, and a steam boiler to provide electricity.

1980S: A DECADE OF ACQUISITIONS AMID REGULATION AND RECESSION

John Hampton led Hampton Affiliates through the tumultuous late 1980s when the environmental movement, the Endangered Species Act, and the Clinton Forest Plan cut Oregon's timber harvest in half. In this new, regulated environment, Hampton, chairman of the Northwest Forest Resource Council, earned the reputation of being a formidable adversary of environ-

mentalists. Although Hampton championed sustainable forest management and self-regulation of the timber industry, he favored giving timberland owners the opportunity to take matters into their own hands through stream restoration and forest management.

Hampton Affiliates also tangled with its employees' union during the early 1980s and lost. When the workers at Willamina Lumber struck during a contract fight in 1983, the company hired non-union replacements. However, despite the fact that more than 30 percent of the workforce petitioned for a decertification election and many strikers crossed the picket line, the International Woodworkers of America (IWA) won the right in 1984 to remain the bargaining representative for the workers at Willamina. The IWA reluctantly signed a three-year pact with Hampton Affiliates in 1984 that included major reductions in vacations, a loss of paid holidays, and reduced health and pension benefits. The pact also established the company as an open shop.

According to John Hampton in a 1984 *Oregonian* article, "The company has accomplished every single major objective that it set out to achieve at the beginning of negotiations" with the IWA. In fact, following these disputes, the company concentrated on intense education and training for supervisors and managers to teach them how to "'handle their departments in a more effective and communicative manner,'" as Hampton announced in a talk quoted in a 1987 *Oregonian* article. "Our overall people are being encouraged to participate in the decision-making process."

Under John Hampton's leadership, Hampton Affiliates began investing aggressively in timberland acquisitions during the 1980s as well. During this decade, the company purchased: Champion Plywood in 1983; a majority interest in the Smurfit Newsprint Corp. sawmill and Tillamook operations in 1986 (it sold the sawmill in 1987); and the Fort Hill Lumber Company in 1988. The severe industry recession of the first several years of the 1980s caused many mills in the Oregon wood industry to reduce working hours, but Hampton Affiliates grew. By 1985, its overall lumber production was 308 million board feet.

The close of the 1980s and the start of the next decade proved another hard time for the lumber business as a whole. The cost of labor and logs increased while panel prices remained flat, leading many lumber, veneer, and plywood mills throughout the Northwest to close temporarily or permanently. Hampton Affiliates closed two of its mills in the Willamina area temporarily, trimming its number of employees by 150 in 1989. In 1990, it slashed production at its Fort Hill Lumber Company, blaming high log prices and laying off an additional 20 of the remaining 60 Fort Hill workers.

KEY DATES

1942: L. M. "Bud" Hampton founds Willamina Lumber Co.

1950: The company creates Hampton Lumber Sales.

1955: The company creates Hampton Lumber Mills, Ltd.

1960: The company sells Hampton Plywood Co. to Pacific Lumber Co.

1966: John Hampton succeeds L. M. Hampton as president of Willamina Lumber Co.

1970: John Hampton becomes CEO of the company; the company forms Hampton Tree Farms.

1983: The company, now known as Hampton Affiliates, purchases Champion Plywood.

1986: Hampton Affiliates purchases the Tillamook Lumber Co. from Smurfit Newsprint Co.

1988: The company acquires the Fort Hill Lumber Company.

1991: The company acquires 34,000 acres in northwest Oregon.

1993: The company acquires 11,000 acres of timberland in southwest Washington.

1995: Ron Parker becomes president and CEO of the company.

1996: The Ryderwood acquisition adds 94,000 acres of timberland in Southwest Washington.

1997: The company purchases California Builders Supply.

1999: The company acquires Cowlitz Studs.

2000: The company acquires Lane Stanton Vance.

2002: The company acquires a sawmill in Darrington, Washington.

2003: Steven Zika becomes president and CEO of the company.

2004: The company purchases Wilson River Tree Farm; closes Fort Hill sawmill.

2005: The company sells Lane Stanton Vance hardwoods distribution business to BlueLin.

1990S–2005: EMBRACING NEW TECHNOLOGY, CULTIVATING FOREST LAND IN THE FACE OF FINANCIAL CRISES

In the face of tough times for the wood industry, confrontation between environmentalists and timber interests flared. Those in business favored lifting injunctions that strictly limited federal timber sales in the Northwest, while environmentalists argued to support old growth stands as a means of preserving northern spotted owl habitats. In the midst of this period and at the height of the 1991 industry slowdown, Hampton forged an agreement with Portland-based environmentalists, agreeing to sell close to 29 acres of old-growth trees in Northwest Portland to a nonprofit called Friends of Forest Park for $600,000.

Hampton also made significant purchases of timberland in the early 1990s in response to debate over federal forest management practices: 34,000 acres in northwest Oregon, the Big Creek acquisition, in 1991; 11,000 acres of timberland, the Knappton Naselle acquisition, in southwest Washington in 1993; and 94,000 acres of timberland in southwest Washington, the Ryderwood acquisition, in 1996. "We have to depend on private sources of timber now," said Hampton in a 1994 *Business Journal* article. "Our ability to cut public lands has dried up." These purchases increased the company's holdings from 37,000 to 182,000 acres of forest land in Oregon and Washington, which, all told, provided about a third of the company's timber supply. The rest of Hampton's raw materials came from state, federal, and private sources. In 1997, under the direction of Ron Parker, who took the reins as CEO of the company in 1995, Hampton also purchased California Builders Supply, adding to its distribution capabilities.

By the mid-1990s, Hampton Affiliates was averaging $700 million a year in revenues, of which 15 percent came from sales to Japan. By the late 1990s, the company was one of the Northwest's largest privately owned lumber manufacturers. The company owned three sawmills in Oregon: the Willamina Lumber Co., which mainly processed Douglas fir for dimensional lumber; the Tillamook Lumber Co., specializing in kiln-dried hemlock; and the Fort Hill Lumber Co., which produced domestic and specialty items from Douglas fir. Until 1999, Hampton Affiliates also owned Precision Lumber Co. in Pollok, Texas, which manufactured southern yellow pine dimensional lumber.

The year 1999 was another one of growth for Hampton, which then employed about 750 workers and produced 575 million board feet of dimensional lumber each year. The company bought three mills and a reloading facility in the state of Washington from Pacific Lumber & Shipping Co. It also acquired Cowlitz Studs, branching out into stud lumber production and thereby increasing its presence in the home-center and builders markets. Hampton Affiliates now ranked as the third largest lumber manufacturing company in the Northwest behind Simpson Timber Co. and Sierra-Pacific Industries. It remodeled two of its three new mills and expanded its Willamina facility to increase its annual capacity of eight foot-long studs to about 250 million board feet.

The remodeled mills embraced new industry technology: a planning system to cut wood to traditional Japanese construction sizes; new drying kilns; a finger-joint facility for joining scrap wood into domestic two by fours and two by sixes; a small log mill for processing logs less than ten inches in diameter; a curve sawing gang which cut with the grain of the wood; and a 3D computer program that could calculate how to carve the most pieces of lumber from raw wood. The new tools allowed for greater efficiencies that became critical to profits during Oregon's financial crisis of the late 1990s during which manufacturers in the wood industry faced growing pressure from Asia's toppling economies. Despite a thriving domestic economy and record housing sales in 1998, the Asian crisis caused lumber prices to plunge; exports of logs and finished lumber to Japan dropped off while Canadian lumber poured into the United States, pushing lumber prices down further. Sawmills and paper mills shut for weeks or months at a time. About 1,000 jobs were cut throughout the top forest products companies. The sector as a whole at the time employed about 60,000 people.

Just as suddenly, during the first six months of 1999, the recovering Japanese market, record home construction, and less imported wood from Canada led to all-time highs in lumber prices and record sales. Mills ran overtime throughout the summer to take advantage of the 35 percent price increase in Douglas fir prices, and retail lumber costs rose accordingly. Some companies found it hard to reenter the Japanese market, but Hampton Affiliates had continued to devote about 10 percent of its business to Japan, and now, once again, saw its overseas sales increase. By 2000, the company ranked as the sixth largest lumber company in the nation and acquired Lane Stanton Vance, a hardwoods distribution business.

Overproduction throughout the industry and a slowing economy, however, led to a precipitous decline in lumber prices during the second half of 1999, and 2000 was, once again, a very poor year for the lumber market overall with the lowest lumber prices in nine years. U.S. exports to Japan had decreased from 1.15 billion board feet in 1990 to 303 million in 1999 and remained depressed because of competition from countries such as Canada, which exported nearly 95 percent of its lumber. Hampton Affiliates shut down its mill at Willamina.

Japan continued to figure prominently in lumber industry fortunes through 2002. A weaker dollar led to redoubled efforts to sell wood to Japan. Although sales to Japan now accounted for less than 5 percent of Hampton's revenues, its Fort Hill sawmill tailored its lumber for the Japanese market, beams up to 120 mm thick and 360 mm wide.

Moving forward on other fronts as well, the company purchased a Darrington, Washington mill from Summit Timber, which it renovated for a spring 2003 reopening. It exchanged 93,500 acres in Longview, Washington, and Cowlitz counties in southwest Washington for 68,000 acres of forestland in Whatcom, Skagit, and Snohomish counties with Lincoln Timber. Between July 2001 and March 2002, the company successfully bid nearly $10 million on enough standing timber to build 4,000 houses. It owned more than 180,000 acres of softwood timberland and marketed 1.4 billion board feet that year.

In 2003, Hampton ranked ninth in terms of timberland owned, behind North Pacific Group at sixth, Columbia Forest Products at fifth, and Roseburg Forest Products at third. Under the direction of Steven Zika, who became its fourth CEO in 2003, the company purchased Wilson River Tree Farm and closed its Fort Hill sawmill in 2004. In 2005, it sold Lane Stanton Vance hardwoods distribution business to BlueLin. Hampton Affiliates ranked third in the *Oregon Business Private 150* in 2005. As the fourth largest lumber producer in the United States and the second largest in the Northwest, the company continued on its path of growth.

Carrie Rothburd

PRINCIPAL SUBSIDIARIES

Willamina Lumber Co.; Tillamook Lumber Co.; Mid-Valley Resources, Inc.

PRINCIPAL COMPETITORS

Georgia-Pacific Corporation; International Paper Company; Louisiana-Pacific Corporation; Roseburg Forest Products Co.; Sierra Pacific Industries; Simpson Investment Company; TreeSource Industries, Inc.; West Fraser Timber Co. Ltd.; Western Forest Products Inc.; Weyerhaeuser Company.

FURTHER READING

Federman, Stan, "Union Wins Willamina Mill Vote," *Oregonian*, June 22, 1984, p. C2.

Kadera, Jim, "Lumber Executive Shares Management Strategy with Students," *Oregonian*, October 18, 1987, p. D5.

Leeson, Fred, "Portland, Oregon-Based Lumber Firm Buying Three Washington State Mills," *Oregonian*, March 30, 1999.

Louey, Sandy, "Forest Park Group Says Tree Adoption Complete," *Oregonian*, July 10, 1991.

Rivera, Dylan, "Lumbering to Gain Ground," *Oregonian*, January 9, 2005.

Shipley, Sara, "To Survive, Companies Embrace Technology," *Oregonian*, June 27, 1999.

Williams, Christina, "Timber Baron's Art: John Hampton's Love Affair with the Arts Is a Boon for Oregon," *Oregon Business*, December 2005.

❂HermanMiller

Herman Miller, Inc.

———————■———————

855 East Main Avenue Post Office Box 302
Zeeland, Michigan 49464-0302
U.S.A.
Telephone: (616) 654-3000
Toll Free: (888) 443-4357
Fax: (616) 654-5234
Web site: http://www.hermanmiller.com

Public Company
Incorporated: 1960
Employees: 6,234
Sales: $1.52 billion (2005)
Stock Exchanges: NASDAQ
Ticker Symbol: MLHR
NAIC: 337211 Wood Office Furniture Manufacturing;
337214 Office Furniture (Except Wood) Manu-
facturing; 337127 Institutional Furniture Manu-
facturing; 337215 Showcase, Partition, Shelving,
and Locker Manufacturing

■ ■ ■

Herman Miller, Inc. is one of the leading manufacturers of office furniture and furniture systems, second only to Steelcase, Inc. in sales. Ranked since 1986 among the top 20 in *Fortune* magazine's annual list of the 500 most admired companies, Herman Miller is esteemed as an innovator in furniture design, as well as for its unique commitment to employee relations and the environment. The company maintains operations in more than 40 countries, with about 18 percent of net sales coming from outside the United States.

EARLY HISTORY

Herman Miller was founded by D. J. De Pree, who bought the Michigan Star Furniture Company in 1923 with his father-in-law, Herman Miller, and a small group of local businessmen. The company originated in 1905 as Star Furniture Company before adding *Michigan* to its name four years later. It was located in Zeeland, a town in western Michigan near the city of Grand Rapids. Settled primarily by Dutch immigrants, many of whom handed down a legacy of skill in crafting fine furniture, Grand Rapids and its surrounding areas had by 1900 become a hub for American furniture production. Nevertheless, the industry suffered from a lack of innovations, and despite the abilities of its employees, Michigan Star Furniture Company, like most furniture companies in the area, had developed as a manufacturer of high-end traditional style home furnishings, which were modifications of European designs. De Pree had joined the company in 1909 as a general office boy and worked his way up to become president in 1919.

De Pree renamed the company Herman Miller Furniture Company, after his father-in-law, a major shareholder well known in the community, and set about trying to turn the struggling company around. However, both profits and employee morale during this time were low, and this trend continued through the Great Depression. In 1931 Herman Miller was primarily producing traditional furniture for the home, such as bedroom suites, which it marketed to such retailers as Sears, Roebuck and Co. De Pree's company was near bankruptcy.

COMPANY PERSPECTIVES

Our founder, D. J. De Pree, committed Herman Miller to "modern" furniture in 1936 partly because he saw a moral dimension to Gilbert Rohde's clean designs, honest materials, and lack of ornamentation. In 1984, a major impetus behind Bill Stumpf and Don Chadwick's Equa chair was a desire to give a reasonably priced, comfortable, good-looking chair to everybody in offices—not just the higher-ups. These are but two examples of some of the best work done at Herman Miller. Our people and the designers we work with are concerned with larger issues of humanity and equality and bettering the world we work in. What arrives on the truck is furniture. What went into the truck was an amalgam of what we believe in: innovation, design, operational excellence, smart application of technology, and social responsibility.

That year De Pree was approached by the industrial designer Gilbert Rohde, who reportedly entered the Herman Miller showroom unannounced with a plan for a new look in furniture design. De Pree listened to Rohde's ideas and, attracted to the designer's straightforward approach, employed Rohde to design a new line of furniture for Herman Miller.

Rohde speculated that the decreasing size of modern homes would inspire a demand for a smaller, simpler, and lighter furniture style that De Pree referred to as "more honest" than that of traditional pieces. Rohde's first designs, completed in 1933, were exhibited at the Chicago World's Fair, where they met with approval from retail buyers and enthusiasm from the general public. In less than five years, most furniture makers had adopted more functional styles similar to those of Rohde.

During this time De Pree, a profoundly religious man, had begun to regard furniture design as a moral issue, and he admired the simplicity, high quality, and utilitarianism of the modern designs. This sense of moral responsibility also pervaded De Pree's management style. In an often-repeated anecdote regarding the origins of the company's commitment to its employees, De Pree visited the home of a millwright who had died on the job at Herman Miller in 1927. At the request of the widow, De Pree remained to hear some poetry that she read aloud. Profoundly moved by the poems, he inquired as to the author's identity and was told that the millwright had written them. De Pree became intrigued

by the question of whether he had employed a millwright who happened to write poetry, or a poet who worked as a millwright, and after that he sought to realize and encourage the hidden strengths and talents of all of his employees.

DEBUT OF OFFICE FURNITURE IN THE 1940S

After Rohde's first efforts for Herman Miller met with success, he turned his attention to designing office furniture. Seeking to design an office more functional than decorative, he produced several different desktops, pedestals, and drawers, all of which could be interchanged to form a desk that would suit the user's individual needs. The Executive Office Group, the designs for which Rohde completed in 1939, was introduced in 1942. It included a creative L-shaped desk. Rohde also produced a design for a sectional sofa, manufactured by Herman Miller, that would exert a substantial influence on sofa designs in the years to come. With the revolutionary product line, Herman Miller's sales continued to climb and the company experienced considerable growth in the 1940s.

Rohde died in 1944, and one year later George Nelson, a young architect and the editor of the periodical *Architectural Forum,* was contracted as design director. By this time the company had abandoned all of its traditional furniture lines in order to focus solely on the contemporary. Nelson produced several creative and profitable office furniture designs as well as the classic Storagewall shelving and storage system, the "slat bench," the "pretzel armchair," and other residential pieces while also helping the company develop graphic design and advertising departments. Among his most important accomplishments at Herman Miller, however, was bringing the company together with such important design artists as Isamu Noguchi, Alexander Girard, and Charles and Ray Eames, which broadened the company's reputation for quality and innovation.

Charles Eames is widely regarded as a genius in contemporary furniture design. Working in collaboration with his wife, Ray, Eames experimented with new materials, such as molded plywood, fiberglass, aluminum, and wire, producing several distinctive pieces, primarily chairs, for Herman Miller. In 1946 he produced an influential design for a molded plywood side chair, and in 1956 he produced perhaps his most famous piece, known as the 670 swivel lounge chair. Consisting of a molded plywood back shell and seat shell with rosewood veneer padded with down, covered in leather, and supported by a five-prong stand, the 670 chair is known for its support and comfort as well as its light weight and

KEY DATES

1905: Star Furniture Company is founded in Zeeland, Michigan.

1909: Company changes its name to Michigan Star Furniture Company.

1923: D. J. De Pree and his father-in-law, Herman Miller, lead a buyout of Michigan Star Furniture, which is renamed Herman Miller Furniture Company.

1933: Company debuts a new furniture line designed by Gilbert Rohde.

1942: Herman Miller enters the office furniture sector through the Rohde-designed Executive Office Group.

1946: Designer Charles Eames's collaboration with Herman Miller begins.

1950: Company adopts the Scanlon participative management plan.

1960: Company incorporates as Herman Miller, Inc.

1964: The Action Office System is introduced.

1970: Herman Miller goes public.

1976: Company introduces its Ergon chair.

1984: The Equa chair debuts.

1994: Herman Miller introduces the Aeron chair and reenters the residential furniture market.

1999: Geiger Brickel, maker of wood office furniture, is acquired.

2002: Company workforce reductions reach nearly 4,000 in midst of deep industry recession.

2003: Company introduces its Mirra chair.

casual form. The chair, one of Herman Miller's most successful products, was widely copied by other furniture companies.

By 1950 Herman Miller's sales had increased to $1.7 million. That year the company initiated the Scanlon management plan. Named after its inventor, a lecturer at the Massachusetts Institute of Technology, the plan was based on the idea that employees could serve as a valuable source of ideas for operations and cost effectiveness and should therefore be called on to participate in management decisions. The plan called for team organization and provided employees with various incentives, including financial rewards for productivity gains. Revolutionary at the time, the plan proved successful for Herman Miller and has since been adopted by several other major companies.

DEBUT OF ACTION OFFICE SYSTEM IN THE 1960S

In 1960 the company was incorporated as Herman Miller, Inc. Two years later, D. J. De Pree's son Hugh took over operations, and Herman Miller began changing the configuration of the American office floorplan. The Action Office System, introduced in 1964, included freestanding desks, files, and other pieces that could be configured a variety of ways to form work arenas, specific to individual work needs. Then in 1968 Action Office products replaced the traditional construct of individual offices or large rooms with partitions and panels supporting desk components that could be easily moved or added on to, allowing for efficient use of floor space. The concept was created by a newly formed research team, headquartered in Ann Arbor, Michigan, and headed by inventor and sculptor Robert Propst. The team spent four years researching the needs of office workers, finding that the open plan system broke up the monotony of previous plans and provided an illusion of privacy for each employee while also allowing proximity for easy communication with coworkers. Furthermore, the Herman Miller Action Office system had the advantage of being cheaper to manufacture than the heavy wood furniture previously favored. It was the first open plan panel system in the world and subsequently fostered a multibillion-dollar industry.

Herman Miller became a public corporation in 1970, and its stock rose steadily. In 1976 the company made a hit with its Ergon chair, designed by Bill Stumpf and based on the science of ergonomics, in which the worker's physical relationship to his or her environment and duties is given special consideration. The chair, featuring a five-pronged aluminum pedestal on casters and comfortably padded with an adjustable back support and seat, became widely used in American offices.

Although sales of the Action Office components continued to increase during this time, research during the 1970s indicated some drawbacks to the product. Some customers complained that the cubicles lacked privacy while simultaneously engendering a feeling of isolation among employees, who could hear but not see one another. In 1975 Herman Miller contracted Stumpf and designer Don Chadwick to come up with a solution. Chadwick and Stumpf worked for nearly three years on the project, traveling to Europe to study contemporary office buildings in an effort to capture a more humane spirit in their new office designs. In December 1978 they presented their design, entitled Buroplan, to Herman Miller. However, the plan's combination of futuristic windows, archways, balustrades, and windows with traditional freestanding desks was considered too eclectic, and the company rejected it, subsequently offering the two a chance to design a new office chair that was based on the design elements of the project.

Because of special challenges in finding the right materials, the chair took Chadwick and Stumpf five years to design, but the result met with enormous approval. Manufactured in 1984, the Equa chair was designed to provide "seating equity," or equal comfort for both the employee who spends a long period of time in the chair and the employee who sits only between frequent periods of motion. Offering support and comfort, without complicated mechanical adjustment knobs and levers, the Equa chair was offered in two models, a standard model selling for $320 and a high-backed, leather model that retailed for $1,100. *Time* magazine later named the Equa chair one of three best products of the decade. The following year elements of Chadwick and Stumpf's Buroplan resurfaced in Ethospace interiors, an alternative to the Action Office system designed by Stumpf and Jack Kelley, which offered the worker a greater sense of control and more natural light.

Company sales saw unprecedented growth during the 1970s and early 1980s, increasing from $49 million in 1975 to $492 million in 1985. During this time Hugh De Pree stepped down and was replaced by his brother Max. Max De Pree developed a plan in which employees were allowed to become shareholders in the company, a practice that contributed to the company's inclusion in 1984 in *The 100 Best Companies to Work for in America*, by Robert Levering and Milton Moskowitz. Earnings and stock prices fell late in 1985, however, and industry analysts speculated that the decline in orders from the computer and electronics industries and the large number of companies copying and marketing Herman Miller designs were to blame. Some maintained that Herman Miller had focused too long on improving its internal operations and had ignored the increase in competition. Others, including Herman Miller representatives, attributed the decline in earnings to the disappointing sales of the Ethospace system. Nevertheless, the company surprised investors, overcoming the slump by implementing an aggressive program to sway large corporate customers away from their competitors. They reported sales of $714 million in 1988, up 20 percent from the previous year.

The following year Max De Pree published a book on the Herman Miller management style, titled *Leadership Is an Art*. Writing that "everyone has the right and duty to influence decision-making and to understand the results," De Pree emphasized the need to treat all employees as important contributors. He also stressed that in order to promote competence in a staff, a leader needs to form a "covenant" with the employees, attend-

ing carefully to their need for "spirit, excellence, beauty, and joy." Finally, De Pree maintained, the signs of a failing company included a "dark tension" among employees, an increase in the distribution of memos and manuals, and a lack of interest in company anecdotes and extracurricular functions. De Pree's book was well received, providing managers in other companies with insights into Herman Miller's success.

UPS AND DOWNS IN THE 1990S

By 1990 Herman Miller's sales had reached $865 million, and the company began to expand its scope, acquiring other companies as subsidiaries and addressing new issues in the industry. The preceding year Meridian, Inc., a manufacturer of metal file cabinets, storage cases, and desks, was acquired. Other acquisitions included Miltech and Integrated Metal Technology, which fabricated sheet metal parts. Milcare, spun off from Herman Miller in 1985, sought to fill the needs of the healthcare profession, adapting the Action Office equipment for use in nursing stations, medical libraries, and hospital rooms. Also during this time Herman Miller sought to become a leader in conservation. Extensive recycling programs were implemented and the use of endangered tropical hardwoods, including the rosewood in the Eames 670 swivel lounge, was discontinued in favor of walnut, cherry, and other more plentiful hardwoods. The company won several awards for its efforts to protect the natural environment.

In March 1992 Richard H. Ruch retired from his position as Herman Miller CEO, having served in that position since 1987 and having been the first person outside the De Pree family to hold that title. Brought onboard as the company's fifth president and CEO was J. Kermit Campbell, who became the first outsider to be named to either post. Campbell was a 32-year veteran of Dow Corning, most recently serving as group vice-president and president of the U.S. area. He joined Herman Miller at an inauspicious time as the recession of the early 1990s hit the commercial real estate market particularly hard, dampening demand for office furniture. For the fiscal year ending in May 1992 Herman Miller posted its first loss in 22 years as Campbell immediately moved to restructure operations, including closing an assembly plant in California and dropping a low-volume product line. Charges of $48.7 million led to a net loss of $14.1 million, and the company also saw its sales decline from $878.7 million to $804.6 million.

Campbell continued to restructure over the next couple of years, discontinuing additional unprofitable product lines, pushing products to market faster, seeking to make the manufacturing process less costly, and shutting down some showrooms. By fiscal 1994 Herman

Miller was able to report an 11.4 percent jump in net sales, to a record $953.2 million, and net income of $40.4 million, the company's best showing in four years. On the product front, Herman Miller introduced the Aeron chair in 1994, a multi-task chair ergonomically designed with a mechanism that, during inclination, transfers the weight of the user from rear to back. The Aeron won immediate accolades, including being added to the 20th Century Design Collection of New York's Museum of Modern Art. The chair was later given a furniture "Design of the Decade" award by *Business Week* magazine and the Industrial Designers Society of America. Herman Miller also reentered the residential furniture market in 1994 by launching Herman Miller for the Home, a collection comprised of both new designs and reintroduced "classic" home furnishings from the 1940s, 1950s, and 1960s. In addition, the company acquired Geneal GmbH, a German maker of office furniture.

While the company's sales were on the rise, expenses were rising as fast if not faster, leading to the need for further cost-cutting. Late in 1994 Herman Miller announced that it intended to close plants in Fort Worth, Texas, and Dayton, New Jersey. Then in the early months of the next year about 200 white-collar workers were cut from the workforce through either layoffs or early retirement. In May, Campbell added the chairmanship to his duties, succeeding the retiring Max De Pree. Just two months later, however, the board forced Campbell out, apparently displeased with the pace of cost-cutting. Ruch, who had remained on the board as vice-chairman, assumed the chairmanship, while Michael A. Volkema was named CEO. Then 39 years of age, Volkema had served as president and chief operating officer since May, having joined Herman Miller in 1990 through the acquisition of Meridian. Volkema had made a strong impression through his leadership at Meridian, which was growing at a compound annual rate of more than 20 percent, and where he had instituted a number of successful efficiency initiatives.

Volkema took charge just after the conclusion of 1995, when Herman Miller saw its sales surpass $1 billion for the first time but recorded only $4.3 million in profits. While focusing on containing expenses, the new leader also gave the green light to a new office furniture division called SQA, which in 1996 began selling lines not as expensive as Herman Miller's typical premium furniture—SQA standing for simple, quick, affordable. In early 1996 the company settled a four-year-old patent infringement suit that had been brought by competitor Haworth, Inc. Haworth had claimed that Herman Miller had copied its designs for prewired panel systems allowing office workers to plug into outlets built right into

their cubicle walls. While not admitting any wrongdoing, Herman Miller agreed to pay Haworth $44 million.

A turnaround was evident in the results for 1996 as Herman Miller posted net income of $45.9 million on record sales of $1.28 billion. The company in fact rode the strong economy of the late 1990s to ever greater heights, culminating in 1999's $141.8 million in profits on revenues of $1.77 billion. Results overseas were not as strong, leading the company to divest its German manufacturing operations in 1997. The following year Herman Miller began selling its home furnishings over the Internet. In 1999 the company made its first major acquisition in nearly a decade, purchasing Geiger Group Inc., parent of furniture maker Geiger Brickel. Based in Atlanta, Geiger Brickel produced high-quality wood office furniture, including chairs and desks. It operated four manufacturing plants, three in Atlanta and one in Lake Mills, Wisconsin.

EARLY 2000S: SURVIVING A SEVERE INDUSTRY DOWNTURN

In late 2000 Herman Miller went down market again by launching a lower-priced office line dubbed RED that was aimed at small businesses in general but particularly at Internet-based ventures. The line was sold exclusively over the Internet and via a single retail outlet in New York City. While early sales were encouraging, the faltering economy pushed the office furniture industry into one of its deepest downturns in decades, rendering the RED launch ill-timed. Both it and the SQA division were phased out in 2002. Meanwhile, the downturn wreaked havoc at the entire company. After reaching a record $2.24 billion in 2001, sales plunged to just $1.47 billion the following year. In 2001 and first few months of 2002, Herman Miller slashed its workforce by nearly 4,000, a cut of 37 percent, and closed several plants. Pretax restructuring charges of $81.6 million sent Herman Miller into the red for 2002, a net loss totaling $56 million.

While attempting to better position itself for an industry recovery, Herman Miller maintained its level of spending on research and development. One outcome was the introduction in 2003 of the Mirra chair, touted by the company as cheaper, more environmentally friendly, and more comfortable than the Aeron. Of the chair's weight, 42 percent came from recycled content, while 96 percent of the chair's content was recyclable. According to the company, the Mirra, recipient of several awards, was "the first piece of office furniture to be developed from its inception according to cradle-to-cradle principles."

Herman Miller recovered slowly along with the rest of the office furniture industry. By 2005 the company was able to report net earnings of $68 million on revenues of $1.52 billion, its best showing since 2001. During this period, the company leadership was altered. In March 2003 Brian Walker, who had helped shepherd Herman Miller through the downturn as head of the firm's North America operations, was named president and chief operating officer. He had joined Herman Miller in 1989 having previously worked for the accounting firm of Arthur Andersen. Walker was then named the seventh Herman Miller CEO in July 2004, succeeding Volkema, who remained chairman of the board and was also given leadership of a new creative office charged with creating innovations and inventions in furniture products designed for both in the office and outside the workplace.

In 2005 this creative office launched its first new product, Babble, which was codeveloped with a California firm called Applied Minds Inc. Babble was a desktop device designed for open office systems that made telephone conversations unintelligible to those outside the workspace. Babble was the first offering of Herman Miller's new line of sound management products, Sonare Technologies. Moving into new markets such as this one was deemed essential if Herman Miller was to reach a goal that Walker set in 2005: to challenge for the industry's top position by 2010—a daunting undertaking requiring five years of double-digit annual growth. On more familiar new product ground, the company also introduced a new office chair in 2005. Cella was positioned as the firm's low-priced seating entry, retailing for between $450 and $650, depending on the accessories. This compared with the $740 list price for the Mirra, the company's mid-priced market chair. Along with the high-end Aeron, Herman Miller now had "high-performance" chairs at every price point. Its reputation for innovation, quality, and integrity intact, Herman Miller was indeed well positioned to challenge Steelcase for the top position in office furniture.

Tina Grant
Updated, David E. Salamie

PRINCIPAL SUBSIDIARIES

Geiger International, Inc.; Herman Miller (Australia) Pty., Ltd.; Herman Miller B.V. (Netherlands); Herman Miller Canada; Herman Miller Global Customer Solutions, Inc.; Herman Miller Italia S.p.A. (Italy); Herman Miller Japan, Ltd.; Herman Miller, Ltd. (U.K.); Herman Miller Mexico S.A. de C.V.; Integrated Metal Technologies, Inc.; Meridian, Inc.; Milsure Insurance, Ltd. (Barbados); W.B. Wood N.Y., Inc.; Office Pavilion South Florida, Inc.; OP Corporate Furnishings, Inc.; OP Spectrum LLP (90%); OP Ventures, Inc.; OP Ventures of Texas, Inc.; Workstyles, Inc.

PRINCIPAL COMPETITORS

Steelcase, Inc.; Haworth, Inc.; HNI Corporation.

FURTHER READING

Abercrombie, Stanley, "The Company That Design Built," *AIA Journal,* February 1981, pp. 54-57.

Ager, Susan, "Philosopher of Capitalism," *Nation's Business,* March 1986, pp. 77-78.

Bauer, Julia, "Sitting Pretty Again?," *Grand Rapids (Mich.) Press,* June 23, 2005, p. A1.

Berman, Ann E., "Herman Miller—Influential Designs of the 1940s and 1950s," *Architectural Digest,* September 1991, pp. 34-40.

Berry, John, *Herman Miller Is Built on Its People, Research, and Designs,* Zeeland, Mich.: Herman Miller, Inc., 1992.

Brammer, Rhonda, "Not Miller Time? A Furniture Company Loses Some of Its Gloss," *Barron's,* October 7, 1985, p. 18.

Caplan, Ralph, *The Design of Herman Miller,* New York: Whitney Library of Design, 1976, 119 p.

De Pree, Hugh, *Business As Unusual: The People and Principles at Herman Miller,* Zeeland, Mich.: Herman Miller, Inc., 1986, 197 p.

De Pree, Max, *Leadership Is an Art,* East Lansing: Michigan State University Press, 1987, 142 p., reprinted, with a new foreword by the author, New York: Currency, 2004, 148 p.

Ebeling, Ashlea, "Herman Miller: Furnishing the Future," *Forbes,* January 10, 2000, p. 94.

Geber, Beverly, "Herman Miller: Where Profits and Participation Meet," *Training: The Magazine of Human Resources Development,* November 1987, pp. 62-66.

Greenwald, John, "Advice to Bosses: Try a Little Kindness," *Time,* September 11, 1989, p. 56.

Harger, Jim, "New Herman Miller CEO Sees Himself More As a Leader Than a Furniture Man," *Grand Rapids (Mich.) Press,* March 29, 1992, p. D1.

Henderson, Angelo B., "Herman Miller's Campbell Quits Under Pressure," *Wall Street Journal,* July 12, 1995, p. B7.

Khan, Mahvish, "Herman Miller Inc. Has Small Businesses Seeing Red," *Wall Street Journal,* June 18, 2001, p. B4.

Kirkbride, Rob, "CEO Baton Passed at Herman Miller," *Grand Rapids (Mich.) Press,* July 31, 2004, p. A14.

———, "Plunging Profits Spur New Cuts at Herman Miller," *Grand Rapids (Mich.) Press,* September 25, 2001, p. A1.

———, "Sales Batter Herman Miller's Work Force," *Grand Rapids (Mich.) Press,* March 21, 2002, p. A1.

Labich, Kenneth, "Hot Company, Warm Culture," *Fortune,* February 27, 1989, pp. 74-78.

Leith, Scott, "Herman Miller Buys Furniture Company," *Grand Rapids (Mich.) Press,* July 23, 1999, p. B9.

Martin, Justin, "Broken Furniture at Herman Miller," *Fortune,* August 7, 1995, p. 32.

McClory, Robert J., "The Creative Process at Herman Miller," *Across the Board,* May 1985, pp. 8-22.

Mitchell, Jacqueline, "Herman Miller Links Worker-CEO Pay," *Wall Street Journal,* May 7, 1992, p. B1.

Morrison, Ann M., "Action Is What Makes Herman Miller Climb," *Fortune,* June 15, 1981, pp. 161-77.

Nelson-Horchler, Joani, "The Magic of Herman Miller," *Industry Week,* February 18, 1991, pp. 11-17.

Radigan, Mary, "Herman Miller Chiefs Mapping a Rough Route Back to Profitability," *Grand Rapids (Mich.) Press,* December 20, 1992, p. F1.

Sanchez, Mark, "Herman Miller's Restructuring Looks Past Present Downturn," *Grand Rapids (Mich.) Business Journal,* October 1, 2001, p. 21.

Skolnik, Rayna, "Battling for the Power of the Seats," *Sales and Marketing Management,* April 1987, pp. 46-48.

"Three Furniture Giants Acquire Competitors," *Michigan Business,* March 1990, pp. 12-13.

Upbin, Bruce, "A Touch of Schizophrenia," *Forbes,* July 7, 1997, pp. 57+.

Veverka, Amber, "Furniture Makers Settle Patent Battle," *Grand Rapids (Mich.) Press,* January 9, 1996, p. B7.

——, "New CEO Revels in Recovery," *Grand Rapids (Mich.) Press,* July 23, 1996, p. A1.

——, "Sitting Pretty: After Cutting Costs and Reorganizing, Herman Miller Is Healthy Again," *Grand Rapids (Mich.) Press,* May 15, 1994, p. F1.

Wechsler, Dana, "A Comeback in Cubicles," *Forbes,* March 21, 1988, pp. 54, 56.

Hewitt Associates, Inc.

———— ■ ————

100 Half Day Road
Lincolnshire, Illinois 60069-3342
U.S.A.
Telephone: (847) 295-5000
Fax: (847) 295-7634
Web site: http://www.hewitt.com

Public Company
Founded: 1940 as Edwin Shields Hewitt and Associates
Employees: 22,000 Operating Revenues: $2.89 billion (2005)
Stock Exchanges: New York
Ticker Symbol: HEW
NAIC: 541214 Payroll Services; 541612 Human Resources and Executive Search Consulting Services; 561310 Employment Placement Services; 561320 Temporary Help Services; 561330 Professional Employer Organizations

■ ■ ■

The Lincolnshire, Illinois-based Hewitt Associates, Inc. is a global management consulting firm specializing in the outsourcing of corporate human resources (HR) programs such as healthcare benefits, stock options and investment accounts, retirement programs, and severance packages. Hewitt represents many *Fortune* 500 companies, administering their investment and benefit programs and offering their clients a host of related services, many of them online. Hewitt not only pioneered the use of automated benefit programs, but brought the HR industry into the Internet age by launching a series of online programs and software packages.

IN THE BEGINNING: 1940S-70S

Edwin "Ted" Hewitt founded Edwin Shields Hewitt and Associates on October 1, 1940, as a brokerage house focusing on insurance and personal financial services. It was a heady time in the United States; population had grown to 132 million, the economy was robust, and President Franklin Delano Roosevelt was reelected for a record third term. Unfortunately, the war raging in Europe was about to bring the United States into what became World War II.

During and after the war, Hewitt's particular expertise became immensely valuable when the government instituted "pay-as-you-go" income taxes in 1943 and the U.S. cost of living increased more than 25 percent in 1945. Once the war and its rationing ended, Americans returned to work and the economy recovered. Hewitt's clients, many of whom had manufactured goods for the war effort, returned to their customary businesses and thrived. Hewitt began offering its clients statements to track their employee benefits and had pioneered the use of specific financial goals for company investments. Hewitt's programs were the first of their kind to be approved by the Internal Revenue Service; they were so cutting edge the U.S. Department of Labor asked the firm to create forms for the welfare and pension programs of the 1950s.

By the 1960s the Hewitt firm continued to expand its pension and benefit plans, creating more sophisticated programs for its clients. During the decade the firm revolutionized employee benefit packages once again, as the first company to design pension and benefit plans tied to a corporation's revenue and growth projections. While such a practice became commonplace in the pension and employee benefits of larger corporations, it was another in Hewitt's growing list of industry firsts. Hewitt was so respected for its work in the field that it was the only company asked by the U.S. government to consult on the Federal Interagency Task Force from 1964 to 1968. The Task Force was responsible for the design and implementation of the new Employee Retirement Income Security Act.

In the next decade Hewitt began offering its clients an increasing number of innovative products, including its trademarked Benefit Index to track the performance of benefit programs. The Benefit Index was another industry first and soon became the standard to which all aspired. Hewitt also offered its clients several flexible investment strategies for employee benefit packages, which led to the formation of a new consulting firm, the Hewitt Investment Group, in 1974.

SIGNIFICANT GROWTH: 1980S AND 1990S

Never content to be an industry leader, Hewitt continually sought to better its programs. The company began to conduct in-depth surveys to find out which benefit programs worked best and which ones needed improvement. In the 1980s Hewitt researched numerous issues and began issuing its findings industrywide on subjects such as offering benefits to part-time employees, full versus partial hospital reimbursement, fluctuating profit-sharing percentages, mental health benefits, 401(k) programs, and rising health plan deductibles. Another topical issue was computer use for automated benefit calculations.

The use of computers had finally begun to take hold in larger businesses, as Hewitt found automated benefit programs had increased remarkably from 1986 to 1988. In a survey detailed in *PC Week* (November 6,

1989), Hewitt had surveyed 700 companies to find 71 percent had become either fully or partially automated in their administration of benefits plans, up from 48 percent two years before. Hewitt responded to the expanding use of technology by designing computerized benefit programs and software so companies could manage their benefit plans. Hewitt Technologies was created in 1988 to monitor and respond to the industry's rapidly changing technological needs.

By the beginning of the 1990s Hewitt had ventured abroad and offered tailored benefit programs to corporations in the United Kingdom. The firm had brought in more than $250 million in revenues for 1990 and was ranked the fourth largest benefit management and consulting firm in the world, according to *Business Insurance* magazine. Yet many of Hewitt's clients were feeling the pinch of a struggling economy and inflation. As companies began looking for ways to bolster the bottom line, benefits were often the first place executives looked for a quick fix. In a time when few received raises and those who did received only cost-of-living increases, Hewitt started retooling retirement packages and healthcare benefits to keep its customers from making drastic changes. Of particular interest were retirement programs since few seniors could withstand the effects of inflation and soaring healthcare costs. Hewitt also researched other benefit additions such as flextime scheduling, child- and elder-care benefits, and HMOs (health management organizations) versus PPOs (preferred provider organizations).

By 1997 more than 100 large companies outsourced their benefit programs to Hewitt, covering about nine million worldwide employees. Hewitt not only managed these HR services but provided both the companies and their employees with the opportunity to view their benefits with ease. The company ran into controversy, however, when it secured lucrative incentives to open a new benefits management center in Orlando, Florida. Public officials decried the incentives, believing that Hewitt was favored over other firms that could have offered more jobs and revenue for the city. Despite the furor, the new office opened in Orlando in 1997, during a fiscal year (ending in September) in which Hewitt's revenues reached close to $700 million.

Hewitt was ahead of the curve again in 1998 when it partnered with the California-based Financial Engines, an online investment firm, to offer its clients financial advice over the burgeoning "information superhighway" or Internet. Hewitt clients were among the first to view nearly every facet of their company's benefit programs with a few simple keystrokes, and could seek online

KEY DATES

1940: Edwin Shields Hewitt and Associates is founded by Ted Hewitt.

1964: The company begins consulting on the government's Federal Interagency Task Force.

1974: Hewitt forms a consulting firm for investment advice.

1988: Hewitt creates a new division to monitor technological advances.

1997: Hewitt opens a benefits management center in Orlando, Florida, amidst controversy.

1998: Hewitt and Financial Engines form a joint venture to offer clients online investment advice.

2000: Hewitt breaks the billion-dollar mark in revenues for the first time.

2002: Hewitt Associates goes public on the New York Stock Exchange.

2003: The company acquires HR management firm Cyborg Worldwide.

2004: Exult Inc., an HR and consulting firm, is bought by Hewitt and merged into operations.

2005: Hewitt lands lucrative contracts with Thomson Corporation, PepsiCo Inc., Wachovia Corp., and others.

investment advice and make changes in real-time. Such advancements, along with being the first HR industry firm to launch a corporate web site, landed Hewitt among *PC Week*'s Top Ten Most Technologically Innovative Companies. Hewitt also continued its in-depth surveys, developing the Health Value Initiative in 1999 to measure the effectiveness and quality of more than 2,000 healthcare programs worldwide. The Initiative's findings led to testimony for the government and various agencies in an attempt to reform the U.S. healthcare industry.

As the decade closed, Hewitt was poised for further growth both domestically and abroad. Not only was the company broadening the scope of its operations, but it offered clients advanced tools to outdistance their competitors. Hewitt's HR management services had become known for their cutting-edge technology and the company's ongoing commitment to offer newer, faster, and more comprehensive programs would take it to the top of the industry in the next century.

A NEW ERA: 2000 ONWARD

By early 2000 Hewitt's expansion moved forward with new offices near Houston, Texas, and an increased presence in Asia with a new office in Kuala Lumpur, Malaysia. The company also announced the merger of its British and Irish operations with the United Kingdom's Bacon & Woodrow, a leading retirement and HR management consulting firm. Hewitt also unveiled plans for Sageo, a comprehensive online service where participants could compare, choose, and enroll in benefit programs. Sageo was designed for retirees and companies with numerous older employees, to offer this growing population the same benefits provided to Hewitt's 150 corporate clients and their 15 million worldwide employees. Hewitt hoped that Sageo's online format would not only simplify the benefits process but lower employer costs as well. Within a few months of its debut, Sageo had enrolled nearly a dozen companies and represented 500,000 individuals.

With revenues topping the billion-dollar mark in 2000, Hewitt executives pondered the benefits of going public. Funds raised through an initial public offering would spearhead expansion, and Hewitt was eager to conquer more of Europe and Asia. In 2001 Hewitt formally announced its intention to become a publicly traded company after nearly six decades as a private firm. Under the ticker symbol HEW on the New York Stock Exchange, Hewitt went public with an initial offering of 11 million shares (at $19 per share). Share prices rose as high as $23 the following day. Hewitt wasted little time in putting its new funds to work, paying off debt, purchasing France's Finance Arbitage, an investment consultancy firm, and spearheading expansion plans for the United Kingdom and China.

In 2003 Hewitt took over the Cork, Ireland-based Becketts, a benefits consultancy, and bought the software programs and payroll services of Cyborg Worldwide Inc. These moves, along with several others, prompted the Chicago-based *Crain's Chicago Business* to name Hewitt one of the area's fastest growing public firms, with fiscal revenues topping $1.9 billion for the year. In 2004 Hewitt announced the purchase/merger of Irvine, California's Exult Inc., another HR and consulting firm. The deal was valued at close to $700 million and was expected to bring in combined revenues of more than $3 billion by the following fiscal year.

For 2004 Hewitt reached solid revenues of $2.2 billion and the firm sustained its 43rd consecutive year of growth. Employees numbered more than 22,000 in nearly three dozen countries (including Brazil, China, France, India, Ireland, The Netherlands, Puerto Rico, Singapore, and Switzerland) representing more than 18 million employees for its corporate clients. In addition, the company was named one of America's Most Admired Companies in 2004 by *Fortune* magazine, ranked as one of the 100 Best Places to Work for the fourth consecutive year by *Computer World,* and had become the United States' largest and the world's second largest benefits outsourcing company, according to *Business Insurance* magazine.

By early 2005 the newly empowered Hewitt clinched several significant business processing outsourcing (BPO) contracts, signing publisher Thomson Corporation, Sun Microsystems, hospitality leader Marriott International, beverage giant PepsiCo Inc., Wachovia Corporation, and others to a roster of more than 2,500 international clients. As the year came to a close, Hewitt had fallen a bit short of its $3 billion goal, though not much, bringing in revenues of $2.8 billion. With analysts believing the business outsourcing market would top $33 billion or more in 2006, Hewitt continued to dominate the U.S. benefits industry and aimed to be the world's top provider of outsourced business processing.

Nelson Rhodes

PRINCIPAL SUBSIDIARIES

Hewitt Financial Services L.L.C.

PRINCIPAL COMPETITORS

Accenture Ltd.; FMR Corporation; Mercer Inc.; T. Rowe Price Group, Inc.; Towers Perrin; Vanguard Group Inc.; Watson Wyatt & Company Holdings.

FURTHER READING

Ackerman, Matt, "Hewitt Deal to Boost Human Resources Leadership," *American Banker,* June 17, 2004, p. 10.

———, "Hewitt Looks to Organic Growth to Stay No. 1," *American Banker,* September 29, 2005, p. 9.

Babcock, Pamela, "Hewitt and Exult Create Outsourcing Powerhouse," *HR Magazine,* August 2004, p. 29.

Bates, Steve, "Hewitt Goes Public with Stock Offering," *HR Magazine,* August 2002, p. 12.

Cowans, Deborah Shalowitz, "Thomas L. Schmitz: Insider on Benefits Outsourcing Directs Employers to New Frontier," *Business Insurance,* November 3, 1997, p. S108.

Feinberg, Phyllis, "Callan Left Out: Deal Gives Hewitt Foothold in UK," *Pensions & Investments,* October 28, 2000, p. 2.

Geisel, Jerry, "Hewitt Mulls Benefits of IPO," *Business Insurance,* March 5, 2001, p.1.

———, "Hewitt Starts Health Care e-business," *Business Insurance,* March 20, 2000, p. 1.

Gunsauley, Craig, "High Hopes Attend Hewitt's Online Venture for Health Benefits," *Employee Benefit News,* May 1, 2000.

"Hewitt Buy First Step in Pension Market," *South China Morning Post,* October 24, 2001.

"Hewitt to Provide HR Services to PepsiCo," *Westchester County Business Journal (NY),* May 2, 2005, p. 22.

Jacobius, Arlene, "First Steps: Hewitt, Financial Engines Push Advice Trade," *Pensions & Investments,* April 5, 1999, p. 43.

Jacobs, Jennifer, "Hewitt Eyes Projects in Various Sectors," *Business Times (Malaysia),* March 24, 2000.

Kochaniec, Joanne W., "Hewitt Tries Online Bids for Clients' Health Plans," *Business Insurance,* November 29, 1999, p. 3.

Page, Leigh, "Self-Service Systems Empower Workers," *Crain's Chicago Business,* August 7, 2000, p. SR7.

"PCs for Compensation," *PC Week,* November 6, 1989, p. 104.

Rafter, Michelle V., "Hewitt-Marriott Pact Bodes Well for BPO Sector," *Workforce Management,* March 1, 2005, p. 23.

Hilb, Rogal & Hobbs Company

4951 Lake Brook Drive, Suite 500
Glen Allen, Virginia 23060
U.S.A.
Telephone: (804) 747-6500
Fax: (804) 747-6046
Web site: http://www.hrh.com

Public Company
Incorporated: 1982 as Hilb, Rogal and Hamilton Co.
Employees: 3,700
Sales: $609.7 million (2004)
Stock Exchanges: New York
Ticker Symbol: HRH
NAIC: 524126 Direct Property and Casualty Insurance Carriers

∎ ∎ ∎

Hilb, Rogal & Hobbs Company (HRH) is the nation's eighth largest insurance brokerage firm. Much of its growth has come through the acquisition of small insurance agencies. Commissions from insurance companies comprise the majority of the brokerage's revenues and middle market businesses make up its primary market area.

EXECUTIVE BUSINESS: 1982-89

The Rogal Family had begun selling insurance in Pittsburgh early in the 1920s. In 1972, a financial services company purchased Rogal Co., headed by Alvin Rogal, and eight other agencies, mainly based in the southeastern part of the country. The purchaser,

Richmond Corp., formed Insurance Management Corp. (IMC). In 1977, Continental Group acquired Richmond and Robert H. Hilb was hired to run IMC. However, when a new CEO came on the scene at Continental, the conglomerate changed focus and moved to divest itself of the Richmond-based insurance operation.

Hilb, Rogal and Hamilton Co. was established in 1982, by three IMC executives, including Hilb, Rogal, and David W. Hamilton, head of the Birmingham office. The trio borrowed $17 million to buy out the 19-office company. Rogal was the largest agency of the group, producing 25 percent of combined revenue of $16.9 million. During their first eight months in business the new owners lost $1.9 million on $9.8 million in revenue.

By 1985, HRH revenues, primarily from commissions, had reached $25.4 million. Net income was $1.5 million. The company had fueled its growth by adding agencies to the fold. Small enterprises were lured aboard with promises of economies of scale, reduced administrative time, and an expanded range of services. The majority of purchases were funded by transactions consisting of 80 percent cash and 20 percent stock.

The Tax Reform Act of 1986, which resulted in double taxation on cash purchases of agencies prompted HRH to rethink its combination cash and stock acquisition transactions. All stock purchases, called pooling of interests, would move the acquired company's balance sheet to its own without the extra tax burden. An initial public offering in 1987 built up HRH's capital and created the vehicle for the pooling of interest purchases.

From January through October 1988, HRH acquired 14 U.S. insurance agencies: nine in Texas, two in Virginia, and one each in Florida, Georgia, and Maryland. Agencies in Arizona and Colorado were in its sights.

Based on its 1987 revenues of $36.1 million, the company held the number 12 spot among the nation's largest insurance agencies. The original founders continued to guide the company, with Hilb as president and Rogal as executive vice-president and director. Hamilton, who retired as executive vice-president in December 1987, remained on the board.

Profits rose from 1985 to 1987, despite a slump in the property-casualty insurance industry. Climbing from $1.5 million to $3.4 million over the period. But stock traded over the counter below that of comparable companies.

NOT JUST AN AGENCY ANYMORE: 1990-99

By 1990, HRH ranked by *Business Insurance* as the tenth largest U.S. insurance agency system and the 20th worldwide. Revenue in 1989 topped $74 million. The largest insurer, New York broker Marsh & McLennan Cos. Inc., recorded gross revenues of $2.45 billion during 1989 but from 1988 to 1989 HRH's gross revenue had outpaced the giants of the industry, climbing 12.9 percent versus an average of 4.8 percent.

HRH continued to grow despite challenges facing insurers. Elevated competition and depressed pricing had continued in 1989. Moreover, Hurricane Hugo and the World Series quake brought multibillion-dollar losses. The combination resulted in the "industry's worst year ever," according to the *Richmond Times-Dispatch*. HRH, an insurance agency though not an underwriter, did not pay claims on clients' property and casualty losses, but competition put pressure on pricing and profits.

By October 1990, the company operated 40 offices in 15 states and the District of Columbia. Employees, as of mid-September that year, numbered 1,250 with another 150 expected to join the roll by year-end, reported the *Richmond Times-Dispatch*.

About 60,000 independent insurance agencies operated in the United States, leaving more room for consolidation. HRH planned to continue concentrating its efforts in the growing Sunbelt. The Southwest with a struggling economy was of particular interest. Development of new lines of business gained through previous acquisitions was also on the docket.

HRH offered agencies an appealing level of independence in addition to the benefits of merging with a national entity. The company's torrid growth was expected to slow as the climate of the industry improved, driving up the cost of buying agencies. But HRH would see a corresponding upswing in premium prices.

HRH set the stage for development outside the United States in October 1990 with the creation of Hilb, Rogal and Hamilton International Inc. Andrew L. Rogal, president of Hilb, Rogal and Hamilton Co. of Pittsburgh and son of Alvin Rogal, was tapped to take charge of the foreign market development beginning in Britain.

HRH's shift to acquisitions by way of pooling of interests had helped build the company but left some investors scratching their heads about its finances: "The drawback of these transactions is that they force Hilb, Rogal to restate its earnings as if the newly acquired agency had been part of the company all year. While this makes the Internal Revenue Service happy, it can be confusing for potential investors as it tends to lower earnings in the previous year, making the current year's earnings look better in comparison than if the earnings in the previous year had been left alone," W. Dolson Smith, vice-president and analyst with New Jersey-based Firemark Research Inc. told the *Richmond Times-Dispatch*.

Believing its stock was undervalued, HRH began a stock repurchasing plan in 1990.

The company's growth, not only in size but range of activities, had moved it from the ranks of insurance agencies to that of insurance intermediaries, doing broker-like activities, according to the *National Underwriter Property & Casualty—Risk & Benefits Management*.

In early 1993 HRH was planning a secondary offering to fuel the flow of more independent agencies into its fold. On its way to its place among the largest U.S. agencies, the company completed 114 mergers and studied a total of 500, according to the *Richmond Times-Dispatch*.

Typically, the agencies in its network were solid operations that had been weighed down by pricing pressures. Many were stymied by difficulties related to leadership succession. Selling to HRH eased both dilemmas.

KEY DATES

1982: Hilb, Rogal and Hamilton Co. is founded by three insurance executives.

1987: An initial public offering creates a vehicle for more acquisitions.

1990: The company begins looking to foreign markets for business.

1996: The company establishes a regional framework for its agencies.

2000: The company ranks 80th on the Forbes list of the country's best 200 companies.

2003: The name is changed.

2005: The company settles a business practices suit for $30 million.

"The company's strategy is to build a significant market share in small to mid-sized metropolitan areas where it does business. Hilb, Rogal said that it expects its offices to be among the top two or three property and casualty agencies in each market," Mollie Gore wrote for the Richmond newspaper. Slightly more than three-quarters of its revenue was coming from commercial property and casualty account commissions.

HRH had purchased more than 140 agencies by late 1995. Robert H. Hilb, chairman and CEO, bought companies from people he liked and felt he could work with on a daily basis, explained David Ress in the *Richmond Times-Dispatch.* Hilb's business philosophy was straightforward. "The business is real simple. It's selling and it's service. There's no point in making it more complicated," Hilb said.

HRH entered the Canadian market in 1995, with the purchase of a small group of agencies. Also during the year Andrew L. Rogal, son of one of the other founders, was promoted to president and COO.

Looking toward the next century, HRH refocused its strategy. In 1996, the company announced plans to: create a regional framework, shifting away from its decentralized system; increase emphasis on internal growth through sales; and continue to acquire agencies in the United States and Canada. The company had slipped in *Business Insurance* rankings to 18th from 16th among the world's largest brokerages.

Despite the change, HRH maintained that it fared well against its competition, delivering a greater degree of service and expertise than independent agencies. Admittedly, the giants of the industry had the same advantage over HRH, drawing from a deeper well of resources. The regional office concept was introduced to improve service to clients and improve results for HRH. By mid-year 1996, five formal regions had been created in the United States. The Mid-Atlantic region consisted of offices in Maryland, New Jersey, Pennsylvania, and Virginia and was the largest in terms of revenue. The Southeast region encompassed the states of Alabama and Georgia. The California region also included the Nevada offices. Texas and Florida offices formed the remaining two U.S. regions. A separate Canadian region also was established.

HRH, which acted as an intermediary between midsize businesses and the insurance underwriters, experienced a spike in revenue and earnings and was rewarded with a corresponding rise in its price per share in 1997. Hilb retired as CEO during the year but continued as chairman of the board. Andrew Rogal stepped in as the new chief officer.

The waning years of the century were marked by a state of upheaval in the financial services industry, as new laws allowed banks, investment companies, and insurers to cross into each other's territory. As for HRH, it continued on its acquisitive path. But the new century would bring new challenges for the company.

CHALLENGING TIMES: 2000-05

Andrew Rogal, chair and CEO of the parent company, had begun his tenure in Pittsburgh. Rogal, having earned degrees in journalism and law, took interest in the insurance business when HRH was established and began buying up small agencies. He joined the Pittsburgh operation, becoming president in 1987 and senior vice-president of the parent firm in 1990, CEO in 1996, and chair in 2000. The business he headed placed 80th on *Forbes*'s list of the 200 Best Small Companies in America in 2000.

The top ten insurance broker recorded revenues of $262.1 million in 2000. HRH embarked on expansion in the Midwest in the summer of 2001. Prior to the purchase of Ohio's largest independent broker, the company held just five offices in the region. A purchase of significance in 2002 was the Hobbs Group L.L.C., based in Atlanta. The company specialized in property and casualty coverage, risk management, executive compensation, and employee benefits.

Andrew L. Rogal stepped down as chairman and CEO in May 2003 and was succeeded by Martin L. "Mell" Vaughan, company president and COO. Vaughan joined HRH in 1999, when the company he headed was acquired. Rogal led the company during its period of expansion. During Rogal's tenure stock price more than quadrupled, according to the *Richmond Times-Dispatch.*

Net income rose from $13 million in 1997 to $65 million in 2002.

In 2003, the company changed its name to Hilb, Rogal & Hobbs Company, dropping the Hamilton name; David W. Hamilton, one of the original founders, retired from the board in 1994. "Martin L. Vaughan, HRH's chairman and chief executive, said the retooled name recognizes 'the strategic contribution of Hobbs Group to HRH and the equity of its brand identity in the risk-management community,'" the *Richmond Times-Dispatch* reported.

The company continued growth in the Midwest during 2004, acquiring assets from firms in Illinois, Michigan, and Wisconsin. But troubles were on the horizon in 2005. The industry overall was being affected by the specter of investigations into insurance contingency fees by state attorneys general and insurance regulators and a soft pricing market, according to *National Underwriter Property & Casualty—Risk & Benefits Management.*

Specific to HRH were problems with integration of Hobbs and its transition from a middle market player to a mix of middle-market and large-market accounts.

Robert B. Lockhart, HRH president and COO and former head of the Hartford office and Northeast region, resigned in May 2005. Connecticut officials had charged the Hartford office with making improper contingency fee arrangements beginning in 1998. The office was accused of taking payments from insurers in exchange for sending clients their way. The fee was hidden in the premium paid by customers. HRH agreed to set up a $30 million restitution fund as part of the terms to end the action. "This settlement is the first involving insurance agents, the first really to involve product lines that go to 'Joe Main Street insurance consumer'—owners of automobiles, homes and small businesses who purchase insurance," Connecticut Attorney General Richard Blumenthal said in the *Hartford Courant* in September 2005. HRH would continue to collect commissions paid to them by insurance underwriters. The company also agreed to improve its disclosure practices.

Kathleen Peippo

PRINCIPAL COMPETITORS

Arthur Gallagher; Brown & Brown, Inc.; Marsh & McLennan Companies, Inc.

FURTHER READING

Crystal, Charlotte, "Let's Make a Deal; Hilb, Rogal and Hamilton Can't Refuse a Bargain," *Richmond Times-Dispatch* (Richmond, Va.), October 8, 1990, p. B1.

————, "Local Agency Is Becoming Mighty Mite: Hilb, Rogal & Hamilton Growing Fast on Power of Purchases This Year," *Richmond Times-Dispatch* (Richmond, Va.), October 31, 1988, p. B3.

Gannon, Joyce, "Like Father, Like Son; Rogals Help to Build, Maintain Reputation of Virginia-Based Insurance Brokerage," *Pittsburgh Post-Gazette,* December 19, 2000, p. E1.

Gearson, Christopher J., "Beatson Merges with National Chain," *Baltimore Business Journal,* July 9, 1990, p. 8.

Gore, Mollie, "Hilb, Rogal Practices Stock Pitch: Proceeds to Finance Further Expansion," *Richmond Times-Dispatch* (Richmond, Va.), February 19, 1993, p. B13.

"Hamilton Retires," *Richmond Times-Dispatch* (Richmond, Va.), May 5, 1994, p. B10.

Hofmann, Mark A., "Hilb, Rogal & Hamilton Co.," *Business Insurance,* July 22, 1996, p. 66+.

Hoke, Kathy, "BOA Shuns Several Suitors to Merge with Hilb Rogal," *Business First-Columbus,* June 22, 2001, p. A5.

Levick, Diane, "Insurance Broker Settles Suit for $30 Million," *Hartford Courant* (Hartford, Conn.), September 1, 2005.

————, "Insurance Executive Quits amid State Probe," *Hartford Courant* (Hartford, Conn.), May 27, 2005.

Otis, L. H., "Aggressive Acquisitions Drive Hilb Rogal's Growth," *National Underwriter Property & Casualty-Risk & Benefits Management,* March 4, 1991, pp. 29+.

Rayner, Bob, "Richmond, Va., Insurance Broker Changes Name After Atlanta Acquisition," *Richmond Times-Dispatch* (Richmond, Va.), September 19, 2003.

————, "Rogal to Step Down at HRH," *Richmond Times-Dispatch* (Richmond, Va.), March 26, 2003.

Ress, David, "Richmond, Va., Insurance Brokerage Goes on Agency-Buying Quest," *Knight Ridder/Tribune Business News,* November 21, 1995.

"Richmond, Va.-Based Hilb Rogal & Hobbs Makes Name-Change Official," *Richmond Times-Dispatch* (Richmond, Va.), May 5, 2004.

Roberts, Sally, "HRH Settlement Allows Some Contingents," *Business Insurance,* September 5, 2005, p. 3.

Ruquet, Mark E., "Analysts See HRH Report As Negative Bellwether for Brokers," *National Underwriter Property & Casualty-Risk & Benefits Management,* February 14, 2005, p. 40.

————, "HRH President Quits in Fee Controversy: A Second Employee Fired, A Third Suspended After Internal Investigation," *National Underwriter Property & Casualty-Risk & Benefits Management,* June 6, 2005, p. 8.

Slack, Charles, and Virginia Churn, "Hilb, Rogal Not Fearful of Change," *Richmond Times-Dispatch* (Richmond, Va.), May 6, 1998, p. C1.

HomeVestors of America, Inc.

———————— ■ ————————

10670 N. Central Expressway, Suite 700
Dallas, Texas 75231
U.S.A.
Telephone: (972) 761-0046
Fax: (972) 761-9022
Web site: http://www.homevestors.com

Private Company
Founded: 1989
Sales: $27 million (2004 est.)
NAIC: 531390 Other Activities Related to Real Estate

■ ■ ■

HomeVestors of America, Inc. is a privately owned, Dallas-based company that specializes in buying older single-family houses in need of repair at below-market prices. The company then renovates and sells them. Involved in franchising since the mid-1990s, HomeVestors has approximately 250 franchised offices located in 30 states. The company has pursued a "seed concept" in expanding into new markets, starting out with a strong franchisee, which it then supports with local marketing and advertising. HomeVestors has built its marketing around the concept of "ugly," creating slogans such as "We buy Ugly Houses" and "Ugly's OK." The company has successfully sued more than a dozen competitors attempting to copycat the use of "Ugly." Although anyone can buy a home, fix it up, and sell it, HomeVestors offers franchisees a complete program to create and sustain a successful business. HomeVestors helps franchisees to generate leads on houses to buy through an advertising program as well as helping them to conduct research on the owner of a target property; provides proprietary software to help in determining market value of a property, repair costs, and a target purchase price; makes financing available to franchisees for the purchase price and loans to cover renovations; and in order to sell homes quickly it offers financing to homebuyers with small down payments or credit problems through owner-carried financed notes. Franchisees pay a $46,000 franchise fee, a monthly fee, and a royalty to HomeVestors.

COMPANY'S FOUNDING IN THE LATE 1980S

HomeVestors was founded by Ken D'Angelo, who had worked as a real estate agent in Houston and Dallas for Red Carpet Realtors and ERA Realtors for 20 years. Late one night in 1989 he saw an infomercial pitching a two-hour video to teach people everything they needed to know about home buying. It was the inspiration the 40-year-old needed to strike out on his own. "I just took that idea one step further and into a specialized area," D'Angelo told *Dallas Morning News* in 2003. "No one likes to buy ugly houses, so I thought, 'Why not do it myself?'" He set up shop in East Dallas as a one-man business and began buying houses at below-market prices in the Dallas-Fort Worth area, renovating, and selling them. "When I started out, people thought I was crazy," he confessed.

Over the next several years, D'Angelo steadily grew HomeVestors. By 1995 he was buying and turning over more than 150 homes a year. He now decided to franchise his concept, and to help in that effort he hired Dain Zinn in March 1995. Together they put together a franchising program that would distinguish Home-Vestors from the competition and sell the concept to potential franchisees. "Anyone who has ever watched late-night TV has seen the ads hawking real estate investment systems," Zinn explained to *Dallas Business Journal* in a 2001 profile. "People wondered why they should buy a franchise when they could spend $149 on a tape and a weekend seminar." According to *Dallas Business Journal,* "D'Angelo and Zinn focused on creating a brand-name image and developing financing, training and support systems, including Web-based software that helps franchisees determine the value of a home. They got the word out with a memorable slogan—'We buy ugly houses'—slapped on bright yellow billboards." All of these elements were important in turning what had traditionally been a part-time endeavor into a career, because the key to success, as D'Angelo knew from firsthand experience, was locating a lot of properties to buy, having funds available to act quickly and buy target properties, and having a way to quickly resell the houses.

LAUNCH OF FRANCHISING IN 1996

HomeVestors raised $350,000 in a public debt offering to launch its franchising program in 1996. From that point forward, HomeVestors was purely a franchising business, with the company-owned operation providing the foundation for the franchised chain. D'Angelo sold the original HomeVestors business to his manager, who became the first franchisee. Another six franchises would be sold to employees and former business associates of D'Angelo. All told, HomeVestors awarded 17 franchises and generated revenues of about $800,000 in 1996. A year later those numbers would increase to $1.4 million in revenues and 30 franchises. At this point, the company raised another $1.5 million through a private placement of stock, with the money earmarked to pay off debt and provide operating capital to fuel further growth.

In the words of *Franchising World,* "The secret to HomeVestors' success is their focus on a segment of potential sellers who are not contacted by other home buyers and real estate agents. These are sellers who would be willing to accept a discount on their property in exchange for a cash offer and the ability to close within days of purchase... Typically, these homeowners have houses with deferred maintenance because the houses were inherited, they were rental properties that are no longer wanted, or the owner had a financial situation which allowed their house to deteriorate." Other sellers had recently divorced or had grown too old to properly maintain their homes. In short, HomeVestors offered a win-win situation: sellers received cash quickly for their properties, and HomeVestors received a property at a discount and could begin renovations as soon as closing took place. Typically, a homeowner was offered 65 percent of the house's value, less the amount it would cost to repair it. Moreover, the renovated houses proved to be a good value for many first-time homeowners, who had previously rented.

By the end of 2001 HomeVestors was operating in nine states through 84 franchisees, a 50 percent increase over the previous year. The company's strong growth was reflected by its inclusion in *Entrepreneur Magazine*'s listing of the top 500 franchises. In January 2001 HomeVestors ranked 189. A year later the company improved to 125. It would crack the top 100 in the January 2004 issue.

As the economy slipped into recession in the early 2000s, the prospects for HomeVestors improved further. A large number of homeowners, who had been falling behind on mortgages or refinancings, were now looking to quickly unload their properties to avoid foreclosure. By early 2003 HomeVestors had grown to 135 offices in 17 states.

HomeVestors grew on a number of fronts in 2004. It signed an agreement with The Home Depot in February to make the retailer its exclusive building materials provider to HomeVestors franchisees, who would now enjoy the benefit of a price discount. The deal was struck with Home Depot's business to business division, The Home Depot Supply. Later in 2004, HomeVestors moved into a new headquarters to accommodate its steady expansion, and also unveiled a new advertising campaign, which introduced a company mascot, a caveman named Ug. The company's longtime slogan was modified to "Ug Buys Ugly Houses," which now appeared along with his likeness on a new series of billboards. By this stage in its history HomeVestors was spending about $18 million a year on advertising, mostly

KEY DATES

1989: Ken D'Angelo launches HomeVestors in Dallas.
1996: HomeVestors begins franchising.
2004: The company begins buying "Ugly Notes."
2005: D'Angelo dies, and is succeeded by John P. Hayes.

on billboards and some television spots. According to the company, this marketing accounted for 70 percent of its business.

INTRODUCING "UGLY NOTES" IN 2004

HomeVestors also found a new way to drum up new properties for its franchisees. In July 2004 the company launched a real estate-owned (REO) program to buy so-called "ugly notes" on single-family houses. (REOs are in the possession of a lender as a result of foreclosure or forfeiture.) The company was well familiar with the value of homes as collateral and, unlike other companies that bought such notes from banks and other parties and turned around and sold them "as is," HomeVestors planned to buy the notes at a reasonable cost, then turn them over to franchisees, who would renovate and sell the collateral properties. In addition to banks, the program hoped to appeal to holders of owner-financed notes on collateral homes that were on the verge of foreclosure and who did not want to take on the rehabilitation costs, legal fees, and other expenses involved in making good on the loan. Once again, Homevestors was offering a win-win situation: Sellers of the ugly notes benefited, as did the franchisees who picked up additional inventory in their markets.

The year 2004 also was marked by misfortune for HomeVestors. According to *Franchising World,* "D'Angelo moved the company's corporate headquarters to a bigger space. He started hiring more support staff and even dabbled in relinquishing some of his lesser duties so he could concentrate on managing the business as CEO. Things couldn't have been better. Then D'Angelo started having stomach pain. After a battery of tests, doctors concluded that he had terminal cancer of the bile duct." D'Angelo underwent treatments and surgeries at the Mayo Clinic, but it became apparent that he had only a short time to live.

With all hope exhausted in September 2004, D'Angelo met with Dr. John Hayes, a national franchise

consultant and a member of the board of directors, and asked him to take over as president and CEO. Hayes told *Franchise Times Magazine* that D'Angelo said, "I created HomeVestors. It's everything to me; it will be my legacy; and there are lots of people depending on it. You're the person I'd like to come in and take over." Hayes agreed immediately: "He needed to know that he didn't have to worry about this. My gift to him was that he didn't."

Aside from being a consultant, Hayes was an author, public speaker, and seminar leader, who started out as a communications professor at Temple University. He wrote a primer called *Franchising: The Inside Story,* which became a platform for landing consulting assignments from companies such as Aamco transmission shops, the Subway sandwich chain, and Jani King, a cleaning service. D'Angelo originally hired Hayes to help with training and to start a franchise advisory council at HomeVestors. The two men grew closer and were soon in contact on a daily basis. Hayes even bought a Home-Vestors franchise himself. (After becoming an officer of the company, however, he sold his stake to his partner who had been actively running the business.) He also helped to make HomeVestors a more disciplined, professional organization. Strong on intuition and emotion, D'Angelo realized that he fell short in some areas and came to rely on Hayes. For example, D'Angelo had been lax on the enforcement of franchise agreements on payments, allowing some of the franchisees to fall behind and creating a dangerous precedent. Hayes brought stricter enforcement, and although it resulted in the termination of some franchise agreements, the organization as a whole grew stronger.

During his final months of life, D'Angelo took other steps to prepare the business for his departure. The company's current president, David Young, agreed to become a vice-president charged with handling the increasingly important task of maintaining relationships with national vendors. Other executives also received an expanded portfolio of responsibilities. In addition, D'Angelo wrote a letter that was sent to all the franchisees explaining his condition. Then in December 2004, in defiance of his doctors, he traveled to Miami to address the annual HomeVestors Convention. According to *Franchising World,* he "gave a moving speech that he called a personal highlight in his life. He passed away exactly five weeks later. He was 55 years old."

As a testament to its founder, HomeVestors did not miss a beat after D'Angelo's death. The same week as his death, for instance, the company graduated its largest training class of new franchise owners. The successful transition was a testament to the plans D'Angelo put into place as well as to his team of executives, which included his widow, Betty D'Angelo, director of human resources, and brother Paul D'Angelo, director of IT services. HomeVestors continued to grow and in October 2005 began to award franchises in New York, Connecticut, and Massachusetts.

Ed Dinger

PRINCIPAL SUBSIDIARIES

Uglynote.com.

FURTHER READING

Augstums, Ieva M., "Man's Real Estate Investment Firm Has Franchises in 17 States," *Dallas Morning News,* February 9, 2003.

Daniels, Earl, "Even 'Ugly Houses' Have Potential Buyers," *Florida Times Union,* May 20, 2002, p. FB-4.

DeFiglio, "Beauty of Buying Ugly," *Daily Herald* (Arlington Heights, Ill.), October 15, 2004, p. 1.

Dymi, Amilda, "'Ugly Notes' Set for 'Ugly Houses,'" *National Mortgage News,* July 19, 2004, p. 6.

Feid, Monica, "How to Survive the Loss of a Founder," *Franchising World,* May 2005, p. 44.

Larson, Polly, "How Does Your Franchise Grow?," *Franchising World,* November/December 2001, p. 6.

Lupo, Lisa, "Communication, Preparation, Smooth Leadership Transition," *Franchise Times Magazine,* May 1, 2005.

Perez, Christine, "Building a Brand," *Dallas Business Journal,* August 31, 2001, p. 39.

Steiner, Christopher, "Diamonds in the Rough," *Forbes,* October 3, 2005, p. 71.

Vogell, Heather, "HomeVestors Franchisers, Homeowners Makes Pretty Good Profit from 'Ugly Houses,'" *Charlotte Observer,* July 20, 2003.

Zinn, Dain, "HomeVestors Turns Ugly Houses into Pretty Cash," *Franchising World,* November/December 2001, p. 68.

Huntleigh Technology PLC

———— ■ ————

310-312 Dallow Road
Luton,
United Kingdom
Telephone: +44 01582 413104
Fax: +44 01582 402589
Web site: http://www.huntleigh-technology.com

Public Company
Incorporated: 1975 as Huntleigh Group Ltd.
Employees: 2,200
Sales: £198.7 million ($368.6 million) (2004)
Stock Exchanges: London
Ticker Symbol: HTL
NAIC: 334510 Electromedical and Electrotherapeutic Apparatus Manufacturing; 335999 All Other Miscellaneous Electrical Equipment and Component Manufacturing; 423450 Medical, Dental and Hospital Equipment and Supplies Merchant Wholesalers

■ ■ ■

Huntleigh Technology PLC is a leading developer and producer of equipment for the healthcare industry. The company has built up market-leading positions in four core areas: Pressure Area Care (PAC), which includes mattresses, beds, and other equipment used for the prevention of pressure ulcers (i.e., bedsores); Patient Positioning and Transportation, including hospital beds, trolleys, and hoists, as well as couches, lockers, and related hospital and nursing home furniture and furnishings; Intermittent Pneumatic Compression (IPC), and especially equipment used for the prevention of deep vein thrombosis; and Diagnostics equipment, especially ultrasound-based equipment used for monitoring fetal development and blood flow and other vital statistics. Huntleigh distributes to more than 120 countries and operates manufacturing facilities in the United Kingdom, the United States, Australia, and South Africa. Iron lung inventor Rolf Schild founded the company, and the Schild family remains its largest single shareholder. Julian Schild is company chairman of the board. Huntleigh Technology is listed on the London Stock Exchange. In 2004, the company posted revenues of £199 million ($368 million).

ENGINEERING ORIGINS IN THE 1970S

Rolf Schild was born in Cologne, Germany, in 1924, and studied at that city's Jawne Gymnasium in the late 1930s. In 1939, Schild, whose father, a textile merchant, was Jewish, was sent to England as part of the *Kindertransport* rescue effort, arriving in Liverpool. Schild's parents remained behind and were murdered by the Nazis at the Chewnow concentration camp.

With the outbreak of the war, Schild found himself classified as an "alien enemy." As the war progressed, however, Schild, who had spent time in the internment center on the Isle of Man, was later transferred to Manchester. There, Schild was given training operating a capstan lathe. Soon after, Schild moved to London to join an aunt, who found him work at a film projector factory. Schild then began studying physics, engineering, and electronics at night school.

After the war, Schild joined the Allied forces for a time, serving as an interpreter for the U.S. Army, in the hope of discovering the fate of his parents. Returning to England, Schild went to work for New Electronics Products (NEP), under the direction of Zoltan Kellerman. At NEP, Schild developed a "phono cardiograph," a device for measuring and recording the sound of the heart. Schild then became part of the team developing a new "heart-lung" machine for use with polio patients in conjunction with Hammersmith Hospital. That device became more popularly known as the iron lung. Another major innovation was Schild's invention of a catheter-based "pressure transducer," which measured blood pressure within the heart.

While working at NEP, Schild was approached by an aircraft manufacturer, Hawker Siddeley, seeking a means of measuring the airflow pressure with aircraft engines. As Schild told the *Sunday Times*: "An engine is just a pump, similar to the heart, where flow, temperature and pressure are similar, so it was only a matter of adapting our existing system." Schild added: "This is how engineers work. You piece different ideas from various experiences and put them together. The key is to find the application and then create the solution."

Schild approached Kellerman with the idea of developing the project through NEP. Kellerman, however, did not see the potential in expanding into the aerospace industry. "Instinct has taught me that whenever you get a new idea for a product you need a feeling in your fingertips," Schild told the *Sunday Times*. "I felt this. Kellerman thought the potential in the airline market was nonsense, saying we sold only 300 transducers a year. I told him I would do it myself."

At first, Schild was allowed to pursue the project in his spare time, given space in a basement room at NEP. Schild recruited a friend, Peter Epstein, a valve engineer to the project, and set up a business initially called Mechanical Electronic Products (MEP). Soon after, however, Schild was asked to leave NEP. Joined by Epstein, the partners created a new company, SE Laboratories Ltd., with a starting capital of just £100.

Operating out of Schild's home, the company managed to win a number of contracts, from customers including De Havilland and English Electric. With no manufacturing capacity of its own, the company contracted for the manufacture of components, which Schild and Epstein assembled at Schild's home. The company's big break came in the mid-1950s, when the pair was contracted to provide transducers for the Blue Streak missile, the first attempt at building a ballistic missile. Schild and Epstein borrowed £5,000, backed by the mortgage on Epstein's father's house, and rented a nearby factory. By the 1960s, SE Laboratories employed 300 people and had grown into a major producer for the medical and aerospace industries. The company went public in 1963, in one of the London market's most successful initial public offerings of the time.

Thorn EMI acquired SE Laboratories in 1966. Schild at first remained as head of the company, working on the development of the first whole body scanner. EMI remained skeptical of the project until Schild sold 50 of the devices on a single trip to the United States. Nonetheless, Schild and EMI continued to disagree with the direction of Schild's body scanner work. In 1973, therefore, Schild left EMI, and acquired a stake in Hymatic Engineering, originally a producer of military equipment. In 1975, Schild merged Hymatic into Huntleigh Group. That company had been founded in 1969 as Flowtron Aire Ltd., but had been little more than a publicly listed shell company. Schild then performed a management buyout of Huntleigh, and its listing on the Unlisted Securities Market.

HEALTHCARE SECTOR SPECIALIST IN THE 1980S

Huntleigh started strongly, focusing on the healthcare sector. Among the company's earliest products was its development of a new generation of mattresses designed to prevent the formation of pressure ulcers, more popularly known as bedsores, in hospitalized patients. The company's initial design, called the Nimbus, boasted strong initial sales. By 1977, the success of the company's product led it to launch its first international sales effort, opening a sales office in the United States.

In 1979, however, the company was sidetracked when Schild, his wife, and his daughter were kidnapped while vacationing in Italy; the kidnappers had mistaken Schild for a member of the Rothschild family. Schild himself was released after several weeks; his wife and daughter were released several months later.

KEY DATES

1973: Rolf Schild, an engineer and inventor of the iron lung, acquires control of Hymatic Engineering, a producer of military equipment.

1975: Schild merges Hymatic into Huntleigh Group, a shell company with a listing on the Unlisted Securities Market.

1977: Huntleigh establishes a U.S. sales subsidiary.

1985: The company is reincorporated as healthcare specialist Huntleigh Technology and is listed on the London Stock Exchange.

1988: The Nimbus Dynamic Floating System, designed to prevent pressure ulcers, is launched.

1990: The company reorganizes its operations and creates a new Huntleigh Healthcare subsidiary.

1992: A sales subsidiary in Australia is added.

1993: The company acquires hospital bed manufacturer Nesbit Evans; a subsidiary is launched in France.

1996: U.K.-based Hoskins Healthcare is acquired.

2001: The company acquires Joyce Healthcare in Australia, adding its first international manufacturing operations.

2002: The company acquires Hejsani Duncan in South Africa.

2005: The cardiovascular and obstetrics diagnostic equipment division is acquired from Viasys Healthcare.

With that ordeal over, Schild now began building Huntleigh in earnest. In 1985, Schild reincorporated the company as Huntleigh Technology PLC and listed it on the London Stock Exchange. The company now focused its production entirely on the healthcare sector. By 1987, the company's revenues had topped £10 million, with profits of more than £100,000. Joining Schild in the business was son Julian Schild, who became finance director by the early 1990s, before taking over the company's direction at the dawn of the 21st century.

By the early 1990s, Huntleigh's sales had risen past £30 million, and the company's profits had soared to more than £5.5 million. Part of the group's growth came from the successful launch of the new Nimbus Dynamic Flotation System in 1988, which established the company as a leading player in the pressure ulcer prevention market. By the early 1990s, Huntleigh had captured the lead in the U.K. hospital bedding market. In the early 1990s, also, the company reorganized its operations, segmenting the company into its core product areas. These included a range of electronic diagnostic equipment, launched in 1992, and the company's line of compression devices, used for treating lymphatic and vascular problems, and also for the prevention of deep vein thrombosis. The company's operations in this latter category were particularly focused on the U.S. market. As part of its reorganization, the company created a new subsidiary, Huntleigh Healthcare, in 1990.

In support of its sales success, Huntleigh invested strongly in new manufacturing facilities, as well as expanded research and development capacity in the early 1990s. An important boost to the group's operations came with its acquisition, through Huntleigh Healthcare, of hospital bed manufacturer Nesbit Evans. The purchase complemented Huntleigh's own strength in hospital mattresses, and also gave the company an entry into Australia, then Nesbit Evans's most important foreign market. The newly merged operation was renamed HNE Healthcare.

BUILDING INTERNATIONAL SALES IN THE NEW CENTURY

Huntleigh, which relied heavily on the United Kingdom's National Health Care system for its revenues, became more and more interested in building up its international scope through the 1990s and into the 2000s. In 1993, the company established a subsidiary in France, HNE Médical S.A.S. The company also established subsidiaries in Germany, Switzerland, and Austria, and entered the Benelux market in 1996, opening subsidiaries in Holland and Belgium. Also that year, the company made a new acquisition, of Hoskins Healthcare, a U.K.-based maker of equipment for the healthcare industry.

By 1998, Huntleigh's sales had topped £100 million. The company continued in its international development, adding subsidiaries in Denmark, while also entering the Latin American market. In 1999, Huntleigh moved into Singapore, and also established a subsidiary in Sweden. The company also entered South Africa that year. By 2000, the company had expanded its sales network to Spain and India. The group's efforts to rebalance its sales profile paid off; by the end of the decade, some 60 percent of the group's sales came from outside of the United Kingdom.

In the early 2000s, Huntleigh moved to back up its growing global presence with an expansion of its manufacturing network. The company added its first foreign manufacturing plant in 2001, through the acquisition of Australia's Joyce Healthcare. The following year, the company added a production presence in South Africa, buying up that country's Hejsani Duncan.

Rolf Schild remained active in the company's operations until his death at age 78 in 2003. The company's new management, led by Julian Schild, now embarked on a new expansion strategy designed to continue to increase the percentage of the group's international sales, as well as increase its manufacturing base. The company especially targeted growth in the United States, where its market share stood at just 1 percent. As part of that effort, the company boosted its research and development. By 2004, the company's R&D effort led to the development of a new-generation hospital bed, including a model designed specifically for the U.S. market, as well as a budget model to boost the group's presence in developing markets.

Huntleigh also began targeting acquisitions into the mid-2000s. By July 2005, the company had located its first target, paying £4 million ($7.3 million) to acquire Viasys Healthcare's cardiovascular and obstetric analysis and monitoring equipment division. The purchase added the Sonicaid and Medilog brands to Huntleigh's own diagnostic division line. Meanwhile, the company boosted its U.S. presence through a three-year supply agreement with Novation for Huntleigh's deep-vein thrombosis prevention systems. Huntleigh expected to remain a major player in its core healthcare equipment markets into the new century.

M. L. Cohen

PRINCIPAL SUBSIDIARIES

HNE Huntleigh Healthcare Medizinprodukte GmbH (Austria); Huntleigh Healthcare N.V. S.A. (Belgium); Huntleigh Healthcare A/S (Denmark); HNE Médical S.A.S. (France); HNE Huntleigh Nesbit Evans Health-care GmbH (Germany); Huntleigh Healthcare B.V. (Holland); Huntleigh Healthcare SL (Spain); Huntleigh Healthcare AB (Sweden); HNE Médical S.A. (Switzerland); Huntleigh Healthcare Ltd. - Pressure Area Care (U.K.); Huntleigh Healthcare Ltd. - Patient Positioning and Transportation (U.K.); Huntleigh Healthcare Ltd. - Intermittent Pneumatic Compression (U.K.); Huntleigh Healthcare Ltd. - Diagnostics (U.K.); Huntleigh Healthcare Ltd. - Akron (U.K.); Huntleigh Renray Ltd. (U.K.); Huntleigh Healthcare L.L.C. (U.S.A.); Huntleigh Healthcare India Pvt. Ltd.; Huntleigh Healthcare Pty. Ltd. (Australia); Huntleigh Healthcare Ltd. (New Zealand).

PRINCIPAL COMPETITORS

Medtronic Inc.; Baxter HealthcareCorporation; Medtronic AVE Inc.; Gambro AB; B Braun Melsungen AG; Fresenius Medical Care; Amersham Health A.S.

FURTHER READING

Firn, David, "Huntleigh in Move to Reduce NHS Reliance," *Financial Times,* June 11, 2004, p. 22.

Groom, Brian, "Huntleigh Probes Medical Market with New Products," *Financial Times,* September 20, 1999, p. 26.

"Huntleigh Acquires Analysis and Monitoring Business," *Pharma Marketletter,* July 4, 2005.

"Huntleigh Goes Steady," *Birmingham Post,* March 17, 2005, p. 29.

"Huntleigh Technology," *Investors Chronicle,* September 23, 2005.

Levi, Jim, "Huntleigh's Painless Route to Stardom," *Management Today,* August 1993, p. 48.

Pain, Steve, "Medical Systems Group Ups Pace," *Birmingham Post,* September 16, 2004, p. 21.

Richmond, Caroline, "Obituary: Rolf Schild: Businessman and Kidnap Victim," *Independent,* May 3, 2003, p. 26.

"Rolf Schild; Obituary," *The Times,* April 21, 2003, p. 22.

Smith, Caroline, "US Deal Points to Overseas Expansion," *Financial Times,* February 7, 2004.

Steiner, Rupert, "Iron Lung Inventor Got Off to Flying Start," *Sunday Times,* May 30, 1999, p. 14.

Ihr Platz GmbH + Company KG

Postfach 37 40
Osnabrück,
Germany
Telephone: +49 0541 98 55 0
Fax: +49 0541 98 55 267
Web site: http://www.ihrplatz.de

Private Company
Incorporated: 1895 as Osnabrücker Seifenfabrik Frömbling
Employees: 8,000
Sales: EUR 810 million ($1 billion) (2004 est.)
NAIC: 452111 Department Stores (Except Discount Department Stores)

■ ■ ■

Ihr Platz GmbH + Company KG is one of Germany's top three drugstore chain operators, with more than 830 stores throughout the country. Ihr Platz, which means "Your Place" in German, owns nearly 690 stores. The company's network also includes 145 franchised stores. Nearly all of the company's stores operate under the Ihr Platz name; the company operates some 90 stores in the Berlin region under the Drospa name, acquired in 2000. Altogether, the Ihr Platz group's network includes a combined floor space of nearly 275,000 square meters, more than 8,000 employees, and sales of EUR 840 million (approximately $1 billion) in 2004. The company claims an 8 percent share of the total German drugstore market. After several years of losses in the first half of the 2000s, Ihr Platz, formerly owned and operated by the founding Frömbling family, nearly went bankrupt in 2005. Instead, investment banking giant firm Goldman Sachs Group led a buyout of the business, and put into place a rescue plan under the guidance of turnaround specialist Alvarez & Marsal. This involved placing the company into a Chapter 11-styled insolvency in order to restructure the company's debt, something of a revolution in Germany. Within months, Ihr Platz was able to relaunch its expansion. CEO Sankar Krishnan and CFO Michael F. Keppel both came to the company from Alvarez & Marsal.

LATE 19TH-CENTURY ORIGINS AS SOAP BUSINESS

The Frömbling (or Froembling) family founded a business manufacturing soap, opening the Osnabrücker Seifenfabrik Frömbling in Osnabruck, in the northeast of Germany, in 1895. The company prospered and by 1911 was able to expand its production, opening a second factory in Osnabruck, called the Osnabrücker Stärkefabrik. The company began marketing its soaps on an international level, and by 1920 the company's soaps, including its top seller "Frömblings Beste," had found their way to store shelves in a number of markets, especially markets such as Argentina with growing German immigrant communities.

The Frömbling family made the leap to the retail market in the 1930s with the acquisition of Wilhelm Stützer, based in Wilhelmshaven, also in Lower Saxony, in 1931. That purchase also added Stützer's own soap production capacity to that of Frömbling. The following year, the company reincorporated as

KEY DATES

1895: Osnabrücker Seifenfabrik Frömbling, a soap factory, is founded in Osnabruck.
1911: A second factory, Osnabrücker Stärkefabrik, is opened.
1931: The company acquires Wilhelm Stützer, in Wilhelmshaven, and its soap production and retail operations.
1932: The company changes its name to Seifen-Specialgeschäfte Wilhelm Puls.
1962: The company changes its name to Der Seifen-Platz.
1969: The first franchise operations are launched.
1973: The company changes its name to Ihr Platz.
1990: Sales top DEM 1 billion for the first time.
1999: The 250-store Dropsa drugstore chain is acquired.
2000: Sales begin to drop and the group slips into losses.
2005: Goldman Sachs takes over the company by acquiring its debt, then leads it into an insolvency and restructuring program.

Seifen-Specialgeschäfte Wilhelm Puls and moved its headquarters to Oldenburg. The company's stores then traded under the name Seifen-Puls. The company began opening new stores and, by World War II, operated more than ten stores in the region.

The company rebuilt its operations following the war, raising its store network to 18 by the end of the 1940s. In 1950 the company moved its headquarters to Rastede. In the early years of the 1950s, the company began emphasizing its retail network, opening a number of new stores. The company's initial focus remained on a regional level. By the end of the decade, however, the family-owned company began to develop national aspirations, boosting its store network to nearly 250 by the beginning of the 1960s. The company also changed the names of its stores, to Der Seifen-Platz (the Soap Place) in 1962. By then, the company's revenues had risen to the equivalent of EUR 25 million, compared with less than EUR 1 million just ten years earlier.

The company underwent a steady expansion through the 1960s, expanding its network to more than 400 stores. The company's expansion was further aided by the introduction of a franchise network in 1969. At the same time, the Frömbling family continued to expand their retail concept, developing a wider range of goods and sundries and embracing a true European-style drugstore format. By 1973, the company decided to relaunch its retail network under a new brand, "Ihr Platz," German for "Your Place." Revenues by then had grown to more than EUR 110 million.

EXPANSION AND REBUILDING

Ihr Platz expanded steadily through the 1970s, developing a national notoriety in part through sponsorships of popular soccer teams. By 1980, the company's store network included all of West Germany, with the sole exception of the Berlin and Hannover markets, where competition was most intense. By then, the company's network topped 550 stores. The German reunification at the end of the 1980s opened new expansion opportunities for Ihr Platz. Into the 1990s, as its store network topped 600, the company's revenues passed the DEM 1 billion mark (EUR 600 million) for the first time.

Through the 1990s, the company renewed its expansion effort. A new generation of the Frömbling family now led the company beyond Germany for the first time, as the company added retail operations in Switzerland, under the Estorel name. That operation launched its own expansion drive at the end of the 1990s, doubling in size to 13 stores by 1999. Estorel nonetheless remained only a small part of Ihr Platz's overall business, accounting for less than EUR 15 million of the Ihr Platz group's nearly EUR 1.2 billion by decade's end.

A larger diversification effort came with the company's entry into the perfumery market, through its control of a chain of Yaska-branded perfumeries. By the end of the 1990s, Ihr Platz had opened nearly 100 Yaska stores, generating turnover of approximately EUR 90 million. Also in the late 1990s, the company overhauled its flagship Ihr Platz chain, refurbishing its store network with a more modern design. As part of the refurbishing effort, the company added a number of new technological features, such as an in-store shopping channel, "ShopTV."

Trouble had begun to loom for the company as the 21st century neared, prompting *Business Week* to refer to "blunders" committed by the newest generation of Frömblings who had taken leadership of the company. Making matters worse, the company went through a series of CEOs in the early 2000s, as it tried to put a halt to a steady drop in sales.

Nonetheless, the company appeared to have made a roaring start to the new decade. In 1999, the company agreed to sell off its perfumery business in order to concentrate on its core drugstore operation. The nearly

100-store Yaska chain was sold to fast-rising Douglas Group, which held several retail formats, including bookstores, clothing stores, and cafes, and especially a chain of more than 600 perfume shops. In return, Douglas agreed to transfer its own drugstore operation, Dropsa, to Ihr Platz.

The addition of the Dropsa chain added 250 stores, including 100 in the Berlin market alone, as well as more than EUR 350 million to Ihr Platz's revenues. The company, now boosted to the position of the number three drugstore chain in Germany, planned to maintain the Dropsa name in the Berlin market, while converting the rest of its new stores to the Ihr Platz signage. Yet the addition of Dropsa proved too much for Ihr Platz to swallow, with the integration of that operation compounded by the group's management troubles. By 2000, Ihr Platz's sales appeared to have entered a free fall, from nearly EUR 1.2 billion in 2000, sales slid below EUR 1.1 billion by 2000, and slipped under the EUR 1 billion mark by 2003.

By 2004, the company's fortunes appeared to be sputtering to an end. As sales continued to slip, the group's debt levels rose, nearing EUR 150 million. The company found itself unable to pay its debts, and neared bankruptcy by the end of the year. Temporary rescue came from its main bank, Deutsche Bank, which led a consortium bank into the acquisition of the group's debt, giving the company a reprieve of several months in order to put into place a restructuring of its operations. As part of that process, the group agreed to sell off its Swiss retail operation to the Muller Group in December 2004. Nonetheless, the Deutsche Bank rescue was seen as something of a formality toward the company's inevitable declaration of bankruptcy, and the complete dissolution of the business.

In the meantime, Ihr Platz's distress had caught the attention of investment banking powerhouse Goldman Sachs. In January 2005, the U.S. company bought up all of Ihr Platz's bank debt, and then brought in Alvarez & Marsal, a group that specialized in turning around failing companies. With two Alvarez & Marsal executives, Sankar Krishnan and Michael F. Keppel, taking over Ihr Platz's top management positions, the company began negotiating with its remaining creditors to restructure the company's debt. The company also began negotiations with labor unions in an effort to shut down 80 of the group's poorest performing stores, a move which would have entailed the elimination of some 10 percent of the group's staff.

Negotiations on both fronts quickly broke down, in part because of the extremely negative German cultural attitude toward bankruptcy. Indeed, the use of bankruptcy as a mechanism for restructuring and rescuing struggling companies, as seen in the Anglo Saxon corporate world, had been unheard of in Germany, and had been legally possible in the country only since 1999. Having failed in its negotiations with the company's creditors, the Goldman Sachs-backed team decided to take advantage of the new bankruptcy laws, and declared Ihr Platz to be insolvent in May 2005.

The move raised eyebrows in the country, and was viewed as something of a revolution in the corporate world. As an insolvent company, however, Ihr Platz enjoyed a greater latitude of movement; for example, the company quickly received a court order allowing it to shut down its 80 money-losing stores, as well as one of the group's warehouses. The insolvency filing also enabled Goldman Sachs to buy out the group's creditors within a week, allowing the company, now debt-free, to put into place a new and more favorable line of credit. Meanwhile, under the new bankruptcy code, the German government agreed to take over salary payments for a three-month period, allowing Ihr Platz to use its cash flow to make payments to its suppliers and similar critical creditors. As a further concession, the company received an exemption from some EUR 5 million in trade taxes.

Meanwhile the Alvarez & Marsal team, led by CEO Krishnan and CFO Keppel, also put into a place a public relations campaign intended to remove the stigma of insolvency by focusing on the fact that the "restructuring" of the company was meant to save more than 8,000 jobs across the country.

Krishnan and Keppel backed up the group's financial restructuring with a revitalization of the Ihr Platz stores themselves. The company revamped store interiors, placing greater emphasis on so-called "lifestyle" promotions, including the introduction of a line of art supplies and the addition of seasonal features such as barbecue grills. The company also added a section for organic cosmetics and beauty and skin care products.

By the end of 2005, Ihr Platz's resurrection appeared well in hand. By December of that year, the company announced that it was once again prepared to launch an expansion of its retail network, intending to open three new stores. The new stores were also to feature a new format, with an emphasis on organic goods. In 2006, Ihr Platz had hopes of returning to profitability, putting its difficulties behind it to focus on a future as one of Germany's leading drugstore groups.

M. L. Cohen

PRINCIPAL SUBSIDIARIES

Globus Holding GmbH and Company KG.

PRINCIPAL COMPETITORS

METRO AG; KarstadtQuelle AG; Real - SB-Warenhaus GmbH; AVA Allgemeine Handelsgesellschaft der Verbraucher AG; Kaufhof Warenhaus AG; Quelle AG and Co.; Wal-Mart Germany GmbH and Company KG; PRO Verbraucher-Betriebsgesellschaft GmbH.

FURTHER READING

Drier, Melissa, "Douglas to Buy Yaska Chain," *WWD,* December 10, 1999, p. 17.

Edmondson, Gail, "Goldman's German Revolution," *Business Week,* October 24, 2005. p. 54.

"Glaubiger unterstutzen Rettung von Ihr Platz," *Financial Times Deutschland,* November 18, 2005.

"Ihr Platz expandiert wieder," *Borsen-Zeitung,* December 9, 2005.

"Ihr Platz on Form," *European Cosmetic Markets,* May 2000, p. 172.

"Ihr Platz Plans Expansion," *European Cosmetic Markets,* June 1999, p. 223.

Krishnan, Sankar, "Ihr Platz: Prescription for Recovery," *INSOL World,* December 1, 2005.

Weber, Stefan, "Neue Hoffnung fur Drogeriekette Ihr Platz," *Suddeutsche Zeitung,* December 23, 2004.

INTERMET

INTERMET Corporation

5445 Corporate Drive, Suite 200
Troy, Michigan 48098-2683
U.S.A.
Telephone: (248) 952-2500
Fax: (248) 952-1512
Web site: http://www.intermet.com

Private Company
Incorporated: 1984
Employees: 5,200
Sales: $837.2 million (2004)
NAIC: 331511 Iron Foundries; 331312 Primary Aluminum Production; 331524 Aluminum Foundries (Except Die-Casting); 336330 Motor Vehicle Steering and Suspension Components (Except Spring) Manufacturing; 336340 Motor Vehicle Brake System Manufacturing; 336350 Motor Vehicle Transmission and Power Train Parts Manufacturing; 336360 Motor Vehicle Seating and Interior Trim Manufacturing

■ ■ ■

INTERMET Corporation (Intermet) is one of the largest independent foundry companies in the world, involved in producing ferrous and non-ferrous casting products for automotive and industrial manufacturers. Intermet produces ductile iron, aluminum, magnesium, and zinc castings at more than a dozen locations in the United States, Germany, and Portugal, deriving approximately 95 percent of its revenue from sales to the automotive market. The company's products include castings for steering and suspension components, camshafts, crankshafts, brake parts, electronic housing and enclosures, and instrument panel beams used in passenger and commercial vehicles. Soaring costs, particularly of scrap metal, forced Intermet to seek Chapter 11 bankruptcy protection in September 2004. The firm emerged from bankruptcy as a private entity in November 2005.

19TH-CENTURY ORIGINS

Intermet's lineage winds its way through a tangle of subsidiaries and predecessor companies to one of the oldest chartered companies in the United States, Columbus Iron Works, established in 1846. As a founding predecessor, Columbus Iron Works lent Intermet the type of prestige only history can impart: Aside from manufacturing armor plate for military applications, the 19th-century metalworker was involved in the development of the first breech-loading cannon, and later, manufactured the cast iron pipe used in Manhattan Island's water system.

Intermet's modern-day origins begin in 1971, when Columbus Foundries, Inc. was founded, incorporating the link to the past, the 19th-century Columbus Iron Works. During its first decade of operation, Columbus Foundries' internal growth was augmented by a methodical acquisition campaign. A machinery facility was acquired in 1976, followed by the purchase in 1980 of a foundry located in Germany, and the acquisition of the Lynchburg Foundry Company in 1983, which owned three Virginia-based foundries. Intermet, founded by George Mathews, Jr., was formed a year after Columbus

Foundries acquired the three Virginia foundries. The new company, which was based in Columbus, Georgia, assumed control over Columbus Foundries.

More than a century after Columbus Iron Works' pioneering military work, Intermet geared itself for an entirely different sort of existence. The company manufactured cast iron pieces for the automobile industry, operating as an automotive parts supplier to original equipment manufacturers (OEMs) such as Ford Motor Company, General Motors Corporation, and Chrysler Corporation. In 1985, a year after its formation, Intermet's stock began trading on the public market, touching off an energetic acquisition spree. In 1986 the company purchased Northern Castings Company, based in Hibbing, Minnesota, and New River Castings Company, based in Radford, Virginia. Two years later, Intermet acquired the Ironton Iron foundry in Ironton, Ohio, completing an initial surge of welcome additions to the company's fold. However, with the good came the bad. In an effort to extend its geographic reach and strengthen its capabilities and capacity, Intermet became involved in deals its management would later regret. Although the company eventually would rank as the largest concern of its kind in the world, its path to future dominance would not prove an easy road.

INTERNATIONAL MISTAKES OF THE LATE 1980S

As Intermet pursued an aggressive expansion campaign during its first decade of business, its zeal resulted in two acquisitions that represented notable failures. Intermet purchased a foundry in Sweden, intent on bolstering its international presence, but slackening demand by European automobile manufacturers delivered a fatal blow to the new acquisition. The foundry failed to attract sufficient business to remain profitable and, consequently, the entire facility was shuttered, save a machinery division.

Intermet's progress was hobbled by another misguided overseas adventure, a joint venture named INTAT Precision. The company was formed through a partnership agreement between Intermet and a Japanese concern named Aisin Takaoda. Together, Intermet and Aisin Takaoda invested $25 million in an automotive

parts facility located in Indiana, with Intermet controlling 60 percent of the joint venture and Aisin Takaoda controlling the remainder. Through INTAT Precision, automotive parts were to be manufactured first for Toyota, then for Honda Motor Co., Ltd., Mitsubishi Motors Corporation, and Nissan Motor Co., Ltd., and finally for Japanese brake manufacturers. Under the terms of the agreement, Aisin Takaoda assumed control over the marketing and sales of the products manufactured by INTAT Precision, convincing Intermet officials that Aisin Takaoda's management possessed a greater understanding of the Japanese market and business customs governing trade in Japan. Ceding control to Aisin Takaoda proved to be a costly mistake, as Mathews later acknowledged in a March 1992 interview with *Business Atlanta,* saying, "We were asleep at the switch when we made the rudiments of that transaction." Projected sales of the new joint venture failed to materialize, but Intermet's partners preached patience, promising that sales would recover. Mathews and his staff waited, but eventually the losses became too significant to endure, forcing Intermet to withdraw from the joint venture with only financial losses to show for its efforts. "It drained our money from the company and drained theirs, too," Mathews explained in his interview with *Business Atlanta.* "Only thing, it was draining 40 percent of theirs and 60 percent of ours," he added.

Despite the costly miscues, Intermet's stature within the industry was impressive. By the early 1990s, the company was generating in excess of $320 million a year in sales through its worldwide operations. Intermet employed 3,600 workers spread among 12 foundries and two machining operations, primarily involving itself in ductile iron casting, which was stronger and lighter than traditional gray iron. Although the company manufactured housings, hubs, gear boxes, and other parts for farm and construction equipment, as well as parts for industrial manufacturers, the overwhelming majority of its sales were derived from OEM car and truck manufacturers. The company's major customers included Ford, Chrysler, General Motors, Toyota, Honda, Caterpillar Inc., and Bendix Corporation. For these and other customers, Intermet manufactured casting products such as brake parts, steering and transmission components, camshafts, and crankshafts, earning distinction not so much for the particular products it produced but more for the manufacturing processes it employed. The company was capable of producing a broad range of casting products, from small castings to castings weighing up to 400 pounds, which enabled Intermet to pursue a commensurately broad range of contracts.

KEY DATES

1846: Intermet's earliest predecessor company, Columbus Iron Works, is founded.

1971: Columbus Foundries, Inc. is formed.

1984: Intermet Corporation is formed and assumes control of Columbus Foundries.

1985: Company goes public.

1995: Bodine-Robinson Aluminum Foundry is acquired, ushering Intermet into the aluminum castings business.

1996: Sudbury, Inc. is acquired, substantially increasing production capacity of iron castings and lifting sales by $300 million.

1999: Company's aluminum business is bolstered with the acquisition of Ganton Technologies, Inc. and Diversified Diemakers, Inc.

2004: Sharply rising prices for scrap metal force Intermet to seek Chapter 11 bankruptcy protection.

2005: The company emerges from bankruptcy as a private entity.

The opportunities available to Intermet promised to increase significantly as the company's management surveyed the industry during the early 1990s. Domestically, the automotive market was mired in a decisive slump during the early years of the decade. In 1991 the industry sold 12.3 million cars and light trucks, 11 percent less than it had sold the previous year. Further, the one-year drop in sales appeared to be part of an unwelcome trend: unit sales had peaked at 16.3 million in 1987, then began a five-year decline that intensified during the economically recessive early 1990s. At first blush, the anemic performance of Intermet's mainstay market pointed toward a commensurate decline in Intermet's business; a likely scenario considering OEM suppliers would suffer along with the manufacturers they supplied products to. For Intermet, however, the recessive conditions worked to the company's benefit. Because of the economic decline, major automobile manufacturers were forced to implement sweeping measures to improve efficiency and reduce costs. As they scaled down their operations, the automobile manufacturers increasingly turned to outside suppliers for the components they had traditionally produced on their own, using outsourcing as a means to reduce costs. For Intermet, the trend toward outsourcing not only led to an increase in business but also reduced the strength of some of the

company's largest competitors. In addition to competing against other independent foundry companies, Intermet battled for market share with companies such as General Motors' Central Foundries, which dramatically reduced the scope of its operations in the midst of the recessive early 1990s. Accordingly, while the automotive market suffered, Intermet increased its market share, exuding a vitality that was exemplified by the announcement in 1992 of a three-year, $100 million capital expenditure program.

DIVERSIFICATION INTO ALUMINUM: EARLY 1990S

From an early 1990s vantage point, there were other positive developments that pointed toward promising growth for Intermet in the years ahead. The company was searching to add to its already formidable market position in iron casting by diversifying into aluminum, which was expected to be a high-growth segment of the automotive market in the future. During the early 1990s, a typical car manufactured in the United States contained 175 pounds of aluminum, a proportion that was expected to double to 350 pounds per vehicle by 2000 as automobile manufacturers sought to reduce the weight of their various models. Intermet was intent on tapping into the burgeoning aluminum castings market and took its first steps into the business during the early 1990s. In 1992 the company formed a new division, Intermet Aluminum Inc., to produce cast aluminum chassis parts and signed a joint venture agreement with Australia-based Comalco Ltd. The joint venture, named ICA Castings, comprised a pilot plant and a smelting and rolling facility in Kentucky, which were to be used to make cast aluminum cylinder heads and engine blocks for U.S. automobile manufacturers. The agreement was terminated two years later, however, primarily because manufacturers were reluctant to place orders until further competition in the industry ensured competitive prices. Although its initial foray into aluminum suffered a setback, Intermet was determined to push ahead. In 1995 the company achieved its goal.

Midway through the decade, Intermet's iron castings business was growing robustly, enabling it to reach the half-billion-dollar mark in sales, which ranked the company as one of the largest independent foundry concerns in the world. In late 1995 Intermet added to its massive iron castings business by acquiring the Bodine-Robinson Aluminum Foundry, marking the company's formal entry into aluminum castings production. Based in Alexander City, Alabama, the foundry, which was renamed Alexander City Casting Company, Inc., was equipped to make automotive intake manifolds, transmission clutch parts, marine engine components, and castings for lawn and garden engines, possessing an annual capacity of more than 12 million pounds of light-alloy castings. For Intermet, the Bodine-Robinson acquisition represented an important first step into aluminum, touching off further aluminum acquisitions to follow, but the company's acquisitive activities were not restricted to building a presence in the fast-growing light-alloy market. The 1990s were heady years for Intermet, highlighted by an aggressive expansion campaign that cemented the company's standing as a global giant, particularly after a significant transaction in 1996 was completed.

Roughly a year after the Bodine-Robinson acquisition, Intermet struck again, purchasing Cleveland, Ohio-based Sudbury, Inc. for a reported $195 million. The acquisition lifted Intermet past all rivals, pushing its annual sales to $845 million and making it the largest independent ferrous castings foundry in the United States. Sudbury, a manufacturer of castings and machined parts and a provider of powder coating services primarily to the automotive industry, comprised five operating companies employing 2,300 workers, the largest of which, Wagner Castings Company, made the same kind of ductile iron castings as Intermet. Aside from adding substantially to Intermet's casting capacity, the Sudbury acquisition also expanded Intermet's product lines and capabilities to include zinc and aluminum die-casting, cantilevered cranes, and specialty service truck bodies.

LATE 1990S EXPANSION

During the late 1990s, Intermet continued with its prevailing theme of the decade: expansion through acquisition. In May 1998 the company entered a joint venture for PortCast, a foundry company located in Portugal. In December 1998 the company completed another strengthening move overseas when it purchased an iron foundry in Eastern Germany, but the biggest development of the month was Intermet's announcement that it was acquiring the Minnesota-based Tool Products division belonging to Quadion Corp. The purchase represented another important step toward the expansion of Intermet's aluminum business, giving the company the capacity to produce an additional 17 to 18 million pounds of aluminum castings annually. Tool Products, with plants in New Hope, Minnesota, and Jackson, Tennessee, manufactured precision die-castings for automotive and industrial electronic products, as well as small castings for anti-skid braking systems, fuel pumps, and steering wheel cores, deriving 60 percent of its annual revenue from the automotive market.

Intermet ended its most prolific decade of growth with yet another aluminum acquisition, leading some industry observers to speculate that the company would

eventually abandon ferrous castings. The acquisition, announced in November 1999, included two companies, Ganton Technologies, Inc. and Diversified Diemakers, Inc., which, combined, were expected to generate $235 million in sales in 1999. Ganton Technologies, one of North America's largest aluminum die casters, operated three manufacturing facilities, two located in Wisconsin and another in Tennessee, and an engineering center in Wisconsin. Diversified Diemakers specialized in magnesium die-cast products such as brake pedal brackets, instrument panel frames, and housings used by automotive, commercial, and electronics industries, operating three production facilities in Michigan. With the addition of the two companies, Intermet's annual revenues were expected to reach $1.3 billion by the end of 2000, four times the total generated eight years earlier. The growth, however, was not being achieved at the expense of the company's longstanding involvement in the iron castings business, according to Intermet officials. Although the company announced the closure of its Ironton Iron foundry in December 1999 because of declining business, Intermet management scotched rumors that it was pursuing a long-term strategy that excluded the company's involvement in ferrous castings. Instead, the company declared it was pursuing a growth strategy that would shape Intermet into a full-service metal caster.

TROUBLED TIMES IN THE NEW CENTURY

The heady years of the 1990s gave way to darker days in the early 2000s. Tragedy struck Intermet in March 2000 when a gas explosion at the New River foundry cost the lives of three workers and injured several others. Casting production halted for several months. A serious fire at the Neunkirchen, Germany, foundry in May disrupted production there for more than three months. Further impacting financial results for the year was the botched launch of two new products for automotive engines at Intermet's Alexander City, Alabama, aluminum casting plant. Intermet still managed to post strong results—$40.9 million in net income on revenues of $1.04 billion, the firm's first billion-dollar-plus year—but the various difficulties led investors to pummel Intermet's stock price.

The North American auto industry fell into one of its periodic downturns starting in 2001 as production dropped sharply, by almost two million vehicles. This downturn, coupled with continued production problems stemming from the aftermath of the New River explosion, led to a sharp reduction in revenue at Intermet: $843.2 million for the year. The operational difficulties at the Alexander City plant continued into 2001 as well, and Intermet elected to close down that facility late in the year. A $12.9 million charge taken in connection with this closure contributed to a net loss for the year of $8.7 million. Intermet slashed its workforce by 25 percent as part of an effort to shore up profits.

The struggles continued in 2002 as the company eked out a profit of $9 million on still lower sales of $814.9 million. In June 2003 Gary F. Ruff was promoted from president and chief operating officer to CEO, succeeding John Doddridge, who remained chairman until the following year, when Ruff took on the chairmanship as well. Seeking to shore up its long-term profitability, Intermet further rationalized its production portfolio in 2003, closing plants in Radford, Virginia, and Havana, Illinois, and selling off Frisby PMC, Inc., which operated a machining plant. Charges for the year of more than $61 million led to a net loss of $98.9 million on sales of $731.2 million. Also during the year, Intermet bought out its joint venture partner in Portugal.

In 2004 Intermet fell victim to sharply rising prices for scrap metal. The company's cost of ferrous scrap had risen from $160 a ton to $210 a ton during 2003, but then the cost skyrocketed to $395 a ton by the end of August 2004. As a result, Intermet was forced to seek protection under Chapter 11 of the bankruptcy code, making its filing in September. Operating under Chapter 11, the company closed several more facilities in 2005: its machining plant in Midland, Georgia; its die-casting and machining plants in Sturtevant, Wisconsin; and its Decatur, Illinois, foundry. Intermet also renegotiated metal surcharges with its customers in order to insulate itself from renewed raw material price spikes. Having secured $285 million in new loans, Intermet emerged from bankruptcy in November 2005 as a private company with two hedge funds as its primary owners: R2 Investments L.D.C. and Stanfield Capital Partners L.L.C.

Jeffrey L. Covell
Updated, David E. Salamie

PRINCIPAL SUBSIDIARIES

Lynchburg Foundry Company; Northern Castings Corporation; Ironton Iron, Inc.; Intermet International, Inc.; Columbus Foundry, L.P.; SUDM, Inc.; Alexander City Casting Company, Inc.; Tool Products, Inc.; Sudbury, Inc.; Cast-Matic Corporation; Frisby P.M.C., Incorporated; Transnational Indemnity Company; Wagner Castings Company; Wagner Havana, Inc.; Diversified Diemakers, Inc.; Ganton Technologies, Inc.; Intermet Netherlands, B.V.; Intermet European Foreign Holdings Corporation, B.V. (Netherlands); Intermet

Holding, B.V. (Netherlands); Intermet Europe GmbH (Germany); Intermet Neunkirchen Foundry GmbH (Germany); Fundico Nodular, SA (Portugal; 75%).

PRINCIPAL COMPETITORS

Citation Corporation; Grede Foundries, Inc.; Worthington Industries, Inc.

FURTHER READING

"Alvin W. Singleton, Intermet President, Dies," *Foundry Management and Technology,* February 1991, p. 9.

Barrett, Rick, "Intermet to Amend Some Contracts," *Milwaukee Journal Sentinel,* January 5, 2005.

——, "Intermet to Close Sturtevant Plants," *Milwaukee Journal Sentinel,* December 16, 2004.

Burgert, Philip, "Intermet Blames Scrap Costs for Ch. 11 Filing," *American Metal Market,* October 1, 2004, p. 5.

——, "Intermet Files Ch. 11 Reorganization Plan," *American Metal Market,* June 29, 2005, p. 4.

Corbett, Brian, "Master Caster," *Ward's Auto World,* May 2003, pp. 28+.

——, "Intermet Restructures, Emerges from Chapter 11 As Private Entity," *American Metal Market,* November 14, 2005, p. 7.

"Ductile Iron As Good As Steel," *Ward's Auto World,* May 1999, p. 3.

"Just-in-Time Manufacturing Is Working Overtime," *Business Week,* November 8, 1999, p. 36.

Kingman, Nancy, "Drive for Lighter Cars Sets Intermet on Expansion Path," *American Metal Market,* April 26, 1993, p. 14.

Kosdrosky, Terry, "Foreign Competition Spurs Intermet to Look at Regions with Cheap Labor," *Crain's Detroit Business,* August 25, 2003, p. 4.

——, "Funds Pilot Intermet Out of Ch. 11," *Crain's Detroit Business,* October 3, 2005, p. 45.

Palmer, Jay, "Intermet Corp.: A Shining Standout in the Rust Belt," *Barron's,* November 9, 1987, pp. 100+.

Rodgers, Robert C., "Intermet's Strategy for Worldwide Growth," *Foundry Management and Technology,* July 1988, pp. 46+.

Savage, Mark, "Die-Casting Firm Agrees to Sale," *Milwaukee Journal Sentinel,* November 18, 1999.

Sherefkin, Robert, "Supplier Seeks Chapter 11 Protection," *Automotive News,* September 27, 2004, p. 16.

Smith, Faye McDonald, "Self-Inflicted Wounds All Healed," *Business Atlanta,* March 1992, p. 72.

Stundza, Tom, "In a Squeeze," *Purchasing,* December 9, 2004, pp. 24B1+.

Teel, Leonard Ray, "Turning Iron into Gold," *Georgia Trend,* November 1986, p. 44.

Vanac, Mary, "Ohio-Based Automobile, Industrial Parts Manufacturer to Be Bought Out," *Knight-Ridder/Tribune Business News,* November 20, 1996.

Wrigley, Al, "Aluminum Castings Deal Canceled," *American Metal Market,* December 29, 1994, p. 5.

———, "Intermet Gets Deeper into Aluminum," *American Metal Market,* December 29, 1998, p. 7.

———, "Intermet Moves to Aluminum," *American Metal Market,* October 4, 1995, p. 2.

Irwin Union Bank

Irwin Financial Corporation

500 Washington Street
Columbus, Indiana 47201
U.S.A.
Telephone: (812) 376-1909
Toll Free: (888) 879-5900
Fax: (812) 376-1709
Web site: http://www.irwinfinancial.com

Public Company
Founded: 1871 as Irwin's Bank
Employees: 3,145 Total Assets: $5.23 billion (2004)
Stock Exchanges: New York
Ticker Symbol: IFC
NAIC: 522110 Commercial Banking; 551111 Offices of
Bank Holding Companies

■ ■ ■

The businesses of holding company Irwin Financial Corporation engage in consumer and small business lending. The community bank, founded more than 130 years ago, was eclipsed by a mortgage banking business acquired in 1981 and then expanded outside Indiana. The company entered into home equity loan origination to help balance out the company's revenue flow during downturns in the real estate market. About 40 percent of the holding company is owned by the company's chairman, a member of the founding family.

INDIANA ROOTS RUNNING DEEP: 1870S-1970S

Twenty-two-year-old Joseph Ireland Irwin already had a decade of work experience under his belt before he left the farm and family in 1846. In Columbus, Indiana, Irwin would use $150 saved from his job in a dry goods store plus a $500 loan to strike out on his own. Real estate activities allowed him to pay off the loan, the only loan made in his lifetime, and buy a mercantile store in 1850.

As he grew the dry goods business he gained a reputation for honesty among his fellow merchants, who, in the early 1860s, began asking him to hold their money in his safe. Upon this bedrock, he established an informal banking business out of the store. He founded Irwin's Bank in 1871 after a local bank failed, a common occurrence in the post-Civil War years. Decades before federal deposit insurance, Irwin's personal funds backed deposits made in the bank.

Irwin completed renovations on the building housing the bank and store in 1882. In 1889, his son, William G. Irwin (W. G.) came aboard as a cashier. In 1895, the family exited the dry goods business, concentrating solely on the banking operation. By the start of the 20th century, assets totaled $690,000, "an immense sum of money" for 1900, according to the *Indiana Business Magazine*.

Upon his father's death, W. G. took over the presidency of the bank in 1910 and used the business to help Columbus move into the industrial age. In 1919, he backed local inventor Clessie Cummins, who would found Cummins Engine Company. In the 1920s, he helped bring Indianapolis-based Noblitt-Sparks Industries (later Arvin Industries) to Columbus.

W. G. also drove the 1928 merger between Irwin's Bank and Union Trust, creating Irwin-Union Trust Company. The deal reduced the family ownership to about 50 percent. The Columbus entity remained solvent as others around it folded following the 1929 stock market crash: W.G. had the foresight to convert investment portfolios to cash. In 1937, Irwin-Union held deposits of slightly less than $4.2 million and netted $40,000 in earnings, during a time when many banks still struggled to stay afloat.

W.G. Irwin died in 1943. He was succeeded by his nephew Hugh Miller as bank president. Hugh's tenure was short. His death put son J. Irwin Miller at the helm in 1947, when net earnings were $105,000. The younger Miller pulled double duty, continuing to hold his management role with the Cummins Engine Co.

During the 1950s, the bank introduced a range of innovative services. A growing commercial banking business prompted a name change in 1954, to Irwin Union Bank and Trust Company. In 1956, the purchase of another bank pushed total deposits to more than $36 million.

Total assets more than doubled in the 1960s, reaching $100 million in 1969. Anticipating new directions, in 1972, holding company Irwin Union Corporation was formed. Later, during 1979, a small business investment company was created.

The banking family continued to make its mark on the town of Columbus as well. "Like his great uncle W.G., J. Irwin was a visionary but also a philanthropist and patron of the arts. In 1957 he spearheaded the campaign to cover architectural fees of public buildings," Bill Beck wrote for *Indiana Business Magazine*. The move would put Columbus on the map in terms of architecture and earned Miller the accolades of *Esquire* magazine in 1967.

MORTGAGE BUSINESS FUELING GROWTH: 1980S-90S

With total assets of $280 million in 1981, the holding company purchased Inland Mortgage Corporation. Inland had one office in Indianapolis and held a servicing portfolio of $140 million, according to the *Indianapolis Business Journal.*

During 1985, Indiana granted banks the right to operate in more than one county in the state. But quickly the company recognized that its greater opportunity laid with expanding the mortgage business. By 1990, Inland Mortgage operated in 14 states, originating $1.2 billion in mortgages annually.

William I. Miller, the fifth generation to own Irwin, bought out the family in 1990. Miller joined the board of the holding company, Irwin Union Corporation, in 1985, during which time he was also president of Irwin Management Corp., a family business not affiliated with the bank. The holding company, with revenues of $43 million, net income of $4.6 million, 700 employees, and offices in 11 states, changed its name in 1990 to Irwin Financial Corporation.

The mortgage concern, Inland, had benefited from the savings and loan collapse, as consumers turned to mortgage bankers for home loans in affected markets such as Arizona. The servicing portfolio, those mortgages on which Inland collected payments, climbed to $2.7 billion by the end of 1991, up from $1.9 billion a year earlier. Even though the mortgage origination business was operating at a loss, the profitable servicing business took up the slack. The company retained the servicing rights on about two-thirds of the residential mortgages it originated.

Inland Mortgage, closing in on the earnings generated by Irwin Union Bank, was instrumental in driving up the holding company's price per share during 1991. Credited for its good management, the company also had benefited from declining long-term interest rates, which brought more people in seeking home loans.

Irwin's success and the trend toward consolidation in the industry fueled talk of a sale. But according to the *Indianapolis Business Journal,* Miller believed that both Inland Mortgage and Irwin Union Bank still had growth potential. Moreover, the company looked to complementary businesses for sources of revenue and earnings. The company established a small investment firm in 1984 and a leaser of small ticket medical equipment in 1990. Miller held about 47 percent of the company's stock.

In 1992, Inland Mortgage Corp. produced about 80 percent of Irwin's earnings, according to *American Banker.* Its mortgage activities, atypical among com-

KEY DATES

1871: Joseph I. Irwin founds a private bank in Columbus, Indiana.

1889: William G. Irwin joins his father's bank business.

1910: The founder dies, succeeded by his son as president.

1919: Financier W. G. Irwin backs the founding of Cummins Engine Company.

1928: Irwin's Bank merges with another Columbus entity, Union Trust, creating Irwin-Union Trust Company.

1943: The Miller family line enters into leadership of the company with the death of W. G. Irwin.

1954: The name is changed to Irwin Union Bank and Trust Company.

1969: Irwin Union Bank assets reach $100 million.

1972: Holding company Irwin Union Corporation is formed.

1979: A small business investment corporation is formed.

1981: Inland Mortgage Corporation is acquired.

1984: An entity is formed to offer investment management services.

1990: The name is changed to Irwin Financial Corporation.

1995: Irwin Home Equity Corporation is established.

2000: The company enjoys its 11th consecutive year of record earnings.

2001: The holding company moves to the New York Stock Exchange.

2004: A decline in mortgage generation hurts profits.

munity banks, had helped Irwin become one of the most profitable in the Midwest.

During 1993 its business segments included the $439 million in assets Irwin Union Bank and Trust Co., Inland Mortgage Corp. with a $5.5 billion servicing portfolio, Irwin Union Investor Services, and Affiliated Capital Corp., the leasing business.

By 1995, Inland Mortgage ranked among the nation's 30 largest lenders, originating more than $3 billion in loans annually. Its servicing portfolio had topped $10 billion. Irwin Union Bank and Trust Co.'s 15

branches primarily served nonmetropolitan areas, competing with local banks.

Irwin Home Equity, established in 1995 in San Ramon, California, lost $3.2 million its first year. With three-quarters of revenue derived from mortgage banking, rising interest rates were hurting stock, prompting the company to begin developing new business areas. "Irwin, in many respects, is the bank of the future," Joseph Stieven, analyst with Stifel Nicolaus in St. Louis, said in a *Knight Ridder/Tribune Business News* article. It believed its success would come from well-developed niches. In 1996, the company sold off part of the investor services business and absorbed the rest into the banking operation.

Inland Mortgage changed its name to Irwin Mortgage Corporation on January 1, 1998. The company originated $9 billion in mortgages during the year, but the home mortgage boom had peaked. By 2000, the company's mortgage generation would fall to half that amount. From 1998 to 2000, the home equity loan niche would be the gainer in revenue and earnings momentum. In 1999 the company established two smaller operations: a reconstitution of the equipment leasing business and a venture capital firm investing in companies involved in technology applicable to financial services.

NICHE PLAYER JUGGLING MANY BALLS: 2000-05

In 2000, Irwin Financial closed in on $300 million in revenue and achieved an 11th straight year of record earnings. Net income was $35.7 million. The company employed 2,500 people, with offices in all 50 states and in Canada, according to *Indiana Business Magazine*.

The Columbus-based bank holding company, with more than $2 billion in assets, was regarded as one of the country's top performers. The holding company's return on average equity (ROE) was 20.7 percent in 2000. For nine straight years the ROE had been 20 percent or more. Miller attributed the company's ROE numbers to diversification. The bank brought in 16 percent of revenue, the mortgage business 46 percent, and home equity loans 35 percent. Across the board the company's target markets were small businesses and consumers.

Typically, community banks expanded through adding branches in their service area and adjacent territory. When Indiana banks were allowed to cross county lines, Irwin chose to grow its small business lending instead. The company sought out high growth markets and offered its best commercial bankers a job. Taking advantage of the upheaval in the industry, Irwin recruited good local talent freed up by consolidation. A familiar face gave credibility to the new name in town and brought with it knowledge of the credit risk of the customer base. The strategy put Irwin in cities from Kalamazoo to St. Louis to Phoenix and gave it a toehold for its other businesses.

Irwin's business niches were subject to different economic cycles. While the mortgage banking business focused on first-time buyers, peaking with low interest rates, the home equity loan business served people attempting to manage credit card debt. The commercial banking operation served small businesses overlooked by larger banks.

Under Miller, great-great-grandson of Joseph I. Irwin, the financial services company racked up record earnings. Since 1990, earnings per share grew 23 percent and net income rose from slightly less than $5 million to $35.7 million in 2000.

During 2001, Irwin Financial established Irwin Capital Holdings as its commercial finance line of business, encompassing leasing companies in the United States and Canada and a branded franchise financing operation. The 29-location Irwin Union Bank added a federal savings bank. The holding company moved to the New York Stock Exchange.

When Irwin Financial began securitizing and selling its loans, in the late 1990s, the related interest income boosted stock price, rising to about $25 per share in the summer of 2001. But the scandals that rocked the corporate world had created wary investors. When Irwin moved to raise $75 million in a secondary offering in 2002, potential investors went over the prospectus with a fine-tooth comb, wanting further information about accountant firm changes and downturns in key business areas before handing over the cash.

The U.S. real estate market heated up as interest rates fell to record lows in an effort by the federal government to jumpstart the economy following the September 11, 2001 terrorist attacks. Irwin Mortgage Corp. originated a record $22.7 billion worth of mortgage loans in 2003, driving a record profit.

Excess capacity in the mortgage banking industry, as well as internally, hurt Irwin Financial in 2004. The company closed offices to cut expenses. With just $13.1 billion in loans generated during the year, profits plummeted. Performance of the other three core business areas was solid but not enough to completely offset the decline in the mortgage business.

The overcapacity problem continued to plague Irwin Financial into 2005; moreover, the company believed that its mortgage servicing rights were being undervalued by the market. But as 2005 began to wind down, Irwin Financial began to report improvement in its mortgage banking operation.

Kathleen Peippo

PRINCIPAL SUBSIDIARIES

Irwin Mortgage Corporation; Irwin Home Equity Corporation; Irwin Union Bank and Trust Company; Irwin Union Bank, FSB; Irwin Commercial Finance.

PRINCIPAL COMPETITORS

Bank of America Corporation; Countrywide Financial Corporation.

FURTHER READING

Andrews, Greg, "Inland Experiencing Explosive Growth," *Indianapolis Business Journal,* December 2, 1991, pp. 1+.

Beck, Bill, "Irwin's Bank," *Indiana Business Magazine,* March 2001, p. 10.

Beck, Bill, and Kathleen Curley, "Irwin Union Bank & Trust (Centennial Business)," *Indiana Business Magazine,* September 2002, pp. 39+.

Cox, Robert B., "Indiana's Super-Profitable Irwin Doesn't Fear End of Refinancings," *American Banker,* July 9, 1993, p. 9.

Dinnen, S. P., "Indiana's Irwin Financial Producing Fortunes in Stock Splits," *Knight Ridder/Tribune Business News,* December 2, 1996.

Morrison, Pat, "Bank Holding Company Focuses on Niches," *Indianapolis Business Journal,* May 28, 2001, p. 17B.

Quinn, Matthew, "In Brief: Irwin to Post Profit from Mortgage Line," *American Banker,* October 5, 2005, p. 11.

Revell, Janice, "Life in the Danger Zone: Companies Like Irwin Financial Are Getting Punished for Flying Red Flags," *Fortune,* March 4, 2002, p. 206.

Schnitzler, Peter, "Mortgage Dip Forces Irwin to Make Cuts: Lender Closes 120 Branches, Trims Workers As Profits Drop, Housing Market Cools Off," *Indianapolis Business Journal,* April 25, 2005, pp. 3A+.

Watkins, Steve, "Columbus, Indiana Bank Makes Itself at Home, a City at a Time," *Investor's Business Daily,"* March 5, 2001, p. A10.

Jockey International, Inc.

—————■—————

2300 60th Street
Kenosha, Wisconsin 53141
U.S.A.
Telephone: (262) 658-8111
Toll Free: (866) 256-2539
Fax: (262) 658-1812
Web site: http://www.jockey.com

Private Company
Incorporated: 1876 as S.T. Cooper & Sons
Employees: 5,000
NAIC: 315192 Underwear and Nightwear Knitting
Mills; 315221 Men's and Boys' Cut and SewUnder-
wear and Nightwear Manufacturing; 315231 Wo-
men's and Girls' Cut and Sew Lingerie, Loungewear,
and Nightwear Manufacturing

■ ■ ■

Jockey International, Inc. is one of the oldest and best-
known U.S. underwear manufacturers. The company
markets a broad range of underwear for men, women,
and children, along with related products such as sleepwear, tee shirts, clothing for sports activities, hosiery and
socks. Its products are primarily sold under the flagship
Jockey brand, but the company also produces products
under license agreements, such as those with Tommy
Hilfiger and Liz Claiborne. Jockey International's manufacturing facilities include about a dozen plants in Costa
Rica, Honduras, Jamaica, the United Kingdom, and the
southern United States, and it licenses and distributes its
products in more than 120 countries worldwide. Within

the United States, the Jockey brand is distributed
through more than 14,000 department and specialty
stores. Privately owned since its inception, Jockey began
by making socks and branched out to make innovative
designs in men's underwear, pioneering the marketing of
the brief.

EARLY HISTORY

Jockey got its start in 1876, when Samuel T. Cooper
purchased six hand-operated knitting machines. Along
with his sons Charles, Henry, and Willis, he used this
equipment to found S.T. Cooper & Sons, a hosiery
manufacturer located in the small town of Ludington,
Michigan. Cooper sold heavy wool socks to general
stores, which in turn sold them to customers.

Cooper soon expanded its line from wool socks to
men's underwear, adding union suits, the only men's
underwear then manufactured. The union suit was a
long-sleeved, long-legged knit garment that buttoned up
the front. Around 1900, Cooper moved its operations
from Ludington, Michigan, to the slightly larger town
of Kenosha, Wisconsin, which became its headquarters.
In addition Cooper changed its name to Cooper's
Underwear Company.

In 1910, Cooper's introduced a new design for its
union suits which eliminated the need for buttons. The
"Kenosha Klosed Krotch" consisted of two overlapping
pieces of fabric that could be drawn apart to create an
opening. Cooper's patented this design innovation, and
trademarked the "Kenosha" name.

In the following year, Cooper's undertook the first
national advertising campaign for a line of men's

COMPANY PERSPECTIVES

Our values: We commit ourselves, as trusted representatives of Jockey International, to pursue the highest level of personal and collective integrity in our day-to-day dealing with our employees, suppliers, and business partners. We commit ourselves with passion to our people and to their personal development as employees and members of their communities. We commit ourselves to being the market leader in product innovation and to extend this spirit of innovation into every facet of our organization. We commit ourselves to our customers in a relentless drive to satisfy their need for comfort and to secure their undying loyalty. We commit ourselves to an uncompromising approach to quality in our products and in the daily performance of our jobs.

underwear when it took out an ad in the *Saturday Evening Post.* The company hired a well-known illustrator named Leyendecker for the magazine to produce a series of color renderings of Cooper's products. The first of these promotional spots ran in the May 6, 1911, edition of the journal. Three years later, a Leyendecker rendering of a "man on the bag" became a staple of the Cooper's brand identity.

With the entry of the United States into World War I, large numbers of men were inducted into the armed services for the first time in a generation. In the army, servicemen were given woven shorts to wear as underwear in the summer, as opposed to the long johns typically worn in civilian life. After the war ended in 1918, many demobilized soldiers continued to prefer the greater comfort and convenience of boxer shorts, shunning the union suit. By the early 1920s, the more traditional garment had fallen into disfavor. Despite this decline in popularity, Cooper's did not dramatically change its product offerings throughout the 1920s.

In 1926, the company briefly changed its name to Cooper's, Inc., and two years later, Cooper's created an export department to facilitate the eventual marketing of its products outside the United States.

1930S AND EARLY 1940S: JOCKEYS AND BRIEFS

At the end of the decade, Cooper's introduced a new product line, a variation on the union suit called the "Jockey Singleton." This sleeveless, one-piece garment

was made of Durene yarn, and came only to the knees. The company called the snug-fitting underwear "Jockey" to suggest athleticism and flexibility. Cooper's trademarked this name and the construction of the garment, and sold a high volume of this product throughout the 1930s. Three years after the introduction of the singleton, Cooper's rolled out another new product line when it began to sell knit pajamas. In 1934, Cooper's expanded its line of knit products once again, when it started marketing knit sports shirts to retailers.

In 1934, Cooper's made its most important innovation in underwear when it designed the brief. This idea came about after a senior vice-president of Cooper's saw a picture of men on the French Riviera wearing a new type of bathing suit. He saw this garment as a potential prototype for a new kind of men's support underwear. In September 1934, Cooper's produced an experimental prototype, brief style #1001. In response to its introduction, competitors labeled the new underwear style a fad. On January 19, 1935, Marshall Field and Company, the premier Chicago department store, unveiled a window display featuring the new brief. On that day, Chicago was experiencing a severe blizzard, and the skimpy men's underwear in the window made a stark contrast to the wintry conditions outside. Under these circumstances, Marshall Field's managers gave the order to take the brief out of the window display. When the workers who were to carry out this order were delayed, however, the new underwear style stayed on display, and prompted an unexpected surge of demand for the product. More than 600 briefs were sold before noon, at a price of 50 cents apiece.

The brief's popularity remained strong in the following days. Over the next week, more than 12,000 of the new underwear style were sold. In its first three months of sales, Marshall Field's rang up more than 30,000 pairs of the red-hot item. With this runaway success, the brief garnered widespread attention in the underwear industry. In August 1935, Cooper's Underwear Company received a patent on the construction principles of the Y-front brief from the U.S. Patent Office.

Building on the strength of its new underwear style, Cooper's introduced another new line in 1935, when it began to sell a Junior set of products for boys. The first items offered were a brief and an athletic shirt. Cooper's also became the first company to sell men's underwear in packages in that year. In 1936, Cooper's began to market its products outside the United States when it signed a contract for a Canadian firm to manufacture and sell its styles under license. In an effort to further enhance the sales of its brief, Cooper also unrolled an advertising campaign designed to point out the

---

KEY DATES

1876: Samuel T. Cooper purchases six hand-operated knitting machines and with his sons founds S.T. Cooper & Sons, a hosiery manufacturer located in Ludington, Michigan.

1900: Company relocates to Kenosha, Wisconsin, and changes its name to Cooper's Underwear Company.

1911: Cooper's undertakes the first national advertising campaign for a line of men's underwear with an ad in the Saturday Evening Post.

1929: The Jockey brand is first used for a one-piece garment called the "Jockey Singleton."

1934: Cooper's introduces a new underwear style, the brief.

1938: Company presents the first underwear fashion show at an industry convention.

1948: Cooper's begins to use radio advertising to push its products; the company also moves toward the positioning of its products as fashion items with a line of underwear decorated with novelty prints.

1954: Company begins to promote underwear as a gift item by packaging its products in a special Christmas box.

1955: Television advertising is added, with the first spots airing on NBC's Home Show.

1971: Harry Wolf, a company consultant, purchases Cooper's.

1972: Company is reincorporated as Jockey International, Inc.

1978: Wolf dies and ownership passes to his three children; Donna Wolf Steigerwaldt holds controlling interest and becomes chair and CEO.

1980: Baltimore Orioles pitcher Jim Palmer becomes sole spokesperson for the company.

1982: The Jockey for Her line of cotton panties is introduced.

1985: Company establishes its own in-house advertising agency.

1988: Company purchases Nantucket Mills, a hosiery manufacturer.

1993: Steigerwaldt buys out her sister's share to become sole owner of Jockey.

1994: Jockey begins making and marketing a Tommy Hilfiger line of underwear.

1995: Edward C. Emma is named president and COO.

1998: The men's and women's divisions are consolidated into a single unit called Jockey Brand; the Jockey for Her label is replaced by Jockey Intimates; the "Let 'em know you're Jockey" ad campaign is launched.

2001: Debra Waller becomes CEO.

---

disadvantages of boxer shorts. Called the "stop squirming" promotion, this campaign went on to win awards in its field.

Following these efforts, Cooper's in 1937 brought a greater degree of structure to the retail underwear business. In that year, the company introduced a model program for retailers to use in controlling their inventory of Cooper's underwear products, and also produced a manual called "New Era for Underwear Selling" that was designed to instruct retailers in the most effective marketing of Cooper's wares. In addition, the company began to offer special mannequins for use in displaying Cooper's products in stores.

Cooper's move toward greater retailing sophistication continued in February 1938, when the company mounted an innovative display at the National Associa-

tion of Retail Clothiers and Furnishers Convention in Chicago. The company presented the first underwear fashion show, which it called the "Cellophane Wedding." The display consisted of a male and female model, each dressed in evening clothes, as if for a wedding. The trick to the display, however, was that half of the man's coat and pants, and half of the woman's gown, were made of cellophane, displaying the couple's underwear underneath. The woman wore fashionable undergarments of the day, and the man wore a brief and a t-shirt. This fashion show caused a sensation at the convention, and pictures of the couple appeared in every major newspaper and magazine, winning Cooper's a bonanza of free publicity.

Also in 1938, Cooper's introduced another promotional device, the Jockey hip tape. This was used to insure a proper fit for underwear. The company received its second patent on the brief, this one for the "Classic" style #1007, with Y-front construction, on January 2, 1938.

In the following year, Cooper's enhanced its display systems for retailers when it designed a table-top dispenser for its products that customers could use themselves. In the late 1930s and early 1940s, Cooper's also employed a number of sports celebrities to endorse its products, including Babe Ruth, Yogi Berra, Bart Starr, and others. As the 1940s began, Cooper's also introduced a new trademark, the Jockey Boy statue, which it used to differentiate its products from those of its competitors.

To reinforce the consistent impression made by the Jockey Boy trademark, Cooper's introduced a slide and sound film on how to sell underwear in 1941. At the end of that year, the United States entered World War II, and Cooper's, like the rest of the country's industry, switched over to wartime production. The company manufactured flare parachutes and underwear for the armed forces for the duration of the war.

RAPID POSTWAR EXPANSION

At the cessation of hostilities, the U.S. economy entered a period of rapid expansion. In order to help its market share grow, Cooper's began to use radio advertising to push its products in selected major cities in 1948. That year, the company also came up with a new way to make its briefs appealing to customers when it began offering underwear made out of fabrics that had been decorated with novelty prints. These promotions went under the name "fancy pants." By 1953, Cooper's had expanded its "fancy pants" line by adding its most popular item, animal prints. Among the animal skin designs were leopard, tiger, and zebra.

Cooper's also expanded its line of non-underwear products in 1950, when it began to offer men's sportswear. Two years later, the company began to market products for women for the first time, introducing a feminine version of the Jockey short called the "Jockette." The company also stepped up its efforts to sell underwear for boys, taking out advertisements for its Jockey Junior line in *Parent's Magazine.* In a further promotional effort, Cooper's produced two new training tools for salespeople, how-to films entitled "All I Can Do" and "The Big Little Things."

Also in 1953, Cooper's introduced a new fabric which, like the design for the brief, had originated in France. Called "tricot," the French word for "knit," this material was originally made of pure silk thread, knitted into a soft, supple fabric. Cooper's adapted this substance for the U.S. market, manufacturing tricot out of nylon.

In addition, the company moved beyond basic white, offering products made of tricot in a full range of colors.

With the introduction of animal prints and colored tricot underwear, Cooper's moved away from the conception of underwear as a plain, functional item toward a conception of its product as a fashion item, with style and novelty value that extended beyond its basic utility. This process continued in 1954, when the company began to promote underwear as a gift item, packaging its products in a special Christmas box. This trend was expanded to a second holiday in the following year, when Cooper's introduced a special fashion brief as part of a Valentine's Day promotion.

In the following year, Cooper's again expanded the number of fabrics out of which its products were sewn when the company began to offer a line of woven boxer shorts. The company also took another step in its promotional efforts, when it began to advertise underwear on television, running spots on NBC's *Home Show.* In addition to these advances, Cooper's notched yet another patent in its field after it developed a uni-sized hosiery package.

In 1957, Cooper's continued its promotional innovations when it proclaimed the first "National Long Underwear Week." In a further effort in this area, the company became a sponsor of the *Jack Parr Show* on NBC, which later became known as the *TonightShow.* Two years later, Cooper's scored another underwear fad when it introduced "Skants," smaller cut briefs with a no-fly front. In addition, the company extended its line of sportswear and also began to sell men's hosiery, returning to its original roots as a sock manufacturer.

In the 1960s, Cooper's continued to adjust the design of its products to keep pace with trends in fashion. In general, the company's knit and woven underwear became shorter, tighter fitting, and were offered in more bright colors and patterns. Despite the broad variety of offerings, however, 97 percent of the company's sales still came from white underwear. In 1964, Cooper's rolled out "Life," a Lo Rise fashion underwear collection. At the same time, the company began to make its products out of Suprel, a trade name for a blend of polyester and combed cotton.

In the late 1960s, Cooper's returned to its earlier practice of using sports stars and other celebrities to endorse its products. The company's new line of golf sportswear, for instance, was promoted by Bert Yancey and Tom Weiskopf, and ads for Jockey brand products were run on the *Wide World of Sports* television program. For these efforts, Cooper's was named "Brand Names Manufacturer of the Year" in 1969.

1970S AND 1980S: NEW OWNER-SHIP, JIM PALMER, AND JOCKEY FOR HER

Three years later, the Cooper's Underwear Company was purchased by Harry Wolf, who had previously worked as a consultant to the company. At that time, the company was renamed for its trademark, which Cooper's had promoted aggressively over the decades. On May 1, 1972, the company was reincorporated under the new name Jockey International, Inc. In the following year, Jockey expanded its product line further by merging two similar categories of garment, the bathing suit and the brief, into a product called the "DP." In 1974, the company took another step away from strict utility and toward fashion when it hired a New York designer, Alexander Sheilds, to design its sportswear.

When Wolf died in 1978, ownership of Jockey passed on to his three children. Within five years, Wolf's son sold his interest in the firm to his sisters, and Donna Wolf Steigerwaldt, who held a controlling interest in the company, became chair and chief executive officer of Jockey.

Jockey's promotional efforts received a big boost in 1980, when the company selected Jim Palmer, a handsome pitcher for the Baltimore Orioles and an experienced Jockey model, to be sole spokesperson. The image of Palmer wearing a Jockey "Elance" brief became so popular that it was manufactured and distributed as a poster. In 1982, Jockey stepped up its marketing of women's underwear, when it rolled out a new "Jockey for Her" line of cotton panties at a formal fashion show in New York. The company launched the line with three styles, and soon added fashion colors and stripes, and matching tops. Two years later, Jockey added a fourth style, the "French Cut" brief, and in 1985 a line of "Queen Size" underwear for taller and larger women.

In 1985 Jockey also established its own in-house advertising agency to handle all of its promotional campaigns and marketing activities. In that year, the company began to feature "real people," such as a construction worker, an executive vice-president, and a mother, in its advertising, a strategy that won Jockey praise from women's groups.

Three years later, Jockey purchased Nantucket Mills, a hosiery manufacturer. Following this acquisition, the company began to market "Sheer & Comfortable," a collection of women's hosiery with four styles. This line was soon expanded to include "Sheerest Ever" and "Ultra Sheer" products. To promote its hosiery products, the company sponsored a nationwide "Legs Search" for real people to model its stockings.

1990S AND 2000S: EMPHASIS ON STYLE AND COMFORT

Jockey continued to expand its line of product offerings in the early 1990s, adding new styles and fabrics, as well as related products, such as socks. In 1993 Donna Wolf Steigerwaldt bought out her sister's share of Jockey, and thus became its sole owner. That year, and continuing into 1994, the company also worked to address the problem of excess capacity in its manufacturing operations through plant closings. Four U.S. manufacturing plants were closed, including its last factory in Wisconsin. A distribution center in Kenosha was also shuttered, leaving only the corporate headquarters in the town. Nearly 1,000 jobs were eliminated from the company workforce in connection with these closures. These moves culminated a several years long shift of production to lower-wage areas in the southern United States and in offshore areas in Central America and the Caribbean.

In May 1995 Edward C. Emma was named managing director and chief operating officer of Jockey International, assuming responsibility for the company's day-to-day operations. He replaced Thomas J. Bienemann, who had been hired in 1993 to lead the downsizing and restructuring effort. Emma joined Jockey in 1990 as director of the Jockey Menswear division, then was promoted to senior vice-president of retail operations in 1993. In the latter post Emma spearheaded the opening of 37 Jockey retail and manufacturer's outlet stores, a move intended to counter the increasingly difficult task of selling underwear and related items through department stores. In October 1995 Emma was promoted to president and COO. In January of the following year the company reorganized its operations into five independent units—men's, women's, special markets, retail, and international—each of which had its own president reporting to Emma.

In late 1996 Jockey announced that it would purchase from Courtaulds Textiles a long-running licensee operation in the United Kingdom, which manufactured Jockey brand underwear at a plant in northern England and distributed the products in the United Kingdom and Scandinavia. Jockey made another purchase in early 1997 with the acquisition of the Formfit seamless panties division of I. Appel Corp. In mid-1997 Jockey entered into a new licensing agreement, this one with Russell Corporation for the launch of a line of sports underwear for the mass market called Jerzees Sport.

Further reorganizing came in early 1998 when the company consolidated its men's and women's divisions into a single unit called Jockey Brand. At the same time, the company gradually began to phase out the Jockey for Her label in favor of Jockey Intimates, paralleling the Jockey Men's appellation. With designer brands grabbing increasing shares of the underwear market, and with the company fighting an image as an old-fashioned, uptight maker of white underwear, Jockey aimed to capture younger consumers while keeping its longstanding customers through the introduction of new, more fashionable products and a hipper marketing campaign.

In March 1998 Jockey, with the help of its new ad agency, Grey Advertising, launched a campaign dubbed "Let 'em know you're Jockey." Among the products pushed were a new line called Jockey Sport featuring such items as boxer briefs in bright colors. In the ads, male and female models dropped their trousers to show the world that they proudly wore Jockey underwear. David Drescher, vice-president for marketing and advertising, told the *New York Times,* "We want to spark Jockey with a new spirit, breathe new life into the Jockey name, get Jockey talked about." The campaign was the subject of much media attention.

In addition to its new ad campaign, Jockey International also worked to expand through licensing agreements. Most notable was an agreement with Liz Claiborne whereby Jockey would make and market bras, panties, daywear, foundations, and related accessories under a new brand called Liz Claiborne Intimates, which was launched in early 2000. This was Jockey's first license in women's wear. Other turn of the millennium initiatives included the launching in the spring of 1999 of the first line of Jockey bras, an increased use of outside sourcing, and the shift of more operations offshore, specifically packaging facilities.

In December 2000, Donna Wolf Steigerwaldt died, and leadership of the company passed in 2001 to her daughter, Debra Waller. Waller described herself, according to an interview in *WWD* (August 29, 2005), as the "brand soul chairman," and she had been working for the company for the past 19 years. While respecting her mother's vision, the new chief executive had her own plans, specifically to organize the brand image internationally and to expand licensing opportunities. Waller also said she wanted to keep growing the company, but at a moderate pace. "I like steady growth," she told *WWD* (July 2, 2001), "and we plan to be here another 125 years." Under Waller's leadership, the company changed its advertising agency and began sorting out the way Jockey was portrayed in different overseas markets.

Jockey's new advertising agency was a small New York firm called Octopus. Its new campaign ran with the tag line "The next best thing to naked," and it played up both the underwear's comfort and its stylishness. Comfort seemed to be Jockey's overriding theme over the next few years. It used this theme to unify its many products, including licensed products such as bedding and home textiles. The company introduced seamless microfiber women's underwear in 2001, said to be a more comfortable alternative to cotton underwear. The line also answered competition in women's underwear from Hanes. Then in 2002, Octopus designed an "underwear-free" ad campaign for Jockey. This highlighted all the ancillary products Jockey sold, such as sleepwear, activewear, pajamas and bathrobes, and baby clothing.

While comfort was the thread that tied together Jockey's products domestically in the 2000s, in overseas markets the brand's image was more mixed. International marketing increased in the 2000s, with the company moving into China in 2001 and increasing its presence in key European countries. In some markets, such as Germany, Jockey was positioned as a designer line, while in others, it was more of a mid-market line. The company had tried, apparently without much success, to alter its image in the United Kingdom in the late 1990s, trying to project a more youthful face. In the mid-2000s, U.K. marketing pushed Jockey's women's lines. Much British and European marketing of women's underwear seemed actually geared towards men, with some too revealing ads from one of Jockey's competitors actually squelched in France. Jockey's new approach was to stress comfort and quality. Jockey was seen as perhaps precipitating a wholesale change in the way women's undergarments were marketed in Europe. Jockey's U.K. subsidiary picked a new chief of marketing in 2003. Her job was described as specifically to target women and to make the Jockey brand appeal to younger, more style-conscious consumers of either gender.

Jockey continued to close down some of its older facilities in the 2000s, while expanding others. Three plants in Kentucky closed in 2004, while plants in Georgia, North Carolina, and in Honduras took on more production. Meanwhile, the company experimented with new fabrics and designs. In 2005 Jockey came out with a new line of women's underwear called "3-D Contours," made of a stretchy viscose material. It also redesigned its matching bra lines for an improved and simplified fit. The company's 2005 advertising used the tag line "Are you comfortable being …". Jockey emphasized the comfort theme even more by launching a magazine in late 2004 called *Being.* The magazine's credo was "Connecting People with Comfort," and it ran articles on various subjects such as comfort foods, wild horses, and backyard getaways. The magazine continued to appear in 2005. While it contained fashion spreads of models in Jockey underwear and garments, it also pushed what Jockey CEO Waller described (*WWD,* August 29, 2005) as a "stop-and-smell-the-roses approach." This seemed to show the company's expanding vision of what its products were or could represent to consumers.

Elizabeth Rourke
Updated, David E. Salamie; A. Woodward

PRINCIPAL COMPETITORS

Calvin Klein Inc.; Fruit of the Loom, Inc.; Sara Lee Branded Apparel; Intimate Brands, Inc.

FURTHER READING

Abend, Jules, "Jockey Colors Its World," *Bobbin*, February 1999, pp. 50-54.

Askin, Ellen, "Jockey, It Ain't Just Boxers," *Daily News Record*, October 21, 2002, p. 8.

Backmann, Dave, "Emma, 40, Named to Lead Jockey," *Kenosha News*, May 16, 1995, p. 1.

———, "Jockey in National Spotlight," *Kenosha News*, March 5, 1998, p. C6.

———, "Jockey Park Dedicated: Time Capsule Buried During Ceremony," *Kenosha News*, May 22, 1993.

Cardona, Mercedes M., "Player Profile: Lockard Is Eager for Brief Marketing Effort at Jockey," *Advertising Age*, September 3, 2001, p. 18.

Elliott, Stuart, "Jockey Tries to Update the Image of Its Underwear Line," *New York Times*, March 4, 1998, p. D6.

Feitelberg, Rosemary, "Jockey Revamp Splits It into Five Separate Firms," *Women's Wear Daily*, October 9, 1995, p. 11.

Friedman, Arthur, "Liz Claiborne, Jockey Sign Pact for Innerwear," *Women's Wear Daily*, September 24, 1998, p. 4.

Gray, Jacquelyn, "Jockey: Kenosha Firm's History Makes a Splash in New York," *Milwaukee Journal*, June 21, 1992, p. G6.

Guilford, Roxanna, "Understanding the Challenges of Underwear," *Apparel Industry Magazine*, November 1999, pp. 50, 52-53.

Hajewski, Doris, "In Brief, Jockey Aims for Fun," *Milwaukee Journal Sentinel*, April 5, 1998, p. 1.

Hart, Elena, "Hilfiger Launches Ad Campaign and New Underwear Collection: Line Is Licensed to Jockey International," *Daily News Record*, June 28, 1994, p. 8.

———, "Tommy Hilfiger Licenses Jockey for Underwear Line for '94," *Daily News Record*, September 22, 1993, pp. 2+.

"In This Suit, Lawyers Will Argue About Briefs," *New York Times*, June 3, 1993, p. D4.

"Jockey Creates a State of Being," *WWD*, August 29, 2005, p. 10.

"Jockey Picks Ellesse Chief for Top UK Job," *Marketing Week*, July 22, 2004, p. 12.

"Jockey's Field Is Widening in Merchandise Mix," *Daily News Record*, March 17, 1989, p. 7.

Lloyd, Brenda, "Jerzees—Labeled for Undercover Action: Jockey Licenses Russell's Brand for Sports Briefs Line," *Daily News Record*, June 30, 1997, p. 12.

McKinney, Melonee, "Jockey Gallops into Global Marketing: Company Also Set to Battle Designer Lines As Level of Underwear Fashions Rise," *Daily News Record*, January 16, 1998, pp. 4+.

Molaro, Regina, "The Right Fit," *License!* November 2004, p. 16.

Monget, Karyn, "Jockey Acquires Appel's Formfit Seamless Panties," *Women's Wear Daily*, January 8, 1997, p. 23.

———, "Jockey at 125: A Long Journey," *WWD*, July 2, 2001, p. 7.

———, "Jockey Sizes Up a New Line of Bras," *Women's Wear Daily*, March 8, 1999, p. 28.

Munde, Jeannine, "Jockey's Golden Success Story: The Cotton Brief," *Daily News Record*, September 17, 1984, p. 8.

Nolan, Kelly, "This Fall, Intimates Manufacturers Have a Fit," *DSN Retailing Today*, September 12, 2005, p. 19.

Palumbo, Sandra, "Women's Line Is Blooming for Jockey As Division Builds Toward 40% of Firm," *Women's Wear Daily*, February 12, 1987, pp. 10+.

Parr, Jan, "The Woman's Touch," *Forbes*, October 27, 1986, pp. 332+.

Sandler, Larry, "Jockey Will Close Plant in Kenosha," *Milwaukee Sentinel*, October 23, 1993, p. 1A.

Sharoff, Robert, "Jockey Gallops into Mass Market Riding New Brands," *Daily News Record*, December 17, 1990, pp. 18+.

Smarr, Susan L., "Chairman Holds a Steady Rein," *Bobbin*, September 1988, pp. 178+.

———, "Thoroughbred Takes Jockey to the Winner's Circle," *Bobbin*, September 1988, pp. 170+.

Thomas, Daniel, "Can Jockey Gee Up Its Image with the Ladies?" *Marketing Week*, November 20, 2003, p. 20.

"Why Jockey Switched Its Ads from TV to Print," *Business Week*, July 26, 1976, p. 140.

Koch Industries, Inc.

———— ■ ————

4111 East 37th Street North
Wichita, Kansas 67220-3203
U.S.A.
Telephone: (316) 828-5500
Fax: (316) 828-5739
Web site: http://www.kochind.com

Private Company
Incorporated: 1942 as Rock Island Oil & Refining
  Company
Employees: 85,000
Sales: $60 billion (2005 est.)
NAIC: 112111 Beef Cattle Ranching and Farming;
  321211 Hardwood Veneer and Plywood Manu-
  facturing; 321219 Reconstituted Wood Product
  Manufacturing; 322110 Pulp Mills; 322121 Paper
  (Except Newsprint) Mills; 322130 Paperboard Mills;
  322210 Paperboard Container Manufacturing;
  322232 Envelope Manufacturing; 322233 Sta-
  tionery, Tablet, and Related Product Manu-
  facturing; 322291 Sanitary Paper Product Manu-
  facturing; 324110 Petroleum Refineries; 325211
  Plastics Material and Resin Manufacturing; 333999
  All Other Miscellaneous General Purpose Machinery
  Manufacturing; 424710 Petroleum Bulk Stations
  and Terminals; 486110 Pipeline Transportation of
  Crude Oil; 486210 Pipeline Transportation of
  Natural Gas; 486910 Pipeline Transportation of
  Refined Petroleum Products

■ ■ ■

Following its December 2005 purchase of Georgia-Pacific Corporation, Koch Industries, Inc. became the largest privately held firm in the United States. In addition to Georgia-Pacific, a leading producer of tissue and paper products (including the consumer brands Quilted Northern, Dixie, and Brawny) and building materials, Koch (pronounced COKE) controls a diverse array of other companies, many of which are involved in commodity-based industries. Flint Hills Resources, LP, operates refineries in Alaska, Minnesota, and Texas with a combined crude oil processing capacity of nearly 800,000 barrels per day. Koch Pipeline Company, L.P. controls 4,000 miles of pipeline that transport crude oil, refined petroleum products, and natural gas liquids. IN-VISTA B.V. specializes in fibers, intermediates, and polymers and owns several well-known brands, including Lycra and Stainmaster. Matador Cattle Company operates ranches in Montana, Kansas, and Texas comprising a total of 445,000 acres and about 15,000 head of cattle. Other Koch companies are involved in chemicals, minerals, commodity trading, and financial services.

This powerful assortment of assets is owned and run by Charles G. and David Koch, two of the four sons of Fred C. Koch, founder of the company. The various Koch companies operate independently under a homegrown free-market philosophy called market-based management, which essentially encourages employees to think as entrepreneurs, and to constantly question themselves and their colleagues. Another hallmark of Koch's success has been the willingness of the owners to plow 90 percent of earnings each year back into the business, a strategy that yielded an exponential growth rate of

Koch Industries is perhaps best viewed as a collection of capabilities continually searching for new ways to create value in society. Koch companies' ability to apply those capabilities—Market Based Management and operations, trading, transaction, and public sector excellence determines their success in providing superior value to customers and adding real value in society.

Koch companies are focused on long-term value creation in a myriad of industries worldwide. Their employees bring a disciplined, strategic approach to these industries, and strive for continuous improvement in compliance and performance. Underlying the management philosophy and its day-to-day execution is the expectation that each Koch company employee will be both entrepreneur and responsible citizen.

The success achieved in the past—and any future success—is a direct result of Koch companies' commitment to live by a set of Guiding Principles that includes integrity, humility, intellectual honesty and respect for others, as well as a commitment to principled entrepreneurship.

1,600 percent during the period from 1961 to 2005. Koch is tra-ditionally a very secretive company, but the various lawsuits and investigations into the company's practices that proliferated from the 1980s to the early 2000s served to pull away some of its veil. The company was propelled further into the spotlight following its high-profile acquisitions of INVISTA and Georgia-Pacific in 2004 and 2005, respectively.

FOUNDER BATTLING BIG OIL, MAKING INITIAL FORTUNE IN SOVIET UNION

The son of a Texas newspaperman, Fred C. Koch earned an engineering degree at Massachusetts Institute of Technology in the 1920s. In the late 1920s Koch invented a new and more efficient method for the thermal cracking of crude oil, the process by which oil is heated to effect a recombination of molecules yielding higher proportions of usable compounds, especially gasoline. With the dramatic growth in the use of the automobile in the first quarter of the 20th century, refiners were constantly trying to improve their cracking technology, and Fred Koch's innovation was apparently

good enough to draw upon him the wrath of the major oil companies. Protective of their tight control over every aspect of the oil business, the majors began a series of lawsuits against Fred Koch that would last 20 years and involve over 40 separate cases, eventually being resolved in 1952 when Koch won a $1.5 million settlement. Then as now, the international oil business was in the hands of only a few firms, which meant that Fred Koch would encounter the same obstacles wherever oil was bought and sold.

In the late 1920s there was at least one country in the world where oil was not bought and sold in the usual sense: the Soviet Union. The Soviets had been trying to take advantage of their immense oil reserves since gaining power in 1917, and under Joseph Stalin the drive to industrial efficiency was pursued with ruthless speed but without the benefit of Western technology. Fred Koch offered to build oil refineries in the Soviet Union that would be more efficient than those in the West. The young engineer's ideas were welcomed, and he was awarded a large contract to coincide with Stalin's first five-year plan, beginning in 1929. The contract called for construction of 15 refineries for an initial fee of $5 million, from which Koch and his partner, L. E. Winkler, are said to have netted a $500,000 profit. Koch's work in the Soviet Union necessitated sojourns in that country, offering the Texas farmboy an intimate look at the Soviet system while providing the cash he would later need in building his U.S. empire. The Winkler-Koch Engineering venture lasted until 1932.

By the late 1940s Koch had achieved a truce with his adversaries in the oil industry and begun assembling bits and pieces of business in the Midwest. Having been burned severely by the majors the first time around, Koch carefully avoided head-to-head competition with the industry leaders, instead developing a knack for discovering unexploited niches and an ability to turn a profit on even the smallest orders. In an age of massive, worldwide integration in the oil industry, Koch concentrated on service businesses too small to interest the majors and too obscure to attract much competition. While the majors largely controlled oil at the wellhead, they still required an ever growing network of pipelines and trucks to convey the oil to the refinery, thence to the mass of distributors, wholesalers, and retailers involved in its final sale. As the country's dependence on oil grew, so too did the need for more complete systems of oil distribution, and Fred Koch amassed a fortune in providing the equipment and expertise to meet that need.

Koch's main vehicle in the oil business was a company called Rock Island Oil & Refining Company, based in Wichita, Kansas. Rock Island was originally

```
┌─────────────────────────────────────────────┐
│                                               │
│              KEY DATES                        │
│                   ■                           │
│                                               │
│  1940:  Fred C. Koch founds Wood River Oil &  │
│         Refining Company.                     │
│  1942:  Rock Island Oil & Refining Company is │
│         incorporated.                         │
│  1946:  Wood River merges with Rock Island    │
│         Oil & Refining Company.               │
│  1967:  Koch dies, leaving Rock Island and    │
│         various subsidiaries to his sons;     │
│         Charles G. Koch takes over            │
│         leadership.                           │
│  1968:  Company is renamed Koch Industries,   │
│         Inc.                                  │
│  1983:  Charles and David Koch buy out        │
│         William and Frederick Koch's          │
│         interests in the company.             │
│  2004:  Koch acquires DuPont's INVISTA        │
│         textile unit for $4.2 billion.        │
│  2005:  In a deal valued at $21 billion in    │
│         cash and assumed debt, Koch           │
│         acquires the building products and    │
│         paper company Georgia-Pacific         │
│         Corporation.                          │
│                                               │
└─────────────────────────────────────────────┘
```

incorporated in 1942; Koch acquired the firm in 1946, combining it with his own firm, Wood River Oil & Refining Company, founded in 1940. While busy picking up bargains in businesses from trucks to coal mines, Koch fiercely guarded the privacy of his company, ensuring that it would not only remain under family control but also stay far from the prying eyes of government and the media alike. It is reported that a number of Koch's good friends in the Soviet oil industry were liquidated during Stalin's purges of the 1930s, an experience that only confirmed his belief, perhaps originally instilled by the battering he took at the hands of big oil, that business is best conducted silently.

Rock Island Oil & Refining had no public relations department, having no relations with the public, and the Koch family went out of its way to avoid doing business with the government. Fred Koch's particular aversion to Soviet communism took a more direct form in 1958 when he helped found the John Birch Society, an ultraconservative group which soon became notorious for its warnings about the threat of communism to U.S. society. Charles Koch, the second of Fred Koch's four sons, would later pour millions of dollars into the Libertarian Party, a proponent of minimal governmental interference in the affairs of business, and was also a cofounder of the libertarian think tank the Cato Institute.

Like his father, Charles Koch earned an engineering degree at Massachusetts Institute of Technology, and then spent several years working for a business consulting firm before joining Rock Island Oil in 1961. Frederick Koch, Fred Koch's eldest son, did not participate in the oil business. Charles Koch took over leadership of Koch Engineering, one of the family's many concerns, and helped make it into the world's largest manufacturer of mass transfer equipment for the chemical industry. By the time of Fred Koch's death in 1967, sales at Rock Island and the various Koch subsidiaries had reached about $400 million, presenting the 32-year-old Charles Koch with a weighty responsibility. Charles Koch was not only a capable leader in his own right but also enjoyed the continued presence of his father's top aide, Sterling Varner. Varner had already won a reputation as a shrewd buyer of what he referred to as "junk," the bankrupt or unwanted oil and gas properties that Rock Island habitually turned into profitable acquisitions. Under the ambitious administration of Charles Koch, Varner kept a low profile but was widely credited with supplying the savvy behind the company's rapid expansion.

Charles Koch brought a young man's energy to the company. From the new Wichita corporate headquarters of the renamed Koch Industries, Inc. (the name assumed in 1968), Charles Koch oversaw his company's diversification into a number of new areas, including petrochemicals, oil trading services, and ownership of a refinery in St. Paul, Minnesota. In 1969 Koch Industries merged with Atlas Petroleum Limited of the Bahamas, a distributor of crude oil and petroleum products with about $100 million a year in sales. The next few years saw the arrival at Koch of Charles's twin younger brothers, William and David, both of whom took executive positions with the company. While sharing their father's basic preference for privacy, the brothers gradually let it be known that Koch Industries was a far larger concern than imagined. In 1974 the family admitted to owning some 10,000 miles of pipeline in the Midwest and Canada, hundreds of tank trucks, barges, deepwater terminals, and storage facilities of every description. Through this system Koch distributed about 800,000 barrels of oil each day, some of it refined at its St. Paul refinery, some sold via the company's several hundred gas stations, but most of it transported to and from the major oil companies. Koch also participated in the rush to buy supertankers, owning a handful of the huge ships to complement its oil trading offices in eight countries. Finally, the company had begun its own program of oil exploration and drilling, and also owned around 60,000 head of cattle. Sales reached more than $2 billion in

1974, the first full year of post-OPEC price inflation in the oil business.

The OPEC price hikes of the early 1970s effectively killed the supertanker business, however, forcing Koch to sell all but one of its ships at salvage prices. Nevertheless, the dramatic run-up in oil prices during the 1970s helped Koch increase its revenue sevenfold in a matter of years. By 1981 its sales had reached $14 billion, 56 times their level in 1967, Charles Koch's first year as head of the company, and in some quarters Koch was beginning to be called an oil major in its own right. The company picked up a second refinery in 1981, paying $265 million for a Sun Company plant in Corpus Christi, Texas, and had greatly expanded its capacity in gas-liquids fractionating and asphalt production, to name only two of its myriad activities. While Koch had little luck in its exploration efforts, in 1979 the company moved decisively into the real estate business, joining Wichita businessman George Ablah in the formation of Abko Realty Inc. Abko was created specifically to buy Chrysler Realty Corporation and its several hundred Chrysler dealership sites around the country. It is believed that the hard-pressed Chrysler sold the unit for less than $100 million in cash.

FAMILY FEUD IN 1979 CULMINATING IN FIRST OF SEVERAL LAWSUITS

The year 1979 also marked the beginning of the feud that eventually would split the Koch family. William Koch, five years younger than Charles, grew restive with his secondary role at Koch and began pressing his brother for more power, freer access to information, and some means by which a fair market value could be assigned to the company's stock. As a private company, the only likely buyers of Koch stock were other stockholders, who, in the absence of an open market, would pay far less than the shares might otherwise fetch. William Koch gained the support of the oldest brother, Frederick, until then relatively uninvolved in company affairs, and the two of them launched a proxy fight in 1980 aimed at ousting Charles from his leadership. The attempt failed, and after a round of lawsuits and mudslinging, William and Frederick Koch were bought out in 1983 by Charles and David Koch for around $1.1 billion in cash. From that time through 2001, William Koch continued to wage legal and emotional warfare against Charles Koch, going so far as to hire private detectives to gather evidence of wrongdoing by Koch Industries that was subsequently handed over to federal investigators. In 1987 the Justice Department announced it was investigating several companies on price-fixing charges, a Koch unit among them.

Later in the 1980s a U.S. Senate investigation forced Koch Industries further into the limelight. In 1989 the Senate looked into charges that Koch had been stealing oil from Native Americans in Oklahoma by deliberately mismeasuring the crude oil it was buying. A committee concluded that Koch had stolen $31 million in oil over a three-year period. Koch vigorously denied the charges, and hired public relations experts for the first time to fight the battle of public opinion. The committee submitted its findings to the Justice Department, which three years later dropped the case. William Koch did not let the matter drop, however, and subsequently filed yet another lawsuit, this one for $400 million, alleging that Koch Industries had defrauded the federal government by stealing oil on federal land.

The parade of litigation continued for Koch in April 1995 when the Justice Department, the Environmental Protection Agency, and the Coast Guard filed suit against the company for allegedly being responsible for more than 300 separate oil spills since 1990. The government claimed that 55,000 barrels of oil were spilled from Koch pipelines, some of which polluted wetlands and, in the biggest offense, Corpus Christi Bay on the coast of Texas. Koch, which faced a penalty as high as $55 million but was likely to pay only $5 million or $6 million, claimed that more than half of the spills cited by the government had never happened.

MORE DEALMAKING IN THE 1990S AND EARLY 2000S

Meanwhile, Charles Koch continued to build the company through wheeling and dealing in the 1990s. Among the deals were: the $21 million purchase of a marine terminal and other pipeline and oil gathering systems from Ashland Oil Inc.'s Scurlock Permian Corp. in 1991; the 1992 purchase of the 9,271-mile United Gas Pipe Line Co., with annual sales of $370 million and a valuation of $1.1 billion; the early-1995 acquisition of a second refinery in Corpus Christi, Texas, from Kerr-McGee Corp.; the formation of Koch Paper Technology Group in mid-1995 to consolidate Koch's activities in the pulp and paper industry; and the $250 million acquisition in mid-1997 of Glitsch International Inc., a supplier of products and services to the petroleum and chemical industries, from Foster Wheeler Corp.

By 1996 Koch Industries had revenues of about $30 billion, a 300-fold increase in the previous 30 years. It operated more than 40,000 miles of pipeline, refined about 540,000 barrels of crude oil a day, was the largest buyer and seller of asphalt in the country, ranked in the top ten among U.S. calf producers, and was the country's 34th largest landowner (according to *Worth* magazine). These diverse operations, many of which were often overlooked businesses that Koch specialized in making money from, together formed one of the world's great private fortunes. As a private company, Koch had the advantage of being able to move fast to pick up undervalued assets as soon as they became available.

Though private and historically publicity-shy, Koch opened up a bit more in 1997 when it created a company web site. That year the company made an estimated profit of $600 million on revenues of $30 billion. At this time Koch was becoming more heavily involved overseas and was working to beef up its capital services unit, which was involved in oil, commodities, and currency trading through offices in Wichita, London, and Singapore. Further acquisitions in the late 1990s included Purina Mills, Inc., a maker of livestock feed purchased for $670 million in March 1998. This proved to be a brief chapter in Koch's history as economic turmoil in Asia and Latin America undercut U.S. grain and livestock exports, sending the U.S. farm economy into recession. Collapsing hog prices forced Purina Mills to file for bankruptcy protection in late 1999. It emerged from bankruptcy protection the next year, when it also went public, but then Land O'Lakes, Inc. acquired it in 2001.

A more lasting venture also began in 1998 when Koch joined with the Saba family of Mexico to acquire Hoechst AG's Trevira unit, which specialized in advanced polyester resins and synthetic fibers. The acquired assets formed the basis for the 50-50 joint venture KoSa B.V. In 2001 Koch bought out the Saba family, gaining full control of KoSa. Also in 2001, Koch joined with the utility company Entergy Corp. to form an energy marketing and trading company with more than $1 billion in assets. Late in 2004 Merrill Lynch & Co., Inc. bought the Entergy-Koch venture for an undisclosed sum.

In the meantime, the Koch family feud continued, as did the various lawsuits against the company. In 1998 a jury finally heard William Koch's claim that his brothers Charles and David had cheated him out of more than $1 billion in the 1983 buyout deal, but they ruled in favor of the latter. William Koch, however, got a measure of revenge one year later, through his whistle-blower lawsuit against Koch Industries, claiming that the company had underreported the amount and quality of oil it had purchased from federal and Native American leases between 1985 and 1989. A jury found in his favor, leaving the company open to penalties potentially totaling as much as $286 million. After Koch appealed the verdict, the parties settled the lawsuit in May 2001, with the terms not being disclosed. At this time, the

brothers buried their hatchets, agreeing not to sue each other again and even had dinner together for the first time in 20 years.

There were other legal challenges to the company, however, particularly on the environmental front. In 1999 a Koch subsidiary pled guilty to charges that it had negligently allowed aviation fuel to leak into waters near the Mississippi River from its refinery in Rosemount, Minnesota, and that it had illegally dumped a million gallons of high-ammonia wastewater onto the ground and into the Mississippi. The company agreed to pay several million dollars in fines and for remediation. In January 2000 Koch agreed to pay a $30 million fine to settle the lawsuits that had been filed in connection with its involvement in more than 300 oil spills from its pipelines and oil facilities in six states. But this fine, at the time the largest civil environmental penalty in U.S. history, was severely reduced after George W. Bush took office in 2001. In a similar development, Koch in late 2000 faced a 97-count federal indictment charging it with covering up illegal releases of 91 metric tons of benzene, a known carcinogen, from its Corpus Christi refinery. Initially facing possible fines totaling $350 million, Koch reached a deal with Bush's first Attorney General, John Ashcroft, in which all major charges were dropped, and the company pled guilty to falsifying documents and settled the lawsuit for just $20 million.

BLOCKBUSTER DEALS FOR INVISTA AND GEORGIA-PACIFIC: 2004 AND 2005

Already one of the most powerful industrial corporations in the United States, Koch Industries grew substantially and greatly widened its interests with two blockbuster deals, each in turn the largest in company history, completed in 2004 and 2005. In May 2004 Koch acquired the INVISTA textile unit from E. I. du Pont de Nemours and Company for $4.2 billion. INVISTA was comprised of DuPont's nylon, polyester, and Lycra fiber businesses and boasted a number of well-known brand names, including Lycra, Stainmaster, Antron, Coolmax, and Thermolite. Its manufacturing base encompassed the United States, Canada, the Netherlands, Germany, the United Kingdom, Brazil, and Singapore. Annual revenues at INVISTA were approximately $6 billion, and its workforce totaled 18,000 employees worldwide. Koch's KoSa unit was subsequently merged into INVISTA, whose headquarters were shifted to Wichita.

Koch next turned its attention to the pulp and paper industry. In May 2004 the company acquired the nonintegrated fluff and market pulp operations of Georgia-Pacific Corporation for $610 million and began operating them as Koch Cellulose, LLC. Koch then returned the following year with an offer to buy all of Georgia-Pacific, and a deal was struck in November 2005 and completed the following month. The price was a staggering $13.2 billion in cash plus the assumption of $7.8 billion in Georgia-Pacific debt. The Atlanta-based company was a forest-product industry giant, specializing in tissue, packaging, paper, building products, and related chemicals. It was one of the nation's leading suppliers of building products to lumber dealers and major home improvement retailers, and its portfolio included a number of well-known consumer tissue brands—including Quilted Northern, Angel Soft, Brawny, and Vanity Fair—and the Dixie brand of disposable cups, plates, and cutlery. Its workforce was comprised of 55,000 employees in North America and Europe. Following the deal, Koch Cellulose was integrated back into Georgia-Pacific, which continued to operate under the same name as an independently managed company based in Atlanta. A. D. (Pete) Correll, the head of Georgia-Pacific, continued to serve as chairman, but Koch shifted its president and chief operating officer, Joseph W. Moeller, over to be president and CEO of Georgia-Pacific. Dave Robertson, a Koch executive vice-president and former head of Flint Hills Resources, its petroleum and chemicals subsidiary, was named president and COO of Koch Industries.

With the addition of Georgia-Pacific's $20 billion in annual revenues, Koch's revenues were expected to top $80 billion starting in 2006, making the firm the nation's largest private company, surpassing Cargill, Incorporated. This fact, coupled with Koch's ownership of Georgia-Pacific, a high-profile consumer-products company, seemed destined to bring more attention to the traditionally secretive company, but Charles Koch was determined to continue to run Koch Industries in the same way: using market-based management, reinvesting 90 percent of earnings back into the company, and, as a private company that did not need to worry about satisfying Wall Street quarter after quarter, building and investing for the long term.

Jonathan Martin
Updated, David E. Salamie

PRINCIPAL SUBSIDIARIES

The C. Reiss Coal Company; Flint Hills Resources, LP; Georgia-Pacific Corporation; INVISTA B.V.; John Zink Company LLC; KMC Enterprises, LLC; Koch Carbon, LLC; Koch Cellulose, LLC; Koch Exploration Company, LLC; Koch Financial Corporation; Koch Genesis Company, LLC; Koch-Glitsch, LP; Koch Mineral Services, LLC; Koch Nitrogen Company; Koch Pipeline Company, L.P.; Koch Pulp & Paper Trading, LLC; Koch

Supply & Trading, LLC; Matador Cattle Company; Oasis Capital Markets, LP; Flint Hills Resources, S.à r.l. (Belgium); Koch Carbon Belgium BVBA; Koch International B.V. (Belgium); Koch-Glitsch France, S.à r.l.; Koch Membrane Systems GmbH (Germany); Koch-Glitsch Italia, S.à r.l. (Italy); John Zink International, S.àr.l. (Luxembourg); Flint Hills Resources BV (Netherlands); Koch HC Partnership BV (Netherlands); Koch Cellulose GmbH (Switzerland); Koch Minerals S.A. (Switzerland); Koch Engineering Company Ltd. (U.K.).

PRINCIPAL COMPETITORS

International Paper Company; ChevronTexaco Corporation; Kimberly-Clark Corporation; ConocoPhillips; Valero Energy Corporation; The Procter & Gamble Company.

FURTHER READING

Berkowitz, Bill, "The Biggest Company You Never Heard Of," *Global Information Network,* January 5, 2006.

Berman, Dennis K., and Chad Terhune, "Koch Industries to Buy Georgia-Pacific," *Wall Street Journal,* November 14, 2005, p. A3.

Bond, Patti, "The Georgia-Pacific/Koch Deal: Free-Market Management Style on Way," *Atlanta Journal-Constitution,* November 20, 2005, p. Q1.

Grant, Jeremy, "The Private Empire of Koch Industries," *Financial Times,* January 30, 2004.

Griekspoor, Phyllis Jacobs, "Boundless Koch: Downturn Sets Stage for Expansion," *Wichita Eagle,* September 14, 2003.

———, "Koch Industries Subsidiary to Buy Portion of Lumber Giant Georgia-Pacific," *Wichita Eagle,* January 30, 2004.

Herrick, Thaddeus, "DuPont to Sell Textiles Unit to Koch," *Wall Street Journal,* November 18, 2003, p. A6.

"High Profit, Low Profile," *Forbes,* July 15, 1974.

Kilman, Scott, "Koch Industries Expands Its Operations in Agriculture, Seeks More Purchases," *Wall Street Journal,* March 20, 1998, p. B7A.

———, "Koch Industries' Purina Subsidiary Files for Bankruptcy-Court Protection," *Wall Street Journal,* October 29, 1999, p. B12.

"Koch Industries, Inc.: Sons Make a Global Enterprise Flower in Kansas," *Nation's Business,* February 1970.

"Koch Industries to Acquire Georgia-Pacific in $48 Per Share Cash Transaction," *Pulp and Paper,* December 2005, p. 6.

Kraar, Louis, "Family Feud at a Corporate Colossus," *Fortune,* July 26, 1982.

Kratzer, Dave, "Koch at a Crossroads," *Wichita Business Journal,* October 6, 2000, p. 21.

———, "'New Koch' Aims to Be More Competitive," *Wichita Business Journal,* January 14, 2000, p. 1.

Kurt, Kelly, "Jury: Koch Industries Cheated in Oil Buys," *Topeka Capital-Journal,* December 24, 1999, p. A1.

McMillin, Molly, "Koch Has Grown Quickly, Quietly," *Wichita Eagle,* March 23, 1997.

O'Reilly, Brian, "The Curse on the Koch Brothers," *Fortune,* February 17, 1997, pp. 78-84.

Petzinger, Thomas, Jr., "Charles Koch Teaches Staff to Run a Firm Like a Free Nation," *Wall Street Journal,* April 18, 1997, p. B1.

Smith, Rebecca, "Entergy and Koch Industries to Form $1 Billion Energy-Marketing Company," *Wall Street Journal,* April 24, 2000, p. A15.

———, "Merrill Lynch Agrees to Acquire Entergy-Koch Trading Business," *Wall Street Journal,* September 3, 2004, p. C4.

Suber, Jim, "Koch Industries: 'The Kansas Business Connection,'" *Topeka Capital-Journal,* May 5, 1997.

Tomsho, Robert, "Blood Feud: Koch Family Is Roiled by Sibling Squabbling over Its Oil Empire," *Wall Street Journal,* August 9, 1989, pp. A1, A7.

Upbin, Bruce, and Brandon Copple, "Creative Destruction 101," *Forbes,* December 14, 1998, pp. 92, 96, 98.

Wald, Matthew L., "Conglomerate, Accused of Allowing Spills to Cut Costs, Is Fined $30 Million," *New York Times,* January 14, 2000, p. A21.

Wayne, Leslie, "Brother Versus Brother: Koch Family's Long Legal Feud Is Headed for a Jury," *New York Times,* April 28, 1998, p. D1.

———, "Pulling the Wraps Off Koch Industries," *New York Times,* November 20, 1994, pp. F1, F8, F9.

———, "Why an Apparent Mismatch Just Might Be a Perfect Fit," *New York Times,* November 15, 2005, p. C3.

Kohl's Corporation

———■———

N56 W17000 Ridgewood Drive
Menomonee Falls, Wisconsin 53051-5660
U.S.A.
Telephone: (262) 703-7000
Fax: (262) 703-6143
Web site: http://www.kohls.com

Public Company
Incorporated: 1988
Employees: 95,000
Sales: $11.7 billion (2004)
Stock Exchanges: New York
Ticker Symbol: KSS
NAIC: 452112 Discount Department Stores; 454111
   Electronic Shopping

■ ■ ■

Kohl's Corporation is one of the largest discount department store chains in the United States, with more than 730 outlets located in 41 states. Targeting middle-income shoppers buying for their families and homes, the chain maintains low retail prices through a low cost structure, limited staffing, and progressive management information systems, as well as the economical application of centralized buying, distribution, and advertising. This "Kohl's concept" has proven successful in both small and large markets, and in strip shopping centers, regional malls, and freestanding venues. The company's stores, which average 86,500 square feet in size, are designed for convenience in their location, layout, centralized checkouts, and deeply stocked merchandise. Kohl's also offers online shopping through its kohls.com web site.

1962-86: FROM GROCERY OFFSHOOT TO BATUS SUBSIDIARY TO INDEPENDENT, PRIVATE FIRM

The first Kohl's department store opened in Brookfield, Wisconsin, in 1962 as an offshoot of the Kohl's grocery chain, which had been founded in Milwaukee in the late 1920s by Max Kohl. In the mid-1960s the store positioned itself in a niche between higher-end department stores and discounters, the niche that later propelled Kohl's into a major nationwide chain. This positioning effort was led by William Kellogg, a twenty-something, who was hired after gaining experience in budget retailing from a stint at Milwaukee's Boston Store. By 1972 there were five Kohl's department stores.

That year, the chain's association with BATUS Inc., the U.S. division of BAT Industries plc, began. The parent was formed when James Buchanan Duke, founder of the American Tobacco Co., expanded his U.S. tobacco empire to Great Britain. His encroachment on the British market sparked a trade war, provoking several British tobacco companies to join forces as the Imperial Tobacco Group plc. Imperial succeeded in squelching Duke's British effort, then moved to invade the U.S. market. Taking the threat seriously, Duke negotiated a pact with Imperial Tobacco that formed the British-American Tobacco Co. Ltd. (BAT) in 1902 to manufacture and market the two companies' blends and brand names. When the U.S. Supreme Court found that BAT was a monopoly, it compelled American Tobacco to annul its

COMPANY PERSPECTIVES

■

Kohl's mission is to be the leading family-focused, value-oriented, specialty department store offering quality exclusive and national brand merchandise to the customer in an environment that is convenient, friendly and exciting.

territorial agreement with Imperial and divest its interest in BAT. Imperial kept its 33 percent interest in the company until 1972.

Following a tobacco industry trend, BAT began to diversify in the 1960s, purchasing several famous perfume houses. In the 1970s, the company formed a U.S. subsidiary, BATUS Inc., and began to acquire retail department stores. Wisconsin-based Kohl's Food and Department Stores was the British conglomerate's first acquisition in this arena; BATUS bought an 80 percent stake in the two-chain company in 1972 and took full control in 1978. By the early 1980s, BATUS had the 19th largest retail holdings in the United States, including Gimbels, Saks Fifth Avenue, and Marshall Field & Co. BATUS invested expansion capital into two of its acquisitions, Saks and Kohl's department stores.

By the mid-1980s, BATUS had more than doubled the number of Kohl's department stores to 34, but the chain was an anomaly in the upscale retail group with its "value-oriented," "bargain-basement" positioning. BATUS sold the food segment of Kohl's to the Great Atlantic & Pacific Tea Company, Inc. (A&P) in 1983, and began divesting its retail businesses. (A&P closed its remaining Kohl's grocery stores in September 2003.) In 1986 a management-led group of investors took the Kohl's department store chain's 40 stores in Wisconsin and Indiana private. Management spent the following three years refining the "Kohl's concept": moderately priced, quality apparel for middle-income families.

THE "KOHL'S CONCEPT"

The concept incorporated several factors. To set itself apart from mass merchandisers and discounters and become a specialty department store, over 80 percent of Kohl's merchandise carried national brand names recognized for quality. Kohl's also prided itself on stocking "narrow, but deep merchandise assortments," especially where advertised specials were concerned. At the same time, Kohl's eschewed the high-end and designer merchandise that characterized upscale depart-

ment stores. The chain dropped low-volume, low-margin departments such as candy, sewing notions, and hard sporting goods in favor of higher margin goods such as linens and jewelry.

Kohl's was able to price its merchandise more competitively by maintaining a low cost structure. The company kept consumer prices low and margins relatively high through lean staffing, state-of-the-art management information systems, and operating efficiencies that resulted from centralized buying, advertising, and distribution. Promotional and marketing partnerships with vendors also helped hold down overhead. For example, many of Kohl's 200 vendors used electronic data exchange (EDI) to submit advance shipment notices electronically, which made ordering more efficient. The chain used aggressive marketing and promotional events to position Kohl's as the "destination store." Once customers arrived, management hoped the stores' convenient layouts, clear signage, and centralized checkouts would encourage high store productivity.

Kohl's most impressive growth spurt began in 1988, when management and The Morgan Stanley Leveraged Equity Fund II, L.P. formed Kohl's Corporation and acquired Kohl's Department Stores. That same year, Kohl's purchased 26 MainStreet department stores from Federated Department Stores, which expanded the chain geographically into the Detroit, Minneapolis/St. Paul, Chicago, and Grand Rapids, Michigan, metropolitan areas and brought the chain's unit total to 66. The chain continued to grow internally as well, posting 8 to 10 percent store-for-store gains in 1989, 1990, and 1991 despite a recessed retail environment. From 1988 to 1992, sales increased from $388 million to $1 billion.

1990S: GOING PUBLIC, EXPANDING TO MORE THAN 250 STORES

Kohl's did not stop there. In 1992 the corporation prepared for further growth by expanding and upgrading its distribution facilities, automating merchandise handling, and making a public stock offering to finance projected openings of 14 to 16 additional stores annually. Kohl's enlisted the help of consultant group SDI Industries of Pacoima, California, to manage the automation and expansion of the chain's ten-year-old distribution center. The center, which supplied Kohl's stores with 98 percent of their merchandise, was expanded to 500,000 square feet, enough capacity to service 120 stores. Automation was achieved at a cost of $9.7 million. Completed in 1993, it encouraged higher productivity and lower turnaround time, and allowed vendors to send advance ship notices electronically and to pre-ticket merchandise. Construction on a second 650,000-square-foot distribution center was underway

KEY DATES

1962: Kohl's grocery chain opens the first Kohl's department store in Brookfield, Wisconsin.

1972: BATUS Inc., the U.S. division of BAT Industries plc, buys 80 percent stake in Kohl's.

1978: BATUS gains full control of Kohl's.

1986: A management-led group of investors takes Kohl's private.

1988: Company is reorganized as Kohl's Corporation; 26 MainStreet stores are acquired and melded into the now 66-unit chain.

1992: Company goes public.

1997: Kohl's opens a distribution center in Winchester, Virginia, to support an expansion into the Mid-Atlantic region.

1998: To support a westward push, Kohl's opens a distribution center in Blue Springs, Missouri.

2000: Kohl's begins offering online shopping at kohls.com.

2001: Backing expansion into the South Central United States is a new distribution center in Corsicana, Texas.

2002: In anticipation of West Coast store openings, Kohl's builds a distribution center in San Bernardino, California.

2003: With entry into California, Kohl's is now a coast-to-coast chain.

2005: Kohl's moves into the Florida market for the first time.

in Findley, Ohio, in 1993; completed in August 1994, this facility served stores in central Illinois, Ohio, Michigan, Indiana, Kentucky, Tennessee, and West Virginia.

Kohl's advanced toward the 120-store mark with the opening of eight new stores in 1992, expanding its geographical reach to Ohio. The chain added Iowa and South Dakota to its roster in 1993 and opened 11 new stores. Continuing its expansion, Kohl's opened 18 new stores in 1994, and 22 each in the following two years. Kohl's also continued to tinker with its store format, completing its phaseout of electronics in 1995.

To support a planned expansion eastward into the Mid-Atlantic region, the company built a third distribution center in Winchester, Virginia, which opened in the summer of 1997 with an initial capacity of 350,000

square feet (which was later expanded to 400,000). The Winchester center served Kohl's stores in New York, North Carolina, Pennsylvania, Virginia, Maryland, Delaware, and New Jersey. By 1998 Kohl's had stores in 22 states and the District of Columbia.

During 1999 the expansion emphasis was on the West, particularly Missouri and two new states, Colorado and Texas. To support its westward expansion, Kohl's in 1999 was building a fourth distribution center, a 542,000-square-foot facility in Blue Springs, Missouri, to handle 80 to 100 stores and to service units in Colorado, Texas, Kansas, Missouri, Nebraska, and central Iowa; this center opened in 2000. On the management front, William Kellogg, who had served as chairman and CEO since 1979, relinquished the CEO position to Larry Montgomery in February 1999. Montgomery also continued as vice-chairman, a position he assumed in March 1996; previously he served as executive vice-president of stores from February 1993 through February 1996. Also in early 1999 came the purchase of 33 stores previously operated by bankrupt Caldor Corporation. All but one of the stores was in the New York metro area, with the other in the Baltimore area. Kohl's converted the Caldor units to the Kohl's format during 2000. The purchase was funded through the issuance of 2.8 million shares of stock. From its emergence as a public company in 1992 to 1999, Kohl's more than tripled its number of stores, while its revenues quadrupled, from $1.1 billion to $4.56 billion.

EARLY 2000S: COAST TO COAST

In the face of the more uncertain economic climate of the early 2000s, Kohl's nevertheless forged ahead with its aggressive program of expansion. In 2000 the company opened 60 more stores and entered several new markets, particularly in the Northeast, including Connecticut, New Jersey, the New York metropolitan area, and Oklahoma. To support its move into e-commerce, Kohl's opened a 500,000-square-foot fulfillment center in Monroe, Ohio. For the year, the company posted a remarkable same-store sales increase of 9 percent as revenues jumped 35 percent to reach $6.15 billion and net income increased from $255 million to $367 million.

Of the 62 stores opened in 2001, more than a dozen blanketed the new market of Atlanta while other new markets included Oklahoma City, Austin, Fayetteville, and El Paso. To facilitate this drive into the south central United States, Kohl's opened a fifth distribution center, this one built in Corsicana, Texas. Around this time, Kohl's made an effort to upgrade its brand offerings, commissioning special lines from Jones Apparel Group, Inc. (the Nine & Co. brand) and Liz Claiborne, Inc. (Villager) and once again offering children's apparel from OshKosh B'Gosh, Inc.

Once again taking a blanket approach to new markets, Kohl's entered Boston with 13 stores and Houston with 12 stores in 2002. The company also opened its first stores in New Hampshire and Rhode Island, as well as Nashville, Tennessee. Overall, 75 stores were opened that year, bringing the chain total to 457. Sales passed the $9 billion mark, while net income totaled $635 million and same-store sales increased a still strong 5.3 percent. Late in the year Kohl's opened a 575,000-square-foot distribution center in San Bernardino, California, in advance of a West Coast expansion. In March 2003, shortly after Montgomery succeeded Kellogg as chairman, Kohl's stormed into California, opening no fewer than 28 stores in the Los Angeles area and making Kohl's a coast-to-coast retail chain. Later in the year, Kohl's expanded into Sacramento, San Diego, and Fresno, California, as well as San Antonio, and also entered both Nevada and Arizona with stores in Las Vegas, Phoenix, Tucson, and Flagstaff. The store total reached 542 with the opening of 85 more outlets.

Not all was well at Kohl's, however. Competition heated up as department stores, particularly J.C. Penney Corporation, Inc., and specialty apparel stores improved their performances; Kohl's also faced fierce competition in California in the form of entrenched players Mervyn's and Macy's West. Some analysts contended the big push into the Golden State had distracted management, and indeed the company suffered from excess inventory during the year, forcing it to discount heavily, which dented profits. Some shoppers turned to rival retailers when they encountered less-well-kept stores and longer checkout lines than usual. The resulting numbers were certainly disappointing: while revenues were up a still respectable 12.7 percent, surpassing $10 billion for the first time, net income fell for the first time in ten years, dropping 8.5 percent to $581 million, and same-store sales fell 1.6 percent.

During 2004 Kohl's concentrated on turning its performance around. The company reduced inventory levels, improved its in-store operations, and made some minor adjustments to the store design to make it easier for customers to navigate and to highlight various brands. On the merchandise side, Kohl's began introducing new merchandise into its store more frequently and perhaps most importantly moved aggressively to secure exclusive brands that could help differentiate the chain from its growing array of competitors. Seven new exclusive, private or national

brands were added in 2004. In home products, exclusive Laura Ashley Lifestyles and Gloria Vanderbilt lines debuted, as did a new apparel line from celebrity Daisy Fuentes. Kohl's also added a new category to its stores, cosmetics, via a partnership with Estée Lauder Companies Inc. This effort continued in 2005, and in the fall of that year Kohl's became the exclusive U.S. vendor of Candie's apparel as the retailer attempted to lure in young, fashion-conscious female consumers. The turnaround efforts began to pay off in 2004 as same-store sales were up 0.3 percent, and net income was a record $730 million on $11.7 billion in revenues. Kohl's opened 95 new stores during the year, entering several new markets in California along with Salt Lake City, Utah; Memphis, Tennessee; and Rochester, New York. The chain now extended to 637 stores in 40 states.

In 2005 Kohl's opened another 95 stores, most significantly entering the Florida market for the first time late in the year. To support this new southeastern push, the company opened its eighth distribution center, located in Macon, Georgia. Future plans were no less ambitious. Kohl's aimed to open approximately 500 stores between 2006 and 2010, seeking to create a chain of more than 1,200 outlets by the latter year. Plans for 2006 and 2007 included a push into the Northwest through store openings in Portland, Oregon, and Seattle, Washington. Kohl's also aimed to continue pursuing new exclusive merchandise offerings and was working on a new store design it planned to introduce in the fall of 2006.

April Dougal Gasbarre
Updated, David E. Salamie

PRINCIPAL SUBSIDIARIES

Kohl's Department Stores, Inc.; Kohl's Investment Corporation; Kohl's Illinois, Inc.; Kohl's Pennsylvania, Inc.; Kohl's New York DC, Inc.; Kohl's Texas, L.L.C.; Kohl's Texas Limited Partner, L.L.C.; Kohl's Texas, L.P.; Kohl's Indiana, Inc.; Kohl's Indiana, L.P.; Kohl's Michigan, L.P.

PRINCIPAL COMPETITORS

Wal-Mart Stores, Inc.; Target Corporation; J.C. Penney Corporation, Inc.; Sears Holding Corporation; Mervyn's, LLC; The TJX Companies, Inc.; Ross Stores, Inc.; Federated Department Stores, Inc.

FURTHER READING

Alpert, Bill, "Full-Priced Goods: Kohl's Has Charmed Wall Street and Main, but the Company's Growth May Start to Slow," *Barron's*, August 12, 2002, pp. 30-31.

Arbose, Jules, and Daniel Burstein, "BAT Moves Beyond Tobacco," *International Management,* August 1984, pp. 17-20.

"BATUS Battles Chilly Retail Climate," *Chain Store Age General Merchandise Trends,* June 1985, p. 62.

Berner, Robert, "Is Kohl's Coming Unbuttoned?," *Business Week,* July 28, 2003, p. 44.

Brookman, Faye, "Kohl's Updates DC," *Stores,* January 1992, pp. 142, 144.

Coleman, Calmetta, "Kohl's Retail Racetrack," *Wall Street Journal,* March 1, 2001, p. B1.

Croghan, Lore, "Kohl's: Discounted Discounter," *Financial World,* November 21, 1995, p. 22.

Duff, Christina, "Kohl's of the Midwest Maps an Invasion of Both Coasts," *Wall Street Journal,* May 12, 1994, p. B4.

Duff, Mike, "Kohl's Storms into Northeast Market," *Discount Store News,* April 3, 2000, pp. 1, 46.

———, "The Mid-Tier Titan with Discount Appeal," *Discount Store News,* December 14, 1998, p. 78.

Faircloth, Anne, "The Best Retailer You've Never Heard Of," *Fortune,* March 16, 1998, pp. 110-12.

Faust, Fred, "Kohl's to Enter St. Louis Area with Six Department Stores," *St. Louis Post-Dispatch,* August 12, 1999.

Forest, Stephanie Anderson, and Gerry Khermouch, "Don't Tell Kohl's There's a Slowdown," *Business Week,* February 12, 2001, p. 62.

Gentry, Connie Robbins, "Kohl's Goes West," *Chain Store Age,* March 2003, pp. 50F+.

Hajewski, Doris, "Kohl's Copes with Growing Pains," *Milwaukee Journal Sentinel,* October 13, 2003, p. 1D.

———, "Kohl's Corp. Heads into Florida As Part of 95-Store Expansion," *Milwaukee Journal Sentinel,* November 12, 2004.

———, "Kohl's Has Big Plans to Expand," *Milwaukee Journal Sentinel,* August 18, 2005, p. A1.

———, "Kohl's Learns to Say 'Grow' in Spanish: El Paso a Proving Ground for Chain," *Milwaukee Journal Sentinel,* June 23, 2002, p. 1A.

———, "Kohl's Narrows Its Focus," *Milwaukee Journal Sentinel,* October 6, 2002, p. 1D.

———, "Kohl's to Slow Store Openings in 2006," *Milwaukee Journal Sentinel,* November 11, 2005, p. D1.

———, "Kohl's Tweaks Garner Notice," *Milwaukee Journal Sentinel,* November 7, 2004.

Heller, Laura, "Kohl's to Continue Contiguous Growth," *Discount Store News,* June 7, 1999, pp. 7, 159.

Jagler, Steven, "Kohl's Corp. Marches into the South," *Business Journal-Milwaukee,* April 2, 1999, pp. 1+.

"Kohl's First $1 Billion," *Discount Merchandiser,* March 1993, p. 12.

"Kohl's Way: Narrow but Deep," *Discount Merchandiser,* March 1994, p. 20.

Merrick, Amy, "New Game at Kohl's: Dressing Up," *Wall Street Journal,* March 12, 2002, p. B1.

Merrick, Amy, and Sally Beatty, "Kohl's Plans Estée Lauder Counters," *Wall Street Journal,* October 28, 2003, p. A6.

Owens, Jennifer, "Kohl's March to the East Coast," *Women's Wear Daily,* March 12, 1997, pp. 22+.

"Rain Falls on Gimbels' Parade," *Chain Store Age Executive,* August 1986, pp. 59-61.

Reda, Susan, "Kohl's Expands with Hybrid of Discount Store Efficiency, Department Store Ambience," *Stores,* February 1997, pp. 49-50.

Reese, Shelly, "Hybrid Kohl's Weathers Tough Apparel Climate," *Discount Store News,* May 6, 1996, p. A18.

———, "Kohl's Strives for National Status," *Discount Store News,* April 1, 1996, pp. 3, 104.

Robins, Gary, "Lin Allison Keeps Kohl's on the Leading Edge," *Stores,* August 1991, pp. 54-58.

Rublin, Lauren R., "Taylor-Made Portfolio," *Barron's,* June 22, 1992, pp. 16-20.

Samuels, Gary, "Learning by Doing," *Forbes,* February 14, 1994, p. 51.

Scardino, Emily, "Kohl's Makes Sweet Deal for Exclusive Candie's Line," *Discount Store News,* January 10, 2005, pp. 5, 41.

Seckler, Valerie, "Stoking Kohl's," *Women's Wear Daily,* June 12, 1996, pp. 10-11.

Tillotson, Kristin, "Minding the Store: Kohl's Comes Up with Winning Mix of Name Brands and Low Prices," *Minneapolis Star Tribune,* February 11, 1994, p. 1D.

Veverka, Mark, "Kohl's Isn't Just for Cheeseheads," *Crain's Chicago Business,* May 22, 1995, p. 4.

LifeCell Corporation

■

1 Millennium Way
Branchburg, New Jersey 08876
U.S.A.
Telephone: (908) 947-1100
Toll Free: (800) 367-5737
Fax: (908) 947-1200
Web site: http://www.lifecell.com

Public Company
Incorporated: 1986
Employees: 196
Sales: $61.1 million (2004)
Stock Exchanges: NASDAQ
Ticker Symbol: LIFC
NAIC: 541710 Research and Development in the Physical Sciences and Engineering Sciences

■ ■ ■

LifeCell Corporation develops and markets products made from human tissue that are used in a variety of surgical procedures related to grafting and transplantation. The company's patented tissue-processing technology produces a regenerative tissue matrix that can be used in periodontal procedures, urologic and gynecologic procedures, and in plastic reconstructive, general surgical, and burn applications. The company's products, marketed under the names "AlloDerm," "Cymetra," "Repliform," "GraftJacket," and "AlloCraft," grew out of technology developed at The University of Texas Health Science Center in Houston, Texas. The company's first product, AlloDerm, has been used in more than 750,000

grafts and implants. LifeCell's tissue regeneration products are sold in the United States and internationally through distributors.

ORIGINS

LifeCell owed its existence, in part, to a change in policy effected by the Board of Regents of the University of Texas, who for years had prohibited its employees to profit from research conducted under the aegis of the university. In 1986, the board made an exception to the rule, allowing two of its researchers at The University of Texas Health Science Center in Houston to take a stake in a commercial venture that their research efforts helped to create. For its part, the University of Texas gained a 10 percent stake in the venture, a company named Life-Cell to which The Board of Regents gave exclusive license to manufacture and market advanced technology developed by Dr. John Linner and his colleague, Dr. Stephen Livesey. For their part, Linner and Livesey took an equity position in LifeCell as well, spearheading the formation of what would become the first Houston-based biotechnology company to put a product on the open market.

While working at the Health Science Center, Linner and Livesey focused their research efforts on the field of cryobiology, the study of the use and effects of extremely low temperatures on living organisms. Specifically, the pair sought to avoid the structural and biochemical damages caused by traditional cell preservation methods, such as freeze-drying, which formed ice crystals that damaged cells. Linner and Livesey made significant strides in advancing cryobiological technol-

COMPANY PERSPECTIVES

Our mission is to continually expand our offerings with first-in-class products that are distinctly different—and superior—to anything available on the market. Toward this end, we are not only leveraging our existing proprietary technology to develop products that enhance the matrix, but we are also exploring how LifeCell can expand into new realms of biosurgery to provide surgeons a full complement of biologically based products that expedite the body's ability to fully heal. Above all, however, our research efforts are always grounded in our commitment to develop products and applications that fulfill a significant unmet clinical need, so that we can give surgeons and their patients real hope for recovery in cases where few, if any, options exist today.

ogy, developing a patented process that involved a rapid, ultra-cooling system coupled with a molecular dryer that removed the remaining vapor, enabling the preservation of cells and, by extension, tissues. LifeCell acquired the rights to the process, a technology it intended to market to medical schools, hospitals and pathology laboratories, pharmaceutical companies, and to the tissue and organ transplant market. Linner, for example, had developed a method for preserving and regenerating corneas for transplantation by the time LifeCell was commencing operations.

As with any biotechnology start-up, the road ahead for LifeCell promised to include years of financial uncertainty. The company had a process, not a product, to market, a shortcoming that meant annual revenues would be outstripped by annual losses as the company endeavored to turn pioneering work into a marketable product. To shepherd the company through the bleak financial years ahead, Paul M. Frison was chosen, a veteran of the healthcare industry who brought with him more than two decades of experience as a senior executive. He spent 13 years working for American Hospital Supply Corporation, directing the company's corporate activities in Latin America and Western Europe. Next, he joined LifeMark Corporation, a Houston-based hospital management concern where he served as president, chief operating officer, and a director until 1984. During the two-year period between leaving LifeMark and joining LifeCell, he served as chairman, chief executive officer, and president of ComputerCraft, Inc., titles he would hold at LifeCell.

Frison, as he guided LifeCell through its critical first years of development, would be forced to rely on private sales of equity securities, nominal funds from venture capitalists, and government grants to keep the company financially solvent.

Under Frison's stewardship, LifeCell's small scientific staff focused on two broad fields of commercial use, tissue transplantation and blood cell preservation. Federal grants, which began being awarded to the company by the end of the 1980s, highlighted some of the work being performed at LifeCell's headquarters in The Woodlands, north of Houston. In January 1990, the company received its fourth research grant within the year, a grant awarded by the National, Heart, Lung and Blood Institution to develop a method of preserving heart valves for transplantation. LifeCell, which received $50,000 from the contract, also was conducting federally funded research into the preservation of human blood, skin, and cultured mammalian cells. Later in the year, the company was awarded a $500,000 grant from the U.S. Department of Defense to continue development on a method to preserve and store human blood at room temperature for extended periods.

Aside from its research work, LifeCell leveraged its technology and expertise to make its living in other ways. The company earned money from selling equipment designed to preserve tissue samples, relying on Phillips Electronic Instruments Co. to distribute the equipment in the United States and Bio-Rad Microsciences Ltd. to conduct distribution in Europe. In 1990, the company's equipment-selling business gained the support of an important partner when an agreement was signed with a major Japanese trading company, Nissei Sangyo Co. Ltd. Under the terms of the deal, Nissei Sangyo agreed to market LifeCell's equipment in Japan, opening up an important new market for the company. Frison, in a June 11, 1990 interview with the *Houston Business Journal*, commented on the significance of the distribution agreement. "Nissei Sangyo's strong market presence," he said, "will increase usage and acceptance of LifeCell equipment in Japan, where the market for electron microscopy and cryopreservation is at least as large as in the United States."

FIRST PRODUCT DEBUTS IN 1993

As LifeCell eked out a living during the developmental phase of its existence, all expectations for future financial vitality were pinned to the day when the company put its first product on the market. Revenue totaled a paltry $239,102 in 1992, the year LifeCell completed its initial public offering (IPO) of stock, but the debut of the company's product was near, fueling hope that the company soon would generate exponentially larger sums

KEY DATES

1986: LifeCell is formed as a technology transfer spinoff of the University of Texas.

1992: The company completes its initial public offering of stock.

1993: Commercial distribution of AlloDerm begins in December, at first marketed for use in treating burn patients.

1995: LifeCell begins marketing AlloDerm to periodontal and reconstructive plastic surgeons.

1999: LifeCell moves its head offices from Texas to New Jersey; Repliform and Cymetra are introduced.

2002: GraftJacket is introduced for use in orthopedic surgical procedures.

2004: Revenues exceed $60 million and the company records its third consecutive year of profits.

of revenue. Commercial distribution of the company's first product commenced in December 1993, when AlloDerm, a human dermal graft, was introduced to the market.

A landmark achievement for the seven-year-old venture and the first product to be sold by a Houston-based biotechnology firm, AlloDerm initially was targeted for patients with third-degree burns or severe second-degree burns requiring skin grafting. AlloDerm consisted of specially processed skin from organ donors, which was used as an alternative to a patient's skin for grafting in extreme burn cases, a capability that no other company could claim to offer. LifeCell was one of only three or four companies competing in the burn treatment field, and the only one to have progressed beyond the clinical trial stage to sell a skin replacement product on the open market. Frison, after seven years of waiting for the moment, at last possessed a product capable of commercial success. "We knew we had identified a major product that answered a critical need in the wound healing arena," he explained in a March 21, 1994 interview with the *Houston Business Journal*. "We had been sufficiently shown that we had an answer, if fully developed, that almost assuredly would answer the need in a very, very big market. Competition was somewhere between minimal and non-existent."

AlloDerm gave LifeCell a product to rally around. Developing a commercial product represented only part of the battle, however. Financial success hinged on ef-

fectively marketing the product, on educating the medical community about the novel qualities of AlloDerm and promoting its embrace by doctors and surgeons. Frison, having penetrated the commercial marketplace by presenting AlloDerm as a product to treat burn victims, soon began to market the product for other uses, thereby expanding AlloDerm's potential customer base. In September 1995, LifeCell began marketing AlloDerm to periodontists, promoting the use of the tissue graft in periodontal surgery. Subsequently, periodontal surgeons began using AlloDerm to increase the amount of attached gum tissue supporting the teeth, eliminating the need to excise tissue from the roof of the patient's mouth. AlloDerm also was used in periodontal procedures for covering exposed tooth roots. One month after marketing efforts began targeting periodontal surgeons, LifeCell began courting reconstructive plastic surgeons, promoting AlloDerm's use as a soft tissue implant in a variety of procedures such as head and neck aesthetic surgeries, cancer reconstruction, and scar revision.

Despite an expanding potential customer base and nominal competitive pressure, AlloDerm did not deliver immediate financial salvation to LifeCell. Revenues increased substantially, jumping from $816,615 in 1994 to nearly $8 million in 1998, but losses during the period ranged from $3 million to $7 million annually, totaling more than $25 million. The period represented the last years of Frison's day-to-day control over the company, a transition in leadership that passed the reins to Paul G. Thomas, who assumed the responsibilities of president and chief executive officer in October 1998. (Frison stayed on as chairman until Thomas was elected to the office in June 1999.)

Thomas, who earned postgraduate degrees in business and chemistry, joined LifeCell after serving as president of the pharmaceutical products division of Ohmeda, Inc., a global competitor in the anesthetics and acute-care pharmaceuticals markets. Thomas took charge of a company that was struggling financially, but making encouraging progress. The year he took the helm, LifeCell estimated AlloDerm had been transplanted in more than 40,000 patients. Under Thomas's control, AlloDerm's use would increase substantially, as the applications of its use expanded and a greater percentage of the medical community turned to the company's tissue-regenerating technology to complete a variety of surgical procedures.

Not long after Thomas joined the company, LifeCell announced it was moving its headquarters. In 1999, the company began moving its operations to Branchburg, New Jersey, making the geographic leap to place itself in the center of activity related to its field of work.

New Jersey was home to 15 of the 20 largest pharmaceutical companies in the country and the state chosen as the headquarters location for 100 biotechnology companies. "The move to New Jersey will allow us to access a very large pool of folks with experience in the commercialization of healthcare products," Thomas explained in a June 11, 1999, interview with the *Houston Business Journal.* "I think this is an important phase for LifeCell," he added. Indeed, the year of the company's relocation also marked the debut of two new brand names for products incorporating LifeCell's proprietary technology. Since 1997, some surgeons had been using AlloDerm for surgical procedures in the fields of urology and gynecology, which prompted the company to introduce Repliform as the brand name for a tissue-processing product tailored for the urology and gynecology markets. In December 1999, in another branding effort, the company introduced Cymetra, a form of AlloDerm developed for plastic and reconstructive surgeons, as well as for the dermatology market.

A PROFITABLE START TO THE 21ST CENTURY

After years of enduring financial hardship, LifeCell began to demonstrate financial strength as it neared its 20th anniversary. The company registered a $9 million loss in 1999 and a combined loss of another $9 million between 2000 and 2001, but the string of consecutive annual losses, which stretched back to the company's inception, ended in 2001. The company reported a $1.4 million profit in 2002, the year it introduced GraftJacket for use in orthopedic surgical procedures. Revenues, meanwhile, had begun to increase steadily, climbing from $12.6 million in 1999 to $34.4 million in 2002. Underpinning the company's financial vitality was the growing acceptance of its AlloDerm family of products, whose use had proliferated during Thomas's first five years in charge. By 2004, LifeCell estimated that AlloDerm had been used in more than 750,000 grafts and implants, exponentially more than the estimate of 40,000 such uses in 1999. The increasing demand for AlloDerm, particularly for hernia-repair procedures midway through the decade, fueled the company's financial growth, driving revenues from $40.2 million in 2003 to $61.1 million in 2004 and yielding nearly $26 million in profits during the two-year span. Looking ahead, the company was confident that the greater use of AlloDerm and the development of additional products that used LifeCell's

tissue-processing technology would continue to generate positive financial results.

Jeffrey L. Covell

PRINCIPAL SUBSIDIARIES

LifeCell Technologies Inc.

PRINCIPAL COMPETITORS

Genzyme Biosurgery; Integra Lifesciences Holdings Corporation; Smith & Nephew PLC.

FURTHER READING

Birger, Jon, "Seven Stocks to Bet On," *Fortune,* September 5, 2005, p. 83.

Calkins, Laurel Brubaker, "LifeCell Cracks Japanese Market with Agreement," *Houston Business Journal,* June 11, 1990, p. 8.

Darwin, Jennifer, "LifeCell Drops The Woodlands for New Jersey Digs," *Houston Business Journal,* June 11, 1999, p. 5.

Hart, Joe, "UTStarcom Gives Birth to Unique New LifeCell," *Houston Business Journal,* August 4, 1986, p. 1.

"Hospitals Look to One-Stop Shopping for Orthopedic Implants, Tissue Products," *Hospital Materials Management,* August 2003, p. 5.

Lau, Gloria, "A Unique Niche Pays Off Here," *Investor's Business Daily,* October 17, 2005, p. A12.

"LifeCell Corp. Gets $529,000 Grant," *Houston Business Journal,* August 6, 1990, p. 8.

"LifeCell Reports 1999 Product Sales Increase 64% of 1998," *Biotech Financial Reports,* April 2000.

"LifeCell to Set Up Transplant Centre in Mumbai in 2007," *PTI—The Press Trust of India Ltd.,* January 8, 2006.

"LifeCell Voluntarily Recalls Product from One Tissue Recovery Organization," *Asia Africa Intelligence Wire,* October 7, 2005.

McNamara, Victoria, "Heart Research Grant Will Go to Unique Houston Company," *Houston Business Journal,* January 8, 1990, p. 9.

———, "Houston Biotech Companies Picking Up the Business Pace," *Houston Business Journal,* July 8, 1991, p. 22.

Reeves, Kimberly, "Profile of a Partnership: Biotechnology Firm Heads for Market," *Houston Business Journal,* March 21, 1994, p. 31.

Lojas Americanas S.A.

Rua Sacadura Cabral 102
Rio de Janeiro, Rio de Janeiro 20081-902
Brazil
Telephone: (55) (21) 2206-6505
Fax: (55) (21) 2206-6969
Web site: http://www2.lasa.com.br

Public Company
Incorporated: 1940
Employees: 8,491
Sales: BRL 2.28 billion ($948.81 million) (2004)
Stock Exchanges: São Paulo OTC (for ADRs)
Ticker Symbol: LAME3
NAIC: 452112 Discount Department Stores; 454111
  Electronic Shopping

■ ■ ■

Lojas Americanas S.A., or Lasa for short, is one of the largest retailers in Brazil, operating almost 200 discount department stores and selling more than 80,000 items from 4,000 different companies. The company's stores guarantee major brand products at competitive prices and have a major share of the Brazilian trade in toys, chocolates and candies, lingerie, and compact discs. Other areas are household goods, small household appliances, basic clothing lines, convenience foods, and perfumes and cosmetics. Its subsidiaries include the Internet sales company Americanas.com S.A. Comércio Electrônico for shopping online, and the financial services provider Facilita Serviços e Propaganda S.A.,

which offers such products as personal loans, cellular telephones, and its own credit card.

BRAZIL'S FIVE-AND-DIME STORE CHAIN: 1929-89

Lojas Americanas was founded in 1929 by four directors of the F.W. Woolworth Co. who were bound for Buenos Aires with the intention of opening a store in Woolworth's nickel-and-dime tradition. On the ship, they met two Brazilians who invited them to get to know Rio de Janeiro. On their visit to Rio, they noted that people with modest but stable incomes, such as public servants and military personnel, were not being well-served by local merchants, who generally sold expensive and specialized merchandise so that a housewife had to visit a number of establishments to do her shopping. They decided that the city was the ideal place to launch their venture and opened a store there before the year was out. At the end of the first year, there were three other Lojas Americanas as well: two in Rio and one in São Paulo. Lojas Americanas became a joint-stock company in 1940.

Lojas Americanas was the fourth largest retail chain in Brazil, with $300 million in annual sales in 1982, when, at the end of the year, a controlling share of the enterprise was purchased by major stockholders of the Garantia group for $23 million. Unusual for Brazil, the acquisition was made through the stock exchange, using several brokerages to buy stock so as not to alert potential selling shareholders. Considering the chain's sales volume, the purchase price was cheap, but over the next seven years, Garantia invested $220 million in cash flow and depreciation. The *Economist* concluded in 1991

> # COMPANY PERSPECTIVES
>
> Mission: To continuously help people in improving their quality of life, providing them access to quality products, with the best service, saving them time and money.

that "From a financial point, that investment ... has simply disappeared; Garantia would have been better off in cash and gold." In spite of this evaluation, Lasa was profitable throughout the rest of the 1980s. There were 63 stores doing about $570 million worth of business in 1988 and selling 40,000 different items. The stores were carrying so many food items that they resembled supermarkets and, later, some of them were turned into a supermarket chain administered by a subsidiary.

CHALLENGES OF THE 1990S

The early 1990s were a difficult period for the Brazilian economy, but Lojas Americanas lost money only in 1990. Even in 1992, when the chain, consisting of 83 Lojas Americanas stores in 18 states, experienced a decline in revenue for the third consecutive year, it was able to earn a small profit. Only three of the stores were unprofitable. In 1995 Lasa reached maximum annual revenue of BRL 2.34 billion.

In 1994 Lojas Americanas entered into a joint venture with Wal-Mart Stores Inc. This alliance had been under consideration since the beginning of 1983, when, following Garantia's acquisition of the chain, Lasa's chairman had written Sam Walton, founder of Wal-Mart. For Lasa executives, Wal-Mart constituted the gold standard of retailing. Company executives frequently visited Wal-Mart's headquarters in Bentonville, Arkansas, to study modern retailing concepts and techniques and to learn about cash-flow management. They then applied what they learned in order to operate within Brazil's highly inflationary environment. When a new government program wrung hyperinflation out of the economy in 1994, Brazilian retailing executives were faced with new challenges, such as effective cost control and pricing, inventory control, lowering overhead, and making better merchandising selections.

Wal-Mart Brasil S.A. was established in 1994, with Lojas Americanas taking 40 percent of the shares. The new company began to operate in April 1995 with both a warehouse-club format and supercenters selling grocer-

ies and general merchandise. Twelve months later, the joint venture was operating five stores, all in the state of São Paulo. The road was rocky, however. Manufacturers such as Nestlé Brasil Ltda., accustomed to controlling pricing, were angered when Wal-Mart sold their products at deep discounts. Difficulty in implementing just-in-time deliveries resulted in serious inventory shortages of critical products. An attempt to apply Wal-Mart's U.S.-style management-control systems proved to be difficult or inadequate. For its own part, Lojas Americanas made some unwise decisions, such as overextending credit to consumers and entering midsized cities with doubtful profit prospects. At the end of the first year of operation, Wal-Mart Brasil had lost $16.5 million. Lasa, at the end of 1997, sold Wal-Mart its stake in Wal-Mart Brasil.

Even apart from its Wal-Mart Brasil difficulties, Lojas Americanas was running into problems. In spite of investing $35 million in cutting-edge information technology, the company was not coping well with the logistics and distribution of its large number of stock items, 139,000 by one count. Each one of the 99 stores was receiving, in 1996, separate deliveries from the chain's 4,580 suppliers. Twenty percent of basic goods were found to be out of stock in a given store at a given time. Addressing the problem demanded more employees, more invoices, and hence, more bureaucracy. A recent policy of accepting predated checks from customers boosted sales but also uncollectible debts. Moreover, Lojas Americanas was faulted for not entering the lucrative field of home electronics while filling its space with such low-margin goods as groceries, which now accounted for 40 percent of sales. Lasa's shares of stock fell 55 percent in value in less than two years. In late 1996, Jorge Paulo Lemann, founder of Garantia and the principal shareholder in Lasa, fired the company's chief executive after four years on the job.

Lojas Americanas lost money that year and again in 1997. In the following year it cut costs, reducing employment by about 15 percent and renegotiating property leases. Next, it reduced the number of different stock items, focusing on five core areas: housewares; health, beauty, and adornment items; underwear and hosiery; toys; and confectionary. Rather than emphasizing discount sales, the chain decided to rely much more on selling popular brands, declaring a policy of "strong brands, low prices, every day." Centralized distribution centers were established in Rio de Janeiro and São Paulo, with a third to open in Recife in 1999. Finally, unable to compete successfully with food chains, Lasa sold its 23 supermarkets to Comptoirs Modernes S.A., a French group, for $200 million.

```
┌─────────────────────────────────────────────┐
│                                               │
│              KEY DATES                        │
│                   ▪                           │
├───────────────────────────────────────────────┤
```

1929: The first Lojas Americanas opens, in Rio de Janeiro.

1982: The Garantia group buys a controlling share of the enterprise.

1988: The chain, Brazil's fourth largest, has 63 stores selling 40,000 different items.

1994: Lojas Americanas enters an ill-fated joint venture with Wal-Mart Stores Inc.

1998: The company restructures its operations and sells its supermarket division.

1999: Lasa unveils its e-commerce affiliate, Americanas.com.

2003: Americanas.com has become Brazil's leading e-commerce site.

2004: Lojas Americanas adds 36 stores to bring the total to 156.

STAKING ITS FUTURE ON E-COMMERCE: 1999-2005

These measures buttressed the finances of Lojas Americanas, but its critics continued to maintain that the chain was outdated, doomed to lose its customers to bigger general-merchandise stores, especially the hypermarkets cropping up in Brazil's urban areas, and also to Internet commerce. Accordingly, in late 1999 Lasa unveiled its new, virtual enterprise, Americanas.com. A platform of six delivery services offered to bring the chain's merchandise to customers anywhere in Brazil in less than six days. (By 2005 this had been reduced to 48 hours.) Customers in São Paulo could generally count on same-day delivery. The electronic site initially targeted the high-income customers who owned most of the computers in Brazil, then expanded to the middle class through kiosks in Lojas Americanas stores. The first product lines offered were similar to those in which the stores specialized, but in 2000 five new lines were added, including articles generally not available in the stores: computer hardware and software, larger electronic equipment, digital videodiscs, watches, perfumes, and flowers. The site also included content such as news and entertainment by 42 journalists contributing weekly articles. Americanas.com went public in 2000, with private-equity funds taking a one-third share of the enterprise for about $40 million, while Lasa kept a 60 percent stake and Americanas.com executives took the rest.

Lojas Americanas' revenues stabilized at about BRL 1.7 billion a year, or an average of $600 million, in the early years of the 21st century, and after incurring a loss in 2000—perhaps due to development costs needed to get Americanas.com off the ground—the company became increasingly profitable. Under a new chief executive, the stores were expected to meet performance goals not only for the year but every day. "Access to information allows us to resolve the problem in an hour," a company executive told Consuelo Dieguez for the Brazilian business magazine *Exame* in 2003. The centralization of distribution in three warehouses allowed company functionaries to obtain better prices from their suppliers, who could no longer play one store against another. Lasa began opening many new stores, although these were smaller neighborhood ones.

By this time Americanas.com had emerged as Brazil's biggest electronic-commerce business in terms of sales and the only such business in the country to make a profit. Although the Brazilian e-commerce customer base was relatively small, it was wealthy in Brazilian terms, and Americanas.com was able to attract many buyers by offering big-ticket items not available in its stores. It also offered interest-free payment plans extending as long as 12 months, compared to the standard instore three-month installment plan. Americanas.com accounted for almost 9 percent of Lasa's sales in 2002 and 13 percent in 2004. In November 2003, the parent company raised its stake in Americanas.com to 74 percent; subsequently its holding grew to 80 percent. In 2005 Americanas.com was reaching four million customers (half of all Brazilian virtual-store clients) and more than 9,000 businesses with about 160,000 items. Also that year, Americanas.com acquired TV Sky Shop S.A., owner of the pay-TV channel and web site Shoptime.

Established in 1999, Facilita Serviços e Propaganda S.A. was a Lojas Americanas subsidiary that had been operating since 1984 under another name. With the subsequent merger of three other subsidiaries into its operations, it was offering, in 2005, personal loans, financing of consumer goods, a Facilita financing card, cellular telephone services, and payment of accounts at 205 points of sale inside Lasa stores, its own stores, and through the web site http://www.facilitanet.com.br. But in 2005 Lasa announced that a joint venture with the holding company for Banco Itaú S.A., Brazil's second largest private bank, would replace Facilita.

Lojas Americanas added 36 stores in 2004, including its first five Americanas Express outlets, compact neighborhood stores in São Paulo and Rio de Janeiro with a select assortment of goods. This brought the total to 156 in 19 states and the federal district, 65 percent of them in shopping centers. By late 2005, the total number of stores had reached 193. Lojas Americanas claimed to be serving an average of 700,000 customers a day in 2004, some 77 percent of them female. Net consolidated sales for the parent company in 2004 came to BRL 2.78 billion, or $948.81 million at the average currency exchange rate for the year. Net income was BRL 64.1 million ($21.87 million). Lojas Americanas ranked seventh among Brazilian retailers in 2004 and was near the top in terms of adjusted net income and investment in real estate.

Lojas Americanas led all Brazilian retailers in the sale of compact discs. The CD/DVD/entertainment segment of its business was the chain's largest in 2003, accounting for 20.2 percent of gross income; this was followed by clothing, 18.2 percent; convenience foods, 17.7 percent; household goods/electronics, 15.3 percent; perfumes and cosmetics, 14.3 percent; and toys, 9 percent.

Robert Halasz

PRINCIPAL SUBSIDIARIES

Americanas.com (80%); Americanas.com S.A. Comércio Electrónico (80%); Cheyney Financial S.A.; Facilita Serviços e Propaganda S.A.; Klanin Services Ltd.; Lojas Americanas da Amazonia S.A.; Lojas Americanas Home Shopping Ltda.

PRINCIPAL COMPETITORS

Arthur Lundgren Tecidos S.A. - Casas Pernambucanas; Casas Bahia Comercial Ltda.; Globex Utilidades S.A.; Sonae Distribuição Brasil S.A..

FURTHER READING

"Americanas.com," *Institutional Investor,* July 2000, p. 14.

"Americanas.com Raises $40 Million," *Private Equity Week,* September 18, 2000, p. 14.

Caplen, Bruce, "Decision Time for Brazil's Top Bankers," *Euromoney,* May 1998, p. 42

da Rocha, Angela, and Rebecca Arkader, "Horizontal Strategic Alliance and Company Behavior," *Latin America Business Review,* 1998 no. 1, pp. 9-13.

Dieguez, Consuelo, "Mudar ou morrer," *Exame,* March 12, 2003, pp. 48-50.

Karp, Jonathan, "From Bricks to Clicks," *Wall Street Journal,* September 22, 2003, p. R7.

McDermott, Francis, "Lean and Limber," *Business Latin America,* December 7, 1998, p. 3.

Moffett, Matt, and Jonathan Friedland, "Wal-Mart Won't Discount Its Prospects in Brazil, Though Its Losses Pile Up," *Wall Street Journal,* June 4, 1996, p. A15.

"A palavra de ordem agora é reforma," *Exame,* December 14, 1988, p. 118.

"O sol volta a brilhar para a Americanas," *Exame,* April 28, 1993, pp. 54-55.

Vassallo, Cláudia, "ASSUSTADOR Mundo Novo," *Exame,* August 11, 1999, pp. 48-50.

———, "O modelo não era tão modelo assim," *Exame,* September 11, 1996, pp. 38-39.

"Wal-Mart Sets Sam's, Supercenters for Brazil, Argentina," *HFD,* June 13, 1994, p. 6.

"Where the Money Is," *Economist,* December 7, 1991, Brasil supplement, pp. 20-21.

LSB Industries, Inc.

—————— ■ ——————

16 S. Pennsylvania Avenue
Oklahoma City, Oklahoma 73107
U.S.A.
Telephone: (405) 235-4546
Fax: (405) 235-5067
Web site: http://www.lsbindustries.com

Public Company
Incorporated: 1968
Employees: 1,240
Sales: $364.1 million (2004)
Stock Exchanges: American
Ticker Symbol: LXU
NAIC: 325314 Fertilizer (Mixing Only) Manufacturing; 333415 Air Conditioning and Warm Air Heating Equipment and Commercial and Industrial Refrigeration Equipment Manufacturing

■ ■ ■

Listed on the American Stock Exchange, LSB Industries, Inc. is a diversified holding company based in Oklahoma City, Oklahoma, whose subsidiaries are divided among three major categories: Chemical, Climate Control, and Industrial. Within the Chemical Group, LSB maintains three business units. The agricultural products unit produces items such as ammonium nitrate, Urea-Ammonium Nitrate solution, specialty fertilizer chemicals blends, and micronutrients. The industrial products business unit produces nitric acid, sulfuric acid, mixed acids, and low-density ammonium nitrate. LSB is the largest supplier of nitric acid in the United

States. The third chemical group business unit, explosives, manufactures blasting agents and commercial explosives. LSB's Climate Control Group produces water source heat pumps, fan coils, geothermal heating and cooling products, and air purification and dehumidification equipment. Finally, the Industrial Group manufactures machine tools, milling machines, lathes, drills, and fabrication equipment, as well as providing engineering services to help set up industrial plants in the chemical, metal stamping, metal fabricating, air conditioning, bearing manufacturing, and precision machines parts fields.

COMPANY ORIGINS DATING TO WORLD WAR II ERA

LSB Industries grew out of an Oklahoma City company formed in 1946, L&S Bearing Company. It started out rebuilding bearings, which had been commandeered by the military during the recently ended World War II and left a severe shortage of the much needed item. As the economy roared following a brief postwar recession, the demand for bearings remained extremely high, prompting L&S to begin manufacturing its own bearings. In 1961, the founder of LSB, Jack E. Golsen, acquired the company. In that same year, he acquired another Oklahoma City business, International Manufacturing Company, which in the 1950s became involved in the manufacture of heating and air conditioning fan coils. It later changed its name to International Environmental Corporation and remains a key LSB subsidiary. Over the next several years of the 1960s Golsen acquired a dozen more companies, which by 1968 employed about 600 people and generated sales

COMPANY PERSPECTIVES

LSB Industries, Inc. is a manufacturing, marketing, and engineering company with activities on a worldwide basis.

of $17 million. In 1968 he formed LSB Industries, drawing on the L&S Bearing name, to serve as a holding company for his manufacturing interests. He then made an initial public offering of stock a year later.

By the mid-1970s LSB was manufacturing anti-friction bearings, air conditioning and heating equipment, and machine tool products. The workforce had grown to 800 and annual sales totaled some $33 million. Following the construction of a major air conditioning plant, the company maintained 500,000 square feet of manufacturing space in Oklahoma City. Later in the decade LSB, located in oil country, began making oil-field pumping units.

In 1981 LSB topped the $100 million mark for the first time in its history, a 43 percent increase over the prior year's $70.5 million. Net income also improved from $1.6 million in 1980 to more than $2 million in 1981. But business conditions quickly soured and the combination of high interest rates and the cost of keeping higher than normal inventories led to losses in 1982. Of particular concern was a downturn in the oil industry and a softening in demand for pump jacks, which had begun even as LSB became involved in the business. Sales dipped to $63.9 million in 1983 and the company had to contend with a heavy debt load and the discounting of its large inventories.

Forced to cut costs, LSB slashed it workforce from the 1981 peak of 1,400 to 750. Not only was the oil industry suffering, U.S. manufacturers also were enduring difficult times. Many of them had their machine tools repossessed, leading to a surplus of inexpensive used machine tools, putting the products manufactured by LSB at a competitive disadvantage. The company also had to contend with foreign-made bearings, which were subsidized by their governments and sometimes available in the United States at a price less than what LSB paid for raw materials. Moreover, a strong U.S. dollar hurt the company's ability to sell its products overseas. The lone bright spot was the Environmental Control Division, which produced air conditioning equipment for major buildings. In 1984 Golsen told the *Oklaho-*

man that it would likely take two years for the company to work through its inventory, restart major production, and regain its health.

EARLY 1980S RECAPITALIZATION

Despite its difficulties, however, LSB was able to implement a recapitalization plan with its 12 lender banks and arranged a $40 million line of credit with Philadelphia National Bank. As a result LSB completed a major acquisition in 1984, adding El Dorado, Arkansas-based El Dorado Chemical Company. El Dorado would become the heart of LSB's Chemical Group. A year later, LSB acquired Utica, New York-based Friedrich Climate Master Inc., manufacturer of cooling and heating products, to bolster its Environmental Control Division unit and add about $30 million in annual revenues. Also in 1985, LSB acquired Marshall Supply & Equipment Company, a Tulsa distributor of industrial and electronic products and machine tools, but a deal to buy Hyatt Clark Industries, a New Jersey employee-owned manufacturer of roller bearings, fell through when General Motors refused to continue to underwrite loans to the company if it ceased to be employee-owned.

LSB next tried to acquire financial institutions, at a time when the thrift industry was becoming distressed. In 1986 it failed in its bid to buy Home Savings & Loan Association of Bartlesville, Oklahoma, but succeeded in 1988 in acquiring Northwest Federal Savings & Loan Association of Wood, Oklahoma, for $1.5 million. Northwest had combined with three other troubled S&Ls, was renamed Equity Bank for Savings by LSB, and became a major factor in the attempt to salvage Oklahoma's troubled thrift industry. As an inducement to get involved, the Resolution Trust Corporation (RTC), a government agency formed in 1989 to help bail out or merge insolvent S&Ls, gave Equity financial assistance, essentially making up for losses on nonperforming assets. Equity also would include Arrowhead Federal Savings & Loan, bought in 1988 for $317 million. In 1989 it would pay $10.3 million for United BankCard Inc., the largest bank credit card operator in Oklahoma, issuing both Visa and MasterCard credit cards.

LSB enjoyed a strong turnaround in the second half of the 1980s, which ended with the company posting $262.5 million in revenues and net income of $4 million. But the company experienced a downturn with the start of the 1990s, as once again the U.S. economy slipped into recession. Sales fell to $248.2 million in 1990 and LSB lost $9.1 million. The company's industrial products business was particularly hard hit, as was Equity, which by itself lost $8 million in 1990. The financial group

> ## KEY DATES
>
> **1946:** L&S Bearing is launched in Oklahoma City.
> **1961:** Jack E. Golsen acquires L&S.
> **1968:** Golsen incorporates a holding company, LSB Industries, Inc.
> **1984:** El Dorado Chemical Co. is acquired.
> **1992:** Slurry Explosive Corporation is acquired.
> **1994:** The Financial Services unit is sold.
> **2000:** The Automotive Products unit is sold.
> **2002:** Slurry is sold.

returned to profitability in 1991, while the parent company continued to post a net loss.

Business turned around for LSB in 1992, when net income totaled $9.2 million, and LSB was once again looking to expand. In 1992 it acquired Slurry Explosive Corporation, and in 1993 added a number of assets. It bought an Australian explosives manufacturer, Total Energy Systems Limited, for approximately $4.3 million; El Dorado Chemical acquired a concentrated nitric acid plant and other assets from the Joliet, Illinois Army Ammunition Plant; and LSB also added the assets of Memphis, Tennessee-based International Bearings Corporation, a distributor of agricultural and power transmission bearings and roller chains. By this point Equity had sold off much of its original assets and RTC opted to end its assistance agreement, paying the subsidiary $14 million. By the end of 1993, LSB decided to exit the financial services field, selling Equity to Fourth Financial Corp. for $92 million in a deal completed in May 1994.

After realizing net profits of $12.4 million in 1993 and $24.5 million in 1994, LSB lost $3.7 million in 1995 and $3.8 million in 1996, prompting management in 1995 to launch a long-term restructuring effort that would include casting off underperforming businesses. Selling off assets became even more of a priority after 1997, a year that Golsen called in his annual shareholder's letter, "the most disappointing year in the history of LSB Industries." Sales fell to $255 million, compared with $276.4 million in 1996, and the company lost more than $23 million.

MID-1990S FOCUS ON CORE BUSINESSES

With the help of outside advisors, the company came to the conclusion that its core businesses were Chemical and Climate Control. The automotive and industrial

units, on the other hand, were expendable and should either be sold or spun off to shareholders. Divesting the automotive bearing business was not easily achieved, however. It had been a core element of LSB from the start and its operations were tied into the entire infrastructure of LSB. Making it a stand-alone operation required the time-consuming task of building a marketing plan, adding customer relations operations, and in general resizing the workforce. Although the company announced its intention of spinning off the automotive unit, it would be some time before it was actually accomplished.

The divestiture of assets began in March 1998 with the sale of the company's Tower office building for $31 million, the proceeds earmarked for the paying down of debt. This sale helped to improve the balance sheet, but in operational terms failed to make any significant contributions. Not only did the noncore business fail to perform any better, LSB's chemical business struggled because of the agricultural market, which was adversely affected by poor weather. Losses continued to mount in 1998 and 1999, although much of the latter were non-cash losses connected to the sale or discontinuation of businesses, such as the sale of Total Energy Systems in August 1999. The price of LSB stock also tumbled, resulting in the company failing to meet the price or market capitalization requirements of the New York Stock Exchange. LSB was delisted in June 1999 but eventually landed a spot on the American Stock Exchange.

LSB finally dealt with its unprofitable automotive business by selling it in May 2000 to Drive Line Technologies for $8.7 million. Overall, LSB showed marked improvement in 2000, growing revenues to $296.2 million and posting a $6.2 million profit. It also succeeded in trimming operating expenses from $51.7 million in 1999 to $47.8 million in 2000. Moreover, the company cut its annual interest payments by more than $2 million by buying back nearly $30 million of its public bonds in 2000.

LSB's turnaround continued in 2001, as the emphasis on core businesses began to bear fruit. The agricultural segment of the chemical business, for example, benefited from the acquisition of a plant in Cherokee, Alabama, a move that added customers from a number of new states, including Alabama, Mississippi, Georgia, Kentucky, and Indiana. This expansion helped to offset a decline in demand in the overall market. LSB improved sales to $346.6 million in 2001 and increased earnings to $8.6 million.

LSB's momentum was blunted in 2002 by a pair of unforeseen events. In February of that year, the Slurry facility had its license to manufacture high explosives revoked by the Bureau of Alcohol, Tobacco, and Firearms, because of improper storage of finished goods and raw material. LSB lost $3.5 million from the shuttered unit before selling off Slurry in December 2002. The chemical business was dealt a blow in April of that year when the El Dorado plant was severely damaged by high winds, the likely effects of a tornado. As a result, the production of industrial grade ammonium nitrate was shut down. The company's other core business, Climate Control, fared better, producing record earnings. As a whole, however, LSB realized a profit of less than $100,000 for the year.

LSB earned $3.1 million in 2003 and $1.9 million in 2004 on sales of $364.1 million, marking the fifth straight year the company posted a profit. One sore spot was the El Dorado subsidiary, which experienced ongoing losses. In June 2005 LSB announced that it was exploring "numerous alternatives" for the business. Whether that led to another divestiture, and a further refinement of the company's business lines, remained to be seen.

Ed Dinger

PRINCIPAL SUBSIDIARIES

Clime Master International Limited; Summit Machine Tool Manufacturing Corporation; Hercules Energy Mfg.

Corporation; El Dorado Chemical Company; International Environmental Corporation.

PRINCIPAL COMPETITORS

Agrium Inc.; CF Industries Holdings, Inc.; Mississippi Chemical Corporation.

FURTHER READING

Bayless, Glen, "LSB's Full Health Called 2 Years Away," *Oklahoman,* April 8, 1984, p. 34.

"City Firm Plans Offering of Stock," *Oklahoman,* April 5, 1969, p. 46.

Laval, Kevin, "Equity Savings Agrees to Buy United BankCard," *Oklahoman,* June 16, 1989, p. 26.

———, "LSB Industries Agrees to Buy Insolvent Thrift," *Oklahoman,* March 28, 1987, p. 20.

Martin, Stacy, "Equity Bank, RTC Deal to End, Officials Say," *Oklahoman,* September 30, 1992, p. 121.

———, "LSB Buys Australian Company," *Oklahoman,* June 26, 1993, p. 100.

———, "LSB Eyes 'Alternatives' for El Dorado As Losses Continue," *Chemical Week,* June 22, 2005, p. 12.

———, "LSB Planning Restructure, Subunit Sales," *Oklahoman,* September 27, 1995, p. 15.

Sim, Peck Hwee, "LSB's Ammonium Nitrate Production Halted by Tornado," *Chemical Week,* April 24, 2002, p. 13.

Matthews International Corporation

—■—

Two NorthShore Center
Pittsburgh, Pennsylvania 15212-5851
U.S.A.
Telephone: (412) 442-8200
Fax: (412) 442-8290
Web site: http://www.matthewsinternational.com

Public Company
Incorporated: 1972
Employees: 3,600
Sales: $639.8 million (2005)
Stock Exchanges: NASDAQ
Ticker Symbol: MATW
NAIC: 331522 Nonferrous (Except Aluminum) Die-
castings

■ ■ ■

Matthews International Corporation is a leader in the U.S. death-care industry. In addition to its core memorialization business, Matthews engages brand solutions, including packaging graphics and design and marking products. Among the Matthews Bronze products are flush bronze memorials, cremation urns, and monuments. One of the most famous of the company's bronze memorials marks the grave of Elvis Presley.

Matthews Bronze is also the leading American producer of cremation equipment and a leading builder of mausoleums in the United States. For most of its long history, Matthews International was known for its bronze memorial products, but during the middle and late 1990s management made a concerted effort to strengthen its

product base by expanding the brand solutions business through a strategic acquisitions program. Then in 2001, Matthews entered the casket making business through the acquisition of The York Group.

EARLY HISTORY

The founder of the company, John Dixon Matthews, was born and lived most of his early life in Sheffield, England. Although Matthews was not formally educated, he was talented with his hands, and at an early age became an apprentice to learn the intricacies of the engraving profession. The young man learned his trade quickly and soon was designing and making such items as branding irons, stamps for wooden crates, and ornate engravings for small businesses that desired unique signs of identification. As his apprenticeship ended, Matthews decided that the best opportunity for advancement, and for making more money, was to establish his own engraving firm. The likelihood of his achieving this goal in England was minimal, however, because there were many highly skilled engraving firms engaged in intense competition with each other. As a result, Matthews traveled to the United States to establish his own company.

From the time Matthews opened the door of his company for business, it was a thriving concern. Having established his firm in Pittsburgh, Pennsylvania, a growing metropolis with a burgeoning population, the young man was inundated with requests for identification products. Throughout the first 40 years of his business, from 1850 to 1890, his company focused on manufacturing and distributing various products such as branding irons for cattle ranches in the Great Plains and the South, ornate engravings that were used in the decoration of public buildings, military stamping dies used by the U.S. Army, especially during the Civil War and immediately afterward, and stamps for crates, packaging, and different sorts of large bundles. As the company grew and prospered, revenues continued to increase at a steady pace. When John Dixon Matthews passed away during the waning years of the 19th century, his company was on the verge of a major transformation.

During the 1890s, the company established the Bronze Tablet Department, specifically intended to design and prepare patterns for bronze plaques and other items that later would be cast by other firms. Historically, bronze had been used since 2500 B.C.E. when metalsmiths living in the eastern part of the Mediterranean discovered that an addition of very small amounts of tin to molten copper produced bronze. These metal smiths soon learned that this new alloy was castable, allowing it to be widely used in casting and creating swords, helmets, and breastplates for war, as well as for statues and decorative articles such as jewelry. As the skills of metalsmiths developed, they found that cast bronze was ideal for artistic expression, since the metal was malleable, easily cast for detail, easy to work with, and exhibited an attractive natural color. As the centuries rolled onward, hollow casting was discovered and used by many artists to produce bronze statues honoring those men who had become heroes to their nation.

Although the use of bronze in art had declined dramatically and was not widespread either in Europe or the United States during the 19th century, the Bronze Tablet Department at Matthews Company was convinced there was a growing market for such items. Thus, as the company finished and detailed the castings done by other suppliers and shipped them to customers around the United States, its reputation for quality bronze workmanship began to grow. By the start of the

20th century, the company had garnered a national reputation for its identification work using bronze.

GROWTH AND EXPANSION IN THE EARLY 20TH CENTURY

The company's success continued during the early decades of the 20th century, and revenues steadily increased. Yet in 1927 the company developed a product that not only changed the direction of its business but affected the history of what has become known as "Memorialization."

Throughout the ages people from around the world memorialized the dead by constructing ornate tombs that identified the person as someone of importance. Ground burial and mausoleum entombment were the traditionally preferred methods of disposition and, since the rise of Christianity, cemeteries were created for resting places of the deceased and as a place for the living to seek consolation and peace. Memorialization primarily consisted of stone memorials with the date of birth, date of death, and name of the deceased.

American cemeteries, especially during the 19th and early 20th centuries, were filled with and characterized by memorials of stone carving and sculpture, with only an occasional enhancement of bronze. Memorials encompassed all budgets and a wide variety of tastes, from large, ornate, exquisitely decorated private family mausoleums built for wealthier people to simple upright monuments carved with the person's birth and death dates and the first and last names of the deceased.

One of the most important developments in the history of memorialization occurred in 1906, when Dr. Hubert Eaton designed and built Forest Lawn Cemetery in California. A turning point in memorialization, the cemetery combined stone, bronze, and marble to create a revolution in funerary sculpture. Within a few short years, Forest Lawn had become one of the most famous cemeteries in the United States, known for its works of memorialization in a variety of materials.

In 1927 the employees at Matthews Tablet Department were approached by a family that wanted to exhibit its affection and respect for a deceased member by commissioning an entirely bronze memorial. Matthews accepted the commission and cast the very first flush bronze memorial for a gravesite in Oaklawn Cemetery in Jacksonville, Florida. As the first flush bronze memorial designed, cast, and installed in a cemetery within the United States, the piece immediately revolutionized memorialization in American cemeteries. Soon Matthews had garnered a reputation as the preeminent designer and manufacturer of flush bronze memorials for use in cemeteries, and people from across the United States began placing orders with the company.

```
┌─────────────────────────────────────────────┐
│                                             │
│              KEY DATES                      │
│                                             │
├─────────────────────────────────────────────┤
│  1850:  Immigrant John Dixon Matthews       │
│         establishes engraving business.     │
│  1927:  Company produces first flush        │
│         bronze memorial.                    │
│  1989:  Company enters Australian market.   │
│  1999:  Matthews acquires Italian           │
│         mausoleum and statuary company.     │
│  2001:  Matthews enters casket making       │
│         niche of death-care industry.       │
└─────────────────────────────────────────────┘
```

DEVELOPMENTS IN BRONZE MEMORIALIZATION: MID-20TH CENTURY THROUGH THE LATE 1990S

As the company grew, its expertise in bronze memorials grew apace. The men working at Matthews Bronze were recognized as the best in the business for casting bronze for freestanding memorial sculptures. Much more preferable than stone or wood, the durability and lightness of bronze allowed Matthews Bronze a freedom of conception and design that was virtually impossible in stone and other materials. As a natural outgrowth of its work in the field of bronze memorialization, the most important development for the company during the 1940s, 1950s, and 1960s accompanied the rise of interest in the process of cremation.

Cremation goes back to the prehistoric period. The process developed a large following in the major world cultures of Ancient Greece, the Roman Empire, India, and Japan. The first documented cremation in the United States was reported in 1792, but it was not until the late 19th century that the number of cremations began to increase. By 1913, there were more than 50 crematories located throughout the United States and, during the 1950s and 1960s, the number grew rapidly.

For Matthews, the rise in the interest in cremation meant that people wanted permanent placements of the remains of their deceased loved ones, and memorializations assisted in preserving the memories of love, devotion, and respect. People were no longer limited in their choices for cremation memorialization, as in the days of the Ancient Greeks and Roman Empire, because of the wide array of memorialization options that Matthews offered to satisfy an individual's taste, including outdoor Cremorials, unique and distinctive columbarium estates, elegant and uniquely designed handcrafted urns, attractive niches, and highly personalized memorial plaques

that could be set in gardens or parks. By the end of the 1960s, Matthews Bronze was the leading designer and manufacturer of cremation memorializations throughout the United States.

Starting in 1961, the company began designing and casting some of the most notable bronze memorials in the United States. One of the company's high-profile projects included hand-crafting and casting the plaques used in the Major League Baseball Hall of Fame. Matthews Bronze cast the metal plaque situated on the top of Pike's Peak to commemorate the 100th anniversary of the composition of "America the Beautiful." The company cast bronze memorialization tributes for some of the most popular celebrities in the United States, including Lucille Ball, Jack Benny, Humphrey Bogart, Nat King Cole, Sammy Davis, Jr., Alan Ladd, Michael Landon, Liberace, Groucho Marx, and Selena.

One of the most famous Matthews Bronze pieces is the memorial for one of the most famous singers in the world, Elvis Presley. His bronze memorial, which is situated on the southern end of his estate at Graceland in Memphis, Tennessee, is considered to be the most visited piece of work ever cast by Matthews Bronze, with more than 700,000 people visiting the site annually. Another one of Matthews Bronze's creations includes the very famous identification plaque cast for the 1984 Summer Olympics in Los Angeles, California.

The company also completed a significant number of bronze memorials for war veterans dating from World War I to the Gulf War in the early 1990s. Among its bronze memorials was the installation of a tribute to the men and women of the 14th Quartermaster Detachment Unit at the U.S. Army Reserve Center in Greensburg, Pennsylvania, which suffered the most casualties of any unit in the entire Allied Force throughout the duration of the hostilities between the United Nations and Iraq. The memorial included the boots, rifle, and helmet of a fallen soldier, life-sized American soldiers cast in bronze reflecting on the fate of their fallen comrade-in-arms, and an imposing bronze eagle, symbolizing the bravery and honor of American soldiers in battle.

During the 1990s, in addition to its hold on the market for bronze memorializations, Matthews decided to expand its presence in the Graphics Imaging market. Seven acquisitions were made in 1998 alone, the most important including an interest in O.N.E. Color Communications L.L.C., a digital graphics firm located in California, and S+T Gesellschaft fur Reprotechnik mbH, a well respected manufacturer of photopolymer printing plates in Germany. The overseas acquisition, in combination with the bronze casting work done for the Sultan of Brunei and the Saudi Arabia Monetary

Authority, provided the company with approximately 10 percent of its total revenues for the 1998 fiscal year.

Although Matthews International Corporation was clearly the undisputed leader in the bronze memorialization market, and its dominance likely to continue for years to come, management realized the wisdom in a certain amount of diversity when the markets experience a downturn. Therefore, it implemented a long-term strategic plan to enhance the position of its graphics as well as marking products businesses, both of which were showing signs of growth and expansion.

Graphics Imaging, which comprised approximately 35 percent of company revenues, provided pre-press services, printing plates, and imaging systems to the packing industry. The company's printing plates were used by firms within the packaging industry to print corrugated boxes, for example, with lettering and graphics that assist in selling the packaged product. Marking Products comprised about 15 percent of its revenues, designed and manufactured equipment used to mark and identify such items as industrial products and packaging containers.

As the 20th century wound down, Matthews Bronze produced approximately 50 percent of the firm's revenues, focusing primarily on the design and manufacture of cast bronze products used as memorials in cemeteries. But cost-conscious consumers had put pressure on the death-care industry during the late 1990s. In response to pricing pressures national chains began buying up small independent funeral homes. The changes depressed the stock of even solid operations such as Matthews. On the other hand, the rise in popularity of cremation boded well for growth in that business area.

NEW NICHE: 2000-05

Chairman and CEO David M. Kelly, who joined the company in 1995 and directed Matthews' internal growth and acquisition plan in the late 1990s, took the 150-year-old company into the 21st century. Despite 13 consecutive quarters of double-digit earnings growth, Matthews stock traded in the low $20s during the spring of 2000, down from the upper $20s a year earlier. Matthews had been repurchasing its own stock, buying back three million or 15 percent of its shares since its 1994 IPO and authorized to repurchase as much as one million more.

According to the *Pittsburgh-Post Gazette*, Kelly planned to maintain the company's growth through new products, new domestic and international markets for old products, and acquisitions. During 1999, Matthews had acquired Italy's Caggiati S.p.A., Europe's leading

supplier of bronze memorials, expanding the company's mausoleum and statuary offerings.

The U.S. death rate was growing about 1 percent a year as the new millennium began but by 2020, about 53 million Americans would be 65 years of age or older. According to Allentown Pennsylvania's *Morning Call*, bronze funeral memorials continued to make up about half of Matthews' sales, while bringing in 70 percent of profits.

In May 2001, The York Group, the nation's second largest coffin maker, agreed to merge with Matthews. The $11 per share offer followed York's rejection of another suitor, Wilbert Funeral Services, which held 14 percent of $130 million business. York previously sold its metal vault operation to Doric Products Inc.

The York Group was established in 1892 as York Wagon Gear Co., first as a builder of wooden coaches for horse-drawn carriages and then chassis for Ford Motor Co. The company subsequently entered the burial casket business, selling off the auto equipment division in 1958. Following several incarnations during the next few decades, the company became the York Group in 1989 and made an initial public offering in 1996.

In a separate deal Matthews purchased York's commemorative products division for $45 million. The purchase gave Matthews an estimated 75 percent of the bronze memorial market, thought to be about $280 million; other significant players in the market were privately held and did not reveal sales figures. Matthews controlled 20 percent of the overall memorial market, according to *Mergers & Acquisitions*.

A bronze statute commissioned by the Firefighters Association of Missouri sat at JFK International Airport en route from Matthews' Italian facility on September 11, 2001. "Our customers started calling us to find out if we had plaques, anything commemorative," Corinne Laboon, Matthews' public relations director told the *Pittsburgh Business Times*. "We sat down to discuss ideas and someone brought up the firefighter statue. We called the Firefighters Association and without hesitation they decided to dedicate the statue, with Matthews, to the citizens of New York." The memorial was placed in Midtown Manhattan, and New Yorkers graced the base of the statue of a kneeling firefighter with items such as flowers and notes during the weeks following the loss of so many of the city's public servants.

In December 2001, upon closure of a $98 million deal, Houston-based York became a wholly owned subsidiary of Matthews. The purchase of the country's second largest bronze memorial business and second largest casket maker pushed Matthews stock back to the upper $20s, according to an April 2002 *National Post* article. The high-margin, steady growth bronze memorial business had funded the acquisitions and stock repurchase program.

Fiscal 2002 revenue was expected to reach $400 million, according to the *National Post*, 50 percent from the bronze segment, 25 percent from caskets, and 25 percent from the graphics and marking products businesses. Recession hurt the cyclical market and graphics portion of the business but added revenue from acquisitions more than balanced that out.

"Matthews' record of buying mediocre businesses and improving performance is considered a key to its growth. It has purchased 23 businesses over the last five years, but it told investors last week the acquisition program has quieted now as the company absorbs last year's additions," Dinah Wisenberg Brin wrote for the *National Post* in April 2002. The company improved its success rate with acquired companies by culling out underperformers. The leading bronze memorial maker ranked as the second largest producer of caskets in the country, after Hillenbrand Industries. "With pricing power and limited competition Matthews dominates the death-care market—an extremely consistent and predictable industry that earns attractive rates of return, requires very little capital reinvestment and nevertheless is hard to penetrate. Over the longer term the business will benefit from the inevitable demographics of the baby boom (people born between 1946 and 1964). What's more, flat bronze memorials, Matthews' specialty, are increasing in popularity and are making inroads on traditional headstones," John W. Rogers, Jr., wrote for *Forbes* in April 2003.

As the first decade of the new century approached its midpoint, Matthews worked to grow the business areas rooted in its early history. Matthews acquired a U.S. industrial controls manufacturer in the summer of 2004, as part of its growth strategy for the marking products business. The company supplied Matthews with microprocessor controls. In September 2004, the company purchased a leading European player in packaging graphics origination and brand management.

Matthews' sales increased 25.8 percent year over year for fiscal 2005. Costs related to the establishment of a Mexican-based manufacturing facility, a downturn in the graphics business, and higher material costs in the bronze segment put a drag on earnings. But favorable international currency exchange rates, fiscal 2004 acqui-

sitions, and growth of the bronze and marking products businesses helped increase earnings for the year.

Thomas Derdak
Updated, Kathleen Peippo

PRINCIPAL SUBSIDIARIES

The York Group.

PRINCIPAL COMPETITORS

Eastman Kodak Company; Hillenbrand Industries, Inc.; Service Corporation International.

FURTHER READING

Brin, Dinah Wisenberg, "Matthews Finds Growth in Grave Markers," *National Post*, April 30, 2002.

Brown, Monique R., "Preparing for the Hereafter," *Black Enterprise*, March 1999, p. 129.

Cecil, Andra Marie, "Buried in Business," *York Daily Record*, December 14, 2005, p. 8.

Cecil, Mark, "FTC Decides to Reopen Matthews' Takeout of York," *Mergers & Acquisitions Report*, November 25, 2002.

"Company Finds: With Age Comes Business," *Morning Call*, December 11, 2000, p. B7.

"Deal for Coffin Maker," *New York Times*, May 25, 2001, p. C6.

Ellis, Junius, "This Talented Value Hunter Aims for Profits of 51% from Four Obscure Stocks," *Money*, April 1996, p. 183.

Gannon, Joyce, "Death Leads to Growth in This Business," *Pittsburgh Post-Gazette*, April 11, 1999, p. F4.

Gaynor, Pamela, "A Memorable Existence," *Pittsburgh Post-Gazette*, May 5, 2000, p. C1.

"Ink Jet System," *Beverage World*, January 15, 1999, p. 72.

Lenderman, Maxim, "Customers Call, Coders Respond," *Beverage World*, June 1996, p. 86.

"Matthews International Corporation," *Wall Street Journal*, April 28, 1998, p. B26.

Nix-Ennen, Steven, "Ink-Jet Printers Cut Through the Dust," *Packaging Digest*, October 1998, p. 86

Parkin, David, "Wrap Artists InTouch Are a Hit with US Giant," *Yorkshire Post*, September 8, 2004, p. 1.

Rogers, Jr., John W., "Turtle Stocks," *Forbes*, April 14, 2003, p. 246.

Schooley, Tim, "Matthews' Bronze Fireman Honors Those Fallen in N.Y.," *Pittsburgh Business Times*, September 28, 2001, p. 2.

Wooding, Jr., Walker C., "Local Coffin-Maker Completes Merger with Pittsburgh Firm," *Houston Business Journal*, December 7, 2001, p. 8.

McCain Foods Limited

———————————■———————————

107 Main Street
Florenceville, New Brunswick E7L 1B2
Canada
Telephone: (506) 392-5541
Fax: (506) 392-6062
Web site: http://www.mccain.com

Private Company
Incorporated: 1956
Employees: 20,000
Sales: $4.62 billion (2005)
NAIC: 424420 Packaged Frozen Food Merchant Whole-
salers; 311412 Frozen Specialty Food Manufactur-
ing; 311411 Frozen Fruit, Juice and Vegetable
Manufacturing; 311423 Dried and Dehydrated
Food Manufacturing

■ ■ ■

McCain Foods Limited is the largest processor of frozen
potatoes in the world. McCain has a business presence
in 110 countries on six continents and has been expanding its empire steadily over the past 50 years. In addition to its French fry production, McCain has diversified its product lines to include frozen pizzas, juice, and
an array of gourmet/ethnic frozen appetizers and entrees.

1956-69: THE BEGINNING OF A
FRENCH FRY EMPIRE

Frozen foods were a relatively new concept in 1956
when Allison and Wallace McCain introduced their new
business in their native Florenceville, New Brunswick,

Canada. The two set up shop on some old pasture land
but it was only a short time before their frozen potatoes
and other products were found in many freezers
throughout the world.

The company's beginnings were modest. McCain
Foods employed 30 locals to process, freeze, distribute,
and sell its goods. The 1950s saw a surge of growth in
partially processed convenience foods. Space-aged technology influenced the modern household. Frozen
vegetables, canned soups, instant breakfast drinks, and
ready-made meal options with their efficiency and
modern panache held wide consumer appeal.

In a few short years steady growth led to expanded
market options and the Canadian company looked to its
British allies overseas to buy its products. McCain's
"chips" gained a foothold in the United Kingdom in
1965. The British campaign was accompanied by a
quirky advertising plan that made McCain fries a
household name.

By 1968 the company was ready to expand to
another English-speaking member of the commonwealth
and McCain Foods set its sites down under on Australia.
McCain also created subsidiary McCain Great Britain
Ltd. in 1968. The following year, McCain opened its
first British French fry production facility in Scarborough, England.

McCain Foods forged its way south in 1971 when
it entered the U.S. market. The 1970s brought about
significant changes in the American workplace and record
numbers of women went to work outside the home
for the first time. Convenience foods were not only
sought after for their modern appeal but for their time-

COMPANY PERSPECTIVES

Today McCain Foods is a global leader among food processors. It makes nearly one-third of the French fried potatoes produced internationally and is known for appetizers, pizza, vegetables, desserts, entrees, oven meals, and other quality frozen foods on six continents. The remarkable success of McCain Foods is built on cutting edge agronomy, superior technology and a global workforce sharing a unique culture and vision.

saving functions as well. McCain was well poised and capitalized on this newly emerging market.

Continuing to grow in the southern hemisphere in 1971 McCain Foods acquired an existing French fry processing plant in Doylesfood, Australia. The newly acquired plant allowed the company to produce and sell its product without overseas shipping. The same year McCain built a new plant on site at Florenceville and added an additional plant in Grand Falls, New Brunswick.

Demand in Britain led the company to double the capacity of its operation in Scarborough and growth in its European sector brought company leaders to the Netherlands soon after. Belgium, France, and the Netherlands had long established themselves as countries where "Frites" were traditional foods. Fried potato stands were a common sight throughout Belgian city streets where tourists and locals could purchase paper cones full of crisp fries smothered in mayonnaise. Within two years, from 1972 to 1973, McCain Foods added to its holdings and purchased plants in Werkendam and Lewedorp, the Netherlands.

Expansion and acquisition trends continued throughout the decade. In 1975 McCain bought a Washburn, Maine potato processing plant; a year later it purchased another U.S. plant, in Easton, Maine.

In 1976, McCain turned back to Europe, buying a French fry production facility in Whittlesey, England. A third Dutch facility would follow in 1978, this time in the town of Hooffddorys.

McCain took a gamble on a newer frozen food in 1976 when the company built a frozen pizza production facility at its Grand Falls, New Brunswick location. The company made frozen pizzas one of its top priorities in the last part of the 1970s. McCain built pizza production businesses in Doylesfood and Ballarat, Australia; Scarborough, England; and Manitoba.

1980-2000: EXPANSION, ACQUISITION AND A FAMILY FEUD

McCain bought Sunny Orange Juice Limited based in Toronto, Ontario, and entered the frozen beverage business in 1980. In subsequent years the company would increase its frozen juice holdings. In 1983 McCain bought a new juice processing plant in Grand Falls, and in 1987 the company went on to purchase another Canadian juice operation in Calgary.

In addition to the company's new interest in juices, McCain diversified its Australian frozen vegetable business by buying a processing plant for vegetables other than frozen potatoes. McCain further diversified by investing in a frozen fish processing plant in England under the Tater Meal label.

McCain opened a French fry potato processing plant in Haines, France, in 1981 and by 1987 the company added another French plant in Betheune. The decade's additional plant openings included the purchase of a Belgian frozen food company, Frima Viking, in April 1986. Frima Viking, the frozen foods subsidiary of Tractionel, operated plants in Ostend and Grobbendank, Belgium. McCain also developed its operations in South Africa and the United States. McCain bought an existing potato processor's facilities in Othello, Washington, and Clark, South Dakota, in 1988.

To keep up with increasing European demand McCain spent $33 million doubling the production capability of its processing business in Haines, France. The following year capital improvements were made to its Othello, Washington, plant at a cost of $35 million.

If the decade of the 1980s was known for acquisition, the 1990s was highlighted by a series of plant retoolings and expansions. The McCain plant in Prince Edward Island, known for its specialty potato products, was given $36 million in improvements.

The company bought New Zealand-based Alpine Foods Limited in 1990, renaming it McCain Foods New Zealand Ltd.

A fire in 1990 near the company headquarters in Florenceville meant an additional outlay of $25 million in rebuilding costs but resulted in a state-of-the-art facility at the headquarters site. In addition to the production site at Florenceville, McCain added a new $2.4 million data facility.

A significant rift between joint CEOs and brothers Harrison and Wallace McCain developed in the early 1990s. The brothers had worked out a plan to smooth the transition when the two retired at age 75, or in the event that one or both of the two died. The plan failed when Wallace unilaterally appointed his son to lead the

KEY DATES

1956: McCain Foods is incorporated.
1965: McCain enters the British market.
1968: Company begins marketing in Australia.
1969: Company opens U.K. facility in Scarborough.
1971: Company enters U.S. market.
1976: McCain begins producing frozen pizzas.
1997: McCain purchases Ore-Ida Food Service business.
2000: McCain Foods builds $7.2 million potato processing technology center.
2002: Wong Wing Foods is acquired by McCain.
2005: McCain builds $18 million processing plant in India.

company's U.S. subsidiary. This action led to a meeting of the directors and the firing of Wallace as co-CEO and president. A court battle ensued and the fight over the future of the privately held business turned ugly. In an article in the *Financial Times,* Bernard Simon wrote, "Harrison and Wallace thought they were moving the succession process along by giving their sons and nephews an increasingly active role. But it is hard to escape the conclusion that the participation of so many McCain family members in the business hampered rather than helped the process. Harrison says in an affidavit, 'an atmosphere of distrust, intrigue, and maneuvering has existed.'"

The future direction of the company leadership was left up to the courts. A decision in February 1995 upheld the decision of Harrison McCain and the directors to remove Wallace McCain from his position as co-chief executive. Wallace still held a one-third stake in the company and argued for a public offering of McCain stock. The brothers could not reach an equitable agreement regarding a buyout of shares. Wallace McCain went on to take a position with Toronto-based Maple Leaf Foods.

McCain Foods began its South American debut in Argentina. In 1994 the company presented plans to build a potato processing facility in Balarce, Argentina. The plant opened its doors two years later.

The company acquired Everest Foods PLC of Womourne, England, and Growers Foods Limited of Hasting, New Zealand, in 1996. The following year McCain Foods Holland B.V. spent $41 million on a French fry line expansion project at its Lelystad plant.

One of McCain's largest acquisitions also occurred

in 1997 when the company bought the Ore-Ida Food Service frozen French fry and appetizer business for approximately $500 million from the H.J. Heinz Company. The buyout included a major production facility at Burley, Idaho, and four other U.S. plants. Several foodservice brands were part of the transaction, including Ore-Ida and Tator Tots brand potatoes, Rosetto frozen stuffed pasta, and Bagel Bites frozen bagel snacks.

The company introduced a new line of six varieties of snack strips in American Tex Mex and Cajun cuisine flavors. The products were designed to be deep fried and served with dips or as a side dish.

The McCain network expanded into central Europe in 1998 with the construction of a $78.6 million French fry production plant in Wroclaw, Poland. In addition, a host of expansions characterized the year. Besides the company's entry into Central Europe, a third fry plant was built in Matougues, France. The renovated fry line in the Netherlands opened and a $70.8 million expansion was slated for the Easton, Maine business. Further growth was added in a $93.9 million facility in southern Alberta.

Towards the end of the decade McCain had become one of the largest producers of frozen potato products worldwide. The company spent 1999 acquiring assets of Farscheure d'Europe in Vic-sur-Aisne, France, and expanding production with a $68.4 million addition to its Argentinean plant.

McCain Foods made a decision to refuse to buy genetically modified potatoes in November 1999. Harrison McCain commented on the so called "Franken foods," saying, "We think genetically modified material is very good science but at the moment, very bad public relations." He added, "we've got too many people worried about eating the product and we're in the business of giving our customers what they want, not what we think they should have."

McCain embraced the new century with entry into South Africa. The company acquired a French fry plant east of Johannesburg and two frozen vegetable plants nearby. McCain Foods Canada purchased Aloro Foods Inc. of Mississauga, Ontario, in order to increase its frozen pizza product division. The year 2000 also brought plant openings at the newly renovated Easton, Maine expansion and the state-of-the-art French fry plant in Coaldale, Alberta. Capping the year, the company built a $7.2 million potato processing technology center. This research facility illustrated the company's commitment to research agrarian methods and practices devoted to the potato. The facility grew out of the company's interest in developing ongoing research to grow better potatoes with more efficient and economically affordable farming.

In 2001 McCain Foods worked another deal with the H.J. Heinz Company and acquired its frozen foods company in South Africa. The company also bought Heinz Watties Australia for $33 million.

The company broadened its inventory of frozen entrees and appetizers in 2002 when it acquired ethnic Chinese frozen food company Goodman, Fielder International Taiwan from Goodman Fielder Ltd. of Australia. The company also bought Wong Wing Foods of Montreal in 2002, adding Chinese entrees, egg rolls, and dim sum to its Canadian operations.

Business and industry began flooding into China and India in the early part of the 2000s. McCain broke into the Far East in 2004 when it announced plans to open a $43.3 million French fry processing facility in Harbin, Heilongjiang Province, in northeast China.

The following year the company began the process of opening an $18 million plant north of Ahmedagad, Guijarat Province, in India.

McCain Foods Limited stood out as the premier producer of frozen French fries and a growing competitor of ConAgra and other food giants. Its diversified product lines and global presence as well as solid business agreements with McDonald's and various foodservice vendors made it one of the most profitable privately held businesses to date.

Susan B. Culligan

PRINCIPAL SUBSIDIARIES

McCain Foods US, Inc.; McCain Great Britain Ltd.

PRINCIPAL DIVISIONS

McCain Foods Canada; McCain Foods Food Service Products Division.

PRINCIPAL COMPETITORS

ConAgra, Inc.; J.R. Simplot Company; Kraft Foods Inc.

FURTHER READING

Burghardt, John, "Viewpoint; Will Maple Leaf Foods Go the Way of McCain," *Strategy,* May 29, 1995, p. 19.

Chavda, Dharmendrasinh, "Specially for French Fries," *Economic Times of India,* December 3, 2001.

Cheeseright, Paul, "Tractionel Sells Frozen Foods Unit to McCain," *Financial Times,* April 24, 1986, p. 36.

"Giant McCain Poised to Ban Genetically Altered Potatoes," *Toronto Star,* November 29, 1999.

"Heinz Agrees to Sell Its Frozen Foodservice Business to McCain," *Canada Newswire,* March 14, 1997.

Hemstasilpa, Sujintana, "McCain Aims to Lead Thai Market," *Bangkok Post,* September 14, 2005.

"McCain Aims for Strip of Snacks," *Food Manufacture,* January 1997, p. 33.

Simon, Bernard, "Aged Enfants Terribles-The McCain Brothers Seemed to Have the Ideal Succession Plan but They Have Paralysed the Company by Falling Out," *Financial Times,* September 20, 1993, p. 14.

———, "Divided Family Set to Vote on McCain's Future," *Financial Times,* September 13, 1994, p. 30.

———, "Fresh Move in Frozen Foods Feud," *Financial Times,* February 13, 1995, p. 21.

Stern, Avi, "Fifty Jobs Cut at Food Products Firm in Appleton, Wisconsin Area," *Post-Crescent,* November 9, 2001.

Van Alphen, Tony, "Farm Groups Split Over Free Trade with U.S.," *Toronto Star,* September 28, 1988, p. F1.

Medis Technologies Ltd.

— ∎ —

805 Third Avenue, 15th Floor
New York, New York 10022
U.S.A.
Telephone: (212) 935-8484
Fax: (212) 935-9216
Web site: http://www.medisel.com

Public Company
Incorporated: 1992 as Medicell
Employees: 72
Stock Exchanges: NASDAQ
Ticker Symbol: MDTL
NAIC: 335999 All Other Miscellaneous Electrical
    Equipment and Component Manufacturing

∎ ∎ ∎

Medis Technologies Ltd. is a New York City-based company involved in the development of a number of proprietary technologies. Since its founding in 1992, the company has never turned a profit and has generated negligible sales, but it holds out great promise for its disposable micro-fuel cell product, the Power Pack, which it hopes will find a ready market with users of portable electronic devices, such as cell phones, digital cameras, hand-held video games, and PDAs. Roughly the size of a pack of cigarettes, the Power Pack is intended to be used as a recharger or an auxiliary power source. The device itself can be refueled several times before being disposed. In addition to the consumer market, the Power Pack is aimed at the military, to provide the kind of extended-life battery power required by the devices

employed by the modern soldier. Aside from fuel cells, Medis has developed the CellScan, a desktop cytometer used in the early detection of diseases. Other technologies the company has or continues to develop include fuel-efficient engines and environmentally friendly refrigeration and cooling systems.

COFOUNDERS BECOMING BUSINESS PARTNERS IN THE EARLY 1960S

Medis was cofounded in 1992 by CEO and Chairman Robert K. Lifton and Howard Weingrow, president and treasurer of the company. Their partnership, however, stretched back another three decades. Lifton was born in Brooklyn, New York, in 1928. He started out to be an accountant, enrolling at City College in New York, but lacked the necessary mathematical aptitude. Instead, he pursued the law, graduating from Yale Law School in 1951. But he only practiced briefly before turning to real estate, a field in which he succeeded and used as a springboard for other business interests. In 1958 he and Weingrow, who was six years older, first became partners, forming Hechler, Lifton & Weingrow, Inc. Then in 1961 he and Weingrow established Transcontinental Investing Corporation, which they grew into a conglomerate.

Lifton and Weingrow took Transcontinental public in 1969, gaining a listing on the New York Stock Exchange. They then sold the company in 1972. Later ventures included Preferred Health Care, a managed psychiatric care company, and Marcade, an apparel company they ran until 1992 when Medis was launched as a joint venture with Israel Aircraft Industries Ltd.

COMPANY PERSPECTIVES

Medis Technologies develops and produces highly advanced proprietary technologies and products in response to key worldwide needs in the areas of:

Greater and longer-lasting power through proprietary fuel cell technology for portable electronic devices; Improved cell-based medical diagnostics and research systems.

Originally known as Medicell, the company changed its name to Cell Diagnostics Inc. The initial interest of the company was diagnostic cell scan technology that could detect breast cancer with a simple blood test. This technology had been licensed from Bar Ilan University, where it had been developed, and Israel Aircraft Industries now decided to spin it off as a separate enterprise, Medis El Ltd., which became a joint venture with Lifton and Weingrow's Cell Diagnostics. Lifton had a personal interest in the detection of breast cancer, which had touched his family. As the president of the American Jewish Congress from 1988 to 1994, he also wanted to invest in an Israeli company.

The company's cell scan technology had obvious potential. According to *Israel Business Arena,* "Capital market veterans remember an impressive presentation by the company in a prestigious Tel Aviv hotel, with graphs showing enormous potential and astounding profit and revenue forecasts. The presentation helped the company obtain $70 million in a share issue. Medis El took its first steps on Wall Street in 1993, raising $8 million at $8 a share." But turning cell scan technology into a commercial product proved elusive, prompting Medis to look for other opportunities.

In the 1990s Israel experienced an influx of Soviet Jews, including a large number of scientists. Medis tapped into this pool of talent and began pursuing a wide range of ideas, including a linear compressor for use in appliance refrigeration and automotive cooling systems, a "reciprocating electric machine" intended for use in electrical vehicles, and an environmentally friendly internal combustion engine. The company also recruited Gennadi Finkelshtain, an expert in the field of energy who headed a small company called More Energy Ltd., along with colleague Mikhail Khidekel, whose expertise was special materials. It was through More Energy that Medis became involved in fuel cells. It began investing in the company in 1998 and acquired More in 2000 when it developed a viable fuel cell technology.

FUEL CELL ORIGINS DATING TO THE 1800S

The fuel cell was not actually cutting-edge technology. Its origins dated back to 1802 when Sir Humphrey Davy discovered the underlying principle: water decomposed through electrolysis could be reunited with hydrogen and oxygen atoms to produce electricity and water. Although a simple and tantalizing concept, fuel cells proved difficult to harness. It was not until the 1950s that fuel cells began to become a viable power alternative. In the 1960s they appeared to come of age when NASA chose fuel cells over nuclear power to provide electricity and drinking water for the Gemini and Apollo spacecrafts. Most of the research in fuel cells in the ensuing years was in the development of large units, capable of acting as power generators or fuel sources for automobiles. But the economics were not favorable. The combustion engine, a far less elegant device, could produce power far more cheaply than a fuel cell. That equation changed, however, when it came to micro-fuel cells, which faced a different source of competition: batteries, which produced power at a much higher cost per watt and possessed a relatively short life. Given the proliferation of contemporary on-the-go devices and the need for an increasing amount of longer-lasting portable energy supplies, micro-fuel cells were afforded a greater chance to succeed in the marketplace than their much larger companions. "The only hitch," according to *Barron's,* "is that small fuel cells still face monumental hurdles on the way to commercialization—technical ones, like how to deal with heat and microscopic amounts of water, and regulator ones, like developing sufficiently safe packaging to permit methanol, which is flammable, on airplanes."

Medis took an approach to making micro-fuel cells different from that of the competition, however. Instead of relying on platinum or other precious metals to serve as a fuel cell catalyst, Medis developed a catalyst composed of traces of nonprecious metals and a proprietary superconductive polymer coating, the result of work done by Khidekel. As a result, Medis hoped to reduce the cost of making a fuel cell by 50 percent. In addition, Medis eschewed the use of methanol, the fuel used by the vast majority of fuel cell developers, opting instead for a fuel that combined a borohydricle-alkaline solution with alcohols. It was a somewhat caustic substance, but no more so than a number of household products, according to the company.

NAME CHANGE IN 1999

In 1999 Medis announced that its CellScan System was ready for the marketplace and that an entire slate of innovative products were in the pipeline. It was at this

KEY DATES

1992: The company is founded as Medicell.
1993: The joint venture Medis El goes public.
1998: The company begins investments in fuel cell technology.
1999: The name is changed to Medis Technologies.
2000: A stake in More Energy Ltd. is acquired.

point that Cell Diagnostics changed its name to Medis Technologies and traded stock to acquire the rest of Medis El, making it a wholly owned subsidiary. As a result, Israel Aircraft Industries gained a 20 percent stake in Medis Technologies. Although the company held out hope for its other products, it did not have the resources to fund development of them, and as it entered the 2000s it became increasingly committed to the micro-fuel cell field. Its first endeavor, a direct liquid methanol (DLM) fuel cell module, a building block for future commercial products geared toward portable electronic devices, was demonstrated in the laboratory in 2000. It was from the methanol that the fuel cell found the hydrogen it needed to derive electricity. The module was able to operate for eight straight hours at 60 percent of its normal capacity and 20 hours at 50 percent of its nominal capacity, essentially yielding five times more energy on a single fueling than the longest-lasting lithium-ion battery on the market at the time. Moreover, it could be refueled repeatedly, with the plan calling for refueling to be accomplished by the replacement of a disposable fuel cartridge. The company announced that it would have a product in production in 2002. That time frame, however, would be pushed back regularly.

In June 2001 Lifton appeared on CNNfn's *Capital Ideas,* and listed the company's partners, which included General Dynamics, with whom Medis was approaching the Department of Defense and other militaries around the world about buying the micro-fuel cells for military applications. He also explained the advantage fuel cells held over batteries: "When you think of the new forthcoming technology, the 3G phones and the new functionality that they're going to have to offer which is color and music and movies and bank accounts ... and stock accounts. A, they need much more power and fuel cells can give them much more power. B, if you're frustrated today, when your phone goes off, imagine how frustrated you will be when your phone goes off in the middle of your bank statement or in the middle of your movie. They give you much more lasting power. C, they're much more convenient. It takes you three hours

to charge your battery today. You'll be able to use a Medis cartridge in three seconds." Lifton said he hoped to have a commercial product ready for sale in 2003 or 2004, and in the meantime the company was going to demonstrate that the fuel cells were makeable in an effort to convince other companies to manufacture them around the world.

In early 2004 Medis announced that it planned to release a new fuel cell charger at the end of the year, costing $14.99 and offering 15 hours of talk time for cell phone users. The fuel was now different, switched to borohydride (alkaline solutions mixed with alcohols). Unlike methanol it was not flammable or toxic. But some observers, in particular *Barron's* writer Rhonda Brammer, began taking a more critical look at Medis. "The cold, hard reality," she wrote in August 2004, "is that, in spite of these supposedly promising technologies—and Lifton says Medis is still pursuing some of them—Medis Technologies, since inception in April 1992, has generated no earnings and virtually no sales. Indeed, pretty much all it has to show for itself—financially speaking, anyway—is an accumulated deficit that now amounts to more than, get this, $110 million. What Medis has sold in quantity—the only thing, really—is stock."

Displeased with the tenor of the *Barron's* piece, Lifton fired back with a letter to the editor to state his case. He maintained that Medis had much more to show for its efforts than $110 million in debt: "Medis has developed a broadly patented, fuel-cell technology that, in view of its high levels of power, its own cost and safety, suggests it can become an important power source for many portable devices.... The Company has in place a program for bringing those products to high-volume production with companies like Kodak and Flextronics." Lifton also defended the company's CellScan product, which he maintained had "significant business value to Medis." He contended that the company had not spent $110 million in development costs. Rather, "a large part of the accumulated deficit is a result of noncash write-offs of the goodwill accumulated when Medis Technologies acquired part of Medis El, most of whose stock it already owned, as well as other noncash write-offs."

Brammer was not alone in discounting the prospects of Medis bringing a commercially viable fuel cell product to market. The company would also be the target of short-sellers, which Lifton charged were disseminating false information about the company in order to hurt the share price. Nevertheless, Medis still had a lot of interest in its potential. During 2004 it set up distribution arrangements in preparation for the introduction of the Power Pack into the market with companies such as Kensington/Acco Brands, which had access to major office supply and big box retailers; ASE International, with ties to more than 60,000 drugstores, convenience stores, and airport shops; and Superior Communications, which distributed cellular products and controlled branding rights to Cingular/AT&T Wireless, Altel, and T-Mobile USA.

In 2005 Medis made a number of demonstrations of fully operational Power Packs to convince manufacturers to produce the Power Pack as well as drum up future sales. In June 2005 the company announced that it had reached a cooperation agreement with a major, although unnamed, mobile operator to do market testing in preparation for introducing Power Packs as a secondary power source for portable electronic devices. Despite the work of short-sellers, the steps taken by Medis were enough to convince most investors, who bid up the price of the company's stock. As a result, Medis's market cap approached $500 million in 2005. All signs pointed to the company finally fulfilling its promise, but whether that would prove true remained to be seen.

Ed Dinger

PRINCIPAL SUBSIDIARIES

CDS Distributor, Inc.; Medis El Ltd.; Medis Inc. (64%); More Energy Ltd. (44.8%).

PRINCIPAL COMPETITORS

Mechanical Technology Incorporated; Motorola, Inc.; Samsung Electronics Co. Ltd.

FURTHER READING

Brammer, Rhonda, "Sleeper Cell?," *Barron's,* August 2, 2004, p. 23.

Francis, Bruce, "Medis Technologies CEO," *CNNfn: Capital Ideas,* June 27, 2001.

Halper, Mark, "More Power to You," *Time,* December 15, 2003, p. A10.

Manuel, Marlon, "Pocket Power: Battery Industry Surges to Keep Electronic Devices Humming," *Atlanta Journal-Constitution,* January 2005, p. E1.

Pincas, Gitit, "Fueling a $430m Dream," *Israel Business Arena,* January 6, 2005.

——, "Medis Raising $45-60m," *Israel Business Arena,* July 14, 2005.

Scott, Alex, "Medis Develops Nonprecious Metal Catalyst," *Chemical Week,* April 3, 2002, p. 22.

Simou, Alexandra, "Commercializing the 'Next Small Thing,'" *New York Sun,* January 24, 2005.

Mercian Corporation

1-5-8 Kyobashi, Chuo-ku
Tokyo, 104-8305
Japan
Telephone: +81 3 3231 3910
Fax: +81 3 3231 8539
Web site: http://www.mercian.co.jp

Public Company
Incorporated: 1934 as Showa Brewery Co. Ltd.
Employees: 1,290
Sales: $947.0 million (2004)
Stock Exchanges: Tokyo
NAIC: 312130 Wineries; 311119 Other Animal Food
    Manufacturing; 312140 Distilleries

■ ■ ■

Mercian Corporation is Japan's leading wine producer and distributor, and also ranks in the top three, alongside Sapporo and Asahi, of the country's alcoholic beverage groups. Mercian produces and distributes a wide range of wines, including its flagship Chateau Mercian. The company's efforts to develop and refine a Japanese wine based exclusively on grapes grown in Japan has enabled it to win a number of international wine competitions since the late 1990s, including the Japan International Wine Challenge in 2000. In addition to its higher-priced Chateau Mercian line, Mercian produces the economically priced Bon Marché brand, credited with playing a major part in the Japanese wine boom in the 1990s. The company operates wineries in France, Spain, and in the United States. Mercian's overseas holdings include Markham Vineyards, in Napa Valley, California; Chateau Reysson, in the Bordeaux region; as well as several production partnerships in Spain and elsewhere, including Spain's Codorniu and Chile's Vina Concha y Toro. In the traditional Japanese beverages segment, Mercian focuses primarily on Shochu, a white spirit distilled from rice or potatoes. The company also produces Scotch-styled whiskey and Japanese plum brandy, and holds import and/or production and distribution agreements with William Grant, Old Crow, Jim Beam, and Original Peachtree, among others. Using the byproducts of its distillation operations, Mercian has extended into animal feed and pet food production. The company also produces antibiotics, including the cancer-fighting drugs Aclacinomycin and Pinorubin. Mercian's partnership with Japanese food production giant Ajinomoto provides it with sales and distribution and other support services. Mercian is listed on the Tokyo Stock Exchange, and Ajinomoto is the company's largest shareholder, with more than 11 percent of shares. The founding Suzuki family remains active in the company, although former President Tadao Suzuki, grandson of the company's founder, retired from the position of chairman in 2004 at the age of 75. In that year, the company's sales topped $947 million. Wine accounted for 26.8 percent of group sales, followed by Shochu (23 percent) and other Japanese liquors (14.4 percent).

DEVELOPING JAPAN'S WINE LEADER IN THE 20TH CENTURY

Mercian Corporation traces its winemaking history back to the late 19th century, with the founding of Dai-

COMPANY PERSPECTIVES

Established in 1934 as a liquor manufacturer, Mercian Corporation has become one of Japan's leading producers of wine, Oriental liquors and low-alcohol beverages. The Company has also established a strong record of selling a wide range of imported alcoholic beverages. Throughout its history, Mercian has used original fermentation know-how and biotechnology to expand its business horizons. In addition to its alcoholic beverages business, the Company manufactures and markets pharmaceuticals, chemicals and feedstuffs.

Mercian's network consists of five branch offices, eight factories and two research facilities in Japan, as well as one representative office and five production facilities overseas. Two of the overseas production facilities are wholly owned, while the remaining are affiliates in which Mercian's equity participation is less than 50%.

Mercian enjoys a close relationship with the Ajinomoto Group—one of Japan's largest food manufacturers—in such areas as sales, distribution and information processing.

Nihon Yamanashi Budoushu-Gaisha in 1877. Japan's humid climate, however, remained rather hostile to grape-growing, and into the mid-20th century, the country's wine industry relied heavily on imported grapes for production of wines. The Yamanashi-based company began developing new growing techniques and working with domestic grape varieties, adapting traditional grape-growing techniques to the Japanese climate. By 1949, the company had succeeded in launching its Mercian label, which claimed to be the first Japanese wine made wholly from Japanese grapes. The Mercian label quickly became a leading wine label in France, and the Yamanashi company adopted the brand name as its own.

In 1961, Mercian was acquired by the Showa Brewery Co. Ltd. By the mid-1960s, Mercian had begun to earn an international reputation, starting with the winning of a gold medal in an international wine competition in 1966. Following that success, the winemaker began developing a premium wine label, launched as Chateau Mercian in 1970. With this label, the company sought to adapt French winemaking traditions to the Japanese climate. Planting of Merlot grapes began in 1976 at the company's Kikyogahara vineyard. This

was followed by the addition of Cabernet Sauvignon grapes at the company's Jyonohira vineyard in 1984.

An important step in the group's winemaking effort came with the development of its Vertical Shoot Positioned trellis system. Pioneered in Jyonohira, the new method broke with traditional Japanese grape-growing methods, involving the use of an overhead trellis. The company also adapted techniques from other agricultural sectors, such as apple growers' use of plastic bags to cover fruit in order to protect it from the elements.

At the same time, Mercian, under Showa, had begun expanding its wine interests. In the early 1970s, the company began developing its import business, starting with an agreement to import and distribute Tio Pépé brand sherry wines from Spain's Gonzales Byass in 1972. The following year, the company became the importer and distributor for wines made by Germany's Gustav Adolf Schmitt, as well as the Tokay brand of wines from Hungary.

The company's relationship with France began in 1982, when it received the distributorship for Maison Albert Bichot's wines. This was followed by a distribution agreement with Remy-Cointreau, bringing that company's cognac to France, and an agreement with Administration Schloss Reinharshausen, introducing that company's Rhine Wines to the Japanese market. In the late 1980s, the company strengthened its presence in the French wine segment in Japan through import and distribution agreements with champagne-maker Pommery, and wine merchant Crus & Domaines de France, both in 1988.

Into the late 1980s, however, Mercian launched its first efforts to develop its own international wine production component. The company initially turned to the United States, where it acquired Markham Vineyards, in California's Napa Valley, in 1987. This was followed by the purchase of a wine estate in France, Chateau Reysson, in Bordeaux.

Partnerships formed an important part of Mercian's continuing growth strategy into the 1990s. In 1989, the company entered a partnership with seven Italian wine companies, providing Mercian with a portfolio of Italian wine labels for the Japanese market. The following year, the company reached an agreement to begin importing Gu Yue Long Shan branded wine from China's Shaoxing province. In 1993, the company turned to the South American market, and especially the rapidly improving Chilean wine industry, winning the import and distribution agreement for Japan for the wines of Vina Concha y Toro. This was followed by an agreement with Argentinian producer Bodegas Trapiche in 1996.

KEY DATES

1877: Wine grower Dai-Nihon Yamanashi Budoushu-Gaisha is founded.

1934: Showa Brewery is founded.

1937: Showa begins production of Sanraku synthetic sake.

1946: Showa begins production of Shochu liquor.

1949: Yamanashi launches the Mercian label.

1961: Showa Brewery acquires Mercian; Showa merges with Nisshin Brewery Co.

1962: The company merges with Ocean Co., maker of Ocean brand whiskey.

1966: Showa begins production of agricultural antibiotic Kasugamycin.

1969: Showa launches production of Josamycin, a medical antibiotic suitable for human use.

1972: The company initiates an import and distribution agreement for Tio Pépé brand sherry wines from Spain.

1973: The company begins the import and distribution of Gustav Adolf Schmitt wines (Germany) and Tokay wines (Hungary).

1977: The company enters into an import and distribution agreement with Jim Beam Brands of the United States.

1985: Showa changes its name to Sanraku Co.

1987: The company acquires Markham Vineyards in Napa Valley, California, and Chateau Reysson in Bordeaux, France.

1988: The company enters into import and distribution agreements with champagne-maker Pommery, wine merchant Crus & Domaines de France, and William Grant.

1990: Sanraku changes its name to Mercian because of rising wine sales; the company begins importing Gu Yue Long Shan branded wine from China's Shaoxing province.

1993: The company begins an import and distribution agreement for Japan for the wines of Vina Concha y Toro (Chile).

1996: The company enters into an import and distribution agreement with Argentinian producer Bodegas Trapiche.

1998: The company enters into an import and distribution agreement with Roberto Mondavi (U.S.A.).

1999: Import and distribution agreements begin with Marchesi de Frescobaldi (Italy) and Montan Wines Limited (New Zealand).

2001: The company enters into an import and distribution agreement with Piat Pere et Fils (France).

2005: The company acquires 44 percent of Nippon Liquor Ltd.

By the dawn of the 21st century, Mercian had added distribution agreements with Californian wine heavyweight Roberto Mondavi, starting in 1998, and with Marchesi de Frescobaldi, of Italy, and Montan Wines Limited in New Zealand, both in 1999. By 2001, the company had added another French wine partner, Piat Pere et Fils, and several of its Piat d'Or wine labels.

JAPANESE DRINKS LEADER IN THE NEW CENTURY

At the same time it developed its wine business, Showa, which adopted the name Mercian Corporation in 1990, had been building its other interests in the drinks industry. Showa had been founded in 1934 in Tokyo, and began producing alcoholic drinks in 1935. This company expanded its production to include synthetic sake, which led to the launch of a new brand, Sanraku,

in 1937. By 1946, the company had extended its drinks production to include another traditional Japanese spirit, Shochu. In the mid-1950s, Showa's liquor production operations (more specifically, the waste byproducts of the distillation process) gave it an entry into the animal feed industry.

Showa's acquisition drive in the early 1960s went beyond Mercian to include a merger with Nisshin Brewery Co. in 1961 and with Ocean Co. in 1962, a maker of Ocean brand whiskey. Following the latter merger, Showa changed its name to Sanraku Ocean Co. Through the 1960s, the company continued its diversification effort as well, launching production of the agricultural antibiotic Kasugamycin in 1966. This was followed by the launch of production of a medical antibiotic suitable for human use, Josamycin in 1969.

Both antibiotics became strong sellers in Japan and internationally.

Sanraku sought to complement its success developing its portfolio of wine import and distribution agreements in the 1970s. In 1977, for example, the company signed an agreement with Jim Beam Brands of the United States, adding that company's whiskey labels, including Windsor Canadian whiskey and Old Crow bourbon. Later, in 1988, the company added Grant's blended whiskey, from William Grant & Sons. This was followed by the distribution rights to the Original Peachtree Fizz brand in 1989.

The company changed its name to Sanraku Co. in 1985. The growth of its wine business, however, encouraged the company to change its name again, to Mercian, in 1990. By then, Mercian had scored two new successes in the pharmaceuticals market. In 1981, the company launched its successful anticancer antibiotic Aclacinomycin. This was followed by a new cancer-fighting compound, Pinorubin, in 1988. Two years later, the company formed a joint venture, Shenzhen Main Luck Pharmaceuticals Inc., in order to introduce its antibiotics into the mainland Chinese markets.

Pharmaceuticals were to remain just a small part of Mercian's business, however, and by the mid-2000s, with no new products ready for market, the percentage of pharmaceuticals in Mercian's overall revenues had begun to shrink. Yet this was due in part to the development of a boom in Japanese wine consumption in the 1990s.

The discovery of potential health benefits of the polyphenols naturally present in red wine captured the attention of the health-conscious Japanese consumer market. Mercian shrewdly capitalized on the new and growing interest by launching a new wine label, Bon Marche. The new wines were marketed at lower price points than the group's other labels. The result was an upsurge in Japanese wine consumption. Into the mid-2000s, wine consumption in Japan had doubled its level from just a decade earlier. By then, however, the wine boom had ended.

Mercian nonetheless continued to capitalize on the purported health benefits of drinking red wine into the 2000s. The company launched new wine varieties featuring enhanced polyphenol levels, as well as other wines containing other health-promoting ingredients, such as blueberries (for sharpening eyesight) and, in 2004, perilla leaf, said to help suppress allergy symptoms. Meanwhile, rival Sapporo's decision to exit the low-end wine segment in 2003 enabled Mercian to claim the leading position in Japan's wine industry.

Mercian continued to seek new growth opportunities into the second half of the 2000s. In 2005, for example, the company reached an agreement to acquire a 44 percent stake in Nippon Liquor Ltd., which specialized in importing and distributing wine to the Japanese market. Wine remained a driving force for the group's growth, representing nearly 27 percent of its sales. Mercian Corporation prepared to toast further growth into the new century.

M. L. Cohen

PRINCIPAL SUBSIDIARIES

Château Reysson (France); China Shaoxing Yellow Wine Group Co. (PRC); La Jota Vineyard & Winery L.L.C. (U.S.A.); Markham Vineyards (U.S.A.); Marusan Express Co., Ltd.; Mercian Bio Green Co., Ltd.; Mercian Cleantec Corporation; Mercian Feed Corporation; Mercian Karuizawa Museum of Art; MERCOM CORPORATION; Nanki Kushimoto Fisheries Corporation; San'o Corporation; Sanraku Finechem Incorporated; Shenzhen Main Luck Pharmaceuticals Inc. (PRC).

PRINCIPAL COMPETITORS

Taian Taishan Brewery; Sapporo Holdings Ltd.; Asahi Brewers Ltd.; Oenon Holdings Inc.; Yibin Wuliangye Company Ltd.; International Distillers Philippines Inc.

FURTHER READING

Edwards, Ben, "Business in Japan: A Rude Awakening," *Economist*, November 27, 1999.

"Mercian Targeting US$46.5 MLN Group Operating Profit in FY05," *Asia Pulse*, December 16, 2003.

"New Healthy Wine from Mercian," *Japan Food Products & Service Journal*, March 24, 2004.

Robinson, Jancis, "Winning the Struggle Against the Elements," *Financial Times*, May 6, 2000, p. 14.

"Sapporo, Suntory, Mercian to Raise Wine, 'Happoshu' Prices," *Japan Weekly Monitor*, March 25, 2003.

Tsukahara, Mami, "Mercian Toasts the Popularity of Wine in Japan," *Yomiuri Shimbun*, 1998.

Mesa Air Group, Inc.

410 N. 44th Street, Suite 700
Phoenix, Arizona 85008-7608
U.S.A.
Telephone: (602) 685-4000
Toll Free: (800) 637-2247
Fax: (602) 685-4350
Web site: http://www.mesa-air.com

Public Company
Incorporated: 1983 as Mesa Air Shuttle, Inc.
Employees: 5,000
Sales: $1.14 billion (2005)
Stock Exchanges: NASDAQ
Ticker Symbol: MESA
NAIC: 481111 Scheduled Passenger Air Transportation; 481112 Scheduled Freight Air Transportation; 481212 Nonscheduled Chartered Freight Transportation; 481211 Nonscheduled Chartered Passenger Air Transportation

■ ■ ■

More than 13 million passengers a year fly Mesa Air Group, Inc., although they may not know it by name: the company's subsidiaries (Mesa Airlines, Inc.; Air Midwest, Inc.; and Freedom Airlines, Inc.) operate regional feeder flights under the brands America West Express, Delta Connection, US Airways Express, and United Express. Mesa also flies under its own brand. The group's young fleet visits more than 165 cities in the United States, Canada, and Mexico. Its fleet of 184 planes collectively makes more than 1,100 flights every

day. About half of revenues were coming from America West and US Airways.

BEGINNINGS

By his own admission, Larry L. Risley barely graduated from high school, having judged anything above a "C" grade "a wasted effort." He then enlisted in the U.S. Army and eventually obtained an aviation mechanic's license, aspiring to emulate his two older brothers, who were employed as union mechanics for two major airlines. However, following the career path chosen by his brothers proved difficult for Risley, who became a somewhat itinerant worker, securing employment at general aviation fields then quickly losing his job or quitting in anger, as he disliked working under anyone's supervision. In between his stints as an aviation mechanic, Risley found employment where he could get it, including selling burglar alarms and working as a janitor in a baby clothes factory. Later recalling this period of his life, Risley noted, "I was really out of my element."

Risley's prospects brightened in 1970 when he found his first opportunity to work alone, unfettered by a supervisor, opening an aircraft engine shop in Waxahachie, Texas. This comfortable niche, however, soon deteriorated. Several of his customers reneged on payments, debts mounted, and Risley's engine shop dissolved. It would be roughly another decade before an opportunity for success arrived, but when it did, Risley took hold and entrenched himself in the industry that had for so long eluded him.

COMPANY PERSPECTIVES

The turnaround at Mesa Air Group is complete. The focus moving forward is to maintain the carrier's superior operational performance; sustain its strong relationships with its codesharing partners; incorporate more regional jets into the company fleet; work with other carriers on forging new codesharing relationships; and improve profitability and shareholder value.

In 1979, through the efforts of his brother-in-law, Risley was hired by Four Corners Drilling Co., an oil company based in Farmington, New Mexico, to manage its charter airline service. Oil was a plentiful and lucrative commodity in the region during this period, and Risley was kept busy maintaining a fleet of 14 small planes that shuttled oil drillers to and from the desert. The oil boom era in the region was short-lived, however, shuddering to a stop in 1980. The downward spiral of oil prices forced Four Corners Drilling to sharply reduce its drilling activities. The company's fleet was sold as a consequence, but Risley convinced the company to keep one plane, a five-seat Piper, so he could try to establish a shuttle airline service between Farmington and Albuquerque.

With this one small plane, Risley established the foundation from which Mesa Airlines evolved. He advertised on local radio, placed signs along the roads surrounding Four Corners Regional Airport, and, perhaps most importantly, charged half the ticket price of his rival, Frontier Airlines Inc. After two years, during which both Risley and his wife had worked seven days a week maintaining and operating the shuttle service, the couple decided to purchase the plane, offering their pickup truck and house as collateral against a $125,000 loan. The following year, 1983, their fledgling enterprise was incorporated as Mesa Air Shuttle, Inc.

From the beginning Risley's operating philosophy was to fly only small planes between cities and towns in need of additional airline service and to pay close attention to the company's operating costs. Those costs largely resulted from aircraft maintenance, a task for which Risley was particularly well suited. Keeping costs low also carried over into other areas, such as having the pilots of the shuttle service assist in loading passengers' baggage, reducing the number of gate crew at arrival and destination points, and keeping the number of reservation agents to a minimum. Risley's strategy was to have a comparatively small workforce operating small planes

that flew their routes with greater frequency, initially five times a day between Farmington and Albuquerque, than the company's competitors. If all reservation agents were busy booking flights, the incoming calls were directed to other Mesa employees. If the entire staff was busy handling reservations, as they often were during Mesa's first decade of operation, Risley himself would answer the phone and book a passenger's flight.

ACQUISITIONS: 1980S

Very early then, the characteristics that would set Risley's company apart from other regional/commuter airline companies were established, and the shuttle service prospered. From the single, five-seat Piper, the company's fleet gradually grew, with each new plane and each new service route enabling the company to generate greater revenues. With the exception of a small loss in 1984, Mesa recorded a profit throughout the 1980s and reached a financial level that enabled it to begin acquiring other companies, thus broadening its presence in the southwestern United States.

A majority of Mesa's acquisitions in its first decade were not outright purchases of other airline companies, but instead were code-sharing agreements reached with major airline companies, a necessary arrangement for a small airline company following the deregulation of the airline industry in 1978. A code-sharing agreement is a franchise that enables smaller airlines to benefit from the air traffic attracted by larger carriers without incurring their enormous marketing expenses, by operating a shared service on certain routes or reselling seats on another operator's aircraft.

In the mid- and late 1980s, Mesa signed two such agreements, first with Midwest Express, then with United Airlines, and additional agreements followed. Generating nearly $5 million in sales in 1985, Mesa embarked on a five-year period of prodigious growth, elevating itself to the top ranks of regional/commuter airlines in the United States. In 1986 it forced a much larger airline company, Air Midwest, out of the New Mexico region. The following year the company changed its name to Mesa Airlines, Inc., went public, and increased its sales volume to $14.3 million, a nearly 200 percent increase from two years earlier.

That year, 1987, proved to be a busy one for Risley's company and not without its disappointments. Mesa acquired the assets and the Denver, Colorado-based route system of Centennial Airlines, a purchase that resulted in a $250,000 loss for Mesa. The decision to acquire Centennial's service routes emanating from Denver and thereby compete against much larger, more entrenched air carriers represented a step away from Risley's initial corporate strategy to only enter markets suf-

KEY DATES

1982: Mesa Shuttle begins flying between Farmington and Albuquerque, New Mexico.

1985: Company begins a five-year growth spurt that will quadruple its size.

1987: Company goes public as Mesa Airlines, Inc.

1988: *Inc.* magazine names Mesa one of the fastest-growing small companies in the United States.

1992: Acquisition of WestAir doubles Mesa's size.

1994: Mesa Air Group holding company is formed.

1997: United Airlines dumps Mesa, instantly cutting revenues 40 percent.

1998: Jonathan Ornstein succeeds founder Larry Risley as CEO; relocates headquarters to Phoenix.

1999: Mesa buys Charlotte's CCAir Inc.

2003: Mesa begins flying turboprops for United Express again.

2005: Mesa joins Delta Connection, posts revenues of more than $1 billion.

fering from a dearth of established air carriers. Operating as an independent in a market occupied by airline companies possessing much larger financial resources, Mesa found that its approach of offering low air fares and more frequent service was not enough to unseat the larger air carriers.

Despite this setback, Mesa continued to expand. By 1989, the airline's annual sales had reached $22.5 million, more than four times the revenues recorded four years earlier, and the mainstream press began to take notice. A year earlier *Inc.* magazine had named Mesa as one of the country's fastest-growing small public companies. In 1989 Mesa formed Skyway Airlines as a wholly owned subsidiary to fly in conjunction with Midwest Express Airlines out of Milwaukee, Wisconsin, extending Mesa's reach northward. In the same year, the company became the only commuter airline in the world authorized by Pratt & Whitney, an aircraft engine manufacturer, to perform complete overhauls of the PT6, the primary type of engine used by Mesa's planes. Mesa's construction of a $1 million engine shop illustrated Risley's focus on reducing aircraft maintenance costs. Within a year, the costs incurred from building the engine shop were recouped, positioning Mesa as one of the few vertically integrated commuter airlines in the world.

Mesa Airlines quadrupled in size between 1985 and 1990, and doubled in size in roughly the five months preceding the company's tenth anniversary in October 1990 by acquiring Aspen Airways' United Express franchise at United's Denver hub. Risley could look back on a decade of enormous success. By letting each market dictate the size of the particular aircraft serving that market, Mesa had perennially recorded one of the lowest seat-per-mile costs in the industry and could efficiently operate its 33 planes. Mesa planes by this time serviced a considerable portion of the United States: its Skyway planes serviced Iowa, Wisconsin, Illinois, Indiana, Michigan, and New York; its United Express code-sharing agreement took Mesa planes throughout Colorado, Wyoming, Nebraska, and South Dakota; and its original route system, evolving from the company's Farmington-to-Albuquerque flight, now covered New Mexico, Arizona, Texas, and Colorado. All this was enough to make Mesa one of the ten largest commuter/regional airlines in the nation. The airline's greatest growth, however, was still to come at the hands of Jonathan Ornstein, an airline financier who joined the company during its tenth year of operation. Ornstein had originally approached Risley to inquire about purchasing Mesa, an offer Risley declined, but the meeting eventually led to Ornstein's employment by the company. Once Ornstein arrived, he began prodding Risley to pursue purchases of additional airline-related assets and to increase Mesa's influence in the commuter/regional airline industry, aggressively following a course Risley had previously pursued with moderation.

One year after Ornstein's arrival, Mesa acquired Air Midwest, Inc., an airline that operated under a code-sharing agreement with USAir Inc. The purchase extended Mesa's presence into Missouri by virtue of US-Air's base operations in Kansas City and signaled the beginning of an era in which Ornstein and his desire to increase Mesa's magnitude would figure prominently. Later that year, in 1991, Mesa formed a new subsidiary, FloridaGulf Airlines, spreading the company's influence into the southeastern United States. By the conclusion of 1991, a disastrous year for many air carriers, particularly for Eastern, Pan-Am, and Midway Airlines, each of which ceased operation, Mesa continued to exhibit robust performance. The company posted a 39 percent increase in earnings from 1990, a 69 percent increase in revenues to $78 million, and a 50 percent increase in passengers from the previous year.

These positive results were dwarfed by what was to follow. In May 1992, Mesa announced the completion of a merger combining Mesa Acquisition Corp., a wholly owned subsidiary of Mesa, with WestAir Holding Inc., California's largest regional airline. For Mesa the acquisition was enormous, doubling its size and making it the largest regional/commuter airline in the United States. WestAir Holding was organized as a wholly owned subsidiary after the merger and continued to operate under its code-sharing agreement with United Airlines as United Express, based in Fresno, California.

NEW CHALLENGES IN THE 1990S

As Mesa entered the mid-1990s, it continued to look for additional acquisitions, guided by both Risley and Ornstein. In 1994, a year in which the company expected to post $354 million in sales, Risley was contemplating the purchase of CCAir Inc., a commuter airline based in Charlotte, North Carolina, for $32 million, as well as other, smaller, acquisitions, such as a $3 million acquisition of SunAir, an airline serving the Virgin Islands and Puerto Rico, and a 24 percent share in a small commuter carrier based in Britain. As the company continued to expand, succeeding where other airlines had failed, it gained the attention of investors and competitors alike, becoming, for some, the prototype of a regional/commuter airline for the future. *Air Transport World* named it Regional/Commuter Airline of the Year in 1993.

Mesa's corporate holdings were renamed Mesa Air Group in December 1994. However big and powerful it was becoming, Mesa was also developing a reputation for delayed flights and overbooking, particularly at Denver International Airport. The FAA investigated this and allegations of poor maintenance, ultimately fining the carrier and recommending that several of the carrier's operations be merged. In essence, the FAA felt the carrier's operations had not kept pace with its furious growth.

As sales approached the half-billion dollar mark in 1996, Mesa's growth propelled the airline to order 16 Canadair Regional Jets (CRJs) worth $20 million apiece. It sent ten of them to Fort Worth's Meacham International Airport, which had no scheduled passenger service at the time, although American Airlines operated a huge hub at nearby Dallas-Fort Worth International. However, regulations limited Mesa to flights within Texas, traffic did not meet projections, and this operation folded within a year.

An even more devastating setback came when United Airlines replaced Mesa with SkyWest for its West Coast regional feeder services. The loss was severe, as Mesa had garnered 47 percent of its sales from United. Mesa lost $45 million on sales of $423 million in 1998, down from $510 million in 1997, and employment was cut nearly in half.

Risley announced his retirement against this dismal backdrop in early 1998. Ornstein, who had left the company to become CEO of Virgin Express, had led a group of investors that acquired 6.6 percent of Mesa shares and won two board seats. He became CEO of Mesa Air Group himself in May 1998 and set out to reverse the carrier's decline, cutting unprofitable routes, refining Mesa's pricing formula, and disposing of excess aircraft. He also fired 17 of his executives, retaining just one.

Mesa's next largest partner after United was US Airways, which was scrambling to keep up with competitors offering jet service on feeder routes. Although other carriers, Chautauqua and CCAir, also partnered with US Airways on the East Coast, Mesa was the only one operating regional jets at the time. Ornstein planned to expand the US Airways Express operations still further. Mesa Air Group bought CCAir Inc., another US Airways Express partner headquartered in Charlotte, North Carolina, for about $53 million worth of stock. By 1999, Ornstein had succeeded in directing the carrier back toward profitability as he had previously done during a brief tenure at Continental Express. It did not hurt that Bombardier paid Mesa $9 million to settle claims related to aircraft financing and trade-in options. Mesa operated 30 Canadair Regional Jets and 22 de Havilland Dash 8 turboprops at the time, making it one of Bombardier's largest customers.

The company relocated its headquarters to Phoenix from Farmington, New Mexico, in late 1998, and soon afterward, a new corporate logo was unveiled that featured a red sun, which represented a new sun rising for Mesa. As *Forbes* reported, Ornstein's first career as a stockbroker ended with him being fined and suspended for lying to clients. In his career as an airline executive, however, restored profits and on-time performance of better than 90 percent gave him credibility among Mesa's passengers, shareholders, and employees.

GROWING IN 1999 AND BEYOND

A turnaround was in evidence by 1999; however, the company posted a loss for the year due to an accounting charge related to retirement of turboprop aircraft. It was replacing them in part due to expensive new federally mandated training requirements for 19-seat aircraft such as the 1900D that made up most of Mesa's turboprop fleet (it also flew the larger Dash-8). At the same time, major airlines were shifting more of their routes from large airliners to less expensive regional jets operated by their feeder partners. Mesa finally bought Charlotte's CCAir in 1999.

Mesa Air was able to post a profit ($59 million) in 2000 after three years of losses. Revenues were $472 million. The airline was operating a thousand flights a day and its network connected 120 destinations in 38 U.S. states, Canada, and Mexico. It ended the fiscal year with 134 aircraft in its fleet; it had worked out an arrangement to return up to 31 of the 1900D turboprops to their manufacturer, Raytheon Aircraft. At the same time, it was buying more regional jets, adding ones from Embraer of Brazil to its existing Canadian-made CRJs.

Risley retired as Mesa's chairman in 2000. He then ran a small charter operator, Austin Express, for a time and passed away in September 2004 at the age of 59. Mesa announced plans to add the initials "Lima Romeo" to the fleet's tail numbers in honor of Risley.

The company announced plans to double its business with America West Airlines in 2001. By this time, a majority of its contracts with major airlines virtually guaranteed a profit on each flight regardless of fuel costs. Following the expanded America West deal, Mesa formed a new non-unionized subsidiary called Freedom Air.

Mesa stopped doing its own engine maintenance in 2002, selling off its Desert Turbine unit to Pratt & Whitney Canada, Inc. The airline lost about $60 million in 2001 and 2002. Mesa won wage concessions from employees in the difficult aviation environment after the September 11, 2001 terrorist attacks, and there were some temporary layoffs.

In 2003 Mesa was able to rekindle its relationship with United Airlines, whose partner in the Denver area, Air Wisconsin, was retiring its turboprops. Mesa picked up service to medium-sized Colorado cities using ten of its Dash-8s.

The carrier was growing organically and was making bids to buy out others in 2003 and 2004. Looking east, it paid $9 million for assets of bankrupt Midway Airlines while simultaneously attempting a $500 million hostile takeover of Atlantic Coast Airlines (ACA), a United Express carrier on the East Coast.

ACA succeeded in remaining independent, dropping its United Express and Delta Connection feeder contracts and renaming itself Independence Air. However, it failed to take off as a low-cost carrier, and was bankrupt by the end of 2005.

Mesa's Freedom Airlines unit replaced ACA as a Delta Connection carrier in March 2005. Two of Mesa's other partner airlines, America West and US Airways, were merging following US Airways' restructuring. In addition, Mesa's final major airline partner, United Airways, was shifting more volume to Mesa's regional jets as it exited Chapter 11.

While its rivals and partner airlines alike were flying through bankruptcy, Mesa was winging its way to record earnings. Revenues rose from $523 million to $897 million in 2004; the company was profitable again, posting

income of about $25 million a year. Net income was a record $57 million in 2005, while operating revenues of $1.1 billion technically made Mesa a major airline. More than 13 million people flew Mesa a year, and the carrier was looking to set establish a regional jet service in the Hawaiian Islands in 2006.

Jeffrey L. Covell
Updated, Frederick C. Ingram

PRINCIPAL SUBSIDIARIES

Mesa Airlines, Inc.; Air Midwest, Inc.; Freedom Airlines, Inc.; MPD, Inc.; Regional Aircraft Services, Inc.; MAGI Insurance, Ltd. (Barbados); Ritz Hotel Management Corp; Mesa Air Group—Aircraft Inventory Management, LLC.

PRINCIPAL COMPETITORS

Continental Airlines, Inc.; Frontier Airlines, Inc.; MAIR Holdings, Inc.; SkyWest, Inc.; Southwest Airlines Co.

FURTHER READING

Arnoult, Sandra, "Back from the Edge," *Air Transport World,* March 2001, p. 48.

Balzer, Stephanie, "Getting Noticed," *Business Journal—Serving Phoenix & the Valley of the Sun,* April 6, 2001, p. 1.

———, "Ornstein Has Hands Firmly on Controls," *Business Journal—Serving Phoenix & the Valley of the Sun,* April 6, 2001, p. 1.

Barrett, William P., "Second Act," *Forbes,* August 9, 1999, pp. 113-14.

"Commuter Airline of the Year," *Air Transport World,* February 1993, p. 35.

"Flight Leader," *Success,* January 1993, p. 30.

Frink, S., and Jack Hartsfield, "On the Wings of Eagles: The Air Industry," *New Mexico Business Journal,* February 1992, p. 26.

McCartney, Scott, "Mesa Air Consents to an FAA Fine and Improvements," *Wall Street Journal,* September 26, 1996, p. B2.

"Mesa Air Exploring Low-Cost Hub Operation in Charlotte," *Airline Business Report,* March 14, 2005.

"Mesa Airlines Embraces Code Sharing," *Air Transport World,* September 1990, p. 178.

"Mesa Says Aloha to Hawaii," *Air Transport World,* November 2005, p. 22.

"Mesa's Takeover Chase," *Airline Business,* January 1, 2004, p. 10.

Moorman, Robert, "Playing Catch-Up," *Air Transport World,* September 1998, pp. 131-35.

————, "Riches to Rags," *Air Transport World,* April 1998, pp. 66-69.

Phillips, Edward H., "Mesa Seeks to Boost Houston Traffic," *Aviation Week and Space Technology,* August 11, 1997, p. 88.

"Pilots Blast Mesa for Forming Freedom Air," *Airline Financial News,* September 23, 2002.

Reagor, Catherine, "Mesa Airlines Makes Offer to WestAir," *Business Journal,* November 18, 1991, p. 1.

"Regional Airline of the Year: Mesa Air Group," *Air Transport World,* February 2005, p. 28.

Shine, Eric, "Is Mesa Airlines Flying Too High?," *Business Week,* May 9, 1994, p. 82.

Teitelbaum, Richard S., "Mesa Airlines," *Fortune,* May 4, 1992, p. 88.

"Temporary Downdraft," *Forbes,* June 22, 1992, p. 244.

Vuong, Andy, "United, Mesa Air Reunite; Carriers to Resume Mountain-Town Flights This Summer," *Denver Post,* February 28, 2003, p. C2.

"Woes of Big Airlines Mean Boom Times for Mesa, StatesWest," *Business Journal,* October 21, 1991, p. 11.

Yantis, John, "Mesa Air Group, Delta Team Up," *Tribune* (Mesa, Ariz.), May 5, 2005.

Zellner, Wendy, "A Small-Jet Dogfight over Texas," *Business Week,* March 24, 1997, p. 36.

Métro Inc.

———— ■ ————

11011 boul. Maurice-Duplessis
Montreal, Quebec H1C 1V6
Canada
Telephone: (514) 643-1000
Fax: (514) 643-1215
Web site: http://www.metro.ca

Public Company
Incorporated: 1947 as Magasins La Salle Stores Limitée
Employees: 10,500
Sales: CAD 6.69 billion ($5.76 billion) (2005)
Stock Exchanges: Montreal Toronto
Ticker Symbol: MRU.SV.A
NAIC: 445110 Supermarkets and Other Grocery (Except
   Convenience) Stores

■ ■ ■

Métro Inc. has emerged as a driving force in the consolidation of Canada's retail food sector. The Quebec-based company, the number two food retailer in that market, has successfully expanded outside of its home region to become Canada's fifth largest supermarket group. Since its acquisition of The Great Atlantic & Pacific Tea Company of Canada (A&P Canada) in 2005, the company also ranks number two in the Ontario market. Formerly known as Métro-Richelieu, the company's retail network includes nearly 575 stores under the following main banners: Métro, Métro Plus, Loeb, A&P, Dominion, and The Barn Markets, as well as discount store brands Super C and Food Basics. Métro supports its retail operation with its own range of private-label goods, under the Merit Selection, Irresistible, and Super C brands, as well as its own meat processing facility. The company is also a major pharmacy operator, with 256 Brunet, Clini Plus, The Pharmacy, and Drug Basics pharmacies. Métro has set a goal of building its position to number two in Canada during the 2000s. The company is listed on the Ontario and Montreal Stock Exchanges. Métro is led by Chairman Maurice Jodoin, and President and CEO Pierre Lessard. In 2005, the company's revenues reached CAD 6.7 billion ($5.76 billion). Following the integration of the A&P Canada operation, however, Métro's sales were expected to top CAD 11 billion.

COOPERATIVE ROOTS IN THE 1940S

Although Métro-Richelieu has diversified from its historical focus on wholesaling, it retained vestiges of its cooperative roots. Retailers who operated under the Métro and Marché Richelieu marquees were required to invest in Métro-Richelieu Inc. stock. In the early 1990s, more than half of the 480 independent retailers affiliated with its wholesale business were also shareholders with privileged voting rights and a significant enough stake in the company to control its board of directors.

The company was incorporated in 1947 as Magasins la Salle Stores Limitée. Later known as Métro Food Stores Ltd., the firm evolved in the late 1970s and early 1980s into a leading competitor in Quebec's retail food industry through a series of mergers uniting several grocery cooperatives. In 1976, the group merged with Épiceries Richelieu Limitée to form Métro-Richelieu

COMPANY PERSPECTIVES

Our vision is to create, over time, value for our shareholders. Increased earnings, dividends and share value constitute the heart of this vision. Our strategies extend across several axes: Maintaining a retail network ranking among the most modern and competitive in the various segments in which we operate; Establishing management and operational methods to increase both our efficiency and our profitability; Training and developing our employees in order to ensure our continuity and expansion; Aiming for a solid financial position; Remaining poised to take advantage of opportunities to expand our share of the food and pharmaceutical markets.

Inc. The name changed to Métro-Richelieu Group Inc. in 1979. In 1982, Métro-Richelieu acquired and merged with United Grocers Inc. to form United Grocers Métro-Richelieu Group Inc. These amalgamations created Quebec's third largest grocery company, a firm with 75 percent of its volume concentrated in wholesale distribution for its 660 affiliate-shareholders.

The formation of these cooperatives helped independent supermarketers retain their autonomy while enabling them to compete with such larger rivals as Loblaw Co. Ltd. and Provigo Inc. Co-ops pooled warehousing and distribution, thereby eliminating the middleman and cutting overhead. Shared promotions saved money and increased marketing and advertising clout. Since affiliates were required to own stock in the cooperative, they also were entitled to a share of its profits.

The evolution and growth of Métro-Richelieu Inc. (the name was shortened in 1986) was a manifestation of declining population growth in the province, the maturation of the region's food distribution market, and the intensified competition that resulted. By the early 1980s, Métro's merger strategy had earned it a third-place ranking among Quebec's wholesale food companies. By that time, the wholesaler was racking up more than $1 billion in sales and $2.5 million in profits.

In spite of its efforts to build up a strong presence, Métro-Richelieu suffered a stunning reversal in 1985, losing $417,000 on sales of $1.3 billion. Jacques Maltais, a relative newcomer to Métro with only three years' experience, advanced to the wholesaler's presidency that year. Maltais proposed a sweeping "modernization

program" that encompassed Métro's organizational scheme, its operations, and its growth strategy. The first part of Maltais's plan entailed the partial dissolution of the cooperative organizational scheme. The company went public with the sale of $27.5 million in subordinate voting stock, but remained under the control of its grocer-affiliates. Part of this capital infusion went toward technological upgrades, including the installation of electronic point-of-sale systems, store renovations and expansions, and other enhancements.

Following the lead of Quebec grocery industry leader Provigo, Inc., Métro-Richelieu also undertook a diversification program in the late 1980s. Maltais reasoned that geographic and product diversification would shelter the food company from economic cycles and supplement its skinny, but typical, 1 percent profit margins. According to a December 1986 *Globe and Mail* article, the new leader's plan enjoyed "a clear mandate from his controlling shareholders." Over the course of just one year, 1987, the company bought into restaurant and sporting goods chains, pharmaceutical wholesaling and retailing, institutional foodservice, and its own chain of retail supermarkets.

Analysts (who enjoyed the 20-20 vision of hindsight) later characterized the diversification program as a miserable failure. Four of the seven acquisitions were divested within five years of their purchase, and Métro-Richelieu incurred back-to-back losses in fiscal years 1989 and 1990 totaling more than $25 million. The acquisition policy also cost President Maltais his job; he quit early in 1990. Marcel Guertin, who had maintained his position as chairman throughout the crisis, assumed the additional role of interim CEO, and Jacques Obry became president and chief operating officer.

Métro-Richelieu recruited two former executives of its primary competitor, Provigo Inc., and hired them in the fall of 1990. Pierre Lessard had served as Provigo's president for nine years when he resigned in 1985 after being "passed over" when the CEO's position came open. Lessard was characterized as a "cautious, conservative" leader who focused on the basics of the grocery industry: increasing volume and returns. In fact, some industry observers correlated his lack of daring with his lack of progress at Provigo, but by the early 1990s that "flaw" had become a virtue. H. Paul Gobeil formed the other half of the new management team. Gobeil did "double-duty" during the early 1990s, dividing his work week between Métro-Richelieu's vice-chairmanship and his previously held chairmanship of Royal Trust Co. Called "a firm believer in deficit reduction," Gobeil was put in charge of financial planning. Both aged 48, the partners had worked together at Provigo for almost a decade before going their separate ways in 1985.

KEY DATES

1947: Magasins la Salle Stores Limitée is created (later known as Métro Food Stores Ltd.).

1976: The company merges with Épiceries Richelieu Limitée and becomes Métro-Richelieu Inc.

1982: The company acquires United Grocers Inc. and changes its name to United Grocers Métro-Richelieu.

1986: The name is shortened to Métro-Richelieu and the company launches a diversification strategy into the restaurant sector and retail sporting goods, leading to several years of losses.

1987: The company acquires discount grocery chain La Ferme Carnaval, including Super Carnaval stores.

1990: New management ends the diversification effort, selling off the restaurant and sporting goods holdings to refocus the company on food and pharmacy operations.

1992: The company acquires 46 stores from the failed supermarket chain Steinberg.

1994: The company launches private-label brands, including Norois beer.

1999: The company acquires 51 Loeb stores, marking its first entry into the Ontario market.

2000: The name is changed to Métro Inc. as part of a new strategy to develop into a national Canadian supermarket leader.

2002: The company acquires Grossiste Sue Shang, a wholesale distributor in Quebec.

2003: The company acquires Alexandre Gaudet Ltee., a wholesaler serving the small format grocer circuit; the new store format Maxi Plus is launched.

2004: The company acquires 15 Gargon stores in Quebec City area.

2005: A&P Canada is acquired, boosting sales by more than CAD 4.6 billion.

NEW DIRECTION IN THE 1990S

Under new direction, the company divested its restaurant and retail sporting goods interests to concentrate on the food and drug businesses. The companies that Métro retained from its ill-fated diversification evolved into vital contributors to the parent company's bottom line.

La Ferme Carnaval Inc. had been acquired from Burnac Corp. for $135 million (half cash, half shares) in 1987. Founded in Quebec City in 1982, it had previously been a customer of Métro's warehouse operations. Within just five years, the supermarket chain had captured 20 percent of its hometown retail food market and expanded into Montreal. Although La Ferme Carnaval had been partly to blame for Métro's poor performance, Lessard and Gobeil elected to keep the discount grocery chain. Its positive contributions included the addition of 12 Super Carnaval stores. Carnaval also gave Métro a foothold in the fledgling warehouse/discount sector and vaulted over struggling rival Steinberg Inc. to become Quebec's second largest food retailer.

McMahon-Essaim Inc., a wholesale pharmaceutical distributor acquired for $6 million in 1986, also grew under Métro-Richelieu's custody. Over the course of its eight years in the Métro family, the company's sales increased from about $50 million to $186.3 million. An aggressive franchising program for the division's Brunet drugstores helped it evolve into the second largest player in the provincial pharmacy market by the early 1990s.

In 1992, the tough Quebec food market claimed a major victim, number three chain Steinberg Inc. The three largest remaining competitors (according to rank)—Provigo (which was renamed Univa, Inc. that year), Métro-Richelieu, and Oshawa Group Ltd.'s Hudon et Deaudelin Inc.—divided the spoils of the decade-long battle for the provincial market among them. Métro-Richelieu bought 46 of Steinberg's 102 stores for slightly more than $100 million. The new locations were an instant boon; Métro-Richelieu's profit rose 153 percent in the first quarter of 1993.

From 1990 to 1994, in fact, Métro-Richelieu's sales increased 33 percent, from $2.19 billion to $2.91 billion. Net earnings quadrupled during the same period, from a deficit of $9 million to a $37.2 million profit. The company also was able to reduce its long-term debt load by almost 75 percent, from $184.4 million to $46.7 million, thereby freeing up funds for capital investment. Part of the company's success was attributed to an advertising campaign begun in 1991. The ads, which featured the tagline, "Métro, grocers by profession," won numerous accolades from regional, national, and even international industry organizations.

Métro placed increased emphasis on its private label (or house brand) program in the 1990s. Private-label products enable retailers to offer their customers a consistently low-priced product, yet retain higher profit margins for themselves. By the early 1990s, Métro-Richelieu's own-label program included more than 1,500 products. In 1994, the company launched two new private lines: Éconochoix bargain-priced items and the controversial Norois Premium beer. Retailing at 12 percent less than its next-lowest-priced competitor, Métro's brew was the lowest-priced beer in the province. But Canada's beer establishment was quick to counter this incursion. Molson, Labatt, and the Quebec Brewers' Association filed a lawsuit to stop sales of the beer. Although sales of the brew were halted in 1994, an intermediate ruling allowed Métro to resume sales in 1995 pending a final decision. By mid-year, it was estimated that Norois had captured 2 percent of home consumption sales in the province.

CONSOLIDATION LEADER FOR THE NEW CENTURY

Métro-Richelieu entered 1995 with a bankroll of $32 million intended for renovations, store expansions, and construction of new stores. The company was in a strong competitive position, having increased its market share from 25 percent in 1990 to 32 percent in 1995. It appeared poised to capture the top position in the provincial food market from longtime rival Univa, which remained hobbled by heavy diversification-related debt. By the spring of 1995, Lessard was confident enough to reinstate the company's dividend for the first time since 1990.

The company soon faced a new threat, however, as another of Canada's major supermarket groups, Loblaw, based in Toronto, announced its intention to enter the Quebec market. That occurred in 1998, when Loblaw acquired Provigo Inc., which operated under the Maxi and Maxi & Co. banners. Provigo also operated some 90 stores under the Loeb banner outside of Quebec. That same year, another major, Sobeys, took over Quebec's Oshawa Group, and its IGA store network.

Lessard recognized that Métro would have to launch its own expansion effort, and especially position itself as a leading player outside of the Quebec region. This led the company to buy part of the Loeb supermarket chain in 1999, paying Provigo CAD 85 million for 51 stores in Ottawa and northeastern Ontario, as well as the exclusive rights to the Loeb name, and a number of distribution centers in the region. The move represented Métro-Richelieu's first entry into the most populated region in Canada. As a result of the company's expansion outside of Quebec, and in confirmation of its determination to build itself into one of the top Canadian supermarket groups, the company changed its name to Métro Inc. in 2000.

By then, Métro had also expanded its range of private-label foods, rapidly building its portfolio beyond the Norois beer brand to include a range of some 1,000 products. In keeping with the group's national ambitions, the private-label lines, originally branded as Le Choix Evident and Marche Richelieu, were rebranded under the single Merit Selection name. At the same time, Métro began redeveloping the Super Carnaval format as a discount format, Super C. The company began opening Super C stores in the Ontario market as well, converting a number of Loeb stores there.

Into the mid-2000s, Métro emerged as a driving force behind Canada's continuing grocery sector consolidation. In 2002, the company bought up Grossiste Sue Shang Inc., a Quebec-area wholesale grocery distributor serving the independent grocery circuit. The following year, Métro purchased Alexandre Gaudet Ltee., another wholesale distributor serving primarily smaller grocery shops. That acquisition boosted to 2,000 the number of stores supplied by Métro's wholesale division. Meanwhile, Métro launched a new store format in 2003, the Maxi Plus, featuring an "ultra-modern" format including specialty shops, as well as an extensive organic food section. The format proved successful, leading to a rapid rollout, including 12 new Maxi Plus stores in 2004 alone.

Métro continued acquiring scale into the mid-decade. In 2004, for example, the company purchased 15 Gargon stores in the Quebec City area, adding another CAD 165 million in sales to its Quebec operations. While that purchase was relatively modest, the company was already preparing a greater coup. In 2003, the company announced its interest in acquiring the Canadian operation of the Great Atlantic and Pacific Tea Company Ltd., more popularly known as A&P, should its U.S. parent ever consider a sale.

By 2005, Métro had its way, and the company acquired A&P Canada in a deal worth some CAD 1.7 billion. Through that purchase, Métro gained some CAD 4.6 billion in additional turnover, through a nationally operating network of 234 stores. The company's newly expanded operation included 132 Dominion, A&P, and The Barn Markets supermarkets, and 102 stores under the Food Basics discount format. The addition of A&P was expected to boost Métro's total sales past CAD 11 billion, while providing operational synergies of as much as CAD 60 million per year. Métro had emerged as one of Canada's true supermarket leaders for the new century.

April Dougal Gasbarre; M. L. Cohen

PRINCIPAL SUBSIDIARIES

Épiciers Unis Métro-Richelieu Inc.; La Ferme Carnaval Inc.; McMahon-Essaim Inc.; Alimentation Dallaire St.-Romuald Inc.

PRINCIPAL COMPETITORS

Empire Company Ltd.; Sobeys Inc.; Alimentation Couche-Tard Inc.; Costco Wholesale Canada Ltd.; Canada Safeway Ltd.; Westfair Foods Ltd.; North West Company Fund; Calgary Co.-Operative Association Ltd.

FURTHER READING

Clifford, Edward, "Metro-Richelieu Looking Better," *Globe and Mail,* June 17, 1993, p. B11.

"Drama amid Success at Metro," *MMR,* February 24, 2003, p. 13.

Dunn, Brian, "50 and Ready to Fight," *Supermarket News,* March 2, 1998, p. 1.

———, "Metro-Richelieu: Growing Despite Competition," *Supermarket News,* February 10, 1997, p. 9.

———, "Metro-Richelieu to Buy 41 Loeb Supermarkets," *Supermarket News,* May 17, 1999, p. 22.

———, "Metro-Richelieu to Shorten Name," *Supermarket News,* January 31, 2000, p. 4.

Gibbens, Robert, "Métro-Richelieu Buys Major Food Chain," *Globe and Mail,* May 5, 1987, p. B1.

———, "Métro-Richelieu Seeking to Diversify," *Globe and Mail,* December 30, 1986, p. B6.

Gibbon, Ann, "Lessard Returns," *Globe and Mail,* October 1, 1990, p. B1.

———, "Métro-Richelieu Posts Profit Rise," *Globe and Mail,* January 24, 1995, p. B8.

———, "Richelieu Reports Profit," *Globe and Mail,* January 29, 1991, p. B9.

McKenna, Barrie, and Ann Gibbon, "Provigo, Métro-Richelieu, Hudon to Carve up Steinberg," *Globe and Mail,* May 23, 1992, p. B1.

Olijnyk, Zena, "Clean Up, Aisle Two," *Canadian Business,* October 10, 2005, p. 49.

Zwiebach, Elliot, "Metro Drives Synergies with A&P," *Supermarket News,* November 21, 2005, p. 6.

Micrel, Incorporated

———■———

2180 Fortune Drive
San Jose, California 95131
U.S.A.
Telephone: (408) 944-0800
Fax: (408) 944-0970
Web site: http://www.micrel.com

Public Company
Incorporated: 1978
Employees: 877
Sales: $257.5 million (2004)
Stock Exchanges: NASDAQ
Ticker Symbol: MCRL
NAIC: 334413 Semiconductor and Related Device
Manufacturing

■ ■ ■

Micrel, Incorporated is a manufacturer of analog, mixed-signal, and digital semiconductors that are used for power management in telecommunications equipment, networking equipment, and industrial electronics. Micrel ships more than 2,500 products that are characterized by high speed, low noise, and maximum efficiency in the smallest package. The majority of the company's manufacturing activity takes place in San Jose, California. Micrel also owns a design facility in Huxley, Iowa. Internationally, sales and technical facilities are located in Korea, Taiwan, China, Hong Kong, Japan, the United Kingdom, Germany, Norway, and France.

ORIGINS

Micrel's founder, Raymond D. Zinn, left an indelible mark on the company he started in 1978, directing its development and orchestrating its growth during the first 30 years of its existence. Zinn, the eldest of 11 children, grew up in a devoutly Mormon family in the farming community of El Centro, California, where his father worked as a cattle rancher. Zinn and his siblings learned the merits of hard work under the watchful eye of their father, each participating in running the ranch at an early age. By the time he was four years old, Zinn was in charge of carrying home goods from the country store. He baled hay and milked cows before and after school. When his actions did not accord with his father's wishes, his errancy was brought to his attention by an object lesson. One such reprisal occurred in 1958, when Zinn decided to drop out of college and get a job. He left midway through his junior year at Brigham Young University and drove home to California to inform his father of his decision. The news was not welcomed. "First, my father took my car keys," Zinn recounted in an August 9, 2000, interview with *Investor's Business Daily.*

Zinn's father told him to take off his shirt and socks. "Then," Zinn explained, "he marched me into the office restroom and told me to hand my pants through the door." Naked, Zinn waited for his father to return his clothes, spending six hours wrapped in paper towels, trying to determine what his father's message was. "He was saying, 'Well, if you're going to quit school, you're going out in the world the way you came in.' He wanted me to think about living with decisions." Zinn returned to Brigham Young, earned an undergraduate degree in business management, and continued his education, receiving a master's degree from San Jose State University.

Zinn moved to the San Francisco Bay Area at the beginning of the 1960s, the destination the choice of his girlfriend. The region's first high-technology companies were emerging at the time, capturing Zinn's attention. Interested specifically in the space program, which was reaching its greatest intensity of development during the 1960s, Zinn wanted to become an astronaut. The desire directed him toward his first job at a rocket motor manufacturer named United Technologies, where he was hired as an internal ballistician. Zinn spent two years at United Technologies, leaving after his father-in-law, who worked at Fairchild Semiconductor, sparked his interest in the chip-making business. He joined Fairchild as an engineer in 1963, beginning a lifelong fascination with designing semiconductors that led him to found Micrel.

Zinn struggled against the corporate structure and hierarchy at Fairchild, deeming himself to be too fiercely individualistic to enjoy working in the traditional employer-employee setting. Although far from espousing the anti-Establishment views prevalent in the Bay Area during the 1960s (he, like his father, was a devout Mormon), Zinn never was comfortable working for others and, consequently, never held a job for long. After leaving Fairchild, Zinn worked at several chip-making plants, including Electromark and TRE, gaining the experience that would enable him to strike out on his own as an entrepreneur. In 1978, he made his move, forming a partnership with a colleague named Warren Muller to start Micrel. The pair used $300,000 in savings and bank loans to found the company, eschewing the financial support of venture capitalists. "I wanted control of my destiny and to do it my way," Zinn remarked in his interview with *Investor's Business Daily*.

With scant start-up capital at his disposal, Zinn was forced to play a limited role in the semiconductor

industry. Micrel initially operated as a testing facility for other chip manufacturers, offering wafer-test services as a way to fund the development of its own products. A turning point in the company's development occurred in 1981, when it acquired a fabrication facility from German giant Siemens AG, a purchase that gave Zinn the means to begin offering wafer foundry services. The company, duplicating a customer's process, manufactured chips designed by the customer. Entering the production fray failed to spark any meaningful financial growth for the company, however. Throughout the 1980s, Micrel remained, in large part, out of sight, operating on the periphery of its industry. One pundit, as reported in the May 19, 1997 issue of *Electronics News*, criticized the company for its lackluster growth, remarking that Micrel had "glacier-like growth and the sex-appeal of a mud hen."

Zinn, looking back at the period, offered no apologies for his company's diminutive stature, explaining to *Electronics News* that Micrel's slow development was "like an apple tree or an almond tree that doesn't produce for seven years because it takes a long time for it to develop its root structure and its fruit." Micrel eventually recorded growth at a pace that would rank it among the fastest growing companies in the nation, growth that was attributable to the proliferation of products that used the types of chips made by Zinn's company.

Integrated circuits were divided into three broad categories: digital, analog, and mixed-signal. Digital circuits processed information by implementing two values, either zero or one, through on-off electrical surges. Although Micrel later delved into the digital chip market, the majority of its business was based on analog and mixed-signal semiconductors, particularly analog circuits. Analog circuits, which were used in virtually every electronic system, processed information in the form of continuously varying voltages and currents that had an infinite number of values. Mixed-signal chips combined analog and digital functions on one circuit.

ACCELERATED GROWTH IN THE 1990S

Micrel recorded its first meaningful growth after it began designing its own chips in the early 1990s. The company's analog and mixed-signal circuits sold well, as well as a product called a low-voltage dropout regulator, which was a chip designed to control voltages in a circuit that desktop computers used. Sales reached $20 million in 1993 and doubled the following year, when Zinn, for the first time, solicited financial help from outside investors. Micrel filed for an initial public offering (IPO) of stock in October 1994 after recording four years of

---

KEY DATES

1978: Micrel is founded.
1981: Micrel acquires a fabrication facility.
1994: Micrel completes its initial public offering of stock.
2002: A $41 million loss halts 22 years of consecutive profits.
2004: Micrel's product line surpasses 2,500 products.

---

steady growth, seeking to pay down its debt and to finance its expansion with Wall Street's help.

In the wake of its IPO, Micrel flourished, its growth propelled by the proliferation of products in the portable electronics industry. As sales of cellular telephones, laptop computers, and industrial handheld instruments increased, so too did the need for longer battery life and lower power consumption, a trend that played to Micrel's expertise. The company's power management chips, particularly those of the mixed-signal variety, provided it with a rate of financial growth that silenced its critics. Zinn, no longer relegated to the fringe of the industry, began to attract attention from the press, earning accolades for his astute management.

Although Micrel began to record substantial growth during the latter half of the 1990s, the company continued to rank as a small- to medium-sized semiconductor manufacturer, dwarfed by the biggest chip makers. In 1996, the company's sales reached $66 million, a fraction of the total generated by multibillion-in-sales rivals, but Micrel's relatively small size, coupled with Zinn's business savvy, served as an advantage. The company was in a position to react nimbly to changing market conditions, particularly in one important instance that bolstered Zinn's reputation within the semiconductor industry.

In 1997, when Micrel celebrated its 19th consecutive year of profitability, Zinn was credited with being one of the first in his industry to foresee the onset of the Asian financial crisis. Micrel depended on Asia for 40 percent of its sales at the time, a dependence that Zinn realized would cause great damage to the company and end its profit-making streak. He ordered his managers to focus their sales efforts elsewhere, such as original equipment making, and he called a meeting of senior executives, informing them of the severity of the impending crisis. He gave the gathered executives one week to formulate a plan to deal with the collapse of Asian markets. "That meeting lasted a half-hour," the company's executive vice-president said in an August 9, 2000, interview with *Investor's Business Daily.* "We came back a week later and had another half-hour meeting to tell Ray what we could do. Two half-hour meetings recast what we did for 1998."

The Asian economic crisis precipitated one of the most severe downturns in the history of the semiconductor industry, yet Micrel recorded robust financial growth. Between 1997 and 1999, the company's annual sales jumped from $104.5 million to $195.1 million, while its net income more than doubled, leaping from $24.4 million to $54.4 million.

By the end of the 1990s, Zinn was pursuing an ambitious financial goal, one that dictated a much more aggressive approach to growth. Zinn announced his desire to make Micrel a $1 billion-in-sales company by 2003, an objective that would require enormous expansion for the company to meet. The pursuit of the $1 billion mark led Zinn to diversify his business and broaden the company's capabilities, something he would accomplish in large part through acquisitions. In November 1998, the company entered the high-bandwidth telecommunications and data communications market by acquiring Synergy Semiconductor Corp. Synergy, based in Santa Clara, California, posted $37.4 million in sales in 1997 by supplying mixed-signal and digital chips for the communications, high-performance computing, and automated test-equipment industries. One year later, in November 1999, Micrel entered another new market via an acquisition, purchasing Altos Semiconductor, which competed in the thermal management market. Altos provided mixed-signal circuits that accurately measured the temperature at various so-called "hot spots" in electronic systems and initiated system cooling by turning on fans.

FALTERING IN THE 21ST CENTURY

As Zinn pressed toward his financial target, Micrel, for once, showed that it was not immune to negative market forces. In 2000, revenues increased at a record high pace, reaching $346 million, but the following year the company felt the effects of what was regarded as the most severe downturn in the history of the semiconductor industry. A combination of recessive economic conditions, the collapse of the dot-com industry, and excess inventory held by wireless communication customers, delivered a decisive blow, leading to a 37 percent decline in revenues in 2001 to $218 million. Revenues fell the following year, slipping to $205 million, but the most notable financial blemish was a $41 million loss for the year, the first time Micrel had posted an annual loss since its inception.

In the wake of the difficulties experienced during the first years of the decade, Micrel pinned its hopes on the recovery of the semiconductor market. Instead of celebrating its 25th anniversary as a $1 billion company, Micrel pursued less lofty ambitions, striving to restore the stature it attained in 2000, the high watermark of its existence. In 2003, there were signs that the worst was over. Sales increased marginally to $211 million and the company recorded a small profit of $5.1 million, ensuring that the loss in 2002 did not turn into an unwanted streak of losses. More encouraging results were achieved in 2004, when sales increased 22 percent to $257 million and net income swelled to $31.3 million. In the years ahead, with a diverse range of products and Zinn's capable leadership underpinning its progress, the company was expected to factor as a prominent player in its industry and one day reach the $1 billion mark.

Jeffrey L. Covell

PRINCIPAL COMPETITORS

Maxim Integrated Products, Inc.; Texas Instruments Incorporated; National Semiconductor Corporation; Vitesse Semiconductor Corporation; Linear Technology Corporation; Broadcom Corporation; Marvell Technology Group Ltd.

FURTHER READING

Baljko, Jennifer L., "Proactive Strategy Keeps Micrel on Profitable Path," *Electronic Buyers' News,* September 28, 1998, p. 1.

————, "Raymond D. Zinn—Executive's Pithy Sayings Sum Up Successful Business Principles," *Electronic Buyers' News,* December 21, 1998, p. 84.

Hardie, Crista, "Micrel: A Growing Sense of Power," *Electronic News,* May 19, 1997, p. 1.

Tsuruoka, Doug, "Entrepreneur Raymond Zinn: His Hard Work and Independence Built Chip Empire," *Investor's Business Daily,* August 9, 2000, p. A4.

The Mills Corporation

1300 Wilson Boulevard, Suite 400
Arlington, Virginia 22209
U.S.A.
Telephone: (703) 526-5000
Fax: (703) 526-5111
Web site: http://www.millscorp.com

Public Company
Incorporated: 1991
Employees: 1,150
Sales: $832.8 million (2004)
Stock Exchanges: New York
Ticker Symbol: MLS
NAIC: 525930 Real Estate Investment Trusts

■ ■ ■

The Mills Corporation is a real estate investment trust (REIT) listed on the New York Stock Exchange, focusing on shopping malls, which it develops, owns, and manages. The Arlington, Virginia-based company is best known for its mega-malls, combining retail and entertainment elements, that bear the Mills name, such as Potomac Mills in Washington, D.C.; Sawgrass Mills in Ft. Lauderdale, Florida; Franklin Mills in Philadelphia, Pennsylvania; Discover Mills in Atlanta, Georgia; Opry Mills in Nashville, Tennessee; and Gurnee Mills in Chicago, Illinois. In addition, Mills operates more than 20 regional shopping centers across the United States, as well as international centers located in Toronto, Madrid, and Glasgow. All told, Mills controls more than 50 million square feet of leasable space, and its properties at-tract some 370 million visits a year, resulting in $8.7 billion in tenant sales.

PREDECESSOR'S FOUNDING IN THE 1960S

Mills grew out of the portfolio of the Western Development Corporation, founded in Washington, D.C., in 1967 by Herbert S. Miller. According to the *Washington Post,* Miller "shelved the corporation about the time he went to work for Shannon and Luchs. Building a reputation as an idea man not overly concerned with details, Miller brokered what is perhaps the most glamorous ménage a trois in Washington real estate." Miller brought together property owner Mrs. Olga Mazza, a real estate subsidiary of Exxon, and depart-ment store Neiman Marcus to develop Mazza Gallerie. In the process he made extensive contacts in the market. Miller left Shannon and Luchs in 1973 to become eastern regional director for Michigan-based Taubman Company, the nation's largest developer at the time. Less than two years later he struck out on his own and put Western Development to use, taking on partners Richard L. Kramer and Gerald L. Dillon. Kramer was a Wharton School of Finance graduate who managed his family's real estate holdings, which included more than 1,000 acres in the Washington area, while Dillon had been a senior vice-president in charge of construction at Taubman. Over the next few years they developed strip malls and office buildings together.

Miller and Western Development forged a national reputation in the real estate industry with the 1985 opening of Potomac Mills in the Washington, D.C.,

COMPANY PERSPECTIVES

Our mission is to deliver superior shareholder value by creatively developing, acquiring, merchandising and managing a diversified portfolio of exceptional domestic and international retail and entertainment destinations.

market, which broke the accepted model of a regional shopping mall. Instead of department store anchors, it relied on the combination of off-price retailers and factory outlet stores. Bringing the retailers together required some salesmanship on the part of Miller, however. "The outlet people didn't want to be near off-price, and the off-pricers didn't want to be near factory outlets," Miller told *Shopping Centers Today.* "We told the outlet people it would be called Dale City Mall and would be out in the country. With off-price people, we called it the Washington Outlet Mall and emphasized that it was near the city." Potomac Mills proved so popular that construction carried on for several years, as the original 650,000 square feet of space grew to 1.6 million square feet. But it was not just the prices that brought in the patrons to Potomac Mills. According to the *Washington Times,* "It also broke with convention for discount retailing, dressing up Potomac Mills with pricey fixtures such as giant overhead movie screens for shoppers' entertainment and a licensed Elvis Presley museum stocked with the rock 'n' roll king's guns and jewelry." According to *WWD,* "By inviting several mid-sized anchors—rather than major department store anchors—to ground the project, and surrounding retail with family fun and entertainment, the developer created an unusual retail hybrid. Closer to a virtual department store than a regional mall, it was a place where outlets and big-box power stores could cohabit peacefully with price sensitive retailers."

Western Development continued to open strip malls as well, but the Mills concept received greater emphasis over the next several years. In 1989 Franklin Mills opened in Philadelphia, Pennsylvania, followed a year later by Sawgrass Mills in Ft. Lauderdale, and Gurnee Mills, located between Chicago and Milwaukee, in 1991. But even as the Mills concept was expanding, Western Development was experiencing serious difficulties: overdue taxes, property lien foreclosure threats, and a lawsuit filed against it by the Franklin Mills partner. The suit maintained that Miller and Kramer were "embroiled in extensive and protracted negotiations with a view

toward the dissolution and division of their respective interests in Western and Western's various affiliates." To make matters worse, the economy was not doing well, making it a difficult environment for all real estate developers.

GOING PUBLIC AS A REIT IN 1994

Miller and Kramer parted ways, with Miller continuing on with the Mills concept. In 1991 Mills Corporation was incorporated in Virginia and in January 1993 it replaced Western Development as the parent of the four Mills malls. A year later Mills was taken public as a REIT, one of many real estate companies to take advantage of the long-neglected investment vehicle.

With real estate available at distressed prices in the early 1990s, REITs had finally became an attractive mainstream investment option and many real estate firms went public, starting in 1993. Many of them staked out their claims in different sectors, such as office buildings, apartments, and—like Mills Corp.—shopping malls.

One of Miller's chief lieutenants, Laurence C. Siegel, was named Mill's chief executive officer, and he would soon succeed Miller as chairman of the board. In August 1995, Miller resigned. According to press accounts, he clashed with board members as well as investors over policy, especially his plan to take the Mills concept overseas, such as building megamalls in Asia. Given that the company had several other domestic projects that had been stalled for the past couple of years, Miller's foreign ambitions seemed out of place.

Siegel had played a key role in creating the Mills value concept, very much the result of his background in retailing. His father was the head of general merchandising for Philadelphia's John Wanamaker department store, where Siegel began to learn the trade while working part-time in high school. He then earned a degree in marketing and finance from Boston University and went to work for Merrill Lynch Commercial Services, rising to vice-president of leasing for the mid-Atlantic states before joining Western Development in 1983 and becoming executive vice-president of leasing. A major contribution Siegel made in the refinement of the Mills concept was the development of new store divisions with major retailers to fill out the store roster at the Mills properties, including OFF 5th Saks Fifth Avenue Outlet, Last Call from Neiman Marcus, Ann Taylor Loft, ESPN X Games Skatepark, and Bass Pro Shops Outdoor World.

Soon after taking the helm at Mills, Siegel succeeded in bringing to completion Ontario Mills, which opened in November 1996 near Los Angeles. The $190 million, 1.5-million-square-foot mall offered a 30-plex cinema

```
┌─────────────────────────────────────────────┐
│                                               │
│                 KEY DATES                     │
│                      ▪                        │
├───────────────────────────────────────────────┤
│ 1967:  Herbert S. Miller founds Western Develop- │
│        ment Corporation.                      │
│ 1985:  Western opens Potomac Mills in Washington, │
│        D.C.                                   │
│ 1989:  Franklin Mills opens in Philadelphia.  │
│ 1994:  Four Mills malls are packaged into a real │
│        estate investment trust called The Mills │
│        Corporation.                           │
│ 1995:  Laurence Siegel replaces Miller as CEO and │
│        chairman.                              │
│ 2002:  The Shops at Riverside in Hackensack, New │
│        Jersey, becomes the first acquisition. │
│ 2003:  Madrid Xanadu opens.                   │
│ 2005:  St. Enoch Centre is acquired in Glasgow, │
│        Scotland.                              │
│                                               │
└─────────────────────────────────────────────┘
```

and a walk-through simulated nature experience. The mall proved so popular that it was rivaling Disneyland as a tourist destination. Two more Mills malls opened in 1997: Grapevine Mills in Dallas and Arizona Mills near Phoenix.

In November 1998 the company opened a new venture in Orange County, California, pursuing a new concept called "The Block." Essentially, it was an open-air shopping mall with a main street ambiance. It proved popular because of its 30-screen movie theater, bowling alley, restaurants, and microbreweries, but the Block was not a brand that Mills Corp. pursued further, although it continued to develop similar open-air shopping malls. Mills closed out the 1990s with the opening of Katy Mills in Houston and Concord Mills in Charlotte, North Carolina, in 1999. In the second half of the decade, under Siegel's leadership, the company also upgraded its older properties. Potomac Mills and Franklin Mills replaced some tenants with a number of new merchants and added more entertainment options. Sawgrass Mills opened The Oasis, a 300,000-square-foot entertainment zone, while Ontario Mills added 150,000 square feet of additional retail and entertainment space.

GOING INTERNATIONAL IN 2001

Mills Corp. opened a pair of Malls in 2000. The 1.2-million-square-foot Opry Mills opened in May on the site of the former Opryland USA theme park, adjacent to the world famous Grand Old Opry House. Then, in November 2000, the 1.3-million-square-foot Arundel

Mills opened on a site located between Baltimore and Washington, D.C. The company opened just one mall in 2001, Discover Mills in Atlanta. Also in 2001 Mills Corp.'s first international venture took shape, Madrid Xanadu. It would open two years later and feature a 17-story indoor ski and snowboarding slope.

In 2002, Mills Corp. opened Colorado Mills near Denver and also completed its first acquisition: The Shops at Riverside in Hackensack, New Jersey, which the company hoped would be a companion to an envisioned mall in the Meadowlands, the sports complex home to the Giants and Jets in the National Football League, the Nets of the National Basketball Association, and the Devils of the National Hockey League, as well as a harness track. The site was attractively located across the Hudson River from midtown Manhattan, but because it held such great potential it became the battleground for a number of developers. In fact, Miller had begun work on a potential Meadowlands mall in the mid-1980s, and every year in its annual report Mills Corp. touted the project, seemingly on the verge of getting the green light but always delayed. In the meantime, the company made further acquisitions in 2003. It bought five properties from Toronto's Cadillac Fairview Corporation: the Galleria in White Plains, north of New York City; Broward Mall in Fort Lauderdale; Dover Commons in Dover, Delaware; Northpark Mall in Jackson, Mississippi; and The Esplanade in New Orleans. Later in 2003, the company acquired Del Amo Fashion Center in Los Angeles, Great Mall in San Jose, and Gwinnett Place in Atlanta. Mills Corp. also completed construction on a new property in 2003, the 1.1-million-square-foot St. Louis Mills.

The acquisition spree continued in 2004. The company bought Briarwood Mall in Ann Arbor, Michigan; Columbus City Center and the Mall at Tuttle Crossing, both in Columbus, Ohio; The Falls in Miami, Florida; Hilltop Mall in San Francisco; Lakeforest Mall in Washington, D.C.; Marley Station in Baltimore; Meadowland Mall in Reno, Nevada; Stoneridge Shopping Center in San Francisco; and Westland Mall in Miami. In addition, in 2004, Mills Corp. opened a pair of projects it developed: Cincinnati Mills and Vaughn Mills near Toronto, which was the first enclosed retail center built in Canada in 14 years.

The pace slackened in 2005, although the company still added three more properties to its portfolio through acquisition: Southdale Center in Minneapolis; Southridge Center in Milwaukee; and St. Enoch Centre in Glasgow, Scotland. It also opened Pittsburgh Mills, located 16 miles north of Pittsburgh, Pennsylvania. In addition, the company broke ground on a major project in the heart of Chicago's Loop, where it was building a

4.8-million-square-foot retail, entertainment, office, and hotel complex on N. State Street, a long-vacant block.

But Mills Corp. was not adjusting to its rapid growth without some difficulty. In 2005 it announced that it would restate earnings, a development that concerned the investment community. According to the *New York Times,* "Several analysts said the latest difficulties have raised serious questions of whether Mills can handle an ambitious and risky development program. 'My concern is that they took on too much too fast, that they didn't have the systems or the people or the infrastructure in place to handle all the growth,' said Ross Nussbaum, a REIT analyst at Banc of America Securities." Despite concerns about the depth of the organization, Mills Corp.'s slate of properties were not in question, as the malls continued to perform well. What was in doubt, however, was the fate of the projects on the drawing board: Mercati Generali in Rome, the first retail and entertainment complex of its kind to make use of a historical site in the city; Potomac Town Center, to be located across from Potomac Mills; and Meadowlands Xanadu, a project 20 years in the making.

Ed Dinger

PRINCIPAL SUBSIDIARIES

108 North State Street II, L.L.C.; Arizona Mills, L.L.C.; Franklin Mills, L.L.C.; Gurnee Mills L.L.C.; Katy Mills, L.L.C.; Ontario Mills, L.L.C; Potomac Mills Operating Company, L.L.C.; Sawgrass Mills Phase II, L.L.C.

PRINCIPAL COMPETITORS

Developers Diversified Realty Corporation; General Growth Properties, Inc.; Simon Property Group, Inc.

FURTHER READING

Bird, Laura, "Huge Mall Bets on Formula of Family Fun and Games," *Wall Street Journal,* June 11, 1997, p. B1.

Knight, Jerry, "Active New Team; The Team Behind 'Western Who?,'" *Washington Post,* April 9, 1978, p. K1.

Marsh, Lisa, "Mills Outlet Concept Called '90's Direction," *Daily News Record,* January 9, 1992, p. 4.

"Miller's Megamall Combined Outlets, Off-Pricers," *Shopping Centers Today,* May 2004.

Moin, David, "Mills on the Move," *WWD,* April 5, 2004, p. 16.

Pristin, Terry, "March of the Malls (Not Always in Step)," *New York Times,* November 23, 2005, p. C5.

Wallace, David, "Franklin Mills Mall Manager Sued by Partner," *Philadelphia Business Journal,* August 26, 1991, p. 3.

Williams, Elisa, "Western Blazes Maverick Trail to Success with Its 'Mills' Malls," *Washington Times,* October 16, 1990, p. C1.

Modtech Holdings, Inc.

———————————— ■ ————————————

2830 Barrett Avenue
Perris, California 92571
U.S.A.
Telephone: (951) 943-4014
Toll Free: (800) 929-0998
Fax: (951) 940-0427
Web site: http://www.modtech.com

Public Company
Incorporated: 1984 as Modtech, Inc.
Employees: 901
Sales: $185.2 million (2004)
Stock Exchanges: NASDAQ
Ticker Symbol: MODT
NAIC: 321992 Prefabricated Wood Building Manufacturing

■ ■ ■

Based in Perris, California, Modtech Holdings, Inc. specializes in permanent and relocatable modular buildings, especially classrooms. The structures also are used as temporary offices at factories or construction sites; serve various purposes for the military, police, Homeland Security, and other federal, state, and local agencies; act as doctor's offices, rural medical clinics, or small hospital additions; and also have been employed as banks, retail kiosks, strip malls, fast-food restaurants, convenience stores, motel rooms, and remote restrooms. The structures can be built in one- or two-story configurations, and are available in a variety of exterior and interior finishes. They also meet the same strict building codes as site-built structures. The company maintains six factories located in California, Arizona, Florida, and Texas. Modtech is a public company listed on the NASDAQ.

1970S' CALIFORNIA LEGISLATION CREATING MODULAR SCHOOL MARKET

The demand for modular classrooms in the California market grew out of the passage of the Leroy F. Greene State School Building Lease Purchase Act of 1976, which stipulated that 30 percent of all school construction funds had to be spent on relocatable classrooms. The legislation was an answer to what was occurring in many large cities along the coast regions. Area schools were finding themselves increasingly empty as Baby Boomers grew up and moved further inland to raise their families where housing was less expensive, such as in the San Fernando Valley and Riverside area. Furthermore, in 1978, California voters approved Proposition 13, which resulted in the scaling back of property taxes, a traditional source of school funding. School districts, faced with tighter budgets, had to find ways to stretch their resources. Modular classrooms were less expensive to build than traditional brick-and-mortar schools, and had the extra advantage of being able to be moved to where they were needed, due to the state's shifting population. Bonds to finance new school construction were then put on the ballot for voter consideration in 1982, making a greater pool of money available for modular classrooms.

In the same year that funds became available, Gerald B. Bashaw founded Modtech, and incorporated it

COMPANY PERSPECTIVES

We have been manufacturing permanent modular buildings for over two decades. We have six factories with over 1.2 million square feet of manufacturing capacity located on approximately 132 acres in four states.

two years later, in 1984, as Modtech, Inc. Bashaw was no stranger to modular buildings. In 1965 he had cofounded Aurora Modular Industries, which produced modular houses and buildings, mobile homes, and office trailers, as well as modular classrooms. Bashaw served as vice-president of operations, then president of the company, before striking out on his own. He was not alone in viewing modular classrooms as a tremendous business opportunity, as a bevy of companies cropped up during the 1980s hoping to get a share of California's school construction funds. There were a number of other compelling factors that attracted these entrepreneurs. California's student population was growing by more than 200,000 new students a year, a trend that was expected to last well into the 1990s. It meant that California would have to build more than 6,500 new classrooms to meet the need. Not only did the state mandate that 30 percent of all new school construction be relocatable, it required that temporary trailers, which were estimated to number as many as 20,000, be phased out by 1993.

GOING PUBLIC IN 1990

There were many small players in the modular classroom field, none of which stood out until Modtech emerged by the end of the 1980s. In 1989 the company produced just 1,000 classrooms, but Bashaw was setting it up for greater growth. He brought in Evan M. Gruber, a certified public accountant, in January 1989 to serve as his chief financial officer and later in the year Modtech completed its first acquisition, buying Q.E.D. Industries in a deal worth approximately $3.3 million. Gruber then became chief executive officer in January 1990 and prepared Modtech for an initial public offering of stock that would make it the only public company among California's modular classroom builders. Underwritten by Los Angeles-based Seidler Amdec Securities Inc., Modtech went public at $10 a share in July 1990, grossing approximately $40 million.

As the only public company in a highly fragmented industry, Modtech appeared well positioned to prosper

in the 1990s and was embraced by the investment community. The company employed 450 by the end of 1990, and sales for the year totaled $50 million. A reflection of Modtech's strength came in January 1991, when California awarded $14 million in contracts for modular relocatable schools. Modtech was expected to land $3 million to $5 million of that total, but instead was awarded the entire $14 million.

Unfortunately for Modtech and its competitors the California economy was in rapid decline and belt tightening became the order of the day. Because of a state budget crisis, funds for school construction dried up and business soured for Modtech. Sales dropped in 1992 and again in 1993, totaling just $19.6 million, at which level the company remained for the next two years. Modtech had no choice but to cut costs in an attempt to weather the storm. The workforce was slashed from 450 to just 90 in 1993, and its Lathrop plant in northern California was shuttered. In addition, top managers accepted 10 percent reductions in pay. For his part, Gruber cut his own salary in half. The company lost money in 1991, 1992, and 1993, but managed to turn a profit of $602,000 in 1994 and $965,000 in 1995.

California's economy began to rebound in the mid-1990s and the state's finances improved, and as a result Modtech's prospects increased dramatically. Due to several years of limited classroom construction, the state found itself in dire need of new classrooms, since demand by now far outweighed supply. The California Legislature approved a $1 billion increase in school spending for the 1995-96 school year and a $3 billion bond issue earmarked for school construction was approved by voters to help alleviate overcrowded schools. Moreover, California Governor Pete Wilson pushed through the legislature the Class Size Reduction Program, which he signed into law in July 1996. It called for the allocation of $200 million for the construction of new classrooms aimed at reducing classes to 20 students for children in kindergarten through third grade. Schools also would receive a bonus if they achieved that goal, prompting officials to turn to modular classrooms, which could be erected much faster than traditional buildings.

Modtech experienced a surge in school business and was once again a darling of investors, who bid up the price of Modtech stock 100 percent from the summer of 1995 to the summer of 1996. In 1996 alone the price of Modtech surged an impressive 270 percent, from $2.13 a share at the start of the year to $7.88 by the end. Modtech was then able to go back to the public market and ask for $20 a share in a secondary offering of stock in 1997. The company was also more attractive because it had taken steps to diversify beyond the school

KEY DATES

1982: The company is founded by Gerald Bashaw.
1984: The company is incorporated in California.
1990: An initial public offering of stock is completed.
1999: SPI Manufacturing is acquired.
2001: Innovative Modular Structures, Inc. is acquired.
2004: David Buckley is named CEO.

business. In 1996, for example, it completed a $1 million canopy project for Hertz Rent A Car at the San Francisco International Airport. It also began to erect remote cellular telephone equipment shelters for Air-Touch and L.A. Cellular. Nevertheless, the company's bread and butter remained the construction of modular classrooms. Fat state contracts led to an expansion of the workforce and the reopening of the Lathrop facility. In October 1996 Modtech bought another northern California plant, located in the city of Patterson, paying $1.3 million to Elkhart, Indiana-based Miller Building Systems Inc.

Business was booming for Modtech in 1997. Sales more than doubled to $134 million, net income tripled to $13 million, and the company ended the year with a backlog of orders worth $71 million, making it in all likelihood the largest California manufacturer of modular relocatable classrooms. In addition, the company carried almost no debt and had $11 million in cash on hand. Business fell off somewhat in 1998, due in large measure to a delay in passing the state budget. Although revenues slipped to $127.6 million, net income increased to $16.5 million. Modtech also took a step in March 1998 to expand beyond the California borders to neighboring states in an effort to spread some of its risk by acquiring an 80 percent controlling stake in Trac Modular of Glendale, Arizona, a provider of modular buildings to commercial customers. Thus the deal not only provided entry into the Nevada and Arizona markets but it also helped Modtech diversify its product line.

LATE 1990S AND EARLY 2000S: EXTERNAL GROWTH

During 1998 Modtech negotiated another acquisition, which came to completion in 1999, the $90 million cash and stock purchase of SPI Manufacturing Inc., a Rancho Cucamonga-based manufacturer of commercial and light industrial modular buildings that was owned by Colorado-based SPI Holdings, Inc. Again, Modtech added to its nonschool product lines and expanded geographically, taking advantage of SPI's recent acquisitions: Rosewood Industries of Phoenix, Baron Homes in California, and Glenrose, Texas-based Office Master. A month after the SPI acquisition closed, in March 1999, Modtech completed another purchase, picking up St. Petersburg, Florida-based Coastal Modular Buildings, Inc., which designed and manufactured both relocatable classrooms and modular buildings for commercial use. Once more, Modtech moved into a new market while expanding its product lines. Also in 1999 Modtech began the process of acquiring Miller Building Systems, from which it had bought its Patterson plant. Miller was an attractive prospect because it had a telecommunications shelter that customers found acceptable, unlike Modtech, which had struggled to stake out a significant slice of this market. In addition, Miller operated plants in what would be several new markets for Modtech, including Indiana, New York, Pennsylvania, South Dakota, and Vermont. But the merger proved difficult. After being on and off again for several months, the deal was scuttled in August 2000 when Modtech withdrew its offer after a group of Miller shareholders blocked the sale in hopes of finding a better price. Modtech's successful acquisitions, however, helped to boost sales to $167.2 million in 1999, although sales dipped to $8.4 million. Also of note, the company changed its name in February 1999 to Modtech Holdings, Inc. to serve as a holding company for the different subsidiaries.

The future appeared bright for Modtech as it entered the new century. Funds for new school construction were plentiful in California, where money was becoming available from the 1998 California School Construction Bond. In addition, the strong U.S. economy spurred sales for the company outside of the state. As a result, revenues increased in 2000 to $235.7 million and net income climbed to $10.3 million.

Due in large part to a downturn in the economy, business eroded for Modtech in 2001, as sales fell to $201.1 million. The company did manage to increase net income to $11.6 million, and it also completed an acquisition. In March 2001 it bought Innovative Modular Structures, Inc., another St. Petersburg, Florida-based manufacturer of modular structures for both school and commercial use.

The poor economy continued to take its toll on Modtech in 2002 and 2003, as declines in sales of structures for industrial and commercial use resulted in revenues dropping to $168 million in 2002 and $160 million in 2003. The company also lost $29.3 million in 2002, in part due to a switch in the way the company marketed its products. Instead of relying on independent dealers, the company began to sell directly to customers. Modtech returned to profitability, albeit marginally, in 2003, posting net income of $1.5 million.

Although business picked up somewhat in 2004 it was not enough for Gruber to keep his job. In August 2004 he stepped down as CEO, although he stayed on as a director and a consultant. Within a month, the company hired his replacement, David M. Buckley, a Wharton School of Business graduate and General Electric Company executive with expertise in supply-chain management, operations and facilities management, and new business development. Especially keen on viewing the business from the perspective of customers, Buckley quickly took steps to evaluate Modtech and began overhauling the way it did business with its customers. By the end of the year the company was beginning to see a turnaround. All told, sales improved to $185.2 million in 2004, although the company took a loss of $18.5 million, due primarily to the company underbidding on some projects, which ended up costing considerably more than expected because of a spike in the price of steel and other raw materials.

More changes followed in 2005, as Buckley detected inefficiencies and overlap in Modtech's California manufacturing operations. As a result, the Lathrop plant was closed and its business transferred to the Perris facility. Buckley was also successful in renegotiating some contracts, so that the higher cost of raw materials was paid by customers. Although Modtech continued to improve geographic diversification and grew less reliant on the school market, it appeared to be positioning itself under Buckley for a strong future. Unlike a number of competitors, such as Aurora Modular, who went out of business, Modtech had proven to be a survivor and now looked to take advantage of a less crowded marketplace.

Ed Dinger

PRINCIPAL SUBSIDIARIES

Modtech, Inc.; SPI Manufacturing Inc.; Coastal Modular Buildings, Inc.; Innovative Modular Structures, Inc.

PRINCIPAL COMPETITORS

American Modular Systems; Design Mobile Systems; Miller Building Systems, Inc.

FURTHER READING

Hammond, Teena, "Rise in California School Spending Helps Modtech Inc.," *Business Press* (Ontario, Calif.), July 29, 1996.

Katzanek, Jack, "Perris, Calif.-Based Modular Classroom-Maker Modtech Hires GE Executive As CEO," *Press-Enterprise,* September 8, 2004.

Rublin, Lauren R., "Taylor-Made Portfolio," *Barron's National Business and Financial Weekly,* July 8, 1991, p. 71.

Scott, Gary, "In California, Movable-Building Maker Profits from Smaller Class Size," *Business Press* (Ontario, Calif.), May 27, 1997.

———, "Smaller Classrooms Mean Bigger Profits for California Firms," *Business Press* (Ontario, Calif.), February 18, 1997.

Veverka, Mark, "Modtech May Have Stumbled, But the Future Still Looks Strong," *Wall Street Journal,* April 8, 1998, p. CA2.

Molson Coors Brewing Company

311 Tenth Street
Golden, Colorado 80401-0030
U.S.A.
Telephone: (303) 279-6565
Toll Free: (800) 642-6116
Fax: (303) 277-6246
Web site: http://www.molsoncoors.com

Public Company
Incorporated: 1913 as Adolph Coors Brewing and Manufacturing Company
Employees: 14,000
Sales: $4.31 billion (2004)
Stock Exchanges: New York Toronto
Ticker Symbol: TAP
NAIC: 312120 Breweries

■ ■ ■

Molson Coors Brewing Company, the product of the February 2005 merger of the Colorado-based Adolph Coors Company and the Canadian brewer Molson Inc., ranks as the fifth largest brewing company in the world. It holds the number one position in Canada, the number two rank in the United Kingdom, and the number three slot in the United States. Coors Light, the firm's biggest-seller, is the fourth best selling beer in the United States; Molson Canadian is the bestseller in English-speaking Canada; and Carling ranks as the best-selling lager in the United Kingdom. Other key brands include Molson Ice, Molson Golden, Coors, George Killian's Irish Red, Rickard's Red, Zima, Blue Moon, and Keystone.

Although the 2005 amalgamation was billed as a "merger of equals" and Molson Coors maintains twin headquarters in Golden, Colorado, and Montreal, Canada, the company is officially a U.S. firm. The merger brought together two companies with deep roots—Molson Inc., established in 1786, the oldest brewery in North America; and Adolph Coors, established in 1873—both of which were still under control of their respective founding families. Following the merger, the Coors and Molson families jointly controlled Molson Coors, each holding one-third of the voting power.

ORIGINS OF MOLSON IN
MONTREAL BREWERY

The history of Molson brewing began soon after 18-year-old John Molson emigrated from Lincolnshire, England, during the late 18th century. He arrived in Canada in 1782 and became a partner in a small brewing company outside Montreal's city walls on the St. Lawrence River a year later. In 1785 he became the sole proprietor of the brewery, closed it temporarily, and sailed to England to settle his estate and buy brewing equipment. Upon his return in 1786, with a book titled *Theoretical Hints on an Improved Practice of Brewing* in hand, the novice started brewing according to his own formula. By the close of the year, Molson had produced 80 hogsheads (4,300 gallons) of beer. In 1787 Molson remarked, "My beer has been almost universally well liked beyond my most sanguine expectations." His statement in part reflects the quality of the brew, but it also

COMPANY PERSPECTIVES

The time is right. The global beer business is rapidly consolidating, becoming more competitive every day. More than ever, scale is crucial for any brewer to excel. That's why it's the right time for Molson Coors. For two successful players in the world's most profitable beer markets, it's a perfect fit. Together we're financially stronger and more efficient. By dramatically increasing our size overnight, the merger enhances our ability to support aggressive marketing campaigns, innovative product introductions and strategic geographic expansion. Pour it on.

indicates that Molson had excellent timing; he faced little competition in the pioneer community.

Before electrical refrigeration became available, Molson was confined to a 20-week operating season because the company had to rely on ice from the St. Lawrence River. Nevertheless, production grew throughout the 1800s as the Montreal brewery steadily added more land and equipment. Population growth and increasingly sophisticated bottling and packaging techniques also contributed to Molson's profitability in the early days.

It was not long before Molson became an established entrepreneur in Montreal, providing services in the fledgling community that contributed to its growth into a major Canadian city. Molson first diversified in 1797 with a lumberyard on the brewery property. A decade later he launched the *Accommodation,* Canada's first steamboat, and soon thereafter he formed the St. Lawrence Steamboat Company, also known as the Molson Line. The steam line led to Molson's operation of small-scale financial services between Montreal and Quebec City; eventually the services became Molson's Bank, chartered in 1855.

In 1816 John Molson signed a partnership agreement with his three sons—John, Jr., William, and Thomas—ensuring that the brewery would remain under family control. He was elected the same year to represent Montreal East in the legislature of Lower Canada and opened the Mansion House, a large hotel in Montreal that housed the public library, post office, and Montreal's first theater.

The Molsons established the first industrial-scale distillery in Montreal in 1820. Three years later, the youngest brother, Thomas, left the organization after a severe disagreement with his family. In 1824 he moved to Kingston, Ontario, where he established an independent brewing and distilling operation.

The elder John Molson left the company in 1828, leaving John, Jr., and William as active partners. He served as president of the Bank of Montreal from 1826 to 1830, and in 1832 he was nominated to the Legislative Council of Lower Canada. Possibly his most fortuitous venture was his contribution of one quarter of the cost of building Canada's first railway, the Champlain and St. Lawrence. He died in January 1836 at age 72.

Thomas Molson returned to Montreal in 1834 and was readmitted to the family enterprise. Over the next 80 years new partnerships formed among various members of the Molson family, prompting several more reorganizations. The first in the third generation to enter the family business was John H. R. Molson, who joined the partnership in 1848. He became an increasingly important figure in the company as William and John, Jr., devoted more of their time to the operation of Molson's Bank.

In 1844 the Molson brewery, now called Thos. & Wm. Molson & Company, introduced beer in bottles that were corked and labeled by hand. Beer production grew faster than bottle production, though, necessitating the company's purchase of a separate barrel factory at Port Hope, Ontario, in 1851. In 1859 Molson started to advertise in Montreal newspapers, while also setting up a retail sales network and introducing pint bottles.

The company became John H.R. Molson & Bros. in 1861 following the establishment of a new partnership with William Markland Molson and John Thomas Molson. In 1866 the Molsons closed their distillery, citing poor sales, and in 1868 they sold their property in Port Hope.

By 1866, the brewery's hundredth year in Molson hands, its production volume had multiplied 175 times but profit cleared on each gallon remained the same: 26¢. In the early years of the 20th century, the company incorporated pasteurization and electric refrigeration into its methods. In addition, electricity replaced steam power, and mechanized packaging devices sped the bottling process. In 1911 the company became Molson's Brewery Ltd. following its reorganization as a private, limited joint-share company. The Molson family would continue to hold a major stake in the company right through the 2005 merger with Coors. The family's direct interest in banking ended in 1925 when Molson's Bank merged with the Bank of Montreal.

The first half of the 20th century was a period of rapid growth for Molson. Production at the Montreal

KEY DATES

1786: John Molson founds a brewery in Montreal.

1816: Molson signs partnership agreement with his three sons, ensuring continued family control.

1844: Company begins operating as Thos. & Wm. Molson & Company.

1861: Under new partnership arrangement, company becomes John H.R. Molson & Bros.

1873: Adolph Herman Joseph Coors forms a partnership with Jacob Schueler to convert a tannery in Golden, Colorado, into a brewery.

1880: Coors buys out Schueler.

1911: Molson is reorganized as a private, limited joint-share company and renamed Molson's Brewery Ltd.

1913: Coors's firm is incorporated as Adolph Coors Brewing and Manufacturing Company.

1920: During Prohibition era, Coors changes its name to Adolph Coors Company.

1945: Molson's Brewery Limited becomes a public joint-stock company.

1959: The flagship Molson Canadian beer makes its debut; Coors develops the first aluminum can.

1968: In a reflection of a diversification, Molson changes its name to Molson Industries Limited.

1972: Molson acquires Beaver Lumber.

1973: Molson changes its name again, to The Molson Companies Limited.

1975: Coors goes public, offering only nonvoting shares.

1978: Coors Light is introduced; Molson acquires Diversey Corporation and the Montreal Canadiens hockey team.

1981: Coors's distribution area expands across the Mississippi for the first time.

1989: Molson merges its brewery operations with those of Carling O'Keefe, with the resulting company 50-50 owned by Molson Companies and Foster's Brewing Group; Coors's Keystone and Keystone Light brands make their debut.

1991: Coors beer is now available in all 50 states.

1992: Coors introduces Zima, a clear, foam-free malted brew.

1993: For the first time, a nonfamily member, W. Leo Kiely, is selected as president of the Coors brewing business.

1996: Molson sells Diversey.

1997: Coors forms partnership with Molson and Foster's to manage distribution of its brands in Canada.

1998: Molson regains full control of its brewery operations, and also takes over Foster's stake in the partnership formed with Coors the previous year.

1999: The Molson Companies divests Beaver Lumber and renames itself Molson Inc.

2001: Molson and Coors enter into partnership whereby Coors begins importing, promoting, and selling Molson brands in the United States; Molson sells the Montreal Canadiens.

2002: Coors acquires U.K. beer maker Carling; Molson acquires Cervejaria Kaiser of Brazil.

2005: Coors and Molson merge, creating Molson Coors Brewing Company.

2006: Company divests Kaiser.

---

brewery rose from three million gallons in 1920, to 15 million in 1930, to 25 million in 1949. Molson adopted modern marketing and advertising methods to enhance market penetration and in 1930 began producing its first promotional items, despite founder John Molson's contention that "An honest brew makes its own friends." In 1945 shares in the company became available to the public for the first time as Molson's Brewery Limited became a public joint-stock company.

ADDITIONAL BREWERIES BUILT AND ACQUIRED STARTING IN 1955

In the mid-1950s Molson management recognized a need to expand operations significantly. By concentrating their resources, other Canadian breweries had finally begun to compete successfully against perennial leader Molson. Molson decided that the appropriate strategy was to have a brewery operating in each province, as distribution from its base in Quebec to other provinces was subject to strict government regulations. With operations in the other provinces, Molson could further build its market throughout Canada. This large-scale expansion began when Molson announced a second brewery would be built on a ten-acre site in Toronto. Modernizations at the Montreal facility had, it was felt, fully maximized output there. The new Toronto installation opened in 1955 and became the home of Molson's first lager, Crown and Anchor. In the next few years Molson acquired three breweries: Sick's Brewery, bought in 1958; Fort Garry Brewery in Winnipeg, 1959; and Newfoundland Brewery, 1962. This period also saw the introduction of Molson Golden beer, first brewed in 1954, as well as the flagship Molson Canadian, which debuted in 1959. In 1962 the company name was changed to Molson Breweries Limited, reflecting the firm's expansion into multi-brewery operation.

The expansion effort resulted in good returns for Molson investors; between 1950 and 1965 earnings more than doubled. Even so, Molson leaders recognized that expansion potential within the mature brewing industry was limited, and further, that growth rates in the industry would always be slow. It was clear that even the most successful brewing operation soon would reach the limits of its profitability. Thus Molson began an accelerated diversification program in the mid-1960s that heralded in Canada the era of the corporate takeover.

DIVERSIFICATION BEGINNING IN 1968

In 1968 Molson made its first major nonbrewing acquisition in more than a century. Ontario-based Anthes Imperial Ltd. was a public company specializing in steel materials, office furniture and supplies, construction equipment rentals, and public warehousing. The Anthes executive staff was known to be highly talented in acquisitions and strategic management, two areas in which Molson needed expert help to pursue its goal of diversification. However, because the various Anthes companies required different management and marketing strategies, the acquisition did not benefit Molson as much as its directors had hoped. Soon Molson sold off most of the Anthes component companies. The company had learned that future acquisitions should be of firms that were more compatible with Molson's longstanding strengths in marketing consumer products and services. In the meantime, the company in 1968 had changed its name to Molson Industries Limited, a reflection of its diversification; the beer-making operations were renamed Molson Breweries of Canada Ltd.

Molson did retain one important component of Anthes: its president. As Molson's chairman, Donald "Bud" Willmot directed a series of successful acquisitions in the early 1970s. Management felt that the ideal candidate must be a Canadian-based firm and must be involved in above-average growth. The do-it-yourself material supplies market appeared to be the ideal candidate: there seemed to be a new trend, consumers doing their own home improvements, and Molson recognized the potential for rapid growth of this market in urban areas, which at that time had few or no lumberyards or similar outlets. Molson began acquiring small hardware, lumber, and home furnishings companies. In 1972 it spent $50 million buying more than 90 percent of the shares of Beaver Lumber Company Limited, a large Canadian company. During the remainder of the decade Beaver acquired several smaller hardware and lumber operations. Molson's service center division grew to encompass 162 retail stores, most of them franchises, selling everything from paint to home-building supplies. In the mid-1980s Beaver began importing competitively priced merchandise from Asian countries. Meanwhile, in July 1973, the company's name was changed yet again, to The Molson Companies Limited. The brewery operations were bolstered one year later through the acquisition of Formosa Spring Brewery, based in Barrie, Ontario.

Although Beaver's sales climbed steadily throughout the 1970s, rapidly making it a leader in its industry, profits lagged behind what Molson had anticipated, and initially the company considered the Beaver purchase only a modest success. Struggling at first to integrate the brewing and home improvement divisions, Molson eventually learned that the two industries, and marketing therein, are very different. The beer industry operates in a controlled market; governments regulate sale and manufacture of alcoholic products. The hardware industry, on the other hand, operates in a relatively free market. Furthermore, in brewing, manufacturing efficiency is the key to a profitable enterprise, but the success of a home improvement retail operation hinges on the ability to provide a broad variety of products at competitive prices.

The challenge of integrating two companies operating in such different markets led Molson to a careful reassessment of its diversification criteria; in the future, the company would concentrate on marketing specific product brands. W. J. Gluck, vice-president of corporate development, wrote: "We only wanted to go into a business related to our experience—a business in which marketing, not manufacturing, is the important thing." The search for another acquisition began.

EXPANSION INTO CHEMICALS, SPORTS, AND ENTERTAINMENT: 1978

In 1978 Molson offered $28 per share of stock in Diversey Corporation, a manufacturer and marketer of institutional chemical cleansers and sanitizers based in Northbrook, Illinois. Contending that their company, which boasted $730 million in annual sales, was worth more, Diversey stockholders contested the sale, but eventually accepted Molson's original $55 million offer. Diversey was Molson's first large acquisition in the United States, though most of its clients and manufacturing plants were in fact located outside the United States in Europe, Latin America, and the Pacific basin. Molson also bought into sports and entertainment in 1978, buying a share in the Club de Hockey Canadien Inc. (the Montreal Canadiens) and the Montreal Forum, as well as hosting Molson Hockey Night in Canada and other television shows through its production company, Ohlmeyer Communications.

Molson opened the 1980s with the $25 million purchase of BASF Wyandotte Corporation, a U.S. manufacturer of chemical specialties products related to foodservices and commercial laundries. The subsequent merger of BASF and Diversey made Molson's chemical products division its second largest earnings contributor. Prior to the merger, Diversey was a weak competitor in the U.S. sanitation supplies market. BASF Wyandotte, however, was a leader in the U.S. kitchen services market. Thus the marriage was a sound move for Diversey, which had found a relatively inexpensive way to increase its share of its market in the United States.

Having concentrated on diversification, Molson found that it had missed the globalization of the brewing industry that had begun in the 1970s. While other major competitors had expanded internationally through acquisition, Molson had not completed a single foreign acquisition. Although the conglomerate remained profitable throughout the 1980s, it became clear to the board of directors, led by eighth-generation heir Eric Molson, that the company would need to make some international connections to remain a major, independent participant in the beer market.

1989 MERGER OF MOLSON BREWERIES AND CARLING O'KEEFE

In 1988 the board hired Marshall "Mickey" Cohen as president and CEO. A career civil servant who had entered the private sector in 1985, Cohen was brought into Molson with one objective: to raise the 202-year-old company's sagging returns. His first move was to revive ailing merger talks between Molson and Elders IXL Ltd., Australia's largest publicly traded conglomerate. Elders (subsequently renamed for its beer-making subsidiary, Foster's Brewing Group Ltd.) had recently capped off a five-year amalgamation of global brewing companies with the purchase of Canada's number three brewery, Carling O'Keefe. The proposed merger of number two Molson with Carling was called "the biggest and most audacious deal in Canadian brewing history" in a 1989 *Globe and Mail* story, but it required Molson to share control of the resulting company (50-50 between Molson and Foster's). Whereas it had been difficult for Cohen's predecessors to agree to relinquish more than two centuries of control, Cohen had no such compunctions.

The resulting union, consummated in 1989, gave Molson access to Foster's 80-country reach, while Foster's bought entrée into the lucrative U.S. market, where Molson was the second largest importer after Heineken N.V. The merger also helped lower both participants' production costs: the combined operations were pared from 16 Canadian breweries down to nine, and employment was correspondingly cut by 1,400 workers. As a concession to its larger premerger size–Molson's brewery assets were valued at $1 billion, whereas Carling's amounted to only about $600 million—Cohen also managed to wring $600 million cash for Molson Companies out of the deal.

Some analysts surmised that the CEO would use the funds to further supplement the multinational beer business, but he surprised many with the $284 million acquisition of DuBois Chemicals Inc., the United States' second largest distributor of cleaning chemicals, in 1991. The addition boosted Diversey's annual sales by 25 percent to $1.2 billion and augmented operations in the United States, Japan, and Europe. Unfortunately, the merger proved more troublesome than expected, and a subsequent decline in service alienated customers. While Diversey's sales increased to $1.4 billion in 1994 (ended March 1994), its profits declined to $72.6 million and the subsidiary's president jumped ship. Cohen took the helm and began to formulate a turnaround plan.

Hoping to boost the Molson brand's less than 1 percent share of the U.S. beer market, Molson and Foster's each agreed to sell an equal part of their stake in Molson Breweries to Miller Brewing Company, a leader in the U.S. market. Miller's $349 million bought it a 20 percent share of Molson Breweries and effectively shifted control of Canada's leading brewer to foreigners in 1993 (Molson's stake in Molson Breweries having been reduced to 40 percent). Cohen expected the brand to retain its distinctly Canadian character (the beer would continue to be manufactured exclusively in Canada), but hoped that it would benefit from Miller's marketing clout.

Molson's financial results were mediocre at best in the early 1990s. Sales rose from $2.55 billion in 1990 to $3.09 billion in 1993, but earnings vacillated from $117.9 million in 1990 to a net loss of $38.67 million the following year, rebounding to $164.69 million in 1993. The company blamed its difficulties on Diversey's money-losing U.S. operations, which faced strong competition from industry leader Ecolab Inc. The following year's sales and earnings slipped to $2.97 billion and $125.67 million, respectively, as Diversey continued to lose money in the United States.

Nevertheless, Cohen remained determined to turn Diversey's operations around. Late in 1994 he announced a decision to divest Molson's retail home improvement businesses to focus on the brewing and chemicals operations. By this time Molson's retail sector included Beaver Lumber, a 45.1 percent interest in the Quebec-based Réno-Dépôt Inc. chain, and a 25 percent stake in Home Depot Canada. The last of these was rooted in Molson's 1971 purchase of the Ontario-based Aikenhead's Home Improvement Warehouse chain. In 1994 Home Depot Inc. purchased a 75 percent stake in Aikenhead's, whose stores were then converted to Home Depots.

REFOCUSING ON BREWING IN THE MID- TO LATE 1990S

The exit from retailing proved to be a slow one, however, and Molson dramatically shifted course in 1996 when it sold Diversey, jettisoning its troubled chemicals operations. Most of Diversey was sold to Unilever PLC, with the entire chemical unit bringing about $1.1 billion to Molson. Nonetheless, charges related to the sale and for restructuring both Molson Breweries and Beaver Lumber resulted in a net loss of CAD 305.5 million ($225 million) for 1996. Management shakeups led to Cohen's exit from Molson in September 1996 and to Cohen's replacement, former company executive Norman Seagram, lasting only until May 1997, when James Arnett took over as president and CEO. Arnett, a corporate lawyer based in Toronto, had been a director of Molson. Meanwhile, the historic Montreal Forum was replaced in 1996 as the home of the Montreal Canadiens by the newly built Molson Centre, a 21,400-seat state-of-the-art arena, which was wholly owned by the Molson Companies.

Under Arnett's leadership, it quickly became apparent that brewing was once again number one at Molson. The company finally began to unload its retail interests,

starting with the March 1997 sale of its interest in Réno-Dépôt. In April 1998 Molson's stake in Home Depot Canada was sold to Home Depot Inc. for CAD 370 million ($260 million). Two months later Molson announced that it would sell Beaver Lumber as well, and it placed Beaver within its area of discontinued operations.

The long neglected Molson Breweries had suffered from steadily declining market share, falling from 52.2 percent of the Canadian market in 1989 to 45.8 percent in mid-1997. John Barnett had been named president of Molson Breweries in November 1995, and he used his 25-plus years of brewing experience to aggressively attempt to reverse the decline. He decentralized the unit's operations (which included seven Canadian breweries) and began niche marketing, targeting particular brands at specific Canadian regions.

While Barnett moved to shore up Molson Breweries, Arnett acted quickly to regain full control of the unit. In December 1997, Molson Companies, Foster's, and Miller Brewing reached an agreement that restructured their relationships. Molson and Foster's repurchased Miller's 20 percent stake in Molson Breweries, returning each to 50 percent shares in the unit. The deal also had Molson and Foster's purchasing a 24.95 percent stake in Molson USA, with Miller retaining a 50.1 percent interest. Molson USA was charged with distributing Molson and Foster's brands in the United States. The new relationship also called for Molson Breweries to continue to manage the Miller brands in Canada.

Then in June 1998 Molson regained full ownership of Molson Breweries by paying CAD 1 billion ($679.4 million) in cash to Foster's. Through the deal, Molson also gained Foster's stake in Coors Canada, Inc., manager of Coors brands in Canada. Molson's interest in Coors Canada was thus increased to 49.9 percent.

With the Canadian beer market in an extended flat period and with competitor Labatt's share of the market nearly equal to that of Molson's, Arnett was counting on Canadians preferring 100 percent Canadian-owned Molson brands to those of Labatt, which had been purchased by Belgium's Interbrew S.A. in 1995. Molson's return to a focus on brewing was symbolized the following year by yet another name change, this time to simply Molson Inc. Also in 1999, Molson finally sold off Beaver Lumber, and it hired Daniel O'Neill to take over leadership of the brewery operations after Barnett left the company late in 1998. O'Neill, a former executive at Campbell Soup Company and H.J. Heinz Company, led a restructuring of the brewery operations aiming to cut CAD 100 million in annual costs. In September 1999 nearly 300 of Molson's 1,500 salaried workers were laid off, with CAD 36 million in one-time charges incurred as a result. One month later the company announced that it would shut down its brewery in Barrie, Ontario, and consolidate its Ontario beer-making operations at its plant in Toronto. The Barrie brewery was shuttered in August 2000, putting more than 400 people out of work, and Molson took a CAD 188 million charge to cover the costs of the restructuring. The charges led to a net loss of CAD 44 million for the fiscal year ending in March 2000. Revenue that year totaled CAD 2.5 billion, up from the previous year's CAD 2.1 billion.

A GLOBAL STRATEGY IN THE EARLY 2000S

In June 2000 Arnett stepped down as president and CEO, and O'Neill was named to succeed him. O'Neill would lead Molson through the few tumultuous years leading up to the merger with Coors. One of his first moves came in October 2000 when Molson paid Miller and Foster's $133 million to regain 100 percent ownership and control of the Molson brands in the United States. Molson officials felt that Miller and Foster's were not doing enough to promote Molson products in the huge U.S. market. The following January, Molson entered into a partnership with Coors in which the Canadian company retained a 50.1 percent interest and full ownership of the brands themselves. Coors agreed to import, promote, and sell Molson beer brands in the United States. With the Canadian beer market in stagnation, Molson was targeting the U.S. market as a main growth vehicle, but the firm needed to reverse its fortunes there; over the previous two years, Molson had lost about half of its U.S. market share, falling from third to seventh place among import beers. Molson increased its U.S. marketing spending by more than 20 percent, and it decided to concentrate its U.S. efforts on its three top sellers, Molson Golden, Molson Canadian, and Molson Ice. As a second leg of its international growth strategy, Molson entered into its first brewing venture outside North America, purchasing Brazil's number four beer brand, Bavaria, and five breweries from Companhia de Bebidas das Américas (AmBev) for CAD 98 million.

Back home, O'Neill continued to focus on streamlining and improving profitability. In early 2002 Molson shut down another brewery, the small one in Regina, which had been deemed superfluous. O'Neill also unsentimentally closed the final chapter on Molson's days of diversification by selling both the Montreal Canadiens and the Molson Centre (later renamed the Bell Centre) in 2001 to Colorado ski magnate George Gillett. In addition, in a move to cut costs and simplify

marketing efforts, Molson slashed its Canadian product line from 77 beers to just 8 along with a few regional brews. These moves were largely responsible for Molson's operating profits doubling by 2003, to CAD 512 million.

In March 2002 Molson took an even greater leap into the Brazilian market, the fourth largest beer market in the world, when it acquired Cervejaria Kaiser for $765 million. Molson subsequently merged Bavaria into Kaiser, which ranked as the number two beer maker in Brazil, with a market share of approximately 18 percent, a far cry, however, from the dominating 70 percent controlled by AmBev. Molson, which became the 13th largest brewer in the world, sold a 20 percent in Kaiser to Heineken for about $220 million, and it also extended an agreement to produce and distribute Heineken beer in Brazil and to distribute Heineken in Canada.

Unfortunately, soon after the acquisition of Kaiser, Brazil's economy, currency, and beer consumption took a nosedive, and Kaiser suffered from additional problems in its product lineup, promotion, and distribution. By 2004 Molson's Brazilian adventure was widely seen as a costly mistake. At the same time, while Molson had arrested the decline of its import business in the United States, its flagship brands in Canada were in decline, suffering from intense competition from imports, discount and value-price brewers such as Lakeport Brewing, and premium craft brewers such as Sleeman Breweries Ltd. and Moosehead Breweries Limited. One of the few bright spots for the company was the growing popularity of Coors Light, which it was selling as part of its partnership with Coors and which by 2004 was generating about 20 percent of Molson's operating profit in Canada. On a global level, however, Molson had fallen well behind its peers in the late 20th and early 21st centuries when the beer industry went through an unprecedented wave of global consolidation. For example, in the late 1970s, Molson was about the same size as Heineken, but by 2004 the Dutch firm was five times the size of Molson. It was from this position of weakness, then, that Molson pursued the marriage with Coors that was completed in February 2005.

THE FOUNDATION OF THE COORS BREWERY

Adolph Herman Joseph Coors emigrated from Germany to the United States in 1868 at the age of 21. After purchasing a Denver bottling company in 1872, Coors formed a partnership with Jacob Schueler in 1873. Although Schueler invested the lion's share of the $20,000 necessary to purchase and convert an old tannery in nearby Golden into a brewery, Coors was able to buy out his partner in 1880. His acquisition inaugurated more than a century of Coors family control.

The fledgling brewery's sales increased steadily in the ensuing decades. In 1887 the brewery sold 7,049 barrels of beer (31 gallons per barrel). Three years later that figure more than doubled, reaching 17,600 barrels. Over the years Adolph Coors slowly expanded his market. By the time he officially incorporated his brewery in 1913 as Adolph Coors Brewing and Manufacturing Company, Coors beer was being distributed throughout Colorado.

Even at this early point in the company's history, the distinctive Coors philosophy was emerging. The main tenets of this philosophy adhered to by four successive generations of Coors beermakers, each generation further refining the knowledge inherited from the preceding generation, were the following: Adolph Coors believed in sparing no effort or expense in producing the best beer possible. To this end, he believed that only Colorado spring water was good enough for his beer. He also commissioned farmers to grow the barley and hops that he needed for his brewing process. The second tenet of the philosophy was that his family always came first, without exception; the Coors family brewery remained a tight-knit, protective, almost secretive enterprise. The last tenet was that "a good beer sells itself." Until 1980 Coors spent substantially less on advertising than any other brewer.

Prohibition came early to Colorado. In 1916 the state's legislature passed a law banning the production and consumption of alcoholic beverages within the state. Obviously, Prohibition was detrimental to Adolph Coors's brewery; some business historians assert, however, that the legislation strengthened the burgeoning company. The obvious changes in product offerings—Coors manufactured "near beer" and malted milk during this period—were reflected in a name change, in 1920, to Adolph Coors Company. Adolph Coors and his son, Adolph, Jr., also used the opportunity to diversify their company, creating what was eventually to become a small-scale vertical monopoly: Coors acquired all that it needed to produce its beer, from the oil wells that created the energy necessary to run the brewery to the farms that grew the ingredients, and from the bottling plant that made the containers to the trucks used for distribution. This expansion was financed entirely with family money.

ASTOUNDING POST-PROHIBITION GROWTH

The repeal of Prohibition in 1933 did not result in as dramatic a sales increase for Coors as it did for many other producers of alcoholic beverages. Instead, the Adolph Coors Company, under the direction of Adolph, Jr., and his two brothers, expanded its market slowly in the 1930s. Their insistence on the use of all natural ingredients and no preservatives, in accordance with the brewery's founding tenets, made wider distribution prohibitively expensive. The beer had to be brewed, transported, and stored under refrigeration, and its shelf life was limited to one month. But if Coors's growth and development in the decades following the repeal of Prohibition was less dramatic than that of brewing powerhouses such as Anheuser-Busch and Miller, it was no less amazing. For while other regional breweries were squeezed out of the market—the number of independents shrank from 450 in 1947 to 120 in 1967—Coors grew steadily into one of the nation's leading beer brands. Coors's production increased 20-fold, from 123,000 barrels in 1930 to 3.5 million barrels in 1960, as the brewer expanded its reach into 11 western states. Coors's ranking among the nation's beer companies advanced accordingly, from 14th in 1959 to fourth by 1969.

How did Coors grow 1,500 percent between 1947 and 1967, with only one product, made in a single brewery, and sold in only ten states? A quality product was certainly one reason for Coors's success. The company's technological innovations, including the development of both the first cold-filtered beer and the first aluminum can in 1959, also placed it in the vanguard of the beer industry. Another reason was a unique marketing ploy that Coors perfected during the 1960s. When Coors entered a new market, it would lead with draft beer only. The company would sell kegs to taverns and bars at a price under that of its lowest competition. Then Coors would encourage the barkeepers to sell the beer at a premium price. Once Coors's premium image was established, the company would then introduce the beer in retail stores. Since Coors spent so little on advertising, the company was able to offer a better profit margin to its wholesalers. These profit incentives to both wholesalers and retailers worked well. Through the 1970s Coors was the leading beer in nine of the 11 western states in which it was sold. In California, the second largest beer market in the country (New York was first), Coors at one time held an astonishing 43 percent of the market.

1970S THROUGH MID-1980S: CULT STATUS, CONTROVERSIES, AND DECLINING FORTUNES

Marketing, innovation, and product quality, however, could not account for what was later considered one of the strangest phenomena in U.S. business history. Beginning in the late 1960s and culminating in the mid-1970s Coors developed, without any effort by the company, an unusual reputation as a "cult" beer. Limited availability created intense demand on the East Coast. Westerners, keen to flaunt their perceived superiority to Easterners, got caught up in a "we have what you want" syndrome and unwittingly became the company's unpaid advertisers. As a result, Coors virtually eliminated its competition in nine western states. Those nine states provided Coors with all the market it needed to become the fourth largest brewery in the nation.

But all was not well with the company and its enigmatic founding family. The 1960 kidnapping and murder of Adolph III had intensified the clan's already strong tendency toward secrecy. Their cautious, elusive nature produced circumspect hiring practices, including polygraphs and sworn statements of loyalty. Outsiders saw these practices as both unfair and as a means of enforcing racial discrimination: the limited numbers of African Americans and Hispanics employed by the company seemed to support this view. Lawsuits were filed alleging discrimination and, more important, a coalition of minority and labor groups organized a boycott, which intensified the negative publicity surrounding the company. The boycott and lawsuits provoked more public scrutiny of the Coors dynasty. A series of articles appeared in the *Washington Post* in May 1975 documenting Joe Coors's ultraconservative political philosophy. Not only did these revelations exacerbate the boycott, they also influenced the average consumer and generally undermined Coors's market position.

At first, the Coors family's response was retrenchment and litigation. But when sales dropped 10 percent in California in 1975 (at the time that state accounted for 49 percent of total sales), the family changed its tactics. They settled the lawsuits, agreed to a minority hiring plan, and launched advertising campaigns aimed at showing the company's "good side." Television advertisements showed that minorities were happily employed in the brewery. Bill Coors took the initiative on environmental issues and proclaimed that the company was well ahead of the industry and the government in keeping the environment clean. The replacement of pull-tabs with "pop-down" tabs and the first aluminum recycling program were cited as proof of Coors's commitment.

After a decrease in sales through the late 1970s, the company appeared to revive in 1980. Sales volume dropped by one million barrels between 1976 and 1978, bottoming out at 12.5 million barrels before rebounding in 1980 to 13.7 million. Bill and Joe Coors, the third generation of the family to take charge, concluded that their sales problem emanated from their image problem and that they had successfully solved both.

Two separate situations, one in 1975 and the other in 1976, should have signaled that the company's problems went beyond that of image. In 1975 the Coors family was forced for the first time to offer shares to the public to raise $50 million to pay inheritance tax for a family member. The original offering was successful, raising more than $130 million. The stock sold was of a nonvoting class, so the family did not relinquish any control over the company. Analysts suggested, however, that the reluctance with which the company undertook the offering disclosed a disdain for modern methods of capitalization. The second situation involved a Federal Trade Commission ruling, later upheld by the U.S. Supreme Court, striking down Coors's strong-arm distribution tactics. Coors refused to sell its product to distributors that the company regarded as unable to handle the beer properly. Once again, many industry analysts remarked that the company exhibited a disdain for mass marketing techniques.

Indeed, Coors remained committed to its founder's decidedly outdated idea that "a good beer sells itself." In 1975 William Coors claimed, "We don't need marketing. We know we make the best beer in the world." Throughout its entire history, Coors had spent far less than its competitors on advertising. In the 1970s, Coors's ad budget amounted to about $.65 per barrel, compared with the $3.50 per barrel promoting the leading beers. Anheuser-Busch and Miller spent billions on promotion in a market that they continually expanded with new products. Coors, on the other hand, only reluctantly joined the light beer movement, introducing Coors Light in 1978, and grudgingly increased its meager marketing outlay. As a result, Coors's 1982 sales volume declined to less than 12 million barrels for the first time in ten years, and the company relinquished its third-place ranking to Stroh Brewing Company. This decline came in spite of the expansion of Coors's distribution area across the Mississippi for the first time in 1981, when the company began selling its beer in Louisiana, Mississippi, and Tennessee.

Although Coors's sales increased from $1.1 billion in 1983 to $1.8 billion in 1989, profits declined from $89 million to $13 million, and the company's return on sales dropped from 8 percent to less than 1 percent. Some observers blamed the brewery's entrenched family management, which they characterized as reactionary. But larger industrywide trends also contributed to the low earnings. The beer market's customer base began to stagnate in the mid-1980s, forcing brewers to use margin-lowering tactics to build volume and share. These included brand segmentation, increased advertising, international expansion, and heavy discounting.

LATE 1980S INTO THE 21ST CENTURY: CHANGING TIMES UNDER PETER COORS

Under the direction of Peter Coors, the brewery eagerly sought to catch up with its larger rivals. In 1987 Peter Coors, a great-grandson of the founder, was named vice-chairman, president, and CEO of Coors Brewing Company, a new beer-focused subsidiary of Adolph Coors Company (Bill Coors remained chairman of the parent company). The new leader was a driving force behind Coors's groundswell of change and continued on that course in the late 1980s into the early 1990s. Under his direction, the brewery completely reversed its advertising course: by the early 1990s, Coors began to spend more, in terms of advertising per barrel of beer sold, than its bigger rivals. Coors Light became the company's best-selling beer, the third-ranking light beer in the United States, and the number one light beer in Canada. The company embraced the concept of brand segmentation and discounting, introducing the "economy" or "popularly priced" Keystone and Keystone Light in 1989. Ostensibly offering "bottled-beer taste in a can," these beers boosted sales volume, raising overall Coors sales to 10 percent of the beer market and winning back the number three spot. But at the same time, such new products took market share away from other Coors brands, including the family's original label, which lost one-third of its sales volume from the mid-1980s to the mid-1990s.

While Keystone appealed to the budget-minded beer drinker, other new beverages targeted the higher-margin "specialty" and "boutique" markets. The domestic company craftily entered the fast-growing import market with the introduction of "George Killian's Irish Red," a defunct Irish brand licensed by Coors and produced in the United States. Even without the support of television advertising, the faux import was able to compete with the Boston Beer Company, Inc.'s domestically microbrewed Samuel Adams brand for leadership of the specialty beer segment.

In 1992 Coors launched Zima, one of the beer industry's most creative new beverages. The clear, foam-free malted brew created a whole new beverage category. The drink's novelty won it instant popularity that fizzled even before Coors could introduce its first derivative, Zima Gold, in 1995. Analysts noted the telling fact that neither Anheuser-Busch nor Miller, both savvy marketers, followed Coors's lead into the clearmalt category. Zima Gold was pulled from the market after six weeks of disappointing sales.

Peter Coors was not afraid to buck decades of family tradition, chalking up several firsts that had previously been renounced. With Coors running up against

its lone brewery's 20-million-barrel annual capacity, Peter floated the company's first long-term debt offering in 1990. Later in 1990, he tried to negotiate a $425 million acquisition of Stroh Brewing, but ended up buying its three-million-barrel-capacity Memphis, Tennessee, brewery for about $50 million. If, as Peter Coors hinted to a reporter in a March 1991 *Forbes* article, the company wanted to mount a challenge to second-ranking Miller Brewing, it would still need to double its U.S. brewing capacity. Meanwhile, in 1991, the company's distribution area covered all 50 states for the first time.

In 1992 Coors spun off the company's nonbeer assets, including the high-tech ceramics division, as well as the aluminum and packaging businesses, as ACX Technologies, Inc. Coors shareholders received one share of ACX for every three shares of the brewing company. The divestment was considered successful: ACX's sales increased from $544 million in 1991 to $732 million in 1994, and profits multiplied from $1.3 million to $20 million over the same period.

In 1993 Peter Coors broke with 121 years of history by hiring the first nonfamily member for the presidency of the brewing business. His choice, W. Leo Kiely, reflected Coors's new emphasis on marketing. Kiely had been a top marketing executive with Frito-Lay Company, a division of PepsiCo, Inc. The new president was given a straightforward, but arduous mandate: increase Coors's return on investment from less than 5 percent to 10 percent by 1997. A significant cost-cutting move came in the form of a 1993 workforce reduction of 700, which was accompanied by a $70 million charge that led to the company's first full-year loss in ten years.

With the Zima brand faltering, Coors looked for growth from overseas markets and from a new specialty brewing venture. In 1994 the company purchased the El Aquila brewery in Zaragoza, Spain, to manufacture Coors Gold for the Spanish market and Coors Extra Gold and Coors Light for several markets in Europe. That same year Jinro-Coors brewery in Cheong-Won, South Korea, one-third owned by Coors, began operation.

Coors's partner in the venture, Jinro Limited, ran into financial difficulties later in the decade, leading to the sale of the brewery to another company and ending Coors's involvement. In 1995 Coors entered the microbrewery market with the opening of the SandLot Brewery located at Coors Field in Denver, the home of Major League Baseball's Colorado Rockies. Specialty beers under the Blue Moon label began to be crafted at this 4,000-barrel-capacity facility. In 1997 the company entered into a partnership with Foster's Brewing Group Limited of Australia and the Molson Companies Limited of Canada for the distribution of Coors brands in

Canada. The following year Molson gained Foster's stake, giving Molson a 49.9 percent stake and Coors a 50.1 percent stake.

From 1988 to 1997 Coors increased its share of the U.S. market from 8.8 percent to 10.7 percent. Production increased over the same period from 16.5 million barrels to 20.4 million. Coors remained a distant third to Anheuser-Busch and Miller, but it had made strides in improving profitability, in part from an overhaul of what had been a convoluted U.S. distribution system. In 1997 the company reported net income of $82.3 million on sales of $1.82 billion, which translated into a net profit margin of 4.5 percent, a significant increase over the previous year's figure of 2.5 percent.

By 1999 sales had surpassed the $2 billion mark for the first time, and net income reached $92.3 million. Return on average shareholders' equity reached 11.4 percent, a vast improvement over the low single-digit figures of the early 1990s. That year Coors sold 23 million barrels of malt beverages. Surprisingly, a comeback by Zima was a driving force behind the improving results. Zima was repositioning as a refreshing alcoholic beverage, and as an alternative to beer, and its taste was altered to make it less sweet and more tangy. Consequently, sales began rising in 1998 and 1999, although they failed to reattain the peak level of 1994. In 1999 Zima Citrus was introduced, offering a blend of natural citrus flavors. Among other late 1990s new product introductions was Coors Non-Alcoholic, a premium brew with less than 0.5 percent alcohol by volume. In May 2000, on the heels of the record 1999 performance, Peter Coors was named chairman of Coors Brewing Company and president and CEO of Adolph Coors Company, with Bill Coors remaining chairman of the parent company. Kiely was promoted to president and CEO of Coors Brewing.

In the early 2000s Peter Coors and Kiely sought new ways for Coors to compete in a rapidly consolidating global beer industry increasingly dominated by huge multinational players. One of the few growth areas in the U.S. market was import beers, and Coors filled that gap in its lineup by entering into a new partnership with Molson in early 2001. Coors paid Molson $65 million for a 49.9 percent stake in the new venture, through which it began importing, promoting, and selling three key Molson brands—Molson Canadian, Molson Golden, and Molson Ice—in the United States.

Coors also had little presence on the international scene; only 2 percent of revenues were derived outside the United States. This changed dramatically in February 2002 when the company shelled out $1.7 billion for the U.K. beer maker Carling Brewers, thereby gaining one of Britain's leading beer brands, Carling, as well as

the number two position in the U.K. market, Europe's second largest beer market, with an 18 percent share. In addition to Carling, several other British brands were part of the deal, including Worthington's, Caffrey's, and Grolsch, the latter via a joint venture with Grolsch N.V. Under Coors, Carling was transformed into a U.K. subsidiary called Coors Brewers Limited, which by 2004 achieved net sales of $1.82 billion, or 42 percent of overall Adolph Coors Co. sales. This total was aided by the successful introduction of Coors Fine Light Beer into the U.K. market in 2003.

The Carling deal, however, failed to reverse one of Coors's main weaknesses: its overreliance on Coors Light, which accounted for 75 percent of U.S. sales and 40 percent of global profits. The brand was in fact losing market share at a time when sales of premium light beers in the United States were rising by 4 to 5 percent per year, and in 2004 it fell from third to fourth place in the U.S. market, surpassed by a resurgent Miller Lite. In addition to gaining additional scale to better compete against the ever growing global beer giants, another key rationale behind a merger with Molson was that the union would significantly reduce the importance of this one brand to total profits.

CREATION OF MOLSON COORS IN 2005

In late July 2004, then, two midsized players in the worldwide beer sector, both still controlled by their respective founding families and already cooperating through joint ventures in Canada and the United States, announced plans for a merger. The deal, however, soon ran into trouble from disgruntled Molson shareholders, who felt the terms undervalued Molson's more profitable brewery operations. By January 2005 the Molson shareholders had been placated by the inclusion of a special cash dividend totaling $532 million, and the transaction finally closed in early February. Although billed as a "merger of equals," the $3.5 billion deal centered on Coors buying Molson and then renaming itself Molson Coors Brewing Company. Molson Coors was thus a U.S. company, but it maintained dual headquarters in Golden, Colorado, and Montreal, and its stock was listed on both the New York and Toronto Stock Exchanges. The founding families continued to control the company, albeit in joint fashion, with each holding one-third of the voting rights. Kiely remained in charge of day-to-day operations as president and CEO, while Eric Molson was named chairman and Peter Coors was now simply a director. O'Neill initially served as vice-chairman in charge of synergies and integration, but he left the company just a few months later after apparently clashing with Kiely.

Molson Coors began its existence as the fifth largest brewing company in the world, with combined revenues of about $6 billion and annual output of 51 million barrels of beer a year. It ranked number one in the Canadian beer market, number two in the United Kingdom, and number three in the United States. The company aimed to achieve $175 million in annual savings within three years through various synergies, including streamlining its brewery networks, making procurement more efficient, and consolidating administrative functions. Almost immediately after the merger was consummated, Molson Coors announced the first step in its cost-cutting plan, the closure of its brewery in Memphis, Tennessee, scheduled for early 2007. In addition, the company soon put its troubled Brazilian unit up for sale. In January 2006 the company announced it had sold a 68 percent stake in Kaiser to FEMSA Cerveza S.A. de C.V. for just $68 million. Molson Coors retained a 15 percent stake in Kaiser and one seat on its board. In Canada, meanwhile, Molson Coors sought to cash in on the growing popularity of microbrews by acquiring Creemore Springs Brewing Co., an Ontario-based microbrewery turning out what connoisseurs considered one of Canada's best beers. This deal closed in 2005, the same year that Molson Coors ventured into Russia for the first time, introducing Coors Fine Light Beer into that market.

April Dougal Gasbarre
Updated, April Dougal Gasbarre; David E. Salamie

PRINCIPAL SUBSIDIARIES

Coors Brewing Company; Coors Brewers Limited (U.K.); Molson Inc. (Canada).

PRINCIPAL COMPETITORS

Anheuser-Busch Companies, Inc.; SABMiller plc; Pabst Brewing Company; Heineken N.V.; InBev NV/SA.

FURTHER READING

"Adolph Coors: Brewing Up Plans for an Invasion of the East Coast," *Business Week*, September 29, 1980, p. 120.

Adrangi, Sahm, "Molson Revamp Aims to Put Fizz Back into Stalled Major Brands," *Globe and Mail*, August 13, 2003, p. B1.

Atchison, Sandra D., and Marc Frons, "Can Pete and Jeff Coors Brew Up a Comeback?," *Business Week*, December 16, 1985, pp. 86+.

Banham, Russ, *Coors: A Rocky Mountain Legend*, Lyme, Conn.: Greenwich Publishing, 1998, 127 p.

Banks, Brian, "Continental Draft: Molson Brews Up a Strategy to Export Its Canadian Success to the Mighty US," *CA Magazine*, December 1991, pp. 28-31.

Baum, Dan, *Citizen Coors: An American Dynasty*, New York: Morrow, 1999, 352 p.

Berman, Dennis K., Christopher J. Chipello, and Daniel Bilefsky, "Coors Raises Molson Bid 6% in Bid to Save the Merger Plan," *Wall Street Journal*, January 14, 2005, p. A3.

Bertin, Oliver, "Molson Buys Brazil's Kaiser," *Globe and Mail*, March 19, 2002, p. B1.

Brent, Paul, *Lager Heads: Labatt and Molson Face Off for Canada's Beer Money*, Toronto: HarperCollins, 2004, 243 p.

Burgess, Robert J., "Popular Keystone Hurt Other Coors Brands," *Denver Business Journal*, April 30, 1993, p. A1.

————, *Silver Bullets: A Soldier's Story of How Coors Bombed in the Beer Wars*, New York: St. Martin's Press, 1993, 256 p.

Cheers for 200 Years!: Molson Breweries, 1786–1986, Vancouver: Creative House, 1986, 48 p.

Cherney, Elena, "Molson's U.S. Sales Are Left in the Cold," *Wall Street Journal*, December 8, 2000, p. A13.

Chipello, Christopher J., and Robert Frank, "A Canadian-American Beer Bash," *Wall Street Journal*, September 24, 2004, p. C1.

Cloud, John, "Why Coors Went Soft," *Time*, November 2, 1998, p. 70.

Conny, Beth Mende, *Coors, A Catalyst for Change: The Pioneering of the Aluminum Can*, Golden, Colo.: Adolph Coors Company, 1990, 101 p.

"Coors' Bitter Brew," *Financial World*, April 30, 1983, pp. 31+.

"Coors: The Adolph Coors Story," Golden, Colo.: Adolph Coors Company, 1984.

Daly, John, "Miller Time for Molson: The Largest Brewer Gives Up Canadian Control," *Maclean's*, January 25, 1993, p. 30.

Dawson, Havis, "Hey. Beer. Plan.," *Beverage World*, August 15, 1998, pp. 37-38, 40, 42.

DeMont, John, "A Global Brew," *Maclean's*, July 24, 1989, pp. 28+.

Denison, Merrill, *The Barley and the Stream: The Molson Story*, Toronto: McClelland and Stewart, 1955, 398 p.

Edwards, Greg, "After the Merger, Molson Coors Faces a Strange Brew of Hurdles," *Wall Street Journal*, May 11, 2005, p. B14F.

Forsyth, Neil, *The Molsons in Canada: The First 200 Years*, Public Archives Canada, 1986.

Fulscher, Todd James, *A Study of Labor Relations at the Adolph Coors Brewery*, M.A. thesis, Denver: University of Denver, 1994.

Galarza, Pablo, "Molson: Talk About Frothy," *Financial World*, November 7, 1995, p. 18.

Greenberg, Larry M., "Canada's Top Brewers Draft Ways to Fight New Rivals," *Wall Street Journal*, March 16, 1993, p. B4.

————, "Molson Buys Rest of Brewing Unit for $679.4 Million," *Wall Street Journal*, June 24, 1998, p. B6.

Hoffman, Andy, "Molson Coors Ends Ill-Fated Foray into Brazil," *Globe and Mail,* January 17, 2006, p. B1.

Holloway, Andy, "Strange Brew," *Canadian Business,* August 16, 2004, pp. 50+.

Hudson, Kris, "Coors Shuffles Leaders," *Rocky Mountain News,* May 12, 2000, p. 1B.

Hunter, Douglas, *Molson: The Birth of a Business Empire,* Toronto: Viking, 2001, 486 p.

Hunter, Kris, "Battle of the Beers," *Memphis Business Journal,* March 13, 1995, p. 34.

Joslin, Barry, "Anatomy of a Merger," *Business Quarterly,* Autumn 1990, pp. 25-29.

Lane, Randall, "Splitsville in Coors Country," *Forbes,* April 10, 1995, p. 52.

Lang, Tam, *Coors: A Report on the Company's Environmental Policies and Practices,* New York: Council on Economic Priorities, Corporate Environmental Data Clearinghouse, 1992.

Lubove, Seth, "No Fizz in the Profits," *Forbes,* September 7, 1998, pp. 72-74.

Marotte, Bertrand, "Molson Buys Back U.S. Brands," *Globe and Mail,* October 12, 2000, p. B1.

———, "Molson's Mission Hinges on U.S., Brazil," *Globe and Mail,* July 31, 2001, p. B14.

———, "Strictly Suds," *Globe and Mail,* September 27, 2002.

McArthur, Keith, "Coors' Toughest Tasks Are Only Just Beginning," *Globe and Mail,* February 2, 2005, p. B4.

———, "Molson Coors to Shut Plant in Memphis," *Globe and Mail,* February 12, 2005, p. B5.

———, "Molson Puts Cap on the Deal, Buys Creemore," *Globe and Mail,* April 23, 2005, p. B5.

———, "Molson Shuts Ontario Brewery," *Globe and Mail,* October 8, 1999, p. B1.

McArthur, Keith, Bertrand Marotte, and Derek DeCloet, "Merger Golden with Molson Shareholders," *Globe and Mail,* January 29, 2005, p. B2.

McWilliams, Gary, and Philip Shishkin, "Coors Gets Europe Access in Carling Deal," *Wall Street Journal,* December 26, 2001, p. A3.

Melcher, Richard A., "Why Zima Faded So Fast," *Business Week,* March 10, 1997, p. 110.

Miller, Ben, "Coors Buys Carling in U.K., Expanding World Presence," *Denver Business Journal,* March 1, 2002.

Molson, Karen, *The Molsons: Their Lives and Times, 1780–2000,* Willowdale, Ont.: Firefly Books, 2001, 416 p.

Mullin, Rick, "Unilever Pays $568 Million for a Big Piece of Diversey," *Chemical Week,* January 31, 1996, p. 9.

Ortega, Bob, "Zima Goes Cool and Gets Hot, Sells What It Is, Not What It's Not," *Wall Street Journal,* July 2, 1999, p. B6.

Perrault, Michael, "Coors to Acquire Carling," *Rocky Mountain News,* December 25, 2001, p. 1B.

Perreault, Michel G., *The Molson Companies Limited: A Corporate Background Report,* Ottawa: Royal Commission on Corporate Concentration, 1976, 75 p.

Poole, Claire, "Shirtsleeves to Shirtsleeves," *Forbes,* March 4, 1991, p. 52.

The Pre-Prohibition History of Adolph Coors Company, 1873–1933, Golden, Colo.: Adolph Coors Company, 1973, 106 p.

Sellers, Patricia, "A Whole New Ball Game in Beer," *Fortune,* September 19, 1994, p. 79.

Shore, Sandy, "Coors Remains a Family Affair After 125 Years," *Buffalo News,* April 12, 1998, p. B13.

Slater, Michael, "Number One at Last," *Globe and Mail,* November 17, 1989, p. 50.

Sneath, Allen Winn, *Brewed in Canada: The Untold Story of Canada's 350-Year-Old Brewing Industry,* Toronto: Dundurn Press, 2001, 431 p.

Stevenson, Mark, "My Dear, Best Friend," *Canadian Business,* March 1994, pp. 52+.

Theodore, Sarah, "Company of the Year: The Nation's Third-Largest Brewer Puts Focus on Results," *Beverage Industry,* January 2000, pp. 21-22.

"Time in a Bottle: Adolph Coors Company," Golden, Colo.: Adolph Coors Company, 1984.

Verespej, Michael A., "This Coors Is Different," *Industry Week,* July 22, 1985, pp. 53+.

Waal, Peter, "Molson Muscle?," *Canadian Business,* July 31, 1998, p. 18.

Ward, Sandra, "Gains on Tap," *Barron's,* November 8, 2004, pp. 29-30.

Wells, Jennifer, "Thirst for Growth: Molson Tries to Halt a Decline in Beer Sales," *Maclean's,* September 1, 1997, pp. 44+.

Wells, Jennifer, and Ann Brocklehurst, "The End of a Dream: Molson Jettisons a Money-Losing U.S. Subsidiary," *Maclean's,* February 5, 1996, pp. 38-39.

Williamson, Richard, "Century Not Always Kind to Coors," *Rocky Mountain News,* February 16, 1999, p. 16A.

Woods, Shirley F., *The Molson Saga, 1763–1983,* Toronto: Doubleday Canada, 1983, 370 p.

MONSANTO
imagine®

Monsanto Company

800 North Lindbergh Boulevard
St. Louis, Missouri 63167
U.S.A.
Telephone: (314) 694-1000
Fax: (314) 694-8394
Web site: http://www.monsanto.com

Public Company
Incorporated: 2000 as Monsanto Ag Company
Employees: 12,600
Sales: $6.29 billion (2005)
Stock Exchanges: New York
Ticker Symbol: MON
NAIC: 325412 Pharmaceutical Preparations; 325311
Medicinal and Botanical Manufacturing

■ ■ ■

Monsanto Company is a leading global supplier of herbicides and seeds. Monsanto leads the world market for genetically modified (GM) seed; it produces GM varieties for corn, soybeans, and cotton. Monsanto also makes the leading brand of herbicide, Roundup, and has developed genetically engineered seeds for crops to resist Roundup. Monsanto owns one of the world's top suppliers of fruit and vegetable seeds, Seminis, and has acquired a number of regional seed producers through its American Seeds Inc. subsidiary.

The original Monsanto Company spun off its chemical business in 1997 and renamed itself Pharmacia Corporation following a merger with Pharmacia & Up-

john Inc. in 2000. The old Monsanto's agriculture business became the new Monsanto Company.

EARLY 20TH-CENTURY ORIGINS

Monsanto traces its roots to John Francisco Queeny, a purchaser for a wholesale drug house, who formed the Monsanto Chemical Works in St. Louis, Missouri, in order to produce the artificial sweetener saccharin. By 1905 John Queeny's company was also producing caffeine and vanillin and was beginning to turn a profit. In 1908 Queeny felt confident enough about his firm's future to leave his part-time job with another drug house to work full time as Monsanto's president. The company continued to grow, with sales surpassing the $1 million mark for the first time in 1915.

While prior to World War I the United States relied heavily on foreign supplies of chemicals, the increasing likelihood of U.S. intervention meant that the country would soon need its own domestic producer of chemicals. Looking back on the significance of the war for Monsanto, Queeny's son Edgar remarked, "There was no choice other than to improvise, to invent and to find new ways of doing all the old things. The old dependence on Europe was, almost overnight, a thing of the past." Monsanto was forced to rely on its own knowledge and nascent technical ability. Among other problems, Monsanto researchers discovered that pages describing German chemical processes had been ripped out of library books. Monsanto developed several strategic products, including phenol as an antiseptic, in addition to acetylsalicyclic acid, or aspirin.

With the purchase of an Illinois acid company in

1918, Monsanto began to widen the scope of its factory operations. A postwar depression during the early 1920s affected profits, but by the time John Queeny turned over the company to Edgar in 1928 the financial situation was much brighter. Monsanto had gone public, a move that paved the way for future expansion. At this time, the company had 55 shareholders and 1,000 employees and owned a small company in Britain.

Under Edgar Queeny's direction Monsanto, renamed the Monsanto Chemical Company, began to substantially expand and enter into an era of prolonged growth. Acquisitions expanded Monsanto's product line to include the new field of plastics and the manufacture of phosphorus.

By the time the United States entered World War II in 1941, the domestic chemical industry had attained far greater independence from Europe. Monsanto, strengthened by its several acquisitions, was also prepared to produce such strategic materials as phosphates and inorganic chemicals. Most important was the company's acquisition of a research and development laboratory called Thomas and Hochwalt. The well-known Dayton, Ohio, firm strengthened Monsanto at the time and provided the basis for some of its future achievements in chemical technology. One of its most important discoveries was styrene monomer, a key ingredient in synthetic rubber and a crucial product for the armed forces during the war.

EXPANSION AND NEW LEADER-SHIP IN THE POSTWAR PERIOD

Largely unknown by the public, Monsanto experienced difficulties in attempting to market consumer goods. However, attempts to refine a low quality detergent led to developments in grass fertilizer, an important consumer product since the postwar housing boom had created a strong market of homeowners eager to perfect their lawns. In the mid-1950s Monsanto began to produce urethane foam, which was flexible and easy to use; it later became crucial in making automobile interiors. In 1955 Monsanto acquired Lion Oil, increasing its assets by more than 50 percent. Stockholders during this time numbered 43,000.

Having finally outgrown its headquarters in downtown St. Louis, Monsanto moved to the suburban community of Creve Coeur in 1957. Three years later Edgar Queeny turned over the chair of Monsanto to Charles Thomas, one of the founders of the research and development laboratory so important to Monsanto. Charlie Sommer, who had joined the company in 1929, became president. Under their combined leadership Monsanto saw several important developments, including the establishment of the Agricultural Chemicals division, created to consolidate Monsanto's diverse agrichemical product lines. Monsanto's European expansion continued, with Brussels becoming the permanent overseas headquarters in 1962.

In 1964 Monsanto changed its name to Monsanto Company in acknowledgment of its diverse product line. The company consisted of eight divisions, including petroleum, fibers, building materials, and packaging.

According to Monsanto historian Dan Forrestal, "Leadership during the 1960s and early 1970s came principally from ... executives whose Monsanto roots ran deep." In 1964 Edward O'Neal became chairperson. O'Neal, who had come to Monsanto in 1935 with the acquisition of the Swann Corporation, was the first chair in company history who had not first held the post of president. Another company leader was Edward J. Bock, who had joined Monsanto in 1941 as an engineer. He rose through the ranks to become a member of the board of directors in 1965 and president in 1968. Edgar Queeny, who left no heirs, died in 1968.

Although Bock had a reputation for being a committed company executive, several factors contributed to his volatile term as president. High overhead costs and a sluggish national economy led to a dramatic 29 percent decrease in earnings in 1969. Sales were up the following year, but Bock's implementation of the 1971 reorganization caused a significant amount of friction among members of the board and senior management. In spite of the fact that this move, in which Monsanto separated the management of raw materials from the company's subsidiaries, was widely praised by security analysts, Bock resigned from the presidency in February 1972. After a nine-month search, John W. Hanley, a former executive with Procter & Gamble, was chosen as president. Hanley also took over as chairperson in 1975.

Under Hanley, Monsanto more than doubled its sales and earnings between 1972 and 1983. Toward the end of his tenure, Hanley put into effect a promise he had made to himself and to Monsanto when he accepted the position of president, namely, that his succes-

KEY DATES

1901: Monsanto Chemical Works is formed to produce saccharin; caffeine and vanillin are soon added.

1915: Sales exceed $1 million.

1955: Lion Oil is acquired.

1971: Management of raw materials is separated from other subsidiaries in company reorganization.

1972: Monsanto quits making saccharin.

1985: Monsanto acquires G.D. Searle, maker of NutraSweet.

1992: Ortho lawn chemicals business is acquired from Chevron Chemical Co.

1996: Monsanto launches biotech line.

1997: Chemicals business is spun off as Solutia, Inc.

1999: Celebrex anti-inflammatory medication is introduced.

2000: Monsanto Company merges with Pharmacia & Upjohn and is renamed Pharmacia Corporation; agriculture business becomes Monsanto Ag Company, later renamed Monsanto Company.

2004: American Seeds Inc. subsidiary is formed to acquire regional seed producers.

2005: Global fruit and vegetable seed maker Seminis is acquired in $1.4 billion deal.

sor would be chosen from Monsanto's ranks. Hanley and his staff chose approximately 20 young executives as potential company leaders and began preparing them for the head position at Monsanto. Among them was Richard J. Mahoney. When Hanley joined Monsanto, Mahoney was a young sales director in agricultural products. In 1983 Hanley turned the leadership of the company over to Mahoney. Wall Street immediately approved this decision with an increase in Monsanto's share prices.

LEGAL CHALLENGES IN THE 1970S AND 1980S

During this time, public concern over the environment began to escalate. Ralph Nader's activism and Rachel Carson's book *The Silent Spring* had been influential in increasing the American public's awareness of activities within the chemical industry in the 1960s, and Monsanto responded in several ways to the pressure. In 1964 the company introduced biodegradable detergents, and in 1976, Monsanto announced plans to phase out production of polychlorinated biphenyl (PCB).

In 1979 a lawsuit was filed against Monsanto and other manufacturers of Agent Orange, a defoliant used during the Vietnam War. Agent Orange contained a highly toxic chemical known as dioxin, and the suit claimed that hundreds of veterans had suffered permanent damage because of the chemical. In 1984 Monsanto and seven other manufacturers agreed to a $180 million settlement just before the trial began. With the announcement of a settlement Monsanto's share price, depressed because of the uncertainty over the outcome of the trial, rose substantially.

Also in 1984, Monsanto lost a $10 million antitrust suit to Spray-Rite, a former distributor of Monsanto agricultural herbicides. The U.S. Supreme Court upheld the suit and award, finding that Monsanto had acted to fix retail prices with other herbicide manufacturers.

In August 1985, Monsanto purchased G. D. Searle, the "NutraSweet" firm. NutraSweet, an artificial sweetener, had generated $700 million in sales that year, and Searle could offer Monsanto an experienced marketing and sales staff as well as real profit potential. Since the late 1970s the company had sold nearly 60 low margin businesses and, with two important agriculture product patents expiring in 1988, a major new cash source was more than welcome. What Monsanto did not count on, however, was the controversy surrounding Searle's intrauterine (IUD) birth control device called the Copper-7.

Soon after the acquisition, disclosures about hundreds of lawsuits over Searle's IUD surfaced and turned Monsanto's takeover into a public relations disaster. The disclosures, which inevitably led to comparisons with those about A. H. Robins, the Dalkan Shield manufacturer that eventually declared Chapter 11 bankruptcy, raised questions as to how carefully Monsanto management had considered the acquisition. In early 1986 Searle discontinued IUD sales in the United States. By 1988 Monsanto's new subsidiary faced an estimated 500 lawsuits against the Copper-7 IUD. As the parent company, Monsanto was well insulated from its subsidiary's liabilities by the legal "corporate veil."

Toward the end of the 1980s, Monsanto faced continued challenges from a variety of sources, including government and public concern over hazardous wastes, fuel and feedstock costs, and import competition. At the end of the 99th Congress, then President Ronald Reagan signed an $8.5 billion, five-year cleanup superfund reauthorization act. Built into the financing was a surcharge on the chemical industry created through the tax reform bill. Biotechnology regulations were just being formulated, and Monsanto, which already had types of genetically engineered bacteria ready for testing, was poised to be an active participant in that field.

In keeping with its strategy to become a leader in the health field, Monsanto and the Washington University Medical School entered into a five-year research contract in 1984. Two-thirds of the research was to be directed into areas with obviously commercial applications, while one-third of the research was to be devoted to theoretical work. One particularly promising discovery involved the application of the bovine growth factor, a way to greatly increase milk production.

In the burgeoning low-calorie sweetener market, challengers to NutraSweet were putting pressure on Monsanto. Pfizer Inc., a pharmaceutical company, was preparing to market its product, called alitame, which it claimed was far sweeter than NutraSweet and better suited for baking.

In an interview with *Business Week,* Howard Schneiderman, senior vice-president for research and development, commented, "To maintain our markets—and not become another steel industry—we must spend on research and development." Monsanto, which had committed 8 percent of its operating budget to research and development, far above the industry average, hoped to emerge in the 1990s as one of the leaders in the fields of biotechnology and pharmaceuticals that were only then emerging from their nascent stage.

By the end of the 1980s, Monsanto had restructured itself and become a producer of specialty chemicals, with a focus on biotechnology products. Monsanto enjoyed consecutive record years in 1988 and 1989: sales were $8.3 billion and $8.7 billion, respectively. In 1988 the Food and Drug Administration (FDA) approved Cytotec, a drug that prevented gastric ulcers in high-risk cases. Sales of Cytotec in the United States reached $39 million in 1989.

The Monsanto Chemical Co. unit prospered with products including Saflex, a type of nylon carpet fiber. The NutraSweet Company held its own in 1989, contributing $180 million in earnings, with growth in the carbonated beverage segment. Almost 500 new products containing NutraSweet were introduced in 1989, for a total of 3,000 products.

Monsanto continued to invest heavily in research and development, with 7 percent of sales allotted for this area. The investment began to pay off when the research and development department developed an all-natural fat substitute called Simplesse. The FDA declared in early 1990 that the product was "generally recognized as safe" for use in frozen desserts. That year, the Nutra-Sweet Company introduced Simple Pleasures frozen

dairy dessert. Monsanto hoped to see Simplesse used eventually in salad dressings, yogurt, and mayonnaise.

Despite these successes, Monsanto remained frustrated by delays in obtaining FDA approval for bovine somatotropin (BST), a chemical used to increase milk production in cows. Opponents to BST said it would upset the balance of supply and demand for milk, but Monsanto countered that BST would provide high-quality food supplies to consumers worldwide.

The final year of the 1980s also marked Monsanto's listing for the first time on the Tokyo Stock Exchange. Monsanto officials expected the listing to improve opportunities for licensing and joint venture agreements.

EARLY 1990S TRANSITIONAL PERIOD

Monsanto had expected to celebrate 1990 as its fifth consecutive year of increased earnings, but numerous factors—the increased price of oil due to the Persian Gulf War, a recession in key industries in the United States, and droughts in California and Europe—prevented the company from achieving this goal. Net income was $546 million, a dramatic drop from the record of $679 million the previous year. Nonetheless, subsidiary Searle, which had experienced considerable public relations scandals and headaches in the 1980s, had a record financial year in 1990. The subsidiary had established itself in the global pharmaceutical market and was beginning to emerge as an industry leader. Monsanto Chemical, meanwhile, was a $4 billion business that made up the largest percentage of Monsanto's sales.

Monsanto continued to work at upholding "The Monsanto Pledge," a 1988 declaration to reduce emissions of toxic substances. By its own estimates, the company devoted $285 million annually to environmental expenditures. Furthermore, Monsanto and the Environmental Protection Agency agreed to a cleanup program at the company's detergent and phosphate plant in Richmond County, Georgia.

The company restructured during the early 1990s to help cut losses during a difficult economic time. Net income in 1991 was only $296 million, $250 million less than the previous year. Despite this showing, 1991 was a good year for some of Monsanto's newest products. Bovine somatotropin finally gained FDA approval and was sold in Mexico and Brazil, and Monsanto received the go-ahead to use the fat substitute, Simplesse, in a full range of food products, including yogurt, cheese and cheese spreads, and other low-fat spreads. In addition, the herbicide Dimension was approved in 1991, and scientists at Monsanto tested genetically improved plants in field trials.

Furthermore, Monsanto expanded internationally, opening an office in Shanghai and a plant in Beijing, China. The company also hoped to expand in Thailand, and entered into a joint venture in Japan with Mitsubishi Chemical Co.

Monsanto's sales in 1992 hit $7.8 million. However, as net income dropped 130 percent from 1991 due to several one-time aftertax charges, the company prepared itself for challenging times. The patent on NutraSweet brand sweetener expired in 1992, and in preparation for increased competition, Monsanto launched new products, such as the NutraSweet Spoonful, which came in tabletop serving jars, like sugar. The company also devoted ongoing research and development to Sweetener 2000, a high-intensity product.

In 1992, Monsanto denied that it planned to sell G. D. Searle and Co., pointing out that Searle was a profitable subsidiary that launched many new products. However, to decrease losses, Monsanto did sell Fisher Controls International Inc., a subsidiary that manufactured process control equipment. Profits from the sale were used to buy the Ortho lawn-and-garden business from Chevron Chemical Co.

MONSANTO REINVENTING ITSELF: 1990S

Monsanto expected to see growth in its agricultural, chemical, and biotechnological divisions. In 1993, Monsanto and NTGargiulo joined forces to produce a genetically altered tomato. As the decade progressed, biotechnology played an increasingly important role, eventually emerging as the focal point of the company's operations. The foray into biotechnology, begun in the mid-1980s with a $150 million investment in a genetic engineering lab in Chesterfield, Missouri, had been faithfully supported by further investments in the ensuing years. Monsanto's efforts finally yielded tangible success in 1993, when BST was approved for commercial sale after a frustratingly slow FDA approval process. In the coming years, the development of further biotech products moved to the forefront of Monsanto's activities, ushering in a period of profound change. Fittingly, the sweeping, strategic alterations to the company's focus were preceded by a change in leadership, making the last decade of the 20th century one of the most dynamic eras in Monsanto's history.

Toward the end of 1994, Mahoney announced his retirement, effective the following year in March 1995. As part of the same announcement, Mahoney revealed that Robert B. Shapiro, Monsanto's president and chief operating officer, would be elected by Monsanto's board of directors as his successor. Shapiro, who had joined

Searle in 1979 before being named executive vice-president of Monsanto in 1990, did not waver from exerting his influence over the company he now found himself presiding over. At the time of his promotion, Shapiro inherited a company that ranked as the largest domestic acrylic manufacturer in the world, generating $3 billion of its $7.9 billion in total revenues from chemical-related sales. This dominant side of the company's business, representing the foundation upon which it had been built, was eliminated under Shapiro's stewardship, replaced by a resolute commitment to biotech.

Between the mid-1980s and the mid-1990s, Monsanto had spent approximately $1 billion on developing its biotech business. Although biotech was regarded as a commercially unproven market by some industry analysts, Shapiro pressed forward with the research and development of biotech products, and by the beginning of 1996 he was ready to launch the company's first biotech product line. Monsanto began marketing herbicide-tolerant soybeans, genetically engineered to resist Roundup, and insect-resistant cotton, beginning with two million acres of both crops. By the fall of 1996, there were early indications that the first harvests of genetically engineered crops were performing better than expected. News of the encouraging results prompted Shapiro to make a startling announcement in October 1996, when he revealed that the company was considering divesting its chemical business as part of a major reorganization into a life-sciences company.

By the end of 1996, when Shapiro announced he would spin off the chemical operations as a separate company, Monsanto faced a future without its core business, a $3 billion contributor to the company's annual revenue volume. Without the chemical operations, Monsanto would be reduced to an approximately $5 billion company deriving half its sales from agricultural products and the rest from pharmaceuticals and food ingredients, but Shapiro did not intend to leave it as such. He foresaw an aggressive push into biotech products, a move that industry pundits generally perceived as astute. "It would be a gamble if they didn't do it," commented one analyst in reference to the proposed divestiture. "Monsanto is trying to transform itself into a high-growth agricultural and life sciences company. Low-growth cyclical chemical operations do not fit that bill." Spurring Shapiro toward this sweeping reinvention of Monsanto were enticing forecasts for the market growth of plant biotech products. A $450 million business in 1995, the market for plant biotech products was expected to reach $2 billion by 2000 and $6 billion by 2005. Shapiro wanted to dominate this fast-growing market as it matured by shaping Monsanto into what he described as the main provider of "agricultural biotechnology."

As preparations were underway for the spinoff of Monsanto's chemical operations into a new, publicly owned company named Solutia Inc., Shapiro was busy filling the void created by the departure of the company's core business. A flurry of acquisitions completed between 1995 and 1997 greatly increased Monsanto's presence in life sciences, quickly compensating for the revenue lost from the spinoff of Solutia. Among the largest acquisitions were Calgene, Inc., a leader in plant biotech, which was acquired in a two-part transaction in 1995 and 1997, and a 40 percent interest in Dekalb Genetics Corp., the second largest seed-corn company in the United States. In 1998, the company acquired the rest of DeKalb, paying $2.3 billion for the Illinois-based company.

By the end of the 1990s, Monsanto bore only partial resemblance to the company that entered the decade. The acquisition campaign that added dozens of biotechnology companies to its portfolio had created a new, dominant force in the promising life sciences field, placing Monsanto in a position to reap massive rewards in the years ahead. For example, a rootworm-resistant strain under development had the potential to save $1 billion worth of damages to corn crops per year. The company's pharmaceutical business also faced a promising future, highlighted by the introduction of a new arthritis medication named Celebrex in 1999. During its first year, Celebrex registered a record number of prescriptions. As Monsanto entered the 21st century, however, there were two uncertainties that loomed as potentially serious obstacles blocking its future success. The acquisition campaign of the mid- and late 1990s had greatly increased the company's debt, forcing Monsanto to desperately search for cash. Secondly, there was growing opposition to genetically altered crops at the decade's conclusion, prompting the United Kingdom to ban the yields from such crops for a year. A great part of the company's future success depended on the resolution of these two issues.

REORGANIZING IN 2000 AND BEYOND

Three years after the spinoff of the chemicals business, the two remaining Monsanto businesses, agriculture and pharmaceuticals, were separated in 2000 as Monsanto Company merged with Pharmacia & Upjohn Inc., creating a company that, for the moment had a market cap of more than $50 billion. The agricultural products business was incorporated as a Monsanto Company subsidiary in February 2000 named the Monsanto Ag Company.

The merger became effective on March 31, 2000. Pharmacia & Upjohn became another subsidiary of Monsanto Company, which changed its name to Pharmacia Corporation. The agricultural subsidiary, Monsanto Ag Company, then became the new Monsanto Company. Pharmacia Corporation (the old Monsanto Company) offered 15 percent of the new Monsanto's shares to the public in October 2000.

In August 2002, Pharmacia distributed its remaining holdings in the new Monsanto Company to its shareholders through a tax-free stock dividend. Pharmacia was acquired by Pfizer Inc. in April 2003, while the chemicals business, Solutia, filed for Chapter 11 bankruptcy in December 2003, burdened by the cost of settlements related to the old Monsanto's PCB manufacturing (which ended in 1977).

In the meantime, a number of other strategic divestments and acquisitions were made. The sweetener ingredient business (including NutraSweet) was sold to a Boston investment group for $440 million, while Merisant Company acquired the NutraSweet tabletop brand. Roundup's main ingredient, glyphosate, came off patent in 2000, opening its herbicide market share to erosion.

Sales slipped 14 percent to $4.7 billion in 2002. After earning $295 million the previous year, the company posted a horrific $1.7 billion loss, even though it had a 90 percent share of the market for genetically engineered seeds. CEO Hendrik Verfaille, who had taken over from Robert B. Shapiro after the Pharmacia merger, stepped down in December 2002. His position was filled for a time by Chairman Frank Atlee III. Chief Operating Officer Hugh Grant, a native of Scotland, became CEO in May 2003 and chairman in October 2003.

Under Grant, Monsanto's emphasis shifted from agrichemicals to seeds, both conventional and genetically modified. In 2004, the American Seeds Inc. subsidiary was formed to acquire regional seed producers. It soon bought Indiana's Channel Bio Corp. and Nebraska's NC Hybrids. Each had significant corn seed production. Emergent Genetics' cotton seed business was added soon after. Oxnard, California-based fruit and vegetable seed maker Seminis Inc. was acquired in 2005 in a deal worth $1.4 billion (including assumed debt). Seminis's 3,500 types of seed were distributed in 150 countries. Monsanto applied its expertise in studying genes from its GM business to breeding hybrids at Seminis.

The company's genetically modified seeds were by this time sown on nearly 200 million acres, principally in the United States and Argentina. They had gained acceptance in Canada and China, but were a subject of considerable controversy in Europe. Monsanto was promoting the higher yields of its GM products to farmers in developing countries. It was also developing drought resistant crops. For trans-fat conscious consumers in more affluent markets, Monsanto was touting its Vistive soybeans, whose oil did not have to be partially hydrogenated. The company also claimed other functional properties and better taste and shelf life for a range of other genetically modified or hybrid produce.

Monsanto was navigating a number of legal and PR challenges, including the pirating of its genetically modified soybean seeds in Brazil. The Brazilian farmers eventually agreed to pay Monsanto royalties for using the company's seeds. Monsanto, which had been selling the artificial bovine growth hormone Posilac for ten years, was suing a Maine dairy whose packaging allegedly disparaged artificial hormones. The company was also fighting attempts to label products as containing genetically modified ingredients.

PRINCIPAL SUBSIDIARIES

Asgrow Seed Company LLC; Channel Bio Corp.; Corn States Hybrid Service L.L.C.; DEKALB Genetics Corporation; Emergent Genetics, Inc.; Holden's Foundation Seeds L.L.C.; Mahyco-Monsanto Biotech Ltd. (India); Monsanto Ag Products LLC; Monsanto Argentina S.A.I.C.; Monsanto Australia Ltd.; Monsanto Canada, Inc.; Monsanto do Brasil Ltda. (Brazil); Monsanto Europe S.A./N.V. (Belgium); Monsanto India Limited; Monsanto Inter SARL (France); Monsanto Nordeste S.A. (Brazil); Monsanto SAS (France); Monsanto Seeds (Thailand) Ltd.; Monsanto Technology LLC; Semillas y Agroproductos Monsanto, S.A. de C.V. (Mexico); Seminis, Inc.

Marinell Landa
Updated, Jeffrey L. Covell; Frederick C. Ingram

PRINCIPAL DIVISIONS

Seeds and Genomics; Agricultural Productivity.

PRINCIPAL COMPETITORS

BASF Aktiengesellschaft; Bayer CropScience AG; Dow AgroSciences LLC; DuPont Agriculture & Nutrition; Pioneer Hi-Bred International, Inc.; Syngenta AG.

FURTHER READING

Baldwin, Virginia, "Monsanto Shifts Focus of Biotech Sales to Poor Countries; Use of Bioengineered Crops Is Greatest in U.S., China, Argentina, Canada," *St. Louis Post-Dispatch,* February 12, 2002, p. D1.

Barboza, David, "Monsanto Picks Top Executive As It Works Through Slump," *New York Times,* Bus. Sec., May 30, 2003, p. 6.

————, "Monsanto Sues Dairy in Maine Over Label's Remarks on Hormones," *New York Times,* Bus. Sec., July 12, 2003, p. 1.

Crisafulli, Patricia, "Monsanto, EPA Resolve Superfund Cleanup," *Journal of Commerce,* April 12, 1991, p. 13A.

Desloge, Rick, "Is a Divided Monsanto a Target for Purchase?," *St. Louis Business Journal,* December 30, 1996, p. 3.

Donlon, J. P., "After Restructuring, What?," *Chief Executive (U.S.),* March-April, 1988, p. 50.

Ellis, James E., "Monsanto and the Copper-7: A 'Corporate Veil' Begins to Fray," *Business Week,* September 26, 1988, p. 50.

Forrestal, Dan J., *Faith, Hope, and $5,000: The Story of Monsanto: The Trials and Triumphs of the First 75 Years,* New York: Simon and Schuster, 1977.

Gilpin, Kenneth N., "Pharmacia Planning Spinoff of Its 85% Stake in Monsanto," *New York Times,* November 29, 2001, p. 2.

"The Green Gene Giant," *Economist,* April 26, 1997, p. 66.

Henkoff, Ronald, "Monsanto: Learning from Its Mistakes," *Fortune,* January 27, 1992, p. 81.

Jaffe, Thomas, "How Do You Top This?," *Forbes,* June 1, 1998.

Kiesche, Elizabeth S., "Monsanto Cultivates Lawn and Garden Line with Ortho Buy," *Chemical Week,* January 20, 1993, p. 7.

Lambrecht, Bill, "Monsanto Battles Effort to Require Labeling of Genetically Modified Food; Industry Opposes Oregon Ballet Initiative," *St. Louis Post-Dispatch,* September 19, 2002, p. A1.

Melcer, Rachel, "Monsanto Is Delivering on Promises It Made; Its Newest Products Help Foods Taste Better While Being Healthier and Easier to Process, Ship and Store," *St. Louis Post-Dispatch,* November 27, 2005, p. E1.

"Monsanto Pursues Seed Pirates," *New York Times,* June 13, 2003, p. 12.

Smith, Tony, "Brazilian Farmers to Pay Monsanto for Soybean Seeds," *New York Times,* Bus. Sec., January 29, 2004, p. 4.

Steyer, Robert, "Going It Alone," *Knight-Ridder/Tribune Business News,* October 19, 1998.

Stringer, Judy, "Monsanto Poised to Reap BioTech Harvest," *Chemical Week,* November 6, 1996, p. 51.

Stroud, Jerri, "Seminis, Monsanto Scientists See Synergy," *St. Louis Post-Dispatch,* May 1, 2005, p. E1.

NOKIA

Nokia Corporation

■

Keilalahdentie 4 FIN-02150
Espoo,
Finland
Telephone: (358) 7180-08000
Fax: (358) 7180-38226
Web site: http://www.nokia.com

Public Company
Incorporated: 1865
Employees: 55,505
Sales: EUR 29.26 billion (2004)
Stock Exchanges: New York Helsinki Stockholm Frankfurt
Ticker Symbol: NOK
NAIC: 334210 Telephone Apparatus Manufacturing; 334220 Radio and Television Broadcasting and Wireless Communications Equipment Manufacturing; 334310 Audio and Video Equipment Manufacturing; 334419 Other Electronic Component Manufacturing; 517212 Cellular and Other Wireless Telecommunications; 517910 Other Telecommunications; 551112 Offices of Other Holding Companies

■ ■ ■

Nokia Corporation is the world's largest manufacturer of mobile phones, serving customers in 130 countries. Nokia is divided into four business groups: Mobile Phones, Multimedia, Enterprise Solutions, and Networks. The Mobile Phones group markets wireless voice and data products in consumer and corporate markets. The Multimedia segment sells mobile gaming devices, home satellite systems, and cable television set-top boxes. The Enterprise Solutions group develops wireless systems for use in the corporate sector. Wireless switching and transmission equipment is sold through the company's Networks division. Nokia operates 15 manufacturing facilities in nine countries and maintains research and development facilities in 12 countries.

19TH-CENTURY ORIGINS

Originally a manufacturer of pulp and paper, Nokia was founded as Nokia Company in 1865 in a small town of the same name in central Finland. Nokia was a pioneer in the industry and introduced many new production methods to a country with only one major natural resource, its vast forests. As the industry became increasingly energy-intensive, the company even constructed its own power plants. But for many years, Nokia remained an important yet static firm in a relatively forgotten corner of northern Europe. Nokia shares were first listed on the Helsinki exchange in 1915.

The first major changes in Nokia occurred several years after World War II. Despite its proximity to the Soviet Union, Finland has always remained economically connected with Scandinavian and other Western countries, and as Finnish trade expanded Nokia became a leading exporter.

During the early 1960s Nokia began to diversify in an attempt to transform the company into a regional conglomerate with interests beyond Finnish borders. Unable to initiate strong internal growth, Nokia turned its attention to acquisitions. The government, however, hoping to rationalize two underperforming basic industries, favored Nokia's expansion within the country and encouraged its eventual merger with Finnish Rubber Works, which was founded in 1898, and Finnish Cable Works, which was formed in 1912, to form Nokia Corporation. When the amalgamation was completed in 1966, Nokia was involved in several new industries, including integrated cable operations, electronics, tires, and rubber footwear, and had made its first public share offering.

In 1967 Nokia set up a division to develop design and manufacturing capabilities in data processing, industrial automation, and communications systems. The division was later expanded and made into several divisions, which then concentrated on developing information systems, including personal computers and workstations, digital communications systems, and mobile phones. Nokia also gained a strong position in modems and automatic banking systems in Scandinavia.

OIL CRISIS, CORPORATE CHANGES: 1970S

Nokia continued to operate in a stable but parochial manner until 1973, when it was affected in a unique way by the oil crisis. Years of political accommodation between Finland and the Soviet Union ensured Finnish neutrality in exchange for lucrative trade agreements with the Soviets, mainly Finnish lumber products and machinery in exchange for Soviet oil. By agreement, this trade was kept strictly in balance. But when world oil prices began to rise, the market price for Soviet oil rose with it. Balanced trade began to mean greatly reduced purchasing power for Finnish companies such as Nokia.

Although the effects were not catastrophic, the oil crisis did force Nokia to reassess its reliance on Soviet trade (about 12 percent of sales) as well as its international growth strategies. Several contingency plans were drawn up, but the greatest changes came after the company appointed a new CEO, Kari Kairamo, in 1975.

Kairamo noted the obvious: Nokia was too big for Finland. The company had to expand abroad. He studied

the expansion of other Scandinavian companies (particularly Sweden's Electrolux) and, following their example, formulated a strategy of first consolidating the company's business in Finland, Sweden, Norway, and Denmark, and then moving gradually into the rest of Europe. After the company had improved its product line, established a reputation for quality, and adjusted its production capacity, it would enter the world market.

Meanwhile, Nokia's traditional, heavy industries were looking increasingly burdensome. It was feared that trying to become a leader in electronics while maintaining these basic industries would create an unmanageably unfocused company. Kairamo thought briefly about selling off the company's weaker divisions, but decided to retain and modernize them.

He reasoned that, although the modernization of these low-growth industries would be very expensive, it would guarantee Nokia's position in several stable markets, including paper, chemical, and machinery productions, and electrical generation. For the scheme to be practical, each division's modernization would have to be gradual and individually financed. This would prevent the bleeding of funds away from the all-important effort in electronics while preventing the heavy industries from becoming any less profitable.

With each division financing its own modernization, there was little or no drain on capital from other divisions, and Nokia could still sell any group that did not succeed under the new plan. In the end, the plan prompted the machinery division to begin development in robotics and automation, the cables division to begin work on fiber optics, and the forestry division to move into high-grade tissues.

RISE OF ELECTRONICS: 1980S

Nokia's most important focus was development of the electronics sector. Over the course of the 1980s, the firm acquired nearly 20 companies, focusing especially on three segments of the electronics industry: consumer, workstations, and mobile communications. Electronics grew from 10 percent of annual sales to 60 percent of revenues from 1980 to 1988.

In late 1984 Nokia acquired Salora, the largest color television manufacturer in Scandinavia, and Luxor, the Swedish state-owned electronics and computer firm. Nokia combined Salora and Luxor into a single division and concentrated on stylish consumer electronic products, since style was a crucial factor in Scandinavian markets. The Salora-Luxor division was also very successful in satellite and digital television technology. Nokia purchased the consumer electronics operations of Standard Elektrik Lorenz A.G. from Alcatel in 1987,

KEY DATES

1865: Nokia is founded as a maker of pulp and paper.
1898: Finnish Rubber Works is founded.
1912: Finnish Cable Works is formed.
1915: Nokia shares are first listed on the Helsinki exchange.
1967: Nokia merges with Finnish Rubber Works and Finnish Cable Works to form Nokia Corporation.
1979: Mobira Oy is formed as a mobile phone company.
1981: The first international cellular system, the Nordic Mobile Telephone network, comes on line, having been developed with the help of Nokia.
1982: Nokia acquires Mobira, which later becomes the Nokia Mobile Phones division.
1986: Company markets internationally the first Nokia mobile telephone.
1993: The first Nokia digital cellular phone hits the market.
1998: Nokia surpasses Motorola as the world's number one maker of mobile phones.
2002: Nokia introduces the first third-generation compliant mobile phone.
2005: Jorma Ollila announces he will step down as chief executive officer in 2006.

further bolstering the company's position in the television market to the third largest manufacturer in Europe.

In early 1988 Nokia acquired the data systems division of the Swedish Ericsson Group, making Nokia the largest Scandinavian information technology business.

Although a market leader in Scandinavia, Nokia still lacked a degree of competitiveness in the European market, which was dominated by much larger Japanese and German companies. Kairamo decided, therefore, to follow the example of many Japanese companies during the 1960s (and Korean manufacturers a decade later) and negotiate to become an original equipment manufacturer, or OEM, to manufacture products for competitors as a subcontractor.

Nokia manufactured items for Hitachi in France, Ericsson in Sweden, Northern Telecom in Canada, and Granada and IBM in Britain. In doing so it was able to increase its production capacity stability. There were,

however, several risks involved, those inherent in any OEM arrangement. Nokia's sales margins were naturally reduced, but of greater concern, production capacity was built up without a commensurate expansion in the sales network. With little brand identification, Nokia feared it might have a difficult time selling under its own name and become trapped as an OEM.

In 1986 Nokia reorganized its management structure to simplify reporting efforts and improve control by central management. The company's 11 divisions were grouped into four industry segments: electronics; cables and machinery; paper, power, and chemicals; and rubber and flooring. In addition, Nokia won a concession from the Finnish government to allow greater foreign participation in ownership. This substantially reduced Nokia's dependence on the comparatively expensive Finnish lending market. Although there was growth throughout the company, Nokia's greatest success was in telecommunications.

Having dabbled in telecommunications in the 1960s, Nokia cut its teeth in the industry by selling switching systems under license from a French company, Alcatel. The Finnish firm got in on the cellular industry's ground floor in the late 1970s, when it helped design the world's first international cellular system. Named the Nordic Mobile Telephone (NMT) network, the system linked Sweden, Denmark, Norway, and Finland. A year after the network came on line in 1981, Nokia gained 100 percent control of Mobira, the Finnish mobile phone company that would later become its key business interest as the Nokia Mobile Phones division. Mobira's regional sales were vastly improved, but Nokia was still limited to OEM production on the international market; Nokia and Tandy Corporation, of the United States, built a factory in Masan, South Korea, to manufacture mobile telephones. These were sold under the Tandy name in that company's 6,000 Radio Shack stores throughout the United States.

In 1986, eager to test its ability to compete openly, Nokia chose the mobile telephone to be the first product marketed internationally under the Nokia name; it became Nokia's "make or break" product. Unfortunately, Asian competitors began to drive prices down just as Nokia entered the market. Other Nokia products gaining recognition were Salora televisions and Luxor satellite dishes, which suffered briefly when subscription programming introduced broadcast scrambling.

The company's expansion, achieved almost exclusively by acquisition, had been expensive. Few Finnish investors other than institutions had the patience to see Nokia through its long-term plans. Indeed, more than half of the new shares issued by Nokia in 1987 went to foreign investors. Nokia moved boldly into

Western markets; it gained a listing on the London exchange in 1987 and was subsequently listed on the New York exchange.

CRISES OF LEADERSHIP, PROFIT-ABILITY IN THE LATE 1980S AND EARLY 1990S

Nokia's rapid growth was not without a price. In 1988, as revenues soared, the company's profits, under pressure from severe price competition in the consumer electronics markets, dropped. Chairman Kari Kairamo committed suicide in December of that year; not surprisingly, friends said it was brought on by stress. Simo S. Vuorileto took over the company's reins and began streamlining operations in the spring of 1988. Nokia was divided into six business groups: consumer electronics, data, mobile phones, telecommunications, cables and machinery, and basic industries. Vuorileto continued Kairamo's focus on high-tech divisions, divesting Nokia's flooring, paper, rubber, and ventilation systems businesses and entering into joint ventures with companies such as Tandy Corporation and Matra of France (two separate agreements to produce mobile phones for the U.S. and French markets).

In spite of these efforts, Nokia's pretax profits continued to decline in 1989 and 1990, culminating in a loss of $102 million in 1991. Industry observers blamed cutthroat European competition, the breakdown of the Finnish banking system, and the collapse of the Soviet Union. But, notwithstanding these difficulties, Nokia remained committed to its high-tech orientation. Late in 1991, the company strengthened that dedication by promoting Jorma Ollila from president of Nokia-Mobira Inc. (renamed Nokia Mobile Phones Ltd. the following year) to group president.

LEADING THE TELECOMMUNICA-TIONS REVOLUTION: MID-1990S AND BEYOND

Forbes's Fleming Meeks credited Ollila with transforming Nokia from "a moneylosing hodgepodge of companies into one of telecommunications' most profitable companies." Unable to find a buyer for Nokia's consumer electronics business, which had lost nearly $1 billion from 1988 to 1993, Ollila cut that segment's workforce by 45 percent, shuttered plants, and centralized operations. Having divested Nokia Data in 1991, Nokia focused further on its telecommunications core by selling off its power unit in 1994 and its television and tire and cable units the following year.

The new leader achieved success in the cellular phone segment by bringing innovative products to market quickly with a particular focus on ever smaller and easier-to-use phones featuring sleek Finnish design. Nokia gained a leg up in cellphone research and development with the 1991 acquisition of the United Kingdom's Technophone Ltd. for $57 million. The company began selling digital cellular phones in 1993.

Ollila's tenure brought Nokia success and with it global recognition. The company's sales more than doubled, from FIM 15.5 billion in 1991 to FIM 36.8 billion in 1995, and its bottom line rebounded from a net loss of FIM 723 million in 1992 to a FIM 2.2 billion profit in 1995. Securities investors did not miss the turnaround: Nokia's market capitalization multiplied ten times from 1991 to 1994.

In late 1995 and early 1996, Nokia suffered a temporary setback stemming from a shortage of chips for its digital cellular phones and a resultant disruption of its logistics chain. The company's production costs rose and profits fell. Nokia was also slightly ahead of the market, particularly in North America, in regard to the shift from analog to digital phones. As a result, it was saddled with a great number of digital phones it could not sell and an insufficient number of analog devices. Nevertheless, Nokia had positioned itself well for the long haul, and within just a year or two it was arch-rival Motorola, Inc. that was burdened with an abundance of phones it could not sell, analog ones, as Motorola was slow to convert to digital. As a result, by late 1998, Nokia had surpassed Motorola and claimed the top position in cellular phones worldwide.

Aiding this surge was the November 1997 introduction of the 6100 series of digital phones. This line proved immensely popular because of the phones' small size (similar to a slim pack of cigarettes), light weight (4.5 ounces), and superior battery life. First introduced in the burgeoning mobile phone market in China, the 6100 soon became a worldwide phenomenon. Including the 6100 and other models, Nokia sold nearly 41 million cellular phones in 1998. Net sales increased more than 50 percent over the previous year, jumping from FIM 52.61 billion ($9.83 billion) to FIM 79.23 billion ($15.69 billion). Operating profits increased by 75 percent, while the company's skyrocketing stock price shot up more than 220 percent, pushing Nokia's market capitalization from FIM 110.01 billion ($20.57 billion) to FIM 355.53 billion ($70.39 billion).

Not content with conquering the mobile phone market, Nokia began aggressively pursuing the mobile Internet sector in the late 1990s. Already on the market was the Nokia 9000 Communicator, a personal all-in-one communication device that included phone, data, Internet, e-mail, and fax retrieval services. The Nokia 8110 mobile phone included the capability to access the

Internet. In addition, Nokia was the first company to introduce a cellular phone that could be connected to a laptop computer to transmit data over a mobile network. To help develop further products, Nokia began acquiring Internet technology companies, starting with the December 1997, $120 million purchase of Ipsilon Networks Inc., a Silicon Valley firm specializing in Internet routing. One year later, Nokia spent FIM 429 million ($85 million) for Vienna Systems Corporation, a Canadian firm focusing on Internet Protocol telephony.

Acquisitions continued in 1999, when a further seven deals were completed, four of which were Internet-related. Meanwhile, net sales increased a further 48 percent in 1999, while operating profits grew by 57 percent; riding the late 1990s high-tech stock boom, the market capitalization of Nokia took another huge leap, ending the year at EUR 209.37 billion ($211.05 billion). Nokia's share of the global cellular phone market increased from 22.5 percent in 1998 to 26.9 percent in 1999, as the company sold 76.3 million phones in 1999.

Nokia's ascendance to the top of the wireless world by the end of the 1990s could be traced to the company being able to consistently, over and over again, come out with high-margin products superior to those of its competitors and in tune with market demands. The continuation of this trend into the 21st century was by no means certain as the increasing convergence of wireless and Internet technologies and the development of the third generation (3G) of wireless technology (which followed the analog and digital generations and which was slated to feature sophisticated multimedia capability) were predicted to open Nokia up to new and formidable competitors.

Perhaps the greatest threat was that chipmakers such as Intel would turn mobile phones into commodities just as they had previously done with personal computers; the days of the $500 Nokia phone were potentially numbered. Nevertheless, Nokia's 25 percent profit margins were enabling it to spend a massive $2 billion a year on research and development and continue to churn out innovative new products, concentrating on the various standards being developed for 3G wireless networks.

A TWO-PRONGED APPROACH IN THE 21ST CENTURY

Mobile communications developed along two broad fronts during the first years of the century, both of which played to Nokia's advantage, ensuring that the company remained the leader of its industry. The evolution of handsets into multimedia devices ushered in by 3G technology meant that Nokia could continue to rely on marketing expensive, sophisticated handsets. The days of

the $500 Nokia phone gave way to the days of increasingly more expensive phones, such as the Nokia N90, a unit featuring a camera with Carl Zeiss optics, video-recording capabilities, and Internet access. Nokia could count on a substantial share of the high end of the market, a segment that continued to thrive midway through the decade, but the company's greatest strength was in the lower end of the market. In countries such as China, Brazil, and India there was a tremendous demand for inexpensive mobile phones, with analysts expecting 50 percent of the one billion handsets sold between 2005 and 2010 to be sold in developing economies. Industry observers believed there were only two companies in the world that could seriously compete for the estimated 800-million-unit-per year market for inexpensive handsets: Motorola and Nokia. Rivals such as Samsung, Sony Ericsson, and LG Electronics preferred to confine their activities to the high end of the market, while emerging low-cost producers lacked the manufacturing efficiencies enjoyed by Nokia and Motorola.

Against the backdrop of favorable market trends supporting Nokia's entrenched position, the company experienced a rare event in its modern history: a change in leadership. After a decade-and-a-half at the helm, CEO Ollila announced his retirement, effective June 2006. His replacement was a 25-year Nokia veteran named Olli-Pekka Kallasvuo, a lawyer by training whom *Fortune*, in that magazine's October 31, 2005 issue, described as so taciturn that "he can seem like an extra from an Ingmar Bergman movie."

Kallasvuo, who was promoted from his position as the head of the handset division, inherited an impressively capable company whose greatest challenge was contending with Motorola for the low end of the market and beating back competitors for control of the high end of the market. "Nokia is a dynamic company in a fast-changing and fluid environment," Kallasvuo said in a November 29, 2005 interview with the *South China Morning Post*. "I look forward to working together with our team to help Nokia shape the future of mobile communications at a pivotal time for the industry."

PRINCIPAL SUBSIDIARIES

Nokia Holding Inc.; Nokia Products Limited (Canada); Nokia IP Telephony Corporation (Canada); Nokia Telecommunications Inc.; Nokia Inc.; Nokia (China) Investment Co. Ltd.; Nokia (H.K.) Limited (Hong Kong); Nokia (Ireland) Ltd.; Nokia Australia Pty Limited; Nokia Asset Management Oy; Nokia Austria GmbH; Nokia Danmark A/S (Denmark); Nokia Do Brasil Ltda. (Brazil); Nokia Do Brasil Tecnologia Ltda. (Brazil); Nokia Finance International B.V. (Netherlands); Nokia France; Nokia GmbH (Germany); Nokia India

Private Limited; Nokia Italia Spa (Italy); Nokia Korea Ltd.; Nokia Mobile Phones; Nokia Networks; Nokia Norge AS (Norway); Nokia Oyj; Nokia Pte Ltd. (Singapore); Nokia Spain, S.A.; Nokia Svenska AB (Sweden); Nokia U.K. Ltd.; Nokia Ventures Organization; Bave Tartum (U.K.); Beijing Nokia Hangxing Telecommunications Systems Co., Ltd. (China); Doctortel—Assistencia De Telecomunicaes S.A. (Portugal); Funda Ao Nokia De Ensino (Brazil); Instituto Nokia De Tecnologia (Brazil); Nokia (M) Sdn Bhd (Malaysia); Nokia Argentina S.A.; Nokia Belgium NV; Nokia Capitel Telecommunications Ltd. (China); Nokia Ecuador S.A.; Nokia Hellas Communications S.A.; Nokia Hungary Kommunikacios Korlatolt Felelossegu Tarsasag (Hungary); Nokia Israel Ltd.; Nokia Middle East (United Arab Emirates; Nokia Nederland B.V. (Netherlands); Nokia Poland Sp Z.O.O.; Nokia Portugal S.A.; Nokia Private Joint Stock Company (Russia); Nokia Research Center; Nokia River Golf Ry; Nokia S.A. (Columbia); Nokia Servicios, S.A. de C.V. (Mexico); Nokia Technology GmbH (Germany); Nokianvirta Oy; Oy Scaninter Nokia Ltd.; Pointo Nokia Oy.

Updated, April D. Gasbarre; David E. Salamie; Jeffrey L. Covell

PRINCIPAL COMPETITORS

Telefonaktiebolaget LM Ericsson; Motorola, Inc.; Siemens AG; Sony Corporation.

FURTHER READING

Angell, Mike, "Nokia Banking on New Phone Features, Cameras, E-Mail Access," *Investor's Business Daily,* December 3, 2002, p. A7.

Baker, Stephen, and Kerry Capell, "The Race to Rule Mobile," *Business Week,* February 21, 2000, pp. 58-60.

Baker, Stephen, Roger O. Crockett, and Neil Gross, "Nokia: Can CEO Ollila Keep the Cellular Superstar Flying High?," *Business Week,* August 10, 1998, pp. 54-60.

"Bellaby, Mara D., "Nokia Acquires Intellisynch," *America's Intelligence Wire,* November 17, 2005.

Bensinger, Ari, "The Call on Nokia," *Business Week Online,* January 7, 2003.

Berkman, Barbara N., "Brainstorming in the Sauna," *Electronic Business,* November 18, 1991, pp. 71-74.

———, "Sagging Profits Spark Identity Crisis at Nokia," *Electronic Business,* March 4, 1991, pp. 57-59.

Burt, Tim, and Greg McIvor, "Land of Midnight Mobiles: A Former Toilet-Paper Maker from Finland Has Become the World's Largest Manufacturer of Mobile Phones," *Financial Times,* October 30, 1998, p. 18.

Edmondson, Gail, Peter Elstrom, and Peter Burrows, "At Nokia, a Comeback—and Then Some," *Business Week,* December 2, 1996, p. 106.

Fox, Justin, "Nokia's Secret Code," *Fortune,* May 1, 2000, pp. 161-64+.

Furchgott, Roy, "Nokia Signals Desire for Higher Profile," *ADWEEK Eastern Edition,* June 12, 1995, p. 2.

Guth, Robert A., "Nokia Fights for Toehold in Japan's Cell-Phone Market," *Wall Street Journal,* June 26, 2000, p. A26.

Heard, Joyce, and Keller, John J., "Nokia Skates into High Tech's Big Leagues," *Business Week,* April 4, 1988, pp. 102-03.

Jacob, Rahul, "Nokia Fumbles, But Don't Count It Out," *Fortune,* February 19, 1996, pp. 86-88.

Kharif, Olga, "Will New Phones Boost Nokia's Signal?," *Business Week Online,* December 11, 2002.

La Rossa, James, Jr., "Nokia Knocks on U.S. Door," *HFD—The Weekly Home Furnishings Newspaper,* February 10, 1992, pp. 66-67.

Lemola, Tarmo, and Raimo Lovio, *Miksi Nokia, Finland,* Porvoo, Sweden: W. Sööderström, 1996, 211 p.

Lineback, J. Robert, "Nokia's Mobile Phone Unit Is Ringing Bells," *Electronic Business Buyer,* June 1994, pp. 60-62.

Meeks, Fleming, "Watch Out, Motorola," *Forbes,* September 12, 1994, pp. 192-94.

"Nokia and CommTel Expand Broadband in the Pacific," *PR Newswire,* December 28, 2005.

"Nokia Expands Production in China," *TelecomWeb News Digest,* December 1, 2005.

"Nokia Launches New 3G Phones," *eWeek,* December 1, 2005.

"Not Finnished Yet," *Economist,* February 9, 1991, p. 73.

Perez, Bien, "Nokia Adapts to Swift Changes," *South China Morning Post,* November 29, 2005.

Reinhardt, Andy, "Cell Phones for the People," *Business Week,* November 7, 2005, p. 26.

———, "A Whole New Wireless Order," *Business Week,* October 31, 2005, p. MTL2.

Salameh, Asad, "Nokia Repositions for a Major Cellular Marketing Initiative," *Telecommunications,* June 1992, p. 43.

Schwartz, Nelson D., "The Man Behind Nokia's Comeback," *Fortune,* October 31, 2005, p. 39.

Seyfer, Jessie, "Nokia to Acquire Intellisync," *San Jose Mercury News,* November 17, 2005.

Silberg, Lurie, "A Brand Apart," *HFD—The Weekly Home Furnishings Newspaper,* September 5, 1994, pp. 54-55.

"These Sexy Gadgets Will Rock Next Year," *Economic Times of India,* December 20, 2005.

Williams, Elaine, "100-Year-Old Nokia Experiences Fast-Growth Pains," *Electronic Business,* June 26, 1989, pp. 111-14.

Oil States International, Inc.

————— ■ —————

Three Allen Center
333 Clay Street, Suite 4620
Houston, Texas 77002
U.S.A.
Telephone: (713) 652-0582
Fax: (713) 652-0499
Web site: http://www.oilstatesintl.com

Public Company
Incorporated: as CE Holdings, Inc. in 1995
Employees: 3,940
Sales: $1.38 billion (2005)
Stock Exchanges: New York
Ticker Symbol: OSI
NAIC: 213112 Support Activities for Oil and Gas
Operations

■ ■ ■

While its name suggests its business, Oil States International, Inc. does not actually produce oil but helps the drilling and production companies that do. Oil States provides a wide range of products and services to oil and gas drilling firms around the world, conducting business in the oil- and gas-producing regions of Canada, the Gulf of Mexico, South America, the Middle East, West Africa, and Southeast Asia. Oil States operates in three primary business segments—offshore products, tubular services, and well site services—and has established itself as a leader in each of these growing industries.

SERVING THE OIL INDUSTRY: 1930S TO EARLY 1990S

What is today's Oil States International, Inc. (OSI) began with several disparate companies. Henry Zarrow opened the first of these companies in Tulsa, Oklahoma, in 1937 to provide supplies for area oilfield drillers. Many of his products were tubular parts, essential to the local drillers in their ongoing search for oil. As the technology for drilling evolved, so did Zarrow's supplies, always providing customers with a growing range of products. Zarrow's ingenuity became the cornerstone for OSI's tubular products division. By the late 1990s Zarrow's company was a leading distributor of "OCTG," or oil country tubular goods. In 1999 Zarrow's company bought three rivals and merged their operations, becoming the United States' top OCTG manufacturer.

A second company, Oil States Industries of Arlington, Texas, revolved around rubber components and was founded in 1949. This firm designed and manufactured a growing line of innovative marine products, including the first flexible load bearings for bridges and the earliest laminated bearing products used in any building structure in 1955. Next came the Hydro-Couple in 1966, a "coupling" or joining product used to connect pipes underwater, followed by further laminated bearings and seals for flexible pipes used in drill rigs and nuclear submarines in the 1970s. The laminated bearings and joints became part of the very successful Flex-Joint line of products, considered one of the company's most technologically advanced and profitable ventures. In the 1980s came the Merlin, a nonrotating connector, and Hydra-Lock, a locking mechanism, for use in deep sea oil rig platforms.

By the 1990s additional products were developed, including diverless connections for use in undersea structures in depths of over 5,000 feet; the first rigid, extra long free-hanging riser; and the Top Entry Sub, a tool to help divers connect wiring and tubing underwater. The Top Entry Sub was available as a rental to companies worldwide for deep sea operations. Oil States Industries had also segued into portable accommodations as part of its well site services, providing housing and related needs for oil rig workers who put out to sea for either weeks or months at a time. Most of the company's housing could be delivered and set up, either offshore or by new land drilling sites, within 24 hours and often included catering services as well.

INCORPORATION AND CONSOLIDATION: 1995-99

Zarrow's expanding operations were incorporated as CE Holdings, Inc. in July 1995. Soon after, the firm acquired another oilpatch supply store chain called Continental Emsco Company, based in Garland, Texas. The deal included Continental's offshore products subsidiary, Oil States Industries, Inc. The following May, in 1996, Oil States bought the construction unit of Hunting Oilfield Services, Ltd., an offshore oil and gas products and services company. In November, the growing CE Holdings changed its name to Conemsco, Inc., to better reflect its operations. The company's headquarters was established in Houston with SCF Partners, an energy services and equipment investment firm founded and run by L. E. Simmons, owning the majority of the operations.

Conemsco continued to buy compatible companies in 1997 including HydroTech Systems, Inc., a manufacturer of offshore products; Skagit Products and Smatco Industries Inc., deep sea product manufacturers; and Gregory Rig Service & Sales Inc., which supplied drilling equipment and services. By early the following year, Conemsco bought Subsea Ventures, Inc. for its offshore rig work and Klaper (UK) Limited, another firm devoted to preventative maintenance and product supply for offshore drilling.

In 1999 Conemsco sold its tubular goods unit to the Oklahoma-based Sooner, Inc. and prepared to evolve from a privately held collection of companies to a public corporation with worldwide aspirations. To accomplish these goals, Douglas E. Swanson was hired as Conemsco's new president and chief executive officer effective the following January. Swanson had previously served as president of the Houston-based Cliffs Drilling Company, leaving upon its acquisition by R&B Falcon Corporation (itself later sold to offshore drilling giant Transocean Inc.). Conemsco finished 1999 with revenues of $487.4 million and net income of $8.9 million.

EVOLUTION AND EXPANSION: 2000S

In early 2000 Swanson took the reins of Conemsco and dove into several critical projects, including the development of an e-commerce web site for its oil and gas producers to buy tubular products and services online. Launched in February under the Sooner name (soon to become part of the new public company) the online service did extremely well and expanded its offerings throughout the year.

In July the company changed its name from Conemsco, Inc. to Oil States International, Inc. Oil States Industries (part of Conemsco) and three other companies—HWC Energy Services, Inc., PTI Group Inc., and Sooner Inc.—agreed to merge and do business as the soon-to-be public Oil States International, Inc. The deal was partially financed by SCF Partners and Simmons became OSI's chairman of the board. Papers were filed with the Securities and Exchange Commission in August. Oil States International, Inc. completed an initial public offering (IPO) on the New York Stock Exchange under the ticker symbol OSI on February 9, 2001, with shares priced at $9 each. Proceeds were used to pay down accumulated debt and to finance domestic and international expansion plans. For the year 2001, OSI owned and operated four of the highest producing U.S. oil rigs. The company owned 1,156 oil rigs in the United States (1,003 on land and 53 offshore) and an additional 266 in Canada.

KEY DATES

1937: Henry Zarrow opens an oilfield supply store in Tulsa, Oklahoma.

1949: Oil States Industries is founded in Texas.

1995: CE Holdings, Inc. is formed and buys Continental Emsco Company and its subsidiaries.

1996: CE Holdings changes its name to Conemsco, Inc.

1997: Conemsco buys three companies related to offshore marine and oil drilling.

1998: The company buys two deep sea maintenance and component services companies.

2000: Conemsco changes its name to Oil States International, Inc. (OSI).

2001: The company makes its initial public offering on the New York Stock Exchange.

2002: OSI completes six acquisitions to bolster its three business segments.

2003: OSI purchases five additional companies during the year.

2005: The company experiences record revenues and acquires four more companies.

While 2001 had seemed a prudent time to go public, in the months following the IPO business did not boom. Though share prices rose as high as $15 each, they soon fell back to their issue price. The company went ahead with a series of acquisitions, however, to build its three primary business segments: Well Site Services, Tubular Products, and Offshore Products. In 2002 Oil States spent a total of just over $72 million for six acquisitions: Mississippi's Southeastern Rentals LLC, the Louisiana-based Edge Wireline Rentals Inc. and J.V. Oilfield Rentals & Supply, Inc., for its well site services unit; and Oklahoma's Barlow Hunt, Inc., Texas-based Big Inch Marine Services, Inc., and Louisiana's Applied Hydraulic Systems, Inc. for offshore products.

In 2003 OSI continued its acquisitions spree, though to a slightly lesser degree than the previous year. Five businesses were bought for a total of $16.8 million, of which three were well site tool rental companies operating in Texas and Louisiana and the other two were folded into OSI's offshore products unit. During the year OSI's stock fluctuated between a low of $9.95 in the second quarter and a high of $14.84 reached in the fourth quarter.

Oil States continued to bolster its well site services division in 2004 with the purchase of more tool rental businesses in the south Texas area in January and April for a total of $39.6 million, and acquired a tubular goods distribution firm, Hunting Energy Services LP, for $47 million in May. Stock prices climbed throughout the year, responding to OSI's growth, with a low of $12.75 in the first quarter and an all-time high of $21.10 in the fourth quarter. Share prices reflected OSI's strong year with revenues topping $971 million and income surging to $59.4 million for 2004.

In 2005 with robust sales and increased drilling in the United States, OSI's well site services segment was booming with an additional 153 rigs brought into production for the first three months of the year alone. The company had 1,800 rigs throughout North America, with 1,279 in the United States and 521 in Canada, a substantial increase from just five years earlier, when OSI had a total of 1,263 North American rigs (918 in the United States, 345 in Canada). To go with the increased flow, OSI embarked on several strategic acquisitions in 2005 including Elenburg Exploration Company, Inc. ($22 million) and Stinger Wellhead Protection, Inc. ($89 million) for its well site services segment; Phillips Casing and Tubing LP ($31 million) for its tubular services segment; and Noble Structures, Inc. ($9 million) for its offshore products unit.

Near the end of the year OSI announced it would merge Boots & Coots International Well Control, Inc. into its hydraulic products and service sector, part of the well site services unit based in Louisiana. Oil production highs carried OSI through the year, with revenues topping the billion-dollar mark for the first time at $1.38 billion in 2005.

OSI continued to grow at a phenomenal rate through early 2006, as stock prices climbed to over $42 per share. The company remained an industry leader by offering clients an ever expanding array of cutting edge products and services. Still North America's largest distributor of oil country tubular goods, Oil States offered the widest range of specialized rental tools for the oil and gas production industry, and accommodated the industry's workforce with extensive remote-site housing in both Canada and offshore sites in the Gulf of Mexico.

Nelson Rhodes

PRINCIPAL SUBSIDIARIES

Capstar; General Marine Leasing; HydroTech; International Quarters; MCS; Oil States Industries, Inc.; PTI Group, Inc.; Skagit/Smatco; Sooner, Inc.; Specialty Rental Tools & Supply; Subsea Ventures.

PRINCIPAL DIVISIONS

Tubular Services; Wellsite Services; Offshore Products.

PRINCIPAL COMPETITORS

AmClyde Engineered Products Company, Inc.; Dril-Quip, Inc.; Cooper Cameron Corporation; FMC Technologies, Inc.; Stolt Offshore; Coflexip Stena Offshore; Red Man Pipe & Supply; Superior Energy Services, Inc.

FURTHER READING

De Rouffignac, Anne, "Equity Firm Drives Oil Service Consolidation," *Houston Business Journal,* July 2, 1999, p. 1.

Fletcher, Sam, "Sooner Buys Three Firms to Climb the Ranks of Tubular Distributors," *Oil Daily,* June 28, 1999.

Greer, Jim, "Wall Street Renews Energy Interest," *Houston Business Journal,* August 18, 2000, p. 1.

Marcial, Gene G., "Tempting Buys in Oil Drilling and Broadband Gear," *Business Week,* June 19, 2004, p. 92.

Moroney, Richard, "Oil States International," *Medical Economics,* December 2, 2005, p. 81.

Musero, Frank, "Lock-up Selling Down for August Releases," *IPO Reporter,* August 20, 2001.

"Oil and Gas Companies Come Together for IPO," *Corporate Financing Week,* September 4, 2000, p. 6.

"Oil Services Company Plans IPO to Pay Down Debt," *Corporate Financing Week,* October 2, 2000, p. 5.

"Oil States Industries, Inc.," *Oil and Gas Journal,* June 21, 1999, p. 61.

"Oil States International," *Venture Capital Journal,* April 1, 2001.

Rutledge, Tanya, "Continental Emsco of Garland Moving Headquarters to Houston," *Houston Business Journal,* February 9, 1996, p. 6A.

OmnicomGroup Inc.

Omnicom Group Inc.

■

437 Madison Avenue
New York, New York 10022
U.S.A.
Telephone: (212) 415-3600
Fax: (212) 415-3530
Web site: http://www.omnicomgroup.com

Public Company
Incorporated: 1986
Employees: 60,000Gross Billings: $9.7 billion (2004)
Stock Exchanges: New York
Ticker Symbol: OMC
NAIC: 541613 Marketing Consulting Services; 541810
    Advertising Agencies; 541820 Public Relations
    Agencies; 541830 Media Buying Agencies; 541840
    Media Representatives; 541850 Display Advertising;
    541890 Other Services Related to Advertising

■ ■ ■

The largest advertising group in the world, Omnicom Group Inc. operates as the parent company for three separate, independent advertising networks: BBDO Worldwide, DDB Worldwide Communications Group, and TBWA Worldwide. Omnicom also operates numerous independent agencies, interactive marketing firms, and public relations companies around the globe to offer clients a wide range of marketing or communications services. Omnicom was created in 1986 as a holding company, but its history stretches much further back, to the influential roles each of its three major subsidiary

agencies played in the growth and development of the U.S. advertising industry.

ORIGINS OF BATTEN, BARTON, DURSTINE & OSBORN

The agency known as BBDO was the product of a merger. In 1919 Bruce Barton, Roy Durstine, and Alex Osborn opened an advertising agency on West 45th Street in New York City. A few years later, as its business grew, Barton, Durstine & Osborn moved to the seventh floor of a building on 383 Madison Avenue. Three floors above BDO was another advertising agency, the George Batten Company. It seemed odd having competing firms sharing the same address, so a merger was proposed. On May 16, 1928, the George Batten Company joined with BDO to form Batten, Barton, Durstine & Osborn.

The most important man at the Batten agency was William Johns. Johns was more experienced and considerably older than Barton, Durstine, or Osborn. He was therefore made president of BBDO while the job of chairman went to Bruce Barton. Durstine was vice-president and general manager, and Osborn ran a separate BBDO office in his hometown of Buffalo, New York.

Bruce Barton was not a typical advertising man. He admitted on numerous occasions that he and the profession were not well suited. Barton was trained in theology and philosophy, attracted to politics, and committed to his personal writing projects. He wrote two extremely popular books, *The Man Nobody Knew* (a reappraisal of the life of Jesus Christ) and *The Book Nobody Knew* (a similar reappraisal of the Bible). Then, in the mid-1930s,

COMPANY PERSPECTIVES

Omnicom Group (NYSE: OMC) is a strategic holding company that manages a portfolio of global market leaders. Our companies operate in the disciplines of advertising, marketing services, specialty communications, interactive/digital media and media buying services.

Barton ran for Congress. He was elected and held office for two consecutive terms. In 1940 he ran for senator but lost by 400,000 votes. Barton was involved only in the creative aspects of BBDO's enterprises.

Durstine was the opposite of Barton. He was in love with the advertising business and what it could obtain for him. Like a number of other agency heads trying to make money during the Depression, Durstine's workaholism became self-destructive. He began drinking heavily, lost his wife and Long Island estate, and was forced to retire from BBDO in 1939.

The vacancy left by Durstine's departure caused some reshuffling of BBDO's management. William Johns was now too old to handle the day to day operations of the agency. He was "promoted" to chairman, but relieved of all administrative duties. Osborn and Barton were then required to run the agency themselves. The readjustment proved beneficial, for BBDO was in need of a new approach to its advertising. Osborn in particular was instrumental in reorganizing the agency and directing it toward the packaged goods advertising business. From the very beginning BBDO had primarily handled accounts for "institutional" clients such as Du Pont Chemical, Consolidated Edison, and Liberty Mutual. Although they were consistent customers, these companies neither needed nor wanted extensive advertising. If BBDO was going to grow rapidly enough to compete with large and established agencies, it would have to do advertising for packaged goods. Not only were new packaged goods constantly introduced to the market, but also those already on the shelves were always being improved to keep up with the competition. In this environment advertising flourished and it proved to be Osborn's most important insight.

Between 1939 and 1945 BBDO gained a number of important accounts: Lever Brothers, B.F. Goodrich, Chrysler (Dodge Division), MJB Coffee, and the 3M Company. Not even the upheaval of World War II kept BBDO from growing. Billings increased from $20 million at the height of the Depression to $50 million at the end of the war. In 1946 management changes again took place at BBDO. Ben Duffy, a veteran account man with over 15 years experience, was elected president; and Charlie Brower, who was to lead BBDO in the 1950s and 1960s, became executive vice-president in charge of copywriting. Duffy was an excellent salesman who could close a deal quickly. When Foote, Cone & Belding resigned the $11 million American Tobacco Company account in 1948, Duffy went directly to see American Tobacco's George Hill and secured the account after one meeting. In Duffy's ten years at the helm of BBDO, the agency increased its billings from $50 million to over $200 million.

Unfortunately for BBDO, Duffy was prone to ill health. In 1956 he suffered a stroke in Minneapolis while visiting the chairman of General Foods. He could not continue as the head of the agency, and Charlie Brower replaced him as president. Brower had a "no-nonsense" approach to advertising. He felt as president of BBDO he had to do four things: 1) add $1 million to the payroll; 2) hire talent from the outside; 3) fire many of his best friends; and 4) do away with company time clocks, which he thought made the agency a factory instead of a creative enterprise.

When Duffy retired there was confusion at BBDO. Until Charlie Brower established himself as president of the company no one had actually been in charge. Revlon, a $6 million customer, canceled its account as soon as it heard of Duffy's retirement. Other clients followed Revlon's example. The agency was headed toward disaster when Brower won the most lucrative account in its history, Pepsi Cola. Within a matter of weeks BBDO was financially healthy once again.

For BBDO the 1950s and early 1960s was a period marked by more than management readjustments and client shuffling. It was also a period in which BBDO became extensively involved in political advertising. Many agencies avoided politics altogether, but BBDO considered it as a normal part of its business. In 1948 BBDO ran its first ad campaign for a political candidate, Republican Thomas Dewey. Both candidate and agency lost the close election but, though Dewey left the political foreground, BBDO simply waited for the next election and a more marketable candidate. It found one in Dwight D. Eisenhower. In 1952 BBDO signed the Republican National Committee as a regular account, and did the advertising in Eisenhower's successful bid for the presidency. The firm was hired again four years later to handle Eisenhower's re-election campaign. Unfortunately for the Republican Party, and Richard Nixon in particular, BBDO's success ended with Eisenhower.

```
┌─────────────────────────────────────────────┐
│                                               │
│              KEY DATES                        │
│                   ■                           │
│  ───────────────────────────────────────────  │
│                                               │
│  1924:  Maurice H. Needham creates an advertising  │
│         agency.                               │
│  1928:  BBDO is created by a merger of two New  │
│         York City advertising firms.          │
│  1949:  Doyle Dane Bernbach is formed in New York  │
│         City.                                 │
│  1984:  Needham Harper Worldwide is formed.   │
│  1986:  Omnicom is created as a holding company  │
│         for its advertising units.            │
│  1995:  Chiat/Day is merged with TBWA to become  │
│         TBWA International.                    │
│  1997:  Omnicom acquires public relations and direc-  │
│         tory ad firm Ketchum Communications.  │
│  1999:  DDB Needham becomes DDB Worldwide     │
│         Communications Group.                 │
│  2000:  Omnicom wins the huge DaimlerChrysler  │
│         account away from True North          │
│         Communications.                       │
│  2001:  The company buys David Brown Entertain-  │
│         ment, a Hollywood marketing firm.     │
│  2003:  Omnicom buys interactive services firms.  │
│  2006:  Omnicom remains the world's top advertising  │
│         group in revenues.                    │
│                                               │
└─────────────────────────────────────────────┘
```

Outside the political realm BBDO continued to expand and sign new clients. Not only did it increase the number of its institutional customers such as CBS Broadcasting (1959) and the SCM Corporation (1961), but it also won product-oriented accounts such as Tupperware (1959), Autolite (1961), McGregor Sporting Goods (1964), and Pepperidge Farms (1964). To match this domestic growth BBDO began to expand internationally in 1959, opening up offices in London, Paris, Milan, Frankfurt, and Vienna. In 1964 BBDO acquired the Atlanta-based firm of Burke Dowling Adams and with it the accounts of Delta Air Lines and the various governmental agencies of the state of Georgia. The Clyne Maxon firm of New York, with its $60 million in billings, was also merged with BBDO in 1966.

By the time of the worldwide recession during the 1970s, Charlie Brower had retired as president of BBDO. His successor was Tom Dillon, who had been the agency's treasurer since the late 1950s. Like most ad agencies BBDO suffered considerable losses in domestic billings during these years of economic stagnation. Yet because of the way the company was structured, BBDO was able to endure this period without undue strain. By

opening offices in new places around the world, the agency entered advertising markets which had previously been closed to it. This international expansion served to offset losses incurred in the domestic market. In addition, BBDO began selling shares to the public in an effort to diffuse operating costs.

In 1976 Bruce Crawford was named president of BBDO. He had been head of the agency's foreign operations. During his eight-year tenure billings at BBDO tripled to $2.3 billion, and his cost management measures kept the company from misusing the benefits of this growth. As one analyst said of BBDO in 1981, "I've never seen a company so conscious of cost controls."

Crawford retired in 1985 and was succeeded by Allen Rosenshine. Under his tutelage BBDO continued to expand by acquiring subsidiaries, creating a worldwide network. Though BBDO traditionally allowed local entrepreneurs the freedom to run their own offices, this practice came to an end under Rosenshine. A number of foreign and international clients expressed concern over these "local" shops. They thought there was too little direction coming from top management, and became wary of giving business to BBDO subsidiaries. To remedy the problem Rosenshine attempted to tighten the connections within the BBDO network and provide more centralized leadership.

When the question of a merger with Needham Harper Worldwide and Doyle Dane Bernbach came up, many wondered why BBDO was interested particularly when the other two were experiencing financial difficulty. What BBDO had to gain, however, was consistent international growth, something the other two had mastered. A merger with Needham and Doyle Dane Bernbach would provide BBDO with greater international presence, particularly in France, Canada, and Great Britain. According to the policy planning heads at BBDO, this improvement of the agency's foreign business was necessary for BBDO to maintain itself as a formidable worldwide advertising competitor.

ORIGINS OF DOYLE DANE BERN-BACH

When those within the advertising industry are asked which agency most exemplifies innovation and creativity, one firm above all others is mentioned, Doyle Dane Bernbach (DDB). In the world of advertising, where imitation is the rule, the Doyle Dane Bernbach agency has made itself an exception. Most ad firms follow familiar schools of thought, but not DDB. In the words of David Ogilvy, "They just sort of created an original school out of air."

In 1949 Ned Doyle and William Bernbach joined Maxwell Dane in the formation of a new advertising agency. Bernbach and Doyle had been trained at Grey Advertising, and Dane had owned his small ad company for a number of years. DDB's first year billings came to just $500,000, but something about its advertising style suggested it would soon be a major force in the industry. It hired the most creative people it could find, no matter where they came from. Among Max Dane, Ned Doyle, and Bill Bernbach there existed a well-defined division of labor. Doyle was the account executive in charge of winning and retaining clients; Dane took care of administration and financial matters; and Bernbach handled the creative concerns. Rarely did they cross into each other's designated spheres.

What made the firm unique in the ad industry was Bill Bernbach and his preoccupation with the "road not taken." His ideas were fresh, striking, and more often than not, couched in subtle humor. He sympathized with the public at large, which found most advertisements boring. His quest was to make ad campaigns exciting and fun while still focusing on the product's attributes. For him, advertising was an art, and as an artist he was primarily concerned with imagery, impression, and point of view.

Bernbach was also a good teacher. He was patient, precise but gentle in his criticisms, and had the ability to nurture natural ability. His "students" formed the firm's Creative Team: a small group of copywriters, artists, art directors, and photographers who produced the agency's campaigns. Bernbach led the group but not in an authoritarian manner. It was what he called a "horizontal hierarchy."

In the 1950s DDB displayed its style of advertising in four notable campaigns for four nearly unknown companies: Polaroid Cameras, Levy Bakery Goods, Ohrbach's Department Store, and El Al Israel Air Lines. These companies, like DDB, were attempting to establish themselves in their respective markets. Polaroid was overshadowed by Kodak, Ohrbach's by Macy's, and few people had ever heard of Levy's Bread or El Al Air. To compensate for this lack of public recognition, the agency created strikingly different ads featuring everything from a cat dressed in a woman's hat to an American Indian claiming "you don't have to be Jewish to enjoy Levy's real Jewish rye." Not only did the campaigns sell large quantities of cameras, clothes, bread, and airline tickets, they sold DDB advertising as well. In 1954 the Agency's billings were $8 million; by 1959 that figure had increased to $27.5 million.

In the early 1960s the agency won two new accounts that enhanced its reputation: Avis Car Rental Service and Volkswagen. In the rent-a-car business Hertz held the dominant market share. Far behind in second place, Avis wanted to increase its own market share. Most advertising portrayed a client in as favorable and strong a position as possible. DDB, however, disregarded this tradition; its campaign stressed Avis's weak position vis-a-vis Hertz. "We're number two," said the ads, "We try harder. We have to." This strategy worked. In two years Avis increased its market share by over 25 percent.

The Volkswagen advertising campaign was a similar story. These small German cars were not what the American consumer wanted, or so it appeared. Again, DDB converted a liability into a saleable asset. Hoping people had tired of the large and overly embellished American-made cars of the 1950s, the ad simply said: "Think small." The art of the ads was minimalist, usually showing a small picture of the car against a blank white backdrop. The text was equally odd. The short, simple copy was blocked in paragraphs that looked, in the words of copywriter Helmut Krone, "Gertrude Steiny." Not only did Americans purchase these "ugly" Volkswagens by the thousands, but the car became a symbol for an entire nonconformist generation.

Following these successes the agency won accounts from American Airlines, Seagram, International Silver, Heinz Ketchup, Sony, Uniroyal, Gillette, Bristol-Myers, and Mobil Oil. The 1960s were the golden age of advertising and DDB was at its forefront. As the 1960s gave way to the 1970s, the industry witnessed a return to conventional advertising techniques. This trend and the recession spelled trouble for the company. In 1970 DDB lost the $20 million Alka-Seltzer account, even though the "that's a spicy meat-ball" commercial was extremely popular and a favorite of the critics. Other agency clients quickly followed Alka-Seltzer's lead: Lever Brothers, Whirlpool, Sara Lee, Quaker Oats, Cracker Jack, Uniroyal, and Life Cereal canceled their accounts.

Fortunately for the agency, its growth during the 1960s provided it with enough revenue to absorb these losses, at least in the short run. Nonetheless, a company reorganization and reorientation was in order. In 1974 Neil Austrian joined the company as executive vice-president. He gradually transformed the company into a more orderly advertising network. Subsidiaries were acquired to strengthen DDB's worldwide presence and offer more comprehensive client services. In 1975 the agency's billings rose for the first time in the new decade, and this trend continued for seven years.

In October 1982, William Bernbach died of leukemia. His absence left a void at the agency. This raised a difficult question: could DDB continue without Bill Bernbach?

The question haunted the firm and earnings fell 30 percent during the year. This loss was compounded in the next two years by the resignation of important accounts. American Airlines canceled its account in 1983, its spot temporarily filled by Pan Am, which then left the agency itself. In 1984 Polaroid announced it would be taking its business elsewhere. The agency was particularly shocked by this resignation. Its commercials had helped make Polaroid the world's top-selling camera.

In the first half of 1986 Doyle Dane Bernbach was forced to lay off 24 staff members; it had lost almost $113 million in net earnings. The merger with BBDO and Needham Harper Worldwide represented a necessary business decision. The security afforded by the Omnicom umbrella would relieve the agency of its financial difficulties, and allow it to concentrate on what it did best, innovative advertising.

ORIGINS OF NEEDHAM HARPER WORLDWIDE

In 1924 Maurice Needham opened up his own advertising agency in Illinois. It was named The Maurice H. Needham Company. This title was changed in 1929 to Needham, Louis & Brorby, Inc. The firm then merged with Doherty, Clifford, Steers & Shenfield, Inc. in 1964 to become Needham, Harper & Steers. In 1984 the company name was again changed, this time to Needham Harper Worldwide.

As a Chicago-based agency, it traditionally avoided Madison Avenue-type advertising and was generally considered to have a stronger presence in the Midwest than the East. Until becoming part of Omnicom, Needham & Harper had not ranked among the largest worldwide agencies. Its size, however, had contributed to its success as smaller companies, feeling neglected and disrespected by large advertising agencies, often turned to Needham & Harper. These clients were the foundation of the firm's business.

In addition to that of Maurice Needham, the other name associated with the agency was Paul Harper. He came to the company in 1945 when it was Needham, Louis & Brorby. Harper had been educated at Yale and spent four years in the Marine Corps. After his discharge, he walked into Needham's Chicago office looking for employment. He had no resume, no writing experience, and no civilian clothes. Despite his scant qualifications Needham gave him a job as a copywriter, and Harper had soon made a name for himself, primarily in broadcast advertising. Harper gradually moved from copywriter to manager. In 1964 he became president of the company and supervised the acquisition by Needham

of Doherty, Clifford, Steers and Shenfield in 1965. At this time the name of the agency was changed to Needham, Harper & Steers. In 1967 he became chairman and chief executive of the agency, and retained this position until his retirement in 1984.

During the late 1950s and 1960s when companies were substantially increasing their expenditures on advertising, Needham, Harper & Steers, though still only a mid-sized agency, grew along with the industry. It concentrated on smaller accounts but also retained a number of large Midwest clients, such as the Household Finance Corporation and the Oklahoma Oil Company.

In 1972 the firm followed the industry trend of publicly trading its shares. Unlike the larger agencies such as Ogilvy & Mather and Interpublic, Needham, Harper & Steers was unsuccessful in drawing a strong investment interest. Four years after going public Needham & Harper "went private" again. Although it serviced many small and mid-size accounts, Needham & Harper was primarily known for its "blue chip" clients. It won Xerox in 1968, McDonald's in 1970, Honda in 1977, and Sears in 1982. The agency produced the famous "Brother Dominic" commercials for Xerox, and the "you deserve a break today" slogan for McDonald's. Unfortunately for the agency, in 1984 McDonald's took its domestic business away from Needham and turned it over to Leo Burnett. The bad news continued in 1986, when Needham lost the $40 million Xerox account.

Many believed a merger with BBDO and Doyle Dane Bernbach would alter the "personality" of Needham. Even if the three agencies continued to operate as separate divisions of Omnicom, there was more to the merger than a simple name change. Some clients were not happy with the prospect of sharing Needham with competitors and the old conflict of interest problem became particularly pronounced when Campbell's Soup, a Needham client, would not stay with Omnicom if Heinz, a DDB client, remained. Similar difficulties arose between Stroh's and Busch beer, and Honda and Volkswagen automobiles.

The most important question among Needham customers was whether they would continue to receive the same attention to which they had been accustomed. Keith Reinhard, chairman and CEO of Needham Harper Worldwide, maintained the merger with Omnicom would help Needham attract and retain large clients, but claimed the agency would not treat its smaller customers any differently than it had in the past. Reinhard also hoped Omnicom would restore Needham's presence in the New York advertising market, something it had lacked since Xerox withdrew its account.

THE FORMATION OF OMNICOM: 1986

When the final documents were signed and Omnicom was formally created, the task of making sense and profits out of the amalgamation fell to BBDO head Allen Rosenshine. As some had anticipated, the process of combining three competing agencies under one umbrella corporation was a tiresome and fitful chore, sparking further speculation about the prudence of the merger in the first place. Omnicom limped from the starting block. More than $40 million was spent on merger and restructuring-related costs, leaving the company essentially profitless for its first year. Several clients were wholly opposed to the merger, and expressed their displeasure by taking their business elsewhere. One such client was RJR Nabisco, whose chairman stated, "As a client, I see disruption but little value. With very few exceptions, the wave of mergers has benefited the shareholders and managers of the agencies."

By the time the dust had settled after the merger, the three Omnicom agencies lost $184 million in billings directly attributable to the act of the merger itself. The assimilation process did not get any easier after the end of 1986. When Omnicom's 1987 financial totals were announced, they were depressingly low. For the year, the company earned only $32 million from commissions and fees of $785 million, or 4.1 percent in what traditionally was a double-digit margin business. The year did have its highlights, however, including the gain of several large accounts. Omnicom agencies landed a U.S. Navy account, a large portion of new Pepsi business, including Slice soft drinks and Pizza Hut, and the account for NEC Home Electronics. In all, Omnicom registered $280 million in new business during 1987, but this was not enough to offset other difficulties.

Bruce Crawford, who had departed BBDO in 1985, returned to the advertising world and signed on as Omnicom's chief executive officer. He took the helm in early 1989 and immediately began paring away superfluous managerial layers and divesting businesses. "With every merger," Crawford announced, "everybody talks about all these wonderful economies of scale, but it usually amounts to small potatoes. I believe the idea is to build businesses, not worry about the economies of scale to be realized by the joint buying of erasers. My belief is that the management structure is a little too complicated. I believe it is necessary to keep it simple, fast, and that corporate structure and overhead need to be minimized."

OMNICOM IN THE 1990S

Crawford made good on his words, divesting a number of Omnicom businesses while shuttering others. He developed a more concentrated presence in Britain and Europe, where Omnicom lagged behind other U.S.-based, international advertising agencies. By the beginning of the 1990s Crawford's strategy was beginning to work wonders, and Omnicom, after a torpid start, was demonstrating the vitality its creators had envisioned prior to the merger. Despite the effects of a stifling economic recession during the early part of the decade, Omnicom registered robust financial gains. In 1991 revenues increased to $1.2 billion and profits grew consistently. This growth trend continued after the recession, when the company increased revenues to $2.3 billion in 1995.

By mid-decade, any lingering doubt about the prudence of the merger had been thoroughly washed away. Omnicom held sway as a powerful and creative force, buying a number of firms both large and small to integrate into its network. In 1996 Omnicom bought Ketchum Communications, which had three strong business segments: traditional advertising, telephone directory advertising, and public relations. Rather than integrate Ketchum into TBWA, DDB Needham, or BBDO, its three units were divided among the subsidiaries. The company finished 1996 with robust sales of $2.64 billion and net income of $176.3 million. In January 1997 Crawford stepped down as chief executive but remained chairman. He was succeeded as CEO by Omnicom's president, John D. Wren, who would continue Crawford's legacy of success, growth, and creativity in Omnicom's second decade of business.

Wren had barely added the title of chief executive when Omnicom moved decisively into high-tech interactive marketing. Razorfish, Think New Ideas, Agency.com Ltd., Red Sky Interactive, Organic Online, Eagle Interactive, and Interactive Solutions all became part of Omnicom's Diversified Agency Services unit. In addition, Gaskell Associates, Fleishman-Hillard, and Meridian Technology Marketing were bought within a few months. Throughout the acquisition spree Omnicom's three major advertising units earned numerous awards and recognition, but in 1997 it was Omnicom's turn when it was selected as *Fortune* magazine's most respected advertising group. More good news was DDB Needham's winning of the coveted McDonald's account in 1997, which it had lost more than a decade earlier.

Omnicom continued to buy firms in line with its expansion plans in 1998, including London's GGT Group. GGT had been wooed by rival WPP Group, but chose Omnicom. The acquisition helped topple WPP Group from its perch as the world's largest advertising organization as ranked by *Advertising Age* (April 27, 1998). Omnicom's revenues climbed to just under $4.2 billion for 1997 with WPP trailing at $3.7 billion and

Interpublic Group coming in at $3.4 billion. New York City, home to both Omnicom and Interpublic, remained the world's advertising hub.

Omnicom scored another coup in 1998 with its majority stake in I&S Corporation, one of Japan's top ten advertising agencies. Omnicom was the first Western firm to invest in Japan's top agencies, and its purchase of I&S Corporation, ranked eighth, opened the door for further opportunities in Asia. To maintain its edge in the global advertising market and retain its number one ranking ahead of WPP Group, Interpublic Group, and Publicis, Omnicom needed to offer an ever wider array of services to its clients, to be a "full-service" provider. To this end, Wren continued to consolidate some operations while expanding others. In 1999 Omnicom jumped into the burgeoning healthcare marketing field with the creation of Accel Healthcare Communications, part of its Diversified Agency Services division. Omnicom also bought half of the Alberta, Canada-based Critical Mass, all of the Irving, Texas-based M/A/R/C agency, the remaining interest in the United Kingdom's Abbot Mead Vickers for $600 million and merged it into BBDO, while DDB Needham reorganized and christened itself DDB Worldwide Communications Group.

A NEW ERA: 2000S

As the new century took hold, Omnicom lost its rank as the world's largest advertising group in revenues when WPP Group earned the top spot after its acquisition of the mighty Young & Rubicam agency. WPP Group's revenues spiked to over $7.9 billion for 2000, topping Omnicom's $6.9 billion. To its credit, Omnicom had been no slouch in the acquisitions department, buying majority stakes or all of 19 firms during the year. In addition, while WPP Group may have ended its reign, albeit temporarily, Omnicom had the last laugh earning most honors at the International Advertising Festival in Cannes for the third year in a row, and winning the prestigious DaimlerChrysler account.

In the fall of 2001 Omnicom bought the Santa Monica-based David Brown Entertainment, a Hollywood product-placement firm, right before the terrorist attacks of September 11. While the U.S. economy, including advertising, went into a tailspin after the attacks, Omnicom weathered the storm. Wren did not slow down but aggressively pursued such goals as further immersion in Hollywood and its entertainment marketing services, as Omnicom's ad networks continued to create popular, award-winning ads. In the wake of the Enron mess and Arthur Anderson's troubles, Omnicom's board of directors underwent a major shakeup as seven members were ousted. Omnicom termed the shift

as better corporate governance, but an insider cried foul calling it a "board clearance."

Despite a few lawsuits and a temporary stock tumble, Omnicom remained in good shape when its rivals were restructuring and laying off employees. Omnicom finished 2002 with revenues of $7.5 billion and net income of $643.5 million for the year.

In the mid-2000s Omnicom carried on with business as usual, acquiring companies with potential and churning out original, creative advertising. The company had regained its status as the world's largest advertising group, ahead of rivals WPP Group (second), Interpublic gaining ground at third, and Publicis S.A. at fourth. Each conglomerate housed some of the best and brightest advertising agencies, but had branched out to include a myriad of related communication services. Though Interpublic was Omnicom's only major U.S.-based rival, both continually sought international clients closer to the Paris, France-based Publicis and London's WPP Group. Revenues for Omnicom reached a remarkable $9.7 billion for 2004 and net income climbed to an all-time high of $723.5 million.

In 2005 Omnicom continued to best its competitors by gaining blue-chip accounts including Disney, Bank of America, and 7-Eleven stores. The sky truly seemed the limit for this "full-service" marketing and communications behemoth.

Updated, Jeffrey L. Covell; Nelson Rhodes

PRINCIPAL COMPETITORS

Interpublic Group of Companies, Inc.; Publicis Groupe S.A.; WPP Group Plc.

FURTHER READING

Alden, Robert, "Bernbach's Advertising: A Formula or Delicate Art?," *New York Times,* May 7, 1961.

Baar, Aaron, "Bright Beginnings," *ADWEEK,* January 9, 2006, p. 4.

Bidlake, Suzanne, "Omnicom Wants All of UK's Abbot Mead Vickers," *Advertising Age,* November 30, 1998, p. 2.

Comiteau, Jennifer, "Omnicom Continues to Build Empire," *ADWEEK Eastern Edition,* December 9, 1996, p. 5.

"An Empire of Happy Fiefdoms," *Business Week,* April 3, 2000, p. 68.

Endicott, Craig, "Omnicom Storms Past WPP," *Advertising Age,* April 27, 1998, p. S1.

Fahey, Allison, "True Snit," *ADWEEK Southwest,* November 27, 2000, p. 15.

Feuer, Jack, "Omnicom and IPG: A Continental Divide," *ADWEEK,* May 26, 2003, p. 18.

Garcia, Shelly, "Ketchum Brings Diversified Assets to Omnicom," *ADWEEK Eastern Edition,* January 15, 1996, p. 9.

Gleason, Mark, "Big Bang of '86 Is Still Shaping the Ad World," *Advertising Age,* April 22, 1996, p. 3.

Irwin, Tanya, "Maximum Overdrive," *ADWEEK New England Edition,* November 13, 2000, p. 14.

Kilburn, David, "Getting a Foot in the Door," *ADWEEK Eastern Edition,* June 29, 1998, p. 12.

Kindel, Stephen, "It Looked Good on Paper," *Financial World,* March 8, 1988, p. 36.

MacDougall, A. Kent, "Doyle Dane Bernbach: Ad Alley Upstart," *Wall Street Journal,* August 1965.

McCarthy, Michael, "Omnicom-Fleishman Deal Precursor to Mega PR Unit," *ADWEEK Eastern Edition,* April 7, 1997, p. 2.

McCormack, Kevin, "Crawford Managing Omnicom Like the Met: Playing a Leaner Tune," *ADWEEK Eastern Edition,* January 15, 1990, p. 1.

Petrecca, Laura, "Omnicom Group Gains Critical Mass," *Advertising Age,* October 18, 1999, p. 1.

———, "Omnicom Stalks More Acquisitions," *Advertising Age,* February 2, 1998, p. 2.

Rich, Laura, "Mucho Communicado," *ADWEEK Eastern Edition,* October 20, 1997, p. 64.

———, "Omnicom Grows Organically," *ADWEEK Eastern Edition,* February 10, 1997, p. 6.

———, "The Omnicom Shopping Spree: How Wren and Co. Picked Their Targets," *ADWEEK Eastern Edition,* October 14, 1996, p. 32.

Santoli, Michael, "Too Much Hype? Ad Giant Omnicom Is a Good Company with Very Pricey Stock," *Barron's,* June 14, 1999, p. 19.

Sharkey, Betsy, "Omnicom's Operatics," *ADWEEK Eastern Edition,* April 20, 1992, p. 20.

Thomaselli, Rich, "Shakeup at Omnicom," *Advertising Age,* April 15, 2002, p. 1.

Wood, James P., *The Story of Advertising,* New York: Ronald Press, 1958.

Otor S.A.

---

70 Blvd. de Courcelles
Paris,
France
Telephone: +33 01 42 12 80 00
Fax: +33 01 42 27 96 48
Web site: http://www.otor.com

Public Company
Incorporated: 1969 as Cartonneries Menigault
Employees: 2,820
Sales: EUR 422.43 million ($534.3 million) (2004)
Stock Exchanges: Euronext Paris
Ticker Symbol: Sicovam: 006443
NAIC: 322211 Corrugated and Solid Fiber Box Manufacturing; 322121 Paper (Except Newsprint) Mills; 322130 Paperboard Mills; 322213 Setup Paperboard Box Manufacturing; 322231 Die-Cut Paper and Paperboard Office Supplies Manufacturing; 333993 Packaging Machinery Manufacturing

■ ■ ■

Otor S.A. is one of Europe's top manufacturers of corrugated cardboard, paper, and other packaging materials and systems. Headquartered in Paris, Otor operates from 27 sites in France, Germany, Switzerland, the United Kingdom, Finland, and Poland. The company's manufacturing operations include seven paper mills, eight corrugated board mills, and three cardboard box factories. Otor also operates eight recycling centers for the recovery of used paper and cardboard and a factory for the production of the company's own packaging equipment

designs. Together, the group's operations produce more than 1.7 billion packaging items and more than 750 million square meters of corrugated cardboard. The company is also the world's leading producer of lightweight recycled packaging paper. Otor supports its manufacturing and distribution operations with a strong commitment to research and development. The group's R&D effort has enabled it to become a leader in packaging innovation in the European market. Listed on the Euronext Paris Stock Exchange, Otor has changed ownership in 2005 at the end of a long and highly contested battle for control between founder Jean-Yves Bacques and the European wing of U.S.-based investment group, Carlyle. In December 2005, the French courts gave the victory in that battle to Carlyle, which now controls more than 80 percent of the group. Otor generated revenues of EUR 422 million ($534 million) in 2004.

FOUNDING A FRENCH CARDBOARD SPECIALIST IN THE 1980S

In 1969, the Swedish paper group Billerud AB bought two French paper mills, establishing the foundation for the later Otor. Billerud combined the two sites into a single company. The first was a paper mill in Iteuil; the second, Cartonneries Menigault, was a mill specialized in the production of wallpaper and corrugated cardboard that had been in operation since 1907. The new company then took on the Menigault name.

Through the 1970s, Menigault continued to build a presence in France. In 1974, for example, the company built a new cardboard factory in Torigni sur Vire. The plant was called Menigault Normandie (later renamed as Otor Normandie). In 1976, the company added a new cardboard mill, in Carhaix-Plouguer, in the Brittany region. That subsidiary became Menigault Bretagne (later Otor Bretagne). The company also established a reputation for innovation in the paper market. In 1975, for example, Menigault became the first to develop cardboard-based packaging for camembert cheese, traditionally packaged with a wood base.

By the second half of the decade, Menigault had become an important fixture in the French packaging sector. The company added new operations, notably through the 1977 takeover of Cartonneries Velin, a struggling packaging producer based in Remiremont, in the Vosges region. That subsidiary later became known as Otor Velin. The following year, Menigault acquired another company hit hard by the difficult economic period, Minguet & Thomas, located in Amiens. That company was later renamed as Otor Picardie.

Into the early 1980s, Billerud, soon part of what later became Scandinavian paper giant StoraEnso, began restructuring its operations and focusing on its forest products business. As a result, Billerud sold off its Menigault subsidiary to a new company, Cartonneries Associes, founded by Jean-Yves Bacques, in 1981. Joining Bacques was longtime partner Michèle Bouvier.

Bacques and Bouvier set out to build Cartonneries Associes into a French, and later European, cardboard packaging leader. The company quickly made its first growth effort, buying up Cognac-based cardboard maker Godard & Fils in 1983. That company had been founded in 1913 by Eugene Godard, and specialized from the start in the production of boxes and cardboard cases used for shipping sample bottles of cognac. By 1918, Godard had begun using corrugated cardboard as separators inside its boxes, before converting its box production entirely to corrugated cardboard. By the 1950s, Godard had begun shipping its packaging to the

international market. The company expanded in 1970, building a factory in Chateaubernard. Following its acquisition by Cartonneries Associes, Godard was restructured into two businesses, Godard, which took over the company's cardboard production, and Etuis Cognac, which took over its production of luxury packaging for the cognac sector.

Godard also became the site of one of the first implementations of a new innovation by Cartonneries Associes, which had begun developing its own packaging machinery. Those efforts resulted in the launch of the "Flexotor" system, which enabled the pre-printing of packages. The company installed the first Flexotor machine in its Normandy region cardboard mill in 1984. In 1985, the Godard site added the flexotor machine as well, leading to a full-scale rollout of the system to all of the company's mills.

The company's French expansion continued through the 1980s. In 1986, the company built a new corrugated cardboard factory in Cabourg, in the Normandy region. Subsidiary Godard expanded with the formation of a new subsidiary in St. Michel, near Angouleme, which then acquired Papeteries Elji in 1988. This operation marked one of the later Otor's first entries into the market for recuperation of used paper and cardboard and the launch of its own recycled packaging products. The company's machinery division also helped the company grow, notably with the launch of new equipment automating the box-building process for the company's customers.

INTERNATIONAL GROWTH IN THE 1990S

The company changed its name to Otor in 1989, and continued its expansion, acquiring paper mills in Doubs and in Nantes that year. By then, too, the company had made its first move into the international market, through the acquisition of Ashton Corrugated from the United Kingdom's David S. Smith. The acquisition brought Otor two plants in England, located in Portbury, near Bristol, and Claycross, in the British Midlands. These acquisitions helped boost the company's total production to 300,000 tons of corrugated board and 240,000 tons of paper.

Otor maintained its growth pace at the beginning of the 1990s. In 1990, the company launched a new system for the production of eight-paneled boxes, representing another major innovation by the group. The following year, Otor expanded its production capacity, building a new plant in the Dauphine region. In that year, also, Otor made its first entry into the recycling business, buying up its first recycling plant, Delaire Recyclage.

KEY DATES

1907: Cartonneries Menigault, a producer of corrugated cardboard and wallpaper, is founded.

1969: Swedish paper and forest products group Billerud acquires Menigault and merges it with another French paper mill in Itreuil.

1974: Menigault builds a new cardboard mill in Normandy.

1976: A cardboard mill is added in Brittany.

1977: The company acquires Cartonneries Velin, in the Vosges region.

1978: The company acquires Minguet & Thomas, in the Picardy region.

1981: Jean-Yves Bacques and Michel Bouvier form Cartonneries Associes and buy Menigault from Billerud.

1983: The company acquires Godard & Fils, based in the Cognac region.

1987: Two Ashton cardboard plants in England are acquired.

1989: The name is changed to Otor.

1991: The company acquires Delaire Recyclage and enters the paper recycling market.

1994: The U.K. operations are sold.

1997: The company acquires Papeterie de Rouen and the Chapelle d'arbley site and begins a massive investment to upgrade the plant.

1998: Otor goes public on the Paris Stock Exchange.

1999: On the verge of bankruptcy, Otor agrees to sell a 21 percent stake for EUR 45 million to Carlyle.

2000: Carlyle exercises its option to acquire 90 percent of Otor, but Bacques and Bouvier refuse, setting off a five-year court battle.

2005: Bacques and Bouvier resign from the board of directors and Carlyle takes control of Otor.

Otor's initial effort to grow internationally ran aground with the deepening European economic crisis in the early 1990s. By 1994, the company was forced to abandon this strategy, selling off its British plants. The company also restructured parts of its French operations, closing down its Menigault Centre & Ouest subsidiary. In the meantime, Otor's own difficulties had led to the company's agreement to sell 90 percent of its stock to rapidly expanding Svenska Cellulosa Aktiebolaget (SCA).

The deal, worth the equivalent of more than EUR 300 million, would have boosted SCA's French position to more than 16 percent. Yet that deal fell through before the end of the year.

Otor resumed its expansion at mid-decade, launching a new subsidiary, Pinel Recyclage in Periers in 1995, and boosting its share of the recycled papers market in France. The following year, the company once again tested the international waters, this time in Poland, where it acquired the paper mill Silesianpap in Tychy. Otor then opened a cardboard production unit on the site. In that same year, the company added a cardboard plant in Belgium.

NEW OWNERS IN THE NEW CENTURY

The year 1997 marked a new milestone for Otor, as the company developed a strategy designed to transform it into a European corrugated cardboard leader. In that year, the company bought Papeterie de Rouen, based in Chapelle d'arbley, in France, from Finnish paper producer UPM Kymmene. That site, however, already had a troubled history, having gone through a succession of owners. At one point, the French government had been forced to rescue the Chapelle d'arbley mill from financial collapse. The purchase, and subsequent investments made by Otor to expand the mill, left Otor heavily in debt.

In 1998, Otor went public on the Paris Stock Exchange, becoming one of the few publicly owned cardboard producers. In that year, the company opened a new corrugated cardboard plant as part of its expansion of the Papeterie de Rouen. The company also began converting the Chapelle d'arbley site. Yet the massive investment needed for that project brought the group to the edge of a new financial dilemma.

Bacques and Bouvier found themselves under increasing pressure from their bank, Credit Lyonnais. By the end of 1999, the bank had threatened to cut off Otor's credit line if the company did not bring in cash from a new major investor. Credit Lyonnais brought Bacques and Bouvier into contact with American investment giant Carlyle, which had launched a European investment wing just two years earlier. With little room to maneuver, Bacques and Bouvier agreed to sell Carlyle a 21 percent stake in Otor for EUR 45 million. The deal saved Otor from bankruptcy.

The acquisition of a minority stake was a departure for Carlyle, which ordinarily acquired outright control of its investments. Yet under terms of the shareholding agreement, Carlyle also gained the option to acquire up to 90 percent of Otor if the company failed to meet its financial targets in the period between 2000 and 2006. By 2001, after Otor failed to deliver on its promised profit levels, Carlyle decided to exercise its option to gain control of the company. Yet Bacques and Bouvier resisted the takeover; a small clause in the agreement required that authorization for the option had to come from the company's board of directors, which was, of course, controlled by Bacques and Bouvier. This set the stage for a five-year legal battle, in which Bacques and Bouvier sought to overturn the option agreement with Carlyle. In the end, however, Carlyle prevailed. Bacques and Bouvier resigned from the company's board of directors in 2005, and by the end of 2005, the French courts had confirmed Carlyle's right to take over the company.

Despite the uncertainty of its ownership, Otor had in the meantime continued investing in its future. The company added a new corrugated cardboard operation in Brittany in 2001. The company also emerged as a leading innovator in the production of new lightweight cardboards, as well as launching a new generation of its flexotor pre-printing system, enabling up to eight-color printing directly onto even lightweight cardboard and paper. Otor expected to maintain its growth as a European corrugated cardboard leader under its new owners.

M. L. Cohen

PRINCIPAL SUBSIDIARIES

Otor Benelux; Otor Bretagne; Otor Dauphiné; Otor GmbH (Germany); Otor Godard; Otor Normandie; Otor Papeteire de Rouen; Otor Picardie; Otor Riquet; Otor Services; Otor Silesia (Poland); Otor Suisse; Otor Systems; Otor Velin; Otor UK; Etuis Cognac; Delaire Recyclage; Normandie Ondulé; Pinel Recyclage; Sarl Czulow; GIE Otor Investissement.

PRINCIPAL COMPETITORS

Jefferson Smurfit Group Ltd.; Stora Enso Oyj; Container Corporation of America; Kappa Packaging B.V.; D S Smith PLC; Constantia Packaging AG; Empaques de Carton Titan S.A. de C.V.; Samhall AB; Yule Catto and Company PLC; Papierfabrik Palm GmbH and Company KG; S.C.A. Packaging Ltd.

FURTHER READING

"Benefits Stack Up," *Packaging Magazine,* December 9, 2004, p. 24.

Chol, Eric, "Otor-Carlyle: la guerre d'usure," *L'Express,* April 18, 2005.

Cori, Nicolas, "Otor-Carlyle: pas de cadeau dans l'emballage," *Liberation,* March 9, 2004.

Higham, Robert, "Trending Toward Lightweight: From Modest Beginnings 20 Years Ago, Otor Has Become a Leading Innovator in Europe's Box Making Business," *Paperboard Packaging,* September 2003, p. 32.

Leboucq, Valerie, "Le fonds americain Carlyle va pouvoir prendre le controle d'Otor," *Les Echos,* November 23, 2005.

Maiello, Michael, "Boxed In," *Forbes,* August 15, 2005, p. 40.

"Otor Expanding," *Packaging Magazine,* March 6, 2003, p. 5.

"Otor Invests in Plants," *Paperboard Packaging,* March 2003, p. 56.

"Otor Presents Flexotor," *Paperboard Packaging,* August 2004, p. 32b.

Philippon, Thierry, "Qui a peur de Carlyle?," *Nouvel Observateur,* September 30, 2004.

Polaris Industries Inc.

2100 Highway 55
Medina, Minnesota 55340-9770
U.S.A.
Telephone: (763) 542-0500
Toll Free: (800) 765-2747
Fax: (763) 542-0599
Web site: http://www.polarisindustries.com

Public Company
Incorporated: 1945 as Hetteen Hoist & Derrick
Employees: 3,600
Sales: $1.87 billion (2005)
Stock Exchanges: New York Pacific
Ticker Symbol: PII
NAIC: 336999 All Other Transportation Equipment
    Manufacturing; 336991 Motorcycle, Bicycle, and
    Parts Manufacturing; 336322 Other Motor Vehicle
    Electrical and Electronic Equipment Manufacturing

■ ■ ■

Polaris Industries Inc. is the largest manufacturer of snowmobiles in the world and the second largest maker of all-terrain vehicles (ATVs), trailing only Honda Motor Co., Ltd. It introduced a line of motorcycles in 1998, but it no longer makes personal watercraft, having exited from that sector in 2004. The company entered into a partnership with and bought a 24 percent stake in the Austrian motorcycle firm KTM Power Sports AG in 2005. Although best known as a snowmobile maker, Polaris now generates only about 14 percent of its revenues from its line of snow machines; ATVs account

for fully two-thirds of sales, while motorcycles comprise the firm's fastest growing sector though only about 5 percent of overall sales. The remaining revenues come from the sales of parts, garments, and accessories. Headquartered near Minneapolis, Polaris operates manufacturing facilities in Minnesota, Wisconsin, and Iowa; it sells its products through approximately 1,900 North American dealers and a network of five foreign subsidiaries and 40 international distributors that market Polaris products in 126 countries around the world. More than 20 percent of sales are generated outside North America. A pioneering force in the U.S. snowmobile industry, Polaris has since its inception enjoyed a strong reputation for quality and innovation.

ARCTIC ORIGINS

Polaris Industries was born in Roseau, a small community within a few miles of the northernmost point in the contiguous 48 states. This relatively remote area, located closer to Winnipeg, Manitoba, than to Minneapolis, inspired a climate of persistent innovation. Hetteen Hoist & Derrick, the forerunner of Polaris, was established in 1945 not for the manufacture of snowmobiles, however, but as a problem-solving job shop that became known for its fabrication of one-of-a-kind machinery for farmers in the region. Metal supply was at a premium at the end of World War II, and Edgar Hetteen was a skilled and inventive metalworker who could help people make do with what they had. Close friend David Johnson bought into the company while he was still serving in the navy, and Edgar's brother Allan Hetteen became a partner in the early 1950s. The company produced farm equipment, including straw choppers, portable grain elevators, and sprayers, but also depended on welding, grinding, and general repair work in the off-season.

Given the area's climate, the seasonal nature of the original business, and the fact that the founders were avid outdoorsmen, it was perhaps inevitable that the idea of snowmobile production would eventually transform the company. At the time, trips to fishing, hunting, and trapping areas in the winter had to be navigated by cross-country skis or snowshoes. Although inventors had been toying with the concept of snow machines since the 1920s, no reliable machine was readily available that could be used for such utilitarian purposes. Not until the 1950s, in large part because of the work of Johnson, did the general notion of creating a snow-going vehicle steered by skis begin to take shape as an industry in the United States. The company sold its first machine, a rough, virtually untested model, to an eager Roseau lumberyard owner in 1954. There was then no clear development plan to guide the company in this new area. Indeed, Edgar Hetteen was focused principally on selling the company's mainstay straw choppers and was lukewarm on the idea of snow machines until he saw the considerable interest generated when the company's first snowmobile customer demonstrated his powered sled.

Other orders followed that year and the company, which renamed itself Polaris Industries after the Latin name for "north star," worked on improving the original concept with each consecutive model. Five machines were built in the winter of 1954-55 (all of which sold for less than $800), 75 in the winter of 1956-57, and more than 300 in 1957-58. The earliest models were called Sno-Cats, then Sno-Travelers, and were purchased primarily by outdoorsmen and utility companies. The sleds, propelled by a rear-end four-cycle engine, featured a toboggan-style front with a steering wheel and control levers. The early production line yielded one-of-a-kind machines, with components varying from one vehicle to

the next. Skis were fabricated from bumpers of Chevrolets and steering wheels were appropriated from cars and trucks. Not surprisingly, the early machines were heavy and utilitarian. The Ranger rear-engine prototype and the Ranger model, manufactured between 1956 and 1964, formed the basis for Polaris snowmobile development.

When the bulk of the business shifted from fabricating farm equipment to designing, building, and testing snowmobiles, Edgar Hetteen was faced with a marketing problem. The company needed to broaden interest in the machine beyond utilitarian to recreational use. In short, Polaris had to convince people it would be fun to ride around in the middle of winter in a small, open-air vehicle. As Jerry Bassett wrote in *Polaris Partners,* "Edgar Hetteen, as the first president, had to establish a sales network for a product that could only be sold in places which got snow to people who weren't totally certain that they needed his product." During a promotional trip Hetteen made in 1958, according to C. J. Ramstad in *Legend: Arctic Cat's First Quarter Century,* "Hetteen got a real taste of the enormity of the problem that year when he set up an exhibit at a sport and travel show. Full of enthusiasm, he hustled show goers into his booth and eagerly showed them his new 'snow machine.' The curious public thought the machine somehow produced snow. They wanted to know which end the snow came out!"

Then, inspired by a friend's suggestion, Hetteen decided to make a snowmobile trip across Alaska to demonstrate both the durability and recreation his company's product offered. In March 1960 Hetteen and three others covered more than a thousand miles in about three weeks on one Trailblazer and two Rangers. The adventure yielded national publicity, but Hetteen was shocked to find that it had also created dissension at home. The negative response of some of the company's backers to Hetteen's trip, viewed by them as unnecessary, even frivolous, resulted in his selling out his controlling interest in Polaris. After a trip back to Alaska he returned to Minnesota, this time west of Roseau to Thief River Falls, where he started the company that became Arctic Enterprises, later Arctco Inc., and still later Arctic Cat Inc., producer of Arctic Cat snowmobiles. His younger brother Allan, 31 at the time, became president of Polaris.

Running a nearly parallel course to Polaris was another company that contributed to the early industry history. In Canada, Joseph-Armand Bombardier developed and patented the sprocket-and-track assembly in 1937 and developed a one-piece molded rubber track in 1957. In 1958, the first year of Ski-Doo brand manufacturing, his company produced 240 snowmobiles.

KEY DATES

1945: In Roseau, Minnesota, Edgar Hetteen founds Hetteen Hoist & Derrick, later renamed Polaris Industries.
1954: Company sells its first "powered sled."
1960: Edgar Hetteen completes a promotional snowmobile trip across Alaska.
1968: Textron acquires Polaris.
1981: Management buys out the company after a couple of brown winters dry up sales.
1985: Polaris starts making ATVs.
1987: Company goes public.
1992: Polaris introduces its personal watercraft.
1995: Sales pass $1 billion.
1996: For the first time, Polaris makes more money selling ATVs than from snowmobiles.
1998: Victory Motorcycles debut.
2004: Polaris shuts down its personal watercraft business.
2005: Company enters into partnership with the Austrian firm KTM Power Sports AG.

The early 1960s marked the beginning of snowmobiling as a sport with the front-engined Bombardier Ski-Doo. Such vehicles were used for recreation as well as competitive racing. The testing of the first Polaris front-engined machine, the Comet, looked promising, but the 1964 model failed in production. The company's very survival was suddenly at stake.

Polaris cofounder David Johnson later joked, "We made 400 machines and got 500 back." But it was the value of his word and reputation at the time that convinced the creditors to give the company breathing room and a second chance. Johnson and Hetteen redoubled their efforts by converting the Comets to rear-engined machines while they worked on a new front-end model. They hit pay dirt with the front-engined Mustang, which enjoyed successful production from 1965 to 1973 and brought the company into the sporty racing vehicle arena.

CORPORATE IN THE 1970S

After its one stumble, the company grew rapidly in the boom years of the 1960s. So pronounced was the growth that it outstripped the management skills of the owners, who had to decide whether to hire professional managers or sell the company. In 1968 Polaris was sold to Tex-tron Incorporated, a diversified company holding E-Z Go golf carts, Bell helicopters, Talon zippers, and Schaefer pens. The company kept Polaris in Roseau and continued snowmobile manufacturing, but also began limited research and development on watercraft and wheeled turf vehicles. Herb Graves of Textron became president and Johnson stayed on as vice-president to oversee production.

During the 1970s Polaris began to solidify its reputation for high-performance snowmobiles. In pre-Textron years, Polaris had purchased its snowmobile engines from a number of suppliers. With the entry of Textron, Polaris was able to bring on Fuji Heavy Industries as its sole supplier. Fuji engineers went to Roseau to work on building a high-quality engine specifically for Polaris. Increasingly, the Polaris product lines were being noticed. The TX Series set a standard for power and handling in racing and gained popularity with recreational riders. Introduced in 1977, the liquid-cooled TX-L was a strong cross-country racing competitor. Polaris also introduced the RX-L in the mid-1970s, which carried the first independent front suspension (IFS) and produced winners on the racing circuits shortly after its debut. Meanwhile, Polaris shifted its corporate headquarters to Minneapolis, with product development and production staying up north.

The sport of snowmobiling grew by leaps and bounds in the early 1970s; enthusiasts in the snowbelts of the United States and Canada now numbered more than a million. The growth rate for the industry was 35 percent per year, versus 20 percent for other recreation industry manufacturers. In 1970, 63 companies manufactured snowmobiles in the United States, Canada, Europe, and Japan. Bombardier held 40 percent of the market, with an additional 40 percent shared by Arctic Cat, Polaris, Scorpion, and Sno Jet. About one-third of the machines manufactured in North America in the early 1970s were made in Minnesota.

Factory-backed racing teams found Polaris support in the days of Allan Hetteen and Textron, but the death of a Polaris team member in 1978 effectively ended the program. From 1981 on the company sponsored a modified racing program with independent racers. Hill climbs, stock and modified oval racing, snow and grass drag racing, and cross-country endurance racing tested the limits of the machines and appealed to customers. Racing was an important part of engineering research and development as well as public relations and product marketing.

Yet in the late 1970s, despite everything that favored the industry, including regular improvements in safety and an expanding trail system that would eventually rival the U.S. Interstate Highway System in total miles, the snowmobiling boom was about to go bust. Companies began shutting down or selling off their snowmobile divisions in the face of declining sales. Names such as Scorpion, AM, Harley-Davidson, Johnson & Evinrude, Chaparral, and Suzuki would no longer be seen on snowmobile nameplates. By 1980 even Arctic Enterprises, the number one manufacturer, was in trouble. High energy costs, economic recessions, snowless winters, and overexpansion eventually drove all but three manufacturers of snowmobiles out of business. Industry sales slid downhill from 500,000 units annually in the early 1970s to 316,000 in 1975; 200,000 in 1980; 174,000 in 1981; and 80,000 in 1983.

MANAGEMENT BUYOUT IN 1981

Textron wanted out of the snowmobile business, too. Textron President Beverly Dolan, who had been president of Polaris during its first years with Textron, told Polaris's then-president, W. Hall Wendel, Jr., to sell off the company. A deal to sell the Polaris division to Canada's Bombardier fell through, however, because of the threat of antitrust action by the U.S. Department of Justice. Liquidation was on the horizon. This opened the door for a management group leveraged buyout led by Wendel, who believed that there was a market for snowmobiles and that seasonal snowfalls would rise again. Polaris Industries was created in July 1981, and a shutdown of the Roseau plant was avoided. (Still, the company began production with just 100 workers after the buyout.) Also at this time, plant workers voted the union out and Polaris proceeded to establish a Japanese labor model of worker participation, with a crew that had firsthand knowledge of the machines and their capabilities. Times were still tough, though: the 1982 product line consisted of the 1981 model with some detail changes, and barely more than 5,000 machines were built that season. The same year as the buyout, Polaris attempted to purchase Arctic Cat. When the deal failed, Arctic Cat shut down, leaving Polaris, at least for a while, as the only U.S. snowmobile manufacturer.

The first years following the management buyout from Textron were lean and characterized by a skeleton factory crew and tight budgets. But the Textron debt was paid off ahead of schedule and the snowmobile line was expanded and improved. The company also expanded into Canada to become more price competitive and to create a stronger dealer network. Five years after the buyout the company had reached sales of $40 million and employed 450 people. A Polaris innovation of the early 1980s was the "Snow Check" early deposit program. Polaris encouraged its dealers with incentives to make spring deposits on machines for preseason delivery. For the first time snowmobiles were built to

dealer orders rather than manufacturer forecasts, which had been resulting in excess inventory. Other factors helping the industry along at the time were advancements in clothing technology, winter resorts welcoming snowmobilers on winter vacations, and new engineering on the machines producing quieter, more reliable vehicles. By 1984 there were 20 million snowmobilers in the northern snowbelt and mountain regions using the vehicles for rescue and outdoor work as well as recreational and sporting events.

One of the highlights of the 1980s was the introduction of the Indy line of snowmobiles, which became so popular that other high-quality Polaris sleds, such as the Cutlass, were phased out. Good suspension, special features (such as handwarmers and reverse drive), powerful engines, and reliability all pushed Polaris into the number one position in the market. The Indy 500 was named the "sled of the decade" by *Snowmobile* magazine. Another key event occurred in 1987 when Polaris conducted an initial public offering and went public as a master limited partnership.

DIVERSIFYING IN THE EARLY 1990S

Into the 1990s Polaris continued to improve the performance, ride, and reliability of its machines by introducing such features as the triple-cylinder and high-displacement engines, extra-long travel suspensions, and specialized shock absorbers. The machines of the 1990s were a long way from the industry's early noisy, pull-start models, with uncertain braking and questionable reliability. In 1990 Polaris held 30 percent of the snowmobile market, manufacturing 165,000 units. Arctco Inc. held 25 percent of the total market, followed by Yamaha and Ski-Doo (Bombardier, Inc.), both at 22.5 percent.

Just as the snow outside Polaris's doors had provided a proving ground for snowmobiles, the summertime swampland of the far north provided a place for testing wheeled turf vehicles. The company built and sold two-wheel tractor-tired bikes in the middle to late 1960s as it was testing diversification into such areas as lawn and garden products, single and two-person watercraft, and snowmobile-engined go-carts. The Textron acquisition and merger with E-Z Go golf carts ended formal ATV product development, so testing stayed underground until after the buyout. The company then tried but failed to sell private-label ATVs to other large companies. Still hoping to better utilize its manufacturing facilities, the company brought out two ATV designs, a three-wheel and a four-wheel with automatic shifting, which caught the interest and commitment of distributors.

Added features such as racks and trailers appealed to farmers, ranchers, and lawn maintenance workers. ATVs made perfect sense for Polaris in that they shared engines and clutches with snowmobiles, could be marketed through the same dealers, and represented a seasonal line manufactured in fall and winter months for sale in the summer, just the opposite of snowmobiles.

When Polaris entered the ATV market in 1985, all the major manufacturers were Japanese, led by Honda. Polaris ATVs, a combination recreation-utility vehicle, avoided direct competition with the leaders. The majority of the two million ATVs in use in the mid-1980s were in the United States and Canada. The first production run of the Polaris ATVs was a resounding success and quickly sold out to dealers. Eventually, production of three-wheel vehicles would be curtailed by all manufacturers, in response to reports of rising accidents and deaths and action by the Consumer Product Safety Commission. Polaris ceased manufacture of its three-wheel adult version after its first year of ATV production. In 1990 the retail cost of a four-wheel ATV ranged from $2,400 to $4,000 and Polaris controlled about 7 percent of a shrinking market. By the end of 1993, however, ATV sales made up 26 percent of entire sales by product line. ATV manufacture was now year-round, with a dedicated production line, and had the potential to surpass snowmobile production. Because of marketing and distribution that now extended beyond the snowbelt to tractor, lawn and garden, used car, and motorcycle dealers, Polaris had become a key national as well as international player in the broader market of recreational vehicles.

Polaris introduced its first personal watercraft (PWC) in 1992, becoming the first major U.S. company to enter that industry. The recreational vehicle started off with a splash because of its speed and handling. Just as it had in snowmobiles and ATVs, Polaris emphasized machine stability, coming up with an entry in the market that was wider than most and was a sit-down rather than stand-up model, which by then was declining in popularity. In the late 1980s personal watercraft was the growth segment of the marine industry and the trend was toward machines requiring less athletic ability and targeting a broader age range. The recreational vehicle was similar to the snowmobile and the ATVs in terms of engine type and channels of distribution. By testing competitors' products Polaris identified the qualities it wanted in its entry: a machine that was fast and fun to drive, with good handling and stability, as well as better boarding in deep water than the competitors'. The company's first model was a success and drew high-income, first-time buyers. By the end of 1993 PWC made up 9 percent of total Polaris sales.

In 1994 Polaris employed 2,400 people company-wide, had a sister plant in Osceola, Wisconsin, and was planning another plant in Iowa. Polaris Canada, a wholly owned subsidiary, provided 25 percent of total sales, or about $100 million. Since 1991, $70 million had been spent in plant improvements and new product development. David Johnson, the only person to see Polaris through all its incarnations, commented in Bassett's retrospective, "The biggest strength of Polaris is the people .... Everybody who's involved at Polaris, whether it's with the watercraft, or with the ATVs or the snowmobiles, they want to make the best machine they know how." Polaris's partnership with its employees meant not only sharing in making the best product possible, but sharing in the benefits. Profit sharing began in 1982 with an average of $200 per employee. By 1993 employees shared $6.8 million.

In December 1994 Polaris converted from a publicly traded limited partnership to a public corporation for several reasons, including its desire to maximize shareholder value, its need for greater flexibility, and the approaching 1997 deadline for relinquishing its partnership tax status. The small company that began up along the Canadian border 40 years earlier had since transformed itself, through a series of rebirths, into a worldwide leader, with annual sales of more than $800 million.

Polaris had a great year in 1994: sales rose 56 percent to $826 million and profits climbed 66 percent to $55 million. Its share price fell drastically, however, after *Barron's* ran an article in January 1995 wondering whether a light snowfall would affect the company. Sympathetic analysts pointed to the new areas of the company's business that were not snow-related, such as ATVs and watercraft, where the company had captured market shares of 20 and 15 percent, respectively.

In fact, Polaris had become the perfect diversification success story. In spite of *Barron's* worries, all product segments set records in 1995, leading to total sales of more than $1 billion in 1995. Revenues had more than tripled in five years. Snowmobiles accounted for 40 percent, down from 67 percent in 1990.

Polaris opened its own engine plant in Osceola, Wisconsin, in October 1995. The company had previously bought Japanese engines from Fuji Heavy Industries and had set up the Robin ATV engine joint venture in Hudson, Wisconsin, in February 1994. The new plant gave Polaris some flexibility in dealing with currency fluctuations.

VENTURING INTO MOTORCYCLES: LATE 1990S

Another record year followed in 1996, although snowmobile and watercraft sales slipped and, in a dramatic shift, a higher percent of revenue came from ATVs than from snowmobiles for the first time. Still, snowmobiling was reaching new highs in popularity, revitalizing the economy of sleepy Minnesota resorts that would otherwise have closed for the winter. Other related businesses popped up, supplying snowmobile trailers or hauling the finished goods to market. Demographics and a lack of new trails led some to believe that the boom was coming to an end, however. Concurrent with the rediscovery of the snowmobile was an explosion in personal watercraft sales, which tripled between 1991 and 1996. Makers of larger powerboats felt that they were spoiling their business, though.

As the revitalized Harley-Davidson could not make its famous "hogs" fast enough, Polaris decided to develop its own big, heavy cruiser class motorcycle priced below the Harleys. Made in Iowa, the first Victory V92C rolled off the line on July 4, 1998. Wendel noted that the company had already shown it could compete with the Japanese bike makers in other categories. The Harley mystique would be difficult to approach, although the Victory bikes received generally enthusiastic reviews. Others began making American bikes at the same time: Big Dog Motorcycles of Sun Valley, Idaho, the reborn Excelsior-Henderson Motorcycle Mfg. Co. of Minnesota, and numerous smaller shops.

W. Hall Wendel, Jr., stepped down as CEO in May 1999, remaining a major shareholder as well as board chairman. Thomas Tiller, president and chief operating officer since the previous summer, became the new CEO. Tiller had spent 15 years at General Electric Company, learning from its legendary leader, Jack Welch. When appointed, Tiller announced plans to double the company's sales within four years.

EARLY 2000S AND BEYOND

Polaris had made huge strides growing organically, and several record years gave Polaris plenty of cash for acquisitions. But the company stuck with joint ventures instead. In 2000 it contracted with Karts International Inc. to make a line of Polaris mini-bikes and go-carts for children. It also marketed a child-sized snowmobile to compete with Arctic Cat's Kitty Cat and began developing a snowmobile video game for kids to "burn Polaris into their beautiful little brains," as Tiller put it. Polaris took aim at hunters with a special camouflaged ATV co-branded with Remington firearms. Other promotions with DeWalt Industrial Tool Co. and NASCAR helped publicize the brand in the South.

In March 2000 Edgar Hetteen and David Johnson, joined by Tiller and seven others, recreated the epic Alaskan journey Hetteen had taken 40 years earlier to promote the snowmobile. This time the trip raised funds for ALS (Lou Gehrig's disease) research.

Dark clouds were just over the horizon: the Department of the Interior banned snowmobiles from most national parks in May 2000. "The snowmobile industry has had many years to clean up their act and they haven't," said an official. Polaris and Arctic Cat countered that both had been working to cut emissions and noise for years, but were waiting for the Environmental Protection Agency to announce a new emissions standard in September 2000 before retooling their production lines. The Park Service also complained of the potential for disturbing wildlife that snowmobiles offered. This threat, however, seemed to evaporate as quickly as it had arisen following the election of George W. Bush, whose administration led efforts to scuttle or delay environmental regulations inside and outside the parks.

Unfortunately for Polaris, the early 2000s brought new challenges in the form of economic uncertainty and continued bad weather for snowmobile sales. The economic climate forestalled any chance the company had of achieving Tiller's goal of doubling sales within four years. While Polaris remained solidly profitable, revenue gains were in the low single digits each year, translating by 2005 into sales of $1.87 billion. Dragging down this figure was the declining fortune of the snowmobile sector, which by 2005 had seen low-snow winters six of the previous seven seasons. Polaris saw its snowmobile sales fall from $313.6 million in 2000 to $256.7 million in 2005. Snowmobiles now accounted for only 14 percent of revenues, compared to a whopping 66 percent for ATVs. At the same time, the personal watercraft sector was also in decline, under the pressure of heavier regulation and bans on their use, and Polaris's PWC business was operating in the red. In September 2004 the company elected to shut down its money-losing marine business, taking a one-time $36 million before-tax charge to do so.

In June 2002 the Roseau River poured over its banks following heavy rains, flooding the town and destroying many homes. Polaris's plant, however, was saved after company employees worked day and night erecting sandbag barriers around the facility. That same year, the company entered a new sector of the ATV market, sports models aimed at performance riders, with the debut of the Predator. Polaris's motorcycle line, meanwhile, had gotten off to a rather slow start. Sales were lackluster thanks to a less than enthusiastic reaction from riders to the first Victory models. To turn things around, Tiller hired Mark Blackwell, a former motocross champion and motorcycle expert, away from Arctic Cat to head up the motorcycle division. Blackwell assembled a new team focused on producing models tailored to customers' desires and perhaps most importantly hired renowned custom motorcycle designers Arlen and Cory Ness as consultants. The first result was the sleek Victory Vegas, which debuted in late 2002 to stellar reviews and strong sales. Driving interest was the ability of customers to custom design their machines, choosing from more than 500 configurations. Sales of the Victory line surged from $34 million in 2002 to $99 million in 2005, by which time motorcycles were generating 5 percent of Polaris's revenues. Victory also turned a profit for the first time in the fourth quarter of 2005.

The increased emphasis on research and development took concrete form in June 2005 when the company opened a new research facility in Wyoming, Minnesota. The center, located closer to Minneapolis in hopes of attracting a broader range of engineers and designers, initially employed about 200 workers concentrating on testing and developing motorcycles, ATVs, and utility vehicles. That same year the Consumer Product Safety Commission fined Polaris nearly $1 million for failing to promptly report safety problems on six of its ATV models. Bennett Morgan, head of Polaris's ATV division since 2001, was named company president and chief operating officer in mid-2005.

Between 2000 and 2005 Tiller had helped engineer an increase of international sales from 5 percent of the overall total to more than 20 percent. In July 2005 he took a further step overseas by entering into a partnership with KTM Power Sports AG, an Austrian maker of off-road dirt bikes that had recently entered the motorcycle category. Polaris purchased a 25 percent stake in KTM for $82.8 million, and the companies agreed to jointly create new products, share engine technology, and develop distribution, manufacturing, and purchasing arrangements. After an initial two-year period, the agreement called for one of two actions: Polaris purchasing majority control of KTM or KTM's largest shareholder buying out Polaris's stake. A merger of the two companies would create the world's largest non-Japanese manufacturer of power sports equipment.

Jay P. Pederson
Updated, Frederick C. Ingram; David E. Salamie

PRINCIPAL SUBSIDIARIES

Polaris Real Estate Corporation of Iowa, Inc.; Polaris Real Estate Corporation; Polaris Industries Ltd. (Canada); Polaris Acceptance Inc.; Polaris Sales Inc.; Po-laris Industries Manufacturing LLC; Polaris Insurance Services LLC; Polaris Direct Inc.; Polaris Sales Australia Pty Ltd.; Polaris France S.A.; Polaris Britain Limited (U.K.); Polaris Norway AS; Polaris Scandinavia AB (Sweden).

PRINCIPAL COMPETITORS

Honda Motor Co., Ltd.; Yamaha Motor Co., Ltd.; Suzuki Motor Corporation; Arctic Cat Inc.; Bombardier Recreational Products Inc.; Harley-Davidson, Inc.; Kawasaki Heavy Industries, Ltd.

FURTHER READING

Bary, Andrew, "Polaris Industries: A Slippery Slope," *Barron's,* January 30, 1995, p. 17.

Bassett, Jerry, *Polaris Partners,* St. Paul, Minn.: Recreational Publications, Inc., 1994.

Beal, Dave, "Can Roseau County Keep It Up?," *St. Paul Pioneer Press,* March 4, 1991.

———, "For Snowmobile Makers, Storm of Century Timely," *St. Paul Pioneer Press,* November 11, 1991.

Bjorhus, Jennifer, "CEO of Polaris Industries Shifts Company into High Gear," *St. Paul Pioneer Press,* July 4, 2004.

———, "Polaris Pays $950,000 to Settle Claims," *St. Paul Pioneer Press,* January 14, 2005.

———, "Polaris to Abandon Marine Business," *St. Paul Pioneer Press,* September 3, 2004.

Byrnes, Nanette, "Lighting a Fire Under Polaris," *Business Week,* November 15, 2004, p. 78.

Dapper, Michael, "Snow Pioneers," *Snowmobile,* November 1994, pp. 74-93.

DePass, Dee, "Thriving, Not Just Surviving: Buoyant Polaris Charges on Despite a Flood of Difficulties," *Minneapolis Star Tribune,* October 27, 2002, p. 1D.

Feyder, Susan, "Making Waves," *Minneapolis Star Tribune,* January 5, 1998, p. 1D.

Foster, Jim, "Polaris Now a Public Corporation," *Minneapolis Star Tribune,* December 23, 1994, p. 3D.

Geiger, Bob, "What's with Polaris Industries Shifting Among Ad Agencies?," *Minneapolis Star Tribune,* November 13, 1995, p. 2D.

Hallinan, Joseph T., "Polaris Expects to Ride Out Speed Bumps in Economy," *Wall Street Journal,* December 29, 2000, p. A12.

Harris, John, "Noisemakers," *Forbes,* October 29, 1990, pp. 104+.

Hendricks, Dick, "Snowmobiling: The Next Generation," *Snowmobile,* January 1995, p. 13.

Hetteen, Edgar, and Jay Lemke, *Breaking Trail,* Bemidji, Minn.: Focus Publishing, 1998.

Kennedy, Tony, "Polaris Revs Up for Motorcycles," *Minneapolis Star Tribune,* February 20, 1997, p. 1D.

McCartney, Jim, "Polaris Will Dive into Water Scooter Market Next Year," *St. Paul Pioneer Press,* August 2, 1991.

Opre, Tom, "Snowmobiles at 25," *Outdoor Life,* January 1984, pp. 18-20.

"Polaris Snowmobile Celebrates Birthday," *St. Paul Pioneer Press,* July 17, 1989.

Peterson, Susan, "Nature vs. Noise," *Minneapolis Star Tribune,* May 15, 2000, p. 1D.

———, "Revving Up Polaris," *Minneapolis Star Tribune,* May 18, 1999, p. 1D.

Phelps, David, "Toro, Polaris Find Right Product Mix; Two Companies Diversify Successfully While Remaining Strong in Old Lines," *Minneapolis Star Tribune,* January 8, 1996, p. 1D.

"Polaris and KTM Join Forces," *Dealernews,* September 2005, p. 14.

"Polaris History Sets Stage for Future," *Powersports Business,* June 28, 2004, pp. 10+.

"Polaris Industries Inc.," *Wall Street Transcript,* September 30, 2002.

Poole, Wiley, "Built in the U.S.A.," *Trailer Boats,* September 1992, pp. 60-61.

Powers, Kemp, "Polaris Industries: Vroom!," *Forbes,* January 8, 2001, p. 124.

Ramstad, C. J., *Legend: Arctic Cat's First Quarter Century,* Deephaven, Minn.: PPM Books, 1987, 189 p.

Rodengen, Jeffrey L., and Richard F. Hubbard, *The Legend of Polaris,* Fort Lauderdale, Fla.: Write Stuff Enterprises, 2003, 152 p.

Rubenstein, David, "Wheels of Fortune," *Corporate Report Minnesota,* March 1986, pp. 58-62.

"The Ruckus Over Snowmobiles," *Changing Times,* January 1980, p. 16.

Schonfeld, Erick, "Catching a Killer Wave with Polaris," *Fortune,* May 29, 1995, p. 155.

Skorupa, Joe, "Ski-Doo: 50 Years on Snow," *Popular Mechanics,* January 1992, pp. 94-95.

"Splendor in the Snow," *Corporate Report Minnesota,* April 1977, pp. 10-12.

Stevens, Karen, "That Vroom! You Hear May Not Be a Harley," *Business Week,* October 20, 1997, p. 159.

Taylor, John, "Built in Iowa: Polaris Unleashes Victory, a Cruiser-Class Motorcycle," *Omaha World-Herald,* Bus. Sec., July 10, 1998, p. 18.

"Those Wild Snowmobilers—Expensive Fun in More Ways Than One," *Corporate Report Minnesota,* February 28, 1970, pp. 8-10.

"Those Wild Snowmobilers—Where Do They Go from Here?," *Corporate Report Minnesota,* March 14, 1970, pp. 8-10.

Welbes, John, "Polaris Industries to Partner with Austrian Motorcycle Company," *St. Paul Pioneer Press,* July 20, 2005.

Youngblood, Dick, "He Made Winters Fun and Brought Factories to Roseau, Thief River Falls; Edgar Hetteen Formed Polaris and Arctic Enterprises," review of *Breaking Trail* by Edgar Hetteen and Jay Lemke, *Minneapolis Star Tribune,* February 4, 1998, p. 2D.

———, "Hetteen's Back in the Driver's Seat; This Time He's Finding Big Demand for New All-Season Vehicle," *Minneapolis Star Tribune,* October 7, 1996, p. 2D.

Polski Koncern Naftowy ORLEN S.A.

—————— ■ ——————

ul Chemikow 7
Plock,
Poland
Telephone: +48 024 365 0000
Fax: +48 024 365 4040
Web site: http://www.orlen.pl

Public Company
Incorporated: 1999
Employees: 14,398
Sales: PLN 30.57 billion ($9.26 billion) (2004)
Stock Exchanges: Warsaw London
Ticker Symbol: PKN
NAIC: 324110 Petroleum Refineries; 324199 All Other Petroleum and Coal Products Manufacturing; 325188 All Other Inorganic Chemical Manufacturing; 326122 Plastics Pipe and Pipe Fitting Manufacturing; 424720 Petroleum and Petroleum Products Merchant Wholesalers (Except Bulk Stations and Terminals); 447110 Gasoline Stations with Convenience Stores

■ ■ ■

Polski Koncern Naftowy ORLEN S.A. (PKN) is the largest refiner and marketer of petroleum products in the Central European region. The company operates six refineries, three in Poland and three in the Czech Republic, with a total processing capacity of 21.7 million tons per year. The company processes crude oil, producing oil, diesel and gasoline, heating oil, aviation fuel, ethylene, and other petroleum derivatives and plastics. The company, the former state-owned oil monopoly, remains the dominant player in Poland, controlling some 70 percent of the domestic processing market and, depending on the end product, between 40 and 100 percent of the domestic market. PKN is also Poland's largest service station operator, with nearly 2,000 gas stations in Poland operating under the ORLEN, Petrochemia Plock, and Bliska brands. PKN has begun an effort to expand internationally, with 500 ORLEN and Star service stations in northern and northeastern Germany and 300 stations in the Czech Republic. The company intends to become the dominant Central European player, and in pursuit of that goal has been engaging in merger talks with Hungarian counterpart MOL. A merger between the two companies could occur as early as 2006. PKN is listed on the Warsaw and London (ADR) stock exchanges. The Polish privatization agency, Nafta Polska, retains a 17.3 percent stake in PKN. In 2004, the company's revenues topped PLN 30.5 billion ($9.25 billion). Igor Chalupec is company president and CEO.

POST-WORLD WAR II NATIONAL OIL COMPANIES

PKN originated as two companies established by the Polish government following World War II. The first of these was founded in 1944 as Polski Monopol Naftowy and charged with taking control of the country's shattered oil supply and its distribution. The following year, that body was transformed into a state-owned company, Centrala Produktow Naftowych (CPN). By 1948, CPN had been transferred to the Ministry of Industry and Trade, and became the state monopoly for the distribu-

COMPANY PERSPECTIVES

Mission Statement: Aiming to become the regional leader, we ensure long-term value creation for our shareholders by offering our customers products and services of the highest quality. All our operations adhere to "best practice" principles of corporate governance and social responsibility, with a focus on care for our employees and the natural environment.

tion of fuel and petroleum-based lubricants. CPN's oversight was later transferred among various ministries, before being brought under the Ministry of Chemical Industry in 1959. In the meantime, CPN had been building a national network of service stations, introducing electric-powered pumps in 1957. The company also began distributing automotive parts and accessories at this time.

By the 1980s, CPN's service station network had topped 1,000, and the state-owned body employed more than 17,000 people. CPN had also developed facilities for the production of an end-user automotive lubricant oil.

In 1983, CPN's status was changed again, to that of a public utility enterprise with control of the national market. The company now provided oversight to 17 regional directorates, as well as tanker operations, and Naftoprojekt, which provided engineering and design services, as well as construction and assembly operations. Also included under the "new" CPN were Poland's petroleum pipeline operations, including the "Friendship" crude oil pipeline.

With the end of Soviet domination, and the institution of a free market system in Poland, the Polish government launched the privatization process of the country's oil sector in the mid-1990s. CPN was then restructured as a state-owned limited liability company in 1995. By the end of the decade, CPN's operations included more than 1,400 service stations and related facilities, 156 fuel depots, a 600-strong fleet of tanker trucks, port operations, and 22 research laboratories. The next step in CPN's privatization process took place in 1999, when the company was merged into its petroleum refining counterpart, Petrochemia Plock.

Plock had been the result of the Polish government's determination to develop a national petrochemicals industry in the early 1950s. At that time the country had only five small refineries, which produced a combined total of less than one million tons annually.

The decision to construct the country's first large-scale refinery was taken in 1954, when the country's Oil Refining Industry oversight body was given instruction to begin planning a new facility. The original plan called for a facility with a capacity of one million tons. Those plans were scaled upward, however, and the final design boasted an initial capacity of six million tons, with further expansion to reach up to ten million tons. In 1958, Plock was chosen as the site for the new refinery, to be developed under the auspices of a new company, Mazovia Refinery and Petrochemical Plant, which was established in 1960.

Production at the new site was launched in 1964, with an initial capacity of two million tons. Production at first focused on gasoline and diesel oil, before expanding to include a wide range of refined fuels, including automotive and airplane fuels, xylene, diesel oil, oil coke, bitumen, lubricant oil, and hard and soft paraffin. By the late 1960s, the company had begun production of a number of petrochemical products as well, including ethylene oxide, ethylene glycol, phenol, acetone, sulfuric acid, and the like. In 1971, the company initiated polyethylene production and, later, polypropylene and other plastics and plastic component materials. The company's petrochemicals production took off especially after production was launched at a new catalytic cracking plant in 1976, which became the largest single facility on the Plock site.

In 1978, the Plock operation posted its first major milestone, producing its 100 millionth ton since its launch in 1964. The company continued to improve and expand the site, and less than ten years later had produced its 200 millionth ton. In 1993, Mazovia Refinery and Petrochemical Plant became one of the early targets for the Polish government's privatization plans. In that year, the company was restructured as a limited liability company, and changed its name to Petrochemie Plock. By the end of the decade, the Plock site had grown to encompass more than 710 hectares, employing 7,700 people and boasting an annual production of more than 11 million tons per year.

PRIVATIZATION PROCESS IN THE 1990S

In 1996, the Polish government created a new body, Nafta Polsky, to oversee the privatization of the country's oil industry and to serve as an oversight body for the newly liberalized market. Nafta Polsky set into place the restructuring of the industry, which resulted in the merger of Petrochemie Plock and CPN in 1999. That company was then renamed Polski Koncern Naftowy (PKN). In November of that year, the Polish government listed PKN's stock on the Warsaw Stock Exchange,

KEY DATES
∎

1944: Polski Monopol Naftowy, which takes control of the country's oil supply and its distribution, is founded.

1945: The company is renamed as Centrala Produktow Naftowych (CPN).

1948: CPN is placed under the Ministry of Industry and Trade.

1954: The Polish government announces the intention to build the country's first large-scale refinery.

1958: Plock is chosen as the site of the new refinery.

1960: The state-owned Mazovia Refinery and Petrochemical Plant is incorporated.

1964: Crude oil processing is launched.

1971: Polyethylene production is launched.

1983: CPN is restructured as a state utility, taking control of the country's oil and petroleum products retail, wholesale, and logistics operations.

1993: The Mazovia Refinery is reincorporated as a limited liability company and is renamed Petrochemie Plock as the first step in the privatization of the Polish petroleum industry.

1995: CPN is restructured as a limited liability company.

1996: Natfa Polsky is created to oversee the privatization of industry.

1999: Plock and CPN are merged into Polski Koncern Naftowy (PKN); the government sells a 30 percent stake on the Warsaw and London Stock Exchanges.

2000: The ORLEN brand name is launched; PKN changes its name to Polski Koncern Naftowy ORLEN.

2002: The company forms a distribution joint venture with Basell Europe Holdings.

2003: The company acquires 500 service stations in Germany from BP.

2004: Nearly 63 percent of Unipetrol in the Czech Republic is acquired; the company signs a memo of intent to merge with Hungary's MOL.

2005: The acquisition of Unipetrol is completed.

2006: The merger between MOL and PKN is expected before the end of the year.

selling a 30 percent stake. A percentage of that offering was earmarked for foreign investors and placed on the London Stock Exchange in the form of depositary receipts.

In the year 2000, PKN launched a new brand name, ORLEN, which became its flagship service station brand. As part of the branding effort, the company changed its own name, becoming Polsky Koncern Naftowy ORLEN that year. At the same time, the Polish government continued the privatization process, placing an additional 40 percent stake of PKN on the Warsaw Stock Exchange. By the mid-2000s, Nafta Polsky's shareholding in PKN had been reduced to slightly more than 17 percent.

PKN also began a restructuring effort in 2000, as a run-up to its effort to position itself not only as a Polish petroleum products leader, but as a leader in the Central European region. In the meantime, the company began a modernization effort, which included the launch of the Flota Polska fuel card for the corporate market, and a loyalty card, Vitay, for the consumer market. Both schemes were introduced in 2001.

PKN's move into the international market came in 2002, when the company bought nearly 500 service stations in northern and northeastern Germany from British petroleum giant BP (as part of its requirement to reduce its share of the German market to less than 26 percent). The acquisition of the German network, placed under the ORLEN and Star brand names, gave PKN a 7 percent share of the local market and a 3 percent share of the national market.

Back at home, PKN had been investing in its refining capacity as well. In May 2002, the company inaugurated production at its new DRW III crude oil processing facility. That facility, the largest in Central Europe, more than doubled PKN's crude oil capacity to reach 6.7 million tons.

PKN maintained its search for external growth opportunities. In 2003, the company formed a joint venture partnership with polypropylene giant Basell Europe Holdings. The new company, called Basell ORLEN Polyolefins, enabled PKN to begin marketing and distributing its own petrochemicals products on an international level.

CENTRAL EUROPEAN MARKET LEADER IN THE 2000S

At the same time, PKN, in large part restricted from further expansion at home, launched an effort to build itself into the Central European market leader. The company's plans took a major step forward in 2004 when PKN won its bid to acquire nearly 63 percent of

Unipetrol from the Czech Republic government. That purchase gave PKN control of Unipetrol's national network of more than 300 service stations, as well as joint ownership of Unipetrol's three refineries. The company's share of that production boosted its total annual refinery output to nearly 22 million tons; by the end of 2005, PKN celebrated its 400 millionth ton of processed crude oil since the launch of production in 1964.

At the same time, PKN continued to plan for its future expansion. The company launched a new strategy for the second half of the 2000s, confirming its commitment to becoming a true regional leader. The company also launched an effort to expand its production, including the doubling of its ethylene production in mid-2005.

External growth, however, appeared PKN's likeliest path to expansion. In 2004, the company reportedly signed a memorandum of agreement with Hungarian counterpart MOL to merge the two companies. That merger was expected to take place before the end of 2006, and would likely include MOL's control of a majority stake in Slovnaft, a refinery group based in Slovakia, and its 25 percent stake in INA, in the Czech Republic. Meanwhile, PKN continued to scout for other acquisition possibilities in the region, eyeing potential candidates in the Czech Republic, Romania, and Serbia. Although some observers remained skeptical of PKN's expansion strategy, primarily because an enlarged PKN would become a more attractive takeover target for one of the petroleum giants, PKN had shaken off the dust of its Communist past and emerged as one of the European region's most vibrant petrochemical groups in the 2000s.

M. L. Cohen

PRINCIPAL SUBSIDIARIES

ORLEN Deutschland AG; ORLEN Deutschland GmbH; ORLEN Gaz Sp. z.o.o.; ORLEN PetroCentrum Sp. z.o.o.; ORLEN Medica Sp. z.o.o.; ORLEN Budonaft Sp. z.o.o.; ORLEN Powiernik Sp. z.o.o.; ORLEN KolTrans Sp. z.o.o.; ORLEN Transport Szczecin Sp. z.o.o.; ORLEN ASFALT Sp. z.o.o; ORLEN Petro-Tank Sp. z.o.o. (90%); Energomedia Sp. z.o.o.; Euronaft Sp. z.o.o.; Nafto Wax Sp. z.o.o.; RAF-LAB Sp. z.o.o.; RAF-ENERGIA Sp. z.o.o.; RAF-KOLTRANS Sp. z.o.o.; RAF-REMAT Sp. z.o.o. (96%); RAF-EKOLOGIA Sp. z.o.o. (93%).

PRINCIPAL COMPETITORS

SOCAR; RWE AG; Lukoil Oil Co.; Saknavtobi; Ukrtatnafta Joint Stock Co; Kirishinefteorgsintez Ltd.; Tobolsk-Neftekhim; NAFTAN Refinery.

FURTHER READING

Green, Peter S., "Big Decision on Future of Polish Oil Is Looming," *New York Times,* August 31, 2001, p. W1.

Koza, Patricia, "PKN Orlen Buys German Gas Stations," *Daily Deal,* December 12, 2002.

Modrzejewski, Andrzej, "PKN-Orlen: Petrochemical Giant Continues to Refine Strategy to Fuel Its Rise," *Worldlink,* January-February 2002, p. 175.

"MOL and PKN to Merge," *World Refining,* January-February 2004, p. 22.

"Orlen to Expand Cracker," *CAN Asian Chemical News,* January 31, 2005, p. 5.

"PKN Thinks Global," *FSU Energy,* October 4, 2002, p. 13.

"Polish Refiner Eyes Unipetrol," *NEFTE Compass,* August 1, 2002, p. 7.

PolyMedica Corporation

11 State Street
Woburn, Massachusetts 01801
U.S.A.
Telephone: (781) 933-2020
Fax: (781) 938-6950
Web site: http://www.polymedica.com

Public Company
Incorporated: 1988 as Emerging Sciences, Inc.
Employees: 1,900
Sales: $451.4 million (2005)
Stock Exchanges: NASDAQ
Ticker Symbol: PLMD
NAIC: 325412 Pharmaceutical Preparation Manufacturing; 339112 Surgical and Medical Instrument Manufacturing; 454113 Mail-Order Houses

■ ■ ■

PolyMedica Corporation provides healthcare products and services primarily to seniors with Medicare insurance coverage. PolyMedica is best known through its Liberty Healthcare division, which provides blood glucose testing supplies and related services to diabetics. Through Liberty, which is advertised in a national television marketing campaign featuring actor Wilford Brimley and broadcaster Paul Harvey, PolyMedica also operates a mail-order pharmacy that provides a broad range of prescription medications. PolyMedica serves more than 800,000 patients through facilities in Woburn, Massachusetts; Port St. Lucie, Florida; Salem, Virginia; and Deerfield Beach, Florida.

ORIGINS

PolyMedica experienced two distinct periods during its first 15 years in business, enjoying far greater financial success in its second incarnation. The company was founded in 1988 as Emerging Sciences, Inc., a name it kept for two years before adopting the name PolyMedica Industries, Inc. in 1990 (the company made the slight alteration to "PolyMedica Corporation" in 1997). The name change in 1990 was made to reflect more accurately the company's mainstay technology and services, which was the manufacture of polyurethane-based medical products. PolyMedica, using proprietary polymer-based technology, competed in the ethical wound care market, providing dressings prescribed by doctors, a $415 million global market during the early 1990s. The company's first commercial applications of its polyurethane expertise was a group of wound care products marketed under the Mitraflex and Spyroflex names, although, in contrast to the later manifestation of the company, PolyMedica did not engage in any marketing activities. The company's products were sold through exclusive licensing agreements with two pharmaceutical companies, U.S.-based Merck and Germany-based Rauscher, who marketed PolyMedica's products in the United States and in Europe.

PolyMedica, in name and business, changed significantly during its first decades in business. Doctor-prescribed wound dressings continued to define its core business as it began to evolve into a different type of company, but the additions to its business were important, nevertheless. PolyMedica's most meaningful changes were engendered by acquiring other companies, and in 1992 two acquisitions were completed that broadened its scope of operations. PolyMedica completed its initial public offering (IPO) of stock in 1992, the same year it purchased American CDI, Inc., a manufacturer and distributor of consumer home healthcare products, which led to the formation of the company's healthcare division. The division manufactured and distributed nearly 100 products through a distribution network covering the United States and Canada. Although varied, the core of the division's product line comprised branded and private label digital thermometers, a new line of PolyMedica's business that soon accounted for roughly one-fifth of the company's revenue total. Before the end of the year, the company established the foundation for another division, acquiring the WE-BCON line of products from Alcon Surgical, Inc. The acquisition, a $45 million deal, gave PolyMedica products consisting primarily of prescribed and over-the-counter (OTC) urological and suppository remedies, providing the framework of the company's pharmaceutical division.

Through its PolyMedica Healthcare division, the company focused on urinary health maintenance products, beginning with AZO Standard, a urinary pain reliever that initially was limited to regional distribution. In 1993, the company began expanding distribution, seeking to turn the label into a national brand. In 1995, AZO Cranberry, a daily urinary health maintenance product, was introduced to the consumer market, broadening the AZO line. The company, with $27 million in revenue that year, was still reliant on its proprietary polymer-based technology. PolyMedica then comprised three principal business groups. PolyMedica's Technology Group consisted of research and development efforts aimed at patented manufacturing processes that were applied to advanced wound care products. The

company's Materials Group provided new polymers with applications for medical devices and other consumer products. PolyMedica's third facet, its Medical Group, which manufactured pharmaceuticals, wound care, and home healthcare products, became the new home of the company's transforming acquisition, a purchase completed in August 1996.

1996 ACQUISITION OF LIBERTY MEDICAL SUPPLY

The emergence of a new, integrated developer, manufacturer, and marketer of medical products was signaled when PolyMedica revealed it was acquiring Liberty Medical Supply. Based in Palm City, Florida, Liberty Medical was founded in 1989 to serve as a reliable source of diabetic supplies primarily for patients with Medicare insurance coverage. PolyMedica completed the estimated $9 million acquisition largely because changes by Medicare in its reimbursement policy for ethical wound care dressings had reduced PolyMedica's revenue-generating potential in the market. The acquisition of Liberty gave the company a new line of business, one that in later years would account for 80 percent of its revenue and define its corporate identity.

Liberty, in 1996, ranked as one of the largest diabetic healthcare suppliers in the country. It relied almost exclusively on print advertising to attract customers, figuring prominently as a direct-to-consumer provider of diabetic supplies; yet, such providers only controlled a small percentage of the market. During the mid-1990s, there were approximately 1.5 million insulin-dependent diabetics with Medicare insurance, but only 125,000 of the 1.5 million patients obtained their supplies through such companies as Liberty. Seniors were largely unaware of Liberty-type companies and obtained their supplies primarily at drugstores, either unaware that Medicare reimbursed for products such as glucose test machines, test strips, and control solutions or opting to endure the lengthy reimbursement process on their own. PolyMedica greatly heightened the awareness of the mail-order availability of diabetic supplies and reimbursement services, and, remarkably considering its roots as a non-marketing company, it did so with a hugely successful marketing campaign. As the years went by, with PolyMedica promoting and expanding Liberty, the time when direct-to-consumer diabetic supplies providers controlled only a fraction of the market ended. "If you're a senior with diabetes, you know who Liberty is," a PolyMedica executive said in an August 22, 2004 interview with the *Palm Beach Post*.

In many respects, the importance of the Liberty acquisition was not the acquisition itself, but what PolyMedica did with the acquisition in succeeding years.

KEY DATES
■

1988: The company is founded as Emerging Sciences, Inc.

1992: An initial public offering of stock coincides with creation of healthcare and pharmaceutical divisions.

1996: Liberty Medical Supply is acquired.

1999: The company, now known as PolyMedica Corporation, generates more than $100 million in sales for the first time.

2001: Allegations of Medicare fraud followed by a federal investigation into PolyMedica's accounting methods do little to tarnish the company's business.

2004: PolyMedica acquires National Diabetic Assistance Corporation.

2005: PolyMedica sells its Women's Health division to Amerifit Nutrition Inc.

The Liberty of 1996 barely resembled the Liberty of 2006 in scope and stature. When PolyMedica acquired Liberty, approximately 17,000 customers had signed up to receive their diabetic supplies through the company's Palm City operations. The ranks of insulin-dependent patients who turned to Liberty increased exponentially under PolyMedica's control after executives in Woburn decided to abandon Liberty's print advertising marketing approach and develop a national television campaign. Commercials featuring broadcaster Paul Harvey and actor Wilford Brimley began airing and a largely unknown source of diabetic supplies became widely known. PolyMedica also expanded its other lines of business during the second half of the 1990s, building a new pharmaceutical manufacturing facility at its headquarters in Woburn in 1997 and adding AZO Test Strips to its urinary health maintenance line of products in 1998. The expansion coincided with the company's retreat from the wound care market, a move made in 1997 when PolyMedica sold its wound care assets to Innovative Technologies Group PLC.

By the end of the 1990s, the wholesale changes that had occurred during the decade produced a much larger PolyMedica. In 1999, when trading of the company's stock moved from the American Stock Exchange to the NASDAQ, it eclipsed the $100 million-in-sales mark for the first time, a fourfold increase from the total registered five years earlier. Driving the financial growth was the company's Liberty assets, which were expanded during the year by the launch of Liberty Home Pharmacy, a business created to serve seniors suffering from chronic obstructive pulmonary disease (COPD), a chronic lung disease such as asthma or emphysema. The heart of the Liberty assets, and by 1999 the heart of PolyMedica, was the diabetic supplies business. The national television campaign had worked wonders, fueling the expansion of Liberty's customer base to a staggering 265,000 patients by the end of the decade. As PolyMedica entered the 21st century, rapid financial growth continued, despite events that otherwise might have caused the company's collapse.

2001-03: FEDERAL INVESTIGATIONS TAKING CENTER STAGE

PolyMedica's 13th year in business gave credence to the superstition, resulting in perhaps the single most dreaded event any public company could experience. In August 2001, 85 agents from the Federal Bureau of Investigation (FBI) raided four Liberty offices and two executives' homes, spending two days confiscating reams of documents and hard-disk drives as they launched an investigation into Medicare fraud. The FBI acted on information from former employees, who alleged Liberty purposefully shipped diabetic supplies to patients who had not ordered them and then did not reimburse Medicare when the products were returned. Exactly one year after Liberty's offices were raided, PolyMedica announced Liberty was being investigated by the U.S. Attorney's Office for the Southern District of Florida, an investigation that centered around allegations of improper revenue recognition. The Securities and Exchange Commission (SEC) launched a formal inquiry, which was followed by a shareholder lawsuit, portending further disaster. The mounting controversy struck at the heart of Liberty's success: once PolyMedica launched its national marketing campaign, it treated its television commercial expenses as assets instead of subtracting expenses from its revenue total, amortizing the expenses over two to four years. PolyMedica argued that it operated like an insurance company because its customers purchased its product immediately upon viewing a commercial. The SEC approved the unusual accounting method in 2003, resulting in a major victory for PolyMedica.

Remarkably, PolyMedica thrived during the protracted investigation into improper revenue recognition. The company physically expanded and recorded substantial financial growth, exhibiting impressive resilience while undergoing federal scrutiny. In 2000, Liberty's headquarters were moved to Port St. Lucie, Florida, where a new 72,000-square-foot facility was established. In 2001, a new 64,000-square-foot facility was built to accommodate Liberty's expanding respiratory business. The following year, PolyMedica opened the company's first full-service, mail-order pharmacy, launching Liberty Medical Supply Pharmacy, which opened a new 120,000-square-foot building in 2004 to serve its growing business. Annual revenue during this period of physical expansion leaped upward, increasing from $220 million in 2001 to $419 million in 2004.

As PolyMedica neared its 20th anniversary, the company was exuding enviable strength. The strategic moves of the 1990s, particularly the decision to purchase Liberty, had created a more diverse and much larger healthcare products competitor, transforming a company with $25 million in annual sales into an industry leader flirting with the $500 million-in-sales mark, all within the course of decade. In the final years before its 20th anniversary arrived, PolyMedica moved in two directions, shedding some of its assets and acquiring new ones. In 2004, the company acquired National Diabetic Assistance Corporation, a mail-order provider of diabetic supplies based in Deerfield Beach, Florida. In 2005, PolyMedica completed two more acquisitions, but the year also included a pair of divestitures. Reductions in Medicare reimbursement rates prompted PolyMedica executives to put its respiratory business up for sale, which was expected to sell for between $20 million and $25 million. Talks also were underway to sell the company's Women's Health division, which included the AZO line of urinary products. PolyMedica sold the division to Amerifit Nutrition Inc. in October 2005, receiving $45 million from the sale. On the acquisition front, PolyMedica announced an agreement to purchase Salem, Virginia-based National Diabetic Pharmacies in August 2005, adding another mail-order provider of diabetic supplies. PolyMedica closed the year with the purchase of IntelliCare, Inc. in December. IntelliCare provided telephone-based nursing services, offering patients triage advice and helping them to determine whether they required immediate care.

Jeffrey L. Covell

PRINCIPAL SUBSIDIARIES

Liberty Healthcare Group, Inc.; Polymedica Pharmaceuticals USA Inc.; Polymedica Pharmaceuticals Securities Inc.

PRINCIPAL COMPETITORS

Bristol-Myers Squibb Company; Matria Healthcare, Inc.; Medtronic MiniMed, Inc.

FURTHER READING

Adams, Duncan, "Company to Buy Competitor in Salem," *Roanoke Times,* August 13, 2005.

"Advancing Women's Health Care," *MMR,* October 29, 2001, p. 28.

Aoki, Naomi, "SEC to Investigate Woburn, Mass.-Based Home Diabetes-Kit Maker," *Boston Globe,* December 5, 2001.

Becker, Lori, "Despite Federal Probe, Liberty Medical Increases Revenues, Customer Base," *Palm Beach Post,* August 22, 2004.

———, "Liberty Medical Double-Checks Paperwork, Delays Billing," *Palm Beach Post,* February 9, 2005.

———, "Medicare Cuts Spur Sale of Liberty Respiratory Unit," *Palm Beach Post,* August 10, 2005.

Clifford, Lee, "Betting Against the SEC—and Winning," *Fortune,* May 13, 2002, p. 170.

Kerber, Ross, "SEC Approves Unusual Accounting Method Used by Medical-Supply Company," *Boston Globe,* September 5, 2003.

Lipton, Joshua, "Sweet Move," *Corporate Counsel,* August 2005, p. 49.

"Monitoring Polymedica," *Business Week,* April 5, 1999, p. 98.

"The Perennials," *Fortune,* September 3, 2001, p. 75.

"Polymedica Announces Divestiture of Women's Health Division," *Asia Africa Intelligence Wire,* October 3, 2005.

"Polymedica to Pay $35 Million to United States to Resolve False Claims," *America's Intelligence Wire,* December 2, 2004.

Port, Susan, "Parent of Port St. Lucie, Fla.-Based Liberty Medical Reveals Federal Probe," *Palm Beach Post,* August 17, 2002.

———, "President of Port St. Lucie, Fla.-Based Liberty Medical Resigns," *Palm Beach Post,* January 15, 2004.

Rowland, Christopher, "Woburn, Mass.-Based Medical Supply Company PolyMedica Sued by Shareholders," *Boston Globe,* July 8, 2003.

Wickenheiser, Matt, "One of Portland, Maine's Fastest Growing Tech Companies Is Sold," *Portland Press Herald,* December 20, 2005.

Publicis Groupe

133 av des Champs Elysees
Paris,
France
Telephone: +33 01 44 43 70 00
Fax: +33 01 44 43 75 25
Web site: http://www.publicis.com

Public Company
Incorporated: 1926
Employees: 36,384
Sales: EUR 3.83 billion ($4.84 billion) (2004)
Stock Exchanges: Euronext Paris
Ticker Symbol: PUB
NAIC: 541810 Advertising Agencies; 541820 Public
    Relations Services; 541840 Media Representatives;
    551112 Offices of Other Holding Companies

■ ■ ■

Publicis Groupe is one of the world's leading advertising groups: the company claims the fourth spot in the world, the third in Europe, and the fourth in the United States. The company also operates the world's largest media buying and consultancy firm. Publicis has transformed itself from a largely France-focused group to a worldwide advertising empire including such global networks as Saatchi & Saatchi, Leo Burnett, and Publicis itself, as well as a myriad of prominent regional and local companies, such as Fallon Worldwide, 49 percent of Bartle Bogle Hegarty, Burrell Communications, The Kaplan Thaler Group, Cartwright Williams Direct, and, since 2005, Freud Communications. Publicis' Media

Buying and Consultancy division is composed of two global groups, Starcom MediaVest Group and Zenith-Optimedia. The company also operates a third division, Specialized Agencies and Marketing Services, providing direct market, public relations, communications, and other services. Publicis is present in 104 countries, with nearly 200 offices, and more than 36,000 employees. The company is led by Maurice Levy, protégée of the company's founder, Marcel Bleustein-Blanchet. Publicis is listed on the Euronext Stock Exchange. In 2004, the group posted total revenues of EUR 3.83 billion ($4.8 billion).

THE FATHER OF FRENCH ADVERTISING

Marcel Bleustein founded Publicis (a combination of the French word for advertising, "publicité," and the sound of the French "six" to denote the year of the company's formation) in Paris in 1926. Bleustein was then 20 years old. His family had immigrated to France from the Russian-Polish border and built a successful furniture business following World War I; Bleustein was also related to the Lévitan brothers furniture empire (three of Bleustein's sisters married Lévitans). At the age of 14, Bleustein dropped out of school to work in the family's business, before completing his compulsory military service at age 18. Returning from the army, however, Bleustein decided to leave the furniture business and enter advertising, setting up France's fourth advertising agency.

"My son is leaving me to go and sell hot air," was Bleustein's father's reaction. Indeed, by the 1920s,

COMPANY PERSPECTIVES

At the heart of Publicis Groupe, there is La Difference, coming from our networks and our agencies. Each specific approach builds our strength as a Groupe. Across each brand and entity, each team, we dedicate all our energy to the success of our clients, their projects and their campaigns.

advertisers had earned the disdain of French consumers, with ads that displayed little regard for the truth. Nevertheless, Bleustein's father gave his blessing, if only so that his son would not reproach him later. With only 40,000 francs in savings, Bleustein set up shop in a small office above a delicatessen on the Rue Montmartre, and set out to change the nature of French advertising. After studying the market, Bleustein drafted two edicts: the product must be entirely visible, and the product must not be tampered with, but shown as is. Bleustein began to search for clients, literally going from door to door.

Finding clients, however, proved difficult, as potential clients shared consumers' distaste for advertising. Bleustein's first break came through his family. His mother, who was active in many charities, prevailed upon a friend, the owner of the Comptoir Cardinet, who reluctantly agreed to allow Bleustein to draft an advertisement. Bleustein chose two products, a silver set and a clock, and asked his illustrator, Aristide Perré to illustrate them exactly as they were and in detail. Within two days after the advertisement appeared, Comptoir Cardinet sold 15 sets of silver and 12 clocks.

Next, Bleustein lined up Brunswick Furriers (for whom he created the famous slogan: "the furrier that creates a furor") and brother-in-law Wolf Lévitan and the family's Lévitan furniture stores (slogan: "Lévitan furniture is guaranteed to last," a promise few French furniture manufacturers could make in the postwar years). Publicis's first large advertising budget followed by the end of the decade. The owners of André Shoes, a chain of some 100 shoe stores, were equally wary of the need for advertising, but Bleustein managed to persuade them, and won a 600,000 franc full-service budget, and created another famous French advertising slogan: "Andre, le chausser sachant chausser" ("the shoe store that knows how to shoe you").

Bleustein's agency took off. By the age of 23, he was already a millionaire, and by the beginning of the new decade, he had taken the French advertising industry into a new era. Bleustein had traveled to the United States in 1929, where he discovered radio advertising. Returning to France, Bleustein made an arrangement to advertise Brunswick's furs on Radio Eiffel Tower. Brunswick was skeptical, but the radio ads proved immediately successful. Publicis was also gaining momentum. After winning the André contract and a contract with Sools, the largest hatter in Paris, Bleustein began eyeing the national market. He bought a plane—he already had a pilot's license—and began flying across France to sign up advertising contracts with radio stations in other cities. In exchange for exclusive rights to a station's advertising time, he offered a fixed yearly revenue. Twenty of the country's 29 public and private radio stations signed on, and Publicis soon became one of the largest agencies in the country, signing on such major clients as Max Factor, Procter & Gamble's Monsavon, Renault, and others.

In 1934, the government banned advertising from its public radio stations, leaving Publicis with only 11 private stations. These stations quickly demanded a larger share of Publicis's profits, with Radio Lyon, led by M. Pierre Laval, later the premier of Vichy France, among them. After meeting with Laval, Bleustein decided to buy his own station, rather than bow to the private stations' demands. Publicis paid 3.5 million francs for Radio-L.L., located in a Parisian suburb, changed its name to Radio Cité, in homage to Radio City Music Hall in New York, and promptly created a new sensation. Among Radio Cité's innovations was the institution of regular news broadcasts, in a deal with *L'Intransigeant* newspaper, which supplied the news staff in exchange for 25 percent of Radio Cité. Radio Cité would become a Parisian institution in the years leading up to the war and would be responsible for launching the careers of such noted French stars as Edith Piaf and Yves Montand.

REBUILDING AFTER WORLD WAR II

The outbreak of World War II put an end to Publicis's success. Bleustein flew in the French air force, then returned to Paris after France's defeat. He was soon forced to abandon Publicis and Radio Cité, after the German occupation of France and Vichy's France's promulgation of laws barring Jewish ownership of radio stations and other media outlets. Bleustein joined the Resistance, helping to smuggle British pilots back to London. However, when word came that he was wanted by the Gestapo, Bleustein, using the *nom de guerre* Blanchet, was forced to leave France. He spent three months in prison in Spain, then was allowed to leave for London, where he joined De Gaulle and flew as an assistant pilot on U.S. Air Force reconnaissance and bombing runs.

KEY DATES

1926: Marcel Bleustein founds Publicis in Paris, and becomes the "father of French advertising."

1929: Company launches radio advertising, acquiring exclusive rights to much of France's radio network.

1934: Bleustein buys his own radio station, Radio LL.

1940: Bleustein joins French Resistance, adopting nom de guerre Blanchet.

1946: Publicis is resurrected after its destruction during World War II; Bleustein changes name to Blanchet-Bleustein.

1954: Publicis conducts France's first public opinion poll.

1957: Company opens office in New York.

1958: Company opens agency in Germany.

1970: Company goes public on Paris Stock Exchange.

1972: Publicis acquires Intermarco group, entering Belgium, the Netherlands, Sweden, and Spain.

1973: Publicis acquires Switzerland's Farner group, adding offices in Italy and Austria.

1980: Publicis acquires majority control of Media System.

1987: Media buying group Optimedia, based in France, Switzerland, and the United Kingdom, is launched.

1988: Company begins alliance with Foote Cone Belding (FCB) in United States.

1993: Company acquires FCA of France.

1995: Alliance with FCB (later True North) ends.

1996: Marcel Blanchet-Bleustein dies; Maurice Levy takes over as chairman.

1997: Company acquires Mojo Partners in Australia and New Zealand.

1998: Company acquires Hal Riney & Partners and Evans Group (U.S.), Capurro (Argentina), Unitros (Chile), and Casadavell-Pedren (Spain).

1999: Welcomm (South Korea), AMA (Philippines), Gramercy Group, Lobsenz/Stevens, and 49 percent of Burrell Communications (U.S.) are added.

2001: Publicis acquires Saatchi & Saatchi; merges Optimedia and Zenithmedia to form ZenithOptimedia.

2002: Company acquires Bcom3, including Leo Burnett and D'Arcy, becoming world's number four advertising agency; Dentsu (Japan) acquires 15 percent of Publicis as part of Bcom3 deal.

2003: Dentsu and Publicis form iSe sports marketing joint venture.

2005: Publicis acquires Freud Communications (U.K.), Pharmaconsult Healthcare (Spain), and Solutions Integrated Marketing (India).

When Bleustein returned to Paris on the day of that city's liberation, Publicis had been destroyed by the Germans and Radio Cité had been taken over by the new French government, which banned the formation of private French radio stations. Bleustein, who added Blanchet to his surname, was forced to rebuild his business from scratch. In 1946, he won the advertising franchise for the newly created *France-Soir* newspaper, and formed Régie-Presse to operate his media-buying business. Soon after, Bleustein-Blanchet was able to resurrect his agency, as his former clients, also rebuilding their businesses, began to return to Publicis. With advertising banned from radio, Publicis began placing its clients' ads on billboards, buses, subway stations, and in the cinema.

Publicis again rose to the top of the French advertising industry. By the late 1950s, the company was posting yearly billings of more than $15 million per year. Its clients included 50 top French companies, and the French market for such international clients as Shell, General Motors, Dunlop, Colgate-Palmolive, Nestlé, and Singer Sewing Machines. At the same time, Publicis had helped to organize the French advertising industry trade association, which effectively ensured that companies could only use French agencies for the French ad market. Publicis continued its history of innovation as well.

In 1954, the company conducted France's first pubic opinion poll (Bleustein-Blanchet had met George Gallup on a trip to the United States in 1938). In 1957,

Publicis made its first international moves, opening an office in New York (primarily to serve the company's French clients) and forming alliances with agencies in other European countries.

Since his youth, Bleustein-Blanchet's dream had been to own a building at the top of the Champs-Elysées. In 1958 that dream was realized when Publicis bought and moved into the former Astor Hotel (and later General Eisenhower's Paris headquarters) opposite the Arc de Triomphe. In that building, Bleustein-Blanchet introduced another of his American discoveries, the Publicis Drugstore, which quickly became a popular Parisian fixture. The following year, Bleustein-Blanchet, critical of the typical secrecy of French businesses, introduced the concept of institutional advertising, in which a company spoke about its business and manufacturing techniques, rather than its products.

During the 1960s, Publicis established a firm reputation as the most modern of French advertising agencies, particularly with its ad campaign for a panty-hose maker, which was one of the first advertisements to use a symbolic emblem, rather than the product itself, to promote the product. In the late 1960s, Publicis introduced advertising to television. The company also moved into crisis communication, successfully helping French glassmaker Saint-Gobain to defend itself from France's first hostile takeover in 1968.

STARTING AGAIN IN THE 1970S

Publicis's Champs-Elysées headquarters, and all of its records, burned in 1972, and the company was forced to rebuild yet again. Publicis built a new headquarters on the same location, but by then, the company, which had gone public in 1970, was itself evolving. Bleustein-Blanchet named his successor, Maurice Levy, who effectively took over the agency's day-to-day operations, leaving Bleustein-Blanchet as chairman.

During the 1970s, Publicis began to expand its international operations, acquiring Intermarco, which had been formed as the in-house advertising arm of Philips Electronics, and Farner, a leading agency for the Swiss and German markets. The combined Intermarco-Farner subsidiary brought Publicis representation into more than 15 European countries, including, with the acquisition of McCormick Agency, the United Kingdom. Publicis also opened a full-service Intermarco agency in New York. Meanwhile, Publicis was also branching out into the nascent data processing and graphics industry, establishing its S.G.I.P. subsidiary in 1973.

By the 1980s, Publicis had grown to become a worldwide leader in the advertising industry. In 1988, the company grew even stronger, signing an alliance agreement with Chicago-based Foote, Cone & Belding that gave Publicis a 20 percent ownership of FCB and its dominance of the North and Latin American markets. FCB, in turn, received 49 percent of Publicis's European network, which was renamed Publicis-FCB.

During the first half of the 1990s, Publicis, through Publicis-FCB, continued to solidify its dominance of the European market, acquiring, among others, the Dutch agency Overad, and moving into the newly opened Eastern European market with agreements with Hungary's Hungexpo, Czechoslovakia's Mertis, and Poland's Estra. From 1988 to 1996, the company shifted its revenues from 69 percent billed in France to more than 65 percent billed beyond the French border.

The international recession of the 1990s helped dampen Publicis's revenue growth. Despite a series of acquisitions, including the Feldman, Calleux et Associés (FCA) network in 1993, Publicis's revenues remained largely flat during the first half of the decade, hovering around FRF 20 billion, while net income saw steady declines, from FRF 318 million in 1990 to a low of FRF 220 million in 1994. Nevertheless, Publicis remained among the healthiest of advertising agencies, with zero long-term and medium-term debt. The agency also scored a major coup when it was awarded the international advertising account for Coca-Cola's Diet Coke and Coca-Cola Light products. The following year, the agency also won the British Airways account through its alliance with the New Saatchi Agency formed by former Saatchi & Saatchi founder Maurice Saatchi.

The Publicis-FCB alliance ground to a halt in 1995, when FCB changed its name to True North and announced its intention to create its own network of agencies. Publicis demanded to be released from the alliance, and in 1996, the two agencies reached agreement to separate. In 1997, the separation was finalized, with Publicis taking 100 percent ownership of the former Publicis-FCB European network, renamed Publicis Europe. Publicis was also freed to enter True North's Latin American and Asian territories, as well as to consolidate its position in North America. The agency moved quickly, purchasing interests in agencies in Singapore, the Philippines, Brazil, Mexico, and Canada. Marcel Bleustein-Blanchet, the father of French advertising, died in April 1996 at the age of 89.

GLOBAL LEADER IN THE 2000S

Marcel Levy took over as head of the company and launched Publicis on a new expansion drive that raised the company into the top ranks of the global advertising industry. With the end of the True North alliance, Publicis targeted entry into the United States, making a bid for Bozell, Jacobs, Kenyon & Eckhardt. Yet the company quickly found itself in a hotly contested battle with True North, ultimately losing to its one-time partner. The loss, however, set the stage for a flurry of U.S. acquisitions by Publicis, including Hal Riney & Partners and the Evans Group in 1998, Gramercy Group, Lobsenz/Stevens, and a 49 percent stake in Burrell Communications, a specialist in advertising for the African-American population, acquired in 1999.

The company's U.S. push continued into 2000, with the additions of Frankel & Co., Fallon McElligott (later Fallon Worldwide), DeWitt Media, and Winner & Associates. In the meantime, the company had also continued its expansion elsewhere in the world, buying up Mojo Partners in Australia and New Zealand in 1997, Capurro in Argentina, Unitros in Chile, and Casadevall-Pedren in Spain in 1998, and, in 1999, Welcomm (South Korea) and AMA (Philippines). The company also moved into China and India that year, establishing subsidiaries in both countries.

The breakup of Saatchi & Saatchi into Cordiant Communications and the "new" Saatchi & Saatchi set the stage for the tightening of the relationship between the "two Maurices." By 2001, the companies had agreed to merge Saatchi & Saatchi into Publicis, with Saatchi & Saatchi becoming one of Publicis's core global advertising networks. In that year, also, Publicis merged its two media buying groups, Optimedia and Zenithmedia to form a new worldwide powerhouse, Zenith-Optimedia. Publicis then acquired full control of Zenith-Optimedia.

By 2002, Levy was ready to shift Publicis into high gear. In March of that year, Publicis announced that it had reached an agreement to acquire Bcom3 in a deal worth more than $3 billion. The addition of Bcom3 brought two new global advertising networks into the Publicis fold, Leo Burnett and D'Arcy, and also elevated Publicis into the fourth place position in the worldwide advertising industry. As part of that deal, Publicis also entered into a relationship with Japanese leader Dentsu, a major shareholder in Bcom3, which agreed to pay nearly $500 million for a 15 percent stake in Publicis instead. Publicis and Dentsu cemented their relationship the following year, creating an international sports marketing joint venture, International Sports Entertainment, or iSe. That company got off to a good start, landing the contract for the 2006 FIFA World Cup, to be held in Germany.

By 2004, Publicis's revenues neared $5 billion. Yet the company appeared in no hurry to slow down its expansion. In June 2005, Publicis reached an agreement to acquire 50.1 percent of U.K.-based Freud Communications, one of that country's leading independent consumer public relations operations. Also that year, the company expanded its presence in Spain, acquiring the Pharmaconsult Healthcare publishing company. Publicis also stepped up its interest in building a position in the vast Indian market, one of the fastest-growing in the world, behind that of China. In August of that year, the company announced a proposal to buy up Delhi-based Solutions Integrated Marketing. In less than a decade, Publicis had succeeded in joining the top ranks of the worldwide advertising industry.

Updated, M. L. Cohen

PRINCIPAL SUBSIDIARIES

Bartle Bogle Hegarty Limited; Bcom3 (U.S.A.); Burrell Communications Group, LLC; Cartwright Williams Direct; D'Arcy Masius Benton & Bowles (U.S.A.); Fallon Worldwide; Freud Communications (U.K.); The Kaplan Thaler Group, Ltd.; Leo Burnett Worldwide, Inc. (U.S.A.); Mojo Partners (Australia); Publicis Welcomm (South Korea); Saatchi & Saatchi (U.K.); Zenith-Optimedia; Starcom MediaVest.

PRINCIPAL COMPETITORS

McCann-Erickson Worldwide Inc.; Ogilvy and Mather Worldwide Inc.; Aegis Group PLC; WPP Group USA Inc.; Young and Rubicam Inc.; Omnicom Group Inc.; Regian and Wilson/Grey Worldwide; BBDO Worldwide Inc.; WPP Group plc; Leo Burnett Worldwide.

FURTHER READING

Bleustein-Blanchet, Marcel, *The Rage to Persuade*, New York: Chelsea House, 1982.

Bozonnet, Jean Jacques, "Publicis Regie Son Conflit avec L'Americain True North," *Le Monde*, February 21, 1997.

Doyere, Josee, and Yves Marie Labe, "La Mort du Dernier Empereur de la Publicité," *Le Monde*, April 13, 1996.

"France's Marcel Bleustein-Blanchet: The Ad Man Who Built 'Publicis,'" *Printer's Ink*, August 7, 1958, p. 46.

Labe, Yves Marie, "Numero Un Européen, Publicis S'Implante au Mexique et au Bresil," *Le Monde*, August 20, 1996.

Negreanu, Gerard, "Le Point Bas Est Atteint," *La Vie Française*, March 19, 1994.

———, and Virginie Savin, "Publicis–Maurice Levy," *La Vie Française*, December 4, 1993.

Subramanian, Dilip, "A Eulogy for France's Advertising Patriarch," *Marketing (Canada)*, May 6, 1996, p. 5.

Raymond Ltd.

————————————■————————————

Plot 156/H No. 2
ZadgaonRatnagiri, 415 612
India
Telephone: +91 2352 492 1917
Fax: +91 2352 492 3851
Web site: http://www.raymondindia.com

Public Company
Incorporated: 1925
Employees: 10,000
Sales: INR 173.07 billion ($5.8 billion) (2005)
Stock Exchanges: Mumbai London
Ticker Symbol: RYMDQ
NAIC: 313210 Broadwoven Fabric Mills; 315111 Sheer
  Hosiery Mills; 315191 Outerwear Knitting Mills

■ ■ ■

Raymond Ltd. is one of India's, and the world's, leading producers of worsted fabrics, claiming some 60 percent of the Indian worsted suiting market. The company's Textiles division, which accounts for 50 percent of group turnover, produces more than 25 million meters of wool and wool-blended fabrics each year, placing the company at number three worldwide. Raymond is a major supplier to the global textile industry, providing fabrics and completed garments to more than 50 countries, including the North American, European, Middle East, and Japanese markets. The company is also a major fabric innovator, and is one of just two or three manufacturers in the world capable of producing the Super 210s and Super 220s grades of pure wool, made from 13.2 micron

and 12.69 micron wool, respectively. In the mid-2000s, Raymond also has been investing heavily in the production of denim; in 2005, the company raised its installed capacity to more than 30 million meters of ring denim, and boosted capacity by another ten million meters in early 2006. Denim sales accounted for 15 percent of group sales in 2005.

Raymond has long been an integrated textiles group, including production of its own branded clothing—under the Raymond, Parx, and Manzoni names—as well as retail distribution through an India-wide network of more than 320 stores, including nearly 20 Be designer clothing stores. The company also acquired ColorPlus in 2004, giving it control of one of India's leading casual-wear brands. Garment sales contributed more than 20 percent of the company's sales in 2005. Other Raymond operations include a 50 percent stake in the J.K. Ansell joint venture, which produces condoms under the Kama Sutra brand. Raymond also controls J.K. Files & Tools, the world's leading producer of files and rasps. Raymond itself is the flagship of the Singhania Group, a chemicals producer. The company is led by CEO Gautam Hari Singhania, great-grandson of the company's founder. Raymond is listed on several stock exchanges in India, including the Mumbai (Bombay) Stock Exchange.

BRANCHING INTO TEXTILES IN THE 1920S

Raymond stemmed from the founding of the Wadia Woollen Mill along the Thane creek in Maharashtra, near Bombay, in the early part of the 20th century. The

COMPANY PERSPECTIVES

Excellence is a way of life at Raymond that has been manifested in all our endeavours over our entire history. These endeavours have been translated into designing and developing products of international standards, delivering enhanced values through brand building, distribution and customer relationship. Raymond today, is a culmination of untiring human efforts based on the fabric of values.

mill was later acquired by a wealthy industrialist family, the Sassoons, who were based in Bombay. The Sassoons reincorporated the company as Raymond Woollen Mill in 1925. Raymond's production was at the time limited to coarse woolen blankets and low-priced wool fabrics.

The Singhania family entered Raymond's picture in the 1940s. Led by Juggilal Singhania and his son Kamlapat Singhania, the Singhanias had been building their own industrial empire, the J.K. Group of companies, in the Kanpur region. Although involved in a number of activities, chemicals, particularly the production of textile dyes, became something of a family focus. In the 1940s, the family, then led by Kailashpat Singhania, grandson of the company's founder, began looking for further expansion possibilities, particularly in the Bombay area. The company's interest turned to the textile sector, a natural extension of its other operations. In 1944, the Singhanias purchased the Raymond Woollen Mill, keeping its name, and building it into one of the most well-known names in the Indian textile and clothing industry.

Kailashpat Singhania became determined to raise the mill's production beyond its cheap woolen blankets, and began investing in technology improvements through the 1950s. While the company continued to produce blankets, it introduced new wool grades and colors. At the same time, Raymond launched its own research and development to create new wool-based fabrics. This effort resulted in the launch of the company's first new wool type, Terool, a wool-blended yarn, in 1958.

That year also marked Raymond's first venture into the retail market. In 1958, the company opened its first showroom, in Mumbai in the J.K. Building. The first store was called King's Corner. The company's publicity efforts in the 1950s and into the 1960s, based on the "Chess King" motif, reflected the group's focus on a higher-end, upwardly mobile market. Later, in the 1960s and into the 1970s, the company adapted its advertising

for the times, shifting its advertising focus to an "ordinary man" character. The company later enjoyed advertising success with its "Guide to the well dressed male" in the 1980s, which was followed by the launch of a new campaign, for "The Complete Man" in the 1990s and 2000s. The company later changed its retail store name to Raymond Shops. By the 2000s, there were more than 320 Raymond shops in operation in more than 150 cities.

In the late 1960s, Raymond's research and development effort paid off again, with the launch of a new fabric type, Trovine, in 1968. The material represented a breakthrough in the wool industry, providing a lightweight fabric for cooler garments and enabling wool to be worn year-round, including during the hot Indian summers. In the meantime, Raymond, which remained focused especially on the textile market, moved to boost its operations in the clothing sector, founding subsidiary Raymond Apparel in 1969. From this beginning, the Raymond-branded line became one of the biggest-selling clothing brands in India.

INDUSTRIAL GROUP IN THE 1980S

The arrival of a new generation of Singhanias at the head of the family empire signaled a new era for the company. Vijayapat Singhania, who formally took over the company in 1980, became credited with developing the company into a modern, industrial group. The company's new strategy involved building its capacity and its technology to become a world-class textile producer. The company took a first step in this direction in 1979, when it began construction of a new factory in Jalgaon. The company added a third mill, in Chindwara, in 1992. By the 2000s, Singhania's production had topped 25 million meters of worsted fabric per year, placing it as one of the world's top three producers.

While continuing to target growth in the textile sector, Vijayapat Singhania became determined to develop Raymond into a diversified industrial conglomerate. The company entered the cement production market, and later added a unit producing files and rasps, developing that business, J.K. Files & Tools, into a world leader. In 1984, the company added the manufacture of automobile components, later brought together into Ring Plus Aqua Limited, in a joint venture with Osaka Pump Company of Japan, in 1998.

Yet textiles remained at Raymond's heart. In 1985, the company extended its reach in the clothing sector with the launch of the Park Avenue brand. That line initially consisted of formalwear, including suits, jackets, trousers, shirts, woolen knitwear, and accessories. In

KEY DATES

1925: Raymond Woollen Mill, a producer of woolen blankets, is incorporated to take over a wool mill in Thane, Maharashtra, India.

1944: J.K. Singhania Company and the Singhania family acquire Raymond and it begins expanding production into higher-grade wools and textiles.

1958: Raymond opens its first retail store, King's Corner (later Raymond Shops) in Bombay; a new wool blend, Terool, is introduced.

1968: The company introduces a new lightweight wool, Trovine.

1969: A clothing subsidiary, Raymond Apparel, is established.

1980: Vijayapat Singhania becomes head of the company and begins industrial diversification.

1985: The company launches the Park Avenue clothing brand.

1990: The first foreign Raymond shop opens in Oman.

1991: The company launches production of condoms through a subsidiary.

1995: Steel production begins.

1996: Condom production is merged into a joint venture with Ansell International.

1999: The company launches the Parx casualwear brand.

2000: Gautam Hari Singhania becomes head of the company and leads a restructuring to focus on textile and clothing sales.

2002: Raymond sells its steel operations as part of the divestment of much of the company's noncore businesses; the Be ready-to-wear designer retail format is launched.

2003: The ColorPlus casual brand is acquired.

2005: The company opens its first Manzoni and Park Avenue retail stores; production of denim is expanded to 30 million tons.

2006: Denim production is expected to top 40 million tons.

1986, the company expanded the Park Avenue line to include a range of ready-to-wear business clothing. The Park Avenue brand was later broadened with the addition of a casualwear range, under the Parx label, introduced in 1999. The company also took its first step on the international retail scene, opening its first foreign Raymond shop, in Oman, in 1990.

At the same time, Raymond maintained its technological edge, introducing a number of new fabric types in the 1990s. These included the superfine pure wool collection, Lineage, in 1995, which was followed by the Renaissance collection in 1996, featuring merino wool blended with polyester and other specialty fibers. The company added extra-fine cashmere and merino wool blends, called the Chairman's Collection, in 1999. In 2000, Raymond debuted its PV Lycra-based suiting material as well. Then in 2003 and 2004, the company became one of only two or three manufacturers in the world capable of producing the new Super 210s and Super 220s grades of wool.

Raymond in the meantime had begun production of apparel of a different sort. In the early 1990s, the company, through subsidiary J.K. Chemicals, launched production of Kama Sutra-branded condoms. In 1996, Raymond merged its condom production into a new joint venture company, J.K. Ansell. The company's partner in the new operation was Ansell International, one of the world's leading producers of latex-based condoms, gloves, and other products.

By then, too, the company's diversified interests had led it to enter the steel industry. In 1995, the company formed a technical partnership with Allegheny Ludlum Corp., based in the United States, to produce high value-added and specialty cold-rolled close annealed and silicon steel products. For this effort, the company set up a plant at Igatpuri. The company invested heavily in boosting its production, and by 1999, the steel division accounted for 20 percent of Raymond's total revenues.

In the meantime, the company's interests in diversified businesses had taken it to the skies, literally. In 1996, the company formed a new Aviation division, and launched its own air charter service, Million Air. That company then built up a small fleet, including an executive jet and three helicopters.

REFOCUSING ON TEXTILES IN THE 2000S

Vijayapat Singhania retired in 2000, making way for his son, Gautam Hari Singhania. The younger Singhania followed in the family's tradition by immediately steering Raymond into a new direction. In the early 2000s, Singhania restructured the company, selling off most of its diversified interests, including its cement division and, in 2002, its steel operations, to refocus the company as a clothing and textiles business.

Another Raymond textiles operation took center stage at the start of the 21st century, as the company moved to boost its production of denim, and especially high-quality ring denim. Part of this expansion was directed to the launch of the Parx brand in 1999, which featured denim clothing in its collection. The bulk of the group's denim production, however, was meant to fuel the booming global demand for the fabric. Into the mid-2000s, the company launched a strong expansion effort, boosting its denim production capacity to 16 million tons annually.

The ending of export quotas by the World Trade Organization at the beginning of 2005 encouraged Raymond to boost its denim production still further. The company launched a new investment effort, driving up production past 30 million tons by the end of that year. Further investments were expected to boost the group's total denim production capacity to more than 40 million tons by early 2006. Already, the company had begun to position itself for further growth in its international sales, buying out Regency Textile Portuguesa Limitada in 2003. That acquisition gave the company production facilities both in Portugal and in Spain, forming the launch pad for the group's expansion into the European market.

While textile production remained a centerpiece of Raymond's operations, the company's focus fell especially on its determination to transform itself into a leading producer of brand name clothing. As part of this effort, the company launched a new luxury brand, Manzoni. The company supported this launch with the opening of an exclusive Manzoni retail showroom in New Delhi in 2005. Raymond also opened its first Park Avenue shops that year.

In the meantime, the company had continued to develop its brand family, notably with the acquisition of ColorPlus in 2003. That purchase gave the company control of one of India's leading casualwear brands to supplement the Parx brand, which had been struggling to gain a significant share of the Indian market. More successful for the group was its launch of the Be retail designer clothing collection in 2002. By 2005, the company had opened 16 Be stores and had attracted a number of India's prominent designers. Raymond had become one of the most prominent names in the Indian and global textile industries.

M. L. Cohen

PRINCIPAL SUBSIDIARIES

Celebrations Apparel Limited; ColorPlus Fashions Limited (75%); Everblue Apparel Limited; Hindustan Files Limited; J.K. (England) Limited; J.K. Ansell Limited (50%); J.K. Helene Curtis Limited; Jaykayorg AG (Switzerland); P.T. Jaykay Files (Indonesia; 39.20%); Pashmina Holdings Limited; Plugin Sales Limited (60%); Raymond Apparel Limited; Regency Texteis Portuguesa, Limitada Portugal; Silver Spark Apparel Limited; Textiles Regency, Sociedad Limitada (Spain).

PRINCIPAL COMPETITORS

National Textile Corporation Ltd.; Rai Saheb Rekhchand Mohta Spg and Wvg Ltd.; Elgin Mills Ltd.; Ayyappan Textiles Ltd.; Super Polyfabriks Ltd.; APR Ltd.; Grasim Industries Ltd.; Howrah Mills Company Ltd.; Swan Mills Ltd.; Sree Valliappa Textiles Ltd.; Century Textiles and Industries Ltd.; Bombay Silk Mills Ltd.; Arvind Mills Ltd.; Maniyar Plast Ltd.; Birla Corporation Ltd.

FURTHER READING

"The Complete Man: Gautam Hari Singhania," *India Business Insight*, December 9, 2002.

Dobhal, Shailesh, "The Complete Feeling," *Business Today (India)*, October 13, 2002.

"India's Raymond Ltd. Raises Investment in Zambaiti JV," *AsiaPulse News*, April 1, 2005.

Menon, Shyam G., "Raymond Ready to Weave Magic in Foreign Markets," *Business Line*, April 10, 2002.

Mukherjee, Ambarish, "Raymond Exiting Steel," *Business Line*, April 4, 2004.

Peter, Anna, "Raymond Sees Scope in Fabric-to-Garment Biz," *Business Line*, March 12, 2004.

"Raymond Stitches Denim Strategy for International, Local Markets," *India Business Insight*, March 13, 2003.

"Raymond to Buy Auto Parts Co.," *Business Line*, July 13, 2005.

"Raymond to Buy Foreign Women's Wear Brand," *IRIS News Digest*, November 29, 2005.

"Raymond to Invest Rs 100-cr in South Gujarat," *IRIS News Digest*, December 6, 2005.

"Raymond to Set Up Joint Venture with Italian Woollen Fabric Co.," *Business Line*, June 10, 2005.

"Raymond Weaves Overseas Plans," *India Business Insight*, November 19, 2004.

"A Stitch in Time," *India Business Insight*, November 11, 2002.

Verma, Virenda, "Raymond Up on Brand Strength," *Business Line*, September 2, 2003.

Rocawear Apparel LLC

1411 Broadway
New York, New York 10018
U.S.A.
Telephone: (201) 601-4283
Toll Free: (800) 839-6016
Fax: (201) 617-8686
Web site: http://www.rocawear.com

Private Company
Founded: 1999
Employees: 200
Sales: $700 million (2005 est.)
NAIC: 315119 Other Hosiery and Sock Mills; 315191 Outerwear Knitting Mills; 315192 Underwear and Nightwear Knitting Mills; 315211 Men's and Boy's Cut and Sew Apparel Contractors; 315212 Women's, Girls', and Infants' Cut and Sew Apparel Contractors; 315299 All Other Cut and Sew Apparel Manufacturing; 315999 Other Apparel Accessories and Other Apparel Manufacturing; 316219 Other Footwear Manufacturing; 316992 Women's Handbag and Purse Manufacturing; 316993 Personal Leather Good (Except Women's Handbag and Purse) Manufacturing

■ ■ ■

Rocawear Apparel LLC sells urban and upscale clothing for men, women, teens, and children including jeans, jerseys, footwear, outerwear, headwear, sportswear, jewelry, accessories, and loungewear. Once part of the entertainment empire known as The Roc, Rocawear underwent a change in ownership in late 2005 when Damon Dash sold his interest to partners including rap superstar Jay-Z. Rocawear's increasingly popular brands include State Property (fronted by rapper Beanie Sigel), Team Roc sportswear for Foot Locker, C. Ronson by club D.J. Charlotte Ronson, limited edition Pro-Keds with Stride Rite Corporation, and high-end jewelry and watches with Tiffany & Company. Rocawear is sold at department and specialty stores throughout North America, Asia, and Europe.

IN THE BEGINNING: LATE 1990S

The story of Rocawear is deeply embedded in the hip-hop world, with the rise of rapper Jay-Z who wanted unique, stylish clothes to wear on tour and in his music videos. Longtime friend Damon Dash, who had worked with Jay-Z and Kareem Burke to form Roc-A-Fella Records in 1995, believed an urban clothing line with Jay-Z as its front man was a solid business opportunity. Few retailers carried urban clothes; fewer still actually knew what they were. Though designer Tommy Hilfiger had begun designing clothes with an urban appeal, Damon and Jay-Z not only knew the hip-hop style of life but lived it every day. With backing from several investors, Rocawear was established in 1999 as a wholly owned subsidiary of the growing Roc-A-Fella Enterprises.

At Rocawear, Dash handled the business end while Jay-Z and Burke, known as "Biggs" in the rap world, continued to write and perform music, wearing the apparel. A key factor in the success of the firm was Dash and Jay-Z's contacts in the music world and the relatively new use of co-branding. Soon after the company began,

Dash brought singer Charlotte Ronson into the fold. Ronson wanted to design her own clothing line, but had no experience or knowledge of the apparel industry. She signed with Rocawear for financial backing and distribution, so the 21-one-year-old Ronson was able to concentrate on the creative aspects of the business.

HITTING THE STREETS: 2000-03

In 2000 Rocawear signed a deal with Midway Games and Playstation2 (owned by Sony) to design clothing for the "Afro Thunder" character from the popular video game "Ready 2 Rumble." The new apparel line, sold in Macy's stores, debuted late in the year and gained popularity with subsequent Rumble game releases.

Another branding opportunity came with the early 2002 release of the new film *State Property*, starring Roc-A-Fella Records rapper Beanie Sigel. The film, produced by Roc-A-Fella Pictures and Lion's Gate Films, was an urban crime drama featuring a new apparel line by Rocawear. The apparel collection was aptly titled State Property, of which Sigel was offered an interest. The Philadelphia-based Sigel and fellow rappers wore Rocawear's clothing in the film, while performing, and in the announced sequel.

By mid-year Dash and a crew were in Paris shooting an ad campaign, featuring the new State Property line and Rocawear's other apparel. Models, rappers, and former Spice Girl Victoria Beckham shot on locations around the legendary City of Lights, in a campaign Dash hoped would appeal to European consumers. Rocawear also opened an office in Amsterdam to handle its international interests.

While Rocawear had firmly established itself in the United States as an urban "lifestyle" brand, racking up sales of about $120 million, Dash was bent on worldwide domination. To this aim, Rocawear unveiled a new slogan: "It's not where you're from, it's what you Roc," and relocated its offices from Seventh Avenue to a 35,000-square-foot showroom in New York City's garment district at the end of 2002. By the following year,

Charlotte Ronson's apparel line, C. Ronson, shot its first advertising campaign in the Rocawear showroom. Ronson had designed a new menswear line, and brought in her DJ brother Mark and twin sister Samantha, who was finishing an album for Roc-A-Fella Records, as part of the campaign. Rocawear's investment in the C. Ronson line had paid off, as her sales neared the $1 million mark.

Dash was on a roll in 2003 with the success of Rocawear and its various clothing lines (bringing in upwards of $300 million in sales), as well as Roc-A-Fella Records and Roc-A-Fella Films. Roc-A-Fella Records' musicians continually topped the rap charts while Roc-A-Fella Films was shooting *State Property 2* and other films. Ever ambitious, Dash created Roc Music, a new music label for pop, rock, and blues recordings, and launched a new quarterly lifestyle magazine called *America*.

Hoping to take his empire mainstream, Dash likened his magazine to a "multicultural *Vogue*." In addition, the brash entrepreneur told *Crain's New York Business* he planned on being a billionaire and "wanted to rule the world."

Other developments in 2003 included a deal with London's Selfridges department store to sell Rocawear, and signing model Naomi Campbell to join Victoria Beckham and her soccer superstar husband, David Beckham, as Rocawear representatives. Near the end of the year Rocawear formed its own marketing firm called Native/DBG, installing David Gensler as its chief executive. By creating the agency, Dash hoped to give Rocawear a more professional image and to work with more corporate partners.

EXPANSION AND TURMOIL: 2004

Rocawear's new image took several hits in early 2004 when Dash was embroiled in controversy and his carefully constructed Roc empire began to crumble. It had all started with rumors of Jay-Z's retirement and possible hiring as chief executive at Def Jam Recordings, which owned half of Roc-A-Fella Records. During the year, Def Jam offered to buy out Jay-Z, Dash, and Burke's shares of Roc-A-Fella. The partners received $10 million and Roc-A-Fella became a wholly owned subsidiary of Def Jam.

Around the same time as the buyout, Dash was slapped with a lawsuit by a former model who claimed he had raped her. Next came a meltdown of Rocawear's new marketing firm, with Dash firing most of the staff and dissolving the agency after a dispute with Gensler. Dash then hired Roy Edmundson, formerly of Levi Strauss, as a vice-president to handle all of Rocawear's marketing and public relations, not an easy task with

KEY DATES

1995: Roc-A-Fella Records is founded by Damon Dash, Kareem Burke, and Jay-Z.

1999: Rocawear, a hip-hop "lifestyle" brand of apparel, is founded in New York City.

2000: Rocawear launches a new clothing line based on Ready 2 Rumble's Afro Thunder character.

2001: Beanie Sigel fronts a new Rocawear collection called State Property.

2002: The company opens an office in Amsterdam.

2003: Dash, Jay-Z, and Burke sell their interest in Roc-A-Fella Records to Def Jam Recordings.

2004: Rocawear begins selling luxury jewelry, accessories, and specially designed Pro-Keds shoes.

2005: Dash sells his stake in Rocawear, but retains majority ownership of State Property and other ventures.

Dash's legal woes and the upcoming incarceration of Beanie Sigel, front man of the booming State Property apparel line, on federal weapons charges.

Rumors were soon flying about a rift between Dash and Jay-Z, who were still partners of Rocawear. The tension reached a fever pitch when Jay-Z became president and CEO of Def Jam. Part of the deal included a stake in Roc-A-Fella Records, without his founding partners. Jay-Z's new ownership in Roc-A-Fella upset Dash and Burke. To make amends and keep the peace for their other business interests, like Rocawear, it was reported Jay-Z offered his share of Roc-A-Fella back to Dash and Burke if they would give him sole rights to his first album for Roc-A-Fella, *Reasonable Doubt.*

Though it has been said Dash agreed to this offer, Burke did not. The rumored rift was now full blown, with Jay-Z on one side and Dash and Burke on the other. Throughout the drama, however, Rocawear continued to thrive. In 2004 Rocawear expanded its branding to include outerwear through a deal with Brandon Thomas Designs, renowned for its washable suede jackets and coats; introduced its first sock collection with New York's Gina Hosiery; and rolled out a "bling" (jewelry) line called Tiret, consisting of watches and a variety of gem-encrusted accessories selling at New York City's famed Tiffany & Company. This bling, however, was only for high rollers with prices starting at $20,000 or more. In addition, Rocawear acquired the licensing rights to Stride Rite Corporation's Pro-Keds

and planned to design a limited edition collection for the State Property apparel line. Rocawear also prepared for the launch of a sportswear line called Team Roc, to be sold initially at Foot Locker stores in Los Angeles and New York, then at Macy's department stores.

Ironically, Rocawear unveiled an advertising campaign called "La Familia" in mid-year, including Dash's sister Stacey, an actress, his two children, and a roster of rappers from Roc-A-Fella Records. Dash told the *Daily News Record* (May 10, 2004), "In the umbrella of Roc, everyone is family. It's more than just a business, it's more than just friends. All the artists look out for each other."

While his words might have characterized the campaign, Dash's personal and professional relationships were fraught with discord. In November he fired Edmondson, his vice-president of marketing, and a dozen other staff members less than a year after dissolving Rocawear's in-house marketing agency. While some staffers commented to the *Daily News Record* (November 29, 2004) that Dash was difficult to work with and irrational, he told the magazine, "Not many people can understand my business, and I have high expectations."

THE FUTURE OF ROCAWEAR, 2005 AND BEYOND

By early 2005 one of Rocawear's partners, RyanKenny, discontinued their business relationship, less than a year after Rocawear had parted ways with the Nesi Apparel Group. RyanKenny reportedly disapproved of Rocawear's use of Malaysian factories to produce its apparel, though it was never confirmed by either party.

On the positive side, Rocawear's Pro-Keds collection was selling well and Dash announced an apparel and footwear collaboration with Patricia Field. Field's designs would be part of a collection called the House of Rocawear, featuring retro-glam styling. In addition, Rocawear was selling well in the United Kingdom, with slimmer tops and less baggy bottoms to compete with Diesel and other London fashion houses. *State Property 2,* starring Beanie Sigel, hit theaters in April just after his latest album went on sale. Sigel was not making public appearances, since he was behind bars, but his notoriety only increased sales for both the movie and Rocawear's State Property apparel line.

By September 2005 Dash was no longer willing to work with his partners, primarily Jay-Z, at Rocawear. He sold his interest in Rocawear, which had reached sales of over $700 million worldwide, for a total of about $30 million, with $22.5 million in cash and control of the State Property, Team Roc, and other brands. Dash maintained the breakup was due to philosophical differences. He commented to *Daily News Record* (December 15, 2005), "My vision for Rocawear was a colorless one. Jay and the other partners want to cater more to the pure urban demographic, and that's not the direction I wanted to go anymore." When asked if he was bitter, Dash said, "It was a beautiful experience … . I never thought I could have made so much money so quickly, and I have no doubt Rocawear will continue to be successful."

Dash vowed to move on to bigger and better projects, though the remarkable success of Roc-A-Fella Records and Rocawear were a hard act to follow.

Roacwear conducted its business as usual after Dash's departure, showcasing its wares at a mini showroom during New York City's "7th on Sixth" semi-annual fashion extravaganza. Rocawear's partners, Jay-Z, Alex Bize, and Norton Cher, planned further European expansion for 2006, to launch new women's and teen collections, and to promote its RocBox, an alternative to Apple Computer's phenomenally popular iPod.

Nelson Rhodes

PRINCIPAL COMPETITORS

Diesel SpA; FUBU; Phat Fashions LLC; Tommy Hilfiger Corporation; Ecko Unlimited Inc.; TKO Apparel, Inc.

FURTHER READING

Bailey, Lee, "Damon Dash Sells Stake in Rocawear," *Daily News Record*, September 26, 2005, p. 1.

———, "It's Time for Urban Renewal," *Daily News Record*, February 14, 2005, p. 38.

———, "Roc Heads Roll," *Daily News Record*, November 29, 2004, p. 72.

Burney, Ellen, "Hip-Hop Style Hits London Streets," *WWD*, January 22, 2004, p. 13.

Carofano, Jennifer, "Just Dashing," *Footwear News*, April 18, 2005, p. 18.

Croghan, Lore, "Clothing Designers Sew Up Space in Showroom Building," *Crain's New York Business*, August 12, 2002, p. 11.

DeCarlo, Lauren, "Dash Cashes Out of Rocawear," *WWD*, September 26, 2005, p. 11.

———, "Hip-Hop's Rising Heat," *WWD*, September 13, 2004, p. 1.

"Fourteen Innovators," *Fortune*, November 15, 2004, p. 192.

Greenberg, Julie, "Rocawear's Family Affair," *WWD*, May 6, 2004, p. 10.

———, "Ronson's Family Affair," *WWD*, July 17, 2003, p. 10.

Greene, Joshua, "Paris Rocs," *WWD*, August 8, 2002, p. 2B.

"Hip Hop Culture Comes to Town: Interview with Damon Dash," *Marketing*, August 4, 2004, p. 17.

"Hip Hop Impresario Damon Dash Plans UK Assault," *Marketing*, August 4, 2004, p. 1.

Mitchell, Gail, "Dash Sets Goals for Life After Roc," *Billboard*, April 9, 2005, p. 21.

Pallay, Jessica, "All in the Family Business," *Daily News Record*, May 10, 2004, p. 6.

Thompson, Stephanie, "Ex-Levi's Exec Takes Reins at Rocawear Unit," *Advertising Age*, April 19, 2004, p. 3.

———, "Roca Breakout Dogged by Rap's Rap," *Advertising Age*, February 2, 2004, p. 1.

Touré, "The Book of Jay," *Rolling Stone*, December 15, 2005, p. 81.

Rohm and Haas Company

100 Independence Mall West
Philadelphia, Pennsylvania 19106-2399
U.S.A.
Telephone: (215) 592-3000
Fax: (215) 592-3377
Web site: http://www.rohmhaas.com

Public Company
Incorporated: 1917
Employees: 16,691
Sales: $7.3 billion (2004)
Stock Exchanges: New York
Ticker Symbol: ROH
NAIC: 311940 Seasoning and Dressing Manufacturing;
325211 Plastics Material and Resin Manufacturing;
325188 All Other Inorganic Chemical Manufacturing; 325510 Paint and Coating Manufacturing;
325520 Adhesive Manufacturing

■ ■ ■

Positioning itself as a specialty materials company, Rohm and Haas Company focuses on three main areas: specialty chemicals, electronic materials, and salt. Among the company's six business groups, the one focusing on coatings for paints and various consumer goods is the largest, generating about one-third of sales. Performance chemicals, including antimicrobials, ion-exchange resins, and plastic additives, contribute another 22 percent, while monomers, including acrylates and methacrylates, generate about 19 percent of Rohm and Haas's revenues. Approximately 17 percent of sales occur in connection with electronic materials, such as those used in integrated circuits and semiconductor chips. Contributing about 10 percent of revenues each are the adhesives and sealants group and the salt group, the latter of which includes the Morton brand salt business. Perhaps best known historically for the invention of Plexiglas, a product it no longer makes, Rohm and Haas has grown since its early twentieth-century founding into a wide-ranging global business with some 100 manufacturing and 37 research facilities in 27 countries. Nearly half of the company's revenues are booked outside North America, with Europe responsible for 26 percent; the Asia-Pacific region, 18 percent; and Latin America, 4 percent. The Haas family, descendants of one of the company's two founders, continue to control a substantial ownership interest of nearly 30 percent.

ORIGINS IN LEATHER SOFTENING

The story of Rohm and Haas begins in 1904 when a German man named Otto Röhm noticed that the stench from the local tannery was similar to the smell of the gas water produced by the Stuttgart Gas Works, where he was dissatisfied with his job as an analytical chemist. The bad odor of the gas water came from the combination of carbon dioxide and ammonia, and Röhm wondered if these chemicals could be used to soften (bate) leather. At the time, tanners bated leather as they had for centuries, with fermented canine feces which varied in composition and hence yielded inconsistent results. The unpredictability of the bating process, coupled with the inherently disgusting nature of the bating agent, made tanners eager to break with tradition.

COMPANY PERSPECTIVES

At Rohm and Haas imagination means exploring the frontiers of technology—pushing beyond conventional boundaries to create products once thought impossible. Imagination is information racing at the speed of light through electronic devices, microscopic light-reflecting polymers protecting skin from harmful solar rays, and adhesives helping buildings stand firm above violently shaking earthquake ground. These are just glimpses of the imagination of Rohm and Haas.

From extending the freshness in fruits and vegetables to purifying antibiotics, we help customers create products that enhance the way of life for people around the world. Today Rohm and Haas extends to the far corners of the earth, with sales in more than 100 countries. As a global company we meet fast-changing market requirements with advancements in technology and progressive thinking—yet always with respect and understanding for local custom and need.

As the leading producer of specialty materials with revolutionary developments in everything from electronic materials and polymers for paints to personal care products, Rohm and Haas will continue to bring innovation to market, imagining new possibilities to help you succeed in yours. Let us Imagine the Possibilities with you.

Nevertheless, not even the German chemical industry, the most advanced in the world at the time, understood the chemical nature of bating, and no satisfactory replacement for the bating agent had been discovered.

Hoping to make a name for himself in chemistry, Otto Röhm attempted to solve the problem. By 1906 he had developed a solution of gas water and salts that appeared to sufficiently soften leather. He then wrote to his friend Otto Haas, a young German who had immigrated to the United States a few years before. Haas agreed to join Röhm in his venture, with the understanding that Haas would bring the process back to the United States. The new bating agent was christened Oroh, derived from the two owners' initials.

By the time Haas returned to Germany, there was bad news waiting for him. Oroh was not performing as well as expected. The two men went back to the laboratory and studied the chemical process of bating, a process that had been debated a good deal in the leather industry. Röhm eventually concluded that the two prevailing schools of thought, the first, that the bating action was caused by bacteria and the second, that the action was caused by lime reacting with a bate, were both partially correct. Reaction with a bate removed the lime used to dehair the hide, and then something in the organic bate softened the hide. But what?

In 1907 Eduoard Buchner discovered enzymes, the chemical compounds from living cells that caused fermentation. Röhm saw the applicability of Buchner's Nobel prize-winning work to his own research on leather chemistry. He realized that enzymes in organic bate softened leather by decomposing it, while his product merely delimed it.

Röhm set out to isolate enzymes cheaply, and by 1907 had applied for a patent for a bate made with enzymes derived from animal pancreas. Combining his own initials with the Greek word for juice, Röhm called the solution Oropon. He then developed a technique to measure the strength of Oropon so that the solution could be sold in standard strengths.

That year Röhm and Haas legally formed a German company bearing their names and established their first plant in Esslingen, a city outside of Stuttgart. The first order of business was to manufacture large quantities of Oropon, which they made by squeezing animal pancreas in a manual press and collecting the juice.

As more tanneries began to use Oropon, Haas and Röhm were able to hire men to squeeze the pancreas for them, and turned their attention to marketing the product in Germany, England, and France. This early marketing effort established a style of salesmanship that still characterizes Rohm and Haas: technically proficient salesmen working closely with manufacturers. The company did so well that in 1909 Haas was able to return to open a branch in the United States. Because of the large number of tanneries in the area Haas decided to settle in Philadelphia.

By 1914 Haas was able to expand by opening a plant in Chicago in order to serve Midwestern tanners. His product line had increased to leather finishes, fat-liquors, and a mordant for dyeing. The timing of this expansion was fortunate since, with the advent of World War I, there was a dramatic need for leather chemicals to replace the ones that had come from Germany, still the world's leading chemical producer.

FORMATION OF THE U.S. ROHM AND HAAS IN 1917

Röhm and Haas's chemicals were needed for army boots, yet the firm's German origins meant that it was under

KEY DATES

1907: Otto Röhm and Otto Haas form a partnership in Esslingen, Germany, to make and sell a leather bate called Oropon.

1909: Haas, an earlier immigrant to the United States, returns there to open a branch office in Philadelphia.

1917: Haas incorporates the U.S. branch as Rohm and Haas Company, which is now legally separate from the German firm.

1935: A research associate at Röhm's laboratory accidentally discovers Plexiglas.

1982: Rohm and Haas enters the electronic materials field with purchase of 30 percent interest in Shipley Co. Inc.

1992: Company acquires full control of Shipley and also purchases Unocal Corporation's emulsion polymers business.

1998: Company divests its Plexiglas business.

1999: LeaRonal, Inc. and Morton International Inc. are acquired.

2001: Rohm and Haas sells its agricultural chemicals business to the Dow Chemical Company.

surveillance by the U.S. government. This was due to the fact that a few companies run by German-Americans were discovered to be in collaboration with the Kaiser's Germany. Although there was no evidence that Haas was a collaborator, the government nevertheless ordered that 50 percent of the company's stock (held jointly by the two owners) be sold to outsiders. A tanners' group, which was afraid of a disruption in the production of necessary leather chemicals, arranged to buy the shares, Röhm's stake, and become a friendly partner with the firm. At the same time, Haas incorporated the U.S. branch as Rohm and Haas Company, a separate company independent of the German firm (which itself evolved into Röhm GmbH, currently owned by Degussa AG).

While this legal maneuvering was taking place Rohm and Haas diversified into textile chemicals and then, in 1920, acquired one of its suppliers which was going out of business. That same year Haas purchased the North American rights to a German synthetic tanning agent and also supervised his company's expansion into synthetic insecticides. When the Great Depression began Rohm and Haas management's growth policies helped the company through this difficult period. The company expanded its product line but still concentrated on serving the leather and textile industries, which continued to produce goods albeit at a reduced rate throughout the Depression. This, coupled with Haas's policy of high liquidity and low dividend payments, meant that the company not only survived the Depression without layoffs but also managed to grow.

In 1927 Haas established a company called Resinous Products with a German scientist, Kurt Albert, who had developed a synthetic resin that was useful in making varnishes. Like Oropon this new product replaced a variable and unpredictable organic product. The new company was run separately from Rohm and Haas, and from its research into resins came a whole range of chemicals used in the coating and plywood industries.

Haas was satisfied with the success of his two business ventures but unhappy with the ownership agreement, so he arranged to purchase the shares held by the tanners' association and set up a trust for Röhm who had been deprived of his interest in Rohm and Haas Company.

1935 DISCOVERY OF PLEXIGLAS

Haas reaped many benefits from his continued association with Röhm. One of them was the introduction of Plexiglas, which was discovered by accident in Röhm's laboratory located in Darmstadt, Germany. Röhm had started his work with acrylics in 1927. He had originally intended them for use as drying oils in varnishes, but soon realized that they could also be used as a coating for safety glass. In 1935 one of his research associates was experimenting with an acrylic polymer to see if it would bind two sheets of glass. Instead of acting as an adhesive, however, the polymer dried into a lightweight, clear plastic sheet that was immediately considered a promising glass substitute.

It was another three years until Plexiglas could be manufactured inexpensively and applications for it found. Röhm himself experimented with various uses: he replaced the glass in his car and even the glass in his spectacles with Plexiglas. Among the many uses Röhm's researchers explored were musical instruments. One such instrument, the acrylic violin, while striking in appearance produced a terrible sound. The Plexiglas flute was more successful. The most important applications of Plexiglas, however, were not for see-through flutes but for airplanes.

It was through such frivolities as the acrylic violin that company researchers learned how to stretch and shape Plexiglas sheets into cockpit enclosures. By 1934, when these techniques were almost perfected, the Nazi government had placed restrictions on the transmission of technical reports abroad. Haas got around these restrictions by sending one of his own chemists from the United States over to the company's German laboratory and having this man memorize the technology.

The U.S. Army Air Force was immediately interested in Plexiglas because it was lightweight and durable, and the design of war planes was altered to take advantage of this new, shatterproof material. Rohm and Haas, anticipating the entrance of the United States into the war, enlarged its capacity to manufacture Plexiglas so that the discovery made in Nazi Germany could benefit the Allies.

During the war Plexiglas accounted for two-thirds of Rohm and Haas's sales. In the last year before the war, sales had reached $5.5 million and by the end of the war this figure had swelled to $43 million. Nevertheless, Plexiglas was not the company's only contribution to the war effort. In 1934 Herman Bruson, an employee hired by Haas, discovered a synthetic oil additive. It was not until the war that the significance of his discovery was revealed. Designers of military aircraft had difficulty finding a hydraulic fluid that would function at a sufficiently wide temperature range, until a review of potentially useful patents turned up Bruson's formula. Bruson often took credit for the Russian victory at Stalingrad because his hydraulic fluid kept Russian equipment from freezing, unlike the German hydraulic fluid, which was rendered useless by the cold.

When the war ended Rohm and Haas experienced a dramatic decrease in the demand for Plexiglas and, as a result, the company struggled to expand the civilian uses of acrylic polymers. Plexiglas began to be used for illuminated signs and car lights, along with additives for coatings and fuel. The company's major undertaking in the decade following the war was building a huge plant in Houston, Texas, that was used to make the ingredients for acrylics. Along with acrylics the company also attempted to increase its holdings in markets for insecticides and fungicides. Exports, especially fungicides, were used to expand the company's European markets, which Haas had previously left underdeveloped in order not to compete with his friend Röhm.

In 1959, the 50th year of Rohm and Haas's U.S. operation, Otto Haas retired, leaving the company in excellent shape. He was described as a hard-driving administrator who was, by turns, kind and unfair to his employees. One incident that typified Haas's attitude toward his employees took place during World War II when a new guard refused to allow Haas into a company munitions plant without a pass. Haas immediately fired the man and then rehired him the next day with a raise in pay. John Haas, Otto's son, was a less colorful pre-

sident. John's style of administration stressed teamwork among the top executives, while his father's administration had stressed obedience.

ILL-FATED 1960S AND 1970S DIVERSIFICATION

One of the first projects John Haas undertook was the ill-fated diversification into fibers and health products. At the time Rohm and Haas was the main producer of Plexiglas in the country, and had a successful product mix of paper, leather, textile, and agricultural chemicals. The expansion into fibers was motivated by the fear that one of the large chemical companies would challenge the company in the Plexiglas and acrylic emulsion markets that Rohm and Haas dominated. Yet the challenge from the major chemical companies never materialized, and it was the measures taken to prevent the company from being hurt that caused the damage. The new divisions, health and fibers, were profitable in only one of their 14 years of existence.

The fibers division was especially costly. The company intended to enter the crowded field through technological breakthroughs and specialized markets; this was how it had succeeded with leather chemicals and acrylics. The company had high hopes for a new synthetic fiber named Anim/8, which was supposed to give fabrics added stretch without altering their appearance. Anim/8 failed in part because Rohm and Haas misunderstood the nature of the fibers market. While an aerospace manufacturer might pay the higher dollar amount for a superior hydraulic fluid, consumers did not care that Anim/8 had slight advantages over its competitors, Spandex and Lycra, when it was 20 to 30 percent more costly. Secondly, Rohm and Haas entered the field just as women were abandoning girdles and other undergarments that were a major market for stretch fabrics. The coup de grace was the crash of the entire synthetic fabric industry in 1975 when, as company President Vincent Gregory said, "You couldn't give the stuff away."

BRIDESBURG TRAGEDY

Earnings were depressed in the late 1960s and early 1970s as the losses incurred by the two new divisions canceled out the gains made by specialty chemicals. The company's troubles were not only of a financial nature, however. In 1975, just as the synthetic fabric industry was reaching its nadir, Rohm and Haas was deluged with bad publicity surrounding the deaths of workers who were exposed to a carcinogenic chemical called BCME. In 1962 a suspicious pattern of lung cancer deaths emerged at the company's Bridesburg,

Pennsylvania, plant where resins for water purification purposes were produced. The company took measures to minimize employee exposure to chemicals at the plant, but its efforts were not sufficient. In 1974 the Health Research Group, founded by Ralph Nader, accused Rohm and Haas of concealing the dangers at the plant, 54 employees of which had died of cancer, probably induced by BCME.

Vincent Gregory, who had become president in 1970, was confronted with a difficult situation. Not only did he have a public relations fiasco on his hands, but he also had to accept some of the blame for the company's financial situation since he should have divested Rohm and Haas of the fiber and health divisions immediately upon his appointment. By 1975 the company began to lose money and there was speculation that Gregory would be relieved of his duties. However, the chairman of the board, John Haas, assumed his share of the blame for having started the ill-fated diversification into areas that were unfamiliar to the company. The board decided that Gregory had had "an expensive education," and retained him to help revitalize the company.

1980S TURNAROUND

The solution to the company's difficulties turned out to be a combination of cost-cutting (including extensive layoffs), the sale of unprofitable plants, and a few judicious acquisitions. One acquisition was the Borg-Warner PVC modifier plant (the modifiers make PVC more malleable), a business that was inexpensive to purchase but that had not been profitable for a period of time. Rohm and Haas, with its experience in plastics, returned the plant to profitability by 1982, a year after it was purchased for $35 million.

The company decided to keep its slow-growing but profitable staples such as Plexiglas and paint and floor finishes. For faster growth it turned to herbicides, which the company started working with in the 1930s. A herbicide called Blazer, used on soybeans, had the largest sales in its specialized market. By building on its experience with resins Rohm and Haas made coatings for electronic components a part of its product line through the purchase of a 30 percent stake in Shipley Co. Inc. in 1982. These acquisitions marked the company's return to its early strategy: relying on businesses and product lines it was well acquainted with, concentrating on value-added chemicals, and increasing its market share rather than its size. This old-fashioned approach resulted in record profits. In 1985 sales were down slightly, but given the difficult economic conditions that existed that

year for chemical companies the performance of Rohm and Haas was regarded by many industry analysts as satisfactory.

The late 1980s saw revenues increase to $2.66 billion by 1989, while earnings reached a record $230 million in 1988 before falling to $176 million in 1989. In mid-1988 Gregory retired as chairman and CEO, with J. Lawrence Wilson selected to succeed him. The popular Wilson—a cost-cutter quoted by the *Wall Street Journal* as saying, "I'm probably a bit of a cheapskate"—had once been in charge of Rohm and Haas's European operations and had been serving as vice-chairman and director of corporate business.

1990S RESHUFFLING OF PORTFOLIO

The recession of the early 1990s created more difficult conditions for Rohm and Haas, but the company managed to keep its earnings from falling as far as some of its rivals. The tight ship that Wilson ran helped make Rohm and Haas one of the most efficient specialty chemical companies in the industry. A net loss of $5 million in 1992 resulted from a reduction in earnings of $179 million caused by the adoption of a new accounting standard for retirement benefits. That year, sales surpassed the $3 billion mark for the first time, totaling $3.06 billion.

Meanwhile, Rohm and Haas made a number of moves in the 1990s to bolster and extend its existing product areas. In 1992 the company paid $175 million to Unocal Corporation for that firm's emulsion polymers business, which included acrylic polymer lines for paints, coatings, and varnishes. That same year, Rohm and Haas joined with Elf Atochem of France to form AtoHaas Americas, a joint venture that included the Plexiglas business of Rohm and Haas and Elf Atochem's Altuglas operation. In mid-1998, however, Rohm and Haas sold its half-interest in this venture to its partner, thus divesting itself of its most famous product. Though Plexiglas was long a company staple, Rohm and Haas had determined that its future lay in more specialty chemistry. In yet another 1992 move, Rohm and Haas issued $170 million in stock to purchase the 70 percent of Shipley it did not already own, thereby lifting the company's profile in the field of chemicals for the electronics industry.

During 1993, when Rohm and Haas's net earnings fell to $107 million, in part because of the skyrocketing prices of raw materials used to make specialty chemicals, Wilson announced a reengineering effort aimed at further curtailing costs. By 1996 1,300 jobs were eliminated, mainly through attrition. Sales that year reached $3.98 billion, while record net earnings of $363 million reflected both the strength of the economy and the effectiveness of the restructuring. In July 1996 Rohm and Haas formed a 50-50 joint venture with Röhm, its one-time German sister company, called RohMax. The venture, which involved the manufacture and sale of petroleum additives, was short-lived, however, as Rohm and Haas sold its interest to Röhm less than two years later.

In June 1997 Rohm and Haas purchased a 25 percent stake (later increased to 31 percent) in Newark, Delaware-based Rodel, Inc., an expansion of its electronic materials sector. Rodel specialized in precision polishing technology for the semiconductor and other industries. Additional electronic chemicals expansion came in the form of the 1997 acquisition of Pratta Electronic Materials, Inc., of Manchester, New Hampshire, which was involved in wiring board materials; and the January 1998 formation of a joint venture between Shipley and LG Chemical Ltd. of Korea for the manufacture and sale of microelectronic chemicals in Korea. Shipley owned 51 percent of the new entity.

Later in 1998 Rohm and Haas announced that for financial reporting purposes it had reorganized its businesses into three sectors: performance polymers, chemical specialties, and electronic materials. In July 1998 the company purchased a minority stake in Isagro Italia, a subsidiary of Isagro S.p.A. specializing in crop protection products. That same month Rohm and Haas announced a plan of succession to create the management team that would lead the company in the early 21st century. John P. Mulroney, president and chief operating officer since 1986, retired at year-end 1998 and was replaced by J. Michael Fitzpatrick, who previously held the position of vice-president and chief technology officer. Wilson then retired in October 1999, with Rajiv L. Gupta, previously vice-president for electronic materials and Asia-Pacific, taking over as chairman and CEO.

As this management transition unfolded, Rohm and Haas ended the decade with a bang with two acquisitions, one significant and one blockbuster. In January 1999 the company acquired LeaRonal, Inc. of Freport, New York, for about $460 million. This deal bolstered Rohm and Haas's burgeoning electronics materials operations, bringing in new chemical products used to make printed circuit boards, semiconductor packaging, and electronic-connector plating. Then in June 1999, Rohm and Haas paid $4.9 billion in stock and cash for Morton International Inc. Acquiring the Chicago-based Morton vaulted Rohm and Haas from sixth to first place among specialty chemical companies in the United States. Morton was most famous for its flagship consumer salt brand and its well-known umbrella-girl logo—a business comprising 31 percent of the company's

1998 revenues of $2.5 billion—but it was most attractive to Rohm and Haas for its specialty chemicals business, which included adhesives, polymers, coatings, and electronics materials. By 2000 revenues at Rohm and Haas had reached $6.88 billion, with more than $1 billion of the total deriving from the sale of electronics materials.

UPS AND DOWNS IN THE EARLY 2000S

Acquisitions were put on hold while the huge effort to integrate the Morton operations took center stage. A few of the more peripheral Morton assets were divested in 2000, including Morton's industrial coatings unit, thermoplastic polyurethane business, and European salt business. Rohm and Haas retained Morton's U.S. and Canadian salt operations because they provided stable revenue and had strong brand recognition. In 2001 Rohm and Haas sold its agricultural chemicals business to the Dow Chemical Company for approximately $1 billion. The company thus exited from a business it had been in for 70 years, but one that ranked as only the 11th largest worldwide.

In 2001 and 2002, amid an economic downturn, a restructuring effort aiming at shaving $200 million from annual expenses involved a workforce reduction of nearly 2,000, the closure of a couple of plants, and an exit from the liquid polysulfide sealants business. Revenues fell more than 10 percent in 2001 before inching only slightly higher in 2002. During the downturn, Rohm and Haas made a few minor, fill-in acquisitions, including the September 2002 purchase of the European powder coatings business of Ferro Corporation for about $60 million.

In 2003 Rohm and Haas benefited from a recovery in both the electronics and industrial sectors, pushing sales up 12 percent, to $6.42 billion. Late in the year the company announced the elimination of an additional 550 jobs, a reduction stemming from redundancies that followed the implementation of an enterprise-wide resource planning information technology system. In both 2003 and 2004 Rohm and Haas had to contend with skyrocketing raw material costs, but the improved economic environment enabled the company to increase the prices it charged for its products and thus post increasing sales and profits. By 2004 profits had jumped to $497 million (from $280 million the previous year), while revenues surged 14 percent, hitting $7.3 billion.

The story was much the same in 2005 as revenues and earnings were driven upward because of higher selling prices necessitated by higher costs of both raw materials and energy. In this environment, the company continued to restructure, announcing in December 2005 the launch of an initiative to improve its manufacturing operations in Europe. The effort involved the closure or partial shutdown of five manufacturing plants and a research and development facility, the elimination of approximately 400 positions from the payroll, and charges of about $65 million.

Updated, David E. Salamie

PRINCIPAL SUBSIDIARIES

Acima AG fur Chemische Industrie (Switzerland); AgroFresh Inc.; Bee Chemical Company; Beijing Eastern Rohm and Haas Company, Limited (China); Canadian Brine Limited; The Canadian Salt Company Limited; Charles Lennig & Company LLC; Cone Sul Uruguay S.A.F.I.; CVD Incorporated; DISA (UK) LIMITED; Duolite Int. Limited (U.K.); Ecuatoriana de Sal Y Productos Quimicos C.A. (Ecuador); Imperial Thermal Products, Inc.; Japan Acrylic Chemical Co., Ltd. (Japan); Rohm and Haas Chemicals Singapore Pte. Ltd.; Rohm and Haas Electronic Materials Holdings UK Ltd.; LeaRonal Japan K.K.; Lennig Chemicals Limited (U.K.); Leyship S.A. (Switzerland); Morton International, Inc.; Paraplex Industrias Quimicas S.A. (Venezuela); PT. Rohm and Haas Indonesia; Pulverlac Powder Coatings S.A. (Spain); Rohm and Haas Electronic Materials CMP Inc.; Rohm and Haas (Far East) Limited (Hong Kong); Rohm and Haas (India) Pvt. Ltd.; Rohm and Haas (Scotland) Limited; Rohm and Haas (UK) Limited; Rohm and Haas Argentina S.R.L.; Rohm and Haas Australia Pty. Ltd.; Rohm and Haas B.V. (Netherlands); Rohm and Haas Belgium N.V.; Rohm and Haas Benelux N.V. (Belgium); Rohm and Haas Canada Inc.; Rohm and Haas Capital Corporation; Rohm and Haas Centro America, S.A. (Costa Rica); Rohm and Haas Chemical (Thailand) Limited; Rohm and Haas Chile Ltda.; Rohm and Haas Chemical Products Distribution and Trade Joint Stock Corporation (Turkey); Rohm and Haas Co. Contrato 1 Asociacion en Participacion (Mexico); Rohm and Haas Colombia LTDA; Rohm and Haas Credit Corporation; Rohm and Haas de Venezuela, C.A.; Rohm and Haas Denmark ApS; Rohm and Haas Deutschland GmbH (Germany); Rohm and Haas El Salvador S.A.; Rohm and Haas Equity Corporation; Rohm and Haas Espana, S.A. (Spain); Rohm and Haas Establecimiento Permanente (Mexico); Rohm and Haas European Holding ApS (Denmark); Rohm and Haas Far South Pte. Ltd. (Hong Kong); Rohm and Haas France SAS; Rohm and Haas Greater China Technical Center; Rohm and Haas Guatemala S.A.; Rohm and Haas International B.V. (Netherlands); Rohm and Haas International SAS (France); Rohm and Haas International Holdings Inc.; Rohm and Haas International Trading (Shanghai) Co. Ltd. (China); Rohm and Haas Italia S.r.l. (Italy); Rohm and Haas Japan Kabushiki Kaisha; Rohm and Haas Korea Co., Ltd.; Rohm and Haas Malaysia SDN BHD; Rohm and Haas Management Consulting Service (Shanghai) Company Limited (China); Rohm and Haas Mexico, S.A. de C. V.; Rohm and Haas Nederland B.V. (Netherlands); Rohm and Haas New Zealand Limited; Rohm and Haas Nordiska AB (Sweden); Rohm and Haas Peru S.A.; Rohm and Haas Philippines, Inc.; Rohm and Haas Quimica Ltda. (Brazil); Rohm and Haas Shanghai Chemical Industry Co., Ltd. (China); Rohm and Haas (Shanghai) Speciality Coatings Co., Ltd. (China); Rohm and Haas Singapore (Pte.) Ltd.; Rohm and Haas South Africa (PTY) Limited; Rohm and Haas Taiwan, Inc.; Rohm and Haas Texas Inc.; Rohm and Haas Venezuela S.A. (Caracas); Rohm and Haas Vermont Company; Romicon B.V. (Netherlands); Shanghai Eastern Rohm and Haas Company Ltd. (China); Rohm and Haas Electronic Materials LLC; StoHaas Marl GmbH (Germany); Silicon Valley Chemical Laboratories Inc.; The Southern Resin & Chemical Company.

PRINCIPAL COMPETITORS

BASF Aktiengesellschaft; The Dow Chemical Company; E. I. du Pont de Nemours and Company.

FURTHER READING

Basralian, Joseph, "Rohm & Haas: Little Cause for Pricing Panic," *Financial World,* November 8, 1994, p. 18.

Bennett, Elizabeth, "Rohm & Haas Works to Fix Up Morton Mess," *Philadelphia Business Journal,* June 15, 2001, p. 4.

Bishop, Todd, "Rohm Builds on Salt Pillar," *Philadelphia Business Journal,* October 1, 1999.

Challener, Cynthia, "Executive Insight: Rohm and Haas Stresses R&D, Cost-Cutting in Managing for Recovery and Growth," *Chemical Market Reporter,* April 29, 2002, p. 21.

Chang, Joseph, "Rohm and Haas Embarks on Massive Overhaul," *Chemical Market Reporter,* May 7, 2001, p. 3.

Cochran, Thomas N., "Rohm & Haas Co.: Its Key Parts Shine Brighter Than Its Overall Record," *Barron's,* August 15, 1988, pp. 37-38.

Freedman, Alix M., "Rohm & Haas Names Wilson As Next Chief," *Wall Street Journal,* December 3, 1986, p. 16.

Gotlieb, Andy, "Refocused Rohm Cooks Up Growth," *Philadelphia Business Journal,* April 5, 2002.

———, "Rohm & Haas Fortifies Powder Coatings Grip," *Philadelphia Business Journal,* August 16, 2002.

Hochheiser, Sheldon, *Rohm and Haas: History of a Chemical Company,* Philadelphia: University of Pennsylvania Press, 1986, 231 p.

Lane, Randall, "Tough in the Clutch," *Forbes,* January 4, 1993, p. 107.

Peterkofsky, David, "Rohm & Haas Deal Likely to Bolster Emulsions Hand," *Chemical Marketing Reporter,* December 16, 1991, pp. 5, 24-25.

Racanelli, Vito J., "Bad Chemistry?," *Barron's,* May 20, 2002, p. 36.

Randall, Willard S., and Stephen D. Solomon, *Building 6: The Tragedy at Bridesburg,* Boston: Little Brown, 1977, 317 p.

Trommsdorff, Ernst, *Dr. Otto Röhm: Chemiker und Unternehmer,* Düsseldorf: Econ Verlag, 1976, 296 p.

Walsh, Kerri, "Rohm and Haas to Take Charges for Impairment and Maintenance," *Chemical Week,* June 29/July 6, 2005, p. 11.

Warren, Susan, "Dow Agrees to Buy Chemicals Business from Rohm & Haas Co. for $1 Billion," *Wall Street Journal,* March 9, 2001, p. B6.

————, "Rohm & Haas Agrees to Acquire Morton for Total of $4.6 Billion in Cash, Stock," *Wall Street Journal,* February 2, 1999, p. A3.

————, "Rohm & Haas to Buy LeaRonal Inc., Broadening Electronics-Chemicals Role," *Wall Street Journal,* December 22, 1998, p. A10.

Webber, Maura, "The Price May Not Be Right for Rohm and Haas' Taste," *Philadelphia Business Journal,* May 9, 1997, p. 6.

Wood, Andrew, "Rohm and Haas Sees Earnings Bloom, but Returns Disappoint," *Chemical Week,* September 21, 1994, pp. 42, 44.

Wood, Andrew, and David Hunter, "Rohm and Haas: Working on the Margins," *Chemical Week,* April 30, 2003, pp. 18-20.

Sandvik AB

SE-811 81
Sandviken,
Sweden
Telephone: (26) 26 00 00
Fax: (26) 26 10 22
Web site: http://www.sandvik.com

Public Company
Incorporated: 1868 as Sandvikens Jernwerks Aktiebolag
Employees: 39,519
Sales: SEK 54.61 billion ($8.19 billion) (2004)
Stock Exchanges: Stockholm
Ticker Symbol: SAND
NAIC: 331210 Iron and Steel Pipe and Tube Manufacturing from Purchased Steel; 331221 Rolled Steel Shape Manufacturing; 331222 Steel Wire Drawing; 331513 Steel Foundries (Except Investment); 332999 All Other Miscellaneous Fabricated Metal Product Manufacturing; 333120 Construction Machinery Manufacturing; 333131 Mining Machinery and Equipment Manufacturing; 333512 Machine Tool (Metal Cutting Types) Manufacturing; 333515 Cutting Tool and Machine Tool Accessory Manufacturing

■ ■ ■

Sandvik AB is an industrial engineering group based in Sandviken, Sweden, with an international network of more than 200 companies in 130 countries. About 95 percent of Sandvik's sales are from outside Sweden, with 48 percent stemming from Europe as a whole, 20 percent from North America (including Mexico), 21 percent from the Australasian region, 6 percent from Africa and the Middle East, and 5 percent from South America. Originating from a steelworks using the Bessemer method in the 1860s, the company has developed into a group with three main business units, each of which holds world-leading positions in several niches. Sandvik Tooling specializes in tools and tooling systems for metalworking applications, with the products made of cemented carbide and other hard materials such as synthetic diamond, ceramics, and high-speed steel. Sandvik Mining and Construction is a leading global supplier of rock-working equipment, tools, and services for mining and civil engineering. Sandvik Materials Technology is a world leader in the manufacture of products made of stainless steel and of titanium, nickel, and zirconium alloys and in the production of metallic and ceramic resistance materials in the form of wire, strip, and electric heating elements.

STEELWORKS BEGINNINGS

The origins of Sandvik can be traced back to the formation of the Högbo Stål & Jernwerks AB in 1862. The company was set up to build a new steelworks at Sandviken, 150 miles north of Stockholm, the capital of Sweden, by Göran Fredrik Göransson. Sandvik claims that Göransson, who obtained a license to use the Bessemer process, was the first to get the new process to work on an industrial scale. The Bessemer method, unlike earlier methods, allowed the production of heavy castings and forgings in one piece from one melt. In the process, air is blown through molten pig-iron and a vigorous combustion results from the reaction of the

COMPANY PERSPECTIVES

Sandvik shall develop, manufacture and market highly processed products, which contribute to improving the productivity and profitability of our customers. Operations are primarily concentrated on areas where Sandvik is—or has the potential to become—a world leader.

blast and the hot iron in the converter. Sandviken is located in the southeastern corner of the region of Sweden where iron products had been produced for hundreds of years prior to the formation of the new company. The original iron industry was based on local deposits of iron and the ready availability of wood to make charcoal.

Johan Holm, the main financial backer of Göransson's company, however, got into financial difficulties that resulted in his and the company's downfall. The company was declared bankrupt in 1866; after financial restructuring, Sandvikens Jernwerks (Steelworks) Aktiebolag was founded in May 1868. Anders Henrik Göransson, the son of the founder, became the manager of the new company and set Sandvik on the course that would lead to its future success. By international standards, Sweden offered a small home market for the new company. From the start Sandvik exported products that, because of the company's location far from the main industrial markets, had to be highly upgraded steel products. The high quality of Swedish iron ore and the Bessemer process urged the company in the same direction. Even during the first years of the new company, Anders Göransson traveled widely in Europe, taking orders for products and establishing agencies.

By the 1890s the company was making some manufactured products, such as saws, from the steel it produced. In the latter part of the 19th century, the company's specialties included boiler tubes for installation in steamships and railway engines, rock drilling steels, and wire for umbrellas. By the outbreak of World War I, exports accounted for up to 80 percent of Sandvik's output. In 1901, meantime, Sandvik shares were listed on the Stockholm Stock Exchange.

By 1914 employment at Sandviken exceeded 2,200. During World War I the export share shrank, but was offset by the booming domestic market for steel. In the interwar period the company was hit hard by recession, in the early 1920s and again in the early 1930s. The workforce declined, but by 1937 had risen again to

5,380. During this period, the production of steel by the open-hearth process and electro process replaced the Bessemer process that had been instrumental in the foundation of the company. Sweden's cheap hydroelectric power provided an advantage for steelmakers using the electro process.

Between 1918 and 1939 exports as a proportion of sales varied between 60 and 70 percent. Throughout this period, steel was the dominant product group; manufactured products such as saws, conveyor belts, complete conveyors, and razor blades accounted for only 6 percent of sales. Within the area of steel products, tube products were increasingly important; these included seamless stainless tubes for the food, pulp and paper, and chemical industries.

From 1920 until 1958 the dominant figure in the company was Karl Fredrik Göransson, grandson of the company's founder. When he returned to Sweden in 1901 after studying in the United States, he brought with him the company's, and probably Sweden's, first microscope for metallurgical studies. He was managing director from 1920 until 1948 and chairman from 1929 until 1959.

By the beginning of World War II, Sandvik's production amounted to 90,000 tons of steel ingots a year and 65,000 tons of finished products. In terms of ingots, the company accounted for about 10 percent of Sweden's output, but because the final products were highly upgraded this understated the company's relative importance in terms of the value of output. During World War II, exports collapsed again and output was diverted to the home market. During this period, however, an event of immense importance for the development of the company occurred.

INCREASING IMPORTANCE OF CEMENTED-CARBIDE PRODUCTS: 1940S-60S

In 1942 the company entered the cemented-carbide trade. Cemented-carbide is a powder-metallurgical product of which tungsten carbide is the main constituent. It may also contain carbides of other metals such as titanium, tantalum, and niobium. Powders prepared from the various metal carbides are mixed with fine-grained powdered metal, most commonly cobalt. The mix is pressed to the desired shape and is treated at a high temperature; the cobalt melts and functions as a binding agent for the carbide grains which are sintered in. The sintered product has multiple advantages: hardness, ductility, and resistance to wear. A sintered blank can be ground to high edge sharpness, affixed to a holder, and used as a tool for metal cutting.

KEY DATES

1862: Göran Fredrik Göransson forms Högbo Stål & Jernwerks AB to build a new steelworks at Sandviken, Sweden.

1866: Company is declared bankrupt.

1868: Company is reestablished as Sandvikens Jernwerks Aktiebolag, with Anders Henrik Göransson, son of the founder, as general manager.

1901: Shares in the company are listed on the Stockholm Stock Exchange.

1920: Karl Fredrik Göransson, grandson of the founder, becomes managing director.

1942: Company enters the cemented-carbide trade.

1957: Control of the company passes out of the hands of the Göransson family; investment company Kinnevik acquires stake in the firm.

1967: Hugo Stenbeck, chairman of Kinnevik, becomes company chairman; Arne Westerberg, formerly of Kinnevik, becomes managing director.

1971: Sales of cemented-carbide products exceed those of steel products for the first time.

1972: Company changes its name to Sandvik AB; the U.S. rock drilling manufacturing operation of Fagersta is purchased.

1983: Skanska AB acquires Kinnevik's holding and builds up a 37 percent stake in the company; Percy Barnevik, chief executive of ASEA AB, is appointed chairman.

1984: Company's operations are restructured into six core business areas: Sandvik Tooling, Sandvik Rock Tools, Sandvik Hard Materials, Sandvik Steel, Sandvik Saws and Tools, and Sandvik Process Systems.

1987: The Carboloy Division of General Electric Company is acquired.

1991: Bahco Tools Group is acquired and added to Sandvik Saws and Tools.

1993: Company completes acquisition of CTT Tools from AB SKF.

1997: Sandvik takes full control of Tamrock, Kanthal, and Precision Twist Drill; Skanska sells the bulk of its stake in Sandvik, with large portion sold to AB Industrivärden.

1999: Company's operations are concentrated around three core business areas: Sandvik Tooling, Sandvik Mining and Construction, and Sandvik Specialty Steels; Sandvik Saws and Tools unit is sold to Snap-On Incorporated.

2002: Sandvik acquires the German firm Walter AG and the U.S.-based Valenite.

2003: The Sandvik Specialty Steels unit is renamed Sandvik Materials Technology.

Fried. Krupp AG, the German steel and engineering company (which was later subsumed into Thyssen Krupp AG), had invented cemented-carbide tools in the 1920s and was the leading supplier before World War II. The war separated Krupp from many of its markets and provided opportunities for new entrants to the trade.

Sandvik used the name Coromant for its new venture, which was initiated by production manager Carl Sebart. Previously, cemented-carbide had been sold in the form of blanks to be fashioned and sharpened into tools by the users. Sandvik's new approach, to supply ready-made tools, was first applied to rock-drills, which were developed and marketed in collaboration with Atlas Copco AB, another Swedish company, and were an immediate success. The cooperative arrangement with Atlas

Copco continued until 1988. Michael Porter, author of *The Competitive Sources of Power,* suggested that one reason for Sweden's success in producing internationally competitive rock drilling equipment is that its rock is among the hardest in the world. Cemented-carbide metalworking tools were slower to achieve popularity, but development after 1956 was rapid. Sandvik Coromant expanded by building new factories in Sweden and other countries and by acquiring existing producers. Wilhelm Haglund, who had managed the development of Sandvik's cemented-carbide operation from the start in 1942, was appointed managing director of Sandvik in 1957 by K. F. Göransson, and held the position until 1967.

The Göransson family was the company's major shareholder and controlled Sandvik until 1957, when additional capital was raised by an issue of shares, and the investment company Kinnevik acquired a stake in the company. In 1967 Hugo Stenbeck, chairman of Kinnevik, became chairman of Sandvik, and Arne Westerberg, a former manager of a subsidiary of Kinnevik, took over as managing director.

An important change of corporate strategy occurred in 1967 at about the time of the changeover in management from Wilhelm Haglund as managing director and Gustaf Söderlund as chairman to Hugo Stenbeck and Arne Westerberg, respectively. Hitherto, the company's policy had been to market products made by the parent company or by its subsidiaries starting from products made by the parent company. Between 1962 and 1966, parent company sales represented 78 percent of group sales. From 1967 more products, particularly cemented-carbide products, were manufactured by the company's overseas subsidiaries.

In 1971 sales of cemented-carbide products exceeded those of steel products for the first time. In 1972 this was acknowledged by a change in the company's name from Sandvikens Jernwerks Aktiebolag to Sandvik AB.

EXPANSION THROUGH ACQUISITION: 1970S-80S

Sandvik's other divisions were also making progress in developing products and markets while the carbide-tool business took off; they certainly could not afford to be idle in the intensely competitive environment of the steel and engineering industries during the 1970s and 1980s. While other steel companies faced repeated if not terminal crises, Sandvik succeeded as a result of its policies of investment in the latest technology and by developing specialty products to be sold in world markets. In world terms, Sandvik was a small-scale producer of steel; it survived in spite of the existence of large economies of scale for steel production by concentrating on the production of types of specialty steel and making high quality special products, such as surgical needles, scalpels, and probes that require special strength and resistance to corrosion, bone pins, artificial hip-joints, cladding in nuclear reactors, and springs.

The pace of expansion through acquisitions in Sweden and abroad was stepped up after 1967. In 1968 a joint venture, the Saeger Carbide Corporation, was set up in the United States with the Greenleaf Corporation. Between 1970 and 1973, manufacturers of rock drilling equipment in France and Spain were acquired. In 1972 the U.S. rock drilling manufacturing operation of another Swedish steel company, Fagersta, was purchased. In 1973 the U.K.-based Wickman-Wimet group was acquired, and during 1978 and 1979 tool manufacturers in Germany and France were bought. Between 1971 and 1974 the steel division made acquisitions in Spain, West Germany, and the United Kingdom; saw, hand-tool, and conveyor manufacturers were also taken into the group.

Although it was better placed than many other Swedish steel producers, Sandvik took part in the successive rationalizations of the Swedish special steels industry during the early 1980s. The result of the rationalizations was that there were only two principal special steel manufacturers in Sweden, Sandvik and Avesta, with Sandvik specializing in strip, wire, and tube products.

Following the second oil crisis in 1980, Sandvik suffered from the effects of the recession in many of its major markets. In 1983 the company's profits were reduced by SEK 219 million ($30 million) owing to an exchange rate loss brought about by unauthorized foreign-exchange speculation by an employee. In the aftermath of this disaster, Skanska AB, a construction company with diversified interests, acquired Kinnevik's holding and built up a 37 percent stake in Sandvik. In October 1983 Percy Barnevik, the chief executive officer of the Swedish electrical giant ASEA AB, was appointed chairman of Sandvik in succession to Arne Westerberg. In 1984 Per-Olof Eriksson was appointed president. In 1989 Percy Barnevik remained chairman while Per-Olof Eriksson became president and CEO of Sandvik, and Skanska AB controlled 26 percent of shareholders' votes. Meantime, in 1984 the company restructured its operations into six core business areas: Sandvik Coromant, Sandvik Rock Tools, Sandvik Hard Materials, Sandvik Steel, Sandvik Saws and Tools, and Sandvik Process Systems.

Acquisitions continued to be made during the 1980s. An important one was the Carboloy Division of the General Electric Company, of the United States, in 1987. In 1989 Metinox Steel Ltd., a small British company making medical products out of stainless steel, was acquired.

During the years 1987 to 1989, Sandvik's operating profit, after charging depreciation, represented more than 15 percent of sales. Expenditure on research and development was more than 4 percent of sales, while capital expenditure averaged more than 5 percent of sales.

STRENGTHENING AND FOCUSING ON THREE CORE AREAS: 1990S

The early 1990s were difficult years for Sandvik as recession gripped much of the world from 1990 through

1993. Despite declining sales, the company remained profitable thanks to management's heeding signs of the downturn as early as mid-1989. Eriksson began cutting staff around the world, reducing the workforce by 20 percent by the end of 1992. He also held off on making any significant acquisitions in 1989 or 1990, returning the company to its more acquisitive nature starting in 1991, but at a slower pace than in the past. During 1991 Sandvik spent SEK 358 million to acquire ten enterprises in whole or in part. The largest of these was the December purchase of the Bahco Tools Group, which had annual revenue of SEK 700 million and about 1,700 employees. The addition of Bahco bolstered Sandvik Saws and Tools. In late 1992 and early 1993 Sandvik acquired CTT Tools from AB SKF in a two-step transaction. CTT Tools, which was formed in 1990 through the merger of SKF Tools and the German firm Günther & Co., was the world leader in the manufacture of high-speed steel tools for metalworking, such as drills, thread-cutting tools, milling cutters, and reamers. CTT Tools and Sandvik Coromant were grouped into a new Sandvik Tooling business area.

In 1993 Sandvik formed a subsidiary in China, Sandvik China Ltd., which began construction of a cemented-carbide tools factory in Langfang City. The following year Eriksson turned over the reins to a new president and CEO, Clas Åke Hedström. In February 1994 Sandvik reached an agreement to acquire the cemented-carbide operations of Krupp Widia GmbH (the original producer of cemented-carbide products) from Fried. Krupp AG Hoechst-Krupp. German antitrust authorities, however, concluded that Sandvik would gain too dominant a position in particular product segments of the German market and squelched the deal.

From 1993 through 1995 Sandvik recorded steadily rising revenues and profits as the business climate was generally favorable worldwide. With the late 1990s difficulties experienced in Japan, other parts of Asia, Russia, and Latin America, net profits declined from SEK 3.73 billion in 1995 to SEK 2.10 billion in 1998. Revenues, however, moved in the opposite direction, increasing from SEK 29.7 billion to SEK 42.4 billion during the same period, aided by several major acquisitions. During 1997 alone, Sandvik took full control of Tamrock, Kanthal, and Precision Twist Drill. Finland-based Tamrock, which Sandvik acquired in two phases in 1996 and 1997, was a world-leading maker of rock-drilling equipment. The three main operations of Tamrock were combined with Sandvik Rock Tools to form a new Sandvik Mining and Construction business area. This area included four separate business sectors: the newly named Sandvik Tamrock, producer of drilling rigs, loaders, trucks, hydraulic hammers, and cemented-carbide products; Voest-Alpine Eimco, maker of equip-

ment and tools for the mining of coal and other soft minerals; Driltech Mission, maker of drilling rigs and cemented-carbide tools for rotary and down-the-hole drilling; and Roxon, provider of equipment for conveyors and systems for handling of bulk materials.

Also acquired in two steps in 1996 and 1997 was Kanthal AB, a leading maker of high-temperature metallic and ceramic materials in the form of wire, strip, and electric heating elements. Kanthal had strong ties to Sandvik Steel and the two units were grouped within a new business area called Sandvik Specialty Steel. In September 1997 Sandvik acquired Crystal Lake, Illinois-based Precision Twist Drill Co. for SEK 1.06 billion. With annual sales of more than $110 million, Precision was one of the leading manufacturers of high-speed steel twist drills in the world. It became part of CTT Tools.

In mid-1997 Skanska sold the bulk of its significant holding in Sandvik. Skanska sold part of its stake to AB Industrivärden, a Swedish investment company that held an 11.7 percent voting stake at the end of 1998. In April 1999 Sandvik announced that it would sell Sandvik Saws and Tools to Kenosha, Wisconsin-based Snap-On Incorporated. The SEK 3.3 billion ($400 million) deal was completed in September of that year, with Sandvik recording a capital gain of about SEK 1.6 billion. Sandvik Saws and Tools was renamed Bahco Group AB and continued to be based in Sandviken, Sweden. With this divestment pending, Sandvik in May 1999 announced that it would restructure its operations into three main areas. The first was Sandvik Tooling, which continued to include Sandvik Coromant and CTT Tools and also gained Sandvik Hard Materials, producer of cemented-carbide blanks, components, and rolls. The second was Sandvik Mining and Construction. The third was Sandvik Specialty Steels, which comprised Sandvik Steel and Kanthal as well as the newly added Sandvik Process Systems, maker of steel belts and steel-belt-based process plants. Sandvik was now well-positioned for the 21st century, as the firm held leading global positions in specific niches within each of these areas.

FURTHER ACQUISITIONS AND LEADERSHIP CHANGES: EARLY 2000S

Sandvik posted strong sales gains in both 2000 and 2001, but profits began to decline in the latter year and then fell further the next two years amid the generally weak worldwide economy. Sales were flat in both 2002 and 2003. During this period the company closed a number of plants as part of a drive to improve efficiency and productivity. Sandvik also completed a few significant, complementary acquisitions. Over 2001 and 2002 the company purchased a 94 percent controlling stake in the German firm Walter AG, which specialized in tools for metalworking, software systems for tool management, and numerically controlled grinding machines. Walter, whose annual revenues totaled approximately SEK 2.5 billion, became part of Sandvik Tooling. Another addition was made to this same unit in August 2002, when Sandvik acquired Valenite, the North American metal-cutting tools business of Milacron Inc., for SEK 1.65 billion. Valenite was based in Madison Heights, Michigan; maintained manufacturing plants in South Carolina, Michigan, and Texas; and generated annual sales of SEK 1.85 billion. Sandvik touted the acquisition as one that broadened its base, especially in the automotive industry. The deals for Walter and Valenite increased Sandvik's share of the world tool business from 20 percent to 25 percent.

The Valenite deal was the first acquisition completed under Sandvik's new chief executive, Lars Pettersson. Pettersson was promoted to the top position in May 2002, having previously served as executive vice-president and having joined the company in 1979. Hedström was named chairman, succeeding Barnevik. During Barnevik's 19 years as chairman, Sandvik's sales increased 500 percent, its earnings surged 1,000 percent, and its stock price skyrocketed 2,000 percent. Sandvik rounded out 2002 with its first acquisition in Japan. In November, Sandvik Mining and Construction acquired Mazda Earth Technologies and its Toyo brand, thereby gaining a leading maker of machinery and equipment for the Japanese mining and construction industries.

Sandvik started out 2003 by changing the name of its Sandvik Specialty Steels unit to Sandvik Materials Technology. The change was made to highlight the unit's focus on high-value-added products. Among other initiatives during the year, Sandvik continued its push into emerging markets. Sandvik Mining and Construction opened a new plant in India for the assembly of crushers, feeders, and screens, and Sandvik Materials Technology inaugurated a new plant in China for manufacturing process systems and press plates. In 2004 Sandvik rode the stronger world economy to record levels, achieving its highest profits (SEK 6.47 billion) and revenues (SEK 54.61 billion) ever. This trend continued well into 2005 as sales for the first three quarters were up 17 percent over 2004 levels and net profits jumped 26 percent.

Cliff Pratten
Updated, David E. Salamie

PRINCIPAL SUBSIDIARIES

Dormer Tools AB; Edmetson AB; Gusab Holding AB; Gusab Stainless AB; Industri AB Skomab; AB Sandvik Antenn; AB Sandvik Automation; AB Sandvik Bruket; AB Sandvik Calamo; AB Sandvik Coromant; Sandvik Coromant Norden AB; Sandvik Export Assistance AB; AB Sandvik Falken; Sandvik Försäkrings AB; AB Sandvik Hard Materials; Sandvik Hard Materials Norden AB; AB Sandvik Information Technology AB; Sandvik Intellectual Property HB; AB Sandvik International; AB Sandvik Materials Technology; Sandvik Mining and Construction Sverige AB; Sandvik Mining and Construction Tools AB; AB Sandvik Process Systems; Sandvik Raiseboring AB; AB Sandvik Service; AB Sandvik Skogsfastigheter; Sandvik Smith AB; Sandvik Stål Försäljnings AB; Sandvik Systems Development AB; AB Sandvik Tranan; AB Sandvik Vallhoven; AB Sandvik Västberga Service; Sandvik Örebro AB; AB Sandvik Örnen; Seco Tools AB (60%); Sandvik Australian Ltd. Partnership (99%); Dormer Tools S.A. (Brazil); Sandvik do Brasil SA. (Brazil); Sandvik Bulgaria Ltd.; Sandvik China Ltd.; Sandvik International Trading (Shanghai) Co. Ltd. (China); Sandvik Mining and Construction (China) Ltd.; Sandvik Process Systems (Shanghai) Ltd. (China); Sandvik CZ s.r.o. (Czech Republic); Sandvik GmbH (Germany); Sandvik Holding GmbH (Germany); Sandvik A.E. Tools and Materials (Greece); Sandvik KFT (Hungary); Sandvik Asia Ltd. (India; 97%); Sandvik SMC Distribution Ltd. (Ireland); Sandvik Sorting Systems S.p.A. (Italy); Sandvik K.K. (Japan); Sandvik Kenya Ltd. (96%); Sandvik Korea Ltd.; Sandvik Méxicana S.A. de C.V. (Mexico); Sandvik Maroc SARL (Morocco; 94%); Sandvik Finance B.V. (Netherlands); Sandvik del Perú S.A.; Sandvik Baildonit S.A. (Poland); Sandvik Polska Sp.z. o.o. (Poland); Sandvik Slovakia s.r.o.; Minas y Metalurgia Española SA (Spain); Sandvik Endüstriyel Mamüller Sanayi ve Ticaret A.S. (Turkey); Sandvik (Private) Ltd. (Zimbabwe).

PRINCIPAL COMPETITORS

Atlas Copco AB; Kennametal Inc.; Iscar Tools; Gildemeister AG.

FURTHER READING

Aronson, Robert B., "Journey to Sweden," *Manufacturing Engineering,* July 1998, pp. 134-38.

Burt, Tim, "Snap-On Buys Sandvik Unit," *Financial Times,* April 23, 1999, p. 31.

Garnett, Nick, "Carbide Tool Groups Sharpen Up Their Image," *Financial Times,* April 6, 1988.

Hedin, Göran, *Ett Svenskt Jernwerk, Sandviken, 1862-1937,* Uppsala: [n.p.], 1937.

"Lars Pettersson" (CEO interview), *Wall Street Transcript,* August 12, 2005.

Marsh, Peter, "Attention to Detail Engineers Healthy Profits for Sandvik," *Financial Times,* November 16, 2001, p. 34.

———, "Sandvik Plots Precise Route to the Top Spot," *Financial Times,* February 4, 2003, p. 30.

McIvor, Greg, "Skanska to Sell Its Holding in Sandvik," *Financial Times,* April 15, 1997, p. 27.

Reier, Sharon, "Against the Tide," *Financial World,* May 10, 1994, pp. 48-49.

"Sandvik, Inc. to Acquire Precision Twist Drill," *Industrial*

Distribution, August 1997, pp. 16, 23.

Shutte, Lesley, "Sandvik Shows Its Metal," *Director,* December 1996, pp. 54-58.

Transformation: Sandvik, 1862-1987, Sandviken: Sandvik AB, 1987.

Wright, Chris, "Sandvik Ready for the Increase in Competition," *Corporate Finance,* January 1999, p. 29.

Schneider National, Inc.

3101 South Packerland Drive
Green Bay, Wisconsin 54306-2545
U.S.A.
Telephone: (920) 592-2000
Toll Free: (800) 558-6767
Fax: (920) 592-3063
Web site: http://www.schneider.com

Private Company
Incorporated: 1939 as Schneider Transfer and Storage Co.
Employees: 20,000
Sales: $3.2 billion (2004)
NAIC: 484110 General Freight Trucking, Local; 484121 General Freight Trucking, Long-Distance, Truckload; 423110 Automobile and Other Motor Vehicle Merchant Wholesalers; 532120 Truck, Utility Trailer and RV (Recreational Vehicle) Rental and Leasing; 561110 Office Administration Services

■ ■ ■

Schneider National, Inc. is the largest truckload carrier in North America. Privately owned by members of the Schneider family, it was a relatively small player until the 1980s, when the trucking industry was deregulated. In that era when many small trucking firms failed, Schneider instead soared to the forefront, chiefly by deploying advanced communications technology. Schneider's fleet of approximately 14,000 trucks and 48,000 trailers is distinguished by a signature bright orange color. The company also is known for its logistics business, which helps other companies determine efficient ways to ship and distribute goods. A leader in trucking logistics, the holding company canceled plans to spin off Schneider Logistics, Inc. when the IPO market faltered in 2001.

EARLY YEARS

Schneider National was founded in 1935, at the advent of the regulated truck era, by Al Schneider, known as "A. J.," in Green Bay, Wisconsin. Schneider was raised on a farm in east-central Wisconsin, and his education took him through the eighth grade only. He began with one truck, and took shipments through the Green Bay area. The company grew, as did the Schneider family. Eventually there were five sons and a daughter.

The trucking business, named Schneider Transport & Storage following the purchase of Bins Transfer & Storage in 1938, incorporated in Nevada in 1939. The storage aspect of the intrastate trucking business was dropped in 1944, but a corresponding name change would not come about until the 1960s. Schneider Transport was granted its first interstate authority in 1958. The first load in that capacity was for Procter & Gamble. Growth through the acquisition of other trucking companies contributed to growth in the 1960s and the early 1970s. The holding company, Schneider National, Inc., was formed in 1976.

Al's oldest son, Don, worked his way up in the business, becoming president in 1971. Unlike his father, Don had a thorough education to match his homegrown business skills. He graduated from a parochial high school in Green Bay, and then went to St. Norbert College, graduating in 1957. After a period in the Army, Don Schneider entered the University of Pennsylvania's esteemed Wharton School of Finance and Commerce. With this valuable business degree in hand, Don returned to Green Bay in 1961 and became an instrumental Schneider manager. Ten years later, he assumed control of the company, which was then an estimated $80 million business. Don Schneider seemed to have brought his father's company an unusual combination of skills. In a profile of the company in the October 31, 1994, *Milwaukee Journal,* an industry analyst proclaimed Schneider "a trucker who thinks like an economist."

CHANGES AFTER DEREGULATION IN THE 1980S

Until 1980, thinking like a "lawyer" might have been the most valuable skill at a trucking company. Trucking was regulated by a web of state and federal statutes that determined minutiae of the industry's routes, rates, and loads. Thus Schneider was licensed to carry cellulose products, for example, but not paper products, and its lawyers had to negotiate for years in order to reclassify disposable diapers as a cellulose product so it could legally ship them. Both government rules and union contracts dictated much of the business.

Schneider itself seemed versed in legal finagling. From 1978 to 1981 the company claimed its headquarters were in a facility it used in Illinois, thus avoiding a higher licensing fee it would have owed to the state of Wisconsin. The state of Wisconsin sued Schneider for $3.8 million in licensing fees in 1982, and the case was eventually settled on appeal in Schneider's favor.

When the trucking industry was deregulated in 1980, such bureaucratic wrangling became much less a part of the way Schneider and other trucking companies did business. Under deregulation, truckers were freed to compete directly for customers. Around the same time,

many large manufacturers and retailers were changing their business pattern, switching to so-called just-in-time delivery. Just-in-time meant that instead of warehousing huge stocks of common items, factories ordered raw materials as needed, and shipped finished goods directly to retailers. This cut costs associated with large inventories, but it put intense pressure on truckers. A truckers' delay of as little as 20 minutes could cause retailers annoying back-ups as they tried to get their goods out to waiting customers.

Don Schneider was quick to realize that his company had to change massively in order to adapt to the new business climate. Two major changes were in employee relations and in new use of technology. In the early 1980s Schneider began giving its drivers bonuses based on performance, while also eliminating such perks as reserved parking spaces for upper echelon employees. Deregulation allowed the company to hire non-union drivers, which it did, while pledging to keep its union employees. In 1979, all 1,500 drivers belonged to the Teamsters union. As the company grew, the percentage of unionized drivers became smaller. By the early 1990s, only 500 Teamsters were left, out of a crew of roughly 10,000 drivers. Attrition of the union allowed Schneider more freedom to set its own policies for employees. This gave the company more flexibility, which it needed to adapt to the increased demands of its customers.

Schneider also pioneered the use of satellite technology in trucking. Traditionally, drivers on the road would find a phone at a truck stop and call a company dispatcher for a periodic check-in. This was sometimes a frustrating process, as pay phones were often engaged, or the dispatcher busy and unable to accept the call. Schneider National made a large investment in computer and satellite technology in 1988 to give it a new way to communicate with drivers. The company spent an estimated $50 million, and installed a satellite dish and communication console on every truck it owned. Each truck was linked by satellite to the company's home base in Green Bay. Specialized software ran continuous updates on the many variables of the business, not only keeping track of where each truck was, but logging how many hours the driver had slept, fuel use, and average unloading time at each customer's facility. Changes in routes could be beamed directly to the driver on the road, and if a customer needed an empty trailer in half an hour, the computer could determine which driver was nearby and eligible for another load. Schneider was the first major trucker to make use of satellite technology, and soon the rest of the industry was scrambling to keep up.

Meanwhile, Schneider prospered financially. The trucking market in the 1980s was characterized by

KEY DATES

1935: Company is founded in Green Bay.

1958: Company begins interstate shipping.

1976: Schneider National, Inc. is formed as a holding company.

1988: Schneider makes first big investment in satellite technology.

1993: Valuable subsidiary Schneider Logistics is founded.

2000: Company plans, but later cancels, move to spin off Schneider Logistics.

2002: First non-family member takes over leadership.

2004: Company surpasses $3 billion in annual revenue.

intense competition and recessive prices, yet Schneider managed to grow at around 20 percent annually. Revenue in 1981 was a modest $200 million, but by 1992, revenue exceeded $1 billion. Because the company was privately held, it was able to reinvest freely with an eye to long-term profits, and Schneider continued to put money into technology and new ventures.

EXPANSION IN THE 1990S

With its rapid growth, Schneider needed to expand its facilities in the early 1990s in order to accommodate more drivers. The company began work on a huge facility in Memphis in 1990, building a driver service center and operations center and enlarging an existing maintenance center. The driver service center gave drivers a place to relax, rest, and shower while their trucks were being refueled or repaired. Originally planned in the late 1980s as home base for about 600 drivers, by the early 1990s the Memphis site grew into a hub for close to 1,000 truckers. The expansion cost Schneider an estimated $6 million. Schneider also employed its high technology at its new service center. When drivers refueled in Memphis or at any of the company's other major service centers, their mileage was automatically beamed to Schneider's headquarters in Green Bay. If a truck was using an atypical amount of fuel, the computer could note that, and alert personnel of possible maintenance needs on that vehicle. The investment in cutting edge technology let the company save money over the long term, by giving it such tight control over its fleet.

Schneider also began investing in equipment in the early 1990s, specifically truck trailers that could be used on railways. Schneider entered the so-called intermodal transport industry in 1991, working with Southern Pacific railway to serve routes between the Midwest and southern California. Though industrywide far more freight was shipped by road than by rail, being able to combine the two often gave the company more efficient routes. By 1992, Schneider had worked out intermodal shipping agreements with several more railroads, giving it access to most major markets in the United States. Schneider invested approximately $12 million in the early 1990s to replace existing truck trailers with trailers that could be stacked on flatbed rail cars. Then the company spent around $600 million over several years to buy a new kind of convertible trailer called a roadrailer. The roadrailer was a modified truck frame that could use steel rail wheels and travel directly on train tracks. Unlike stackable containers, which required special lifting equipment found only in rail yards to place them onto rail cars, the roadrailers could move onto rail tracks anywhere there was a spur. This gave Schneider the kind of flexibility it liked.

Schneider National was an innovative, fast-growing company in the 1990s. It had surpassed much of its competition by embracing change and new technology. In 1993 the company formed a subsidiary, Schneider Logistics, to sell its shipping expertise to clients. Large manufacturers were working to reduce inventory and streamline operations to improve profits, and Schneider was effective in determining how that could be best done. Schneider Logistics garnered large contracts early on, including one with General Motors to improve the delivery of auto parts to its dealers. By 1995, Schneider Logistics had 140 contracts, ranging in size from about $2 million for small companies to $200 million for such large firms as General Motors and auto parts maker PPG Industries. By the mid-1990s, Schneider was getting 15 percent of its profit from its logistics division, and the subsidiary was the fastest-growing part of the company.

BRANCHING OUT IN THE LATE 1990S

By the late 1990s, Schneider National was the nation's largest full-load trucking firm, with sales approaching $3 billion. The firm had distinguished itself in the 1980s by moving quickly into advanced communications technology. As the Internet changed the face of business in the United States in the late 1990s, Schneider found a way to adapt.

In June 1999, the company launched a new subsidiary, Schneider Brokerage, which handled a web-based service. Schneider Brokerage operated a web site called the Schneider Connection, which posted trucking jobs online and let shippers find available loads. Schneider also found other ways to work with the Internet. In June 2000 Schneider Logistics formed an alliance with an online construction service business, ContractorHub.com. ContractorHub.com brought together businesses looking for construction contractors and contractors looking for jobs. Schneider Logistics provided the new company with its expertise in shipping, order fulfillment, and tracking, and gained exposure through ContractorHub.com's wide marketing.

By the year 2000, Schneider's logistics subsidiary had grown so rapidly and profitably that the parent decided to spin it off to the public. Schneider wanted cash to help pay for more technological development at Schneider Logistics, and to allow the subsidiary to expand into international markets. This was the first time the closely held Schneider considered letting any piece of it fall to investors. However, the company announced it would sell off only a minority share in Schneider Logistics. The majority would still be held by Donald Schneider and other shareholders of the private parent firm. In 2001, the holding company dropped plans to spin off Schneider Logistics, unwilling to risk the deteriorating IPO market.

North America's biggest transportation and logistics concern gained a new leader in 2002. For the first time in company history a non-family member would direct the company. Christopher B. Lofgren, former COO and CIO, succeeded Don Schneider as CEO and president. Schneider continued to serve as chairman of the board.

The company had created an independent board late in the 1980s to address corporate governance issues and leadership transition, according to *Traffic World*. Just the third person to run the company since 1935, Lofgren was named COO, in 2000, a position, designed to groom him as successor to Schneider. That slot would remain unfilled but a six-person executive board would share in the company's oversight. Lofgren joined the company in 1994, as vice-president of engineering and systems for Schneider Logistics. Operating primarily in North America and Europe, Schneider Logistics expanded into China during the new millennium.

Despite the economic recession at home, the company continued to grow its logistics as well as intermodal and brokerage units while maintaining its strong trucking business brand name. "Don will say there are two times when you're well-positioned to grow," Lofgren told *Industry Week*'s David Drickhamer. "One is in a recession. The other is when the economy is growing. So it's really a mindset." In response to the 2001 to 2003 economic downturn, Schneider National cut costs and paid down some debt. A solid market position also helped the company produce double digit gains during 2002 and 2003. The privately held company was "solidly profitable," according to *Traffic World*.

By 2004, Don Schneider had cut back on his hours in his role as chairman, although another family member, his son Paul, served as manager at the Green Bay operating center. Under Lofgren, the once family-run company revealed more of its inner workings and views about the state of the trucking industry. "'We think it's a competitive advantage to be privately held,' said Lofgren. At the same time he has adopted some of the business disciplines that public companies follow, such as forecasting. 'We had a board like a public company, so I said let's put the disciplines in place from the operational and executional level on how we forecast the business,'" he told *Traffic World's* John D. Schulz.

Schneider National topped $3 billion in annual revenue in 2004. Its diversification, including truckload, intermodal, brokerage and non-asset businesses, financial services, and freight payment companies, contributed to ongoing success. Its acquisitions, also part of the story, had been relatively small in size, ones relatively easy to integrate.

External forces pressed the trucking industry during 2005. A shortage of truckers during a time of rising demand drove up wages. Yet oil prices skyrocketed, threatening to propel fuel cost into the top spot among trucking companies' expenses. Moreover, new emission standards for diesel engines, scheduled to go into effect in 2007, meant added equipment related expenditures. Federal changes regarding driver hours and delays on the borders also put pressures on profitability. Schneider National passed along a portion of its added fuel expense with a surcharge. Since the industry was running at capacity, even customers with considerable clout, such as Wal-Mart Stores, Procter & Gamble, and the Detroit automobile makers, had few other options than to pay.

A. Woodward
Updated, Kathleen Peippo

PRINCIPAL SUBSIDIARIES

Schneider Logistics, Inc.

PRINCIPAL COMPETITORS

J.B. Hunt Transport Services Inc.; Swift Transportation Co., Inc.; Werner Enterprises, Inc.

FURTHER READING

Bigness, Jon, "Driving Force," *Wall Street Journal*, September 6, 1995, pp. A1, A11.

Booker, Ellis, "Schneider Looks for 'Deep Visibility,'" *InformationWeek,* October 25, 1999, p. 76.

Brown, Eryn, "Slow Road to Fast Data: For Truck Company Schneider, BI Software Was a Godsend," *Fortune,* March 18, 2002, pp. 170+.

Carey, Bill, "Trucking's Sticker Shock: Rising Costs Threaten Trucking Companies Stuck on Productivity 'Plateau,' Warns Schneider's Lofgren," *Traffic World,* September 5, 2005, p. 22.

Cassidy, William B., "Lofgren Leads Schneider: Former COO, CIO Takes Helm of Nation's Largest Truckload Carrier," *Traffic World,* August 12, 2002, p. 13.

Castillo Mireles, Ricardo, "Going with the Flow in Mexico: A Major U.S. Carrier Has Changed Its Operating Model to Achieve Success in Mexico," *Logistics Today,* July 2005, pp. 10+.

Cohen, Warren, "Taking to the Highway," *U.S. News & World Report,* September 18, 1995, pp. 84-87.

Drickhamer, David, "Rolling on: At Schneider National, a New Leader and an Emphasis on Executive Team Interaction Keep the Focus on 'Low Cost, Low Cost, Low Cost,'" *Industry Week,* December 2002, pp. 47+.

Kenyon, Richard L., "A Long-Distance Mover and Shaker," *Milwaukee Journal,* October 31, 1994, pp. 13-16, 22.

Levenson, Marc, "Riding the Data Highway," *Newsweek,* March 21, 1994, pp. 54-55.

Machalaba, Daniel, "An Industry's Direction Rides on Schneider National," *Wall Street Journal,* May 24, 1993, p. B4.

———, "Truckers Lift Rates for the Long Haul, Citing Surging Traffic and Rising Costs," *Wall Street Journal,* March 31, 1994, p. A4.

———, "Trucking Firms, Amid Heavy Demand, Seek Rate Rise," *Wall Street Journal,* December 9, 1999, p. B6.

Magnet, Myron, "Meet the New Revolutionaries," *Fortune,* February 24, 1992, pp. 94-101.

Mayo, Virginia, "Wisconsin Sues Trucking Firm," *Capital Times* (Madison, Wis.), February 2, 1982, p. 26.

Muller, E. J., "Don Schneider: A Humble Leader," *Distribution,* November 1993, pp. 32-36.

Provost, Richard, "Schneider Expands Facility to Serve As Home Base to 1,000 Truckers," *Memphis Business Journal,* March 5, 1990, pp. 44-46.

"Schneider Drops Logistics IPO," *Fleet Owner,* October 2001, p. 16.

"Schneider Launches Nationwide Intermodal Service," *American Shipper,* December 1992, p. 67.

Schulz, John D. "Legendary Follow Through: 'Analytical' Lofgren Thriving in Profit Mode in Wake of Schneider Transition to Diversification," *Traffic World,* August 23, 2004, pp. 8+.

"A Trailer-Full of Troubles," *Business Week,* June 20, 2005.

The Scoular Company

9401 Indian Creek Parkway, Building 40, Suite 850
Overland Park, Kansas 66210
U.S.A.
Telephone: (913) 338-1474
Toll Free: (800) 487-1474
Fax: (913) 338-2999
Web site: http://www.scoular.com

Private Company
Founded: 1892 as George Scoular Grain and Lumber
    Company
Employees: 340
Sales: $2 billion (2004 est.)
NAIC: 424510 Grain and Field Bean Merchant
    Wholesalers

■ ■ ■

With $2 billion in annual sales, The Scoular Company is one of the largest private companies in the United States. Based in Overland Park, Kansas, Scoular is involved in the grain business in a wide variety of ways. It stores and transports grain, and also provides producers with marketing and risk management services. In addition, Scoular serves end-users who process grains in either manufacturing or feeding operations by acting as a procurement broker. Scoular's Flourmill Markets Division supplies cereal grains to flour millers of all sizes. The company's Industrial Markets Division is engaged in the marketing of processed ingredients to the food and feed industries, both in the United States and internationally. The company also offers dairy marketing services and operates subsidiaries in Canada and Mexico.

ORIGINS DATING TO THE 1890S

The Scoular Company was founded in Superior, Nebraska, in 1892 as the George Scoular Grain and Lumber Company by Scottish immigrant George Scoular. Superior, named for the excellent farmland, was platted in 1875 and incorporated in 1879, but was located so far from rail service it had a difficult time growing until one of the town's key boosters, William Loudon, convinced the Burlington Railroad, after much pleading, that it was in the road's best interest to build an east-west connection through Superior in 1880. Over the next 20 years, three other railroads would intersect Superior, making it a significant regional hub for farmers and the largest town in Nebraska's Nuckolls County. In the early years Scoular's business mostly consisted of hauling goods by horse-drawn wagons between railroad depots.

In 1898 Scoular took a partner named Dennis Bishop and the company changed its name to Scoular and Bishop Lumber and Grain. It was Bishop who several years later established grain commission operations in Omaha and Kansas City. As the lumber business lost prominence, the company became known as Scoular-Bishop Grain Company. George Scoular died in 1930, and then in 1954 his widow and her two sons bought out the Bishop family, although the Bishop name was retained. George Scoular's son Bob Scoular, who had been working for the company since the 1920s, took over as chairman.

COMPANY PERSPECTIVES

A century-old company, Scoular's operations now extend across the North American continent and around the world.

By 1967, however, Bob Scoular came to the conclusion that the business was sorely lacking in youthful energy and needed to expand in order to survive. It was just a 25-person operation at the time, composed of three elevators in Superior, in Lovewell, Kansas, and in Council Bluffs, Iowa, and merchandising offices in Omaha and Kansas City. Scoular sold the company to a group of grain industry executives led by Marshall E. Faith, who had managerial experience at Pillsbury and Bartlett. Faith headed Scoular and assembled an executive team that would transform the little company into a powerhouse a generation later. Vice-President Jim Clinton was a key lieutenant, as was Neal E. Harlan, whom they recruited to join Scoular in 1969. Harlan had been in the grain business since starting his career with West Central Cooperative in 1956. Harlan became president and chief operating officer in 1983 and played an important role in Scoular's growth.

Soon after putting his team in place, Faith began looking to grow Scoular. The first moves were to acquire Omaha's Butler-Welsh Grain Company as well as the Omaha business of Texas-based Flour Mills of America. Scoular then focused on buying and leasing small local elevators, capable of holding 600,000 to 700,000 bushels of grain. Almost as important as the size of the elevators were the communities in which they were located. Scoular wanted to do business in towns that offered good schools and healthcare facilities. The overall goal was to create a network of locally run grain operations that were supported by the corporate parent. In this way, local identity was married to the power of a larger organization, which could bring to bear economies of scale in terms of merchandising expertise, information technology, and quantity shipping.

CHANGES IN AGRICULTURE IN THE 1970S

At the time the new ownership group took control of Scoular, the company was primarily an elevator and storage operation. "Soon the landscape changed," according to the *Omaha World-Herald*. Agriculture Secretary Earl Butz, who served from 1971 to 1976, "called on farmers to plant fence row to fence row, and

the federal government tightened its control of the supply of grain. 'If you wanted to stay in business,' Faith said, 'you had to build storage, where grain could be locked away for three to five years. We took advantage of that program.'" Scoular already had a headstart and added to its storage capacity by leasing elevators all across Nebraska and other grain-producing states, even building temporary bins to accommodate as much of the government largesse as possible.

By the mid-1980s Scoular maintained 72 grain elevators in eight states employing 550 people. With a total of 110 million bushels of licensed storage capacity, Scoular emerged as the United States' fourth largest grain warehouse company. In 1985 the U.S. Congress passed a new Farm Bill, which brought to an end government-subsidized grain storage programs. "Then the bushel bubble burst," wrote the *Omaha World-Herald.* "The federal government decided it didn't want to own what amounted to all of the grain in the world. The storage program ended and grain flowed out of bins and warehouses. Suddenly Scoular had more than 100 million bushels of empty space."

Scoular had benefited from government supports and their removal proved to be a blessing in disguise. As a matter of necessity the company was forced to scale back on storage, focus more attention on grain merchandising and distribution, and become more involved in other aspects of grain-based foods and agribusiness, such as livestock services and trading specialty food ingredients for bakers.

Harlan retired in 1989, and in 1990 Duane "Butch" Fischer succeeded him as president and shepherded Scoular through the 1990s and the next stage of the company's development. A business administration graduate of the University of Nebraska-Lincoln in 1971, Fischer started out as a futures trader with Milton G. Waldbaum Company, a Nebraska egg producer. In 1973 he joined Scoular as a grain trader.

Under Fischer, Scoular emerged as one of the United States' largest merchandisers of corn, wheat, soybeans, and other commodities. About the only thing limiting the company's growth was a lack of experienced personnel. Due to a poor farm economy in the 1980s, few grain traders were needed and trained, and after a decade of neglect the industry was not well prepared for the reinvigorated commodities market. In the mid-1990s, the lack of qualified and experienced traders was so severe that Scoular could not take on as much business as was available. In fact, it was so eager to recruit top-notch traders that it opened offices in places such as Indianola, Iowa; Springfield, Illinois; and Andover, Ohio, simply to accommodate traders who wanted to live in those communities.

KEY DATES

1892: The company is founded by George Scoular in Superior, Nebraska.

1930: George Scoular dies.

1967: An investor group headed by Marshall Faith buys the company from the Scoular family.

1990: Duane Fischer is named president.

1997: Subsidiaries are formed in Canada and Mexico.

2000: The Industrial Markets Division is formed.

2005: Scoular opens an ethanol plant in Sterling, Colorado, and in November, begins development of an ethanol production facility in Plainview, Texas, scheduled to open in 2007.

Scoular prospered by opening a lot of local offices, providing the kind of customer care larger rivals including Cargill did not offer. "We feel like getting as local to that demand as we can be is what makes us different in the marketplace," Fischer explained to the *Omaha-World Herald* in 1997. "We know whether it's raining or the sun is shining because we live there, and we have enough size and resources to serve those customers. Location, location, location, it's more important all the time." But being so local resulted in Scoular becoming unknown in some respects, as many customers did not have a full appreciation for what Scoular had to offer. On the East Coast, for example, the company was seen as a feed ingredient company, with its bulk grain operations unknown to many in the market.

"We tend to be a quiet company," Fischer told the *Omaha-World Herald*. "We're really small when compared to the major companies in our industry. We're a niche player, except we're not in one niche—we're in 30 or 40 of them. We compound that when the only Scoular our customers see is their local office with one or four or seven people. That becomes their picture of the whole company." To combat its image deficiency, in the mid-1990s Scoular began an effort to make itself better known. It hired a public relations firm and launched a web site touting itself. "We're really only coming out of our shell because we felt like it has hurt our business," Fischer explained.

DEVELOPMENTS NORTH AND SOUTH OF THE BORDER IN 1997

Along with self-promotion, Scoular began a major growth spurt. In 1997 Scoular moved beyond the U.S.

borders, established Scoular Canada in Calgary, and began trading barley, feed wheat, and oats in the western part of Canada. Also in 1997, Scoular looked to the south and formed Scoular de Mexico. For decades Scoular had shipped a great deal of grain to Mexico but only to the border, where Mexican buyers took possession and transported the grain to their own facilities. With a Mexican subsidiary in place, Scoular was now able to transport grain, feed, and food ingredients in the country, and also trade in grain in Mexico.

Domestically, Scoular grew on a number of fronts as it closed out the century. In 1998 it teamed up with Ontario, California-based Coast Grain Co. and began construction of a 100-car train receiver facility in Ontario, California. The new 960,000 bushel capacity facility became operational in 1999. Scoular was also active on the acquisitions front. In June 1998 it acquired the trading businesses of International Proteins Corporation. Then, in May 1999, Scoular acquired Foxley Grain Company, adding grain elevators in Fremont and Grainton, Nebraska, and Woodbine, Iowa. In addition, Scoular gained permits to operate five elevators in Nebraska, five in South Dakota, and one in Iowa. Scoular also received Foxley Freight Services, a livestock freight brokerage. All told, Scoular added 12.8 million bushels in capacity. Other developments for Scoular during 1998 and 1999 included the launch of a truck brokering division; the opening of offices in Scottsdale, Arizona, and Jerome, Idaho; an expansion of its Minneapolis office, adding a spring and durum wheat merchandising program; the opening of a warehouse in Thailand; and the opening of fish byproduct plants in Arkansas and Massachusetts.

Furthermore, in 1999, there was a significant change in management. Randal L. Linville was named chief executive officer while Fischer stayed on as president. Linville was well seasoned for the job. After earning bachelor's and master's degrees in agricultural economics from Kansas State University, Linville started his career in Tennessee in 1977 working for Central Soya Co., and then became a corn and oats merchandiser in Fort Wayne, Indiana, before becoming a feed grain merchant for Pillsbury in 1980. He joined Scoular in 1984 as a merchandising manager and four years later relocated to Overland Park, Kansas, to serve as southern region manager. In 1992 he became vice-president of the new grain marketing division, and then in 1997 was named president of the division. Although Scoular continued to maintain its Omaha headquarters, CEO Linville opted to remain in Overland Park.

Expansion continued for Scoular under its new CEO as it entered the new century. In 2000 Scoular opened a new Industrial Markets Division, combining the Commodity Marketing Division and the assets picked up from International Protein. The new division marketed processed ingredients to the food and feed industries, both in the United States and throughout the world. Around the same time, Scoular sold off its businesses involved in livestock marketing and truck freight brokerage. Ground was broken on a 100-car grain shipping facility in Kingfisher, Oklahoma, which would permit local wheat farmers to ship grain directly to millers in Mexico and to the Gulf of Mexico for export. Also in 2000 Scoular opened an office in Portland, Oregon.

Business at the Ontario, California facility was hindered by the bankruptcy of Coast Grain, leading to the facility's purchase in 2003. Scoular also picked up a feed manufacturing facility previously operated by Coast, which it then leased to Tulare, California-based J.D. Heiskell & Company. During this time, Scoular also expanded its grain facility in Venango, Nebraska; assumed the operations of the grain facilities owned by Farmers Grain Cooperative of Idaho; purchased a grain handling facility in Downs, Kansas; and upgraded its grain-loading facility in Alpena, South Dakota. Then, in 2004, Scoular added a new shuttle-train loading facility to Alpena as well as Fremont, Nebraska.

In 2005, Scoular acquired a bulk grain-handling terminal in Helena, Arkansas, a Mississippi River facility that transferred grain directly from trucks to two barge loading locations. In addition to its ongoing commitment to its core grain merchandising business, Scoular took steps to build up one of its newer businesses:

renewable fuels. It opened a 42-million-gallon-per-year ethanol plant in Sterling, Colorado, and in November 2005, Scoular began development of a 100-million-gallon ethanol production facility in Plainview, Texas, scheduled to open in 2007.

Ed Dinger

PRINCIPAL SUBSIDIARIES

Scoular Canada; Scoular de Mexico.

PRINCIPAL COMPETITORS

Archer Daniels Midland Company; Cargill Incorporated; ConAgra Foods, Inc.

FURTHER READING

Hendee, David, "New CEO of Omaha, Neb.-Based Grain-Trading Company to Keep Kansas Office," *Omaha-World Herald,* September 13, 1999.

————, "Quiet Company Making Some Noise," *Omaha-World Herald,* May 24, 1997, p. 1.

Howie, Michael, "Scoular Forms Division, Sells Non-Core Units," *Feedstuffs,* June 12, 2000, p. 6.

Taylor, John, "Omaha, Nev.-Based Scoular Continues Growth Pattern with New Acquisitions," *Omaha-World Herald,* May 26, 1999.

Van Dyke, Jean, "Trade Spaces," *Feed & Grain,* February-March, 2005, p. 8.

SL Industries, Inc.

———— ■ ————

520 Fellowship Road, Suite A114
Mt. Laurel, New Jersey 08054
U.S.A.
Telephone: (856) 727-1500
Fax: (856) 727-1683
Web site: http://www.slpdq.com

Public Company
Incorporated: 1956 as G-L Electronics Company
Employees: 1,406
Sales: $118.8 million (2004)
Stock Exchanges: American
Ticker Symbol: SLI
NAIC: 335931 Current-Carrying Wiring Device
   Manufacturing

■ ■ ■

SL Industries, Inc. is a public company trading on the American Stock Exchange involved in the manufacture of power electronics, power motion, and power protection equipment, mostly sold to original equipment manufacturers for use in aerospace, computer, datacom, industrial, medical, telecommunications, and utility equipment. The Mt. Laurel, New Jersey-based company operates through four main subsidiaries. Condor D.C. Power Supplies, Inc. is an Oxnard, California company that designs and manufactures AC/DC and DC/DC power supplies for medical devices and commercial applications such as elevator controls, test equipment, laboratory instruments, embroidery machines, document feeders, engraving equipment, and money order dispens-

ers and linear power supplies for both medical and commercial applications. New Jersey-based RFL Electronics makes telecommunications protection products, used to protect electric utility transmission lines and equipment by isolating troubled lines from the transmission grid. Operating out of Montevideo, Minnesota, SL Montevideo Technology, Inc. produces high-performance precision AC and DC motors, amplifiers and drives, controllers, and windings for the aerospace, defense, and industrial markets. Teal Electronics Corporation is a San Diego company that manufactures Power Conditioning and Distribution Units (PCDUs), subsystems used to control power-related products. Although SL is involved in mundane businesses, throughout its history it has dabbled in a range of enterprises, bought and sold scores of companies, and been involved in several, sometimes bitter, proxy fights for control of the company.

COMPANY'S FOUNDING IN THE 1950S

SL Industries was incorporated in 1956 by Stephen Girard Lax and Dr. Edward A. Gaugler (holder of a doctorate in physics). Drawing on the first letters of their last names, they called the company G-L Electronics. They took the company public in 1963 as G-L Industries, and the company sought to become a diversified manufacturer. It also began a pattern of buying and casting off companies, forever tinkering with its product mix, which now expanded beyond electrical products to include metalworking. G-L acquired Glaspy Corp. in 1964, followed a year later by B&S Screw Machine Products, Inc., Mercury Packaging Machinery Corp. in 1966, and Modern Hard Chrome Service in 1967. By

---

this time, in 1967, Gaugler left the company, but Lax continued to use the G-L name until November 1970, when he drew on his initials to rename it SGL Industries.

The acquisition spree continued after Gaugler's departure, as the company bought Dependable Printed Circuit Corp. and Galaxie Manufacturing Company in 1968. G-L Microwave Corporation also was organized in 1968. In 1969 the company completed three acquisitions: Dumor Hard Chrome Company, Modern Decorating Company, and Creative Decorating Company (the latter two purchases moved the company into the bottle decorating business). They were merged in 1970 to create Modern Creative Corporation.

In 1970, SGL sold G-L Microwave and bought Waber Electronics. A year later it added General Grinding Wheel Corp. to its metalworking portfolio and also bought the assets of United Chromium Corp. Although the acquisition pace fell off somewhat, SGL completed several more purchases in the 1970s, two of which moved the company into the automotive arena: Detroit's Batteries Manufacturing Company in 1974 and, in 1976, Auburn Spark Plug Company, maker of sparkplugs and igniters used in aircraft and industrial applications. Other acquisitions during the decade included Lube/Systems Corporation, Sculpta Glass Corporation, and the Grinding Wheel division of Michigan General Corp. in 1977. A year later SGL divested its graphics division, which was sold to Pittsburgh-based Pannier Corp.

SGL underwent a number of significant changes in the early 1980s. Lax died and his family sold back their shares in SGL to the company. Then in 1984, to avoid some confusion with Supermarkets General, which traded on the New York Stock Exchange under the SGL symbol, the company changed its name to SL Industries Inc. But according to *Barron's*, "A bigger reason for the switch is that the SL designation is simpler for market-

ing purposes. 'We could name a line of products the "SuperLine" and highlight the SL,' says [CEO John C.] Instone. 'That's just one idea we're considering.'" By now the company divided its businesses into four business groupings: electrical products, metalworking, plastics, and services. By far the largest contributor, accounting for more than half of the company's total revenues and the lion's share of profits, was electrical products, which included spark plugs and igniters, voltage-surge protectors, and multiple-electrical outlet strips.

NUMEROUS ASSETS BOUGHT AND SOLD IN THE MID-1980S

SL elected to exit some of the less promising businesses and buy into areas associated with emerging technologies. Hence, during the two-year period between January 1984 and January 1985, SL was involved in a flurry of buying and selling of assets. In January 1984 it sold its printed circuit division, and two months later divested B&S Screw Machine Products. In November of that year, S&L acquired New Rochelle Manufacturing, Inc. and its affiliate Dynagro Corp., involved in the manufacture of precision thermoplastic products. The Modern Creative division was sold in February 1985, followed by the sale of SL Homalite Corp. in May of the same year, and its Electronics division in August. SL also completed a pair of acquisitions in 1985, adding Montevideo Technology, Inc., producer of avionics components, and the aircraft spark plug product line of Allied Corporation's Autolite division. As a result, SL entered 1986 with a business mix that included electrical products, aviation, metalworking, and plastics, with electrical products and aviation contributing 65 percent of all sales. Now trading on the New York Stock Exchange, SL appeared to be well positioned for ongoing growth, and even moved its corporate headquarters to a new business center after years of dowdy accommodations. But the company was too dependent on defense industries, which went into decline in the late 1980s with the end of the Cold War as the Soviet Union and its Eastern European neighbors abandoned Communism. By the 1990s SL found itself struggling financially, no longer followed by investment analysts.

At the age of 64, Instone turned over the president and CEO roles to Daryl L. Renschler, 20 years younger, in February 1988 in what the company called an orderly transition. The company also launched a restructuring program to eliminate some layers of management, consolidate operations, and streamline the decision-making process. Over the years, SL had granted divisions and subsidiaries a great deal of autonomy while keeping a thin corporate operation, but it now shifted to

KEY DATES

1956: The company is founded as G-L Electronics Company.
1963: The company is taken public as G-L Industries.
1970: The name is changed to SGL Industries.
1984: The company is renamed SL Industries Inc.
1985: Montevideo Technology Inc. is acquired.
1993: Condor D.C. Power Supplies, Inc. is acquired.
1995: Teal Electronics Corporation is acquired.
1999: RFL Electronics, Inc. is acquired.
2002: Warren Lichtenstein is named CEO and chairman.
2005: Lichtenstein turns over the CEO job to James C. Taylor, but retains the chairmanship.

a more direct management approach favored by Renschler. It did not work out as planned, however. The company faltered and in April 1991 Renschler was replaced by Owen Farren. Even before Farren took charge, the company had made attempts once again to adjust its business mix, acquiring Dynatech Computer Power, Inc. and Electrostatic Technology, Inc., while casting off SL Plastics, Inc. and SL Abrasives, Inc. But Farren would find the task of turning around SL further complicated by a series of proxy fights over control of the company, engineered by dissident shareholders, or corporate raiders, in the opinion of management.

In 1992 a group led by Wilmer J. Thomas of Palm Beach, Florida, and Martin L. Solomon of Coconut Grove, Florida, who together owned less than 8 percent of SL, nominated a slate of candidates, including themselves, to the board of directors. If successful, they would seize control of the company, and promised to make changes that they said would be in the best interests of shareholders and the company. The company painted Thomas as little more than a "greenmailer," because in 1990 he had met with SL's chairman and indicated he might be interested in selling back his stock to the company. Thomas accused SL management of attempting to assassinate his character "because they can't run on their record." In the end, the dissidents took three of SL's seven board seats in December 1992, but fell short of gaining control. There was public talk of pulling together for the sake of the company from both factions, but within the year, Thomas and Solomon stepped down from the board, selling back their shares to the

company in a move, according to *Philadelphia Business Journal,* that left "many shareholders shocked and suspicious." Solomon told the publication, "Nothing very mysterious prompted my early retirement," adding, "I just didn't have a large enough economic interest in this to continue putting in all the time and energy I was."

One significant move made by SL during the time Thomas and Solomon served on the board was the February 1992 acquisition of Condor D.C. Power Supplies, Inc. and its Mexican affiliate, Electronica Condor de Mexico S.A. de C.V. In addition, SL hoped to invest more in product development. "We knew a couple of years ago that the defense business would be in rapid decline," Farren told the *Wall Street Journal* in August 1993. "So we had to move aggressively out of that area and create our own proprietary products. We have now become a problem solver and solution creator rather than a build-from-order company." Despite the rosy pictures Farren painted, a new dissident shareholder, Warren Lichtenstein, a 28-year-old partner in a New York investment firm, sought to replace the board but only won a seat on the board of directors for himself. According to *Philadelphia Business Journal,* the annual shareholders meeting "was tense and punctuated by complaints from shareholders about lack of stock performance…. Solomon's and Thomas' resignations and their stock buyout brought allegations of 'greenmail' from shareholder Charles L. Klein…. 'You people keep bleeding us dry,' Klein told the board of directors."

SL launched a restructuring program to transform itself from a mere maker of specialty products, overly dependent on defense and aerospace work, into a designer and producer of proprietary advanced systems and equipment. Customers for such products would be greatly increased because of the incorporation of microprocessors in an expanding number of products, all of which would require power conversion solutions. SL placed a great deal of emphasis on SL Waber, maker of power strips and surge protectors, which now developed surge units for large satellite installations. It was also during this time that SL acquired Teal Electronics (May 1995) while divesting businesses serving old-guard markets, such as SL LUBE/systems, Inc. in 1995 and SL Piping Systems, Inc., fabricator of metallic piping systems, in 1996.

STRONG MID-1990S PERFORMANCE

In the mid-1990s, SL's strategy appeared to be working well. Sales increased from $54.7 million in 1991 to $117.3 million in 1996. In 1997 the company sold SL Auburn, Inc., a move that management said signaled the end of its restructuring effort, and began increasing its investment in product development. In 1998 the company spent a record $6.3 million on engineering and product development, a 16.7 percent jump over the previous year. Also in 1998, SL improved its global presence by acquiring a German company, Elektro-Metall Export GmbH, a designer and manufacturer of PDQ products, such as actuators, motor controllers, and power distribution units used by industrial and aerospace original equipment manufacturers.

As the 1990s came to a close, SL's momentum was blunted; the company was adversely impacted by a recession in Asia and a slump in the semiconductor industry. SL turned to the electric utilities market, which was undergoing deregulation, and management believed offered market opportunities. In May 1999 SL acquired RFL Electronics, a maker of teleprotection systems, high-speed communications equipment, and relaying devices, with a strong base of utility customers. It also acquired Todd Products Corporation, a supplier of power supplies to the datacom, telecommunications, and computer industries, to beef up the Condor subsidiary. The overall strategy was to gear up to meet the anticipated global demand for telecommunications and data communications products. It proved to be the wrong call, as the telecommunications field and semiconductor market entered an extended downturn. Moreover, the company's surge protectors and power strips had become low-profit commodities. In response, SL discontinued these lines and consolidated Condor, Todd Products, and SL Waber into a single division, Power Electronics, a restructuring effort that cost SL more than $1 million.

Due in part to restructuring charges, revenues increased to $167.7 million in 2000, but profits fell from $5.4 million in 1999 to $1.7 million in 2000. SL's financial situation had become precarious, however. Credit Suisse First Boston was hired in February 2001 to help management explore "strategic alternatives." A group of dissident shareholders, again led by Lichtenstein, pressed for a quick sale of the company. Instead only SL Waber and Waber de Mexico were sold. Another proxy fight ensued, and this time Lichtenstein prevailed and he took over as CEO and chairman.

Under Lichtenstein, SL sold Elektro-Metall and SL Surface Technologies, but initially the company did not perform better than under the previous management regime. Sales dipped from $107.9 million in 2002 to $105.3 million in 2003, and the company's net loss grew from $470,000 in 2002 to $1.3 million in 2003. Business improved in 2004, when SL returned to profitability, earning nearly $8.7 million on revenues of $118.8

million. In August 2005, Lichtenstein turned over the CEO job to James C. Taylor, although he retained the chairmanship. Taylor had been the company's chief operating officer and had played a key role in SL's turnaround, which continued in 2005.

Ed Dinger

PRINCIPAL SUBSIDIARIES

Condor D.C. Power Supplies, Inc.; RFL Electronics, Inc.; SL Montevideo Technology, Inc.; Teal Electronics Corporation.

PRINCIPAL COMPETITORS

American Power Conversion Corporation; Emerson Electric Co.; Power-One, Inc.

FURTHER READING

Armstrong, Michael W., "Proxy Fight to Highlight SL Shareholders Meeting," *Philadelphia Business Journal,* November 2, 1992, p. 15.

Brubaker, Harold, "Philadelphia-Area Power Supplies Firm Announces Job Cuts, Financial Warning," *Philadelphia Inquirer,* July 20, 2001.

Helzen, Jerry, "Big—And Bold—Changes Have Bolstered SL Industries," *Barron's National Business and Financial Weekly,* January 6, 1986, p. 45.

———, "Careful Planning: That's Helped SGL Industries Find Profitable Niches," *Barron's National Business and Financial Weekly,* September 3, 1984, p. 64.

Kansas, Dave, "SL Industries Inc. Seeks to Expand into New Fields," *Wall Street Journal,* August 30, 1993, p. B4A.

Key, Peter, "Dissidents Up Their Stake in SL Industries," *Philadelphia Business Journal,* October 26, 2001, p. 4.

———, "SL Industries Facing Fight for Control," *Philadelphia Business Journal,* November 30, 2001, p. 3.

———, "Why Has SL Put Itself Up for Sale?," *Philadelphia Business Journal,* March 23, 2001, p. 3.

Mastrull, David, "Two Directors Quiet SL Industries," *Philadelphia Business Journal,* November 26, 1993, p. 4.

Mastrull, Diane, "Optimism Is the Order of Business at SL Industries," *Philadelphia Business Journal,* November 11, 1994, p. 3.

Reicher, Kent, "'Undervalued' SL Industries Gets a Boost," *Philadelphia Business Journal,* August 31, 1987, p. 20.

Werner, Thomas, "Upturn Ahead: SL Industries Shakes Off Run of Flat Profits," *Barron's National Business and Financial Weekly,* April 27, 1987, p. 67.

Wilen, John, "SL Industries Surges Back with Farren," *Philadelphia Business Journal,* August 23, 1996, p. 13.

Softbank Corporation

24-1, Nihonbashi-Hakozakicho Chuo-ku
Tokyo, 103-8501
Japan
Telephone: (03) 5642-8005
Fax: (03) 5641-3401
Web site: http://www.softbank.co.jp

Public Company
Incorporated: 1981 as Japan Softbank
Employees: 12,950
Sales: ¥8.38 trillion ($7.83 billion) (2005)
Stock Exchanges: Tokyo
Ticker Symbol: 9984
NAIC: 517110 Wired Telecommunications Carriers;
517910 Other Telecommunications; 522298 All
Other Non-Depository Credit Intermediation

∎ ∎ ∎

Softbank Corporation has reinvented itself, again, as the driving force behind Japan's fast-growing broadband market. The company, led by the charismatic Masayoshi Son, controls Yahoo! BB, the country's leading provider of broadband Internet access and related services, with a subscriber base of some six million people at the beginning of 2006. The company is also a leading provider of fixed line and international telecommunications services. Softbank has invested massively in building its own infrastructure and developing its own broadband technologies. As such, the company expects to reach download speeds of as much as 100 Mbps, along a fiber optic network of more than 12,000 kilometers. Having established a thriving broadband base, including the acquisition of Japan Telecom, Softbank has been eyeing an entry into the mobile telecommunications market as well; the company currently does not hold a cellular telephone license, however. In the meantime, the company has acquired Cable & Wireless IDC, the Japanese division of Cable & Wireless, establishing its presence in the fixed line segment. Few doubt Son's ability to conquer new horizons: Having founded the company as a personal computer wholesaler in the 1980s, Son guided its transformation into Japan's leading publisher of computer-oriented magazines, before emerging as one of the world's most ambitious Internet-focused venture capitalists. During that period, Son himself became one of the world's richest people, with a paper-based worth of some $90 billion. The company retains some of its former holdings, including subsidiaries involved in the sale of personal computers, peripherals, and software; magazine publishing; venture capital investments; as well as a stake in Aozora Bank. Softbank is listed on the Tokyo Stock Exchange. In 2005, the company posted revenues of ¥8.38 trillion ($7.83 billion).

1980S ENTREPRENEURIAL ORIGINS

Son was born in 1957 to Japanese citizens of Korean descent. By his own account, his early years were characterized by second-class citizenship and poverty. In a 1992 interview with Alan M. Webber of the *Harvard Business Review*, he acknowledged that, like many other Koreans in Japan, his entire family had assumed a Japanese surname, Yasumoto, in order to better assimilate into society. Son's family was able to move out of a squatter town and into the middle class by the time he reached the age of 13. At 16, Son traveled to the United States to attend high school.

The youngster flourished in his new environment, resuming his Korean surname and breezing through three grades to graduate from his California high school within a couple of weeks. Son attended Holy Names College for two years, then transferred to the University of California at Berkeley. It was there that, with the help of some professors of microcomputing, he made his first $1 million at the age of 19 by developing a pocket translator. Son sold the patent for his device to Sharp Corp., which marketed it as the Sharp Wizard. By the time he was 20, Son had earned another million importing used video game machines from Japan.

Although Son realized that it would be relatively easy to launch a business in the United States, the budding entrepreneur also knew that the Japanese culture tended to produce employees who were likely to be more loyal and work harder than their American counterparts. Consequently, he decided to return to his homeland upon his graduation from college. He spent the next 18 months researching 40 different business options ranging from software development to hospital management. Using a matrix, Son ranked each one against 25 of his own "success measures." He described a few of these to Webber in the *Harvard Business Review* interview: "I should fall in love with [the] business for the next 50 years at least," "the business should be unique," and "within 10 years I wanted to be number one in that particular business." The field he chose, wholesaling personal computer (PC) software, met the majority of his criteria. At the time, most software developers did not have the capital to promote their products to hardware manufacturers, and most hardware manufacturers and retailers did not have software to run on their machines. Son hoped to carve out a profitable niche as a liaison between the two groups.

At first, his 1981-formed company, Japan Softbank, was more spectacle than substance. Using a combination of previously earned and borrowed funds, Son purchased one of the biggest display areas available at a 1981 consumer electronics show in Tokyo. Having absolutely no product to offer, Son called all 12 of the software vendors he knew at the time and offered to display their wares at his booth *gratis*. Not surprisingly, many jumped at the opportunity. Although his exhibit, which featured a large banner proclaiming a "revolution in software distribution," caught many attendees' attention, most already had their own contacts with software vendors. The show earned the fledgling entrepreneur only one contact; luckily, it was with Japan's foremost PC retailer, Joshin Denki Co. Son negotiated exclusive rights to purchase software for the chain, then parlayed that top-notch industry connection into exclusive contracts with other firms, including Hudson Software, the country's largest vendor. Over the course of its first year in business, Japan Softbank's monthly sales increased from $10,000 to $2.3 million. By 1983, the company served more than 200 dealer outlets.

By that time, Son was pursuing additional business interests in the broader field he called "computing infrastructure." He first diversified into publishing in 1982. His original two magazine titles, *Oh!PC* and *Oh!MZ*, lost hundreds of thousands of dollars in their inaugural months due to lack of interest. But Son feared that if he dropped these sidelines clients would smell trouble, so instead he revamped the layout and threw the weight of an expensive television advertising campaign behind the project. By the early 1990s, the flagship *Oh!PC* enjoyed a circulation of about 140,000 and had become the forerunner of a stable of 20 Softbank-published periodicals, including the Japanese edition of *PC Magazine*, launched in 1989. Writing for *Forbes* in 1992, Andrew Tanzer noted that "the magazines rather shamelessly promote products Son distributes," an accepted practice in Japan. By the early 1990s, the division also had put out more than 300 computing books and become Japan's leading publisher of high-tech magazines.

A lengthy bout with hepatitis sidelined Son from 1983 through 1986. Although he gave up Japan Softbank's presidency during this period, Son kept tabs on the company via computer and telecommunications equipment installed in his hospital room. His prolonged recuperation apparently gave him time to conjure up new ideas. Upon his return to Japan Softbank's helm, Son invented a "least-cost routing device" that came to form the basis of the company's DATANET telephone data division. The idea evolved when Japan's telephone monopoly, Nippon Telegraph & Telephone Corp. (NTT), was joined by three new common carriers—DDI Corporation, Teleway Japan, and Japan Telecom—in 1986. Although they offered lower long-

KEY DATES

1981: Masayoshi Son founds Japan Softbank as a wholesaler of PC software.

1982: The company diversifies into publishing.

1989: The company launches the Japanese edition of PC Magazine.

1990: The company is renamed Softbank Corporation.

1994: Softbank is taken public; the trade show division of Ziff Communications is acquired.

1995: The company purchases 17 computer trade shows, including Comdex, from Interface Group.

1996: Ziff-Davis Publishing Co. is acquired; Softbank gains a controlling stake in Yahoo! Inc., which goes public later in the year; an 80 percent stake in memory board maker Kingston Technology Company is acquired.

1999: Softbank transforms itself into a holding company focusing on the Internet; a stake in Kingston Technology is divested.

2000: Ziff-Davis is sold off; ZD Events is spun off as Key3Media Group, with Softbank retaining a significant stake; ZDNet is sold to CNET Networks; the NASDAQ Japan Market, partially owned by Softbank, is launched; a Softbank-led consortium purchases Nippon Credit Bank, Ltd., which is renamed Aozora Bank Ltd.; Softbank's stock plunges 90 percent as the Internet stock bubble bursts.

2001: The company launches Yahoo! BB broadband service.

2002: Yahoo! BB launches Japan's first VoIP telephone service.

2003: Yahoo! BB launches online gaming services.

2004: Softbank acquires Japan Telecom, becoming the leading broadband provider in Japan; Cable and Wireless IDC is acquired.

2005: Softbank announces a partnership with Yahoo! Japan to launch an Internet television broadcasting service in 2006.

distance rates, the inconvenience of dialing the three newcomers' additional four-digit prefixes deterred many customers from signing on. Son's computerized invention, which he described as about "the size of two cigarette packs," would automatically choose the cheapest carrier and route, then dial the appropriate number. Periodic online updates kept the routers' rate information current. Japan Softbank offered the devices free to telephone customers and made money by collecting royalties on common carriers' increased billings. In the early 1990s, Son expanded the business by offering routers installed in new telephones and fax machines.

EARLY 1990S: VENTURE CAPITAL-IST AND CORPORATE MATCHMAKER

Son renamed his company Softbank Corp. in 1990. Seeking ways to invest his profits, and perhaps to erect a bulwark against getting bypassed in the distribution chain, Son soon earned renown as a venture capitalist and corporate "matchmaker." Early deals paired U.S. software vendors with Japanese partners who modified American computer applications for sale in Japan. Softbank made commissions on the matchmaking, then distributed the newly modified products.

The "marriages" got bigger in the early 1990s. In 1991, Son arranged two major computer networking alliances that combined the resources of a coterie of well-known rivals. The lead company in the first venture was BusinessLand Inc., a top systems integrator in the United States. It owned 54 percent of the $20 million venture, appropriately named BusinessLand Japan Co. Softbank held another 26 percent of the equity, while Toshiba Corp., Sony Corp., Canon Inc., and Fujitsu Ltd. each controlled 5 percent. Unlike its California-based majority partner, BusinessLand Japan eschewed the retail market in favor of corporate customers. While some analysts observed that the new venture's Japanese participants would give it a leg up on pre-existing competitors such as America's Electronic Data Systems (EDS), IBM Corp., and Digital Equipment Corp., others noted a conflict of interest in having computer manufacturers among BusinessLand Japan's investors. In fact, the venture failed and was liquidated within a year.

Nonetheless, Son had no trouble convincing many of those same corporations to invest in a second endeavor that same year, Novell Japan Ltd., in which Novell took a 54 percent stake. Softbank held 26 percent of the new company, while hardware manufacturers NEC, Toshiba Corp., Fujitsu Ltd., Canon Inc., and Sony Corp. each chipped in 4 percent of the equity. Although each of the latter five partners produced its own version of the networking system, all were compatible. The coalition sold network operating systems, peripherals, cables, transceivers, boards, and other network-related products. Since, according to Son's estimate, less than 5 percent of

Japan's PCs were networked in 1990, the allies expected to make Novell's NetWare the industry standard there. Son predicted that the Japanese computer networking industry would "grow like hell" in a 1992 interview for the *Harvard Business Review.* This prediction came true: by 1994, Novell Japan Ltd. boasted $130 million in annual sales.

That same year, Son engineered what *Business Week* called a "sweeping alliance" involving Cisco Systems Inc., Fujitsu Ltd., Toshiba Corp., and a dozen other Japanese firms. The partners anted up a total of $40 million to fund the launch of Nihon Cisco Systems, which planned to distribute internetworking systems in Japan.

Although he was widely hailed as a "whiz kid," Son was not infallible. Within just six months in 1991, he allegedly lost $10 million in a bungled online shopping venture. Systembank, a joint venture with Perot Systems, was intended to provide systems integration for large Japanese corporations. According to a February 1995 article in the *New York Times,* Systembank was "quietly disbanded." In 1994, Son convinced NTT to invest $200,000 in a "video on demand" alliance. The proposed interactive system would allow subscribers to request movies and other media at their leisure. Son boldly predicted that the joint venture would have ten million customers by the start of the 21st century. But NTT, which had a similar agreement with Microsoft Corporation, did not plan to have the necessary infrastructure (i.e., fiber optic cable to households) ready for another five to ten years, which pushed back Son's anticipated timetable substantially.

Son's first postgraduate American venture, Softbank Inc., was formed in 1993 with the cooperation of Merisel Inc., Phoenix Technologies Ltd., and telemarketer Alexander and Lord. The new subsidiary planned to distribute software through the interactive Softbank On-Hand Library service. Softbank Inc.'s vice-president, Meg Tuttle, described the demo discs as "adware." Reviewer Steve Bass of *PC World* "fell in love" with the $10 CD-ROMs, which allowed users to "test-drive" more than 100 programs, then order and pay for the selected software online. Several big-league computer companies, including Apple Computer, IBM, and Ingram Micro, had already launched similar promotions. But other analysts and competitors nixed the idea. For example, David Goldstein, president of Channel Marketing, told *PC Week*'s Lawrence Aradon that offering software on compact discs would become "the Edsel of the computer industry." The venture's direct competition with one of Softbank's most important consumer groups, software retailers, broke what Steve Hamm of *PC Week* called one of Son's golden rules: "Don't compete with clients or

suppliers." By early 1995, in fact, a number of industry analysts pronounced the venture defunct for that very reason.

MID-1990S: EXPANDING INTO "DIGITAL INFORMATION INFRASTRUCTURE"

Son took Softbank Corp. public in 1994 in an offering that valued the company at $3 billion. The founder retained a 70 percent interest in his company. Coming off the late 1994 loss of a bidding war for the U.S. magazine publishing operations of Ziff Communications Co., Son acquired that firm's trade show division for $202 million. The subsidiary's name was changed from ZD Expos to Softbank Expos. Early in 1995, Softbank made a major addition to that interest with the $800 million purchase of a package of 17 computer trade shows from Sheldon Adelson's Interface Group.

The acquisition, which was financed with at least $500 million in debt and a new offering of Softbank Corp. shares, nearly doubled Softbank's U.S. operations.

The acquisition included the Las Vegas Comdex show, which was characterized in a 1995 *Wall Street Journal* article as "a huge draw in the computer industry." Launched in 1979, Comdex attracted 195,000 attendees and 2,200 exhibitors to its November 1994 show. Although the event remained popular, its high prices had come under criticism. Some major exhibitors, including Compaq, Packard Bell, Oracle, and Seagate Technologies, had already opted out of the show by the time Softbank took over. Son expressed confidence that he could revitalize the event without a total revamp, citing the fact that exhibit space for the 1995 show was already 90 percent booked by the previous spring. Expansion plans for the new businesses included the first French Softbank Expo in 1995 and the premier Japanese and British Comdexes in 1996.

Son's aggressive approach to acquisitions continued in 1996. In February Softbank was able to secure Ziff-Davis Publishing Co., which Son had failed to acquire in late 1994, through a $1.8 billion purchase price, paid to Forstmann Little & Co. (the firm that had outbid it the first time around). Ziff-Davis was the leading publisher of computer and high-tech magazines in the United States and had a several-years-long relationship with Softbank involving licensing deals to publish Japanese versions of Ziff computer magazines, including *PC Magazine.*

Son's expansion into trade shows and publishing was part of his aim to become the world's leading provider of "digital information infrastructure." Along these lines were two additional 1996 developments. In

1995 Softbank had already purchased a 5 percent stake in Yahoo! Inc., initially the provider of a directory for the Internet before evolving into the premier Internet portal. In April 1996 Softbank increased this stake to a controlling 37 percent, marking the firm's first major investment in the Internet; later in 1996 Yahoo! was taken public. Son was aggressive not only with acquisitions but also in exploiting synergies between his burgeoning holdings. For example, the new Ziff-Davis magazine title *Internet Life* was recast as *Yahoo! Internet Life*; positioned as the "*TV Guide* of the Internet," this title's advertising rate base reached 200,000 by the end of 1996. Softbank and Yahoo! also set up a joint venture called Yahoo! Japan Corporation, 60 percent owned by Softbank, which created a Japanese-language version of Yahoo! that quickly became the most visited web site in Japan.

Consummated in September 1996 was the $1.51 billion purchase of an 80 percent stake in Kingston Technology Company, a privately held maker of PC memory boards based in Fountain Valley, California. The acquisitions and investments in Softbank, Ziff-Davis, Yahoo!, and Kingston were part of a clear and rapid expansion outside of Japan, concentrating on the world's key technology market, that of the United States. Yet another 1996 development, meanwhile, was centered on Japan as Softbank entered the field of digital satellite broadcasting through the establishment of Japan Sky Broadcasting Co., Ltd., a joint venture with Rupert Murdoch's News Corporation Limited.

Softbank's spectacular series of acquisitions resulted in the doubling of net sales from 1996 to 1997, from ¥171.1 billion ($1.61 billion) to ¥359.74 billion ($2.9 billion), and a 94 percent jump in pretax profits, from ¥15.98 billion ($150.3 million) to ¥29.57 billion ($238.3 million). At the same time, long-term debt used to fund the company's expansion was ballooning, reaching ¥595.03 billion ($4.79 billion) by the end of 1997. Concern about the debt load, coupled with slower sales growth and falling margins, as well as allegations of improprieties in the company's financial disclosures (which were widely disseminated in a best-selling book in Japan called *Inside Revelation: Softbank's Warped Management,* whose publisher, Yell Books, was sued by Softbank), sent Softbank's stock plunging from ¥8,450 in early 1997, its peak for the year, to a low of ¥1,670 by November of that year. Another setback for Softbank in 1997 was a serious dilution of its initial 50 percent stake in Japan Sky Broadcasting when Sony Corporation and Fuji TV joined the venture followed by the merging of it with a competitor, Japan Digital Broadcasting Services. Softbank's stake was reduced to 11.4 percent.

To raise much needed cash, Son began seeking listings for some of his subsidiary companies. In November 1997 Yahoo! Japan was taken public on the Japanese over-the-counter (OTC) market, with Softbank keeping a 51 percent stake. Then in April 1998, 26 percent of stock in the renamed Ziff-Davis Inc. was sold through an initial public offering (IPO) on the New York Stock Exchange, raising $400 million. Prior to its listing, Ziff-Davis was given ownership of Softbank's exhibits operations, which were initially called ZD Comdex and Forums Inc. but were soon renamed ZD Events Inc., as well as ZDNet, a web site featuring online versions of a number of Ziff-Davis publications. Meanwhile, Softbank's stock began trading on the first section of the Tokyo Stock Exchange in January 1998.

"JAPAN'S BILL GATES" IN THE LATE 1990S

The late 1990s saw Softbank increase its investments in the Internet significantly, during what would eventually be viewed as the Internet stock bubble. By mid-1999, Softbank had significant stakes in Yahoo!, Yahoo! Japan, ZDNet, community-oriented portal GeoCities, e-commerce "superstore" Buy-com Inc., consumer loan specialist E-Loan Inc., and online broker E*Trade Group Inc. Through joint ventures, Softbank had helped establish several more Japanese versions of successful American web sites, including E-Loan Japan, E*Trade Japan, GeoCities Japan, and Morningstar Japan, the latter a venture with Morningstar Inc. that set up a web site providing Japanese financial news and market analysis. Although not all of Son's Internet investments were successful, he was able to ride the $338 million he had invested in Yahoo! to spectacular heights. Yahoo!'s soaring stock price led Softbank's investment to be worth more than $10 billion by mid-1999. Overall, the $2 billion that Son had invested in 100 Internet companies was worth more than $17 billion by this time. In March 1999 Ziff-Davis created a tracking stock for ZDNet and sold 16 percent of the unit to the public through an IPO. In the topsy-turvy world of the Internet stock bubble, by mid-1999 ZDNet had a market capitalization greater than that of Ziff-Davis, despite Ziff-Davis's 84 percent stake in ZDNet.

In June 1999 Softbank Corp. transformed itself into a holding company focusing on the Internet. The finance-oriented Internet holdings, including E*Trade and Morningstar Japan, were combined within a new subsidiary called Softbank Finance Corporation. Softbank's technology services related to e-commerce were bundled within Softbank Technology Corp., which was taken public in July 1999 on the Japanese OTC market. That same month, Softbank sold its stake in Kingston

Technology back to the company's founders for $450 million, in a move to divest non-Internet assets. Also in July, Softbank began exploring strategic options related to Ziff-Davis, including the possible sale of the company in what would be a further concentration on the Internet. One month earlier, Softbank joined with the National Association of Securities Dealers (NASDAQ) to create a joint venture called NASDAQ Japan, Inc. to set up a Japanese version of the NASDAQ. In June 2000 the NASDAQ Japan Market commenced operations with eight listed companies.

In early 2000 Softbank began selling off Ziff-Davis piecemeal, initially planning to retain ZDNet. In April 2000 the magazine unit was sold for $780 million to a partnership headed by Willis Stein & Partners, L.P., emerging as Ziff Davis Media Inc. The ZD Events unit was spun off to shareholders as a new company called Key3Media Group, Inc., in which Softbank retained a sizable stake. ZDNet would have then become a stand-alone, publicly traded company 45 percent owned by Softbank. But CNET Networks Inc., ZDNet's arch-rival, stepped in with a takeover offer, which was accepted, resulting in a $1.6 billion-in-stock acquisition later in 2000.

By February 1999, Son's emphasis on the Internet had helped send his company's share price soaring to ¥60,667 ($592). At that point, Softbank's market value was $190 billion. By late November, the share price had plunged more than 90 percent to ¥5,970 ($53.87). The company's market value dropped by $172 billion in just nine months, reaching $17.9 billion. During this precipitous decline, Softbank was forced to abandon plans to sell shares in five of its main subsidiaries: Softbank E-Commerce Corp., Softbank Finance, Softbank Media & Marketing Corp., Softbank Broadmedia Corporation, and Softbank Networks Inc. Later in 2000, faced with continued stock market doldrums, Softbank put the brakes on joint ventures in Europe with News Corporation and Vivendi, both of which aimed at creating European versions of U.S. Internet companies. In September 2000, a Softbank-led consortium purchased Nippon Credit Bank, Ltd., which had collapsed in late 1998, from the Japanese government for $932 million. Softbank held a 49 percent stake in the bank, which was renamed Aozora Bank Ltd., as Softbank became the first nonfinancial company to enter the Japanese banking sector. Both NASDAQ Japan and Aozora Bank were viewed by Son as underpinnings of a new financial infrastructure in Japan that might foster the development of the Internet-centered economy—and in turn, Softbank—by remedying the chronic shortage of capital faced by the nation's venture firms.

BROADBAND LEADER IN THE 2000S

At the lowest point during the crash of the dot-com market and the subsequent collapse of the international telecommunications market, Softbank's market valuation had dropped back to just $15.5 billion. Son's personal net worth dropped accordingly, and by 2001 had slipped to as low as $1.1 billion. Son's difficulties continued into the new decade, particularly after his partners moved to shut down NASDAQ Japan. Although Softbank's own investment in the exchange had been minimal, the company lost a much needed outlet for its rapidly devaluing holdings. As a result, the company was forced to write off huge portions of its investments, which included stakes in some 600 companies, while selling off parts of its other investments, including some of its stake in Yahoo!, to finance its continuing operations.

Yet Son remained resilient. Indeed, Son even seemed somewhat relieved that the dot-com bubble had burst. As he told *Forbes*: "The market became filled with people who had no understanding of the Internet. They had no passion for the Internet, they just had a passion for making money. It was a boom without belief. With the market correction, those who are passionate just about making money are leaving. Now it is a better situation in which to make investments. Prices are more realistic."

Even as the venture capital market was in the process of self-destructing, Son had already found a new avenue for Softbank's future growth: broadband. At the beginning of the 2000s, Japan had fallen behind most of the world's developed markets in the rollout of broadband technologies, in large part because of a lack of interest from NTT. Son recognized the opportunity to build Softbank's own high-speed network, leading the development of proprietary technology that enabled the deployment of broadband speeds of 10 Mbps, the fastest in the world at the time, and which was capable of being scaled up to 100 Mbps.

Son did not hesitate to invest billions in the construction of the company's network, selling off large swathes of its shares in Yahoo! especially in order to finance the infrastructure development. Nonetheless, the company carefully maintained control of Yahoo! Japan, redeveloping that brand into Japan's first commercial broadband service, Yahoo! BB. Son's passion for the company's new broadband strategy was evident in his own devotion to the network's creation. Leaving his office at Softbank's headquarters behind, Son went to work alongside the Yahoo! BB engineering team, putting in 15-hour days, including weekends, with no break for vacation for some 18 months. The company also supported the rollout of its new services through strong advertising spending, and even, at one point, handed out free modems on the street to passersby.

Yahoo! BB was slow in taking off, until Son recognized the potential of new voice-over-Internet protocols (VoIP), and of offering broadband-based telephone services. NTT remained a major stumbling block for the company, in its refusal to connect the company's network to the country's telephone system, despite the government's orders that it do so. Famously, Son had his way by threatening to immolate himself during a meeting with Japan's communications ministry, and the company launched its VoIP service in 2002.

Subscribers flocked to Yahoo! BB to take advantage of its telephone services, which included free calls among Yahoo! BB subscribers and low dialing rates to NTT's fixed line network and internationally as well. Before long, NTT was forced to respond with their own broadband offers. By the mid-2000s, Son was credited with having transformed Japan from an Internet "backwater" to the world's most vibrant telecommunications market. By 2004, the company had signed up more than four million subscribers.

Yet Softbank was soon overtaken by its rivals, which, backed by NTT's muscle, quickly expanded their networks beyond Softbank's own somewhat limited, mostly coaxial-based network. Son struck back, however, with the acquisition of Japan Telecom in 2004. Paying some $3.1 billion, Softbank acquired Japan's third largest fixed line telecommunications group, with more than 600,000 residential subscribers, 150,000 corporate clients, and, most important, a national network of more than 12,000 kilometers of fiber optic cable. The addition of Japan Telecom once again placed Softbank at the head of the country's fast-growing broadband market.

Softbank continued to roll out new services to attract new customers and raise spending of its existing customers. The company added online gaming services in 2003, and its own broadband-based television services, including video-on-demand and pay-per-view movie offerings. Nonetheless, the cost of building its network remained high, and the company continued to post massive losses into the mid-2000s, forcing it to continue sales of parts of its other investments, including much of its remaining stake in Yahoo!.

In the meantime, Son began lobbying the Japanese government to allow new entrants to the country's mobile telecommunications market, including, Son hoped, Softbank. Son even went so far as to file a lawsuit against the communications ministry. Challenging the ministry in this way was not without risks, not the least because of the risk of creating a new Softbank rival. As Son told *Business Week*: "I'm getting smarter. It's still business suicide, but it's better than physically killing myself." In the meantime, Son remained committed to expanding Softbank's fixed line presence. At the end of 2004, the company acquired Cable & Wireless IDC, the Japanese subsidiary of international telecom group Cable & Wireless. That acquisition gave Son control of Japan's second largest international voice and data telecommunications business.

Into 2006, Softbank continued to seek new means of expanding its service offering, and its subscriber revenues. In December 2005, for example, the company announced the formation of a partnership with Yahoo! Japan to launch Internet-based television broadcasts. The two companies expected to launch the service as early as March 2006. Masayoshi Son had successfully established himself as a leading fixture in Japan's telecommunications market.

April D. Gasbarre
Updated, David E. Salamie; M. L. Cohen

PRINCIPAL SUBSIDIARIES

Abovenet Japan, Inc.; Alps Mapping K.K.; Asia Vision Japan Inc.; Bb Backbone Corporation; Bb Cable Corporation; Bb Marketing Corporation; Bb Mobile Corporation; Bb Serve, Inc.; Bbix, Inc.; Best Broadband Corporation; Blue Planet Corporation; Bridalnet, Inc.; Broadband Japan Corporation; Carview Corporation; Cj Internet Japan Corporation; Cmnet Corporation; Creativebank Inc.; Deecorp Limited; Diamond.Com Corporation; Ebest Corporation; Greenfield Corporation; Gungho Online Entertainment, Inc.; Hr Solutions Corporation; Investoria Inc.; Ip Revolution, Inc.; Japan Telecom America, Inc.; Japan Telecom China Co., Ltd.; Japan Telecom Co., Ltd.; Japan Telecom Information Service Co., Ltd.; Japan Telecom Network Information Service Co., Ltd.; Japan Telecom Singapore Pte. Ltd.; Japan Telecom UK Ltd.; Jtos Co., Ltd.; Laox Bb Corporation; Macs Broadband Corporation; Nc Japan K.K.; Net Culture Kk; Netrust, Ltd.; Overseas Human Resources, Inc.; Oy Gamecluster Ltd.; Sb China Holdings Pte Ltd; Seven and Y Corporation (formerly E-Shopping! Books Corporation); Softbank Bb Corporation; Softbank Bb Corporation; Softbank Broadmedia Corporation; Softbank Capital Partners; Softbank Frameworks Corporation; Softbank Human Capital Corporation; Softbank Idc Corporation; Softbank Korea Co., Ltd.; Softbank Logistics Corporation; Softbank Media & Marketing Corporation; Softbank Publishing Inc.; Softbank Technology Corporation; Softbank Technology Ventures Iv L.P.; Softbank Technology Ventures V L.P.; Tavigator, Inc.; Te Co. Ltd.; Technoblood Inc.; Tmsw Corporation; Trustguard Co., Ltd.; Vector Inc.; Xdrive Japan K.K.; Yahoo! Japan Corporation; Yahoo! Deutschland GmbH; Yahoo! France S.A.S.; Yahoo! Korea Corporation; Yahoo! UK Limited; Yamada Broadband Corporation; Y's Insurance Inc.

PRINCIPAL COMPETITORS

Nippon Telegraph and Telephone Corporation; Tokyo Electric Power Company Inc.; Vodafone Holdings K.K.; NTT Communications Corporation; Hikari Tsushin Inc.; Commuture Corporation; Bellsystem 24 Inc.; Kanda Tsushinki Company Ltd.; Seibu Electric Industry Company Ltd; Okinawa Cellular Telephone Co.; TTK Company Ltd.; Oi Electric Company Ltd.

FURTHER READING

"After the Party," *Economist,* May 18, 1996, p. 65.

Aragon, Lawrence, "Off and Running," *PC Week,* March 14, 1994, p. A1.

Bass, Steve, "Hot Picks for the Home Office," *PC World,* March 1995, p. 241.

"The Best Entrepreneurs," *Business Week,* January 9, 1995, p. 112.

Bickers, Charles, "Japan's Mr. Internet: Softbank's Bold Moves Cause Ripples in Japan Inc.," *Far Eastern Economic Review,* July 29, 1999, pp. 11-12.

Bremner, Brian, "Hard Truths for Softbank," *Business Week,* August 9, 2004, p. 38.

———, "Is Softbank Sinking? Don't Bet on It," *Business Week,* April 24, 2000, p. 144.

———, "Why Softbank Is Shouting 'Yahoo!,'" *Business Week,* September 7, 1998, p. 48.

Bremner, Brian, and Amy Cortese, "Cyber-Mogul: To Conquer the Net, Masayoshi Son Takes to the High Wire," *Business Week,* August 12, 1996, pp. 56-62.

Bremner, Brian, and Linda Himelstein, "Softbank's Cyber Keiretsu," *Business Week,* April 5, 1999, p. 24.

Bulkeley, William M., Jim Carlton, and Norihiko Shirouzu, "Japanese Firm to Buy Comdex Computer Show," *Wall Street Journal,* February 14, 1995, p. A3.

Burke, Steven, "$20 Million Joint Venture Gives BusinessLand Foothold in Japan," *PC Week,* June 11, 1990, p. 119.

Butler, Steven, "Empire of the Son: The Bill Gates of Japan Controls a Huge Chunk of the Internet," *U.S. News and World Report,* July 5, 1999, pp. 48, 50.

Desmond, Edward W., "Japan's Top Technology Investor Takes a Hit," *Fortune,* September 8, 1997, pp. 150-52.

Gilley, Bruce, Chester Dawson, and Dan Biers, "Internet Warrior on the Defensive," *Far Eastern Economic Review,* November 16, 2000, pp. 54+.

"Grounded Internet High Flyer Takes on NTT," *Business Asia,* August 2003, p. 21.

Hamilton, David P., "Comdex Owner Doesn't Plan to Alter Show," *Wall Street Journal,* February 21, 1995, p. A13B.

Hamilton, David P., and Norihiko Shirouzu, "Softbank to Buy Memory Board Maker," *Wall Street Journal,* August 16, 1996, p. A3.

Hamlin, Kevin, "Son Rise, Son Set?," *Institutional Investor International Edition,* June 2001, p. 29.

Hamm, Steve, "The Rising Son," *PC Week,* April 10, 1995, p. A1.

"Heat Turns Up on the Rising Son," *Financial Times,* November 13, 1997, p. 39.

Holyoke, Larry, "Japan's Hottest Entrepreneur Hits the U.S.," *Business Week,* February 27, 1995, p. 118G.

Ip, Greg, and Bill Spindle, "NASDAQ Plans to Set Up a New Stock Market in Japan: Softbank to Invest in Proposed Project," *Wall Street Journal,* June 16, 1999, p. A19.

Kunii, Irene M., "Get Those Stun Guns Ready: Here Comes Masayoshi Son," *Business Week,* August 4, 2003, p. 24.

Landers, Peter, "Prodigal Son: For 'Japan's Bill Gates,' Last Year Was Daunting. Can Masayoshi Son Come Back?," *Far Eastern Economic Review,* January 22, 1998, pp. 42+.

Lipin, Steven, "Persistence Pays Off in Second Sale of Ziff-Davis," *Wall Street Journal,* December 29, 1995, p. C1.

———, "Ziff-Davis Unit of Forstmann Set to Be Sold," *Wall Street Journal,* November 9, 1995, p. A3.

McCartney, Laton, "The Rising Son," *Upside,* April 1997, pp. 108-10.

Moffett, Sebastian, "The Entrepreneur: Softbank's Masayoshi Son Builds an Unconventional Empire," *Far Eastern Economic Review,* November 7, 1996, p. 206.

———, "A Whole New Ballgame," *Far Eastern Economic Review,* July 4, 1996, p. 70.

Ono, Kazuyuki, "Fortunate Son: A One-of-a-Kind Success Story," *Tokyo Business Today,* October 1995, pp. 26+.

Patch, Kimberly, "'Virtual Shopping' Via CD-ROM," *PC Week,* July 12, 1993, p. 6.

Pollack, Andrew, "A Japanese Gambler Hits the Jackpot with Softbank," *New York Times,* February 19, 1995, Sec. 3, p. 10.

Rocks, David, "Setting Fire to the Cell-Phone Market," *Business Week,* November 1, 2004, p. 22.

Rowley, Ian, and Hiroko Tashiro, "Where the Net Has Telecom on the Run," *Business Week,* June 27, 2005, p. 28.

"Setting Son," *Economist,* August 24, 2002.

Shirouzu, Norihiko, and David P. Hamilton, "Softbank's Buying Spree May Be Hard Act to Follow," *Wall Street Journal,* August 19, 1996, p. B4.

Smith, Dawn, "Demo Disk Double-Take," *Marketing Computers,* October 1993, pp. 18-19.

"Softbank, Yahoo Start Internet Television Service," *Reuters,* December 27, 2005.

Spindle, Bill, "Japan's Softbank Hits Some Rough Road," *Wall Street Journal,* October 17, 1997, p. A16.

Strom, Stephanie, "Its Own Stock Battered, Softbank Abandons Spinoff Plan," *New York Times,* August 2, 2000, p. C4.

Sugawara, Sandra, "Masayoshi Son Was Among the First to Flout Japan's Business Establishment," *Washington Post,* May 9, 1999, p. H1.

Tanzer, Andrew, "Hot Hands," *Forbes,* May 11, 1992, p. 182.

Umezawa, Masakuni, "The New Golden Age of Wireless," *Tokyo Business Today,* November 1994, pp. 10-12.

Webber, Alan M., "Japanese-Style Entrepreneurship: An Interview with Softbank's CEO, Masayoshi Son," *Harvard*

Business Review, January-February 1992, pp. 93-103.

Weinberg, Neil, "Overreaction," *Forbes,* February 9, 1998, pp. 47-48.

Weinberg, Neil, and Amy Feldman, "Bubble, Bubble ... ," *Forbes,* March 11, 1996, p. 42.

Sonic Automotive, Inc.

—■—

6415 Idlewild Road, Suite 109
Charlotte, North Carolina 28212
U.S.A.
Telephone: (704) 566-2400
Fax: (770) 536-4665
Web site: http://www.sonicautomotive.com

Public Company
Incorporated: 1997
Employees: 11,600
Sales: $7.4 billion (2004)
Stock Exchanges: New York
Ticker Symbol: SAH
NAIC: 441110 New Car Dealers

■ ■ ■

Charlotte, North Carolina-based Sonic Automotive, Inc. is the third largest automobile retailer in the United States, a *Fortune* 300 company, and a member of the Russell 2000 index. It is composed of some 200 dealership franchises and 40 collision repair centers located in 15 mostly Sunbelt states, preferring middle markets where dealerships are cheaper to acquire, profits are higher, and the competition for customers is not as steep. Sonic has grown from just a handful of dealerships in the mid-1990s by adopting a "hub and spoke" approach. Sonic enters a market by acquiring a "hub" dealership, one that is well respected in a market, enjoys strong customer satisfaction, and a strong market share. Underperforming dealerships in the area are then added as spokes, and the expertise of the managers of the hub

operation is used to help the underperformers achieve their potential. Overall, Sonic sells more than 35 brands of cars and light trucks. Although a public company listed on the New York Stock Exchange, Sonic is 74 percent owned by Chairman and Chief Executive Officer O. Bruton Smith.

FOUNDER, A 1960S FORD DEALER

Before launching Sonic, Bruton Smith became better known to the public as a leader in the NASCAR racing circuit, the head of publicly traded Speedway Motorsports Inc., which operated several NASCAR racetracks. He first became an automobile dealer with a Ford franchise in Rockford, Illinois, in 1969. He prospered and added two more Ford dealerships, but at the time three was the maximum number of dealerships Ford would allow. Hence, he branched out to open Chrysler, Toyota, BMW, and Mercedes franchises in North Carolina, Texas, and Georgia. Smith moved his operations to Charlotte in 1978. He eventually soured on auto retailing because of manufacturers' rules and the capital-intensive nature of the business. Smith dropped out and concentrated on his racetrack operations, but when automakers loosened their restrictions allowing ownership of multiple stores, he regained his interest in the business.

Automobile retailing was traditionally a highly fragmented industry, dominated by family-owned dealerships spread across the country. As was the case in many industries, however, businessmen, including Wayne Huizenga of Waste Management and Blockbuster Video fame, in the 1990s began looking to consolidate, to build a large portfolio of dealerships and gain a competitive edge through the benefits achieved from economies of scale, especially in terms of advertising. To fuel these ambitions they turned to Wall Street to engineer public offerings, not only to provide cash to buy dealerships but also to have stock to use in lieu of cash for acquisitions. There was also a large pool of willing sellers, families who had established their dealerships in the boom years of the 1940s just after World War II. Many of them lacked a second or third generation willing to carry on the business and were looking for an exit strategy. Cash was welcomed, but so was stock, which at least gave the sellers a chance to cash in at an opportune time.

Bruton Smith was one of those businessmen who wanted to be a consolidator in auto retailing. In February 1997 he incorporated Sonic Automotive, Inc. and began building up its portfolio of dealerships before tapping the equity markets. Smith got a head start with the 1996 purchase of Fort Mill Ford in South Carolina for $5.7 million. Then in June 1997 Sonic paid about $3.7 million for Fort Mill Chrysler-Plymouth-Dodge. More acquisitions followed in the fall of 1997. Sonic paid $18.3 million for Lake Norman Dodge and its affiliates in September. A pair of acquisitions were completed in October: $1.8 million for Williams Motors, Inc. located in Rock Hill, South Carolina, and $25.5 million for Clearwater, Florida-based Ken Marks Ford, Inc. Then, in November 1997, Sonic paid $18 million in cash to acquire Atlanta's Dyer & Dyer Volvo, and another $27.6 million for the Bowers Dealerships and affiliates located mostly in Chattanooga and Nashville, Tennessee.

With 23 dealerships in five states as well as four stand-alone used-vehicle lots and seven collision-repair centers, altogether generating close to $900 million in sales, Sonic went public in November 1997 at $12 a share, with the initial stock offering underwritten by a group of firms led by Merrill Lynch. The stock did not, however, flourish after it began trading, enjoying a high of $12.37 before it soon dipped below the $10 mark. Investors were generally optimistic about Sonic's business plan and respected the ability of Smith and his team, which included his son and heir apparent, Scott

Smith, but were mistrustful of the industry in general, believing that car sales were too cyclical. According to *Barron's,* "IPO investors reasonably ask: How much better will it get over time?" Indeed, Group 1 Automotive, backed by another Wall Street heavyweight in Goldman Sachs, experienced a similar fate after going public two weeks earlier than Sonic.

Despite the tepid response from investors in the aftermarket, Sonic forged ahead with a business plan and continued to apply its "hub and spoke," middle market strategy in 1998. To assuage fears of shareholders concerned that it could not support and control its growth, Sonic beefed up senior management by adding a president and vice-president of retail operations. The company also looked to achieve some geographic diversity, so that it was not vulnerable to downturns in local and regional economies. In 1998 Sonic entered new markets such as Columbus, Ohio; Montgomery, Alabama; Daytona Beach, Florida; and Greenville, South Carolina. Moreover, Sonic diversified its brands, adding balance to the mix to ensure that the company was not overly dependent on any one brand. Over the course of the year Sonic bought dealerships representing brands such as Chevrolet, Mercedes, Hyundai, Subaru, Isuzu, Lincoln, Mercury, and Mitsubishi. All told, Sonic acquired 19 dealerships representing 20 brands. In addition, the acquisitions completed in 1997 were successfully integrated and their operations improved, resulting in a 25 percent increase in operating income for these dealerships over the prior year. Sonic also was beginning to enjoy the benefits of size as interest costs and insurance expenses were lowered, resulting in greater profits and larger dividends to shareholders. For 1998 Sonic generated revenues of more than $1.6 billion, netting $18.6 million, or 74 cents per share. Even before the results were announced, Sonic had clearly outperformed its rivals and gained the respect of Wall Street, which by the end of the year bid up the price to more than $34 a share. Sheldon Sandler, head of investment banking firm Bel Air Partners, told *Automotive News,* "Sonic has raised the chinning bar for anybody else that wants to be public." The stock price soon topped $36 and in January 1999 the company engineered a 2-for-1 stock split.

Sonic closed the 1990s with another strong year, marked by the largest acquisition, to date, in the history of automotive retailing: FirstAmerica Automotive. The deal provided Sonic entry into the highly coveted, high-growth California market, as well as giving it a coast-to-coast footprint. Moreover, Sonic added several luxury brands and picked up the services of FirstAmerica's talented and seasoned management team. In addition, in 1999 Sonic acquired another 44 dealerships and expanded into ten new metropolitan markets including Las Vegas, Nevada; Washington, D.C.; Mobile, Alabama;

```
┌─────────────────────────────────────────────┐
│                                               │
│              KEY DATES                        │
│                  ■                            │
├───────────────────────────────────────────────┤
│  1969:  O. Bruton Smith opens his first car   │
│         dealership.                           │
│  1978:  Smith moves operations to Charlotte,  │
│         North Carolina.                       │
│  1997:  Sonic is launched in Charlotte and    │
│         taken public.                         │
│  1999:  FirstAmerica Automotive is acquired.  │
│  2002:  Don Massey Dealerships is acquired.   │
└───────────────────────────────────────────────┘
```

Panama City, Florida; Monroe, North Carolina; Florence, South Carolina; and a number of cities in Texas, including Houston, Baytown, Richardson, and Stafford. To help pay the price tag, Sonic raised $85 million in a secondary stock offering held in April 1999 and raised another $280 million in debt financing while increasing its available credit lines by $250 million. As a result of these acquisitions, Sonic's revenues soared to $3.35 billion and net income approached $45 million in 1999.

ACQUISITIONS CONTINUING IN THE NEW CENTURY

In 2000 Sonic acquired 11 dealerships, representing 16 different brands and accounting for nearly $800 million in annual sales. The company also took stock of its dealership portfolio, which included a number of dealerships that were essentially acquisition throw-ins. Many of these were weeded out, resulting in the 2000 sale of eight dealerships representing some $65 million in annual sales. Overall 2000 was a strong year for Sonic, despite sluggish new vehicle sales in the final months of the year.

Sonic continued to expand through acquisitions in 2001, adding a dozen dealerships representing $1 billion in annual sales. These purchases included Buena Park Honda, HarborCity Honda, and Coast Cadillac in the Los Angeles area, and Lawrence Marshall Chevrolet in Houston. Sonic was even more active in 2002, acquiring 31 dealerships representing $1.8 billion in annual sales. The most important deal took place early in the year with the purchase of Michigan-based Don Massey Dealerships, a seven-state chain of 16 dealerships with $1 billion in annual revenue. After the acquisition, Sonic did background checks on Massey personnel and fired 200 of the 1,550 employees. The company's caution was understandable, given that two of its Clearwater dealerships were under investigation in Florida for fraudulent sales practices in the finance and insurance

departments, problems the company blamed on rogue employees at some of Sonic's early acquisitions before policies and training were implemented to curb unethical practices.

It was also during 2002 that the 75-year-old Bruton Smith was reported to be on the verge of retirement. In November 2002 Scott Smith was promoted to the post of vice-chairman and chief strategic officer along with other managerial changes that the younger Smith told the press was "really kind of a prelude to our successorship." Bruton Smith quickly told the *Charlotte Observer,* "I'm not going to retire, period. We have no successorship plan." Scott Smith, according to the *Observer,* told board member William Belk that he had misspoken. "He was probably forecasting 20 years down the road, not the next year or two," Belk explained.

TAKING STOCK AFTER A DISAP-POINTING 2003

Sonic experienced a disappointing year in 2003, when it failed to keep pace with its peer group and failed to live up to its own expectations. The company continued to grow through acquisitions, adding dealerships in existing markets such as Atlanta, Dallas, San Francisco, and Detroit, many of them representing luxury brands such as Porsche, BMW, Jaguar, and Mercedes. But Sonic's sluggish performance in 2003 prompted management to take stock of its operating strategies, including its aggressive acquisition program. Much of Sonic's success had been based on buying and turning around underperforming dealerships. But such an approach put a great deal of pressure on the managers, who were now buckling under the strain. As a result, management decided to put on the brakes somewhat, limiting acquisitions to no more than 10 percent of annual revenues. Moreover, management looked to improve profitability by better controlling costs, in particular advertising and sales compensation.

Many of the recommended changes implemented by Sonic began to show progress in 2004. The company cut back on acquisitions, allowing recent purchases to be integrated into the company. At the same time, management came to the conclusion that acquisitions had to remain a key part of company strategy in light of the automotive industry, which remained highly fragmented and offered great opportunities. Hence, Sonic began to adopt a concept it called "enriching our dealership portfolio." In a nutshell it meant selling off underperforming dealerships and replacing them with other dealerships offering greater long-term potential. They would mostly be luxury and import dealerships that offered higher profits and required lower inventory levels. On other fronts, Sonic was able to cut advertising expenses as a percentage of gross profit from 6.5 percent in 2003 to 5.4 percent in 2004. Concerning sales compensation, Sonic introduced a variable compensation structure tied to key performance metrics, which reduced compensation expense as a percentage of gross profit from 36.4 percent in 2003 to 35.3 percent in 2004. Sonic closed 2004 posting sales of nearly $7.4 billion and net income of $86.1 million. Its founder, now approaching 80 years of age, remained very much in charge.

Ed Dinger

PRINCIPAL SUBSIDIARIES

FirstAmerica Automotive, Inc.; Don Massey Cadillac, Inc.

PRINCIPAL COMPETITORS

AutoNation, Inc.; CarMax, Inc.; United Auto Group, Inc.

FURTHER READING

Bonnie, Fred, "Rapid But Disciplined Growth at Sonic," *Ward's Dealer Business,* September 1998, p. 47.

———, "Sonic's Growth Continues," *Ward's Dealer Business,* April 2000, p. 33.

Dyer, Leigh, "Charlotte, N.C.-Based Auto Group to Purchase 18 More Dealerships," *Charlotte Observer,* August 1, 2003.

Geist, Laura Clark, "On Wall Street, Sonic Looks Bionic," *Automotive News,* January 4, 1999, p. 6.

Lamm, Marcy, "Sonic Rides into Town," *Atlanta Business Chronicle,* December 19, 1997, p. 1A.

Lundegaard, Karen, "Sonic Automotive Acquires Chain of 16 Dealerships," *Wall Street Journal,* January 16, 2002, p. B7.

Moore, Pamela L., "No Boom in Stock of Charlotte, N.C.-Based Sonic Auto Dealerships," *Charlotte Observer,* January 9, 1998, p. 109.

Postman, Lore, "Charlotte, N.C., Sonic Automotive to Buy More Dealerships," *Charlotte Observer,* April 28, 1998.

Reeves, Scott, "Offerings in the Offing: Auto Sellers Don't Zoom Out of the IPO Showroom," *Barron's,* November 17, 1997, p. 51.

Williams, Audrey Y., "Buyout Plan Drives Charlotte, N.C., Automotive Firm's High Performance," *Charlotte Observer,* June 6, 1999.

SRA International, Inc.

—■—

4300 Fair Lakes Court
Fairfax, Virginia 22033
U.S.A.
Telephone: (703) 803-1500
Fax: (703) 803-1509
Web site: http://www.sra.com

Public Company
Incorporated: 1976 as Systems Research and Applications
    Corp.
Employees: 4,800
Sales: $881.8 million (2005)
Stock Exchanges: New York
Ticker Symbol: SRX
NAIC: 511210 Software Publishers; 541511 Custom
    Computer Programming Services; 541512
    Computer Systems Design Services

■ ■ ■

SRA International, Inc. offers information technology
(IT) services to clients in three principal markets:
national security, civil government, and healthcare and
public health. Its services, which span the IT life cycle,
include: strategic consulting; systems design, development, and integration; and outsourcing and managed
services. The company offers text mining, data mining,
and warehousing software to enable clients to sort
through growing data collections. The company
primarily serves the U.S. government, with customers
including the Departments of the Army, Navy, and Air
Force; the Joint Chiefs of Staff; the Department of the
Treasury; the Federal Emergency Management Agency;
the Department of Defense, the Food and Drug
Administration, the Internal Revenue Service, and the
Federal Deposit Insurance Company, among others.

1978-95: STEADY GROWTH IN
RELATIVE OBSCURITY

Ernst Volgenau started Systems Research and Applications Corp. (SRA) in the basement of his Reston,
Virginia, home. Because venture capitalists were not
investing heavily in Washington's government-oriented
businesses at that time, Volgenau funded his start-up,
which was incorporated in 1976 and began operations
in 1978, with money he had saved and loans he took
out against his family home. Prior to founding SRA,
Volgenau had completed a 20-year career in the Air
Force, during which time he earned a doctorate in
electrical engineering. He had also worked for several
years during the 1960s under Robert S. McNamara and
his team of tech-savvy "whiz kid" aides on computer applications that would maximize the use of the nation's
military dollars. Later, he worked for two years directing
the inspection and enforcement activities of the Nuclear
Regulatory Commission.

    SRA started out as a subcontractor, offering con-
sulting services as a means of building its track record as
an IT services provider. Recalled Volgenau in a 2004
Washington Post article: "My contracts were small
contracts of $10,000 to $20,000 each. Our objective
was to do a good job on a little job and then maybe the
customer would give us some more." SRA's first contract
was with American Management Services, Inc., a

company founded by members of McNamara's old team. Its first year, SRA had six employees.

By the mid-1980s, SRA was bidding on and winning its own contracts with the U.S. government. But for SRA, as for much of the defense-contracting industry, these were lean times. The Cold War and the Persian Gulf War had ended, and military spending had fallen off. Still, SRA continued to grow, as Volgenau worked for civilian as well as government agencies. Keeping its focus on technology, the company went from installing early computer systems in the 1980s to developing data-mining software by the mid-1990s. According to company management, by 1995, 85 percent of SRA's 1,000 employees were information technology professionals whose job it was to customize systems for clients.

Volgenau first began thinking of taking the company public in 1996, but Wall Street was not interested in the company at the time. "We valued our shares pretty highly," recalled Volgenau in the *Washington Post*, "so we decided against it." As a result, SRA continued to grow in relative obscurity. During the second half of the 1990s, it developed retrieval software for corporate intranets. With its NameTag and NetOwl, companies and government offices could index, find, and distribute internal documents, photos, stock quotes, and incoming news feeds as well as limit access to sensitive documents. Intermezzo, another SRA product, also allowed NetOwl users to conduct searches through other types of search engines. SRA's Photofile software employed deep linguistic knowledge and artificial intelligence techniques to analyze users' natural language queries and search through, for example, captions written years ago. In so doing, it avoided the "brittleness" or narrowness of key word searches.

The Smithsonian began using Intermezzo, which had the capacity of polling the various databases to which it was connected, to catalog its extensive collection of related artifacts and documents. Publishing house Simon & Schuster hired SRA to build its Corporate Digital Ar-

chive, a single, integrated archive to serve all 30 of its business units. In 1996, the company formed a subsidiary called IsoQuest Inc. to handle its data retrieval software.

Two years later, in 1998, SRA branched off into a slightly new direction with Assentor, the first automated e-mail message screening system designed for the financial services industry. Using a sophisticated, linguistics-based natural language pattern matching system and highly refined compliance patterns, Assentor evaluated not just specific words but the context in which they were used. It ensured broker compliance with regulatory guidelines in written communications with clients. Also in 1998, the United States Postal Service awarded a contract jointly to SRA and partner Unisys for year 2000 verification and validation services.

1999-2003: EXTERNAL EVENTS LEADING TO INCREASED DEMAND FOR SERVICES

The end of the 1990s was a busy time for companies involved in technology and computer applications. As the Internet frenzy climaxed, many of SRA's younger employees left to join dot.com start-ups. However, times changed with the bursting of the dot.com bubble and the terrorist attacks of September 11, 2001. Encouraged by prospects of growth, in 2001, SRA and Safeguard Scientifics, a holding company, launched SRA Ventures to act as an incubator for technology start-ups. SRA Ventures' goal was to bring the technology SRA had developed to market, building companies from scratch to meet proven technology needs.

With greater demand for technology in the defense, intelligence, and homeland security markets, SRA chose this period to hold its initial public offering, and, in 2002, raised $103.5 million in sales of stock. Also that year, it purchased Marasco Newton Group, gaining services and capabilities in the environmental area, and adding the EPA as a client. It sold its Assentor division so that it could concentrate in the areas of national security, civil government, and healthcare and public health.

About 60 percent of SRA's revenue came from defense-related programs in 2003, up from 43 percent in 1999; 15 to 20 percent came from healthcare and public sector health businesses or agencies. The remainder occurred in the area of civil government, such as its contract (with partner General Dynamics) to design and integrate command centers for the Pentagon, and to develop systems to improve the military's ability to track people and supplies.

The company won three government contracts worth more than $100 million in 2003, further expand-

KEY DATES

1978: After incorporating two years earlier, Ernst Volgenau starts operations at Systems Research and Applications Corp.

1996: The company forms a subsidiary, called Iso-Quest Inc.

2001: SRA and Safeguard Scientifics launch SRA Ventures.

2002: The company sells its Assentor division.

2003: SRA acquires Adroit Systems, Inc.

2004: SRA acquires ORION Scientific Systems.

2005: The company acquires Touchstone Consulting Group and Spectrum Solutions Group.

ing a well-diversified client base. In 2003, SRA had about 70 active contracts, and no single contract accounted for more than 4 percent of its total revenue. When, in January 2003, SRA purchased Adroit Systems, it opened the doors to the surveillance and reconnaissance realm of the Department of Defense and took a step toward its goal of ongoing, controlled growth through one acquisition each year. The rest of the company's growth would occur, according to management, organically.

Increasingly, SRA became known as a well-managed company. In 1999, and for each of the six years following, *Fortune* magazine named it one of the 100 best companies in the United States to work for. The company also began to make a name for itself in the workforce management realm after implementing its Nurse Advocacy Program. To offset increasing health insurance premiums, SRA instituted an in-house healthcare program with onsite clinic. The program managed to save nearly $1 million a year by proactively managing the cases of employees who sought care, regularly checking the blood pressure of employees with hypertension; suggesting diet, exercise, and lifestyle changes in response to other chronic conditions; working out on-the-job accommodations for injured employees who wished to return to work or for those caring for family members.

The clinic was just one instance of the ways in which SRA attempted to tap into the attitudes and values of workers. The company also responded to the basic desires and needs of workers through flextime, education reimbursements, and by ensuring that the nature of employees' work assignments suited their interests and capabilities. "People are motivated by an ideal. They want to have meaning in their lives, and they want to be part of an organization that's special," was the way Volgenau described his company's workforce ideal in a 2005 *Newsbytes* article.

Throughout the years 2003 to 2005, SRA's workforce grew steadily. By 2004, the company had 2,600 employees; the following year, it employed about 3,300, and by the end of the year, 4,800. This was in part because in 2004, although much of the tech world had not yet recovered from dot.com melt-down, Virginia was a hot bed for employment. The Federal government was looking for help in developing surveillance software, assistance in integrating agencies brought together to make the Department of Homeland Security, and aid in analyzing reams of foreign intelligence data. SRA had the tools to respond to these needs. According to Di-Pentima, who took over as head of the company from Volgenau in 2005, in a 2005 *U.S. News & World Report* article, "We are in an information-technology revolution, and in certain areas we are running out of knowledge workers."

SRA also grew in 2004 and 2005 through acquisitions. In 2004, it acquired ORION Scientific Systems, a leading provider of counterintelligence, counterterrorism, and law enforcement services and solutions. In 2005, it purchased Touchstone, a management company that helped senior government executives develop, launch, and manage strategies, and SRA's fourth government services acquisition. Touchstone's customers included the Department of Homeland Security and Defense, intelligence agencies, and the Office of Management and Budget. Also in 2005, in its largest acquisition yet, SRA purchased Galaxy, a provider of systems engineering, information technology, and tactical communications services and solutions to the federal government whose customers included the departments of Defense and Homeland Security and the Federal Aviation Administration.

All told, SRA served more than 250 government clients on more than 750 active contracts, a 32 percent increase from the year before. Revenues increased accordingly, jumping 43 percent to $882 million in 2005. The company had averaged organic growth of 15 percent annually since its start, with significantly higher increases of 25 percent in 2003, 37 percent in 2004, and 43 percent in 2005.

Ernst Volgenau retired as CEO after 26 years heading the company in 2005, and Renny DiPentima assumed the responsibilities of CEO as well as president. Under DiPentima, SRA continued to strive "not just to build shareholder value, but to serve society," befitting its corporate culture of honesty and service, according to Volgenau in a 2005 *Newsbytes* article. Preparing itself for future growth, SRA implemented a new financial system for billing and collections in 2005. Others, outside the company, also seemed convinced that the company would continue to grow: *BusinessWeek* selected SRA as one of its Hot Growth companies for 2005, and *GovernmentVAR* named SRA the Government Solution Provider of the Year.

Carrie Rothburd

PRINCIPAL SUBSIDIARIES

SRA Technical Services Center, Inc.; SRA Ventures, LLC; Systems Research and Applications Corp.; The Marasco Newton Group Ltd.

PRINCIPAL COMPETITORS

Accenture Ltd.; Affiliated Computer Services Inc.; Anteon International Corporation; BearingPoint, Inc.; Booz Allen Hamilton Inc.; CACI International Inc.; Computer Sciences Corp.; Electronic Data Systems Corporation; General Dynamics Corporation; Inter-national Business Machines Corporation; Keane, Inc.; Lockheed Martin Corporation; The MITRE Corporation; Northrop Grumman Corporation; Raytheon Company; SAIC, Inc.; Unisys Corporation.

FURTHER READING

Biesecker, Calvin, "SRA Expects National Security Needs Will Continue to Fuel Growth," *Defense Daily*, March 13, 2003.

Jacobs, April, "Smithsonian's Suite Search Through History," *Computerworld*, June 24, 1996, p. 45.

Kiger, Patrick J., "Healthy, Wealthy, and Wise," *Workforce Management*, July 1, 2003, p. 41.

Lavelle, Marianne, "Government Spawns a Tech Boom," *U.S. News & World Report*, March 21, 2005, p. 36.

LeSueur, Steve, "Large Contractor Executive of the Year (Co-winner): Ernst Volgenau," *Newsbytes*, November 2, 2005.

McCarthy, Ellen, "Contracting Pioneer at Ease; Ernst Volgenau Steps Away from SRA International's Daily Grind," *Washington Post*, November 1, 2004, p. E1.

Verity, John W., "'Key Words' for Graphics?," *BusinessWeek*, December 23, 1996, p. 80.

Starbucks Corporation

2401 Utah Avenue South
Seattle, Washington 98134-1436
U.S.A.
Telephone: (206) 447-1575
Toll Free: (800) 782-7282
Fax: (206) 447-0828
Web site: http://www.starbucks.com

Public Company
Incorporated: 1985 as Il Giornale
Employees: 115,000
Sales: $6.37 billion (2005)
Stock Exchanges: NASDAQ
Ticker Symbol: SBUX
NAIC: 722213 Snack and Nonalcoholic Beverage Bars;
311920 Coffee and Tea Manufacturing; 311520 Ice
Cream and Frozen Dessert Manufacturing; 312111
Soft Drink Manufacturing; 422490 Other Grocery
and Related Products Wholesalers; 454110 Elec-
tronic Shopping and Mail-Order Houses; 533110
Lessors of Nonfinancial Intangible Assets (Except
Copyrighted Works)

■ ■ ■

Starbucks Corporation is the leading roaster, retailer,
and marketer of specialty coffee in the world. Its operations include upwards of 7,300 coffee shops and kiosks
in the United States, and nearly 3,000 in 34 other
countries, with the largest numbers located in Japan,
Canada, the United Kingdom, China, Taiwan, South
Korea, the Philippines, Thailand, Malaysia, Mexico,
Australia, Germany, and New Zealand. In addition to a
variety of coffees and coffee drinks, Starbucks shops also
feature Tazo teas; pastries and other food items; espresso
machines, coffee brewers, and other coffee- and tea-
related items; and music CDs. The company also sells
many of these products via mail-order and online at
starbucks.com. It also wholesales its coffee to restaurants,
businesses, education and healthcare institutions, hotels,
and airlines. Through a joint venture with Pepsi-Cola
Company, Starbucks bottles Frappuccino beverages and
the Starbucks DoubleShot espresso drink and sells them
through supermarkets and convenience and drugstores.
Through a partnership with Kraft Foods, Inc., the
company sells Starbucks whole bean and ground coffee
into grocery, warehouse club, and mass merchandise
stores. A third joint venture, with Dreyer's Grand Ice
Cream, Inc., develops superpremium coffee ice creams
and distributes them to U.S. supermarkets. From a single
small store that opened in 1971 to its status as a 21st-
century gourmet coffee giant, Starbucks has led a coffee
revolution in the United States and beyond.

ROOTS IN COFFEE RETAILING
AND WHOLESALING

Starbucks was founded in Seattle, Washington, a haven
for coffee aficionados. The city was noted for its coffee
before World War II, but the quality of its coffee had
declined so much by the late 1960s that resident Gordon Bowker made pilgrimages to Vancouver, British
Columbia, to buy his beans there. His point of reference
for the beverage was dark, delicious coffee he had
discovered in Italy. Soon Bowker, then a writer for *Seattle*
magazine, was making runs for friends as well. When

COMPANY PERSPECTIVES

Starbucks mission statement: Establish Starbucks as the premier purveyor of the finest coffee in the world while maintaining our uncompromising principles while we grow. The following six guiding principles will help us measure the appropriateness of our decisions: Provide a great work environment and treat each other with respect and dignity. Embrace diversity as an essential component in the way we do business. Apply the highest standards of excellence to the purchasing, roasting and fresh delivery of our coffee. Develop enthusiastically satisfied customers all of the time. Contribute positively to our communities and our environment. Recognize that profitability is essential to our future success.

Seattle folded, two of Bowker's friends, Jerry Baldwin, an English teacher, and Zev Siegl, a history teacher, also happened to be seeking new ventures; the three banded together and literally built their first store, located in Seattle's Pike Place Market, by hand. They raised $1,350 apiece, borrowed another $5,000, picked the name Starbucks, for the punchy "st" sound and its reference to the coffee-loving first mate in *Moby Dick,* then designed a two-tailed siren for a logo and set out to learn about coffee.

Siegl went to Berkeley, California, to learn from a Dutchman, Alfred Peet, who ran Peet's Coffee, which had been a legend among local coffee drinkers since 1966. Peet's approach to coffee beans became the cornerstone for Starbucks' reputation: high-grade arabica beans, roasted to a dark extreme by a trained perfectionist roaster. Starbucks bought its coffee from Peet's for its first nine months, giving away cups of coffee to hook customers. The plan worked. By 1972 the three founders had opened a second store in University Village and invested in a Probat roaster. Baldwin became the young company's first roaster.

Within its first decade, Starbucks had opened stores in Bellevue, Capitol Hill, and University Way. By 1982 the original entrepreneurs had a solid retail business of five stores, a small roasting facility, and a wholesale business that sold coffee primarily to local restaurants. The first of the company's growth-versus-ethos challenges came at this stage: how does one maintain a near fanatical dedication to freshness in wholesale? Starbucks

insisted that the shelf life of coffee is less than 14 days after roasting. As a result, they donated all eight-day-old coffee to charity.

In 1982 Starbucks hired Howard Schultz to manage the company's retail sales and marketing. While vice-president of U.S. operations for Hammarplast, a Swedish housewares company, and working out of New York, Schultz met the Starbucks trio and considered their coffee a revelation. (He had grown up on instant.) He and his wife packed up and drove 3,000 miles west to Seattle to join Starbucks.

There were other changes taking place at Starbucks at the same time. Siegl had decided to leave in 1980. The name of the wholesale division was changed to Caravali, out of fear of sullying the Starbucks name with less than absolute freshness. Blue Anchor, a line of whole-bean coffees being prepackaged for supermarkets, was relinquished. Starbucks learned two lessons from their brief time in business with supermarkets: first, supermarkets and their narrow profit margins were not the best outlet for a coffee roaster who refused to compromise on quality in order to lower prices, and second, Starbucks needed to sell directly to consumers who were educated enough to know why the coffee they were buying was superior.

MID-1980S: THE SHIFT TO COFFEE BARS

In 1983 Starbucks bought Peet's Coffee, which had by then become a five-store operation itself. That same year, Schultz took a buying trip to Italy, where another coffee revelation took place. Wandering the piazzas of Milan, Schultz was captivated by the culture of coffee and the romance of Italian coffee bars. Milan had about 1,700 espresso bars, which were a third center for Italians, after work and home. Schultz returned home determined to bring Italian coffee bars to the United States, but found his bosses reluctant, being still more dedicated to retailing coffee. As a result, Schultz left the company to write a business plan of his own. His parting with Starbucks was so amicable that the founders invested in Schultz's vision. Schultz returned to Italy to do research, visiting hundreds of espresso and coffee bars.

In the spring of 1986, he opened his first coffee bar in the Columbia Seafirst Center, the tallest building west of Chicago. Faithful to its inspiration, the bar had a stately espresso machine as its centerpiece. Called Il Giornale, the bar served Starbucks coffee and was an instant hit. A second was soon opened in Seattle, and a third in Vancouver. Schultz hired Dave Olsen, the proprietor of one of the first bohemian espresso bars in Seattle, as a coffee consultant and employee trainer.

KEY DATES

1971: Gordon Bowker, Jerry Baldwin, and Zev Siegl open the first Starbucks in Seattle's Pike Place Market.

1982: Howard Schultz is hired to manage retail sales and marketing.

1983: Peet's Coffee is acquired.

1985: Schultz leaves the company to found Il Giornale, an operator of coffee bars.

1987: Schultz buys the six-unit Starbucks chain from the original owners for $4 million, merges them into Il Giornale, renames his company Starbucks Corporation, and begins a national expansion; Baldwin remains president of the now separate Peet's Coffee and Tea business.

1988: A mail-order catalog is introduced.

1992: Company goes public.

1993: First East Coast store opens, in Washington, D.C.

1995: Frappuccino beverages are introduced.

1996: Overseas expansion begins with units in Japan, Hawaii, and Singapore; partnership with Dreyer's begins selling Starbucks Ice Cream; partnership with Pepsi-Cola begins selling bottled Frappuccino beverages.

1998: U.K.-based Seattle Coffee Company is acquired; partnership with Kraft Foods is formed for the distribution of Starbucks coffee into supermarkets.

1999: Pasqua Coffee Co. and Tazo Tea Company are acquired.

2000: Schultz steps aside as CEO to become chief global strategist, while remaining chairman; Orin Smith takes over as CEO.

2001: Starbucks expands to continental Europe with opening of stores in Switzerland and Austria.

2005: The 10,000th Starbucks opens.

A year later, Schultz was thriving while Starbucks was encountering frustration. The wholesale market had been reconfigured by the popularity of flavored coffees, which Starbucks resolutely refused to produce. The company's managers were also increasingly aggravated by the lack of wholesale quality control, so they sold their wholesale line, Caravali, to Seattle businessman Bart Wilson and a group of investors. In addition,

Bowker was interested in leaving the company to concentrate on a new project, Red Hook Ale. Schultz approached his old colleagues with an attractive offer: how about $4 million for the six-unit Starbucks chain? They sold, with Olsen remaining as Starbucks' coffee buyer and roaster; the Starbucks stores were merged into Il Giornale. Baldwin remained president of the now separately operated Peet's Coffee and Tea. In 1987 the Il Giornale shops changed their names to Starbucks, and the company became Starbucks Corporation and prepared to go national.

In August 1987 Starbucks Corporation had 11 stores and fewer than 100 employees. In October of that year it opened its first store in Chicago, and by 1989 there were nine Chicago Starbucks, where employees trained by Seattle managers served coffee roasted in the Seattle plant.

Their methods were costly, using high-grade arabica beans and expensive dark roasting, while suffering the financial consequences of snubbing the supermarket and wholesale markets. Nevertheless, Starbucks' market was growing rapidly: sales of specialty coffee in the United States grew from $50 million in 1983 to $500 million five years later.

In 1988 Starbucks introduced a mail-order catalog, and by the end of that year, the company was serving mail-order customers in every state and operating a total of 33 stores. Because the company's reputation grew steadily by word of mouth, it spent little on ads. Schultz's management philosophy, "hire people smarter than you are and get out of their way," fed his aggressive expansion plans. Industry experts were brought in to manage Starbucks' finances, human resources, marketing, and mail-order divisions. The company's middle ranks were filled with experienced managers from such giants as Taco Bell, Wendy's, and Blockbuster. Schultz was willing to lose money while preparing Starbucks for explosive growth. By 1990 he had hired two star executives: Howard Behar, previously president of a leading developer of outdoor resorts, Thousand Trails, Inc.; and Orin Smith, chief financial and administrative officer for Danzas, USA, a freight forwarder.

Starbucks installed a costly computer network and hired a specialist in information technology from McDonald's Corporation to design a point-of-sale system via PCs for store managers to use. Every night, stores passed their sales information to Seattle headquarters, which allowed planners to spot regional buying trends almost instantly. Starbucks lost money while preparing for its planned expansion, including more than $1 million in 1989 alone. In 1990 the headquarters expanded and a new roasting plant was built. Nevertheless, Schultz resisted both the temptation to franchise and to flavor the beans. Slowly, the chain developed near-cult status.

RAPID EARLY 1990S GROWTH AS A PUBLIC COMPANY

Starbucks also developed a reputation for treating its employees well. In 1991 it became the first privately owned company in history to establish an employee stock option program that included part-timers. Starbucks also offered health and dental benefits to both full- and part-time employees. As a result, the company had a turnover rate that was very low for the food service industry. Employees were rigorously trained, completing at least 25 hours of coursework on topics including the history of coffee, drink preparation, and how to brew a perfect cup at home. The company went public in 1992, the same year it opened its first stores in San Francisco, San Diego, Orange County, and Denver. Its stores totaled 165 by year's end. The company began special relationships with Nordstrom, Inc. and Barnes & Noble, Inc., offering coffee to shoppers at both chains.

Growth mandated the opening of a second roasting plant, located in Kent, Washington, by 1993. After 22 years in business, Starbucks had only 19 individuals it deemed qualified to roast coffee. One of the 19 was Schultz, who considered it a tremendous privilege. Roasters were trained for more than a year before being allowed to roast a batch, which consisted of up to 600 pounds of coffee roasted for 12 to 15 minutes in a gas oven. The beans made a popping sound, like popcorn, when ready, but roasters also used sight and smell to tell when the beans were done to perfection. Starbucks standards required roasters to test the roasted beans in an Agron blood-cell analyzer to assure that each batch was up to standards. If not, it was discarded.

Starbucks' first East Coast store opened in 1993, in a premier location in Washington, D.C. The chain had 275 stores by the end of 1993 and 425 one year later. Sales had grown an average of 65 percent annually over the previous three years (reaching $284.9 million in 1994), with net income growing 70 to 100 percent a year during that time. Starbucks broke into important new markets in 1994, including Minneapolis, Boston, New York, Atlanta, Dallas, and Houston, and purchased the Coffee Connection, a 23-store rival based in Boston, for $23 million, making it a wholly owned subsidiary. Smith was promoted to president and COO and Behar became president, international. Starbucks also announced a partnership with Pepsi-Cola to develop new ready-to-drink coffee beverages. After Starbucks debuted a frozen coffee drink called Frappuccino in its stores in the summer of 1995, resulting in a sales bonanza, the partnership with Pepsi began rolling out a bottled ver-

sion in grocery, convenience, and drugstores the following year. Starbucks broke into new markets in 1995, including Pittsburgh, San Antonio, Las Vegas, and Philadelphia. That same year, Starbucks began supplying coffee for United Airlines flights and launched a line of Starbucks compilation music CDs, which were sold in its coffeehouses.

LATE 1990S: INTERNATIONAL EXPANSION AND NEW VENTURES

The following year, in addition to continued North American expansion into Rhode Island, Idaho, North Carolina, Arizona, Utah, and Ontario, the company ventured overseas for the first time. Its initial foreign forays were launched through joint venture and licensing arrangements with prominent local retailers. With the help of SAZABY Inc., a Japanese retailer and restaurateur, the first market developed in 1996 was Japan; through other partnerships, Hawaii and Singapore also received their first Starbucks that year. The Philippines followed in 1997. Meantime, Starbucks entered into a partnership with Dreyer's Grand Ice Cream, Inc. in 1996 to develop and sell Starbucks Ice Cream. Within eight months of introduction, the product became the number one coffee ice cream in the United States. Starbucks' expansion into Florida, Michigan, and Wisconsin in 1997 helped the total number of units reach an astounding 1,412 by year-end, more than double the previous two-year total. Sales approached the $1 billion mark that year, while net income hit $57.4 million, more than five times the result for 1994.

As this rapid growth continued, the company began to be needled by late night talk show hosts for its seeming Starbucks-on-every-corner expansion strategy, while a number of owners and patrons of local coffee shops began speaking out and demonstrating against what they considered overly aggressive and even predatory moves into new territory. Critics complained that the company was deliberately locating its units near local coffee merchants to siphon off sales, sometimes placing a Starbucks directly across the street. In 1996 and 1997 residents in Toronto, San Francisco, Brooklyn, and Portland, Oregon, staged sidewalk protests to attempt to keep Starbucks out of their neighborhoods. One of the company's responses to the scattered resistance was to try to enhance its image through stepped-up advertising. Still, like Wal-Mart Stores, Inc. and its reputation in some quarters as a destroyer of Main Street, Starbucks remained the object of snickers from comedians and derision from a vocal minority of protesters. This undercurrent of hostility burst into the spotlight in late 1999 when some of the more aggressive protesters against a World Trade Organization meeting took their anger out on several Starbucks stores in the company's hometown of Seattle, tagging a number of the 26 downtown locations with graffiti and inflicting more serious vandalism on three stores, which were then temporarily closed.

The anti-multinational protesters in Seattle also singled out stores operated by McDonald's Corporation and Nike, Inc. The lumping of the once modest purveyor of gourmet coffee in with these global giants was in part an outgrowth of the company's aggressive overseas expansion in the late 1990s. Growth in the Pacific Rim continued with the opening of locations in Taiwan, Thailand, New Zealand, and Malaysia in 1998 and in China and South Korea in 1999. By early 2000 the number of Starbucks in Japan had reached 100. The company aimed to have 500 stores in the Pacific Rim by 2003. The Middle East was another target of global growth, with stores opened in Kuwait and Lebanon in 1999, but it was the United Kingdom that was the object of the company's other big late 1990s push. In 1998 Starbucks acquired Seattle Coffee Company, the leading U.K. specialty coffee firm, for about $86 million in stock. Starbucks began rebranding Seattle Coffee's locations under the Starbucks name. Aggressive expansion in the United Kingdom yielded more than 100 units by late 1999. Starbucks hoped to use its U.K. base for an invasion of the Continent, aiming for 500 stores in Europe by 2003.

Growth was not slowing back home either. Areas receiving their first Starbucks in 1998 and 1999 included New Orleans, St. Louis, Kansas City, and Memphis and Nashville, Tennessee. The number of North American locations approached 2,200 by early 2000. Always searching for new revenue streams, Starbucks in 1998 entered into a long-term licensing agreement with Kraft Foods, Inc. for the marketing and distribution of Starbucks whole bean and ground coffee into grocery, warehouse club, and mass merchandise stores. The company also began experimenting with a full-service casual restaurant called Café Starbucks. A further move into food came in early 1999 through the purchase of Pasqua Coffee Co., a chain of coffee and sandwich shops with 56 units in California and New York. Starbucks had already developed its own in-house tea brand, Infusia, but it was replaced following the early 1999 acquisition of Tazo Tea Company, a Portland, Oregon-based maker of premium teas and related products with distribution through 5,000 retail outlets.

Starbucks had also launched a web site featuring an online store in 1998, and Schultz began talking about Starbucks becoming a mega-cybermerchant offering everything from gourmet foods to furniture. To this end, the company attempted, but failed, to acquire

Williams-Sonoma, Inc., a specialty retailer of high-end kitchenware. Wall Street analysts began questioning the wisdom of moving so far afield from the company's core coffee business. In mid-1999, following Starbucks' announcement of an earnings shortfall, the company's stock plunged 28 percent, leading Schultz to pull back on his ambitious cyber plans.

Other developments included an agreement with Albertson's, Inc. to open more than 100 Starbucks coffee bars in Albertson's supermarkets in the United States; and the acquisition of the five-store San Francisco-based Hear Music chain, in an extension of Starbucks' music retailing ventures. Image problems continued to crop up for the rapidly growing company, whose 1999 revenues of $1.68 billion were nearly six times the figure of five years earlier. In April 2000 a San Francisco-based human rights group called Global Exchange was readying a large protest at Starbucks in 29 cities to publicize its allegations that the coffee company was buying its beans from wholesalers who were paying farmers what amounted to poverty wages. In a preemptive move, which staved off the protests and the resultant bad publicity, Starbucks announced that it would buy more coffee certified as "fair trade," meaning that the farmers who grew it received more than market price for their crop, sometimes as high as three times the 30 cents per pound they typically received.

ACCELERATING GROWTH IN THE EARLY 21ST CENTURY

In the early 21st century, Starbucks was working to achieve Schultz's ambitious goals of 500 stores in both Japan and Europe by 2003, as well as his ultimate goal of 20,000 units worldwide. With about half of that total envisioned to be located outside North America, Schultz decided to spend more time on the company's overseas operations. In June 2000 he stepped down as CEO of the company to become its chief global strategist, while remaining chairman. Schultz began working closely with Peter Maslen, who had taken charge of the international division in late 1999, following the retirement of Howard Behar. Assuming the CEO title was Orin Smith, who retained his previous responsibility for domestic retail and wholesale operations, alliances, and coffee roasting and distribution.

Starbucks' rate of expansion accelerated in the early 2000s: after opening about 1,200 new stores each year from 2001 to 2004, the company added nearly 1,700 new outlets in 2005, pushing the chain past the 10,000 unit mark. About 1,150 of the units opened in 2005 were located in the United States, bringing the domestic total to 7,300. Even this figure did not represent a saturated market, as Starbucks was now aiming to eventually have 15,000 stores in the U.S. market alone. It also expected to eventually increase its international outlets from the approximately 3,000 that were operating in late 2005 to 15,000. Starbucks debuted in continental Europe in 2001 when stores were opened in Switzerland and Austria, and further new territories were entered in each of the following years: Oman, Indonesia, Germany, Spain, Mexico, and Greece in 2002; Turkey, Chile, Peru, and Cyprus in 2003; Paris, France, in 2004; and Jordan in 2005. In addition, the Starbucks unit in Japan was taken public in 2001. During this same period, the company's revenues skyrocketed, surging from $2.17 billion in 2000 to $5.39 billion in 2005. Net earnings increased more than fivefold, from $94.6 million to $494.5 million.

Among the new initiatives during this period, the company in 2001 introduced the Starbucks Card, a stored-value card that customers could use and reload, and also began offering high-speed wireless Internet access at its stores. In 2002 the beverage line was extended to include the first noncoffee/nontea blended concoction, the Crème Frappuccino, a cold, creamy vanilla drink. The Starbucks Card in 2003 was extended into a combined credit and stored-value card. That same year, the company acquired Seattle Coffee Company from AFC Enterprises, Inc. for $72 million, thereby gaining the Seattle's Best Coffee and Torrefazione Italia coffee brands. Starbucks' music endeavors expanded in 2004 with the launch of the first Hear Music media bars at select Starbucks locations. These media bars enabled customers to burn unique compilation CDs from an initial selection of 200,000 songs. Also in 2004 the company entered into an agreement with Jim Beam Brands Co. to develop and market a superpremium coffee liqueur, and the following year Jim Beam began distributing Starbucks Coffee Liqueur to licensed establishments, not to Starbucks outlets. A further expansion of the outlets' beverage offerings came in 2005 when Chantico drinking chocolate debuted in the United States and Canada and the company acquired Ethos Water.

In March 2005 Smith retired as CEO and was succeeded by Jim Donald, who had been president of the firm's North America unit and had been hired away from Pathmark Stores, Inc. in 2002. Donald was a main force behind a drive to broaden Starbucks outlets beyond coffee—not only into music but also into food. Lunch items, typically sandwiches, began to be offered at many North American Starbucks, and testing of hot breakfasts, such as ham, egg, and cheese on a muffin, began in 2004. Rather than morphing into a restaurant chain, however, Schultz (who remained chairman) and Donald aimed to reshape Starbucks into a retailer with a broader array of products and services. At the same time, the

global expansion continued toward the eventual goal of 30,000 outlets worldwide and with China potentially rivaling the United States as Starbucks' largest market. In 2006 alone, the company planned to open another 1,800 stores.

Carol I. Keeley
Updated, David E. Salamie

PRINCIPAL SUBSIDIARIES

Olympic Casualty Insurance Company; Seattle Coffee Company; Starbucks Capital Asset Leasing Company, LLC; Starbucks Coffee Company (Australia) Pty. Ltd.; Starbucks Coffee Canada, Inc.; Starbucks Coffee Holdings (UK) Limited; Seattle Coffee Company (International) Limited (U.K.); Starbucks Coffee Company (UK) Limited; Torz & Macatonia Limited (U.K.); Starbucks Coffee International, Inc.; Coffee Concepts (Southern China) Ltd. (Hong Kong); Coffee Concepts (Guangdong) Ltd. (China); Coffee Concepts (Shenzhen) Ltd. (China); Rain City C.V. (Netherlands); Emerald City C.V. (Netherlands); Starbucks Coffee EMEA B.V. (Netherlands); Starbucks Manufacturing EMEA B.V. (Netherlands); Starbucks Coffee (Deutschland) GmbH (Germany); Starbucks Coffee (Ireland) Limited; Starbucks Coffee Trading Company Sarl (Switzerland); Starbucks Coffee Agronomy Company S.R.L. (Costa Rica); Qingdao American Starbucks Coffee Company Limited (China); Starbucks Coffee (Dalian) Company Limited (China); Chengdu Starbucks Coffee Company Limited (China); Starbucks Card Europe, Limited (U.K.); Starbucks Coffee Asia Pacific Limited (Hong Kong); Starbucks Coffee Singapore Pte. Ltd.; Sur-Andino Café S.A. (Chile); Starbucks Coffee (Thailand) Ltd.; Starbucks Global Card Services, Inc.; Starbucks Manufacturing Corporation; Urban Coffee Opportunities, LLC.

PRINCIPAL COMPETITORS

Caribou Coffee Company, Inc.; Diedrich Coffee, Inc.; Dunkin' Brands, Inc.; Peet's Coffee & Tea, Inc.; Panera Bread Company; Cosi, Inc.; ABP Corporation; Tully's Coffee Corporation.

FURTHER READING

Abramovitch, Ingrid, "Miracles of Marketing: How to Reinvent Your Product," *Success,* April 1993, pp. 22-26.

Anders, George, "Starbucks in Pact with Kozmo.com on Using Stores," *Wall Street Journal,* February 14, 2000, p. A34.

Barron, Kelly, "The Cappuccino Conundrum," *Forbes,* February 22, 1999, p. 54.

Brammer, Rhonda, "Grounds for Caution," *Barron's,* August 15, 1994, p. 20.

Browder, Seanna, "Starbucks Does Not Live by Coffee Alone," *Business Week,* August 5, 1996, p. 76.

Cuneo, Alice, "Starbucks' Word-of-Mouth Wonder," *Advertising Age,* March 7, 1994, p. 12.

Daniels, Cora, "Mr. Coffee," *Fortune,* April 14, 2003, pp. 139-40.

Doherty, Jacqueline, "Make It Decaf," *Barron's,* May 20, 2002, pp. 20-21.

Ebenkamp, Becky, "This Java Joint Is Jumpin'," *Brandweek,* October 10, 2005, pp. M42-M45, M66.

Fitch, Stephane, "Latte Grande, Extra Froth," *Forbes,* March 19, 2001, p. 58.

Fitzpatrick, Eileen, "Starbucks Buy Hear Music Chain," *Billboard,* December 4, 1999, p. 10.

Frank, Stephen, "Starbucks Brews Strong Results Analysts Like," *Wall Street Journal,* July 14, 1994, p. C1.

Gibson, Richard, "Some Meatloaf with That Decaf Latte?," *Wall Street Journal,* March 16, 1999, p. B1.

———, "Starbucks Cyberspace Mission Returns to Earth After Big Bang on Wall Street," *Wall Street Journal,* July 23, 1999, p. B4.

———, "Starbucks Holders Wake Up, Smell the Coffee and Sell," *Wall Street Journal,* July 2, 1999, p. B3.

Gray, Steven, "Starbucks Brews Broader Menu," *Wall Street Journal,* February 9 2005, p. B9.

Gray, Steven, and Amy Merrick, "Latte Letdown: Starbucks Set to Raise Prices," *Wall Street Journal,* September 2, 2004, p. B1.

Gray, Steven, and Ethan Smith, "In Latest Music Move, Starbucks Will Blend Hot Java, CD Burning," *Wall Street Journal,* October 14, 2004, p. D1.

———, "New Grind: At Starbucks, a Blend of Coffee and Music Creates a Potent Mix," *Wall Street Journal,* July 19, 2005, p. A1.

Hamstra, Mark, "Starbucks' Pasqua Purchase Dovetails with Food-Caf Tests," *Nation's Restaurant News,* January 4, 1999, pp. 3, 104.

Harris, John, "Cuppa Sumatra," *Forbes,* November 26, 1990, pp. 213-14.

Holmes, Stanley, "First the Music, Then the Coffee," *Business Week,* November 22, 2004, p. 66.

———, "Strong Lattes, Sour Notes," *Business Week,* June 20, 2005, pp. 58, 60.

Holmes, Stanley, Drake Bennett, Kate Carlisle, and Chester Dawson, "Planet Starbucks: To Keep Up the Growth, It Must Go Global Quickly," *Business Week,* September 9, 2002, pp. 100-05+.

Holmes, Stanley, Irene M. Kunii, Jack Ewing, and Kerry Capell, "For Starbucks, There's No Place Like Home," *Business Week,* June 9, 2003, p. 48.

Jones Yang, Dori, "The Starbucks Enterprise Shifts into Warp Speed," *Business Week,* October 24, 1994, pp. 76-78.

Kaplan, David A., "Trouble Brewing," *Newsweek,* July 19, 1999, pp. 40-41.

Kim, Nancy J., "Starbucks Weighing European Growth Strategies," *Puget Sound Business Journal,* August 20, 1999, p. 9.

Kugiya, Hugo, "Seattle's Coffee King," *Seattle Times,* December 15, 1996, p. 20.

Leung, Shirley, "Starbucks May Indeed Be a Robust Staple," *Wall Street Journal,* July 26, 2002, p. B4.

Meyers, William, "Conscience in a Cup of Coffee," *U.S. News and World Report,* October 31, 2005, p. 48.

Ordonez, Jennifer, "Starbucks' Schultz to Leave Top Post, Lead Global Effort," *Wall Street Journal,* April 7, 2000, p. B3.

Pressler, Margaret Webb, "The Brain Behind the Beans," *Washington Post,* October 5, 1997, p. H1.

Reese, Jennifer, "Starbucks: Inside the Coffee Cult," *Fortune,* December 9, 1996, pp. 190-92+.

Robinson, Kathryn, "Coffee Achievers," *Seattle Weekly,* August 2, 1989.

Schultz, Howard, "By Way of Canarsie, One Large Hot Cup of Business Strategy," *New York Times,* December 14, 1994, pp. C1, C8.

Schultz, Howard, and Dori Jones Yang, *Pour Your Heart into It: How Starbucks Built a Company One Cut at a Time,* New York: Hyperion, 1997, 351 p.

Schwartz, Nelson D., "Still Perking After All These Years," *Fortune,* May 24, 1999, pp. 203+.

Serwer, Andy, "Starbucks to Go," *Fortune,* January 26, 2004, pp. 60-64+.

Simons, John, "A Case of the Shakes: As Starbucks Cafes Multiply, So Do the Growing Pains," *U.S. News and World Report,* July 14, 1997, pp. 42-44.

Spector, Amy, "Starbucks Launches Lunch Tests in Seven Major Markets," *Nation's Restaurant News,* October 18, 1999, p. 32.

Strauss, Karyn, "Howard Schultz," *Nation's Restaurant News,* January 2000, pp. 162-63.

Theodore, Sarah, "Expanding the Coffee Experience," *Beverage Industry,* October 2002, pp. 57, 60-62.

Weiss, Naomi, "How Starbucks Impassions Workers to Drive Growth," *Workforce,* August 1998.

Whalen, Jeanne, "Starbucks, Pepsi Tackle Coffee Venture," *Advertising Age,* August 1, 1994, p. 44.

StarHub Ltd.

————————■————————

51 Cuppage Road, Suite 07-00
StarHub Centre
Singapore
Telephone: +65 6825 5000
Fax: +65 6721 5000
Web site: http://www.starhub.com.sg

Public Company
Incorporated: 1998
Employees: 2,702
Sales: SGD 1.35 billion (2004)
Stock Exchanges: Singapore
Ticker Symbol: SRHBF
NAIC: 517110 Wired Telecommunications Carriers; 517212 Cellular and Other Wireless Telecommunications; 518111 Internet Service Providers

■ ■ ■

StarHub Ltd. is the fast-rising challenger in the Singapore telecommunications market, placing second behind former government monopoly Singapore Telecom (SingTel). StarHub is also that market's only telecommunications group capable of providing the full range of telecommunications services, combining fixed and wireless telephone networks, cable television service, and broadband Internet access. As such, 75 percent of Singapore's population of one million households subscribes to at least one of StarHub's services, and nearly 30 percent of the population subscribes to two of the company's services. The company offers fixed line digital telephone service, as well as its own GSM and high-speed 3G cellular phone service, through StarHub

Mobile. StarHub also has put into place international roaming agreements with some 13 countries worldwide. StarHub's share of the Singapore mobile market tops 30 percent. The company's cable television network is available to 99 percent of Singapore's population, and features some 50 channels, most of which are international channels. StarHub launched a digital television package in 2004 and, on a more limited scale, a Digital Terrestrial Television system, available to corporate customers. The only cable TV supplier in Singapore (which has banned satellite television services), the company boasts more than 400,000 customers. StarHub's broadband Internet access service piggybacks on its cable television network, offering the island's highest download speeds of up to 30 Mbps. The company holds more than 46 percent of Singapore's broadband market. The company also offers dial-up Internet access. Formed in 1998, and listed on the Singapore Stock Exchange since 2000, StarHub is led by CEO and Chairman Terry Clontz. In 2004, the company posted revenues of SGD 1.35 billion.

LATE 1990S START-UP

The Singapore government's resolve to transform the city-state into a southeast Asian technology hub in the 1990s set the scene for the emergence of new players in the country's telecommunications and media markets. The government's decision to abolish Singapore Telecom's monopoly on the telecommunications sector brought interest from a number of groups, both domestic and foreign, eager to grab a share of one of the country's most promising industries. In its drive to privatize and deregulate the telecommunications market, the Singapore government went farther than nearly all of its counterparts, both in Asia and in the West, taking bids not only for the license to operate cellular telephone services, but also for the license to establish basic services. A factor behind this initiative was the relatively small size of Singapore's population, with just two million people. Yet the government to transform Singapore into one of the world's most "wired" cities played a major factor in the introduction of competition to the telecommunications sector.

In 1998, a consortium led by ST Telemedia, a unit of the Singapore state-owned investment agency Temasek Holdings, won its license bid and established StarHub Holdings. Other shareholders in the new company included BT Group, Nippon Telegraph & Telephone Corp., Singapore Press Holdings, and Medicorp, although ST Telemedia remained the controlling partner with a 50 percent stake. StarHub began setting up its cellular and fixed line networks, including building its own fiber optic network. The company's investment in this effort topped $1.5 billion. StarHub expected to launch its cellular network by 2000; the fixed line telephone sector was not expected to be deregulated until 2002.

In 1999, StarHub brought in a new CEO, Steven Terrell (Terry) Clontz, an American who had entered the telecommunications industry as an engineer for Southern Bell in 1973. Clontz later joined BellSouth International, rising to president of that company's Asia Pacific region division before taking the president and CEO positions at IPC Information Systems. Clontz led StarHub to its first acquisition, Cyberway Pte., one of only three Internet service providers (ISPs) in Singapore. The company rebranded its Internet service under the StarHub brand, and then jump-started the market by offering the city's first free dial-up service. This move helped establish the StarHub brand among customers for the first time. The addition of Internet service added an important component to its "hub" concept, that of providing the full array of telecommunications services.

StarHub officially launched its cellular phone operations in 2000. The company quickly established itself as an aggressive competitor, introducing customer services such as free incoming calls and per-second billing. The company also benefited from the decision by the government to step up the pace of the telecommunications sector's liberalization, ending SingTel's fixed line monopoly in 2000. Another focus for the company at the beginning of the new decade was the extension of its international service agreement networks. By the end of 2000, the company had signed agreements with partners in 16 countries, including mainland China, as well as the United States and the United Kingdom. The company expected to build out this network to more than 50 partners worldwide into the mid-decade.

COMPLETING THE HUB IN THE 2000S

StarHub began preparing for its future expansion in 2001, bidding for and winning one of the city's 3G cellular phone licenses. In the meantime, the company also had begun negotiations that would bring a major extension to its "hub" concept. Those negotiations resulted in the company's announcement that it had reached a merger agreement with Singapore Cable Vision (SCV), the city's only pay-TV provider. (Satellite television remained banned by the Singapore government, concerned over its potential use by terrorist organizations, whereas the cable television network allowed the government to impose content controls.)

SCV had been founded in 1991 and was granted the license to build the city's cable television network. In exchange for building the network, which was to reach 99 percent of Singapore's homes and businesses, SCV was granted a monopoly on the city's pay-television market lasting into the early 1990s. By 1995, SCV had completed much of its network and officially launched its service with 12 channels. The cable service started with a base of 15,000 subscribers.

Yet SCV grew only slowly, in part because of the novelty of a pay-TV service in Singapore. By 1996, with more than 155,000 homes made cable-ready, the company counted only 22,000 subscribers. The late 1990s saw a more massive adoption of the service, however, as SCV built out its network to reach more than 930,000 homes, or 99 percent of the market, at a cost of some SGD 600 million ($348 million). The company also had made strides in improving its customer

KEY DATES

1991: Singapore Cable Vision (SCV) is founded.
1995: SCV cable television service is launched.
1998: StarHub is founded to bid for fixed line and mobile telephone licenses.
1999: StarHub acquires CyberWay, one of three Singapore Internet service providers; SCV launches broadband Internet access via cable television network.
2000: StarHub launches its mobile telephone and fixed line networks.
2001: StarHub and SCV agree to merge.
2002: SCV is rebranded as StarHub Cable TV.
2004: StarHub goes public on the Singapore Stock Exchange; the company launches a 3G mobile telephone network.
2005: I-mode mobile Internet service is launched.

base, topping 225,000 subscribers by 2000. Aiding its surge in subscribers was the launch of cable-based broadband Internet access in 1999. By 2000, the company's MaxOnline broadband service counted more than 50,000 subscribers.

While the rest of the telecommunications world had been buzzing around the future "convergence" of telecommunications and media technologies, the newly enlarged StarHub became one of the first to turn the concept into reality. With sales of nearly SGD 700 million ($400 million), the new company combined broadband Internet with cellular and fixed line telephone and television, with a coverage of nearly 100 percent of the market. As the next step toward its convergence, the company rebranded its broadband and cable television operations under the StarHub brand.

By 2003, StarHub Cable TV's subscriber base had topped 300,000, with a penetration rate of nearly one-third. In that year, the company's cable television operation received a new boost when the Singapore government announced that the Singapore market was most likely not large enough to support two pay-TV services. As a result, StarHub retained a de facto monopoly on that market. By the end of that year, the company's cable television service neared 400,000, lured by its expanded offering of 50 channels.

StarHub continued to develop new technologies toward the middle of the decade. The company rolled

out a digital television service in 2004, adding 11 digital channels as well as a series of interactive services. The company hoped that the launch of digital services would help it push its penetration to as high as 70 percent of the market before the end of the decade. Meanwhile, the company's cellular phone operations also had been performing strongly, capturing nearly one-third of the market. The company remained the third-place player, however, behind leader SingTel and rival M1.

StarHub went public in October 2004, listing its stock on the Singapore Stock Exchange. The maturity of the country's mobile telephone market, however, with bruising competition and near total penetration, as well as a lack of understanding of the cable television market by Asian investors, kept the company's initial share price low. In the end, the offering raised nearly SGD 460 million, valuing the company at more than SGD 2 billion. Nonetheless, the company's "hub" model remained attractive to many investors.

The company added a new link to its hub at the end of 2004, launching its first 3G mobile telephone service. The high-speed mobile telephone standard was complemented by the launch of next-generation high-speed broadband services, with a top speed of 30 Mbps through the company's cable lines. StarHub also launched a new pay-as-you-go broadband service, in an effort to step up its subscribers' adoption of multiple services.

The hub concept also enabled StarHub to post some impressive market penetration rates into the second half of the decade. By the end of 2005, the company was able to claim that some 75 percent of Singapore's population had adopted at least one of its services. More than two-thirds had signed up for two of the group's offerings. A minor percentage had adopted all of the group's cable TV/mobile/broadband fixed line services, and StarHub targeted this segment for its future growth.

In July 2005, for example, the company rolled out a special offering bundling broadband Internet access with free unlimited outgoing calls using its fixed line digital network. The company also launched a new interactive SMS/MMS channel for its cable system. Although the channel was provided free to StarHub cable subscribers, the company charged a fee for sending SMS and MMS messages to the channel. The company also planned to launch a channel for interactive video gaming, while also introducing television-based games to its mobile handsets. In November 2005, the company's 3G network offerings grew even more robust with the launch of the I-mode cellular telephone Internet service pioneered by Japan's NTT DoCoMo. StarHub appeared to have clear plans to remain a major player in the Singapore telecommunications and media market.

M. L. Cohen

PRINCIPAL SUBSIDIARIES

StarHub Cable Vision Ltd.; StarHub Internet Pte. Ltd.; StarHub Mobile Pte. Ltd.; StarHub Online Pte. Ltd.

PRINCIPAL COMPETITORS

Singapore Telecommunications Ltd.; Singapore Telecom Mobile Private Ltd.; Keppel Land Ltd.; Pacific Century Regional Developments Ltd; Reditech Services (S) Private Ltd.; Cable and Wireless Singapore; Singapore Telecom Paging Private Ltd.; Inno-Pacific Holdings Ltd.

FURTHER READING

Clark, Robert, "Challenger Looking for Glory," *Telecom Asia,* July 13, 2002, p. 28.

———, "Duopoly Rising," *Telecom Asia,* July 13, 2002, p. 10.

"Hub Scouts: The Converged Cable TV-Telephone-Internet 'Hubbing' Concept Has Huge Room for Growth in Singapore," *Television Asia,* October 2004, p. 20.

Osborne, Magz, "Starhub Gets Overactive," *Variety,* March 28, 2005, p. 22.

———, "Starhub's Getting It Together," *Variety,* January 13, 2003, p. 39.

———, "Two's a Crowd in Territory's Pay TV Market," *Variety,* March 24, 2003, p. 24.

"Starhub Begins Offering I-Mode," *Tarifica Alert,* November 22, 2005.

"Starhub Can Only Price Low As Investors Remain Cautious," *Euroweek,* October 8, 2004, p. 23.

"Starhub Outlines Singapore Strategy," *Network Briefing,* December 1, 1998.

"Starhub Reveals Multiple Discount Offers," *Tarifica Alert,* July 26, 2005.

"Starhub Revives IPO with Integrated Telephone/Pay TV Story," *Euroweek,* August 27, 2004, p. 18.

"Starhub Rolls Out Digital Cable Platform," *Television Asia,* June 2004, p. 6.

"Telecoms Deal of the Year: Starhub," *Project Finance,* January 2000, p. 40.

State Auto Financial Corporation

518 East Broad Street
Columbus, Ohio 43215
U.S.A.
Telephone: (614) 464-5000
Toll Free: (800) 444-9950
Fax: (614) 464-5325
Web site: http://www.stateauto.com

Public Company
Incorporated: 1991
Employees: 2,029 Total Assets: $2.02 billion (2004)
Stock Exchanges: NASDAQ
Ticker Symbol: STFC
NAIC: 524126 Direct Property and Casualty Insurance
Carriers; 551112 Offices of Other Holding
Companies

■ ■ ■

State Auto Financial Corporation is an insurance holding company for five regional insurance subsidiaries: State Auto Property and Casualty Insurance Company, Milbank Insurance Company, Farmers Casualty Insurance Company, State Auto Insurance Company of Ohio, and State Auto National Insurance Company. Through its insurance subsidiaries, State Auto Financial writes personal and commercial automobile, homeowners, commercial multi-peril, fire, and general liability insurance, serving customers in 26 states through 22,500 independent insurance agents. The company's insurance operations are supported through ten regional and branch offices. State Auto Financial also controls three non-insurance subsidiaries: Stateco Financial Services, Inc., which provides investment management services to all of the holding company's subsidiaries; Strategic Insurance Software, Inc., a developer of software that is marketed in the insurance agency management system market; and 518 Property Management and Leasing, LLC, a subsidiary that owns and leases real and personal property to other State Auto Financial subsidiaries. Policyholder-owned State Auto Mutual Insurance Company controls 67 percent of State Auto Financial.

ORIGINS

The company at the center of a billion-dollar tug-of-war in the early 21st century began operating nearly a century earlier, formed with modest resources that hardly suggested the birth of one of the country's largest insurance companies. In 1921, Robert S. Pein borrowed $30,000 and started the State Automobile Insurance Company, the first home-office casualty company in Columbus, Ohio. Pein, motivated by his displeasure at the exorbitant rates charged by other insurers and their inept settlement of claims, promised to give Columbus residents a better alternative for their insurance needs, but it was doubtful he could have foreseen the expansion of his business into a billion-dollar corporation with operations covering more than half of the United States.

Pein's start-up capital was enough to hire three employees and rent a room in downtown Columbus. The company's trappings could not have been more humble, but Pein registered almost immediate success, enabling him and his small staff to occupy larger quarters within a short time. State Automobile Insurance, which wrote auto insurance during its first years in business, moved its headquarters twice by 1925, the year it began writing non-assessable policies, under which policyholders could not be assessed additional fees if the losses became too great. Perhaps the most notable aspect of the company's first years in business was Pein's decision to use only independent insurance agents to distribute his company's insurance products. It was a decision that became the company's policy, one that was strictly adhered to years after Pein's death, representing one of the defining characteristics of the State Auto Financial group of companies in the 21st century.

The 1930s presented a formidable challenge to virtually every type of business in the United States, presenting an exacting, determinative test of a company's durability. For State Automobile Insurance, the crucible arrived early in the company's development, making its chances at survival all that more tenuous, but the company responded to the harsh economic conditions of the Great Depression with remarkable resilience. Pein's company, it could be easily argued, thrived during the disastrous decade. As if setting the tone for the robustness the company would demonstrate during the 1930s, a new, larger headquarters building was occupied at the decade's start, the company's third move to grander quarters in nine years. Pein began expanding operations the following year, entering Kentucky, West Virginia, and Tennessee, giving State Automobile Insurance a four-state operating territory that relied on more than 700 agents.

Midway through the decade, as the Great Depression reached its trough, State Automobile Insurance exhibited even greater strength, expanding its product portfolio and its operating territory. The company was aided somewhat by the passage of two laws in Ohio, the first of which, promulgated in 1935, was a statute assigning financial responsibility to drivers. The following year, the state passed the Driver's License Law, making driving a privilege rather than a right. Because of the two laws, the number of drivers buying liability insurance increased markedly, but Ohio was not the only source of growth for Pein's enterprise. On the heels of the expansion achieved early in the decade, the company entered Maryland, South Carolina, and Michigan midway through the decade. State Automobile Insurance's growing customer base had more products to choose from as well, as the company began offering an early version of homeowners insurance and general liability coverage.

In some ways, the 1940s presented a bigger challenge than the Great Depression to State Auto Insurance, but again the company persevered, ensuring that it was well positioned to share in the explosive growth of the national economy following World War II. Several months after the United States entered the conflict, every automobile manufacturer in the country halted production of civilian passenger cars to direct their efforts fully toward the prosecution of the war. For insurers such as State Automobile Insurance who were heavily reliant on writing automobile insurance, the nation's new priorities cut off the supply of new business that would have come from the purchase of new automobiles. State Automobile Insurance withstood the shock to its operations and, by the end of the 1940s, when new automobile production soared to a near record level, the company reigned as a formidable regional force. State Automobile Insurance had $20.4 million in assets by the 1940s, issuing more than 250,000 policies and recording gross premium writings of $14.5 million during the final year of the decade.

POST-WORLD WAR II EXPANSION

State Automobile Insurance's postwar growth was highlighted by the expansion of the company's selection of insurance offerings, vigorous geographic expansion, numerous acquisitions, and, for the first time in its history, changes in leadership. Pein began to cede control of his company in 1954, when Paul Gingher, who joined State Automobile Insurance in 1931, was named executive vice-president. Gingher was named president two years later by Pein, who assumed the role of chairman, but he occupied his new post for only a matter of months, passing away before the end of 1956. During this transition in leadership, the company added fire insurance and inland marine coverage in Ohio and certain other states in its operating territory. Once State Automobile Insurance was firmly under Gingher's control, the company began capitalizing on a new,

1921: Robert Pein opens an insurance office in Columbus, Ohio.

1931: State Automobile Insurance expands beyond Ohio's borders for the first time.

1949: The company's assets exceed $20 million.

1958: State Automobile Insurance completes its first acquisitions.

1971: Assets reach $370 million during the company's 50th anniversary.

1991: State Auto Financial is created to facilitate an initial public offering of stock.

1993: Milbank Insurance Co. is acquired.

1998: Farmers Casualty Co. is acquired.

2001: State Auto Financial completes the largest acquisition in its history, purchasing Meridian Insurance Group.

2003: Gregory Shepard launches a takeover attempt of State Auto Financial.

2004: Takeover specialist Carl Icahn purchases half of Shepard's State Auto Financial stock.

figure increased to $185 million by the end of the decade, when State Automobile Insurance maintained operations in 14 states.

In contrast to the expansionist mindset directing the company's movements during the 1960s and 1970s, the 1980s were characterized by streamlining efforts undertaken by the executive staff in Columbus. In 1983, Robert L. Bailey, who was named director of product services and distribution four years earlier, was named president of State Automobile Insurance, the third change in leadership after Gingher's tenure. Bailey would lead the company for the next two decades, and under his stewardship, cost-cutting measures were effected and underwriting efforts were strengthened. Bailey also emphasized a more balanced business mix, seeking to increase the company's involvement in the commercial sector. In 1984, the company derived 80 percent of its revenue from personal business, relying on commercial work for the other 20 percent. Bailey set a goal of increasing the company's commercial business to 40 percent of revenues. A decade later, he reorganized the company to achieve an even split between personal and commercial business.

PUBLIC DEBUT IN THE 1990S AND UNCERTAINTY IN THE 21ST CENTURY

Although each decade brought some sort of change to the company, the 1990s stood out from the rest. Expansion resumed in earnest, touched off by a move into Mississippi in 1989, but the decade's most profound event was the public debut of the enterprise Pein had created 70 years earlier. In 1991, the company completed its initial public offering (IPO) of stock, a corporate maneuver that required the formation of State Auto Financial Corporation as a holding company for all companies either formed internally or acquired during the previous decades. Policyholder-owned State Auto Mutual Insurance Co., in turn, was given a 67 percent stake in State Auto Financial. To this new structure, new assets were added throughout the decade, joining subsidiaries such as the 1958 acquisition of Southern Home, which changed its name to State Auto Property & Casualty Co., and Stateco, Inc., which lengthened its name to Stateco Financial Services, Inc. One year after the IPO, the State Auto group of companies began to grow. State Auto National was launched in Ohio to compete in the non-standard automobile market, a new venture that registered quick success, expanding into seven other states within its first four years of operation. In 1993, the group gained another member when State Auto Financial acquired Milbank Insurance Co., a Milbank, South Dakota-based insurer that provided the

expedient means of rounding out its product portfolio and expanding geographically by acquiring other insurers. In 1958, the company purchased two companies based in Greer, South Carolina, Dixie Fire and Casualty Co. and the Southern Home Insurance Co. The acquisitions paved the company's entry into Alabama, Georgia, Mississippi, North Carolina, South Carolina, and Virginia.

State Automobile Insurance's actions during the 1950s set the tone for the company's development in succeeding decades. The emphasis was on expansion, which often was achieved via acquisition. In 1962, the year the company began offering health insurance, its product selection was broadened further with the purchase of Columbus Mutual Life Insurance Co. The following year, the company formed a non-insurance subsidiary, Stateco, Inc., which facilitated the financing of insurance premiums. By the time State Automobile Insurance celebrated its 50th anniversary, its stature as an insurer had been elevated substantially by postwar economic growth. The $20 million in assets supporting the company at the end of the 1940s had swelled to $370 million by 1971. The company's volume of business as measured by the amount of premiums written in a year had increased exponentially as well, jumping from $14.5 million in 1949 to $127.7 million in 1971. The company with entry into markets in North Dakota, South Dakota, Minnesota, and Utah. In 1997, the acquisition of Midwest Security Insurance Co., an insurer based in Onalaska, Wisconsin, established State Auto Financial's presence in its 24th state, a purchase that was followed one year later by the addition of Des Moines, Iowa-based Farmers Casualty Co., which added two more states, Kansas and Iowa, to State Auto Financial's geographic coverage. By the end of the decade, the string of acquisitions lifted the company's annual revenues to $440 million.

In retrospect, the series of acquisitions completed during the 1990s represented a mere prelude to what would be both Bailey's masterstroke and his swan song. In October 2000, two months before Bailey's retirement, State Auto Financial announced it was acquiring Meridian Insurance Group, one of Indiana's largest insurers with $302 million in revenue. State Auto Financial's announcement ended a hostile takeover, a "bitter battle" as described by the October 26, 2000 edition of the *Indianapolis Star,* led by Gregory Shepard, who owned an Illinois-based insurer named American Union Insurance Co. and ranked as Meridian Insurance's largest shareholder. Shepard, who had launched his bid in August, was beaten to the punch by State Auto Financial, withdrawing his offer in December. State Auto Financial completed the transaction in June 2001, a deal that made it the 48th largest property/casualty insurer in the United States with more than $1 billion in written premiums and $2 billion in assets. The acquisition of Meridian Insurance and its largest insurance arm, Meridian Security Insurance Co., which operated in 18 states, provided an enormous boost to State Auto Financial's stature, increasing the group's penetration in a number of important Midwest states. "In virtually every respect the fit is perfect in terms of marketing systems, products, people, and philosophy," Bailey said in an October 26, 2000 interview with the *Indianapolis Star*. "We intend to utilize fully the skills and experience of the entire Meridian staff."

As State Auto Financial prepared for the future, a cloud of uncertainty hung over the company, representing virtually the only wrinkle in an otherwise stalwart organization. Shepard, evidently, was not as enthusiastic as Bailey about the Meridian Insurance deal. In 2003, Shepard launched a bid to acquire State Auto Financial, proposing a $256 million deal that reportedly would use State Auto Financial's existing assets as the means to finance the transaction. State Auto Financial firmly opposed the offer and urged shareholders to reject Shepard's advances, describing the takeover attempt as a "scheme" that "makes no economic sense," according to Robert Moone, Bailey's replacement, in the September 3, 2003 issue of *A.M. Best Newswire*. Shepard was not to be deterred, however, responding to the company's rejection by extending his bid five more times. The battle between Shepard and State Auto Financial carried on until mid-2004, when the saga gained a new protagonist. Carl Icahn, whose personal fortune eclipsed $7 billion, entered the fray, acquiring half of Shepard's two million shares for $13 per share at a time when State Auto Financial's stock was trading at $27 per share. Icahn was a well-known takeover specialist who earned his reputation during the 1980s when he spearheaded takeovers of Texaco, TWA, and USX. His intervention did little to resolve questions concerning State Auto Financial's future ownership, nor did it end speculation about Shepard's involvement in a hostile takeover attempt. "I don't know what game Shepard is playing," an analyst remarked in a May 17, 2004 interview with *Mergers & Acquisitions Report*, "but I know he is playing a game. The fact that one million shares in this stock are exchanging hands at $13 is so absurd I don't think anyone knows what to do with it. I just don't understand the sale."

As State Auto Financial plotted its course for the second half of the decade, industry observers continued to ponder the implications of Icahn's stock purchase.

Jeffrey L. Covell

PRINCIPAL SUBSIDIARIES

State Auto Property and Casualty Insurance Company; Stateco Financial Services, Inc.; Milbank Insurance Company; Farmers Casualty Insurance Company; State Auto Insurance Company of Ohio; State Auto National Insurance Company; Strategic Insurance Software, Inc.; 518 Property Management and Leasing, LLC; State Automobile Mutual Insurance Company; State Auto Insurance Company of Wisconsin; State Auto Florida Insurance Company; BroadStreet Capital Partners, Inc.; Meridian Citizens Mutual Insurance Company; Meridian Insurance Group, Inc.; Meridian Security Insurance Company.

PRINCIPAL COMPETITORS

The Allstate Corporation; Prudential Financial, Inc.; State Farm Mutual Automobile Insurance Company.

FURTHER READING

Cornejo, Rick, "Softening Insurance Market Is Finished Thanks to Katrina, State Auto CEO Says," *A.M. Best Newswire,* October 25, 2005.

Grocer, Stephen, "Icahn Drives into State Auto for a Nice Price," *Mergers & Acquisitions Report,* May 17, 2004.

Mehlman, William, "State Auto Combines Safety, Risk into Winning Combination," *Insiders' Chronicle,* June 15, 1992, p. 1.

O'Malley, Chris, "Ohio Insurer Will Acquire Indianapolis-Based Insurance Firm," *Indianapolis Star,* October 26, 2000.

Stammen, Ken, "CEO Set to Retire from Columbus, Ohio-Based State Auto Financial," *Columbus Dispatch,* May 12, 2005.

"State Auto Financial Corp.," *Business First-Columbus,* August 14, 1995, p. 15.

"State Auto Financial Corp.," *Business First-Columbus,* October 19, 1992, p. 23.

"State Auto Financial Rejects Takeover Proposal As 'Illusory,'" *A.M. Best Newswire,* September 3, 2003.

"State Auto, Meridian Complete Merger," *A.M. Best Newswire,* June 1, 2001.

Wolf, Barnet D., "Corporate Takeover Giant Buys Stake in State Auto Financial," *Columbus Dispatch,* May 13, 2004.

———, "State Auto Financial Urges Shareholders to Reject Bid," *Columbus Dispatch,* September 3, 2003.

Symyx Technologies, Inc.

—————— ■ ——————

310 Central Expressway
Santa Clara, California 95051
U.S.A.
Telephone: (408) 764-2000
Fax: (408) 748-0175
Web site: http://www.symyx.com

Public Company
Incorporated: 1994
Employees: 275
Sales: $83.1 million (2004)
Stock Exchanges: NASDAQ
Ticker Symbol: SMMX
NAIC: 541710 Research and Development in the Physical Sciences and Engineering Sciences

■ ■ ■

Symyx Technologies, Inc. acts as a partner in research and development efforts, serving customers in the chemical, energy, pharmaceutical, and electronics industries. Symyx uses what is known as combinatorial chemistry to discover new compounds with potential commercial applications. Through high-speed, automated techniques in a mass-production approach to chemistry discovery, the company helps customers such as Dow Chemical Company, ExxonMobil Company, Eli Lilly and Company, and Merck & Co., Inc. improve or discover products. The first company to apply combinatorial techniques to materials research in a commercial context, Symyx owns the largest portfolio of patents in its field, with 280 patents issued and 370 patent applications on file. The company is supported by more than $600 million in strategic relationships with its customers, relying heavily on collaborative agreements with Dow and ExxonMobil. Symyx maintains that its methodology is 100 times faster than traditional research methods, at a dramatically lower cost per experiment.

ORIGINS

Symyx's founders, Alejandro Zaffaroni and Peter Schultz, helped shape a revolution during the late 20th century, developing and promoting a new approach to scientific research that promised to play a prominent role in the advancement of science in the 21st century. Their work centered on combinatorial chemistry, a new methodology in chemistry discovery that took the conventional process of research and development and replaced it with something akin to what Henry Ford might have done had he been a chemist instead of a pioneer in mass-producing automobiles. Traditionally, chemists in search of a new compound analyzed the properties of molecules one compound at a time, using carefully thought-out recipes to synthesize compounds and, with hope and a rationalized premise to support their hope, discover something useful: a new type of compound that presented characteristics superior to those of existing compounds. Combinatorial chemistry took a different approach, but its architects, Zaffaroni and Schultz included, did not look to Ford for the inspiration for their work. A form of combinatorial chemistry had been on display for millennia, but it took millennia for the show to be witnessed. Once scientists were able to observe the intricacies of the human body's functions, a model of combinatorial chemistry was available to

Traditional materials discovery relies on an expensive and time-consuming process of trial and error, making and testing one material at a time. A typical project can take years to complete, often with low probabilities of success. This approach cannot keep pace with current product life cycles and growth expectations in the chemical and electronics industries, nor can it address rising costs, manufacturing challenges, and increasing competitive pressures. Symyx's high-throughput technologies enable researchers to generate hundreds to thousands of unique materials at a time, and rapidly screen those materials for desired properties. Our approach delivers results an order of magnitude faster than traditional research methods at a fraction of the cost. Symyx pioneered high-throughput experimentation for materials discovery, applying the same concepts of automation, miniaturization and parallel processing that have been employed successfully to discover new pharmaceutical compounds.

replicate. The research into mimicking the body's strategy began in the early 1980s, establishing the scientific foundation that gave birth to Symyx.

The way in which the immune system functioned offered one example of a combinatorial approach to discovering a solution to a problem. The immune system responds to diseases by unleashing billions of antibodies and selecting the one that best combats the disease. The process taps into the ability of cells to create a wide variety of molecules by only using a limited number of building blocks. Cells create a vast number of DNA and protein molecules by arranging a common, relatively small number of building blocks in different order. In contrast to the way chemistry research was traditionally conducted, there was a certain randomness in the human body's approach to discovery. By using a small library of information, the body created an exponentially larger selection of answers to a problem by rearranging, or recombining, its library of information, producing billions of potential answers to arrive at one "correct" solution. Traditional chemistry research dictated unearthing one potential answer at a time before moving on to the next potential answer, repeating the process until a solution was found. Combinatorial chemistry took its cue from the human body, relying on high-

speed, automated techniques in a mass-production approach to produce vast numbers of potential answers in a short period of time.

During the early 1980s, the first attempts to use combinatorial chemistry were applied to the pharmaceutical industry. The approach, which to some eliminated the science of drug discovery, drew heavy criticism from some elements of the scientific community. "There was enormous resistance from medicinal chemists in the beginning," a founder of a combinatorial start-up venture noted in the May-June 1998 issue of *Technology Review.* "They felt it was completely inelegant and ugly." Combinatorial chemistry's supporters felt differently, claiming that the new methodology would transform drug discovery and genetic screening "from a plodding one-at-a-time business to a high-technology bingo game," as quoted by *Technology Review.*

One of the supporters of combinatorial chemistry was Zaffaroni, a drug and biotechnology entrepreneur with a remarkable record of success dating to the 1960s. Zaffaroni, described as a "serial entrepreneur" in the September 28, 2005 issue of *Forbes,* had more than a basic understanding of the science in which he was investing, having earned a Ph.D. in biochemistry from the University of Rochester. In 1987, intrigued by the potential of using combinatorial chemistry to discover new drugs, he approached a biochemist at the University of California in Berkeley named Peter Schultz. At the time, Schultz was conducting pioneering work on the antibodies produced by the immune system, which Zaffaroni believed could benefit drug discovery. Schultz later conceded that he had little idea about the commercial implications of his work (Zaffaroni was the entrepreneurial wizard), but the meeting eventually led to the formation of Affymax, the first company committed exclusively to using combinatorial chemistry to discover new drugs. Affymax flourished, adding another success story to Zaffaroni's list of achievements. In 1993, Affymax spun off Affymetrix, creating a separate company that used combinatorial methods to create DNA chips for drug screening. In 1995, in a deal that confirmed the legitimacy of combinatorial chemistry in the pharmaceutical industry, U.K.-based GlaxoSmithKline PLC, one of the five largest drug companies in the world, paid $538 million for Affymax.

The commercial success of combinatorial chemistry in the pharmaceutical industry led Schultz to explore other applications. Back in the laboratory, Schultz, with Affymax thriving in the marketplace and deepening his convictions, became convinced that the methods of miniaturization, high-speed automation, and parallel processing could be applied to materials research. Schultz believed combinatorial chemistry could be used to

KEY DATES

1994: Symyx is incorporated.
1997: Hoechst AG invests $43 million in Symyx.
1999: Symyx completes its initial public offering of stock.
2003: Symyx signs a $200 million technology agreement with ExxonMobil.
2004: Dow Chemical commits $120 million to Symyx, extending the six-year relationship between the two companies.

discover new polymers, superconductors, catalysts, phosphors, and any of a number of new materials. In what was something of a role reversal, he approached Zaffaroni about the idea, perceiving commercial uses that were not discernible to Zaffaroni. "He's not a materials scientist," Schultz said of Zaffaroni in his interview with *Technology Review,* "but he is a person who is always looking for new scientific ideas. When he sees something with tremendous potential, he's not afraid to go after it. It's just damn the torpedoes, full speed ahead."

To make his case and trigger Zaffaroni's entrepreneurial zeal, Schultz enlisted the help of Xiao Dong Xiang, a physicist at the Lawrence Berkeley National Laboratory. Together, the pair created combinatorial libraries of materials, first making an array of 128 different compounds on a one-inch chip, each a potential high-temperature semiconductor. Schultz and Xiang went on to create collections of phosphors, polymers, data storage materials, and catalysts, but Zaffaroni already was convinced. With $1 million in start-up capital, Symyx was formed in 1994, becoming the first company to attempt to apply combinatorial techniques to materials research commercially.

EARNING RESPECT IN THE LATE 1990S

Zaffaroni took the managerial helm at Symyx, serving as its chairman and chief executive officer during its first four years—the period critical to the company's development. As the company worked to put Schultz's theory to the test, it subsisted on research deals and investments from private and venture sources such as Aventis Research and Technology, Bayer Innovation, and Chemical and Materials Enterprise Associates. A break-

through moment occurred in 1997, when Germany's Hoechst AG, one of the world's largest chemical makers, signed a five-year, $43 million deal with Symyx, an agreement that industry observers touted as combinatorial chemistry's entry into mainstream industrial research. Symyx grew from an organization with 23 scientists to a research and development firm with 85 scientists during the year. At the company's laboratories (there were seven in operation by mid-1998) the carpet-bombing approach to materials discovery was well underway, pursuing research in several different directions. In one room of Symyx's two-story office building, a robotic arm moved side to side across a tabletop, depositing drops into scores of wells arranged on plastic trays slightly larger than a CD jewel box. Each well contained a different mixture of chemicals, which, once the robotic arm finished its work, would represent entirely new types of plastic. With an array of novel polymers to screen, Symyx's scientists hoped to discover at least one polymer with desirable attributes and strike upon a new plastic that would become the preferred material for use in high-strength structures, electrical insulation, biological implants, or sundry other applications.

Symyx caused a stir in the materials industry as it entered the late 1990s, attracting admirers who saw great promise in the company's research efforts. The major obstacle for the company was turning the potential inherent in its research into the discovery of a compound that was commercially viable. One shortcoming of using combinatorial methodology in materials research was the lack of a screening process to vet compounds with potential and determine which one possessed superior properties. Rapid screening methods existed in drug discovery research, but materials research technology had no way of quickly determining physical properties. "It doesn't make a lot of difference if you can make 100,000 compounds at once if you have to test them one by one," conceded a chemist in *Technology Review*'s May-June 1998 issue. A consultant to combinatorial firms reiterated the chemist's point in the same issue, asking, "How do you measure the strength of a nanogram of material? Nobody has developed that technology yet. There's a whole new technology that has to be built."

Schultz and his team of scientists were working on software to enable rapid screening, but funds were necessary to finance such research, as well as to support the company's combinatorial research efforts. To obtain the necessary capital, Symyx turned to Wall Street, completing its initial public offering of stock in November 1999. The company sold 5.4 million shares at $14 per share in its public debut, raising nearly $80 million to continue its pioneering work.

SYMYX IN THE 21ST CENTURY

As Symyx progressed toward the end of its first decade of business, the company was hitting its stride, both financially and scientifically. Annual revenues nearly doubled between 2000 and 2004, jumping from $43 million to $83 million, while profits began to come in on a consistent basis. After losing $922,000 in 2000, the company recorded four consecutive years of profitability, with net income increasing from $6.3 million in 2001 to $12.8 million in 2004. On the research side, three of the company's discovered materials made the all-important leap into the commercial marketplace: a catalyst used by Dow, a phosphor used by Belgian-owned Agfa-Gevaert N.V., and a polymer used in electronic applications by Tokyo-based JSR Corp. Commercial success heightened the company's appeal among its research partners, convincing massive, global concerns to increase their investment in combinatorial materials research. In mid-2003, the company signed the largest agreement in its history, forging a technology alliance with ExxonMobil. The $200 million, five-year agreement called for the incorporation of Symyx's technology into ExxonMobil's research and development program. "It's hugely significant," an analyst explained in a May 12, 2004 interview with *Investor's Business Daily*. "It's like Merck or Pfizer saying they're going to modify their research around a little company. It's a profound vote of confidence." The deal with ExxonMobil was followed in late 2004 by a $120 million, five-year agreement with Dow, extending their six-year alliance.

As Symyx plotted its course for its second decade of business, the company reigned as the leader in its field, having carved a lasting place for combinatorial chemistry's contributions to materials research. In November 2004, the company strengthened the screening capabilities it offered to customers by acquiring IntelliChem, a Bend, Oregon-based developer of electronic laboratory notebooks used in the pharmaceutical, biotechnology, and chemical industries. On the heels of the $28.9 million acquisition, Symyx announced that sales had increased between 26 percent and 35 percent during the previous three fiscal quarters, a pace of growth that was eclipsed by the company's earnings per-

formance. During the same period, Symyx's earnings per share increased between 150 percent and 300 percent. As the company looked ahead, standing on firm financial footing, there was every expectation that the great promise of its research techniques would yield lucrative discoveries in the materials industry in the coming years.

Jeffrey L. Covell

PRINCIPAL SUBSIDIARIES

Symyx Technologies, AG (Switzerland); Symyx Discovery Tools, Inc.; Symyx Technologies International, Inc.; Symyx IntelliChem, Inc.

PRINCIPAL COMPETITORS

Avantium Technologies B.V.; Bayer AG; E.I. du Pont de Nemours and Company; hte Aktiengesellschaft.

FURTHER READING

Alva, Marilyn, "Symyx Technologies Inc.," *Investor's Business Daily*, May 12, 2004, p. A10.

Carlsen, Clifford, "Symyx Spinoff Draws $8M in VC Funds," *Daily Deal*, May 12, 2003.

Fairley, Peter, "Symyx Lands BFGoodrich in First U.S. Alliance," *Chemical Week*, October 14, 1998, p. 10.

Haines, Mark, "Symyx Technologies," *America's Intelligence Wire*, July 4, 2003.

Kher, Unmesh, "Doing It Nature's Way," *Time*, August 7, 2000, p. 70.

Moukheiber, Zina, "The World's Fastest Chemists," *Forbes*, September 28, 2005, p. 63.

Stalter, Katharine, "Symyx Pays $28.9 Mil to Acquire IntelliChem," *Investor's Business Daily*, December 7, 2004, p. B8.

"Symyx Acquires IntelliChem," *R&D Directions*, January 2005, p. 29.

Van Arnum, Patricia, "Symyx Raises the Bar in R&D," *Chemical Market Reporter*, June 6, 2005, p. 29.

——, "Symyx Technologies Goes Public," *Chemical Market Reporter*, November 22, 1999, p. 25.

TAG Heuer S.A.

14a Avenue des Champs-Montants
Marin-Epagnier,
Switzerland
Telephone: +41 032 755 60 00
Fax: +41 032 755 64 00
Web site: http://www.tagheuer.com

Wholly Owned Subsidiary of LVMH Moët Hennessy Louis Vuitton S.A.
Incorporated: 1860 as Heuer Watchmaking Company
Employees: 689
Sales: EUR 496 million ($560 million) (2004 est.)
NAIC: 334518 Watch, Clock, and Part Manufacturing

■ ■ ■

TAG Heuer S.A. is one of the world's leading manufacturers of luxury and sports performance watches and other high-end and high-precision timepieces. Since 1999, the company, founded in 1860 in Switzerland's Jura mountain region, has also been the cornerstone of the LVMH luxury products empire's Watches and Jewelry Division. As part of LVMH, TAG Heuer has grown strongly in the 2000s, expanding its range beyond a traditional emphasis on sports-oriented timepieces to establish itself as a highly sought-after luxury watch brand. The company produces a variety of models, ranging in price from $600 to $15,000. TAG Heuer has long been a synonym for innovation in the watch industry, a tradition the company has continued to the present. An example of the group's commitment to innovation is its launch of a revolutionary new belt-driven mechanical movement system, featured in the Monaco V4 watch, released in 2004. In that year, also, the company released the world's first timepiece capable of 1/10,000th second timing. Traditionally sold through a limited network of retailers, TAG Heuer has launched its own boutique concept, with a first store opened in New York's SoHo in 2002. LVMH's Watches and Jewelry Division posted revenues of EUR 496 million ($560 million) in 2004.

THE PARIS EXHIBITION OF 1889

The first TAG Heuer workshop was founded by Edouard Heuer in 1860 in the small St. Imier town high in the Swiss Jura mountains. While his competitors at that time concentrated on the production of luxury pocket watches, Heuer began by making a name for himself in timing devices for sports. In 1869 he patented his first stem-winding system. Heuer displayed his wares at the 1889 Paris Exhibition, which unveiled the Eiffel Tower as its main exhibit, heralding the advent of modern society, and won a silver medal for his pocket chronographs. In 1908 Heuer invented and patented the Pulso-meter dial division, still in use for medical applications, and introduced the first dashboard timer for automobiles with a journey-time indicator. Then, in 1916, Heuer laid the basis for a new and modern dimension to sport with his invention of the high precision "Micrograph," capable of measuring time to an accuracy of 1/100th of a second. The introduction of a precise timing device was considered a turning point that marked the beginning of modern sport since athletes no longer competed against one another, but against their own time records.

Heuer chronographs were used at all three Olympic Games in the 1920s. By 1930 Heuer developed its first water-resistant case, followed by a new period of emphasis on the development of the wristwatch. Continuing in its efforts toward innovative uses for timing devices, in 1949 the company patented its invention of the Mareograph chronograph, the first watch fabricated for the purpose of measuring ocean tides.

THE 1960S-70S: TIMEKEEPING IN THE WORLD OF MOTOR SPORTS

In the 1960s the company developed the "Carrera," a stylish chronograph sporting a high-legibility dial, named after a world-renowned motor race of the 1950s, and the "Monaco," which featured an automatic winding mechanism. Heuer's other introductions during this time included the patented "Microsplit," the first solid-state pocket-timer with a digital readout; the first miniaturized, electronic sports timer with readings down to 1/100th of a second; and a new Microsplit timer with LCD (liquid-crystal display) readout. Actor Steve McQueen wore the "Monaco" throughout the filming of *Le Mans,* reflecting the growing association between Heuer products and the motor sport industry. The company's prominence was evidenced by its performance as Official Timekeeper for the Scuderia Ferrari in training and races. As Official Timekeeper, the company was responsible for providing times and details such as information about top speeds, split times, and fastest laps. In 1970 Heuer equipped all of the competing sailing vessels in the American Cup sailing event with timing instruments.

Heuer also was the timekeeper at the 1980 Moscow Olympic Games and at Lake Placid. During this period

the watch industry was revolutionized by the introduction of the new quartz mechanisms. Heuer introduced the first analog quartz chronograph with a 12-hour, 30-minute, and second elapsed-time register.

In a far-reaching move toward technological expansion the TAG group (Techniques d'Avant-Garde) acquired a majority stake in the Heuer company in 1985, forming TAG Heuer. Under the new management team the revitalized company almost immediately began realizing a significant rate of growth. The new company designed and produced its biggest-selling watch when it launched the S/cl series, an unusual design still considered a benchmark in the sports watch sector. The new management team determined to tighten control over the brand's international distribution network to better manage its image, and they began to raise the average retail price of their products, targeting an upscale market. By 1988 the company sold more than 420,000 timepieces, significantly outperforming the Swiss watch industry.

TAG HEUER IN THE 1980S: FORM FOLLOWING FUNCTION

According to company reports, a careful philosophical criterion informs the creation of Heuer watches. In order to create the ultimate sports watch, TAG Heuer started with the premise that all its products had to be capable of high performance and reliability in extreme conditions. The brand strategy focused on the development of a well-defined product style and the implementation of distinctive centralized marketing, advertising, sponsoring, and merchandising. Heuer aimed to attract a broad cross-section of upscale consumers from around the world. It drew up a list of six design features that each of its watches would include: water resistance to 200 meters; unidirectional bezel; screw-in crown; sapphire crystal; double-security clasp; and luminous markings. Within this framework Heuer expected its designers to find different ways to add unique form. Most of its watches took two or three years to design, during which time technical feasibility studies and design work evolved cooperatively. Watches were subjected to tension and torsion tests, as well as exposure to chemicals, ultraviolet light, and extremes of temperature. State-of-the-art computer-aided design and manufacturing techniques were utilized during product development and the machining of precise tolerances.

A large part of the company's marketing strategy involved recognition as sponsors of major sporting events (its sponsorship amounted to approximately $15 million per annum), along with official recognition as professionals implementing the use of their equipment for these events. The company primarily concentrated on

KEY DATES

1860: Edouard Heuer opens a watchmaking workshop in St. Imier, in the Swiss Jura mountain region.

1869: Heuer patents the first stem-winding system.

1916: Heuer introduces a stopwatch capable of timing to 1/100th of a second.

1920: The company becomes the official timekeeper of the Olympics for the first time.

1964: The Carrera chronograph, inspired by the famous race, is launched.

1985: The company merges with Techniques d'Avant Garde, forming TAG Heuer.

1992: The company becomes the official timekeeper of Formula One races.

1996: The company is listed on the Swiss and New York Stock Exchanges.

1999: The company agrees to be acquired by LVMH.

2002: The company opens its first boutique in New York.

2004: The company debuts the Monaco V4, featuring a new belt-driven movement; the company launches the world's first chronometer capable of 1/10,000th of a second accuracy.

2005: The first full haute couture watch collection, including the Diamond Fiction watch, is launched.

three sports: sailing, Formula One racing, and skiing. In Formula One TAG Heuer had been associated with the sponsorship of many great names of the sport: Niki Lauda, Emerson Fittipaldi, Jacky Ickx, Michael Schumacher, and Ayrton Senna, with an especially close association with the McLaren team since 1986 (in 1990 the McLaren team won the world title for constructors and drivers in Formula One racing with Ayrton Senna). In 1988 Heuer launched the S/el chronographs with a 1/10th-second register. In the following year the company became the Official Timekeeper at the Ski World Cup events in the United States and Canada. In skiing, the company sponsored champions such as Marc Girardelli, Harti Weirather, Helmut Hoeflehner, Pedra Kronberger, Kristian Ghedina, and Ole K. Furuseth. Heuer created the Tag Heuer Maxi Yacht World Cup competition in tandem with the release of its 1500 and 4000 Series timepieces.

To ensure high brand recognition Heuer stressed a nontraditional form of vitality and originality in its designs as well as its advertising campaigns. Its 1995 advertising campaign, "Success. It's a Mind Game," won major advertising awards globally and emphasized the relationship between competitive sports and success. To capture the attention of buyers, the exclusive boutiques and galleries featuring TAG Heuer products tended to promote an ambiance of Modernistic minimalism that contrasted starkly with the busy cosmopolitan cityscapes. The discriminating buyer was appealed to rather than the masses. The image of museumlike showcasing presented an atmosphere of artful quality. Setting itself apart from other watch manufacturers, Heuer combined the casual image of the sports watch with the design and substance of opulence when it offered the TAG Heuer Gold Series—sports watches in 18-carat gold, featuring a sophisticated case and bezel design and a unique bracelet of more than 200 elements assembled by hand.

INITIAL PUBLIC OFFERING IN 1996

The company reported that since 1988, TAG Heuer had seen its sales climb by an annual compounded growth rate of 26 percent, rising from CHF 66 million in 1988 to CHF 420 million in 1996, with gross margins rising from 42 percent to 55 percent during that same period. Free cash flow rose by 13 percent for the year. In September 1996 TAG Heuer made its initial public offering with simultaneous listings on the Swiss and New York Stock Exchanges, where it traded under the symbols "TAGN" and "THW," respectively. A large portion of the proceeds from the offering were used to reduce long-term debt for the purpose of decreasing significant future interest expenses. As of December 1996 Heuer had reduced its net debt level to $86.2 million, down from $241.0 million the previous year. The company organized a stock program providing that Heuer would purchase stock on the open market as incentive awards to key executives consisting of about 30 managers.

The company worked to strengthen its presence in geographical markets such as Japan, southeast Asia, Europe, and North America, while increasing brand awareness in areas where its products were less well known. Early in 1997 the company announced that it agreed to acquire its U.K. distributor, Duval, a company instrumental in the successful development of the Heuer brand in the United Kingdom. The purchase had the advantage of allowing Heuer to control distribution of its products in its most important European market. In July 1997 Heuer made another move toward controlling higher yields in the marketplace when it took over the distribution of its sports watches in Japan, after signing an agreement with World Commerce Corporation of Tokyo. At that time Japan represented 20 percent of Heuer's overall sales, making it one of the company's most important markets.

Approximately three quarters of Heuer's business, represented by ten key markets, came under the direct control of the company by this time. A new wholly owned subsidiary, TAG Heuer Japan K.K., was formed, which included 100 World Commerce employees and was headed by a new management team. CEO Christian Viros commented on the transaction, "This development is an extremely important step in TAG Heuer's strategy to increase its downstream integration in order to improve margins and exercise better control over distribution worldwide." He added, "Following the acquisition of our U.K. distributor in February, this transaction further consolidates TAG Heuer's potential to obtain higher returns from our key markets." Continuing in like fashion, Heuer took over the distribution of its prestige sports watches in Australia and New Zealand after signing an agreement with Swiss Time Australia Pty. Ltd., the distributor for Heuer in both countries. A new wholly owned subsidiary named TAG Heuer Australia Pty. Ltd. was formed, incorporating nine employees from the previous ownership and bringing Heuer's direct control of worldwide sales up to approximately 80 percent.

Heuer phased out watch models that were unpopular and added new models in segments such as women's watches, an area with considerable growth potential. From 1991 to 1996 the average factory price of Heuer timepieces had risen by nearly 40 percent, representing a compound annual growth rate of nearly 9 percent. Sales growth was fastest in the North American segment in 1996, accounting for one-third of the company's sales. European sales were up more than 15 percent during the same period, followed by strong performance in Spain, the Benelux countries, and Scandinavia. In its home market of Switzerland, the company also performed well. Sales were down slightly in Japan for the year because of the weakness of the Japanese yen, impacting sales in the region's duty-free outlets, and also because of inventory imbalances.

NEW OWNER FOR THE NEW CENTURY

The company had begun cutting back on the number of retailers selling Heuer watches, with the intention of focusing on presentation solely in upscale markets. Heuer preferred to offer its watches exclusively through premium retailers in premium locations, alongside other prestigious brands. The company continued to update its product range through the design of newer models

and line extensions. Most of its timepieces had been refined over the years to encompass what the company reconsidered as core features of a sports watch, namely, unidirectional turning bezel, water resistance to a depth of at least 200 meters, screw-in crown, scratch-resistant sapphire crystal, luminous hands and dial, and bracelet with a double safety clasp. The company had relaunched its classic 1964 model Heuer Carrera chronograph in 1996 and produced limited editions of high-performance specialty timepieces designed to display its technological expertise, including a limited edition platinum watch of its 6000 series. Following a two-year developmental process and the expansion of its engineering, product development, and quality control departments, Heuer released its 1997 Kirium watch series, designed by world-renowned stylist Jorg Hysek. It featured a band made of the company's patented link system that followed a uniquely rigid yet flexible bracelet design. The watch sold especially well in Germany, and especially well with women, where advertising featured German sports hero Boris Becker. The company regarded Germany, a relatively new geographical area for Heuer, as a potentially lucrative market.

Sales for 1997 dipped in Japan, Hong Kong, Thailand, Indonesia, and South Korea in large part due to the financial turmoil in those regions. Sales increased by 22 percent in North America, aided in part by the appreciation of the U.S. dollar versus the Swiss franc. Revenues in South America, Canada, the Middle East, Singapore, Malaysia, Taiwan, and the Caribbean were also impressive, although overall total unit sales dropped by 6 percent from the previous year, which the company attributed to changes made in product mix and the move toward selling more high-end items. Lower-priced products were phased out during this time.

Heuer announced in May 1998 that consolidated net sales for the first quarter were almost identical to those of 1997, with the most promising results in Europe and the Americas. In a press release, CEO Christian Viros stated, "We are very confident that our strong growth in Europe and in the Americas, the global success of the Kirium and the planned launch of new products will enable the company to more than offset the difficult sales environment in some parts of Asia."

Heuer continued to pare down its number of retail outlets, with the goal of reducing the number of retailers carrying its models to just 1,000 worldwide. In this way, the company hoped to build TAG Heuer into a truly global, and lasting, luxury brand. As Susan Nicholas, then president of TAG Heuer USA, told *Jewelers Circular Keystone*: "We don't want to be so hot that tomorrow we're cold... . It's always a delicate balance of being very much in demand and not being a fad. I feel our success has been calculated. We've been on this steady march. Maybe it was a new kid on the block marching boldly with a little luck. But now we're marching as one of the new leaders. We're in the big leagues. It's a position of strength not to be abused. We'll probably never say we've made it."

TAG Heuer's international ambitions led the company to give up its prized independence in 1999, after luxury goods giant LVMH approached the company with a friendly takeover offer. By the end of that year, LVMH had bought out nearly 100 percent of the Swiss company. Under LVMH, TAG Heuer benefited from the company's extensive global presence. The association with the luxury goods group also encouraged TAG Heuer to continue in its drive to move into the more up-scale watch categories, with its top-priced watch selling for some $15,000. The company also extended its range of models beyond its traditional emphasis on sports-oriented timepieces, adding watches designed to establish the brand as a fashion leader as well. As part of this effort, the company brought in a new range of celebrity sponsors, including Brad Pitt and Uma Thurman.

TAG Heuer dipped its toes into the retail market as well, opening its first boutique in New York's fashionable SoHo district. At the same time the company continued in its tradition of innovation and commitment to technological advancement. In 2004, for example, the company debuted a new professional chronometer capable of measuring within 1/10,000th of a second. At mid-decade, the company also debuted its Monaco V4 wristwatch, featuring a revolutionary new mechanical movement using miniature belts, based on an automotive transmission system. At the same time, TAG Heuer prepared its entry into the haute couture segment, launching its first full collection, including the Diamond Fiction watch, featuring nearly 900 diamonds. TAG Heuer appeared to have found the balance between its sports-oriented past and its luxury goods future.

Terri Mozzone
Updated, M. L. Cohen

PRINCIPAL SUBSIDIARIES

TAG Heuer International S.A. (Luxembourg); Tag Heuer Ltd. (U.K.).

PRINCIPAL COMPETITORS

Seiko Epson Corporation; Slava Joint Stock Co.; Chayka Watch Factory Ltd.; Matrix Systems Inc.; Compagnie Financiere Richemont AG; SWATCH Group AG; Citizen Watch Company Ltd.; Diehl Stiftung and Company KG; Bulgari S.p.A.; Fossil Inc.

FURTHER READING

Askin, Ellen, "Tag's New Take on Time," *Daily News Record,* February 16, 2004, p. 28.

Christopher, Warren, "Race Against Time," *Men's Fitness,* September 2004, p. 72.

"It's Arnault Time Again As LVMH Launches Bid for Tag Heuer Watches," *WWD,* September 14, 1999, p. 1.

Kletter, Melanie, "Tag Heuer Launches First US Unit in SoHo," *WWD,* March 21, 2002, p. 12.

Maillard, Pierre, and D. Malcolm Lakin, "Tag Heuer: The Living Legend," *American Time,* June-July 2003, p. 18.

O'Loughlin, Sandra, "TAG Heuer Makes Time for New Marketing Tactics," *Brandweek,* May 9, 2005, p. 16.

Shuster, William George, "TAG Heuer Makes 'Bold' Expansion in Women's Watches," *Jewelers Circular Keystone,* March 2005, p. 72.

"Success Is a Tag Heuer Game," *Jewelers Circular Keystone,* May 1998, p. 54.

"Tag Heuer International SA," *Wall Street Journal,* June 10, 1997, p. B11.

"Tag Heuer Net Rises 15.7 Percent for 1996 As Sales Gain 10.6 Percent," *Clock and Watch Industry,* April 3, 1997, p. 14.

"Tag Heuer Profits Climb 60 Percent," *Daily News Record,* September 12, 1997, p. 9.

"The Timing Couldn't Have Been Worse," *Business Week,* November 4, 2002, p. 28.

"With the Help of Spokeswoman Uma Thurman, the Usually Sporty Tag Heuer Has Launched Its First Haute Couture Collection, Which Includes the Over-the-Top Diamond Fiction Watch with, Count 'em, 879 Rocks," *Variety,* August 15, 2005, p. S36.

Tanox, Inc.

———■———

10555 Stella Link
Houston, Texas 77025
U.S.A.
Telephone: (713) 578-4000
Fax: (713) 578-5000
Web site: http://www.tanox.com

Public Company
Incorporated: 1986 as Tanox Biosystems, Inc.
Employees: 127
Sales: $20.5 million (2004)
Stock Exchanges: NASDAQ
Ticker Symbol: TNOX
NAIC: 541710 Research and Development in the Physical Sciences and Engineering Sciences; 325412 Pharmaceutical Preparation Manufacturing

■ ■ ■

Tanox, Inc. is a biotechnology company engaged in the development of monoclonal antibodies that treat unmet medical needs related to asthma, allergy, inflammation, autoimmune disease, and other conditions stemming from an overactive immune system. Working with Novartis AG and Genentech, Inc., the company has developed Xolair, the first biological therapy for allergic asthma, which is marketed by Novartis and Genentech. Tanox's collaborative agreement with Novartis and Genentech includes research and development work on other treatments undergoing Food and Drug Administration-mandated clinical trials, such as TNX-355, which is a monoclonal antibody designed to combat human immunodeficiency virus (HIV). Other applications of the company's technology target conditions such as severe peanut allergy and acute inflammation in chemotherapy patients. Tanox's main manufacturing facility is located in San Diego, California.

ORIGINS

Tanox began its efforts to bring a product to market in the late 1980s, embarking on the long road toward commercialization that virtually every start-up biotechnology company was forced to endure. The lengthy struggle to develop a marketable therapeutic outlasted the marriage of the company's founders, Nancy Chang and Tse Wen Chang, who formed the company, initially named Tanox Biosystems, Inc., in March 1986. Nancy Chang stayed with the company, guiding it through its formative years and leading it toward its ultimate objective of selling a product on the market. The process took nearly 20 years. For Chang, who received her doctorate degree in biological chemistry from Harvard University, Tanox became her life's work, a career devoted to the development of therapeutic monoclonal antibodies.

Chang, along with her then-husband, was employed by the Baylor College of Medicine when she started Tanox, serving as an associate professor in the institution's molecular virology division. She remained at Baylor until 1992, but took an active role in running Tanox, serving as its president and chairwoman upon inception and adding the title of chief executive officer in 1990, a significant year in the company's development. The year marked Tanox's first partnership

COMPANY PERSPECTIVES

We are committed to becoming a world leader in providing effective therapies for immune-mediated diseases, infectious disease, inflammation and cancer. Through the development and use of innovative technologies, we will create products that address unmet medical needs by treating the underlying cause of disease.

agreement with a larger company, a necessity for any small biotechnology company that gave Tanox essential financial and technical help in its research and development endeavors. Chang and her small staff of scientists attracted the attention of a deep-pocketed partner because of their work in developing monoclonal antibodies, a nascent and promising field of science during the late 1980s.

The human immune system has several general mechanisms to combat infections, toxins, and cancers. Tanox focused on one such mechanism, the ability of the body to produce proteins called antibodies that attack and help remove foreign agents, known as antigens, from the body. Each antibody is tailor made for the antigen it is intended to attack, possessing particular attributes that enable it to complete its task, much like a particular key that matches a particular lock. In some cases, cases ranging from allergic diseases to autoimmune diseases such as HIV, the immune system is at fault, essentially instigating or fanning hostilities within the body instead of fighting to protect it. With asthma or seasonal allergic rhinitis (hay fever), for instance, the immune system responds to the antigen, an allergen in the case of allergic diseases, by producing an immunoglobulin E, or IgE, form of antibody, which only serves to trigger the symptoms of the disease. In a more severe case of malfunction, the immune system becomes the body's own worst enemy, mistakenly identifying normal cells as foreign agents, which triggers an immune response against the body resulting in autoimmune disease and associated tissue destruction. One way scientists helped the immune system when it faltered in its mission was by using monoclonal antibodies, genetically engineered antibodies designed to target a specific antigen. Such was the focus of Tanox's research and development efforts, specifically monoclonal antibodies that targeted the IgE antigen, an immune system pathway.

Not long after the company was incorporated, a small group of Tanox scientists discovered a novel approach for the treatment of allergic disease by reducing the levels of IgE in the blood. The company's discovery of an anti-IgE antibody attracted the attention of Ciba-Geigy Ltd., later to become the Swiss pharmaceutical giant, Novartis AG. The two companies agreed to collaborate in 1990, a deal that provided essential financial support to the fledgling company and marked the beginning of a relationship that would endure for more than 15 years. Under the terms of partnership, the two companies agreed to develop anti-IgE antibodies to treat allergic diseases. Tanox's research and development efforts were focused on monoclonal antibodies for the treatment of allergy, asthma, HIV infection, inflammation, and other related diseases, but at the forefront of the company's work was a treatment for allergic asthma, a therapeutic initially referred to as "E25." The treatment, based on the company's discovery made in 1987, would take years of further work and more time still to gain approval from the Food and Drug Administration (FDA), a lengthy and costly process that was not without controversy.

As Tanox's research staff concentrated on developing E25, a legal dispute erupted that threatened to make their work irrelevant. The problem arose from meetings Tanox had with Genentech, Inc., a major U.S. biotechnology company. Forming partnerships with larger companies was vital to Tanox's existence, prompting it to broker a deal with Novartis and enter discussions with Genentech in 1989 and 1990. After the two companies discussed collaborating on the development of an antibody for the treatment of allergies and asthma, they were unable to agree on terms to work together on commercializing the discovery, ending their discussions in 1990. Several years passed before Tanox filed a lawsuit against Genentech, alleging that one month after discussions between the two companies ended, Genentech launched a competing allergy program that violated an agreement between the two companies. Tanox filed its lawsuit in December 1993 and Genentech was quick to respond, filing its own lawsuit against Tanox in January 1994, alleging patent infringement. Remarkably, after the legal salvos were fired, the dispute resulted in a partnership between the two companies, providing additional support to Chang's pioneering work. In 1996, Genentech signed a collaborative agreement with Tanox and Novartis, forming a trio committed to commercializing monoclonal antibodies that addressed afflictions occurring along the IgE pathway.

Despite the backing of billion-dollar partners, Tanox endured bleak financial times throughout the 1990s. E25 was granted "fast-track" status by the FDA, a designation reserved for promising drugs that targeted

KEY DATES

1986: Tanox is formed.
1990: Tanox signs a collaborative agreement with Ciba-Geigy Ltd., later to become Novartis AG.
1996: Genentech, Inc. joins the partnership between Tanox and Novartis.
2000: Tanox completes its initial public offering of stock, raising $244 million.
2003: The company's first product, Xolair, is introduced on the market.
2006: Founder Nancy Chang steps down as chief executive officer.

critical, unmet medical needs, but an accelerated approval process did little to improve the company's financial condition. Tanox, like virtually every small biotechnology company, was forced to endure years of mounting losses and meager revenue totals as it struggled to bring its first product to market. The company's financial results at the end of the decade epitomized the hardships of operating as a therapeutic pioneer: Tanox generated $1.4 million in revenue in 1999, a year in which losses totaled more than $23 million.

INITIAL PUBLIC OFFERING IN 2000

For Chang and her staff, hopes for a financially successful future were pinned to the release of E25. To obtain some financial help and cash in on the growing expectations of E25's effectiveness in treating allergic asthma, Tanox turned to Wall Street, filing for an initial public offering (IPO) of stock in 2000. The company originally had planned to complete its IPO in 1993, an offering that was expected to raise roughly $30 million in proceeds, but the offering was withdrawn. The seven-year wait proved to be financially prudent, resulting in exponentially higher proceeds for the company. The IPO was completed in May 2000, when Tanox's shares debuted at $28.50 per share, raising $244 million in proceeds in what ranked as one of the largest public debuts in the history of the biotechnology industry. At the time of the offering, E25 had completed Phase III clinical trials in both allergic asthma and hay fever, with regulatory approval expected to be granted sometime between 2002 and 2003. As Chang prepared for the long-awaited release of the company's first commercial product, she did what she could to keep costs at

minimum. In 2001, the company's research operations in Taiwan, the Netherlands, and the United States were consolidated at the company's headquarters in Houston. Revenue by the end of the year had slipped to a paltry $419,000. The company's losses in 2001 amounted to more than $21 million.

Tanox's mission to offer a product to sufferers of allergic asthma ended 17 years after it was begun. In June 2003, the FDA approved E25, which had been given the trade name Xolair, to treat moderate-to-severe persistent asthma in adults and adolescents. Xolair, marketed by Novartis and Genentech, was introduced the following month, the first humanized monoclonal antibody evaluated for asthma and the first therapeutic to target the IgE antibody. For its part, Tanox received a royalty on net sales of Xolair of between 8 and 12 percent, which, according to Chang's estimates, would enable the company to begin turning a profit by 2007. Analysts expected Xolair to generate $750 million in annual revenue by 2008.

A PRODUCT PIPELINE FOR THE FUTURE

As Tanox neared its 20th anniversary, the company was still a work in progress, a company with one marketable product that arguably was still in the developmental phase of its existence. Consistent profits, something that had eluded the company during its first two decades in business, depended on the market success of Xolair and the commercialization of other therapeutics in Tanox's development pipeline. Midway through the first decade of the 21st century, there were two promising treatments buoying hopes for improved financial performance in the near future. One was given the preliminary name "TNX-901," a monoclonal antibody developed to treat those with severe peanut allergies, the most common food allergy. An estimated 1.5 million Americans suffered from the condition, and each year between 50 and 100 of the afflicted died after eating just one or two peanuts. TNX-901, which targeted the IgE pathway, was in Phase II clinical trials by the time Xolair was approved, registering encouraging results. Tests demonstrated that TNX-901 raised the average threshold at which patients had an allergic reaction from half a peanut to nearly nine peanuts. Tanox's other promising monoclonal antibody was dubbed "TNX-355," a treatment for HIV that was undergoing clinical trials midway through the decade. TNX-355, another antibody that targeted the IgE pathway, worked by coating the cells that HIV targeted to prevent HIV from entering them. Data collected during clinical trials showed TNX-355 reduced the amount of HIV in the body by an estimated 95 percent. "As a company," Chang said in a January

11, 2006 interview with the *Houston Chronicle,* "we are very excited. This is our second home-run opportunity to take this drug to the market for thousands and thousands of people who can benefit from this drug. We see a real product opportunity in this drug."

As Tanox prepared for the years ahead, the true merit of the work completed during its first 20 years of business would be determined during its next two decades of business.

The commercial success of Xolair, which was approved for sale in Europe in October 2005, TNX-901, TNX-355, and other treatments in the company's product pipeline offered potential financial rewards that would validate years of research and development efforts. As the company headed toward this new, conclusive era of existence, it did so under new leadership. Chang relinquished day-to-day control over the company in February 2006, passing the reins of command to Danong Chen, whom she had groomed for the chief executive officer role for the previous four years. Chang remained Tanox's chairwoman. Chen, who had met Chang at Baylor College, assumed responsibility for shepherding the company's products towards commercial success and fulfilling Chang's pledge of making Tanox profitable between 2007 and 2009.

Jeffrey L. Covell

PRINCIPAL SUBSIDIARIES

Tanox Pharma International, Inc.; Tanox West, Inc.

PRINCIPAL COMPETITORS

Biogen Idec Inc.; Medarex, Inc.; PDL BioPharma, Inc.

FURTHER READING

Arnst, Catherine, "Delayed Help for Peanut Allergy Sufferers," *Business Week Online,* March 11, 2003.

Brune, Brett, "Chief Is Stepping Down As Tanox Drug Steps Up," *Houston Chronicle,* January 11, 2006.

Fowler, Tom, "Houston-Based Drug Company Tanox Narrows Its Losses, Increases Revenues," *Houston Chronicle,* February 2, 2001.

"Funds for Development of Drugs Push Tanox into Fast Tech 50," *Houston Business Journal,* November 30, 2001, p. 10B.

"Genentech, Novartis and Tanox Settle Disputes Surrounding Xolair and TNX-901," *Asia Africa Intelligence Wire,* February 26, 2004.

Gorner, Peter, "Tanox Shares Surge As FDA Panel Backs Asthma Drug," *America's Intelligence Wire,* May 16, 2003.

Krause, Carey, "Genentech Gains Approval for Xolair," *Chemical Market Reporter,* June 30, 2003, p. 7.

Lau, Gloria, "Biotech Finds Right Formula by Partnering with Ex-Rival," *Investor's Business Daily,* October 6, 2003, p. A9.

McNamara, Victoria, "Biotech Chiefs Make Changes in Boardrooms," *Houston Business Journal,* March 4, 1991, p. 1A.

———, "Private Firms Fight AIDS Out of Financial Necessity," *Houston Business Journal,* July 2, 1990, p. 13A.

"Monoclonal Antibody Among HIV Therapies Discussed at Human Virology Meeting," *Medical Letter on the CDC & FDA,* December 12, 2004, p. 51.

Musero, Frank, "Biotech IPOs Remain Absent from Market," *IPO Reporter,* May 14, 2001.

Osborne, Randall, "With Xolair Approved, Trio Sorts Options for Peanut Allergy Drug," *Bioworld Financial Watch,* July 7, 2003, p. 1.

Schelegel, Darrin, "Tanox Assembles New Legal Team in Biotech Battle with Genentech," *Houston Business Journal,* August 19, 1994, p. 1.

"Tanox, Inc. Announces Initial Public Offering," *AsiaPulse News,* April 10, 2000, p. 515.

"Tanox to Expand Manufacturing Capacity with Facility in San Diego," *Asia Africa Intelligence Wire,* December 15, 2004.

"Xolair Is Being Evaluated in Patients Suffering from Peanut Allergy," *Asia Africa Intelligence Wire,* July 7, 2004.

THOMSON

™

The Thomson Corporation

Toronto Dominion Bank Tower, Suite 2706
Wellington Street West
Toronto, Ontario M5K 1A1
Canada
Telephone: (416) 360-8700
Fax: (416) 360-8812
Web site: http://www.thomson.com

Public Company
Incorporated: 1977
Employees: 40,000
Sales: $8.1 billion (2004)
Stock Exchanges: New York Toronto
Ticker Symbol: TOC
NAIC: 511110 Newspaper Publishers; 511120 Periodi-
cal Publishers; 511130 Book Publishers; 511140
Database and Directory Publishers; 514199 All
Other Information Services; 551112 Offices of
Other Holding Companies; 611710 Educational
Support Services

■ ■ ■

The Thomson Corporation is a publishing and information services powerhouse serving businesses, libraries,
and individuals worldwide. Its electronic information
databases are second to none, and Thomson publishing
includes the reference, educational, and trade markets.
With operations in 40 countries worldwide, Thomson
is organized into four divisions, each a leader in its
field: Legal & Regulatory (serving the legal, tax,
accounting, professional, and governmental markets);

Learning (serving higher education, corporate, professional, and governmental clients); Financial (serving
investment, banking, and financial planning markets);
and Scientific & Healthcare (serving the research, healthcare, scientific, and academic markets).

BIRTH OF AN EMPIRE: 1890S TO 1950S

Born in Toronto in 1894, Roy Thomson left school at
14 to become a bookkeeper and, later, branch manager
of a cordage company. After an unsuccessful attempt at
farming in Saskatchewan, he returned to Ontario in
1920 to establish an automotive parts distributorship,
which also proved unsuccessful. In 1930 Thomson
agreed to a franchise arrangement to sell radios in the
remote town of North Bay. As Susan Goldenberg
reported in *The Thomson Empire*: "Only someone with
Thomson's optimism, stamina, and ebullient salesmanship would have accepted such an assignment under the
odds he faced." Not only was it the Depression, but
radio reception in North Bay was dismal. Thomson
solved the problem of feeble radio sales by borrowing
money and opening his own radio station, CFCH, in
1932.

Thomson's avowed ambition was to become a millionaire by the time he was 30 but, nearing the age of
40, he was nearly penniless. His decision to capitalize on
advertising revenue in his current venture, however,
helped him to belatedly achieve his goal several hundred
times over. Within two years of CFCH's debut, Thomson had bought additional stations in Kirkland Lake and
Timmins. The latter purchase coincided with Thom-

COMPANY PERSPECTIVES

The Thomson Corporation is a leading global provider of integrated information solutions to business and professional customers. Thomson provides value-added information, with software tools and applications that help its customers make better decisions, faster. We serve more than 20 million information users in the fields of law, tax, accounting, higher education, reference information, corporate e-learning and assessment, financial services, scientific research, and healthcare.

son's entry into newspaper publishing, another source of advertising revenue and what would become the cornerstone of his empire, via the *Timmins Press*, a paper whose offices were in the same building as his newest station. By 1944 his holdings included five newspapers and eight radio stations. Newspapers became Thomson's primary concern, while Jack Kent Cooke, with whom he formed a partnership in 1940, assumed management of the radio end of the business. Their partnership ended in 1949, just as Thomson began buying newspapers outside Ontario.

In 1952 Thomson bought his first newspaper outside Canada, the *Independent* of St. Petersburg, Florida, to add to the 12 he already owned. A turning point came in 1953 when Thomson moved to Great Britain, leaving his North American operations under the control of his son Kenneth, then 30. Thomson's first U.K. acquisition was the *Scotsman*, a prestigious Scottish daily founded in 1817. Owning Scotland's leading newspaper put Thomson in an excellent position to make a bid for a commercial television franchise covering central Scotland when it became available in 1957. Famous for his frugality as well as for his quotes on the topic of wealth, he called this coup "a license to print money."

The enormous profits from Scottish Television (STV) made it possible for Thomson to buy London's leading Sunday paper, the *Sunday Times,* as well as 17 other local newspapers from the Kemsley family in 1959. This was the first "reverse takeover" in U.K. business history. Kemsley Newspapers bought Thomson's STV company in return for Kemsley shares, which gave Thomson majority control of the group and allowed him to indirectly retain STV as well, with 70 percent control of the total business (stricter government controls later led to a forced reduction in Thomson's holdings).

ADDING PUBLISHING, TRAVEL, AND PETROLEUM: 1960S-70S

Thomson did not restrict himself to newspapers and television. Thomson Publications, the forerunner of what became Thomson's largest and most profitable group, was established in 1961 to publish books and magazines. The subsidiary began with the acquisition of the Illustrated London News Company, which owned not only the magazine of that name and the *Tatler*, but trade book publisher Michael Joseph. To this base Thomson Publications added educational publisher Thomas Nelson & Sons; George Rainbird, specializing in illustrated books; Hamish Hamilton in trade books; and Derwent Publications in scientific and technical information, all in the early 1960s.

Thomson moved into consumer, professional, and business press publishing in the United Kingdom, Australia, and Africa. It also revamped its regional newspaper group, launched four newspapers, started new magazines, including *Family Circle* and *Living,* to be distributed through supermarkets (a novel concept that proved highly successful in the United Kingdom), and started the *Sunday Times* color magazine, which by 1963 was an unqualified success. In addition, Thomson Publications created a paperback imprint, Sphere, in 1966, aiming its titles at confectioners, news agents, and tobacconists rather than established bookshops. This venture suffered losses, in part because it could not secure the paperback rights of books published by other Thomson companies, since most of these had already been bought by rival paperback publishers.

In 1964 Roy Thomson made it clear that Britain rather than Canada was now his base by taking British citizenship and accepting a seat in the House of Lords as Lord Thomson of Fleet, an honor sponsored by Prime Minister Harold Macmillan. From television, newspapers, books, and magazines, Thomson next extended his empire into the travel business starting in 1965, when foreign travel was just beginning to become a popular activity in Britain. Three existing package tour companies and a small airline, Britannia Airways, were bought and formed the basis for Thomson Travel. After an initial period of good profits, the company encountered intense competition in the early 1970s which resulted in the failure of several competing companies. Thomson Travel survived as the largest operator due to a reconstruction of its management, organizational, and commercial policies.

In 1972 the group moved into travel retailing with the acquisition of Lunn Poly. Thomson introduced Yellow Pages to the United Kingdom as a long-term profit venture. Once he had won the contract from the Post

KEY DATES

1932: Roy Thomson begins operating a radio station in North Bay, Ontario.

1934: Thomson acquires his first newspaper, the *Timmins Press.*

1949: Thomson exits the radio field to concentrate on newspapers.

1952: Thomson buys the *Independent* of St. Petersburg, Florida, his first American newspaper.

1953: Thomson moves from Canada to Great Britain.

1961: Thomson Publications is established.

1966: The *London Times* and its associated weeklies are acquired.

1978: International Thomson Organisation Ltd. is formed; headquarters is moved to Toronto.

1980: Thomson Newspapers Ltd. acquires a group of Canadian newspapers, including the *Globe & Mail.*

1989: ITOL and Thomson Newspapers merge to become The Thomson Corporation.

1994: Thomson acquires Information Access Company and the healthcare database firm Medstat Group.

1995: The company divests numerous U.K. newspaper holdings.

1996: West Publishing Company is acquired, and most North American daily newspapers are sold.

1998: Thomson sells its leisure and travel firm.

2000: The company divests more newspaper interests, maintaining a stake in the *Globe & Mail.*

2001: Reed Elsevier Plc and Thomson buy Harcourt General's assets.

2002: Kenneth Thomson retires and Thomson offers shares on the New York Stock Exchange.

2004: Thomson sells print assets from its Financial and Scientific & Health divisions.

2005: Seattle-based NexCura, Inc. is acquired by Thomson Scientific & Health.

Office to sell advertising in its telephone directories, Thomson persuaded the agency of the need for a classified directory in all 64 telephone regions. From this enterprise the company learned the constraints and dif-

ficulties of working in a commercial venture with a public utility. In 1980 Thomson relinquished the Yellow Pages contract and start its own local directory operation in partnership with the American firm Dun & Bradstreet.

Thomson had been looking for a national daily newspaper to put together with the *Sunday Times,* and in 1966 he bought the *London Times* and its associated weeklies, *Times Literary Supplement* and *Times Educational Supplement,* from the Astor family. Thomson described the acquisition as the summit of a lifetime's work, and cheerfully bore the continuing financial losses as his one extravagance. Perhaps even more to his credit than his financial commitment was Thomson's pledge of complete freedom and independence for his papers' editorial staff.

In 1971 the company went into its single most profitable area of business when it joined with Occidental Petroleum, Getty Oil, and Allied Chemical as the sole U.K. partner in a bid for oil exploration licenses in the North Sea. The consortium's first strike, in 1973, was in the Piper field, containing more than 800 million barrels of oil. Thomson rejected the U.S. partners' offer to buy his 20 percent stake, and his investment turned out even wiser than expected when a second strike, in the Claymore field in 1974, brought the consortium another 400 million barrels. Within a decade the International Thomson Organisation was gaining most of its overall profits from North Sea oil on the basis of an initial stake of just CAD 5 million and bank loans using the oil itself as collateral. In 1977 International Thomson showed a trading profit of almost CAD 190 million, compared with less than CAD 20 million in 1971.

EXPANSION THROUGH ACQUISITIONS: LATE 1970S-80S

When Kenneth Thomson succeeded his father in 1976, he inherited control of a CAD 750 million media monolith. British government policy on monopolies prevented expansion of newspaper holdings in the United Kingdom, and exchange controls, since abolished, would have made overseas investment from a base in London very costly. The decision was made to concentrate on expanding in North America by investing oil profits into publications and publishers with proven track records. In 1978 International Thomson Organisation Ltd. (ITOL) was established and corporate headquarters were moved back to Toronto. ITOL's philosophy, according to a 1988 *Forbes* article, became: "Buy the market leader, even in a specialized field, and then you can afford to pay for the acquisition."

In 1979 ITOL's first acquisition in North America was U.S. college textbook publisher Wadsworth Inc., followed quickly by others in business and professional publishing and information services, such as Callaghan & Company, Van Nostrand Reinhold, Research Publications, and Warren, Gorham & Lamont, as well as numerous business magazines. By 1983 a quarter of ITOL's sales were to the United States and nearly 20 percent of its workforce was employed there. Acquisitions continued over the next several years, bringing in such companies as Gale Research, South-Western Publishing Company, and Mitchell International.

Back in the United Kingdom, Times Newspapers had become a source of continual trouble for the group. By 1978 strikes over pay and conditions were seriously disrupting the publication of both titles. The situation continued to deteriorate until the company suspended publication for 11 months. Not long after the papers' operations resumed, International Thomson gave up the unequal struggle to introduce new technology on terms acceptable to the company and, in 1981, sold the titles to Australian media magnate Rupert Murdoch.

The Canadian company Thomson Newspapers Ltd., which was separate from ITOL, had long restricted itself to owning small Canadian and U.S. newspapers with circulations below 20,000; the strategy was in keeping with Roy Thomson's drive to contain costs while nonetheless being assured of near monopolies in local advertising. During the 1950s under Kenneth Thomson, the group published the largest number of newspaper titles in Canada. In the following decade a bold U.S. acquisition program was launched. In 1967 the company acquired 16 daily and six weekly newspapers, mainly from the purchase of the Brush Moore Newspaper, Inc., and was publishing more daily newspapers in the United States than in Canada. By 1974 the group owned more than 100 newspapers.

In 1980 its profile was transformed through the acquisition of FP Publications and its chain of newspapers in most of the big cities of Canada, including Toronto's *Globe & Mail,* which Thomson attempted to turn into a national newspaper along U.K. lines. By this time, Thomson Travel ranked as the largest inclusive tour operator based in the United Kingdom (about three times the size of its nearest rival), owning the country's biggest charter airline, and was one of the world's largest travel retailers. Within a few years of entering the U.S. market it became one of the top three U.S. tour operators, although by 1988 it had withdrawn completely in order to concentrate on its activities based in the United Kingdom. This same year Thomson strengthened its U.K. leadership in tour operating, charter airlines, and travel retailing with the acquisition of the Horizon Travel Group, one of its major competitors.

For ITOL, expansion continued throughout the 1980s in Britain and the United States alike. With the 1986 acquisition of South-Western, the largest American publisher of business textbooks, ITOL became second overall in U.S. college textbook publishing. The following year saw one of ITOL's biggest British purchases, when it acquired Associated Book Publishers (ABP), a group including legal publisher Sweet & Maxwell and academic publisher Routledge, Chapman & Hall. Purchased for $323 million, ABP represented a major advance for ITOL in legal, scientific, technical, and academic publishing in the United Kingdom, North America, and Australia.

The 1986 fall in oil prices dragged the company's North American petroleum subsidiaries into losses and they were sold off in 1987. By reducing its oil interests, ITOL was able to concentrate even more resources and attention on its core activities of publishing and information services. In 1988 subsidiary Thomson & Thomson launched a database containing over 300,000 trademarks and logos and ITOL acquired 36 free newspapers in Britain. By the end of 1988, after 54 years of growth, Thomson Newspapers published 40 daily and 12 weekly newspapers in Canada, and 116 daily and 24 weekly newspapers in the United States, representing the largest number of daily newspapers of any publishing group in either country with a daily circulation exceeding three million.

In 1989 ITOL exited the petroleum business completely, selling its remaining interests. Next, in a dawning era of megamergers among media conglomerates (Time Inc. and Warner Communications Inc. had proposed such a landmark merger, which was completed in early 1990), ITOL and Thomson Newspapers announced preparations to merge as the Thomson Corporation, a CAD 4.7 billion entity which began operations a few months later. Thus empowered, the new company then bought the Lawyers Cooperative Publishing Company for CAD 815 million, at the time the largest acquisition ever by a Thomson company. In 1990 Thomson purchased five daily newspapers and several associated weekly publications in the United States, its largest ever single purchase. Eight more Canadian local papers and the *Financial Times* were also bought. Thomson newspapers were now being published in 32 of the 50 American states and in eight of the ten Canadian provinces.

TRANSITION TO A SINGLE FOCUS ON INFORMATION, 1990S

From 1990 to 1992 Thomson saw its revenues and profits rise from $5.36 billion to $5.98 billion; its operating profits, however, stumbled from $726 million to $692 million before partially rebounding to its 1992 figure of $714 million. Two straight years of double-digit profit declines for Thomson Newspapers were caused by recession-influenced decreases in advertising and the introduction of 400 new products, including the first corporation-generated project, an entertainment weekly entitled *CoverSTORY,* whose circulation, primarily through Thomson newspapers, approached one million. While newspaper profits fluctuated, Thomson invested in Internet-based services, including ownership of 190 online services, 161 CD-ROM products, and a large number of other software offerings, all part of subsidiary Thomson Information/Publishing Group (TIPG). Thomson further accelerated its entry into information services with the $210 million purchase of New York-based JPT Publishing, to acquire its data provider Institute for Scientific Information (ISI). ISI enjoyed over 300,000 customers worldwide and was believed to be generating healthy annual profits estimated at $15 million.

During the mid-1990s Thomson completed several more acquisitions, three of which were particularly important. In 1994 the company paid about $465 million for the Foster City, California-based Information Access Company (IAC), a former division of Ziff-Davis Communications. IAC was a leading provider of reference and database services for academic and public libraries, corporations, hospitals, and schools. Thomson also added the $339 million purchase of the Medstat Group to its healthcare information portfolio, but lost out to rival Reed Elsevier in the bidding for information database Lexis-Nexis. Two years later, in 1996, Thomson completed the largest acquisition in its history when it paid $3.4 billion for the Minnesota-based West Publishing Company, which maintained more than 6,000 electronic databases on law, medicine, and insurance.

Thomson and West were the two largest U.S. legal publishers, which prompted close antitrust scrutiny and objections from competitors in the field, most notably Reed Elsevier. To gain antitrust approval, Thomson and West sold off more than 50 legal publications, some of which went to Reed Elsevier. In early 1997 West and Thomson Legal Publishing were merged as West Group. At the same time, Thomson had reduced its newspaper holdings by divesting numerous U.K. papers in 1995 and U.S. and Canadian daily newspapers in 1996.

Michael Brown was named deputy chairman in 1998 and replaced as president and CEO by Richard Harrington. The early 1998 acquisition of Computer Language Research Inc. for about $325 million bolstered Thomson's existing tax and accounting information operations, which centered on its Research Institute of America Group. By this time, Thomson's information services operations were the core of the company, with overall information revenue increasing by more than 75 percent over a five-year period to $4.8 billion. The company took another major step to further its focus on information in May 1998, when it spun off Thomson Travel through a public offering that generated net proceeds of $2 billion. As a result more than 83 percent of 1998 revenues were derived from Thomson's information businesses.

GOING GLOBAL, ELECTRONIC- ALLY: 2000-01

Given Thomson's historic roots in the newspaper industry, its February 2000 announcement to sell its newspaper interests was dramatic. Thomson Newspapers included 55 daily newspapers and more than 75 non-daily newspapers and had generated $810 million in 1999 revenues. The company's flagship, the *Globe & Mail,* was sold to Bell GlobeMedia, with Thomson retaining a stake of 20 percent. Proceeds from the sales bolstered Thomson's growing portfolio of electronic databases. Acquisitions remained a key strategy for its business units, especially Thomson Learning, which purchased test provider Prometric, Alliance Press, Wave Technologies, Dialog Corporation, Greenhaven Press, and Lucent Books. In addition, Thomson inked a deal with Reed Elsevier Plc to buy Harcourt General's higher education and professional units for $2.06 billion during Reed's $5.7 billion acquisition of Harcourt.

Thomson Financial planned an aggressive international campaign to knock rival Reuters Group Plc from its perch as the global leader in financial information services. During 2000 and 2001 Thomson Financial made several purchases along this line including Primark Corporation, a European electronic data distributor; Brazil's Invest Tracker Technologia, a data provider; the remaining interest in Wall Street data firm First Call Corporation; and put its business publications, including *American Banker* and *Bond Buyer,* up for sale. This repositioning was a prime example of Thomson's strategy for the future, to be electronic and global, not print and local. Thomson finished 2000 with revenues of $5.9 billion and income of $1.1 billion.

As expected in the Reed Elsevier/Harcourt deal, the Department of Justice (DOJ) was concerned about antitrust issues and ordered Thomson to sell 38 college titles before approval would be given for the acquisitions. Thomson complied, having expected interference from the DOJ, and the Reed Elsevier/Harcourt deal became final in July 2001.

A NEW ERA: 2002 AND BEYOND

In 2002 Thomson was poised for a new era, not only in leadership, since Chairman Kenneth Thomson was planning to retire, but as the company considered a public offering on the New York Stock Exchange. With the vast majority of the company's shares retained by the Thomson family (more than 70 percent), many believed the future of the electronic information powerhouse was in having a more diversified shareholder base. Others speculated the fund-raising was for a sizeable acquisition. In May 2002, before its planned offering on the New York Stock Exchange (NYSE), Kenneth Thomson stepped down as chairman and was succeeded by his son, David Thomson, a fellow director on the board. In June Thomson floated 32 million shares on the NYSE, raising over $1 billion from the offering.

Other news included Thomson Learning's acquisition of McGraw-Hill's Lifetime Learning unit; Thomson Scientific & Healthcare's purchase of the U.K.-based Current Drugs, Ltd., an e-services provider; Thomson Legal's acquisitions of Brazil's leading legal publisher, Sinese, and the United Kingdom's Lawtel in 2002 and the purchase of Elite Information Group in early 2003. Despite a weakened economy, Thomson Corp. finished 2002 with revenues of $7.2 billion and climbed slightly to $7.6 billion for 2003.

Thomson continued to acquire electronic data providers and launch new services in 2004, including the purchase of Information Holdings Inc. and Techstreet Inc.; the rollout of Thomson Learning subsidiary Gale's Virtual Reference Library of numerous reference books and series; and the purchase of dozens of texts and titles for its Learning unit. Late in the year, Thomson finally sold its Media unit to Investcorp for $350 million. Thomson Media, which held the company's financially themed print assets (*American Banker, Bond Buyer, Accounting Today,* and others), was originally put up for sale in 2001, then taken off the market. Thomson Scientific & Health also divested its print assets, selling 15 healthcare magazines to Boston-based Advanstar Communications for $135 million.

Thomson posted strong results for 2004 with revenues hitting $8.1 billion, led by Thomson's Legal & Regulatory division with CAD 3.3 billion in revenues. Thomson Learning ranked as the company's second revenue producer with $2.2 billion, Thomson Financial weighed in at $1.7 billion, and Thomson Scientific & Health brought in $934 million for the year, which the company hoped would be bolstered by the acquisition of the Seattle-based NexCura, Inc., a healthcare information services firm, in 2005.

By the mid-2000s Thomson's transformation from a newspaper publishing empire to a global Web-based information services provider was complete. With more than 20 million users in an unparalleled number of disciplines—including law, tax, accounting, higher education, reference, corporate, assessment, scientific, and healthcare—Thomson's reach was far beyond what its founder ever believed possible. Led by the third generation of the Thomson family, the sky was truly the limit for the multibillion-dollar firm.

Jay P. Pederson; Patrick Heenan
Updated, David E. Salamie; Nelson Rhodes

PRINCIPAL SUBSIDIARIES

AutEx; BETA; Creative Solutions; Current Drugs; Datastream; Derwent World Patents Index; Elite; Find-Law; First Call; IR Channel; ISI Web for Science; Micromedex; Medstat; Thomson Delmar Learning; Thomson Gale; Thomson NETg; Thomson ONE; Thomson Peterson's; Thomson Prometric; Thomson Wadsworth; TradeWeb; Westlaw, Sweet & Maxwell.

PRINCIPAL DIVISIONS

Thomson Legal & Regulatory; Thomson Financial; Thomson Scientific & Healthcare; Thomson Learning.

PRINCIPAL COMPETITORS

Bell & Howell Company; Dow Jones & Company, Inc.; Dun & Bradstreet Corporation; Gannett Company, Inc.; Hearst Corporation; Hollinger Inc.; Hoover's, Inc.; Info-USA Inc.; John Wiley & Sons, Inc.; Knight Ridder; LEXIS-NEXIS; McGraw-Hill Companies, Inc.; News Corporation Limited; Reed Elsevier Plc; Reuters Group Plc; Times Mirror Company; Tribune Company; United News & Media plc; W.W. Norton & Company, Inc.

FURTHER READING

Beard, Alison, "Thomson Finds the Grass Is Greener Next Door," *Financial Times,* February 25, 2002, p. 25.

Berss, Marcia, "Greener Pastures," *Forbes,* October 23, 1995, p. 56.

Braddon, Russell, *Roy Thomson of Fleet Street,* London: Collins, 1965, 396 p.

Chung, Mary, and Ken Warn, "Thomson IPO May Be First Step to Acquisition," *Financial Times,* June 12, 2002, p. 26.

Coffey, Michael, "Thomson Pays $210M for Electronic Database, Journals," *Publishers Weekly,* April 20, 1992, p. 6.

Cohen, Judith R., "Will Harcourt Deal Clear Antitrust Hurdles?," *Mergers & Acquisitions,* November 13, 2000.

Craig, Susanne, "Thomson and Globe Shift Gears: Flagship Publication Will Be Centre of Information Powerhouse," *Globe and Mail,* February 16, 2000, p. A1.

Daneshkhu, Scheherazade, "Thomson to Float Travel Business Valued at EUR 1.5bn," *Financial Times,* March 19, 1998, p. 25.

Fabrikant, Geraldine, "2 Thomson Companies in a Proposal to Merge," *New York Times,* March 16, 1989, p. D22.

Faustmann, John, "Buying Legal History: Thomson's Biggest Takeover Draws Mixed Reaction," *Maclean's,* March 11, 1996, p. 36.

Goldenberg, Susan, *The Thomson Empire,* New York: Beaufort Books, Inc., 1984.

Greenberg, Larry M., "Thomson Pushes to Get Customers to Use Online Data," *Wall Street Journal,* March 9, 2000, p. B14.

Hane, Paula J., "Reed, Thomson Negotiate Two-Step Deal to Buy Harcourt General," *Information Today,* December 2000, p. 18.

Harding, James, "Why B2B Is the Place to Be," *Financial Times,* November 13, 2000, p. 16.

Heinzl, Mark, "Thomson Decides to Stop the Presses," *Wall Street Journal,* February 16, 2000, pp. A3, A6.

"Industry Speculation Swirls As Clock Ticks, Thomson Puts Thirty-Eight Titles on the Block," *Educational Marketer,* July 9, 2001.

Jereski, Laura, "Profits by the Numbers," *Forbes,* September 19, 1988, p. 104.

Lipin, Steven, et al., "Thomson to Purchase West Publishing for $3.43 Billion," *Wall Street Journal,* February 27, 1996, p. A3.

"Lord Thomson Dies; Built Press Empire," *New York Times,* August 5, 1976, pp. 1, 32.

"Mid-Life Makeover," *Canadian Business,* June 26-July 10, 1998, p. 85.

Milliot, Jim, "From Harcourt to Reed to Thomson," *Publishers Weekly,* July 23, 2001, p. 18.

———, "Thomson Companies Make Niche Buys," *Publishers Weekly,* April 19, 2004, p. 8.

———, "Thomson, Reed Coping with Challenging Market," *Publishers Weekly,* August 18, 2003, p. 20.

Milner, Brian, and Susanne Craig, "Thomson Targets New Media," *Globe and Mail,* February 16, 2000, p. B1.

Morantz, Alan, "The Power Elite: Kenneth Roy Thomson," *Canadian Business,* November 1989, p. 49.

Moskowitz, Milton, et al., "Thomson," in *Everybody's Business: A Field Guide to the 400 Leading Companies in America,* New York: Doubleday, 1990.

Newman, Peter C., "Celebrating Success—Very, Very Privately," *Maclean's,* June 1, 1998, p. 48.

———, "The Private Life of Canada's Richest Man," *Maclean's,* October 14, 1991, p. 44.

O'Leary, Mike, "Gale Virtual Reference Library Supersizes Reference," *Information Today,* May 2004, p. 41.

Pritchard, Timothy, "Thomson Jumps Head First into an Electronic Future," *New York Times,* February 21, 2000, p. C11.

Roman, Monica, "Thomson: A Billion-Dollar Debut," *Business Week,* June 24, 2002, p. 51.

Rudolph, Barbara, "Good-bye to All That," *Forbes,* March 2, 1981, p. 108.

Schachter, Harvey, "Information Overlord," *Canadian Business,* November 1995, p. 34.

Sheppard, Robert, "No News Here," *Maclean's,* February 28, 2000, p. 44.

Simon, Bernard, "Investcorp Buys Thomson Media," *Financial Times,* October 9, 2004, p. 8.

Smith, Desmond, "Thomson: Media's Quiet Giant," *Advertising Age,* May 14, 1984, p. 4.

Symonds, William C., "Lord of the Cyberpress: Thomson Charges Online with His West Publishing Purchase," *Business Week,* March 11, 1996, p. 36.

"Thomson Acquires Brazil's Largest Electronic Legal Publisher," *Information Today,* January 2002, p. 49.

"Thomson Acquires Current Drugs, Lawtel," *Information Today,* October 2002, p. 55.

"Thomson Corp. Purchases Greenhaven Press and Lucent Books," *Business Publisher,* December 22, 2000, p. 6.

"Thomson Corporation to Sell Noncore Businesses Within Thomson Financial," *Canadian Corporate News,* February 27, 2001.

Thomson of Fleet, Lord *After I Was Sixty: A Chapter of Autobiography,* London: Hamilton, 1975.

"Thomson Set to Buy Sylvan's Prometric in $775 Million Deal," *Wall Street Journal,* January 27, 2000, p. B21.

Weidner, David, "Thomson Buys Remaining First Call Stake," *Daily Deal,* June 21, 2001.

Wickens, Barbara, "Highway Patrol: Thomson Gathers Speed on the Infobahn," *Maclean's,* November 14, 1994, p. 86.

The Toro Company

8111 Lyndale Avenue South
Bloomington, Minnesota 55420-1196
U.S.A.
Telephone: (952) 888-8801
Toll Free: (800) 348-2424
Fax: (952) 887-8258
Web site: http://www.thetorocompany.com

Public Company
Incorporated: 1914 as the Toro Motor Company
Employees: 5,185
Sales: $1.78 billion (2005)
Stock Exchanges: New York
Ticker Symbol: TTC
NAIC: 333112 Lawn and Garden Tractor and Home Lawn and Garden Equipment Manufacturing; 332919 Other Metal Valve and Pipe Fitting Manufacturing; 336220 Rubber and Plastics Hoses and Belting Manufacturing

■ ■ ■

The Toro Company is a leading manufacturer of premium-priced lawnmowers, snowblowers, and irrigation systems. An industry frontrunner in both turf maintenance and underground irrigation capacities for golf courses, sports fields, and other "professional" establishments, Toro in addition markets products to landscape contractors under the Toro, Exmark, and Lawn-Boy brands and holds a strong position in the homeowner and consumer markets with such brand-name lines as Toro, Lawn-Boy, and Lawn Genie. A significant portion

of the consumer business, more than 10 percent of overall sales, is channeled through home improvement retailer The Home Depot, Inc. An increasingly diversified Toro now generates approximately 64 percent of its revenue from professional turf maintenance products, with residential products accounting for most of the balance. The company also generates an increasing share of its total revenues outside the United States, nearly 25 percent in fiscal 2005. Toro distributes its products in more than 90 countries worldwide through approximately 50 domestic and 100 foreign distributors, along with a number of hardware retailers, home centers, and mass retailers. A longstanding player in the turf maintenance sector, Toro produced its first mower for golf course use in 1921 and its first mower for home use in 1939, began making snow-removal equipment in 1951, and diversified into irrigation equipment in 1962.

EARLY HISTORY

Founded in Minneapolis in 1914, the Toro Motor Company was established by executives of the Bull Tractor Company, among them J. S. Clapper, Toro's first president, primarily to manufacture engines and other machined parts for use in the parent company's line of Bull tractors. When Bull Tractor folded in 1918, approximately the same time that Deere & Company and other competitors were fortifying their positions in the agricultural market, Toro was forced to fend for itself. The United States' entry into World War I in 1917, however, created a demand for steam engines for merchant supply ships, a need that Toro helped to fill through the conclusion of the war. In 1920 Toro Motor became Toro Manufacturing Company. The first product

COMPANY PERSPECTIVES

We emphasize quality and innovation in our customer service, products, manufacturing, and marketing. We strive to provide well-built, dependable products supported by an extensive service network. We have committed funding for engineering and research in order to improve existing products and develop new products. Through these efforts, we seek to be responsive to trends that may affect our target markets now and in the future. A significant portion of our revenue has historically been attributable to new and enhanced products. Our mission is to be the leading worldwide provider of outdoor beautification products, support services, and integrated systems that help customers preserve and beautify their outdoor landscapes with environmentally responsible solutions of customer-valued quality and innovation.

to carry the company's name was the Toro (two-row) cultivator that converted to a tractor. A widespread economic depression among American farmers during the early 1920s, however, left the company overstocked and in need of new products to sell. In 1921 the opportunity came for Toro to reinvent itself and become profitable for the long term. The greens committee chairman for an exclusive Minneapolis country club had approached the company with an unusual request: could a specialized tractor replace the horse-powered system then used for cutting the greens and fairways? The solution was a tractor equipped with five 30-inch lawnmowers, which enabled the groundskeeper to cut a 12-foot wide swath in a third of the time required by the earlier method. This relatively simple invention led directly to the machine-driven, gang-reel mower, the forerunner of the modern power mower industry.

By 1925 the Toro name had become synonymous with turf maintenance among nearly all of the major golf courses in the nation. Business was booming. The rapid growth of the company was due in large part to the establishment of a distributorship system in which regional business owners/sales representatives promoted quality Toro products while offering knowledgeable advice and service. In 1929, 13 distributorships were in place and Toro decided to go public, realizing that its research and development edge had to be maintained to thwart rising competition. The October 1929 stock market crash impeded the company's progress, but only temporarily.

In 1935 the company was incorporated as Toro Manufacturing Corporation of Minnesota; two years later its engineers unveiled its most important product to date, the 76-inch Professional, an ingenious compromise between the maneuverability of walk-behind mowers and the speed and capacity of the large gang-reel units. The popular product was replaced ultimately by the Super-Pro and the 58-inch Pro.

In the years prior to World War II, the company succeeded in forming several overseas distributorships and in introducing its first power mower for the domestic consumer market, which debuted in 1939. By 1942 sales had grown to $2 million and the company's commercial line, its mainstay, now served not only golf courses, but parks, schools, cemeteries, and estates. Like most American manufacturers during that period, Toro concentrated its resources on the war effort, contributing parts for tanks and other machinery. When 1945 came, Toro retooled under new owners.

AGGRESSIVELY TARGETING CONSUMER MARKET FOLLOWING WORLD WAR II

Robert Gibson, Whitney Miller, and David Lilly, all veterans and all friends since their days at Dartmouth College, purchased the company in 1945 and fueled it for the next several years with youthful ambition and systematic expansion. To maintain the loyalty of their workers, who then numbered around 50, they named longtime employee Kenneth Goit as president. Following much-needed plant reorganization and modernization, the three owners led the company aggressively into the homeowner mower business, which market studies had shown to be a particularly promising area. From 1946 to 1950 sales climbed from $1.4 million to $7 million. Several factors contributed to this remarkable increase. The solid expansion of Toro's distribution network, which had grown to 88 members, who in turn sold to approximately 7,000 retailers, made the company a large-scale presence. In addition, the company developed and marketed Sportlawn, a popular walk-power reel mower. Finally, and most importantly, Toro acquired Milwaukee-based Whirlwind, Inc. in 1948. Whirlwind was a prominent manufacturer of a consumer rotary mower, a new design that Toro proceeded to enhance with safety features.

In 1950 Lilly succeeded Goit as president. A number of firsts highlighted the decade, including Toro's pioneering lawn and garden television advertisements, the erection of a test facility in Bloomington, Minnesota, and the creation of the Wind Tunnel housing for its Whirlwind mower, which made rear-bagging feasible for the first time. Sales increases uniformly reached double-digit percentages, despite a lukewarm entry into snow-removal equipment in 1951 and a poor performance by the Tomlee Tool Company, acquired in 1954.

Toro indisputably came of age in the 1960s, aided by the power of its ad campaigns and the strength of its research and development department. Its power mower line was widely regarded by the public as the standard in engineering excellence. After achieving this goal, the half-century-old company was ready for a new dynamism. The retirement of "Mr. Toro," a charismatic salesman named "Scotty" McLaren, also augured a change in direction. The invention of the single-stage Snow Pup snow thrower in 1962 signaled the company's recommitment to establishing a winter product line, but the results were less than satisfactory (Toro would suc-

ceed eventually, years later, with the Snow Master). Further diversification within the golf market was another possibility. One campaign centered on the production of a deluxe golf car, the Golfmaster, that would utilize all of the company's significant design expertise. As Trace James reported in *Toro: A Diamond History,* "Toro had purchased the materials and manufactured the parts to build 1,000 Golfmasters. However, by the time the first 250 of these beauties came off the assembly line, they were so loaded with features that golf courses could not afford to buy them. Toro was left with work in progress for 750 cars." Through persistent sales efforts, however, the company was able to rid itself of all but four cars and turn a profit.

EXPANDING INTO IRRIGATION PRODUCTS IN 1962

Finally, in 1962, Toro purchased a company that would virtually ensure Toro's lasting preeminence in the golf course industry. California-based Moist O'Matic, Inc., a manufacturer of irrigation products, brought sales above the $20 million mark that year and ultimately gave Toro the number one position in golf course irrigation equipment. This same year the company relocated to its present headquarters in Bloomington. By the end of the decade, with a greatly strengthened commercial division and the introduction in 1968 of the electric start feature for its consumer mowers, Toro's sales surpassed $50 million.

The 1970s began with David McLaughlin assuming the presidency from Lilly. Growth during the decade for The Toro Company (so named in 1971) was phenomenal. The consumer snow-removal business, after persistent reengineering and remarketing, began to thrive. Commercial turf maintenance, with the introduction of the all-hydraulic Greensmaster and Groundsmaster, experienced a renaissance. As a flurry of new products went on line, the Toro workforce swelled to substantially more than 1,000 employees. Net earnings from 1977 to 1979 almost tripled and sales reached an all-time high of $357.8 million. McLaughlin forged ahead with greatly expanded production of snowblowers. Suitable weather in which buyers could utilize the new product line proved elusive, however. Snow was a relative scarcity during the winters of 1980 and 1981 and, consequently, so were snowblower sales. Because Toro had positioned a full 40 percent of its business in this market, it suffered devastating losses, a total of $21.8 million between fiscal 1981 and fiscal 1982. To make matters worse, McLaughlin had moved Toro into the mass merchandising arena and away from its reliance on the dealer network, where lower sales but greater profits were the norm.

DIVERSIFYING FURTHER IN THE 1980S

Ken Melrose replaced McLaughlin in 1983 and went to work quickly, cutting salaried staff by nearly half, closing plants, and instituting a "just-in-time" inventory system to prevent future overproduction. During the mid-1980s he systematically diversified, acquiring two lighting manufacturers and establishing an outdoor electrical appliance division. The 1986 purchase of Wheel Horse (a manufacturer of lawn tractors) and Toro's entry into the lawn aeration business helped push sales to more than $500 million the following year. Rounding out the decade was the company's 1989 purchase of one of its chief lawnmower competitors, Outboard Marine Corporation's Lawn-Boy, for $98.5 million. Melrose, along with recently elected President Morris, had succeeded in reducing the company's dependency on snow thrower sales, which fell to just 9 percent of revenues, while maintaining the Toro name as the industry market leader.

The investment community, however, remained oblivious, in large part, to the dramatic turnaround, and this was reflected in Toro's depressed stock price. Robert Magy, in his article "Toro's Second Season," recounted Melrose's befuddlement at the sluggish reaction of the investment community to Toro's recovery. This puzzlement led to the hiring in 1989 of a Chicago-based investor relations firm. "In October, the agency surveyed analysts and institutional investors in several major markets and discovered that few of them had any knowledge of Toro, and that among those who believed they did know something about the company, several thought it had collapsed early in the last decade." Thus work of a different sort, higher-profile public and investor relations, awaited Melrose. Although he quickly proved to be an effective and energetic company spokesperson, Melrose did err with overly optimistic earnings predictions.

EARLY 1990S STRUGGLES

Toro's 1990 introduction of the Toro Recycler (a high-performance mulching mower) and its high expectations for Lawn-Boy as a lower-priced complement to the existing product line were among the many reasons why Melrose anticipated the company would achieve billion-dollar status by 1992. Instead, the company saw sales drop from $750 million in 1990 to $711 million in 1991 to $635 million in 1992. A series of profit projections, all of which had to be revised downward, seriously dampened the company's credibility during the early part of this period. Particularly harsh criticism came from *Minneapolis Star Tribune* writer Tony Carideo. "With each piece of negative news, Toro has trotted out

explanations: A bad economy. Not enough rain. Too much rain. Not enough snow. A really bad economy. Well, maybe. But how about this? Toro makes a product that costs too much because there's a lot of R&D and advertising cost in it and because it's sold through an antiquated distributor-dealer network that raises the price even higher." Carideo's article appeared January 28, 1992, just after Toro had announced a major consolidation and restructuring of its Lawn-Boy and Toro businesses, including a plant closing and some 450 layoffs.

Restructuring charges for fiscal 1992 led to a net loss of $21.7 million for the year. Recognizing that its current mix of products left it vulnerable to the cyclicality of the consumer market (not to mention the weather), Toro executives determined to place a greater emphasis on a wide range of professional turf-related product areas. Expanding upon its irrigation lines, Toro entered the fertilizer market in 1992 with the Toro BioPro brand environmentally friendly liquid fertilizer. A further step into this arena came in 1996 when the company acquired Liquid Ag Systems Inc., a pioneer in "fertigation" systems that simultaneously watered and fertilized tuft areas, including farmland. In 1994 Toro began manufacturing recycling equipment for landscape contractors and housing developers when it acquired Olathe Manufacturing and formed a new Recycling Equipment Division. Among the initial products offered by the division was a grinding machine that turned tree stumps into sawdust, which could simply be plowed right into the ground.

Toro significantly bolstered its irrigation lines during this period through acquisitions. In December 1996 the company acquired the James Hardie Irrigation Group from James Hardie Industries Limited of Australia for $118 million, one of Toro's largest acquisitions ever. The acquired product lines were soon relaunched under the Irritrol brand. Hardie's irrigation business was strongest in agricultural markets and commercial markets other than golf courses, which was Toro's major market. Hardie also made drip irrigation systems, a rapidly growing area and one that expanded upon Toro's irrigation lines. Another positive aspect of the acquisition was Hardie's strong international presence. The purchase made Toro the world's largest supplier of irrigation products and systems. The February 1998 acquisition of Drip In Irrigation further expanded Toro's drip irrigation lines.

Two additional 1997 acquisitions expanded Toro's professional product offerings still further. In September Toro bought the manufacturing, sales, and distribution rights to Dingo Digging Systems; the Dingo utility loader, designed for landscape contractors, was a versatile and compact product featuring more than 35 attachments. In November the company purchased Beatrice, Nebraska-based Exmark Manufacturing Company, Inc., a maker of mid-sized walk-behind power mowers and zero-turning-radius (ZTR) riding mowers for professional landscape contractors.

FOCUSING ON IMPROVING PROFITS IN THE LATE 1990S AND EARLY 2000S

The increasing emphasis on professional turf maintenance products provided the company with a steady income and profit generating force not nearly as susceptible to the vicissitudes of the consumer market—in particular, the consumer market for such seasonal items as lawnmowers and snow throwers. Thanks to this shift and a more aggressive pursuit of overseas markets, Toro rebounded nicely from the dark days of the early 1990s. By fiscal 1997 net sales surpassed $1 billion for the first time and net earnings were a healthy $36.5 million. The 1998 fiscal year, however, did not start out so rosy, primarily because of its consumer product lines, the sales of which fell 8.5 percent in 1997. In May 1998 Toro initiated a "profit improvement plan" aimed mainly at overhauling its struggling consumer business. In addition to scaling back significantly on the number of models it offered in the areas of mowers, tractors, and other garden equipment, Toro closed a manufacturing plant in Sardis, Mississippi, and sold its recycling equipment business to Leeds, Alabama-based Precision Husky Corporation, having determined that this particular product line was incompatible with the company's core products. Perhaps the most dramatic change came in the form of the expansion of Toro's distribution network for Toro-branded lawnmowers to include selected home improvement retailers for the first time. This shift was likely long overdue given consumers' increasing preference for shopping at mass merchant outlets.

Toro ended the 1990s on a positive note as its residential operations showed a 12.7 percent increase in sales in 1999 and an operating profit of $21.2 million compared to an operating loss of $15.1 million in fiscal 1998. A lack of snow during the year did not hurt the company as much as in previous light-snow years because snow throwers now accounted for only about 4 percent of total sales, compared to 10 percent in 1995. By this time, too, the firm's professional product lines were generating fully two-thirds of revenues, compared to 41 percent in 1990. Overall revenues of $1.28 billion for 1999 represented a 15 percent increase over 1998. Also in 1999, the company introduced its Toro Personal Pace lawnmower, and it divested another noncore product line, its fertilizer business.

Further divestments came in 2000, when Toro jettisoned its outdoor lighting and gas handheld product lines. After another solid year of growth, the sluggish economy, poor snowfall, and a slowdown in golf course construction hampered both earnings and revenues in 2001 and 2002. Toro took additional steps to improve its profitability, shutting down plants in Riverside and Madera, California, and Evansville, Indiana, in 2002 and 2003. Production was shifted to a newly acquired plant in Beatrice, Nebraska, and two new facilities in Mexico. The Beatrice plant came to Toro in 2001 through the acquisition of Beatrice-based Goossen Industries, Inc., maker of debris vacuums and blowers for the commercial market. Also acquired in 2001 was Electronic Industrial Controls, Inc., a provider of irrigation computer control systems based in Englewood, Colorado. In 2002 Toro adopted a new strategy for bolstering its consumer business. It introduced a line of moderately priced walk-behind mowers for sale principally through Home Depot outlets but also available at Toro dealers. The relationship with Home Depot helped push residential sales up 9.8 percent in 2002 to about $474 million. The Home Depot line was augmented in 2003 with a new line of ZTR riding mowers. Sales to Home Depot quickly grew to comprise more than 10 percent of overall sales.

Toro's various efforts to improve profitability began to pay off in fiscal 2003 when the company achieved its goal of increasing its net profit margin to more than 5 percent. That year's net income of $81.6 million on revenues of $1.5 billion translated into a 5.5 percent margin. Results the following two years were even better, with the net profit margin increasing to 6.4 percent by 2005. During this period, having completed the bulk of its restructuring moves, Toro boosted its new product development expenditures by more than 20 percent in order to maintain the level of innovation that was one of the key hallmarks of the company's success. Toro also shut down an engine manufacturing plant in Oxford, Mississippi, during fiscal 2004 and completed two more minor but strategic acquisitions. R & D Engineering, a producer of wireless rain and freeze switches for both the residential and commercial irrigation markets, was acquired in fiscal 2003, and then in February 2005 Toro purchased Hayter Limited, a U.K. manufacturer of mowing products for the sports fields and municipal markets.

The Hayter deal was the last significant event of Melrose's 21-year reign as Toro CEO. He stepped aside in March 2005, remaining chairman, having shepherded Toro through a remarkable comeback, a significant shift in the product mix, and a period of exponential growth. From 1983 to 2004, sales increased an average 8 percent annually, on a compounded basis, and net income jumped 15 percent per year. Most importantly, Melrose transformed a company highly vulnerable to recessions because of its focus on the consumer market into a diversified manufacturer predominantly targeting the professional market and thereby cushioned from the impact of downturns, as happened during the recession of the early 2000s. The person selected to follow this impressive act was Michael J. Hoffman, who had climbed the corporate ladder since joining Toro in 1977, eventually being named president and chief operating officer in October 2004.

Jay P. Pederson
Updated, David E. Salamie

PRINCIPAL SUBSIDIARIES

Electronic Industrial Controls, Inc.; Exmark Manufacturing Company Incorporated; Hayter Limited (U.K.); Irritrol Systems Europe, S.r.L. (Italy); Irritrol Systems Europe Productions, S.r.L. (Italy); MTI Distributing, Inc.; Red Iron Insurance, Limited (Bermuda); Toro Australia Pty. Limited; Toro Australia Group Sales Pty. Ltd; Toro Briggs & Stratton LLC (50%); Toro Credit Company; Toro Europe BVBA (Belgium); Toro Factoring Company Limited (U.K.); Toro Finance Company; Toro Foreign Sales Corporation (Barbados); Toro Hayter LLP (U.K.); Toro Hayter (Guernsey) Limited (U.K.); Toro Holdings Limited (U.K.); Toro LLC; Toro Mexico Holdings, LLC; Toro International Company; Toro Manufacturing LLC; Toro Purchasing Company; Toro R&D Company; Toro Receivables Company; Toro Sales Company; Toro Warranty Company; Turf Professionals Equipment Company.

PRINCIPAL COMPETITORS

Deere & Company; Kubota Corporation; Textron Inc.; Ariens Corporation; Sears, Roebuck & Co.; Simplicity Manufacturing, Inc.; Honda Motor Co., Ltd.; The Black & Decker Corporation; Scag Power Equipment; Ransomes Jacobsen Ltd.; Rain Bird Corporation, Inc.; Hunter Industries Incorporated.

FURTHER READING

Black, Sam, "Hoffman Gets Behind the Wheel at Toro," *Minneapolis/St. Paul Business Journal,* March 25, 2005.

———, "Toro to Launch New Line at Home Depot Stores," *Minneapolis/St. Paul Business Journal,* January 10, 2003, p. 1.

Brezonick, Mike, "Toro Charges Toward New Markets," *Diesel Progress Engines and Drives,* July 1995, pp. 26+.

Carideo, Anthony, "It's Not All Sunshine for 3 Minnesota Firms," *Minneapolis Star Tribune,* May 6, 1991, p. 1D.

———, "Toro Tackles Question of Luring Buyers Seeking a Cheaper Lawn Mower," *Minneapolis Star Tribune,* January 28, 1992, p. 2D.

Gibson, Richard, "Toro Charges into Greener Fields with New Products," *Wall Street Journal,* July 22, 1997, p. B4.

Howatt, Glenn, "Toro Has First Quarterly Profit in Year; Retail Sales Still Weak," *Minneapolis Star Tribune,* May 22, 1992, p. 7D.

James, Trace, *Toro: A Diamond History,* Bloomington, Minn.: The Toro Company, 1989.

Kirsch, Sandra L., "Toro Co.," *Fortune,* November 20, 1989, p. 106.

Kurschner, Dale, "Toro Battles Snapper for Similar Turf," *Minneapolis-St. Paul City Business,* September 9, 1991, pp. 1, 24.

Magy, Robert, "Toro's Second Season," *Corporate Report Minnesota,* May 1990, pp. 57-63.

Marcial, Gene G., "Who's After Toro's Green Pastures?," *Business Week,* June 27, 1988, p. 80.

Meeks, Fleming, "Throwing Away the Crystal Ball: Most Chief Executives Shy from Making Profit Projections. Toro Co.'s Ken Melrose Now Knows Why," *Forbes,* July 22, 1991, p. 60.

Melrose, Ken, *Making the Grass Greener on Your Side: A CEO's Journey to Leading by Serving,* San Francisco: Berrett-Koehler, 1995, 239 p.

"Mulching Mowers Cutting an Ever-Widening Swath," *Minneapolis Star Tribune,* May 17, 1991, p. 1D.

Myers, Randy, "Mowing Down Losses: Revamping Puts Toro on Path to Another Year of Rising Profits," *Barron's,* February 10, 1986, pp. 37+.

Osborne, Richard, "Company with a Soul," *Industry Week,* May 1, 1995, pp. 20-22+.

Padley, Karen, "Toro, World's Largest Lawnmower Maker, Reforms Itself to Beef Up Stock Price," *St. Paul Pioneer Press,* September 10, 2000.

Peterson, Susan E., "Toro Moving Mississippi Work to State," *Minneapolis Star Tribune,* June 19, 1998, p. 3D.

———, "Toro Plans to Close Distribution Center and 2 Plants," *Minneapolis Star Tribune,* July 31, 1992, p. 1D.

———, "Toro Restructuring Will Shut Down Mississippi Plant, Cut 450 Workers," *Minneapolis Star Tribune,* January 22, 1992, p. 1D.

"Toro: Coming to Life After Warm Weather Wilted Its Big Plans," *Business Week,* October 10, 1983, p. 118.

"The Toro Company," *Wall Street Transcript,* January 31, 2005.

"Toro: Transforming Itself to Dominate Home-Care Products," *Business Week,* September 10, 1979, p. 116.

Welbes, John, "Toro Looks to Maintain Golf-Course Equipment Sales," *St. Paul Pioneer Press,* August 17, 2002.

TriPath Imaging, Inc.

---

780 Plantation Drive
Burlington, North Carolina 27215
U.S.A.
Telephone: (336) 222-9707
Toll Free: (800) 426-2176
Fax: (336) 222-8819
Web site: http://www.tripathimaging.com

Public Company
Incorporated: 1999
Employees: 280
Sales: $68.5 million (2004)
Stock Exchanges: NASDAQ
Ticker Symbol: TPTH
NAIC: 334510 Electromedical and Electrotherapeutical Apparatus Manufacturing; 334517 Irradiation Apparatus Manufacturing; 339111 Laboratory Apparatus and Furniture Manufacturing; 339112 Surgical and Medical Instrument Manufacturing; 339113 Surgical Appliance and Supplies Manufacturing

■ ■ ■

TriPath Imaging, Inc. develops, manufactures, markets, and sells products for cancer screening. The company's SurePath Pap test and PrepStain slide processor, formerly known as the AutoCyte PREP system, form one of only two FDA-approved alternatives to the traditional Pap smear. Its FocalPoint slide profiler utilizes visual intelligence technology to increase accuracy in distinguishing between normal Pap smears and those that have the highest likelihood of abnormality. TriPath Oncology develops and manages the market introduction of molecular diagnostic and pharmaceutical products and services for treating cervical, breast, ovarian, and prostate cancer.

1999: A NEW SORT OF TECHNOLOGY FOR SLIDE PREPARATION AND ANALYSIS

In September 1999, AutoCyte, Inc. merged with Neo-Path, Inc. to form TriPath Imaging, Inc. AutoCyte had its roots in the Burlington-based Laboratory Corporation of America (LabCorp), a medical testing company, from which it spun off in 1996. LabCorp, in turn, was created by the merger of the former Roche Biomedical Laboratories Inc. and National Health Laboratories Holdings Inc. in 1995. Dr. James B. Powell, of LabCorp, took the reins at AutoCyte at its inception.

The new company, TriPath Imaging, acquired the technology and intellectual property of Neuromedical Systems, Inc. in 1999 and focused on cervical cancer screening. Neuromedical Systems, along with AutoCyte and NeoPath, was a pioneer in applying computerized image processing and analysis to detect the often subtle cellular abnormalities associated with cancer and its precursor conditions. TriPath's goal, as James B. Powell, TriPath's new president and chief executive, announced in a press release, was to combine thin-layer slide preparation technology with computerized cell image analysis to lower screening costs and improve patient outcomes. The company began trading on the NASDAQ.

TriPath's first two products, the AutoCyte PREP and the AutoPap, aimed to improve upon the conventional Pap test, which delivered a substantial number of inconclusive results and false negatives. The reason for this inaccuracy lay in part on the Pap's collection method, which stacked cells one on top of the other on the slide. It was also the byproduct of human error since individual technicians visually scanned scores of slides for as few as ten abnormal cells among the thousands in each smear. TriPath's system, by contrast, was an automated liquid-based cytology sample preparation system, one of only two FDA-approved alternatives to the traditional Pap smear. It used a brush to collect cervical cells instead of the traditional Pap test's cotton swab. The brush with the harvested cells was inserted into a vial of ethanol-based preservative. Once the collected cells were disaggregated, mixed, and freed from the mucus and proteinaceous material, they were applied in a homogeneous, thin layer of cervical cells to a slide, and the automated AutoPap screening system reviewed the slide for abnormal cervical cells.

TriPath also hoped to move beyond cervical cancer screening. To this end, it joined with Bayer Diagnostics in 1999 in a research project to detect patients at risk of lung cancer. The joint project combined Bayer's proprietary molecular probes with TriPath's automated cell analysis technology. Also in 1999, TriPath acquired Cell Analysis Systems (CAS) from Becton Dickinson and Company, a company that had pioneered computerized microscopic image analysis beginning in the 1980s. CAS's method of analyzing the information on slides held a wide range of research-oriented applications, including DNA measurement and specific cell marker quantification. With the acquisition of CAS, TriPath became the holder of 100 issued U.S. patents and more than 30 U.S. patents pending. These patents pertained to every aspect of microscopic-based image analysis and increased the possibility that TriPath would be able to leverage its technological advantages for product applications beyond cervical cancer screening.

As one of only two FDA-approved alternatives to the traditional Pap smear, TriPath vied fiercely with its competitor, Cytyc Corporation, for market share. Cytyc marketed the ThinPrep System, which, like the AutoCyte PREP, was an automated method for preparing microscope slides of cervical cell specimens that relied on computer imaging technology to examine slides. In

1999, Cytyc sued TriPath for alleged patent infringement. TriPath responded to Cytyc's suit in 2000 with a number of counterclaims, among them illegal anticompetitive conduct. The two companies settled their dispute in 2001 without admission of liability by either party. Cytyc again sued TriPath in 2003, however, claiming that certain of TriPath's patents were invalid and not infringed upon by Cytyc's imaging system.

2000-01: GROWTH IN SALES AND PRODUCTS

Powell handed over the reins at TriPath to Paul Sohmer in mid-2000. Sohmer, a clinical pathologist, had been the president and chief executive of the former Neuromedical Systems. A native of New York, Sohmer was a graduate of Chicago School of Medicine and had begun his career at the largest trauma center in the United States in Baltimore. He next took a job in a research lab with the Army where he developed a way to extend the shelf life of blood to 46 days. While later teaching as an associate professor at Vanderbilt University, he completed a master's in business, then moved on to work with small biotechnology companies in California, among them the Pathology Institute in Berkeley, California, Chiron Reference Laboratory, Nichols Institute, and Genetrix. While in California, Sohmer met up with TriPath's investors.

Throughout 2000, an increasing number of labs began to use TriPath's products. To accommodate the company's growth, TriPath expanded its customer service, sales, and marketing activities. It entered into an agreement with Nelson Professional Sales to augment direct sales efforts focused on the physician's office—specifically, obstetricians, gynecologists, and primary care physicians—and boosted its sales and marketing staff by 70 positions. The company also instituted a regional structure for its technical services, laboratory sales, reimbursement management, and marketing teams.

Also in 2000, TriPath released the next-generation AutoPap Primary Screener for use outside the United States. This equipment incorporated a user interface and a motorized microscopic stage to direct the cytologist to fields of view determined by the AutoPap to be the most likely to contain abnormal cells. The company also concluded its early lung cancer detection development agreement with Bayer Diagnostics; the collaboration resulted in new analytical tools to more rigorously assess molecular probes and qualify them for commercialization.

Further changes took place for the company in 2001. TriPath created TriPath Oncology to develop and manage the market introduction of its molecular

KEY DATES

1999: AutoCyte, Inc. and NeoPath, Inc. merge to form TriPath Imaging, Inc., which acquires the technology and intellectual property of Neuromedical Systems, Inc.
2000: Paul Sohmer replaces James B. Powell as chief executive officer.
2001: TriPath Imaging creates subsidiary TriPath Oncology.
2003: The company receives FDA approval to advertise its SurePath Pap test as more accurate than the conventional Pap test.
2004: The company turns its first profit.

diagnostic and pharmaceutical products and services for cancers of the cervix, breast, ovary, and prostate. In another major move, the FDA approved TriPath's PREPmate accessory, which automated several steps in preparing thin-layer slides for the Autocyte PREP system. The PREPmate mixed and removed specimen cells from the collection vial and layered them onto a proprietary reagent located in a test tube for automated slide preparation and staining. Soon afterward, TriPath received a Canadian Medical Device License to market the AutoCyte PREP and PREPmate accessory in Canada where approximately four to five million Pap tests were performed each year. By 2004, AutoCyte PREP tests (then called SurePath Pap tests) accounted for approximately 36 percent of all conventional and liquid-based Pap tests in Canada. By 2005, there were more than 1.6 million SurePath Pap tests per year, greater than 90 percent of all the liquid-based Pap tests in Canada.

2002-05: INCREASED MARKET SHARE

In 2002, TriPath renamed its products. The collection and preservative vials for gynecological applications were renamed SurePath. Together with the PrepStain slide processor, these two components took the place of the AutoCyte PREP and PREPmate accessory. The AutoPap Primary Screening System became the FocalPoint slide profiler.

Back in the United States in 2003, TriPath won regulatory approval from the U.S. Food and Drug Administration (FDA) to market its liquid Pap smear as more than 64 percent more accurate at detecting signs of cervical cancer than the traditional Pap test. The approval put TriPath, which held about 8 percent of the

domestic Pap smear market at the end of 2002, in a stronger position to battle Cytyc for market share. With the approval came the possibility of analyzing the SurePath specimen using the only automated, slide-based human papilloma virus (HPV) detecting system on the market, manufactured by Ventana Medical Systems of Tucson, Arizona. HPV is a major contributor to cervical cancer and a possible contributor to cancers of the anus, vulva, vagina, and penis, and oropharynx as well. Cytyc, which had won approval from the FDA to announce its greater efficacy in 2001, had 64 percent of the market for Pap tests in the United States by 2003 and had been coupling its specimen collection system with equipment manufactured by Ventana to test for HPV for several years.

TriPath's share price soared 38 percent to close to $6 in response to the news of the FDA decision. In 2003, 150 new laboratory customers came on board, 88 of them in the United States, bringing the total number of SurePath customers worldwide to 600. Still, TriPath had yet to turn a profit and lost $8.5 million on revenues of $53.8 million in 2003. This loss notwithstanding, the company remained optimistic and laid plans to build an addition to its building.

TriPath continued to add new domestic and international customers and grossed $56 million in revenues in 2004, its first year to turn a profit. Its SurePath had about 14 percent of the domestic Pap test market and 36 percent of the Canadian market that year. The company signed an agreement with Ventana for the latter to market a brand of its interactive histology imaging system. *Business Week* announced late in 2004 that analysts were "upbeat" on the company, whose stock they considered undervalued. Also in 2004, TriPath Oncology released two new molecular tests to help research cervical and breast cancer. In 2005, it received FDA approval for a third test.

In the future, TriPath expected to expand its business by providing next-generation clinical solutions through soon-to-be developed novel molecular oncology products. It also intended to develop proprietary reagents to screen and assist in diagnosing the presence of disease, to assist doctors in patient prognosis and outcome more accurately, and to guide their choices in selecting therapies for managing cancers of the cervix, breast, ovary, and prostate, as well as melanomas. With one in three women in the United States at risk of developing cancer in her lifetime, according to the American Cancer Society, TriPath's market presence seemed assured.

Carrie Rothburd

PRINCIPAL SUBSIDIARIES

TriPath Oncology, Inc.

PRINCIPAL COMPETITORS

Applied Imaging Corp.; Bio-Reference Laboratories, Inc.; Clarient Inc.; Cytyc Corporation; Digene Corporation; Molecular Diagnostics, Inc.; Ortho-Clinical Diagnostics, Inc.; Quest Diagnostics Incorporated; Ventana Medical Systems, Inc.; Vysis, Inc.

FURTHER READING

Campbell, Doug, "TriPath's Stock Surging amid Breakthroughs," *Business Journal,* June 6, 2003, p. 2.

"Entrepreneur of the Year: Dr. Paul Sohmer," *Business Journal,* June 18, 2004, p. A17.

Hall, Terry, "TriPath Will Step Aside; A New York Pathologist Will Become President and CEO As TriPath Shifts Gears and Starts to Aggressively Market Its Products," *News & Record,* June 8, 2000, p. B8.

Tosczak, Mark, "TriPath Expanding Space to Consolidate Staff, Grow," *Business Journal,* December 17, 2004, p. 6.

"TriPath Sees Opportunity Ahead," *News & Observer,* December 24, 2003.

"TriPath to Begin Targeting Doctors: The Medical Manufacturer Broadens Its Sales Efforts Beyond Laboratories," *Greensboro News & Record,* August 1, 2000.

"U.S. FDA Grants 510 Clearance for Image Analysis System with HER-2/neu Stain," *Telemedicine Business Week,* September 14, 2005, p. 66.

Unica Corporation

Reservoir Place North 170
Tracer Lane
Waltham, Massachusetts 02451-1379
U.S.A.
Telephone: (781) 839-8000
Fax: (781) 890-0012
Web site: http://www.unicacorp.com

Public Company
Incorporated: 1992 as Unica Technologies Inc.
Employees: 241
Sales: $63.5 million (2005)
Stock Exchanges: NASDAQ
Ticker Symbol: UNCA
NAIC: 511210 Software Publishers

■ ■ ■

Unica Corporation is a leading provider of analytical client relationship management (CRM) and marketing automation solutions. It develops, manufactures, and distributes enterprise marketing management (EMM) software that businesses use to help identify, measure, and predict customer behaviors and preferences. Unica's software suite enables users to conduct large-sized, personalized marketing campaigns, to incorporate enterprise data, and to analyze the effectiveness of marketing efforts. Unica also offers consulting, installation, integration, and training services. The company has six international offices and global customers in more than 25 countries.

1992-97: THE ESTABLISHMENT OF ENTERPRISE MARKETING MANAGEMENT

In 1992, Massachusetts Institute of Technology graduate school classmates Yuchun Lee, Ruby Kennedy, and David Cheung founded Unica Technologies Inc., which developed software to help companies' marketing operations. The three men had met while at MIT, where each specialized in data mining, predictive modeling, and statistics. Avoiding the rapid growth models of other tech start-ups, the company funded its product development through 1997 with consulting services, a rare occurrence among technology companies who more generally sought and secured venture capital. "A billion-dollar company is built one brick at a time, and it's built as a company that knows how to make money," said Lee retrospectively in a 2002 *DM Review* article supporting his company's independent position.

Lee, who became chief executive of the company, had as a child in Taiwan decided to pursue a career in art and architecture. After his family immigrated to the United States when he was 13, he earned both undergraduate and graduate degrees from MIT as well as a masters in business from Babson College. Prior to founding Unica, Lee held senior-level positions at Digital Equipment Corp. and MIT's Lincoln and Media Labs. Lee did not believe that his science-related degrees meant he had abandoned his earliest calling. "I wasn't really introduced to software until high school. However, after I started programming, I realized that it is the ultimate, purest form of design. I consequently became very enthusiastic about computer science," he explained in a 2002 *DM Review* article.

Our direction is simple. We are satisfying the demand of directors of marketing and the IT staffs that support the marketing operations. Through the ups and downs, we are very careful to ensure that we identify our customers and provide a product that clearly adds value and can be differentiated from a core-competency standpoint in the market. The truth is that we haven't shifted the direction of the company at all, even through the CRM cycle and the dot-com cycle. We're focusing on the areas in the market where we're adding value. For this reason, we're in sharp contrast to the foundations of many of the companies born in the dot-com era.

In 1995, Unica introduced a line of software that simplified the task of building data-driven and statistical financial models. The Pattern Recognition Workbench (PRW) integrated a spreadsheet and an experiment manager that let users build nonlinear neural network models from data. Unlike dedicated neural network software packages, which supplied only a learning engine, the PRW integrated all the ordinary pre- and post-processing tasks that other tools left up to the user. PRW automatically evaluated every possible combination of input variables and came with an accompanying book by Lee, *Solving Pattern Recognition Problems,* to help users take full advantage of the PRW software.

Many of the customers for Unica's initial product were financial institutions that relied on network models to predict market price movements, volatility, and other market factors, such as interest rate fluctuations. Using the PRW, users could perform a "forward search," which started with one-variable models, from which it chose the best option and then added on variables, or a "backward search," starting with all variables and pruning off the worst until only one best option was left. At almost $7,000 for the PC version and $12,000 for the workstation platform, only larger, well-established companies could afford the cost.

1998-2000: NEW PRODUCTS, NEW CUSTOMERS, AND STRATEGIC PARTNERSHIPS

In 1998, Unica added to its product offerings with the Model 1, data mining software which offered four data mining modules and which ran all the standard statistical and nonstatistical techniques to develop a data mining algorithm. Model 1, distributed by Group 1 Software in partnership with Unica, quickly became the premier data mining software for database marketing in the *Fortune* 1000, used by organizations in a wide variety of industries, such as banking, marketing consulting, retailing, telecommunications, insurance, catalog, and healthcare.

Also in 1998, Unica introduced Impact!, a predictive marketing campaign management system that could deploy high-volume marketing campaigns. Impact! tapped directly into a companies' customer information and worked with data in whatever form available, whether flat files or database information.

In order to help customers integrate advanced data mining technology into their marketing campaigns, Unica also formed a consulting division in 1998. Unica Consulting Division consisted of a team of specialists skilled in the technology of data mining and the application of data mining to real world problems. This division began to offer training courses to teach data mining techniques and to apply them to real world marketing situations, such as targeted customer acquisition, customer retention, and cross-selling.

Unica grew as planned, "one brick at a time," and its revenues increased tremendously from 1992 to 1999, starting at $100,000 and increasing to $4 million. In 1999, the company raised $12 million from investment partners, including Summit Accelerator Fund, the venture capital arm of Summit Partners, and from JMI Equity Fund, all of which it saved. "Our venture partners provided us with security, connections, and helped get us organized more like a public company," according to Lee in a 2002 *Boston Herald* article.

Unica also grew through forming a series of strategic technology alliances. Starting in 1999, it partnered with marketing services companies to market Unica's software, and with software companies, to integrate products and thereby expand the usefulness and applicability of each partner's tools. The partnerships contributed to Unica's steady expansion, and, by 2000, the company, now based in Lincoln, Massachusetts, had 200 client companies, offices throughout the United States, and a network of distribution partners in Europe, South Africa, and South America. With close to 75 employees, it was adding about two employees per week. In recognition of the company's steady performance, Ernst & Young chose Lee as a finalist for its Entrepreneur of the Year in 2000.

```
┌─────────────────────────────────────────────┐
│                                             │
│              KEY DATES                      │
│              ──────■──────                   │
│                                             │
│   1992:  Yuchun Lee, Ruby Kennedy, and David Che- │
│          ung found Unica Technologies Inc.  │
│   1998:  The company forms Unica Consulting │
│          Division.                          │
│   1999:  Summit Accelerator Fund, the venture capital │
│          arm of Summit Partners, and JMI Equity │
│          Fund Summit Partners invest $12 million in │
│          Unica.                             │
│   2001:  Unica receives two patents for technology. │
│   2002:  Unica holds its first annual Global Customer │
│          Conference; the company moves to new │
│          corporate headquarters in Waltham, │
│          Massachusetts.                     │
│   2003:  Unica acquires Marketic SA of France; the │
│          company receives another patent for │
│          technology.                        │
│   2004:  Unica opens an office in Munich.   │
│                                             │
└─────────────────────────────────────────────┘
```

2000-05: RAPID GROWTH, INDUSTRY RECOGNITION, AND A FOCUS ON CUSTOMER RELATION MANAGEMENT

Lee and Unica's other managers made a decision in 2000 prior to the release of the company's next round of software. They changed Unica's focus from that of a data mining company to a company focused on customer relation management (CRM) in order to ensure its continued expansion. During the late 1990s, the data mining bubble having burst, those software applications that formerly had been devoted to mining became embedded in CRM and supply/demand planning. The idea behind CRM was to discover as much about a customer in real-time, regardless of the point of contact, and to suggest products or services based on customer responses to questions.

Affinium was Unica's first fully-automated marketing, or CRM, software suite, designed to help marketing professionals understand and track purchasing and other business-related behaviors; it was released in 2000 and represented an amalgamation of Unica's earlier products, including Model 1 and Impact! Affinium had four different applications: Affinium Model, a data mining tool; Affinium Campaign, a campaign management system; Affinium Interact, a personalized permission-based e-mail communications system; and Affinium Report, a business intelligence reporting and web portal.

With the addition of Affinium, the company also received a number of industry awards, including a ranking among the elite New England Technology Fast 50 for 2000, based on five-year revenue growth. Unica was named 174th of the 500 fastest growing companies in the country by *Inc. Magazine*, and 262nd on Deloitte & Touche's Technology Fast 500. The company opened new offices in Denver and San Francisco, the fast-growing centers for CRM, in 2000 and began its Alliance Program to guide successful collaboration between itself and its technology partners on CRM initiatives for joint customers.

The year 2001 saw Unica's 10th consecutive record quarter and an increase in revenues of greater than 2,000 percent from 1998. The company's outstanding performance resulted in its again being named to the New England Technology Fast 50 and moving up to 137th among the country's 500 entrepreneurial growth leaders as ranked by *Inc.* magazine. Between 1998 and 2002, the company successfully bucked the nation's economic downturn, with revenues that declined in only two of 15 quarters.

Unica received a patent in 2001 for technology that provided a unique, graphical presentation of complex modeling results. This technology replaced the traditional "life chart," a graph depicting the predictive value of a single model over random chance, and permitted users to monitor the predictive value of the best models as they were being built. The company received a second patent that same year for its optimization technology and methodologies that allowed users to break with the traditional approach of sending a marketing offer with the highest average response rate to all potential customers. Instead each individual received a targeted product offer as part of an "optimal" marketing campaign.

In 2002, Unica continued to develop its emphasis on customer support with its first annual two-day Global Customer Conference in Boston. "This conference enabled us to continue our dialog without customers and gather valuable insights and ideas, which will help Unica continue to develop and deliver leading-edge products and services that meet the specific needs of marketing organizations." It also met with its newly formed customer advisory board to discuss key business challenges and to learn more about how organizations execute marketing initiatives on the strategic and tactical level.

More awards arrived in 2002. Unica was named one of the ten most influential e-business leaders in New England by the Mass Electronic Commerce Association and the editors of *CMP's Intelligent Enterprise* chose it to be seventh in their list of the 12 best IT solutions providers that turned data into intelligence, along with IBM, Microsoft, PeopleSoft, SAP AG, and BEA Systems. The company expanded into Europe, the Middle East, Africa, and the Asian-Pacific market with offices in London and Singapore. It opened regional sales offices and employed technical teams as well as instituting around-the-clock support in nine languages. The company, whose revenues had increased another 340 percent since 2000, served about 250 customers. In 2002, it moved to new corporate headquarters in Waltham, Massachusetts.

In 2003, Unica received another patent for creating data mining and modeling technologies that allowed for more accurate predictive models for expected customer behavior. This technology was a part of a move to focus on marketing planning rather than analytics and campaign management as marketers, faced with the continued economic downturn, were returning to direct marketing strategies to generate specific measurable returns on campaigns.

Unica acquired Marketic of France, which focused solely on campaign management in mid-2003. This acquisition conferred an immediate foothold in southern Europe and strengthened the company in the areas of financial services, retail services, and telecommunications. The company now counted ten of the top 20 U.S. banks, three of the top Canadian financial institutions, Europe's leading telecom companies, leading hotel and leisure companies, and key retailers, auto manufacturers, publishers, and insurers worldwide among its customers. Affinium was the product of choice by as many as four times the number of companies as any other EMM software suite. Unica enjoyed an estimated 33 percent share of new EMM customer sales worldwide and had 52 percent revenue growth per year, leading industry analysts to announce that it held the top slot among EMM providers.

Unica's revenues in 2004 reached $48 million, almost 40 percent higher than the year before, while the marketing software category as a whole grew 15 to 20 percent. The company had a three-year record of profitable growth. By 2005, it employed more than 250 people (up from 130 just two years before), including 67 outside the United States. More than 300 organizations used its Affinium Suite. Total revenue grew more than 30 percent to $63.5 million, and the company held its initial public offering, joining the NASDAQ. It opened an office in Munich as its activities increased overseas.

Looking to the future, Lee shared his view with *DM Review* that "[i]n the long run, Unica will be successful because our mission is to build Unica as a billion-dollar company.... . We know the technology space and we know it's in its infancy in terms of what it can do in enterprise marketing software. We're confident of the opportunity out there." He was referring to the fact that 40 percent of companies surveyed in 2004 had raised their marketing budgets three to 11 percent that year, but most businesses had not yet automated their marketing functions. Unica believed that EMM was a needed alternative to ineffective, manual marketing solutions, a tool to understand customers, create and execute marketing campaigns, coordinate activities, and optimize resources. Its growth seemed to indicate that the companies it aimed to serve agreed with this view.

Carrie Rothburd

PRINCIPAL COMPETITORS

Applix, Inc.; Art Technology Group, Inc.; Blue Martini Software, Inc.; BroadVision, Inc.; CA, Inc.; E.piphany, Inc.; KANA Software, Inc.; MarketSoft Corporation; Marketswitch Corporation; Onyx Software Corporation; Oracle Corporation; Pivotal Corporation; SAP Aktiengesellschaft; Siebel Systems, Inc.; thinkAnalytics.

FURTHER READING

Evans, Bruce R., "When It's Time to Think About an IPO," *Inc. 500 Alumni Network*, www.inc.com/resources, inc500alumni/articles/20051101/evans.html.

French, Matthew, "Unica Makes Move from Mining Data to CRM Software," *Mass High Tech*, June 12, 2000, p. 10.

Hollander, Geoffrey, "Model 1 Deftly Parses Customer Characteristics," *InfoWorld*, May 25, 1998, p. 148.

Johnson, R. Colin, "Tool Automates Neural-Net-Variables Analysis," *Electronic Engineering Times*, May 27, 1996.

Latzke, Val, "Unica—The Grand Design," *DM Review Magazine*, May 2002, www.dmreview.com/articlesub. .cfm?articleId=5143.

Schubarth, Cromwell, "Steadiness Is the Secret Behind Firm's Tech Success," *Boston Herald*, July 4, 2002, p. 19.

Slavens, Roger, "Campaign Management Technology Comes of Age," *B to B*, April 14, 2003, p. 23.

"Unica Goes Public and Sees Its Shares Rise," *Mass High Tech*, August 4, 2005, www.masshightech.com/displayarticle detail.asp?Art_ID=69268.

Usinas Siderúrgicas de Minas Gerais S.A.

Rua Prof. Vieira de Mendonça 3011
Belo Horizonte, Minas Gerais 31310-260
Brazil
Telephone: (55) (31) 3499-8000
Fax: (55) (31) 3499-8899
Web site: http://www.usiminas.com.br

Public Company
Incorporated: 1956
Employees: 8,363
Sales: BRL 6.68 billion ($2.28 billion) (2004)
Stock Exchanges: São Paulo OTC (for ADRs)
Ticker Symbol: USNZY
NAIC: 331111 Iron and Steel Mills; 331112 Electro-
metallurgical Ferroalloy Products Manufacturing;
331221 Cold-Rolled Steel Shape Manufacturing

■ ■ ■

Usinas Siderúrgicas de Minas Gerais S.A., universally known as Usiminas, has long been one of the leading steel producers in Brazil. With the completion in 2005 of the restructuring of Companhia Siderúrgica Paulista (Cosipa) into its subsidiary, Usiminas became Brazil's largest steelmaker and one of the largest in the world. Like other Brazilian steelmakers, Usiminas is attractive to buyers abroad because of the low cost of its basic product: flat, or slab, steel. Steel products yield higher profit margins, and so the company seeks to raise its sales of such products as a variety of specialized plates, including hot-rolled high-carbon ones, and cold-rolled plates, among them enameled plates, plates for stamp-

ing, and galvanized plates, including ones coated with zinc and nickel-zinc.

PUBLICLY OWNED GIANT: 1956-91

Usiminas was the creation of business interests in Minas Gerais who wanted an integrated steel complex in their state. The company was founded in 1956. The following year a Japanese consortium, Horikoshi, agreed to build the mill in exchange for a 40 percent stake in the operation taken by a holding company, Nippon Usiminas Cia. Ltda., which was led by Nippon Steel Corp. Brazil's development bank, BNDES, provided capital in exchange for a 25 percent share, the state of Minas Gerais took another 24 percent for their contribution, and Companhia Vale do Rio Doce (CVRD), the nation's publicly owned chief source of iron ore, assumed a 9 percent stake. A metallurgy professor, Amaro Lanari, Jr., negotiated the agreement with the Japanese and became the first president of Usiminas, serving until 1977. A new town, Ipatinga, was built from scratch to house the mill, which was located not far from CVRD's ore deposits. CVRD's rail line would transport the ore from the mines to the mill, then haul the finished steel to the port of Vitória. Rail cars would return from the port to the mill with the imported coal needed to produce coke for the blast furnaces. Headquarters were in Belo Horizonte, the capital of Minas Gerais.

Because of cost overruns, the federal holding company for the steel industry, Siderbrás, had to provide more funds and consequently became the majority stockholder of Usiminas, with Nippon Usiminas's share of the enterprise falling first by half, later by even more. However, some 400 Japanese technicians were brought over to bear a lasting influence on Usiminas, from an emphasis on long-range planning to the oriental gardens in the corridors of the mill. This influence was particularly strong in human resources. A massive effort was made to involve all personnel in decision making, with weekly assessments in each department. Almost all the employees had a brother, son, or spouse working in the company, and this was considered an asset. Larani's investment in personnel and research and development was credited for the 140 Brazilian patents that Usiminas held in 1991 and the significant income it thereby earned from the sale of technology.

This rosy view of labor relations at Usiminas, expressed in the Brazilian business magazine *Exame,* ignored the 1963 strike during which policemen opened fire against demonstrating strikers at the mill, killing, according to a company spokesperson, seven workers and hospitalizing 49. Twenty years of ensuing military rule in Brazil blocked further investigation, but a 1986 article claimed that the strikers were unarmed, that the death toll was perhaps more than 100, including uninvolved passersby, and that over 3,000 people were wounded.

Small-scale operations began in 1962. The company was employing 8,867 workers in 1965. The following year production reached 500,000 metric tons of ingot steel and nearly 390,000 tons of flat-rolled products, making it second in Brazil in steel production, with about 15 percent of the national total. By 1979, thanks to $5 billion in total investment by its owners, Usiminas had raised its annual capacity to 3.6 million metric tons. In that year its income came to 30.33 billion cruzeiros (about $1.05 billion), but it lost money.

The 1980s were mostly a lost decade for Usiminas. It operated in the red in most years, and its debt climbed as high as $900 million. By 1989, however, the company's fortunes were definitely on the mend. It earned $239 million on record sales of $2.03 billion, and its debt fell to a manageable $218 million. Steel production reached a record 3.8 million metric tons, of which 40 percent was exported. Its average productivity

per employee/hour was twice as high as Brazil's other steelmakers and compared favorably with similar enterprises in Japan and Germany. Moreover, Usiminas had not suffered a strike since 1963 and was said always to pay the maximum salary permitted by the government. Nevertheless, the company was selected to be the first of a series of state-owned enterprises to be privatized by the incoming president of Brazil, Fernando Collor de Mello. A longtime Usiminas functionary, Rinaldo Campos Soares, was appointed president of the company with the mandate of preparing it for sale. "The greatest difficulty," he later recalled to Ricardo Galuppo of *Exame,* "was to convince the employees that privatization wouldn't lead to mass layoffs."

THRIVING IN THE 1990S AFTER PRIVATIZATION

The auction was twice delayed before being held in October 1991 and was marked by violent demonstrations outside the Rio de Janeiro stock exchange. The Brazilian government sold 75 percent of the company's voting shares for about $1.1 billion, with a controlling group taking 51 percent of these shares. This consortium was led by the investment bank Banco Bozano Simonsen S.A. and included at least three other banks and four steel distributors. It also had the support of Nippon Usiminas, which still held almost 14 percent, and Usiminas's own workers and executives, who had been allotted 10 percent. Two government-controlled entities: CVRD and Previ, the pension fund run by Brazil's biggest bank, state-owned Banco do Brasil S.A., took another 10 percent each.

Because Usiminas was an efficiently run operation, the number of workers fell only 14 percent over two years, through retirement and buyouts rather than outright dismissals. Soares retained his job. Managers found they had more freedom to make decisions in matters such as purchasing and finance.

Freed from state control, Usiminas began to compete for the first time in the production and sale of high-quality, high-value steel products. Some $200 million was invested, for example, to begin manufacturing galvanized steel products. In 1995 Usiminas was making 65 percent of the thick plates used by the Brazilian naval industry, 63 percent of the needs of the machinery and electrical equipment sectors, 58 percent of the steel used by automakers, and 56 percent of the steel used by manufacturers of home appliances. One important customer, Rockwell-Fumagalli, a major manufacturer of automobile wheels, was receiving steel shipments from Usiminas 10 days after the order, compared to 90 days before privatization.

KEY DATES

1957: A Japanese consortium agrees to build the Usiminas steel mill.

1966: Usiminas is ranked Brazil's second largest steel producer.

1979: The company raises its annual capacity to 3.6 million metric tons of raw steel.

1991: The Brazilian government sells most of Usiminas's shares to private investors.

1993: Usiminas buys half of another privatized steelmaker, Cosipa.

1999: Usiminas opens Usicentro, a complex to serve automakers, distributors, and end-users.

2005: By absorbing Cosipa, Usiminas makes itself Brazil's leading steel producer.

Working for private investors, Usiminas became an investor itself. It purchased, in 1993, a half-share in another privatized steelmaker, Companhia Siderúrgica Paulista (Cosipa), a company founded in 1953 to serve business interests in the state of São Paulo. It also acquired a share of the Argentine steelmaker Siderar S.A. I.C. Another purchase was a half-share of Companhia Paulista de Ferro Ligas, Brazil's main producer of ferroalloys, which was on the verge of bankruptcy. Together with CVRD, which took the other half, Usiminas issued preferred shares to the creditors of Ferro Ligas and obtained a 12-year grace period for $50 million in debts. (It sold its share of the company to CVRD in 1999.)

Between 1991 and 1995 Usiminas purchased shares in 11 companies with total annual revenue of $5 billion and employment of 35,000. It also joined with the Italian automaker Fiat S.p.A. in 1993 to build Usistamp, a $40 million plant next to the Usiminas steel mill. This plant pressed the company's steel into small shapes, mostly suspension parts.

Usiminas was chosen by the Brazilian business magazine *Exame* in 1995 as its enterprise of the year. The company recorded a net profit of $422.8 million in 1994 on sales of about $2 billion, a profit margin exceeded by only five Brazilian companies. About a third of the year's profits were passed on to shareholders in the form of dividends.

Usiminas and Fiat in 1998 opened Usicort, a service center for turning steel coils into Fiat blanks for stamping. A year later, it opened Usicentro, a $45 million complex in São Paulo state that included Rio Negro,

a new auto-service center; a plant, Usilight, to electro weld structural shapes; and a logistics center. Rio Negro, like Usicort, was intended to supply blanks for stamping, this time chiefly to the Brazil subsidiaries of automakers General Motors Corp. and Volkswagen AG. The Usilight plant for electrowelding hot-rolled coil I and H beams was intended for the civil construction industry. The logistics center transferred Usiminas products arriving from the mill by railroad to trucks for delivery to distributors and end-users in São Paulo and nearby states.

21ST CENTURY-POWERHOUSE

The ownership of Usiminas was still heterogenous as the 21st century opened. In 2001 a controlling group in which Nippon Usiminas and the employees had the largest stakes held 53 percent of its voting capital. Among other shareholders, CVRD held 23 percent of the voting capital and Previ, 15 percent. Soares was still the chief executive of the enterprise. Cosipa became more closely tied to Usiminas in 2001, when the latter converted its holdings of the former's debentures into stock, thereby raising its ownership to about 93 percent.

Usiminas continued to augment its level of production, which reached 4.74 million metric tons of raw steel in 2004. Revenue and profits continued to rise as well, and the company reduced its debt during the year.

In 2005 Usiminas completed the integration of Cosipa into its orbit by purchasing the remaining stock. Cosipa ceased to be a public corporation and became a wholly owned subsidiary of Usiminas. Its production of raw steel, 4.21 million metric tons in 2004, was almost as high as Usiminas's own output. Usiminas was now the leader company of Usiminas System, which included 13 other companies, of which Cosipa was the most important. Taken as a whole, the system's revenues of BRL 12.23 billion in 2004 (or $4.17 billion, based on the average currency rate for the year), were 83 percent higher than those of Usiminas as a stand-alone company. The system accounted for one-third of Brazil's production of flat steel. Its market share in major sectors included large-diameter tubes, 74 percent; auto parts, 55 percent; electrical-electronic equipment, 52 percent; automobile industry, 48 percent; civil construction, 36 percent; industrial equipment and machinery, 36 percent; and home appliances, 27 percent. Export revenue came to 24 percent of the total. The United States was by far the main foreign market, taking 35 percent of the system's exports.

In August 2005 Usiminas announced that it would take a share, together with the Techint Group, in a large steel company named Ternium. Ternium intended to hold a controlling interest in three major steel producers: Siderar (Argentina), CVG Siderúrgica del Orinoco C.A., or Sidor (Venezuela), and Hylsamex S.A. de C.V. (Mexico). The Techint Group was an international group of companies focused mainly on power and steel. Usiminas was to take a 16 percent stake in Ternium's overall share capital. It would, separately, take stock interests in Siderar (5.3 percent) and Sidor (16.6 percent).

Robert Halasz

PRINCIPAL SUBSIDIARIES

Companhia Siderúrgica Paulista - Cosipa; Rncentro Participações Ltda.; Unigal Ltda. (95 percent); Usiminas International Ltd.; Usiminas Mecánica S.A.

PRINCIPAL COMPETITORS

Companhia Siderúrgica Nacional; Gerdau S.A.

FURTHER READING

Baer, Werner, *The Development of the Brazilian Steel Industry,* Nashville: Vanderbilt University Press, 1969.

Barros, Guilherme, "A Usimas já está pronta," *Exame,* September 18, 1991, pp. 66-69.

"Brazilian Steelmaker Usiminas Inaugurates $45M Service Center," *American Metal Market,* March 21, 2000, p. 4.

"Dozen Firms, Banks Claim to Gain Control of Brazil's Usiminas," *Wall Street Journal,* October 28, 1991, p. B9C.

Galuppo, Ricardo, "A vitória da ização," *Exame,* August 30, 1995, pp. 93-98.

Instituto Brasileiro de Análises Sociais e Econômicas, "Usiminas continua sendo sinónimo de velha república," *Vozes,* May 1986, pp. 307-09.

Kamm, Thomas, "Brazil Sells Off Big Steelmaker to the Public," *Wall Street Journal,* October 25, 1991, p. A10.

Kepp, Michael, "Usiminas Sells Ferro Ligas Stake," *American Metal Market,* December 17, 1999, p. 4.

Onis, Juan de, "Goulart Cancels Bid for Powers," *New York Times,* October 8, 1963, p. 8.

Ponce de Leon, Gustavo, "A barra ficou mais leve e melhor," *Exame,* May 27, 1992, pp. 52-54.

UTStarcom, Inc.

1275 Harbor Bay Parkway
Alameda, California 94502
U.S.A.
Telephone: (510) 864-8800
Fax: (510) 864-8802
Web site: http://www.utstar.com

Public Company
Incorporated: 1991 as Unitech Telecom, Inc.
Employees: 8,200
Sales: $2.7 billion (2004)
Stock Exchanges: NASDAQ
Ticker Symbol: UTSI
NAIC: 334119 Other Computer Peripheral Equipment Manufacturing; 334290 Other Communication Equipment Manufacturing; 541512 Computer Systems Design Services

■ ■ ■

UTStarcom, Inc. designs and manufactures telecommunications equipment, selling its gear to telephone companies primarily in China. The company's products and services, which aid in the installation and operation of its gear, are designed to work with existing infrastructure to provide low-cost voice, data, and video services to underserved customers in fast-growing markets. UTStarcom's success in China has encouraged the company to target other vast markets such as India where substantial percentages of the population do not have access to telecommunications services. The company historically has generated approximately 90

percent of its revenues from China, but expansion into Africa, India, Central and Latin America, and the Middle East is expected to reduce its dependence on China. UTStarcom maintains research and design operations in North America, China, India, and Korea.

ORIGINS

Hong Liang Lu found inspiration from a trip abroad, turning his impressions of his ancestral home into a billion-dollar entrepreneurial creation. The UTStarcom founder was born in Taiwan, but spent much of his youth in Japan before moving to the United States, where he earned an undergraduate degree in civil engineering at the Berkeley campus of the University of California. Lu founded a software development firm in Berkeley named Unison World, Inc., starting the company in 1983. In 1986, Unison was acquired by Kyocera International, Inc., the U.S. arm of Japan-based Kyocera Corp., a technical ceramic producer that manufactured a diverse range of components. After the acquisition, Lu became president and chief executive officer of the majority-owned subsidiary created by the deal, Kyocera Unison. Lu was serving in this capacity when he took a trip to China in 1990, a trip that led to the formation of UTStarcom. "It was very eye-opening," Lu said of his trip to China in an October 15, 1999 interview with *Inc.* magazine. "I never thought China was so lively," he continued. "Everyone seemed happy, very busy, full of energy, walking quickly, riding bicycles, smiling, hurrying to do something."

Lu was in Shenzhen, a city near Hong Kong in the midst of phenomenal growth that saw its population

UTStarcom has made great strides in its strategy to become a preeminent supplier of leading edge telecommunications products in high growth markets worldwide. While we continue to focus on the tremendous opportunities in Mainland China, we have been able to leverage our success there to promote our products in markets throughout the world.

swell from 100,000 to three million in little more than a decade. The city was a bustle of activity, but as Lu discovered, Shenzhen, like the rest of China, lacked the telecommunications infrastructure to support its surging growth. "China had only five or six digits for telephone numbers," Lu recalled in his interview with *Inc.* "If you wanted to make a call from Beijing to Shenzhen, you'd have to hire a secretary to keep dialing until a call went through." Lu sensed a great business opportunity, an opportunity he would take advantage of once he returned to the United States.

Lu set out to serve the underserved, deciding to sell telecommunications access equipment and services to the most populated country in the world. He recruited ten former Bell Labs engineers who were willing to help him start a business and formed Unitech Telecom, Inc. in 1991, basing the start-up venture in Oakland, California. Lu attempted to gain his first foothold in China by entering Beijing, but his small company was overwhelmed by bureaucratic barriers and overshadowed by much larger competitors such as Lucent Technologies Inc., Siemens AG, and Motorola, Inc. who were battling against one another in Beijing. Unable to stand out from the crowd in the country's capital, Lu turned his focus elsewhere, deciding in 1993 to establish an initial presence in a mid-coastal city named Hangzhou. With a population of one million, Hangzhou was an ideal proving ground for Lu's start-up venture, boasting an educated workforce, 30 universities, and less restrictive bureaucratic barriers. Unitech Telecom completed its first full year of production the following year, in 1994, selling $4 million worth of telecommunications gear primarily to China's two massive telephone companies, China Telecommunications Corp. and China Netcom Corp.

Not long after carving a niche for itself in Hangzhou, Unitech Telecom joined forces with another company, a transaction that gave birth to the UTStarcom name. In 1995, the company merged with Starcom,

Inc., a telecommunications software company founded by Ying Wu and a colleague. Wu, raised in China and educated in the United States at the New Jersey Institute of Technology, became vice-chairman of the combined entity, UTStarcom, and chairman and chief executive officer of its UTStarcom (China) subsidiary. Lu served as chairman, chief executive officer, and president of UTStarcom.

Although Lu was able to establish a presence in China, it would be years before his firm began to generate substantial revenues. UTStarcom suffered because of its diminutive size, struggling to secure deals with big Chinese telephone companies and unable to assert itself as a rival to the big telecommunications gear providers, particularly Lucent Technologies. "[Lucent Technologies] could go in with a private jet and see the President of China," Lu recalled in his interview with *Inc.* "We were nobody," he said. Lu was forced to look for business outside the big cities, where he eked out an existence by soliciting business from rural telecommunications officials. Because venture capitalists had little regard for UTStarcom, capital was hard to come by as well, but Lu benefited from a relationship cultivated during his college years. In Oakland, he had worked at an ice cream parlor with Masayoshi Son, who went on to become chief executive officer of Softbank Corp. During the 1990s, Softbank contributed $166 million of the $220 million raised by Lu, giving his company enough cash to expand at a moderate pace.

GROWTH ACCELERATING IN THE LATE 1990S

UTStarcom's stature began to increase during the late 1990s, giving Lu his first sense of leading a company that factored in the telecommunications industry. UTStarcom's fortunes improved after Lu decided to concentrate his efforts on Personal Access System (PAS) technology, which had been introduced in Japan earlier in the 1990s but failed to secure a lasting place in the market. PAS, essentially a scaled-down version of a cellular network, offered telephone service ideally suited to China's population. PAS equipment, which included handsets, towers, and antennas, was roughly half the cost of traditional cellular gear and provided wireless service with limited mobility, enabling a customer to have wireless service within a particular area, a city, for example, but not outside a particular area. Considering that most of China's population rarely strayed far from work or home—UTStarcom figured that 95 percent of people in China never left their geographic area 95 percent of the time—PAS provided a relatively cheap solution to the country's telecommunications inadequacies. UTStarcom marketed the service as "Xiaol-

KEY DATES

1991: UTStarcom's predecessor, Unitech Telecom, Inc., is founded by Hong Liang Lu.

1993: After failing to penetrate the Beijing market, Lu sets his sights on Hangzhou.

1994: Unitech Telecom completes its first full year of production, generating $4 million in revenues.

1995: Unitech Telecom and Starcom, Inc. merge, creating UTStarcom, Inc.

2000: UTStarcom completes its initial public offering of stock.

2003: Revenues reach $2 billion, a tenfold increase since the company's initial public offering.

2005: Lu sets a financial goal of $10 billion in revenues by the end of the decade.

ingtong," or "Little Smart," a name borrowed from a Chinese comic strip character in the 1940s who used futuristic gadgets, selling the service for one cent per minute. By comparison, Global System for Mobile (GSM) cellular service, the leading type of mobile phone service in China, sold for five cents per minute.

The combination of low-end technology and a vast, underserved market enabled UTStarcom to emerge from obscurity. The company's sales began to grow, reaching $105 million in 1998 and increasing to $187 million in 1999. Once his strategy began to deliver results, Lu could turn to Wall Street for the capital needed to expand his business, no longer forced to subsist on the trickle of cash supplied by only a few investors. UTStarcom completed its initial public offering (IPO) of stock in March 2000, ushering in a period of phenomenal growth that made the company the darling of its industry. In 2000, UTStarcom generated $368 million in revenue, nearly double the previous year's total. Lu's decision to build UTStarcom's foundation in China proved increasingly astute as the company entered a new decade. China's telecommunications industry was growing at twice the rate of the overall economy, fueling UTStarcom's growth. In 2001, China passed the United States as the largest market of fixed line subscribers, a year that also saw the country surpass the United States as the largest mobile telephone market. UTStarcom reaped the rewards, reaching nearly $1 billion in revenues in 2001 and, remarkably, doubling the total the following year, when sales reached $1.96 billion.

UTStarcom's financial gains during the first years of the 21st century were astounding. The company went from being a little-known upstart unable to attract anyone's interest to asserting itself as the next telecommunications equipment giant in the space of a few years. Between its IPO and 2003, UTStarcom's revenues increased tenfold, a feat made even more remarkable when the company's results were compared with those of its rivals, the industry behemoths whose sway had once presented formidable obstacles to Lu's small outfit. Lucent, for example, suffered a 78 percent decline in revenues during the period, its sales volume shrinking to $8.5 billion during one of the industry's worst downturns. Lu sailed through the period, marketing a low-cost alternative to telecommunications in a fast-growing market while the industry elite hawked next-generation technology in established markets in Europe and North America. By 2003, he controlled 60 percent of the PAS market for network gear in China, with substantial expansion opportunities being created with each passing year. Major cities, which had once been inaccessible to UTStarcom, were becoming fertile territories for Lu to expand his company's presence. In 2003, for example, Beijing and Chongqing approved the deployment of PAS technology after being convinced that the service did not necessitate obtaining a cellular license.

LOOKING BEYOND CHINA FOR THE FUTURE

By all measures, Lu played the leading role in one of the most successful business stories of his time, but if there was one criticism of his company it was its dependence on China. UTStarcom derived nearly 90 percent of its revenue from China, a reliance that raised the eyebrows of skeptics. Lu had an answer to such pundits, however, proposing to move UTStarcom into other markets where much of the population lacked access to telecommunications services. He forged deals in Vietnam, Panama, and India, where a population of 1.1 billion people relied on 35 million telephones. Before the end of the decade, Lu hoped to generate half of UTStarcom's revenue from outside of China, pursuing geographic diversification that would provide a base for the company to become one of the world's largest equipment providers to the telecommunications industry.

Lu's attempts to provide a more stable foundation for UTStarcom went further than guiding the company into other markets. Between 2002 and 2004, he completed a half-dozen acquisitions that moved UTStarcom into the manufacture and sale of PAS handsets, equipment that enabled high-speed Internet access, and into telecommunications services that competed with

PAS. Code division multiple access (CDMA) technology, for instance, ranked as the second most popular cellular technology in China. In April 2004, Lu acquired the CDMA infrastructure business for markets outside Korea belonging to Hyundai Syscomm, Inc., paying roughly $12 million to complete the deal. In November 2004, he obtained additional CDMA assets by acquiring the wireless handset division of Audiovox Communications Corporation, paying $165 million for the property with the hopes of taking the business international, particularly into China and India.

As Lu plotted his course for the second half of the decade, he was expecting to draw alongside his largest rivals, matching their stature with the size and capabilities of UTStarcom. By geographically expanding and broadening the company's selection of products and services, he hoped to reach $10 billion in annual revenues, a volume that would make UTStarcom a formidable telecommunications equipment company. In the years ahead, the company was expected to graft his success in China onto other large, underserved countries and to build a greater presence in established markets, developing a balanced stance to battle against its competitors. With revenues nearing $3 billion in 2004, UTStarcom had the size and the potential to become the driving force of its industry, pursuing a goal thought to be unattainable a decade earlier.

Jeffrey L. Covell

PRINCIPAL SUBSIDIARIES

ACD Labs Inc.; UTStarcom International Products, Inc.; UTStarcom International Services, Inc. (China); UTStarcom (China), Co. Ltd.; Universal Communication Technology (Hangzhou) Company Limited (China); UTStarcom Telecom Co. Ltd. (China); Hangzhou Starcom Telecom Co. Ltd.; (China); UTStarcom (Chongqing) Telecom Co. Ltd. (China); UTStarcom Hong Kong Ltd.; UTStarcom Ltd. (Thailand); UTStarcom Japan KK; UTStarcom, S.A. de C.V. (Mexico); UTStarcom GmbH (Germany); UTStarcom Canada Company; UTStarcom Ireland Limited; Rolling-Streams Systems, Ltd. (Cayman Islands); UTStarcom Singapore PTE.LTD; UTStarcom Taiwan Ltd.; UTStarcom Network Solutions—Redes de Nova Geracao Ltda.; UTStarcom Australia Pty. Ltd.; UTStarcom France S.A.R.L.; UTStarcom Korea Limited; UTStarcom Honduras, S. de R.L.; UTStarcom Chile Soluciones De Redes Limitada; UTStarcom Argentina S.R.L.; Telecom Sales and Marketing K.K. (Japan); UTStarcom India Telecom Pvt.; UTStarcom UK Limited; UTStarcom Personal Communication L.L.C.; UTStarcom CDMA Technologies Korea Limited; Hangzhou Starcom CEC Telecom Company Limited (China).

PRINCIPAL COMPETITORS

Lucent Technologies Inc.; Zhongxing Telecom; Huawei Technologies Co., Ltd.

FURTHER READING

Angell, Mike, "UTStarcom Making Smart Wireless Move," *Investor's Business Daily,* September 9, 2003, p. A6.

———, "With Its Growth on the Wane, UTStarcom Broadens Its Focus for '05," *Investor's Business Daily,* October 12, 2004, p. A5.

Burrows, Peter, "Ringing Off the Hook," *Business Week,* June 9, 2003, p. 20.

Detar, James, "How KFC, UTStarcom Learned to Operate Profitably in China," *Investor's Business Daily,* February 13, 2002, p. A1.

"Great Leap into China," *Inc.,* October 15, 1999, p. 29.

Grugal, Robin M., "UTStarcom Inc.," *Investor's Business Daily,* January 8, 2002, p. A8.

Kuo, Kaiser, "UTStarcom: Wu Ying," *Time,* July 28, 2003, p. A18.

Lyons, Daniel, "Call to Action," *Forbes,* November 15, 2004, p. 142.

"UTStarcom to Acquire Audiovox's Wireless Handset Business," *Wireless News,* June 15, 2004.

"Why UTStarcom Is a Telecom Star," *Business Week Online,* March 4, 2004.

Valspar

The Valspar Corporation

1101 Third Street South
Minneapolis, Minnesota 55415-1211
U.S.A.
Telephone: (612) 332-7371
Fax: (612) 375-7723
Web site: http://www.valspar.com

Public Company
Incorporated: 1832 as Valentine and Company
Employees: 7,540
Sales: $2.71 billion (2005)
Stock Exchanges: New York
Ticker Symbol: VAL
NAIC: 325510 Paint and Coating Manufacturing;
     325211 Plastics Material and Resin Manufacturing

■ ■ ■

The Valspar Corporation is the world's sixth largest manufacturer of paints and coatings, a business it has engaged in for more than two centuries. Its sterling reputation was built on the Valspar varnish, which was unveiled in 1906 as the first coating for wood that retained its clear finish when exposed to water. Nonetheless, until formative mergers with Rockcote Paint Company in 1960 and Minnesota Paints, Inc. in 1970, Valspar was a relatively small manufacturer with limited possibilities for growth. During the last three decades of the 20th century and the beginning years of the 21st, however, it rose to *Fortune* 500 status and Wall Street favor through an aggressive acquisition campaign in

which dozens of smaller paint and coatings companies entered the Valspar fold.

The company's product line is diverse, encompassing consumer interior and exterior paints, stains, primers, and varnishes sold through home improvement, mass-merchant, and other retailers; automotive refinish paints; industrial coatings for building products, appliances, automotive applications, furniture, and other areas; and coatings and inks for rigid packaging containers, particularly tin and aluminum cans. Valspar operates more than 50 manufacturing plants in the United States, Canada, Mexico, Brazil, the United Kingdom, France, Germany, Ireland, the Netherlands, Switzerland, Australia, China, Malaysia, Singapore, and South Africa; is involved in joint ventures in China, South Africa, and Japan; and markets branded product lines that include American Tradition, Cabot, De Beer, House of Kolor, McCloskey, Mr. Spray, Plasti-Kote, Signature Colors, Tempo, and Valspar. In the mid-1990s Valspar began an aggressive international expansion, which over the following ten years increased its overseas sales from 3 percent to more than 30 percent of overall sales.

19TH-CENTURY ORIGINS

In 1820 two businessmen in Cambridge, Massachusetts, began the first commercial production of varnishes in the United States, a business that was to become Valspar's forte for more than a century. Fourteen years earlier, on Boston's Broad Street, Samuel Tuck opened a paint dealership that led directly to the formation of Valspar. Tuck's business, Paint and Color, changed names and hands several times during the next 50 years. With

COMPANY PERSPECTIVES

The Valspar Corporation's mission is to be the best coatings company in the world as judged by our customers, shareholders, employees, suppliers and the communities in which we operate. To become the best, we must: Be in the top five in global sales. Be #1 or #2 and a technology leader in each of our target markets. Be the leader in sales growth, earnings growth and return on investment. Be the lowest cost supplier through integrating technology and productivity improvements. Be environmentally responsible. Establish an accident-free work environment. And above all else, always act with integrity and comply with ethical codes of business conduct.

Augustine Stimson's assumption of the Broad Street business and Lawson Valentine's incorporation of Boston varnish manufacturer Valentine and Company in 1832, the formation of Valspar was made possible. These two businesses soon merged to become Stimson & Valentine. In 1855 Otis Merriam joined Stimson & Valentine as the other principal owner. Merriam, interestingly, had for the previous six years been associated with the original varnish plant in Cambridge. Although popularly known as "varnish manufacturers," these men also conducted an import and retail trade in paints, oils, glass, and beeswax. Around 1860 Valentine's brother, Henry, joined the firm. By 1866, both Stimson and Merriam had retired and left the Valentine brothers the sole partners in the business, which was then renamed Valentine & Company.

Shortly thereafter, Lawson Valentine made a singularly important decision: he hired a chemist at a time when there were fewer than 100 such specialists in the country, a first for the American varnish industry. More important than the creation of the position, however, was the candidate selected for the job. That person was Charles Homer, brother of famed New England artist Winslow Homer and an expert craftsman in the mixing of varnishes. According to the *Valspar History,* he "made varnishes so perfect they could be poured from the can to the back or side of a carriage.... Varnishes that flow out smoothly and evenly, dry perfectly." Following Lawson's relocation of the business to New York City in 1870, the same year in which the firm acquired Minnesota Linseed Oil Paint Company, Valentine & Company began to specialize in vehicle finishing varnishes that were competitive with widely prized English

varnishes. At the time, the company operated a West Coast office with Whittier, Fuller & Company (later renamed W.P. Fuller & Company) as its representative. In 1878 Valentine & Company entered the Midwest market via a Chicago branch office. Four years later Henry Valentine succeeded his brother as president and the company renewed its Boston ties by reopening a plant there. By 1900, Valentine & Company had established additional operations in Pennsylvania as well as Paris, and had won dozens of international medals for its high-quality varnishes.

EARLY 20TH CENTURY: VALSPAR VARNISH

Lawson Valentine's grandson, L. Valentine Pulsifer, joined the company in 1903 after receiving his degree in chemistry from Harvard University. Working under Homer, Pulsifer was allowed to conduct experiments to discover why varnishes always turned white when exposed to water. From Homer's standpoint, the experiments would be edifying, though not otherwise profitable. Pulsifer believed, however, that the formula for a clear varnish existed; it simply had yet to be discovered. Three years later Pulsifer produced Valspar, the first clear varnish. Factory production began within two years, accompanied by promotional stunts designed to highlight the product's unique features. The first such exhibition involved a boiling water test at the Grand Rapids Furniture Show in 1908. The following year, at the New York Motor Boat Show, Valspar and eight of the best competing brands were applied to a submarine in alternating stripes; the vessel was then submerged and "gradually took on the appearance of a sea-going zebra, as the other varnishes whitened and Valspar remained clear."

For the next few decades the company rode on the coattails of Valspar, supported by a strong national advertising campaign during the 1920s that made the product a household word with the tagline "the varnish that won't turn white." Pulsifer's invention, by virtue of its unparalleled appearance, durability, and ease of application, became a willing participant in a number of historic events. These included Admiral Robert Peary's expedition to the North Pole in 1909, U.S. involvement in World War I, and Charles Lindbergh's nonstop solo flight from New York to Paris in 1927. In each of these cases, Valspar finishes were employed as a protective coating on exposed wood surfaces. The varnishing of airplanes, in particular, became synonymous with Valspar during this period. The unveiling of new products and the acquisition of other paint and varnish manufacturers helped Valentine & Company to successfully weather the Great Depression. Among the new products were Super Valspar, Four-Hour Valspar, Val-Oil

KEY DATES

1806: Samuel Tuck opens a Boston paint dealership called Paint and Color, which is later acquired by Augustine Stimson.

1820: First commercial production of varnishes in the United States begins in Cambridge, Massachusetts.

1832: Valentine and Company, a varnish manufacturer, is incorporated in Boston by Lawson Valentine, and soon merges with Paint and Color to become Stimson & Valentine.

1866: Valentine and his brother, Henry, become sole partners in the business, renaming it Valentine & Company.

1870: Company relocates to New York City and acquires Minnesota Linseed Oil Paint Company. 1882: Henry Valentine succeeds his brother as president.

1903: Chemist L. Valentine Pulsifer, grandson of Lawson Valentine, joins company.

1906: Pulsifer develops Valspar, the first clear varnish.

1932: Valentine & Company begins operating as a subsidiary of newly formed Valspar Corporation.

1960: Valspar merges with Rockcote Paint Company, with new headquarters in Rockford, Illinois.

1970: Valspar merges with Minnesota Paints, Inc., with new headquarters in Minneapolis.

1973: C. Angus Wurtele becomes company chairman.

1984: Mobil Corporation's chemical coatings business is acquired for $100 million.

1994: Company acquires Cargill Inc.'s resin products division, combines it with part of existing resin business, and spins it off to shareholders as McWhorter Technologies, Inc.

1995: Richard Rompala becomes CEO

1996: Four-stage acquisition of the Coates Coatings unit of TOTAL S.A. is begun.

1997: Sales reach $1 billion.

1999: The packaging coatings business of Dexter Corporation is acquired.

2000: Valspar acquires Lilly Industries, Inc., for more than $1 billion.

2001: Final stage of the Coates Coatings acquisition is completed.

2005: William L. Mansfield succeeds Rompala as CEO.

Clear, Valenite Clear, Valenite Enamel, Three V Floor Varnish, and French Formula Enamel. Among the acquired paint and varnish manufacturers were Con-Ferro Paint and Varnish Company and Detroit-Graphite Company (both acquired in 1930) and Edward Smith & Company (acquired in 1938).

FORMATIVE MERGERS: ROCK-COTE (1960), MINNESOTA PAINTS (1970)

Prior to the stock market crash, in 1927 the seed for another important predecessor to the Valspar Corporation was planted. It was in this year that Ralph J. Baudhuin entered the paint business as a salesman. Within a short time, he helped found the Baudhuin-Anderson Company in Rockford, Illinois. In 1932, the same year that Valentine & Company began to operate as a subsidiary of the newly formed Valspar Corporation, Baudhuin-Anderson became Rockford Paint

Manufacturing Company. Four years later, after Ralph Baudhuin had gained sole ownership of the Illinois firm, Rockford Paint was renamed Rockcote Paint Company. During the 1950s Rockcote formed two important subsidiaries. The first, Color Corporation of America, was created to license and sell color systems and related equipment to paint manufacturers; the second, Midwest Synthetics, was formed to develop synthetic resins and resin-based varnishes. Like Valspar, Rockcote also grew by steady acquisitions during this period. By 1958, Baudhuin had taken special notice of Valspar; two years later, he succeeded in merging Rockcote with the old-line firm, then headquartered in Ardmore, Pennsylvania, and consolidated headquarters in Rockford.

Under the direction of the Baudhuin brothers, Ralph and F. J., the 1960s represented a heavy period of growth for Valspar. From the time of the merger until the end of the decade, the company averaged almost two acquisitions per year. Among the businesses purchased were Norco Plastics of Milwaukee, McMurtry Manufacturing of Denver, Keystone Paint and Varnish of Brooklyn, and the Trade Sales Division of Mobil Corporation. Fittingly, the company inaugurated the 1970s with even more phenomenal growth, this time through a historic merger. In June 1970, privately held Minnesota Paints, Inc., of Minneapolis, with annual sales of $24 million, merged with Valspar, with annual sales of $27 million; once again, Valspar's headquarters changed, this time to Minneapolis. The deal came at a propitious time, for the old Valspar had suffered a loss of $148,500 while Minnesota Paints had posted a gain of $200,000. Furthermore, Minnesota Paints boasted a strong, cash-heavy financial position to support further acquisitions. In the first fiscal year following the merger, earnings were $226,000 on revenues of $47.6 million. Within two years, Valspar's earnings had grown to $1.53 million and it was again ready to expand. The consecutive acquisitions of Phelan Faust Paint, Speed-O-Lac Chemical, Conchemco's Detroit Chemical Coatings, Elliott Paint and Varnish, and Conchemco's Coatings Division increased initial annual revenues by another $74 million during the decade.

1980S AND EARLY 1990S: ACQUISITIONS CONTINUE

Overseeing much of this expansion was C. Angus Wurtele, former president of Minnesota Paints and chairman of Valspar starting in 1973. At the time of Wurtele's succession approximately 60 percent of Valspar's sales came from its consumer business; the remainder came from industrial coatings. This alignment changed dramatically in the 1980s following the $100 million purchase of Mobil's chemical coatings business in 1984. Among those setting the stage for this acquisition, unprecedented both in size and nature, was Mike Meyers, who reported in June 1984 that "in the last 10 years Valspar's net profits have soared 13-fold, while sales have tripled. However, its formula for prosperity may be about to face a severe test, when Valspar in August is expected to complete the most ambitious acquisition in its history." For Valspar the test was unusually challenging, but not severe.

In effect, the company more than doubled in size through a bargain purchase: 1983 revenues for Valspar were $161 million while revenues for the Mobil division were around $180 million. Valspar's profit margin, at 6 percent, had been leading the industry, while Mobil's coatings margin lagged at just 3 percent. When Wurtele was asked by Meyers why Mobil was willing to sell, he responded that the Mobil division represented "less than half of 1 percent of the total corporation." In other words, Mobil, with such a minute investment, could

well afford to let the business go and Valspar, with such an established track record in the industry, could ill afford to pass it by. Virtually overnight, the deal elevated Valspar from the tenth to the fifth largest coatings company in North America. In addition, it gave the manufacturer ready access to potentially high-margin markets, including packaging coatings and industrial metal finishes, which it had previously been unable to capitalize on. By 1986, Valspar had successfully integrated the Mobil operations, thereby proving its adeptness at acquiring even the largest paint and chemical plants and instituting means for improving efficiency and profitability. The buy-low, raise-efficiency strategy remained particularly effective for the company, for the tactic tended to postpone costly new construction and allow for a greater investment in research and development.

To achieve its standing objective of remaining among the top three participants within any of the markets it sought, Valspar prudently divested itself of plants and businesses in the 1980s and early 1990s. Yet, for much the same reason, Valspar acquisitions still continued apace. In 1987 Enterprise Paint Companies, maker of Enterprise Paint and the Federal floor care line, was purchased for $60 million. In July 1989 the McCloskey Corporation, with $42 million in sales, was acquired. The purchase was especially significant for the growth of Valspar's resin business, conducted through its McWhorter Inc. subsidiary. In October 1990 the company acquired certain assets of DeSoto, Inc., which had combined revenues of approximately $45 million. This purchase strengthened the company's market-leading packaging coatings group, and elevated it to a leader in coil and extrusion coatings for the construction industry.

Following the much smaller purchases of container coatings and powder coatings businesses, Valspar acquired Hi-Tek Polymers, Inc., from Rhône Poulenc in May 1991. The Hi-Tek purchase was among the key factors in Valspar's 18 percent increase in packaging coatings sales for 1992. During that year, the company spent a record $19.6 million on such capital improvements as a new resin manufacturing plant, a new consumer coatings research facility, and various capacity enhancements. In addition, nearly $25 million was spent on research and development and quality process training.

In May 1993 the company announced a definitive agreement to acquire Cargill Inc.'s resin products division, which had $190 million in revenues for the year ended May 31, 1992. By contrast, Valspar's resin sales then ranged somewhere between $60 million and $85 million. This deal would have moved Valspar into the number two position in the resin industry, trailing Reichhold Chemicals, but it would not be consummated as an outright acquisition. The Federal Trade Commission investigated the acquisition and concluded that the deal would result in Valspar holding too great a share of the resin market in the Midwest. Rather than abandoning the endeavor, Valspar went ahead with the purchase, a $76 million in cash deal concluded in February 1994, and divided the combined resin operations into two separate companies: McWhorter Technologies, Inc. and Engineered Polymer Solutions, Inc. McWhorter, the larger of the two entities, was then spun off to Valspar shareholders in April 1994. McWhorter began its life as an independent public company with all of the resin assets and plants of Cargill plus three of Valspar's resin plants. What Valspar gained from this complicated deal was new technology for its own coatings business.

KEY ACQUISITIONS OF ROMPALA ERA (1995 TO 2005): COATES, DEXTER, LILLY INDUSTRIES

During 1994 Richard Rompala was brought in as the new president, becoming CEO the following year, and chairman in 1998. The key to hiring Rompala was his experience running global coatings and specialty chemicals businesses at competitor PPG Industries, Inc. Through the mid-1990s, Valspar remained an essentially North American-oriented firm. Only 3 percent of revenues came from overseas. Under Rompala's leadership, the company would dramatically increase this figure to nearly 30 percent by 2004, forming joint ventures in China, Hong Kong, Brazil, South Africa, and Mexico and making a number of acquisitions.

A number of these moves were centered within Valspar's packaging coatings unit. In 1996 and 1997 Valspar completed the first two stages of a four-stage acquisition of the Coates Coatings unit of TOTAL S.A., which included packaging coatings and metal decorating inks operations in the United Kingdom, France, Norway, Germany, Spain, Australia, Hong Kong, and China. The third and fourth stages, completed in 2000 and 2001, included operations in Singapore, Malaysia, Indonesia, and Thailand. During 1998 the company purchased Anzol Pty. Ltd., a maker of packaging and industrial coatings and resins based in Australia. Then in February 1999 Valspar completed its largest acquisition yet, that of the packaging coatings business of Dexter Corporation. The operations acquired from Dexter, which were particularly strong in Europe, had 1998 revenues of $212 million, vaulting Valspar into the number one position worldwide in packaging coatings with a global market share of between 35 and 40 percent. Valspar's consumer unit, meantime, also expanded internationally,

through the 1998 acquisition of Plasti-Kote Co., Inc., a maker of consumer aerosol and specialty paint products in the United Kingdom and Scandinavia.

In December 2000 Valspar completed its largest acquisition ever, the purchase of Lilly Industries, Inc. for $1.04 billion, including the assumption of $218 million in debt. Based in Indianapolis, Lilly specialized in wood, metal, and glass coatings for furniture, appliances, building products, and transportation, agricultural, and construction equipment. Lilly's strength in wood and aluminum coatings meshed well with Valspar's focus on steel coatings. Lilly, which reported net sales of $670 million for fiscal 2000, was also attractive to Valspar for its more extensive international business: 27 percent of its sales were international compared to 20 percent for Valspar. Lilly operated 26 manufacturing plants, and these facilities and its sales offices were located in the United States, Canada, Mexico, the United Kingdom, Ireland, Germany, China, Malaysia, Taiwan, Singapore, and Australia. For the deal to pass antitrust muster, Valspar had to divest its mirror coatings business, which was replaced by Lilly's mirror coatings unit. The deal vaulted Valspar from eighth to sixth place among global players in paints and coatings.

In integrating Lilly, Valspar initially aimed at saving $70 million per year through cutbacks. By September 2001 the company had closed seven of its plants, but difficult economic conditions prompted it to go further. That month, Valspar announced plans to shut down seven more plants, reduce production at four others, and cut its global workforce by about 350, or 5 percent. These moves were expected to add as much as $30 million more in annual savings. The company incurred a $39.3 million restructuring charge, which coupled with the weak economy, increasing raw material prices, and higher debt servicing costs translated into net income for fiscal 2001 of $51.5 million, down from the previous year's $86.5 million. This marked the end of 26 consecutive years of earnings growth.

Valspar rebounded in 2002 with revenues surpassing the $2 billion mark for the first time and profits jumping to $120.1 million, despite continued softness in the U.S. industrial economy. Over the next few years, rising raw material costs, stemming primarily from steadily increasing oil prices, were one of the company's main challenges, and the firm responded with aggressive cost-containment efforts. Acquisition opportunities were less plentiful during this period, so additional growth was secured organically. For example, Valspar began developing exclusive lines of brand-name paint for home improvement retailer Lowe's Companies, Inc., including the American Tradition and Signature Colors brands. Overseas, Valspar was particularly targeting China for growth, and with that country's furniture manufacturing sector exploding with growth, Valspar moved quickly to secure a strong position in China's furniture coatings market. In the meantime, there were two smaller acquisitions completed in 2004: De Beer Lakfabrieken B.V., a maker of automotive refinish coatings based in the Netherlands, and certain assets of the forest products business of Associated Chemists, Inc., including a facility manufacturing wood coatings in Orangeburg, South Carolina.

In February 2005 the Rompala era ended at Valspar, with the CEO having grown sales from $795 million to $2.44 billion. Sales outside the United States had increased exponentially, hitting $705.3 million by 2004. Taking on the unenviable task of succeeding Rompala was William L. Mansfield, who had led Valspar's packaging coatings business for many years before being named chief operating officer in April 2004. Rompala stayed on as board chairman until August 2005, when he retired and was replaced by Thomas McBurney, serving as nonexecutive chairman.

The new CEO picked up where his predecessor had left off, completing his first acquisition in June 2005. Valspar acquired Samuel Cabot Incorporated, a maker of premium quality exterior and interior stains and finishes. Family owned since 1877, Cabot was based in Newburyport, Massachusetts, and recorded 2004 sales of approximately $58 million. Continuing to be squeezed by high raw material costs, Valspar in August 2005 announced a major restructuring whereby seven plants were to be closed as the first step in a plan to reduce the firm's worldwide manufacturing capacity by 10 percent. Another challenge for the new leader was to decide what to do with Valspar's packaging business. Valspar was the world leader in rigid packaging, particularly coatings for the inside and outside of tin and aluminum cans, but this sector of the market was in stagnation, even decline, as manufacturers were increasingly switching to flexible packaging, for instance, selling chili in boxes rather than cans. Given the company's absence from the flexible-packaging coatings market, some analysts suggested that Valspar needed to enter that sector either from scratch or via acquisition. Nevertheless, given the firm's remarkable track record for growth and solid profitability, Valspar seemed likely to successfully negotiate these challenges. It remained a perennially exciting company in a longstanding and often overlooked industry.

Jay P. Pederson
Updated, David E. Salamie

PRINCIPAL SUBSIDIARIES

Engineered Polymer Solutions, Inc.; Plasti-Kote Co., Inc.; Valspar Coatings Finance Corporation; Valspar Finance Corporation; Valspar Inc. (Canada); Valspar Refinish, Inc.; Valspar Sourcing, Inc.; The Valspar Corporation Limitada (Brazil); Samuel Cabot Incorporated; The Valspar (Australia) Corporation Pty Limited; The Valspar (Nantes) Corporation, S.A.S. (France); The Valspar (France) Corporation, S.A.S.; Valspar Industries GmbH (Germany); The Valspar (Germany) GmbH; The Valspar (H.K.) Corporation Limited (Hong Kong); Valspar Mexicana, S.A. de C.V. (Mexico); Valspar Rock Co., Ltd. (Japan); The Valspar (Singapore) Corporation Pte Ltd; The Valspar (South Africa) Corporation (Pty) Ltd.; The Valspar (UK) Corporation, Limited; The Valspar (Vernicolor) Corporation AG (Switzerland); The Valspar (Malaysia) Corporation Sdn Bhd; Dongguan Lilly Paint Industries Limited (China); Lilly Industries (Shanghai) Limited (China).

PRINCIPAL COMPETITORS

Akzo Nobel N.V.; The Sherwin-Williams Company; Imperial Chemical Industries PLC; PPG Industries, Inc.; BASF AG.

FURTHER READING

Autry, Ret, "Valspar," *Fortune,* July 16, 1990, p. 75.

Black, Sam, "Valspar Expands in Southeast Asia," *Minneapolis/St. Paul Business Journal,* August 30, 2002.

———, "Valspar's New CEO Follows a Tough Act," *Minneapolis/St. Paul Business Journal,* January 21, 2005.

Byrne, Harlan S., "Valspar Corp.: A Paint Maker Makes Headway Against Rising Material Prices," *Barron's,* May 8, 1989, pp. 57-58.

Cahill, William, "Fresh Coat: Industrial Business Is New Focus for Valspar," *Barron's,* August 4, 1986, pp. 39-40.

Carlson, Scott, "Smart Acquisitions Brush Up Valspar," *Pioneer Press and Dispatch,* July 17, 1989.

Chang, Joseph, "Valspar Corp. to Acquire Lilly Industries in $975M Deal," *Chemical Market Reporter,* July 3, 2000, pp. 1, 16.

Cottrill, Ken, "Strategies for World Domination," *Journal of Business Strategy,* May/June 1998, pp. 36-40.

Fattah, Hassan, "Valspar Paints a Brighter Picture," *Chemical Week,* February 12, 1997, p. 36.

Feyder, Susan, "Valspar Earnings Paint Pretty Picture," *Minneapolis Star Tribune,* February 19, 1990, pp. 1D, 6D.

Kiesche, Elizabeth S., "Valspar Settles with FTC over Cargill Resins Acquisition," *Chemical Week,* November 3, 1993, p. 9.

Meyers, Mike, "Valspar Announces Plan to Buy Cargill Division," *Minneapolis Star Tribune,* May 21, 1993, p. 3D.

———, "Valspar Formula Facing Its Biggest Test," *Minneapolis Star and Tribune,* June 18, 1984, pp. 1M, 4M.

————, "Valspar Plans to Buy Global Packaging Coatings Maker," *Minneapolis Star Tribune,* August 26, 1998, p. 1D.

160 Years of Valspar History: 1806-1966, Minneapolis: The Valspar Corporation, 1966.

Peterson, Susan E., "Valspar Will Acquire Lilly Industries," *Minneapolis Star Tribune,* June 27, 2000, p. 1D.

Plishner, Emily S., "Valspar Plan Calls for Going Global," *Chemical Week,* April 15, 1992, p. 21.

Scheraga, Dan, "Sovereign to Buy Valspar's Flexible Packaging Coatings," *Chemical Market Reporter,* April 5, 1999, p. 31.

Tevlin, Jon, "Valspar Seeks Keys to Competence," *Minneapolis Star Tribune,* June 7, 1998, p. 1D.

"Valspar Acquiring Total's Coates Unit," *Chemical Marketing Reporter,* March 4, 1996, p. 9.

"The Valspar Corporation," *Wall Street Transcript,* November 2002.

"Valspar in Massive Restructuring," *Chemical Market Reporter,* August 22–September 4, 2005, p. 4.

"Valspar Winds Up Last Steps to Consolidate Operations," *Corporate Report Minnesota,* April 1973, p. 11.

Walden, Gene, "Valspar Corp.," *The 100 Best Stocks to Own in America,* 2nd ed., Chicago: Dearborn Financial Publishing, 1991.

Warren, Susan, "Valspar Agrees to Buy Lilly Industries, a Rival Paint Maker, for $762 Million," *Wall Street Journal,* June 26, 2000, p. A42.

Weinberg, Neil, "Compound Growth," *Forbes,* January 2, 1995, p. 135.

Weintraub, Adam, "Valspar Buys into Global Markets," *Minneapolis/St. Paul CityBusiness,* July 5, 1999.

Westervelt, Robert, "Valspar Nabs Dexter's Packaging Coatings," *Chemical Week,* August 26, 1998, p. 16.

Vertrue Inc.

———■———

680 Washington Boulevard
Stamford, Connecticut 06901
U.S.A.
Telephone: (203) 324-7635
Fax: (203) 674-7080
Web site: http://www.vertrue.com

Public Company
Incorporated: 1989 as Card Member Publishing
Employees: 1,600
Sales: $579.8 million (2005)
Stock Exchanges: NASDAQ
Ticker Symbol: VTRU
NAIC: 514199 All Other Information Services

■ ■ ■

Vertrue Inc., known as MemberWorks for much of its history, is a leading consumer services marketing company. Vertrue enrolls consumers in a variety of cost-saving membership programs, offering discounted shopping and travel, for example, as well as health insurance, healthcare products and services, financial privacy enhancement, and other programs for which consumers pay monthly or annual fees. Vertrue claims some 18 million members combined in its more than 20 membership programs. Fees are typically between $60 and $120 annually. Vertrue solicits consumers through a variety of channels including over the Internet, through telephone sales calls, and through television. The company typically targets customers by partnering with banks, credit card issuers, and other third parties, paying

royalties for access to lists of millions of people. Vertrue also operates a subsidiary called The Bargain Network, a membership-based Internet search tool that allows consumers access to listings of discounted used cars and bargain houses, including foreclosed properties. Vertrue also owns the Canadian Internet dating service Lavalife, Inc. Lavalife is a leading lister of online personal ads, available in major metropolitan areas across the United States, Canada, and Australia. Lavalife counts more than 1.2 million subscribers.

IDENTIFYING A NEW MARKET OPPORTUNITY

Gary Johnson founded the company that became Vertrue Incorporated in Omaha, Nebraska, in 1989. Johnson had been a vice-president of product development for what was then the largest membership services marketing company, CUC International, in the 1980s. Membership marketing began in the late 1960s and grew hand-in-hand with the credit card industry. The first such company was SafeCard Services Inc., which began soliciting credit cardholders in 1967. Several companies, including CUC International and Signature Group, evolved around the same time, working with credit card issuers to offer their credit cardholders additional services such as insurance. By the late 1980s, the market potential for such companies seemed huge and relatively untapped. There were some 300 million credit cardholders at the time, all potential customers for membership services, who could be solicited once a month as their bill arrived. Membership fees were typically $25 annually, with a high rate of renewal, which added up, according to an interview with Gary Johnson

COMPANY PERSPECTIVES

Vertrue is an integrated marketing services company that gives consumers unrivaled opportunities to improve their lives through exclusive access to significant discounts and unique services. Our consumer-based membership and loyalty programs, as well as proprietary Internet and telephone-based technologies, create multi-channel venues for our clients and marketing partners to generate incremental revenue and enjoy enhanced loyalty.

in *American Banker* (April 10, 1997), to a potential market worth from $4 billion to $5 billion. Existing membership services firms tapped only a small percentage of that market in the late 1980s, and Johnson was convinced that the industry could easily hold another player. Consequently, in 1989 he quit CUC International and founded his own company, which was at first called Card Member Publishing.

Card Member Publishing debuted at a time when the credit card industry was both growing and changing. The number of credit cardholders surged in the 1990s, from approximately 300 million in the late 1980s to about 900 million a decade later. Whereas many credit cards had carried an annual fee from the 1960s to the 1980s, competition forced issuers to both lower interest rates and drop annual fees in the 1990s. Credit card issuers thus became more fond of membership service firms such as Johnson's Card Member Publishing, because these companies were a stable source of revenue. Card Member Publishing paid royalties to card issuers in exchange for access to lists of millions of potential customers. As credit card issuers dropped their own fees, they made up for it by selling information to these third-party marketing firms. Since credit card customers were reaping savings by not paying an annual fee to their card issuer, they were perhaps more likely to consider paying other fees for the services Card Member Publishing offered. Services were first closely tied to credit cards, offering insurance against theft and loss, or other financial services. But over the 1990s, the industry began offering other services, such as travel discounts, dental insurance, or legal services.

Card Member Publishing was at first a small player in the industry, though it grew at a rate of 40 percent a year. Finally in 1996, the company linked up with one of the nation's leading credit card issuers, Citicorp. Citicorp issued more Visa and MasterCard credit cards than

any other bank, so taking it on as a client was a coup for Card Member Publishing. Card Member Publishing offered a financial services membership package called Maximum Dividends to Citicorp cardholders. The company also had other major card issuers as clients, including BancOne, Capital One, Mellon Bank, and Bank of New York. By 1997, Card Member Publishing worked with 13 of the top 20 credit card issuers in the United States.

PUBLIC COMPANY IN THE MID-1990S

By 1996, Card Member Publishing had grown to a company employing 500 people and enrolling as many as 1.7 million customers in its eight membership programs. It was still small compared to its more established rivals. Signature Group had 15.6 million members and CUC had 66 million, but revenue had grown to $57 million, and founder Gary Johnson estimated that the market was still largely untapped. With a lot of potential growth ahead of it, Card Member Publishing went public in October 1996, selling shares on the NASDAQ. The company changed its name to MemberWorks, Inc., and moved its headquarters to Stamford, Connecticut. MemberWorks enrolled customers in varied programs. Some, like Maximum Dividends (which also went by the name MoneyMaster) were financial services packages, long a staple of membership programs allied to credit card issuers. But MemberWorks also had two dental insurance membership programs, a travel discount plan, sports and entertainment packages, and other programs related to health and computers. It brought out several new programs shortly after going public. The company's customers were principally young families with children, who might need additional insurance or were avid bargain hunters, and recent retirees. This second group was often keen for discounted services that might make up for benefits they had had while still employed. MemberWorks customers were promised that they could save an amount worth ten times the membership fee they paid if they enrolled in MemberWorks programs.

In the mid-1990s, the company seemed poised for tremendous growth, as it hoped to ink deals with the remaining seven banks in the top 20 with whom it did not already have a relationship. But the late 1990s saw the start of a string of lawsuits brought against MemberWorks and affiliated banks. While revenue continued to climb, the company attracted negative publicity, and some banks altered the type of business relationship they had with MemberWorks and other membership marketing companies.

KEY DATES

1989: Company is founded as Card Member Publishing.
1996: Company goes public, changes name to MemberWorks.
1999: First of a series of lawsuits is brought against the company.
2004: Company acquires Lavalife, changes name to Vertrue Inc.

In June 1999, the state of Minnesota sued a division of U.S. Bancorp, alleging that the bank violated its citizens' privacy by turning over their personal and financial data to MemberWorks for $4 million plus commissions. The bank quickly settled the suit, but Minnesota then targeted MemberWorks directly. The new suit claimed that MemberWorks had solicited business, using the customer list it bought from U.S. Bancorp, and asked consumers to sign up for a 30-day free trial of a membership plan. Sales calls were made by telephone, and MemberWorks did inform customers that they would be billed after the 30 days was up. But Minnesota claimed MemberWorks misled consumers by not revealing that the firm already had the customer's credit card data on file. MemberWorks could automatically begin withdrawing the membership fee from the consumer's credit card account unless the consumer actively contacted the company at the end of the free trial period and resigned from the program.

The Minnesota lawsuit set off a ripple through the credit card industry, prompting some issuers such as Bank of America to promulgate new rules about how and whether to give out customer information. U.S. Bancorp ended its relationship with MemberWorks and with three other companies in the member services industry as a result of the legal action. A proliferation of consumer complaints about member services companies even led to talk of financial privacy reform in Congress.

The spotlight on the company's marketing practices was doubtless unpleasant for MemberWorks. The effect on the company's growth and financial picture was mixed. Bad news about MemberWorks continued to come out over the next few years. For example, the company had to reimburse the State of New York Attorney General's office the $75,000 the office spent investigating MemberWorks, in addition to agreeing to double refunds to New York customers who complained

about unauthorized billing to their credit cards. Member-Works also agreed to change the way it asked for and recorded customer consent to pay for its services. While this kind of public wrist-slapping might have seemed dire to a company that depended on good customer service to keep going, nevertheless MemberWorks' revenue climbed by more than 50 percent in 2000, to just over $330 million, and its profits were four times what they had been in 1999. MemberWorks lost money in the fourth quarter of 2000, related to its purchase of an online financial services company that year, eNeighborhoods Inc. Even as it recorded another loss in the fourth quarter of 2001, again related to online business, MemberWorks' share price went up. Its membership rose to eight million by 2001, and the company was offering as many as 20 different programs.

CHANGES IN THE 2000S

The company addressed its ongoing legal and public relations problems proactively, engaging a consumer advisory board in 2001 made up of respected figures such as a former Michigan attorney general and the former heads of three state consumer protection divisions. The advisory board was meant to add weight to MemberWorks pledges to offer the best customer service and to reign in practices that had irked consumers and sparked the lawsuits. A number of consumer complaints against the company had led the Better Business Bureau in Omaha, the city where the company had been founded, to suspend MemberWorks from the Bureau in 1999. But in 2001, the Omaha Better Business Bureau reinstated MemberWorks, declaring itself convinced that the company was now upholding high standards of customer service and fair business practices. The company continued to attract complaints in some communities, including a class-action lawsuit brought by several Florida consumers in 2001. Yet the company's revenue and membership continued to grow. Revenue for 2002 was more than $427 million. MemberWorks also sold an Internet business in 2002 that had been a drag on earnings previously. Revenue grew to almost $457 million the next year.

One of the most significant changes the company underwent in the 2000s was its acquisition of a leading online dating company, Lavalife. MemberWorks paid $313 million for the company, adding a new dimension to the kind of business MemberWorks was involved in. Lavalife was founded by a small crew of entrepreneurs and technology buffs in Toronto in the early 1980s. The company at that time was called Phoneworks, and it was basically an interactive voice-mail system at a time when such a service was rare. Phoneworks began offering several information line services, so that customers could call in, pick an option using their phone's keypad, and access restaurant reviews, entertainment calendars, and other information.

Eventually Phoneworks' principals noticed that many of its customers were using an option that allowed people to leave messages for each other, essentially a telephone dating service. They reorganized the company in 1990 under the name Telepersonals, focusing on the dating service. Telepersonals was very successful, and expanded quickly to other Canadian cities. By the late 1990s, Telepersonals was operating in 40 cities in North America and Australia. Revenue rose to $80 million, and the company expanded its staff and infrastructure.

Just as Telepersonals was taking off, the Internet threatened to overtake the telephone as a quick and satisfying way to post and answer personal ads. Telepersonals decided to acquire one Internet dating service in 1996, called Webpersonals. Over the next four years, the telephone side of Telepersonals held steady or contracted, while the Internet side became much more active. In 2000, the Canadian company changed its name and its focus again. It became an Internet dating service called Lavalife, a name picked for its young, hip flavor. The company marketed itself to urban singles with trendy ads in print and on billboards. The company grew quickly, adding an unbelievable 10,000 new users a day in the early 2000s. By late 2003, its service was available in 65 cities in Canada, the United States, and Australia, and revenue reached $125 million. The following year MemberWorks bought Lavalife. The dating service continued to run out of Toronto.

With the addition of this new division, Member-Works was a more diversified company. In 2004, the company decided on a major rebranding, and it changed its name to Vertrue Inc. The new name was supposed to represent "our focus on consumer value," according to founder Gary Johnson (*Fairfield Business Journal*, October 18, 2004). The company also adopted a tag line, used on its web site and in its promotional materials, "Get more out of life every day." By 2004, the company counted approximately 18 million people as members of its various programs.

Vertrue did not leave its problems behind with the change of name. It saw lawsuits in Pennsylvania and Florida in 2003 and 2004, related to consumer complaints of unauthorized withdrawals from credit card accounts for membership in Vertrue's clubs and programs. The company maintained that it had tougher consumer protection policies than any other company in its industry. Vertrue paid a $5.5 million penalty in 2005 relating to a suit in Connecticut. Meanwhile, the Lavalife division seemed to be growing in new directions. It

began cross-marketing programs with the movie theater conglomerate Loews Cineplex Entertainment Corp. in 2004, hosting singles parties at Loews theaters. Lavalife also updated its technology with a new phone service, making use of the growing popularity of cell phone-cameras. Revenue for Vertrue rose to $579.8 million in 2005, up from $488.7 million a year earlier.

A. Woodward

PRINCIPAL SUBSIDIARIES

Lavalife, Inc.; MyChoiceMedical, Inc.; The Bargain Network.

PRINCIPAL COMPETITORS

TRL Group; CoolSavings, Inc.

FURTHER READING

Barancik, Scott, and Dean Anason, "U.S. Bancorp Charged with Selling Data on Consumers," *American Banker*, June 10, 1999, p. 1.

Bittar, Christine, "Movie Date," *Brandweek*, August 9, 2004, p. 28.

"Connecticut-Based Telemarketing Firm $13.8 Million Loss," *Omaha World-Herald*, July 29, 2000.

"Lavalife Finds a Mate," *America's Intelligence Wire*, March 5, 2004.

"Lavalife Offers Mobile 'Click' Dating Service," *Wireless News*, February 6, 2004.

Lee, W. A., "Marketer Mimics Household Approach on Consumer Issues," *American Banker*, August 27, 2001, p. 8.

Meece, Mickey, "Fertile Sales Turf," *American Banker*, April 10, 1997, p. 15.

"MemberWorks Becomes Vertrue Inc.," *Fairfield County Business Journal*, October 18, 2004, p. 43.

"MemberWorks Revises Estimates for Two Quarters," *Fairfield County Business Journal*, April 28, 2003, p. 5.

"MemberWorks Settles with New York AG," *Direct*, November 1, 2000, p. 11.

"Minnesota Sues U.S. Bank on Privacy Data," *New York Times*, June 11, 1999, p. C8.

O'Brien, Timothy L., "Big Bank Says It Won't Share Customer Data," *New York Times*, June 12, 1999, p. C1.

"Omaha, Neb., Better Business Bureau Reinstates Local Firm," *Omaha World-Herald*, January 31, 2001.

Saunders, John, "Online Dating Pioneers Strike It Rich," *Globe & Mail* (Toronto, Canada), March 5, 2004, p. A1.

Spring, Tom, "Fees Surprise Unwary Web Shoppers," *PC World*, August 2004, p. 34.

Strempel, Dan, "MemberWorks Pays $40,000 to Consumers," *Fairfield County Business Journal*, April 26, 2004, p. 10.

———, "Tele-Charge Suits Target Local Firms," *Fairfield County Business Journal*, July 9, 2001, p. 1.

"Telemarketer Is Sued," *New York Times*, July 20, 1999, p. B8.

Weaver, David, "The Matchmaker," *Toronto Life*, October 2003, p. 61.

Vision Service Plan Inc.

3333 Quality Drive
Rancho Cordova, California 95670
U.S.A.
Telephone: (916) 851-5000
Toll Free: (800) 852-7600
Fax: (916) 851-4858
Web site: http://www.vsp.com

Private Company
Incorporated: 1955 as California Vision Services
Employees: 1,900
Sales: $2.06 billion (2004)
NAIC: 524114 Direct Health and Medical Insurance Carriers

■ ■ ■

Vision Service Plan Inc. (VSP) is the largest eye-care insurer in the United States, providing vision health coverage to one out of every eight people in the country. VSP boasts a network of more than 22,000 doctors that serves the company's 41 million members. VSP doctors provide both eye exams and eyewear, with some of the eyewear provided to VSP patients made at the company's optometry lab in Sacramento. VSP covers the gamut of eye-care services, ranging from eye exams to surgical procedures. Through the company's subsidiary Eyefinity, which, unlike VSP is a for-profit entity, the company provides independent doctors a full range of services via the Internet. The company also operates Sight for Students, a program that provides eye exams and eye-

glasses to low-income, uninsured children. VSP has 21,000 corporate and business clients.

ORIGINS

What became the largest eye-care insurer in the country began with more modest intentions during the mid-1950s. In 1954, two organizations were formed, the Alameda Contra Costa Optometric Society and the Joint Council on Vision Care. One year later, in September, the two entities merged, creating California Vision Services (CVS), the nonprofit eye-care provider that 20 years later became VSP.

The impetus for the formation of CVS was drawn from a group of optometrists in the San Francisco Bay Area, who, with help from the California Optometric Association, decided to offer prepaid vision benefits, an undertaking they launched in a small shopping center in Oakland, California. The effort began as an employee benefits program that drew its first members primarily from labor and management trust funds and school districts, a business concept that was novel and limited in its reach. The novelty of the program offered by the founding group of optometrists held the development of CVS in check to some extent. Organizations and their employees needed to be educated about the concept of prepaid vision care and persuaded to become members. Perhaps more of hindrance to the program's acceptance was the general perception of vision care as a benefit. When discussions of benefit packages were discussed, the topic of eye-care services rarely came up, relegating coverage of eye exams to the backwater of insurance-related discussions. Employers, labor unions, and parties involved in collective bargaining arrangements generally focused first on medical coverage before moving down the line to employee benefits related to death, disability, dental, pharmaceutical, pensions, profit sharing, and vacations. Eye care, if the subject was broached at all, typically was at the end of the line. CVS, in this context, became a champion of vision care coverage, a company with a pioneering mission that was forced to wait for its innovative message to change conventional thought.

The vision plan that debuted under the CVS name and later flourished under the VSP name become a model emulated by other states, but the rise in acceptance of eye-care coverage took decades to take root. Group trusts that derived their power from the Taft-Hartley Labor Act and other union-sponsored, collective bargaining arrangements helped foster the inclusion of vision care coverage during CVS's first decades in business, making the coverage a more common facet of the benefit packages offered by *Fortune* 500 companies. CVS during this period celebrated its development with the achievements that represented the milestones charting its development from a Bay Area program, to a statewide program, and eventually into the national giant it later became.

Led by its founding president, Bernhardt N. Thal, a doctor of optometry, CVS initially focused on labor unions to promote its prepaid program for eye care. Within three years of its founding, the organization offered itself to the American Optometric Association, but the national body perceived no need for an entity of CVS's ilk and declined to purchase the company. Undeterred by the lack of interest, CVS pursued its own path, signing its first multistate contract in 1958. Under the terms of the agreement with the Masters, Mates, and Pilots Local 90 Union, CVS paid claims in the port cities of Boston, New York, Philadelphia, New Orleans, Galveston, Seattle, and Portland. The next important contract was signed seven years later after numerous

smaller agreements added to the legitimacy of the company's concept. In 1965, CVS signed a contract with the Western Conference of Teamsters, who agreed to include the company's vision care program in its benefits package. With the acceptance of its program exceeding initial expectations, CVS was forced to move to larger headquarters by the end of the decade. In 1968, the company moved its central offices from Oakland to Sacramento, where its operations would be based into the 21st century.

By the time CVS moved to larger quarters in Sacramento, the company was beginning to see itself as more than just a northern California organization. By the late 1960s, efforts were underway to expand beyond California's borders. These efforts would pay off during the 1970s, a decade of significant maturation for CVS. In 1968, the company signed an agreement with Hawaii for future work in the state. In 1974, it assumed control over the administration of Nevada Vision Service, an arrangement that soon led to CVS signing its first client in the state. In 1976, the year CVS officially became VSP, the company widened its operating territory to a four-state area by assuming responsibility for Oregon Vision Service Plan. The decade also included two significant events that broadened its capabilities and its exposure to the vision care market. In 1972, the company opened its own optical laboratory in Sacramento, vertically integrating its operations in a bid to keep its costs down. In later years, the Sacramento lab would produce more than 2,000 pairs of eyeglasses a day. In 1979, under the VSP name, the company signed its first contract with a health maintenance organization (HMO), marking its entry into the managed care market, which represented a major market for VSP at the end of the century. By the end of the 1970s, VSP stood as a rising force in the vision care market, boasting 2.4 million members.

A NATIONAL FORCE TAKING SHAPE IN THE 1980S

VSP completed its first steps toward becoming a multistate insurer during the 1970s. During the 1980s, the company expressed its intention to become a national company, the first time a vision care specialist made a concerted bid to develop a 50-state membership base. VSP made its objective known in 1984, one year after it reached the $100 million mark in revenue. A major expansion and acquisition program was launched in 1984, the year the company created the State Professional Representative program, which consisted of a group of doctors selected from across the country who would advise VSP on issues pertinent to eye care. By this point, VSP's network of professionals included 5,000

KEY DATES

1955: Vision Service Plan is incorporated as California Vision Services.

1968: Company executives begin to explore expansion beyond California's borders.

1972: A wholly owned optometry laboratory is established in Sacramento.

1976: California Vision Services changes its name to Vision Service Plan.

1979: Vision Service Plan signs its first contract with a health maintenance organization.

1984: Vision Service Plan announces its intention to become a national company.

1990: Managed Eyecare is formed to offer complex eye treatment services.

1993: Roger Valine is appointed president and chief executive officer.

1997: Sight for Students, a program aimed at providing vision care to low-income children, is launched.

2000: A for-profit, Internet-based subsidiary, Eyefinity, is formed.

2004: Revenues surpass $2 billion, a record high.

doctors, a number that would increase as the company began its march across the country, establishing a presence in new regions by either opening its own offices or gaining entry into markets through acquisitions. The expansion program touched off in 1985, when a regional office was opened to serve New York, New Jersey, Connecticut, and Rhode Island. The following year, an office was opened in Atlanta, which served as the company's southeastern hub for a six-state region. In 1987, St. Louis became the center of the company's business in the Midwest, presiding over a six-state area. The following year, VSP merged with Mid-Atlantic Vision Service Plan, which spread the company's presence into Washington, D.C., and neighboring Virginia and Maryland. After adding an office in Wisconsin in 1989, VSP ended the decade with eight million members, more than three times its membership base at the start of the decade.

VSP's expansion during the 1980s represented the most prolific period of growth in the company's history, but the record was soon broken. During the 1990s, the company's expansion efforts, in terms of both geography and the breadth of its services, made it the clear leader in the country, fulfilling the mission articulated in 1984.

The company had nearly 1,000 employees when it unleashed its most ambitious expansion program, but one employee, the 30th employee hired by the company, stood out from the rest, earning much of the credit for the formidable sway it held at the beginning of the 21st century. Roger Valine was hired as a management trainee in 1973, the year after he earned an undergraduate degree in sociology from California State University. Valine, who was raised on a 40-acre farm near Sacramento, was named president and chief executive officer in January 1993, taking the helm as major efforts to expand the company already were underway. In 1990, the company created a program named Managed Eyecare that encompassed the spectrum of vision care services, including complex eye treatment that required surgery. The year also marked the establishment of a regional office in Seattle that governed a four-state territory in the Pacific Northwest. In 1992, the company formed a subsidiary named Altair Eyewear, which was created to sell private-label frames to VSP's network of doctors.

VALINE GUIDING VSP TO ITS 50TH ANNIVERSARY

Valine used the momentum built up during the 1980s and the first years of the 1990s and guided VSP toward greater heights. One of the most important achievements of his tenure occurred at the beginning of his term, when VSP merged with Northeast Vision Service Plan and Midwest Vision Service Plan, the second and third largest eye-care insurers in the country. The merger grew out of joint venture agreements among the three companies that preceded Valine's appointment as president and chief executive officer. The three companies had joined forces to provide coverage to large national corporations that operated in numerous locations, leaving their employees scattered across the country. Midwest Vision Service Plan, which had one million members in a two-state territory, was acquired first, joining VSP's operation in 1993, the same year the company moved to the suburbs of Sacramento, settling into a $20 million headquarters facility in Rancho Cordova. The deal with Northeast Vision Service Plan was completed in early 1994, adding 1.4 million members in an eight-state region. Combined, the two transactions added $72 million in annual revenue.

When Valine took control of VSP, the company was coming off a year in which it generated $443 million in revenue. The company provided insurance to ten million members in 38 states during the year and extended its coverage to all 50 states by early 1994, when revenues eclipsed $500 million. "Our goal," Valine said in a May 23, 1994 interview with *Business Journal Serving Greater Sacramento,* "is to become a national company." The company already operated in every state by the time Valine made his declaration, but the bulk of its business, even after years of geographic expansion, was derived from California. VSP relied on revenues from California for nearly 70 percent of its business volume, a percentage that would decrease as Valine fleshed out the company's presence in other regions and made VSP more of a well-rounded, national company.

Considerable progress was made during Valine's first five years in charge. After the 1997 launch of Sight for Students, a charity that provided free eye-care services to underprivileged children, Valine's five-year anniversary as chief executive officer coincided with revenues surpassing the $1 billion mark for the first time, a total drawn from the company's 25 million members. By the end of the 1990s, membership stood at 27 million, with enrollment having more than tripled during the decade.

VSP entered the 21st century as the industry giant, providing coverage to 12 percent of Americans and 31 percent of Californians. The company formed a new e-commerce subsidiary named Eyefinity in 2000 to provide independent doctors services over the Internet. "We started to talk to doctors regarding utilization of the Internet three or four years ago," Valine explained in a September 22, 2000 interview with the *Sacramento Business Journal.* "We have worked very hard on incentives to come on the Internet because it saves us money. A customer-service call by phone costs a few dollars, while it costs a few cents to go on the Internet."

Aside from branching out into new areas to stimulate growth—Eyefinity was established as a for-profit entity—Valine continued to look to the company's primary business for growth opportunities. Despite VSP's ever expanding membership rolls, only 25 percent of U.S. businesses offered eye-care benefits to their employees. Such data fueled Valine's confidence that VSP would continue to grow well into the future. In 2004, when the company's revenues eclipsed $2 billion, Valine projected that the company would generate $3 billion in revenues by 2012. As VSP celebrated the end of its first half-century of business in 2005, Valine's forecast boded well for the company, but the goal, if reached, was to be met without Valine occupying his posts as president and chief executive officer. Valine, who had orchestrated a fourfold increase in revenues during his first dozen years, announced his intention to retire by the end of the decade. VSP, as it made its way through its second half-century of business, would have to navigate its course without the capable leadership of one of its most influential executives.

Jeffrey L. Covell

PRINCIPAL SUBSIDIARIES

Eyefinity; Altair Eyewear.

PRINCIPAL COMPETITORS

EyeMed Vision Care L.L.C.; Cole Managed Vision; Davis Vision, Inc.; PacifiCare Health Systems, Inc.; Spectera, Inc.

FURTHER READING

Clark, Shelby, "Vision Service Plan Has Its Eyes on More Growth," *Business Journal Serving Greater Sacramento,* May 23, 1994, p. 17.

Kalb, Loretta, "Rancho Cordova, Calif., CEO Runs Vision Service Plan on Respect, Innovation," *Sacramento Bee,* June 13, 2004.

Pulley, Mike, "Vision Plan Grows to Dominate," *Business Journal Serving Greater Sacramento,* March 22, 1993, p. 1.

Roberson, Kathy, "VSP Expands HQ," *Sacramento Business Journal,* April 16, 1999, p. 1.

———, "VSP Expands in Rancho," *Sacramento Business Journal,* April 27, 2001, p. 5.

———, "Vision Service Plan's Growth Prompts Building," *Business Journal Serving Greater Sacramento,* April 29, 1996, p. 8.

Volcom, Inc.

1740 Monrovia Avenue
Costa Mesa,
California 92627
U.S.A.
Telephone: (949) 646-2175
Fax: (949) 999-1253
Web site: http://www.volcom.com

Public Company
Incorporated: 1991 as Stone Boardwear, Inc.
Employees: 171
Sales: $113.2 million (2004)
Stock Exchanges: NASDAQ
Ticker Symbol: VLCM
NAIC: 315223 Men's and Boys' Cut and Sew Shirt (Except Work Shirt) Manufacturing; 315224 Men's and Boys' Cut and Sew Trouser, Slack, and Jean Manufacturing; 315228 Men's and Boys' Cut and Sew Other Outerwear Manufacturing; 315232 Women's and Girls' Cut and Sew Blouse and Shirt Manufacturing; 315239 Women's and Girls' Cut and Sew Other Outerwear Manufacturing; 315299 All Other Cut and Sew Apparel Manufacturing; 315991 Hat, Cap, and Millinery Manufacturing; 315992 Glove and Mitten Manufacturing; 315999 Other Apparel Accessories and Other Apparel Manufacturing; 339920 Sporting and Athletic Goods Manufacturing; 512110; Motion Picture and Video Production; 512120 Motion Picture and Video Distribution; 512220 Integrated Record Production/Distribution; 448110 Men's Clothing Stores; 448120 Women's Clothing Stores

∎∎∎

Volcom, Inc. makes popular clothing and accessories for snowboarders, skateboarders, and surfers. The firm's wares are sold in the United States at independent surf and skate shops or chains including Pacific Sunwear and Zumiez, and in 40 countries abroad through licensing agreements. Volcom also operates a small Los Angeles retail outlet and music and film divisions, and sponsors board sports teams and professional athletes including surfer Bruce Irons, skateboarder Geoff Rowley, and snowboarder Shaun White. Cofounder and CEO Richard Woolcott and his father, chairman Rene Woolcott, own a sizable minority stake in the company, which went public in June 2005.

BEGINNINGS

Volcom was founded in 1991 by Richard Woolcott and Tucker Hall to make clothing for surfers and snowboarders. Both were avid participants in the sports, Woolcott having joined the Quiksilver, Inc. surfing team at 14 and later gone into marketing and producing videos for the clothing manufacturer. After breaking his neck on a Quiksilver-sponsored surfing trip to Mexico he spent a year slowly recovering, and then decided to study business at Pepperdine University, where he earned a B.S.

In March 1991 Woolcott and Hall went snowboarding at Tahoe, and the experience had an unexpect-

COMPANY PERSPECTIVES

We are an innovative designer, marketer and distributor of premium quality young men's and young women's clothing, accessories and related products under the Volcom brand name. Our products, which include t-shirts, fleece, bottoms, tops, jackets, boardshorts, denim and outerwear, incorporate distinctive combinations of fashion, functionality and athletic performance. We were founded in 1991 by Richard Woolcott and Tucker Hall in Orange County, California, the epicenter of boardsports culture. Since that time, Richard has led a committed and talented management team to create one of the leading boardsport brands in the world.

edly profound impact on both of them. Shortly afterwards Woolcott quit his job, and he and the already unemployed Hall decided to found a company that would make t-shirts for boarders, while they surfed and snowboarded on the side. To start the business they borrowed $5,000 from Woolcott's father Rene, who headed investment firm Clarenden House Advisors. The company would officially be called Stone Boardwear, Inc., and use the brand name Volcom.

Working with McElroy Designs, they created a distinctive diamond-shaped "Volcom Stone" logo to use on the company's products. Knowing little about the clothing business, they stuck to t-shirts at first, but added shorts after a year. The tiny firm was headquartered in Woolcott's bedroom in Newport Beach, California, and sales were handled out of Tucker's place in Huntington Beach. At first they were only marginally engaged by the business and spent much of their time on boarding trips, and as a result sales for the first year totaled just $2,600.

As funds began to run dry, the senior Woolcott decided to step in. As Richard Woolcott later recounted to *Transworld Business* magazine, one Saturday morning he got a call from his father, who said, "Son, looking at your numbers, if you don't get your act together, you're going to be out of business in less than three months. I'm not going to help you or bail you out. So you better figure it out." The company had no inventory and was basically out of money, and the suddenly chastened duo began working to get it back on track. As they took the business more seriously, its financial picture began to improve.

In 1993 Volcom released a film called *Alive We Ride*. The company's first video production featured footage of surfers, skaters, and snowboarders from around the world, and a new unit, Veeco Productions, was formed to market it. Two years later another new division, Volcom Entertainment, was founded to produce music CDs. By this time the firm had begun sponsoring surfing and skateboarding teams, as well as an amateur surfing competition called the Volcom Starfish Summer Surf Series, and its clothing was being sold in a number of independent surf shops in Southern California.

In 1995 Volcom designer Neil Harrison introduced the Featured Artist series of t-shirts, which were printed in four colors and used imaginative designs. They would go on to become one of the company's most popular offerings. The next year saw Volcom reach an agreement for its clothing to be produced and sold in Europe under license by an outside firm, which would pay a royalty on each item. In 1997 the company bought a 49 percent stake in the licensee, Volcom Europe, and also reached an agreement for another firm to make and sell its clothing in Australia and New Zealand. Volcom subsequently acquired a small stake in the latter as well.

PACIFIC SUNWEAR ADDING VOLCOM SHIRTS IN 1997

In 1997 major boardwear retailer Pacific Sunwear (PacSun) began selling Volcom's t-shirts at a few of its stores. They sold well, and several months later PacSun added the company's shorts, and then began stocking Volcom clothing at all of its outlets. At the retailer's urging, in the fall of 1998 Volcom also introduced lines of cargo pants, jeans, and other trousers, and the company's sales soon shot through the roof.

By 1999 Volcom, whose motto was "Youth against establishment," had become one of the hottest brands among boarders, ranking in the top five "coolest t-shirts" in the boarding category, according to the 1999 BoardTrac WaveRider Survey. The firm's primary market continued to be Southern California, though its products were also sold in other areas where board sports were popular.

Volcom's staff came largely from the board sports community, and its distribution facility had a half-pipe skateboard ramp onsite. Promotional efforts were similarly unconventional. The firm used tactics including sending a battered sailboat emblazoned with the Volcom logo up and down the beach during a surfing competition, or having a large Volcom-sponsored recreational vehicle "break down" in traffic in front of the U.S. Open of Surfing after which staffers emerged to hand out Volcom gear until the police arrived. Company

KEY DATES

1991: Richard Woolcott and Tucker Hall found Stone Boardwear, Inc. to make t-shirts.

1993: Video division Veeco Productions is launched with film Alive We Ride.

1995: Featured Artist t-shirts debut, music unit Volcom Entertainment is formed.

1996: European licensing deal starts firm's foreign expansion.

1997: Pacific Sunwear begins distributing Volcom clothing.

1999: Firm moves into 86,000-square-foot headquarters/distribution facility.

2002: First company-owned store opens in Los Angeles.

2005: Initial public stock offering brings firm nearly $80 million.

President Woolcott even got into the act, showing up at a skateboard competition dressed in a banana costume.

In 1999 Volcom's surging sales made it necessary to move from the 10,000-square-foot space it had been sharing with several other businesses into an 86,000-square-foot site that had most recently been home to Woolcott's former employer, Quiksilver, Inc. The new location would serve as a combined headquarters/distribution facility, as most of the company's clothing was manufactured in such countries as China and India and only t-shirt screen-printing was done in the United States.

In 2000 Volcom's Totally Crustaceous Tour debuted. An international surfing competition that allowed amateurs to participate without a registration fee, it also included music performances and many product giveaways. For the year, the firm recorded sales of $36.6 million and a profit of $1.5 million.

In early 2001 Volcom signed a deal with MCA Records to create a new joint venture record label. The company's music activities also included sponsoring a stage on the annual Vans Warped Tour, which was popular with the boarding crowd.

VOLCOM STORE OPENING: 2002

The year 2002 saw Volcom open a retail outlet in Los Angeles, which would carry clothing, music, videos, and limited-edition items including a boxed set of jeans and a t-shirt that was priced at $110. The 1,200-square-foot store on La Brea Boulevard was set up in consultation with Billy Stade, owner of a sportswear retailer that sold Volcom products, and it quickly became popular with the young, mostly male surfer crowd. Several other Volcom stores had earlier been licensed to operate overseas at surfing hotspots in France and Indonesia.

As the company grew, its management took pains to ensure that its clothing never reached mass marketers, which could cause it to lose its status as an elite brand. Volcom's clothes were seen by boarders as "core," or a part of the hardcore boarding lifestyle, but if they started to be seen on "wannabe" surfers, the party would soon be over. Hot brands including Jimmy-Z and Mossimo had expanded into mass-market outlets and quickly lost their cachet among their primary audience, then found it difficult to regain momentum or lost it altogether as a result. To steer clear of such problems, Volcom limited sales to independent surf and skateboard shops, such select surfwear chains as PacSun, and such high-end retailers as Nordstrom.

The firm continued to operate in a grass-roots way, using its own 26-person design team and doing advertising in-house to keep it consistent with the look of its clothing.

Founder, President, and CEO Richard Woolcott (known to many as "Wooly") showed little sign that he was now a successful corporate executive, and continued to live in a trailer near his favorite surfing spot, though he was drawing a salary of several hundred thousand dollars per year. Partner Tucker Hall had retired (though he retained a small stake in the firm), and Rene Woolcott served as board chair, with father and son owning controlling interest in the business. Despite the idiosyncratic nature of the company's founder and the firm's anti-establishment image, Volcom was known within the industry as one of the best-managed firms of its type, with a strong reputation for on-time shipments and a well-regarded ability to build and protect its brand.

With sales continuing to grow dramatically, in 2004 Volcom recorded a net profit of $24.4 million on revenues of $113.2 million, a jump of 49 percent from the year before. Menswear was outselling women's by a factor of close to two to one, and top customer PacSun accounted for 27 percent of total sales. Volcom products were now available in nearly 3,000 stores, representing 1,100 separate clients. Some 85 percent of sales took place in the United States, with Canada and Japan accounting for most of the remainder.

VOLCOM GOES PUBLIC: 2005

After reaching a certain point in their growth many companies like Volcom sold out to larger firms such as

Nike or Quiksilver to help fund expansion, but rather than follow this path Woolcott decided to go public. The money raised would go to pay $20 million owed to existing shareholders; improve infrastructure, marketing, and advertising; and to start bringing the company's foreign sales under its own control. The license to sell Volcom goods in Europe expired at the end of 2006, and $4 million would be dedicated to setting up the company's own operations there. Licenses for other foreign territories would end over the next decade as well, and the firm planned to take those back when they became available.

Volcom's June 29 initial public offering (IPO) was a huge success, with the share price jumping from the offering amount of $19 to $26.77 by day's end. The company took in nearly $80 million for 4.2 million shares, with another 500,000 sold by existing shareholders. A few months later existing shareholders sold another five million shares for $178 million at an offering price of $34. After the IPO the 39-year-old Woolcott and his father would continue to hold a large minority stake in the firm, which had officially become known as Volcom, Inc. before it went public.

The year 2005 also saw the premiere of a new film from Veeco Productions, The Bruce Movie, which featured Volcom-sponsored surfer Bruce Irons. After a free public screening at the firm's headquarters it was made available on DVD. The company offered a total of 14 DVDs and about 40 music releases by such acts as Pepper, Single Frame, and ASG, but entertainment products were a small part of the company's mix and accounted for less than 5 percent of revenues.

Volcom's clothing line included a wide range of men's and women's apparel and accessories, ranging from t-shirts and shorts to socks, underwear, jeans, sweaters, jackets, hats, belts, wallets, luggage, and logo items including keychains and even a ping-pong set. The firm continued to sponsor skateboard, snowboard, and surfing athletes and teams, and some products were endorsed with the names of stars including surfer Irons, skateboarder Geoff Rowley, and snowboarder Shaun White. Growth continued to be strong during its first months as a public company, and in 2006 the firm began laying plans to open several more stores, though a large retail presence was not foreseen.

In just 15 years Volcom, Inc. had grown from a bedroom-based t-shirt company into one of the hottest clothing brands in the surf/skate/snowboard market.

Though now publicly owned, it was continuing to follow its own path under the leadership of cofounder Richard Woolcott, and further growth looked certain.

Frank Uhle

PRINCIPAL SUBSIDIARIES

Volcom Entertainment; Veeco Productions.

PRINCIPAL COMPETITORS

Quiksilver, Inc.; Billabong International Ltd.; Burton Snowboards; Stussy, Inc.; Pacific Sunwear of California, Inc.

FURTHER READING

Bailey, Lee, "Volcom Files for Public Offering," *DNR*, May 9, 2005, p. 1A.

Bellantonio, Jennifer, "Apparel Maker Volcom Opening Hip Los Angeles Store," *Orange County Business Journal*, October 28, 2002, p. 6.

———, "Retail Slows, But Analysts Stay Hot on Volcom," *Orange County Business Journal*, October 24, 2005, p. 1.

———, "Volcom's 'Wooly': Mixing Tequila, Wall Street," *Orange County Business Journal*, May 9, 2005, p. 1.

Deemer, Susan, "Volcom Moving to Quiksilver's Costa Mesa Site," *Orange County Business Journal*, May 10, 1999, p. 1.

Greenfield, Karl Taro, "Killer Profits in Velcro Valley," *Time*, January 25, 1999, p. 50.

Koteen, Casey, "Inside the Volcom Stone: A Rare Look into the World of Volcom and its Founder, Richard Woolcott," *Transworld Business*, October 12, 2004.

Luna, Nancy, "Volcom Makes Millions," *Orange County Register*, July 1, 2005, p. 1.

Montgomery, Tiffany, "Volcom Files for Stock Offering Monday," *Orange County Register*, May 2, 2005, p. 1.

———, "Volcom Stock Up 79 Percent Since June IPO," *Orange County Register*, August 9, 2005, p. 1.

———, "Volcom Thinking Globally with IPO Plans," *Orange County Register*, May 3, 2005, p. 1.

Price, Shawn, "Volcom Puts Fun, Money into Its Surf Tour," *Orange County Register*, May 18, 2005, p. 1.

Sage, Alexandria, "Volcom Shuns Diversification, Hews to Edgy Vibe," *Reuters News*, September 9, 2005.

"The Seven Most Influential People in the Surf Industry," *Transworld Business*, April 28, 2004.

vtech

VTech Holdings Ltd.

— ● —

23/F Block 1-Tai Ping Ind Centre
57 Ting Kok Road, Tai Po
Hong Kong,
Hong Kong
Telephone: +852 2680 1000
Fax: +852 2680 1300
Web site: http://www.vtech.com

Public Company
Incorporated: 1976 as Video Technology Ltd.
Employees: 20,700
Sales: $1.02 billion (2005)
Stock Exchanges: Hong Kong London OTC (ADRs)
Ticker Symbol: VTKHY
NAIC: 334111 Electronic Computer Manufacturing; 334119 Other Computer Peripheral Equipment Manufacturing; 334210 Telephone Apparatus Manufacturing; 334310 Audio and Video Equipment Manufacturing

■ ■ ■

VTech Holdings Ltd. is a world-leading manufacturer of cordless and corded telephones, electronic learning products, and other consumer electronics products. Based in Hong Kong, VTech produces "mini-PCs," gaming consoles, and other toys and products targeting the 3- to 12-year-old market. Among the company's products are the Smart Start toys, and the V-Smile game console for young children, launched to great commercial success in 2004. VTech also has announced its plans to release a console developed for children under three years of age in 2006. In support of its products, VTech holds licensing agreements for a number of major children's characters from Disney, Marvel, Brainy Baby, Nickelodeon, Sesame Street, HIT Entertainment, and Joester Loria - American Greetings. The company is one of the world's largest producers of cordless telephones, marketed under its own brand name, as well as the AT&T brand; the company is also a major original equipment manufacturer (OEM) for brands such as Sony and Phillips. The company launched a new Internet-based VoIP (voice-over-Internet-protocol) telephone in partnership with Vonage in 2005. In addition to telephones, the company produces pagers, personal digital assistants, e-mail readers, and modems, as well as set-top satellite television devices. Telephones accounted for nearly 60 percent of the group's revenues of $1.02 billion in 2005, while educational products added 27.5 percent. The North American market is the company's primary market, representing nearly 61 percent of sales, compared with nearly 33 percent in Europe. VTech is led by founder, Chairman, and CEO Allan Wong and is listed on both the Hong Kong and London Stock Exchanges.

CHILDREN'S ELECTRONICS IN THE 1980S

VTech was founded in 1976 as Video Technology Ltd. in Hong Kong by Allan Wong, an electrical engineer with a master's degree from the University of Wisconsin. Wong began his professional career as an engineer for electronics giant NCR, before leaving to found his own company. VTech, with just 40 employees, began developing its first electronics products, using

COMPANY PERSPECTIVES

Mission: VTech's mission is to be the most cost effective designer and manufacturer of innovative, high quality consumer electronics products and to distribute them to markets worldwide in the most efficient manner.

microprocessors to produce small-scale versions of the video arcade games just becoming popular at that time. By 1978, VTech, as the company came to be called, had launched its first product, a handheld copy of the original video game, "Pong."

The company quickly expanded its electronics business, in particular by acting as an OEM for others. From the start, VTech targeted the international market, and especially the North American market, where demand for the new low-cost electronics goods arriving from the Far East ran high in the late 1970s and early 1980s.

An important milestone for the company came in 1981, when U.S. department store giant Sears commissioned the company to develop an electronic children's educational toy. VTech responded with the Lesson One, designed to teach basic reading and math skills. The toy was a big success for Sears, and established the VTech name as a pioneer in the children's electronics sector.

VTech's children's toy development benefited from the company's expansion into the personal computer (PC) market as well. In 1981, the company released its first computer-hybrid product, the CreatiVision. Soon after, the company introduced its first computer, the Laser 110. By 1983, the company introduced a more robust computer, the Laser 200 series. The new series established the company on the OEM computer market, and Laser 200 computers were soon sold worldwide under a variety of brand names, including Texet, Salora, and Dick Smith in Australia and New Zealand.

VTech caught onto Apple's fast-rising coattails, releasing the Laser 3000 in 1985. That computer represented a first attempt to clone the highly popular Apple IIc. With the launch of the Laser 128 in 1988, VTech succeeded in releasing a computer that was nearly 100 percent compatible with the Apple IIc. The company later won the lawsuit challenge by Apple, proving that it succeeded in developing the Laser 128 through its own reverse engineering efforts, without violating any of Apple's patents and copyrights.

Parallel to its attempt to produce Apple clones, the company also produced IBM-based PCs. By the late

1980s, while continuing to produce computers under a variety of brand names, including as a private-label producer for Sears and other department stores, the company also had begun marketing its PCs under the VTech brand name. In the meantime, the company had become an early entrant into the market for satellite receivers, producing its first receiver in 1984.

REVISING THE PRODUCT MIX IN THE 1990S

VTech went public during the 1980s, listing its stock on the Hong Kong Stock Exchange in order to fuel its expansion. While the company continued producing electronic learning aids and satellite receivers, the PC market became its main target. In 1988, the company became one of the first to shift its production to the Chinese mainland, opening production facilities in the Guangdong province. Taking advantage of the low wage scale in China, VTech set out to conquer the global PC market.

VTech had early success in Japan, where it became a market leader in the early 1990s. The North American market provided a strong growth area for the company as well, where it acquired the rights to the Leading Technology brand name. VTech began plans to expand its PC sales, targeting an entry into the European market. As part of that effort, the company delisted its stock from the Hong Kong Stock Exchange, and instead launched a new public offering in 1991, placing its shares on the London Stock Exchange as well.

The company's computer sales, under the VTech, Laser, and Leading Technology brand names, depended primarily on mass-market retailers. Yet the company became caught up in a brutal price war, and especially in a battle for shelf space, at the beginning of the 1990s. As it began experiencing difficulties getting its PCs on stores' shelves, VTech attempted to convert its PC sales to a direct sales model similar to that of Dell. Yet the company proved unable to make its mark in that sales channel. With sales tumbling, VTech attempted to restructure its money-losing PC division in 1993, announcing that it was abandoning sales of complete branded computer systems and instead planned to produce computer components for the OEM market.

By 1997, however, VTech was forced to abandon this operation, too, and in that year the company sold off its computer components division in a management buyout joined by a number of its OEM customers. VTech retained only a small, Hong-Kong focused PC division.

Elsewhere, the company operations also were struggling into the early 1990s. The satellite receiver market

KEY DATES

1976: Allan Wong founds Video Technology Ltd. in Hong Kong.

1978: The company releases its first product, a portable video game system.

1981: The company launches its first personal computer product; the first electronic learning aid is developed for Sears.

1988: A production plant is established in Guangdong province in mainland China.

1991: Production of cordless telephones is launched.

1997: The company abandons the personal computer market.

2000: The company acquires Lucent's telephone production unit and the rights to the AT&T brand name.

2001: The company shuts down Lucent's plant in Mexico and shifts production to expanded plants in China.

2004: The company launches the V.Smile game console for three- to seven-year-olds.

2005: The company launches the handheld V. Smile console; a VoIP telephone is launched in partnership with Vonage.

had failed to take off, in part because of delays in the launch of satellite television services. VTech ended its satellite receiver production in 1993. The company also had attempted to enter the market for cellular telephone handsets in the early 1990s, but was forced to abandon that production by 1995.

ANSWERING THE PHONE IN THE NEW CENTURY

VTech's problems in these product areas were more than offset by the company's entry into the production of corded and cordless telephones in the early 1990s. Combining its experience in radio frequency technology gained through its production of satellite receivers, and its electronics expertise, VTech launched its first 900 Mhz cordless telephone in 1991.

The new technology significantly increased the roaming distance of cordless telephones, as well as offering higher-quality reception. At first, the company produced telephones primarily for the OEM market, producing telephones for brand names such as AT&T, Radio Shack, Sony, and Panasonic through the 1990s.

In the mid-1990s, however, the company began a push to establish sales of its own line of higher-end, VTech-branded telephones. Toward the end of the decade, the company complemented these models with a more expensive range, becoming one of the first to break the $99 price barrier.

Amid the economic crises that swept the Asian region in the late 1990s, VTech appeared to be one of the few Hong Kong-based companies to post rising sales and rising profits. The company's focus on two core markets, cordless telephones and electronic learning aids, coupled with the fact that the Asian markets accounted for less than 5 percent of its total sales, shielded the group from the disastrous financial climate at home. By 1998, at the height of the crisis, VTech sales had soared to $842 million, with profits climbing to $69 million.

Buoyed by its success, VTech began adding new products to its mix in the late 1990s and early 2000s, such as pagers, personal digital assistants, e-mail readers, and modems. Nonetheless, cordless phone sales continued to drive the company's growth through the end of the decade. By the late 1990s, the company had added OEM production for a number of the United States' regional Bell carriers, which had been allowed to begin marketing telephones under their own brands for the first time since the breakup of AT&T.

That company, or, more accurately, the AT&T brand formed the basis of the next expansion move. In 2000, VTech reached agreement with Lucent, which had inherited the rights to the AT&T brand, to purchase Lucent's own telephone manufacturing unit, including a plant in Mexico, some 4,800 employees, as well as exclusive rights to the AT&T brand for the next ten years. Under the agreement, VTech paid $133 million for the deal. The addition of Lucent's operations boosted the company's sales past $1 billion, and gave it more than 50 percent of the entire U.S. cordless phone market.

VTech quickly rolled out a new line of AT&T-branded telephones, reserving its VTech brand for lower-priced telephones. The company also turned its expanded production capacity toward a drive to move the VTech brand into the European cordless phone market, unveiling a new line of DECT-based telephones for the United Kingdom and Germany.

Yet the Lucent deal quickly turned sour. Soon after taking over Lucent's operations, VTech discovered that it also had been overloaded with Lucent's inventory. (VTech sued Lucent for $170 million, claiming it had concealed the extent of the telephone manufacturing operation's problems.) VTech, which also was struggling with quality control issues, made its problems even worse when it began marketing its low-priced telephones under the AT&T brand as well.

VTech's woes were compounded by the economic slump in its core markets in the United States and Europe. By 2001, VTech had slipped into losses for the first time in its history. In that year, VTech announced that it had decided to shut down the plant in Mexico, lay off some 4,500 workers, and transfer all of its telephone production to its newly expanded production plants in mainland China.

VTech restructured its product mix, shifting its focus to higher-margin items. In 2002, the company achieved a new success, becoming the first in the U.S. market to launch a new generation of 5.8 GHz cordless telephones. The company also renegotiated the terms of its AT&T brand agreement, securing the exclusive rights to the brand in China, and non-exclusive rights to market AT&T branded telephones in Europe and the Latin American region.

VTech returned to profitability into the mid-2000s, rebuilding its sales past $1 billion by 2005. Although the company's telephone production continued to account for nearly 60 percent of its sales, the company owed much of its renewed health to its electronic learning aid division. Through the early 2000s, the company had come under increasing pressure from competitors, particularly with the rising use of video game consoles in its core youth market. In August 2004, the company countered with its own game console, dubbed a "TV Learning System" called the V.Smile. Targeting the three- to seven-year-old market, the V.Smile featured licensing agreements with Disney, Marvel, Warner Brothers, Hit Entertainment, and others. The console became a huge success.

VTech quickly moved to capitalize on the V.Smile's success, releasing a new handheld console in 2005. In that year, as well, the company announced to some controversy that it intended to release a new console targeting children under three years of age in 2006. In addition, in 2005, VTech unveiled a new telephone, in partnership with U.S. provider Vonage, providing VoIP capability. As it approached its 30th anniversary, VTech had positioned itself as a worldwide leader in its two core product categories.

M. L. Cohen

PRINCIPAL SUBSIDIARIES

Dongguan VTech Electronics Industries (China); Dongguan VTech Electronics Telecommunication Industries (China); VTech (China) Trading Ltd.; VTech (Dongguan) Electronics and Communications Ltd. (China); VTech (OEM), Inc. (U.S.A.); VTech Communications Limited (Hong Kong); VTech Communications Ltd. (U.K.); VTech Communications, Inc. (U.S.A.); VTech de Mexico Reynosa S.A.; VTech Electronics (Hong Kong) Ltd.; VTech Electronics Europe B.V. (Netherlands); VTech Electronics Europe GmbH (Germany); VTech Electronics Europe PLC (U.K.); VTech Electronics Europe S.A.S. (France); VTech Electronics Europe S.L. (Spain); VTech Electronics Limited (Hong Kong); VTech Electronics North America, L.L.C. (U.S.A.); VTech Holdings Limited (Hong Kong); VTech Telecom, L.L.C. (U.S.A.); VTech Telecommunications Canada Ltd.; VTech Telecommunications Limited (Hong Kong).

FURTHER READING

"Allan Wong: Toy Story," *Businessweek,* January 11, 1999.

Doebele, Justin, "Good-bye, Good Times," *Forbes,* May 28, 2001.

Lewis, Peter, "Let (Cordless) Freedom Ring," *Fortune,* August 22, 2005, p. 120.

Serant, Claire, "Vtech Prepares for OEM Windfall—Will Double Size of China Plant in Response to Growing Demand," *EBN,* March 19, 2001, p. 66.

Silberg, Lurie, "Fueling a Brand," *HFN The Weekly Newspaper for the Home Furnishing Network,* October 9, 1995, p. 129.

Tanzer, Andrew, "The Vtech Phenomenon," *Forbes,* October 19, 1998, p. 88.

"VTech Develops Handheld Console for Pre-Teens," *Marketing,* April 20, 2005, p. 6.

"V-Tech Plans Controversial Games Console for Toddlers," *Marketing Week,* November 17, 2005, p. 15.

"VTech to Shift Mexico Production to China," *EBN,* April 2, 2001, p. 88.

Youbet.com, Inc.

5901 De Soto Avenue
Woodland Hills, California 91367
U.S.A.
Telephone: (818) 668-2100
Toll Free: (888) 968-2388
Fax: (818) 668-2101
Web site: http://www.youbet.com

Public Company
Incorporated: 1987 as PC Totes, Inc.
Employees: 81
Sales: $65.2 million (2004)
Stock Exchanges: NASDAQ
Ticker Symbol: UBET
NAIC: 713990 All Other Amusement and Recreation
Industries

■ ■ ■

Youbet.com, Inc. is a leading provider of services related to online parimutuel horse race wagering through its web-based application, Youbet Express. Through the company's advanced deposit wagering system, subscribers can place bets on more than 100 domestic and international horse tracks and, on its web site, watch live video and audio feeds of racing events. Youbet.com operates only as an information web site. The state-licensed wagering companies actually place the bets of Youbet.com's customers. Youbet.com generates revenues from transaction fees (typically 5.5 cents for every dollar wagered), subscription fees, and merchandise sales. Through a relationship with TVG, a subsidiary of

Gemstar-TV Guide International, Inc., Youbet.com is able to offer its subscribers the ability to place wagers on TVG's 24-hour horse racing network.

ORIGINS

Youbet.com had a difficult start in the business world, enduring years of heavy financial losses as it attempted to develop a viable technological approach to attract the customers it sought. Like any innovator, the company experienced the hardships of having to blaze its own trail, an effort that at times made the company a spectacle, as it realized the path it was taking was leading it in the wrong direction. The potential rewards were massive, however, providing the incentive for several groups of owners and several different management teams to press ahead despite occasionally discouraging circumstances. Youbet.com was chasing the billions of dollars spent on off-track horse race wagering, a form of horse track betting introduced in the late 1970s that became the driving force of the industry. Off-track betting, which included inter-track simulcasts, off-track betting facilities, and telephone account wagering, grew more than 600 percent between the mid-1980s and the end of the 1990s, becoming the principal source of horse racing's growth and accounting for approximately 80 percent of all horse wagering conducted in the United States.

Youbet.com's mission at the end of the 1990s was to become the first online provider of off-track betting services, but the company's predecessor began pursuing bettors well before the Internet became a hub of com-

COMPANY PERSPECTIVES

Youbet.com, Inc. is a technology company that facilitates live events and is focused on entertainment services, network deployment, and event management via a cross-platform environment. Youbet's mission is to be the premier technology and service provider for interactive wagering worldwide. Our goal is to create a widely accessible interactive race and sports environment, filled with rich and exciting content, and to provide unsurpassed service to our clients.

mercial activity. The company began as PC Totes, Inc., a venture formed in 1987 that became a pioneer in developing wagering systems based on personal computer (PC) technology. PC Totes was one of the first companies in the world to use PC-based technology in a real-time, transaction-processing environment, developing what it referred to as a "totalisator" system to operate the parimutuel wagering systems at horse and dog racing tracks, the only types of sports wagering, aside from jai alai, permitted outside Nevada. The company's system, branded as "PC Tote," included facilities for infield scoreboards, closed circuit television, and various types of customer ticket-issuing systems. PC Tote registered its greatest commercial success at racing facilities in the Far East, but the company behind the system drew the attention of a corporate suitor because of the perceived potential of a PC-based wagering system in off-track applications. By the mid-1990s, PCs were proliferating in the consumer marketplace, presenting a new tool for the public to participate in off-track wagering, which was the theory held by the backers of Continental Embassy Acquisition, Inc. In December 1995, Continental Embassy acquired PC Totes and, concurrent with the acquisition, changed its name to You Bet International, Inc.

You Bet International's first years in business were devoted to developing a product it later abandoned, one of the consequences of playing the part of a pioneer. During the mid-1990s, the Internet had yet to develop into a substantially sized marketplace and the technologies to exploit electronic commerce had yet to mature. The company, using PC Totes' totalisator technology, began developing an online interactive program to permit the transmission of parimutuel wagering information. Dubbed "You Bet!," the software package consisted of a CD-ROM intended to "bring the race track to the desktop" as its 1995 annual filing with the Securities

and Exchange Commission noted. The company hoped to attract dedicated horse racing enthusiasts and customers with only a moderate interest in horse racing who were characterized as PC enthusiasts, endeavoring to obtain a percentage of the $10 billion spent in off-track wagering in 1995.

LAUNCHING THE FIRST PRODUCT IN 1998

Development of the company's You Bet network commenced in mid-1995, beginning what would be a lengthy research and development phase. A final, systemwide test was completed in December 1997, leading to a limited release of You Bet! in January 1998, when 400 subscribers (primarily computer-savvy handicappers) gained access to the network, enabling You Bet International to further its research work and study marketing issues such as pricing and packaging. In July 1998, the network became fully operational. Beginning in February 1999, one month after You Bet International changed its name to Youbet.com, Inc., subscribers were charged a monthly subscription fee of $5.95. To open an account, a potential subscriber contacted Youbet.com through its web site or a toll-free telephone number and opened an account that was used for the customer's subscription fee and to purchase handicapping information. To access the You Bet network, the subscriber installed CD-ROM software, provided by the company at no charge, and, once the software was installed, gained access to simulcasts from horse tracks, as well as real-time handicapping information. The company made money from its network through subscription fees, fees from licensed account wagering entities, and from the sale of handicapping information. In June 1999, after generating $1 million in revenue during the first half of the year, Youbet.com formally ended the developmental stage of its existence and declared the beginning of its operating stage. The company ended the year with $3.7 million in revenue, but it could hardly claim to be financially healthy. Between 1997 and 1999, the company lost more than $40 million, including a $23 million loss in 1999. Youbet.com ended the decade with an accumulated net loss of $62 million.

The end of Youbet.com's development stage and the beginning of its operating stage did not herald a turning point in its financial health. The company would continue to suffer financially in the coming years as it struggled to find a viable business model and tackled technological issues. Youbet.com also faced legal issues, which either were ambiguously defined or undefined as they related to gambling on the Internet. In late 1999, for instance, the company was dealt a stinging blow by the Los Angeles County District Attorney, when

KEY DATES

1987: PC Totes, Inc. is founded.
1995: PC Totes is acquired by another company and changes its name to You Bet International, Inc.
1998: A software package using a CD-ROM is released to the public, enabling computer users to place bets on horse races.
1999: The company changes its name to Youbet .com, Inc.
2001: Youbet.com launches its web-based application, Youbet Express.
2002: Charles Champion is appointed president and chief executive officer.
2004: Youbet.com posts its first annual profit.

authorities forced the company to stop accepting wagers from California residents in what was perceived by industry observers as a strict interpretation of California law. Youbet.com paid $1.3 million to resolve the problem and moved its server equipment from California to Nevada, but the debacle stripped the company of the momentum it had built up since entering its operating stage. "It came at a time when our company was performing well, growing subscribers well, and more and more were beginning to embrace us," said Bob Fell, Youbet.com's chairman and chief executive officer, in a May 12, 2000 interview with the *Baltimore Business Journal.* "In that regard, it was hurtful to us."

Although its financial woes and its battle with Los Angeles authorities painted a bleak picture of Youbet .com at the start of the 21st century, several positive developments offered encouragement to the company's management team. Youbet.com, with approximately 15,000 subscribers by mid-2000, ruled the market for online, horse racing wagering in large part on its own, possessing technology that was regarded as more advanced than its best-known competitor, Television Games Network (TVG), a television-based wagering service owned by Gemstar-TV Guide International. Further, the company had decided to abandon CD-ROMs as the means to access its network, deciding instead to offer access through a web-based application, Youbet Express, launched in March 2001, which promised to spur subscriber growth. In May 2001, a significant agreement between TVG and Youbet.com gave the public even more incentive to subscribe to the company's service. Under the terms of the agreement,

Youbet.com gave TVG, which owned a 24-hour horse racing channel available to cable and satellite customers, the right to buy warrants convertible to a 51 percent stake in Youbet.com. In exchange, Youbet.com gained the rights to broadcast races carried on the TVG network, a deal that added 81 racetracks in 35 states to Youbet.com's service. Before the agreement, Youbet.com had access to roughly half the racetracks in the country. After the agreement, it had access to virtually every racing facility in the country.

The balance between the positive and the negative factors describing Youbet.com's status was tipped decidedly toward the negative as the company entered the new century. In 2000, its losses narrowed to $1.7 million, but inflated the following year to $14.8 million on $6.3 million in revenue. The company ended the year facing insolvency, teetering on the brink of bankruptcy and in desperate need of sweeping changes. Help arrived early in 2002 in the form of new management, ushering in a new era in the company's development that offered the first signs of financial success.

CHAMPION TAKING THE HELM IN 2002

Charles F. Champion arrived at Youbet.com in March 2002, when he was appointed president and chief operating officer. Formerly president and publisher of *Access* magazine and a senior executive at Philadelphia Newspapers, Inc., Champion immediately saw a need for wholesale changes at the beleaguered company. "The problem with Youbet was a cultural problem and a leadership one," he recalled in an October 10, 2005 interview with the *San Fernando Valley Business Journal.*

"It wasn't the engineers. It wasn't the people answering the phone. It was focus at the top," he said. Champion knew he had little time to effect a turnaround (Youbet.com was losing $550,000 per month when he joined the company) and he informed his employees of the urgency at hand, declaring at a companywide meeting that everyone would lose their jobs if the company's condition did not improve within three months. He reigned in expenses by renegotiating contracts and he ordered a marketing study of the company's subscribers. The study convinced Champion to target middle to upscale clientele and abandon the mass-market approach employed by his predecessors. An additional fee was charged, which was credited to a subscriber's account once wagering reached a certain level. "We wanted people to be economically viable for us when they were here," Champion explained in May 16, 2003 interview with *Daily Deal.* "We skew more upscale to the heavier user. Our people are likely to be more sophisticated handicappers; six percent of our customers generate 65 percent of the handle and revenue."

Champion's efforts produced almost immediate results, earning him a promotion to the chief executive officer post in September 2002. By the end of 2002, Youbet.com's revenues reached $25.9 million, a fourfold increase in one year, and its subscriber base doubled to 80,000. The company posted another loss for the year, recording a $9 million deficit, but the overall operation of the company was regarded by industry observers as vastly improved, particularly the company's gains against offshore entities that circumvented U.S. laws on wagering. "It just became easier and cheaper to use us than to go to some offshore operation that you didn't know much about," Champion said in a September 1, 2003 interview with the *San Fernando Valley Business Journal.* "We were more reliable and people knew who they were dealing with."

As Champion continued to refine Youbet.com's operations, his efforts yielded the result for which industry pundits had been clamoring, greatly brightening the company's prospects for the future. After registering another loss in 2003 (the year Champion was elected chairman of the board), Youbet.com posted $1.3 million in net income, the first annual profit in its history. Revenue for the year reached $65.2 million, a 930 percent increase from the total recorded five years earlier. Looking ahead, the company hoped to turn 2004's financial results into a consistent pattern and, as it had expressed interest in since its founding, use its horse racing foundation as a springboard for the gamut of sports wagering, including football, soccer, basketball, baseball, boxing, and golf. One of the most important objectives pursued by Champion was the international expansion of Youbet, which promised to deliver exponential growth to the company. "International represents at least half of our potential moving forward," he explained in his October 10, 2005 interview with the *San Fernando Valley Business Journal.* "Horse racing in the world is at least five times larger than it is in the United States alone. There is also sports out there and casino gaming. International opportunity is very important to us and we're prosecuting it aggressively. Hopefully, you'll see us acquire more international companies like IRG and also some outside horse racing."

Jeffrey L. Covell

PRINCIPAL SUBSIDIARIES

Youbet Oregon, Inc.

PRINCIPAL COMPETITORS

World Gaming PLC; Magna Entertainment Corporation; Penn National Gaming, Inc.

FURTHER READING

Berke, Jonathan, "Youbet.com in American Wagering Race," *Daily Deal,* October 7, 2004.

Biddle, RiShawn, "With Gambling Site on a Roll, Gemstar Deals Suit to Youbet," *Los Angeles Business Journal,* September 22, 2003, p. 50.

Bronstad, Amanda, "Gemstar Deal Gives Internet Firm a Leg Up in Wagering," *Los Angeles Business Journal,* August 27, 2001, p. 34.

"In the Race," *San Fernando Valley Business Journal,* October 10, 2005, p. 23.

Kercheval, Nancy, "Youbet.com Looking Like a Sure Bet," *Daily Record,* May 16, 2003.

Liberman, Noah, "Off-Track Betting Goes to World Wide Web," *Baltimore Business Journal,* May 12, 2000, p. 19.

Martinez, Carlos, "Gambling on Youbet.com Success Beginning to Pay Off," *San Fernando Valley Business Journal,* September 1, 2003, p. 12.

Palmeri, Christopher, "Hold Your Horses!," *Forbes,* April 5, 1999, p. 62.

Thuresson, Michael, "Youbet.com Sees Early Results in Online Horse Racing Gambit," *Los Angeles Business Journal,* March 10, 2003, p. 26.

Zoran Corporation

———————■———————

1390 Kifer Road
Sunnyvale, California 94086
U.S.A.
Telephone: (408) 523-6500
Fax: (408) 523-6501
Web site: http://www.zoran.com

Public Company
Incorporated: 1981
Employees: 1,071
Sales: $378.8 million (2004)
Stock Exchanges: NASDAQ
Ticker Symbol: ZRAN
NAIC: 334413 Semiconductor and Related Device
  Manufacturing; 511210 Software Publishers

■ ■ ■

Zoran Corporation develops integrated circuits and embedded software used in digital videodisc players, digital video recorders, digital cameras, and in high-definition television sets. The company also provides processors and products to serve the multimedia mobile telephone market. Zoran focuses its efforts on technologies that allow customers to connect and to share video and audio files. The company serves original equipment manufacturers (OEMs) such as Apex Digital, Samsung, Sanyo, Sharp, JVC, Sony, and Toshiba. Zoran operates offices in North America, China, England, Germany, Japan, Korea, Taiwan, and Israel. Its subsidiary in Haifa, Israel, is of particular importance, employing many of the engineers that develop the company's products. Zo-

ran derives nearly 60 percent of its sales from DVD hardware products.

ORIGINS

Zoran experienced two distinct periods of development during its first two decades in business, changing its strategic stance to adapt to changing market conditions seen by its founder, Levy Gerzberg. A dual citizen of Israel and the United States, Gerzberg pursued his academic career in both countries, attending the Technion-Israel Institute of Technology in Haifa and Stanford University in Palo Alto, California. In Haifa, he earned a bachelor's degree in electronic engineering and a master's degree in medical electronics, completing his studies in Palo Alto, where he earned a doctorate in electrical engineering. After receiving his Ph.D., Gerzberg stayed at Stanford, becoming the associate director of the university's electronics laboratory.

Gerzberg left the academic world to join the business world in 1981, founding Zoran, "silicon" in Hebrew, in December. From its Santa Clara, California, headquarters, Zoran began the first chapter of its history, using Gerzberg's expertise in digital signal processing to provide sophisticated and expensive semiconductors to industrial and military customers. The company focused on developing digital signal processors (DSPs), chips that allowed devices to translate sound, pictures, and light into strings of binary code, the zeros and ones that formed basic number systems used by computers. Gerzberg found his footing and did well with his debut as an entrepreneur, developing technology that found a receptive audience among companies involved in industrial automation, medical imaging, and manufacturing broadcast equipment. Defense contractors, in particular, favored Zoran's DSPs, using the chips to process analog data from radar images and turn the data into digital form. By the mid-1980s, after venture capitalists had invested nearly $30 million in Zoran, companies such as Magnavox Electronics Systems were designing defense products to use Gerzberg's chips, fueling the growth of the small Santa Clara start-up. Sales, which totaled $2 million in 1986, jumped to more than $10 million the following year and continued to climb until the end of the Cold War forced Gerzberg to reassess his market strategy. With more than half of its annual revenue coming from defense-related work, the company felt the pinch of reduced military spending. The market for DSPs fell into a slump, Zoran's sales wilted, and Gerzberg decided that the company's future lay elsewhere.

A CHANGE IN STRATEGY FOR THE 1990S

Zoran entered the 1990s essentially as a start-up venture, forced to reinvent itself and start over. Gerzberg wanted to use the company's expertise and technology in the consumer market, believing that the ability to convert analog data into digital information might have applications in consumer electronics. The dramatic change in strategy represented a gamble because nothing comparable to DSPs existed in consumer applications at the start of the decade, but Gerzberg sensed that just as vinyl records gave way to compact discs (CDs), CDs would be replaced by some other technology that offered multichannel digital sound. He based his thoughts on the likely premise that manufacturers would want to give consumers the purest kind of sound and pictures, which could be achieved only by converting information to digital form. There was a major challenge facing

Gerzberg, however, the same obstacle that had prevented other companies from achieving what Gerzberg contemplated. "Whenever you have to deal with digitized video and audio, it turns out there is one enormous barrier," Gerzberg explained in the May-June 1998 issue of the *Journal of Business Strategy.* "That barrier is the amount of data you have to store. It takes a tremendous amount of memory to store a picture, for example." Given the limited amount of storage on a computer hard drive and on a compact disc, a solution needed to be found.

Gerzberg's search for a solution to the dilemma ended Zoran's years of financial comfort. The company, in pursuit of establishing a new foundation, began to lose money, sustaining its operations only by turning repeatedly to venture capitalists willing to gamble on Gerzberg's technological vision. Gerzberg decided to solve the storage capacity problem by concentrating on developing technology to compress data. He worked on ways to compress information, remove certain parts, store the information, and then reconstruct it mathematically during playback. He began designing integrated circuits that could compress audio and video data, and his company, bearing all the financial characteristics of a start-up venture, began to lose money. In 1992, Zoran generated $7.3 million in revenue and lost $2.6 million. The following year, the company lost more than it grossed, posting a $7.7 million loss on $4.7 million in sales. "There was a lot of money lost in those years," an analyst reflected in the *Journal of Business Strategy's* article about Zoran. "Just look at the list of people who invested in the company. It's an incredibly long list."

Investors' faith in Gerzberg began to be rewarded by the mid-1990s. In 1995, the company posted nearly $1 million in net income, recording $23.4 million in sales for the year. The turnaround effort, five years in the making, was celebrated by Zoran's debut as a public company at the end of the year following an initial public offering of stock, giving the company's private investors the chance to cash in on their belief that Gerzberg would create a second, more powerful Zoran. A technological maverick, Gerzberg represented the vanguard of the coming digital revolution, helping to usher in a new age that ended decades of transmitting, editing, and storing data in analog formats. His digital compression techniques would find numerous uses in the proliferation of digital versatile disc (DVD) players, digital video recorders (DVRs), digital cameras, and other consumer electronics products that emerged at the century's end.

Zoran's greatest growth would come once digital media components began selling in large numbers. The

KEY DATES

1981: Zoran is incorporated.
1989: Zoran's founder, Levy Gerzberg, changes the market orientation of the company, courting multimedia customers instead of military customers.
1995: Zoran completes its initial public offering of stock.
1996: CompCore Multimedia, Inc., is acquired.
2003: Oak Technology, Inc., is acquired, providing entry into the high-definition television market.
2004: Emblaze Semiconductor Ltd., a designer of chips for the multimedia mobile telephone market, is acquired.

company's chips found their greatest use in DVD players, which did not begin to enter the mainstream market until the price of such devices began to drop shortly after the start of the 21st century. In the interim, Gerzberg built the infrastructure to support the company's operations and enhance its capabilities, something he would do in a much more aggressive fashion during the first years of the 21st century.

In 1996, the company acquired CompCore Multimedia, Inc., a developer of software-based decompression technology and software cores for audio and video decoder integrated circuits. CompCore was involved in providing the same solutions as Zoran, but it used software instead of hardware to address the problem of digital compression. Its addition to Zoran's operations gave Gerzberg two ways of approaching decompression problems, either through silicon or through software.

Also of note during the latter half of the 1990s was the company's subsidiary in Haifa, which served as the principal research and development center for Zoran's activities. By establishing itself in Haifa, Zoran was allowed to participate in research and development agreements with Israel's Ministry of Industry and Trade and the Israel-United States Binational Industrial Research and Development Foundation. Under the terms of the agreements, the two organizations funded up to 50 percent of project costs in return for a percentage of product sales and licensing revenue. By the end of the decade, Zoran employed 102 research and development personnel, 98 of whom were based in Haifa.

Zoran's financial stature increased substantially during the first years of the 21st century. The growth was attributable to the mass-market appeal of digital multimedia devices and to strategic acquisitions completed by Gerzberg that broadened the company's capabilities. Gerzberg had attempted to develop chips for digital cameras in the late 1980s, but he abandoned the effort several years later when it became apparent that the cameras were too expensive to attract large numbers of consumers. As the price of digital cameras began to drop in the late 1990s, he renewed his efforts to enter the market, taking a more aggressive stance at the dawn of the 21st century, when Zoran could help reduce costs by developing and selling inexpensive chips. In 2000, he acquired PixelCam in an effort to expand Zoran's digital camera business. PixelCam produced low-power image sensors and lenses for digital cameras, making components that were roughly one-tenth the cost of standard industry prices. Gerzberg also acquired another company in 2000, purchasing Nogatech Inc., which made chips that connected video devices with computers.

As Zoran concluded its first 20 years in business, it was beginning to reap the financial rewards of its shift from military to multimedia components. Much of the company's business, and consequently much of its growth, was related to DVD players, the sales of which were growing at a rapid rate. Industry analysts likened the popularity of DVD players to other groundbreaking consumer electronics products such as color televisions, videocassette recorders, and the Sony Walkman, a commonality that translated into vibrant growth for Zoran. The company's sales doubled between 2001 and 2003, jumping from $107 million to $216 million thanks in large part to its chips that decompressed digital information in DVD players, which accounted for 70 percent of the sales recorded in 2003. Gerzberg estimated that he controlled 30 percent of the DVD chip market in 2003, enough to make his company the leader in its field. Of the six largest DVD player manufacturers in the world, four companies—Pioneer Corp., Sharp Electronics Corp., Toshiba Corp., and Sony Corp.—used chips made by Zoran.

ENTRY INTO THE HIGH-DEFINITION TELEVISION MARKET IN 2003

Gerzberg, having established a solid business foundation with DVD hardware products, began to build the company's presence in other markets, both to reduce its dependence on a single market and to provide new avenues of growth. One area Gerzberg wanted to explore was the fast-growing market for high-definition televisions. He particularly was interested in a company named TeraLogic, Inc., which made chips for high-definition televisions, offering Gerzberg entry into the lucrative market. TeraLogic was up for sale in 2001, and Gerzberg leaped at the opportunity to buy the company, but his efforts were thwarted by the advances of another suitor. In late 2002, Oak Technology, Inc., one of Zoran's rivals, acquired TeraLogic for $50 million. Gerzberg did not give up the fight for TeraLogic, however. TeraLogic controlled 50 percent of the market for high-definition television chips, a business that Gerzberg was intent on obtaining. In August 2003, he achieved his goal by acquiring Oak Technology, paying $358 million for the TeraLogic division and Oak Technology's semiconductor design operations, which supplied chips to OEMs of digital printers and scanners.

As Gerzberg looked to the future, the increasing use of digital compression technology in consumer electronics offered a wealth of opportunities for his company to exploit. He hoped to take full advantage of the opportunities before him by remaining on the technological forefront and by expanding Zoran's breadth and depth of capabilities by acquiring other companies. In July 2004, he acquired Emblaze Semiconductor Ltd., paying $54 million for the Ra'anana, Israel-based company. Emblaze provided semiconductor-based solutions for the multimedia mobile telephone market. Roughly a year later, he signed an agreement to purchase another Israeli company, Oren Semiconductor, a Yoqne'am-based company that he had purchased 17 percent of in August 2003, the same month he acquired Oak Technology. Oren Semiconductor designed integrated circuits for high-definition televisions. Further acquisitions were likely as the company pressed ahead, attempting to fulfill Gerzberg's goal of providing digital solutions on a chip for every type of consumer electronics on the market and those to be developed in the years ahead.

Jeffrey L. Covell

PRINCIPAL SUBSIDIARIES

Zoran Microelectronics Ltd. (Israel); Zoran International, Inc.; Zoran Asia Pacific Ltd. (Hong Kong); Zoran Japan Co. Ltd.

PRINCIPAL COMPETITORS

Cirrus Logic, Inc.; ESS Technology, Inc.; STMicroelectronics N.V.

FURTHER READING

Detar, James, "DVD Chip Sales May Hit Pause Button amid Glut," *Investor's Business Daily,* September 16, 2002, p. A6.

———, "Zoran Writes DVD Player Script," *Investor's Business Daily,* August 6, 2003, p. A5.

Domis, Olaf de Senerpont, "Zoran Gets Oak on Second Try," *Daily Deal,* May 6, 2003.

Elliott, Christopher, "Chips Off a New Block," *Journal of Business Strategy,* May-June 1998, p. 47.

Greenberg, Shlomo, "Thu: Waking Up to Zoran," *Asia Africa Intelligence Wire,* September 8, 2005.

———, "Wed: Right About Zoran," *Asia Africa Intelligence Wire,* July 27, 2005.

Reeves, Amy, "Zoran Corp. Santa Clara, California Focus on Hot Markets Keeps Chip Maker Fit," *Investor's Business Daily,* March 20, 2002, p. A10.

Velshi, Ali, "Zoran Shares Soar As Results Top Estimates," *America's Intelligence Wire,* July 27, 2004.

"Zoran Buys Emblaze Semiconductor," *UPI NewsTrack,* June 7, 2004.

"Zoran Buys Oak Technology of California for $358M," *Asia Africa Inelligence Wire,* May 5, 2003.

"Zoran Buys Oren Semiconductor," *Asia Africa Intelligence Wire,* May 9, 2005.

"Zoran Corp.," *Fortune,* August 4, 1986, p. 138.

"Zoran Establishes Joint Development Laboratory with Chinese Company," *Israel Business Today,* January 2000, p. 13.

Zumiez, Inc.

6300 Merrill Creek Parkway, Suite B
Everett, Washington 98203
U.S.A.
Telephone: (425) 551-1500
Toll Free: (877) 828-6929
Fax: (425) 551-1555
Web site: http://www.zumiez.com

Public Company
Incorporated: 1978 as Above the Belt
Employees: 2,135
Sales: $153.6 million (2004)
Stock Exchanges: NASDAQ
Ticker Symbol: ZUMZ
NAIC: 448110 Men's Clothing Stores; 448120 Women's
Clothing Stores; 448210 Shoe Stores; 451110
Sporting Goods Stores; 448150 Clothing Acces-
sories Stores

■ ■ ■

Zumiez, Inc. operates a chain of more than 170 stores
in about 20 states that sell clothing, footwear, equipment, and accessories to young people interested in
"extreme sports" including skateboarding, snowboarding,
surfing, and bicycle motocross racing. The firm's outlets
offer well-known brands as well as Zumiez's own private
labels, and are staffed with employees drawn from its
target demographic and laid out to mimic the chaotic
bedroom of a teen, complete with thrift-store couches
and video game stations. Zumiez went public in 2005,

but cofounder and Chairman Tom Campion and CEO
Richard Brooks retained sizable stakes.

BEGINNINGS

Zumiez was founded in 1978 by Thomas Campion and
Gary Haakenson as Above the Belt, a young men's and
women's clothing store located in Northgate Mall in
Seattle, Washington. Both were graduates of Seattle
University, Campion in political science and Haakenson
in business administration, and both had worked for
J.C. Penney in a variety of management positions. Their
new venture was soon declared a success, and over the
next few years several additional outlets were added.

In 1988 Campion sensed a new opportunity in the
area of "extreme sports," which was a broadly defined
category that included skateboarding, snowboarding,
and surfing. These sports were becoming especially
popular among teenagers, and clothing associated with
them was developing a distinctive, somewhat edgy look.
As more and more of his customers began seeking out
such fashions, he decided to shift the stores' focus to offer these styles exclusively. His intuition paid off, and by
1990 the company was successfully operating eight stores
in the Seattle area.

In 1993 cofounder Haakenson left the firm (he
would later become the mayor of Edmonds, Washington)
and new CFO Richard Brooks bought part of his stake,
with Campion retaining controlling interest. The following year the company changed its corporate name to
Zumiez, Inc. and began using the new name for its latest stores while gradually renaming the old ones. Zumiez
(pronounced "zoomies") was intended to evoke the

excitement of the sports the company's customers enjoyed. The year 1994 also saw the firm move into a new 49,000-square-foot headquarters and distribution center in Everett, Washington.

By 1995 the rapidly expanding Zumiez had a total of 25 stores in shopping malls in the Pacific Northwest. Their offerings were considered a bit too trendy for malls by some observers, but Campion saw this as an asset, telling *SportStyle* magazine, "Up here, there aren't a lot of hip shopping districts for kids to go to. They have to go to the mall. But they don't want to. So we give them a place that's theirs inside the mall."

The fact that the firm's products were not sold at any other stores in their immediate vicinity gave it a unique advantage, and same-store sales grew steadily year after year.

Zumiez outlets, typically 2,500 to 3,000 square feet in size, were designed with an edgy style that featured green-stained cement floors, industrial-looking fixtures, thrift-store sourced furniture, video screens, and eye-catching displays from vendors. The eclectic, intentionally chaotic look was intended to evoke a teen's cluttered bedroom. The firm deliberately sought out sales employees who were actively engaged in the boarding lifestyle and dressed the part at work, though all had been extensively trained on customer service techniques.

Products were selected by Campion and the firm's buyer, Art Aquino, who went to great lengths to find the hottest trends among boarders. Because the company's employees were drawn from the subculture, their input was considered valuable, and store managers (who had typically been promoted from the ranks of

sales staff) were given relative freedom in deciding how to arrange products and operate stores.

The company's promotional efforts were also different from those of many conventional retailers. Zumiez sponsored a team of 15 snowboarders who competed in four states, and each store hosted autograph parties and screenings of boarding films to draw in new customers. Ads were purchased in such publications as *Transworld Snowboarder* magazine and on MTV.

LAUNCHING A WEB SITE IN 1999

In 1999 Zumiez, now with 50 stores in nine states, launched a web site that offered more than 400 products for sale along with informational features. A national advertising campaign was introduced at the same time that featured a contest called "Day in the Life of," with prizes that included a day with one of ten participating athletes. Contestants could enter in stores or online. In 2000 the firm also signed a revenue-sharing pact with Internet content provider iFuse, which would enhance the content of the firm's web site in exchange for a percentage of online sales.

In 2000 CFO Richard Brooks was named president and CEO, with Campion retaining the post of chairman. The year also saw the debut of the Zumiez Couch Tour, which combined music acts and skating demonstrations. It would travel to as many as a dozen cities each year to promote the firm's stores to its target audience.

By the fall of 2000 Zumiez had 62 locations in ten states. Most were in the western and northwestern United States, but the firm had also recently begun expanding eastward into Minnesota and New York. Over the next several years a push was made to increase its presence in the latter state, with nearly ten outlets open there by mid-2002. For the fiscal year ended in 2001 the company recorded sales of $86 million.

Zumiez needed additional funds to continue its expansion efforts, and after looking at offers for more than a year, in November 2002 Campion and Brooks sold a 41 percent stake to Los Angeles-based investment firm Brentwood Associates for $25.3 million, after which two Brentwood managers were appointed to sit on the board. The company now had 102 stores in 12 states, and was planning to open as many as 300 more. Its outlets continued to do well, racking up 25 percent more sales per square foot than the $300-$350 average for all retailers.

Zumiez's product mix now included brand names such as Billabong, Burton, DC Shoe, DVS Shoes, Element, Etnies, Hurley, Quiksilver, Roxy, and Volcom, along with its own private brands, which accounted for

KEY DATES

1978: The first Above the Belt store opens in a Seattle, Washington, shopping mall.

1988: The company begins shifting focus to teenage "extreme sports" enthusiasts.

1993: Cofounder Tom Campion and CFO Richard Brooks buy Gary Haakenson's stake.

1994: The corporate name is changed to Zumiez, Inc.; the firm begins renaming stores.

1995: Expansion is ramped up; the 25th outlet opens.

2000: Richard Brooks is named president and CEO.

2002: Brentwood Associates buys 41 percent of the firm for $25.3 million.

2005: An initial public offering raises $29.7 million; locations top 170.

12 percent of total sales. Although most stores offered the same items, those in snow-free or landlocked locations had a different mix, with some goods added or deleted as appropriate for the local environment. The firm made a good margin on its products, as they were not typically sold by discount chains and some lines were exclusive to Zumiez. In addition to clothing and related equipment, the company also sold Jones Soda, which was added to all of its outlets in 2004.

To continue to attract and retain the best possible employees, the company had over the years begun offering a variety of incentive programs, including the Zumiez 100K event, in which top sales and company management gathered in Colorado each winter for a snowboarding retreat that combined recreation and education. The firm also ran "Zumiez University" in Everett to train its store managers, who averaged 23 years of age.

SUCCESSFUL IPO IN 2005

In 2004 Zumiez opened 27 new outlets and recorded sales of $153.6 million and a profit of $7.3 million, and at the start of 2005 the company moved into a new headquarters/warehouse facility that doubled its distribution capacity and offered the possibility of further expansion. In February the firm also announced plans for an initial public stock offering (IPO) on the NASDAQ, which would help fund future growth.

From its debut in early May the stock rose swiftly, with the opening price of $18 increasing by almost $7 the first day and doubling by year's end. The offering

raised $29.7 million for the firm and another $28.8 million for existing shareholders. After the offering Chairman Campion would own 29.1 percent of the company and Brooks about half that amount.

By mid-2005 the chain of stores had reached 150 in number, up from 53 at the end of 1999, and net sales per location increased from $882,000 to $1.2 million during the same period. Zumiez was constantly tweaking its stores to strengthen their appeal, seeking out locations near busy teen-friendly areas of malls such as food courts and movie theaters, as well as adding features including free video game stations that caused customers to linger. The company's market was a substantial one, with total U.S. sales of snowboard, skateboard, and surfing-related clothing and equipment put at $11.5 billion during 2003 by market research firm Board-Trac.

In addition to working on its retail stores, Zumiez continued to stock its web site with new features, though these were mostly of an informational and brand-building nature, intended to drive customers to the stores. Online sales were negligible, comprising less than 1 percent of total revenues.

During the latter half of 2005 the company continued to open new outlets, and by year's end the total had topped 170. Plans were in place to add 42 more during fiscal 2006, with some to be opened in southern states, including Texas. Zumiez management was now looking at a long-term goal of 800 stores, with 20 percent annual growth predicted for the foreseeable future. In November the firm, which had eliminated all of its outstanding debt, completed a secondary stock offering of 2.7 million shares, most of which came from existing shareholders.

More than 25 years after its founding, Zumiez, Inc. had become a leading retailer of clothing and equipment for bicycle motocross racers and snow-, skate-, and surfboarders. Future growth appeared certain as the company's management worked to make Zumiez a nationally known brand.

Frank Uhle

PRINCIPAL SUBSIDIARIES

Zumiez Nevada L.L.C.

PRINCIPAL COMPETITORS

Pacific Sunwear of California, Inc.; Abercrombie & Fitch Co.; American Eagle Outfitters, Inc.; Old Navy, Inc.; The Sports Authority; Big 5 Sporting Goods Corporation; Dick's Sporting Goods, Inc.

FURTHER READING

Atkinson, William, "Specialty Apparel Retail Survivors," *Shopping Center World,* May 1, 2002.

Bowers, Katherine, "Zumiez, iFuse Ink Revenue Deal," *Women's Wear Daily,* September 20, 2000, p. 20.

Christinat, Joe, "Brentwood Invests in Action Sports Retailer," *Buyouts,* November 18, 2002.

"Hang Ten at the Mall," *Chain Store Age,* March 2003, p. 45.

Holman, Kelly, "Zumiez Plans IPO," *TheDeal.com,* February 21, 2005.

Ouchi, Monica Soto, "Trendy Sports Chain Zumiez Files to Go Public," *Seattle Times,* February 18, 2005.

————, "Zumiez's IPO Impressive As Stock Jumps 38 Percent," *Seattle Times,* May 7, 2005, p. E1.

Richman, Dan, "Zumiez Prepares to Go Public," *Seattle Post-Intelligencer,* February 18, 2005, p. C1.

Ryan, Thomas J., "Surf/Skate Retailer Zumiez Inc. Plans to Raise $57.5 Million in an Initial Public Offering," *Sporting Goods Business,* May 1, 2005.

Tice, Carol, "Zumiez Rides Boards, Gear to Steady Growth," *Puget Sound Business Journal,* March 16, 2001, p. 7.

————, "Zumiez Zooming: Teen-Trend Retailer Is Set for a Big Spurt of Growth," *Puget Sound Business Journal,* March 14, 2003.

Virgin, Bill, "Zumiez Stock Jumps on First Day," *Seattle Post-Intelligencer,* May 7, 2005, p. E1.

Witt, Debra, "Legends of the Mall: Hardcore Snowboarding Is One Flight Up at Zumiez," *SportStyle,* March 1, 1995, p. 74.

Index to Companies

Agrilusa, Agro-Industria, **51** 54
Agrium Inc., 73 21–23
Agrobios S.A., **23** 172
Agroferm Hungarian Japanese Fermentation Industry, **III** 43
Agrologica, **51** 54
Agromán S.A., **40** 218
AGTL *see* Alberta Gas Trunk Line Company, Ltd.
Agua de la Falda S.A., **38** 231
Agua Pura Water Company, **24** 467
Agusta S.p.A., **46** 66
AgustaWestland N.V., 75 18–20
Agway, Inc., 7 17–18; **21** 17–19 **(upd.);**
   36 440
Aherns Holding, **60** 100
AHI Building Products *see* Carter Holt Harvey Ltd.
AHL Services, Inc., 26 149; **27** 20–23;
   45 379
Ahlstrom Corporation, 53 22–25
Ahmanson *see* H.F. Ahmanson & Company.
AHMSA *see* Altos Hornos de México, S.A. de C.V.
Ahold *see* Koninklijke Ahold NV.
AHP *see* American Home Products Corporation.
AHS *see* American Hospital Supply Corporation.
AHSC Holdings Corp. *see* Alco Health Services Corporation.
Ahtna AGA Security, Inc., **14** 541
AI Automotive, **24** 204
AIC *see* Allied Import Company.
AICA, **16** 421; **43** 308
AICPA *see* The American Institute of Certified Public Accountants.
Aid Auto, **18** 144
Aida Corporation, **11** 504
AIG *see* American International Group, Inc.
AIG Global Real Estate Investment Corp., **54** 225
AIG Latin America Equity Partners, Ltda., **74** 48
AIG/Lincoln International L.L.C., **54** 225
Aigner *see* Etienne Aigner AG.
Aiken Stores, Inc., **14** 92
Aikenhead's Home Improvement Warehouse, **18** 240; **26** 306
AIL Technologies, **46** 160
AIM Create Co., Ltd. *see* Marui Co., Ltd.
AIM Management Group Inc., **65** 43–45
AIMCO *see* Apartment Investment and Management Company.
Ainsworth Gaming Technologies, **54** 15
Ainsworth National, **14** 528
AIP *see* American Industrial Properties; Amorim Investimentos e Participaço.
Air & Water Technologies Corporation,
   6 441–42 *see also* Aqua Alliance Inc.
Air Berlin GmbH & Co. Luftverkehrs
   KG, 71 15–17
Air BP, **7** 141
Air By Pleasant, **62** 276
Air Canada, 6 60–62; **23** 9–12 **(upd.);**
   29 302; **36** 230; **59** 17–22 **(upd.)**

Air China, 46 9–11
Air Compak, **12** 182
Air de Cologne, **27** 474
Air Express International Corporation,
   13 19–20; **40** 138; **46** 71
Air France *see* Groupe Air France; Societe Air France.
Air Global International, **55** 30
Air-India Limited, 6 63–64; **27** 24–26
   (upd.); **41** 336–37; **63** 17–18; **65** 14
Air Inter *see* Groupe Air France.
Air Inuit, **56** 38–39
Air Jamaica Limited, 54 3–6
Air La Carte Inc., **13** 48
Air Lanka Catering Services Ltd. *see* Thai Airways International.
Air Liberté, **6** 208
Air Liquide *see* L'Air Liquide SA.
Air London International, **36** 190
Air Mauritius Ltd., 63 17–19
Air Methods Corporation, 53 26–29
Air Midwest, Inc. *see* Mesa Air Group, Inc.
Air New Zealand Limited, 14 10–12; **24**
   399–400; **27** 475; **38** 24–27 **(upd.)**
Air NorTerra Inc., **56** 39
Air Pacific Ltd., 70 7–9
Air Products and Chemicals, Inc., I
   297–99; 10 31–33 **(upd.); 74** 6–9
   (upd.)
Air Pub S.à.r.l., **64** 359
Air Russia, **24** 400
Air Sahara Limited, 65 14–16
Air Sea Broker AG, **47** 286–87
Air Southwest Co. *see* Southwest Airlines Co.
Air Taser, Inc. *see* Taser International, Inc.
Air Transport International LLC, **58** 43
Air Wisconsin Airlines Corporation, 55
   10–12
Airborne Freight Corporation, 6
   345–47; **13** 19; **14** 517; **18** 177; **34**
   15–18 **(upd.); 46** 72
Airbus Industrie, **7** 9–11, 504; **9** 418; **10**
   164; **13** 356; **21** 8; **24** 84–89; **34** 128,
   135; **48** 219 *see also* G.I.E. Airbus Industrie.
AirCal, **I** 91
Airco, **25** 81–82; **26** 94
Aircraft Modular Products, **30** 73
Aircraft Turbine Center, Inc., **28** 3
Airex Corporation, **16** 337
AirFoyle Ltd., **53** 50
Airgas, Inc., 54 7–10
Airguard Industries, Inc., **17** 104, 106; **61**
   66
AirLib *see* Société d'Exploitation AOM.
Airline Interiors Inc., **41** 368–69
Airlines of Britain Holdings, **34** 398; **38**
   105–06
Airlink Pty Ltd *see* Qantas Airways Ltd.
Airmark Plastics Corp., **18** 497–98
Airopak Corporation *see* PVC Container Corporation.
Airpax Electronics, Inc., **13** 398
Airport Leather Concessions LLC, **58** 369
Airrest S.A., **64** 359
Airshop Ltd., **25** 246

Airstream *see* Thor Industries, Inc.
AirTouch Communications, 11 10–12
   see also Vodafone Group PLC.
Airtours Plc, 27 27–29, 90, 92
AirTran Holdings, Inc., 22 21–23; **28**
   266; **33** 302; **34** 32; **55** 10–11
AirWair Ltd., **23** 399, 401–02
AirWays Corporation *see* AirTran Holdings, Inc.
Aisin Seiki Co., Ltd., III 415–16; **14** 64;
   48 3–5 **(upd.)**
AIT Worldwide, **47** 286–87
Aitchison & Colegrave *see* Bradford & Bingley PLC.
Aitken, Inc., **26** 433
AITS *see* American International Travel Service.
Aiuruoca, **25** 85
Aiwa Co., Ltd., 28 360; **30** 18–20
Ajax Iron Works, **II** 16
Ajax Repair & Supply, **58** 75
Ajinomoto Co., Inc., II 463–64, 475; **III**
   705; **28** 9–11 **(upd.)**
AJS Auto Parts Inc., **15** 246
AK Steel Holding Corporation, 19 8–9;
   41 3–6 **(upd.)**
Akamai Technologies, Inc., 71 18–21
Akane Securities Co. Ltd., **II** 443
AKAY Flavours & Aromatics Ltd., **70** 56
Akemi, **17** 310; **24** 160
Aker RGI, **32** 99
AKG Acoustics GmbH, 62 3–6
AKH Co. Inc., **20** 63
Akin, Gump, Strauss, Hauer & Feld,
   L.L.P., 18 366; **33** 23–25; **47** 140
Akorn, Inc., 32 22–24
Akro-Mills Inc., **19** 277–78
Akron Brass Manufacturing Co., **9** 419
Akron Extruders Inc., **53** 230
Akroyd & Smithers, **14** 419
Aktia Sparbank Abp, **69** 177, 179
Aktiebolaget Electrolux, 22 24–28
   (upd.) *see also* Electrolux A.B.
Aktiebolaget SKF, III 622–25; **38** 28–33
   (upd.)
Aktieselskabet Dampskibsselskabet Svendborg, **57** 3, 5
Akzo Nobel N.V., 13 21–23; **41** 7–10
   (upd.)
Al-Amin Co. For Securities & Investment Funds *see* Dallah Albaraka Group.
Al Copeland Enterprises, Inc., **7** 26–28;
   32 13–15
Al-Tawfeek Co. For Investment Funds Ltd. *see* Dallah Albaraka Group.
Alaadin Middle East-Ersan, **IV** 564
Alabama Bancorp., **17** 152
Alabama Farmers Cooperative, Inc., 63
   20–22
Alabama Gas Corporation, **21** 207–08
Alabama National BanCorporation, 75
   21–23
Alabama Power Company, **38** 445,
   447–48
Alabama Shipyards Inc., **21** 39–40
Aladdin Industries, **16** 487
Aladdin Mills Inc., **19** 276; **63** 300
Alagasco, **21** 207–08

Alagroup, **45** 337

Alain Afflelou SA, **53** 30–32

Alain Manoukian *see* Groupe Alain Manoukian.

Alamac Knit Fabrics, Inc., **16** 533–34; **21** 192

Alamito Company, **6** 590

Alamo Engine Company, **8** 514

Alamo Group Inc., **32** 25–28

Alamo Rent A Car, Inc., **6** 348–50; **24** 9–12 (upd.); **25** 93; **26** 409

Alamo Water Refiners, Inc. *see* The Marmon Group, Inc.

Alania, **24** 88

ALANTEC Corporation, **25** 162

ALARIS Medical Systems, Inc., **65** 17–20

Alarm Device Manufacturing Company, **9** 413–15

Alaron Inc., **16** 357

Alascom, Inc. *see* AT&T Corporation.

Alaska Air Group, Inc., **6** 65–67; **11** 50; **29** 11–14 (upd.); **48** 219

Alaska Commercial Company, **12** 363

Alaska Junk Co., **19** 380

Alaska Native Wireless LLC, **60** 264

Alaska Railroad Corporation, **60** 6–9

Alaska Steel Co., **19** 381

Alatas Mammoet, **26** 279

Alba Foods, **27** 197; **43** 218

Alba-Waldensian, Inc., **30** 21–23

Albany Cheese, **23** 219

Albany International Corporation, **8** 12–14; **51** 11–14 (upd.)

Albany Molecular Research, Inc., **77** 9–12

Albaugh Inc., **62** 19

Albemarle Corporation, **59** 23–25

Alberici Corporation, **76** 12–14

Albert E. Reed & Co. Ltd. *see* Reed International PLC.

The Albert Fisher Group plc, **41** 11–13

Albert Heijn NV, **II** 641–42; **38** 200, 202

Albert Nipon, Inc., **8** 323

Albert Willcox & Co., **14** 278

Albert's Organics, Inc. *see* United Natural Foods, Inc.

Alberta Energy Company Ltd., **16** 10–12; **43** 3–6 (upd.)

Alberta Gas Trunk Line Company, Ltd. *see* Nova Corporation of Alberta.

Alberto-Culver Company, **II** 641–42; **8** 15–17; **36** 23–27 (upd.); **60** 258

Albertson's, Inc., **II** 601–03; **7** 19–22 (upd.); **30** 24–28 (upd.); **65** 21–26 (upd.)

Albion Industries, Inc., **16** 357

Albright & Wilson Ltd., **12** 351; **16** 461; **38** 378, 380; **50** 282; **59** 25

Albuquerque Gas & Electric Company *see* Public Service Company of New Mexico.

Albuquerque Gas, Electric Light and Power Company, **6** 561–62

Alcan Aluminium Limited, **IV** 9–13; **31** 7–12 (upd.); **45** 337

Alcan Inc., **60** 338

Alcatel S.A., **9** 9–11; **36** 28–31 (upd.)

Alchem Capital Corp., **8** 141, 143

Alchem Plastics *see* Spartech Corporation.

Alco Capital Group, Inc., **27** 288

Alco Health Services Corporation, **III** 9–10 *see also* AmeriSource Health Corporation.

Alco Office Products Inc., **24** 362

Alco Standard Corporation, **I** 412–13

ALCO Trade Show Services, **26** 102

Alcoa Inc., **56** 7–11 (upd.)

Alcon Laboratories, **10** 46, 48; **30** 30–31

Alden Merrell Corporation, **23** 169

Alderwoods Group, Inc., **68** 11–15 (upd.)

Aldi Group, **13** 24–26

Aldila Inc., **46** 12–14

Aldine Press, **10** 34

Aldiscon, **37** 232

Aldus Corporation, **10** 34–36

Alenia, **7** 9, 11

Alert Centre Inc., **32** 373

Alert Management Systems Inc., **12** 380

Alessio Tubi, **IV** 228

Alestra, **19** 12

Alex & Ivy, **10** 166–68

Alex Lee Inc., **18** 6–9; **44** 10–14 (upd.)

Alexander & Alexander Services Inc., **10** 37–39; **13** 476

Alexander & Baldwin, Inc., **10** 40–42; **29** 307; **40** 14–19 (upd.)

Alexander and Lord, **13** 482

Alexander Hamilton Life Insurance Co., **II** 420; **29** 256

Alexander Howden Group, **10** 38–39

Alexander-Schroder Lumber Company, **18** 514

Alexander Smith, Inc., **19** 275

Alexander's, Inc., **10** 282; **12** 221; **26** 111; **45** 14–16

Alexandria Petroleum Co., **51** 113

Alexis Lichine, **III** 43

Alfa Corporation, **59** 210; **60** 10–12

Alfa-Laval AB, **III** 417–21; **8** 376; **53** 328; **64** 13–18 (upd.)

Alfa Romeo, **I** 163, 167; **11** 102, 104, 139, 205; **13** 27–29, 218–19; **36** 32–35 (upd.), 196–97

Alfa, S.A. de C.V., **11** 386; **19** 10–12; **37** 176

Alfa Trading Company, **23** 358

Alfalfa's Markets, **19** 500–02

alfi Zitzmann, **60** 364

Alfred A. Knopf, Inc., **13** 428, 429; **31** 376–79

Alfred Bullows & Sons, Ltd., **21** 64

Alfred Dunhill Limited, **19** 369; **27** 487–89

Alfred Marks Bureau, Ltd. *see* Adia S.A.

Alfred McAlpine plc, **51** 138

Alfred Ritter GmbH & Co. KG, **58** 3–7

Alfried Krupp von Bohlen und Halbach Foundation, **IV** 89

ALG *see* Arkla, Inc.

Alga, **24** 83

Algamar, S.A., **64** 91

Algemeen Burgerlijk Pensioenfonds, **26** 421

Algemeen Dagbald BV, **53** 273

Algemene Bank Nederland N.V., **II** 183–84, 185, 239, 527

Algerian Saudi Leasing Holding Co. *see* Dallah Albaraka Group.

Algo Group Inc., **24** 13–15

Algoma Steel Corp., **8** 544–45

Algonquin Gas Transmission Company, **14** 124–26

ALI *see* Aeronautics Leasing, Inc.

Aliança Florestal-Sociedade para o Desenvolvimento Agro-Florestal, S.A., **60** 156

Alicia S.A. *see* Arcor S.A.I.C.

Alico, Inc., **63** 23–25

Alidata SpA *see* Alitalia—Linee Aeree Italiana, S.P.A.

Aligro Inc., **II** 664

Alimenta (USA), Inc., **17** 207

Alimentation Couche-Tard Inc., **77** 13–16

Alimentos Indal S.A., **66** 9

Alimondo, **17** 505

Alitalia–Linee Aeree Italiana, S.p.A., **6** 68–69; **24** 311; **29** 15–17 (upd.)

Alkor-Oerlikon Plastic GmbH, **7** 141

All American Airways *see* USAir Group, Inc.

All American Communications Inc., **20** 3–7

All American Gourmet Co., **12** 178, 199

All American Sports Co., **22** 458–59

All British Escarpment Company LTD, **25** 430

All-Clad Metalcrafters Inc., **34** 493, 496–97

The All England Lawn Tennis & Croquet Club, **54** 11–13

All-Glass Aquarium Co., Inc., **58** 60

All Nippon Airways Co., Ltd., **I** 106; **6** 70–71; **38** 34–37 (upd.)

All Seasons Vehicles, Inc. *see* ASV, Inc.

All Woods, Inc., **18** 514

Allami Biztosito, **III** 209; **15** 30

Allcom, **16** 392

Alldays plc, **49** 16–19

Allders plc, **37** 6–8

Alleanza Assicurazioni S.p.A., **65** 27–29

Alleghany Corporation, **10** 43–45; **19** 319; **22** 494; **60** 13–16 (upd.)

Allegheny Airlines *see* USAir Group, Inc.; US Airways Group, Inc.

Allegheny Beverage Corp., **7** 472–73

Allegheny Energy, Inc., **38** 38–41 (upd.)

Allegheny International, Inc., **8** 545; **9** 484; **22** 3, 436

Allegheny Ludlum Corporation, **8** 18–20; **9** 484; **21** 489

Allegheny Power System, Inc., **V** 543–45 *see also* Allegheny Energy, Inc.

Allegheny Steel and Iron Company, **9** 484

Allegheny Steel Distributors, Inc. *see* Reliance Steel & Aluminum Company.

Allegiance Life Insurance Company, **22** 268; **50** 122

Allegis, Inc. *see* United Airlines.

Allegretti & Co., **22** 26

Allen & Co., **12** 496; **13** 366; **25** 270

Allen & Ginter, **12** 108

Bay Shipbuilding Corporation, **18** 320; **59** 274, 277

Bay State Gas Company, 38 79–82

Bay State Iron Manufacturing Co., **13** 16

Bay State Tap and Die Company, **13** 7

Bay West Paper Corporation *see* Mosinee Paper Corporation.

Bayard SA, 49 46–49

BayBanks, Inc., 12 30–32

Bayer A.G., I 309–11; **13** 75–77 (upd.); **41** 44–48 (upd.)

Bayer S.p.A., **8** 179

Bayerische Hypotheken- und Wechsel-Bank AG, II 238–40 *see also* HVB Group.

Bayerische Landesbank, **14** 170; **47** 83

Bayerische Motoren Werke A.G., I 138–40; **11** 31–33 (upd.); **38** 83–87 (upd.)

Bayerische Vereinsbank A.G., II 241–43 *see also* HVB Group.

Bayerische Wagnisbeteiligung GmbH, **27** 192

Bayerische Zellstoff, **IV** 325

Bayernwerk AG, V 555–58, 698–700; **23** 43–47 (upd.); **39** 57

Bayliner Marine Corporation, **22** 116

Bayou Steel Corporation, 31 47–49

Bayox, Inc. *see* Union Carbide Corporation.

Baystate Corporation, **12** 30

Baytree Investors Inc., **15** 87

Bayview Water Company, **45** 277

Bazaar & Novelty *see* Stuart Entertainment Inc.

Bazar de l'Hotel de Ville, **19** 308

BB Holdings Limited, 77 50–53

BBA *see* Bush Boake Allen Inc.

BBAG Osterreichische Brau-Beteiligungs-AG, 38 88–90

BBC *see* British Broadcasting Corp.

BBC Brown, Boveri Ltd. *see* ABB Ltd.

BBDO Worldwide *see* Omnicom Group Inc.

BBGI *see* Beasley Broadcast Group, Inc.

BBME *see* British Bank of the Middle East.

BBN Corp., 19 39–42

BBO & Co., **14** 433

BBVA *see* Banco Bilbao Vizcaya Argentaria S.A.

BC Development, **16** 481

BC Natural Foods, Inc., **68** 91

BC Partners, **51** 322; **53** 138; **76** 305, 307

BC Property Management Inc., **58** 23

BC Rail Ltd., **71** 82, 88

BC TEL *see* British Columbia Telephone Company.

BCal *see* British Caledonian Airways.

BCC, **24** 266, 270

BCE, Inc., V 269–71; **7** 333; **12** 413; **18** 32; **36** 351; **44** 46–50 (upd.)

BCI *see* Banca Commerciale Italiana SpA.

Bcom3 Group, Inc., **40** 142; **76** 254

BCOP *see* Boise Cascade Office Products.

BCP Corporation, **16** 228–29

BCPA *see* British Commonwealth Pacific Airways.

BDB *see* British Digital Broadcasting plc.

BDB Corp., **10** 136

BDDP *see* Wells Rich Greene BDDP.

BE&K, Inc., 73 57–59

Be Free Inc., **49** 434

BEA *see* Bank of East Asia Ltd.

BEA Systems, Inc., 36 80–83

Beach Hill Investments Pty Ltd., **48** 427

Beach Patrol Inc., **29** 181

Beacon Communications Group, **23** 135

Beacon Education Management LLC *see* Chancellor Beacon Academies, Inc.

Beacon Manufacturing Company, **19** 304–05

Beacon Roofing Supply, Inc., 75 59–61

Beall-Ladymon, Inc., **24** 458

Bealls, **24** 456

Beamach Group Ltd., **17** 182–83

Beaman Corporation, **16** 96; **25** 390

Bean Fiberglass Inc., **15** 247

Bear Automotive Service Equipment Company, **10** 494

Bear Creek Corporation, 12 444–45; **38** 91–94; **39** 361

Bear Instruments Inc., **48** 410

Bear Stearns Companies, Inc., II 400–01, 450; **10** 144–45 (upd.), 382; **20** 313; **24** 272; **52** 41–44 (upd.)

Bearings, Inc., 13 78–80

Beasley Broadcast Group, Inc., 51 44–46

Beasley Industries, Inc., **19** 125–26

Beatrice Company, II 467–69 *see also* TLC Beatrice International Holdings, Inc.

Beatrice Foods, **21** 322–24, 507, 545; **25** 277–78; **38** 169; **43** 355

Beatrix Mines Ltd., **62** 164

Beaulieu of America, **19** 276

Beauté Prestige International S.A. *see* Shiseido Company Limited.

BeautiControl Cosmetics, Inc., 21 49–52

Beauty Biz Inc., **18** 230

Beauty Systems Group, Inc., **60** 260

Beaver Lake Concrete, Inc. *see* The Monarch Cement Company.

Beazer Homes USA, Inc., 17 38–41

Beazer Plc., **7** 209

bebe stores, inc., 31 50–52

BEC Group Inc., **22** 35; **60** 133

BEC Ventures, **57** 124–25

Bechstein, **56** 299

Bechtel Group, Inc., I 558–59; **24** 64–67 (upd.)

Beck & Gregg Hardware Co., **9** 253

Beck's North America, Inc. *see* Brauerei Beck & Co.

Becker Drill, Inc., **19** 247

Becker Group of Germany, **26** 231

Beckett Papers, 23 48–50

Beckley-Cardy Group *see* School Specialty, Inc.

Beckman Coulter, Inc., 22 74–77

Beckman Instruments, Inc., 14 52–54

BECOL *see* Belize Electric Company Limited.

Becton, Dickinson & Company, I 630–31; **11** 34–36 (upd.); **36** 84–89 (upd.)

Bed Bath & Beyond Inc., 13 81–83; **41** 49–52 (upd.)

Bedcovers, Inc., **19** 304

Beddor Companies, **12** 25

Bedford Chemical, **8** 177

Bedford-Stuyvesant Restoration Corp., **II** 673

Bee Chemicals, **I** 372

Bee Discount, **26** 476

Bee Gee Shoe Corporation, **10** 281

Beech Aircraft Corporation, II 87; **8** 49–52, 313; **11** 411, 413; **27** 98; **38** 375; **46** 354

Beech Holdings Corp., **9** 94

Beech-Nut Nutrition Corporation, 21 53–56; **46** 290; **51** 47–51 (upd.)

Beecham Group PLC, **I** 668; **9** 264; **14** 53; **16** 438

Beechcroft Developments Ltd., **51** 173

Beechwood Insurance Agency, Inc., **14** 472

Beeck-Feinkost GmbH, **26** 59

ZAO BeeOnLine-Portal, **48** 419

Beerman Stores, Inc., **10** 281

Beers Construction Company, **38** 437

Befesa *see* Abengoa S.A.

Behr GmbH & Co. KG, 72 22–25

Behr-Manning Company, **8** 396

Behring Diagnostics *see* Dade Behring Holdings Inc.

Behringwerke AG, **14** 255; **50** 249

BEI Technologies, Inc., 65 74–76

Beiersdorf AG, 29 49–53; **41** 374–77

Beijing Contact Lens Ltd., **25** 56

Beijing Dentsu, **16** 168

Beijing-Landauer, Ltd., **51** 210

Beijing Liyuan Co., **22** 487

Beijing Yanshan Petrochemical Company, **22** 263

Beijing ZF North Drive Systems Technical Co. Ltd., **48** 450

Beirao, Pinto, Silva and Co. *see* Banco Espírito Santo e Comercial de Lisboa S.A.

Bejam Group PLC *see* The Big Food Group plc.

Bekins Company, 15 48–50; **26** 197

Bel *see* Fromageries Bel.

Bel Air Markets, **14** 397; **58** 290

Bel Fuse, Inc., 53 59–62

Bel/Kaukauna USA, 76 46–48

Belco Oil & Gas Corp., 23 219; **40** 63–65; **63** 440

Belcom Holding AG, **53** 323, 325

Belden CDT Inc., 19 43–45; **76** 49–52 (upd.)

Beldis, **23** 219

Beldoch Industries Corp., **17** 137–38

Belgacom, 6 302–04; **63** 371–72

Belgian Rapid Access to Information Network Services, **6** 304

Belglas, **16** 420; **43** 307

Belgo Group plc, **31** 41

Calumatic Group, **25** 82
Calumet Electric Company, **6** 532
Calvert Insurance Co. *see* Gryphon Holdings, Inc.
Calvin Klein, Inc., 22 121–24; **55** 84–88 (upd.)
Calyx & Corolla Inc., **37** 162–63
Camaïeu S.A., 72 54–56
Camargo Foods, **12** 531
Camas *see* Aggregate Industries plc.
CamBar *see* Cameron & Barkley Company.
Camber Corporation, **25** 405
Camberley Enterprises Limited, **59** 261
Cambex, **46** 164
Cambrex Corporation, 16 67–69; **44** 59–62 (upd.)
Cambrian Wagon Works Ltd., **31** 369
Cambridge Applied Nutrition Toxicology and Biosciences Ltd., **10** 105
Cambridge Biotech Corp., **13** 241
Cambridge Electric Co., **14** 124, 126
Cambridge Gas Co., **14** 124
The Cambridge Instrument Company, **35** 272
Cambridge Interactive Systems Ltd., **10** 241
Cambridge SoundWorks, 36 101; Inc., **48** 83–86
Cambridge Steam Corp., **14** 124
Cambridge Technology Partners, Inc., 36 105–08
Cambridge Tool & Mfg. Co. Inc., **48** 268
Cambridge Water, **51** 389
Camden Property Trust, 77 80–83
Camden Wire Co., Inc., **7** 408; **31** 354–55
Cameco Corporation, 77 84–87
Camelot Barthropp Ltd., **26** 62
Camelot Community Care, Inc., **64** 311
Camelot Group plc, **34** 140
Camelot Music, Inc., 26 52–54
Cameron & Barkley Company, 13 79; **28** 59–61; **63** 288–89
Cameron Ashley Inc., **19** 57
Cameron-Brown Company, **10** 298
Cameron Iron Works, **II** 17
Camintonn, **9** 41–42
Campagnia della Fede Cattolica sotto l'Invocazione di San Paolo, **50** 407
Campbell Cereal Company *see* Malt-O-Meal Company.
Campbell, Cowperthwait & Co., **17** 498
Campbell Hausfeld *see* Scott Fetzer Company.
Campbell Industries, Inc., **11** 534
Campbell-Mithun-Esty, Inc., 16 70–72
Campbell Scientific, Inc., 51 62–65
Campbell Soup Company, II 479–81; **7** 66–69 (upd.); **26** 55–59 (upd.); **71** 75–81 (upd.)
Campeau Corporation, V 25–28
Camping World, Inc., **56** 5
Campo Electronics, Appliances & Computers, Inc., 16 73–75
Campo Lindo, **25** 85
Campofrío Alimentación S.A, 18 247; **59** 101–03

CAMPSA *see* Compañia Arrendataria del Monopolio de Petróleos Sociedad Anónima.
Campus Services, Inc., **12** 173
Canada Cable & Wire Company, **9** 11
Canada, Limited, **24** 143
Canada Packers Inc., II 482–85; **41** 249
Canada Safeway Ltd., **II** 650, 654
Canada Surety Co., **26** 486
Canada Trust *see* CT Financial Services Inc.
Canadair, Inc., 16 76–78
Canadian Ad-Check Services Inc., **26** 270
Canadian Airlines International Ltd., **6** 61–62, 101; **12** 192; **23** 10; **24** 400; **59** 20
The Canadian Broadcasting Corporation (CBC), 37 55–58
Canadian Electrolytic Zinc Ltd., **64** 297
Canadian Football League, **12** 457
Canadian Forest Products *see* Canfor Corporation.
Canadian Freightways, Ltd., **48** 113
Canadian General Electric Co., **8** 544–45
Canadian Imperial Bank of Commerce, II 244–46; **7** 26–28; **10** 8; **32** 12, 14; **61** 47–51 (upd.)
Canadian Industrial Alcohol Company Limited, **14** 141
Canadian Keyes Fibre Company, Limited of Nova Scotia, **9** 305
Canadian National Railway Company, 6 359–62; **71** 82–88 (upd.)
Canadian Niagara Power Company, **47** 137
Canadian Odeon Theatres *see* Cineplex Odeon Corporation.
Canadian Overseas Telecommunications Corporation, **25** 100
Canadian Pacific Limited, V 429–31; **8** 544–46
Canadian Pacific Railway Limited, 45 78–83 (upd.)
Canadian Steel Foundries, Ltd., **39** 31
Canadian Telephones and Supplies *see* British Columbia Telephone Company.
Canadian Tire Corporation, Limited, 71 89–93 (upd.)
Canadian Utilities Limited, 13 130–32; **56** 53–56 (upd.)
Canadian Vickers, **16** 76
Canal Bank, **11** 105
Canal Digital, **69** 344–46
Canal Electric Co., **14** 125–26
Canal Plus, III 48; **7** 392; **10** 195–97, 345, 347; **23** 476; **29** 369, 371; **31** 330; **33** 181; **34** 83–86 (upd.)
CanalSatellite, **29** 369, 371
CanAmera Foods, **7** 82
Canandaigua Brands, Inc., 34 87–91 (upd.) *see also* Constellation Brands, Inc.
Canandaigua Wine Company, Inc., 13 133–35
Cananwill, **III** 344
Canary Wharf Group Plc, 30 107–09
Canatom NPM Inc. *see* SNC-Lavalin Group Inc.

Candela Corporation, 48 87–89
Candie's, Inc., 31 81–84
Candle Corporation, 64 62–65
Candle Corporation of America *see* Blyth Industries, Inc.
Candle-Lite Inc., **61** 172
Candlewood Hotel Company, Inc., 41 81–83
Candover Partners Limited, **70** 310
Candy SpA *see* Arcor S.A.I.C.
Canfor Corporation, 42 59–61
Cannapp Pty Limited, **56** 155
Cannell Communications, **25** 418
Cannon Design, 63 90–92
Cannon Express, Inc., 53 80–82
Cannon Mills, Co., **9** 214–16
Cannondale Corporation, 21 88–90
Canon Inc., III 120–21; **18** 92–95 (upd.)
Canpotex Ltd., **18** 432
Canrad-Hanovia, **27** 57
Canstar Sports Inc., 16 79–81
Canteen Corp., **II** 679–80; **13** 321
Cantel Corp., **11** 184; **18** 32; **20** 76; **30** 388
Canterbury Park Holding Corporation, 42 62–65
Canterra Energy Ltd., **47** 180
Cantine Giorgio Lungarotti S.R.L., 67 88–90
Canton Railway Corp., **IV** 718; **38** 320
Cantor Fitzgerald Securities Corporation, **10** 276–78
CanWest Global Communications Corporation, 35 67–70; **39** 13
Canyon Cafes, **31** 41
Cap Gemini Ernst & Young, 37 59–61
Cap Rock Energy Corporation, 6 580; **46** 78–81
Capacity of Texas, Inc., **33** 105–06
CAPCO *see* Central Area Power Coordination Group; Custom Academic Publishing Company.
Capco Energy, Inc., **33** 296
Capcom Co., **7** 396
Cape and Vineyard Electric Co., **14** 124–25
Cape Cod-Cricket Lane, Inc., **8** 289
Cape Cod Potato Chip Company, Inc., **41** 233
Cape PLC, **22** 49
Capel Incorporated, 45 84–86
Capezio/Ballet Makers Inc., 62 57–59
Capita Group PLC, 69 79–81
AB Capital & Investment Corporation, **6** 108; **23** 381
Capital Advisors, Inc., **22** 4
Capital Bank N.A., **16** 162
Capital Cities/ABC Inc., II 129–31 *see also* ABC, Inc.
Capital Concrete Pipe Company, **14** 250
Capital Controls Co., Inc. *see* Severn Trent PLC.
Capital Distributing Co., **21** 37
Capital Factors, Inc., **54** 387
Capital-Gazette Communications, Inc., **12** 302
Capital Grille, **19** 342

The Dun & Bradstreet Corporation, IV
604–05; 19 132–34 (upd.); 61 80–84
(upd.)
Dun & Bradstreet Software Services
Inc., 11 77–79
Dunavant Enterprises, Inc., 54 88–90
Dunbar-Stark Drillings, Inc., 19 247
Duncan Toys Company, 55 132–35
Duncanson & Holt, Inc., 13 539
Dundee Acquisition Corp., 19 421
Dundee Bancorp, 36 314
Dundee Cement Co., III 702; 8 258–59
Dunfey Brothers Capital Group, 12 368
Dunfey Hotels Corporation, 12 367
Dunhill Staffing Systems, Inc., 52 397–98
Dunkin' Donuts, II 619; 21 323; 29
18–19
Dunkirk Specialty Steel, LLC *see* Universal
Stainless & Alloy Products, Inc.
Dunlop Coflexip Umbilicals Ltd. *see* Duco
Ltd.
Dunlop Ltd., 25 104
Dunlop Tire Corporation *see* Sumitomo
Rubber Industries, Ltd.
Dunn Bennett, 38 401
Dunn Bros., 28 63
Dunn-Edwards Corporation, 56 97–99
Dunn Manufacturing Company, 25 74
Dunnes Stores Ltd., 58 102–04
Dunning Industries, 12 109
Dunphy Holding Pty. Ltd., 64 349
Dunwoodie Manufacturing Co., 17 136
Duo-Bed Corp., 14 435
Dupey Enterprises, Inc., 17 320
Duplainville Transport, 19 333–34
Duplex Products, Inc., 17 142–44, 445
Dupont *see* E.I. du Pont de Nemours &
Company.
Duquesne Light Company *see* DQE.
Duquesne Systems, 10 394
Dura Automotive Systems Inc., 53 55; 65
282, 284
Dura Convertible Systems, 13 170
Duracell International Inc., 9 179–81;
71 127–31 (upd.)
Durachemie *see* Hexal AG.
Duraflame Inc., 58 52
Duramed Research Inc. *see* Barr Pharma-
ceuticals, Inc.
Durametallic, 21 189–91
Durango-Mapimi Mining Co., 22 284
Duravit AG, 51 196
Duray, Inc., 12 215
D'Urban, Inc., 41 169
Duriron Company Inc., 17 145–47
Durkee Famous Foods, 7 314; 8 222; 17
106; 27 297
Dürkopp Adler AG, 65 131–34
Duro-Matic Products Co., 51 368
Duron Inc., 72 91–93
Dürr AG, 44 158–61
Durr-Fillauer Medical Inc., 13 90; 18 97;
50 121
Dürrkopp Adler AG, 62 132
Dutch Boy, II 649; 10 434–35
Dutch Crude Oil Company *see* Neder-
landse Aardolie Maatschappij.
Dutch State Mines *see* DSM N.V.

Dutchland Farms, 25 124
Duttons Ltd., 24 267
Duty Free International, Inc., 11 80–82
see also World Duty Free Americas, Inc.
Duval Corp., 7 280; 25 461
DVI, Inc., 51 107–09
DVM Pharmaceuticals Inc., 55 233
DVT Corporation *see* Cognex Corpora-
tion.
DWG Corporation *see* Triarc Companies,
Inc.
Dyas B.V., 55 347
Dyckerhoff AG, 35 151–54
Dycom Industries, Inc., 57 118–20
Dyersburg Corporation, 21 192–95
Dyke and Dryden, Ltd., 31 417
Dylex Limited, 29 162–65
Dymed Corporation *see* Palomar Medical
Technologies, Inc.
DYMO *see* Esselte Worldwide.
Dynaction S.A., 67 146–48
Dynalectric Co., 45 146
DynaMark, Inc., 18 168, 170, 516, 518
Dynamem Corporation, 22 409
Dynamic Capital Corp., 16 80
Dynamic Controls, 11 202
Dynamic Foods, 53 148
Dynamic Health Products Inc., 62 296
Dynamic Homes, 61 125–27
Dynamic Microprocessor Associated Inc.,
10 508
Dynamics Corporation of America, 39
106
Dynamit Nobel AG, III 692–95; 16 364;
18 559
Dynamix, 15 455
Dynapar, 7 116–17
Dynaplast, 40 214–15
Dynascan AK, 14 118
Dynasty Footwear, Ltd., 18 88
Dynatech Corporation, 13 194–96
Dynatron/Bondo Corporation, 8 456
DynCorp, 45 145–47
Dynea, 68 125–27
Dynegy, Inc., 47 70; 49 119–22 (upd.)
Dyno Industrier AS, 13 555
Dyson Group PLC, 71 132–34
Dystrybucja, 41 340

E

E&B Company, 9 72
E&B Marine, Inc., 17 542–43
E. & J. Gallo Winery, I 242–44; 7
154–56 (upd.); 28 109–11 (upd.)
E&M Laboratories, 18 514
E & S Retail Ltd. *see* Powerhouse.
E! Entertainment Television Inc., 17
148–50
E-Mex Home Funding Ltd. *see* Cheshire
Building Society.
E-mu Systems, Inc., 57 78–79
E-Pet Services, 74 234
E-Stamp Corporation, 34 474
E-Systems, Inc., 9 182–85
E*Trade Financial Corporation, 20
206–08; 60 114–17 (upd.)
E-II Holdings Inc. *see* Astrum Interna-
tional Corp.

E-Z Haul, 24 409
E-Z Serve Corporation, 17 169–71
E A Rosengrens AB, 53 158
E.B. Badger Co., 11 413
E.B. Eddy Forest Products, II 631
E.C. Snodgrass Company, 14 112
E.C. Steed, 13 103
E. de Trey & Sons, 10 270–71
E.F. Hutton Group, II 399, 450–51; 8
139; 9 469; 10 63
E.F. Hutton LBO, 24 148
E.H. Bindley & Company, 9 67
E.I. du Pont de Nemours and Com-
pany, I 328–30; 8 151–54 (upd.); 26
123–27 (upd.); 73 128–33 (upd.)
E.J. Brach & Sons *see* Brach and Brock
Confections, Inc.
E.J. Longyear Company *see* Boart Long-
year Company.
E. Katz Special Advertising Agency *see*
Katz Communications, Inc.
E.M. Warburg Pincus & Co., 7 305; 13
176; 16 319; 25 313; 29 262
E. Missel GmbH, 20 363
E.On AG, 50 165–73 (upd.); 51 217; 59
391; 62 14
E.piphany, Inc., 49 123–25
E.R.R. Enterprises, 44 227
E. Rabinowe & Co., Inc., 13 367
E. Rosen Co., 53 303–04
E.S. International Holding S.A. *see* Banco
Espírito Santo e Comercial de Lisboa
S.A.
E.V. Williams Inc. *see* The Branch Group,
Inc.
E.W. Howell Co., Inc., 72 94–96
The E.W. Scripps Company, IV 606–09;
7 157–59 (upd.); 28 122–26 (upd.);
66 85–89 (upd.)
E. Witte Verwaltungsgesellschaft GmbH,
73 326
EADS N.V. *see* European Aeronautic De-
fence and Space Company EADS N.V.
EADS SOCATA, 54 91–94
Eagel One Industries, 50 49
Eagle Airways Ltd., 23 161
Eagle Credit Corp., 10 248
Eagle Distributing Co., 37 351
Eagle Family Foods, Inc., 22 95
Eagle Floor Care, Inc., 13 501; 33 392
Eagle Gaming, L.P., 16 263; 43 226; 75
341
Eagle Global Logistics *see* EGL, Inc.
Eagle Hardware & Garden, Inc., 16
186–89
Eagle Industries Inc., 8 230; 22 282; 25
536
Eagle Managed Care Corp., 19 354, 357;
63 334
Eagle-Picher Industries, Inc., 8 155–58;
23 179–83 (upd.)
Eagle Plastics, 19 414
Eagle Sentry Inc., 32 373
Eagle Thrifty Drug, 14 397
Eagle Trading, 55 24
Eagle Travel Ltd., IV 241
Earl Scheib, Inc., 32 158–61
Early American Insurance Co., 22 230

Farmer Bros. Co., **52** 117–19
Farmer Jack, **16** 247; **44** 145
Farmer Mac *see* Federal Agricultural Mortgage Corporation.
Farmers and Mechanics Bank of Georgetown, **13** 439
Farmers Insurance Group of Companies, 25 154–56
Farmers National Bank & Trust Co., **9** 474
Farmers Petroleum, Inc., **48** 175
Farmland Foods, Inc., IV 474; **7** 17, **7** 174–75
Farmland Industries, Inc., 39 282; **48** 172–75
Farmstock Pty Ltd., **62** 307
Farrar, Straus and Giroux Inc., 15 158–60
FAS Acquisition Co., **53** 142
FASC *see* First Analysis Securities Corporation.
Fasco Consumer Products, **19** 360
FASCO Motors *see* Tecumseh Products Company.
Fashion Bar, Inc., **24** 457
Fashion Bug, **8** 97
Fashion Fair Cosmetics *see* Johnson Publishing Company, Inc.
Fashion Resource, Inc. *see* Tarrant Apparel Group.
Fasint Ltd., **72** 128
Fasson *see* Avery Dennison Corporation.
Fast Air, **31** 305
Fast Fare, **7** 102
Fast Trak Inc. *see* Ultimate Electronics, Inc.
Fastenal Company, 14 185–87; **42** 135–38 (upd.)
Fat Bastard Wine Co., **68** 86
Fat Face Ltd., 68 147–49
FAT KAT, Inc., **51** 200, 203
Fata European Group, **IV** 187; **19** 348
Fatburger Corporation, 64 122–24
Fate S.A., **74** 10
Fateco Förlag, **14** 556
FATS, Inc., **27** 156, 158
Faugere et Jutheau, **III** 283
Faultless Starch/Bon Ami Company, 55 142–45
Fauquet, **25** 85
Faurecia S.A., 70 91–93
Favorite Plastics, **19** 414
FAvS *see* First Aviation Services Inc.
Fawcett Books, **13** 429
Fay's Inc., 17 175–77
Faydler Company, **60** 160
Fayette Tubular Products, **7** 116–17
Faygo Beverages Inc., 55 146–48
Fayva, **13** 359–61
Fazoli's Management, Inc., 27 145–47; **76** 144–47 (upd.)
FB&T Corporation, **14** 154
FBC *see* First Boston Corp.
FBO *see* Film Booking Office of America.
FBR *see* Friedman, Billings, Ramsey Group, Inc.
FBS Fuhrpark Business Service GmbH, **58** 28

FC Holdings, Inc., **26** 363
FCA Ltd. *see* Life Time Fitness, Inc.
FCC *see* Federal Communications Commission.
FCI *see* Framatome SA.
FDIC *see* Federal Deposit Insurance Corp.
Feather Fine, **27** 361
Featherlite Inc., 28 127–29
Feature Enterprises Inc., **19** 452
FECR *see* Florida East Coast Railway, L.L.C.
Fedders Corporation, 18 172–75; **43** 162–67 (upd.)
Federal Agricultural Mortgage Corporation, 75 141–43
Federal Bicycle Corporation of America, **11** 3
Federal Cartridge, **26** 363
Federal Coca-Cola Bottling Co., **10** 222
Federal Deposit Insurance Corp., **12** 30, 79
Federal Express Corporation, V 451–53 *see also* FedEx Corporation.
Federal Home Life Insurance Co., **IV** 623
Federal Home Loan Mortgage Corp. *see* Freddie Mac.
Federal Insurance Co., **III** 220–21; **14** 108–109; **37** 83–85
Federal Laboratories, **57** 230
Federal Light and Traction Company, **6** 561–62
Federal-Mogul Corporation, I 158–60; **10** 292–94 (upd.); **26** 139–43 (upd.)
Federal National Mortgage Association, II 410–11 *see also* Fannie Mae.
Federal Pacific Electric, **9** 440
Federal Packaging and Partition Co., **8** 476
Federal Packaging Corp., **19** 78
Federal Paper Board Company, Inc., 8 173–75
Federal Power, **18** 473
Federal Prison Industries, Inc., 34 157–60
Federal Reserve Bank of New York, **21** 68
Federal Savings and Loan Insurance Corp., **16** 346
Federal Signal Corp., 10 295–97
Federal Trade Commission, **6** 260; **9** 370
Federated Department Stores Inc., 9 209–12; **31** 190–94 (upd.)
Federated Development Company, **8** 349
Federated Livestock Corporation, **64** 306
Fédération Internationale de Football Association, 27 148–51
Federation Nationale d'Achats des Cadres *see* FNAC.
Federation of Migro Cooperatives *see* Migros-Genossenschafts-Bund.
Federico Paternina S.A., 69 164–66
FedEx Corporation, 18 128, 176–79 (upd.), 535; **33** 20, 22; **34** 474; **42** 139–44 (upd.); **46** 71
FEE Technology, **29** 461–62
Feed-Rite, Inc., **16** 270; **62** 307
Feed The Children, Inc., 68 150–52
Feffer & Simons, **16** 46
Feikes & Sohn KG, **IV** 325

Felco *see* Farmers Regional Cooperative.
Feld Entertainment, Inc., 32 186–89 (upd.)
Feldmühle Nobel AG, III 692–95; **IV** 142, 325, 337; **36** 449 *see also* Metallgesellschaft.
Felixstowe Ltd., **18** 254
Fellowes Manufacturing Company, 28 130–32
Felten & Guilleaume, **IV** 25
Femsa *see* Formento Económico Mexicano, S.A. de C.V.
Femtech, **8** 513
Fendall Company, **40** 96, 98
Fendel Schiffahrts-Aktiengesellschaft, **6** 426
Fender Musical Instruments Company, 16 200–02; **43** 168–72 (upd.)
Fendi S.p.A., **45** 344
Fenicia S.A., **22** 320; **61** 175
Fenn, Wright & Manson, **25** 121–22
Fenton Hill American Limited, **29** 510
Fenway Partners, **47** 361
Fenwick & West LLP, 34 161–63, 512
Ferembal S.A., **25** 512
Ferfin, **24** 341
Fergus Brush Electric Company, **18** 402
Ferguson Enterprises, **64** 409, 411
Ferguson Machine Co., **8** 135
Ferguson Manufacturing Company, **25** 164
Fermec Manufacturing Limited, **40** 432
Fermentaciones Mexicanas S.A. de C.V., **III** 43; **48** 250
Fernando Roqué, **6** 404; **26** 243
Ferolito, Vultaggio & Sons, 27 152–55
Ferragamo, **63** 151
Ferranti Business Communications, **20** 75
Ferrari S.p.A., 13 218–20; **36** 196–200 (upd.)
Ferrellgas Partners, L.P., 35 173–75
Ferrero SpA, 54 103–05
Ferrier Hodgson, **10** 170
Ferris Industries, **64** 355
Ferro Corporation, 8 176–79; **56** 123–28 (upd.)
Ferro Engineering Co., **17** 357
Ferrocarril del Noreste, S.A. de C.V. *see* Grupo Transportación Ferroviaria Mexicana, S.A. de C.V.
Ferrolux Metals Co., **63** 360
Ferrovial *see* Grupo Ferrovail
Ferroxcube Corp. of America, **13** 397
Ferrum Inc., **24** 144
Ferruzzi Agricola Finanziario, **7** 81–83
Ferruzzi Finanziaria S.p.A., **24** 341; **36** 186
Fertisere SAS, **58** 221
Fetzer Vineyards, **10** 182
FFI Fragrances *see* Elizabeth Arden, Inc.
F5 Networks, Inc., 72 129–31
FFM Bhd, **57** 292–95
FHP International Corporation, 6 184–86
Fiamm Technologies *see* Valeo.
Fianzas Monterrey, **19** 189
Fiat SpA, I 161–63; **11** 102–04 (upd.); **50** 194–98 (upd.)

Gran Central Corporation, **8** 487

Gran Dorado, **48** 315

Granada Group PLC, II 138–40; 24 192–95 (upd.)

Granada Royale Hometels, **9** 426

Granaria Holdings B.V., 23 183; **66 151–53**

GranCare, Inc., 14 209–11

Grand Bazaar Innovations Bon Marché, **13** 284; **26** 159–60

Grand Casinos, Inc., 20 268–70

Grand Department Store, **19** 510

Grand Home Furnishings *see* Grand Piano & Furniture Company.

Grand Hotel Krasnapolsky N.V., 23 227–29

Grand Magasin de Nouveautés Fournier d'Annecy, **27** 93

Grand Metropolitan plc, I 247–49; 14 212–15 (upd.) *see also* Diageo plc.

Grand Ole Opry *see* Gaylord Entertainment Company.

Grand Piano & Furniture Company, 72 151–53

Grand Prix Association of Long Beach, Inc., **43** 139–40

Grand Rapids Carpet Sweeper Company, **9** 70

Grand Rapids Gas Light Company *see* MCN Corporation.

Grand Rapids Wholesale Grocery Company, **8** 481

Grand Union Company, 7 202–04; 28 162–65 (upd.)

Grand Valley Gas Company, **11** 28

Grand-Perret, **39** 152–53

Grandes Superficies S.A., **23** 247

Les Grands Magasins Au Bon Marché, **26** 159–60

GrandVision S.A., 43 198–200

Grandy's, **15** 345

Grange *see* Aga Foodservice Group PLC.

Granger Associates, **12** 136

Gränges, **III** 480; **22** 27; **53** 127–28

Granite Broadcasting Corporation, 42 161–64

Granite City Steel Company, **12** 353

Granite Construction Incorporated, 61 119–21

Granite Furniture Co., **14** 235

Granite Industries of Vermont, Inc., 73 169–72

Granite Rock Company, 26 175–78

Granite State Bankshares, Inc., 37 173–75

Grant Oil Tool Co., **III** 569; **20** 361

Grant Prideco, Inc., 57 162–64

Grant Thornton International, 57 165–67

Grantham, Mayo, Van Otterloo & Co. LLC, **24** 407

Grantree Corp., **14** 4; **33** 398

Granville PLC *see* Robert W. Baird & Co. Incorporated.

Graphic Controls Corp., **IV** 678

Graphic Industries Inc., 25 182–84

Graphic Research, Inc., **13** 344–45

Graphics Systems Software, **8** 519

Graphix Zone, **31** 238

Grass Valley Group, **8** 518, 520

Grasselli Chemical Company, **22** 225

Grasso Production Management Inc., **37** 289

Grattan Plc *see* Otto-Versand (Gmbh & Co.).

The Graver Company, **16** 357

Gray Communications Systems, Inc., 24 196–200

Gray Line, **24** 118

Gray Matter Holdings, L.L.C., **64** 300

Gray, Siefert & Co., Inc., **10** 44; **33** 259–60

Graybar Electric Company, Inc., 54 139–42

Grays Harbor Mutual Savings Bank, **17** 530

Greaseater, Ltd., **8** 463–64

Great Alaska Tobacco Co., **17** 80

Great American Bagel and Coffee Co., **27** 482

Great American Broadcasting Inc., **18** 65–66; **22** 131; **23** 257–58

Great American Cookie Company *see* Mrs. Fields' Original Cookies, Inc.

Great American Entertainment Company, **13** 279; **48** 194

Great American First Savings Bank of San Diego, **II** 420

Great American Insurance Company, **48** 9

Great American Lines Inc., **12** 29

Great American Management and Investment, Inc., 8 228–31; 49 130

Great American Reserve Insurance Co., **IV** 343; **10** 247

Great American Restaurants, **13** 321

The Great Atlantic & Pacific Tea Company, Inc., II 636–38; 16 247–50 (upd.); 55 164–69 (upd.)

Great Bagel and Coffee Co., **27** 480–81

Great Harvest Bread Company, 44 184–86

Great Lakes Bancorp, 8 232–33

Great Lakes Carbon Corporation, **12** 99

Great Lakes Chemical Corp., I 341–42; 8 262; **14 216–18 (upd.)**

Great Lakes Dredge & Dock Company, 69 194–97

Great Lakes Energy Corp., **39** 261

Great Lakes Steel Corp., **8** 346; **12** 352; **26** 528

Great Lakes Transportation LLC, **71** 82

Great Lakes Window, Inc., **12** 397

Great Land Seafoods, Inc., **II** 553

Great Northern Nekoosa Corp., **IV** 282–83; **9** 260–61; **47** 148

Great Northern Railway Company, **6** 596

Great Plains Energy Incorporated, 65 156–60 (upd.)

Great Plains Software Inc., **38** 432

Great Plains Transportation, **18** 226

Great Rigs, Inc., **71** 8–9

Great River Oil and Gas Corporation, **61** 111

Great Shoshone & Twin Falls Water Power Company, **12** 265

The Great Universal Stores plc, V 67–69; 19 181–84 (upd.) *see also* GUS plc.

Great-West Lifeco Inc., III 260–61; 21 447 *see also* Power Corporation of Canada.

The Great Western Auction House & Clothing Store, **19** 261

Great Western Bank, **47** 160

Great Western Billiard Manufactory, **III** 442

Great Western Financial Corporation, 10 339–41

Great Western Foam Co., **17** 182

Great World Foods, Inc., **17** 93

Greatbatch Inc., 72 154–56

Greb Industries Ltd., **16** 79, 545

Grebner GmbH, **26** 21

Grede Foundries, Inc., 38 214–17

Greeley Beef Plant, **13** 350

Greeley Gas Company, **43** 56–57

Green Acquisition Co., **18** 107

Green Bay Food Company, **7** 127

The Green Bay Packers, Inc., 32 223–26

Green Capital Investors L.P., **23** 413–14

Green Giant, **14** 212, 214; **24** 140–41

Green Island Cement (Holdings) Ltd. Group, **IV** 694–95

Green Line Investor Services, **18** 553

Green Mountain Coffee, Inc., 31 227–30

Green Power & Light Company *see* UtiliCorp United Inc.

Green River Electric Corporation, **11** 37

Green Siam Air Services Co., Ltd., **51** 123

Green Tree Financial Corporation, 11 162–63 *see also* Conseco, Inc.

The Greenalls Group PLC, 21 245–47

Greenbacks Inc., **62** 104

Greenberg Traurig, LLP, 65 161–63

The Greenbrier Companies, 19 185–87

Greene King plc, 31 223–26

Greene, Tweed & Company, 55 170–72

Greenfield Healthy Foods, **26** 58

Greenfield Industries Inc., **13** 8

Greenham Construction Materials, **38** 451–52

Greenman Brothers Inc. *see* Noodle Kidoodle.

Greenpeace International, 74 128–30

GreenPoint Financial Corp., 28 166–68

Greensboro Life Insurance Company, **11** 213

Greenville Tube Corporation, **21** 108

Greenwich Air Services Inc., **73** 43

Greenwich Associates, **19** 117

Greenwood Mills, Inc., 14 219–21

Greenwood Publishing Group *see* Reed Elsevier.

Greenwood Trust Company, **18** 478

Greg Manning Auctions, Inc., 60 145–46

Greggs PLC, 65 164–66

Gregory Mountain Products *see* Bianchi International.

Greif Inc., 15 186–88; 66 154–56 (upd.)

Greiner Engineering Inc., **45** 421

Grupo Financiero Banorte, S.A. de C.V., 51 149–51

Grupo Financiero BBVA Bancomer S.A., 54 147–50

Grupo Financiero Galicia S.A., 63 178–81

Grupo Financiero Inbursa, 21 259

Grupo Financiero Inverlat, S.A., 39 188; 59 74

Grupo Financiero Serfin, S.A., 19 188–90, 474; 36 63

Grupo Gigante, S.A. de C.V., 34 197–99

Grupo Hecali, S.A., 39 196

Grupo Herdez, S.A. de C.V., 35 208–10; 54 167

Grupo Hermes, 24 359

Grupo ICA, 52 394

Grupo IMSA, S.A. de C.V., 44 193–96

Grupo Industrial Alfa, S.A. de C.V. *see* Alfa, S.A. de C.V.

Grupo Industrial Atenquique, S.A. de C.V., 37 176

Grupo Industrial Bimbo, 19 191–93; 29 338

Grupo Industrial Durango, S.A. de C.V., 37 176–78

Grupo Industrial Maseca S.A. de C.V. (Gimsa) *see* Gruma, S.A. de C.V.

Grupo Industrial Saltillo, S.A. de C.V., 54 151–54

Grupo Irsa, 23 171

Grupo Leche Pascual S.A., 59 212–14

Grupo Lladró S.A., 52 147–49

Grupo Marsans, 69 9, 11–12

Grupo Martins, 59 361

Grupo Mexico, S.A. de C.V., 40 220–23, 413

Grupo Modelo, S.A. de C.V., 29 218–20

Grupo Nacional Provincial, 22 285

Grupo Pipsamex S.A., 37 178

Grupo Portucel Soporcel, 60 154–56

Grupo Posadas, S.A. de C.V., 57 168–70

Grupo Protexa, 16 210

Grupo Pulsar *see* Pulsar Internacional S.A.

Grupo Quan, 19 192–93

Grupo Salinas, 39 196

Grupo Sanborns S.A. de C.V., 35 118

Grupo Servia, S.A. de C.V., 50 209

Grupo TACA, 38 218–20

Grupo Televisa, S.A., 9 429; 18 211–14; 19 10; 24 515–17; 39 188, 398; 54 155–58 (upd.); 57 121

Grupo TMM, S.A. de C.V., 50 208–11

Grupo Transportación Ferroviaria Mexicana, S.A. de C.V., 47 162–64

Grupo Tribasa, 34 82

Grupo Tudor, IV 471

Grupo Xtra, 39 186, 188

Gruppo Banco di Napoli, 50 410

Gruppo Buffetti S.p.A., 47 345–46

Gruppo Coin S.p.A., 41 185–87

Gruppo Editoriale L'Espresso S.p.A., 54 19–21

Gruppo GFT, 22 123

Gruppo IRI, V 325–27

Gryphon Development, 24 237

Gryphon Holdings, Inc., 21 262–64

GS Financial Services L.P., 51 148

GSD&M Advertising, 44 197–200

GSG&T, Inc. *see* Gulf States Utilities Company.

GSG Holdings Ltd., 39 87

GSI *see* Geophysical Service, Inc.

GSI Acquisition Co. L.P., 17 488

GSI Commerce, Inc., 67 204–06

GSR, Inc., 17 338

GSU *see* Gulf States Utilities Company.

GT Bicycles, 26 183–85, 412

GT Global Inc. *see* AMVESCAP PLC.

GT Interactive Software, 19 405; 31 237–41 *see also* Infogrames Entertainment S.A.

GTE Corporation, V 294–98; 15 192–97 (upd.) *see also* British Columbia Telephone Company; Verizon Communications.

GTE Northwest Inc., 37 124–26

GTECH Holdings, Inc., 27 381

GTI Corporation, 29 461–62

GTM-Entrepose, 23 332

GTM Group, 43 450, 452; 54 392

GTO *see* Global Transport Organization.

GTS Duratek, Inc., 13 367–68

GTSI *see* Government Technology Services Inc.

GTSI Corp., 57 171–73

GU Markets, 55 83

Guangzhou Kurabo Chemicals Co. Ltd., 61 229

Guangzhou M. C. Packaging, 10 130

Guangzhou Pearl River Piano Group Ltd., 49 177–79

Guangzhou Railway Corporation, 52 43

Guarantee Life Cos., 69 368

Guarantee Reserve Life Insurance Company, 59 246

Guaranty Bank & Trust Company, 13 440

Guaranty Federal Bank, F.S.B., 31 441

Guaranty Federal Savings & Loan Assoc., IV 343

Guaranty Properties Ltd., 11 258

Guaranty Savings and Loan, 10 339

Guaranty Trust Co. *see* J.P. Morgan & Co. Incorporated.

Guardforce Limited, 45 378

Guardian Bank, 13 468

Guardian Federal Savings and Loan Association, 10 91

Guardian Financial Services, 64 171–74 (upd.)

Guardian Media Group plc, 53 152–55

Guardian Mortgage Company, 8 460

Guardian Refrigerator Company *see* Frigidaire Home Products.

Guardian Royal Exchange Plc, 11 168–70; 33 319 *see also* Guardian Financial Services.

Guardsmark, L.L.C., 77 171–174

Gubor Schokoladen, 15 221

Gucci Group N.V., 45 343–44; 50 212–16 (upd.); 54 320; 57 179

Guccio Gucci, S.p.A., 12 281; 15 198–200; 27 329; 57 180

GUD Holdings, Ltd., 17 106; 61 66

Gudang Garam Tbk, PT, 62 96–97

Guerbet Group, 46 214–16

Guerdon Homes, Inc., 41 19

Guerlain, 23 240–42; 33 272

Guess, Inc., 15 201–03; 68 187–91 (upd.)

Guest, Keen and Nettlefolds plc *see* GKN plc.

Guest Supply, Inc., 18 215–17

Guida, 63 151

Guidant Corporation, 58 149–51

Guideoutdoors.com Inc., 36 446

Guilbert S.A., 42 169–71

Guild Press, Inc., 13 559

Guild Wineries, 13 134; 34 89

Guilford Industries, 8 270–72

Guilford Mills Inc., 8 234–36; 40 224–27 (upd.)

Guilford of Maine, Inc., 29 246

Guilford Transportation Industries, Inc., 16 348, 350

Guillemot Corporation, 41 188–91, 407, 409

Guillin *see* Groupe Guillin SA

Guinness Mahon, 36 231

Guinness Overseas Ltd., 25 281

Guinness Peat Aviation, 10 277; 36 426

Guinness plc, I 250–52, 268, 272, 282; II 610; 9 100, 449; 10 399; 13 454; 18 62, 501; 29 84; 33 276; 36 405–06 *see also* Diageo plc.

Guinness/UDV, 43 212–16 (upd.); 61 324–25

Guitar Center, Inc., 29 221–23; 68 192–95 (upd.)

Guittard Chocolate Company, 55 183–85

Guizhou Tyres Inc., 71 393

Gulco Industries, Inc., 11 194

Gulf + Western Inc., I 451–53 *see also* Paramount Communications.

Gulf Air Company, 56 146–48

Gulf Canada Ltd., I 262, 264; IV 721; 6 478; 9 391; 13 557–58

Gulf Canada Resources Ltd., 63 110

Gulf Coast Sportswear Inc., 23 65

Gulf Energy Development, 22 107

Gulf Engineering Co. Ltd., IV 131

Gulf Island Fabrication, Inc., 44 201–03

Gulf Marine & Maintenance Offshore Service Company, 22 276

Gulf Oil Chemical Co., 13 502

Gulf Oil Corp. *see* Chevron.

Gulf Power Company, 38 446, 448

Gulf Printing Company, 70 67

Gulf Public Service Company, Inc, 6 580; 37 89

Gulf Resources & Chemical Corp., 15 464

Gulf States Steel, I 491

Gulf States Utilities Company, 6 495–97; 12 99

GulfMark Offshore, Inc., 49 180–82

Gulfstream Aerospace Corporation, 7 205–06; 28 169–72 (upd.)

Gulfwind Marine USA, 30 303

Gulistan Holdings Inc., 28 219

Gulton Industries Inc., 7 297; 19 31

Kay-Bee Toy Stores, **15** 252–53 *see also* KB Toys.
Kay Home Products, **17** 372
Kay Jewelers Inc., **61** 327
Kaydon Corporation, 18 274–76
Kaye, Scholer, Fierman, Hays & Handler, **47** 436
Kayex, **9** 251
Kaynar Manufacturing Company, **8** 366
Kayser Aluminum & Chemicals, **8** 229
Kayser Roth Corp., **8** 288; **22** 122
Kaytee Products Incorporated, **58** 60
KB Home, 45 218–22 **(upd.)**
AO KB Impuls, **48** 419
KB Investment Co., Ltd., **58** 208
KB Toys, 35 253–55 **(upd.)**
KBLCOM Incorporated, **V** 644
KC *see* Kenneth Cole Productions, Inc.
KC Holdings, Inc., **11** 229–30
KCI Konecranes International, **27** 269
KCK Tissue S.A., **73** 205
KCPL *see* Kansas City Power & Light Company.
KCS Industries, **12** 25–26
KCSI *see* Kansas City Southern Industries, Inc.
KCSR *see* Kansas City Southern Railway.
KD Acquisition Corporation, **34** 103–04; **76** 239
KD Manitou, Inc. *see* Manitou BF S.A.
KDI Corporation, **56** 16–17
KDT Industries, Inc., **9** 20
Keane, Inc., 38 431; **56** 182–86
Keck's *see* Decorator Industries Inc.
The Keds Corp., **37** 377, 379
Keebler Foods Company, 36 311–13
Keegan Management Co., **27** 274
Keene Packaging Co., **28** 43
KEG Productions Ltd., **IV** 640; **26** 272
Keil Chemical Company, **8** 178
Keio Teito Electric Railway Company, V 461–62
The Keith Companies Inc., 54 181–84
Keith Prowse Music Publishing, **22** 193
Keithley Instruments Inc., 16 299–301
Kelco, **34** 281
Kelda Group plc, 45 223–26
Keliher Hardware Company, **57** 8
Kelkoo S.A. *see* Yahoo! Inc.
Keller Builders, **43** 400
Keller-Dorian Graveurs, S.A., **17** 458
Kelley & Partners, Ltd., **14** 130
Kelley Drye & Warren LLP, 40 280–83
Kellock, **10** 336
Kellogg Brown & Root, Inc., 62 201–05 **(upd.)**
Kellogg Company, II 523–26; **13** 291–94 **(upd.)**; **50** 291–96 **(upd.)**
Kellogg Foundation, **41** 118
Kellwood Company, 8 287–89; **59** 268; **62** 210
Kelly & Cohen, **10** 468
Kelly-Moore Paint Company, Inc., 56 99, 187–89
Kelly Nason, Inc., **13** 203
Kelly Services, Inc., 6 35–37; **26** 237–40 **(upd.)**

The Kelly-Springfield Tire Company, 8 290–92; **20** 260, 263
Kelsey-Hayes Group of Companies, 7 258–60; **27** 249–52 **(upd.)**
Kelso & Co., **12** 436; **19** 455; **21** 490; **33** 92; **63** 237; **71** 145–46
Kelty Pack, Inc., **10** 215
Kelvinator Inc., **17** 487
Kelvinator of India, Ltd., **59** 417
KemaNobel, **9** 380–81; **13** 22
Kemet Corp., 14 281–83
Kemi Oy, **IV** 316
Kemira Oyj, 70 143–46
Kemper Corporation, III 269–71, 339; **15** 254–58 **(upd.)**; **22** 495; **33** 111; **42** 451
Kemper Financial Services, **26** 234
Kemper Snowboards, **22** 460
Kencraft, Inc., **71** 22–23
Kendall International, Inc., IV 288; **11** 219–21; **14** 121; **15** 229; **28** 486
Kendall-Jackson Winery, Ltd., 28 111, 221–23
Kenetech Corporation, 11 222–24
Kenhar Corporation *see* Cascade Corporation.
Kenmore Air Harbor Inc., 65 191–93
Kennametal, Inc., 13 295–97; **68** 212–16 **(upd.)**
Kennecott Corporation, 7 261–64; **27** 253–57 **(upd.)** *see also* Rio Tinto PLC.
Kennedy Automatic Products Co., **16** 8
Kennedy-Wilson, Inc., 60 183–85
Kenner Parker Toys, Inc., **9** 156; **12** 168; **14** 266; **16** 337; **25** 488–89
Kenneth Cole Productions, Inc., 25 256–58
Kenneth O. Lester, Inc., **21** 508
Kenny Rogers' Roasters, **22** 464; **29** 342, 344
Kenroy International, Inc., **13** 274
Kensey Nash Corporation, 71 185–87
Kensington Associates L.L.C., **60** 146
Kent Electronics Corporation, 17 273–76
Kentrox Industries, **30** 7
Kentucky Electric Steel, Inc., 31 286–88
Kentucky Fried Chicken *see* KFC Corporation.
Kentucky Institution for the Education of the Blind *see* American Printing House for the Blind.
Kentucky Utilities Company, 6 513–15; **11** 37, 236–38; **51** 217
Kenwood Corporation, 19 360; **23** 53; **31** 289–91
Kenwood Silver Company, Inc., **31** 352
Kenwood Winery, **68** 146
Kenyon & Eckhardt Advertising Agency, **25** 89–91
Kenyon Corp., **18** 276
Kenzo, **25** 122
Keo Cutters, Inc., **III** 569; **20** 360
Keolis SA, 51 191–93
Kepco *see* Korea Electric Power Corporation; Kyushu Electric Power Company Inc.
Keppel Corporation Ltd., 73 201–03

Keramik Holding AG Laufen, 51 194–96
Kern County Land Co., **10** 379
Kernite SA, **8** 386
Kernkraftwerke Lippe-Ems, **V** 747
Kerr Concrete Pipe Company, **14** 250
Kerr Corporation, **14** 481
Kerr Drug Stores, **32** 170
Kerr Group Inc., 10 130; **24** 263–65; **30** 39
Kerr-McGee Corporation, IV 445–47; **13** 118; **22** 301–04 **(upd.)**; **63** 441; **68** 217–21 **(upd.)**
Kerry Group plc, 27 258–60
Kerry Properties Limited, 22 305–08; **24** 388
Kerzner International Limited, 69 222–24 **(upd.)**
Keski-Suomen Tukkukauppa Oy, **8** 293
Kesko Ltd (Kesko Oy), 8 293–94; **27** 261–63 **(upd.)**
Kessler Rehabilitation Corporation *see* Select Medical Corporation.
Ketchikan Paper Company, **31** 316
Ketchum Communications Inc., 6 38–40
Kettle Chip Company (Australia), **26** 58
Kettle Foods Inc., 26 58; **48** 240–42
Kettle Restaurants, Inc., **29** 149
Kewaunee Scientific Corporation, 25 259–62
Kewpie Kabushiki Kaisha, 57 202–05
Key Computer Laboratories, Inc., **14** 15
Key Industries, Inc., **26** 342
Key Pharmaceuticals, Inc., **11** 207; **41** 419
Key Safety Systems, Inc., 63 224–26
Key Tronic Corporation, 14 284–86
KeyCorp, 8 295–97; **11** 110; **14** 90
Keyes Fibre Company, 9 303–05
KeyLabs, **65** 34–35
Keypage *see* Rural Cellular Corporation.
Keypoint Technology Corporation *see* ViewSonic Corporation.
KeySpan Energy Co., 27 264–66
Keystone Consolidated Industries, Inc., **19** 467
Keystone Foods Corporation, **10** 443
Keystone Frozen Foods, **17** 536
Keystone Health Plan West, Inc., **27** 211
Keystone Insurance and Investment Co., **12** 564
Keystone International, Inc., 11 225–27; **28** 486
Keystone Life Insurance Co., **III** 389; **33** 419
Keystone Paint and Varnish, **8** 553
Keystone Portland Cement Co., **23** 225
Keystone Savings and Loan, **II** 420
Keystone Tube Inc., **25** 8
Keytronics, **18** 541
KFC Corporation, 7 265–68; **10** 450; **21** 313–17 **(upd.)**; **23** 115, 117, 153; **32** 12–14; **58** 383–84
KFF Management, **37** 350
Kforce Inc., 71 188–90
KHBB, **16** 72

Knife River Corporation, **42** 249, 253
Knight-Ridder, Inc., IV 628–30, 670; **15**
262–66 (upd.); 18 323; **38** 307; **63**
394; **67 219–23 (upd.)**
Knight Trading Group, Inc., 70 147–49
Knight Transportation, Inc., 64 218–21
Knightsbridge Capital Corporation, **59**
192
Knightsbridge Partners, **26** 476
Knightway Promotions Ltd., **64** 346
KNILM, **24** 397
Knogo Corp., **11** 444; **39** 78
Knoll Group Inc., I 202; **14 299–301**
Knorr-Bremse, **11** 31
Knorr Co *see* C.H. Knorr Co.
Knorr Foods Co., Ltd., **28** 10
The Knot, Inc., 74 168–71
Knott's Berry Farm, 18 288–90; 22 130
Knowledge Learning Corporation, 51
197–99; 54 191
Knowledge Systems Concepts, **11** 469
Knowledge Universe, Inc., 54 191–94
KnowledgeWare Inc., 9 309–11; 27 491;
31 296–98 (upd.); 45 206
Knox County Insurance, **41** 178
Knox Reeves Advertising Agency, **25** 90
Knoxville Glove Co., **34** 159
Knoxville Paper Box Co., Inc., **13** 442
KNP BT *see* Buhrmann NV.
KNP Leykam, **49** 352, 354
KNSM *see* Koninklijke Nederlandsche
Stoomboot Maatschappij.
Knudsen & Sons, Inc., **11** 211
Knudsen Foods, **27** 330
Knutson Construction, **25** 331
KOA *see* Kampgrounds of America, Inc.
Koala Corporation, 44 260–62
Kobacker Co., **18** 414–15
Kobe Hankyu Company Ltd., **62** 170
Kobe Shipbuilding & Engine Works, **II**
57
Kobe Steel, Ltd., I 511; **IV** 16, **129–31,**
212–13; **8** 242; **11** 234–35; **13** 297;
19 238–41 (upd.); 38 225–26
Kobelco America Inc., **19** 241
Kobelco Middle East, **IV** 131
Kobold *see* Vorwerk & Co.
Kobrand Corporation, **24** 308; **43** 402
Koç Holding A.S., I 478–80; **27** 188; **54**
195–98 (upd.)
Koch Enterprises, Inc., 29 215–17
Koch Industries, Inc., IV 448–49; **20**
330–32 (upd.); 77 224–230 (upd.)
Koch-Light Laboratories, **13** 239; **38**
203–04
Kockos Brothers, Inc., **II** 624
Kodak *see* Eastman Kodak Company.
Kodansha Ltd., IV 631–33; **38 273–76**
(upd.)
Koehring Company, **8** 545; **23** 299
Koehring Cranes & Excavators, **7** 513
Koei Real Estate Ltd. *see* Takashimaya
Co., Limited.
Koenig & Bauer AG, 64 222–26
Koenig Plastics Co., **19** 414
Kogaku Co., Ltd., **48** 295
Kohl's Corporation, 9 312–13; **30**
273–75 **(upd.); 77 231–235 (upd.)**

Kohl's Food Stores, Inc., **I** 426–27; **16**
247, 249
Kohlberg Kravis Roberts & Co., 24
272–74; **56 190–94 (upd.)**
Kohler Company, 7 269–71; **10** 119; **24**
150; **32 308–12 (upd.); 53** 176
Kohler Mix Specialties, Inc., **25** 333
Kohn Pedersen Fox Associates P.C., 57
213–16
Kokkola Chemicals Oy, **17** 362–63
Kokomo Gas and Fuel Company, **6** 533
Kokudo Corporation, **74** 301
Kokusai Kigyo Co. Ltd., **60** 301
Kolb-Lena, **25** 85
Kolker Chemical Works, Inc., **7** 308
The Koll Company, 8 300–02
Kollmorgen Corporation, 18 291–94
Kölnische Rückversicherungs- Gesellschaft
AG, **24** 178
Komag, Inc., 11 234–35
Komatsu Ltd., III 545–46; **16 309–11**
(upd.); 52 213–17 (upd.)
Kompass Allgemeine Vermögensberatung,
51 23
Konan Camera Institute, **III** 487
KONE Corporation, 27 267–70; 76
225–28 (upd.)
Kongl. Elektriska Telegraf-Verket *see* Swed-
ish Telecom.
Konica Corporation, III 547–50; **30**
276–81 (upd.); 43 284
König Brauerei GmbH & Co. KG, 35
256–58 (upd.)
Koninklijke Ahold N.V., II 641–42; **16**
312–14 (upd.)
Koninklijke Bols Wessanen, N.V., **29**
480–81; **57** 105
Koninklijke Grolsch BV *see* Royal Grolsch
NV.
Koninklijke Hoogovens NV *see* Konin-
klijke Nederlandsche Hoogovens en
Staalfabrieken NV.
Koninklijke Java-China Paketvaart Lijnen
see Royal Interocean Lines.
NV Koninklijke KNP BT *see* Buhrmann
NV.
Koninklijke KPN N.V. *see* Royal KPN
N.V.
Koninklijke Luchtvaart Maatschappij
N.V., I 107–09, 119, 121; **6** 105,
109–10; **14** 73; **28 224–27 (upd.)**
Koninklijke Nederlandsche Hoogovens
en Staalfabrieken NV, IV 132–34; **49**
98, 101
Koninklijke Nederlandsche Stoomboot
Maatschappij, **26** 241
N.V. Koninklijke Nederlandse Vlieg-
tuigenfabriek Fokker, I 54–56; **28**
327–30 (upd.)
Koninklijke Nedlloyd N.V., 6 403–05;
26 241–44 (upd.)
Koninklijke Numico N.V. *see* Royal Nu-
mico N.V.
Koninklijke Paketvaart Maatschappij, **26**
242
Koninklijke Philips Electronics N.V., 50
297–302 (upd.)

Koninklijke PTT Nederland NV, V
299–301; **27** 471–72, 475 *see also*
Royal KPN NV.
Koninklijke Van Ommeren, **22** 275
Koninklijke Vendex KBB N.V. (Royal
Vendex KBB N.V.), 62 206–09 (upd.)
Koninklijke Wessanen nv, II 527–29; **54**
199–204 (upd.)
Koninklijke West-Indische Maildienst, **26**
242
Konishiroku Honten Co., Ltd., **III** 487,
547–49
Konrad Hornschuch AG, **31** 161–62
Koo Koo Roo, Inc., 25 263–65
Kookmin Bank, 58 206–08
Koop Nautic Holland, **41** 412
Koor Industries Ltd., II 47–49; **22** 501;
25 266–68 (upd.); 54 363; **68 222–25**
(upd.)
Koors Perry & Associates, Inc., **24** 95
Koortrade, **II** 48
Kop-Coat, Inc., **8** 456
Kopin Corp., **13** 399
Köpings Mekaniska Verkstad, **26** 10
Koppel Steel, **26** 407
Koppers Industries, Inc., I 354–56; **26**
245–48 (upd.)
Koracorp Industries Inc., **16** 327
Koramic Roofing Products N.V., **70** 363
Korbel Champagne Cellers *see* F. Korbel
& Bros. Inc.
Körber AG, 60 190–94
Korea Automotive Fuel Systems Ltd., **13**
555
Korea Automotive Motor Corp., **16** 436;
43 319
Korea Electric Power Corporation
(Kepco), 56 195–98
Korea Ginseng Corporation *see* KT&G
Corporation.
Korea Independent Energy Corporation,
62 175
Korea Steel Co., **III** 459
Korea Tobacco & Ginseng Corporation *see*
KT&G Corporation.
Korean Air Lines Co. Ltd., 6 98–99; **24**
443; **27 271–73 (upd.); 46** 40
Korean Development Bank, **III** 459
Korean Life Insurance Company, Ltd., **62**
175
Koret of California, Inc., 62 210–13
Kori Kollo Corp., **23** 41
Korn/Ferry International, 34 247–49
Koro Corp., **19** 414
Korrekt Gebäudereinigung, **16** 420; **43**
307
KorrVu, **14** 430
Kortbetalning Servo A.B., **II** 353
Kortgruppen Eurocard-Köpkort A.B., **II**
353
Korvettes, E.J., **14** 426
Kos Pharmaceuticals, Inc., 63 232–35
Koss Corporation, 38 277–79
Kosset Carpets, Ltd., **9** 467
Kotobukiya Co., Ltd., V 113–14; **56**
199–202 (upd.)
Kowa Metal Manufacturing Co., **III** 758
Koyland Ltd., **64** 217

National Mobility Corp., **30** 436
The National Motor Bearing Company *see* Federal-Mogul Corporation.
The National Motor Club of America, Inc., **33** 418
National Mutual Life Assurance of Australasia, **III** 249
National Office Furniture, **12** 297
National Oil Corporation, 66 233–37 **(upd.)**
National Oilwell, Inc., 54 247–50
National Old Line Insurance Co., **III** 179
National Organization for Women, Inc., 55 274–76
National Paper Co., **8** 476
National Parks Transportation Company, **25** 420–22
National Patent Development Corporation, 13 365–68 *see also* GP Strategies Corporation.
National Periodical Publications *see* DC Comics Inc.
National Permanent Mutual Benefit Building Society, **10** 6
National Petroleum Refiners of South Africa, **47** 340
National Pharmacies, **9** 346
National Picture & Frame Company, 24 345–47
National Pig Development Co., **46** 84
National Postal Meter Company, **14** 52
National Power Corporation, **56** 214–15
National Power PLC, 11 399–400; **12** 349–51; **13** 458, 484 *see also* International Power PLC.
National Presto Industries, Inc., 16 382–85; **43** 286–90 **(upd.)**
National Processing, Inc., **24** 394
National Propane Corporation, **8** 535–37
National Public Radio, 19 280–82; **47** 259–62 **(upd.)**
National Publishing Company, **41** 110
National Quotation Bureau, Inc., **14** 96–97
National R.V. Holdings, Inc., 32 348–51
National Railroad Passenger Corporation (Amtrak), 22 375–78; **66** 238–42 **(upd.)**
National Ready Mixed, **70** 343
National Realty Trust *see* NRT Incorporated.
National Record Mart, Inc., 29 348–50
National Register Publishing Co., **17** 399; **23** 442
National Reinsurance Corporation *see* General Re Corporation.
National Research Corporation, **8** 397
National Restaurants Management, Inc., **38** 385–87
National Revenue Corporation, **22** 181
National Rifle Association of America, 37 265–68
National Rubber Machinery Corporation, **8** 298
National Sanitary Supply Co., 16 386–87
National Satellite Paging, **18** 348

National School Studios, **7** 255; **25** 252
National Science Foundation, **9** 266
National Sea Products Ltd., 14 339–41
National Security Containers LLC, **58** 238
National Semiconductor Corporation, II 63–65; **6** 261–63; **26** 327–30 **(upd.); 69** 267–71 **(upd.)**
National Service Industries, Inc., 11 336–38; **54** 251–55 **(upd.)**
National Shoe Products Corp., **16** 17
National Slicing Machine Company, **19** 359
National-Southwire Aluminum Company, **11** 38; **12** 353
National Stamping & Electric Works, **12** 159
National Standard Co., IV 137; **13** 369–71
National Starch and Chemical Company, 32 256–57; **49** 268–70
National Steel and Shipbuilding Company, **7** 356
National Steel Corporation, IV 163, 236–37, 572; **V** 152–53; **8** 346, 479–80; **12** 352–54; **26** 527–29 *see also* FoxMeyer Health Corporation.
National Student Marketing Corporation, **10** 385–86
National System Company, **9** 41; **11** 469
National Tea, **II** 631–32
National Technical Laboratories, **14** 52
National TechTeam, Inc., 41 280–83
National Telecommunications of Austin, **8** 311
National Telephone and Telegraph Corporation *see* British Columbia Telephone Company.
National Telephone Co., **7** 332, 508
National Thoroughbred Racing Association, 58 244–47
National Trading Manufacturing, Inc., **22** 213
National Transcommunications Ltd. *see* NTL Inc.
National Union Electric Corporation, **12** 159
National Utilities & Industries Corporation, **9** 363
National Westminster Bank PLC, II 333–35; **13** 206
National Wine & Spirits, Inc., 49 271–74
Nationale-Nederlanden N.V., III 308–11; **50** 11
Nationar, **9** 174
NationsBank Corporation, 10 425–27 *see also* Bank of America Corporation
NationsRent, **28** 388
Nationwide Cellular Service, Inc., **27** 305
Nationwide Credit, **11** 112
Nationwide Group, **25** 155
Nationwide Income Tax Service, **9** 326
Nationwide Logistics Corp., **14** 504
Nationwide Mutual Insurance Co., **26** 488
NATIOVIE, **II** 234
Native Plants, **III** 43

NATM Buying Corporation, **10** 9, 468
Natomas Company, **7** 309; **11** 271
Natref *see* National Petroleum Refiners of South Africa.
Natrol, Inc., 49 275–78
Natronag, **IV** 325
NatSteel Electronics Ltd., **48** 369
NatTeknik, **26** 333
Natudryl Manufacturing Company, **10** 271
Natura Cosméticos S.A., 75 268–71
Natural Alternatives International, Inc., 49 279–82
Natural Gas Clearinghouse *see* NGC Corporation.
Natural Gas Corp., **19** 155
Natural Gas Pipeline Company, **6** 530, 543; **7** 344–45
Natural Gas Service of Arizona, **19** 411
Natural Ovens Bakery, Inc., 72 234–36
Natural Selection Foods, 54 256–58
Natural Wonders Inc., 14 342–44
NaturaLife International, **26** 470
Naturalizer *see* Brown Shoe Company, Inc.
The Nature Company, **10** 215–16; **14** 343; **26** 439; **27** 429; **28** 306
The Nature Conservancy, 26 323; **28** 305–07, 422
Nature's Sunshine Products, Inc., 15 317–19; **26** 470; **27** 353; **33** 145
Nature's Way Products Inc., **26** 315
Naturin GmbH *see* Viscofan S.A.
Naturipe Berry Growers, **62** 154
Natuzzi Group *see* Industrie Natuzzi S.p.A.
NatWest Bancorp, **38** 393
NatWest Bank *see* National Westminster Bank PLC.
Naugles, **7** 506
Nautica Enterprises, Inc., 18 357–60; **44** 302–06 **(upd.)**
Nautilus International, Inc., **13** 532; **25** 40; **30** 161
Navaho Freight Line, **16** 41
Navajo LTL, Inc., **57** 277
Navajo Refining Company, **12** 240
Navajo Shippers, Inc., **42** 364
Navan Resources, **38** 231
Navarre Corporation, 22 536; **24** 348–51
Navigant International, Inc., 47 263–66
Navigation Mixte, **III** 348
Navire Cargo Gear, **27** 269
Navisant, Inc., **49** 424
Navistar International Corporation, I 180–82; **10** 428–30 **(upd.)** *see also* International Harvester Co.
NAVTEQ Corporation, 69 272–75
Navy Exchange Service Command, 31 342–45
Navy Federal Credit Union, 33 315–17
Naxon Utilities Corp., **19** 359
Naylor, Hutchinson, Vickers & Company *see* Vickers PLC.
NBC *see* National Broadcasting Company, Inc.
NBC Bankshares, Inc., **21** 524

Old Quaker Paint Company, **13** 471

Old Republic International Corporation, 11 373–75; **58** 258–61 (upd.)

Old Spaghetti Factory International Inc., 24 364–66

Old Stone Trust Company, **13** 468

Old Town Canoe Company, 74 222–24

Oldach Window Corp., **19** 446

Oldcastle, Inc., **60** 77; **64** 98

Oldover Corp., **23** 225

Ole's Innovative Sports *see* Rollerblade, Inc.

Olean Tile Co., **22** 170

Oleochim, **IV** 498–99

OLEX *see* Deutsche BP Aktiengesellschaft.

Olex Cables Ltd., **10** 445

Olin Corporation, I 379–81; **13** 379–81 (upd.)

Olinkraft, Inc., **11** 420; **16** 376

Olive Garden Italian Restaurants, **10** 322, 324; **16** 156–58; **19** 258; **35** 83

Oliver Rubber Company, **19** 454, 456

Olivetti S.p.A., 34 316–20 (upd.); **38** 300; **63** 379

Olivine Industries, Inc., **II** 508; **11** 172; **36** 255

Olmstead Products Co., **23** 82

OLN *see* Outdoor Life Network.

Olsten Corporation, 6 41–43; **29** 362–65 (upd.); **49** 265 *see also* Adecco S.A.

Olympia & York Developments Ltd., IV 720–21; **6** 478; **8** 327; **9** 390–92 (upd.); **30** 108

Olympia Arenas, Inc., **7** 278–79; **24** 294

Olympia Brewing, **11** 50

Olympia Entertainment, **37** 207

Olympiaki, **III** 401

Olympic Courier Systems, Inc., **24** 126

Olympic Fastening Systems, **III** 722

Olympic Insurance Co., **26** 486

Olympic Packaging, **13** 443

Olympic Property Group LLC *see* Pope Resources L.P.

Olympic Resource Management LLC *see* Pope Resources L.P.

Olympus Communications L.P., **17** 7

Olympus Optical Company, Ltd., **15** 483

Olympus Partners, **65** 258

Olympus Sport *see* Sears plc.

Olympus Symbol, Inc., **15** 483

OM Group, Inc., 17 362–64

OM Gruppen, **59** 154

Omaha Public Power District, **29** 353

Omaha Steaks International Inc., 62 257–59

Omega Gas Company, **8** 349

Omega Group *see* MasterBrand Cabinets, Inc.

Omega Protein Corporation, **25** 546

OmegaTech Inc. *see* Martek Biosciences Corporation.

O'Melveny & Myers, 37 290–93

OMI Corporation, **IV** 34; **9** 111–12; **22** 275; **59** 321–23

Omnes, **17** 419

Omni ApS, **56** 338

Omni Construction Company, Inc., **8** 112–13

Omni Hotels Corp., 12 367–69

Omni-Pac, **12** 377

Omni Services, Inc., **51** 76

Omnibus Corporation, **9** 283

Omnicad Corporation, **48** 75

Omnicare, Inc., 13 49 307–10

Omnicom Group Inc., I 28–32; **22** 394–99 (upd.); **77** 318–325 (upd.)

Omnipoint Communications Inc., **18** 77

OmniSource Corporation, 14 366–67

OmniTech Consulting Group, **51** 99

Omnitel Pronto Italia SpA, **38** 300

OMNOVA Solutions Inc., 59 324–26

Omron Corporation, 28 331–35 (upd.); **53** 46

Omron Tateisi Electronics Company, II 75–77

ÖMV Aktiengesellschaft, IV 485–87

On Assignment, Inc., 20 400–02

On Command Video Corp., **23** 135

On Cue, **9** 360

On-Line Systems *see* Sierra On-Line Inc.

Onan Corporation, **8** 72

Onbancorp Inc., **11** 110

Once Upon A Child, Inc., **18** 207–8

Ondulato Imolese, **IV** 296; **19** 226

1-800-FLOWERS, Inc., 26 344–46; **28** 137

1-800-GOT-JUNK? LLC, 74 225–27

1-800-Mattress *see* Dial-A-Mattress Operating Corporation.

180s, L.L.C., **64** 299–301

One For All, **39** 405

One Price Clothing Stores, Inc., 20 403–05

17187 Yukon Inc., **74** 234

One Stop Trade Building Centre Ltd. *see* Gibbs and Dandy plc.

O'Neal, Jones & Feldman Inc., **11** 142

OneBeacon Insurance Group LLC, **48** 431

Oneida Bank & Trust Company, **9** 229

Oneida County Creameries Co., **7** 202

Oneida Gas Company, **9** 554

Oneida Ltd., 7 406–08; **31** 352–55 (upd.)

ONEOK Inc., 7 409–12

Onex Corporation, 16 395–97; **65** 281–85 (upd.)

OneZero Media, Inc., **31** 240

Ong First Pte Ltd., **76** 372, 374

Onion, Inc., 69 282–84

Onitsuka Co., Ltd., **57** 52

Online Financial Communication Systems, **11** 112

Only One Dollar, Inc. *see* Dollar Tree Stores, Inc.

Onoda Cement Co., Ltd., III 717–19 *see also* Taiheiyo Cement Corporation.

Onomichi, **25** 469

OnResponse.com, Inc., **49** 433

Onsale Inc., **31** 177

Onstead Foods, **21** 501

OnTarget Inc., **38** 432

Ontario Hydro Services Company, 6 541–42; **9** 461; **32** 368–71 (upd.)

Ontario Power Generation, **49** 65, 67

Ontario Teachers' Pension Plan, 61 273–75

OnTrack Data International, **57** 219

OnTrak Systems Inc., **31** 301

Onyx Acceptance Corporation, 59 327–29

Onyx Software Corporation, 53 252–55

O'okiep Copper Company, Ltd., **7** 385–86

Opel AG *see* Adam Opel AG.

Open *see* Groupe Open.

Open Board of Brokers, **9** 369

Open Cellular Systems, Inc., **41** 225–26

Open Market, Inc., **22** 522

OpenTV, Inc., **31** 330–31

OPENWAY SAS, **74** 143

Operadora de Bolsa Serfin *see* Grupo Financiero Serfin, S.A.

Operation Smile, Inc., 75 297–99

Operon Technologies Inc., **39** 335

Opinion Research Corporation, 46 318–22

Opp and Micolas Mills, **15** 247–48

Oppenheimer *see* Ernest Oppenheimer and Sons.

Oppenheimer & Co., Inc., **17** 137; **21** 235; **22** 405; **25** 450; **61** 50

The Oppenheimer Group, 76 295–98

Oppenheimer Wolff & Donnelly LLP, 71 262–64

Opryland USA, **11** 152–53; **25** 403; **36** 229

Opsware Inc., 49 311–14

Optel S.A., **17** 331; **71** 211

OPTi Computer, **9** 116

Opti-Ray, Inc., **12** 215

Optical Corporation *see* Excel Technology, Inc.

Optical Radiation Corporation, **27** 57

Optilink Corporation, **12** 137

Optima Pharmacy Services, **17** 177

Option Care Inc., 48 307–10

Optische Werke G. Rodenstock, 44 319–23

OptiSystems Solutions Ltd., **55** 67

Opto-Electronics Corp., **15** 483

Optus Communications, **25** 102

Optus Vision, **17** 150

Opus Group, 34 321–23

Oracle Corporation, 6 272–74; **24** 367–71 (upd.); **67** 282–87 (upd.)

Orange *see* Wanadoo S.A.

Orange and Rockland Utilities, Inc., **45** 116, 120

Orange Glo International, 53 256–59

Orange Julius of America, **10** 371, 373; **39** 232, 235

Orange Line Bus Company, **6** 604

Orange PLC, **24** 89; **38** 300

Orange Shipbuilding Company, Inc., **58** 70

OraSure Technologies, Inc., 75 300–03

Orb Books *see* Tom Doherty Associates Inc.

Orb Estates, **54** 366, 368

ORBIS Corporation, **59** 289

Orbis Entertainment Co., **20** 6

Purolator Courier, Inc., **6** 390; **16** 397;
18 177; **25** 148
**Purolator Products Company, 21
416–18; 74 253–56 (upd.)**
Puros de Villa Gonzales, **23** 465
Purup-Eskofot, **44** 44
Push Records, Inc., **42** 271
Putnam Investments Inc. *see* Marsh &
McLennan Companies, Inc.
Putnam Management Co., **III** 283
Putnam Plastics Corporation *see* Memry
Corporation.
**Putt-Putt Golf Courses of America, Inc.,
23 396–98**
PVC Container Corporation, 67 312–14
PW Eagle, Inc., 48 333–36
PWA Group, IV 323–25; 28 446 *see also*
Svenska Cellulosa.
PWS Holding Corporation, **13** 406; **26**
47
PWT Projects Ltd., **22** 89
PWT Worldwide, **11** 510
PYA/Monarch, **II** 675; **26** 504
Pyramid Breweries Inc., 33 353–55
Pyramid Communications, Inc., **IV** 623
Pyramid Companies, 54 303–05
Pyramid Electric Company, **10** 319
Pyramid Electronics Supply, Inc., **17** 275
Pyramid Technology Corporation, **10** 504;
27 448
Pyxis Innovations *see* Alticor Inc.
PZ Cussons plc, 72 288–90

Q

Q&B Foods Inc., **57** 202–03
Q Lube, Inc., **18** 145; **24** 339
Q.A.S. Quality Airport Services Israel
Ltd., **70** 311
Q.E.P. Co., Inc., 65 292–94
**Qantas Airways Ltd., 6 109–13; 24
396–401 (upd.); 68 301–07 (upd.)**
Qantas Airways Limited,
**Qatar General Petroleum Corporation,
IV 524–26**
Qiagen N.V., 39 333–35
Qingdao Haier Refrigerator Co., Ltd., **65**
167, 169
Qintex Australia Ltd., **II** 150; **25** 329
QLT Inc., 71 291–94
QMS Ltd., **43** 284
QO Chemicals, Inc., **14** 217
QSC Audio Products, Inc., 56 291–93
QSP, Inc. *see* The Reader's Digest Associa-
tion, Inc.
Qtera Corporation, **36** 352
Quad/Graphics, Inc., 19 333–36
Quad Pharmaceuticals, Inc. *see* Par Phar-
maceuticals Inc.
Quail Oil Tools, **28** 347–48
Quaker Alloy, Inc., **39** 31–32
Quaker Fabric Corp., 19 337–39
**Quaker Foods North America, 73
268–73 (upd.)**
**Quaker Oats Company, II 558–60; 12
409–12 (upd.); 34 363–67 (upd.)**
**Quaker State Corporation, 7 443–45;
21 419–22 (upd.)** *see also* Pennzoil-
Quaker State Company.

**QUALCOMM Incorporated, 20 438–41;
47 317–21 (upd.)**
Qualcore, S. de R.L. de C.V., **51** 116
Qualipac, **55** 309
QualiTROL Corporation, **7** 116–17
Quality Assurance International, **72** 255
Quality Aviation Services, Inc., **53** 132
Quality Bakers of America, **12** 170
Quality Chekd Dairies, Inc., 48 337–39
Quality Courts Motels, Inc. *see* Choice
Hotels International, Inc.
Quality Dining, Inc., 18 437–40; 63 80
Quality Food Centers, Inc., 17 386–88
Quality Inns International *see* Choice Ho-
tels International, Inc.
Quality Markets, Inc., **13** 393
Quality Oil Co., **II** 624–25
Quality Paperback Book Club (QPB), **13**
105–07
Quality Products, Inc., **18** 162
Qualix S.A., **67** 347–48
**Quanex Corporation, 13 422–24; 62
286–89 (upd.)**
Quanta Computer Inc., 47 322–24
Quanta Display Inc., **75** 306
Quanta Systems Corp., **51** 81
Quanterra Alpha L.P., **63** 347
Quantex Microsystems Inc., **24** 31
Quantronix Corporation *see* Excel Tech-
nology Inc.
**Quantum Chemical Corporation, 8
439–41; 11** 441; **30** 231, 441
Quantum Computer Services, Inc. *see*
America Online, Inc.
**Quantum Corporation, 10 458–59; 62
290–93 (upd.)**
Quantum Health Resources, **29** 364
Quantum Marketing International, Inc.,
27 336
Quantum Offshore Contractors, **25** 104
Quantum Overseas N.V., **7** 360
Quantum Restaurant Group, Inc., **30** 330
Quarex Industries, Inc. *see* Western Beef,
Inc.
Quark, Inc., 36 375–79
Quarrie Corporation, **12** 554
Quebec Credit Union League, **48** 290
Québec Hydro-Electric Commission *see*
Hydro-Québec.
Quebecor Inc., 12 412–14; 19 333; **26**
44; **29** 471; **47 325–28 (upd.)**
Queen City Broadcasting, **42** 162
Queens Isetan Co., Ltd. *see* Isetan Com-
pany Limited.
Queensborough Holdings PLC, **38** 103
Queensland Alumina, **IV** 59
Queensland and Northern Territories Air
Service *see* Qantas Airways Limited.
Queensland Mines Ltd., **III** 729
Quelle Group, V 165–67 *see also*
Karstadt Quelle AG.
Quesarias Ibéricas, **23** 219
Quest Aerospace Education, Inc., **18** 521
Quest Diagnostics Inc., 26 390–92
Quest Education Corporation, **42** 212
Quest Pharmacies Inc., **25** 504–05
Questa Oil and Gas Co., **63** 408

**Questar Corporation, 6 568–70; 26
386–89 (upd.)**
Questor Management Co. LLC, **55** 31
Questor Partners, **26** 185
The Quick & Reilly Group, Inc., 18
552; **20 442–44; 26** 65
Quick Pak Inc., **53** 236
Quicken.com *see* Intuit Inc.
The Quigley Corporation, 62 294–97
Quik Stop Markets, Inc., **12** 112
Quiksilver, Inc., 18 441–43; 27 329
QuikTrip Corporation, 36 380–83
Quill Corporation, 28 375–77; 55 354
Quillery, **27** 138
Quilmes Industrial (QUINSA) S.A., 57
74, 76–77; **67 315–17**
Quilter Sound Company *see* QSC Audio
Products, Inc.
Quimica Geral do Nordeste S.A., **68** 81
Química y Farmacia, S.A. de C.V., **59**
332
Quimicos Industriales Penoles *see* Indus-
trias Penoles, S.A. de C.V.
Quincy Family Steak House, **II** 679; **10**
331; **19** 287; **27** 17, 19
Quiñenco S.A., **69** 56–57; **70** 61–62
Quintana Roo, Inc., **17** 243, 245; **25** 42
Quintel Communications, Inc., **61** 375
Quintex Australia Limited, **25** 329
**Quintiles Transnational Corporation, 21
423–25; 68 308–12 (upd.)**
Quintron, Inc., **11** 475
Quintus Computer Systems, **6** 248
Quixote Corporation, 15 378–80
Quixtar Inc. *see* Alticor Inc.
Quixx Corporation, **6** 580
The Quizno's Corporation, 32 444; **42
295–98**
Quoddy Products Inc., **17** 389, 390
Quotron Systems, Inc., **IV** 670; **9** 49,
125; **30** 127; **47** 37
Quovadx Inc., 70 243–46
QVC Inc., 9 428–29; 10 175; **12** 315;
18 132; **20** 75; **24** 120, 123; **58
284–87 (upd.); 67** 206
**Qwest Communications International,
Inc., 37 312–17**
QwikSilver II, Inc., **37** 119

R

R&B Falcon Corp. *see* Transocean Sedco
Forex Inc.
R&B, Inc., 51 305–07
R & B Manufacturing Co., **III** 569; **20**
361
R&D Systems, Inc., **52** 347
R&O Software-Technik GmbH, **27** 492
R&S Home and Auto, **56** 352
R&S Technology Inc., **48** 410
R. and W. Hawaii Wholesale, Inc., **22** 15
R-Anell Custom Homes Inc., **41** 19
R-B *see* Arby's, Inc.
R-Byte, **12** 162
R-C Holding Inc. *see* Air & Water Tech-
nologies Corporation.
R.B. Pamplin Corp., 45 350–52
R.C. Bigelow, Inc., 49 334–36

R.C. Willey Home Furnishings, 72 291–93
R. Cubed Composites Inc., **I** 387
R.E. Funsten Co., **7** 429
R.G. Barry Corp., 17 389–91; 44 364–67 (upd.)
R.G. Dun-Bradstreet Corp. *see* The Dun & Bradstreet Corp.
R. Griggs Group Limited, 23 399–402; 31 413–14
R.H. Donnelley Corporation, **61** 81–83
R.H. Macy & Co., Inc., V 168–70; 8 442–45 (upd.); **30** 379–83 (upd.)
R.H. Stengel & Company, **13** 479
R.J. Reynolds, **I** 261, 363; **II** 544; **7** 130, 132, 267, 365, 367; **9** 533; **13** 490; **14** 78; **15** 72–73; **16** 242; **21** 315; **27** 125; **29** 195; **32** 344 *see also* RJR Nabisco.
R.J. Reynolds Tobacco Holdings, Inc., 30 384–87 (upd.)
R.J. Tower Corporation *see* Tower Automotive, Inc.
R.K. Brown, **14** 112
R.L. Crain Limited, **15** 473
R.L. Manning Company, **9** 363–64
R.L. Polk & Co., 10 460–62
R-O Realty, Inc., **43** 314
R.P.M., Inc., **25** 228
R.P. Scherer Corporation, I 678–80
R.R. Bowker Co., **17** 398; **23** 440
R.R. Donnelley & Sons Company, IV 660–62; 38 368–71 (upd.)
R.S.R. Corporation, **31** 48
R.S. Stokvis Company, **13** 499
R. Scott Associates, **11** 57
R-T Investors LC, **42** 323–24
R. Twining & Co., **61** 395
R.W. Beck, **29** 353
R.W. Harmon & Sons, Inc., **6** 410
RABA PLC, **10** 274
Rabbit Software Corp., **10** 474
Rabobank Group, 26 419; 33 356–58
RAC *see* Ravenswood Aluminum Company; Roy Anderson Corporation.
Racal-Datacom Inc., 11 408–10
Racal Electronics PLC, II 83–84; 11 408, 547; **42** 373, 376; **50** 134
Race Z, Inc. *see* Action Peformance Companies, Inc.
Rachel's Dairy Ltd., **37** 197–98
Racine Hidraulica, **21** 430
Racine Threshing Machine Works, **10** 377
Racing Champions *see* Action Performance Companies, Inc.
Racing Champions Corporation, 37 318–20
Racing Collectables Club of America, Inc. *see* Action Performance Companies, Inc.
Racket Store *see* Duckwall-ALCO Stores, Inc.
Rada Corp., **IV** 250
Radeberger Gruppe AG, 75 332–35
Radian Group Inc., 42 299–301 *see also* Onex Corporation.
Radiant Lamp Corp., **13** 398
Radio & Television Equipment Company (Radio-Tel), **16** 200–01; **43** 168–69

Radio Austria A.G., **V** 314–16
Radio Cap Company *see* Norwood Promotional Products, Inc.
Radio City Productions, **30** 102
Radio Corporation of America *see* RCA Corporation.
Radio Flyer Inc., 34 368–70
Radio-Keith-Orpheum, **9** 247; **12** 73; **31** 99
Radio One, Inc., 67 318–21
Radio Receptor Company, Inc., **10** 319
Radio Shack, **II** 106–08; **12** 470; **13** 174
Radio Vertrieb Fürth *see* Grundig AG.
Radiocel, **39** 194
Radiometer A/S, **17** 287
Radiometrics, Inc., **18** 369
RadioShack Canada Inc., **30** 391
RadioShack Corporation, 36 384–88 (upd.)
Radiotelevision Española, **7** 511
Radisson Hotels Worldwide, **22** 126–27
Radius Inc., 16 417–19
Radix Group, Inc., **13** 20
Radman Inc., **56** 247
RadNet Managed Imaging Services, Inc., **25** 382–84
Radnor Venture Partners, LP, **10** 474
Raet, **39** 177
Raffinerie Tirlemontoise S.A., **27** 436
Raffineriegesellschaft Vohburg/Ingolstadt mbH, **7** 141
RAG AG, 35 364–67; 60 247–51 (upd.)
Rag Shops, Inc., 30 365–67
Ragan Outdoor, **27** 280
Ragazzi's, **10** 331
Ragdoll Productions Ltd., 51 308–11
Ragnar Benson Inc., **8** 43–43
Rail Link, Inc., **27** 181
Rail Van Global Logistics, **54** 276
Railroad Enterprises, Inc., **27** 347
Railtech International *see* Delachaux S.A.
RailTex, Inc., 20 445–47
Railtrack Group PLC, 39 238; 50 369–72
Railway Maintenance Equipment Co., **14** 43
Rainbow Home Shopping Ltd. *see* Otto-Versand (GmbH & Co.).
Rainbow Media, **47** 421
Rainbow Programming Holdings, **7** 63–64
Rainbow Valley Orchards, **54** 257
RainbowBridge Communications, Inc., **25** 162
Raincoast Book Distribution, **34** 5
Rainer Pulp & Paper Company, **17** 439
Rainfair, Inc., **18** 298, 300
Rainforest Café, Inc., 25 386–88
Rainier Brewing Company, 23 403–05
Rainier Pulp and Paper Company *see* Rayonier Inc.
Rainy River Forest Products, Inc., **26** 445
Rajastan Breweries, Ltd., **18** 502
Raky-Danubia, **IV** 485
Ralcorp Holdings, Inc., **13** 293, 425, 427; **15** 189, 235; **21** 53, 56; **22** 337; **36** 238; **43** 438; **50** 294; **55** 96; **63** 251
Raleigh UK Ltd., 65 295–97

Raley's Inc., 14 396–98; 58 288–91 (upd.)
Ralli International, **IV** 259
Rally's, 25 389–91; 68 313–16 (upd.)
Rallye SA, 12 154; 54 306–09; 59 107
Ralph & Kacoo's *see* Piccadilly Cafeterias, Inc.
Ralph Lauren *see* Polo/Ralph Lauren Corportion.
The Ralph M. Parsons Company *see* The Parsons Corporation.
Ralph Wilson Plastics, **III** 610–11
Ralph's Industries, **31** 191
Ralphs Grocery Company, 35 368–70
Ralston Purina Company, **I** 608, **II** 561–63; **13** 425–27 (upd.) *see also* Ralcorp Holdings, Inc.
Ramada International Hotels & Resorts, **IV** 718; **9** 426; **11** 177; **13** 66; **21** 366; **25** 309; **28** 258; **38** 320; **52** 281
Rambol, **25** 84
Rampage Clothing Co., **35** 94
Ramparts, Inc., **57** 159
Ramsay Youth Services, Inc., 41 322–24
Ranbar Packing, Inc. *see* Western Beef, Inc.
Ranbaxy Laboratories Ltd., 70 247–49
Ranchers Packing Corp. *see* Western Beef, Inc.
Rand Capital Corp., **35** 52–53
Rand McNally & Company, 28 378–81; 53 122
Randall's Food Markets, Inc., 40 364–67
Randgold & Exploration, **63** 182–83
Random House, Inc., 13 113, 115, 178, 428–30; 14 260; **31** 375–80 (upd.); **42** 287; **54** 17, 22
Randon Meldkamer, **43** 307
Randstad Holding n.v., 16 420–22; 43 307–10 (upd.)
Range Resources Corporation, 45 353–55
The Rank Group plc, II 157–59; 14 399–402 (upd.); 64 317–21 (upd.)
Ranks Hovis McDougall Limited, II 564–65; 28 382–85 (upd.)
Ransburg Corporation, **22** 282
Ransom and Randolph Company, **10** 271
Ransom Industries LP, **55** 266
RAO Unified Energy System of Russia, 45 356–60
Rapala-Normark Group, Ltd., 30 368–71
Rapides Bank & Trust Company, **11** 107
Rapidforms, Inc., **35** 130–31
Rare Hospitality International Inc., 19 340–42
RAS *see* Riunione Adriatica di Sicurtà SpA.
Rascal House, **24** 243
Raskas Foods, Inc. *see* Shearer's Foods, Inc.
Rathbone Brothers plc, 70 250–53
Ratin A/S, **49** 376
Rational GmbH, **22** 354
Ratner Companies, 72 294–96
Ratti Vallensasca, **25** 312

Rio Grande Servaas, S.A. de C.V., **23** 145

Rio Sportswear Inc., **42** 269

Rio Sul Airlines *see* Varig, SA.

Rio Tinto plc, IV 58–61, 189–91, 380; **19** 349–53 (upd.) **50** 380–85 (upd.)

Riocell S.A. *see* Klabin S.A.

Riordan Freeman & Spogli, **13** 406

Riordan Holdings Ltd., **10** 554; **67** 298

Ripley Entertainment, Inc., 74 273–76

Ripotot, **68** 143

Riser Foods, Inc., 9 451–54; **13** 237–38

Risk Management Partners Ltd., **35** 36

Risk Planners, II 669

Ritchie Bros. Auctioneers Inc., 41 331–34

Rite Aid Corporation, V 174–76; **19** 354–57 (upd.); **63** 331–37 (upd.)

Rite-Way Department Store, II 649

Riteway Distributor, **26** 183

Rittenhouse Financial Services, **22** 495

Ritter Co. *see* Sybron Corp.

Ritter Sport *see* Alfred Ritter GmbH & Co. KG.

Ritter's Frozen Custard *see* RFC Franchising LLC.

Ritz Camera Centers, **18** 186; **34** 375–77

The Ritz-Carlton Hotel Company, L.L.C., 9 455–57; **29** 403–06 (upd.); **71** 311–16 (upd.)

Ritz Firma, **13** 512

Riunione Adriatica di Sicurtà SpA, III 345–48

Riva Group Plc, **53** 46

The Rival Company, 19 358–60

Rivarossi, **16** 337

Rivaud Group, **29** 370

River Boat Casino, **9** 425–26

River City Broadcasting, **25** 418

River Metals Recycling LLC, **76** 130

River North Studios *see* Platinum Entertainment, Inc.

River Oaks Furniture, Inc., 43 314–16

River Ranch Fresh Foods—Salinas, Inc., **41** 11

River Thames Insurance Co., Ltd., **26** 487

Riverdeep Group plc, **41** 137

Riverside Chemical Company, **13** 502

Riverside Furniture, **19** 455

Riverside Insurance Co. of America, **26** 487

Riverside Iron Works, Ltd., **8** 544

Riverside National Bank of Buffalo, **11** 108

Riverside Press, **10** 355–56

Riverside Publishing Company, **36** 272

Riverwood International Corporation, 7 294; **11** 420–23; **48** 340–44 (upd.)

Riviana Foods, 27 388–91

Riviera Holdings Corporation, 75 340–43

Riyadh Armed Forces Hospital, **16** 94

Rizzoli Publishing, **23** 88

RJMJ, Inc., **16** 37

RJR Nabisco Holdings Corp., V 408–10 *see also* R.J Reynolds Tobacco Holdings Inc., Nabisco Brands, Inc.; R.J. Reynolds Industries, Inc.

RK Rose + Krieger GmbH & Co. KG, **61** 286–87

RKO *see* Radio-Keith-Orpheum.

RKO-General, Inc., **8** 207

RLA Polymers, **9** 92

RMC Group p.l.c., III 737–40; **34** 378–83 (upd.)

RMH Teleservices, Inc., 42 322–24

RMP International, Limited, **8** 417

Roadhouse Grill, Inc., 22 464–66; **57** 84

Roadmaster Industries, Inc., 16 430–33

Roadmaster Transport Company, **18** 27; **41** 18

RoadOne *see* Miller Industries, Inc.

Roadstone-Wood Group, **64** 98

Roadway Express, Inc., V 502–03; **25** 395–98 (upd.)

Roanoke Capital Ltd., **27** 113–14

Roanoke Electric Steel Corporation, 45 368–70

Roanoke Fashions Group, **13** 532

Robb Engineering Works, **8** 544

Robbins & Myers Inc., 13 273; **15** 388–90

Robeco Group, **26** 419–20

Roberds Inc., 19 361–63

Robert Allen Companies, III 571; **20** 362

Robert Benson, Lonsdale & Co. Ltd. *see* Dresdner Kleinwort Wasserstein.

Robert Bosch GmbH, I 392–93; **16** 434–37 (upd.); **43** 317–21 (upd.)

Robert E. McKee Corporation, **6** 150

Robert Fleming Holdings Ltd., I 471; **11** 495

Robert Gair Co., **15** 128

Robert Garrett & Sons, Inc., **9** 363

Robert Half International Inc., 18 461–63; **70** 281–84 (upd.)

Robert Hall Clothes, Inc., **13** 535

Robert Hansen Trucking Inc., **49** 402

Robert Johnson, **8** 281–82

Robert McLane Company *see* McLane Company, Inc.

Robert McNish & Company Limited, **14** 141

Robert Mondavi Corporation, 15 391–94; **39** 45; **50** 386–90 (upd.); **54** 343

Robert Skeels & Company, **33** 467

Robert Stigwood Organization Ltd., **23** 390

Robert W. Baird & Co. Incorporated, III 324; **7** 495; **67** 328–30

Robert Watson & Co. Ltd., I 568

Robert Wood Johnson Foundation, 35 375–78

Robertet SA, 39 347–49

Roberts Express, V 503

Roberts Pharmaceutical Corporation, 16 438–40

Roberts Trading Corporation, **68** 99

Robertson Animal Hospital, Inc., **58** 355

Robertson Building Products, **8** 546

Robertson-Ceco Corporation, 8 546; **19** 364–66

Robertson, Stephens & Co., **22** 465

Robin Hood Flour Mills, Ltd., **7** 241–43; **25** 241

Robin International Inc., **24** 14

Robinair, **10** 492, 494

Robinson & Clark Hardware *see* Clarcor Inc.

Robinson Helicopter Company, 51 315–17

Robinson Industries, **24** 425

Robinson Smith & Robert Haas, Inc., **13** 428

Robinson Way, **70** 160–61

Rogue Wave Software, Inc. *see* Quovadix Inc.

Robinson's Japan Co. Ltd. *see* Ito-Yokado Co., Ltd.

Robinsons Soft Drinks Limited, **38** 77

Robot Manufacturing Co., **16** 8

Robotic Simulations Limited, **56** 134

Robotic Vision Systems, Inc., **16** 68

ROC *see* Royal Olympic Cruise Lines Inc.

Rocawear Apparel LLC, 77 355–358

Roccade, **39** 177

Roch, S.A., **23** 83

Roche Biomedical Laboratories, Inc., 8 209–10; **11** 424–26 *see also* Laboratory Corporation of America Holdings.

Roche Bioscience, 14 403–06 (upd.)

Roche Holding AG, **30** 164; **32** 211, 213–14; **37** 113; **50** 421

Rocher Soleil, **48** 315

Rochester Gas And Electric Corporation, 6 571–73

Rochester Group, Inc., **60** 267

Rochester Instrument Systems, Inc., **16** 357

Rochester Telephone Corporation, 6 332–34

Röchling Industrie Verwaltung GmbH, **9** 443

Rock Bottom Restaurants, Inc., 25 399–401; **68** 320–23 (upd.)

Rock Island Plow Company, **10** 378

Rock of Ages Corporation, 37 329–32

Rock Systems Inc., **18** 337

Rock-Tenn Company, 13 441–43; **59** 347–51 (upd.)

Rockcor Inc., I 381; **13** 380

Rockcote Paint Company, **8** 552–53

The Rockefeller Foundation, 34 384–87; **52** 15

Rockefeller Group International Inc., 58 303–06

Rocket Chemical Company *see* WD-40 Company.

Rockford Corporation, 43 322–25

Rockford Products Corporation, 55 323–25

Rockhaven Asset Management, LLC, **48** 18

Rocking Horse Child Care Centers of America Inc. *see* Nobel Learning Communities, Inc.

Rockland Corp., **8** 271

Rockland React-Rite, Inc., **8** 270

Rockower of Canada Ltd., II 649

Rockport Company *see* Reebok International Ltd.

Roxoil Drilling, **7** 344

Roy and Charles Moore Crane Company, **18** 319

Roy Anderson Corporation, 75 344–46

Roy F. Weston, Inc., 33 369–72

Royal & Sun Alliance Insurance Group plc, 55 329–39 **(upd.)**

Royal Ahold N.V. *see* Koninklijke Ahold N.V.

Royal Appliance Manufacturing Company, 15 416–18

The Royal Bank of Canada, II 344–46; **21** 445–48 **(upd.)**

Royal Bank of Ireland Ltd., **16** 13

The Royal Bank of Scotland Group plc, 12 421–23; **38** 392–99 **(upd.)**

Royal Bankgroup of Acadiana, Inc., **37** 201

Royal Canin S.A., 39 354–57

Royal Caribbean Cruises Ltd., 22 470–73; **74** 277–81 **(upd.)**

Royal China and Porcelain Companies Inc. *see* The Porcelain and Fine China Companies Ltd.

Royal Copenhagen A/S, **9** 99

Royal Crown Company, Inc., 8 536–37; **14** 32–33; **23** 418–20; **52** 97 *see also* Cott Corporation.

Royal Data, Inc. *see* King Kullen Grocery Co., Inc.

Royal Doulton plc, 14 413–15; **38** 400–04 **(upd.)**

Royal Dutch Petroleum Company, IV 530–32 *see also* Shell Transport and Trading Company p.l.c.

Royal Dutch/Shell Group, 49 340–44 **(upd.)**

Royal Exchange Assurance Corp., **III** 369–71, 373

Royal Farms, **24** 528

Royal Food Products, **24** 528–29; **36** 163

Royal Gist-brocades NV, **56** 95

Royal Grolsch NV, 54 315–18

Royal Group Technologies Limited, 73 287–89

Royal Industries, Inc., **19** 371

Royal Insurance Holdings plc, III 349–51

Royal International Optical Inc. *see* U.S. Vision, Inc.

Royal Interocean Lines *see* Koninglijke Nedlloyd N.V.

Royal Jackson, **14** 236

Royal KPN N.V., 30 393–95, 461, 463

Royal Mail Group, **6** 416; **19** 198

Royal Nedlloyd *see* Koninglijke Nedlloyd N.V.

Royal Nepal Airline Corporation, 41 335–38

Royal Netherlands Steamship Company *see* KNSM.

Royal Numico N.V., 33 145, 147; **37** 340–42

Royal Olympic Cruise Lines Inc., 52 297–99

Royal Orchid Holidays *see* Thai Airways International.

Royal Ordnance plc, **13** 356; **24** 87–88

Royal Packaging Industries Van Leer N.V., 9 305; **30** 396–98; **64** 188

Royal Pakhoed N.V., **9** 532

Royal PTT Post, **30** 463

Royal Robbins, Inc. *see* Phoenix Footwear Group, Inc.

Royal Securities Company, **6** 585

Royal Sporting House Pte. Ltd., **21** 483

Royal Ten Cate N.V., 68 324–26

Royal Vendex KBB N.V. *see* Koninklijke Vendex KBB N.V. (Royal Vendex KBB N.V.).

Royal Vopak NV, 41 339–41

Royal Wessanen *see* Koninklijke Wessanen.

Royal Worcester Spode Ltd. *see* The Porcelain and Fine China Companies Ltd.

Royale Belge, **III** 177, 200, 394

Royale Inns of America, **25** 307

Royce Electronics, **III** 569; **18** 68; **20** 361

Royce Laboratories Inc., **56** 375

Royster-Clark, Inc., **13** 504

RPB Venture Capital Corporation, **72** 217

RPG (Aventis) S.A. *see* Ranbaxy Laboratories Ltd.

RPI *see* Research Polymers International.

RPISA *see* Refinaria de Petróleo Ipiranga S.A.

RPM Inc., 8 454–57; **36** 394–98 **(upd.); 51** 369

RSA Security Inc., 46 365–68; **47** 430

RSC *see* Rental Service Corporation.

RSI Corp., **8** 141–42; **30** 160

RSO Records, **23** 390

RSV, **26** 496

RTI Group, **58** 366

RTL Group SA, 44 374–78

RTM Restaurant Group, 58 322–24

RTR Funding LLC, **70** 275

RTS Packaging, LLC, **59** 347, 350

RTW Air Service(s) Pte. Ltd., **51** 123

RTZ Corporation PLC, IV 189–92; **7** 261, 263; **27** 256 *see also* Rio Tinto plc.

Rubber Latex Limited, **9** 92

Rubbermaid Incorporated, III 613–15; **12** 168–69; **13** 317–18; **19** 407; **20** 262, 454–57 **(upd.); 21** 293; **28** 479; **31** 160–61; **34** 369 *see also* Newell Rubbermaid Inc.

Rubicon Group plc, **32** 50

Rubio's Restaurants, Inc., 35 379–81

Rubo Lederwaren, **14** 225

Ruby Tuesday, Inc., 18 464–66; **71** 317–20 **(upd.)**

Rubyco, Inc., **15** 386

La Ruche Meridionale, **12** 153

Ruddick Corporation, **23** 260; **72** 163, 165

Rudolf Wolff & Co. Ltd., **64** 297

Ruel Smith Transportation Services, Inc., **39** 66

Ruff Hewn, **25** 48

Rug Corporation of America, **12** 393

The Rugby Group plc, 31 398–400; **34** 380

Ruger Corporation, **19** 431

Ruhrgas AG, V 704–06; **38** 405–09 **(upd.)**

Ruhrkohle AG, IV 193–95 *see also* RAG AG.

Ruiz Food Products, Inc., 53 287–89

Rumasa, **69** 165

Runnymede Construction Co., **8** 544

Runo-Everth Treibstoff und Ol AG, **7** 141

Rural Cellular Corporation, 43 340–42

Rural/Metro Corporation, 28 396–98; **39** 22

Rural Press Ltd., 74 282–85

Rush Communications, 33 373–75 *see also* Phat Fashions LLC.

Rush Enterprises, Inc., 64 336–38

Russ Berrie and Company, Inc., 12 424–26

Russell Associates Inc. *see* Pall Corporation.

Russell Corporation, 8 458–59; **30** 399–401 **(upd.)**

Russell Electric, **11** 412

Russell Kelly Office Services, Inc. *see* Kelly Services Inc.

Russell Reynolds Associates Inc., 38 410–12

Russell Stover Candies Inc., 12 427–29

Russian Avionics Design Bureau CJSC, **68** 204

Rust Craft Greeting Cards Incorporated, **12** 561

Rust International Inc., 6 599–600; **11** 435–36

Rust-Oleum Corporation, **36** 396

Rütgers AG, **60** 250

Rütgerswerke AG, **8** 81

Ruth's Chris Steak House, 28 399–401; **37** 297

Rutherford Hill Winery, **48** 392

RWD Technologies, Inc., 76 320–22

RWE Group, V 707–10; **50** 396–400 **(upd.); 59** 135–37

RxAmerica, **22** 40; **25** 297

Ryan Aeronautical, **I** 525; **10** 522; **11** 428

Ryan Aircraft Company, **9** 458

Ryan Beck & Co., Inc., 66 273–75

Ryan Homes, Inc. *see* NVR Inc.

Ryan Insurance Company, **III** 204; **45** 26

Ryan Milk Company of Kentucky, **7** 128

Ryan's Family Steak Houses, Inc., 15 419–21; **19** 287; **22** 464

Ryan's Restaurant Group, Inc., 68 327–30 **(upd.)**

Ryanair Holdings plc, 35 382–85

Ryder System, Inc., V 504–06; **24** 408–11 **(upd.)**

Ryecroft Foods Limited, **61** 387–88

Ryerson Tull, Inc., 19 216; **40** 269, 381–84 **(upd.)**

Rykoff-Sexton, Inc., **21** 497; **26** 503, 505; **74** 350

The Ryland Group, Inc., 8 460–61; **19** 126; **37** 343–45 **(upd.)**

Ryobi Ltd., **I** 202

Ryobi US, **73** 332

Ryohin Keikaku Co., Ltd., **36** 420

Ryoshoku Ltd., 72 300–02

Rypper Corp., **16** 43

Springer Verlag GmbH & Co., **IV** 611, 641
Springfield Bank, **9** 474
Springfield Gas Light Company, **38** 81
Springhouse Corp. *see* Reed Elsevier.
Springmaid International, Inc., **19** 421
Springs Industries, Inc., V 378–79; 19 419–22 (upd.); 29 132; **31** 199
Sprint Canada Inc., **44** 49
Sprint Communications Company, L.P., 9 478–80 *see also* Sprint Corporation; US Sprint Communications.
Sprint Corporation, 46 373–76 (upd.)
Sprint PCS, **33** 34, 36–37; **38** 433
Sprocket Systems, **50** 320
Sprout Group, **37** 121
Sprout-Matador A.S., **51** 25
SPS Technologies, Inc., 30 428–30
SPSS Inc., 64 360–63
SPT Telecom *see* Cesky Telecom, a.s.
Spun Yarns, Inc., **12** 503
Spur Oil Co., **7** 362
SPX Corporation, 10 492–95; 47 374–79 (upd.)
SPZ, Inc., **26** 257
SQ Software, Inc., **10** 505
SQL Solutions, Inc., **10** 505
Square D Company, **18** 473
Square Industries, **18** 103, 105
Squibb Beech-Nut *see* Beech-Nut Nutrition Corp.
Squibb Corporation, I 695–97 *see also* Bristol-Myers Squibb Company.
Squire Fashions Inc. *see* Norton McNaughton of Squire, Inc.
SR *see* Southern Railway.
SRA International, Inc., 77 400–403
SRAM Corporation, 65 325–27
SRC Holdings Corporation, 67 358–60
SRI International, Inc., 10 139; **57** 309, 311, **333–36**
SRI Strategic Resources Inc., **6** 310
SS&C Technologies Inc., **66** 225
SS Cars, Ltd. *see* Jaguar Cars, Ltd.
SS Lazio *see* Societá Sportiva Lazio SpA.
SSA *see* Stevedoring Services of America Inc.
Ssangyong Cement Industrial Co., Ltd., III 747–50; 61 339–43 (upd.)
Ssangyong Motor Company, **34** 132
SSC Benelux & Company, **52** 310–11
SSDS, Inc., **18** 537; **43** 433
SSI Medical Services, Inc., **10** 350
SSL International plc, 49 378–81
SSMC Inc., **II** 10
SSOE Inc., 76 333–35
SSP Company, Inc., **17** 434
St. *see under* Saint
Staal Bankiers, **13** 544
STAAR Surgical Company, 57 337–39
Stackpole Fibers, **37** 427
Stadia Colorado Corporation, **18** 140
Stadt Corporation, **26** 109
Staefa Control System Limited *see* Elektrowatt AG.
Staff Builders Inc. *see* ATC Healthcare, Inc.
Staff International, **40** 157

StaffAmerica, Inc., **16** 50
Stafford-Lowdon, **31** 435
Stage Stores, Inc., 24 456–59
Stagecoach Holdings plc, 30 431–33; 55 103
Stags' Leap Winery, **22** 80
Stahl-Urban Company, **8** 287–88
Stahlwerke Südwestfalen AG, **IV** 89
Stainless Fabrication Inc., **65** 289
Stakis plc, **49** 193
Stamford Drug Group, **9** 68
Stamford FHI Acquisition Corp., **27** 117
Stamos Associates Inc., **29** 377
Stamps.com Inc., **34** 474
Stanadyne Automotive Corporation, 37 367–70
Stanadyne, Inc., **7** 336; **12** 344
StanCorp Financial Group, Inc., 56 345–48
Standard & Poor's Corp., **IV** 482, 636–37; **12** 310; **25** 542
Standard Aircraft Equipment, **II** 16
Standard Alaska, **7** 559
Standard Bank, **17** 324
Standard Box Co., **17** 357
Standard Brands, **7** 365, 367; **18** 538
Standard Car Truck, **18** 5
Standard Chartered plc, II 357–59, 386; **10** 170; **47** 227; **48 371–74 (upd.)**
Standard Commercial Corporation, 13 490–92; 62 333–37 (upd.)
The Standard Companies, Inc., **58** 374
Standard Electric Time Company, **13** 233
Standard Electrica, **II** 13
Standard Federal Bank, 9 481–83
Standard Fruit and Steamship Co. of New Orleans, **31** 168
Standard Gauge Manufacturing Company, **13** 233
Standard Gypsum Corp., **19** 77
Standard Insert Co., **28** 350
Standard Kollsman Industries Inc., **13** 461
Standard Life & Accident Insurance Company, **27** 47–48
Standard Life Assurance Company, III 358–61
Standard Life Insurance Company, **11** 481
The Standard Life Insurance Company of New York, **56** 345
Standard Microsystems Corporation, 11 462–64
Standard Motor Products, Inc., 40 414–17
Standard of America Life Insurance Co., **III** 324
Standard of Georgia Insurance Agency, Inc., **10** 92
Standard Oil Co., **7** 169–72, 263, 414; **8** 415; **10** 110, 289; **14** 21; **25** 230; **27** 129 *see also* Exxon Corporation; Mobil Corporation.
Standard Oil Co. (California) *see* ChevronTexaco Corporation
Standard Oil Co. (Indiana) *see* Amoco Corporation.
Standard Oil Co. (New York), **IV** 485, 504, 537, 549, 558; **7** 171 *see also* Mobil Corporation.

Standard Oil Co. of New Jersey, **IV** 415–16, 419, 431–33, 438, 460, 463–64, 488, 522, 531, 537–38, 544, 558, 565, 571; **7** 170–72, 253, 351; **13** 124; **17** 412–13; **24** 521
Standard Oil Co. of Ohio, **IV** 452, 463, 522, 571; **7** 171, 263; **12** 309; **24** 521
Standard Pacific Corporation, 52 319–22
Standard Plastics, **25** 312
Standard Printing Company, **19** 333
Standard Process & Engraving, Inc., **26** 105
Standard Products Company, **19** 454
Standard Rate & Data Service, **7** 286
Standard Register Co., 15 472–74
Standard Screw Co., **12** 344
Standard Shares, **9** 413–14
Standard Steel Propeller, **9** 416; **10** 162
Standard Telephone and Radio, **II** 13
Standard Telephones and Cables, Ltd., **6** 242
Standard Tin Plate Co., **15** 127
Standard-Vacuum Oil Co. *see* Mobil Corporation.
Standex International Corporation, 17 456–59; 44 403–06 (upd.)
Standish Industries Inc., **61** 295
Stanhome Inc., 9 330; **11 94–96; 15 475–78**
Stanhome Worldwide Direct Selling, **35** 262, 264
STANIC, **69** 145, 148
Stankiewicz GmbH *see* Phoenix AG
Stanley Furniture Company, Inc., 34 412–14
Stanley Home Products, Incorporated *see* Stanhome Inc.
Stanley Leisure plc, 66 310–12
Stanley Mining Services, Ltd., **19** 247
Stanley Smith Security *see* Initial Security.
The Stanley Works, III 626–29; 20 476–80 (upd.)
StanMont, Inc., **24** 425
Stant Corporation, **15** 503, 505
StanWest Equities, Inc., **56** 348
Staples, Inc., 10 496–98; 55 351–56 (upd.)
Star, **10** 287–88
Star Air Service *see* Alaska Air Group, Inc.
Star Alliance, **26** 113; **33** 51; **38** 36
Star Banc Corporation, 11 465–67; 13 222; **31** 206 *see also* Firstar Corporation.
Star Broadcasting Network Pty. Ltd. *see* Rural Press Ltd.
Star Building Systems, Inc., **19** 366
Star Cruises Ltd. *see* Genting Bhd.
Star Engraving, **12** 471
Star Enterprises, Inc., **6** 457
Star Finishing Co., **9** 465
Star Laboratories Inc., **24** 251
Star Markets Company, Inc., **23** 169; **56** 317
Star Medical Europe B.V., **56** 338
Star Medical Technologies, Inc., **22** 409; **31** 124
Star Paper Tube, Inc., **19** 76–78

Tampa Electric Company, **6** 582–83

Tampax Inc. *see* Tambrands Inc.

Tampimex Oil, **11** 194

TAMSA *see* Tubos de Acero de Mexico, S.A.

Tandem Computers, Inc., 6 278–80

Tandon, **25** 531

Tandy Corporation, II 106–08; **12** 468–70 **(upd.)** *see also* RadioShack Corporation.

Tandycrafts, Inc., 31 433–37

Tangent Industries, **15** 83; **50** 124

Tanger Factory Outlet Centers, Inc., 49 386–89

Tangiers International *see* Algo Group Inc.

Tangram Rehabilitation Network, Inc., **29** 401

Tanimura & Antle, **54** 257

Tanks Oil and Gas, **11** 97; **50** 178

Tanne-Arden, Inc., **27** 291

Tanner-Brice Company, **13** 404

Tanox, Inc., 77 429–432

Tantalum Mining Corporation, **29** 81

TAP—Air Portugal Transportes Aéreos Portugueses S.A., 46 396–99 **(upd.)**

Tapemark Company Inc., 64 373–75

Tapiola Insurance, **IV** 316

Tapis-St. Maclou, **37** 22

Tappan *see* White Consolidated Industries Inc.

Tara Foods, **II** 645

Target Corporation, 10 515–17; **27** 451–54 **(upd.); 61** 352–56 **(upd.)**

Target Marketing and Promotions, Inc., **55** 15

Target Marketing Systems Inc., **64** 237

Target Rock Corporation, **35** 134–36

Tarkett Sommer AG, 25 462–64

Tarmac America, **64** 379–80

Tarmac plc, III 751–54; **14** 250; **28** 447–51 **(upd.); 36** 21

Taro Pharmaceutical Industries Ltd., 65 335–37

TAROM S.A., 64 376–78

Tarragon Oil and Gas Ltd. *see* Unocal Corporation.

Tarragon Realty Investors, Inc., 45 399–402

Tarrant Apparel Group, 62 351–53

Tarsa, **63** 151

TASC *see* Analytical Sciences Corp.

Taser International, Inc., 62 354–57

Tasman Pulp and Paper Co. Ltd. *see* Fletcher Challenge Ltd.

Tastee Freeze, **39** 234

Tasty Baking Company, 14 485–87; **35** 412–16 **(upd.)**

Tasukara Company Ltd., **62** 170

TAT European Airlines, **14** 70, 73; **24** 400

Tata Airlines *see* Air-India Limited.

Tata Enterprises, **III** 43

Tata Industries, **20** 313; **21** 74

Tata Iron & Steel Co. Ltd., IV 217–19; **44** 411–15 **(upd.)**

Tata Tea Ltd., 76 339–41

Tate & Lyle PLC, II 580–83; **7** 466–67; **13** 102; **42** 367–72 **(upd.)**

Tatham Corporation, **21** 169, 171

Tatham/RSCG, **13** 204

Tati SA, 25 465–67

Tatneft *see* OAO Tatneft.

Tattered Cover Book Store, 43 406–09

Tatung Co., 23 469–71

Taubman Centers, Inc., 75 364–66

Taurus Exploration, **21** 208

Taurus Programming Services, **10** 196

TaurusHolding GmbH & Co. KG, 46 400–03

Tax Management, Inc., **23** 92

Taylor & Francis Group plc, 44 416–19

Taylor Aircraft Corporation, **44** 307

Taylor Corporation, 36 465–67; **37** 108

Taylor Guitars, 48 386–89

Taylor Made Golf Co., 23 270, 472–74; **33** 7

Taylor Material Handling, **13** 499

Taylor Medical, **14** 388

Taylor Nelson Sofres plc, 34 428–30; **37** 144

Taylor Petroleum, Inc., **17** 170

Taylor Publishing Company, 12 471–73; **36** 468–71 **(upd.)**

Taylor Woodrow plc, I 590–91; **13** 206; **38** 450–53 **(upd.)**

Tayto Ltd., **22** 515

Tazo Tea Company, **50** 450

TB Wood's Corporation, 56 355–58

TBC Corp., **20** 63

TBS *see* Turner Broadcasting System, Inc.

TBWA/Chiat/Day, 6 47–49; **43** 410–14 **(upd.)** *see also* Omnicom Group Inc.

TC Advertising *see* Treasure Chest Advertising, Inc.

TC Debica, **20** 264

TCA *see* Air Canada.

TCBC *see* Todays Computers Business Centers.

TCBY Enterprises Inc., 17 474–76

TCF *see* Tokyo City Finance.

TCF Financial Corporation, 47 399–402

TCH Corporation, **12** 477

TCI *see* Tele-Communications, Inc.

TCI Communications, **29** 39

TCI Inc., **33** 92–93

TCI International Inc., **43** 48

TCJC *see* Charisma Brands LLC

TCM Investments, Inc., **49** 159

TCO *see* Taubman Centers, Inc.

TCPL *see* TransCanada PipeLines Ltd.

TCS Management Group, Inc., **22** 53

TCW Capital, **19** 414–15; **76** 330

TD Bank *see* The Toronto-Dominion Bank.

TD Brasil, Ltda., **74** 338

TDC A/S, 63 371–74

TDK Corporation, II 109–11; **17** 477–79 **(upd.); 49** 390–94 **(upd.)**

TDL Group Ltd., 46 404–06

TDL Infomedia Ltd., **47** 347

TDS *see* Telephone and Data Systems, Inc.

Teachers Insurance and Annuity Association-College Retirement Equities Fund, III 379–82; **45** 403–07 **(upd.)**

Teachers Service Organization, Inc., **8** 9–10

Team America, **9** 435

Team Penske *see* Penske Corporation.

Team Rental Group *see* Budget Group, Inc.

Teams, Inc., **37** 247

Teamsters Central States Pension Fund, **19** 378

Teamsters Union, **13** 19

TearDrop Golf Company, 32 445–48

Tech Data Corporation, 10 518–19; **74** 335–38 **(upd.)**

Tech/Ops Landauer, Inc. *see* Landauer, Inc.

Tech Pacific International, **18** 180; **39** 201, 203

Tech-Sym Corporation, 18 513–15; **44** 420–23 **(upd.)**

Tech Textiles, USA, **15** 247–48

Techalloy Co., **IV** 228

Techgistics, **49** 403

Techint Group, **63** 385

Technair Packaging Laboratories, **18** 216

TECHNE Corporation, 52 345–48

Technical Ceramics Laboratories, Inc., **13** 141

Technical Coatings Co., **13** 85; **38** 96–97

Technical Materials, Inc., **14** 81

Technical Olympic USA, Inc., 75 367–69

Technicare, **11** 200

Technicolor Inc., **28** 246

Technicon Instruments Corporation, **III** 56; **11** 333–34; **22** 75

Technifax, **8** 483

Techniques d'Avant-Garde *see* TAG Heuer International SA.

Technisch Bureau Visser, **16** 421

Technitrol, Inc., 29 459–62

Technology Management Group, Inc., **18** 112

Technology Resources International Ltd., **18** 76

Technology Venture Investors, **11** 490; **14** 263

Technophone Ltd., **17** 354

Techserviceavia, CJSC, **68** 204

Techsource Services, Inc., **60** 185

TechTeam Europe, Ltd., **41** 281

Techtronic Industries Company Ltd., 73 331–34

Teck Corporation, 9 282; **27** 455–58

Tecnacril Ltda, **51** 6

Tecnamotor S.p.A. *see* Tecumseh Products Company.

Tecneco, **IV** 422

Tecnipapel-Sociedade de Transformaçao e Distribuiçao de Papel, Lda, **60** 156

Tecnipublicaciones, **14** 555

Tecnost S.p.A., **34** 319

TECO Energy, Inc., 6 582–84

Tecom Industries, Inc., **18** 513–14

Tecomar S.A., **50** 209

Tenet Healthcare Corporation, 55 368–71 (upd.)

TenFold Corporation, 35 421–23

Tengelmann Group, 27 459–62 164

Tengelmann Warenhandelsgesellschaft OHG, 47 107

Tennant Company, 13 499–501; 33 390–93 (upd.)

Tenneco Inc., I 526–28; 10 526–28 (upd.)

Tennessee Book Company, 11 193

Tennessee Eastman Corporation *see* Eastman Chemical Company.

Tennessee Gas Pipeline Co., 14 126

Tennessee Gas Transmission Co., 13 496; 14 125

Tennessee Insurance Company, 11 193–94

Tennessee Paper Mills Inc. *see* Rock-Tenn Company.

Tennessee Restaurant Company, 9 426; 30 208–9; 72 141–42

Tennessee River Pulp & Paper Co., 12 376–77; 51 282–83

Tennessee Trifting, 13 169

Tennessee Valley Authority, 50 473–77

Tennessee Woolen Mills, Inc., 19 304

Teoma Technologies, Inc., 65 51–52

TEP *see* Tucson Electric Power Company.

TEPCO Cable Television Inc., 74 348

TEPPCO Partners, L.P., 73 335–37

Tequila Sauza, 31 91

Tequilera de Los Altos, 31 92

Tera Computer Company, 75 119

TeraBeam Networks Inc., 41 261, 263–64

Teradata Corporation *see* NCR Corporation.

Teradyne, Inc., 11 502–04

Terex Corporation, 7 513–15; 8 116; 40 430–34 (upd.)

Teril Stationers Inc., 16 36

The Terlato Wine Group, 48 390–92

Terminix International, 11 433; 25 16

Terra Industries, Inc., 13 277, 502–04

Terra Lycos, Inc., 43 420–25; 46 416

Terracor, 11 260–61

Terragrafics, 14 245

Terrain King, 32 26

Terre Haute Electric, 6 555

Terre Lune, 25 91

Terrena L'Union CANA CAVAL, 70 320–22

Territory Ahead, Inc., 29 279

Terumo Corporation, 48 393–95

Tesa, S.A., 23 82

TESC *see* The European Software Company.

Tesco plc, II 677–78; 24 473–76 (upd.); 68 366–70 (upd.)

Tesoro Petroleum Corporation, 7 516–19; 45 408–13 (upd.)

Tessenderlo Group, 76 345–48

Tesseract Inc., 11 78; 33 331

Tessman Seed, Inc., 16 270–71

The Testor Corporation, 8 455; 51 367–70

Tetley Group *see* Tata Tea Ltd.

Tetra Pak International SA, 53 327–29

Tetra Plastics Inc. *see* NIKE, Inc.

Tetra Tech, Inc., 29 463–65

Tettemer & Associates *see* The Keith Companies.

Teva Pharmaceutical Industries Ltd., 22 500–03; 47 55; 54 362–65 (upd.)

Tex-Mex Partners L.C., 41 270

Texaco Canada Inc., 25 232

Texaco Inc., IV 551–53; 14 491–94 (upd.); 41 391–96 (upd.) *see also* ChevronTexaco Corporation.

Texas Air Corporation, I 123–24

Texas Almanac, 10 3

Texas Bus Lines, 24 118

Texas Coffee Traders, 60 210

Texas Eastern Corp., 11 97, 354; 14 126; 50 179

Texas Eastern Transmission Company, 11 28

Texas Gas Resources Corporation, 22 166

Texas Homecare, 21 335

Texas Industries, Inc., 8 522–24

Texas Instruments Incorporated, II 112–15; 11 505–08 (upd.); 46 418–23 (upd.)

Texas International Airlines, 21 142

Texas Metal Fabricating Company, 7 540

Texas-New Mexico Utilities Company, 6 580

Texas Pacific Group Inc., 36 472–74

Texas Public Utilities, II 660

Texas Rangers Baseball, 51 371–74

Texas Roadhouse, Inc., 69 347–49

Texas Super Duper Markets, Inc., 7 372

Texas Timberjack, Inc., 51 279–81

Texas Trust Savings Bank, 8 88

Texas United Insurance Co., III 214

Texas Utilities Company, V 724–25; 25 472–74 (upd.)

Texasgulf Inc., 13 557; 18 433

Texboard, IV 296; 19 226

Texstar Petroleum Company, 7 516

Texstyrene Corp., IV 331

Têxtil Santa Catarina Ltda., 72 68

Textile Diffusion, 25 466

Textile Paper Tube Company, Ltd., 8 475

Textile Rubber and Chemical Company, 15 490

Textron Inc., I 529–30; 34 431–34 (upd.)

Textron Lycoming Turbine Engine, 9 497–99

Texwood Industries, Inc., 20 363

TFC *see* Times Fiber Communications, Inc.

TFH Publications, Inc., 58 60

TFM *see* Grupo Transportación Ferroviaria Mexicana, S.A. de C.V.

TFN Group Communications, Inc., 8 311

TF1 *see* Télévision Française 1

TFP, Inc., 44 358–59

TFS *see* Total Filtration Services, Inc.

TG Credit Service Co. Ltd., 55 375

TGEL&PCo *see* Tucson Gas, Electric Light & Power Company.

TH:s Group, 10 113; 50 43

Tha Row Records, 69 350–52 (upd.)

Thai Airways International Public Company Limited, 6 122–24; 27 463–66 (upd.)

Thai Lube Blending Co., 56 290

Thai Nylon Co. Ltd., 53 344

Thai Union Frozen Products PCL, 75 370–72

Thalassa International, 10 14; 27 11

Thales S.A., 42 373–76

Thames Trains, 28 157

Thames Water plc, 11 509–11; 22 89

Thameslink, 28 157

THAW *see* Recreational Equipment, Inc.

Theatrical Syndicate, 24 437

Thelem SA, 54 267

Therm-o-Disc, II 19

Therm-X Company, 8 178

Thermacore International Inc., 56 247

Thermador Corporation, 67 82

Thermadyne Holding Corporation, 19 440–43

Thermal Dynamics, 19 441

Thermal Energies, Inc., 21 514

Thermal Power Company, 11 270

Thermal Snowboards, Inc., 22 462

Thermal Transfer Ltd., 13 485

ThermaStor Technologies, Ltd., 44 366

Thermo BioAnalysis Corp., 25 475–78

Thermo Electron Corporation, 7 520–22

Thermo Fibertek, Inc., 24 477–79

Thermo Instrument Systems Inc., 11 512–14

Thermo King Corporation, 13 505–07

Thermoform Plastics, Inc., 56 378–79

Thermoforming USA, 16 339

Thermogas Co., 35 175

Thermolase Corporation, 22 410

Thermos Company, 16 486–88

TheStreet.com, 34 125

THHK Womenswear Limited, 53 333

ThiemeMeulenhoff BV, 53 273

Thies Companies, 13 270

Thiess Dampier Mitsui, IV 47

Things Remembered *see* Cole National Corporation.

Think Entertainment, II 161

Think Technologies, 10 508

Thiokol Corporation, 9 500–02 (upd.); 22 504–07 (upd.)

Third Age Inc., 71 137

Third Coast Capital, Inc., 51 109

Third National Bank *see* Fifth Third Bancorp.

Third National Bank of Dayton, 9 475

Third Wave Publishing Corp. *see* Acer Inc.

ThirdAge.com, 49 290

Thirteen/WNET *see* Educational Broadcasting Corporation.

Thistle Group, 9 365

Thistle Hotels PLC, 54 366–69

THM Biomedical Inc. *see* Kensey Nash Corporation.

Thom McAn *see* Melville Corporation.

Thomas & Betts Corporation, 11 515–17; 14 27; 54 370–74 (upd.)

Thomas & Howard Co., II 682; 18 8

Thomas and Judith Pyle, 13 433

Trans-Mex, Inc. S.A. de C.V., **42** 365
Trans-Natal Coal Corp., **IV** 93
Trans Ocean Products, **8** 510
Trans-Pacific Airlines *see* Aloha Airlines Incorporated.
Trans-Resources Inc., **13** 299
Trans Thai-Malaysia, **56** 290
Trans Union Corp., **IV** 137; **6** 25; **28** 119
Trans Western Publishing, **25** 496
Trans World Airlines, Inc., I 125–27; **12** 487–90 (upd.); **35** 424–29 (upd.)
Trans-World Corp., **19** 456; **47** 231
Trans World Entertainment Corporation, 24 501–03; **68** 374–77 (upd.)
Trans World International, **18** 262–63
Trans World Life Insurance Company, **27** 46–47
Trans World Music, **9** 361
Trans World Seafood, Inc., **13** 244
Transaction Systems Architects, Inc., 29 477–79
Transaction Technology, **12** 334
TransAlta Utilities Corporation, 6 585–87
Transamerica—An AEGON Company, 41 400–03 (upd.)
Transamerica Corporation, I 536–38; **13** 528–30 (upd.) *see also* TIG Holdings, Inc.
Transamerica Pawn Holdings *see* EZCORP Inc.
Transamerica Retirement Services, **63** 176
TransAmerican Waste Industries Inc., **41** 414
Transat *see* Compagnie Générale Transatlantique (Transat).
Transatlantic Holdings, Inc., III 198; **11** 532–33; **15** 18
Transatlantische Gruppe, **III** 404
Transax, **63** 102
TransBrasil S/A Linhas Aéreas, 31 443–45; **46** 398
TransCanada PipeLines Limited, V 737–38
Transco Energy Company, V 739–40; **18** 366 *see also* The Williams Companies.
Transcontinental and Western Air Lines, **9** 416; **12** 487
Transcontinental Gas Pipe Line Corporation *see* Transco Energy Company.
Transcontinental Services Group N.V., **16** 207; **76** 149
TransCor America, Inc., **23** 154
Transelco, Inc., **8** 178
Transfer Drivers, Inc., **46** 301
Transfracht, **6** 426
Transiciel SA, 48 400–02
Transit Homes of America, Inc., **46** 301
Transit Mix Concrete and Materials Company, **7** 541
Transitions Optical Inc., **21** 221, 223
Transitron, **16** 332
Transkaryotic Therapies Inc., **54** 111
Transking Inc. *see* King Kullen Grocery Co., Inc.
Transkrit Corp., **IV** 640; **26** 273
Translittoral, **67** 353

Transmanche-Link, **13** 206–08; **37** 135
Transmedia Network Inc., 20 494–97 *see also* Rewards Network Inc.
Transmedica International, Inc., **41** 225
Transmisiones y Equipos Mecanicos, S.A. de C.V., **23** 171
Transmitter Equipment Manufacturing Co., **13** 385
TransMontaigne Inc., 28 470–72
Transmontane Rod and Gun Club, **43** 435–36
Transnet Ltd., 6 433–35
Transocean Sedco Forex Inc., 45 417–19; **59** 368
Transpac, **IV** 325
Transport Corporation of America, Inc., 49 400–03
Transport International Pool, **58** 239
Transportacion Ferroviaria Mexicana, **50** 209
Transportacion Maritima Mexicana S.A. de C.V., **12** 279; **26** 236; **47** 162; **50** 208
Transportation Technologies Industries Inc., **51** 155
Transportation.com, **45** 451
Transportes Aéreas Centro-Americanos *see* Grupo TACA.
Transportes Aereos Portugueses, S.A., 6 125–27 *see also* TAP—Air Portugal Transportes Aéreos Portugueses S.A.
Transportes Aeromar, **39** 188
TransPro, Inc., 71 356–59
Transrack S.A., **26** 363
Transue & Williams Steel Forging Corp., **13** 302
Transway International Corp., **10** 369
Transworld Communications, **35** 165
Transworld Corp., **14** 209
Transworld Drilling Company Limited *see* Kerr-McGee Corporation.
The Tranzonic Companies, 8 512; **15** 500–02; **37** 392–95
Trapper's, **19** 286
Trasgo, S.A. de C.V., **14** 516; **50** 493
Travel Air Manufacturing Company, **8** 49; **27** 97
Travel Inc., **26** 309
Travel Information Group, **17** 398
Travel Ports of America, Inc., 17 493–95
Travelers/Aetna Property Casualty Corp., **63** 14
Travelers Bank & Trust Company, **13** 467
Travelers Book Club, **13** 105
Travelers Corporation, III 387–90; **15** 463 124 *see also* Citigroup Inc.
Travelers/Aetna Property Casualty Corp., **21** 15
Travelocity.com, Inc., 46 434–37; **58** 118–20
Travers Morgan Ltd., **42** 183
Travis Boats & Motors, Inc., 37 396–98
Travis Perkins plc, 34 450–52
Travocéan, **25** 104
TRC *see* Tennessee Restaurant Company.
TRC Companies, Inc., 32 461–64
TRE Corp., **23** 225

Treadco, Inc., **19** 454–56
Treasure Chest Advertising Company, Inc., 21 60; **32** 465–67
Treasure House Stores, Inc., **17** 322
Treatment Centers of America, **11** 379
Trebuhs Realty Co., **24** 438
Tredegar Corporation, 10 291; **52** 349–51; **59** 24
Tree of Life, Inc., 29 480–82
Tree Sweet Products Corp., **12** 105; **26** 325
Tree Tavern, Inc., **27** 197
Tree Top, Inc., 76 357–59
TreeHouse Foods, Inc., **73** 108
Trefoil Capital Investors, L.P., **8** 305
Trego Systems Inc., **64** 190
Trek Bicycle Corporation, 16 493–95
Trelleborg A.B., **IV** 166
Tremec *see* Transmisiones y Equipos Mecanicos, S.A. de C.V.
Tremont Corporation, **21** 490
Trencherwood Plc, **45** 443
Trend International Ltd., **13** 502
Trend-Lines, Inc., 22 516–18
Trends Magazine NV, **48** 347
Trendwest Resorts, Inc., 12 439; **33** 409–11 *see also* Jeld-Wen, Inc.
TrentonWorks Limited *see* The Greenbrier Companies.
Tresco, **8** 514
Trevor Sorbie of America, Inc., **60** 287
Trex Company, Inc., 71 360–62
Tri-City Federal Savings and Loan Association, **10** 92
Tri-City Utilities Company, **6** 514
Tri-County National Bank, **9** 474
Tri-Marine International Inc., **24** 116
Tri-Miller Packing Company, **7** 524
Tri-Sonics, Inc., **16** 202; **43** 170
Tri-State Baking, **53** 21
Tri-State Improvement Company *see* Cincinnati Gal & Electric Company.
Tri-State Publishing & Communications, Inc., **22** 442
Tri-State Recycling Corporation, **15** 117
Tri-Union Seafoods LLC, **24** 116
Tri Valley Growers, 32 468–71
Tri-Village Developments BV, **58** 359
Triad, **14** 224
Triad Artists Inc., **23** 514
Triad International Maintenance Corp., **13** 417
Triad Nitrogen, Inc., **27** 316, 318
Triad Systems Corp., **38** 96
The Triangle Group, **16** 357
Triangle Industries Inc., **I** 614; **14** 43
Triangle Pharmaceuticals, Inc., **54** 131
Triangle Publications, Inc., **12** 359–60
Triangle Sheet Metal Works, Inc., **45** 327
Triarc Companies, Inc., 8 535–37; **34** 453–57 (upd.)
Triax Midwest Associates L.P. *see* Mediacom Communications Corporation.
Tribe Computer Works *see* Zoom Technologies, Inc.
Tribune Company, IV 682–84; **22** 519–23 (upd.); **63** 389–95 (upd.)
Tricap Restructuring Fund, **59** 162

Universal Studios, Inc., **33** 429–33
Universal Tea Co., Inc., **50** 449
Universal Telephone, **9** 106
Universal Textured Yarns, **12** 501
Universe Tankships, **59** 198
UNIVERSELLE Engineering U.N.I.
   GmbH, **60** 194
University HealthSystem Consortium, **53**
   346
University of Phoenix, **24** 40
Univisa, **24** 516
Univision Communications Inc., 18
   213; **24 515–18; 41 150–52; 54**
   72–73, 158
Unix System Laboratories Inc., **25** 20–21;
   38 418
UNM *see* United News & Media plc.
Uno-e Bank, **48** 51
Uno Restaurant Holdings Corporation,
   18 538–40; 70 334–37 (upd.)
Uno-Ven, **IV** 571; **24** 522
Unocal Corporation, IV 569–71; 24
   519–23 (upd.); 71 378–84 (upd.)
Unova Manufacturing Technologies Inc.,
   72 69, 71
UNR Industries, Inc. *see* ROHN Indus-
   tries, Inc.
Unterberg Harris, **25** 433
UNUM Corp., 13 538–40
UnumProvident Corporation, 52
   376–83 (upd.)
Uny Co., Ltd., V 209–10; 49 425–28
   (upd.)
UO Fenwick, Inc., **74** 370
UOB *see* United Overseas Bank Ltd.
UPC *see* United Pan-Europe Communica-
   tions NV.
UOD Inc. *see* Urban Outfitters, Inc.
UPI *see* United Press International.
Upjohn Company, I 707–09; 8 547–49
   (upd.) *see also* Pharmacia & Upjohn
   Inc.
UPM-Kymmene Corporation, 19
   461–65; 50 505–11 (upd.)
UPN *see* United Paramount Network.
Upper Deck Company, LLC, **34** 448; **37**
   295
Upper Peninsula Power Co., **53** 369
UPS *see* United Parcel Service, Inc.
UPS Aviation Technologies, Inc., **60** 137
UPSHOT, **27** 195
Urban Outfitters, Inc., 14 524–26; 74
   367–70 (upd.)
Urbaser SA, **55** 182
Urbium PLC, 75 389–91
URS Corporation, 45 420–23
URSI *see* United Road Services, Inc.
Urwick Orr, **II** 609
US *see also* U.S.
US Airways Group, Inc., 28 506–09
   (upd.); 52 24–25, 384–88 (upd.)
US Industrial Chemicals, Inc., **8** 440
US Industries Inc., **30** 231
US Monolithics, **54** 407
US 1 Industries, **27** 404
US Order, Inc., **10** 560, 562
US Repeating Arms Co., **58** 147

US Sprint Communications Company *see*
   Sprint Communications Company, L.P.
US Telecom, **9** 478–79
US West Communications Services, Inc.
   see Regional Bell Operating Companies.
USA Cafes, **14** 331
USA Floral Products Inc., **27** 126
USA Interactive, Inc., 47 418–22 (upd.);
   58 117, 120
USA Networks Inc., **25** 330, 411; **33**
   432; **37** 381, 383–84; **43** 422
USA Security Systems, Inc., **27** 21
USA Truck, Inc., 42 410–13
USAA, 10 541–43; 62 385–88 (upd.)
USAir Group, Inc., I 131–32; 6 131–32
   (upd.) *see also* US Airways Group, Inc.
USANA, Inc., 27 353; 29 491–93
USCC *see* United States Cellular Corpora-
   tion.
USCP-WESCO Inc., **II** 682
Usego AG., **48** 63
USF&G Corporation, III 395–98 *see also*
   The St. Paul Companies.
USFL *see* United States Football League.
USFreightways Corporation, **27** 475; **49**
   402
USG Corporation, III 762–64; 26
   507–10 (upd.)
USH *see* United Scientific Holdings.
Usinas Siderúrgicas de Minas Gerais
   S.A., 77 454–457
Usinger's Famous Sausage *see* Fred Usinger
   Inc.
Usinor SA, 42 414–17 (upd.)
Usinor Sacilor, IV 226–28
USLD Communications Corp. *see* Billing
   Concepts Corp.
USM, **10** 44
USO *see* United Service Organizations.
Usource LLC, **37** 406
USPS *see* United States Postal Service.
USSC *see* United States Surgical Corpora-
   tion.
USSI *see* U.S. Software Inc.
UST Inc., 9 533–35; 42 79; 50 512–17
   (upd.)
UST Wilderness Management Corpora-
   tion, **33** 399
Usutu Pulp Company, **49** 353
USV Pharmaceutical Corporation, **11** 333
USWeb/CKS *see* marchFIRST, Inc.
USX Corporation, IV 572–74; 7
   193–94, **549–52 (upd.)** *see also* United
   States Steel Corporation.
UT Starcom, **44** 426
Utag, **11** 510
Utah Construction & Mining Co., **14**
   296
Utah Federal Savings Bank, **17** 530
Utah Gas and Coke Company, **6** 568
Utah Medical Products, Inc., 36 496–99
Utah Mines Ltd., **IV** 47; **22** 107
Utah Power and Light Company, 9 536;
   12 266; **27 483–86** *see also* PacifiCorp.
UTI Energy, Inc. *see* Patterson-UTI En-
   ergy, Inc.
Utilicom, **6** 572

Utilicorp United Inc., 6 592–94 *see also*
   Aquilla, Inc.
UtiliTech Solutions, **37** 88
Utility Constructors Incorporated, **6** 527
Utility Engineering Corporation, **6** 580
Utility Fuels, **7** 377
Utility Line Construction Service, Inc., **59**
   65
Utility Service Affiliates, Inc., **45** 277
Utility Services, Inc., **42** 249, 253
Utility Supply Co. *see* United Stationers
   Inc.
Utopian Leisure Group, **75** 385
UTStarcom, Inc., 77 458–461
UTV *see* Ulster Television PLC.
Utz Quality Foods, Inc., 72 358–60
UUNET, 38 468–72
UV Industries, Inc., **7** 360; **9** 440
Uwajimaya, Inc., 60 312–14

V

V.L. Churchill Group, **10** 493
VA Linux Systems, **45** 363
VA TECH ELIN EBG GmbH, 49
   429–31
VA Technologie AG, **57** 402
Vacheron Constantin, **27** 487, 489
Vaco, **38** 200, 202
Vaculator Division *see* Lancer Corpora-
   tion.
Vacuum Metallurgical Company, **11** 234
Vacuum Oil Co. *see* Mobil Corporation.
Vadoise Vie, **III** 273
VAE AG, **57** 402
VAE Nortrak Cheyenne Inc., **53** 352
Vail Associates, Inc., 11 543–46; 31 65,
   67
Vail Resorts, Inc., 43 435–39 (upd.)
Vaillant GmbH, 44 436–39
Val Corp., **24** 149
Val-Pak Direct Marketing Systems, Inc.,
   22 162
Val Royal LaSalle, **II** 652
Valassis Communications, Inc., 8
   550–51; 37 407–10 (upd.); 76
   364–67 (upd.)
ValCom Inc. *see* InaCom Corporation.
Valdi Foods Inc., **II** 663–64
Vale do Rio Doce Navegacao
   SA—Docenave, **43** 112
Vale Harmon Enterprises, Ltd., **25** 204
Vale Power Company, **12** 265
Valenciana de Cementos, **59** 112
Valentine & Company, **8** 552–53
Valentino, **67** 246, 248
Valeo, 23 492–94; 66 350–53 (upd.)
Valero Energy Corporation, 7 553–55;
   71 385–90 (upd.)
Valhi, Inc., 10 435–36; **19 466–68**
Valid Logic Systems Inc., **11** 46, 284; **48**
   77
Vality Technology Inc., **59** 56
Vallen Corporation, 45 424–26
Valley Bank of Helena, **35** 197, 199
Valley Bank of Maryland, **46** 25
Valley Bank of Nevada, **19** 378
Valley Crest Tree Company, **31** 182–83
Valley Deli Inc., **24** 243

Vereinigte Stahlwerke AG, **14** 327
Verenigde Bedrijven Bredero, **26** 280
Verenigde Nederlandse Uitgeverijen *see* VNU N.V.
Verenigde Spaarbank Groep *see* VSB Groep.
Veri-Best Baking Co., **56** 29
Veridian Corporation, 54 395–97
Verifact Inc. (IVI), **46** 251
VeriFone, Inc., 18 541–44; **76** 368–71 **(upd.)**
Verilyte Gold, Inc., **19** 452
Verint Systems Inc., 73 370–72
VeriSign, Inc., 47 430–34
Verispan LLC, **68** 308
Veritas Capital Fund L.P., **44** 420, 423; **59** 192
Veritas Capital Management, L.L.C., **54** 178
Veritas Capital Partners, **26** 408
Veritas Software Corporation, 45 427–31
Veritec Technologies, Inc., **48** 299
Veritus Inc., **27** 208–09
Verity Inc., 68 388–91
Verizon Communications, 43 443–49 **(upd.)**
Verizon Wireless, Inc., **42** 284; **63** 131
Verlagsgruppe Georg von Holtzbrinck GmbH, 35 450–53
Verlagsgruppe Märkische Verlags- und Druckgesellschaft mbH, **66** 123
Vermeer Manufacturing Company, 17 507–10
Vermont General Insurance Company, **51** 248
Vermont Pure Holdings, Ltd., 51 394–96
The Vermont Teddy Bear Co., Inc., 36 500–02
Verneuil Holding Co, **21** 387
Vernitron Corporation, **18** 293
Vernon and Nelson Telephone Company *see* British Columbia Telephone Company.
Vernon Savings & Loan, **9** 199
Vernors, Inc., **25** 4
Verreries Brosse S.A.S., **67** 210, 212
Verreries Pochet et du Courval, **55** 309
Versace *see* Gianni Versace SpA.
Versatec Inc., **13** 128
Versatile Farm and Equipment Co., **22** 380
Versax, S.A. de C.V., **19** 12
Verson Allsteel Press Co., **21** 20, 22
Vert Baudet, **19** 309
Vertex Data Science Limited, **52** 372, 374–75
Vertical Technology Industries, **14** 571
Verticom, **25** 531
Vertrue Inc., 77 469–472
Verve Records, **23** 389
Vesa Energy, **57** 397
Vessel Management Services, Inc., **28** 80
Vestas Wind Systems A/S, 73 373–75
Vestek Systems, Inc., **13** 417
Vestro, **19** 309
Vesuvius USA Corporation, **8** 179

Veszpremtej, **25** 85
Veterinary Cos. of America, **III** 25
VEW AG, 39 412–15
Vexlar, **18** 313
VF Corporation, V 390–92; **17** 511–14 **(upd.); 54** 398–404 **(upd.)**
VH Serviços e Construçoes Ltda., **72** 68
VHA Inc., 53 345–47
VHA Long Term Care, **23** 431
VH1 Inc., **23** 503
VI-Jon Laboratories, Inc., **12** 388
Via Cariane *see* Keolis SA.
Via-Générale de Transport et d'Industrie SA, **28** 155
Via Verde, **64** 57
ViaAfrika *see* Naspers Ltd.
Viacao Aerea Rio Grandense of South America *see* VARIG, SA.
Viacom Inc., 7 560–62; **23** 500–03 **(upd.); 67** 367–71 **(upd.)**
Viad Corp., 73 376–78
Viag AG, IV 229–32 *see also* E.On AG.
Viajes El Corte Inglés, S.A., **26** 129
VIASA *see* Iberia.
ViaSat, Inc., 54 405–08
Viasoft Inc., 27 490–93; **59** 27
VIASYS Healthcare, Inc., 52 389–91
Viasystems Group, Inc., 67 372–74
Viatech Continental Can Company, Inc., 25 512–15 **(upd.)**
Vibracoustic GmbH & Co. KG, **68** 289
Vicat S.A., 70 341–43
Vickers Inc., **III** 640, 642; **13** 8; **23** 83
Vickers plc, 21 435; **27** 494–97; **47** 9
VICOM, **48** 415
Vicon Industries, Inc., 44 440–42
VICORP Restaurants, Inc., 12 510–12; **48** 412–15 **(upd.)**
Victoire Delage, **62** 229
Victor Company, **10** 483
Victor Company of Japan, Ltd., II 118–19; **26** 511–13 **(upd.)**
Victor Equipment Co., **19** 440
Victor Value, **II** 678
Victoria & Co., **39** 247
Victoria Coach Station *see* London Regional Transport.
Victoria Creations Inc., **13** 536
Victoria Group, 44 443–46 **(upd.)**
VICTORIA Holding AG, III 399–401 *see also* Victoria Group.
Victoria Ward, Limited, **57** 157
Victoria's Secret *see* The Limited, Inc.
Victorinox AG, 21 515–17; **74** 375–78 **(upd.)**
Victory Refrigeration Company, **22** 355
Victory Savings and Loan, **10** 339
Victory Supermarket *see* Big V Supermarkets, Inc.
Vidal Sassoon, **17** 110
Video Concepts, **9** 186
Video Independent Theatres, Inc., **14** 86
Video Library, Inc., **9** 74
Video News International, **19** 285
Video Superstores Master Limited Partnership, **9** 74
Video Trend, **60** 84
VideoFusion, Inc., **16** 419

Videotex Network Japan, **IV** 680
Videotron, **25** 102
VideV, **24** 509
Vidrala S.A., 67 375–77
La Vie Claire, **13** 103
Vie de France Yamazaki Inc., **58** 380–82
Viel & Cie, 76 372–74
Vielle Montaign, **22** 285
Vienna Sausage Manufacturing Co., 14 536–37
Viessmann Werke GmbH & Co., 37 411–14
Vietnam International Assurance Co., **64** 280
Vietnam LPG Co., Ltd., **56** 290
View-Master/Ideal Group, **12** 496
Viewer's Edge, **27** 429
Viewlogic, **11** 490
Viewpoint International, Inc., 66 354–56
ViewSonic Corporation, 72 365–67
ViewStar Corp., **20** 103
Viewtel, **14** 36
ViewTrade Holding Corp., **46** 282
Vigilant Insurance Co., **III** 220; **14** 108; **37** 83
Vigoro, **22** 340
Viking, **IV** 659
Viking Building Products, **22** 15
Viking Computer Services, Inc., **14** 147
Viking Consolidated Shipping Corp, **25** 470
Viking Direct Limited, **10** 545
Viking Foods, Inc., **8** 482; **14** 411
Viking Industries, **39** 322, 324
Viking Office Products, Inc., 10 544–46
Viking Penguin, **IV** 611
Viking Press, **12** 25
Viking Pump Company, **21** 499–500
Viking Range Corporation, 66 357–59
Viking Star Shipping, Inc. *see* Teekay Shipping Corporation.
Viktor Achter, **9** 92
Village Inn *see* VICORP Restaurants, Inc.
Village Roadshow Ltd., 58 356–59
Village Super Market, Inc., 7 563–64
Village Voice Media, Inc., 38 476–79
Villager, Inc., **11** 216; **39** 244
Villazon & Co., **27** 139
Villeroy & Boch AG, 37 415–18
Vilmorin Clause et Cie, 70 344–46
VILPAC, S.A., **26** 356
AO VimpelCom, 48 416–19
Vimto *see* Nichols plc.
Vin & Spirit AB, 31 458–61; **58** 197
Viña Concha y Toro S.A., 45 432–34
Vina San Pedro S.A., **70** 62–63
Vinci, 27 54; **43** 450–52; **49** 44
Vincor International Inc., 50 518–21
Vinedos Baron de Ley SL *see* Baron de Ley S.A.
Viner Bros., **16** 546
Vinewood Companies, **53** 232
Vingaarden A/S, **9** 100
Vining Industries, **12** 128
Viniprix SA, **10** 205; **19** 309; **27** 95
Vinita Rock Company, **50** 49
Vinland Web-Print, **8** 360

Welch's, **25** 366
Welco Feed Manufacturing Company, **60** 316
Welcome Wagon International Inc., **16** 146
Weldless Steel Company, **8** 530
Wella AG, III 68–70; **48** 420–23 **(upd.)**
Welland Pipe Ltd., **51** 352
Wellborn Paint Manufacturing Company, **56** 98
Wellby Super Drug Stores, **12** 220
WellChoice, Inc., 67 388–91 **(upd.)**
Wellcome Foundation Ltd., I 713–15 *see also* GlaxoSmithKline plc.
Weller Electric Corp., **II** 16
Wellington Management Company, **14** 530–31; **23** 226
Wellington Sears Co., **15** 247–48
Wellman, Inc., 8 561–62; **21** 193; **52** 408–11 **(upd.)**; **64** 86
Wellmark, Inc., **10** 89
Wellness Co., Ltd., **IV** 716
WellPath Community Health Plans, Inc., **59** 140
WellPoint Health Networks Inc., 25 525–29
Wellrose Limited, **53** 333
Wells Aircraft, **12** 112
Wells Fargo & Company, II 380–84; **12** 533–37 **(upd.)**; **38** 483–92 **(upd.)** *see also* American Express Company.
Wells Fargo HSBC Trade Bank, **26** 203
Wells-Gardner Electronics Corporation, 43 458–61
Wells Rich Greene BDDP, 6 50–52
Wells' Dairy, Inc., 36 511–13
Wellspring Associates L.L.C., **16** 338
Wellspring Resources LLC, **42** 429
Welsh Associated Collieries Ltd., **31** 369
Welsh, Carson, Anderson & Stowe, **65** 128–30; **71** 117–19
Welsh Water *see* Hyder plc.
Wendel Investissement, **57** 381
Wendy's International, Inc., 8 563–65; **23** 504–07 **(upd.)**; **47** 439–44 **(upd.)**
Wenger S.A., **21** 515; **74** 375–77
Wenmac Corp., **51** 368
Wenner Media, Inc., 32 506–09
Werco, Inc., **54** 7
Werkhof GmbH, **13** 491; **62** 336
Werknet, **16** 420; **43** 308
Werner Baldessarini Design GmbH, **48** 209
Werner Die & Stamping, **69** 38
Werner Enterprises, Inc., 26 531–33
Werner International, **III** 344; **14** 225
Wertheim Schroder & Company, **17** 443
Weru Aktiengesellschaft, 18 558–61; **49** 295
Wesco Financial Corp., **III** 213, 215; **18** 62; **42** 32–34
Wesco Food Co., **II** 644
Wescot Decisison Systems, **6** 25
Weseley Software Development Corp. *see* RedPrairie Corporation.
Wesley Jessen VisionCare Inc., **65** 274
Wesper Co., **26** 4
Wesray and Management, **17** 213

Wesray Capital Corporation, **13** 41; **17** 443; **47** 363
Wesray Corporation, **22** 55
Wesray Holdings Corp., **13** 255
Wesray Transportation, Inc., **14** 38
Wessanen *see* Koninklijke Wessanen nv.
Wessanen USA, **29** 480
Wesson/Peter Pan Foods Co., **17** 241
West Australia Land Holdings, Limited, **10** 169
West Bend Co., 14 546–48
West Coast Entertainment Corporation, 29 502–04
West Coast Grocery Co., **II** 670; **18** 506; **50** 456
West Coast Machinery, **13** 385
West Coast Power Company, **12** 265
West Coast Restaurant Enterprises, **25** 390
West Coast Savings and Loan, **10** 339
West Company, **53** 298
West Corporation, 42 435–37
West End Family Pharmacy, Inc., **15** 523
West Fraser Timber Co. Ltd., 17 538–40
West Georgia Coca-Cola Bottlers, Inc., **13** 163
West Group, 34 438, 502–06 **(upd.)**
West Harrison Gas & Electric Company *see* Cincinnati Gas & Electric Company.
West Los Angeles Veterinary Medical Group, Inc., **58** 355
West Lynn Creamery, Inc., **26** 450
West Marine, Inc., 17 541–43; **37** 398
West Missouri Power Company *see* UtiliCorp United Inc.; Aquilla, Inc.
West Newton Savings Bank, **13** 468
West Newton Telephone Company, **14** 258
West One Bancorp, 11 552–55; **36** 491
West Penn Electric *see* Allegheny Power System, Inc.
West Penn Power Company, **38** 38–40
West Pharmaceutical Services, Inc., 42 438–41
West Point-Pepperell, Inc., 8 566–69 *see also* WestPoint Stevens Inc.; JPS Textile Group, Inc.
West Publishing Co., 7 579–81 *see also* The West Group.
West Side Printing Co., **13** 559
West Shore Pipe Line Company, **70** 35
West TeleServices Corporation *see* West Corporation.
West Texas LPG Pipeline Limited Partnership, **70** 35
West Texas Utilities Company, **6** 580
West Union Corporation, **22** 517
West Virginia Bearings, Inc., **13** 78
West Virginia Pulp and Paper Co. *see* Westvaco Corporation.
Westaff Inc., 33 454–57
WestAir Holding Inc., **11** 300; **25** 423; **32** 336
Westamerica Bancorporation, 17 544–47
Westar Energy, Inc., 57 404–07 **(upd.)**

Westbrae Natural, Inc., **27** 197–98; **43** 218
Westburne Group of Companies, **9** 364
Westchester County Savings & Loan, **9** 173
Westchester Specialty Group, Inc., **26** 546
Westclox Seth Thomas, **16** 483
WestCoast Hospitality Corporation, 59 410–13
Westcon Group, Inc., 67 392–94
Westcor Realty, **57** 235
Westcorp Financial Services *see* WFS Financial Inc.
Westcott Communications Inc., **22** 442
Westdeutsche Landesbank Girozentrale, II 385–87; **33** 395; **46** 458–61 **(upd.)**; **47** 83
Westec Corporation *see* Tech-Sym Corporation.
Westell Technologies, Inc., 57 408–10
Westerbeke Corporation, 60 332–34
Western Aerospace Ltd., **14** 564
Western Air Express, **9** 17
Western Air Lines, **I** 98, 100, 106; **21** 142; **25** 421–23
Western Areas Ltd., **61** 292
Western Atlas Inc., 12 538–40
Western Australian Specialty Alloys Proprietary Ltd., **14** 564
Western Auto, **19** 223; **57** 11
Western Auto Supply Co., **8** 56; **11** 392
Western Automatic Machine Screw Co., **12** 344
Western Bank, **17** 530
Western Beef, Inc., 22 548–50
Western Bingo, **16** 471
Western Company of North America, 15 534–36
Western Crude, **11** 27
Western Data Products, Inc., **19** 110
Western Digital Corp., 25 530–32
Western Edison, **6** 601
Western Electric Co., **II** 57, 66, 88, 101, 112; **7** 288; **11** 500–01; **12** 136; **13** 57; **49** 346
Western Electric Manufacturing Company, **54** 139
Western Empire Construction *see* CRSS Inc.
Western Equities, Inc. *see* Tech-Sym Corporation.
Western Family Foods, **47** 457; **53** 21
Western Federal Savings & Loan, **9** 199
Western Fire Equipment Co., **9** 420
Western Forest Products Ltd., **59** 161
Western Gas Resources, Inc., 45 435–37
Western Geophysical, **12** 538–39
Western Glucose Co., **14** 17
Western Graphics Corporation, **58** 314
Western Hotels Inc. *see* Westin Hotels and Resorts Worldwide.
Western Inland Lock Navigation Company, **9** 228
Western International Communications, **35** 68
Western International Media, **22** 294
Western International University, **24** 40

Index to Industries

Accounting

American Institute of Certified Public
 Accountants (AICPA), 44
Andersen, 29 (upd.); 68 (upd.)
Automatic Data Processing, Inc., 47
 (upd.)
Deloitte Touche Tohmatsu International,
 9; 29 (upd.)
Ernst & Young, 9; 29 (upd.)
FTI Consulting, Inc., 77
Grant Thornton International, 57
KPMG International, 33 (upd.)
L.S. Starrett Co., 13
McLane Company, Inc., 13
NCO Group, Inc., 42
Paychex, Inc., 46 (upd.)
Plante & Moran, LLP, 71
PRG-Schultz International, Inc., 73
PricewaterhouseCoopers, 9; 29 (upd.)
Robert Wood Johnson Foundation, 35
Univision Communications Inc., 24

Advertising & Other Business Services

ABM Industries Incorporated, 25 (upd.)
Ackerley Communications, Inc., 9
ACNielsen Corporation, 13; 38 (upd.)
Acosta Sales and Marketing Company,
 Inc., 77
Acsys, Inc., 44
Adecco S.A., 36 (upd.)
Adia S.A., 6
Administaff, Inc., 52
The Advertising Council, Inc., 76
Advo, Inc., 6; 53 (upd.)
Aegis Group plc, 6
Affiliated Computer Services, Inc., 61

AHL Services, Inc., 27
Alloy, Inc., 55
Amdocs Ltd., 47
American Building Maintenance Indus-
 tries, Inc., 6
The American Society of Composers, Au-
 thors and Publishers (ASCAP), 29
Amey Plc, 47
Analysts International Corporation, 36
The Arbitron Company, 38
Ariba, Inc., 57
Armor Holdings, Inc., 27
Ashtead Group plc, 34
The Associated Press, 13
Avalon Correctional Services, Inc., 75
Bain & Company, 55
Barrett Business Services, Inc., 16
Barton Protective Services Inc., 53
Bates Worldwide, Inc., 14; 33 (upd.)
Bearings, Inc., 13
Berlitz International, Inc., 13
Big Flower Press Holdings, Inc., 21
Billing Concepts, Inc., 72 (upd.)
The BISYS Group, Inc., 73
Boron, LePore & Associates, Inc., 45
The Boston Consulting Group, 58
Bozell Worldwide Inc., 25
BrandPartners Group, Inc., 58
Bright Horizons Family Solutions, Inc., 31
Broadcast Music Inc., 23
Buck Consultants, Inc., 55
Bureau Veritas SA, 55
Burns International Services Corporation,
 13; 41 (upd.)
Cambridge Technology Partners, Inc., 36
Campbell-Mithun-Esty, Inc., 16
Cannon Design, 63
Capita Group PLC, 69

Career Education Corporation, 45
Carmichael Lynch Inc., 28
Cazenove Group plc, 72
CCC Information Services Group Inc., 74
CDI Corporation, 54 (upd.)
Central Parking Corporation, 18
Century Business Services, Inc., 52
Chancellor Beacon Academies, Inc., 53
ChartHouse International Learning Cor-
 poration, 49
Chiat/Day Inc. Advertising, 11
Chicago Board of Trade, 41
Chisholm-Mingo Group, Inc., 41
Christie's International plc, 15; 39 (upd.)
Cintas Corporation, 21
COMFORCE Corporation, 40
Command Security Corporation, 57
Computer Learning Centers, Inc., 26
Concentra Inc., 71
Corporate Express, Inc., 47 (upd.)
CoolSavings, Inc., 77
CORT Business Services Corporation, 26
Cox Enterprises, Inc., 22 (upd.)
Creative Artists Agency LLC, 38
CSG Systems International, Inc., 75
Cyrk Inc., 19
Dale Carnegie Training, Inc., 28
D'Arcy Masius Benton & Bowles, Inc., 6;
 32 (upd.)
Dawson Holdings PLC, 43
DDB Needham Worldwide, 14
Deluxe Corporation, 22 (upd.); 73 (upd.)
Dentsu Inc., I; 16 (upd.); 40 (upd.)
Deutsch, Inc., 42
Deutsche Post AG, 29
DHL Worldwide Network S.A./N.V., 69
 (upd.)
DoubleClick Inc., 46

Bio-Technology

STERIS Corporation, 29
Stratagene Corporation, 70
Tanox, Inc., 77
TECHNE Corporation, 52
TriPath Imaging, Inc., 77
Waters Corporation, 43
Whatman plc, 46
Wisconsin Alumni Research Foundation, 65
Wyeth, 50 (upd.)

Chemicals

A. Schulman, Inc., 8
Aceto Corp., 38
Air Products and Chemicals, Inc., I; 10 (upd.); 74 (upd.)
Airgas, Inc., 54
Akzo Nobel N.V., 13
Albemarle Corporation, 59
AlliedSignal Inc., 22 (upd.)
American Cyanamid, I; 8 (upd.)
American Vanguard Corporation, 47
ARCO Chemical Company, 10
Asahi Denka Kogyo KK, 64
Atanor S.A., 62
Atochem S.A., I
Avecia Group PLC, 63
Baker Hughes Incorporated, 22 (upd.); 57 (upd.)
Balchem Corporation, 42
BASF Aktiengesellschaft, I; 18 (upd.); 50 (upd.)
Bayer A.G., I; 13 (upd.); 41 (upd.)
Betz Laboratories, Inc., I; 10 (upd.)
The BFGoodrich Company, 19 (upd.)
BOC Group plc, I; 25 (upd.)
Brenntag AG, 8; 23 (upd.)
Burmah Castrol PLC, 30 (upd.)
Cabot Corporation, 8; 29 (upd.)
Calgon Carbon Corporation, 73
Caliper Life Sciences, Inc., 70
Cambrex Corporation, 16
Catalytica Energy Systems, Inc., 44
Celanese Corporation, I
Celanese Mexicana, S.A. de C.V., 54
Chemcentral Corporation, 8
Chemi-Trol Chemical Co., 16
Church & Dwight Co., Inc., 29
Ciba-Geigy Ltd., I; 8 (upd.)
The Clorox Company, 22 (upd.)
Croda International Plc, 45
Crompton Corporation, 9; 36 (upd.)
Cytec Industries Inc., 27
Degussa-Hüls AG, 32 (upd.)
DeKalb Genetics Corporation, 17
The Dexter Corporation, I; 12 (upd.)
Dionex Corporation, 46
The Dow Chemical Company, I; 8 (upd.); 50 (upd.)
DSM N.V., I; 56 (upd.)
Dynaction S.A., 67
E.I. du Pont de Nemours & Company, I; 8 (upd.); 26 (upd.)
Eastman Chemical Company, 14; 38 (upd.)
Ecolab Inc., I; 13 (upd.); 34 (upd.)
Elementis plc, 40 (upd.)
Engelhard Corporation, 72 (upd.)

English China Clays Ltd., 15 (upd.); 40 (upd.)
Enterprise Rent-A-Car Company, 69 (upd.)
Equistar Chemicals, LP, 71
ERLY Industries Inc., 17
Ethyl Corporation, I; 10 (upd.)
Ferro Corporation, 8; 56 (upd.)
Firmenich International S.A., 60
First Mississippi Corporation, 8
Formosa Plastics Corporation, 14; 58 (upd.)
Fort James Corporation, 22 (upd.)
G.A.F., I
The General Chemical Group Inc., 37
Georgia Gulf Corporation, 9; 61 (upd.)
Givaudan SA, 43
Great Lakes Chemical Corporation, I; 14 (upd.)
Guerbet Group, 46
H.B. Fuller Company, 32 (upd.); 75 (upd.)
Hauser, Inc., 46
Hawkins Chemical, Inc., 16
Henkel KGaA, 34 (upd.)
Hercules Inc., I; 22 (upd.); 66 (upd.)
Hoechst A.G., I; 18 (upd.)
Hoechst Celanese Corporation, 13
Huls A.G., I
Huntsman Chemical Corporation, 8
IMC Fertilizer Group, Inc., 8
Imperial Chemical Industries PLC, I; 50 (upd.)
International Flavors & Fragrances Inc., 9; 38 (upd.)
Israel Chemicals Ltd., 55
Kemira Oyj, 70
Koppers Industries, Inc., I; 26 (upd.)
L'Air Liquide SA, I; 47 (upd.)
Lawter International Inc., 14
LeaRonal, Inc., 23
Loctite Corporation, 30 (upd.)
Lonza Group Ltd., 73
Lubrizol Corporation, I; 30 (upd.)
Lyondell Chemical Company, 45 (upd.)
M.A. Hanna Company, 8
MacDermid Incorporated, 32
Mallinckrodt Group Inc., 19
MBC Holding Company, 40
Melamine Chemicals, Inc., 27
Methanex Corporation, 40
Minerals Technologies Inc., 52 (upd.)
Mississippi Chemical Corporation, 39
Mitsubishi Chemical Corporation, I; 56 (upd.)
Mitsui Petrochemical Industries, Ltd., 9
Monsanto Company, I; 9 (upd.); 29 (upd.)
Montedison SpA, I
Morton International Inc., 9 (upd.)
Morton Thiokol, Inc., I
Nagase & Company, Ltd., 8
Nalco Chemical Corporation, I; 12 (upd.)
National Distillers and Chemical Corporation, I
National Sanitary Supply Co., 16
National Starch and Chemical Company, 49

NCH Corporation, 8
Nisshin Seifun Group Inc., 66 (upd.)
NL Industries, Inc., 10
Nobel Industries AB, 9
NOF Corporation, 72
Norsk Hydro ASA, 35 (upd.)
Novacor Chemicals Ltd., 12
NutraSweet Company, 8
Occidental Petroleum Corporation, 71 (upd.)
Olin Corporation, I; 13 (upd.)
OM Group, Inc., 17
OMNOVA Solutions Inc., 59
Penford Corporation, 55
Pennwalt Corporation, I
Perstorp AB, I; 51 (upd.)
Petrolite Corporation, 15
Pioneer Hi-Bred International, Inc., 41 (upd.)
Praxair, Inc., 11
Quantum Chemical Corporation, 8
Reichhold Chemicals, Inc., 10
Rhodia SA, 38
Rhône-Poulenc S.A., I; 10 (upd.)
Robertet SA, 39
Rohm and Haas Company, I; 26 (upd.); 77 (upd.)
Roussel Uclaf, I; 8 (upd.)
RPM, Inc., 36 (upd.)
RWE AG, 50 (upd.)
The Scotts Company, 22
SCP Pool Corporation, 39
Sequa Corp., 13
Shanghai Petrochemical Co., Ltd., 18
Sigma-Aldrich Corporation, 36 (upd.)
Solutia Inc., 52
Solvay S.A., I; 21 (upd.); 61 (upd.)
Stepan Company, 30
Sterling Chemicals, Inc., 16
Sumitomo Chemical Company Ltd., I
Takeda Chemical Industries, Ltd., 46 (upd.)
Terra Industries, Inc., 13
Tessenderlo Group, 76
Teva Pharmaceutical Industries Ltd., 22
Tosoh Corporation, 70
Total Fina Elf S.A., 24 (upd.); 50 (upd.)
Ube Industries, Ltd., 38 (upd.)
Union Carbide Corporation, I; 9 (upd.); 74 (upd.)
United Industries Corporation, 68
Univar Corporation, 9
The Valspar Corporation, 32 (upd.); 77 (upd.)
Vista Chemical Company, I
Witco Corporation, I; 16 (upd.)
Yule Catto & Company plc, 54
Zeneca Group PLC, 21

Conglomerates

A.P. Møller - Maersk A/S, 57
Abengoa S.A., 73
Accor SA, 10; 27 (upd.)
AEG A.G., I
Alcatel Alsthom Compagnie Générale d'Electricité, 9
Alco Standard Corporation, I
Alexander & Baldwin, Inc., 40 (upd.)

Construction

Obrascon Huarte Lain S.A., 76
Ohbayashi Corporation, I
Opus Group, 34
Orleans Homebuilders, Inc., 62
The Parsons Corporation, 56 (upd.)
PCL Construction Group Inc., 50
The Peninsular & Oriental Steam Naviga-
    tion Company (Bovis Division), I
Perini Corporation, 8
Peter Kiewit Sons' Inc., 8
Philipp Holzmann AG, 17
Post Properties, Inc., 26
Pulte Homes, Inc., 8; 42 (upd.)
Pyramid Companies, 54
Redrow Group plc, 31
Rinker Group Ltd., 65
RMC Group p.l.c., 34 (upd.)
Rooney Brothers Co., 25
The Rottlund Company, Inc., 28
Roy Anderson Corporation, 75
The Ryland Group, Inc., 8; 37 (upd.)
Sandvik AB, 32 (upd.)
Schuff Steel Company, 26
Seddon Group Ltd., 67
Shorewood Packaging Corporation, 28
Simon Property Group, Inc., 27
Skanska AB, 38
Skidmore, Owings & Merrill LLP, 69
    (upd.)
SNC-Lavalin Group Inc., 72
Standard Pacific Corporation, 52
Stone & Webster, Inc., 64 (upd.)
Sundt Corp., 24
Swinerton Inc., 43
Taylor Woodrow plc, I; 38 (upd.)
Technical Olympic USA, Inc., 75
Thyssen Krupp AG, 28 (upd.)
Toll Brothers Inc., 15; 70 (upd.)
Trammell Crow Company, 8
Tridel Enterprises Inc., 9
Turner Construction Company, 66
The Turner Corporation, 8; 23 (upd.)
U.S. Aggregates, Inc., 42
U.S. Home Corporation, 8
VA TECH ELIN EBG GmbH, 49
Veit Companies, 43
Walbridge Aldinger Co., 38
Walter Industries, Inc., 22 (upd.)
The Weitz Company, Inc., 42
Willbros Group, Inc., 56
William Lyon Homes, 59
Wilson Bowden Plc, 45
Wood Hall Trust PLC, I
The Yates Companies, Inc., 62

Containers

Ball Corporation, I; 10 (upd.)
BWAY Corporation, 24
Clarcor Inc., 17
Continental Can Co., Inc., 15
Continental Group Company, I
Crown Cork & Seal Company, Inc., I; 13
    (upd.); 32 (upd.)
Gaylord Container Corporation, 8
Golden Belt Manufacturing Co., 16
Greif Inc., 15; 66 (upd.)
Grupo Industrial Durango, S.A. de C.V.,
    37

Hanjin Shipping Co., Ltd., 50
Inland Container Corporation, 8
Kerr Group Inc., 24
Keyes Fibre Company, 9
Libbey Inc., 49
Liqui-Box Corporation, 16
The Longaberger Company, 12
Longview Fibre Company, 8
The Mead Corporation, 19 (upd.)
Metal Box PLC, I
Molins plc, 51
National Can Corporation, I
Owens-Illinois, Inc., I; 26 (upd.)
Packaging Corporation of America, 51
    (upd.)
Primerica Corporation, I
PVC Container Corporation, 67
Reynolds Metals Company, 19 (upd.)
Royal Packaging Industries Van Leer N.V.,
    30
Sealright Co., Inc., 17
Shurgard Storage Centers, Inc., 52
Smurfit-Stone Container Corporation, 26
    (upd.)
Sonoco Products Company, 8
Thermos Company, 16
Toyo Seikan Kaisha, Ltd., I
U.S. Can Corporation, 30
Ultra Pac, Inc., 24
Viatech Continental Can Company, Inc.,
    25 (upd.)
Vidrala S.A., 67
Vitro Corporativo S.A. de C.V., 34

Drugs/Pharmaceuticals

A. Nelson & Co. Ltd., 75
A.L. Pharma Inc., 12
Abbott Laboratories, I; 11 (upd.); 40
    (upd.)
Akorn, Inc., 32
Albany Molecular Research, Inc., 77
Allergan, Inc., 77 (upd.)
Alpharma Inc., 35 (upd.)
ALZA Corporation, 10; 36 (upd.)
American Home Products, I; 10 (upd.)
American Pharmaceutical Partners, Inc.,
    69
AmerisourceBergen Corporation, 64
    (upd.)
Amersham PLC, 50
Amgen, Inc., 10
Amylin Pharmaceuticals, Inc., 67
Andrx Corporation, 55
Astra AB, I; 20 (upd.)
AstraZeneca PLC, 50 (upd.)
Barr Pharmaceuticals, Inc., 26; 68 (upd.)
Bayer A.G., I; 13 (upd.)
Berlex Laboratories, Inc., 66
Biovail Corporation, 47
Block Drug Company, Inc., 8
Boiron S.A., 73
Bristol-Myers Squibb Company, III; 9
    (upd.); 37 (upd.)
C.H. Boehringer Sohn, 39
Caremark Rx, Inc., 10; 54 (upd.)
Carter-Wallace, Inc., 8; 38 (upd.)
Celgene Corporation, 67
Cephalon, Inc., 45

Chiron Corporation, 10
Chugai Pharmaceutical Co., Ltd., 50
Ciba-Geigy Ltd., I; 8 (upd.)
D&K Wholesale Drug, Inc., 14
Discovery Partners International, Inc., 58
Dr. Reddy's Laboratories Ltd., 59
Elan Corporation PLC, 63
Eli Lilly and Company, I; 11 (upd.); 47
    (upd.)
Endo Pharmaceuticals Holdings Inc., 71
Eon Labs, Inc., 67
Express Scripts Inc., 44 (upd.)
F. Hoffmann-La Roche Ltd., I; 50 (upd.)
Fisons plc, 9; 23 (upd.)
Forest Laboratories, Inc., 52 (upd.)
FoxMeyer Health Corporation, 16
Fujisawa Pharmaceutical Company Ltd., I
G.D. Searle & Co., I; 12 (upd.); 34
    (upd.)
GEHE AG, 27
Genentech, Inc., I; 8 (upd.); 75 (upd.)
Genetics Institute, Inc., 8
Genzyme Corporation, 13, 77 (upd.)
Glaxo Holdings PLC, I; 9 (upd.)
GlaxoSmithKline plc, 46 (upd.)
Groupe Fournier SA, 44
H. Lundbeck A/S, 44
Hauser, Inc., 46
Heska Corporation, 39
Hexal AG, 69
Hospira, Inc., 71
Huntingdon Life Sciences Group plc, 42
ICN Pharmaceuticals, Inc., 52
IVAX Corporation, 55 (upd.)
Johnson & Johnson, III; 8 (upd.)
Jones Medical Industries, Inc., 24
The Judge Group, Inc., 51
King Pharmaceuticals, Inc., 54
Kos Pharmaceuticals, Inc., 63
Kyowa Hakko Kogyo Co., Ltd., 48 (upd.)
Laboratoires Arkopharma S.A., 75
Leiner Health Products Inc., 34
Ligand Pharmaceuticals Incorporated, 47
Marion Merrell Dow, Inc., I; 9 (upd.)
Matrixx Initiatives, Inc., 74
McKesson Corporation, 12; 47 (upd.)
Medicis Pharmaceutical Corporation, 59
MedImmune, Inc., 35
Merck & Co., Inc., I; 11 (upd.)
Miles Laboratories, I
Millennium Pharmaceuticals, Inc., 47
Monsanto Company, 29 (upd.), 77 (upd.)
Moore Medical Corp., 17
Murdock Madaus Schwabe, 26
Mylan Laboratories Inc., I; 20 (upd.); 59
    (upd.)
National Patent Development Corpora-
    tion, 13
Natrol, Inc., 49
Natural Alternatives International, Inc., 49
Novartis AG, 39 (upd.)
Noven Pharmaceuticals, Inc., 55
Novo Nordisk A/S, I; 61 (upd.)
Omnicare, Inc., 49
Par Pharmaceutical Companies, Inc., 65
Perrigo Company, 59 (upd.)
Pfizer Inc., I; 9 (upd.); 38 (upd.)
Pharmacia & Upjohn Inc., I; 25 (upd.)

PLIVA d.d., 70
PolyMedica Corporation, 77
QLT Inc., 71
The Quigley Corporation, 62
Quintiles Transnational Corporation, 21
R.P. Scherer, I
Ranbaxy Laboratories Ltd., 70
Roberts Pharmaceutical Corporation, 16
Roche Bioscience, 14 (upd.)
Rorer Group, I
Roussel Uclaf, I; 8 (upd.)
Sandoz Ltd., I
Sankyo Company, Ltd., I; 56 (upd.)
The Sanofi-Synthélabo Group, I; 49
   (upd.)
Schering AG, I; 50 (upd.)
Schering-Plough Corporation, I; 14
   (upd.); 49 (upd.)
Sepracor Inc., 45
Serono S.A., 47
Shionogi & Co., Ltd., 17 (upd.)
Sigma-Aldrich Corporation, I; 36 (upd.)
SmithKline Beecham plc, I; 32 (upd.)
Solvay S.A., 61 (upd.)
Squibb Corporation, I
Sterling Drug, Inc., I
Sun Pharmaceutical Industries Ltd., 57
The Sunrider Corporation, 26
Syntex Corporation, I
Takeda Chemical Industries, Ltd., I
Taro Pharmaceutical Industries Ltd., 65
Teva Pharmaceutical Industries Ltd., 22;
   54 (upd.)
The Upjohn Company, I; 8 (upd.)
Virbac Corporation, 74
Vitalink Pharmacy Services, Inc., 15
Warner-Lambert Co., I; 10 (upd.)
Watson Pharmaceuticals Inc., 16; 56
   (upd.)
The Wellcome Foundation Ltd., I
Zila, Inc., 46

Electrical & Electronics

ABB ASEA Brown Boveri Ltd., II; 22
   (upd.)
ABB Ltd., 65 (upd.)
Acer Incorporated, 16; 73 (upd.)
Acuson Corporation, 10; 36 (upd.)
ADC Telecommunications, Inc., 30 (upd.)
Adtran Inc., 22
Advanced Micro Devices, Inc., 30 (upd.)
Advanced Technology Laboratories, Inc., 9
Agere Systems Inc., 61
Agilent Technologies Inc., 38
Agilysys Inc., 76 (upd.)
Aiwa Co., Ltd., 30
AKG Acoustics GmbH, 62
Akzo Nobel N.V., 41 (upd.)
Alliant Techsystems Inc., 30 (upd.); 77
   (upd.)
AlliedSignal Inc., 22 (upd.)
Alpine Electronics, Inc., 13
Alps Electric Co., Ltd., II
Altera Corporation, 18; 43 (upd.)
Altron Incorporated, 20
Amdahl Corporation, 40 (upd.)
American Power Conversion Corporation,
   24; 67 (upd.)

American Technical Ceramics Corp., 67
Amkor Technology, Inc., 69
AMP Incorporated, II; 14 (upd.)
Amphenol Corporation, 40
Amstrad plc, 48 (upd.)
Analog Devices, Inc., 10
Analogic Corporation, 23
Anam Group, 23
Anaren Microwave, Inc., 33
Andrew Corporation, 10; 32 (upd.)
Anritsu Corporation, 68
Apex Digital, Inc., 63
Apple Computer, Inc., 36 (upd.); 77
   (upd.)
Applied Power Inc., 32 (upd.)
Arrow Electronics, Inc., 10; 50 (upd.)
Ascend Communications, Inc., 24
Astronics Corporation, 35
Atari Corporation, 9; 23 (upd.); 66 (upd.)
Atmel Corporation, 17
AU Optronics Corporation, 67
Audiovox Corporation, 34
Ault Incorporated, 34
Autodesk, Inc., 10
Avnet Inc., 9
AVX Corporation, 67
Ballard Power Systems Inc., 73
Bang & Olufsen Holding A/S, 37
Barco NV, 44
Bell Microproducts Inc., 69
Benchmark Electronics, Inc., 40
Bicoastal Corporation, II
Blonder Tongue Laboratories, Inc., 48
BMC Industries, Inc., 59 (upd.)
Bogen Communications International,
   Inc., 62
Bose Corporation, 13; 36 (upd.)
Boston Acoustics, Inc., 22
Bowthorpe plc, 33
Braun GmbH, 51
Broadcom Corporation, 34
Bull S.A., 43 (upd.)
Burr-Brown Corporation, 19
C-COR.net Corp., 38
Cabletron Systems, Inc., 10
Cadence Design Systems, Inc., 48 (upd.)
Cambridge SoundWorks, Inc., 48
Canon Inc., 18 (upd.)
Carbone Lorraine S.A., 33
Carl-Zeiss-Stiftung, 34 (upd.)
CASIO Computer Co., Ltd., 16 (upd.);
   40 (upd.)
CDW Computer Centers, Inc., 52 (upd.)
Checkpoint Systems, Inc., 39
Chi Mei Optoelectronics Corporation, 75
Chubb, PLC, 50
Chunghwa Picture Tubes, Ltd., 75
Cirrus Logic, Inc., 48 (upd.)
Cisco Systems, Inc., 34 (upd.); 77 (upd.)
Citizen Watch Co., Ltd., 21 (upd.)
Clarion Company Ltd., 64
Cobham plc, 30
Cobra Electronics Corporation, 14
Coherent, Inc., 31
Cohu, Inc., 32
Compagnie Générale d'Électricité, II
Concurrent Computer Corporation, 75
Conexant Systems, Inc., 36

Cooper Industries, Inc., II
Cray Inc., 75 (upd.)
Cray Research, Inc., 16 (upd.)
Cree Inc., 53
CTS Corporation, 39
Cubic Corporation, 19
Cypress Semiconductor Corporation, 20;
   48 (upd.)
Dai Nippon Printing Co., Ltd., 57 (upd.)
Daktronics, Inc., 32
Dallas Semiconductor Corporation, 13; 31
   (upd.)
De La Rue plc, 34 (upd.)
Dell Computer Corporation, 31 (upd.)
DH Technology, Inc., 18
Digi International Inc., 9
Discreet Logic Inc., 20
Dixons Group plc, 19 (upd.)
Dolby Laboratories Inc., 20
DRS Technologies, Inc., 58
Dynatech Corporation, 13
E-Systems, Inc., 9
Electronics for Imaging, Inc., 15; 43
   (upd.)
Emerson, II; 46 (upd.)
Emerson Radio Corp., 30
ENCAD, Incorporated, 25
Equant N.V., 52
Equus Computer Systems, Inc., 49
ESS Technology, Inc., 22
Everex Systems, Inc., 16
Exabyte Corporation, 40 (upd.)
Exar Corp., 14
Exide Electronics Group, Inc., 20
Fisk Corporation, 72
Flextronics International Ltd., 38
Fluke Corporation, 15
Foxboro Company, 13
Frequency Electronics, Inc., 61
FuelCell Energy, Inc., 75
Fuji Electric Co., Ltd., II; 48 (upd.)
Fujitsu Limited, 16 (upd.); 42 (upd.)
Funai Electric Company Ltd., 62
Gateway, Inc., 63 (upd.)
General Atomics, 57
General Dynamics Corporation, 40 (upd.)
General Electric Company, II; 12 (upd.)
General Electric Company, PLC, II
General Instrument Corporation, 10
General Signal Corporation, 9
GenRad, Inc., 24
GM Hughes Electronics Corporation, II
Goldstar Co., Ltd., 12
Gould Electronics, Inc., 14
Grundig AG, 27
Guillemot Corporation, 41
Hadco Corporation, 24
Hamilton Beach/Proctor-Silex Inc., 17
Harman International Industries Inc., 15
Harris Corporation, II; 20 (upd.)
Hayes Corporation, 24
Herley Industries, Inc., 33
Hewlett-Packard Company, 28 (upd.); 50
   (upd.)
Holophane Corporation, 19
Hon Hai Precision Industry Co., Ltd., 59
Honeywell Inc., II; 12 (upd.); 50 (upd.)
Hubbell Incorporated, 9; 31 (upd.)

Engineering & Management Services

Entertainment & Leisure

Financial Services: Banks

Huntington Bancshares Inc., 11
HVB Group, 59 (upd.)
IBERIABANK Corporation, 37
The Industrial Bank of Japan, Ltd., II
Irish Life & Permanent Plc, 59
Irwin Financial Corporation, 77
J Sainsbury plc, 38 (upd.)
J.P. Morgan & Co. Incorporated, II; 30 (upd.)
J.P. Morgan Chase & Co., 38 (upd.)
Japan Leasing Corporation, 8
Julius Baer Holding AG, 52
Kansallis-Osake-Pankki, II
KeyCorp, 8
Kookmin Bank, 58
Kredietbank N.V., II
Kreditanstalt für Wiederaufbau, 29
Krung Thai Bank Public Company Ltd., 69
Lloyds Bank PLC, II
Lloyds TSB Group plc, 47 (upd.)
Long Island Bancorp, Inc., 16
Long-Term Credit Bank of Japan, Ltd., II
Macquarie Bank Ltd., 69
Malayan Banking Berhad, 72
Manufacturers Hanover Corporation, II
Marshall & Ilsley Corporation, 56
MBNA Corporation, 12
Mediolanum S.p.A., 65
Mellon Bank Corporation, II
Mellon Financial Corporation, 44 (upd.)
Mercantile Bankshares Corp., 11
Meridian Bancorp, Inc., 11
Metropolitan Financial Corporation, 13
Michigan National Corporation, 11
Midland Bank PLC, II; 17 (upd.)
The Mitsubishi Bank, Ltd., II
The Mitsubishi Trust & Banking Corporation, II
The Mitsui Bank, Ltd., II
The Mitsui Trust & Banking Company, Ltd., II
Mizuho Financial Group Inc., 58 (upd.)
Mouvement des Caisses Desjardins, 48
N M Rothschild & Sons Limited, 39
National Bank of Greece, 41
The National Bank of South Carolina, 76
National City Corp., 15
National Westminster Bank PLC, II
NationsBank Corporation, 10
NBD Bancorp, Inc., 11
NCNB Corporation, II
Nippon Credit Bank, II
Nordea AB, 40
Norinchukin Bank, II
North Fork Bancorporation, Inc., 46
Northern Rock plc, 33
Northern Trust Company, 9
NVR L.P., 8
Old Kent Financial Corp., 11
Old National Bancorp, 15
PNC Bank Corp., II; 13 (upd.)
The PNC Financial Services Group Inc., 46 (upd.)
Popular, Inc., 41
PT Bank Buana Indonesia Tbk, 60
Pulte Corporation, 8
Rabobank Group, 33

Republic New York Corporation, 11
Riggs National Corporation, 13
The Royal Bank of Canada, II; 21 (upd.)
The Royal Bank of Scotland Group plc, 12; 38 (upd.)
The Ryland Group, Inc., 8
St. Paul Bank for Cooperatives, 8
Sanpaolo IMI S.p.A., 50
The Sanwa Bank, Ltd., II; 15 (upd.)
SBC Warburg, 14
Sberbank, 62
Seattle First National Bank Inc., 8
Security Capital Corporation, 17
Security Pacific Corporation, II
Shawmut National Corporation, 13
Signet Banking Corporation, 11
Singer & Friedlander Group plc, 41
Skandinaviska Enskilda Banken AB, II; 56 (upd.)
Société Générale, II; 42 (upd.)
Society Corporation, 9
Southern Financial Bancorp, Inc., 56
Southtrust Corporation, 11
Standard Chartered plc, II; 48 (upd.)
Standard Federal Bank, 9
Star Banc Corporation, 11
State Bank of India, 63
State Financial Services Corporation, 51
State Street Corporation, 8; 57 (upd.)
Staten Island Bancorp, Inc., 39
The Sumitomo Bank, Limited, II; 26 (upd.)
Sumitomo Mitsui Banking Corporation, 51 (upd.)
The Sumitomo Trust & Banking Company, Ltd., II; 53 (upd.)
The Summit Bancorporation, 14
SunTrust Banks Inc., 23
Svenska Handelsbanken AB, II; 50 (upd.)
Swiss Bank Corporation, II
Synovus Financial Corp., 12; 52 (upd.)
The Taiyo Kobe Bank, Ltd., II
TCF Financial Corporation, 47
The Tokai Bank, Limited, II; 15 (upd.)
The Toronto-Dominion Bank, II; 49 (upd.)
TSB Group plc, 12
Turkiye Is Bankasi A.S., 61
U.S. Bancorp, 14; 36 (upd.)
U.S. Trust Corp., 17
UBS AG, 52 (upd.)
Unibanco Holdings S.A., 73
Union Bank of California, 16
Union Bank of Switzerland, II
Union Financière de France Banque SA, 52
Union Planters Corporation, 54
UnionBanCal Corporation, 50 (upd.)
United Overseas Bank Ltd., 56
USAA, 62 (upd.)
Wachovia Bank of Georgia, N.A., 16
Wachovia Bank of South Carolina, N.A., 16
Washington Mutual, Inc., 17
Wells Fargo & Company, II; 12 (upd.); 38 (upd.)
West One Bancorp, 11
Westamerica Bancorporation, 17

Westdeutsche Landesbank Girozentrale, II; 46 (upd.)
Westpac Banking Corporation, II; 48 (upd.)
Whitney Holding Corporation, 21
Wilmington Trust Corporation, 25
The Woolwich plc, 30
World Bank Group, 33
The Yasuda Trust and Banking Company, Ltd., II; 17 (upd.)
Zions Bancorporation, 12; 53 (upd.)

Financial Services: Excluding Banks

A.B. Watley Group Inc., 45
A.G. Edwards, Inc., 8; 32 (upd.)
ACE Cash Express, Inc., 33
Advanta Corporation, 8; 38 (upd.)
Ag Services of America, Inc., 59
Alliance Capital Management Holding L.P., 63
Allmerica Financial Corporation, 63
Ambac Financial Group, Inc., 65
America's Car-Mart, Inc., 64
American Express Company, II; 10 (upd.); 38 (upd.)
American General Finance Corp., 11
American Home Mortgage Holdings, Inc., 46
Ameritrade Holding Corporation, 34
AMVESCAP PLC, 65
Arthur Andersen & Company, Société Coopérative, 10
Avco Financial Services Inc., 13
Aviva PLC, 50 (upd.)
Bear Stearns Companies, Inc., II; 10 (upd.); 52 (upd.)
Benchmark Capital, 49
Bill & Melinda Gates Foundation, 41
Bozzuto's, Inc., 13
Bradford & Bingley PLC, 65
Capital One Financial Corporation, 52
Carnegie Corporation of New York, 35
Cash America International, Inc., 20; 61 (upd.)
Cattles plc, 58
Cendant Corporation, 44 (upd.)
Certegy, Inc., 63
Cetelem S.A., 21
The Charles Schwab Corporation, 8; 26 (upd.)
Cheshire Building Society, 74
Chicago Mercantile Exchange Holdings Inc., 75
CIT Group Inc., 76
Citfed Bancorp, Inc., 16
Coinstar, Inc., 44
Comerica Incorporated, 40
Commercial Financial Services, Inc., 26
Concord EFS, Inc., 52
Coopers & Lybrand, 9
Cramer, Berkowitz & Co., 34
Credit Acceptance Corporation, 18
Cresud S.A.C.I.F. y A., 63
CS First Boston Inc., II
Dain Rauscher Corporation, 35 (upd.)
Daiwa Securities Group Inc., II; 55 (upd.)

Food Products

Health & Personal Care Products

Health Care Services

Insurance

SCOR S.A., 20
Skandia Insurance Company, Ltd., 50
StanCorp Financial Group, Inc., 56
The Standard Life Assurance Company, III
State Auto Financial Corporation, 77
State Farm Mutual Automobile Insurance Company, III; 51 (upd.)
State Financial Services Corporation, 51
Sumitomo Life Insurance Company, III; 60 (upd.)
The Sumitomo Marine and Fire Insurance Company, Limited, III
Sun Alliance Group PLC, III
SunAmerica Inc., 11
Svenska Handelsbanken AB, 50 (upd.)
Swiss Reinsurance Company (Schweizerische Rückversicherungs-Gesellschaft), III; 46 (upd.)
Teachers Insurance and Annuity Association-College Retirement Equities Fund, III; 45 (upd.)
Texas Industries, Inc., 8
TIG Holdings, Inc., 26
The Tokio Marine and Fire Insurance Co., Ltd., III
Torchmark Corporation, 9; 33 (upd.)
Transatlantic Holdings, Inc., 11
The Travelers Corporation, III
UICI, 33
Union des Assurances de Pans, III
United National Group, Ltd., 63
Unitrin Inc., 16
UNUM Corp., 13
UnumProvident Corporation, 52 (upd.)
USAA, 10
USF&G Corporation, III
Victoria Group, 44 (upd.)
VICTORIA Holding AG, III
Vision Service Plan Inc., 77
W.R. Berkley Corporation, 15; 74 (upd.)
Washington National Corporation, 12
The Wawanesa Mutual Insurance Company, 68
WellChoice, Inc., 67 (upd.)
Westfield Group, 69
White Mountains Insurance Group, Ltd., 48
Willis Corroon Group plc, 25
Winterthur Group, III; 68 (upd.)
The Yasuda Fire and Marine Insurance Company, Limited, III
The Yasuda Mutual Life Insurance Company, III; 39 (upd.)
Zürich Versicherungs-Gesellschaft, III

Legal Services

Akin, Gump, Strauss, Hauer & Feld, L.L.P., 33
American Bar Association, 35
American Lawyer Media Holdings, Inc., 32
Amnesty International, 50
Andrews Kurth, LLP, 71
Arnold & Porter, 35
Baker & Hostetler LLP, 40
Baker & McKenzie, 10; 42 (upd.)
Baker and Botts, L.L.P., 28

Bingham Dana LLP, 43
Brobeck, Phleger & Harrison, LLP, 31
Cadwalader, Wickersham & Taft, 32
Chadbourne & Parke, 36
Cleary, Gottlieb, Steen & Hamilton, 35
Clifford Chance LLP, 38
Coudert Brothers, 30
Covington & Burling, 40
Cravath, Swaine & Moore, 43
Davis Polk & Wardwell, 36
Debevoise & Plimpton, 39
Dechert, 43
Dewey Ballantine LLP, 48
Dorsey & Whitney LLP, 47
Fenwick & West LLP, 34
Fish & Neave, 54
Foley & Lardner, 28
Fried, Frank, Harris, Shriver & Jacobson, 35
Fulbright & Jaworski L.L.P., 47
Gibson, Dunn & Crutcher LLP, 36
Greenberg Traurig, LLP, 65
Heller, Ehrman, White & McAuliffe, 41
Hildebrandt International, 29
Hogan & Hartson L.L.P., 44
Holland & Knight LLP, 60
Holme Roberts & Owen LLP, 28
Hughes Hubbard & Reed LLP, 44
Hunton & Williams, 35
Jenkens & Gilchrist, P.C., 65
Jones, Day, Reavis & Pogue, 33
Kelley Drye & Warren LLP, 40
King & Spalding, 23
Kirkland & Ellis LLP, 65
Latham & Watkins, 33
LeBoeuf, Lamb, Greene & MacRae, L.L.P., 29
The Legal Aid Society, 48
Mayer, Brown, Rowe & Maw, 47
Milbank, Tweed, Hadley & McCloy, 27
Morgan, Lewis & Bockius LLP, 29
O'Melveny & Myers, 37
Oppenheimer Wolff & Donnelly LLP, 71
Orrick, Herrington and Sutcliffe LLP, 76
Patton Boggs LLP, 71
Paul, Hastings, Janofsky & Walker LLP, 27
Paul, Weiss, Rifkind, Wharton & Garrison, 47
Pepper Hamilton LLP, 43
Perkins Coie LLP, 56
Pillsbury Madison & Sutro LLP, 29
Pre-Paid Legal Services, Inc., 20
Proskauer Rose LLP, 47
Ropes & Gray, 40
Saul Ewing LLP, 74
Shearman & Sterling, 32
Sidley Austin Brown & Wood, 40
Simpson Thacher & Bartlett, 39
Skadden, Arps, Slate, Meagher & Flom, 18
Snell & Wilmer L.L.P., 28
Southern Poverty Law Center, Inc., 74
Stroock & Stroock & Lavan LLP, 40
Sullivan & Cromwell, 26
Vinson & Elkins L.L.P., 30
Wachtell, Lipton, Rosen & Katz, 47
Weil, Gotshal & Manges LLP, 55

White & Case LLP, 35
Williams & Connolly LLP, 47
Wilson Sonsini Goodrich & Rosati, 34
Winston & Strawn, 35
Womble Carlyle Sandridge & Rice, PLLC, 52

Manufacturing

A-dec, Inc., 53
A. Schulman, Inc., 49 (upd.)
A.B.Dick Company, 28
A.O. Smith Corporation, 11; 40 (upd.)
A.T. Cross Company, 17; 49 (upd.)
A.W. Faber-Castell Unternehmensverwaltung GmbH & Co., 51
AAF-McQuay Incorporated, 26
AAON, Inc., 22
AAR Corp., 28
Aarhus United A/S, 68
ABB Ltd., 65 (upd.)
ABC Rail Products Corporation, 18
Abiomed, Inc., 47
ACCO World Corporation, 7; 51 (upd.)
Accubuilt, Inc., 74
Acme United Corporation, 70
Acme-Cleveland Corp., 13
Acorn Products, Inc., 55
Acushnet Company, 64
Acuson Corporation, 36 (upd.)
Adams Golf, Inc., 37
Adolf Würth GmbH & Co. KG, 49
Advanced Circuits Inc., 67
Advanced Neuromodulation Systems, Inc., 73
AEP Industries, Inc., 36
Ag-Chem Equipment Company, Inc., 17
Aga Foodservice Group PLC, 73
AGCO Corporation, 13; 67 (upd.)
Agfa Gevaert Group N.V., 59
Agrium Inc., 73
Ahlstrom Corporation, 53
Airgas, Inc., 54
Aisin Seiki Co., Ltd., III
AK Steel Holding Corporation, 41 (upd.)
AKG Acoustics GmbH, 62
Aktiebolaget Electrolux, 22 (upd.)
Aktiebolaget SKF, III; 38 (upd.)
Alamo Group Inc., 32
ALARIS Medical Systems, Inc., 65
Alberto-Culver Company, 36 (upd.)
Aldila Inc., 46
Alfa Laval AB, III; 64 (upd.)
Allen Organ Company, 33
Allen-Edmonds Shoe Corporation, 61
Alliant Techsystems Inc., 8; 30 (upd.); 77 (upd.)
The Allied Defense Group, Inc., 65
Allied Healthcare Products, Inc., 24
Allied Products Corporation, 21
Allied Signal Engines, 9
AlliedSignal Inc., 22 (upd.)
Allison Gas Turbine Division, 9
Alltrista Corporation, 30
Alps Electric Co., Ltd., 44 (upd.)
Alticor Inc., 71 (upd.)
Aluar Aluminio Argentino S.A.I.C., 74
Alvis Plc, 47
Amer Group plc, 41

Cavco Industries, Inc., 65
CEMEX S.A. de C.V., 59 (upd.)
Central Garden & Pet Company, 58 (upd.)
Central Sprinkler Corporation, 29
Centuri Corporation, 54
Century Aluminum Company, 52
Cenveo Inc., 71 (upd.)
Cepheid, 77
Ceradyne, Inc., 65
Cessna Aircraft Company, 27 (upd.)
Champion Enterprises, Inc., 17
Chanel SA, 12; 49 (upd.)
Charisma Brands LLC, 74
The Charles Machine Works, Inc., 64
Chart Industries, Inc., 21
Chittenden & Eastman Company, 58
Chris-Craft Industries, Inc., 31 (upd.)
Christian Dalloz SA, 40
Christofle SA, 40
Chromcraft Revington, Inc., 15
Ciments Français, 40
Cincinnati Lamb Inc., 72
Cincinnati Milacron Inc., 12
Cinram International, 43
Circon Corporation, 21
Cirrus Design Corporation, 44
Citizen Watch Co., Ltd., III
CLARCOR Inc., 17; 61 (upd.)
Clark Equipment Company, 8
Clayton Homes Incorporated, 13; 54 (upd.)
The Clorox Company, 22 (upd.)
CNH Global N.V., 38 (upd.)
Coach, Inc., 45 (upd.)
Coachmen Industries, Inc., 77
COBE Cardiovascular, Inc., 61
Cobra Golf Inc., 16
Cochlear Ltd., 77
Cockerill Sambre Group, 26 (upd.)
Cognex Corporation, 76
Cohu, Inc., 32
Colas S.A., 31
The Coleman Company, Inc., 30 (upd.)
Colfax Corporation, 58
Collins & Aikman Corporation, 41 (upd.)
Collins Industries, Inc., 33
Colorado MEDtech, Inc., 48
Colt's Manufacturing Company, Inc., 12
Columbia Sportswear Company, 19
Columbus McKinnon Corporation, 37
CommScope, Inc., 77
Compagnie de Saint-Gobain, 64 (upd.)
CompuDyne Corporation, 51
Conair Corporation, 69 (upd.)
Concord Camera Corporation, 41
Congoleum Corp., 18
Conn-Selmer, Inc., 55
Conrad Industries, Inc., 58
Conso International Corporation, 29
Consorcio G Grupo Dina, S.A. de C.V., 36
Constar International Inc., 64
Converse Inc., 9
Cooper Cameron Corporation, 58 (upd.)
The Cooper Companies, Inc., 39
Cooper Industries, Inc., 44 (upd.)
Cordis Corporation, 46 (upd.)

Corning Inc., 44 (upd.)
Corrpro Companies, Inc., 20
Corticeira Amorim, Sociedade Gestora de Participaço es Sociais, S.A., 48
Crane Co., 8; 30 (upd.)
Cranium, Inc., 69
Creative Technology Ltd., 57
Creo Inc., 48
CRH plc, 64
Crosman Corporation, 62
Crown Equipment Corporation, 15
CTB International Corporation, 43 (upd.)
Cuisinart Corporation, 24
Culligan Water Technologies, Inc., 12; 38 (upd.)
Cummins Engine Company, Inc., 40 (upd.)
CUNO Incorporated, 57
Curtiss-Wright Corporation, 10; 35 (upd.)
Custom Chrome, Inc., 74 (upd.)
Cutter & Buck Inc., 27
Cybex International, Inc., 49
Cymer, Inc., 77
Dade Behring Holdings Inc., 71
Daewoo Group, III
Daikin Industries, Ltd., III
Daisy Outdoor Products Inc., 58
Danaher Corporation, 7; 77 (upd.)
Daniel Industries, Inc., 16
Daniel Measurement and Control, Inc., 74 (upd.)
Danisco A/S, 44
Day Runner, Inc., 41 (upd.)
DC Shoes, Inc., 60
DCN S.A., 75
De'Longhi S.p.A., 66
Dearborn Mid-West Conveyor Company, 56
Decora Industries, Inc., 31
Decorator Industries Inc., 68
DeCrane Aircraft Holdings Inc., 36
Deere & Company, III; 42 (upd.)
Defiance, Inc., 22
Delachaux S.A., 76
Dell Inc., 63 (upd.)
Deluxe Corporation, 73 (upd.)
DEMCO, Inc., 60
Denby Group plc, 44
Denison International plc, 46
DENSO Corporation, 46 (upd.)
Department 56, Inc., 14
DePuy Inc., 37 (upd.)
Detroit Diesel Corporation, 10; 74 (upd.)
Deutsche Babcock A.G., III
Deutz AG, 39
Devro plc, 55
Dial-A-Mattress Operating Corporation, 46
Diebold, Incorporated, 7; 22 (upd.)
Diesel SpA, 40
Dixon Industries, Inc., 26
Dixon Ticonderoga Company, 12; 69 (upd.)
Djarum PT, 62
DMI Furniture, Inc., 46
Donaldson Company, Inc., 49 (upd.)
Donnelly Corporation, 12; 35 (upd.)
Dorel Industries Inc., 59

Douglas & Lomason Company, 16
Dover Corporation, III; 28 (upd.)
Dresser Industries, Inc., III
Drew Industries Inc., 28
Drexel Heritage Furnishings Inc., 12
Drypers Corporation, 18
Ducommun Incorporated, 30
Duncan Toys Company, 55
Dunn-Edwards Corporation, 56
Duracell International Inc., 9; 71 (upd.)
Durametallic, 21
Duriron Company Inc., 17
Dürkopp Adler AG, 65
Duron Inc., 72
Dürr AG, 44
Dynea, 68
Dyson Group PLC, 71
EADS SOCATA, 54
Eagle-Picher Industries, Inc., 8; 23 (upd.)
The Eastern Company, 48
Eastman Kodak Company, III; 7 (upd.); 36 (upd.)
Easton Sports, Inc., 66
Eaton Corporation, 67 (upd.)
ECC International Corp., 42
Ecolab Inc., 34 (upd.)
Eddie Bauer Inc., 9
EDO Corporation, 46
EG&G Incorporated, 29 (upd.)
Ekco Group, Inc., 16
Elamex, S.A. de C.V., 51
Elano Corporation, 14
Electrolux AB, III; 53 (upd.)
Eljer Industries, Inc., 24
Elkay Manufacturing Company, 73
Elscint Ltd., 20
Encompass Services Corporation, 33
Encore Computer Corporation, 74 (upd.)
Energizer Holdings, Inc., 32
Energy Conversion Devices, Inc., 75
Enesco Corporation, 11
Engineered Support Systems, Inc., 59
English China Clays Ltd., 40 (upd.)
Enodis plc, 68
Ernie Ball, Inc., 56
Escalade, Incorporated, 19
Esselte, 64
Esselte Leitz GmbH & Co. KG, 48
Essilor International, 21
Esterline Technologies Corp., 15
Ethan Allen Interiors, Inc., 12; 39 (upd.)
The Eureka Company, 12
Everlast Worldwide Inc., 47
Excel Technology, Inc., 65
EXX Inc., 65
Fabbrica D' Armi Pietro Beretta S.p.A., 39
Facom S.A., 32
FAG—Kugelfischer Georg Schäfer AG, 62
Faiveley S.A., 39
Falcon Products, Inc., 33
Fanuc Ltd., III; 17 (upd.); 75 (upd.)
Farah Incorporated, 24
Farmer Bros. Co., 52
Fastenal Company, 42 (upd.)
Faultless Starch/Bon Ami Company, 55
Featherlite Inc., 28
Fedders Corporation, 18; 43 (upd.)
Federal Prison Industries, Inc., 34

Materials

Mining & Metals

Personal Services

Petroleum

Publishing & Printing

Real Estate

Textiles & Apparel

Naf Naf SA, 44
Nautica Enterprises, Inc., 18; 44 (upd.)
New Balance Athletic Shoe, Inc., 25; 68 (upd.)
NIKE, Inc., V; 8 (upd.); 75 (upd.)
Nine West Group, Inc., 39 (upd.)
Nitches, Inc., 53
The North Face, Inc., 18
Oakley, Inc., 18
OshKosh B'Gosh, Inc., 9; 42 (upd.)
Oxford Industries, Inc., 8
Pacific Sunwear of California, Inc., 28
Peek & Cloppenburg KG, 46
Pendleton Woolen Mills, Inc., 42
Pentland Group plc, 20
Perry Ellis International, Inc., 41
Phat Fashions LLC, 49
Phoenix Footwear Group, Inc., 70
Pillowtex Corporation, 19; 41 (upd.)
Plains Cotton Cooperative Association, 57
Pluma, Inc., 27
Polo/Ralph Lauren Corporation, 12; 62 (upd.)
Prada Holding B.V., 45
PremiumWear, Inc., 30
Puma AG Rudolf Dassler Sport, 35
Quaker Fabric Corp., 19
Quiksilver, Inc., 18
R.G. Barry Corporation, 17; 44 (upd.)
Raymond Ltd., 77
Recreational Equipment, Inc., 18
Red Wing Shoe Company, Inc., 30 (upd.)
Reebok International Ltd., V; 9 (upd.); 26 (upd.)
Rieter Holding AG, 42
Rocawear Apparel LLC, 77
Rollerblade, Inc., 15
Royal Ten Cate N.V., 68
Russell Corporation, 8; 30 (upd.)
St. John Knits, Inc., 14
Salant Corporation, 51 (upd.)
Salvatore Ferragamo Italia S.p.A., 62
Sao Paulo Alpargatas S.A., 75
Saucony Inc., 35
Schott Brothers, Inc., 67
Shaw Industries, Inc., 40 (upd.)
Shelby Williams Industries, Inc., 14
Skechers U.S.A. Inc., 31
Sophus Berendsen A/S, 49
Springs Industries, Inc., V; 19 (upd.)
Starter Corp., 12
Stefanel SpA, 63
Steiner Corporation (Alsco), 53
Steven Madden, Ltd., 37
Stirling Group plc, 62
Stoddard International plc, 72
Stone Manufacturing Company, 14; 43 (upd.)
The Stride Rite Corporation, 8; 37 (upd.)
Stussy, Inc., 55
Sun Sportswear, Inc., 17
Superior Uniform Group, Inc., 30
Tamfelt Oyj Abp, 62
Tarrant Apparel Group, 62
Teijin Limited, V
Thomaston Mills, Inc., 27
Tilley Endurables, Inc., 67
The Timberland Company, 13; 54 (upd.)

Tommy Hilfiger Corporation, 20; 53 (upd.)
Too, Inc., 61
Toray Industries, Inc., V
Tultex Corporation, 13
Under Armour Performance Apparel, 61
Unifi, Inc., 12; 62 (upd.)
United Merchants & Manufacturers, Inc., 13
United Retail Group Inc., 33
Unitika Ltd., V
Vans, Inc., 16; 47 (upd.)
Varsity Spirit Corp., 15
VF Corporation, V; 17 (upd.); 54 (upd.)
Volcom, Inc., 77
Walton Monroe Mills, Inc., 8
The Warnaco Group Inc., 12; 46 (upd.)
Wellman, Inc., 8; 52 (upd.)
West Point-Pepperell, Inc., 8
WestPoint Stevens Inc., 16
Weyco Group, Incorporated, 32
Williamson-Dickie Manufacturing Company, 14
Wolverine World Wide, Inc., 16; 59 (upd.)
Woolrich Inc., 62

Tobacco

Altadis S.A., 72 (upd.)
American Brands, Inc., V
B.A.T. Industries PLC, 22 (upd.)
British American Tobacco PLC, 50 (upd.)
Brooke Group Ltd., 15
Brown & Williamson Tobacco Corporation, 14; 33 (upd.)
Culbro Corporation, 15
Dibrell Brothers, Incorporated, 12
DIMON Inc., 27
800-JR Cigar, Inc., 27
Gallaher Group Plc, V; 19 (upd.); 49 (upd.)
General Cigar Holdings, Inc., 66 (upd.)
Holt's Cigar Holdings, Inc., 42
Imasco Limited, V
Imperial Tobacco Group PLC, 50
Japan Tobacco Incorporated, V
KT&G Corporation, 62
Nobleza Piccardo SAICF, 64
North Atlantic Trading Company Inc., 65
Philip Morris Companies Inc., V; 18 (upd.)
R.J. Reynolds Tobacco Holdings, Inc., 30 (upd.)
RJR Nabisco Holdings Corp., V
Rothmans UK Holdings Limited, V; 19 (upd.)
Seita, 23
Souza Cruz S.A., 65
Standard Commercial Corporation, 13; 62 (upd.)
Swisher International Group Inc., 23
Tabacalera, S.A., V; 17 (upd.)
Taiwan Tobacco & Liquor Corporation, 75
Universal Corporation, V; 48 (upd.)
UST Inc., 9; 50 (upd.)
Vector Group Ltd., 35 (upd.)

Transport Services

Abertis Infraestructuras, S.A., 65
Aéroports de Paris, 33
Air Express International Corporation, 13
Airborne Freight Corporation, 6; 34 (upd.)
Alamo Rent A Car, Inc., 6; 24 (upd.)
Alaska Railroad Corporation, 60
Alexander & Baldwin, Inc., 10
Allied Worldwide, Inc., 49
AMCOL International Corporation, 59 (upd.)
Amerco, 6
AMERCO, 67 (upd.)
American Classic Voyages Company, 27
American President Companies Ltd., 6
Anderson Trucking Service, Inc., 75
Anschutz Corp., 12
APL Limited, 61 (upd.)
Aqua Alliance Inc., 32 (upd.)
Arriva PLC, 69
Atlas Van Lines, Inc., 14
Attica Enterprises S.A., 64
Avis Group Holdings, Inc., 75 (upd.)
Avis Rent A Car, Inc., 6; 22 (upd.)
BAA plc, 10
Bekins Company, 15
Berliner Verkehrsbetriebe (BVG), 58
Bollinger Shipyards, Inc., 61
Boyd Bros. Transportation Inc., 39
Brambles Industries Limited, 42
The Brink's Company, 58 (upd.)
British Railways Board, V
Broken Hill Proprietary Company Ltd., 22 (upd.)
Buckeye Partners, L.P., 70
Budget Group, Inc., 25
Budget Rent a Car Corporation, 9
Burlington Northern Santa Fe Corporation, V; 27 (upd.)
C.H. Robinson Worldwide, Inc., 40 (upd.)
Canadian National Railway Company, 71 (upd.)
Canadian National Railway System, 6
Canadian Pacific Railway Limited, V; 45 (upd.)
Cannon Express, Inc., 53
Carey International, Inc., 26
Carlson Companies, Inc., 6
Carolina Freight Corporation, 6
Celadon Group Inc., 30
Central Japan Railway Company, 43
Chargeurs, 6
CHC Helicopter Corporation, 67
Chicago and North Western Holdings Corporation, 6
Christian Salvesen Plc, 45
Coach USA, Inc., 24; 55 (upd.)
Coles Express Inc., 15
Compagnie Générale Maritime et Financière, 6
Consolidated Delivery & Logistics, Inc., 24
Consolidated Freightways Corporation, V; 21 (upd.); 48 (upd.)
Consolidated Rail Corporation, V
CR England, Inc., 63

Utilities

Waste Services

Geographic Index

Matsushita Electric Industrial Co., Ltd., II; 64 (upd.)
Matsushita Electric Works, Ltd., III; 7 (upd.)
Matsuzakaya Company Ltd., V; 64 (upd.)
Mazda Motor Corporation, 9; 23 (upd.); 63 (upd.)
Meiji Milk Products Company, Limited, II
Meiji Mutual Life Insurance Company, The, III
Meiji Seika Kaisha Ltd., II; 64 (upd.)
Mercian Corporation, 77
Millea Holdings Inc., 64 (upd.)
Minolta Co., Ltd., III; 18 (upd.); 43 (upd.)
Mitsubishi Bank, Ltd., The, II
Mitsubishi Chemical Corporation, I; 56 (upd.)
Mitsubishi Corporation, I; 12 (upd.)
Mitsubishi Electric Corporation, II; 44 (upd.)
Mitsubishi Estate Company, Limited, IV; 61 (upd.)
Mitsubishi Heavy Industries, Ltd., III; 7 (upd.); 40 (upd.)
Mitsubishi Materials Corporation, III
Mitsubishi Motors Corporation, 9; 23 (upd.); 57 (upd.)
Mitsubishi Oil Co., Ltd., IV
Mitsubishi Rayon Co., Ltd., V
Mitsubishi Trust & Banking Corporation, The, II
Mitsui & Co., Ltd., 28 (upd.)
Mitsui Bank, Ltd., The, II
Mitsui Bussan K.K., I
Mitsui Marine and Fire Insurance Company, Limited, III
Mitsui Mining & Smelting Co., Ltd., IV
Mitsui Mining Company, Limited, IV
Mitsui Mutual Life Insurance Company, III; 39 (upd.)
Mitsui O.S.K. Lines, Ltd., V
Mitsui Petrochemical Industries, Ltd., 9
Mitsui Real Estate Development Co., Ltd., IV
Mitsui Trust & Banking Company, Ltd., The, II
Mitsukoshi Ltd., V; 56 (upd.)
Mizuho Financial Group Inc., 58 (upd.)
Mizuno Corporation, 25
Morinaga & Co. Ltd., 61
Nagasakiya Co., Ltd., V; 69 (upd.)
Nagase & Co., Ltd., 8; 61 (upd.)
NEC Corporation, II; 21 (upd.); 57 (upd.)
NGK Insulators Ltd., 67
NHK Spring Co., Ltd., III
Nichii Co., Ltd., V
Nichimen Corporation, IV; 24 (upd.)
Nichirei Corporation, 70
Nidec Corporation, 59
Nihon Keizai Shimbun, Inc., IV
Nikko Securities Company Limited, The, II; 9 (upd.)
Nikon Corporation, III; 48 (upd.)
Nintendo Co., Ltd., III; 7 (upd.); 28 (upd.); 67 (upd.)

Nippon Credit Bank, II
Nippon Express Company, Ltd., V; 64 (upd.)
Nippon Life Insurance Company, III; 60 (upd.)
Nippon Light Metal Company, Ltd., IV
Nippon Meat Packers, Inc., II
Nippon Oil Corporation, IV; 63 (upd.)
Nippon Seiko K.K., III
Nippon Sheet Glass Company, Limited, III
Nippon Shinpan Co., Ltd., II; 61 (upd.)
Nippon Steel Corporation, IV; 17 (upd.)
Nippon Suisan Kaisha, Limited, II
Nippon Telegraph and Telephone Corporation, V; 51 (upd.)
Nippon Yusen Kabushiki Kaisha (NYK), V; 72 (upd.)
Nippondenso Co., Ltd., III
Nissan Motor Company Ltd., I; 11 (upd.); 34 (upd.)
Nisshin Seifun Group Inc., II; 66 (upd.)
Nisshin Steel Co., Ltd., IV
Nissho Iwai K.K., I
Nissin Food Products Company Ltd., 75
NKK Corporation, IV; 28 (upd.)
NOF Corporation, 72
Nomura Securities Company, Limited, II; 9 (upd.)
Norinchukin Bank, II
NTN Corporation, III; 47 (upd.)
Odakyu Electric Railway Co., Ltd., V; 68 (upd.)
Ohbayashi Corporation, I
Oji Paper Co., Ltd., IV; 57 (upd.)
Oki Electric Industry Company, Limited, II
Okuma Holdings Inc., 74
Okura & Co., Ltd., IV
Omron Corporation, II; 28 (upd.)
Onoda Cement Co., Ltd., III
ORIX Corporation, II; 44 (upd.)
Osaka Gas Company, Ltd., V; 60 (upd.)
Paloma Industries Ltd., 71
Pioneer Electronic Corporation, III; 28 (upd.)
Rengo Co., Ltd., IV
Ricoh Company, Ltd., III; 36 (upd.)
Roland Corporation, 38
Ryoshoku Ltd., 72
Sankyo Company, Ltd., I; 56 (upd.)
Sanrio Company, Ltd., 38
Sanwa Bank, Ltd., The, II; 15 (upd.)
SANYO Electric Company, Ltd., II; 36 (upd.)
Sanyo-Kokusaku Pulp Co., Ltd., IV
Sapporo Breweries, Ltd., I; 13 (upd.); 36 (upd.)
SEGA Corporation, 73
Seibu Department Stores, Ltd., V; 42 (upd.)
Seibu Railway Company Ltd., V; 74 (upd.)
Seiko Corporation, III; 17 (upd.); 72 (upd.)
Seino Transportation Company, Ltd., 6
Seiyu, Ltd., The, V; 36 (upd.)
Sekisui Chemical Co., Ltd., III; 72 (upd.)

Sharp Corporation, II; 12 (upd.); 40 (upd.)
Shikoku Electric Power Company, Inc., V; 60 (upd.)
Shimano Inc., 64
Shionogi & Co., Ltd., III; 17 (upd.)
Shiseido Company, Limited, III; 22 (upd.)
Shochiku Company Ltd., 74
Showa Shell Sekiyu K.K., IV; 59 (upd.)
Snow Brand Milk Products Company, Ltd., II; 48 (upd.)
Softbank Corp., 13; 38 (upd.)
Sony Corporation, II; 12 (upd.); 40 (upd.)
Sumitomo Bank, Limited, The, II; 26 (upd.)
Sumitomo Chemical Company Ltd., I
Sumitomo Corporation, I; 11 (upd.)
Sumitomo Electric Industries, Ltd., II
Sumitomo Heavy Industries, Ltd., III; 42 (upd.)
Sumitomo Life Insurance Company, III; 60 (upd.)
Sumitomo Marine and Fire Insurance Company, Limited, The, III
Sumitomo Metal Industries, Ltd., IV
Sumitomo Metal Mining Co., Ltd., IV
Sumitomo Mitsui Banking Corporation, 51 (upd.)
Sumitomo Realty & Development Co., Ltd., IV
Sumitomo Rubber Industries, Ltd., V
Sumitomo Trust & Banking Company, Ltd., The, II; 53 (upd.)
Suntory Ltd., 65
Suzuki Motor Corporation, 9; 23 (upd.); 59 (upd.)
Taiheiyo Cement Corporation, 60 (upd.)
Taiyo Fishery Company, Limited, II
Taiyo Kobe Bank, Ltd., The, II
Takara Holdings Inc., 62
Takashimaya Company, Limited, V; 47 (upd.)
Takeda Chemical Industries, Ltd., I; 46 (upd.)
TDK Corporation, II; 17 (upd.); 49 (upd.)
Teijin Limited, V; 61 (upd.)
Terumo Corporation, 48
Tobu Railway Co Ltd, 6
Toho Co., Ltd., 28
Tohoku Electric Power Company, Inc., V
Tokai Bank, Limited, The, II; 15 (upd.)
Tokio Marine and Fire Insurance Co., Ltd., The, III
Tokyo Electric Power Company, The, 74 (upd.)
Tokyo Electric Power Company, Incorporated, The, V
Tokyo Gas Co., Ltd., V; 55 (upd.)
Tokyu Corporation, V; 47 (upd.)
Tokyu Department Store Co., Ltd., V; 32 (upd.)
Tokyu Land Corporation, IV
Tomen Corporation, IV; 24 (upd.)
Tomy Company Ltd., 65
TonenGeneral Sekiyu K.K., IV; 16 (upd.); 54 (upd.)

United States

GEOGRAPHIC INDEX